Legal Aspects of Health Care Administration

Eighth Edition

George D. Pozgar, MBA, CHE
Consultant and Healthcare Surveyor
Gp Health Care Consulting, Int'l
Annapolis, Maryland

Legal Review

Nina M. Santucci, JD
General Counsel
The Windermere Group
Annapolis, Maryland

AN ASPEN PUBLICATION®
Aspen Publishers, Inc.
Gaithersburg, Maryland
2002

This publication is designed to provide accurate and authoritative information in regard to the Subject Matter covered. It is sold with the understanding that the publisher is not engaged in rendering legal, accounting, or other professional service. If legal advice or other expert assistance is required, the service of a competent professional person should be sought. (From a Declaration of Principles jointly adopted by a Committee of the American Bar Association and a Committee of Publishers and Associations.)

Library of Congress Cataloging-in-Publication Data

Pozgar, George D.
Legal aspects of health care administration/George D. Pozgar; legal and editorial review, Nina Santucci Pozgar.—8th ed.
p. cm.
Includes bibliographical references and index.
ISBN 0-8342-1911-5
1. Medical laws and legislation—United States.   2. Medical personnel—Malpractice—United States.   I. Pozgar, Nina S.   II. Title.
KF3821.P69 2002
344.73'041—dc21
2001034124

About Aspen Publishers • For more than 40 years, Aspen has been a leading professional publisher in a variety of disciplines. Aspen's vast information resources are available in both print and electronic formats. We are committed to providing the highest quality information available in the most appropriate format for our customers. Visit Aspen's Internet site for more information resources, directories, articles, and a searchable version of Aspen's full catalog, including the most recent publications: www.aspenpublishers.com
Aspen Publishers, Inc. • The hallmark of quality in publishing
Member of the worldwide Wolters Kluwer group

Editorial Services: Denise Hawkins Coursey
Library of Congress Catalog Card Number: 2001034124
ISBN: 0-8342-1911-5

Printed in the United States of America

1 2 3 4 5

Contents

Preface

Legal Aspects of Health Care Administration, Eighth Edition, lays a strong foundation of health law, enabling health care providers to deal knowledgeably with common legal and practical problems facing their industry. Because the law is continually evolving, health care professionals must possess a basic understanding of the law as it relates to their particular areas of responsibility. Moreover, they must stay current with the changes in law and learn from others' mistakes and misjudgments to better serve their patients' needs. The cases, supplementary text, and explanations, in addition to the questions following each chapter, are designed to help readers analyze situations more carefully and approach their jobs with increased awareness and questioning. The reader will become a more effective practitioner, focused on the best care he or she can provide for the patient. Most anyone can learn the mechanics of the technical aspects of his or her job, just as one can learn how to ride a bike, drive a car, or fly a plane. The more difficult task, however, is reaching a destination and being prepared for any emergency or crisis. This is also true in the health care field. Any person can learn policies, procedures, rules, and regulations, but it takes a creative, questioning mind to apply the concepts presented in this book.

This eighth edition guides the reader on a comfortable and easily understood tour through the complicated maze of the legal system as it impacts health care organizations. To assist the reader in applying the substantive material to his or her daily professional life, stops are made to consider actual court cases that bring the information to life.

The text begins with a broad discussion of the structure of the legal system and the sources of its statutory laws, rules,

Author's Note: This text is educational in nature and should not be considered a substitute for legal advice on any particular issue. Moreover, each chapter presents an overview, rather than an exhaustive treatment, of the various topics.

regulations, and guidelines. It then describes the organization of our government and the various federal administrative departments that are relevant to the health care industry. The tour continues through a basic review of tort law, criminal law, contract law, civil procedure, and trial practice. Throughout the text readers are presented with an examination of the numerous issues that confront professionals working in health care organizations.

New to this edition are a fully revised chapter titled "Health Care Ethics," a chapter on zero tolerance, and several new features, including "It's Your Gavel" boxes that give readers the opportunity to make decisions on actual court cases, detailed case reviews, and self-tests. The chapter on zero tolerance provides a self-assessment tool for evaluating the quality of care in health care organizations, which should generate lively discussion and provide innovative insight into the cases reviewed in this and similar texts.

IT'S YOUR GAVEL

Chapters 2 through 20 each begin with a case that has been reviewed by courts in state or federal jurisdictions. After reviewing each case and subsequent relevant material, readers should take on the role of fact-finder and render a decision. The actual court finding and reasoning for each case can be found at the end of its respective chapter under the subtitle "The Court's Decision."

CASE REVIEWS

Incorporated into this new edition is a more detailed review of pertinent health law cases. After reading each fact pattern, decision, and reasoning by the court, readers are presented with discussion questions. The questions are intended to allow readers to demonstrate their understanding of the issues. Moreover, readers will be able to apply what they learn when problem solving in professional situations. Each case and subsequent decision has had an effect on the health care system. Therefore, readers should understand and apply political, social, and economic factors when analyzing the cases. The cases selected have relevance to and are reflective of case law from the majority of states.

The general format of each case review is as follows:

- Title—Each case is given a title that signals the type of case to be reviewed.
- Citation—Students may wish to research cases discussed in this text to gain a deeper understanding of the topics covered. A case citation describes the identity of the parties in the case, the text in which the case can be found, and the year in which the case was decided, for example: *Bouvia v. Superior Court (Glenchur)*, 225 Cal. Rptr. 297 (Cal. Ct. App. 1986).
  - *Bouvia v. Superior Court (Glenchur)*—Identifies the basic parties involved in the lawsuit.
  - 225 Cal. Rptr. 297—Identifies the case as being reported in volume 225 of the California Reporter at page 297.
  - Cal. Ct. App. 1986—Identifies the case as being decided in the California Court of Appeals in 1986.

  Students who decide to research a specific case should visit a law library, which will contain various federal, state, and regional reporters.
- Facts—A review of the facts of the case is presented.
- Issues—The issues discussed in any given case are selected for review on the basis of medical and legal pertinence to the health care professional. Although any one case in this text may have multiple issues, emphasis is placed on those issues considered to be most relevant for the reader.
- Holding—The court's ruling based on the facts, issues, and applicable laws pertaining to a case is summarized.
- Reason—The rationale for the court's decision based on the facts, issues, and relevant laws surrounding a case is presented. Several cases in the text require students to analyze the case themselves and determine the facts, issues, holding, and reason for that case.
- Discussion—Discussion questions, although prompted by a particular case, may not necessarily be germane to the facts of the case. The questions are merely presented as opportunities for discussion and in no way add to the facts of a specific case.

SELF-TESTS

For review and reinforcement of case issues, self-administered tests are provided under separate cover. An attempt has been made to make the multiple-choice questions a learning tool for both beginning and intermediate students, as well as for seasoned professionals.

Each of the questions or incomplete sentences is followed by four to six suggested answers. Although two or more answers may be or appear to be correct, students should select the best answer.

The questions have been designed to provide an opportunity for further discussion of the instant case, as well as to provide a springboard for discussion of what lessons can be gleaned and transferred to one's own work environment. The multiple-choice questions test the student's

- Knowledge. Students are required to recognize or recall specific legal facts, terminology, classifications, principles, and theories (answers to these questions do not require reasoning, only remembering the material involved).
- Comprehension. Students are required to demonstrate not only their knowledge about the law but also a degree of understanding of the material issues involved in each case. This is accomplished by posing questions that have been designed to have more than one right answer, thus requiring the student to select the best answer.

HEALTH CARE IN THE MEDIA

As a result of ever-increasing media attention, the public has lost trust in the ability of health care professionals to provide quality health care. As noted below, the news media continues to feature distressing headlines about the negative side of health care.

HMOs EXERCISING RIGHT TO SUE PATIENTS
Health experts say a drive for more revenue has prompted HMOs and other managed care plans to demand reimbursement from patients who receive settlements or court awards for injuries that require medical care.
—*USA Today*, July 19, 2001

HOSPITAL MISTAKES MUST BE DISCLOSED
Accreditation at Risk if Patients Aren't Told
—*USA Today*, June 28, 2001

NURSING SHORTAGE IS RAISING WORRIES ON PATIENTS' CARE
—*The New York Times*, April 8, 2001

IS CALIFORNIA HOSPITAL WORKER "ANGEL OF DEATH"?
Suspect Confessed, Then Recanted; But Police Say Respiratory Therapist May Have Killed Hundreds
—*National News*, February 4, 2001

New York Surgeon Cleared of Treating Wrong Side of Brain

Among the allegations, beyond those that he operated on the wrong side of a patient's brain, were that he botched a number of spinal surgeries, used inappropriate tools during one procedure, failed to order proper tests and kept poor records.

—*The New York Times,* January 5, 2001

U.S. Toughens Enforcement of Nursing Home Standards

In a new crackdown on substandard care, federal officials have imposed fines on hundreds of nursing homes across the country.

—*The New York Times,* December 4, 2000

State Files Suit against Four HMOs

The horror stories about managed care are not random or isolated…. They are part of a pattern and practice that we have been investigating for some time.

—*The Hartford Courant,* September 8, 2000

Medicare Fraud Case Settled for $1.4 Million

Home health care company Tender Loving Care paid $1.4 million to settle Medicare fraud charges, the Justice Department said…kickbacks to doctors for referrals, and salaries and expenses for relatives who weren't in the business.

—*USA Today,* September 6, 2000

Ohio Leads Nation in Hospital Closures, New Report Says

…all blamed financial loss.

—*Healthcare Monitor,* August 28, 2000

Frustrated Doctors Rebel against Insurers

—*USA Today,* July 20, 2000

U.S. Task Force To Find Ways To Reduce Medical Errors

President Clinton cited what he called the "disturbing report" issued last week that as many as 98,000 Americans lose their lives each year due to medical mistakes.

—CNN.com, December 7, 1999

Medical Mistakes 8th Top Killer

Medical errors kill more Americans than traffic accidents, breast cancer or AIDS, Institute of Medicine officials said Monday as they called for a sweeping "systems approach to make medicine safer."

"These horrific cases that make the headlines are just the tip of the iceberg," says the institute's report, *To Err Is Human.* Estimates range from 44,000 to 98,000 deaths a year attributed to medical mistakes, making it the eighth leading cause of death.

The errors include giving the wrong drug to incorrect diagnoses. The report estimates that such errors cost the nation $8.8 billion a year.

—*USA Today,* November 30, 1999

Doctor Held Liable for Fatal Handwriting Mix-up

—*USA Today,* October 21, 1999

On the Watch in Nursing Homes

Coalition wants "granny cams" to protect elderly from neglect.

—*USA Today,* September 14, 1999

Taken as a whole, the contents of this book should stand as a reminder to its readers that they must learn from the mistakes and tragedies experienced by others to avoid repeating them.

Acknowledgments

The author especially acknowledges Aspen Publishers, Inc., whose guidance and assistance was so important in making this publication a reality. Many thanks to Aspen for permitting use of special adaptations from *Long-Term Care and the Law*, *Hospital Contracts Manual*, *Managed Care Law Manual*, and *Case Law in Health Care Administration, Second Edition*.

Many thanks to those whom I have instructed in the legal aspects of health care administration from the New School for Social Research, Molloy College, Long Island University-C.W. Post College, Saint Francis College, and Saint Joseph's College, as well as those whom I have instructed through the years at various conferences and seminars, for their inspiration. Many thanks to you all.

Also, thanks to the staff at the Library of Congress for their guidance in locating research materials.

Introduction to Law

Laws are the very bulwarks of liberty; they define every man's rights, and defend the individual liberties of all men.

J.G. Holland (1819–1881)

This chapter introduces the health care professional to the development of American law, the functioning of our legal system, and the roles of the different branches of government in creating, administering, and enforcing the law in the United States. It is important to understand the foundation of our legal system before one can appreciate or comprehend the specific laws and principles relating to health care.

Supreme Court Justice Oliver Wendell Holmes said that the law "is a magic mirror, wherein we see reflected not only our own lives but also the lives of those who went before us."[1] "The government of the United States has been emphatically termed a government of laws, and not of men. It will certainly cease to deserve this high appellation, if the laws furnish no remedy for the violation of a vested right."[2]

Most definitions of law describe it as a system of principles and processes by which people in a society deal with their disputes and problems, seeking to solve or settle them without resorting to force. Simply stated, laws are general rules of conduct that are enforced by government, which imposes penalties when prescribed laws are violated.

Laws govern the relationships between private individuals and organizations and between both of these parties and government. *Public law* deals with the relationships between individuals and government; *private law* deals with relationships among individuals. Laws regulate the activities and behaviors of individuals in international, federal, state, local, and municipal settings.

One important segment of public law is criminal law, which prohibits conduct deemed injurious to public order and provides for punishment of those proven to have engaged in such conduct. Public law also consists of countless regulations designed to advance societal objectives by requiring private individuals and organizations to adopt specified courses of action in their activities and undertakings. The thrust of most public law is to attain what society deems to be valid public goals.

Private law is concerned with the recognition and enforcement of the rights and duties of private individuals and organizations. Tort and contract actions are two basic types of private law. In a *tort action*, one party asserts that the wrongful conduct of another has caused harm, and the injured party seeks compensation for the harm suffered. Generally, a *contract action* involves a claim by one party that another party has breached an agreement by failing to fulfill an obligation. Either remuneration or specific performance of the obligation may be sought as a remedy. It is clear that without an organized, clear system of laws that regulate society, anarchy would be the result.

SOURCES OF LAW

The basic sources of law are *common law,* which is derived from judicial decisions; *statutory law,* which emanates from the federal and state legislatures; and *administrative law,* prescribed by administrative agencies. In those instances in which written laws are either silent, vague, or contradictory to other laws, the judicial system often is called on to resolve those disputes until such time as appropriate legislative action can be taken to clear up a particular legal issue. In the following sections the sources of law that formed the foundation of our legal system are discussed.

Common Law

The term *common law* refers to the body of principles that has evolved and expanded from judicial decisions that arise during the trial of court cases. Many of the legal principles and rules applied today by courts in the United States have their origins in English common law.

Because it is impossible to have a law that covers every potential human event that might occur in society, the judicial system is thus doubly necessary. It not only serves as a mechanism for reviewing legal disputes that arise in the written law, but it is also an effective review mechanism for those issues on which the written law is silent or in instances of a mixture of issues involving both written law and common-law decisions. For example, in the *Cruzan* case, discussed in Chapter 16, the decision by the U.S. Supreme Court was based on the consideration of existing statutory law and prior judicial decisions.[3]

Common Law in England

Law reflects to a large degree the civilization of those that live under it. Its progress and development are mirrors not merely of material prosperity but of the method of thought and of the outlook of the age.[4]

The common law of England is much like its language. It is as varied as the nations that have peopled its land in different locations and different periods. Some of it is derived from the Britons, the Romans, the Saxons, the Danes, and the Normans.

To recount what innovations were made by the succession of these different nations, or estimate what proportion of the customs of each go to the composing of our body of common law, would be impossible at this distance of time. As to a great part of this period, we have no monuments of antiquity to guide us in our inquiry; and the lights which gleam upon the other part afford but dim prospect. Our conjectures can only be assisted by the history of the revolutions effected by these several nations.[5]

The Romans governed the island, as a province, from the time of Claudius, A.D. 43, and did not leave until A.D. 448. It was a time of peace and cultivation of the arts. Roman laws were administered as laws of the country. When the Romans left Britain to attend to their own domestic safety, the Picts and the Scots clashed with inhabitants of southern England. Unable to oppose the attack, these southern inhabitants appealed to the Saxons for assistance. The Saxons, who came from German lands, drove the northern invaders back inside their own borders.[6] The Saxons contended with Danish raiders from the eighth to the eleventh centuries.

The law in England before the Norman Conquest in A.D. 1066 was dispensed primarily by tradition and local customs and mostly dealt with violent crimes. The kings during this period were concerned more with enforcing customary law than with amending it. The courts mainly consisted of open-air meetings where no records were maintained. "For the Anglo-Saxons justice was a local matter, administered chiefly in the shire courts, and was largely dependent upon local customs, preserved in the memory of those persons who declared the law in the court."[7] The Saxons turned against the Britons and forced great numbers of them into the mountains of Wales, dividing the remainder of the dominion into seven independent kingdoms.[8]

The circumstances of this revolution are related to be of a kind differing from most others. The Saxons are described as a rude and bloody race, who beyond any other tribe of northern people, set themselves to exterminate the original inhabitants, and destroy every monument and remains of their establishment. In so general a ruin, it cannot be imagined that the customs of the native Britons, or the laws ingrafted upon them by the Romans, could meet with any favour.[9]

The kingdoms were, for a time, independent of one another and a variety of laws grew among the Saxons themselves. During the reign of Alfred, issues with the Danes, who had long harassed the kingdom, were settled by treaty in Northumberland. The Danes were considered in some measure to be part of the nation. They enjoyed their own laws within their district. When their own kings sat on the English throne, their laws pervaded, in some degree, all parts of the country. Toward the latter part of the Saxon times, the kingdom was governed by a variety of laws and local customs.[10]

The most general of these were the three following: the Mercian Law, the West-Saxon Law, and the Danish Law. If any of the British or Roman customs still subsisted, they were sunk into and lost in one of these laws, which governed the whole kingdom and have since received the general appellation of The Common Law.[11]

The Normans, after their conquest in A.D. 1066, had little regard for Anglo-Saxon laws. They considered themselves apart from such laws.

It is obviously impossible to attempt an adequate picture of Anglo-Saxon life. It was a wild time. Men lived in terror of the vast forests, where it was easy to be lost and succumb to starvation, of their fellow man who would plunder and slay, and above all of the Unknown, whose inscrutable ways seemed constantly to be bringing famine and disaster. The uncertainties of modern life pale into insignificance when regarded from the standpoint of these men. It is natural, therefore, that their law should reflect their reaction against the environment. It was conservative and harsh. Violence, robbery and death formed its background.[12]

Land disputes involved the Saxons who held the land before the conquest and the Normans who dispossessed them. Evidence in such disputes was often the result of oral testimony from neighboring landowners.

The principal change introduced by the Norman Conquest, so far as the central jurisdiction was concerned, was that the King's court now became, for the first time, the court in which disputes relating to land-tenure among the King's tenants-in-chief were regularly decided . . . there is no hint of any professional judiciary at this period. The trials were held locally in the presence of the county court or several county courts by the King's representatives, sent out from Curia Regis (the King's Court) and the tenants-in-chief. The presiding officer was often a cleric.[13]

A system of national law began to develop based on custom, foreign literature, and the rule of strong kings. The first royal court was established in A.D. 1178. This court, enlisting the aid of a jury, heard the complaints of the kingdom's subjects. Because there were few written laws, a body of principles evolved from these court decisions, which became known as "common law." Judges used these court decisions to decide subsequent cases. As Parliament's power to legislate grew, the initiative for developing new laws passed from the king to Parliament.

Common Law in the United States

During the colonial period, English common law began to be applied in the colonies. According to John Dickinson in his *Letters from a Farmer in Pennsylvania* in 1768:

The common law of England is generally received. . .; but our courts EXERCISE A SOVEREIGN AUTHORITY, in determining what parts of the common and statute law ought to be extended: For it must be admitted, that the difference of circumstances necessarily require us, in some cases to REJECT the determination of both. . . . Some of the English rules are adopted, others rejected.[14]

Joseph Story, in an 1829 U.S. Supreme Court decision, wrote, "The common law of England is not to be taken in all respects to be that of America. Our ancestors brought with them its general principles, and claimed it as their birthright but they brought with them and adopted only that portion which was applicable to their situation."[15]

The size of the country and the abundance of its natural resources made impossible the importation of the common law exactly as it had been developed in England. Measured by English standards, America had superabundant land, timber, and mineral wealth. American law had to serve the primary need of the new society to master the vast land areas of the American continent. The decisive facts upon which the law had to be based were the seemingly limitless expanses of land and the wealth and variety of natural resources.[16]

After the Revolution, each state, with the exception of Louisiana, adopted all or part of the existing English common law and added to it as needed. Louisiana civil law is based to a great extent on the French and Spanish laws and, especially, on the Code of Napoleon. As a result, there is no national system of common law in the United States, and common law on specific subjects may differ from state to state.

Case law court decisions did not easily pass from colony to colony. There were no printed reports to make transfer easy, though in the 18th century some manuscript materials did circulate among lawyers. These could hardly have been very influential. No doubt custom and case law slowly seeped from colony to colony. Travelers and word of mouth spread knowledge of living law. It is hard to say how much; thus it is hard to tell to what degree there was a common legal structure.[17]

Judicial review started to become part of the living law during the decade before the adoption of the federal Constitution. During that time American courts first began to assert the power to rule on the constitutionality of legislative acts and to hold unconstitutional statutes void.[18]

Cases are tried applying common-law principles unless a statute governs. Even though statutory law has affirmed many of the legal rules and principles initially established by the courts, new issues continue to arise, especially in private-law disputes, which require decision making according to common-law principles. Common-law actions are initiated mainly to recover money damages and/or possession of real or personal property.

When a higher state court has enunciated a common-law principle, the lower courts within the state where the decision was rendered must follow that principle. A decision in a case that sets forth a new legal principle establishes a precedent. Trial courts or those on equal footing are not bound by the decisions of other trial courts. Also, a principle established in one state does not set precedent for another state. Rather, the rulings in one jurisdiction may be used by the courts of other jurisdictions as guides to the legal analysis of a particular legal problem. Decisions found to be reasonable will be followed.

The position of a court or agency, relative to other courts and agencies, determines the place assigned to its decision in the hierarchy of decisional law. The decisions of the U.S. Supreme Court are highest in the hierarchy of decisional law with respect to federal legal questions. Because of the parties or the legal question involved, most legal controversies do not fall within the scope of the Supreme Court's decision-making responsibilities. On questions of purely state concern—such as the interpretation of a state statute that raises no issues under the U.S. Constitution or federal law—the highest court in the state has the final word on proper interpretation. The following are explanations of some of the more important common-law principles:

- *Res Judicata.* In common law, the term *res judicata*—which means "the thing is decided"—refers to that which has been previously acted on or decided by the courts. According to Black's Law Dictionary, it is a rule where "a final judgment rendered by a court of competent jurisdiction on the merits is conclusive as to the rights of the parties and their privies, and, as to them, constitutes an absolute bar to subsequent action involving the same claim, demand, or cause of action."[19]
- *Stare Decisis.* The common-law principle *stare decisis* ("let the decision stand") provides that when a decision is rendered in a lawsuit involving a particular set of facts, another lawsuit involving an identical or substantially similar situation is to be resolved in the same manner as the first lawsuit. The resolution of future lawsuits is arrived at by applying rules and principles of preceding cases. In this manner, courts arrive at comparable rulings. Sometimes slight factual differences may provide a basis for recognizing distinctions between the precedent and the current case. In some cases, even when such differences are absent, a court may conclude that a particular common-law rule is no longer in accord with the needs of society and may depart from precedent. It should be understood that principles of law are subject to change, whether they originate in statutory or in common law. Common-law principles may be modified, overturned, abrogated, or created by new court decisions in a continuing process of growth and development to reflect changes in social attitudes, public needs, judicial prejudices, or contemporary political thinking.

Medical Malpractice. The first common-law case in the United States in which physicians were held legally responsible for a negligence-related action occurred as early as 1794. Since that time, physicians have experienced recurring periods of substantial increases in the number of malpractice cases. The first such increase occurred in the 15 years before the Civil War.[20] Increases in malpractice cases and concern about them occurred at the beginning of this century and also in the years before World War II.

In 1941, The Journal of the American Medical Association published studies showing that 1,296 malpractices had occurred between 1900 and 1940, with more than 500 between 1930 and 1940. The explanations for these increases in malpractice cases are similar to opinions expressed about the current malpractice situation: increased patient expectations, improvements in diagnostic procedures, and erosion of the physician–patient relationship, particularly in large urban centers.[21]

The Harvard Medical Malpractice Study, commissioned by New York State to determine the rate of medical injury in New York hospitals, revealed that 3.7 percent of patients entering New York hospitals in 1984 were injured by the care provided. A tenth of those who were treated negligently filed malpractice suits.[22] The research group conducting the study suggested that "only one claim makes its way into the tort system for every eight cases of injury caused by medical negligence."[23] The study, which cost $3.1 million and ran 1,200 pages, was funded by New York State and a grant from the Robert Wood Johnson Foundation. It involved four years of research and included the review of more than 30,000 medical records.[24]

The current number of malpractice suits is staggering. Critics say that the system fails by making too little information known.[25] A report by the Physicians Insurers of America, which represents 50 malpractice insurance companies covering 50 percent of private physicians in the United States, claims that breast cancer accounts for more medical malpractice claims than any other medical condition. Delayed diagnosis is common among both younger and older women. The report, which summarizes cases from 1994, focuses on 487 lawsuits in which damages were awarded for delayed diagnosis. The most common reasons for delay were misdiagnosis, failure to follow up, and false negative mammograms. The next most common medical diagnoses involving malpractice suits were infant brain damage, pregnancy, and heart attack.[26]

The presidential "Advisory Commission on Consumer Protection and Quality in the Health Care Industry" issued its report on March 12, 1998. The Commission, charged with reviewing the $1 trillion health care system, estimated that 180,000 people die each year from medical mishaps and errors and about one million are injured. One in five surgeries and tests was considered unnecessary or inappropriate and approximately 80,000 women have unnecessary hysterectomies every year. The Commission called for the development of national health care quality improvement goals and the use of measurement standards that will empower consumers and businesses to make informed purchasing decisions based on health plans' quality performance records. President Clinton directed the Secretary of the Department of Health and Human Services (HHS) to establish a "Quality Interagency Coordination Task Force" with responsibility, wherever feasible, to collaborate on goals, models, and timetables that are consistent with the Commission's six "National Aims for Improvement," which are

1. reducing the underlying causes of illness, injury, and disability
2. reducing health care errors
3. ensuring the appropriate use of health care services
4. expanding research on the effectiveness of treatments
5. addressing oversupply and undersupply of health care resources
6. increasing patient participation in their care[27]

Statutory Law

Statutory law is written law emanating from a legislative body. Although a statute can abolish any rule of common law, it can do so only by express words. The principles and rules of statutory law are set in hierarchical order. The Constitution of the United States adopted at the Constitutional Convention in Philadelphia in 1787 is highest in the hierarchy of enacted law. Article VI of the Constitution declares:

> This Constitution, and the Laws of the United States which shall be made in Pursuance thereof; and all Treaties made, or which shall be made, under the Authority of the United States, shall be the supreme Law of the Land; and the Judges in every State shall be bound thereby, any Thing in the Constitution or Laws of any State to the Contrary notwithstanding.[28]

The clear import of these words is that the U.S. Constitution, federal law, and federal treaties take precedence over the constitutions and laws of specific states and local jurisdictions.

Statutory law may be amended, repealed, or expanded by action of the legislature. States and local jurisdictions can only enact and enforce laws that do not conflict with federal law. Statutory laws may be declared void by a court; for example, a statute may be found unconstitutional because it does not comply with a state or federal constitution, because it is vague or ambiguous, or, in the case of a state law, because it is in conflict with a federal law.

In many cases involving statutory law, the court is called on to interpret how a statute applies to a given set of facts. For example, a statute may state merely that no person may discriminate against another person because of race, creed, color, or sex. A court may then be called on to decide whether certain actions by a person are discriminatory and therefore violate the law.

Administrative Law

Administrative law is the extensive body of public law issued by administrative agencies to direct the enacted laws of the federal and state governments. It is the branch of law that controls the administrative operations of government. Congress and state legislative bodies realistically cannot oversee their many laws; therefore, they delegate implementation and administration of the law to an appropriate administrative agency. Health care organizations in particular are inundated with a proliferation of administrative rules and regulations affecting every aspect of their operations.

The *Administrative Procedures Act*[29] describes the different procedures under which federal administrative agencies must operate.[30] The Act prescribes the procedural responsibilities and authority of administrative agencies and provides for legal remedies for those wronged by agency actions. The regulatory power exercised by administrative agencies includes power to license, power of rate setting (e.g., Health Care Financing Administration (HCFA)), and power over business practices (e.g., National Labor Relations Board (NLRB)).

Rules and Regulations

Administrative agencies have legislative, judicial, and executive functions. They have the authority to formulate rules and regulations considered necessary to carry out the intent of legislative enactments.

> [A] "rule" means the whole or a part of an agency statement of general or particular applicability and future effect designed to implement, interpret, or prescribe law or policy or describing the organization, procedure, or practice requirements of an agency and includes the approval or prescription for the future of rates, wages, corporate or financial structures or reorganizations thereof, prices, facilities, appliances, services or allowances therefore or of valuations, costs, or accounting, or practices bearing on any of the foregoing. . . .[31]

Regulatory agencies have the ability to legislate, adjudicate, and enforce their own regulations in many cases. Normally this would be unconstitutional because of the *separation of powers doctrine*. However, the combination of these powers in one government entity has been reconciled by considering these activities as quasi-powers. That is, although the agencies have legislative, judicial, and executive power, these powers are not as complete as those of the respective branches of government. Thus, such powers are quasi-legislative, quasi-judicial, and quasi-executive and the separation of powers doctrine is not violated.

Rules and regulations established by an administrative agency must be administered within the scope of authority delegated to it by Congress. Although an agency must comply with its own regulations,[32] agency regulations must be consistent with the statute under which they are promulgated. An agency's interpretation of a statute cannot supersede the language chosen by Congress. An executive regulation that defines some general statutory term in a too restrictive or unrealistic manner is invalid.[33] Agency regulations and administrative decisions are subject to judicial review when questions arise as to whether an agency has overstepped its bounds in its interpretation of the law.

§ 702: Right To Review

A person suffering legal wrong because of agency action, or adversely affected or aggrieved by agency action within the meaning of a relevant statute, is entitled to judicial review thereof. An action in a court of the United States seeking relief other than money damages and stating a claim that an agency or an officer or employee thereof acted or failed to act in an official capacity or under color of legal authority shall not be dismissed nor relief therein be denied on the grounds that it is against the United States or that the United States is an indispensable party. The United States may be named as a defendant in any action, and a judgment or decree may be entered against the United States: Provided, That any mandatory or injunctive decree shall specify the Federal officer or officers (by name or by title), and their successors in office, personally responsible for compliance. Nothing herein (1) affects other limitations on judicial review or the power or the duty of the court to dismiss any action or deny relief on any other appropriate legal or equitable ground; or (2) confers authority to grant relief if any other statute that grants consent to suit expressly or impliedly forbids the relief which is sought.[34]

§ 703: Form and Venue of Proceeding

The form of proceeding for judicial review is the special statutory review proceeding relevant to the subject matter in a court specified by statute or, in the absence or inadequacy thereof, any applicable form of legal action. . . . If no special statutory review proceeding is applicable, the action for judicial review may be brought against the United States, the agency by its official title, or the appropriate officer.[35]

§ 704: Actions Reviewable

Agency action made reviewable by statute and final agency action for which there is no other adequate remedy in a court are subject to judicial review. A preliminary, procedural, or intermediate agency action or ruling not directly reviewable is subject to review on the review of the final agency action. Except as otherwise expressly required by statute, agency action otherwise final is final for the purposes of this section. . . .[36]

§ 705: Relief Pending Review

When an agency finds that justice so requires, it may postpone the effective date of action taken by it, pending judicial review. On such conditions as may be required and to the extent necessary to prevent irreparable injury, the reviewing court, including the court to which a case may be taken on appeal from or on application for certiorari or other writ to a reviewing court, may issue all necessary and appropriate process to postpone the effective date of an agency action or to preserve status or rights pending conclusion of the review proceedings.[37]

§ 706: Scope of Review

To the extent necessary . . . the reviewing court shall decide all relevant questions of law, interpret constitutional and statutory provisions, and determine the meaning or applicability of the terms of an agency action. The reviewing court shall

(1) compel agency action unlawfully withheld or unreasonably delayed; and

(2) hold unlawful and set aside agency action, findings, and conclusions found to be

(A) arbitrary, capricious, an abuse of discretion, or otherwise not in accordance with law;

(B) contrary to constitutional right, power, privilege, or immunity;

(C) in excess of statutory jurisdiction, authority, or limitations, or short of statutory right;

(D) without observance of procedure required by law;

(E) unsupported by substantial evidence in a case subject to sections 556 and 557 of this title or otherwise reviewed on the record of an agency hearing provided by statute; or

(F) unwarranted by the facts to the extent that the facts are subject to trial de novo by the reviewing court.

In making the foregoing determinations, the court shall review the whole record or those parts of it cited by a party, and due account shall be taken of the rule of prejudicial error.[38]

Recourse to an administrative agency for resolution of a dispute is generally required prior to seeking judicial review. The Pennsylvania Commonwealth Court held in *Fair Rest Home v. Commonwealth, Department of Health*[39] that the Department of Health was required to hold a hearing before it ordered revocation of a nursing home's operating license. The Department of Health failed in its responsibility when "in a revocation proceeding it does not give careful consideration to its statutorily mandated responsibility to hear testimony."[40]

Regulations and decisions of administrative agencies reviewed by the courts may be upheld, modified, overturned, or reversed and remanded for further proceedings. For example, the owner and operator of a licensed residential care facility brought an action challenging regulations, promulgated by HHS through its Office of Long-Term Care (OLTC), governing administration of medicines in residential care facilities.[41] The owner challenged two OLTC regulations that required:

3. Under no circumstances shall an operator or employee or anyone solicited by an operator or employee be permitted to administer any oral medications, injectable medications, eye drops, ear drops, or topical ointments (both prescription and non-prescription drugs).

4. In addition, any owner and/or operator of a Residential Care Facility who is a licensed nurse who administers any medication to a resident will be in violation of operating an unlicensed nursing home.[42]

The circuit court held that the regulations were invalid and HHS appealed. The Supreme Court, reversing the circuit court's decision, held that the regulations were reasonable in light of the distinctions between residential care facilities and nursing homes.

In reviewing the adoption of regulations by an agency under its informal rule making procedures, a court is limited to considering whether the administrative action was arbitrary, capricious, an abuse of discretion or otherwise not in accordance with the law.

. . . .

A court will not attempt to substitute its judgment for that of the administrative agency.

. . . .

A rule is not invalid simply because it may work a hardship, create inconveniences, or because an evil intended to be regulated does not exist in a particular case.[43]

Although the appellee was not victorious in this particular case, there are many instances where those who challenge the decisions of administrative agencies have been successful.

Besides the many federal agencies regulating health care, each state has its own system of administrative law. Health care organizations, both public and private, that fail to comply with state law, as with federal law, can be subject to civil penalties.

Conflict of Laws

The following case illustrates how federal and state laws may be in conflict. The plaintiff in *Dorsten v. Lapeer County General Hospital*[44] brought an action against a hospital and certain physicians on the medical board alleging wrongful denial of her application for medical staff privileges. The plaintiff asserted claims under the U.S. Code for sex discrimination, violations of the Sherman Antitrust Act, and pendent claims for defamation and interference with advantageous business relations. The plaintiff filed a motion to compel discovery of peer review reports to support her case. The U.S. District Court granted the motion, holding that the *plaintiff was entitled to discovery of peer review reports despite a Michigan state law* purporting to establish an absolute privilege for peer review reports conducted by hospital review boards.

GOVERNMENT ORGANIZATION

The three branches of the federal government are the legislative, executive, and judicial branches (Figure 1–1). Figure 1–2 illustrates a typical example of a state government organization. A vital concept in the constitutional framework of government on both federal and state levels is the separation of powers. Essentially, this principle provides that no one branch of government is clearly dominant over the other two; however, in the exercise of its functions, each may affect and limit the activities, functions, and powers of the others.

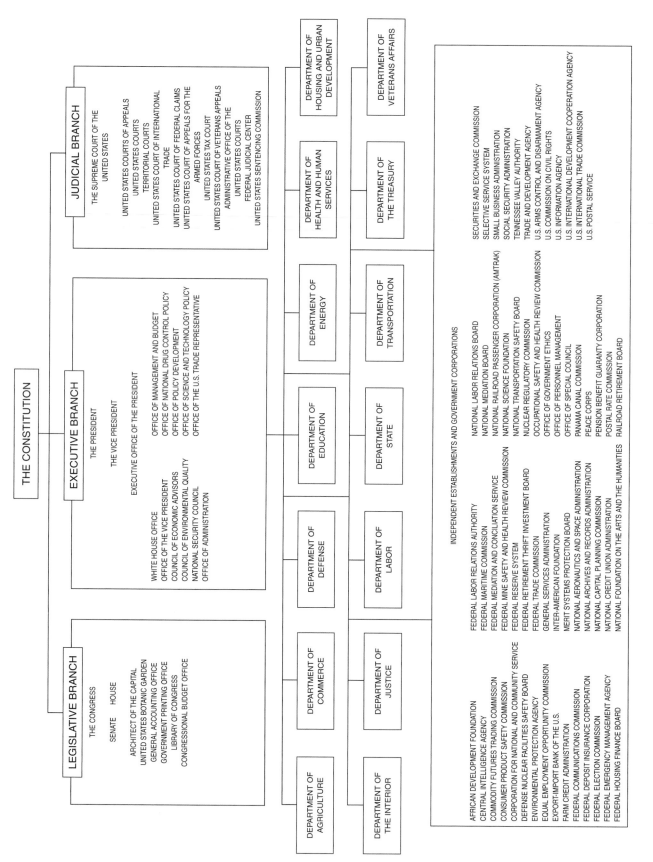

Figure 1-1 The Government of the United States

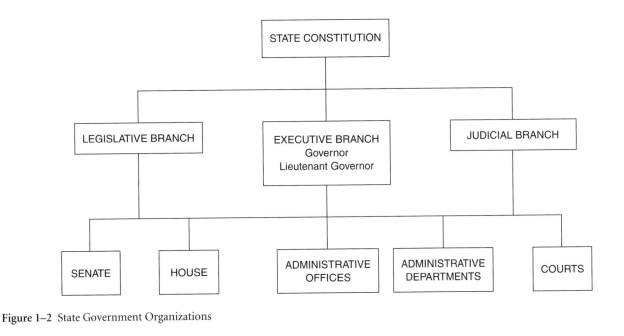

Figure 1–2 State Government Organizations

Legislative Branch

On the federal level, legislative powers are vested in the Congress of the United States, which consists of a Senate and a House of Representatives. The function of the legislative branch is to enact laws that may amend or repeal existing legislation and to create new legislation. It is the legislature's responsibility to determine the nature and extent of the need for new laws and for changes in existing laws. The work of preparing federal legislation is the responsibility of the various committees of both houses of Congress. There are 16 standing committees in the Senate and 19 in the House of Representatives. "The membership of the standing committees of each house is chosen by a vote of the entire body; members of other committees are appointed under the provisions of the measure establishing them."[45]

Legislative proposals are assigned or referred to an appropriate committee for study. The committees conduct investigations and hold hearings where interested persons may present their views regarding proposed legislation. These proceedings provide additional information to assist committee members in their consideration of proposed bills. A bill may be reported out of a committee in its original form, favorably or unfavorably; it may be reported out with recommended amendments; or the bill might be allowed to lie in the committee without action. Some bills eventually reach the full legislative body, where, after consideration and debate, they may be approved or rejected.

The U.S. Congress and all state legislatures are bicameral (consisting of two houses), except for the Nebraska legislature, which is unicameral. Both houses in a bicameral legislature must pass identical versions of a legislative proposal before the legislation can be brought to the chief executive.

Executive Branch

The primary function of the executive branch of government on the federal and state level is to administer and enforce the law. The chief executive, either the President of the United States or the governor of a state, also has a role in the creation of law through the power to approve or veto legislative proposals.

The U.S. Constitution provides that "the executive Power shall be vested in a President of the United States of America. He shall hold his Office during the Term of four Years, . . . together with the Vice President, chosen for the same Term."[46] The President serves as the administrative head of the executive branch of the federal government, which includes 14 executive departments (see Figure 1–1), as well as a variety of agencies, both temporary and permanent.

> The Cabinet, a creation of custom and tradition dating back to George Washington's administration, functions at the pleasure of the President. Its purpose is to advise the President upon any subject on which he requests information (pursuant to Article II, section 2, of the Constitution).[47]

The Cabinet is composed of the 14 executive departments. Each department is responsible for a different area of public affairs, and each enforces the law within its area of responsibility. For example, HHS administers much of the federal health law enacted by Congress. Most state executive branches also are organized on a departmental basis. These departments administer and enforce state law concerning public affairs.

On a state level, the governor serves as the chief executive officer. The responsibilities of a state governor are provided for in the state's constitution. The Massachusetts State Constitution, for example, describes the responsibilities of the governor as

- presenting an annual budget to the state legislature
- recommending new legislation
- vetoing legislation
- appointing and removing department heads
- appointing judicial officers
- acting as Commander-in-Chief of the state's military forces (the Massachusetts National Guard)[48]

Judicial Branch

As I have said in the past, when government bureaus and agencies go awry, which are adjuncts of the legislative or executive branches, the people flee to the third branch, their courts, for solace and justice.[49]
Justice J. Henderson, Supreme Court
of South Dakota

The function of the judicial branch of government is adjudication—resolving disputes in accordance with law. As a practical matter, most disputes or controversies that are covered by legal principles or rules are resolved without resort to the courts.

Alexis de Tocqueville, a foreign observer commenting on the primordial place of the law and the legal profession, stated, "Scarcely any political question arises in the United States that is not resolved, sooner or later, into a judicial question."[50]

It is emphatically the province and duty of the judicial branch to say what the law is. Those who apply the rule to particular cases must of necessity expound and interpret that rule. If two laws conflict with each other, the courts must decide on the operation of each.

So if a law be in opposition to the constitution; if both the law and the constitution apply to a particular case, so that the court must either decide that case conformably to the law, disregarding the constitution; or conformably to the constitution, disregarding the law; the court must determine which of these conflicting rules govern the case. This is the very essence of judicial duty.

•   •   •   •

..., it is apparent, that the framers of the constitution contemplated that instrument, as a rule for the government of courts, as well as of the legislature.

Why otherwise does it direct the judges to take such an oath to support it?[51]

The decision as to which court has jurisdiction—the legal right to hear and rule on a particular case—is determined by such matters as the locality in which each party to a lawsuit resides and the issues of a lawsuit. Each state in the United States provides its own court system, which is created by the state's constitution and/or statutes. The oldest court in the United States, established in 1692, is the Supreme Judicial Court of Massachusetts.[52] Most of the nation's judicial business is reviewed and acted on in state courts. Each state maintains a level of trial courts that have original jurisdiction. This jurisdiction may exclude cases involving claims with damages less than a specified minimum, probate matters (i.e., wills and estates), and workers' compensation. Different states have designated different names for trial courts (e.g., superior, district, circuit, or supreme courts). Also on the trial court level are minor courts such as city, small claims, and justice of the peace courts. States such as Massachusetts have consolidated their minor courts into a statewide court system.

There is at least one appellate court in each state. Many states have an intermediate appellate court between the trial courts and the court of last resort. Where this intermediate court is present, there is a provision for appeal to it, with further review in all but select cases. Because of this format, the highest appellate tribunal is seen as the final arbiter in cases that possess importance in themselves or for the particular state's system of jurisprudence. (Figure 1–3 depicts a typical state court system.)

The trial court of the federal system is the U.S. District Court. There are 89 district courts in the 50 states (the larger states having more than one district court) and one in the District of Columbia. The Commonwealth of Puerto Rico also has a district court with jurisdiction corresponding to that of district courts in the different states. Generally, only one judge is required to sit and decide a case, although certain cases require up to three judges. The federal district courts hear civil, criminal, admiralty, and bankruptcy cases. The Bankruptcy Amendments and Federal Judgeship Act of 1984[53] provided that the bankruptcy judges for each judicial district shall constitute a unit of the district court to be known as the bankruptcy court.[54]

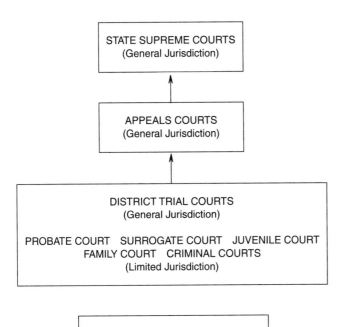

Figure 1–3 State Court System

The U.S. Courts of Appeals (formerly called Circuit Courts of Appeals) are appellate courts for the 11 judicial circuits. Their main purpose is to review cases tried in federal district courts within their respective circuits, but they also possess jurisdiction to review orders of designated administrative agencies and to issue original writs in appropriate cases. These intermediate appellate courts were created to relieve the U.S. Supreme Court of deciding all cases appealed from the federal trial courts.

The Supreme Court, the nation's highest court, is the only federal court created directly by the Constitution.

> The Judicial Power of the United States, shall be vested in one supreme Court, and in such inferior Courts as the Congress may from time to time ordain and establish. The Judges, both of the supreme and inferior Courts, shall hold their offices during good Behaviour, and shall, at stated Times, receive for their Services, a Compensation, which shall not be diminished during their Continuance in Office.[55]

Eight associate justices and one chief justice sit on the Supreme Court. The Court has limited original jurisdiction over the lower federal courts and the highest state courts. In a few situations, an appeal will go directly from a federal or state court to the Supreme Court, but in most cases today, review must be sought through the discretionary writ of certiorari, an appeal petition. In addition to the aforementioned courts, there are special federal courts that have jurisdiction over particular subject matters. The U.S. Court of Claims has jurisdiction over certain claims against the government. The U.S. Court of Appeals for the Federal Circuit has appellate jurisdiction over certain customs and patent matters. The U.S. Customs Court reviews certain administrative decisions by customs officials. Also, there is a U.S. Tax Court and a U.S. Court of Military Appeals. (The federal court system is illustrated in Figure 1–4.)

Separation of Powers

The concept of *separation of powers,* in effect, a system of checks and balances, is illustrated in the relationships among the branches of government with regard to legislation. On the federal level, when a bill creating a statute is enacted by Congress and signed by the President, it becomes law. If the President vetoes a bill, it takes a two-thirds vote of each house of Congress to override the veto. The President also can prevent a bill from becoming law by avoiding any action while Congress is in session. This procedure, known as a pocket veto, can temporarily stop a bill from becoming law and may permanently prevent it from becoming law if later sessions of Congress do not act on it favorably.

A bill that has become law may be declared invalid by the Supreme Court, if the law violates the Constitution. "It is not entirely unworthy of observation, that in declaring what shall be the Supreme law of the land, the Constitution itself is first mentioned; and not the laws of the United States generally, but those only made in pursuance to the Constitution, have that rank."[56]

Even though a Supreme Court decision is final regarding a specific controversy, Congress and the President may generate new, constitutionally sound legislation to replace a law that has been declared unconstitutional. The procedures for amending the Constitution are complex and often time consuming, but they can serve as a way to offset or override a Supreme Court decision.

ADMINISTRATIVE DEPARTMENTS AND AGENCIES

The following sections review a variety of the federal administrative agencies and departments that affect the health care industry. Besides the federal-level departments and agencies described below, many departments and agencies on the state and local levels address many matters also considered on the federal level (e.g., public health, finance, edu-

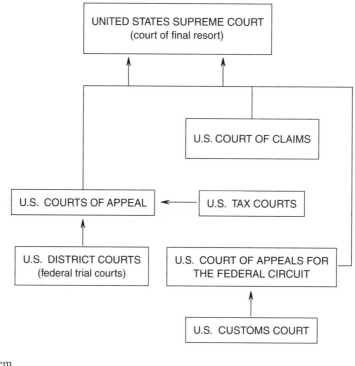

Figure 1–4 Federal Court System

cation, welfare, labor, housing, and other needs and concerns of state residents).

Department of Health and Human Services

HHS (Figure 1–5), a cabinet-level department of the executive branch of the federal government, is concerned with people and is most involved with the nation's human concerns. HHS is responsible for developing and implementing appropriate administrative regulations for carrying out national health and human services policy objectives. It is also the main source of regulations affecting the health care industry. The Secretary of HHS, serving as the Department's administrative head, advises the President with regard to health, welfare, and income security plans, policies, and programs. Within HHS are five operating divisions: (1) the Social Security Administration, (2) HCFA, (3) the Office of Human Development Services, (4) the Public Health Service (PHS), and (5) the Family Support Administration.

HHS also is responsible for many of the programs designed to meet the needs of senior citizens, including Social Security benefits (e.g., retirement, survivors, and disability), Supplemental Security Income (which ensures a minimum monthly income to needy persons and is administered by local Social Security offices), Medicare, Medicaid, and programs under the Older Americans Act (e.g., in-home services such as home health and home delivered meals, and commu-

nity services such as adult day care, transportation, and ombudsman services in long-term care facilities).

Medicare

Medicare is a federally sponsored health insurance program for persons older than 65 years of age and certain disabled persons. It has two complementary parts. Medicare Part A helps cover the costs of inpatient hospital care and, with qualifying preadmission criteria, skilled nursing facility care, home health care, and hospice care. Medicare Part B Medical Insurance helps pay for physicians' services, outpatient hospital services, and so forth.

Medicare is funded through Social Security contributions (Federal Insurance Contributions Act (FICA) payroll taxes), premiums, and general revenue. The program is administered through private contractors, referred to as "intermediaries" under Part A and "carriers" under Part B. The financing of the Medicare program has received much attention by Congress because of its rapidly rising costs and drain on the nation's economy. Even though enormous benefits have been paid out under the Medicare program, the program requires substantial deductibles as well as coinsurance and, unfortunately, limits coverage for long-term care services.

Medicaid

The Medicaid program, Title XIX of the Social Security Act Amendments of 1965, is a government program admin-

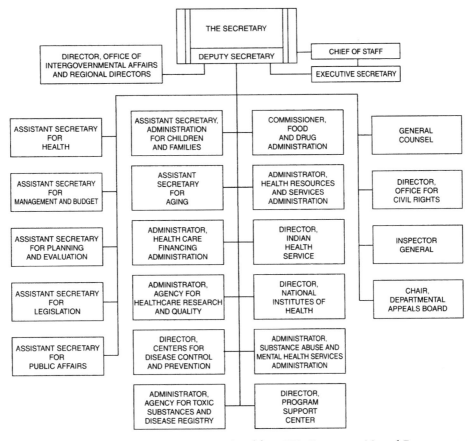

Figure 1–5 Department of Health and Human Services. *Source:* Reprinted from *U.S. Government Manual,* Department of Health and Human Services.

istered by the states providing medical services (both institutional and outpatient) to the medically needy. Federal grants, in the form of matching funds, are issued to those states with qualifying Medicaid programs. In other words, Medicaid is jointly sponsored and financed by the federal government and several states. Medical care for needy persons of all ages is provided under the definition of need established by each state. Each state has set its own criteria for determining eligibility for services under its Medicaid program.

Because Medicaid has been designed for the poor, the elderly must often deplete a major part of their assets before they can become eligible for Medicaid benefits. Medicaid benefits provide for a variety of long-term care services for the elderly that are limited or not provided under Medicare regulations.

Health Care Financing Administration

HCFA was created as a principal operating component of HHS to combine under one administration the oversight of the Medicare and Medicaid programs. HCFA serves approximately 67 million people, or one in four elderly, disabled, and poor Americans through Medicare and Medicaid.

HCFA also is responsible for the related medical care quality assurance provisions of Medicare and Medicaid. Under the Medicare program, HCFA develops and implements policies and procedures and provides guidance related to program recipients, including nursing facilities, hospitals, physicians, and the contractors who process claims, such as Blue Cross and Blue Shield. Under the Medicaid program, HCFA provides grants to the states for medical care services for those who are unable to pay. HCFA also is responsible for working with the states under the Medicaid program to develop approaches toward meeting the needs of the indigent.

Public Health Service

The mission of the PHS is to promote the protection of the nation's physical and mental health. The PHS accomplishes its mission by coordinating with the states in setting and implementing national health policy and pursuing effective intergovernmental relations; generating and upholding cooperative international health-related agreements, policies, and programs; conducting medical and biomedical research; sponsoring and administering programs for the development of health resources, the prevention and control of diseases, and alcohol and drug abuse; providing resources and expertise to the states and other public and private institutions in the planning, direction, and delivery of physical and mental health care services; and enforcing laws to ensure drug safety and protection from impure and unsafe foods, cosmetics, medical devices, and radiation-producing projects.

Within the PHS are smaller agencies responsible for carrying out the purpose of the division and HHS, such as the National Institutes of Health (NIH) and the Food and Drug Administration (FDA). NIH is the principal federal biomedical research agency. It is responsible for conducting, supporting, and promoting biomedical research. The FDA supervises and controls the introduction of drugs, foods, cosmetics, and medical devices into the marketplace and protects society from impure and/or hazardous items. The FDA regulates nearly every consumer product.

> A departmental reorganization order of October 31, 1995, established the Food and Drug Administration (FDA) as an operating division of the Public Health Service. FDA's mission is to ensure that food is safe, pure, and wholesome; human and animal drugs, biological products, and medical devices are safe and effective; and electronic products that emit radiation are safe.[57]

Social Security Administration

The Social Security Administration oversees the nation's social insurance program. Social Security provides retirement income to most citizens older than age 65 years. (Persons aged 62 years may qualify under certain conditions.) The program is funded by contributions from both employers and employees. When the earnings of an employee are reduced or discontinued because of death or disability, Social Security benefits are paid to assist the employee and his or her family.

Federal Council on Aging

The Federal Council on Aging (FCoA) is responsible for advising and assisting the President on matters relating to the special needs of older Americans. Funds appropriated for the council are included in the overall appropriations of HHS. The council

- reviews and evaluates, on a continuing basis, federal policies regarding the elderly and programs and other activities affecting the elderly conducted or assisted by all federal departments and agencies for the purpose of appraising their value and their impact on the lives of older Americans

- serves as a spokesperson on behalf of older Americans by making recommendations to the President, to the Secretary, to the commissioner, and to Congress with respect to federal policies regarding the elderly and federally conducted or assisted programs and other activities relating to or affecting them
- informs the public about the problems and needs of the elderly by collecting and disseminating information, conducting or commissioning studies and publishing the results thereof, and by issuing publications and reports
- provides public forums for discussing and publicizing the problems and needs of the elderly and obtains related information by conducting public hearings, and conducting or sponsoring conferences, workshops, and other such meetings[58]

The council is required by law to prepare an annual report for the President regarding FCoA activities, public meetings, and recommendations. Copies of the FCoA annual report are distributed to members of Congress, governmental and private agencies, institutions of higher education, and others interested in FCoA activities.

National Institute on Aging

The National Institute on Aging (NIA) is one of 13 institutes of the NIH. The NIA is responsible for the conduct and support of biomedical, social, and behavioral research and training related to the aging process and the diseases and other special problems and needs of the aged. The NIA collaborates with other NIH institutes and federal agencies. Research is conducted through interventions and other clinical trials, where appropriate. The priorities of the NIA are as follows:

- Alzheimer's disease and related dementias
- understanding aging
- frailty, disability, and rehabilitation
- health and effective functioning
- long-term care for older people
- special older populations
- training and career development
- international activities (e.g., cross-cultural and cross-national comparative studies involving diverse populations)[59]

Department of Justice

The Department of Justice is responsible for enforcing the laws of the United States. The Attorney General is the administrative head of the department, which consists of various offices, divisions (e.g., the Antitrust, Civil, Criminal, Civil Rights, and Tax Divisions), bureaus (e.g., the Federal Bureau of Investigation and the Drug Enforcement Administration), and boards (e.g., the Executive Office for Immigration Review). In addition to its prosecuting function, the Antitrust Division of the Department of Justice produces general antitrust guidelines including health care and merger guidelines.

Presently the Department of Justice has become more concerned with health care fraud, which affects every type of health care provider. As a result, investigating and prosecuting health care fraud are among the department's highest priorities. Because health care fraud and abuse cost the nation millions of dollars annually and degrade the quality of the health care system, many Americans are deprived of obtaining the quality health care they need.

Department of Labor

The Department of Labor is the ninth executive department of the executive branch of government. The Secretary of Labor advises the President on labor policies and issues. The functions of the Department of Labor are to

> foster, promote, and develop the welfare of wage earners of the United States, to improve working conditions, and to advance opportunities for profitable employment. In carrying out this mission, the department administers a variety of federal labor laws guaranteeing workers' rights to safe and healthful working conditions, a minimum hourly wage and overtime pay, freedom from employment discrimination, unemployment insurance, and workers' compensation. The department also protects workers' pension rights; provides for job

training programs; helps workers find jobs; works to strengthen free collective bargaining; and keeps track of changes in employment prices and other national economic measurements. As the department seeks to assist all Americans who need and want to work, special efforts are made to meet the unique job market problems of older workers, youths, minority group members, women, the handicapped, and other groups.[60]

Within the Department of Labor are various agencies responsible for carrying out the purpose of the department (e.g., Occupational Safety and Health Administration).

National Labor Relations Board

The NLRB is an agency, independent of the Department of Labor, responsible for preventing and remedying unfair labor practices by employers and labor organizations or their agents. It also conducts secret ballot elections among employees in appropriate collective bargaining units to determine whether they desire to be represented by a labor organization and among employees under union-shop agreements to determine whether they wish to revoke their union's authority.

The general counsel of the NLRB has final authority to investigate charges of unfair labor practices, issue complaints, and prosecute such complaints before the NLRB. There are regional directors, under the direction of the general counsel, who are responsible for processing representation, unfair labor practice, and jurisdictional dispute cases.

CHAPTER REVIEW

1. A law is a general rule of conduct that is enforced by the government. When a law is violated, the government imposes a penalty.
   - *Public laws* deal with the relationships between individuals and the government. Criminal law is a segment of public law.
   - *Private laws* deal with relationships among individuals. Two types of private law are tort and contract actions. In a tort action, one person holds that wrongful conduct caused another person harm, and the victim seeks compensation. Contract action deals with the accusation of a breach of agreement between two parties. Compensation can come in the form of remuneration or performance of the contracted obligation.
2. Common law is derived from judicial decisions. U.S. common law has as its roots the English common-law system. The first English royal court was established in A.D. 1178. There were few written laws at the time and a collection of principles evolved from the decisions of the court. These principles, known as "common law," were used to decide subsequent cases. During the colonial period, the United States based its law on English common law, but states had the authority to modify their legal systems. As a result, there is no uniform system of common law among the states.
3. A common-law principle established in a higher state court must be followed by the lower courts in that state. However, trial courts or those otherwise on equal footing are not bound by the decisions of other trial courts, and a principle established in one state does not set precedent within another state. Common-law principles can be modi-

fied, overturned, abrogated, or created by new court decisions. These changes help the law keep pace with changes in society.

4. Statutory law is a written law that emanates from a legislative body. Using express words, a statute can abolish any rule of common law. The Constitution is the highest level of enacted law; it takes precedence over the constitutions and laws of specific states and local jurisdictions.

5. Statutory law can be amended, repealed, or expanded by the legislature. States and local jurisdictions can only enact and enforce laws that do no conflict with federal laws.

6. Administrative law is public law issued by administrative agencies to administer the enacted laws of the federal and state governments. This branch of law controls the administrative operations of the government.

7. Administrative agencies implement and administer the administrative law. The rules and regulations established by an agency must be administered within the scope of the authority delegated to the agency by Congress. Agency regulations and decisions can be subject to judicial review. The effective date of an action taken by an agency may be postponed pending judicial review.

8. Each state has its own system of administrative law. Health care organizations that fail to comply with state or federal law may be subject to civil penalties.

9. The concept of separation of powers provides that no one branch of the government—legislative, executive, or judicial—will be clearly dominant over the other two. The legislative branch, composed of the House of Representatives and the Senate, both enacts laws that can amend or repeal existing legislation and creates new legislation. The executive branch administers and enforces the law. The chief executive can approve or veto legislative proposals. The judicial branch resolves disputes in accordance with the law.

10. The Department of Health and Human Services (HHS) develops and implements administrative regulations for carrying out national health and human services policy objectives. It is the main source of regulations that affect the health care industry. Its five operating divisions include (1) the Social Security Administration, (2) the Health Care Financing Administration, (3) the Office of Human Development Services, (4) the Public Health Service (which includes the National Institutes of Health and the Food and Drug Administration), and (5) the Family Support Administration.

11. The Department of Justice enforces U.S. law and has, as its head, the Attorney General.

12. The Department of Labor fosters, promotes, and develops the welfare of wage earners, improves working conditions, and advances opportunities for profitable employment. The Secretary of Labor advises the President on labor policies and issues.

REVIEW QUESTIONS

1. Define the term *law* and describe the sources from which law is derived.
2. Describe and contrast the legal terms *res judicata* and *stare decisis*.
3. Describe the function of each branch of government.
4. What is the meaning of *separation of powers*?
5. What is the function of an administrative agency?
6. Generally, how does the legal system address the violations of a party's rights?
7. Describe the responsibilities of HHS.

NOTES

1. B. Schwartz, The Law in America 1 (1974).
2. *Marbury v. Madison,* 5 U.S. (Cranch) 137, 163 (1803).
3. *Cruzan v. Director of the Mo. Dept. of Health,* 496 U.S. 261, 110 S.Ct. 2841 (1990).
4. A.K.R. Kiralfy, Potter's Historical Introduction to English Law 9 (1962).
5. J. Reeves, History of the English Law 2 (1814).
6. *Id.*
7. G.W. Keeton, English Law 70 (1974).
8. *Id.*
9. *Id.*
10. *Id.*
11. *Id.*
12. Kiralfy, *supra note* 3, at 9–10.
13. Keeton, *supra note* 6, at 70.
14. Schwartz, *supra note* 1, at 29.

15. *Id.*

16. *Id.* at 30–31.

17. L. FRIEDMAN, A HISTORY OF AMERICAN LAW 92 (1985).

18. SCHWARTZ, *supra* note 1, at 51.

19. BLACK'S LAW DICTIONARY 1305 (6th. ed. 1990).

20. U.S. DEP'T OF HEALTH & HUMAN SERVS., TASK FORCE ON MEDICAL LIABILITY AND MALPRACTICE 3 (1987).

21. *Id.*

22. Zinman, *Study Finds Hospitals "Harm" Some,* NEWSDAY, March 1, 1990, at 17.

23. The Robert Wood Johnson Foundation, *The Tort System for Medical Malpractice: How Well Does It Work, What Are the Alternatives?,* ABRIDGE, Spring 1991, at 2.

24. The Robert Wood Johnson Foundation, *Negligent Medical Care: What Is It, Where Is It, and How Widespread Is It?,* ABRIDGE, Spring 1991, at 6.

25. D. Sharp, *Errors Renew the Call for Doctor Review,* USA TODAY, March 27, 1995, at 2.

26. K. Painter, *Breast Cancer Top Cause of Malpractice Complaints,* USA TODAY, June 15, 1996, at 1.

27. The White House, Office of the Press Secretary, *Establishment of the Quality Interagency Coordination Task Force,* March 13, 1998.

28. U.S. CONST. art. VI, § 1, cl. 2.

29. 5 U.S.C.S. §§ 500–576 (Law. Co-op. 1989).

30. An "agency means each authority of the Government of the United States, . . . but does not include (A) the Congress; the Courts of the United States; . . ." 5 U.S.C.S. § 551(1) (Law. Co-op. 1989).

31. 5 U.S.C.S. § 551 (Law. Co-op. 1989).

32. Lipp v. United States, 181 Ct. Cl. 355 (1967).

33. Tacker v. United States, 178 Ct. Cl. 56 (1976).

34. 5 U.S.C.S. § 702 (Law. Co-op. 1989).

35. 5 U.S.C.S. § 703 (Law. Co-op. 1989).

36. 5 U.S.C.S. § 704 (Law. Co-op. 1989).

37. 5 U.S.C.S. § 705 (Law. Co-op. 1989).

38. 5 U.S.C.S. § 706 (Law. Co-op. 1989).

39. 401 A.2d 872 (Pa. Commw. Ct. 1979).

40. *Id.* at 873.

41. Department of Human Serv. v. Berry, 764 S.W.2d 437 (Ark.1989).

42. *Id.* at 439.

43. *Id.* at 438.

44. 88 F.R.D. 583 (E.D. Mich. 1980).

45. OFFICE OF THE FEDERAL REGISTER, NATIONAL ARCHIVES AND RECORDS ADMINISTRATION, THE UNITED STATES GOVERNMENT MANUAL 2000/2001 29 (2000) [hereinafter MANUAL].

46. U.S. CONST. art. II, §1, cl. 1.

47. MANUAL, *supra note* 45, at 87.

48. D. LEVITAN, YOUR MASSACHUSETTS GOVERNMENT 14 (10th ed. 1984).

49. Heritage of Yankton, Inc. v. South Dakota Dep't of Health, 432 N.W.2d 68, 77 (S.D. 1988).

50. SCHWARTZ, *supra* note 1, at 15.

51. Marbury v. Madison, 5 U.S. (Cranch) 137, 177–180 (1803).

52. LEVITAN, *supra* note 46, at 32.

53. 28 U.S.C. § 151.

54. MANUAL, *supra* note 45, at 73.

55. U.S. CONST. art. III, § 1.

56. Marbury v. Madison, 5 U.S. (Cranch) 137, 180 (1803).

57. MANUAL, *supra* note 45, at 231.

58. Fed. Council on Aging, Ann. Rep. To the President, 1989, at 12.

59. Nat'l Inst. on Aging, Ann. Rep. To the President, 1988, at 17.

60. MANUAL, *supra* note 45, at 284–285.

It's Your Gavel...

THE COURT WAS APPALLED

The plaintiff, while in the custody of the defendant-penal institution, alleged that because the defendant's employees failed to timely diagnose her breast cancer, her right breast had to be removed. The defendant contended that even if its employees were negligent, the plaintiff's cancer was so far developed when discovered that it would nevertheless have required removal of her breast.[1]

Pursuant to the defendant's policy of medically evaluating all new inmates, on May 26, 1989, Dr. Evans gave the plaintiff a medical examination. He testified that his physical evaluation included an examination of the plaintiff's breasts. However, *he stated that his examination was very cursory.*

The day following her examination, the plaintiff examined her own breasts. At that time she discovered a lump in her right breast, which she characterized as being about the size of a pea. The plaintiff then sought an additional medical evaluation at the defendant's medical clinic. Testimony indicated that fewer than half of the inmates who sign the clinic list are actually seen by medical personnel the next day. Also, those not examined on the day for which the list is signed are given no preference in being examined on the following day. In fact, their names are simply deleted from the daily list and their only recourse is to continually sign the list until they are examined.

The preponderance of evidence indicated that after May 27, 1989, the plaintiff constantly signed the clinic list and listed the reason for the requested treatment. Medical personnel did not see the plaintiff until June 21, 1989.

A nurse examined the plaintiff on June 21, 1989. The nurse noted in her nursing notes that the plaintiff had a "moderate large mass in right breast." The nurse recognized that the proper procedure was to measure such a mass but she testified that this was impossible because no measuring device was available. The missing measuring device to which she alluded was a simple ruler. The nurse concluded that Dr. Evans should again examine the plaintiff.

On June 28, 1989, Dr. Evans again examined the plaintiff. He recorded in the progress notes that the plaintiff had "a mass on her right wrist. Will send her to hospital and give her Benadryl for allergy she has."[2] Dr. Evans meant to write "breast" not "wrist." He again failed to measure the size of the mass on the plaintiff's breast.

The plaintiff was transferred to the Franklin County Prerelease Center (FCPR) on September 28, 1989. On September 30, 1989, a nurse at FCPR examined the plaintiff; the nurse recorded that the plaintiff had a "golf ball"-sized lump in her right breast.

The plaintiff was transported to the hospital on October 27, 1989, where Dr. Walker treated her.

The plaintiff received a mammogram examination, which indicated that the tumor was probably malignant. This diagnosis was confirmed by a biopsy performed on November 9, 1989. The plaintiff was released from confinement on November 13, 1989.

On November 16, 1989, Dr. Lidsky, a surgeon, examined the plaintiff. Dr. Lidsky noted the existence of the lump in the plaintiff's breast and determined that the size of the mass was approximately four to five centimeters and somewhat fixed. He performed a modified radical mastectomy upon the plaintiff's right breast, by which nearly the plaintiff's entire right breast was removed.

What is your verdict?

INTRODUCTION

Every instance of a man's suffering the penalty of the law, is an instance of the failure of that penalty in effecting its purpose, which is to deter from transgression.

Whately

This chapter introduces the health care professional to the study of tort law. A *tort* is a civil wrong, other than a breach of contract, committed against a person or property (real or personal) for which a court provides a remedy in the form of an action for damages. Tort actions touch an individual both on a personal and a professional level, which is why those involved in the health care field should be armed with the knowledge necessary to make them aware of their rights and responsibilities.

The basic objectives of tort law are preservation of peace—between individuals by providing a substitute for retaliation; culpability—to find fault for wrongdoing; deterrence—to discourage the wrongdoer (tort-feasor) from committing future torts; and compensation—to indemnify the injured person(s) of wrongdoing.

Adverse medical outcomes often result in some financial damage. The effect of finding fault by the court is to determine who shall bear the cost of an unfavorable outcome—the provider or the recipient of health care. To avoid cost, the plaintiff must prove the negligence of the provider. Conversely, the provider fights to avoid fault determination. Underlying this adversarial proceeding is the assumption that if the provider is forced to bear the cost, then it will discourage further acts of negligence by the provider and by other similarly situated providers of health care. Although "professional liability insurance insulates the individual physician's wallet from the actual cost of claims,"[3] the fear is ever present that the monetary award may exceed the amount of the insurance coverage.

The three basic categories of tort law are (1) negligent torts; (2) intentional torts; and (3) torts where strict liability is assessed regardless of fault (e.g., against manufacturers of defective products).

Although most incidents that raise issues of liability concern harm allegedly resulting from negligence, a person also may be liable for intentional wrongs. Intentional tortious conduct (conduct implying civil wrong) that may arise in the context of patient care includes assault, battery, false imprisonment, invasion of privacy, and infliction of mental distress. Liability, irrespective of fault, may be imposed in certain situations in which the activity, regardless of intentions or negligence, is so dangerous to others that public policy demands absolute responsibility on the part of the tort-feasor.

INTENTIONAL AND NEGLIGENT WRONGDOING

There are two main differences between intentional and negligent wrongs. The first is intent, which is present in intentional but not in negligent wrongs. For a tort to be considered intentional, not only must the act be committed intentionally, but also the wrongdoer must realize to a substantial certainty that harm would result. The second difference is less obvious. An intentional wrong always involves a willful act that violates another's interests; a negligent wrong may or may not involve committing an act at all. It simply may be the failure to act when there is a legal duty to act.

NEGLIGENCE

Negligence is a tort—a civil or personal wrong. It is the unintentional commission or omission of an act that a reasonably prudent person would or would not do under given circumstances.

Commission of an act would include, for example,

- administering the wrong medication
- administering the wrong dosage of a medication
- administering medication to the wrong patient
- performing a surgical procedure without patient consent
- performing a surgical procedure on the wrong patient
- surgically removing the wrong body part
- failing to assess and reassess a patient's nutritional needs

Omission of an act would include, for example,

- failing to administer medications
- failing to order diagnostic tests
- failing to follow up on abnormal test results

Negligence is a form of conduct caused by heedlessness or carelessness that constitutes a departure from the standard of care generally imposed on reasonable members of society. Negligence can occur

- where one has considered the consequences of an act and has exercised his or her best possible judgment
- where one fails to guard against a risk that should be appreciated
- where one engages in certain behavior expected to involve unreasonable danger to others

Malpractice is the negligence or carelessness of a professional person (e.g., a nurse, pharmacist, physician, or accountant). Criminal negligence is the reckless disregard for the safety of another (e.g., willful indifference to an injury that could follow an act).

Forms of Negligence

The basic forms of negligence are

- *malfeasance*—execution of an unlawful or improper act (e.g., performing an abortion in the third trimester when such is prohibited by state law)
- *misfeasance*—improper performance of an act, resulting in injury to another (e.g., wrong-sided surgery)
- *nonfeasance*—failure to act, when there is a duty to act, as a reasonably prudent person would in similar circumstances (e.g., failing to order diagnostic tests or prescribe medications that should have been ordered or prescribed under the circumstances)

Degrees of Negligence

There are basically two degrees of negligence:

1. *ordinary negligence*—failure to do what a reasonably prudent person would or would not do, under the circumstances of the act or omission in question
2. *gross negligence*—intentional or wanton omission of care that would be proper to provide or the doing of that which would be improper to do

Elements of Negligence

The four elements that must be present in order for a plaintiff to recover damages caused by negligence are

1. *duty to care*
   – There is an obligation to conform to a recognized standard of care.
2. *breach of duty*
   – There must be a deviation from a recognized standard of care.
   – There must be a failure to adhere to an obligation.
3. *injury*
   – Actual damages must be established.
   – If there is no injury, then no damages are due.
4. *causation*
   – The act or conduct in departing from the recognized standard of care must be the cause of the plaintiff's injury.
   – The injury was caused by a breach of duty.
   – The injury was foreseeable.

All four elements must be present in order for a plaintiff to recover for damages suffered as a result of a negligent act. When the four elements of negligence have been proven, the plaintiff is said to have presented a *prima facie* case of negligence, which will enable the plaintiff to prevail in his or her lawsuit.

The burden of proof in a negligence case is not as great as the "beyond a reasonable doubt" standard borne by a prosecutor in a criminal case. Therefore, if a plaintiff supports his or her negligence claim with evidence sufficient to outweigh the evidence presented by the defendant, the defendant will be found liable for the negligent act. The defendant then will be ordered by the court, in accordance with the verdict rendered by the jury or by the court itself, to compensate the plaintiff monetarily for the harm that the plaintiff suffered. The purpose of compensatory damages is to put the injured party in the same financial situation he or she was in before he or she suffered harm. Punitive damages can be awarded to the plaintiff, for pain and suffering caused by conduct that would be considered egregious.

Duty To Use Due Care

The first requirement in establishing negligence is for the plaintiff to prove the existence of a legal relationship between him- or herself and the defendant. *Duty* is defined as a legal obligation of care, performance, or observance imposed on one to safeguard the rights of others. This duty may arise from a special relationship such as that between a physician and a patient. The existence of this relationship implies that a physician–patient relationship was in effect at the time an alleged injury occurred. The duty to care can arise from a simple telephone conversation. It can arise out of a physician's voluntary act of assuming the care of a patient. Duty also can be established by statute or contract between the plaintiff and the defendant.

In *O'Neill v. Montefiore Hospital*,[4] the duty owed to a patient was clear. The plaintiff sought recovery against the hospital for failure to render necessary emergency treatment and against a physician for his failure and refusal to treat her spouse. The deceased, Mr. O'Neill, while experiencing pains in his chest and arms, had walked with his wife to the hospital at 5 A.M. He claimed that he was a member of the Hospital Insurance Plan (HIP). The emergency department nurse stated that the hospital had no connection with HIP and did not take HIP patients. After reflecting a few moments, the nurse indicated that she would try to get a HIP physician for O'Neill. The nurse called Dr. Graig, a HIP physician, and explained the patient's symptoms. She then handed the phone to O'Neill, who said, "Well, I could be dead by 8 o'clock." O'Neill concluded his phone conversation and spoke to the nurse, indicating that he had been told to go home and come back when HIP was open. Mrs. O'Neill asked that a physician see her husband. The nurse again requested that they return at 8 o'clock. O'Neill again commented that he could be dead by 8 o'clock. He then left with his wife to return home, pausing occasionally to catch his breath. On arriving at home, O'Neill began to undress with the assistance of his wife, and he suddenly fell to the floor and died. Dr. Graig claimed that he had offered to come to the emergency department, but that O'Neill had said that he would wait and see another HIP physician at 8 o'clock that morning.

The New York Supreme Court for Bronx County, New York, entered a judgment dismissing the complaint, and the plaintiff appealed. The New York Supreme Court, Appellate Division, reversed the lower court and held that a physician who undertakes to examine or treat a patient and then abandons him or her can be held liable for malpractice. The proof of the record in this case indicated that the physician undertook to diagnose the ailments of the deceased by telephone, thus establishing at least the first element of negligence—duty to use due care. The finding of the trial court was reversed, and a new trial was ordered.

The surviving parents in *Hastings v. Baton Rouge Hospital*[5] brought a medical malpractice action for the wrongful death of their 19-year-old son. The action was brought against the hospital; the emergency department physician, Dr. Gerdes; and the thoracic surgeon on call, Dr. McCool. The patient had been brought to the emergency department at 11:56 P.M. because of two stab wounds and weak vital signs. Gerdes decided that a thoracotomy had to be performed. He was not qualified to perform the surgery and called McCool, who was on call that evening for thoracic surgery. Gerdes described the patient's condition, indicating he had been stabbed in a major blood vessel. At trial, McCool claimed that he did not recall Gerdes saying that a major blood vessel could be involved. McCool asked Gerdes to transfer the patient to the Earl K. Long Hospital. Gerdes said, "I can't transfer this patient." McCool replied, "No. Transfer him." Nurse Kelly, an emergency department nurse on duty, was not comfortable with the decision to transfer the patient and offered to accompany him in the ambulance. Gerdes reexamined the patient, who exhibited marginal vital signs, was restless, and was draining blood from his chest. The ambulance service was called at 1:03 A.M., and by 1:30 A.M. the patient had been placed in the ambulance for transfer. The patient began to fight wildly, the chest tube came out, and the bleeding increased. An attempt to revive him from a cardiac arrest was futile, and the patient died after having been moved back to the emergency department. The patient virtually bled to death.

The duty to care in this case cannot be reasonably disputed. Louisiana, by statute, imposes a duty on hospitals licensed in Louisiana to make emergency services available to all persons residing in the state regardless of insurance coverage or economic status. The hospital's own bylaws provided that no patient should be transferred without due consideration for his or her condition and the facilities existing for his or her care. The Nineteenth Judicial District Court directed a verdict for the defendants, and the plaintiffs appealed. The court of appeals affirmed the district court's decision. On further appeal, the Louisiana Supreme Court held that the evidence presented to the jury could indicate the defendants were negligent in their treatment of the victim. The findings of the lower courts were reversed, and the case was remanded for trial.

Some duties are created by statute, which occurs when a statute specifies a particular standard that must be met.

Many such standards are created by administrative agencies under the provisions of a statute. For liability to be established, based on a defendant's failure to follow the standard of care outlined by statute, the following elements must be present: (1) the defendant must have been within the specified class of persons outlined in the statute; (2) the plaintiff must have been injured in a way that the statute was designed to prevent; and (3) the plaintiff must show that the injury would not have occurred if the statute had not been violated.

Duties can be created by an institution through its internal rules and regulations. The courts hold that such internal rules are indicative of the organization's knowledge of the proper procedure to follow and, hence, create a duty. Thus, if an institutional employee fails to follow an operating rule of that institution and, as a result, a patient is injured, then the employee who violated the rule would be considered negligent.

Texas courts recognize that an employer has a duty to hire competent employees, especially if they are engaged in an occupation that could be hazardous to life and limb and requires skilled or experienced persons. For example, the appellant in *Deerings West Nursing Center v. Scott*[6] was found to have negligently hired an incompetent employee that it knew or should have known was incompetent, thereby causing unreasonable risk of harm to others. In this case, an 80-year-old visitor had gone to Deerings to visit her infirm older brother. She had a habit of visiting at all hours, even though it was contended that she was asked to restrict her visitation to certain hours. During one visit, Nurse Hopper, a six-foot-four-inch male employee of Deerings, confronted the visitor to prevent her from visiting. The visitor recalled that: "He was so angry and his face just stared with—looked like hate to me. He looked like—He looked like, I might have said, crazy man at one time." She stated that upon his approach she had thrown up her hands to protect her face but he hit her on the chin, slapped her down on the concrete floor and got on top of her, pinning her to the floor.

Hopper testified that he was hired sight unseen over the telephone by the Deerings' Director of Nursing. Even though the following day he went to the nursing facility to complete an application, he still maintained that he was hired over the phone. In his application he falsely stated that he was a Texas licensed vocational nurse (LVN). Additionally, he claimed that he had never been convicted of a crime. In reality, he had been previously employed by a bar, was not a LVN, and had committed more than 56 criminal offenses of theft, and was on probation at the time of his testimony.

The trial court had awarded the plaintiff a judgment of $35,000 for actual damages and $200,000 in punitive damages. The Court of Appeals held that there was evidence supporting findings that the employee's failure to obtain a nursing license was the proximate cause of the visitor's damages and that the hiring was negligent. It also was found to be a heedless and reckless disregard of the rights of others.

It is common knowledge that the bleakness and rigors of old age, drugs, and the diseases of senility can cause people to become confused . . . and cantankerous. It is predictable that elderly patients will be visited by elderly friends and family. It is reasonable to anticipate that a man of proven moral baseness would be more likely to commit a morally base act on an 80-year-old woman. Fifty-six convictions for theft is some evidence of mental aberration. Hopper was employed not only to administer medicine but also to contend with the sometimes erratic behavior of the decrepit. The investigative process necessary to the procurement of a Texas nursing license would have precluded the licensing of Hopper. In the hiring of an unlicensed and potentially mentally and morally unfit nurse, it is reasonable to anticipate that an injury would result as a natural and probable consequence of that negligent hiring.[7]

The duty of care in this case is clear. The appellant violated the very purpose of Texas licensing statutes by failing to validate whether or not Hopper had a current LVN license. The appellant then placed him in a position of authority and not only allowed him to dispense drugs, but also made him a shift supervisor. This negligence eventually resulted in the inexcusable assault on an elderly woman.

A duty may be created by a contract. Where there is a contractual duty of care and an injury occurs, patients have a choice of theories to use to determine which type of lawsuit to pursue—breach of contract or tort. In some jurisdictions, the statute of limitations for breach of contract is longer than for negligence actions. In such cases, the existence of a contractual duty of care may extend the liability of a health care facility for several years.

Standard of Care

A duty of care carries with it a corresponding responsibility not only to provide care, but also to provide it in an acceptable manner. The plaintiff must show that the defendant failed to meet the prevailing standard of care. The fact that an injury is suffered is not sufficient for imposing liability without proof that the defendant deviated from the practice of competent members of his or her profession.

Duty requires that all health care workers conform to a specific standard of care to protect others. A nurse, for example, who assumes the care of a patient has the duty to exercise that degree of skill, care, and knowledge ordinarily possessed and exercised by other nurses in the care and treatment of the patient. A nurse must be reasonable in the exercise of professional judgment as to the care rendered. Reasonable judgment must not represent a departure from the requirements of accepted nursing practice.

Duty is often difficult to establish. "In common law lies the concept that although one individual need do nothing to rescue another from peril not of that individual's own making, nevertheless, a person who undertakes to do an act must do it with reasonable care."[8] Once a duty to care has been established the standard required of the person owing the duty to avoid potential liability must be determined.[9]

The standard of care describes what conduct is expected of an individual in a given situation. The general standard of care that must be exercised is that which a reasonably prudent person would do acting under the same or similar circumstances.

> The standard of conduct of a reasonable person may be: (a) established by a legislative enactment or administrative regulation which so provides, (b) adopted by the court from a legislative enactment or an administrative regulation which does not so provide, or (c) established by judicial decision, or, (d) applied to the facts of the case by the trial judge or jury, if there is no such enactment, regulation or decision.[10]

The "reasonably prudent person" concept describes a nonexistent, hypothetical person who is put forward as the community ideal of what would be considered reasonable behavior. It is a measuring stick representing the conduct of the average person in the community, under the circumstances facing the defendant at the time of the alleged negligence. The reasonableness of conduct is judged in light of the circumstances apparent at the time of injury and by reference to different characteristics of the actor (e.g., age, sex, physical condition, education, knowledge, training, mental capacity).

> Persons who are known to have mental or physical disabilities, or who are young and inexperienced, are entitled to a degree of care exercised by others proportioned to their incapacity to protect themselves. They are not to be accorded the same treatment as persons of mature years and of sound mentality. No general rule can be articulated, for the standard of care in situations involving victims having these characteristics requires that a determination of what constitutes "reasonable care" be made in each individual case, taking into consideration the victim's known mental and physical condition. Generally the greater the disability, the greater is the degree of care required. The rationale for this principle of law is that natural justice requires that greater consideration and care are due to persons known to be unable to care for themselves than to those who are fully able to do so.[11]

The actual performance of an individual in a given situation will be measured against what a reasonably prudent person would or would not have done. Deviation from the standard of care will constitute negligence if there are resulting damages.

Traditionally, in determining how a reasonably prudent person should perform in a particular situation, courts use the services of an expert witness to testify regarding the professional standard of care required in the same or similar communities. The plaintiff's expert witness in *Stogsdill v. Manor Convalescent Home, Inc., and Hiatt, MD*,[12] who practiced about 12 miles from the convalescent home where the defendant physician treated the plaintiff, was found competent to testify. The defendant objected, stating the expert never practiced in the county where the malpractice occurred. The court overruled this objection on the grounds that locality cannot be construed so narrowly as to be determined by county lines.

Expert testimony generally is necessary because the jury is not trained or qualified to determine what the reasonably prudent professional's standard of care would be under similar circumstances. Essentially, the expert testifies to aid the judge and the jury by providing a measure for properly assessing the actual conduct required of the professional. "Expert testimony is required to establish the specific standard of care for professionals, and to assist in the determination of a professional's conformity to the relevant standard."[13]

To prove a *prima facie* case of malpractice, the plaintiff must produce expert testimony to establish the recognized standard of care attributable to physicians under like circumstances and that the physician whose conduct is being challenged departed from the requisite standard when the patient was treated. Most states hold those with special skills (e.g., physicians, nurses, and dentists) to a standard of care that is reasonable in the light of their special abilities and knowledge.

The courts have been moving away from reliance on a community standard and have applied an "industry" or "national" standard. This trend has developed as a result of a more reasonable belief that the standard of care should not vary with the locale where an individual receives care. The conduct of health care professionals and health care organizations is generally compared with what is considered reasonable in the industry in view of current professional practice. It would be unreasonable for any one health care facility and/or health care professional to set the standard simply because there is no local basis for comparison. Geographical proximity rules have increasingly given way to a national standard, with the standard in the professional's general locality becoming a factor in determining whether the professional has exercised that degree of care expected of the average practitioner in the class to which he or she belongs.[14]

The ever-evolving advances in medicine, mass communications, the availability of medical specialists, the development of continuing education programs, and the broadening scope of governmental regulations continue to raise the standard of care required of health care professionals and health care organizations. Many courts have adopted the view that the practice of medicine should be national in scope. In *Dickinson v. Mailliard*, the court stated:

> Hospitals must now be licensed and accredited. They are subject to statutory regulation. In order to obtain approval they must meet certain standard requirements. . . . It is no longer justifiable, if indeed it ever was, to limit a hospital's liability to that degree of care which is customarily practiced in its own community. . . . [M]any communities have only one hospital. Adherence to such a rule, then, means the hospital whose conduct is assailed, is to be measured only by standards which it has set for itself.[15]

The Court of Appeals of Maryland, in *Shilkret v. Annapolis Emergency Hospital Association*, stated:

> [A] hospital is required to use that degree of care and skill which is expected of a reasonably competent hospital in the same or similar circumstances. As in cases brought against physicians, advances in the profession, availability of special facilities and specialists, together with all other relevant considerations, are to be taken into account.[16]

Evidence of the standard of care applicable to professional activities may be found in a variety of documents, such as regulations of governmental agencies (e.g., state licensure laws) and standards established by private organizations, such as the Joint Commission on Accreditation of Healthcare Organizations. The personnel of a health care organization, subject to such regulations or standards, are responsible for meeting the standards of care prescribed. A professional's failure to do so provides a basis for finding the professional and the facility liable for negligence.

Although the courts tend to favor a broader standard of care, the community standard can be extremely important in any given situation.

> Assume for a moment that the question is whether a doctor in a remote area of Alaska has placed patients at an unnecessarily high risk by receiving telephone inquiries from nurses in Eskimo villages at even more remote areas and attempting to prescribe by phone. Clearly, such conduct would violate the standard of care in San Francisco, and in San Francisco, would place his patients in an "unnecessarily" high-risk situation. For the doctor in Alaska, on the other hand, this

method of consultation may be the only possible one, and thus not at all unnecessary or a gross and flagrant violation.[17]

The parents in *Wickliffe v. Sunrise Hospital*[18] sued the hospital for the wrongful death of their teenage daughter who suffered respiratory arrest while recovering from surgery. The Nevada Supreme Court held that the level of care to which the hospital must conform is a nationwide standard. The hospital's level of care is no longer subject to narrow geographic limitations under the so-called locality rule; rather, the hospital must meet a nationwide standard.

Further, the Georgia Court of Appeals in *Hodges v. Effingham*[19] held that application of the locality rule was erroneous in an action against the hospital. The alleged failure of nurses to take an accurate medical history of the patient's serious condition and convey the information to the physician drew into question the professional judgment of the nurses. The jury should have been instructed as to the general standard of nursing required.

> There are no degrees of care in fixing responsibility for negligence, but the standard is always that care which a prudent person should use under like circumstances. The duty to exercise reasonable care is a standard designed to protect a society's members from unreasonable exposure to potentially injurious hazards; negligence is conduct that falls short of the reasonable care standard. Perfection of conduct is humanly impossible, however, and the law does not exact an unreasonable amount of care from anyone.[20]

Specialists in particular are held to a higher standard of care than nonspecialists. Generally, the reliance of the public upon the skills of a specialist and the wealth and sources of his or her knowledge are not limited to the geographic area in which he or she practices. Rather, his or her knowledge is a specialty. He or she specializes so that he or she may keep abreast. Any other standard for a specialist would negate the fundamental expectations and purpose of a specialty.

Breach of Duty

Once a duty to care has been established, the plaintiff must demonstrate that the defendant breached that duty by failing to comply with the accepted standard of care required. Breach of duty is the failure to conform to or the departure from a required duty of care owed to a person. The obligation to perform according to a standard of care may encompass either doing or refraining from doing a particular act. Evidence of a breach of duty can be offered through direct testimony, circumstantial evidence, *res ipsa loquitur*, etc. The breach of duty can be established by: (1) malfeasance; (2) misfeasance; or (3) nonfeasance.

The court in *Hastings v. Baton Rouge Hospital*,[21] discussed earlier, found a severe breach of duty when hospital regulations provide that when a physician cannot be reached or refuses a call, the chief of service is to be notified so that another physician can be obtained. This was not done. It is not necessary to prove that a patient would have survived if proper treatment had been administered, but only that the patient would have had a chance of survival. As a result of Dr. Gerdes' failure to make arrangements for another physician and Dr. McCool's failure to perform the necessary surgery, the patient had no chance of survival. The duty to provide for appropriate care under the circumstances was breached.

In *Dunahoo v. Brooks*,[22] the court stated that because the defendant nursing facility operator had been aware of the 94-year-old plaintiff's infirmities and had agreed to provide her nursing care, the nursing facility assumed an obligation to exercise care commensurate with her physical condition. While the plaintiff was getting out of bed, she tripped and fell over a light cord that was loose on the floor in an area that the defendant knew the plaintiff frequently used. The cord was plugged into a socket on the floor five inches from the baseboard. The court was impressed with the ease with which the situation could have been corrected. It noted that the cord could have been fastened down with a few nails and the outlet placed on the baseboard instead of almost in the middle of the floor.

The nursing facility in *Booty v. Kentwood Manor Nursing Home, Inc.*[23] was found negligent in permitting a 90-year-old resident to wander outside the facility where he fell and suffered a hip fracture. The resident's physical condition deteriorated and he eventually died. The staff was aware of the resident's confusion and tendency to stray. The court found that the facility was responsible for taking reasonable steps to prevent injury to a mentally confused and physically fragile resident. The facility's alarm system might have alerted the staff of unauthorized resident departures, but it had been deactivated and the doors were propped open for the convenience of the staff. The record demonstrated that inadequate supervision of the resident had been the cause in fact of his departure and that he probably would not have suffered injury but for the nursing facility's breach of duty owed to the resident.

In *Roberson v. Provident House*,[24] a resident brought a personal injury action against the nursing facility, claiming that while he was at Provident House a Foley catheter was improperly implanted, causing infection, bleeding, and impaired urine output. The trial court ruled that the plaintiff did not carry his burden of proving a breach in the standard of care. The plaintiff appealed. The appellate court reversed, holding that there was a lack of expert testimony as to the applicable standard of care, which precluded a finding that the nursing facility was not negligent in implanting the Foley catheter.

One justice dissented, however, stating that careful review of the record revealed that the pleadings were enlarged to include the issue of whether the catheter was inserted without the resident's consent. The catheter was inserted despite the plaintiff's protests. Such an action constitutes a battery (see the discussion of battery later in this chapter). There was testimony that no emergency existed to precipitate the insertion of the catheter. In addition, there was no attempt by the defendants to prove that the resident was of unsound mind.

Injury/Actual Damages

A defendant may be negligent and still not incur liability if no injury or actual damages result to the plaintiff. The term *injury* includes more than physical harm. Without harm or injury, there is no liability. Injury is not limited to physical harm but includes loss of income or reputation and compensation for pain and suffering.

The mere occurrence of an injury "does not establish negligence for which the law imposes liability, since the injury may be the result of an unavoidable accident, or an act of God, or some cause so remote to the person sought to be held liable for negligence that he cannot be charged with responsibility for the injury."[25]

Injury was obvious in *Lucas v. HCMF Corp.*,[26] where the patient had been transferred to a nursing facility following hospitalization for several ailments including early decubitus ulcers. The resident was returned to the hospital 24 days later. "At that time the ulcer on her hip had become three large ulcers that reached to the bone and tunneled through the skin to meet one another. The ulcer on her buttocks that had been one inch in diameter had grown to eight inches in diameter and extended to the bone. Additional ulcers had developed on each of her ribs, on her left arm and wrist, and on the left side of her face."[27] The standard of care required in preventing and treating decubitus ulcers required that the resident be mobilized and turned every two hours to prevent deterioration of tissue. The treatment records reflected that the resident was not turned at all from September 22 through October 1; nor was she turned on October 4, 7, or 12. Failure to periodically turn the resident and move her to a chair had caused the deterioration in her condition.

Proximate Cause/Causation

The fourth element necessary to establish negligence requires that there be a reasonable, close, and causal connection or relationship between the defendant's negligent conduct and the resulting damages suffered by the plaintiff. In other words, the defendant's negligence must be a substantial factor causing the injury. *Proximate cause* is a term referring to the relationship between a breached duty and the injury. The breach of duty must be the proximate cause of the resulting injury. The mere departure from a proper and recognized procedure is not sufficient to enable a patient to recover damages unless the plaintiff can show that the departure was unreasonable and the proximate cause of the patient's injuries.

Causation in the *Hastings v. Baton Rouge Hospital*[28] case was well established. In the ordinary course of events, a person does not bleed to death in a hospital emergency department over a two-hour period without some surgical intervention to save his or her life.

In *Robinson v. Group Health Association, Inc.,*[29] the District of Columbia Court of Appeals held that there was a genuine issue of material fact as to whether the failure of a group health provider to treat a patient's diabetes aggressively resulted in the amputation of his leg below the knee. The testimony of the plaintiff's expert, as it related to the issue of proximate cause, was sufficient to allow the case to go to the jury. According to the expert, the failure of the provider to refer the patient for vascular evaluation resulted in his below-the-knee amputation. The expert testified to a reasonable degree of medical certainty, which he equated to a greater than 50 percent chance, that if there had been an early vascular consult, followed by an angioplasty and perhaps a partial foot amputation, a below-the-knee amputation could have been avoided. Although the provider presented contrary testimony, the plaintiff's expert testimony was found sufficient to permit a reasonable juror to find that there was a direct and substantial causal relationship between the provider's breach of the standard of care and the patient's injuries.

> The primary wrong upon which a cause of action for negligence is based consists in the breach of a duty on the part of one person to protect another against injury, the proximate result of which is an injury to the person to whom the duty is owed. These elements of duty, breach, and injury are essentials of actionable negligence, and in fact most judicial definitions of the term "negligence" or "actionable negligence" are couched in those terms. In the absence of any one of them, no cause of action for negligence will lie.[30]

Can one establish a causal relationship through the process of eliminating other possible causes of a plaintiff's injury? The answer is yes—one of the ways to establish the causal relationship between the particular conduct of a defendant and a plaintiff's injury is through the process of eliminating causes other than the defendant's conduct. For example, in *Shegog v. Zabrecky,*[31] Mr. Pereyra sought treatment for back pain from Dr. Zabrecky, a chiropractor at the Life Extension Center, in January 1987. Zabrecky ordered X-rays. The X-rays revealed that Pereyra was suffering from a fractured vertebra caused by a malignant tumor. Pereyra was referred to a surgeon who performed two surgical procedures to remove the tumor. Pereyra underwent a series of radiation treatments, which were supervised by Dr. Usas. A CT scan revealed that the cancer had spread to Pereyra's lungs. Dr. Usas and other consulting physicians recommended that chemotherapy be considered following the course of radiation treatments. Pereyra was advised that his chance of survival following chemotherapy was 50 percent or better. During the summer of 1987, Pereyra consulted with a number of physicians as to the best course of treatment. Pereyra continued to see Zabrecky throughout the summer and fall of 1987. Zabrecky recommended that Pereyra reject the chemotherapy treatments and undergo a course of treatment with neytumorin and neythymin (two compounds manufactured in Germany). The Food and Drug Administration (FDA) had not approved either drug. Pereyra agreed to undergo the treatment. Zabrecky had performed an initial enzyme study prior to treatment, but did not perform further tests after the course of treatment began. During the course of treatment, the cancer continued to spread. Additional radiation treatments were given. Pereyra's condition worsened, and he was admitted to the hospital. The physicians at the hospital had not been aware that Pereyra was injecting himself with drugs given to him by Zabrecky. Upon urging from his wife, Pereyra revealed this information to the physicians at the hospital. Pereyra died on December 17, 1987, approximately six weeks after he had begun treatment with neytumorin and neythymin. An autopsy revealed that Pereyra had died from necrosis of the liver caused by a toxic reaction to a foreign substance. Pereyra was taking only the drugs (neytumorin and neythymin) between July 1987 and his death. No cancer was found in the liver.

A lawsuit was filed against the defendants, seeking damages for negligent treatment and care. The negligent acts alleged included the following:

- administering drugs statutorily prohibited for use
- withholding information from treating physicians
- failing to follow patient's blood work
- advising the patient to use drugs that had expired
- engaging in the unlicensed practice of medicine
- inducing the patient to forgo appropriate therapy

The jury delivered verdict for the plaintiff. The defendants appealed, claiming that the evidence introduced at trial did not support the jury's finding as to causation.

The Appellate Court held that Zabrecky's grossly negligent actions and the circumstantial evidence introduced supported the jury's finding of causation. Zabrecky had violated a recognized standard of care by prescribing statutorily prohibited drugs. There was no evidence presented that would have supported another cause of the patient's liver failure. Reports from treating physicians indicate that the plaintiff died of liver failure and not from cancer. The defendant's expert testified that necrosis of the liver can be caused by the injection of foreign substances. He also testified that the normal reaction time of the human liver to a foreign protein is, on average, six weeks. "One of the ways to establish the causal relationship between particular conduct of a defendant and a plaintiff's injury is the expert's deduction, by the process of eliminating causes other than the conduct, that the conduct was the cause of injury. . . . The submitted reports indicate that each physician deduced that the German drugs were the most probable cause of Pereyra's liver failure, even without analysis of the drugs."[32]

Patients who are requested and agree to participate in a research project should be notified of the potential risks, benefits, alternatives, and outcomes of the proposed and agreed-upon treatment plan. An appropriate consent form should be signed, witnessed, and dated.

Failure to order tests or to prescribe treatment can be sufficient to establish causation. Failure to order tests or to prescribe treatment is a common cause of malpractice suits. For example, in *Alexander v. Department. of Health & Hospitals,*[33] Ms. Alexander was treated on December 4, 1988, in the emergency department of the Lafayette University Medical Center for complaints of chills, fever, vomiting, and weakness. Her spleen had been removed, which reduced the effectiveness of her immune system and increased the risk of bacterial infection. Her treating physician, Dr. Prejean, was aware that her spleen had been removed, but he diagnosed her malady as acute viral illness because her symptoms were consistent with that diagnosis, and he detected no symptoms of bacterial infection other than fever. Without performing any tests to corroborate this diagnosis, he sent her home with prescriptions for pharmaceuticals and instructions to return if her symptoms persisted. She died early the next morning. According to the autopsy report by Dr. Laga, Ms. Alexander's death was caused by bilateral adrenal infarction (bleeding and death of the adrenal glands). The plaintiff filed a malpractice suit against the Medical Center.

A medical review panel found that the evidence supported the conclusion that Prejean had failed to meet the applicable standard of care. The trial court found for the plaintiff in a bench trial. The defendant appealed, claiming that there was no causal relationship between Prejean's actions and Ms. Alexander's death.

The appeals court held that the evidence supported a finding that the physician's treatment of the patient's condition as a viral infection rather than a possible bacterial infection constituted substandard care. Evidence supported a finding that the physician's failure to treat the patient for bacterial infection caused her death even though the coroner's report designated the cause of death as bilateral adrenal infarction without reference to stimulus for such a condition.

Three members of the medical review panel believed that Ms. Alexander should have been placed on antibiotics prior to her discharge and that a blood culture should have been performed. There was testimony that Dr. Prejean was negligent in: (1) failing to perform blood culture tests and (2) failing to place the patient, whose spleen had been removed and who complained of chills, vomiting, and weakness, on antibiotics. The trial court's decision to credit the plaintiff's interpretation of the evidence was not manifest as an error.

A death certificate is proof only of death itself. It is not proof as to the cause of death and is therefore not admissible for the purpose of showing the cause of death. Laga, who was the only physician to examine Ms. Alexander's body postmortem, could not rule out bacterial infection because he did not perform a culture of her adrenal glands. Further, he stated that bacterial infection is one of the most common causes of bilateral adrenal infarction. There was testimony that it is a very rare occurrence in the United States for a viral infection to cause an adrenal infarction. The appeals court found that there was sufficient evidence in the record to support a finding that Ms. Alexander died as a result of a bacterial infection. Even though the contrary contention is well supported, the trial court did not commit manifest error in finding that Prejean's failure to treat Ms. Alexander for a bacterial infection caused her death.

Diagnostic testing is a necessary medical tool for determining a patient's health care needs. Staff members should integrate medical information from various assessments of the patient in order to identify and assign priorities to his or her care needs.

Foreseeability

Foreseeability is the reasonable anticipation that harm or injury is likely to result from an act or an omission to act. The test for foreseeability is whether one of ordinary prudence and intelligence should have anticipated the danger to others caused by his or her negligent act. "The test is not what the wrongdoer believed would occur; it is whether he or she ought reasonably to have foreseen that the event in question, or some similar event, would occur."[34]

If the action of a defendant meets or surpasses the recognized standard of care and injury results, there has been no negligence or carelessness—just an unavoidable accident. There is no expectation that the actor can guard against events that cannot reasonably be foreseen or that are so unlikely to occur that they would be disregarded. For example, in *Haynes v. Hoffman,*[35] the plaintiff had brought a medical malpractice action against the defendant physician for his alleged negligence in prescribing a medication to which the plaintiff suffered an allergic reaction. The trial court returned a verdict in favor of the defendant, and the plaintiff appealed. The evidence at trial had revealed that the plaintiff had not disclosed her history of allergies to the physician. The physician testified that, at the time of the physical examination of the plaintiff, she denied having any allergies. The physician testified that he would not have prescribed the drug had he known the plaintiff's complete history. By failing to disclose her allergies to the physician, the plaintiff was contributorily negligent. Foreseeability involves guarding against that which is probable and likely to happen, not against that which is only remotely and slightly possible.

When a defendant's actions fail to meet the standard of care, negligence has occurred and the jury must make two determinations. First, was it foreseeable that harm would occur from the failure to meet the standard of care? Second, was the carelessness or negligence the proximate or immediate cause of the harm or injury to the plaintiff? "The broad test of negligence is what a reasonably prudent person would foresee and would do in the light of this foresight under the circumstances."[36]

The question of foreseeability was an issue in *Ferguson v. Dr. McCarthy's Rest Home*.[37] The plaintiff, a resident in the defendant's nursing facility, suffered from paralysis of the left side but was able to roll toward the left side in bed. The defendant had knowledge of this ability. A radiator, which was approximately the same height as the bed, was next to the plaintiff's bed on the left side. During the night, the plaintiff's left foot came in contact with the radiator and she suffered third-degree burns. She had been placed too close to the left side of the bed in an effort to prevent her from rolling out of the bed, which had not been equipped properly with bed rails. The court held that this type of accident was foreseeable with respect to a person in the plaintiff's condition, particularly because the defendant had knowledge of the plaintiff's condition. The defendant should have shielded the radiator or not placed the plaintiff next to it.

Generally, the issue of foreseeability is for the trial court to decide. Harm can be said to be foreseeable if a health care facility becomes aware of facts indicating that patients had previously been exposed to an unreasonable risk of harm. A duty to prevent a wrongful act by a third party will be imposed only where those wrongful acts can be reasonably anticipated.

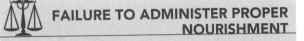

FAILURE TO ADMINISTER PROPER NOURISHMENT

Citation: *Caruso v. Pine Manor Nursing Ctr., 538 N.E.2d 722 (Ill. App. Ct. 1989)*

Facts

In Illinois, a nursing facility by statute has a duty to provide its residents with proper nutrition. Under the Nursing Home Care Reform Act: The owner and licensee of a nursing home are liable to a resident for any intentional or negligent act or omission of their agents or employees that injured the resident. The Act defines neglect as a failure in a facility to provide adequate medical or personal care or maintenance, which failure results in physical or mental injury to a resident or in the deterioration of the resident's condition. Personal care and maintenance include providing food and water and assistance with meals necessary to sustain a healthy life.

The nursing facility in this case maintained no records of the resident's fluid intake and output. A nurse testified that such a record was a required standard nursing facility procedure that should have been followed for a person in the resident's condition, but was not. The resident's condition deteriorated after a stay at the facility of six and one-half days. Upon leaving the facility and entering a hospital emergency department, the treating physician diagnosed the resident as suffering from severe dehydration caused by an inadequate intake of fluids. The nursing facility offered no alternative explanation for the resident's dehydrated condition. As a result of the facility's failure to maintain adequate records, the resident suffered severe dehydration that required hospital treatment.

Causation

The evidence presented clearly demonstrated that the proximate cause of the resident's dehydration was the nursing facility's failure to administer proper nourishment to him. It was not unreasonable for the jury to conclude that the resident suffered dehydration and that the nursing facility's treatment of him caused the dehydration. The trial court found that the record supported a finding that the resident had suffered from dehydration as a result of the nursing facility's negligence. The defendant appealed the jury verdict awarding $65,000 in damages. The trial court increased this amount to $195,000 (three times the actual damages).

Issue

Did the nursing facility resident suffer harm as a result of the facility's negligence?

Holding

The Illinois Appellate Court upheld the trial court's finding that the resident suffered dehydration.

Reason

The evidence presented clearly demonstrated that the proximate cause of the resident's dehydration was the nursing facility's failure to administer proper nourishment to him. It was not unreasonable for the jury to conclude that the resident suffered dehydration and that the nursing facility's treatment of him caused the dehydration.

Discussion

1. What is the importance of timely nutritional screenings and assessments?
2. What is the mechanism for screening and assessing the nutritional needs of patients in your organization?

Summary Case

All the elements necessary to establish negligence were well established in *Niles v. City of San Rafael.*[38] On June 26, 1973, at approximately 3:30 P.M., Kelly Niles, a young boy, got into an argument with another boy on the ball field. He was hit on the right side of his head. He rode home on his bicycle and waited for his father who was to pick him up for the weekend. At approximately 5:00 P.M., his father arrived to pick him up. By the time they arrived in San Francisco, Kelly appeared to be in a great deal of pain. His father then decided to take him to Mount Zion Hospital, which was a short distance away. He arrived at the hospital emergency department at approximately 5:45 P.M. On admission to the emergency department, Kelly was taken to a treatment room by a registered nurse. The nurse obtained a history of the injury and took Kelly's pulse and blood pressure. During his stay in the emergency department, he was irritable, vomited several times, and complained that his head hurt. An intern who had seen Kelly wrote "pale, diaphoretic, and groggy" on the patient's chart. Skull X-rays were ordered and found to be negative except for soft tissue swelling that was not noted until later. The intern then decided to admit the patient. A second-year resident was called, and he agreed with the intern's decision. An admitting clerk called the intern and indicated that the patient had to be admitted by an attending physician. The resident went as far as to write "admit" on the chart and later crossed it out. A pediatrician who was in the emergency department at the time was asked to look at Kelly. The pediatrician was also the paid director of the Mount Zion Pediatric Out-Patient Clinic. The pediatrician asked Kelly a few questions and then decided to send him home. The physician could not recall what instructions he gave the patient's father, but he did give the father his business card.

The pediatrician could not recall giving the father a copy of the emergency department's Head Injury Instructions, an information sheet that had been prepared for distribution to patients with head injuries. The sheet explained that an individual should be returned to the emergency department should any of the following signs appear: a large, soft lump on the head; unusual drowsiness (cannot be awakened); forceful or repeated vomiting; a fit or convulsion (jerking or spells); clumsy walking; bad headache; and/or one pupil larger than the other.

Kelly was taken back to his father's apartment at about 7:00 P.M. A psychiatrist friend stopped by at approximately 8:45 P.M. He examined Kelly and noted that one pupil was larger than the other. Because the pediatrician could not be reached, the patient was taken back to the emergency department. A physician on duty noted an epidural hematoma during his examination and ordered that a neurosurgeon be called.

Today, the patient can move only his eyes and neck. A lawsuit against Mount Zion and the pediatrician for $5 million was instituted. The city of San Rafael and the public school district also were included in the lawsuit as defendants. Expert testimony by two neurosurgeons during the trial indicated that the patient's chances of recovery would have been very good if he had been admitted promptly. This testimony placed the proximate cause of the injury with the hospital. The final judgment was $4 million against the medical defendants, $2.5 million for compensatory damages, and another $1.5 million for pain and suffering.

Case Lessons

Each case presented in this textbook illustrates actual experiences of plaintiffs and defendants. It is anticipated that the reader will learn from these experiences and apply them to real-life situations. The many lessons in *Niles v. City of San Rafael* include

- An organization can improve the quality of patient care rendered in the facility by establishing and adhering to policies, procedures, and protocols that facilitate the delivery of quality care across all disciplines.
- The provision of quality health care requires collaboration across disciplines.
- A physician must conduct a thorough and responsible examination and order the appropriate tests for each patient, evaluating the results of those tests prior to discharging the patient.
- A patient's vital signs must be monitored closely and documented in the medical record.
- Corrective measures must be taken when a patient's medical condition signals a medical problem.

- A complete review of a patient's medical record must be accomplished before discharging a patient. Review of the record must include review of test results, nurses' notes, residents' and interns' notes, and the notes of any other physician or consultant who may have attended the patient.
- An erroneous diagnosis leading to the premature dismissal of a case can result in liability for both the organization and physician.

INTENTIONAL TORTS

Assault and Battery

It has long been recognized by law that a person possesses a right to be free from aggression and the threat of actual aggression against one's person. The right to expect others to respect the integrity of one's body has roots in both common and statutory law. The distinguishing feature between assault and battery is that assault effectuates an infringement on the mental security or tranquility of another whereas battery constitutes a violation of another's physical integrity.

Assault

An *assault* is defined as the deliberate threat, coupled with the apparent present ability, to do physical harm to another. No actual contact is necessary. It is the deliberate threat or attempt to injure another or the attempt by one to make bodily contact with another without his or her consent. To commit the tort of assault, two conditions must exist. First, the person attempting to touch another unlawfully must possess the apparent present ability to commit the battery; second, the person threatened must be aware of or have actual knowledge of an immediate threat of a battery and must fear it.

Battery

A *battery* is the intentional touching of another's person, in a socially impermissible manner, without that person's consent. It is intentional conduct that violates the physical security of another. An act that otherwise would be considered to be an assault may be permissible if proper consent has been given or if it is in defense of oneself or of a third party. The receiver of the battery does not have to be aware that a battery has been committed (e.g., a patient who is unconscious and has surgery performed on him or her without his or her consent, either expressed or implied, is the object of a battery). The unwanted touching may give rise to a cause of action for any injuries brought about by the touching. No actual damages need be shown to impose liability.

The law provides a remedy to the individual if consent to a touching has not been obtained or if the act goes beyond the consent given. Therefore, the injured person may initiate a lawsuit against the wrongdoer for damages suffered. In *Peete v. Blackwell,*[39] punitive damages in the amount of $10,000 were awarded to a nurse in her action against a physician for assault and battery. Evidence showed that the physician struck the assisting nurse on the arm and cursed at her when the physician ordered her to turn on the suction. Although there were no injuries, $1 in compensatory damages and $10,000 in punitive damages were awarded by the jury.

In the health care context, the principle of law concerning battery and the requirement of consent to medical and surgical procedures is critically important. Liability of organizations and health care professionals for acts of battery is most common in situations involving lack of or improper patient consent to medical and surgical procedures. It is inevitable that patients will be touched by many persons for many reasons. Procedures ranging from bathing to surgery involve some touching of a patient. Therefore, the patient must authorize medical and surgical procedures. If such procedures are not authorized, the person performing a procedure could be subject to an action for battery.

It is of no legal importance that a procedure constituting a battery has improved a patient's health. If the patient did not consent to the touching, the patient may be entitled to such damages as can be proved to have resulted from commission of the battery. In *Perna v. Pirozzi,*[40] the New Jersey Supreme Court held that a patient who consents to surgery by one surgeon and is actually operated on by another has an action for medical malpractice or battery. Proof of unauthorized invasion of the plaintiff's person, even if harmless, entitles one to nominal damages.

Not only must individual staff members be aware of potential assault and battery hazards by fellow employees, as well as themselves, but they also must be alert to potential problems between patients (e.g., problems caused by smoking, racial or religious bias, and emotional conflicts). A health care facility has a particular duty to supervise especially closely those patients whose mental conditions make it probable that they will injure themselves or others.

This is especially true of long-term nursing facilities. The nursing facility in *Sayes v. Pilgrim Manor Nursing Home, Inc.,*[41] was found liable to a police officer who was injured while rescuing a suicidal nursing facility resident. The injuries were found to be the result of the facility's negligent lack of supervision of the resident. The resident was discovered missing from the premises and was reportedly threatening to commit suicide in a nearby sewage waste reservoir. The fourth police officer to arrive on the scene, believing the suicide to be imminent, dove into the water. He carried the resident to the shore and the resident then experienced an epileptic grand mal seizure. During the ensuing struggle, the police officer suffered a broken elbow. He underwent five operations and eventually had an artificial elbow implanted, which placed severe restrictions on his physical activity. The 41-year-old police officer was forced to resign as Chief of Police and enter early retirement.

The defendants appealed the trial court's finding for the plaintiff. The defendants claimed that the trial court erred in determining that: (1) Pilgrim Manor was negligent in supervising the resident; (2) Pilgrim Manor breached a duty to the plaintiff; and (3) the plaintiff was not contributorily negligent or assumed the risk of the accident. The plaintiff also appealed, asking the court to increase the award for pain and suffering and the award for loss of future income.

The Louisiana Court of Appeals held that by accepting a mentally retarded epileptic resident with violent tendencies, the nursing facility had a higher duty to protect the resident and public from harm. By accepting the resident with full knowledge of her condition, the nursing facility was obligated to take extra care, over and above that given other residents, to protect her and other residents. Pilgrim Manor presented no evidence that extra care was given to the resident. Evidence showed that she was treated like any other resident who had nominal physical or mental disabilities. The resident's treating physician testified that a person with her problems should not have been given freedom to leave the nursing facility at will. Despite the physician's opinion and the documented serious mental and physical problems of the resident, the director of nursing and the administrator testified that the resident had complete freedom to leave the nursing facility premises, either alone or in the company of other residents. Police officers and firefighters cannot be expected to expose themselves to injury from negligent conduct that has occurred on a repeated basis and that could have been prevented. The appeals court found no contributory negligence on the part of the plaintiff. An award of $60,000 for pain and suffering was not considered an abuse of discretion. The judgment of the district court was amended to increase the plaintiff's award for loss of future earnings from $150,000 to $200,000.

False Imprisonment

False imprisonment is the unlawful restraint of an individual's personal liberty or the unlawful restraining or confining of an individual. The personal right to move freely and without hindrance is basic to our legal system. Any intentional infringement on this right may constitute false imprisonment. Actual physical force is not necessary to constitute false imprisonment. All that is necessary is that an individual who is physically confined to a given area experience a reasonable fear that force, which may be implied by words, threats, or gestures, will be used to detain the individual or to intimidate him or her without legal justification. Excessive force used to restrain a patient may produce liability for both false imprisonment and battery.

A patient does not actually have to be in restraints to be falsely imprisoned. A threat of restraint that a patient may reasonably expect to be carried out may be enough to constitute false imprisonment. To recover for damages, a plaintiff must be aware of the confinement and have no reasonable means of escape. Availability of a reasonable means of escape may bar recovery. To lock a door when another is reasonably available to pass through is not imprisonment. However, if the only other door provides a way of escape that is dangerous, the law may consider it an unreasonable way of escape, and, therefore, false imprisonment may be a cause of action. Whether false imprisonment has taken place will be a matter for the courts to decide. No actual damage need be shown for liability to be imposed.

Where legal justification is absent and an arrest or imprisonment is false, the person denied free movement will be permitted to seek a remedy at law for any injury. There are occasions and circumstances when a person must be confined, such as when a person presents a danger to him- or herself or others. Criminals are incarcerated, as are sometimes the mentally ill who may present a danger to themselves or others. Long-term care residents are sometimes restrained to prevent falls. Children are retained after school for disciplinary reasons. In these examples, the right to move about freely has been violated, but the infringement occurs for reasons that are justifiable under the law.

False Arrest

In *Desai v. SSM Healthcare,*[42] Dr. Desai was walking across a hospital parking lot, a shortcut to the St. Louis University Medical School's Institute of Molecular Virology, where Desai worked as part of his graduate studies. He was stopped by two security guards, Mr. Mealey and Mr. Windam, and was asked to show identification. Desai said that he was a doctor and that he did not have his identification with him. Following an argument, the two security guards grabbed Desai's arms and Windam slammed Desai's head against the trunk of a car. After handcuffing him, the security guards escorted Desai back to the security office where they were joined by the security guard supervisor. The handcuffs were eventually removed after the security guards received verification that Desai was affiliated with the Institute and confirmation from a nurse supervisor that he was a physician. Shortly thereafter, the University campus police arrived. One of the officers asked Desai to apologize to Mealey. Desai refused and said that he wanted the St. Louis City police called, as he wanted to file an official complaint because he had been assaulted. At the request of the security guards, Desai was rehandcuffed and arrested by the St. Louis police for trespassing. The security guards later admitted that they had Desai arrested in order to avoid getting themselves into trouble. Desai was not released from jail until noon the following day. While in jail he suffered headaches and seizures. Desai brought suit against the hospital and security guards for false imprisonment, battery, and malicious prosecution.

The defendants moved to have the malicious prosecution count dismissed, and the motion was granted. The jury had returned a verdict totaling $75,000 in damages for the false imprisonment claim and found in favor of the defendants on the battery claim. The trial court sustained the defendants' motions for judgment notwithstanding the verdict. The plaintiff appealed.

Did the plaintiff meet his burden of establishing his case by substantial evidence? The Missouri Court of Appeals held that the evidence supported a finding that the security guards falsely imprisoned the physician, and that the physician was entitled to punitive damages on the false imprisonment claim. The defendants' own testimony provided the jury with sufficient evidence to establish that the plaintiff had been held against his will. The testimony supported a finding that the arrest was self-serving and resulted in the false imprisonment. The trial court erred in dismissing the punitive damages as to the false imprisonment claim and, therefore, prevented it from being submitted to the jury.

Physically Violent Persons

In *Celestine v. United States*,[43] the right to move about freely had been violated; however, the infringement was permissible for reasons justifiable under the law. In the instant case, the plaintiff had brought an action alleging battery and false imprisonment because security guards had placed him in restraints. The plaintiff-appellant sought psychiatric care at a Veterans Administration (VA) hospital. He became physically violent while waiting to be seen by a physician. The VA security guards found it necessary to place the him in restraints until a psychiatrist could examine him. The U.S. Court of Appeals for the Eighth Circuit held that the record supported a finding that the hospital was justified in placing the patient under restraint. Under Missouri law, no false imprisonment or battery occurred in view of the common-law principle that a person believed to be mentally ill could be restrained lawfully if such was considered necessary to prevent immediate injury to that person or others.

Contagious Diseases

Protocols should be instituted for handling patients diagnosed as having contracted a highly contagious disease. Detaining such patients, without statutory protection, constitutes false imprisonment. State health codes generally provide guidelines for caring for such patients. Statutes in many states allow mentally ill and intoxicated individuals to be detained if they are found to be dangerous to themselves or others. Those who are mentally ill, however, can be restrained only to the degree necessary to prevent them from harming themselves or others. If a mentally ill patient cannot be released, procedures should be followed to provide commitment to an appropriate institution for the patient's care.

Intoxicated Persons

The patient in *Davis v. Charter by the Sea*[44] was found not entitled to a directed verdict on a false-imprisonment claim. The claim arose from her overnight, involuntary detention at a hospital. Evidence that the patient was highly intoxicated, confused, incoherent, and experiencing a low diastolic blood pressure raised a jury question as to the existence of a medical emergency authorizing her detention.

Restraints

Restraints generally are used to control behavior when patients are disoriented or may cause harm to themselves (e.g., from falling, contaminating wounds, or pulling out intravenous (IV) lines) or to others. The use of restraints raises many questions of a patient's rights in the areas of autonomy, freedom of movement, and the accompanying health problems that can result from continued immobility. In general, a patient has a right to be free from any physical restraints imposed or psychoactive drugs administered for purposes of discipline or convenience and that are not required to treat a patient's medical symptoms.

A study of skilled nursing facilities in Connecticut concluded that "restraint use involves a choice between safety and independence. Unfortunately, the decision is made with an almost complete lack of data concerning the effectiveness of restraints on reducing injury or improving behavior."[45] Although the motivations for using restraints appear sound, there has been a tendency toward overuse. The fear of litigation over injuries sustained because of the failure to apply restraints further compounds the problem of overuse. As a result, regulations governing the use of restraints under the Omnibus Budget Reconciliation Act of 1987 (OBRA '87) make it clear that restraints are to be applied as a last resort rather than as a first option in the control of a resident's behavior. Because prescription drugs are sometimes used to restrain behavior, these regulations represent the first time that prescription drugs must by law "be justified by indications documented in the medical chart."[46]

Health care organizations should implement policies aimed at eliminating or reducing the use of restraints. Principles that should be followed in implementing a program for the effective use of restraints include the following:

- written policies that conform to federal and state guidelines (e.g., a policy that prescribes that the least restrictive device will be utilized to maintain the safety of the patient, a policy requiring the periodic review of patients under restraint, and a policy requiring physician orders for restraints)

- procedures for implementing organizational policies (e.g., alternatives to follow before restraining a patient may include family counseling to encourage increased visitations, environmental change, activity therapies, and patient counseling)
- periodic review of policies and procedures, with revision as necessary
- education and orientation programs for the staff to be conducted inside and outside the organization
- education programs for patients and their families
- a sound appraisal of each patient's needs
- informed consent from the patient, and when and where appropriate from the legal guardian
- the application of the least restrictive restraints
- constant monitoring of the patient to determine the continuing need for restraints, injury to the patient, and complaints by the patient
- documentation that includes:
  - the need for restraints
  - time-limited orders ("as needed" (PRN) orders are not acceptable)
  - consents for the application of restraints
  - patient monitoring
  - reappraisal of the continuing need for restraints

In *Big Town Nursing Home, Inc. v. Newman,*[47] the court held there was sufficient evidence to support a finding that a 67-year-old male resident had been falsely imprisoned in a facility against his will. He had attempted to leave the facility three days after he arrived at the facility. He was caught by the facility's employees and forcibly returned. He was placed in a wing with persons who were addicted to drugs and alcohol and those who were mentally disturbed. He asked during the ensuing weeks that he be permitted to leave and attempted to leave five or six times. He was eventually confined to a restraint chair. He was not allowed to use the telephone, and his clothes had been taken from him. The actions of the staff were described as being in utter disregard of the resident's legal rights. There was no court order for his commitment and the agreement for his admission stated that he was not to be kept against his will. The court stated that the staff acted recklessly, willfully, and maliciously by unlawfully detaining him.

Discharge against Medical Advice

A patient's insistence on leaving against medical advice should be so noted on the medical record. The patient also should be informed of the possible harm in leaving against medical advice. If a patient ultimately decides to leave against medical advice, he or she should be requested to sign a discharge against advice and release form. Should a patient refuse to sign such a form, such refusal should be so documented in the patient's medical record.

Defamation of Character

Defamation of character consists of a false oral or written communication to someone other than the person defamed that tends to hold that person's reputation up to scorn and ridicule in the eyes of a substantial number of respectable people in the community. *Libel* results from the written word, and *slander* is from the spoken word. Libel can be presented in signs, photographs, letters, cartoons, etc. To be an actionable wrong, defamation must be communicated to a third person. Defamatory statements communicated only to the injured party are not grounds for an action.

Defamation "on its face" is actionable without proof of special damages. Special damages typically consist of economic losses, such as loss of business or employment. In certain cases, a court will presume that the words caused injury to the person's reputation. There are four generally recognized exceptions where no proof of actual harm to reputation is required to recover damages: (1) accusing someone of a crime, (2) accusing someone of having a loathsome disease, (3) using words that affect a person's profession or business, and (4) calling a woman unchaste. Professionals are legally protected against libel when complying with a law that requires the reporting of venereal or other diseases, which could be considered loathsome.

Libel

Performance Appraisals Not for General Publication. A statement in a hospital newsletter regarding the discharge of a nursing supervisor constituted libel *per se* in *Kraus v. Brandsletter.*[48] The newsletter indicated that the hospital's medical board had discharged the nursing supervisor after a unanimous vote of no confidence. Couching the board's determination in terms of a vote gave the impression that the board's determination had been based on facts that justified the board's opinion. The statement tended to injure the nurse's reputation as a professional because it did not refer to specifics of her performance but rather referred to her abilities as a professional in general. The reasonable interpretation of the statement in the newsletter was that the supervisor was incompetent in her professional capacity, thus giving rise to a cause of action for libel *per se.* An alleged statement that a physician said, "You nurses will receive your Christmas bonus early, your boss is going to get fired," was not slander *per se* in that it did not injure the nurse in her professional capacity.[49] In addition, the statement that she was going to be fired was true.

Performance Appraisal Statements Found Not Libelous: In *Schauer v. Memorial Care System,*[50] the plaintiff applied for and was given a supervisory position at Memorial Hospital's new catheterization laboratory. In March 1989, she received an employment appraisal for the period June 1988 through December 1988. At that time, Schauer's supervisor rated her performance as "commendable" in two categories and "fair" in eight categories, with an overall rating of "fair." Although Schauer did not lose her job as a result of the appraisal, she brought an action against the hospital and her former supervisor for libel and emotional distress as a result of the appraisal. The hospital moved for summary judgment on the grounds that the employment appraisal was not defamatory as a matter of law; the hospital had qualified privilege to write the performance appraisal; and the claim for emotional distress did not reach the level of severity required for a claim for intentional infliction of emotional distress. The trial court granted the hospital's motion for summary judgment, and Schauer appealed.

Did the plaintiff state a claim for defamation and the intentional infliction of emotional distress? The Texas Court of Appeals held that the statements contained in the performance appraisal were not libelous and that the appraisal was subject to qualified privilege. Moreover, the hospital's conduct and the statements contained in the appraisal did not support the claim for intentional infliction of emotional distress.

To sustain her claim of defamation, Schauer had to show that the hospital published her appraisal in a defamatory manner that injured her reputation in some way. A statement can be unpleasant and objectionable to the plaintiff without being defamatory. The hospital argued that the statements contained in the appraisal were truthful, permissible expressions of opinion, and not capable of a defamatory meaning. Schauer's supervisor prepared the appraisal as part of her supervisory duties. The appraisal was not published outside the hospital and was prepared in compliance with the hospital policy for all employees. Schauer disputed her overall rating of "fair" as being libelous. "Clearly, this is a statement of her supervisor's opinion and is not defamatory as a matter of law."[51]

In her performance appraisal, Schauer objected to the statement, "Ms. Schauer was not sensitive to employee relations."[52] Schauer conceded in her deposition that there were a number of interpersonal problems in the catheterization laboratory and that she did not get along with everyone. The court found that given these admissions, the statement was not defamatory.

As to the plaintiff's claim of emotional distress, the plaintiff failed to show that the hospital acted intentionally and recklessly. The *Restatement of Torts, Second,* § 46 (1977) provides:

> Liability has been found only where the conduct has been so outrageous in character, and so extreme in degree, as to go beyond all possible bounds of decency, and to be regarded as atrocious, and utterly intolerable in a civilized community. . . . The liability clearly does not extend to mere insults, indignities, threats, annoyances, petty oppressions, or other trivialities. Complete emotional tranquility is seldom attainable in this world, and some degree of transient and trivial emotional distress is part of the price of living among people. The law intervenes only where the distress is so severe that no reasonable man could be expected to endure it.

Newspaper Articles. A libel suit was brought against the Miami Herald Publishing Company more than two years after its publication of an editorial cartoon depicting a nursing facility in a distasteful manner.[53] The cartoon was described in the following manner:

> On October 29, 1980, The Herald published an editorial cartoon which depicted three men in a dilapidated room. On the back wall was written "Krest View Nursing Home," and on the side wall there was a board which read "Closed by Order of the State of Florida." The room itself was in a state of total disrepair. There were holes in the floor and ceiling, leaking water pipes, and exposed wiring. The men in the room were dressed in outfits resembling those commonly appearing in caricatures of gangsters. Each man carried a sack with a dollar sign on it. One of the men was larger than the other two and was more in the forefront of the picture. One of the others addressed him. The caption read: "Don't Worry, Boss, We Can Always Reopen It As a Haunted House for the Kiddies."[54]

The court held that the newspaper's editorial cartoon depicting persons resembling gangsters in a dilapidated building, identified as a particular nursing facility that had been closed by state order, was an expression of pure opinion and was protected by the First Amendment against the libel suit alleging that the cartoon defamed the owner of the facility.

The court in *Wisconsin Association of Nursing Homes*[55] would not compel the newspapers to accept and print an advertisement in the exact form submitted by the Wisconsin Association of Nursing Homes and various individual homes.

> Plaintiffs allege in their complaint that the defendants published a series of "investigative reports" in the Milwaukee Journal which dealt with the quality of care and services in several nursing

homes. Plaintiffs further characterized the conclusions of the article as being false and erroneous. As a result, the plaintiffs prepared a full page advertisement which purported to respond to, and refute the allegations set out in the above mentioned "reports." The defendant newspaper refused to publish the advertisement in the form presented, and referred the question of possibly libelous matter to the attention of plaintiffs' attorneys.[56]

The court held that it was within the newspaper's journalistic discretion to reject the advertisement on the ground that it contained possibly libelous material. "[T]he clear weight of authority has not sanctioned any enforceable right of access to the press. In sum, a court can no more dictate what a privately owned newspaper can print than what it cannot print."[57]

> Unlike broadcasting, the publication of a newspaper is not a government conferred privilege. As we have said, the press and the government have had a history of disassociation. We can find nothing in the United States Constitution, any federal statute, or any controlling precedent that allows us to compel a private newspaper to publish advertisements without editorial control merely because such advertisements are not legally obscene or unlawful.[58]

The appellee in *Stevens v. Morris Communications Corp.*[59] alleged that a newspaper article, which identified her as a representative of a convalescent center at a city council meeting, had defamed her. She claims that the article implies that she has responsibility for the convalescent center's problems of maintenance and disrepair. The court held that the appellee was not defamed by the article. Using the reasonable person test, the court found that it was highly unlikely that a reasonable person could have read the newspaper article as being defamatory.

Slander

There are few slander lawsuits because of the difficulty in proving defamation, the small awards, and the high legal fees.

The Georgia case of *Barry v. Baugh*[60] involved a nurse who brought a defamation action, charging that a physician had slandered her in the course of a consultation concerning the commitment of her husband to a mental institution. The nurse requested damages for mental pain, shock, fright, humiliation, and embarrassment. The nurse alleged that if the physician's statement were made known to the public, her job and reputation would be affected adversely. The court held that the physician's statement concerning the nurse did not constitute slander because the physician was not referring to the nurse in a professional capacity.[61]

With slander, the person who brings suit generally must prove special damages; however, when any allegedly defamatory words refer to a person in a professional capacity, the professional need not show that the words caused damage. It is presumed that any slanderous reference to someone's professional capacity is damaging; the plaintiff therefore has no need to prove damages. In this case, however, because the court held that the physician's statement did not refer to the nurse in her professional capacity, the plaintiff had to demonstrate damages in order to recover. The plaintiff was unable to show damages.

Professionals who are called incompetent in front of others have a right to sue to defend their reputation. However, it is difficult to prove that an individual comment was injurious. If the person making an injurious comment cannot prove that the comment is true, then that person can be held liable for damages. Therefore, health care professionals should avoid making disparaging remarks about other health care professionals.

An administrator's statements made to a physician's supervisor regarding the physician's alleged professional misconduct is not grounds for a defamation action so long as the statements are made in good faith. A hospital administrator has a duty to report complaints about alleged professional misconduct of physicians working in the hospital. The administrator has qualified privilege to report such complaints to the physician's supervisor and other hospital officials as necessary.[62]

ACCUSATORY STATEMENTS NOT DEFAMATORY

Citation: *Chowdhry v. North Las Vegas Hospital., Inc., 851 P.2d 459 (Nev. 1993)*

Facts

On October 2, 1985, a young woman entered the emergency department of a hospital complaining of chest pain and shortness of breath. Dr. Lapica, the emergency physician on duty, saw her. Lapica diagnosed the patient as suffering from a possible pneumo-hemothorax, which required the placement of a chest tube to drain accumulated fluids. Lapica contacted Dr. Chowdhry, a physician who had recently performed surgery on the young woman and who was also the on-call thoracic surgeon at the hospital, and informed Chowdhry that his services were required at the hospital. The record revealed that Chowdhry refused to return to the hospital to treat the patient because he had recently left there, and would treat her only if she were transferred to University Medical Center (UMC). Chowdhry testified that he could not return to the hospital because of a conflicting emergency at UMC.

Lapica then contacted the hospital's chief of staff, Dr. Wilchins, and told him that Chowdhry refused to come to the hospital and attend to the patient. Both physicians concluded that if the patient could be safely transported to UMC, the transfer should be affected so that Chowdhry could treat her.

Lapica contacted the emergency department physician at UMC, explained the nature and basis of the problem, and received permission to transfer the patient. The patient was ultimately transported to UMC. Lapica and Ms. Crow, the supervising nurse at the hospital, prepared incident reports detailing the events and submitted them to the hospital administrator, Mr. Moore.

On October 3, 1985, Moore informed Dr. Silver, UMC's chief of surgery, that Chowdhry had refused to come to the hospital emergency department to treat the patient. The matter was directed to the hospital's surgery committee, which recommended summary suspension of Chowdhry's staff privileges.

On November 1, 1985, in response to Chowdhry's request, a hearing was held before the medical executive committee. As a result of the hearing, Chowdhry's staff privileges were reinstated, but a reprimand was placed in his file for jeopardizing himself, the patient, and the hospital. The hospital denied Chowdhry's subsequent request to have the reprimand expunged from his record, thus prompting Chowdhry to file an action against the hospital, Silver, Moore, Wilchins, and Lapica.

Chowdhry's complaint alleged theories of liability based upon negligence, breach of contract, conspiracy, defamation, and negligent and intentional infliction of emotional distress. The district court concluded that Chowdhry had no reasonable basis for bringing the action and awarded $209,376 in attorneys' fees and $69,835 in costs to the hospital, Silver, Moore, and Wilchins. Lapica was awarded $47,566 in attorneys' fees and $9,428 in costs. Chowdhry appealed.

Issue

Did the district court err in (1) dismissing the claims of defamation, punitive damage, and inflic-

tion of emotional distress; and (2) awarding respondent attorneys' fees? Did the appellant abandon his patient?

Holding

The Nevada Supreme Court held that the statements accusing Chowdhry of abandoning his patient were not, in context, capable of a defamatory construction. Moreover, the surgeon had reasonable grounds for his action and thus was not liable for statutory attorney fees, even though he did not prevail.

Reason

Chowdhry's emotional distress claims are premised upon respondents' accusations of patient abandonment. Chowdhry testified that as a result, "he was very upset" and could not sleep. Insomnia and general physical or emotional discomfort are insufficient to satisfy the physical impact requirement for emotional distress. Thus, Chowdhry failed, as a matter of law, to present sufficient evidence to sustain verdicts for negligent or intentional infliction of emotional distress.

To establish a prima facie case of defamation, a plaintiff must prove: (l) a false and defamatory statement by defendant concerning the plaintiff, (2) an unprivileged publication to a third person, (3) fault amounting to at least negligence, and (4) actual or presumed damages. Whether a statement is capable of a defamatory construction is a question of law. The actual statements made by the various respondents were not that Chowdhry "abandoned" his patient but that he "failed to respond" or "would not come" to the hospital to treat his patient. Although these statements cannot themselves be deemed defamatory, the court recognized that "words do not exist in isolation." The record reflected that the respondents made the statements to hospital personnel and other interested parties (e.g., the patient's mother), in the context of reporting what was reasonably perceived to be Chowdhry's refusal to treat the patient at the hospital. The statements attributable to the respondents, taken in context, are not reasonably capable of a defamatory construction.

Chowdhry, however, had reasonable grounds upon which to bring this action. Thus, the award of attorneys' fees was reversed.

Discussion

1. Explain what a plaintiff must prove in order to establish an action for defamation.
2. How does libel differ from slander?

Defenses to a Defamation Action

Essentially, the two defenses to a defamation action are *truth* and *privilege*. When a person has said something that is damaging to another person's reputation, the person making the statement will not be liable for defamation if it can be shown that the statement is true. A privileged communication is one that might be defamatory under different circumstances but is not defamatory under the circumstances in which it was made because of a higher duty with which the person making the communication is charged. For example, many states have statutes providing immunity to physicians and health care institutions in connection with peer review proceedings. The person making the communication must do so in good faith, on the proper occasion, in the proper manner, and to persons who have a legitimate reason to receive the information.

There are two types of privilege that may provide a defense to an action for defamation. *Absolute privilege* attaches to statements made during judicial and legislative proceedings as well as to confidential communications between spouses. *Qualified privilege*, however, which attaches to statements such as those made as a result of a legal or moral duty to speak in the interests of third persons, may provide a successful defense only when such statements are made in the absence of malice. If it can be shown that a statement was made as a result of some monetary gain, hatred, ill will, or spite on the part of the speaker, the law will not permit that speaker to hide behind the shield of privilege and avoid liability for defamation.

The defense of privilege is illustrated in the case of *Judge v. Rockford Memorial Hospital*,[63] where a nurse brought an action for libel based on a letter written to a nurses' professional registry by the director of nurses at the hospital to which the nurse had been assigned by the registry. In the letter, the director of nurses stated that the hospital did not wish to have the nurse's services available to them because of certain losses of narcotics during times when this particular nurse was on duty. The court refused the nurse recovery. Because the director of nurses had a legal duty to make the communication in the interests of society, the director's letter constituted a privileged communication. Therefore, the court held that the letter did not constitute libel because it was privileged.

Public figures have more difficulty in pursuing defamation litigation than the average individual. One who occupies a position of considerable public responsibility is considered a public figure for the purposes of the law of defamation and is generally more vulnerable to public scrutiny. Legal action against a defendant generally will be denied in the absence of any showing of actual malice in connection with alleged defamatory references to a plaintiff. Actual malice applies only in cases involving public figures and encompasses knowledge of falsity or recklessness as to truth.

The chairman of a publicly owned and operated county hospital in *Drew v. KATV Television*[64] brought a suit against a television station for defamation. It had been reported during a news broadcast that the board chairman had been charged with a felony when, in fact, he had been charged with two misdemeanor counts of solicitation to tamper with evidence. These charges were dismissed at trial. The second news report implied that he was involved in a drug investigation being conducted at the hospital where he served as chairman of the board. The plaintiff occupied a position of considerable public responsibility, and he was considered a public figure for the purposes of the law of defamation. The circuit court dismissed the case on the defendant's motion for summary judgment, and the plaintiff appealed. The Arkansas Supreme Court held that the trial court properly ordered summary dismissal of the plaintiff's action against the television station in the absence of any showing of malice in connection with the allegedly defamatory references to the plaintiff during the news broadcasts.

Fraud

Fraud is defined as the willful and intentional misrepresentation that could cause harm or loss to a person or property. Intentional misrepresentation can give rise to an action for fraud.

The plaintiff in *Robinson v. Shah*[65] was a long-time patient of defendant, Dr. Shah, and placed her physical well-being in the hands of that physician from 1975 to 1986. During that period of time, the defendant treated the plaintiff for various gynecological disorders. On November 9, 1983, the defendant performed a total abdominal hysterectomy and bilateral salpingo-oophorectomy on the plaintiff. Approximately one week following surgery, the plaintiff was discharged from the hospital and was assured that there were no complications or potential problems that might arise as a result of the surgery. On the day after the plaintiff was discharged from the hospital, she began to experience abdominal distress. She consulted the defendant about these symptoms, and the defendant ordered X-rays to be taken of the plaintiff's kidneys, ureter, and bladder in an effort to explain her discomfort.

The X-rays were taken at St. Joseph Memorial Hospital and were read and interpreted by Dr. Cavanaugh, presumably a radiologist associated with that facility. Cavanaugh was of the opinion, after reading the X-rays, that they showed the presence of surgical sponges that had been left in the plaintiff's abdomen after surgery. Cavanaugh called the defendant and reported the findings of the X-rays and, in addition, sent to the defendant a copy of a written report that also reflected those findings.

The defendant fraudulently concealed from the plaintiff the findings of these X-rays. Instead of being truthful, the defendant intentionally lied to the plaintiff and told her the X-rays were negative and that there were no apparent or unusual complications from the recent abdominal surgery, and she assured the plaintiff that she did not require further treatment. At no time did the defendant reveal to the plaintiff the fact that she had left surgical sponges in the plaintiff's abdomen after the most recent surgery.

Over the next several years, the plaintiff continued to see the defendant for gynecological check-ups. She continued to experience abdominal pain and discomfort. The defendant, however, continued to conceal from the plaintiff the existence of the surgical sponges left in the plaintiff's abdomen. The plaintiff ceased seeing the defendant as her physician in 1986. However, she consulted other physicians and continued to experience frequent pain and discomfort in her abdomen as well as intestinal, urological, and gynecological problems. Although the plaintiff brought her complaints to the attention of other physicians, no one was able to diagnose the source of her problems.

In 1993, one of the physicians attending to the plaintiff's problems diagnosed a pelvic mass, which he felt could be causing some discomfort. The plaintiff underwent pelvic sonograms and X-rays, which revealed the existence of retained surgical sponges. The plaintiff contended that the defendant, from and after November 18, 1983, had actual knowledge of the presence of retained surgical sponges in the plaintiff's abdomen and well knew the potential of future complications that could arise from this condition. Despite this knowledge, the plaintiff contended, the defendant fraudulently concealed the existence of this condition from the plaintiff.

The trial court found that the plaintiff was unable to discover the fact that the defendant had negligently left surgical sponges in her abdomen and that this fact was fraudulently concealed from the plaintiff, who did not discover the defendant's fraud until August 11, 1993.

The appeals court held that where a patient has a cause of action against a physician for malpractice and has been misled by the intentional and knowing lies of the physician to the extent that the patient in reliance on the fraudulent misrepresentation permits the statute of limitations to bar his or her action, the patient can maintain an action for fraud against the physician. The action is not based on the original negligence or malpractice, but rather because of the fraudulent

actions of the physician, which deceived the patient, with the consequence that the time bar ran against the original action.

The broad outlines of fraud are said to include any cunning, deception, or artifice used, in violation of legal or equitable duty, to circumvent, cheat, or deceive another. The forms it may assume and the means by which it may be practiced are as multifarious as human ingenuity can devise, and the courts consider it unwise or impossible to formulate an exact, definite, and all-inclusive definition of the action.

To prove fraud, the following facts must be shown:

- an untrue statement known to be untrue by the party making it and made with the intent to deceive
- justifiable reliance by the victim on the truth of the statement
- damages as a result of that reliance

The plaintiff's petition was found to have set forth sufficient allegations to state a cause of action for actual fraud against the defendant. The appeals court refused to recognize any distinction between the fraud that separates the victim from his or her money and the fraud that deprives a victim of a cause of action for malpractice.

The action in this case was filed more than 10 years after the fraud was perpetrated. The question is whether the statute of repose was also tolled by the defendant's concealment of the cause of action. It is a relatively simple matter to conclude that the running of the statute of limitations is tolled by concealment of the fraud. To hold that a physician may successfully blunt a malpractice cause of action by fraudulently misrepresenting facts to a patient would be to encourage such fraudulent behavior.

Invasion of Privacy

The right to privacy is implied in the Constitution. It is recognized by the law as the right to be left alone—the right to be free from unwarranted publicity and exposure to public view, as well as the right to live one's life without having one's name, picture, or private affairs made public against one's will. Health care organizations and professionals may become liable for invasion of privacy if, for example, they divulge information from a patient's medical record to improper sources or if they commit unwarranted intrusions into a patient's personal affairs.

Patients have a right to personal privacy and a right to the confidentiality of their personal and clinical records. The information in a patient's medical record is confidential and should not be disclosed without the patient's permission. Those who come into possession of the most intimate personal information about patients have both a legal and an ethical duty not to reveal confidential communications. The legal duty arises because the law recognizes a right to privacy. To protect this right, there is a corresponding duty to obey. The ethical duty is broader and applies at all times. There are, however, occasions when there is a legal obligation or duty to disclose information. The reporting of communicable diseases, gunshot wounds, child abuse, and other matters is required by law.

Invasion of privacy is a wrong that invades the right of a person to personal privacy. Absolute privacy has to be tempered with reality in the medical or nursing care of any patient, and the courts recognize this fact. Disregard for a patient's right to privacy is legally actionable, particularly when patients are unable to protect themselves adequately because of unconsciousness or immobility.

Unfortunately, familiarity with an organization's health care environment tends to diminish the conscious concern personnel should have for the protection of patient privacy. The plaintiff, a former hospital employee, in *Vernuil v. Poirier*[66] was awarded $15,000 in a legal action against her supervisor and hospital for invasion of privacy. The plaintiff claimed that while she was a patient and in the postoperative recovery room, her supervisor lifted her sheet in an attempt to view her abdominal incision. The court of appeals held that evidence sustained a finding of invasion of privacy. Because the supervisor's conduct occurred during the time and place of his employment, the hospital was jointly liable for damages. "Ensuring a patient's well being from all others, including staff, while the patient is helpless under the effects of anesthesia is part of its normal business."[67]

The liberty extended to the publication of personal matters, names, or photographs varies. Many public figures will not be heard to complain if their lives are given publicity, and ordinary citizens who voluntarily adopt a newsworthy course of conduct have no grounds for complaint if the activity is reported along with their names and pictures. Generally, the subject of a newsworthy occurrence cannot complain if his or her identity is exposed and exploited by unwarranted publication.

The news media should be accommodated within the limitations placed on such communications by the hospital and applicable statutes and/or regulations pertaining to the release of information. In any event, a patient's right of privacy must be protected. Professionals should restrict their interviews and news releases to avoid any injury to the reputation of a patient.

The press should not be given detailed statements about the physical condition of a patient. Health care professionals are in no position to make any comments concerning the occurrence that led to a patient's hospitalization. Comments concerning a patient's physical condition should come from the physician.

Because such matters do involve protected information, disclosure should be with the patient's permission.

Intentional Infliction of Mental Distress

The *intentional or reckless infliction of mental distress* is characterized by conduct that is so outrageous that it goes beyond the bounds tolerated by a decent society. It is a civil wrong for which a tort-feasor can be held liable for damages. Mental distress includes mental suffering resulting from painful emotions such as grief, public humiliation, despair, shame, and wounded pride. Liability for the wrongful infliction of mental distress may be based on either intentional or negligent misconduct. A plaintiff may recover damages if he or she can show that the defendant intended to inflict mental distress, and knew or should have known that his or her actions would give rise to it. Recovery generally is permitted even in the absence of physical harm.

The circuit court in *Johnson v. Women's Hospital*[68] found that a physician and a hospital, through certain of its employees, committed an intentional infliction of emotional distress. The mother of a premature infant who died shortly after birth had gone to her physician for a six-week check-up. She noticed a report in her medical chart that stated that the child was past the fifth lunar month in development and that hospital rules and state law prohibited disposal of it as a surgical specimen. The mother had understood that the body had been disposed of by common traditions of human dignity. On questioning her physician, he requested that his nurse take her to the hospital. At the hospital, a hospital employee took her to a freezer. The freezer was opened, and she was handed the jar containing her premature infant.

The circuit court entered a judgment in favor of the plaintiffs, and the defendants appealed. The court of appeals held that the jury could find that the hospital agreed to handle the infant's body properly and failed to do so. The jury could properly find that the hospital's conduct in displaying the infant was outrageous. There was no proof that the physician or his nurse was guilty of outrageous conduct. The award of compensatory damages in the amount of $100,000 was not so excessive as to shock the conscience of the court.

An action in *Greer v. Medders*[69] was brought by a patient and his wife against a physician for the intentional infliction of emotional distress. The defendant physician was covering for the attending physician who was on vacation. The plaintiff was in the hospital and had not seen the covering physician for several days, so he called the physician's office to complain. The physician later entered the patient's room, in an agitated manner, and became verbally abusive in the presence of the patient's wife and a nurse. He said to the patient,

"Let me tell you one damn thing, don't nobody call over to my office raising hell with my secretary . . . I don't have to be here every damn day checking on you because I check with physical therapy. . . . I don't have to be your damn doctor."[70] When the physician left the room, the plaintiff's wife began to cry, and the plaintiff experienced episodes of uncontrollable shaking for which he had psychiatric treatment. The superior court entered summary judgment for the physician, and the plaintiff appealed. The Georgia Court of Appeals held that the physician's abusive language willfully caused emotional upset and precluded summary judgment for the defendant.

PRODUCTS LIABILITY

Products liability is the liability of a manufacturer, seller, or supplier of chattels to a buyer or other third party for injuries sustained because of a defect in a product. An injured party may proceed with a lawsuit against a seller, manufacturer, or supplier on three legal theories: (1) negligence, (2) breach of warranty (express or implied), and (3) strict liability.

Negligence

Negligence, as applied to products liability, requires the plaintiff to establish duty, breach, injury, and causation. The manufacturer of a product is not liable for injuries suffered by a patient if they are the result of negligent use by the user. Product users must conform to the safety standards provided by the manufacturers of supplies and equipment. Failure to follow proper safety instructions can prevent recovery in a negligence suit if injury results from improper use.

Manufacturers are liable for injuries that result from the unsafe design of their products. To reduce the risks of liability, they generally provide detailed safety instructions to the users of their products. Failure to provide such instructions could be considered negligence on the part of the manufacturer.

An action in *Airco v. Simmons National Bank, Guardian, et al.*[71] was brought against a physician partnership that provided anesthesia services to the hospital and Airco, Inc., the manufacturer of an artificial breathing machine used in the administration of anesthesia. It was alleged that the patient suffered irreversible brain damage because of the negligent use of the equipment and its unsafe design. The machine had been marketed despite prior reports that there was a foreseeable danger of human error brought about by the presence of several identical black hoses and the necessity of connecting them correctly to three ports of identical size placed closely together. The machine lacked adequate labels and warnings, according to the reports. The jury awarded $1,070,000 in compensatory damages against the physician partnership and Airco, Inc. Punitive damages in the amount of $3 million were awarded against Airco, Inc. On appeal of the punitive damages award, the Arkansas Supreme Court held that the evidence for punitive damages was sufficient for the jury. The manufacturer had acted in a persistent reckless disregard of the foreseeable dangers in the machine by continuing to sell it with the known hazardous design.

Negligence, as well as breach of warranty and strict liability, was not established in the well-publicized case of the 1980s involving a woman who had died from the ingestion of Tylenol capsules tainted with potassium cyanide. The decedent's estate *in Elsroth v. Johnson & Johnson*[72] sued the manufacturer and the retail grocery store that sold the over-the-counter drug. The defendants moved for a summary judgment. The U.S. district court held that the retailer did not have a "duty" to protect the decedent from acts of tampering by an unknown third party. The manufacturer was not liable under an inadequate warning theory. Manufacturers are under a duty to warn of the dangers that may be associated with the normal and lawful use of their products. However, they need not warn that their products may be susceptible to criminal misuse.

The negligent use of a Bovie plate led to liability in *Monk v. Doctors Hospital*.[73] The patient was admitted to the hospital for abdominal surgery. Before surgery, the patient asked the surgeon also to remove three moles from the right arm and one from the right leg. The surgeon instructed a hospital nurse to prepare a Bovie machine but was not present while the machine was set up. The nurse placed the contact plate of the Bovie machine under the patient's right calf in a negligent manner, and the patient suffered burns. Instruction manuals, issued by the manufacturer, supported the claim that the plate was placed improperly on the patient. These manuals had been available to the hospital. The trial court directed a verdict in favor of the hospital and the physician. The appellate court found that there was sufficient evidence from which the jury could conclude that the Bovie plate was applied in a negligent manner. There also was sufficient evidence, including the manufacturer's manual and expert testimony, from which the jury could find that the physician was independently negligent.[74]

This case demonstrates the necessity for an organization to require conformity to the safety standards provided by the manufacturers of supplies and equipment. As evidenced in the above case, such failure can cause an organization and its staff to be held liable for negligence. This case should alert manufacturers of the necessity to provide appropriate safety instructions to the users of their products. It can be assumed that failure to provide such instructions could be considered negligence on the part of the supplier.

Breach of Warranty

To recover under a cause of action based on a breach of warranty theory, the plaintiff must establish first whether there was an express or implied warranty.

Express Warranty

An express warranty includes specific promises or affirmations made by the seller to the buyer, such as that expressed in *Crocker v. Winthrop Laboratories.*[75] The patient, Mr. Crocker, had been admitted to the hospital for a hernia operation. His physician prescribed both Demerol and Talwin for pain. After discharge from the hospital, Crocker developed an addiction to Talwin and was able to obtain prescriptions from several physicians to support his habit. He was eventually admitted to the hospital for detoxification. After six days, Crocker walked out of the hospital and went home. He became agitated and abusive, threatening his wife, and she eventually called a physician at his request. The physician arrived and gave Crocker an injection of Demerol. Crocker then retired to bed and died. Action was brought against the drug company for the suffering and subsequent wrongful death that occurred as the proximate result of the decedent's addiction to Talwin.

The district court rendered a judgment for the plaintiff, and the court of appeals reversed. On further appeal, the Texas Supreme Court held that when a drug company positively and specifically represents its product to be free and safe from all dangers of addiction and when the treating physician relies on such representation, the drug company is liable when the representation proves to be false and injury results.

A blow to the cigarette industry occurred when the U.S. Supreme Court in *Cipollone v. Liggett Group, Inc., et al.* held that the 1965 Federal Cigarette Labeling and Advertising Act did not preempt state law damage actions.

Implied Warranty

Implied warranties are in effect when the law implies that one exists by operation of law as a matter of "public policy" for the protection of the public. *Jacob E. Decker & Sons v. Capps*[76] is a case involving the question of the liability of a manufacturer of food products to the consumer for damages sustained by ingestion of contaminated sausage. One member of a family died, and others became seriously ill, as a result of eating contaminated food. The jury found that the sausage had been contaminated before being packaged by the defendant and that it was unfit for human consumption. The Texas Supreme Court decided that the defendant was liable for the injuries sustained by the consumers of the contaminated food under an implied warranty. Liability in such a case is based neither on negligence nor on a breach of the usual implied contractual warranty. It is based on the broad principle of the public policy to protect human health and life.

Strict Liability

Strict liability refers to liability without fault. Neither care nor negligence nor ignorance will save the defendant from liability. Strict liability makes possible an award of damages without any proof of negligence on the part of the manufacturer. The plaintiff needs only to show that he or she suffered injury while using the manufacturer's product in the prescribed way.

The following elements must be present for a plaintiff to proceed with a case on the basis of strict liability:

- The product must have been manufactured by the defendant.
- The product must have been defective at the time it left the hands of the manufacturer or seller. The defect in the product normally consists of a manufacturing defect, a design defect in the product, and/or an absence or inadequacy of warnings for the use of the product.
- The plaintiff must have been injured by the specific product.
- The defective product must have been the proximate cause of injury to the plaintiff.

A blood bank in *Weber v. Charity Hospital of Louisiana at New Orleans*[77] was held strictly liable to a hospital patient who developed hepatitis from a transfusion of defective blood during surgery. Evidence established that the blood bank collected, processed, and sold the blood to the hospital. Although the hospital administered the blood, absent any negligence in its handling or administration, it was not liable for the patient's injury. Many states have enacted statutes to exempt blood from the product category and thus remove blood products from the theory of strict liability.

Strict liability may be imposed on the manufacturer of a device that causes injury to a plaintiff, even though he or she was not the purchaser of the product, if that product was defective and the defect was the actual and proximate cause of the injuries or damages. A case in point is *Kimberly Gerringer v. Gordon A. Runnells,*[78] in which a seven-year-old child suffered permanent brain damage as a result of convulsions caused by the leaking of an intravascular dose of a local anesthetic, Xylocaine, beyond the cuff (a medical device, similar to a blood pressure cuff, used to control the flow of blood). This leaking was allegedly a hazard of the procedure about which the manufacturer failed to notify the medical public.

Damages awarded against the manufacturer of the automatic cuff amounted to $30,000.

Liability also may be based on the concept of *res ipsa loquitur* ("the thing speaks for itself") by showing all of the following:

- The product did not perform in the way intended.
- The product was not tampered with by the buyer or third persons.
- The defect existed at the time it left the defendant manufacturer.

Blood a Service—Not a Product

The patient in *Perlmutter v. Beth David Hospital*[9] contracted serum hepatitis from a blood transfusion. She relied on an implied sales warranty as the basis of her suit. The court denied recovery, pointing out that even though a separate charge of $60 was made for the blood, the charge was incidental to the primary contract with the hospital for services. Because there was no claim of negligence, the pronouncement of the court that blood provided by the hospital was a service, rather than a sale, barred recovery by the patient. The rationale of this case did not extend to relieve commercial blood banks from liability on the basis of strict liability warranty theories. Action could have been instituted against the hospital if it had been shown that the hospital was negligent in handling the blood.

Products Liability Defenses

Defenses against recovery in a products liability case include

- assumption of the risk (e.g., voluntary exposure to such risks as radiation treatments and chemotherapy treatments)
- intervening cause (e.g., an intravenous solution contaminated by the negligence of the product user, rather than that of the manufacturer)
- disclaimers (e.g., manufacturers' inserts and warnings regarding usage and contraindications of their products)
- contributory negligence (e.g., use of a product in a way that it was not intended to be used)
- comparative fault (e.g., injury is the result of the concurrent negligence of both the manufacturer and the plaintiff)

Successful products liability cases tend to have a negative impact on the development and use of new drugs. In addition, manufacturers tend to remove older technologies from the marketplace to decrease their exposure to liability and potential financial risks.

On the positive side, the slipshod manufacture of products is discouraged. This is increasingly evident in the sale of food products where consumers are demanding full disclosure of the contents of packaged products.

DEFECTIVE SYRINGE

Citation: *Cotita v. Pharma-Plast, U.S.A., Inc., 974 F.2d 598 (5th Cir. 1992)*

Facts

While providing nursing services to a patient with acquired immune deficiency syndrome (AIDS), Mr. Cotita, a registered nurse, was stuck by a syringe manufactured by the defendant-appellee, Pharma-Plast. The syringe, although still in its sterile packaging, was missing the protective cap that normally covers the tip of the needle. This improper packaging allowed the needle to pierce its sterile plastic covering and penetrate the protective gloves that Cotita was wearing. Because of the presence of the patient's blood on his gloves at the time of the needle stick, Cotita feared that he had been exposed to the human immunodeficiency virus (HIV). Subsequent tests revealed that Cotita was not HIV-positive; nevertheless, he sued Pharma-Plast, seeking damages for mental anguish stemming from his fear of contracting AIDS.

Pharma-Plast admitted defective packaging, and the district court granted summary judgment for the plaintiff on the issue of the defective state of the syringe. The issue of damages was specifically reserved for trial. Pharma-Plast moved for leave to amend its answer to assert the defense of Cotita's negligence. With the trial set for the following month, the district court denied this motion. Later, the trial in this matter was continued. Pharma-Plast resubmitted its motion for leave to amend, which was granted over Cotita's objection. Cotita also objected to the introduction of evidence concerning his negligence, contending that the issue of fault was closed by the court's previous entry of summary judgment on the issue of Pharma-Plast's liability as the manufacturer of the defectively packaged syringe.

The damage issue was tried before a jury that returned a verdict for $150,000 in Cotita's favor. This amount was reduced by 30 percent, a figure that the jury found reflected his negligence. Cotita maintained that the issue of his negligence should not have been considered by the jury, nor used to reduce the amount of his award.

Issue

Did the district court err in allowing Pharma-Plast to amend its answer to assert the nurse's negligence?

Holding

The U.S. Court of Appeals found no error in the district court's application of comparative fault.

Reason

Pharma-Plast presented evidence that the procedures used by the nurse were in violation of the universal precautions and procedures that are standard in the health care field. The district court here was entitled to determine that the application of comparative fault would ultimately encourage workers in the health care field to follow the established procedures for handling syringes.

The actions of Cotita in his use of the defective syringe were properly considered in evaluating the damages awarded. The damage phase of the proceeding was separate and apart from the previously decided liability phase.

Discussion

1. Do you agree with the court's decision? Explain your answer.
2. What procedures has your organization implemented to reduce the likelihood of exposing staff, visitors, and patients to infectious diseases?

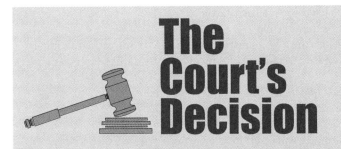

The Court's Decision

The Ohio Court of Appeals held that the delay in providing the plaintiff treatment fell below the medically acceptable standard of care. *The court was "appalled"* that the physician had characterized his evaluation as a medical examination or to imply that what he described as a "cursory breast examination" should be considered a medically sufficient breast examination. It seemed incredible to the court that a physician would deliberately choose not to expend the additional few minutes or seconds to thoroughly palpitate the sides of the breasts, which is a standard minimally intrusive cancer detection technique. His admission that he merely "pressed" on plaintiff's breasts, coupled with the additional admission that such acts would not necessarily disclose lumps in the breasts, constituted poor medical care.

It was probable that an earlier procedure would have safely and reliably conserved a large part of the plaintiff's right breast. Through these inexcusable delays, the plaintiff lost this option and, instead, was medically required to have the entire breast removed. The court concluded that the defendant's negligence was the sole and proximate cause of all of the plaintiff's losses in excess of the basic lumpectomy procedure. The court found the plaintiff's total damages to be $85,000.

CHAPTER REVIEW

1. A *tort* is a civil wrong, not including breach of contract, that is committed against a person or property for which a court provides a correction in the form of an action for damages. Tort actions can affect someone on personal and professional levels, and are therefore highly relevant to those in medical professions. Three categories of torts are *negligent torts*, *intentional torts*, and *torts where strict liability is assessed regardless of fault*.

2. *Intentional wrongdoing* involves a willful act that violates another person's interests. Not only must the action be intentional, but also the perpetrator must realize that the action will, with virtual certainty, result in harm to the person against whom it is committed. A *negligent wrongdoing*, however, may not involve the commission of an act, but merely the failure to act when there is a legal duty to do so. *Malpractice* is negligence or carelessness of a professional person. *Criminal negligence* is the reckless disregard for another's safety.

3. *Negligence* has three basic forms:
   - *Malfeasance* is the execution of an unlawful of improper act.
   - *Misfeasance* is the improper performance of an act that results in injury to another.
   - *Nonfeasance* is a failure to act when there is a duty to do so.

4. There are two basic degrees of negligence:
   - *Ordinary negligence* is the failure to do what a reasonably prudent person would or would not do under the circumstances of the act or omission in question.
   - *Gross negligence* is the intentional or wanton omission of care that should be provided or the performance of an improper act.

5. To recover damages caused by negligence, four elements must be present—duty to care, breach of duty, injury, and causation.
   - *Duty to care* exists when there is a legal obligation of care, performance, or observance imposed on one party to guard the rights of others.
   - *Breach of duty* is the failure to meet a prevailing standard of care. Expert witnesses often are used to help determine what a reasonably prudent person would or would not have done in such a case.
   - Without proof or harm or *injury*, a defendant cannot be found liable.
   - *Causation* refers to the idea that the defendant's negligence must be a substantial factor in having caused an injury.

6. For liability to be established based on failure to follow a specified standard of care outlined by statute, three elements must be present:
   - The defendant must have been within the specified class of persons outlined in the statute.
   - The plaintiff must have been injured in a way that the statute was designed to prevent.
   - The plaintiff must show that the injury would not have occurred had the statute not been violated.

7. *Foreseeability* is the reasonable anticipation that harm or injury will result from an act or a failure to act. The test for foreseeability is whether or not one should have reasonably anticipated that the event in question or a similar event would occur.

8. *Assault* is the infringement on the mental security or tranquility of another person; *battery* is the violation of another person's physical integrity. No actual physical harm need have occurred for an individual to be guilty of assault. Instead, assault is the threat of physical harm coupled with an apparent and present ability to commit the battery. Battery is defined as the intentional act of touching another's person, in a socially impermissible manner, without that person's consent. Damage does not have to be shown to impose liability. Assault and battery are highly relevant to medical professionals because of the amount and degree of physical touching required to provide care.

9. A basic tenant of the U.S. legal system is the personal right to move freely and without hindrance. *False imprisonment* is the unlawful restraint of an individual's personal liberty or the unlawful restraint or confinement of an individual. For a false imprisonment charge to warrant recovery, the plaintiff must be aware of the confinement and have no reasonable means of escape. Damage does not have to be shown to impose liability. In cases in which individuals are confined to prevent harm to themselves or others, the confinement may be justifiable under the law.

10. *Defamation of character* is a false oral or written communication to someone other than the individual defamed that subjects that individual's reputation to scorn and ridicule in the eyes of a substantial number of respectable people in the community. Two aspects of defamation of character are *libel*, which results from the written word, and *slander*, which results from the spoken word.

11. *Fraud* is a willful and intentional misrepresentation that could cause harm or loss to an individual or property. To prove fraud, the following three facts must be shown:
   - An untrue statement known to be untrue by the party making it and made with the intent to deceive;
   - A justifiable reliance by the victim on the truth of that statement;
   - Damages as a result of that reliance.

12. Patients have a right to privacy and to the confidentiality of their personal and clinical records. Health care organizations and professionals can be found in violation of these rights if, for example, they reveal information from a

patient's medical record to improper parties or if they commit unwarranted intrusions into a patient's personal affairs. *Invasion of privacy* is a wrong that interferes with the right of an individual to personal privacy.

13. The *intentional or reckless infliction of mental distress* is conduct that is so outrageous that it goes beyond the bounds tolerated by a decent society. Mental distress can include mental suffering from painful emotions such as grief, public humiliation, despair, shame, and wounded pride. The commission of intentional or negligent misconduct can be grounds for liability, even in the absence of physical harm.

14. *Products liability* is the liability of the manufacturer, seller, or supplier of products to a buyer or other third party for injury sustained because of a defect in a product. The product manufacturer, seller, or supplier is not liable for injuries sustained by a patient if the injuries are the result of negligent use. A plaintiff will not recover unless an express or implied warranty is established. *Strict liability* refers to liability without fault. When strict liability is applied, damages can be awarded without proof of negligence on the part of the manufacturer if the patient used the product in the prescribed way.

REVIEW QUESTIONS

1. Describe the objectives of tort law.
2. Discuss the distinctions among negligent torts, intentional torts, and strict liability.
3. What forms of negligence are described in this chapter?
4. How does one distinguish between negligence and malpractice?
5. What are the elements that must be proven in order to be successful in a negligence suit? Illustrate your answer with a case (the facts of the case can be hypothetical).
6. Can a "duty to care" be established by statute or contract? Discuss your answer.
7. Describe the categories of intentional torts.
8. How does slander differ from libel? Give an example of each.
9. Is "blood" considered a product? Discuss your answer.
10. Describe the defenses that are often used in a products liability case.

NOTES

1. Tomcik v. Ohio Dep't of Rehabilitation & Correction, 598 N.E.2d 900 (Ohio Ct. App. 1991).
2. *Id.* at 904.
3. The Robert Wood Johnson Foundation, *The Tort Systems for Medical Malpractice: How Well Does It Work, What Are the Alternatives?* ABRIDGE, Spring 1991, at 2.
4. 11 A.2d 132 (N.Y. App. Div. 1960).
5. 498 So.2d 713 (La. Ct. App. 1986).
6. 787 S.W.2d 494 (Tex. Ct. App. 1990).
7. *Id.* at 496.
8. 57A AM JUR. 2D *Torts* § 208 (1989).
9. 57A AM. JUR. 2D *Torts* § 143 (1989).
10. 57A AM. JUR. 2D *Torts* § 148 (1989).
11. 57A AM. JUR. 2D *Torts* § 199 (1989).
12. 343 N.E.3d 589 (Ill. 1976).
13. 57A AM. JUR. 2D *Torts* § 193 (1989).
14. *Id.*
15. 175 N.W.2d 588, 596 (Iowa 1970).
16. 349 A.2d 245 (Md. 1975).
17. Greene v. Bowen, 639 F. Supp. 544, 561 (E.D. Cal. 1986).
18. 706 P.2d 1383 (Nev. 1985).
19. 355 S.E.2d 104 (Ga. Ct. App. 1987).
20. 57A AM. JUR. 2D *Torts* § 26 (1989).
21. 498 So.2d 713 (La. Ct. App. 1986).
22. 128 So.2d 485 (Ala. 1961).
23. 483 So.2d 634 (La. Ct. App. 1985).
24. 559 So.2d 838 (La. Ct. App. 1990).
25. 57A AM. JUR. 2D *Torts* § 78 (1989).
26. 384 S.E.2d 92 (Va. 1989).
27. *Id.*
28. 498 So.2d 713 (La. Ct. App. 1986).
29. 691 A.2d 1147 (D.C. App. 1997).
30. 57A AM. JUR. 2D *Torts* § 80 (1989).
31. 654 A.2 771 (Conn. App. 1995).
32. *Id.* at 777.
33. 648 So.2d 11 (La App. 3d Cir. 1994).
34. *Clark v. Wagoner* 452 S.W.2d 437, 440 (Tex. 1970).
35. 296 S.E.2d 216 (Ga. Ct. App. 1982).
36. 57A AM. JUR. 2D *Torts* § 134 (1989).
37. 142 N.E.2d 337 (Mass. 1957).
38. 116 Cal. Rptr. 733 (Cal. Ct. App. 1974).
39. 504 So.2d 22 (Ala. 1986).

40. 457 A.2d 431 (N.J. 1983).

41. 536 So.2d 705 (La. Ct. App. 1988).

42. 865 S.W.2d 833 (Mo. Ct. App. 1993).

43. 841 F.2d 851 (8th Cir. 1988).

44. 358 S.E.2d 865 (Ga. Ct. App. 1987).

45. Tinetti, Liu, Marottoli, & Ginter, *Mechanical Restraint Use among Residents of Skilled Nursing Facilities*, 265(4) JAMA 471 (1991).

46. Garrard, *Evaluation of Neuroleptic Drug Use by Nursing Home Elderly under Proposed Medicare and Medicaid Regulations*, 265(4) JAMA 463 (1991).

47. 461 S.W.2d 195 (Tex. Ct. App. 1970).

48. 562 N.Y.2d 127 (N.Y. App. Div. 1990).

49. *Id.* at 129.

50. 856 S.W.2d 437 (Tex Ct. App. 1993).

51. *Id.* at 447.

52. *Id.*

53. *Keller v. Miami Herald Publishing Company* 778 F.2d 711 (11th Cir. 1985).

54. *Id.* at 713.

55. 285 N.W.2d 891 (Wis. Ct. App. 1979).

56. *Id.* at 893.

57. *Id.* at 894.

58. Associates and Aldrich Co. v. Times Mirror Co., 440 F.2d 133, 136 (9th Cir. 1971).

59. 317 S.E.2d 652 (Ga. Ct. App. 1984).

60. 143 S.E.2d 489 (Ga. Ct. App. 1965).

61. *Id.*

62. Miller-Douglas v. Keller, 579 So.2d 491 (La. Ct. App.1991).

63. 150 N.E.2d 202 (Ill. App. Ct. 1958).

64. 739 S.W.2d 680 (Ark. 1987).

65. 936 P.2d 784 (Kans. App. 1997).

66. 589 So.2d 1202 (La. Ct. App. 1991).

67. Id. at 1204.

68. 527 S.W.2d 133 (Tenn. Ct. App. 1975).

69. 336 S.E.2d 329 (Ga. App. 1985).

70. *Id.*

71. 638 S.W.2d 660 (Ark. 1982).

72. 700 F. Supp. 151 (S.D.N.Y. 1988).

73. 403 F.2d 580 (D.C. Cir. 1968).

74. *Id.*

75. 514 S.W.2d 429 (Tex. 1974).

76. 164 S.W.2d 828 (Tex. 1942).

77. 487 So.2d 148 (La. Ct. App. 1986).

78. (Cal. Sup. Ct. Sacramento City, Nov. 13, 1973.).

79. 123 N.E.2d 793 (N.Y. 1955).

Criminal Aspects of Health Care

NURSE SENTENCED FOR DIABOLICAL ACTS

From 1993 to 1995, Majors worked as a licensed practical nurse (LPN) in the intensive care unit (ICU) of a county hospital. Although he may have been a competent nurse, he had one problem: an incredibly high number of elderly patients died under his watch. By 1995, after rumors started to circulate that he was euthanizing patients, the hospital suspended him, and the State Board of Nursing suspended his license.

During 1994, 100 of the 351 people admitted to the hospital's four-bed ICU died. A large percentage of those who died were elderly. In comparison, during the previous four years, an average of only 27 patients per year passed away, out of an average of 354 admitted to the ICU each year.

In early 1995, spurred on by her suspicions (and those of other nurses), registered nurse Stirek did a correlation, based on work attendance charts, between Majors' presence in the ICU and patient deaths. Her rough analysis showed that Majors was present for more deaths than any other nurse, almost twice as many as the nearest contender.

On March 7, 1995, Stirek showed her analysis to Ling, the president and chief executive officer of the hospital. Two days later, Ling called Majors into his office and suspended him from work, with pay. Ling refused to give Majors a reason for the suspension. Later, Ling went to the police and asked them to investigate.

Although the hospital apparently tried to keep the controversy low keyed, leaks developed. Some nurses, who were afraid of being fired if they spoke publicly about the issue, wrote an anonymous "letter to the editor" accusing Majors of being a "Dr. Kevorkian" and the hospital of covering it up. Majors was subsequently prosecuted.[1]

What is your verdict?

INTRODUCTION

Laws are made to restrain and punish the wicked; the wise and good do not need them as a guide, but only as a shield against rapine and oppression; they can live civilly and orderly, though there were no law in the world.

John Milton (1608–1674)

This chapter presents the procedural aspects of criminal law, as well as a variety of criminal cases that have occurred in the health care industry. The cases reviewed are by no means exhaustive for a particular health care organization or profession. The purpose of this chapter is to provide students and health care professionals with a general review of criminal law as it applies to the health care industry.

CRIMINAL PROCEDURE

Criminal law is society's expression of the limits of acceptable human and institutional behavior. A *crime* is any social harm defined and made punishable by law. The *objectives of criminal law* are to maintain public order and safety, to protect the individual, to use punishment as a deterrent to crime, and to rehabilitate the criminal for return to society.

Crimes are generally classified as misdemeanors or felonies. The difference between a misdemeanor and a felony revolves around the severity of the crime. A *misdemeanor* is an offense punishable by less than one year in jail and/or a fine (e.g., petty larceny). A *felony* is a much more serious crime (e.g., rape, murder) and is generally punishable by imprisonment in a state or federal penitentiary for more than one year.

Peculiar to health care organizations is the fact that patients are often helpless and at the mercy of others. Health care facilities are far too often places where the morally weak and mentally deficient prey on the physically and sometimes mentally helpless. The very institutions designed to make the public well and feel safe can provide the setting for criminal conduct.

The U.S. Department of Justice and state and local prosecutors are vigorously pursuing and prosecuting health care institutions and individuals for what they allege constitutes criminal conduct. Fraud and abuse of billing systems, patients, and other organizations have caused these law enforcement agencies to assume a *zero-tolerance level*. This new reality makes awareness of the rights, responsibilities, and duties of health care professionals more important than ever.

Arrest

Prosecutions for crimes generally begin with the arrest of a defendant by a police officer or with the filing of a formal action in a court of law and the issuance of an arrest warrant or summons. On arrest, the defendant is taken to the appropriate law enforcement agency for processing, which includes paperwork and fingerprinting. The police also prepare accusatory statements, such as misdemeanor complaints and felony complaints. Detectives are assigned to cases when necessary to gather evidence, interview persons suspected of committing a crime and witnesses to a crime, and assist in preparing a case for possible trial. After processing has been completed, a person is either detained or released on bond.

A felony complaint or an indictment commences a criminal proceeding; however, an individual may be tried for a felony after indictment by a grand jury unless the defendant waives presentment to the grand jury and pleads guilty by way of a superior court. Felony cases are presented to a grand jury by a district attorney or an assistant district attorney. The grand jury is presented with the prosecution's evidence and then charged that they may indict the target if they find reasonable cause to believe from the evidence presented to them that all the elements of a particular crime are present. The grand jury may request that witnesses be subpoenaed to testify. A defendant may choose to testify and offer information if he or she wishes. Actions of a grand jury are handed up to a judge, after which the defendant will be notified to appear to be arraigned for the crimes charged in the indictment.

Arraignment

The arraignment is a formal reading of the accusatory instrument and includes the setting of bail. The accused should appear with counsel or have counsel appointed by the court if he or she cannot afford his or her own. After the charges are read, the defendant pleads guilty or not guilty. A not guilty plea is normally offered on a felony. On a plea of not guilty, the defense attorney and prosecutor make arguments regarding bail. After arraignment of the defendant, the judge sets a date for the defendant to return to court. Between the time of arraignment and the next court date, the defense attorney and the prosecutor confer about the charges and evidence in the possession of the prosecutor. At that time, the defense will offer any mitigating circumstances it believes will convince the prosecutor to lessen or drop the charges.

Conference

If the defendant does not plead guilty, both felony and misdemeanor cases are taken to conference, and plea bargaining commences with the goal of an agreed-upon disposition. If no disposition can be reached, the case is adjourned, motions are made, and further plea bargaining takes place. Generally after several adjournments, a case is assigned to a trial court.

Prosecutor

The role of the prosecutor in the criminal justice system is well defined in *Berger v. United States*:

> The United States Attorney is the representative not of an ordinary party to a controversy, but of a sovereignty whose obligation to govern impartially is compelling as its obligation to govern at all; and whose interest, therefore, in a criminal prosecution is not that it shall win a case, but that justice will be done. As such, he is in a peculiar and very definite sense the servant of the law, the twofold aim of which is that guilt shall not escape or innocence suffer.[2]

The potential of the prosecutor's office is not always fully realized in many jurisdictions. In many cities the combination of the prosecutor's staggering caseload and small staff of assistants prevents sufficient attention being given to each case.[3]

Defense Attorney

The defense attorney generally sits in the proverbial hot seat, being perceived as the "bad guy." Although everyone seems to understand the attorney's function in protecting the rights of those represented, the defense attorney often is not very popular.

> There is a substantial difference in the problem of representing the "run-of-the-mill" criminal defendant and one whose alleged crimes have aroused great public outcry. The difficulties in providing representation for the ordinary criminal defendant are simple compared with the difficulties of obtaining counsel for one who is charged with a crime which by its nature or circumstances incites strong public condemnation.[4]

Criminal Trial

Most of the processes of a criminal trial are similar to that of a civil trial and include jury selection, opening statements, presentation of witnesses and other evidence, summations, instructions to the jury by the judge, jury deliberations, verdict, and opportunity for appeal to a higher court. In a criminal trial, the jury verdict must be unanimous, and the standard of proof must be beyond a reasonable doubt. A criminal trial generally is conducted in the following manner:

- jurors are selected
- jury is sworn
- prosecutor (representing the people) opens (mandatory)
- defense attorney opens (optional)
- prosecutor calls witnesses and presents evidence
- defense attorney cross-examines
- defense attorney calls witnesses and presents evidence
- prosecutor cross-examines
- defense attorney sums up
- prosecutor sums up
- judge charges the jury by explaining the legal aspects of the case
- jury deliberates and returns a verdict
- appeals go to a higher court

Many areas of criminal law can have an impact on health care employees. The following sections present some of the more common areas where health care employees have been confronted with criminal charges. Following, some of the issues that could bring health care providers into the criminal arena are explored.

CASE REVIEWS

Drugs

It is no surprise that health care organizations and professionals are affected by the theft, abuse, and illegal sale of drugs. There appears to be no end to the stream of cases entering the nation's courtrooms.

Physician Conspiracy to Distribute Dilaudid. The ophthalmologist in *Bouquett v. St. Elizabeth's Corp.*[5] brought an action to challenge suspension of his medical staff privileges after a felony conviction in a federal court for conspiracy to distribute Dilaudid. He later was sentenced to five years of incarceration. On appeal, the Ohio Supreme Court held that the conviction of the ophthalmologist justified summary suspension of his staff privileges pursuant to a hospital bylaw permitting summary suspension in the best interest of patient care in the hospital. The governing body of a private organization has broad discretion in determining who shall be granted medical staff privileges. Unless an organization has been arbitrary and capricious or has abused its discretion, the courts generally will not interfere with its decision to suspend physicians convicted on drug-related felony charges. Summary suspension of a physician extends beyond technical skills and medical competence. It encompasses the perceived integrity of a physician, which becomes suspect after conviction of a felony.

Pharmacist's Illegal Use and Sale of Marijuana. The pharmacist in *Brown v. Idaho State Board of Pharmacy*[6] had admitted to using marijuana approximately twice per week. During a hearing by the Idaho State Board of Pharmacy, the hearing officer admitted into evidence a copy of a judgment of a conviction on Brown's plea of guilty to a criminal charge of possession of drug paraphernalia. The Idaho State Board of Pharmacy suspended Brown's license. On appeal, the Idaho Court of Appeals held that revocation of his license was supported by evidence that he engaged in the illegal use of marijuana and that he also had participated in the sale and delivery of a misbranded drug.

Child Abuse

Child abuse statutes have been enacted in most states to provide civil immunity for those making or participating in good-faith reports of suspected child abuse. Most states also provide immunity from criminal liability. The New York State Social Services Law provides that "[a]ny person, official, or institution participating in good faith in the making of a report, the taking of photographs, or the removal or keeping of a child pursuant to this title shall have immunity from any liability, civil or criminal, that might otherwise result by reason of such actions."[7] Even in states that do not provide immunity, it is unlikely that anyone making a good-faith report of suspected child abuse would be subject to criminal liability. State laws generally specify what persons (e.g., physicians, nurses, and social workers) are required to report suspected child abuse that comes before them in their official capacities. In some states, failure to report a case of suspected child abuse carries criminal penalties, as well as civil liability for the damages resulting from such failure.[8]

Good-Faith Reporting

The pediatrician in *Satler v. Larsen*[9] had reported the possibility of child abuse to the Bureau of Child Welfare. The report of suspected child abuse was held not actionable in the absence of a persuasive showing that the report was made in bad faith. Summary dismissal was found appropriate with respect to defamation claims brought against the pediatrician for reporting suspected child abuse. The four-month-old infant in this case had been brought to the physician's office in a comatose state with a bilateral subdural hematoma. This occurred one day after the child had been discharged from the hospital.

The psychologist in *E.S. by D.S. v. Seitz*[10] was immune from liability in a suit charging her with negligence in formulating and reporting her professional opinion to a social worker that a father had sexually abused his three-year-old daughter. It was undisputed that the psychologist had made the report in compliance with the Wisconsin statute, after having examined the child in the course of her professional duties as a mental health professional.

Failure To Report

The criminal and civil risks for health care professionals do not lie in good-faith reporting of suspected incidents of child abuse, but in failing to report such incidents. Most states have legislated a variety of civil and criminal penalties for failure to report suspected child abuse incidents. New York, for example, provides:

> 1) Any person, official or institution required by this title to report a case of suspected child abuse or maltreatment who willfully fails to do so shall be guilty of a class A misdemeanor.
> 2) Any person, official or institution required by this title to report a case of suspected child abuse or maltreatment who knowingly and willfully fails to do so shall be civilly liable for the damages proximately caused by such failure.[11]

The Minnesota Board of Psychology was found to have acted properly when it placed the license of a psychologist on conditional status.[12] The psychologist had argued that he was not required to report past abuse that was not ongoing, that a report made five weeks after the incident was not untimely, and that the reporting laws were unconstitutional because they violated the privacy rights of clients and the privilege against self-incrimination. The psychologist had failed to report incidents of sexual child abuse. The court held there was no merit to the psychologist's contentions that the child abuse reporting laws were unclear and that they did not apply to one patient who was a grandfather, responsible for the child's care at the time of the incident in question.

Criminal Negligence

Criminal negligence is the reckless disregard for the safety of others. It is the willful indifference to an injury that could follow an act.

The defendants in *State v. Brenner*[13] were charged with cruelty to the infirm. The defendants brought a challenge stating that the criminal statutes under which they were charged were constitutionally vague. According to the court, Section 14.12 of Louisiana Revised Statutes defines criminal negligence as follows:

> Criminal negligence exists when, although neither specific nor general criminal intent is present, there is such disregard of the interest of others that the offender's conduct amounts to a gross deviation below the standard of care expected to be maintained by a reasonably careful man under like circumstances.[14]

Criminal negligence requires

> a gross deviation below the standard of care expected to be maintained by a reasonably careful man under like circumstances. It calls for substantially more than the ordinary lack of care which may be the basis of tort liability, and furnishes a more explicit statement of that lack of care which has been variously characterized in criminal statutes as "gross negligence" and "recklessness."[15]

In the bill of particulars, the state alleged that the administrator of the nursing facility neglected and/or mistreated residents by failing to ensure that: the facility was maintained in a sanitary manner; necessary health services were performed; staff was properly trained; there were adequate medical supplies and sufficient staff; records were maintained properly; and the residents were adequately fed and cared for. There were allegations that the director of nursing neglected and/or mistreated the residents and also failed to properly train the staff at the facility in correct nursing procedures. The controller was alleged to have failed to purchase adequate medical supplies for proper treatment. The admissions director allegedly failed to exercise proper judgment regarding admissions procedures, and the physical therapist allegedly failed to provide adequate physical therapy services. The defendants asserted that the term "neglect" was unconstitutionally vague. The Louisiana Supreme Court, on appeal by the defendants from two lower courts, held that the phrases "intentional or criminally negligent mistreatment or neglect" and "unjustifiable pain and suffering" were not vague and that they were sufficiently clear in meaning to afford a person of ordinary understanding fair notice of the conduct that was prohibited.[16]

Criminal Trespass

When an employee is the victim of a criminal act committed on hospital property, what does the employee have to prove in order to establish negligence? What action should an organization take when it becomes aware of significant security hazards on its property? The plaintiff in *Mundy v. Department of Health and Human Resources*[17] was an LPN who worked for 11 years for the Department of Health and Human Resources at Charity Hospital. In November 1986, she arrived for work on the evening shift at 11:17 P.M. As she approached the elevators, which were also used by the general public, she noticed that the two guards who were usually stationed at that location were not there. She entered the elevator to go to the eleventh floor, and a man jumped in as the doors were closing. He pressed the second floor button, but when the elevator stopped at that floor, he pulled a knife and

attacked the plaintiff. Thinking that the alarm would frighten her attacker and alert someone, she pressed the emergency button, but it was not operating. She was then stabbed repeatedly before her attacker fell out of the elevator.

The trial court found the hospital negligent in the maintenance and operation of the premises, and awarded the plaintiff $125,000. On appeal, judgment of the trial court was reversed in favor of the defendant hospital.

Security personnel routinely patrolled the floors of the hospital during shift changes and after visiting hours were over. Moreover, at times they would escort people from the building. Escort services were also provided for employees leaving the building at night, but not entering it. The hospital police captain testified that he had no knowledge of criminal acts having been committed near the elevators. When he learned that incidents had taken place near the emergency department, he always posted a guard there.

There was no duty to protect the plaintiff as she came into the hospital. Further, the risk of harm was not related to her employment, nor was it any greater to her than to the general public. At the time and place of her attack, she was not under the supervision and control of her employer. Even if the hospital owed a general duty to provide security for the general public, there was no showing that the hospital was negligent in its security operations. There was no evidence that the hospital knew or should have known that the elevators posed an unreasonable risk of harm to anyone, thereby imposing a duty to provide security guards at the elevators on a permanent basis. There was no legal duty to foresee the attack and, as a result, provide security measures to prevent it.

Falsification of Records

Falsification of medical and/or business records is grounds for criminal prosecution. Civil liability for damages suffered as a result of falsification of records is available to those damaged by such actions. Falsification of records can result in the loss of accreditation and, as a result, lead to the loss of Medicare and Medicaid funding.

Two of the defendants, orthopaedic surgeons, Dr. Lipton and Dr. Massoff, in *People v. Smithtown General Hospital*[18] on the morning of July 3, 1975, performed an orthopaedic procedure on a patient. The prosthesis used during surgery was supplied by a general sales manager, Mr. MacKay, who was present in the operating room during most of the operation, which began at 8:00 A.M. and ended at 11:30 A.M. After completion of the operation, an X-ray of the patient revealed that the "head of the femur popped out of the acetabulum."[19] At the request of Lipton, the salesman was located at a golf course and requested to return to the hospital. On arriving back in the operating room, he found Massoff reopening the hip. Massoff attempted to remove the prosthesis. MacKay offered his assistance and successfully removed the prosthesis. Massoff then left and returned to his office. With the consent of Lipton, MacKay removed the cement from the bone shaft and reinserted the prosthesis. An indictment charged Lipton with the intent to defraud and to conceal crimes of "Unauthorized Practice of Medicine and Assault," for omitting a true entry in his operative report in that he did not indicate that a nonphysician assisted in the patient's surgery. A similar indictment was returned against a supervising nurse and the hospital for failure to make a true entry in the operating room register.

The state supreme court held that the salesman could be found guilty of unlawfully engaging in the practice of medicine without the prior informed consent of a patient under circumstances that did not constitute an emergency. Lipton should have sought the assistance of another surgeon before turning a surgical case over to a layperson. A motion to dismiss the indictments against the physicians and nurse charged with falsifying business records in the first degree was denied. A motion to dismiss the indictments for assault in the second degree was granted.

Fraud

Medicare fraud alone is estimated to have cost the nation more than one trillion dollars since its inception. Scams are growing dramatically bolder and more sophisticated. Hospitals have been provided with incentives for reporting errors or suspected Medicare fraud. They will get more lenient treatment if they report within 60 days of a suspected fraud.

The following elements must be established for a plaintiff to recover damages in a fraud action:

- a representation to the plaintiff with the intent that he or she rely on it
- knowledge on the part of the defendant that the representation is false
- belief by the plaintiff that the representation is true
- reliance on such representation that resulted in injury to the plaintiff

Office of Inspector General

The Office of Inspector General (OIG) was established at the Department of Health and Human Services (HHS) by Congress in 1976 to identify and eliminate fraud, abuse, and waste in HHS programs and to promote efficiency and economy in departmental operations. It carries out this mission through a nationwide network of audits, investigations, and inspections. To help reduce fraud in the Medicare and Medicaid programs, the OIG investigates violations of the Medicare and Medicaid anti-kickback statute.[20] Violators are subject to criminal penalties or exclusion from participation in the Medicare and Medicaid programs.[21] This statute is very broad and, among other things, it penalizes anyone who knowingly and willfully solicits, receives, offers, or pays anything of value as an inducement in return for

- referring an individual to a person for the furnishing or arranging for the furnishing of any item or service payable under the Medicare or Medicaid programs
- purchasing, leasing, or ordering or arranging for or recommending purchasing, leasing, or ordering any good, facility, service, or item payable under the Medicare or Medicaid programs[22]

The following are examples of questionable features, identified by the Inspector General, that separately or taken together could be construed as a business arrangement that violates the antikickback statute:

- Investors are chosen because they are in a position to make referrals.
- Physicians who are expected to make many referrals may be offered a greater investment opportunity in the joint venture than are those anticipated to make fewer referrals.
- Physician investors may be actively encouraged to make referrals to the joint venture and may be encouraged to divest their ownership interest if they fail to sustain an "acceptable" level of referrals.
- The joint venture tracks its source of referrals and distributes this information to investors.
- Investors may be required to divest their ownership interest if they cease to practice in the service area; for example, if they move, become disabled, or retire.[23]

Health Insurance Portability and Accountability Act of 1996

Many forms of health care fraud and abuse pose a threat to the health and safety of countless Americans, including many of the most vulnerable members of our society. To respond to this serious problem, Congress passed, and President Clinton signed into law, the Health Insurance Portability and Accountability Act of 1996 (HIPAA). HIPAA provides new criminal and civil enforcement tools and funding dedicated to the fight against health care fraud. In addition, HIPAA required the Attorney General and the Secretary of HHS, acting through the Inspector General, to establish a coordinated national Health Care Fraud and Abuse Control Program. The Program provides a coordinated national framework for federal, state, and local law enforcement agencies; the private sector; and the public to fight health care fraud.

Fraud in the United States' health care system is a serious problem that has an impact on all health care payers, and indeed affects every person in this country. Dollars alone do not fully measure the impact of health care fraud on the nation. Fraudulent billing practices also may disguise inadequate or improper treatment for patients.

HHS and the Department of Justice, along with other federal, state, and local agencies, are committed to aggressive efforts to enforce the law and prevent health care fraud. Ongoing efforts to attack fraud and abuse in federal health programs were consolidated and strengthened under HIPAA and provided powerful new criminal and civil enforcement tools as well as expanded resources for the fight against health care fraud.

During 1997, the first full year of antifraud and abuse funding under HIPAA, HHS and the Department of Justice Health Care Fraud and Abuse Control Program recorded its most successful year ever in the nation's efforts to detect and punish fraud and abuse against federal health programs, in particular the Medicare and Medicaid programs. Not only were collections and enforcement actions at an all-time high, but much greater amounts were returned to the Medicare Trust Fund. During 1997

- $1.087 billion was collected in criminal fines, civil judgments and settlements, and administrative impositions.
- $968 million was returned to the Medicare Trust Fund, and $31 million was recovered as the federal share of Medicaid restitution.
- More than 2,700 individuals and entities were excluded from federally sponsored health care programs—a 93 percent increase over 1996.
- Federal prosecutors opened 4,010 civil health care matters, an increase of 61 percent over 1996.[24]

Investigation and prosecution of some of the most far-reaching and costly health care fraud schemes in 1997 include

- *Independent Clinical Laboratories:* During 1997, the federal government achieved significant successes in its three-year task force effort targeting unbundling schemes whereby the nation's three largest independent clinical laboratories routinely billed Medicare for medically unnecessary tests and for tests that the physician never ordered. The three laboratories agreed to pay a total of $642 million to settle potential civil and/or criminal liability to the federal and state governments. The federal government also required each corporation to enter a corporate integrity agreement to help safeguard against future fraud in laboratory billing practices.
- *Diagnosis-Related Groups (DRG) 72-Hour Window Project:* A series of audits conducted by HHS/OIG disclosed that many hospitals were improperly billing Medicare for outpatient services rendered within 72 hours prior to and during a hospital admission, in addition to billing for the set fee (the DRG) Medicare pays for each admission (which is supposed to include the outpa-

tient services rendered within 72 hours prior to the admission). In response, HHS/OIG and the Department of Justice launched a national initiative to recover these duplicate payments, and to compel hospitals to institute corrective measures to prevent such improper claims in the future. As of October 1, 1997, more than $46 million had been returned to the federal government.[25]

As the Federal Bureau of Investigation (FBI) has increased the number of agents assigned to health care fraud investigations, the caseload has increased dramatically from 591 cases in 1992, to 2,582 cases through 1997. The FBI caseload is divided between those health plans receiving government funds and those that are privately funded. Criminal health care fraud convictions resulting from FBI investigations have risen from 116 in 1992, to 485 in 1997.[26]

Joint Ventures

The heavy dependence on government funding and related programs (e.g., Medicare and Medicaid) and the continuous shrinkage occurring in such revenues have forced some health care providers to seek alternative sources of revenue. Competition has contributed to the need to seek alternative revenue sources. The traditional corporate structures for health care organizations no longer may be appropriate to accommodate both normal long-term care activities and those additional activities that may need to be undertaken to provide alternative sources of revenue.

Joint ventures with certain features could be construed as business arrangements that violate the antikickback statute. The OIG has become aware of a proliferation of arrangements known as joint ventures between those in a position to refer business and those providing items or services for which Medicare or Medicaid pays.

Health Care Frauds

The following cases describe several areas in which health care professionals have been involved in criminal fraud.

Home Care Fraud. Today, more Americans are living longer, into older age than ever before. As medicine has advanced, the average life expectancy has increased by 50 percent. There is an ever-escalating number of elderly persons receiving in-home care, dependent upon family and health care providers to attend to their physical, financial, emotional, and health care needs. Medicare home health benefits allow individuals with restricted mobility to remain noninstitutionalized by providing for home care. Home care services and supplies are generally provided by nurses, home nursing aides, speech therapists, and physical therapists under a physician-certified plan of care.

Home care is rapidly being recognized as a breeding ground for abuse. The numerous scams in home care fraud are caused by the difficulty in supervising services provided in the home, Medicare's failure to monitor the number of visits per patient, beneficiaries paying no co-payments except for medical equipment, and the lack of accountability to the patient by failing to explain services provided.

Home care fraud generally is not easy to detect. It involves charging insurers for more services than patients received, billing for more hours of care than were provided, falsifying records, and charging higher nurses' rates for care given by aides. The trend toward shorter hospital stays has created a multibillion dollar market in home care services. This new market is attracting opportunities for fraud.

HHS announced Operation Restore Trust, an antifraud enforcement initiative targeted at home care agencies, nursing homes, and durable equipment suppliers. HHS has provided a toll-free telephone number (800-HHS-TIPS) in order to gather allegations of health care fraud from the public as well as organizational whistle-blowers. The OIG is targeting the following billing practices:

- claims for services not provided
- claims for beneficiaries not homebound
- claims for visits not made
- claims for visits not authorized by a physician

Physician and Office Manager—False Medicaid Claims. In *United States v. Larm,*[27] a physician and his office manager were convicted on charges that they violated 42 U.S.C. § 139h(a)1 by submitting false Medicaid claims for medical services they never rendered to patients. Claims sometimes were submitted even when patients administered allergy injections themselves. In addition, sometimes more expensive serums were billed rather than those that were actually given.

Physician—Billing/Services Not Rendered. A physician in *State v. Cargille*[28] was found to have submitted false information for the purpose of obtaining greater compensation than was otherwise permitted under the Medicaid program. Sufficient evidence was presented to sustain a conviction of Medicaid fraud. The physician had argued that he felt justified for multiple billings for single office visits because of the actual amount of time that he saw a patient. He believed that his method of reimbursement was more equitable than Medicaid. The court disagreed with the physician's reasoning.

Pharmacist—False Drug Claims. The pharmacist in *State v. Heath*[29] was convicted on three counts of Medicaid fraud in which the pharmacist had submitted claims for reimbursement on brand name medications rather than on the less expensive generic drugs that were actually dispensed. A licensed pharmacist and former employee of the defendant had contacted the Medicaid Fraud Unit of the Louisiana Attorney General's office and reported the defendant's conduct

in substituting generic drugs for brand name drugs. As a result of the complaint, the Medicaid Fraud Unit conducted a *call out.*

> In a recipient call out, the Medicaid Fraud Unit sends letters to Medicaid recipients in the general area of the pharmacy involved and asks them to bring all their prescription drugs to the welfare office on a specific date. The call out revealed that some of the prescription vials issued by the aforesaid pharmacies contained generic drugs while the labels indicated that they should contain brand name drugs.[30]

The court of appeals in *State v. Beatty*[31] upheld the superior court's finding that the evidence submitted against a defendant pharmacist was sufficient to sustain a conviction for Medicaid fraud. The state was billed for medications that had never been dispensed, for more medications than some patients received, and in some instances for the more expensive trade name drugs when cheaper generic drugs had been dispensed.

Falsification of Records by Nursing Facility Stockholder. The principal stockholder of a nursing home corporation in *Chapman v. United States, Department of Health and Human Services*[32] was convicted of making 19 false line-item cost entries in reports to the Kansas Medicaid agency. The U.S. Court of Appeals found that HHS did not act unreasonably when it imposed a $2,000 penalty for each of the 19 false Medicaid claims and proposed an additional settlement of $118,136 even though the state had already recovered the $21,115 in excessive reimbursement by setoff. The court concluded that "the penalty reflects a fair amount of leniency on the part of the Inspector General and the Administrative Law Judge (ALJ)."[33]

> On the aggravating side of the balance, the record shows that Chapman acted deliberately to submit false data to the Kansas Medicaid agency so that nursing homes owned by him would be reimbursed for goods and services they did not provide. Further, when an audit was scheduled that threatened to reveal the false claims, Chapman had false invoices prepared and checks issued, but not signed, in an effort to cover up the discrepancies that the state audit would reveal.[34]

Kickback Arrangements. Kickbacks are criminal acts punishable under federal and state laws. The Social Security Amendments of 1972 and those expanded in 1977 describe prohibited practices that constitute kickbacks. The Medicare Fraud and Abuse Anti-Kickback Law provides that whoever knowingly and willfully solicits or receives a kickback, bribe, or rebate "shall be guilty of a felony and upon conviction thereof, shall be fined not more than $25,000 or imprisoned for not more than five years or both."[35] Health care provides many opportunities for kickbacks for steering business to pharmacies, laboratories, and medical-equipment suppliers.

Kickback arrangements with suppliers generally occur under one of the following three arrangements:

> First, arrangements could be made for inflated billings, in which case invoices exceeded the actual price of the goods purchased. The operator could then receive a cash kickback and proceed to submit the inflated bills in his Medicaid cost reports. Second, arrangements could be made with a supplier for phony billings; that is, the operator could pay bills for nonexistent goods or services and then receive an under-the-table cash kickback. Finally, phony items could be submitted along with regular invoices, with the same method of sharing the spoils.[36]

Referral Fees. In *United States v. Greber,*[37] an osteopathic physician, board-certified in cardiology, was president of Cardio-Med, Inc., an organization that he formed. The company provided physicians with diagnostic services, one of which was Holter monitoring, a method of recording a patient's cardiac activity on tape, generally for a period of 24 hours. Cardio-Med billed Medicare for the monitoring service and, when payment was received, forwarded a portion to the referring physician. The government charged that the referral fee exceeded that permitted by Medicare and that there was evidence that physicians received interpretation fees even though the defendant actually evaluated the monitoring data. After a trial by jury, the physician was convicted on 20 of 23 counts in an indictment charging mail fraud, Medicare fraud, and false statement. On appeal the physician contended that the evidence was insufficient to support the guilty verdict. The court of appeals held that to the extent that payments made to a physician were made to induce referrals by that physician of Medicare patients to use payer laboratory services, Medicare fraud was established even if the payments also were intended to compensate the physician for professional services in connection with tests performed by the laboratory. Even if only one purpose of the payment was to induce future referrals, the Medicare statute had been violated.

Laboratory Kickback. In the case of *United States v. Katz,*[38] the owner of Tech Diagnostic Medical Lab agreed to kickback 50 percent of the Medicare payments received by Tech-Lab as a consequence of referrals from Total Health Care, a medical service company. Under the scheme, Total Health Care collected blood and urine samples from medical offices and clinics in southern California and sent them to Tech-Lab for testing. Tech-Lab billed Total Health Care, which in turn billed the private insurance carrier or the government-funded insurance programs Medi-Cal and Medicare for reimbursement. Tech-Lab then kicked back half of its receipts to Total Health Care. The owners of Tech-Lab and Total Health Care arranged an identical scheme with a community medical clinic; Katz, the appellant, subsequently purchased a 25 percent interest in the clinic and began collecting payments under the scheme. Katz was convicted of conspiracy to commit Medicare fraud and of receipt of kickbacks in exchange for referral of Medicare patients. He appealed the decision. The court of appeals, however, affirmed the charges against him.

Kickbacks from Suppliers. Revocation of a physician's license in *In re Alaimo v. Ambach*[39] was not considered to be an excessive sanction for his conviction of perjury when he denied that he was receiving kickbacks from suppliers to his three nursing homes. The physician had denied falsely under oath to a grand jury that he had received cash rebates from vendors, when in fact he had received approximately $800 from a pharmacist between December 15, 1974, and January 15, 1975.

Architectural Contract Kickback/Governing Body. In *United States v. Thompson,*[40] three members of a county council, which served as the governing body of a county hospital, were convicted by a jury for soliciting and receiving a $6,000 kickback from architects. The architects had testified that the appellants and others sought a 1 percent kickback on a hospital project, financed by federal funds, in return for being awarded the architectural contract. Mr. Galloway, of the architectural firm of Galloway and Guthrey, delivered the $6,000 to appellant Campbell at the Knoxville airport. The architects had informed the FBI, and an investigation was conducted. After the investigation, indictments, and trial by jury, the defendants were each sentenced to one year in prison. On appeal, the U.S. Court of Appeals for the Sixth Circuit held that the receipt of a kickback constituted an overt act in furtherance of a conspiracy to obstruct lawful government function and was a violation of the general conspiracy statute and a crime against the United States. It had been previously observed that "[t]o conspire to defraud the United States means primarily to cheat the government out of property or money, but it also means to interfere with or obstruct one of its lawful governmental functions by deceit, craft or trickery, or at least by means that are dishonest."[41] Proof that part of the architects' fee was reimbursed with federal funds was not necessary for a conviction. The criminal convictions were affirmed.

Ambulance Service Kickback. In *United States v. Bay State Ambulance and Hospital Rental Services*[42] a city official was convicted in a federal district court for conspiring to commit Medicare fraud along with other defendants who were also convicted of making illegal payments. Bay State Ambulance and Hospital Rental Services, a privately owned ambulance company, had given cash and two automobiles to an official of a city-owned hospital. The gifts were given as an inducement to the city official for his recommendation that Bay State be awarded the Quincy City Hospital ambulance service contract, for which Bay State received some Medicare funds as reimbursement. The defendants appealed, and the U.S. Court of Appeals for the First Circuit held that the evidence was sufficient to sustain a conviction.

Nursing Home Fraud. A two-year probe of proprietary nursing homes in New York City completed in 1960 by Louis I. Kaplan, Commissioner of Investigations, painted a gloomy picture of the industry. The report that resulted from the probe included the following observations: many operators were attracted by the opportunity to make substantial returns on capital investments and were neither socially motivated nor professionally equipped for the undertaking; public regulation, because of the profit incentive, had to become more vigorous if the public interest was to be served; and nursing home operators had committed crimes by filing false reports and false instruments. Many freely admitted to Kaplan's investigators that they had committed such crimes.

Although no prosecution resulted from the investigation, it did prompt changes in the city's nursing home code that later served as a model for changes in the state's nursing home code. Passage of Article 28 in New York State, as well as Medicare and Medicaid regulations in 1965, increased scrutiny of the nursing home industry. In 1975, the governor of New York State appointed a special prosecutor to investigate nursing homes and vendors to the industry. The activities of the Office of the Special Prosecutor (OSP) quickly attracted federal attention. Section 17 of the Medicare-Medicaid Fraud and Abuse Bill of 1977 uses it as a model for developing legislation to encourage other states to create long-term fraud control units. The Secretary of HHS established the Health Care Financing Administration (HCFA) on March 8, 1977. HCFA placed under one administration the oversight of the Medicare and Medicaid programs and related federal medical care quality control staffs.

Fraud against Physicians. The detection, investigation, and prosecution of financial crimes against physicians are not uncommon occurrences. They involve such areas as computer billing crime, bookkeeper/office manager theft, insurance fraud, cash larceny, checkbook scams, and patient record tampering.

Physicians should be aware of how to analyze larcenous transactions, identify embezzled funds, and recognize the criminal employee. Physicians should be wary of bookkeepers who make themselves indispensable because of their per-

ceived ability to operate the office computer system. To avoid being victimized by employee fraud, physicians should

- familiarize themselves with patient-billing and record-keeping practices
- avoid having one individual in charge of billing and collection procedures
- arrange for an annual audit of office procedures and records by an outside auditor

Murder

Administration of Medication

The tragedy of murder in institutions that are dedicated to the healing of the sick has been an all too frequent occurrence.

Fatal Injection of Pavulon. In a case involving Richard Angelo, a registered nurse on the cardiac/intensive care unit at a Long Island, New York, hospital, the defendent was found guilty of second-degree murder on December 14, 1989, for injecting two patients with the drug Pavulon. He was found guilty of the lesser charges of manslaughter and criminally negligent homicide in the deaths of two other patients. Angelo had committed the murders in a bizarre scheme to revive the patients and be thought of as a hero. The attorney for the estate of one of the alleged victims had filed a wrongful death suit against Angelo and the hospital a day before the verdict was rendered by the jury.[43]

Fatal Injection of Lidocaine. In another case, *Hargrave v. Landon,*[44] a nurse's aide was convicted of murder in the first degree when he was found to have injected an elderly patient with a fatal dose of the drug Lidocaine. He was sentenced to life imprisonment by the circuit court. The nurse's aide appealed the judgment of the circuit court, alleging that his due process rights were violated during the trial, in that

- The trial court failed to grant his motion for change of venue.
- Because of a "carnival atmosphere" surrounding the trial, the trial court should have, but did not, sequester the jury.
- The trial court improperly admitted evidence of other crimes.
- The evidence was insufficient as a matter of law to sustain the conviction.[45]

The U.S. district court held that the nurse's aide failed to establish that he was denied an impartial jury because of adverse pretrial publicity, especially because the tenor of newspaper articles before his trial was primarily informative and factual and the articles treated the story objectively. The evidence was found to have been sufficient to support the petitioner's conviction for murder.

As pointed out in the following case, indictments for murder by health care professionals are not limited to the hospital setting.

Lethal Doses of General Anesthesia. A licensed dentist and an oral surgeon in *People v. Protopappas*[46] were convicted in the superior court of second-degree murder for the deaths of three patients, who died after receiving general anesthesia. The record revealed that the three patients received massive doses of drugs, which resulted in their deaths. The dosages had not been tailored to the patients' individual conditions. The dentist had also improperly instructed surrogate dentists, who were neither licensed nor qualified to administer general anesthesia, to administer preset dosages for an extended time with little or no personal supervision, and the dentist had been habitually slow in reacting to resulting overdoses. In one case, the patient's general physician informed the defendant that the 24-year-old, 88-pound patient suffered from lupus, total kidney failure, high blood pressure, anemia, heart murmur, and chronic seizure disorder and should not be placed under anesthesia even for a short time. The defendant consciously elected to ignore that medical opinion. On appeal, the court of appeals found that there was sufficient evidence of implied malice to support the jury's findings that the dentist and the oral surgeon were guilty of second-degree murder.

> This is more than gross negligence. These are the acts of a person who knows that his conduct endangers the life of another and who acts with conscious disregard for life. . . . Many murders are committed to satisfy a feeling of a hatred or grudge, it is true, but this crime may be perpetrated without the slightest trace of personal ill-will.[47]

To illustrate this point, Professors Perkins and Boyce supplied a number of examples, including the mother who kills an illegitimate infant out of shame even though she may be filled with maternal love, a mercy killing carried out at the victim's own request, and the shooting of a person with the intent to wound, but not to kill, without justification or provocation. The conduct of the defendant in this case

> is not meaningfully distinguishable from any of the acts described above. No reasonable person, much less a dentist trained in the use of anesthesia, could have failed to appreciate the risk of death posed by the procedures he utilized. It is not a question of whether a fatality would occur, only a question of when; and ultimately there were three of them.[48]

Not every charge of suspected murder ends in a conviction; however, there is a heavy price to be paid in the mental anguish suffered by those charged with the crime.

Injection of Pavulon. Two government nurses in *United States v. Narciso*[49] were indicted for and convicted of certain offenses arising out of multiple cardiopulmonary arrests in a two-month period at Ann Arbor Veterans Administration (VA) Hospital. During the months of July and August of 1975, 35 patients suffered 51 cardiac arrests. After an intensive investigation, the defendants were charged in June 1976 with five counts of murder by injecting a powerful muscle relaxant, Pavulon, into the patients' intravenous apparatus. The government presented 89 witnesses over a nearly three-month period. The massive set of proofs was entirely circumstantial in nature. The government sought to show through many witnesses that certain breathing failures were criminal in nature, that the defendants had the opportunity to commit these crimes, that they were present during a critical period, that the drug had to have been injected to produce the observed effect, and that this presence during the critical period was exclusive. There was no direct proof of guilt on any count. No witnesses testified that the defendants had Pavulon in their possession, nor was there any testimony that the defendants injected anything into the patients. The district court granted the defendants' motion for a new trial in the interests of justice. The defendants were eventually found not guilty of the murders of which they were accused.

A Lethal Dose of Codeine. Evidence supported a finding that a nurse killed the plaintiff's decedent in *Harvum v. United States*.[50] After a bench trial in an action brought under the Federal Tort Claims Act, the trial court concluded that a nurse at a VA hospital killed veteran Elzie Havrum. On appeal, the government challenged the sufficiency of the evidence.

Ms. Havrum was required to show that the VA hospital had a duty to protect Mr. Havrum from injury and that its failure to perform that duty caused his death. The government did not challenge the trial court's conclusion that the hospital breached its duty to protect Havrum from the nurse, who presented a danger to patients. The government contends, however, that Havrum failed to establish causation because the evidence did not support the court's finding that the nurse killed Havrum.

The trial court found that Williams, the nurse in question, gave Havrum a lethal dose of codeine and, alternatively, that even disregarding the evidence of codeine poisoning, the circumstantial evidence indicated that Williams killed Havrum.

The trial court relied, in part, on a study by the hospital's epidemiologist, Dr. Christensen, who investigated a suspected link between Williams and an increase in deaths on the ward where Williams customarily worked. The study concluded that patients who were under Williams's care were nearly 10 times more likely to die as were other patients.

In addition, Williams was associated with many unexpected deaths that occurred in private rooms. Christensen also testified that he had never seen anything so unusual as the number of patients who died on the relevant ward from May through July, 1992, between 1:00 A.M. and 3:00 A.M. (a period when fewer deaths generally occur). Williams was present for 11 of the 13 deaths in that interim, although he worked on only one-third of the shifts.

Christensen concluded that there was only one chance in a million that the pattern of deaths on the ward was random, and that there was a compelling correlation between the deaths and Williams for which Christensen could find no benign explanation. Although the court agreed with the government, the statistical evidence alone does not establish that Williams caused Havrum's death; that evidence is nevertheless probative. It was, moreover, only one aspect of the circumstantial evidence upon which the trial court relied in finding causation.

With regard to Havrum specifically, the court noted that his death was among those that Christensen found highly unusual. Havrum died on the ward in question at 1:15 A.M. in a private room with Williams present. Havrum was not expected to die, and the government offered no evidence that he faced death as part of some short-term natural progression. Although Havrum suffered from a serious illness, the admitting physician did not place him in intensive care and did not believe that his death was imminent. Havrum actually reported feeling better while he was in the hospital, but 16 hours after his admission he was pronounced dead.

The trial court also referred to suspicious inconsistencies and alterations in the medical records. According to the records, Williams was the last nurse to see Havrum alive. A physician called to the bedside by Williams stated in her progress note that Havrum had no pulse, respiration, heart rate, or blood pressure and that she pronounced him dead at 1:15 A.M. Although the physician's note further states that Havrum was found unresponsive by nursing, Williams's medical note states that he found Havrum in "severe respiratory distress," a description that Williams frequently used in his medical notes on a patient's death. Respiratory distress, according to several nurses, indicates that the patient is struggling to breathe and is inconsistent with being "unresponsive."

The trial court also remarked that Mr. Williams first wrote a medical note indicating that he found Havrum in severe respiratory distress at about 1:15 A.M., the same time that the physician pronounced him dead. The time in the note was then changed to 1:10 A.M., a line was drawn through the note, and the note was marked "error R.W." Williams then wrote another medical note; this time he stated that he found Havrum in severe respiratory distress at about 1:10 A.M. and that the physician arrived at about 1:15 A.M., just as Havrum stopped breathing. Although the government suggests pos-

sible innocent explanations for the changed entries and omissions, the trial court, which noted that Williams had been fired by another hospital for inserting a false entry into a patient's chart, was free to draw its own less innocent inferences from Havrum's hospital records. And one permissible inference is that Williams's evident uncertainty about what to say and to note in the records indicates that there was in fact nothing particularly wrong with Havrum and that Williams took his life.

With regard to the government's complaint that the trial court improperly relied on a physician's hearsay statement to find causation, the appeals court concluded that the trial court relied on other evidence that was admissible and sufficient to support its findings, and the court's opinion clearly indicates that it would have reached the same conclusion without the challenged evidence. The government also contends that the trial court erred in finding causation based on circumstantial evidence because Mrs. Havrum's pathologist did not find that a homicide had occurred until he received a report indicating that Havrum had died of codeine poisoning. Even before he received the report, however, the pathologist specifically stated that Havrum's death could not be classified as natural. Although, excluding codeine poisoning, the evidence does not establish a specific cause of his death, the government's own pathologist testified about several ways to induce a death that cannot be detected post-mortem. The court fails to see how the opinion of Ms. Havrum's expert precluded the trial court as the fact-finder from considering all of the circumstantial evidence, drawing reasonable inferences from that evidence, and concluding that, more likely than not, Williams killed Havrum. The trial court's findings are not clearly erroneous.

 NURSE INJECTS PATIENTS WITH LIDOCAINE

Citation: *People v. Diaz, 834 P.2d 1171 (Cal. 1992)*

Facts

The defendant, a registered nurse, was working on the night shift at a community hospital. In three and one-half weeks, 13 patients on that shift had seizures, cardiac arrest, and respiratory arrest. Nine died. The unit closed, and the defendant went to work at another hospital. Within three days, a patient died after exhibiting the same symptoms while the defendant was on duty. The defendant was arrested and tried for 12 counts of murder.

The testimony revealed that the defendant had injected the patients with massive doses of Lidocaine (a rhythm-controlling drug). Evidence showed that the defendant had assisted the patients before they exhibited seizures, giving her the opportunity to administer the drug; she was observed acting strangely on the nights of the deaths; and high concentrations of Lidocaine were found in the patient's syringes and in the hospital. Moreover, Lidocaine syringes and vials were discovered in the defendant's home.

The pretrial investigation revealed that 26 other patients had died at the defendant's first hospital while under the nurse's care. All had the same symptoms. The defendant, who waived her right to trial by jury, was found guilty of the 12 counts of murder. The nurse appealed the judgment of death.

Issue

Did the expert testimony support the finding that an overdose of Lidocaine caused the patients' deaths? Did the evidence prove that the defendant had the opportunity to give patients overdoses of Lidocaine?

Holding

The California Supreme Court upheld the convictions.

Reason

The expert testimony about the levels of Lidocaine in the patients' tissue, coupled with the nurses' testimony concerning the symptoms prior to the deaths, confirmed that the patients died from overdoses given to them by the defendant. Also, the evidence proved that the defendant murdered 12 patients. Testimony showed that the defendant was the only nurse on duty the night each patient was poisoned, other nurses were there on only some of the nights, and only the defendant had the opportunity to administer the fatal doses.

Discussion

1. Examine how the evidence showed, when there were no eyewitnesses, that the defendant was the one who killed the 12 patients.
2. What is the difference between preponderance of evidence and evidence beyond a reasonable doubt?

Removal of Life-Support Equipment

Although there may be a duty to provide life-sustaining equipment in the immediate aftermath of cardiopulmonary arrest, there is no duty to continue its use once it has become futile and ineffective to do so in the opinion of qualified medical personnel. Two physicians in *Barber v. Superior Court*[51] were charged with the crimes of murder and conspiracy to commit murder. The charges were based on their acceding to requests of the patient's family to discontinue life-support equipment and intravenous tubes. The patient had suffered a cardiopulmonary arrest in the recovery room after surgery. A team of physicians and nurses revived the patient and placed him on life-support equipment. The patient had suffered severe brain damage, which placed him in a comatose and vegetative state from which, according to tests and examinations by other specialists, he was unlikely to recover. On the written request of the family, the patient was taken off life-support equipment. The family, his wife and eight children, made the decision together after consultation with the physicians. Evidence had been presented that the patient, before his incapacitation, had expressed to his wife that he would not want to be kept alive by a machine. There was no evidence indicating that the family was motivated in their decision by anything other than love and concern for the dignity of their loved one. The patient continued to breathe on his own. Showing no signs of improvement, the physicians again discussed the patient's poor prognosis with the family. The intravenous lines were removed, and the patient died sometime thereafter.

A complaint then was filed against the two physicians. The magistrate who heard the evidence determined that the physicians did not kill the deceased because their conduct was not the proximate cause of the patient's death. On motion of the prosecution, the superior court determined as a matter of law that the evidence required the magistrate to hold the physicians to answer and ordered the complaint reinstated. The physicians then filed a writ of prohibition with the court of appeals. The court of appeals held that the physicians' omission to continue treatment, although intentional and with knowledge that the patient would die, was not an unlawful failure to perform a legal duty. The evidence amply supported the magistrate' decision. The superior court erred in determining that, as a matter of law, the evidence required the magistrate to hold the physicians to answer. The preemptory writ of prohibition to restrain the Superior Court of Los Angeles from taking any further action in this matter, other than to vacate its order reinstating the complaint and to enter a new and different order denying the People's motion, was granted.

PATIENT ABUSE

Gale . . . wasn't prepared for the rough treatment and cruel taunts she says her ailing mother suffered at the nursing home. She cried as a nurse's aide upbraided her mother for failing to straighten her arthritis-stricken legs. And she watched in disbelief as an assistant jerked her mother off her rubber bed pad and pushed her into the bed's metal rails.

All of these images were caught . . . by a "granny cam"—a camera hidden in her mother's room.
                                    USA Today, September 14, 1999

Patient abuse is the mistreatment or neglect of individuals who are under the care of a health care organization. Abuse is not limited to an institutional setting and may occur in an individual's home as well as in an institution. Abuse can take many forms. It can be physical, psychological, medical, financial, etc. It is not always easy to identify because injuries often can be attributed to other causes. Elderly patients present particular problems because of their advanced age and failing health. In the hospital setting, patients are not generally as dependent upon the facility operator in the same manner as a resident in a nursing facility is. Persons are usually hospitalized for only brief periods of time, whereas nursing facility residents may be dependent upon the facility operator for a period of years. Thus, the potential for long-term abuse and neglect is far greater for nursing facility residents than it is for hospital patients.[52]

According to a 1990 report by the Chairman of the Subcommittee on Health and Long-Term Care of the Senate Select Committee on Aging, approximately 1.5 million older Americans are victims of abuse each year. About 5 percent or 1 out of 20 older Americans may be victims of abuse from moderate to severe.[53] The abuse of the elderly is not a localized or isolated problem. Unfortunately, it permeates our society. *Behind Closed Doors*, a landmark book on family violence, stated that the first national study of violence in American homes estimated that one in two homes was the scene of family violence at least once a year.[54]

> We have always known that America is a violent society. . . . What is new and surprising is that the American family and the American home are perhaps as much or more violent than any other single institution or setting (with the exception of the military, and only then in the time of war). Americans run the greatest risk of assault, physical injury and even murder in their own homes by members of their own families.[55]

It is difficult to determine the extent of elder abuse because the abused elderly are reluctant to admit that their children or loved ones have assaulted them. Unfortunately, the abuse of the elderly remained hidden from the public. It is of interest that the findings of the 1990 report are as current today as

when they were first published in 1990. The Senate Select Committee on Aging reported that

- Elder abuse is less likely to be reported than child abuse. Although one out of three child abuse cases is reported, only one out of every eight elder abuse cases is reported.
- A majority of states (43, including the District of Columbia) have enacted state statutes or adult protective services laws to require the mandatory reporting of elder abuse.
- Absent the passage of legislation providing assistance to the states, the states are severely hampered in channeling monies into this area. Some states, such as Louisiana, have simply stopped providing elder abuse protective services because of financial constraints.
- Physical violence, including negligence, and financial abuse appear to be the most common forms of abuse, followed by abrogation of basic constitutional rights and psychological abuse.
- Most instances of elder abuse are recurring events rather than one-time occurrences.
- Victims are often 75 years of age or older and women are more likely to be abused than men.
- Older people are often ashamed to admit that their children or loved ones abuse them or they may fear reprisals if they complain.
- Many middle-aged family members, finally ready to enjoy time to themselves, are resentful of a frail and dependent elderly parent.
- The majority of the abusers are relatives.[56]

The plaintiffs in *In re Estate of Smith v. O'Halloran*[57] instituted a lawsuit in an effort to improve deplorable conditions at many nursing homes. The court concluded that

> The evidentiary record . . . supports a general finding that all is not well in the nation's nursing homes and that the enormous expenditures of public funds and the earnest efforts of public officials and public employees have not produced an equivalent return in benefits. That failure of expectations has produced frustration and anger among those who are aware of the realities of life in some nursing homes which provide so little service that they could be characterized as orphanages for the aged.[58]

The abuse to which nursing facilities and their residents are susceptible is well known and documented by the Senate Subcommittee on Long-Term Care.

> Nursing home patients present particular problems because of several factors: (1) their advanced

age (average 82); (2) their failing health (average four disabilities); (3) their mental disabilities (55 percent are mentally impaired); (4) their reduced mobility (less than half can walk); (5) their sensory impairment (loss of hearing, vision or smell); (6) their reduced tolerance to heat, smoke and gases; and (7) their greater susceptibility to shock.[59]

One of this subcommittee's findings revealed that nursing home residents frequently suffer from neglect or are the targets of intentional abuse.[60] With only 4 to 19 percent of those entering a nursing home departing alive,[61] it is a tragedy that the elderly must be exposed to physical and mental abuses.

It is noteworthy that although Congress recognized the growing crisis and passed legislation in 1988 to provide assistance to the states to curb identified abuse, the subcommittee's 1990 report found that funds were never appropriated to carry out the intent of Congress. Thus, absent congressional action to provide financial assistance, the states failed to finance efforts to address this horrifying disgrace.[62]

Policy recommendations of the Subcommittee on Health and Long-Term Care include

- A need for a coordinated national effort to confront the issue of elder abuse. The federal government should assist the states in dealing with this problem.
- Amendments to the Older Americans Act provided for a program of elder abuse identification and prevention as well as increased authorities for ombudsmen. These programs, however, were never fully funded. Congress should fund these programs.
- A need to provide long-term care services in the home to the chronically ill, elderly, disabled, and children.
- States should consider enacting mandatory reporting legislation.
- Congress should authorize the state Medicaid Fraud Control Units to investigate and prosecute all resident abuse and neglect complaints involving violations of state criminal laws for residents of nursing homes and board and care homes.[63]

Abuse of nursing facility residents in the past gave impetus to the strengthening of resident rights under the Omnibus Budget Reconciliation Act of 1989 (OBRA '89). "The resident has the right to be free from verbal, sexual, physical, or mental abuse, corporal punishment, and involuntary seclusion."[64] Although resident rights have been significantly strengthened, resident abuse continues to be in the headlines. For example, the headline "Nurse's Aide Jailed for Punching Patient" topped a story about a nurse's aide who was jailed for punching a 91-year-old senile man in the nose.[65] The aide had been previously convicted of resident abuse. In response to the seriousness of the ongoing prob-

lem, the National Association of Attorney Generals and the National Association of Medicaid Fraud Control Units have developed model state legislation to prohibit patient and resident abuse. They are strongly urging both its adoption and the prosecution of abuse cases.[66]

The Office of Evaluations and Inspections, one of three major offices within the OIG, conducted a major study on resident abuse in nursing facilities. The study involved 232 interviews with representatives from federal, state, and national organizations that either are involved in receiving, investigating, and/or resolving nursing home abuse complaints; or are knowledgeable and concerned about nursing homes and resident issues. Major findings of the study revealed the following:

- Nearly all respondents indicate that abuse is a problem in nursing homes.
- Respondents differ, however, regarding the severity of the problem. A majority of the state oversight agencies and resident advocates for nursing homes perceive abuse as a serious problem, while many nursing home administrators and industry representatives perceive the problem as minor.
- Physical neglect, verbal and emotional neglect, and verbal or emotional abuse are perceived as the most prevalent forms of abuse.
- Nursing home staff, medical personnel, other patients, and family or visitors all contribute to abuse. However, aides and orderlies are the primary abusers for all categories of abuse except medical neglect.
- Respondents believe that nursing home staff lack training to handle some stressful situations.
- Most respondents believe that staff certification and training will help to deter resident abuse.
- Administrative or management factors also contribute to nursing home resident abuse (e.g., inadequate supervision of staff, high staff turnover, low staff-to-resident ratios).[67]

As a result of this study, it was recommended that (1) ongoing training programs be conducted for nurse's aides, with nursing homes documenting staff training and understanding of abuse and reporting responsibilities; (2) new residents to nursing homes be informed about the differences between living in a nursing home environment and their own homes, possible problems that they may encounter, and ways to deal with such problems; (3) HCFA support research concerning long-term care policies that promote staff stability and provide for adequate staff-to-patient ratios necessary to control stress and abuse; and (4) the Administration on Aging collect and disseminate information about nursing home practices that avoid stress and abuse, and promote staff stability and adequate supervision.[68] HCFA was in agreement with these recommendations and believes that implementation of the Omnibus Budget

Reconciliation Act and the Social Security Act will fulfill the recommendations in the report.[69] Surveyors of health care organizations can look for signs of patient abuse by watching for

- physician's order for restraints
- time-limited orders
- the number of patients that are physically restrained
- the type of restraints being used
- whether or not the restraints are applied correctly
- the apparent physical and mental condition of the restrained patients
- whether restraints are released as required by law and whether exercise is provided for the patient
- whether the staff responds to requests for water, assistance to the bathroom, etc., from a patient who is restrained, and the interval of time between the request and the response
- how often restrained patients are observed by the staff
- the effect of restraints on patients and signs of overmedication
- the frequency of overmedication
- signs of mental and physical abuse of patients
- any signs of harassment, humiliation, or threats from staff or patients
- whether patients are comfortable with the staff
- the numbers of patients with bruises or other injuries (because the skin of the elderly bruises easily, abuse or injury should not be assumed automatically)
- patient-to-patient interactions and staff response to any physical or mental abuse of one patient by another
- evidence of patient neglect or patients left in urine or feces without cleaning

Wanton Neglect of Residents

The defendant in *State v. Cunningham*,[70] the owner and administrator of a residential care facility, housed 30 to 37 mentally ill, mentally retarded, and elderly residents. The Iowa Department of Inspections and Appeals conducts routine inspections of health care facilities. All inspections are unannounced and deficiency statements are sent to the administrator of the facility surveyed.

Various surveys were conducted at the defendant's facility between October 1989 and May 1990. All of the surveys except for one resulted in a $50 daily fine assessed against the defendant for violations of the regulations. On August 16, 1990, a grand jury filed an indictment charging the defendant with several counts of wanton neglect of a resident in violation of Iowa Code section 726.7 (1989), which provides "A person commits wanton neglect of a resident of a health care facility when the person knowingly acts in a manner likely to be injurious to the physical, mental, or moral welfare

of a resident of a health care facility. . . . Wanton neglect of a resident of a health care facility is a serious misdemeanor."

The district court held that the defendant had knowledge of the dangerous conditions that existed in the health care facility but willfully and consciously refused to provide or exercise adequate supervision to remedy or attempt to remedy the dangerous conditions. The residents were exposed to physical dangers, unhealthy and unsanitary physical conditions, and were grossly deprived of much-needed medical care and personal attention. The conditions were likely to and did cause injury to the physical and mental well-being of the facility's residents. The defendant was found guilty on five counts of wanton neglect. The district court sentenced the defendant to one year in jail for each of the five counts, to run concurrently. The district court suspended all but two days of the defendant's sentence and ordered him to pay $200 for each count, plus a surcharge and costs, and to perform community service. A motion for a new trial was denied, and the defendant appealed.

The Iowa Court of Appeals held that there was substantial evidence to support a finding that the defendant was responsible for not properly maintaining the nursing facility, which led to prosecution for wanton neglect of the facility's residents. "Substantial evidence" means evidence that would convince a rational fact finder that the defendant was guilty beyond a reasonable doubt. The defendant was found guilty of knowingly acting in a manner likely to be injurious to the physical or mental welfare of the facility's residents by creating, directing, or maintaining the following five hazardous conditions and unsafe practices:

1. There were fire hazards and circumstances that impeded safety from fire.
   - cigarette stubs found in a cardboard box
   - burn holes found in patient clothing
   - burn holes found in furniture
   - cigarette burns noted in nonsmoking areas
   - a rusted fire door that was bent and would not close or latch
   - exposed electrical wiring
2. The facility was not properly maintained.
   - broken glass in patients' rooms
   - excessively hot water in faucets
   - dried feces on public bathroom walls and grab bars
   - insufficient towels and linens
   - dead and live cockroaches and worms in the food preparation area
   - debris, bugs, and grease throughout the facility
   - no soap available in the kitchen
   - at one point only one bar of soap and one container of shampoo found in the entire facility
   - entire facility in a general state of disrepair

3. Dietary facilities were unsanitary and inadequate to meet the dietary needs of the residents.
   - an ordered "no concentrated sweets" diet for a diabetic patient not followed, subjecting him to life-threatening blood sugar levels
4. There were inadequate staffing patterns and supervision in the facility.
   - no funds spent on employee training (only one of three kitchen employees was properly trained)
   - defendant did not spend the minimum amount of time at the facility, as required by administrative standards
5. Improper dosages of medications were administered to the residents.
   - distributing an ongoing overdose of heart medication to one resident
   - failure to administer medication, resulting in one resident suffering a seizure
   - failure to treat residents' skin lesions and herpes[71]

The defendant argued that he did not "create" the unsafe conditions at the facility. The court of appeals disagreed. The statute does not require that the defendant create the conditions at the facility to sustain a conviction. The defendant was the administrator of the facility and responsible for the conditions that existed. The defendant also argued that some of the deficiencies cited had been corrected. The statute, however, does not require failure or refusal to remedy the found conditions in order to sustain a conviction.

Abuse and Revocation of License

The operator of a nursing facility appealed an order by the Department of Public Welfare revoking his license because of resident abuse in *Nepa v. Commonwealth Department of Public Welfare*.[72] Substantial evidence supported the department's finding. Three former employees testified that the nursing facility operator had abused residents in the following incidents:

- He unbuckled the belt of one of the residents, causing his pants to drop, and then grabbed a second resident, forcing them to kiss (petitioner's excuse for this behavior was to shame the resident because of his masturbating in public).
- On two occasions he forced a resident to remove toilet paper from a commode after she had urinated and defecated in it (denying that there was fecal matter in the commode, petitioner's excuse was that this was his way of trying to stop the resident from filling the commode with toilet paper).
- He verbally abused a resident who was experiencing difficulty in breathing and accused him of being a fake as he attempted to feed him liquids.[73]

The nursing facility operator claimed that the findings of fact were not based on substantial evidence and that even if they were, the incidents did not amount to abuse under the code. The defendant attempted to discredit the witnesses with allegations from a resident and another employee that one of his former employees got into bed with a resident, and that another had taken a picture of a male resident while in the shower and had placed a baby bottle and a humiliating sign around the neck of another resident. The court was not impressed. Although these incidents, if true, were reprehensible, they were collateral matters that had no bearing on the witnesses' reputation for truthfulness and therefore could not be used for impeachment purposes. The court held that there was substantial evidence supporting the department's decision and that the activities committed by the operator were sufficient to support revocation of his license.

We believe Petitioner's treatment of these residents as found by the hearing examiner to be truly disturbing. These residents were elderly and/or mentally incapacitated and wholly dependent on Petitioner while residing in his home. As residents, they are entitled to maintain their dignity and be cared for with respect, concern, and passion.

Petitioner testified that he did not have adequate training to deal with the patients he received who suffered from mental problems. Petitioner's lack of training in this area is absolutely no excuse for the reprehensible manner in which he treated various residents. Accordingly, DPW's order revoking Petitioner's license to operate a personal care home is affirmed.[74]

Abusive Search

A nurse in *People v. Coe*[75] was charged with a willful violation of the Public Health Law in connection with an allegedly abusive search of an 86-year-old resident at a geriatric center and with the falsification of business records in the first degree. The resident, Mr. Gersh, had heart disease and difficulty in expressing himself verbally. Another resident claimed that two $5 bills were missing. Nurse Coe assumed that Gersh had taken them because he had been known to take things in the past. The nurse proceeded to search Gersh, who resisted. A security guard was summoned, and another search was undertaken. When Gersh again resisted, the security guard slammed a chair down in front of him and pinned his arms while the defendant nurse searched his pockets, failing to retrieve the two $5 bills. Five minutes later, Gersh collapsed in a chair gasping for air. Nurse Coe administered cardiopulmonary resuscitation but was unsuccessful, and Gersh died.

Nurse Coe was charged with violation of Section 175.10 of the New York Penal Law for falsifying records, because of the defendant's "omission" of the facts relating to the search of Gersh. These facts were considered relevant and should have been included in the nurse's notes regarding this incident. "The first sentence states, 'Observed resident was extremely confused and talks incoherently. Suddenly became unresponsive. . . .' This statement is simply false. It could only be true if some reference to the search and the loud noise was included."[76] A motion was made to dismiss the indictment at the end of the trial.

The court held that the search became an act of physical abuse and mistreatment, the evidence was sufficient to warrant a finding of guilt on both charges, and the fact that searches took place frequently did not excuse an otherwise illegal procedure.

It may well be that this incident reached the attention of the criminal justice system only because, in the end, a man had died. In those instances which are equally violative of residents' rights and equally contrary to standards of common decency but which do not result in visible harm to a patient, the acts are nevertheless illegal and subject to prosecution. A criminal act is not legitimized by the fact that others have, with impunity, engaged in that act.[77]

Physical Abuse

The revocation of a personal care home license was found to be proper in *Miller Home, Inc. v. Commonwealth, Department of Public Welfare*,[78] because of repeated medication violations and resident abuse. Evidence was presented that the son of the personal care home's manager was hired as a staff member after having acted as a substitute, even though he had physical altercations with residents of the home. On one occasion, the manager's son had punched a female resident, resulting in her hospitalization for broken bones around the eye, and on two prior occasions he had been involved in less physical altercations that required police intervention.

A nursing facility orderly challenged a determination by the commissioner of the State Department of Health finding him guilty of resident abuse in *Reid v. Axelrod*.[79] The orderly maintained that the resident struck him with his cane, and that he merely pushed the cane away to avoid being struck a second time. A co-employee testified that the orderly struck the resident in the chest after being hit with the cane. The court held that the determination was supported by substantial evidence and that the three-year delay in conducting the hearing did not warrant dismissal of the petition charging the orderly with resident abuse. Public policy requires that residents must be protected from abusive health care workers.

According to allegations in Count I of a two-count petition, the resident in *Stiffelman v. Abrams*[80] died from

"blows, kicks, kneeings, or bodily throwings intentionally, viciously, and murderously dealt him from among the facility's staff over a period of approximately two to three weeks prior to his death"; that the "beatings were repeated and were received by the decedent at ninety years of age and in a frail, defenseless, and dependent condition"; that the beatings so administered to the decedent were "physically and mentally tortuous; that he was caused by them to live out his final days in agony and terror; and that his physical injuries included thirteen fractures to his ribs, subpleural hemorrhaging, and marked lesions to his chest, flanks, abdomen, legs, arms, and hands; that during and following the period of the beatings the decedent lay at the facility for days unattended and unaided as to the deterioration and grave suffering he was undergoing."[81]

The executors of the estate had brought suit against the operator and individual and corporate owners of the facility for damages for personal injuries resulting in the death of the resident. The executors were requesting under Count I, $1.5 million in survival damages because of the physical and mental pain and suffering of the decedent, as well as $3 million for punitive damages, and under Count II, $1,504,084 in contractual breaches of the resident's admission contract with the facility. The executors claimed that certain standards of care and personal rights contained in the contract were violated. The trial court sustained the nursing facility's motion for dismissal of the case on the grounds that the plaintiffs failed to state a claim on which relief could be granted. On appeal, the judgment of the trial court was reversed with respect to Count I, and the dismissal of Count II was sustained. The case was remanded, requiring the executors to proceed under appropriate statutory authority and not under contract.

Forcible Administration of Medications

The medical employee in *In re Axelrod*[82] sought review of a determination by the commissioner of health that she was guilty of resident abuse. Evidence showed that the employee, after a resident refused medication, "held the patient's chin and poured the medication down her throat."[83] There was no indication or convincing evidence that an emergency existed that would have required the forced administration of the medication. The court held that substantial evidence supported the commissioner's finding that the employee had been guilty of resident abuse.

The commissioner properly found that the notation in the record that "staff are asked to, please, make every effort to make sure that she [the patient] takes them [her medication]"[84] does not authorize the forcible administration of medication. This is particularly so when a medical doctor did not make the notation authorized to prescribe medication and when the written policy of the facility was that the head nurse was to be notified if a patient refused medication.

Intimidation of Abusive Resident/Disciplinary Overkill

A difficult and abusive 80-year-old resident of a veterans home in *Beasley v. State Personnel Board*[85] slapped the face of an aide who was assisting him. The resident, referring to his inability to have sex, said that he might as well have it cut off. The aide responded by indicating that if he did not behave then she might accommodate him. A nursing supervisor who passed by at that moment noted that a nursing assistant and a hospital aide who were standing nearby laughed and did nothing to intervene. The aide was fired and the other two employees were suspended for 10 days. After the State Board upheld the overkill, the three employees went by mandate to the superior court where Beasley's dismissal was ruled too severe. The trial court found that action against the nursing assistant and hospital aide, although harsh, was within discretion. On appeal, the court held that the aide's comments did not constitute misconduct and the veterans home nursing assistant and hospital aide did not commit actionable conduct by "sort of laughing." When this incident was viewed in its context and in light of the whole record, it did not support the state personnel board's finding that the aide's attitude toward patients was poor.

ABUSE OF STROKE PATIENT

Citation: *State v. Houle, 642 A.2d 1178 (Vt. 1994)*

Facts

The defendant, an LPN, had criminal charges brought against her stemming from her treatment of a stroke patient. It was alleged that she had slapped the patient's legs repeatedly and shackled him to his bed at the wrists and ankles. By the time of trial, the patient had died of causes unrelated to the charged conduct. During the trial, the state presented the testimony of eyewitnesses, including the patient's wife, hospital employees, and an investigator from the Office of the Attorney General. The defendant did not deny that she had restrained the patient, but claimed that her actions were necessary for the patient's protection, as well as her own, and that her actions were neither assaultive nor cruel.

The defendant produced the testimony of another nurse who was familiar with the patient's medical condition and his need for restraint. This nurse was also used to impeach the credibility of one of the state's witnesses.

The defendant's first claim was that the trial court improperly admitted, over objection, evidence that the patient gave consistent accounts of the incidents underlying the charges to Ms. Herrick, a hospital employee. The defendant contended that the testimony was not relevant.

Issue

Was the evidence that the patient gave consistent accounts of the incidents underlying the charges to the defendant relevant and admissible in prosecution of the defendant?

Holding

The Vermont Supreme Court held that the evidence that the victim gave consistent accounts of the incidents underlying the charges to the defendant was relevant and admissible.

Reason

The patient's awareness of what happened to him was relevant to the state's case because the trial court, in its instruction to the jury, defined cruelty as "intentional and malicious infliction of physical or emotional pain or suffering upon a person." By showing that the patient was aware of what had happened to him, the state allowed the jury to infer that he had suffered physical or emotional pain. The state presented a witness who was present when the incident occurred and who was able to describe the acts of abuse in detail. The credibility of this eyewitness testimony, and not what the patient's testimony would have been, was the focus of the trial.

Discussion

1. Do you agree with the court's findings? Why?
2. At what point does the application of restraints become a cruelty?

Petty Theft

Health care organizations must be alert to the potential ongoing threat of theft by unscrupulous employees, physicians, patients, visitors, and trespassers. The theft of patient valuables, supplies, and equipment is substantial and costs health care organizations millions of dollars each year.

The evidence presented in *People v. Lancaster*[86] was found to have provided a probable cause foundation for information charging felony theft of nursing home residents' money by the office manager. Evidence showed that on repeated occasions the residents' income checks were cashed or cash was otherwise received on behalf of residents; that the defendant, by virtue of her office, had sole responsibility for maintaining the residents' ledger accounts; and that cash receipts frequently were never posted to the residents' accounts.

Nursing Facility

Criminal charges of theft were imposed because of misapplication of property in *State v. Pleasant Hill Health Facility*.[87] The facility had commingled the residents' personal funds (Social Security checks and personal allowances) in a corporate account. There were times that the residents' funds remained in the corporate account for three to six months before being transferred to the residents' accounts, during which time the combined funds were used to pay corporate expenses. The facility had described its relationship with the residents as debtor-creditor and not a trust relationship. The facility claimed that the funds were always available to residents, and they were never denied a request for their funds. The Maine Supreme Judicial Court held that the facility's handling of the residents' funds was not a debtor-creditor relationship but a trust relationship. Pleasant Hill's commingling of patients' personal need funds with corporate funds and use of the combined funds to pay corporate expenses constituted dealing with the money as its own and a violation of the corporation's trust agreement. The facility argued that it ultimately transferred all the residents' personal funds from a transfer account to the residents' accounts. The court concluded that a violation occurred at the moment the residents' personal funds were deposited without segregating them from the corporation's own funds.

Trespass/Antiabortion Demonstrations

The First Amendment rights of a Catholic priest in *Markley v. State*[88] were found not to have been violated when the circuit court placed him on conditional probation and prohibited his antiabortion protest activities during his period of probation, after his conviction on charges of burglary in the second degree and criminal mischief in the first degree. The charges stemmed from antiabortion demonstrations, which took place at a medical clinic specializing in pregnancy testing, counseling, and abortions. The court of criminal appeals held that limitation of protest activities as a term of probation did not violate the priest's First Amendment rights.

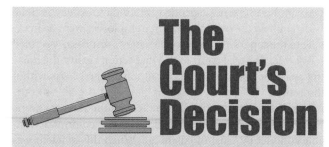

Majors was sentenced to spend the rest of his life in prison for murdering six elderly patients, a crime the judge called *a paragon of evil at its most wicked*. Judge Elton said, "He was entrusted with these people's care. In response he committed diabolical acts that extinguished the frail lives of six people." Investigators suggest that Majors gave lethal injections to dozens of patients at the hospital.

CHAPTER REVIEW

1. The *objectives of criminal law* are fourfold:
   - To maintain public order and safety.
   - To protect individuals.
   - To use punishment as a deterrent to crime.
   - To rehabilitate criminals for return to society.
2. A *crime*—a social harm defined and made punishable by law—is generally either a misdemeanor or a felony. A *misdemeanor* is an offense punishable by less than one year in jail and/or a fine. A *felony*, however, is generally punishable by imprisonment in a state or federal prison for a period of more than one year.
3. After an arrest has been processed, the individual is either detained or released on bond. Following the arrest, the individual is arraigned—the accusatory instrument is read formally and the bail is set. If the defendant does not plead guilty and no agreed-upon disposition can be reached, the case is assigned to the trial court.

4. Health care professionals can face criminal and civil risks not for good-faith reporting of suspected incidents of child abuse, but instead for failing to report such incidents.

5. *Criminal negligence* is the reckless disregard for the safety of others and is the willful indifference to an injury that could result from an act. It differs from tort liability in that it provides for a more specific lack of care commonly characterized as "gross negligence" and "recklessness."

6. The Office of Inspector General, which operates within the Department of Health and Human Services (HHS), conducts nationwide audits, investigations, and inspections with the goals of identifying fraud, abuse, and waste in HHS programs and promoting efficiency and economy in departmental operations.

7. The Health Insurance Portability and Accountability Act of 1996 (HIPAA) was created to help fight health care fraud. HIPAA provides a coordinated national framework for federal, state, and local law enforcement agencies, the private sector, and the public.

8. *Patient abuse* is the mistreatment or neglect of persons under the care of a health care organization. Abuse can occur in an institutional or home setting and can be in the form of physical, psychological, medical, financial, or other harm. Elder abuse is one of the most common forms of patient abuse.

REVIEW QUESTIONS

1. What are the objectives of criminal law?
2. Describe the difference between a "misdemeanor" and a "felony." Give an example of each.
3. List the processes of a criminal trial.
4. Why has health care fraud been so costly to the nation?
5. Discuss why physicians have been so reluctant to remove a patient's life support systems.
6. Based on the cases reviewed above, discuss why patients are reluctant to complain about their health care.

NOTES

1. Majors v. Engelbrecht, 149 F.3d 709 (1998).
2. 295 U.S. 78, 88 (1935).
3. J. Kaplan, Criminal Justice: Introductory Cases and Materials 228 (1973).
4. *Id.* at 259.
5. 538 N.E.2d 113 (Ohio 1989).
6. 746 P.2d 1006 (Idaho Ct. App. 1987).
7. N.Y. Soc. Serv. Law § 419 (McKinney 1992).
8. N.Y. Soc. Serv. Law § 420 (McKinney 1992).
9. 520 N.Y.S.2d 378 (N.Y. App. Div. 1987).
10. 413 N.W.2d 670 (Wis. Ct. App. 1987).
11. N.Y. Soc. Serv. Law § 420 (McKinney 1992).
12. 415 N.W.2d 436 (Minn. Ct. App. 1987).
13. 486 So.2d 101 (La. 1986).
14. *Id.* at 103.
15. *Id.*
16. *Id.* at 101, 104.
17. 609 So.2d 909 (La. Ct. App. 1992).
18. 402 N.Y.S.2d 318 (N.Y. Sup. Ct. 1978).
19. *Id.* at 320.
20. 42 U.S.C. § 1320a-7b(b).
21. Office of the Fed. Register, Nat'l Archives & Records Admin., The United States Government Manual 1988/89, at 307 (1994) [hereinafter Manual].
22. Office of Inspector General, Dep't of Health & Human Servs., Special Fraud Alert, Joint Venture Arrangements 1(1) (May 1989).
23. *Id.* at 2(2).
24. The Department of Health and Human Services and The Department of Justice Health Care Fraud and Abuse Control Program Annual Report for FY 1997, at 1 (1998).
25. *Id.* at 8.
26. *Id.* at 29.
27. 824 F.2d 780 (9th Cir. 1987).
28. 507 So.2d 1254 (La. Ct. App. 1987).
29. 513 So.2d 493 (La. Ct. App. 1987).
30. *Id.* at 495.
31. 308 S.E.2d 65 (N.C. Ct. App. 1983).
32. 821 F.2d 523 (10th Cir. 1987).
33. *Id.* at 530.
34. *Id.* at 529.
35. 42 U.S.C. § 1396h(b)(1) (1977).
36. D.B. Smith, Long-Term Care in Transition, 91–92 (1981).
37. 760 F.2d 68 (3d Cir. 1985).
38. 871 F.2d 105 (9th Cir. 1989).
39. 457 N.Y.S.2d 955 (N.Y. App. Div. 1982).
40. 366 F.2d 167 (6th Cir. 1966).
41. 265 U.S. 182, 188 (1924).
42. 874 F.2d 20 (1st Cir. 1989).
43. Collwell, *The Verdict of Angelo*, 50(103) Newsday 1989, at 3.
44. 584 F. Supp. 302 (E.D. Va. 1984).

45. *Id.* at 305.

46. 246 Cal. Rptr. 915 (Cal. Ct. App. 1988).

47. *Id.* at 927.

48. *Id.* at 928.

49. 446 F. Supp. 252 (E.D. Mich. 1977).

50. 204 F.3d 815 (8th Cir. 2000).

51. 195 Cal. Rptr. 484 (Cal. Ct. App. 1983).

52. Harris v. Manor Healthcare Corp., 49 N.E.2d 1374 (Ill. 1986).

53. SENATE SUBCOMM. ON HEALTH & LONG-TERM CARE, ELDER ABUSE: A DECADE OF SHAME AND INACTION, COMM. PUB. NO. 752, x-xiv (1990).

54. RICHARD J. GELLES, MURRAY A. STRAUSS, & SUZANNE K. STEINMETZ, BEHIND CLOSED DOORS: VIOLENCE IN THE AMERICAN FAMILY (1980).

55. *Id.*

56. SENATE SUBCOMM. ON HEALTH AND LONG-TERM CARE, *supra* note 53.

57. 557 F. Supp. 289 (D. Colo. 1983).

58. *Id.* at 293.

59. SENATE SUBCOMM. ON LONG-TERM CARE OF THE SPECIAL COMM. ON AGING, FAILURE IN PUBLIC POLICY, SUPPORTING PAPER No. 7, 94th Cong., 2d Sess. (1976).

60. *Id.* at 165–173.

61. *Nursing Home Access: Making the Patient Bill of Rights Work*, 54 J. URB. L. 473, 474 (1977).

62. *Id.* at v.

63. *Id.* at xiv–xv.

64. 42 C.F.R. § 483.13 (1989).

65. *Nurse's Aide Jailed for Punching Patient*, THE BALTIMORE SUN, June 29, 1990, §D, at 2.

66. Boggs, *OBRA Requirements Spotlight Resident/Provider Rights Issues*, LEGAL CURRENTS 16, 21 (May 1990).

67. OFFICE OF INSPECTOR GENERAL, OFFICE OF INSPECTIONS & EVALUATIONS, PUB. No. OEI-06–88–00360, RESIDENT ABUSE IN NURSING HOMES, ii–iii (1990).

68. *Id.* at iii.

69. *Id.* at 22.

70. State v. Cunningham, 493 N.W.2d 884 (Iowa Ct. App. 1992).

71. *Id.* at 887–888.

72. 551 A.2d 354 (Pa. Commw. Ct. 1988).

73. *Id.* at 355.

74. *Id.* at 357.

75. 501 N.Y.S.2d 997 (N.Y. Sup. Ct. 1986).

76. *Id.* at 1001.

77. *Id.*

78. 556 A.2d 1 (Pa. Commw. Ct. 1989).

79. 559 N.Y.S.2d 417 (N.Y. App. Div. 1990).

80. 655 S.W.2d 522 (Mo. 1983).

81. *Id.*

82. 560 N.Y.S.2d 573 (N.Y. App. Div. 1990).

83. *Id.*

84. *Id.* at 573–74.

85. 178 Cal. Rptr. 564 (Cal. Ct. App. 1981).

86. 683 P.2d 1202 (Colo. 1984).

87. 496 A.2d 306 (Me. 1985).

88. 507 So.2d 1043 (Ala. Crim. App. 1987).

Contracts and Antitrust

It's Your Gavel...

CONTRACT ENFORCEMENT

The plaintiff, a hospital, sued its former director of physical medicine and rehabilitation to enforce a restrictive covenant in the employment contract precluding the director from accepting similar employment in the same county within one year of termination of employment. The plaintiff filed a complaint against the defendant seeking preliminary and permanent injunctive relief to uphold the covenant. The defendant filed a motion to dismiss the plaintiff's motion for the preliminary injunction and the complaint.

On or about February 27, 1991, the parties to the complaint had entered into a contract whereby the defendant was employed as plaintiff's director of physical medicine. The con-

tract provided that during the director's employment and for a period of one year thereafter, the director would not, directly or indirectly, invest in, own, manage, operate, control, be employed by, participate in, or be connected in any manner with the ownership, management, operation, or control of any person, firm, or corporation engaged in competition with the hospital in providing health services or facilities within Coles County, including the provision of services in a private office, without prior written consent of the hospital.

On or about September 6, 1991, following the termination, the defendant engaged in the business of providing physical medicine and rehabilitation services in Coles County. The plaintiff argued that unless the defendant was enjoined, the hospital would suffer irreparable injury. The circuit court granted the hospital's motion for preliminary injunction. Complaining that the hospital made no sufficient showing that the defendant was in breach of the covenant, the defendant appealed.[1]

What is your verdict?

INTRODUCTION

One of the many areas of law that affects health care providers is contracts. The subject of contracts is a course in and of itself. The intention here is to give the reader an introduction to contracts, focusing on providing a general understanding of the concepts, elements, and importance of them as they pertain to health care organizations and professionals.

PURPOSE OF A CONTRACT

A contract is a special kind of agreement, either written or oral, that involves legally binding obligations between two or more parties. A contract serves to provide one or more of the parties with a legal remedy if another of the parties does not perform its obligations pursuant to the terms of the contract. The major purpose of a contract is to specify, limit, and define the agreements that are legally enforceable. A contract forces the participants to be specific in their understandings and expectations of each other. Contracts, particularly those in writing, serve to minimize misunderstandings and offer a means for the parties of a contract to resolve any disputes that may arise. To achieve this goal, it is important to formulate a contract that is as simple as possible.

TYPES OF CONTRACTS

It is important to be aware of the various types of contracts that exist. The following is a general description of the major types of contracts and a brief definition of each.

- *Express.* An express contract is one in which the parties have an oral agreement or have reduced their agreements to writing.
  - *Written.* It is always desirable to reduce any important contract to writing. In certain instances, the courts can enforce only written contracts.
  - *Oral.* Under the parol (oral) evidence rule, the court will not consider oral negotiations and agreements made before or at the same time a written contract is signed if the parties intended the document to be their complete and final agreement. However, both written and oral contracts are recognized and, generally, are equally legal and binding.
- *Implied.* An implied contract is one that is inferred by law. It is based on the conduct of the parties, such as a handshake or similar conduct. Much of the litigation concerning excesses of corporate authority involves questions of whether a corporation has the implied authority—incidental to its express authority—to perform a questioned act. For example, even though its certificate of incorporation did not authorize such an act

specifically, a hospital was permitted to construct a medical office building on land that had been donated for maintaining and carrying on a general hospital. The court, in recognizing a trend to encourage charitable hospitals to provide private offices for rental to staff members, held that such an act was within the implied powers of the hospital and that such offices aid in the work of a general hospital even though it went beyond the hospital corporation's express powers.[2]

- *Voidable.* A voidable contract is one in which one party, but not the other, has the right to escape from its legal obligations under the contract. It is considered a voidable contract at the option of that party. For example, a minor, not having the capacity to enter into a contract, can void the contract. However, the competent party to the contract may not void the contract.
- *Executory.* An executory contract is one in which something remains to be done (performed) by one or more of the parties.
- *Executed.* An executed contract is one in which all of the obligations of the parties have been performed fully.
- *Enforceable.* An enforceable contract is one that is a valid, legally binding agreement. If one party breaches it, the other will have an appropriate legal remedy.
- *Unenforceable.* An unenforceable contract is one in which, because of some defect, no legal remedy is available if breached by one of the parties to the contract.
- *Contracts for Realty, Goods, or Services.* The subject of a contract will always generate special considerations.
  - *Realty.* Contracts for the purchase or sale of real estate, or any interest in real estate (i.e., easement, license, or the like), are in this category. Forms for such contracts are commonly used but generally deal with the basic special considerations only, either ignoring or leaving blank spaces for individual concerns.
  - *Goods.* All things that are movable—with exceptions such as money and securities—require special considerations of a different sort.
  - *Services.* This involves a unique subject: human energy. There are service contracts for professional services, management agreements, and relationships with health maintenance organizations.

The following case illustrates how contract issues impact on health care providers.

On February 29, 1984, the defendant hospital in *Cogan v. Harford Memorial Hospital,*[3] owned by Upper Chesapeake Health Systems, Inc. (UCHS), contracted with Dr. Cogan to act as the Chief of Radiology for five years. In 1988, the hospital and Cogan renegotiated the contract. Cogan's compensation was increased and the contract extended until May 25, 1993, subject to termination by either party providing a 120-day written notice. During the renegotiation, Cogan sought compensation on a fee-for-service basis. However, the hospital was uncomfortable with such an arrangement.

In December 1990, Cogan began discussing with NMR of America the possibility of opening a radiology clinic to provide testing with magnetic resonance imaging (MRI) separate from the hospital. The hospital expressed opposition to such an arrangement. In response, Cogan tied discussions of a new MRI clinic to renegotiation of his contract on a fee-for-service arrangement. The hospital agreed to discuss a fee-for-service contract. Under the proposed contract Cogan's radiology group would not maintain any financial or professional interest with any competing medical facility within 20 miles of a hospital owned by UCHS. The parties failed to reach an agreement.

On March 1, 1991, the hospital informed Cogan of its intention to terminate his employment contract as of June 28, 1991. In October 1991, Cogan formed Cogan & Smith, a partnership with Dr. Steven Smith, his former associate at the hospital.

In November 1991, Cogan & Smith signed a contract in which it agreed to act as the managing director of a radiology clinic. The clinic had a lower volume of business than anticipated, and Cogan filed suit against UCHS. He contended that the hospital's policy against sending patients to facilities not accredited by the Joint Commission on Accreditation of Healthcare Organizations impeded the clinic's business. The hospital claimed that the policy affected no more than seven patients. Cogan contended it affected 15,000 patients. He characterized this policy as a "group boycott" against the clinic. Under the Sherman Antitrust Act, group boycotts may be considered anticompetitive.

Cogan contended that the defendants violated the Sherman Act, breached the contract between himself and UCHS, interfered with his contractual relations, wrongfully discharged him, and deprived him of his constitutional rights in violation of 42 U.S.C. § 1983, as amended, 15 U.S.C.A. §§ 1, 2.

The U.S. District Court held that the harm suffered by Cogan because he was unable to continue working at the hospital was not compensable under the Sherman Act. The court found no evidence showing that competition in any relevant market had been harmed, reduced, or impacted by the termination of Cogan's contract or the alleged group boycott of the MRI clinic by the implementation of the hospital's policy. The only harm asserted was Cogan's inability to continue working at the hospital. The injury he incurred as a competitor of the hospital was not the "type the antitrust laws were intended to prevent."[4]

ELEMENTS OF A CONTRACT

Whether contracts are executed in writing or agreed to orally, they must contain the following elements to be enforceable:

- Offer/Communication
- Consideration
- Acceptance

Offer/Communication

An offer must be communicated to the other party so that it can be accepted or rejected. Unless the offeror specifically requires that the acceptance be received before a contract is formed, communication of the acceptance to the offeror is not necessary.

Consideration

An *offer* is a promise by one party to do (or not to do) something if the other party agrees to do (or not do) something. Not all statements or promises are offers. Generally, advertisements of goods for sale are not offers but are invitations to the public to come to the place of business, view the merchandise, and be made an offer. An opinion is not an offer. Preliminary negotiations are not offers.

Legal Consideration

The law will not enforce every meeting of the minds as if it were a contract. Only when legal consideration has been given will a court treat the agreement as a contract. There is no commonly accepted definition of consideration but its essence is captured in the term price. Consideration usually is described in terms of legal detriment and legal benefit. Legal detriment is one's performance of an act not required by law, or the forbearing from an act one has a right to do. The party who enjoys the result of another party's act or forbearance to act is said to have received a legal benefit.

Adequacy

Normally the adequacy or inadequacy of the consideration, or the price paid, will not affect the formation of a contract.

Acceptance

Upon proper acceptance of an offer, a contract is formed.

- *Meeting of the Minds.* Acceptance requires a "meeting of the minds" (mutual assent). The parties must understand and then agree on the terms of the contract.
- *Definite and Complete.* Acceptance requires mutual assent to be found between the parties. The terms must be so complete that both parties understand and agree to what has been proposed.
- *Duration.* Generally, the other party may revoke an offer at any time prior to a valid acceptance. When the offeror

does revoke the proposal, the revocation is not effective until the offeree (the person to whom the offer is made) receives it. Once the offeree has accepted the offer, any attempt to revoke the agreement is too late and is invalid.

- *Complete and Conforming.* The traditional rule is that the acceptance must be the mirror image of the offer. In other words, the acceptance must comply with all the terms of the offer and not change or add any terms.

COMPETENT PARTIES

The law will enforce contracts only when they are executed between persons who are competent, that is, those with the legal and mental capacity to contract. Certain classes of persons such as minors, the insane, and prisoners traditionally have been considered unable to understand the consequences of their actions and have been deemed incompetent, or lacking in legal capacity, to make a binding contract.

Corporations

- *Powers.* The ability of a corporation to enter into contracts is limited by its powers as contained in or inferred from its articles of incorporation (sometimes called a charter), or conferred upon it by general corporation law.
- *Approval Requirement.* Whenever a contract of any consequence is made with a corporation, appropriate corporate approval and authorization must be obtained.
- *Ratification.* In the event that a contract is entered into with a corporation without the appropriate authority, the contract nevertheless may be ratified and made binding on the corporation by subsequent conduct or statements made on its behalf by its representatives.

An organization's chief executive officer (CEO) is not personally liable for contracts entered into on behalf of the organization. When the CEO exceeds the limits of his or her authority, the question of whether the organization will be responsible for the CEO's acts may arise. Questions of this nature most often occur when the CEO purports to enter into agreements on behalf of the institution with third parties. If the actions of the governing body give rise to a third party's reasonable belief that the CEO acts with the authority of the institution, and such belief causes the third party to enter into an agreement with the CEO, expecting that the institution will be obligated under the contract, then the institution generally is responsible under the concept of *apparent authority*. However, if a third party deals with the CEO in the absence of indications of the CEO's authority created by the governing body and thereby unreasonably assumes that the

CEO possesses the authority to bind the institution to a contract, then such third party deals with the CEO in an individual capacity and not as an agent of the organization. Thus, the CEO, not the organization, will be personally responsible. There are times when the CEO clearly may exceed the limitations of his or her authority, but the governing body subsequently may approve such actions through *ratification* by accepting any resulting responsibility as though it had been authorized previously.

Generally, the CEO possesses the authority to enter into a contract for a needed piece of equipment, such as a medication cabinet. The contract of sale by the CEO as the agent of the organization becomes the obligation of the organization. However, if the governing body had imposed a limitation on purchases that could be made without specific prior approval of the governing body, the price of the medication cabinets would determine whether the governing body was bound under the contract. If the cabinets were $7,000 and the limitation on purchases without specific governing body approval was $5,000, then the CEO would have no authority to bind the organization for the purchase of the cabinets. The CEO generally would be liable to the supplier of the medication cabinets. As previously discussed, the two legal concepts of apparent authority and ratification may operate to alter the personal liability of the administrator.

Partnerships

A partnership comprises two or more persons who agree to carry on a business for profit and to share profits and losses in some proportions. A partnership, unlike a corporation, can be created by the parties' actions without a written or oral agreement.

Agents

An agent is one who has the power to contract for and bind another person, who is known as the principal. Corporations can act only through agents (e.g., their officers).

Independent Contractor

An independent contractor is an individual who agrees to undertake work without being under the direct control or direction of another, and is personally responsible for his or her negligent acts. This doctrine has been used by health care organizations as a defense to avoid liability caused by a physician's negligence. However, the mere existence of an independent contractual relationship is not sufficient to remove a facility from liability for the acts of certain of its professional personnel where the independent contractor status is not readily known to the injured party.

Emergency Department Physician

The appellate division of the New York State Supreme Court in *Mduba v. Benedictine Hospital*[5] held that the hospital was liable for the emergency department physician's negligence, whether or not the physician was an independent contractor or, even if under contract, the physician was considered to be an independent contractor. The court held that the patient had no way of knowing of the existence of a contract and relied on the relationship between the hospital and the physician in seeking treatment in the emergency department.

The appellant hospital in *Garcia v. Tarrio*[6] claimed that the evidence presented did not establish that Dr. Garcia, a surgeon, was the hospital's agent and that the negligence established was attributable to Dr. Garcia alone. The district court of appeals held that the appellant surgeon was the hospital's agent in that he had an agreement with the hospital guaranteeing him at least 50 percent of the work at the hospital.

Whether a physician is an employee or an independent contractor is of primary importance in determining liability for damages. Generally, a health care facility is not liable for injuries resulting from negligent acts or omissions of independent physicians. There is no liability on the theory of *respondeat superior* where a physician is an independent contractor so long as the physician is not an employee of the facility, is not compensated, maintains a private practice, and is chosen directly by his or her patients.

Independent Nurse Contractor—Alleged Negligent Hiring by Agency

The employer, Patient Support Services, Inc. (PSS), in *Maristany v. Patient Support Services, Inc.,*[7] was found not liable under the negligent hiring theory for injuries received by a patient under the care of an independent contractor.

By contract dated January 29, 1994, plaintiff Margarita Maristany retained the services of PSS to furnish an independent nurse to care for her husband Santiago, a post-operative brain surgery patient at defendant Presbyterian Hospital.

Pursuant to the contract, PSS arranged with defendant Terry to attend Santiago the night of February 29, 1994. Although Margarita contends that she informed PSS that her husband was "confused and combative" after the surgery, Terry denies that this information was transmitted to her either by PSS or the hospital nursing staff.

At approximately 10 P.M. Terry assisted a hospital nurse in placing Santiago into a Posey restraining vest. At approximately 3:30 A.M. Terry returned from a break to find Santiago extremely agitated. Terry sought assistance and tried to restrain the patient physically, but he escaped from the vest, clambered over the rails, and fell onto the floor, sustaining serious injury.

Plaintiffs do not seriously contest that Terry's status was that of an independent contractor, and not an employee. Although an employer is generally not liable for the torts or negligent acts of an independent contractor under the doctrine of *respondeat superior*, the common law has developed certain recognized exceptions that fall roughly into three categories:

1. negligence of an employer in selecting, instructing, or supervising the contractor
2. employment for work that is especially or "inherently" dangerous
3. instances in which the employer is under a nondelegable duty

Plaintiffs' contention that this case comes under the first exception is without merit. Because an employer has the right to rely on the supposed qualifications and good character of the contractor, and is not bound to anticipate misconduct on the contractor's part, the employer is not liable on the ground of its having employed an incompetent or otherwise unsuitable contractor unless it also appears that the employer either knew or, in the exercise of reasonable care, might have ascertained that the contractor was not properly qualified to undertake the work.

Here there is no competent proof that PSS had any reason to question Terry's qualifications. Despite plaintiffs' disparagement, Terry was neither inexperienced nor untrained. At the time of the incident, Terry had her qualifying certificate for more than 10 years. She had received training in the use of Posey restraints, and had previously cared for patients whose condition required these restraints. More importantly, she had been working with PSS for almost two years. Because she had previously worked for PSS and had given no indication that she was incompetent, there is no viability to the claim that PSS was negligent in assigning her to the care of Santiago.

LEGALITY OF OBJECT

To be a valid contract, the purpose or object of the contract must not be against state or federal policy and must not violate any statute, rule, or regulation. If the subject or purpose of the contract becomes illegal by some statute, rule, or regulation before actual formation of the contract, the parties no longer can form the contract.

STATUTE OF FRAUDS

The Statute of Frauds mandates that some types of contracts be put in writing and be signed by the party against whom the contract is sought to be enforced. Common contracts required under the Statute of Frauds to be in writing include those for the sale of an interest in land.

CONDITIONS

A *condition precedent* is an act or event that must happen or be performed by one party before the other party has any responsibility to perform under the contract. An *express condition* is formally written into the contract in specific terms. An *implied condition* is one that, although the parties may not have specifically mentioned it, it can reasonably be assumed that they intended the condition to be enforced.

PERFORMANCE

Ordinarily, substantial performance by one party to a contract will obligate the other parties to perform their function. Many, if not most, performance problems can be avoided by adequate drafting of contract terms.

NONPERFORMANCE DEFENSES

Under some circumstances the law gives a person a right not to perform under a contract. Defenses permitting nonperformance of a contract include

- *Fraud.* A victim of fraud will not have to perform under a contract. Fraud occurs when one party intentionally misrepresents a material fact or term of the contract and intends that the other party rely on that misrepresentation. The second party must, in fact, rely on the misrepresentation and suffer some damage before it will be excused from performing.
- *Mistakes.* Mistakes occur in contracts just as they do in everything else. However, a party will be allowed to claim mistake as a defense in only certain instances.
  - *Mistake of Fact.* A mistake of fact is an incorrect belief regarding a fact. Generally, both parties must have made the mistake. If only one is in error (and it is not known to the other), mistake of fact is not a defense.
  - *Mistake of Law.* A mistake of law is an incorrect judgment of the legal consequences of known facts. If the parties to a suit make a mistake as to the law involved, they usually must accept their plight without any remedy.
- *Duress.* Duress is the use of unlawful threats or pressure to force an individual to act against his or her will. An act performed under duress is not legally binding.
- *Illegal Contract.* No individual can recover damages when a contract is formed for illegal purposes.
- *Impossibility.* Contracts that are impossible to perform do not have to be carried out by the parties.
- *Statute of Limitations.* A party who does not, within a period of time known as the statute of limitations, take action to enforce contract rights by suing for damages caused by a breach of contract or taking other action will be barred permanently from doing so.

REMEDIES

What can a party do when another has breached the contract and refuses to or cannot perform? The general rule is that legal redress will attempt to "make the injured party whole again."

Specified Performance

When an aggrieved party has subsequently complied with his or her obligations pursuant to the agreed-upon terms of a contract, that party might seek specific performance as a remedy, rather than monetary remuneration. The most satisfactory remedy available to an injured party may be to require specific performance by the other entity.

Monetary Damages

Money damages, sometimes called compensatory damages, are awarded in an attempt to restore to the aggrieved party the money that it would have had if the other side had not breached the contract. This can include the cost of making a substitute contract with another party and the expense of delays caused by the breach.

General and Consequential Damages

General damages are those that can be expected to arise from a breach of a contract. They are foreseeable and common in the circumstances. *Consequential damages* are those that occur because of some unexpected, unusual, or strange development involved in the particular contract in dispute. The distinction between the two types is one of foreseeability. If it is found that the party who breached the contract could have foreseen the damages that followed, that person could be liable for consequential as well as general damages.

Duty To Mitigate Damages

Once someone has breached a contract, the other party cannot stand idly by and let damages build indefinitely. Every injured party has a duty to mitigate (lessen) damages caused by the breach of another person or entity. Failure to do so will prevent the aggrieved party's full recovery of damages that could have been mitigated.

Arbitration

Under the modern view of contract law, agreements in contracts to arbitrate subsequent disputes are valid.

STATE LAWS/UNIFORM COMMERCIAL CODE

Each state has a somewhat different set of laws on contracts. For some contracts, the state differences have little effect on day-to-day activities. In other contracts, such as commercial transactions, the state differences are critical.

CONTRACTS OF ADHESION

Contracts of adhesion are agreements in which one party has an obviously superior bargaining position, such as in a typical insurance contract. Contracts on prepared and pre-printed forms presented to the other party on a take-it-or-leave-it basis might also be contracts of adhesion.

GUARANTY AND WARRANTY

A *guaranty* is a promise or pledge by an individual to fulfill the obligation(s) of another in the event that person should default on his or her obligation(s). A *warranty* is a promise that certain facts are true. It is a binding type of guaranty or assurance given by the seller to the buyer about the goods sold. A warranty made by the vendor may be expressed or implied.

EMPLOYMENT CONTRACTS

Express Agreement

An employer's right to terminate an employee can be limited by express agreement with the employee or through a collective bargaining agreement to which the employee is a beneficiary. No such agreement was found to exist in *O'Connor v. Eastman Kodak Co.*,[8] in which the court held that an employer had a right to terminate an employee at will at any time and for any reason or no reason. The plaintiff did not rely on any specific representation made to him during the course of his employment interviews, nor did he rely on

any documentation in the employee handbook, which would have limited the defendant's common-law right to discharge at will. The employee had relied on a popular perception of Kodak as a "womb-to-tomb" employer.

BREACH OF EMPLOYMENT CONTRACT

Citation: *Dutta v. St. Francis Reg'l Med. Ctr.*, 850 P.2d 928 (Kan. Ct. App. 1993)

Facts

On July 1, 1987, Dr. Dutta, a radiologist, began working in the radiology department of the hospital as an employee of Dr. Krause, the medical director of the hospital's radiology department. On August 5, 1988, the hospital terminated Krause's employment as medical director but encouraged Dutta to remain with the hospital. On August 8, 1988, Dutta and the hospital entered into a written employment contract with a primary term of 90 days. The contract provided that if a new medical director had not been hired by the hospital within the 90-day period, the agreement was to be automatically extended for a second 90-day period.

Following a period of recruitment and interviews, the hospital offered Dr. Tan the position. Tan and the hospital executed a contract making him the medical director of the radiology department. The contract granted Tan the right "to provide radiation oncology services on an exclusive basis subject to the exception of allowing Dutta to continue her practice of radiation oncology at the hospital." On April 24, 1989, the hospital notified Dutta that the 90-day contract had expired and that Tan was appointed as the new medical director. The letter provided in part:

> It is our intent at this time to establish an exclusive contract with Dr. Donald C-S Tan for medical direction and radiation therapy at SFRMC. Your medical staff privileges to practice radiation therapy at SFRMC will not be affected by this action. You will be allowed to maintain your current office space for radiation oncology activities; however, you should make alternative arrangements for your billing and collection activities. *Id.* at 931.

Dutta and Tan then practiced independently of each other in the same facility. On October 13, 1989,

Tan became unhappy with this arrangement and requested exclusive privileges, stating he could not continue as medical director without exclusivity. On February, 2, 1990, an exclusive contract was authorized by the hospital. Dutta was notified that she would no longer be permitted to provide radiation therapy services at the hospital after May 1, 1990. By letter, Dutta twice requested a hearing on the hospital's decision to revoke her right to use hospital facilities. Both requests were denied.

Dutta sued the hospital for breach of employment contract after the hospital entered into an exclusive agreement with Tan, thereby denying Dutta the use of the hospital's radiology department and equipment. Dutta presented evidence about the purpose of the requirement in her contract with the hospital that provided that the new medical director be mutually acceptable to both parties. A hospital administrator testified that the hospital and Dutta included the phrase "mutually acceptable" in the contract because "[w]e both agreed that we wanted the person being recruited to be compatible with Dutta." *Id.* at 932.

Issue

Was the language "mutually acceptable" in paragraph four of the employment contract between the hospital and Dutta ambiguous?

Holding

The Kansas Court of Appeals held that substantial evidence supported the jury's verdict that the hospital breached its written employment contract with Dutta by hiring a medical director who was not mutually acceptable to both the hospital and Dutta.

Reason

The language in the contract is ambiguous if the words in the contract are subject to two or more possible meanings. The determination of whether a contract is ambiguous is a question of law. Paragraphs four and five of the hospital's employment agreement with Dutta, dated August 8, 1988, read as follows:

4. During the term of this Agreement the Medical Center shall be actively recruiting for a full-time Medical Director for the Ra-

diation Therapy department or a one-half time radiation therapist. Dr. Dutta shall be involved in the interviewing process. The person selected for either of the above positions shall be mutually acceptable to the Medical Center and Dr. Dutta. Dr. Dutta may discuss potential business arrangements with each individual interviewed.

5. Once the full-time Medical Director or part-time radiation therapist is selected, Dr. Dutta will, in good faith, attempt to reach a satisfactory business arrangement with the selected individual. *Id.* at 936.

The jury would be justified in finding that Dutta could have rejected Tan on the basis that he failed to enter into a business agreement, if there was evidence to support that point of view. The testimony of Dutta, the hospital administrator, and the attorney who represented Dutta in contract negotiations, when viewed in the light most favorable to Dutta, provides a factual basis for the jury to find the phrase "mutually acceptable" in the contract was intended by Dutta to ensure that the hospital would select a medical director who indicated a willingness to form a partnership or otherwise acceptable business relationship.

Discussion

1. What protective elements should each party to an employment contract negotiate?
2. What are the elements necessary to make a contract valid?

Implied Contracts

The rights of employees have been expanding through judicial decisions in the different states. Court decisions have been based on verbal promises, historical practices of the employer, and documents such as employee handbooks and administrative policy and procedure manuals that describe employee rights. The following are a few of the many cases that involve published personnel policies and procedures.

Employee Handbooks

For an employee handbook to constitute a contract, thereby giving enforceable rights to the employee, the following elements must be present:

1. The policy must be expressed in language that clearly sets forth a promise that the employee can construe to be an offer.

2. The statement must be distributed to the employee, making him or her aware of it as an offer.
3. After the employee learns about the offer, he or she must "begin" or "continue" to work.

An employee brought suit against his employer for wrongful termination in *Weiner v. McGraw-Hill.*[9] The court held that although the defendant did not engage the plaintiff for a fixed term of employment, the plaintiff pleaded a good cause of action for breach of contract. The plaintiff allegedly was discharged without the "just and sufficient cause" or the rehabilitative efforts specified in the defendant's handbook and allegedly promised at the time the plaintiff accepted employment. Further, on several occasions when the plaintiff had recommended that certain of his subordinates be dismissed, he allegedly was instructed to proceed in strict compliance with the handbook and policy manuals. The employment application that the plaintiff had signed stated that his employment would be subject to the provisions of McGraw-Hill's *Handbook on Personnel Policies and Procedures.*

An employee handbook or other policy statement may modify an at-will employment contract. The provisions of an employee handbook were held binding in *Dulduloo v. St. Mary of Nazareth Hospital Center.*[10] The Illinois Supreme Court held that

- A presumption that an employee hired for an indefinite term was an employee at will could be rebutted by evidence that the parties contracted to the contrary.
- Language in the employee handbook to the effect that a nonprobationary employee could be discharged after written notice was sufficient to modify the at-will nature of the plaintiff's employment.
- The plaintiff qualified as a "nonprobationary employee," for purpose of the language in the handbook.[11]

In *Watson v. Idaho Falls Consolidated Hospitals, Inc.,*[12] a nurse's aide was awarded $20,000 for damages when the hospital, as employer, violated the provisions of its employee handbook in the manner in which it terminated her employment. Evidence that the employee was making $1,000 a month at the time of her discharge and was not able to find suitable employment after her discharge supported the award of $20,000 in her favor for wrongful discharge. Although the nurse's aide had no formal written contract, the employee handbook and the hospital policies and procedures manual constituted a contract in view of evidence to the effect that these documents had been intended to be enforced and complied with by both employees and management. Employees read and relied on the handbook as creating terms of an employment contract and were required to sign for the handbook to establish receipt of a revised handbook that explained hospital policy, discipline, counseling, and termination. A policy and procedure manual placed on each floor of the hospital also outlined termination procedures.

In *Churchill v. Waters,*[13] a nurse brought a civil rights action against the hospital and hospital officials after her discharge. The federal district court held for the defendants on motion for summary judgment, finding that the hospital employee handbook did not give the nurse a protected property interest in continued employment. "Absent proof that the handbook contained clear promises which indicated the intent to bind the parties, no contract was created."[14] The handbook contained a disclaimer expressly disavowing any attempt to be bound by it and stated that its contents were not to be considered conditions of employment. The handbook was presented as a matter of information only and the language contained herein was not intended to constitute a contract between McDonough District Hospital and the employee. Although an employee handbook may delineate specific disciplinary procedures, that fact does not in and of itself constitute an enforceable contract.[15]

The above cases point out the importance of drafting appropriate personnel guidelines and manuals. Employment guidelines and manuals are very helpful in obtaining employee good will and maintaining good employee relations. They also can be excellent tools in maintaining a union-free environment. Therefore, the use, drafting, and implementation of an employment manual should be taken seriously. When drafting such manuals, employers should keep in mind the legal consequences of each provision and take care to avoid restrictive or tightly worded language.[16]

EXCLUSIVE CONTRACTS

An organization often enters into an exclusive contract with physicians and/or medical groups for the purpose of providing a specific service to the organization. Exclusive contracts generally occur within the organization's ancillary services (e.g., radiology, anesthesiology, and pathology).

Physicians who seek to practice at organizations in these ancillary areas but who are not part of the exclusive group have attempted to invoke the federal antitrust laws to challenge these exclusive contracts. These challenges generally have been unsuccessful.

In *Jefferson Parish Hospital v. Hyde,*[17] the defendant hospital had a contract with a firm of anesthesiologists that required that all anesthesia services for the hospital's patients be performed by that firm. Because of this contract, the plaintiff anesthesiologist's application for admission to the hospital's medical staff was denied. Dr. Hyde commenced an action in the federal district court, claiming the exclusive contract violated Section 1 of the Sherman Antitrust Act. The district court rejected the plaintiff's complaint, but the U.S. Court of Appeals for the Fifth Circuit reversed, finding the contract illegal *per se*. The Supreme Court reversed the Fifth Circuit, holding that the exclusive contract in question does not violate Section 1 of the Sherman Antitrust Act. The Supreme Court's holding was based on the fact that the defendant hospital did not possess "market power" and therefore patients were free to enter a competing hospital and to use another anesthesiologist instead of the firm. Thus, the Court concluded that the evidence was insufficient to provide a basis for finding that the contract, as it actually operates in the market, had unreasonably restrained competition.

Similarly, the anesthesiologists in *Belmar v. Cipolla*[18] brought an action challenging a hospital's exclusive contract with a different group of anesthesiologists. The New Jersey Supreme Court held that under state law the hospital's exclusive contract was reasonable and did not violate public policy.

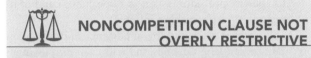

NONCOMPETITION CLAUSE NOT OVERLY RESTRICTIVE

Citation: *Dominy v. National Emergency Servs., 451 S.E.2d 472 (Ga. App. 1994)*

Facts

The appellee, National Emergency Services (NES), assigned appellant, Dr. Dominy, to the emergency department at Memorial Hospital and Manor (MHM) in Bainbridge, Georgia, where he was working in 1987 when that hospital terminated its contract with NES and contracted with another provider, Coastal Emergency Services, for emergency department physicians. Dominy continued to perform emergency medical services at MHM under contract with Coastal until 1989.

The contract provided: "The period of this Agreement shall be for one (1) year from the date hereof, automatically renewable for a like period upon each expiration thereof. . . ." The only reasonable construction of this provision was that the parties intended to contract for Dominy's employment for automatically renewable one-year terms upon the mutual assent of the parties. The fact that the agreement did not set out mechanics by which mutual assent may be communicated does not invalidate the contract.

Dominy challenged the contract's noncompetition clause as overly restrictive. The covenant in this case provides, in pertinent part: "for a period of two (2) years after the termination of this agreement . . . Physician shall not directly or indirectly solicit a contract to perform nor perform nor have any own-ership or financial interest in any corporation, partnership, or other entity soliciting or contracting to perform emergency medical service *for any medical institution at which Physician has performed the same or similar services under this Agreement or any prior Agreement between Physician and Corporation. Id.* at 474.

Dominy also maintained that the contract's $10,000 liquidated damages provision constituted an unenforceable penalty. "[A] contract provision will be treated as one for liquidated damages only if all of the following questions are answered affirmatively: First, was the injury caused by the breach difficult or impossible of accurate estimation; second, did the parties intend to provide for damages rather than a penalty; and third, was the stipulated sum a reasonable pre-estimation of the probable loss from the breach. In determining whether a designated sum that is to be paid to one party in the event that the other breaches the contract is a penalty, we must ascertain whether it was inserted for the purpose of deterring the party from breaching the contract, and of penalizing him in the event he should do so, or whether it was a sum which the parties in good faith agreed upon as representing those damages which would ensue if the contract should be breached." *Id.* at 474.

Issue

Was the contract's noncompetition clause overly restrictive? Was the liquidated damages provision of $10,000 in relation to the noncompetition clause enforceable?

Holding

The Court of Appeals held that (1) the noncompetition clause was not overly restrictive, and (2) the liquidated damages provision of $10,000 in relation to the noncompetition clause was enforceable.

Reason

The record reveals no attempt by either party to terminate the contract, and it is undisputed that Dominy received payment for his services at MHM and other benefits from NES consistent with the agreement until the hospital terminated its contract with NES. By their conduct, the parties assented to each of the contract's yearly renewals. Accordingly, the trial court properly granted summary judgment to NES.

As to the contract's noncompetition clause, this restriction prohibits Dominy from performing emergency medical services in only Memorial Hospital and Manor in Bainbridge, Georgia, where he worked pursuant to a contract with NES, and from having an ownership or financial interest in an entity contracting to provide emergency medical services to that one hospital. He is not precluded from all practice of medicine, with staff privileges at MHM, nor is he prohibited from providing emergency medical services, directly or under contract to a provider of such services, to other hospitals in the immediate vicinity. The court found that such a restriction is reasonably limited in duration and territorial effect while it protects NES's interest in preventing Dominy from becoming its competitor immediately after termination of its contract with MHM.

At the time the parties entered into contract, they limited NES's consequential damages to $10,000 for any breach of the following noncompetition provisions: whether Dominy forms a competing corporation to provide physicians to a hospital, or individually performs emergency medical services for a hospital where he had worked under contract with NES. According to NES, $10,000 represents the estimated cost of locating and verifying the credentials of a replacement for the breaching party rather than merely reassigning him to another client hospital in continuation of his contract with NES.

The contract entitles NES to liquidated damages "in addition to any and all remedies available to Corporation under any and all other agreements, and under this Agreement. . . ." Retention of the right to seek injunctive relief and other remedies for other breaches of the contract does not render the liquidated damages provision a penalty. Accordingly, the provision for liquidated damages is enforceable.

Discussion

1. Was the contract's noncompetitive clause overly restrictive? Why?
2. Why was the $10,000 liquidated damages provision enforceable in relation to the noncompetition clause?

Nurse Practitioner and Noncompetition Clause

The respondent in *Washington County Memorial Hospital v. Sidebottom*[19] employed the appellant as a nurse practitioner from October 1993 through April 1998. The respondent is a not-for-profit hospital located in a medically underserved area, an area where the ratio of patients to physicians is abnormally high.

Prior to beginning her employment, the appellant entered into an employment agreement with the respondent. The agreement included a noncompetition clause providing in part that the appellant ". . . during the term of [the] Agreement and for a period of one (1) year after the termination of her employment with [Respondent] . . . will not, anywhere within a fifty (50) mile radius of [Respondent], directly or indirectly engage in the practice of nursing . . . without the express direction or consent of [Respondent]."

In February 1994, the appellant acknowledged the existence of this clause when she requested the respondent's permission to work for the Washington County Health Department doing prenatal nursing care. Because the respondent was not then doing prenatal care, the respondent gave her permission to accept that employment, but reserved the ability to withdraw the permission if the services that the appellant was providing later came to be provided by the respondent.

In January 1996, the appellant and the respondent entered into a second employment agreement that continued the parties' employment relationship through January 9, 1998. This agreement included a noncompetition clause identical to the 1993 employment agreement. It also provided for automatic renewal for an additional two years, unless either party gave written termination notice no less than 90 days prior to the expiration of the agreement.

On March 11, 1998, the appellant gave the respondent written notice of her resignation effective April 15. On April 16, 1998, the appellant began working as a nurse practitioner with Dr. David Mullen at his office in St. Francois County. The office is within 50 miles from the respondent. The appellant ceased working with Mullen on May 11, 1998, due to a temporary restraining order issued by the Washington County Circuit Court. The court granted a preliminary injunction on June 1. On October 16, 1998, the court entered a Permanent Injunction and Final Judgment and Order prohibiting the appellant from practicing nursing within a 50-mile radius of the respondent for a period of one year from April 15, 1998.

One point of the appellant's appeal contended that the circuit court erred by enforcing the noncompetition clause contained in the appellant's employment agreement because there was no threat of significant patient loss to the respondent from the appellant's employment in the noncompete region because the respondent is located in a medically underserved area and the appellant had agreed not to treat any of the respondent's patients.

Generally, because a covenant not to compete is considered to be a restraint on trade, specific enforcement of such a covenant requires the covenant to be reasonable. The burden of demonstrating the covenant's validity is on the party seeking to enforce it. First, the covenant must be reasonable in scope as to geography and time. The appellant does not debate this aspect of the noncompetition clause in her employment agreement. Second, the covenant must be reasonably necessary to protect certain narrowly defined and well-recognized employer interests.

The respondent's interest lies in protecting its patient base, as income from patient billings constitutes its primary source of revenue. A patient base is a protectable interest under covenants not to compete. Further, the specific enforcement of the appellant's noncompetition clause is reasonably necessary to protect the respondent's interest. Actual damage need not be proven to enforce a covenant not to compete. Rather, the employee's opportunity to influence customers justifies enforcement of the covenant. Thus, the quality, frequency, and duration of an employee's exposure to an employer's customers are crucial in determining the covenant's reasonableness.

The appellant had the opportunity to influence the respondent's patients. Prior to her employment with the respondent, the appellant had never worked in Washington County nor did she have a patient base there. The appellant helped to establish two rural health care clinics for the respondent, one of which she managed for her first year of employment. During her almost five years of employment with the respondent, the appellant saw more than 3,000 patients. Pursuant to a collaborative practice agreement with a physician, the appellant treated patients, diagnosed illnesses and injuries, prescribed and dispensed medications (excluding narcotics), and ordered and interpreted laboratory tests. The appellant got to know the patients and families to whom she provided these services. At the clinic, she had her own telephone number, receptionist, appointment book, medical assistant, patient charts, laboratory, and examination rooms. Her offices were physically separated from the other medical practitioner at the clinic. Further, during her employment, the respondent promoted the appellant as a nurse practitioner in the community by paying for advertisements with her picture and telephone number in the newspaper. In general, the appellant had a good rapport with her patients, and she had patients who requested her for medical services.

Additionally, in the approximate one-month period that the appellant worked with Mullen, she actually saw at least six of the respondent's patients. The respondent also received three requests for medical record transfers to Mullen's office, and four of the respondent's patients voiced displeasure with the termination of the appellant's employment. Thus, although the respondent is located in a medically underserved area, its patient base was affected nonetheless by the appellant's violation of the noncompetition clause.

Further, although there may be no case law dealing with the enforcement of a covenant not to compete against a nurse practitioner, covenants not to compete are enforceable against physicians. The appellant, as a nurse practitioner, performed many of the medical services traditionally performed by a family practice physician. This role gave the appellant the opportunity to influence the respondent's patients. Thus, the physician cases provide support for the enforcement of a covenant not to compete against a nurse practitioner.

The cases also support the reasonableness of prohibiting the appellant from engaging "in the practice of nursing" as opposed to only work as a nurse practitioner. The appellant's violation of the noncompetition clause occurred because of her work as a nurse practitioner, not because of work as a nurse in general.

Moreover, the reasonableness of the noncompetition clause is unaffected by the appellant's offer to refrain from treating any patients treated by her during her employment with the respondent during the term of the noncompetition clause. By the time the appellant made this offer, her violation of the clause already had occurred. The appellant already had treated some of the respondent's patients. Her opportunity to influence the respondent's patients already had occurred. In fact, prior to leaving the respondent, the appellant told several patients where she was going. Additionally, the appellant testified at the preliminary injunction hearing that were it not for the temporary restraining order, she would have continued to work with Mullen and to see any patient who had an appointment.

The noncompetition clause in the appellant's employment agreement was clear and unambiguous. The appellant was aware of the clause. The appellant obtained legal advice before signing her original employment agreement and before resigning. The respondent notified the appellant before her last day that the noncompetition clause would be enforced. The judgment of the circuit court was affirmed.

RESTRAINT OF TRADE

Health care expenditures are a major segment of the nation's economy and are considered a significant cause of inflation. This has resulted in a demand from both the public and the private sectors for the development of more cost-effective approaches to the delivery of health care. This, in turn, has led to significant competition for health care dollars and is changing the very nature of how health care delivery is viewed by the courts.

Probably the most dramatic example of this is in the area of antitrust. Antitrust litigation and enforcement in the health care field were nearly nonexistent before 1975; since then, it has become a major legal issue with health care providers.

The increasing number of health care professionals and alternative delivery systems and the resultant competition create the potential for illegal activities to restrain trade. The emphasis on free enterprise and a competitive marketplace have resulted in careful scrutiny by the Federal Trade Commission (FTC), the federal agency responsible for monitoring the marketplace and enforcing federal antitrust laws.

The Antitrust Division of the Department of Justice has primary responsibility for enforcing federal antitrust laws, which includes investigation of possible violations of both the criminal and the civil provisions of the Sherman, Clayton, and Robinson-Patman Acts.

Federal Trade Commission

The FTC is authorized to enforce Section 5 of the FTC Act, which prohibits unfair methods of competition and unfair or deceptive acts or practices. Together with the Department of Justice, the FTC also enforces the Clayton Act sections that prohibit discrimination (e.g., in price), exclusive dealings and similar arrangements, certain corporate acquisitions of stock or assets, and interlocking directorates.

Sherman Antitrust Act

The primary federal law that comes into play in the health care area is the Sherman Antitrust Act. The Sherman Act proscribes the following:

> Section 1. Every contract, combination in the form of trust or otherwise, or conspiracy, in restraint of trade or commerce among the several states . . . is declared to be illegal.
>
> Section 2. Every person who shall monopolize, or attempt to monopolize, or combine or conspire with any other person or persons, to monopolize any part of the trade or commerce among the several states . . . shall be deemed . . . guilty of a felony. . . .[20]

Areas of concern for health care organizations include reduced market competition, price fixing, actions that bar or limit new entrants to the field, preferred provider arrangements, and exclusive contracts.

For example, a health care organization must be cognizant of the potential problems that may exist when limiting the number of physicians that it will admit to its medical staff. Because closed staff determinations can effectively limit competition from other physicians, medical groups, managed care organizations, etc., the governing body must ensure that the decision-making process in granting privileges is based on legislative, objective criteria and is not dominated by those who have the most to gain competitively by denying privileges.

Physicians have attempted to use state and federal antitrust laws to challenge determinations denying or limiting medical staff privileges. Generally, these actions claim that the organization conspired with other physicians to ensure that the complaining physician would not get privileges so that competition among the physicians would be reduced. To date, physicians generally have been unsuccessful in pursuing these antitrust claims.

However, in *Patrick v. Burget*,[21] the U.S. Supreme Court upheld a $2 million jury verdict in favor of a surgeon practicing in Astoria, Oregon, who claimed that other physicians had conspired to terminate his staff privileges at the only hospital in town and thus drove him out of practice. The defendant physicians argued that their conduct should be immune from liability under the state action doctrine because Oregon, like many states, has state agencies that generally regulate the procedures that hospitals may use to grant or deny staff privileges. The Supreme Court rejected this state action defense in the light of the egregious facts of the case (the defendant physicians were also participants in the state processes) and the fact that Oregon's statutory scheme did not supervise medical staff determinations actively. Significantly, however, the *Patrick* case was decided before the effective date of the Federal Health Care Quality Improvement Act of 1986.[22]

Physician Agreement for Professional Services/Too Restrictive

In *Emergicare Systems Corporation v. Bourdon*,[23] Emergicare Systems Corporation (ESC) provided emergency department physicians to the Longview Regional Hospital for several years, and Dr. Bourdon was one of those physicians. On October 23, 1991, ESC sent a letter to Bourdon confirming that its contract with Longview Regional Hospital would terminate on November 8, 1991, and that "pursuant to your agreement for professional services with ESC, that agreement terminates coincidentally." Bourdon then talked to the hospital administrator and to Metroplex Emergency Physicians, PA. Arrangements were made for him to continue his work at the emergency department as an employee of Metroplex.

ESC sued Bourdon and Metroplex. ESC alleged that Bourdon breached a covenant not to compete and that Metroplex tortiously interfered with its contractual agreement with Bourdon. Following a nonjury trial, judgment was rendered on February 15, 1996, that ESC take nothing from these defendants. ESC appealed. The covenant purports to restrict the physician from working within five miles of "any" clinic operated by ESC, whether the physician ever worked in that clinic or not. Also, the covenant purports to restrict the physician from working in any emergency department where ESC provides emergency department physicians for one year "following termination of such contract." This could be at some indefinite future date, more than one year following the physician's termination of employment by ESC.

The law in Texas as to covenants not to compete was discussed by the state supreme court in *Weatherford Oil Tool Company v. Campbell*.[24]

An agreement on the part of an employee not to compete with his employer after termination of the employment is in restraint of trade and will not be enforced in accordance with its terms unless the same are reasonable. . . . [T]he test usually stated for determining the validity of the covenant as written is whether it imposes upon the employee any greater restraint than is reasonably necessary to protect the business and good will of the employer.[25]

TEX. BUS. & COM. CODE ANN. § 15.51 (Vernon Supp. 1997) provides that, if a covenant not to compete contains "limitations as to time, geographical area, or scope of activity to be restrained that are not reasonable," the trial court can reform the covenant "to the extent necessary to cause the limitations . . . to be reasonable." This section also provides that the court cannot award "damages for a breach of the covenant before its reformation and the relief granted to the promisee shall be limited to injunctive relief." ESC did not seek injunctive relief; it sought liquidated damages.

There are cases, such as those involving sale of a business or goodwill, where a restrictive covenant has been enforced although its sole objective is the elimination of competition. But a restrictive covenant in connection with the sale of a business or goodwill is quite different from a postemployment restriction. The trial court also was correct in rendering the take-nothing judgment on appellant's claim against Metroplex.

The appeals court held that covenants not to compete that are unreasonable restraints of trade and unenforceable on grounds of public policy cannot form the basis of an action for tortious interference.

CONTRACT VIOLATES ANTITRUST LAWS

Citation: *Oltz v. St. Peter's Community Hosp., 19 F.3d 1312 (9th Cir. 1994)*

Facts

Mr. Oltz, a nurse anesthetist, brought an antitrust action against physician anesthesiologists and St. Peter's Community Hospital after he was terminated. Oltz had a billing agreement with the hospital, which provided 84 percent of the surgical services in the rural community that it served. The anesthesiologists did not like competing with the nurse anesthetist's lower fees and, as a result, entered into an exclusive contract with the hospital on

April 29, 1980, in order to squeeze the nurse anesthetist out of the market. This resulted in cancellation of the nurse anesthetist's contract with the hospital. Oltz was faced with a decision to either work for the anesthesiology group or leave the community and find another job. He and his wife decided to leave the community. Oltz found a job two months later working for the University of Iowa. He filed a suit against the anesthesiologists and hospital for violation of the Sherman Antitrust Act, 15 U.S.C. § 1. The anesthesiologists settled for $462,500 before trial.

The case against the hospital proceeded to trial. The jury found that the hospital had conspired with the anesthesiologists and awarded the plaintiff $212,182 in lost income up to November 5, 1986, the date of the trial, and $209,649 in future damages. The trial judge considered the damage award to be excessive and ordered a new trial. The hospital appealed on the issue of "liability" and Oltz appealed the order for a new trial based on excessive "damages."

The trial court's judgment on liability was affirmed, as well as its order for a new trial on damages. The hospital moved the court to exclude all damages after June 26, 1982, which was the date that the hospital had renegotiated its exclusive contract with the anesthesiology group. The court decided that Oltz failed to prove that the renegotiated contract also violated antitrust laws, thus ruling that Oltz was not entitled to damages after June 26, 1982. Because Oltz conceded that he could not prove damages greater than those offset by his settlement with the physicians, his claim for damages against the hospital was disposed of by summary judgment.

The judge who presided over Oltz's request for attorneys' fees restricted the amount that he could claim. Because Oltz had been denied damages from the hospital, the judge refused to award attorneys' fees or costs for work performed after the 1986 liability trial.

Issue

Was Oltz entitled to seek recovery for all damages resulting from destruction of his business after June 26, 1982?

Holding

The United States Court of Appeals for the Ninth Circuit held that Oltz was entitled to seek recovery for all damages.

Reason

Oltz had introduced evidence that the initial exclusive contract violated the antitrust laws and that such violation destroyed his practice. "Because the initial conspiracy destroyed his practice, Oltz is entitled to seek recovery for all damages resulting from the destruction of his business in Helena. . . . The legality of any subsequent agreements between the conspirators is irrelevant, because the April 29, 1980, contract severed the lifeline to Oltz's thriving practice in Helena." *Id.* at 1314.

Discussion

1. What should parties to a contract be aware of when negotiating exclusive contracts?
2. What remedies are available when one party breaches a contract by refusing to perform an agreed-upon service?

HOSPITAL STAFF PRIVILEGES

Staff privileges are both professionally and economically important to health care professionals in the practice of their chosen professions. Health care organizations must be selective in the granting of staff privileges to maintain quality standards. Every effort must be made to prevent anticompetitive abuses. As competition increases between podiatrists and orthopaedic surgeons, psychologists and psychiatrists, nurse midwives and obstetricians, nurse anesthetists and anesthesiologists, chiropractors and orthopaedic surgeons, nurse practitioners and family practice physicians, etc., it must be understood that there is a clear difference in denying staff privileges to an individual on a quality basis and denying such privileges to an entire group of professionals; the latter will serve only to raise a red flag and increase the chances of scrutiny by the courts. The stage has been set for tough competition for a dwindling number of patients, which in turn increases the potential for denial of privileges to prevent competitors from effectively entering the marketplace and practicing their respective professions.

Restricting Privileges

Moratoriums and closed medical staffs, as used in the health care field, describe an organization's policy of prohibiting further appointments to its medical staff. Generally, a moratorium is for a specified period. It is lifted at such time as the purpose for which it was instituted no longer exists. A closed staff is of a more permanent nature and relates to the mission of the institution, such as a commitment to teaching and research. Such institutions are very selective in their medical staff appointments. Generally, physicians who are appointed have both high academic interests and abilities as well as national recognition for expertise in their specialties.

Organizations have adopted a moratorium policy in certain instances because of a high inpatient census and the difficulties that would be encountered in accommodating new physicians. If left unchecked, the closing of an organization's medical staff eventually could have the effect of discouraging a competitive environment in the physician marketplace.

Governing bodies that adopt a closed-staff policy must do so on a rational basis and take the following into consideration before closing the medical staff to new applicants:

- effect on the organization's census
- organization and community needs for additional physicians in certain medical and surgical specialties and subspecialties
- strain that additional staff will put on the organization's supporting departments (e.g., radiology and laboratory services)
- effect of denying medical staff privileges to applicants who presently are located within the geographic area of the organization and serving community residents
- effect on any contracts the organization may have with other health care delivery systems, such as health maintenance organizations
- effect a moratorium will have on physician groups that may desire to add a partner
- effect additional staff may have on the quality of care rendered at the organization
- whether closing the staff will confine control of the organization's beds to the existing medical staff, allowing them to enhance their economic interests at the expense of their patients and other qualified physicians
- effect of a limited moratorium by specialty as opposed to a comprehensive one involving all specialties (Indiscriminately closing a staff in all departments and sections without a review could be considered an action in restraint of trade.)
- existence of a mechanism for periodic review of the need to continue a moratorium
- effect that medical staff resignations during the moratorium may have on the organization's census
- existence of a mechanism for notifying potential medical staff candidates at such time that the organization determines that there is a need for an expanded medical staff
- characteristics of the medical staff (e.g., is the staff aging and in need of new membership?)
- potential for restraint of trade legal action under the antitrust laws

- effect of increasing competition from free-standing surgicenters, emergency care centers, hospice programs, nursing facilities, etc., on the organization's census
- long-term effects
- effect on physicians without staff privileges whose patients are admitted to the organization's emergency department
- formation of a committee composed of representatives from the governing body, medical staff, administration, and legal counsel to develop an appropriate moratorium policy
- selection of a consultant who would study the demographics marketplace, physician referral patterns, literature, and organization use; conduct a medical staff opinion poll; develop patient-physician population ratios; determine population shifts; develop a formula to determine optimal staffing levels by department and section; and provide this information to the governing body for use in determining the appropriateness of closing the staff in selected departments

The continuing pressure of new technology, government, third-party payers, a host of regulations (e.g., utilization reviews, length-of-stay reviews, appropriateness-of-care reviews, alternate levels of care, diagnosis-related groups, and professional review organizations), and an increasing number of physicians demand that organizations review the fast-changing health care delivery systems and seriously consider ways that they can expand effectively and compete in the marketplace. In light of this, the imposition of a moratorium or the closing of an organization's medical staff may prove to be counterproductive to the long-term survival of an institution.

A moratorium must be applied with consistency and non-discrimination. In *Walsky v. Pascack Valley Hospital*,[26] the New Jersey Supreme Court held that the moratorium discriminated against newly admitted members of the staff who were required to agree not to seek staff privileges elsewhere, whereas those admitted to the staff before the moratorium were not subject to the same restriction, and that the moratorium represented an arbitrary and capricious exercise of discretion on the part of the governing body and defendant hospital.

In *Desai v. St. Barnabas Medical Center*,[27] medical staff privileges were closed to new applicants with the exception of physicians who had become affiliated with current staff members. This was considered arbitrary and discriminatory against otherwise competent physicians. The hospital argued that the exception was necessary to help cover the practices of physicians who were already on the hospital's medical staff. It was decided that such arguments involved mere supposition.

In *Berman v. Valley Hospital*,[28] the New Jersey Supreme Court held that a policy denying medical staff privileges to physicians who practiced in the hospital's service area for more than two years was arbitrary and not enforceable. The

hospital claimed that it was overcrowded and overused and that this was attributable to physicians from surrounding areas obtaining medical staff privileges. The hospital stated that its medical/surgical bed occupancy rate in 1977 had reached 89 percent and that the number of physicians increased from 172 in 1968 to 260 in 1977. The hospital conceded that it would have empty beds if it limited admissions to its primary service area.

The governing body must ensure that any proposed action to close an organization's medical staff is based on objective criteria. In several states, state agencies monitor the actions of an organization's governing body with respect to the granting or denial of clinical privileges. Unless the organization can show that its actions are based on legitimate patient care concerns or concerns related to the objectives of the organization, physicians may be successful in using antitrust and tort law to challenge the organization's actions.

PATIENT TRANSFER

Transfer Agreements

Health care organizations should have a written transfer agreement in effect with one or more facilities to help ensure the smooth transfer of patients from one institution to another when such is determined appropriate by the attending physician(s). Generally speaking, a transfer agreement is a written document that sets forth the terms and conditions under which a patient may be transferred to a facility that more appropriately provides the type of care required by the patient. It also establishes procedures to admit patients of one facility to another when their condition warrants a transfer.

Transfer agreements should be written in compliance with and reflect the provisions of the many federal and state laws, regulations, and standards affecting health care organizations. The parties to a transfer agreement should be particularly aware of applicable federal and state regulations.

Agreements should be established that will aid in bringing about the maximum use of the services of each organization and in ensuring the best possible care for patients. The basic elements of a transfer agreement include

- identification of each party to the agreement, including the name and location of each organization to the agreement
- purpose of the agreement
- policies and procedures for transfer of patients (Language in this section of the agreement should make it clear that the patient's physician makes the determination as to the patient's need for the facilities and services of the receiving organization. The receiving organization should agree that, subject to its admission requirements and availability

of space, it will admit the patient from the transferring organization as promptly as possible.)

- organizational responsibilities in arranging and making the transfer (Generally, the transferring organization is responsible for making transfer arrangements. The agreement should specify who will bear the costs involved in the transfer.)
- exchange of information (The agreement must provide a mechanism for the interchange of medical and other information relevant to the patient.)
- retention of autonomy (The agreement should make clear that each organization retains its autonomy and that the governing bodies of each facility will continue to exercise exclusive legal responsibility and control over the management, assets, and affairs of the respective facilities. It also should be stipulated that neither organization assumes any liability by virtue of the agreement for any debts or obligations of a financial or legal nature incurred by the other.)
- procedure for settling disputes (The agreement should include a method of settling disputes that might arise over some aspect of the patient transfer relationship.)
- procedure for modification or termination of the agreement (The agreement should provide that it can be modified or amended by mutual consent of the parties. It also should provide for termination by either organization on notice within a specified time period.)
- sharing of services (Depending on the situation, cooperative use of facilities and services on an outpatient basis [e.g., laboratory and X-ray testing] may be an important element of the relationship between organizations. The method of payment for services rendered should be carefully described in the agreement.)
- publicity (The agreement should provide that neither organization will use the name of the other in any promotional or advertising material without prior approval of the other.)
- exclusive versus nonexclusive agreement (In this age of patient rights, it is advisable for organizations—when and where possible—to have transfer agreements with more than one organization. The agreement may include language to the effect that either party has the right to enter into transfer agreements with other organizations.)

INAPPROPRIATE TRANSFER OF A PATIENT

Citation: *J.B. v. Sacred Heart Hosp. of Pensacola, 635 So.2d 945 (Fla. 1994)*

Facts

J.B., his wife, and their three minor children filed suit in Florida District Court against a hospital based on the following facts:

V. That on [or] about April 17, 1989, Sacred Heart Hospital was requested by their medical staff to arrange transportation for L.B., a diagnosed AIDS patient, to another treatment facility in Alabama.

VI. That the social services for the hospital were unable to arrange ambulance transport and so took it upon themselves to contact L.B.'s brother in Mississippi, namely J.B., requesting that he come to the hospital and provide the transportation.

VII. J.B., having visited L.B. at the hospital when he was first admitted, was under the impression that his brother's diagnosis was Lyme disease. He had not been notified that there was a change in diagnosis after his visit.

VIII. The patient, L.B., was released from the hospital with excessive fever and a heparin lock in his arm to the plaintiff, J.B., a layman providing a service without the benefit of training in the field of medical treatment and transport.

X. The complainant could not provide adequate care for the transferee in an emergency situation, as he was the operator of the vehicle.

XI. That during the trip, L.B. began to thrash about and accidentally dislodged the dressing to his heparin lock causing J.B. to reach over while driving in an attempt to prevent the lock from coming out of L.B.'s arm. In doing so, J.B. came in contact with fluid around the lock site. J.B.'s hand had multiple nicks and cuts due to a recent fishing trip. *Id.* at 947.

The complaint alleged that the hospital was negligent in arranging for J.B. to transport L.B. in that it knew of L.B.'s condition, the level of care that would be required in transporting him, and the risk involved. J.B. alleged that because he contracted the AIDS virus, his wife was exposed to it through him and his children have suffered a loss of relationship with him. The Florida District Court ruled that J.B.'s complaint stated a claim for medical malpractice and was thus subject to the presuit notice and screening procedures set out in Chapter 766,

Florida Statutes (1989). Because J.B. did not follow those procedures, the court dismissed the complaint. On appeal, the Florida Circuit Court declined to rule on J.B.'s claim, concluding that the issues are appropriate for resolution by the Florida Supreme Court.

Issue

Was the claim of the patient's brother a claim for medical malpractice, and therefore subject to a two-year statute of limitations?

Holding

The Florida Supreme Court answered that the claim was not a claim for medical malpractice for purposes of the two-year statute of limitations or presuit notice and screening requirements.

Reason

Chapter 95, Florida Statutes (1989), sets a two-year limitation period for medical malpractice actions. J.B.'s injury arose solely through the hospital's use of him as a transporter. Accordingly, this suit is not a medical malpractice action and the two-year statute of limitations is inapplicable. According to the allegations in J.B.'s complaint, the hospital was negligent in using J.B. as a transporter. The complaint does not allege that the hospital was negligent in any way in the rendering of, or the failure to render, medical care or services to J.B. Accordingly, the complaint does not state a medical malpractice claim for Chapter 766 purposes, and the notice and presuit screening requirements are inapplicable.

Discussion

1. Why was the claim made by the plaintiff not an action in malpractice?
2. Do you agree with the court's decision?
3. What precautions should the hospital have taken to help prevent the patient's brother from contracting the virus?
4. What is the importance of patient-family education as it relates to this case?
5. What are the confidentiality issues in cases of this nature?
6. Were the transfer arrangements for the patient appropriate?

PREEXISTING CONDITION

Citation: *Truett v. Community Mut. Ins. Co., 633 N.E.2d 617 (Ohio Ct. App. 1993)*

Facts

Mr. Truett brought an action against the insurer to recover medical expenses. In June 1991, Truett was treated for migraine headaches. As of August 1, 1991, Truett was covered under an employee benefit plan through a group health insurance contract with Community Mutual Insurance Co. On August 29, 1991, Truett was hospitalized for dizziness, vomiting, and weakness on his left side. After extensive testing, Dr. Moorthy diagnosed Truett as suffering from a complicated migraine. Truett sought reimbursement for medical expenses he incurred during the course of his illness.

Community Mutual concluded on January 20, 1992, that Truett's medical expenses were not covered because the expenses were for the care of a preexisting condition. Under the insurance policy, conditions that existed prior to the effective date of the policy were not covered if health problems related to the conditions were manifested after the effective date. Truett challenged this assessment to a Community Mutual appeals board. Dr. Morrow was recruited by Community Mutual to provide an expert assessment of Truett's case. The Community Mutual appeals board found that Truett's condition was preexisting because he had been treated in June 1991 for migraine headaches. Therefore, Community Mutual denied his coverage for his expenses.

On September 1, 1992, the Truetts filed a complaint against Community Mutual to recover Truett's medical expenses. The Court of Common Pleas entered summary judgment for Community Mutual, and Truett appealed.

Issue

Was the insurer's denial of coverage arbitrary or capricious?

Holding

The Ohio Court of Appeals held that the insurer's denial of coverage was not arbitrary or capricious.

Reason

The appeals board had all of Truett's medical records from before and after the incident in question. It obtained Morrow's expert opinion that the complicated migraine was a continuation from Truett's previous bouts with normal migraines. The appeals board and Morrow relied on medical evidence in making their decisions and neither overlooked nor ignored relevant information. Thus, the decision was not arbitrary or capricious.

Discussion

1. Why was the insurer's denial of coverage neither arbitrary nor capricious?
2. Under what circumstances does the law give a person a right not to perform under a contract?

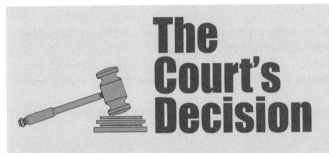

The Illinois Appellate Court held that the grant of the preliminary injunction was proper. That the defendant was engaging in the business of providing physical medicine and rehabilitation service in Coles County was sufficient. The court also found that the plaintiff's allegation of damages was sufficient. The interest the plaintiff sought to protect by the covenant was his interest in his clients. In bringing the defendant into the association, plaintiff was thereby bringing him in contact with a clientele that the plaintiff had established over a period of years. The plaintiff was naturally interested in protecting his clients from being taken over by defendant as a result of these contacts.

CHAPTER REVIEW

1. A *contract* is a written or oral agreement that involves legally binding obligations between two or more parties. The purpose of a contract is to provide legal recourse should one or more of the parties not perform its obligations as set forth under the contract.
2. There exist various types of contracts:
   - *Express* contracts are those in which the parties have an oral agreement or have reduced agreements to writing.
   - *Written* contracts are always the most desirable form.
   - Although *oral* contracts are generally recognized, they cannot always be enforced by the courts.
   - *Implied* contracts are those that are inferred by law and are based on parties' conduct.
   - *Voidable* contracts allow one party, but not the other, to escape from legal obligations under the contract.
   - An *executory* contract allows that something remains to be done by one or more of the parties.
   - *Executed* contracts are those in which obligations have been performed fully.
   - Contracts that are valid and legally binding are *enforceable.*
   - *Unenforceable* contracts allow for no legal remedy if they are breached by one or more parties concerned.
   - There are also contracts for *realty* (real estate or interests in real estate), *goods* (movable objects, with the exception of money and securities), and *services* (human energy).
3. To be enforceable, contracts must contain an offer or communication, consideration, and acceptance. If one or more of the parties who have entered into the contract are not considered competent, the contract will not be enforceable. Examples of those often found incompetent include minors, the mentally insane, and prisoners.
4. *Independent contractors* agree to perform work without being under the direct control or direction of another party. An employer is liable for the torts or negligence of an independent contractor in only certain circumstances; these

include negligence of the employer in selecting, instructing, or supervising the contractor; employment for work that is especially or inherently dangerous; and instances in which the employer is under a duty that is nondelegable.

5. Among the permissible defenses for not performing under a contract are fraud, mistake of fact or law, duress, lack of legality of the contract, impossibility to perform the contract, and expiration of the statute of limitations.

6. Forms of legal redress for breach of contract include specified performance of the duties set forth in the contract, the award of monetary (or compensatory) damages, and the award of general or consequential damages. General damages could be expected to result from the breach of the contract, while consequential damages are do to unforeseen damages.

7. A *guaranty* is a promise to fulfill an obligation of another in the event that the individual defaults on his or her obligation. A *warranty* is a binding guaranty given to the buyer by the seller about goods sold and is a promise that certain facts are true.

8. The right of an employer to terminate an employee can be limited through an *employment contract*—an express agreement with the employee or a collective bargaining agreement to which the employee is the beneficiary.

9. *Exclusive contracts* allow organizations to contract with physicians and/or medical groups to provide specific services to the organization.

10. The *Federal Trade Commission* is a federal agency that monitors the marketplace and enforces federal antitrust laws with the goals of maintaining free enterprise and a competitive marketplace.

11. Moratoriums—which prohibit further appointments to an organization's medical staff—must be applied with consistency and without discrimination. Although a moratorium is usually lifted at some point, a closed staff is more permanent in nature.

12. *Transfer agreements* are written documents that set forth terms and conditions under which patients may be transferred to facilities that more appropriately provide the required type of care.

REVIEW QUESTIONS

1. What is a contract?
2. Describe the differences between an express and an implied contract.
3. What are the elements of a contract?
4. Discuss the remedies available for nonperformance of a contract.
5. What are the benefits of an employment contract?
6. Why should employment disclaimers be included in employee handbooks?
7. Describe why exclusive contracts are so controversial.
8. Describe the advantages and disadvantages of closing a medical staff to new physicians.

NOTES

1. Sarah Bush Lincoln Health Ctr. v. Perket, 605 N.E.2d 613 (Ill. App. Ct. 1992).
2. Hungerford Hosp. v. Mulvey, 225 A.2d 495 (Conn. 1966).
3. 843 F. Supp. 1013 (D. Md. 1994).
4. *Id.* at 1018.
5. 384 N.Y.S.2d 527 (N.Y. App. Div. 1976).
6. 380 So. 2d 1068 (Fla. Dist. Ct. App. 1980).
7. 693 N.Y.S.2d 143 (N.Y. App. Div. 1999).
8. 492 N.Y.S.2d 9 (N.Y. 1985).
9. 457 N.Y.S.2d 193 (N.Y. 1982).
10. 505 N.E.2d 314 (Ill. 1985).
11. *Id.*
12. 720 P.2d 632 (Idaho 1986).
13. 731 F. Supp. 311 (D. Ill. 1990).
14. *Id.* at 321–322.
15. Chesnick v. Saint Mary of Nazareth Hosp., 570 N.E.2d 545 (Ill. App. Ct. 1991).
16. P.I. WEINER, S.H. BOMPEY, & M.G. BRITTAIN, JR., WRONGFUL DISCHARGE CLAIMS 98 (1986).
17. 466 U.S. 2 (1984).
18. 475 A.2d 533 (N.J. 1984).
19. 7 S.W.3d 542 (Mo. App. 1999).
20. 15 U.S.C. § 1 (1982).
21. 108 S. Ct. 1658 (1988).
22. 42 U.S.C.A. §§ 11101–11152 (1986).
23. 942 S.W.2d 201 (Tex. App. 1997).
24. 340 S.W.2d 950 (Tex. 1960).
25. *Id.* at 951.
26. 367 A.2d 1204 (N.J. 1976).
27. 510 A.2d 662 (N.J. 1986).
28. 510 A.2d 673 (N.J. 1986).

Civil Procedure and Trial Practice

PATIENT LEFT IN PERSISTENT VEGETATIVE STATE

Birdie Watkins, a 60-year-old woman, went to the appellant complaining of a sinus infection. Watkins was referred to Dr. Eliachar, an attending surgeon, who diagnosed a deviated septum and advised that a surgical procedure should be performed. When asked by the patient whether he would be performing the procedure, Eliachar testified that he would operate with the assistance of residents.

On the morning of Watkins' surgery, Eliachar was scheduled to perform four elective surgeries in two adjoining operating rooms. The anesthesiologist was Dr. Popovich, who was also involved in more than one surgery at the time and, like Eliachar, moved between operating rooms during the patients' procedures. The nurse anesthetist, who assisted Popovich in Popovich's absence, was Woods. The chief resident of the Ear,

Nose, and Throat (ENT) Department, Dr. Guay, performed the surgery on Watkins. Eliachar, who was listed in the operative records and discharge summary as the performing surgeon, allegedly supervised Guay's work as he moved between the adjoining operating rooms.

Guay testified that he first met the patient on the day of the surgery in the preoperation holding area minutes before the patient was transported to the operating room. He also testified that Eliachar assigned the surgery to him and that Eliachar did not scrub up that morning. Guay, upon meeting the patient, told the patient that he would be operating on her with Eliachar.

During the operation, which began at 7:30 A.M. and ended at 11:10 A.M., the patient was under a general anesthesia and was intubated by the nurse anesthetist to ensure normal breathing. According to Popovich, he did not inform the patient that a nurse anesthetist would perform the intubation and extubation and did not indicate that he, the anesthesiologist, would not be present throughout the operation. According to Eliachar, it was the surgeon's ultimate responsibility to ensure that the patient maintained an adequate airway during and after the operation. Yet Eliachar could not recall whether he was present when the patient was extubated. He believed that the nurse anesthetist extubated the patient. Popovich was not present for the extubation and did not evaluate the patient between the operating room and the postanesthesia care unit (PACU). The nurse anesthetist stated that the patient was extubated at approximately 10:30 A.M. in the operating room and that he and Guay then transported the patient to the PACU. On the way to the PACU at 10:35 A.M., the patient's heart rate was 85 beats per minute according to nurse Woods's records. Yet the nurse's notes from PACU indicate that at 10:35 A.M., when the patient was admitted to the PACU, her heart rate was 50 beats per minute. The nurse anesthetist's records also indicate

that the patient was awake and responsive when he transported her to the PACU, yet the PACU records indicate that the patient was unresponsive, emitting a large amount of clear urine, and not moving. At 10:40 A.M., the nurse anesthetist's records indicate that the patient's heart rate was 78 to 80 beats per minute, while the PACU nurse's record states 30 beats per minute, a rate that is admittedly life-threatening, according to the nurse anesthetist. When the heart rate hit 30 beats per minute, the nurse anesthetist recalls, resuscitative measures were begun on the patient. The patient was given cardiopulmonary resuscitation and was reintubated at 10:50 A.M. The patient was left in a persistent vegetative state.[1]

What is your verdict?

INTRODUCTION

For many students and health care practitioners, this book will be their only formal introduction to the legal aspects of health care administration. This chapter in particular is valuable to both students and health care professionals in understanding the law and its application in the courtroom. Although many of the procedures leading up to and followed during a trial are discussed in this chapter, civil procedure and trial practice are governed by each state's statutory requirements. Cases on a federal level are governed by federal statutory requirements.

PLEADINGS

The pleadings of a case (e.g., summons and complaint), which include all the allegations of each party to a lawsuit, are filed with the court. The pleadings may raise questions of both law and fact. If only questions of law are at issue, the judge will decide the case based on the pleadings alone. If questions of fact are involved, the purpose of a trial is to determine those facts.

Summons and Complaint

The *parties* to a controversy are the plaintiff and the defendant. The *plaintiff* is the person who initiates an action by filing a complaint; the *defendant* is the person against whom

a suit is brought. Many cases have multiple plaintiffs and defendants. Filing an order with a court clerk to issue a writ or summons commences an action.

Although the procedures for beginning an action vary according to jurisdiction, there are procedural common denominators. All jurisdictions require service of process on the defendant (usually through a summons) and a return to the court of that process by the person who served it. Where a summons is not required to be issued directly by a court, an attorney, as an officer of the court, may prepare and cause a summons to be served without direct notice to or approval of a court. Notice to a court occurs when an attorney files a summons and complaint in a court, thereby indicating to the court that an action has been commenced.

The first pleading filed with the court in a negligence action is the *complaint*. The complaint identifies the parties to a suit, states a cause of action, and includes a demand for damages. It is filed by the plaintiff and is the first statement of a case by the plaintiff against the defendant. In some jurisdictions, a complaint must accompany a summons (an announcement to the defendant that a case has been commenced). The essential elements contained in a complaint are: (1) a short statement of the grounds on which the court's jurisdiction depends (the court's authority to hear the case), (2) a statement of the claim demonstrating that the pleader is entitled to relief, and (3) a demand for judgment for the relief to which the plaintiff deems him- or herself entitled. All these elements apply to any counterclaim, cross-claim, or third-party claim.

The complaint can be served on the defendant either with the summons or within a prescribed time after the summons has been served. Specific formalities must be observed in the service of a summons so that appropriate jurisdiction over a defendant is obtained. Such formalities dictate the manner in which a summons is to be delivered, the time period within which service must be effected, and the geographic limitations within which service must be made. For example, a summons to commence an action in a local municipal court generally would require service within the particular municipality in order for the court to obtain jurisdiction. Where such service is not possible, the action may have to be brought in a different court.

In the preliminary motions, the defendant cites possible errors that would defeat the plaintiff's case. For example, the defendant may object that a summons or a complaint was served improperly, that the action was brought in the wrong jurisdiction, or that there was something technically incorrect about the complaint.

IMPROPER SERVICE OF A SUMMONS

Citation: *Collins v. Park, 621 A.2d 996 (Pa. Super. Ct. 1993)*

Facts

In this medical malpractice action, the trial court dismissed a complaint against Dr. Park because of improper service upon him. The plaintiff, Mr. Collins, appealed.

On March 14, 1989, the sheriff attempted to serve the writ on Park by leaving a copy with the receptionist at the hospital. On February 22, 1988, however, Park had terminated his relationship with the hospital, and he did not thereafter maintain an office or place of business at the hospital.

Issue

Was the sheriff's attempt at service of the writ of summons upon Park in a medical malpractice action by leaving a copy with the receptionist at the hospital defective?

Holding

The Pennsylvania Superior Court held that the sheriff's attempt at service of the writ of summons upon the physician by leaving a copy with the receptionist at the hospital was defective, as Park did not

have a proprietary interest in the hospital and, at the time of service, was no longer affiliated with the hospital. The service of a complaint by leaving a copy with the nurse at the intensive care unit was inadequate to confer jurisdiction over him.

Reason

The plaintiff's attempted service of the writ of summons was defective. Because Park was not affiliated with the hospital at which service was attempted, it seems clear that the hospital cannot be deemed his "office" or "usual place of business." A copy of the complaint was left with a nurse at the intensive care unit of the hospital, where Park was then a patient. The intensive care unit of a hospital, however, cannot be deemed the patient's place of residence, nor can it be said that the patient resides there. Park did not voluntarily leave his place of residence to establish a new residence at the hospital.

Discussion

1. What is the proper procedure for serving a summons in your state?
2. What is the difference between a summons and a complaint?
3. Why was the service of the summons determined to be improper?

Demurrer

On receiving a copy of the plaintiff's complaint, the defendant can file preliminary objections before answering the complaint. A *demurrer* is a formal objection by one of the parties to a lawsuit that the evidence presented by the other party is insufficient to sustain an issue or case.

Answer

After service of a complaint, a response is required from the defendant in a document called the *answer*. In the answer, the defendant responds to each of the allegations contained in the complaint by stating his or her defenses and by admitting to or denying each of the plaintiff's allegations. If the defendant fails to answer the complaint within the prescribed time, the plaintiff can seek judgment by default against the defendant. However, in certain instances a default judgment will be vacated if the defendant can demonstrate an acceptable excuse for failing to answer. Even if a plaintiff has been granted judgment by default, he or she could be required to present the basis for damages at a hearing before a court. A defaulting defendant may be entitled to oppose the evidence presented by the plaintiff at such a hearing, at least to the extent of the damages claimed.

Personal appearance of the defendant to respond to a complaint is not necessary. To prevent default, the defendant's attorney responds to the complaint with an answer. The defense attorney attempts to show through evidence that the defendant is not responsible for the negligent act. The answer generally consists of a denial of the charges made and specifies a defense or argument justifying the position taken. The defense may show that the claim is unfounded for such reasons as the following: (1) the period within which a suit must be instituted has run out, (2) there is contributory negligence on the part of the plaintiff, (3) any obligation has been paid, (4) a general release was presented to the defendant, or (5) the contract was illegal and therefore canceled by mutual agreement. The original answer to the complaint is filed with the court having jurisdiction over the case, and a copy of the answer is forwarded to the plaintiff's attorney.

Counterclaim

In some cases the defendant may have a claim against the plaintiff and therefore may file a *counterclaim*. For example, the plaintiff may have sued an organization for personal injuries and property damage caused by the negligent operation of an organization's ambulance. The organization may file a counterclaim on the ground that its driver was careful and that it was the plaintiff who was negligent and is liable to the organization for damage to the ambulance.

Bill of Particulars

Because a complaint may provide very little information regarding the claim, the defense attorney may request a *bill of particulars*, which limits the scope and generality of the pleadings. This document requests more specific and detailed information than is provided in the complaint. If a counterclaim has been filed, the plaintiff's attorney may request a bill of particulars from the defense attorney. More specifically, a bill of particulars for a malpractice suit may request the following from the plaintiff's attorney:

* Specify the date and time of day when the alleged malpractice occurred. Does the malpractice claim include:
  – misdiagnosis or failure to diagnose correctly
  – failure to perform a test or diagnostic procedure

  – failure to medicate, treat, or operate
  – a contraindicated test given or a contraindicated test or surgical procedure performed
  – administration of a medicine or treatment or performance of a test or surgical procedure in a manner contrary to accepted standards of medical practice
* Specify where the alleged malpractice occurred.
* Specify how the occurrence of the malpractice is claimed.
* Specify all the commissions and/or omissions constituting the malpractice claimed.
* List all injuries claimed to have been caused by the defendant's alleged malpractice.
* List any witnesses to the alleged malpractice.
* State the length of time the plaintiff was confined to bed.
* State the weekly earnings of the plaintiff.
* State the name and address of the employer.

A death action rider also may be attached if the malpractice allegedly caused death. The rider may request such information as the length of time the decedent experienced pain; the date, time, and place of death; and a statement setting forth the cause of death.

DISCOVERY AND EXAMINATION BEFORE TRIAL

Discovery is the process of investigating the facts of a case before trial. The objectives of discovery are to: (1) obtain evidence that might not be obtainable at the time of trial; (2) isolate and narrow the issues for trial; (3) gather knowledge of the existence of additional evidence that may be admissible at trial; and (4) obtain leads to enable the discovering party to gather further evidence.

The discovery process is available to promote more just trials by preventing unfair surprise. "Discovery rules were promulgated to prevent trial by ambush. To deny a party the right to know absolutely at some meaningful time before trial the names and addresses of all witnesses the opposing side proposes to call in its case-in-chief is an insult to this principle."[2]

Discovery may be obtained on any matter that is not privileged and that is relevant to the subject matter involved in the pending action. The parties to a lawsuit have the right to discovery and to examine witnesses before trial. Examination before trial (EBT) is one of several discovery techniques used to enable the parties of a lawsuit to learn more regarding the nature and substance of each other's case. An EBT consists of oral testimony under oath and includes cross-examination. A deposition, taken at an EBT, is the testimony of a witness that has been recorded in a written format. Testimony given at a deposition becomes part of the permanent record of the case. Each question and answer is transcribed by a court stenographer and may be used at the subsequent trial. Truthfulness and consistency are important because answers that differ from those given at trial will be used to attack the credibility of the witness.

Either party may obtain a court order permitting the examination and copying of books and records, such as medical records, as well as the inspection of buildings and equipment. A court order also may be obtained allowing the physical or mental examination of a party when the party's condition is important to the case.

In certain instances, it may be desirable to record a witness's testimony outside the court before the time of trial. In such a case, one party, after giving proper notice to the opposing party and to the prospective missing witness, may require a witness to appear before a person authorized to administer oaths in order to answer questions and submit to cross-examination. The testimony is recorded and filed with the court and is entered in evidence as the testimony of the missing witness. This procedure may be used when a witness is aged or infirm or too ill to testify at the time of trial.

Attorney-Client Privilege

Confidential communications made by a client and an attorney to one another are protected by attorney-client privilege. There are three elements required to successfully assert attorney-client privilege:

1. Both parties must contemplate that the attorney-client relationship does or will exist.
2. The client must seek advice from that attorney in his or her capacity as a legal advisor.
3. Communication between the attorney and client must be identified to be confidential.

Incident and Investigation Reports

Hospital incident and investigation reports are generally not protected from discovery. The burden rests upon the hospital to demonstrate that incident and investigation reports are protected from discovery under attorney-client privilege and work product doctrine. Attorney-client privilege is intended to ensure that a client remains free from apprehension that consultations with a legal advisor will be disclosed. Such privilege further encourages a client to talk freely with his attorney so that he or she may receive quality advice. Likewise, with regard to the work product doctrine, not even the most liberal of discovery theories can justify unwarranted inquiries into the files and the mental impressions of an attorney. Courts are required to protect the integrity and fairness of the fact-finding process by requiring full disclosure of all relevant facts connected with the impending litigation while, at the same time, promoting full and frank consultation between a client and a legal advisor by removing the fear of compelled disclosure of information.

If in connection with an accident or an event, a business entity, in the ordinary course of business, conducts an investigation for its own purposes, the resulting investigative report is producible in civil pretrial discovery. The distinction between whether defendant's in-house report was prepared in the ordinary course of business or was work product in anticipation of litigation is an important one. The fact that a defendant anticipates the contingency of litigation resulting from an accident or event does not automatically qualify an in-house report as work product. A document that is not privileged does not become privileged by the mere act of sending it to an attorney.

Preparation of Witnesses

The manner in which a witness handles questioning at a deposition or trial is often as important as the facts of the case. Each witness should be well prepared before testifying. Preparation should include a review of all pertinent records. Helpful guidelines for witnesses undergoing examination in a trial or a court hearing include the following:

- Review the records (e.g., medical records and other business records) on which you might be questioned.
- Do not be antagonistic in answering the questions. The jury may already be somewhat sympathetic toward a particular party to the lawsuit; antagonism may only serve to reinforce such an impression.
- Be organized in your thinking and recollection of the facts regarding the incident.
- Answer only the questions asked.
- Explain your testimony in simple, succinct terminology.
- Do not overdramatize the facts you are relating.
- Do not allow yourself to become overpowered by the cross-examiner.
- Be polite, sincere, and courteous at all times.
- Dress appropriately, and be neatly groomed.
- Pay close attention to any objections your attorney may have as to the line of questioning being conducted by the opposing counsel.
- Be sure to have reviewed any oral deposition in which you may have participated during EBT.
- Be straightforward with the examiner. Any answers designed to cover up or cloud an issue or fact will, if discovered, serve only to discredit any previous testimony that you may have given.

- Do not show any visible signs of displeasure regarding any testimony with which you are in disagreement.
- Be sure to have questions that you did not hear repeated and questions that you did not understand rephrased.
- If you are not sure of an answer, indicate that you are not sure or that you just do not know the answer.

MOTIONS

The procedural steps that occur before trial are specifically classified as pretrial proceedings. After the pleadings have been completed, many states permit either party to move for a judgment on the pleadings. When this motion is made, the court will examine the entire case and decide whether to enter judgment according to the merits of the case as indicated in the pleadings. In some states, the moving party is permitted to introduce sworn statements showing that a claim or defense is false or a sham. This procedure cannot be used when there is substantial dispute concerning the facts presented by the affidavits.

In many states, a pretrial conference will be ordered at the judge's initiative or on the request of one of the parties to the lawsuit. The pretrial conference is an informal discussion during which the judge and the attorneys eliminate matters not in dispute, agree on the issues, and settle procedural matters relating to the trial. Although it is not the purpose of the pretrial conference to compel the parties to settle the case, it often happens that cases are settled at this point.

Dismissal

A defendant may make a motion to dismiss a case, alleging that the plaintiff's complaint, even if believed, does not set forth a claim or cause of action recognized by law. A motion to dismiss can be made before, during, or after a trial. Motions made before a trial may be made on the basis that the court lacks jurisdiction, that the case is barred by the statute of limitations, that another case is pending involving the same issues, and other similar matters. A motion during trial may be made after the plaintiff has presented his or her case, on the grounds that the court has heard the plaintiff's case and the defendant is entitled to a favorable judgment as a matter of law. In the case of a motion made by the defendant at the close of the plaintiff's case, the defendant normally will claim that the plaintiff has failed to present a *prima facie* case (i.e., that the plaintiff has failed to establish the minimum elements necessary to justify a verdict even if no contrary evidence is presented by the defendant). After the trial has been completed, either party may move for a directed verdict on the grounds that he or she is entitled to such verdict as a matter of law.

A plaintiff has the right to appeal a lower court's decision to an appellate court if a defendant's motion for dismissal is granted. If the court rules against the defendant's motion for dismissal, as well as any other preliminary objections and motions that the defendant may have made, the defendant then will be required to file an answer to the plaintiff's complaint.

Summary Judgment

Either party to a suit may believe that there are no triable issues of fact and only issues of law to be decided. In such event, either party may make a motion for summary judgment. This motion asks the court to rule that there are no facts in dispute and that the rights of the parties can be determined as a matter of law, on the basis of submitted documents, without the need for a trial. Although the courts are reluctant to look favorably on motions for summary judgments, they will grant them if the circumstances of a particular case warrant it.

A motion for summary judgment is a means for the efficient disposition of a cause of action where there is no genuine issue of material fact and the moving party is entitled to judgment as a matter of law. The courts should exercise caution in deciding issues involving policy considerations. Excessive caution, however, would undercut the purpose of a motion for summary judgment, which provides a means for piercing the allegations of the pleadings to determine whether there are issues requiring disposition at trial. If, after drawing all inferences of doubt against the movant, a court finds that there is no genuine basis of material fact, it should enter summary judgment.[3]

NOTICE OF TRIAL

The examination before a trial may reveal sufficient facts that would discourage the plaintiff from continuing the case, or it may encourage one or both parties to settle out of court. Once a decision to go forward is reached, the case is placed on the court calendar. Postponement of the trial may be secured with the consent of both parties and the consent of the court. A case may not be postponed indefinitely without being dismissed by the court. Where one party is ready to proceed and another party seeks a postponement, a valid excuse must be shown. An example of a valid excuse is that the attorney for the party seeking the postponement is engaged in another case. Should a defendant fail to appear at trial, the judge can pass judgment against the defendant by default. A case also can be dismissed if the plaintiff fails to appear at trial.

MEMORANDUM OF LAW

Each attorney prepares a *memorandum of law* (or trial brief) for the court. It presents the nature of the case, cites case decisions to substantiate arguments, and aids the court regarding points of law. Trial briefs are prepared by both the plaintiff's and the defendant's attorneys. A trial brief is not required, but it is a recommended strategy. It provides the court with a basic understanding of the position of the party submitting the brief before the commencement of the trial. It also focuses the court's attention on specific legal points that may influence the court in ruling on objections and on the admissibility of evidence in the course of the trial.

THE COURT

A case is heard in the court that has jurisdiction over the subject of controversy. The judge decides questions of law and is responsible for ensuring that a trial is conducted properly in an impartial atmosphere and that it is fair to both parties of a lawsuit. He or she determines what constitutes the general standard of conduct required for the exercise of due care. The judge informs the jury of what the defendant's conduct should have been, thereby making a determination of the existence of a legal duty.

The judge plays the dominant role in a trial. He or she decides whether evidence is admissible, charges the jury (defines the jurors' responsibility in relation to existing law), and may take a case away from the jury (by directed verdict or judgment notwithstanding the verdict) when he or she believes that there are no issues for the jury to consider or that the jury has erred in its decision. This right on the part of the judge with respect to the role of the jury narrows the jury's responsibility with regard to the facts of the case. The judge maintains order throughout the suit, determines issues of procedure, and is generally responsible for the conduct of the trial.

THE JURY

A Jury Cries

A New York City jury awarded $26 million to a boy injured during surgery. What was it that so disturbed the jury that caused it to grant such a huge award? According to an article written by an alternate juror, who had invited the jurors to his home three weeks after the trial:

The defense lawyers were on their feet objecting they didn't want the jury to see Stephen. But that just raised a question for us: If his injuries were as slight as the defense had been insisting, why the resistance? The judge agreed that it was proper for Stephen to appear at his own trial, and the rear doors to the courtroom were opened.

Most of the jurors had begun to cry. But we were also angry. The defense lawyers it seemed, had been trying to put one over on us, claiming that Stephen was a normal teenage boy with a few minor handicaps.

For seven weeks, the jury had sat in that courtroom listening to the defense lawyers belittle Stephen's problems. We saw the doctors refuse to acknowledge Stephen's handicaps or to accept responsibility for them. To the jury at least, it seemed that the doctors had made mistakes, refused to admit them, and then tried to cover them up.[4]

The right to a trial by jury is a constitutional right in certain cases. Not all cases entitle the parties to a jury trial as a matter of right. For example, in many jurisdictions, a case in equity (a case seeking a specific course of conduct rather than monetary damages) may not entitle the parties to a trial by a jury. An example of an equity case would be one that seeks a declaration as to the title to real property.

An individual may waive the right to a jury trial. If this right is waived, the judge acts as judge and jury and becomes the trier of facts and decides issues of law.

Members of the jury are selected from a jury list. They are summoned to court by a paper known as the jury process. Impartiality is a prerequisite of all jurors. The number of jurors who sit at trial is 12 in common law. If there are fewer than 12, the number must be established by statute.

Counsel for both parties of a lawsuit question each prospective jury member for impartiality, bias, and prejudicial thinking. This process is referred to as the *voir dire*, the examination of jurors. Once members of the jury are selected, they are sworn in to try the case.

The jury makes a determination of the facts that have occurred, evaluating whether the plaintiff's damages were caused by the defendant's negligence and whether the defendant exercised due care. The jury makes a determination of the particular standard of conduct required in all cases in which the judgment of reasonable people might differ. The jury must pay close attention to the evidence presented by both sides to a suit in order to render a fair and impartial verdict. Jurors who fall asleep during the trial can be replaced with an alternate juror, as was the case in *Richbow v. District of Columbia*.[5]

Although the verdict must be based on the theory of wrongdoing, it is not always easy for a jury to determine which side is telling the truth and which is masking the truth with rhetoric.

The jury also determines the extent of damages, if any, and the degree to which the plaintiff's conduct may have contributed to his or her injury, thereby mitigating the responsibility of the defendant (contributory negligence).

SUBPEONAS

A *subpoena* is a legal order requiring the appearance of a person and/or the presentation of documents to a court or administrative body. Attorneys, judges, and certain law enforcement and administrative officials, depending on the jurisdiction, may issue subpoenas. Subpoenas generally include

- reference number
- names of plaintiff and defendant
- date, time, and place to appear
- name, address, and telephone number of opposing attorney
- documents requested if a subpoena is for records

Some jurisdictions require the service of a subpoena at a specified time in advance of the requested appearance (e.g., 24 hours). In other jurisdictions, no such time limitation exists. A court clerk, sheriff, attorney, process server, or other person as provided by state statute can serve a subpoena.

A *subpoena ad testificandum* orders the appearance of a person at a trial or other investigative proceeding to give testimony. Witnesses have a duty to appear and may suffer a penalty for contempt of court should they fail to appear. They may not deny knowledge of a subpoena if they simply refused to accept it. The court may issue a bench warrant, ordering the appearance of a witness in court, if a witness fails to answer a subpoena. Failure to appear may be excused if extenuating circumstances exist.

A subpoena for records, known as a *subpoena duces tecum,* is a written command to bring records, documents, or other evidence described in the subpoena to a trial or other investigative proceeding. The subpoena is served on one able to produce such records. Disobedience in answering a *subpoena duces tecum* is considered contempt of court and carries a penalty of a fine or imprisonment.

OPENING STATEMENTS

During the opening statement, the plaintiff's attorney attempts to prove the wrongdoing of the defendant by presenting credible evidence favorable to his or her client. The opening statement by the plaintiff's attorney provides in capsule

form the facts of the case, what he or she intends to prove by means of a summary of the evidence to be presented, and a description of the damages to his or her client.

Opening statements can leave lasting impressions on jury members. They are prepared so that each jury member can sympathize with the plaintiff and relate to the injustice and see it happening to themselves. The opening statement must be concise and to the point.

> Jurors typically do not decide the case on the basis of the opening statements. But pulling for one side or another—even just slightly—gives them a point of view. From then on, they tend to view the evidence from the vantage point of the side they favor.[6]

The defense attorney makes his or her opening statement indicating the position of the defendant and the points of the plaintiff's case he or she intends to refute. The defense attorney explains the facts as they apply to the case for the defendant.

BURDEN OF PROOF

The *burden of proof* in a civil lawsuit is the obligation of the plaintiff to persuade the jury regarding the truth of his or her case. The burden of proof in a criminal case lies with the prosecution. Proof of guilt beyond a reasonable doubt is required to convict a criminal defendant. This is a higher standard than that used in a civil case (which is a fair preponderance of the credible evidence presented).

A *preponderance of the credible evidence* must be presented in order for a plaintiff to recover damages. "Credible evidence" is evidence that in the light of reason and common sense is worthy of belief. A preponderance of credible evidence requires that the prevailing side of the case carry more weight than the evidence on the opposing side. If one would envision the "scales of justice," with the evidence presented by the plaintiff on one scale and that presented by the defendant on the opposite scale, the side tipping the scale in their favor would most likely prevail. If the evidence is evenly balanced between the plaintiff and the defendant, the required burden of proof will not have been met and the plaintiff will not prevail.

The burden of proof in a criminal case requires that the evidence presented against the defendant must be beyond a reasonable doubt. Note the terminology: *reasonable doubt—* not *all doubt.* In the civil suit, the evidence presented need only tip the scales of justice.

The burden of proof requires that the plaintiff's attorney show that the defendant violated a legal duty by not following an acceptable standard of care and that the plaintiff suffered injury because of the defendant's breach. If the evidence presented does not support the allegations made, the case is dismissed. Where a plaintiff, who has the burden of proof, fails to sustain such burden, the case may be dismissed despite the failure of the defendant to present any evidence to the contrary on his or her behalf. The burden of proof in some states shifts from the plaintiff to the defendant when it is obvious that the injury would not have occurred unless there was negligence.

The burden of proving negligence requires that the plaintiff show by evidence that outweighs the evidence offered by the defense that each and every component of negligence is present. This rule is well illustrated in the following case, in which the plaintiff failed to establish the standard of care to be imposed on the facility. In *Montgomery v. American Nursing Centers*[7] a resident fell and injured herself in a nursing facility while recuperating from a fractured hip. An incident report prepared by the facility indicated that the woman thereafter complained of knee and hip pain. The attending physician, not having read the report, treated her knee but not her hip, because she complained of no such pain during the examination. Two weeks later during a follow-up examination, the physician observed symptoms of a possible hip injury and ordered X-rays, which disclosed a hip fracture. The resident sued the nursing facility for negligence and the physician for malpractice. In her complaint, the resident alleged that the nursing facility had been negligent in failing to supervise her adequately and in failing to report her condition fully to the attending physician. The trial court entered judgment against the nursing facility and a directed verdict for the physician. The resident appealed.

The appeals court noted that patients generally have the burden of proving, through the use of expert testimony, the proper standard of care that is to be imposed on physicians and health care organizations in medical malpractice cases. The appeals court noted an absence of expert testimony as to the proper standard of care required. Because the resident failed to satisfy the burden of proof, the appeals court upheld the trial court's verdict for the physician.

Violation of a Statute

Violation of a statute may constitute direct evidence of negligence, or it simply may voice a duty that is owed to a particular class of persons who are protected by the statute, ordinance, or regulation. For example, a regulation that specifies a certain nurse-patient ratio requires compliance by health care organizations covered under the statute. The same regulation is an expression of the duty imposed on the facility to provide adequate nursing care to patients. The patients are, therefore, a class of persons identified within the regulation who are to have the benefits of the protection to be gained by having a predetermined minimum standard nurse-patient ratio. Such ratios were taken into account in *Nichols v. Greenacres Rest Home*,[8] where it was shown that the

nursing facility was in full compliance with all the requirements for the minimum standards for nursing facilities in Louisiana. The rest home had 64 residents, with a total of 19 employees providing 150 hours of nursing care for each 24-hour period. According to applicable standards, only 128 hours of nursing care actually were necessary for compliance. The action was brought for the death of a resident of the defendant nursing home. On an appeal by the plaintiff from a lower court's decision, the appeals court held that evidence establishing that the plaintiff's decedent was seen in his room at approximately 2:55 P.M. and was discovered missing shortly after 3:00 P.M. by an attendant, who immediately reported the decedent missing, and that the decedent was found face down in a puddle of water 25 to 45 feet from a river, supported a finding that the nursing home was not negligent and that the decedent, who was 81 years of age, did not expire from drowning. Although nursing facilities have a duty to provide reasonable and prudent care for their residents, taking into consideration their mental and physical conditions, that duty does not include having an employee following each resident around at all times.

Violation of Internal Policy and Procedures

Internal policy and procedures or rules of conduct of a health care facility are set for the day-to-day operation of the institution. A violation of a facility's policy and procedures can give rise to evidence for negligence.

Res Ipsa Loquitur

Res ipsa loquitur ("the thing speaks for itself" or "circumstances speak for themselves") is the legal doctrine that shifts the burden of proof from the plaintiff to the defendant. It is an evidentiary device that allows the plaintiff to make a case legally adequate to go to the jury on the basis of well-defined circumstantial evidence even though direct evidence is lacking. This does not mean that the plaintiff has proven fully the defendant's negligence. It merely shifts the burden of going forward to the defendant who must argue to dismiss the circumstantial evidence presented as "speaking for itself."

An inference of negligence is permitted from the mere occurrence of an injury when the defendant owed a duty and possessed the sole power of preventing the injury by exercise of reasonable care. For example, the presence of severe burns on a patient's body after being bathed by an employee raises the question of negligence without the need for expert testimony. Negligence is considered so obvious that expert testimony is not necessary. It lies within a layperson's realm of knowledge that people generally do not suffer burns from a bath. That alone is sufficient to require a defendant to come forward with a rebuttal. The three elements necessary to shift the burden of proof from the plaintiff to the defendant under the doctrine of *res ipsa loquitur* are as follows:

1. The event would not normally have occurred in the absence of negligence.
2. The defendant must have had exclusive control over the instrumentality that caused the injury.
3. The plaintiff must not have contributed to the injury.

Negligence commonly can be inferred when individuals suffer burns from hot water bottles, heat lamps, steam vaporizers, chemicals, and bedside lamps and when physicians fail to order X-rays to diagnose possible fractures.

An action was brought against the nursing facility in *Franklin v. Collins Chapel Correctional Hospital*[9] to recover damages for the wrongful death of an 82-year-old resident. The resident was admitted to the nursing facility with senility, high blood pressure, and incontinence. Extensive thermal burns were discovered soon after an attendant bathed the resident. The complaint sought to invoke the doctrine of *res ipsa loquitur* because the injuries suffered by the resident do not occur in a nursing facility in the absence of negligence, and the deceased was in the defendant's "sole care, custody and control." The plaintiffs alleged, among other things, that

- The decedent was placed in scalding hot water sufficient to cause second- and third-degree burns.
- The resident was in the care, custody, and control of the defendants.
- The defendants failed to secure prompt medical treatment for the resident.
- The defendant failed to maintain proper water temperatures.
- The defendant failed to discover the burns within a reasonable time after they had been sustained by the resident.
- The defendant failed to exercise reasonable and ordinary care under the circumstances.

The trial court entered a judgment for the nursing facility pursuant to a jury verdict, and the administrators of the estate appealed. The appeals court held that proof that the nursing facility had exclusive control over the bath wherein burns were allegedly suffered and that the burns normally would not occur absent negligence entitled the administrators to a jury instruction on the doctrine of *res ipsa loquitur*. The case was reversed and remanded for a new trial.

The general rule for all cases of circumstantial evidence, both ordinary negligence cases and *res ipsa loquitur* cases, is that, to make his or her case, the plaintiff does not have to eliminate all other possible causes or inferences other than that of the defendant's negligence, and it is enough for him or her if the evidence makes such negligence more probable than any other cause.[10]

The patient in *Mack v. Lydia E. Hall Hospital*[11] was properly permitted to invoke the doctrine of *res ipsa loquitur* in her suit to recover damages for a third-degree burn on the side of her left thigh caused by an electro-coagulator used during surgery. The prerequisites for application of the doctrine were satisfied by evidence that the injury was unusual, the surgeon had exclusive control over the electro-coagulator, and the patient could not have contributed to the injury. The plaintiff's award of $75,000 was not considered excessive.

A major problem with the doctrine of *res ipsa loquitur* is abuse. To permit an inference of negligence under the doctrine of *res ipsa loquitur* solely because an uncommon complication develops would place too heavy a burden on the medical profession and might result in an undesirable limitation on the use of operations or new procedures involving inherent risks of injury despite due care. Abuse can occur when *res ipsa loquitur* is applied to cases in which the facts show no more than a mistake in diagnosis (e.g., surgery for presumed appendicitis) or an adverse result of a medical procedure known to produce some poor results even when all precautions have been taken.

EXPERT TESTIMONY OK IN *RES ISPA* THEORY

Citation: *Seavers v. Methodist Medical Center of Oak Ridge*, 9 S.W.3d 86 (Tenn. 1999)

Facts

Seavers stayed in the medical center's intensive care unit (ICU) for approximately one month, during which time she was heavily sedated and unable to care for herself. In addition, she was unable to speak during most of her stay in the ICU due to the insertion of an endotracheal tube. The ICU nursing staff monitored the appellant and was responsible for turning, positioning, and restraining her body in the hospital bed.

While in the ICU, a nurse's note indicated for the first time that the grip in Seavers's right hand was weaker than that in her left hand. Both of her hands had been placed in wrist restraints, fastened to bed rails, to prevent her from pulling the endotracheal tube. When the endotracheal tube was removed and the appellant could speak, she complained that her right arm was numb. Dr. Lynch, a neurologist at the medical center, administered an electromyelogram (EMG), which revealed that Seavers had suffered severe damage to her right ulnar nerve. The appellant and her husband filed suit against the medical center, alleging that the injury was the result of the nurses negligently restraining her arm. She later amended her complaint to include the theory of *res ipsa loquitur*.

The medical center filed a motion for summary judgment, supported by the affidavits of Dr. Blumenkopf, a neurosurgeon, and Elizabeth Lewis, a registered nurse who worked in general care and intensive care units. Both experts opined that the nerve damage in appellant's right arm was "of unknown etiology," and that the injury could have developed during her stay in the ICU without any deviation from standards of professional care. In addition, they concluded that the medical center staff had not deviated from the recognized standard of care in treating the appellant, including the manner in which they restrained her arms.

The appellant opposed the medical center's motion for summary judgment, arguing that there were genuine issues of material fact. The appellant's response was supported by the deposition of Dr. Natelson, a neurosurgeon, and the affidavits of both Natelson and Sharon Woodworth, a registered nurse who worked in the ICU at St. Mary's Medical Center in Knoxville. Natelson had been the appellant's neurologist since 1978, and he treated her right arm after she left the medical center. Natelson testified in his deposition that the appellant's injury occurred as a result of prolonged pressure on the ulnar nerve in her right elbow. Although he could not offer conclusive proof of causation, he stated that the nerve injury could have occurred if a member of the ICU nursing staff failed to pad the appellant's elbow or failed to prevent her arm from becoming pressed against a hard object such as a bed rail.

Both Natelson and Woodworth opined that the appellant was under the exclusive control and care of the medical center's nursing staff when the nerve injury occurred. Natelson and Woodworth stated that when treating ICU patients who are unconscious or under heavy sedation or restraint, the standard of professional care requires the protection of the patients' extremities so that injuries to the ulnar nerves do not occur. Based upon their independent review of appellant's medical records and the EMG results, they opined that the injury was the type that would not have occurred if the nursing staff had upheld the standard of care.

The trial court concluded that the theory of *res ipsa loquitur* was unavailable and that the appellant's claim was otherwise insufficient as a matter of law. Finding no genuine issues of material fact, the trial court granted the medical center's motion for summary judgment.

A majority of the Court of Appeals affirmed the trial court's order granting summary judgment for the medical center. Relying upon prior decisions, the Court of Appeals held that *res ipsa loquitur* did not apply because the appellant's injury was not within the common knowledge of laypersons.

Issue

This appeal was granted to address whether the doctrine of *res ipsa loquitur*, as codified in Tennessee Code, is applicable in medical malpractice cases where the plaintiffs must rely upon expert testimony to prove the elements of causation, standard of care, and that the injury does not ordinarily occur in the absence of negligence.

Finding/Holding

Upon review of Tennessee's medical malpractice law and authority in other jurisdictions, the doctrine of *res ipsa loquitur* may be applied in this case.

Reason

Under Tennessee Code, the appellant was required to demonstrate by a preponderance of the evidence that the instrumentality of the nerve injury was under the medical center's exclusive control and that the injury would not have ordinarily occurred in the absence of negligence. The parties agreed that the appellant was under the exclusive control and care of the medical center when the nerve injury occurred. The record further shows that the appellant's right arm and hand were fully functional when she entered the medical center's ICU and that no problem was detected until the ICU nurses noticed that the grip in her right hand was not as strong as the grip in her left hand. During that time, the appellant was heavily sedated, restrained, and under the complete care of the ICU nurses.

Based upon the EMG results, the appellant has shown that the dysfunction in her right arm resulted from damage to her right ulnar nerve. According to Natelson, this injury was likely caused by prolonged pressure on the nerve from a hard object such as a bed rail. This theory was corroborated by evidence that the appellant's arms were strapped to the hospital bed during her stay in the ICU. In addition, the appellant's husband testified in his deposition that he noticed abrasion marks under the appellant's arms while she was confined to the bed in the ICU.

Although experts for the medical center testified that the nerve injury was of "unknown etiology," and that there was no deviation from the standard of professional care, this evidence was insufficient as a matter of law to overcome the testimony provided by Natelson and other witnesses for the appellant. The appellant satisfied the *res ipsa* requirements under Tennessee Code and had raised a genuine issue of material fact on the allegation of negligence. Summary judgment in favor of the medical center was improper in this case.

Discussion

1. Was the appellant's injury within the common knowledge of laypersons? Discuss your answer.
2. What procedures should the medical center implement to reduce the likelihood of similar occurrences?

EVIDENCE

Evidence consists of the facts proved or disproved during a lawsuit. The law of evidence is a body of rules under which facts are proved. The rules of evidence govern the admission of items of proof in a lawsuit. A fact can be proven by either circumstantial or direct evidence. Evidence must be competent, relevant, and material to be admitted at trial.

Direct Evidence

Direct evidence is proof offered through direct testimony. It is the jury's function to receive testimony presented by witnesses and to draw conclusions in the determination of facts.

Demonstrative Evidence

Demonstrative (real) evidence is evidence furnished by things themselves. It is considered the most trustworthy and preferred type of evidence. It consists of tangible objects to which testimony refers (e.g., medical instruments and broken infusion needles) that can be requested by a jury. Demonstrative evidence is admissible in court if it is relevant, has probative value, and serves the interest of justice. It is not admissible if it will prejudice, mislead, confuse, offend, in-

flame, or arouse the sympathy or passion of the jury or if it is indecent. Other forms of demonstrative evidence include photographs, motion pictures, X-ray films, drawings, human bodies as exhibits, pathology slides, fetal monitoring strips, safety committee minutes, infection committee reports, medical staff bylaws, rules and regulations, nursing policy and procedure manuals, census data, and staffing patterns. The plaintiff's attorney uses all pertinent evidence to reconstruct chronologically the care and treatment rendered.

When presenting photographs as a form of evidence, the photographer or a reliable witness who is familiar with the object photographed must testify that the picture is an accurate representation and a fair likeness of the object portrayed. The photograph must not exaggerate a client's physical condition or show coloring of injuries that is prejudicial. Photographs can be valuable legal evidence when they illustrate graphically the nature and extent of a medical injury. Motion pictures also are valuable evidence. The same principles that apply to photographs apply to motion pictures. Motion pictures must not be fraudulently portrayed by destroying continuity (by either cutting or rearranging). Videotape is admissible in court, assuming appropriate authentication of the matter being taped, the time of the taping, and the manner in which such taping took place.

X-ray films are considered pictures of the interior of the object portrayed and are admitted under the same requirements as photographs and motion pictures. The attorney must show competent evidence that the X-rays taken are the object or body part under consideration, that the X-ray was made in a recognized manner, taken by a competent technician, and interpreted by a competent physician trained to read X-rays. The value of X-rays is that they illustrate fractures, foreign objects, etc.

The plaintiff's injuries are admissible as an exhibit if the physical condition of the body is material. The human body is considered the best evidence of the nature and extent of the plaintiff's injury. If there is no controversy about either the nature or the extent of the injury, such evidence can be considered prejudicial material to which the defendant's attorney could object.

Demonstrations are permitted in some instances to illustrate the extent of injuries. The resident in *Hendricks v. Sanford*[12] had developed serious bed sores on her back. The defendant objected to the offer of the plaintiff to display her back to the jury. The court found that the plaintiff's injuries, which had healed, were completely relevant as evidence. Even though the injuries had healed and a skin graft had been performed, a declivity of about three-and-one-half inches in diameter and about the depth of a shallow ashtray was still discernible on the plaintiff's back.

Where an issue as to personal injuries is involved, an injured person may be permitted to exhibit to the jury the wound or injury, or the member or portion of his body upon which such wound or injury was inflicted, and if relevant, the exhibition is allowable in the discretion of the court where there is no reason to expect that the sympathy of the jury will be excited.[13]

Documentary Evidence

Documentary evidence is written evidence capable of making a truthful statement (e.g., drug manufacturer inserts, autopsy reports, birth certificates, and medical records). Documentary evidence must satisfy the jury as to authenticity. Proof of authenticity is not necessary if the opposing party accepts its genuineness. In some instances, concerning wills, for example, witnesses are necessary. In the case of documentation, the original of a document must be produced unless it can be demonstrated that the original has been lost or destroyed, in which case a properly authenticated copy may be substituted.

A sampling of preliminary questions that a witness might be asked on entering a medical record into evidence includes the following:

- Please state your name.
- Where are you employed?
- What is your position?
- What is your official title?
- Did you receive a subpoena for certain records?
- Did you bring those records with you?
- Can you identify these records?
- Did you retrieve the records yourself?
- Are these the complete records?
- Are these the original records or copies of the originals?
- How were these records prepared?
- Are these records maintained under your care, custody, and control?
- Were these records made in the regular course of business?
- Was the record made at the time the act, condition, or event occurred or transpired?
- Is this record regularly kept or maintained?

A manufacturer's drug insert or manual describing the use of equipment is generally admissible. In *Mueller v. Mueller*,[14] a physician was sued by a patient who charged that as a result of the administration of cortisone over an extended period, she had suffered needlessly a deterioration of bone structure and ultimately a collapsed hip. The jury decided that the physician's prolonged use of cortisone was negligent, and the physician appealed. The appeals court held that the manufacturer's recommendations are not only admissible but also essential in determining a physician's possible lack of proper care.

In another case, *Mulligan v. Lederle Laboratories*,[15] the plaintiff, a medical laboratory technician, brought an action against the drug manufacturer as the result of the side effects of the drug Varidase. The plaintiff developed several chronic health problems including mouth sores, microscopic hematuria, and red cell cast, indicating kidney disease. The trial court awarded $50,000 in compensatory damages and $100,000 in punitive damages for the drug manufacturer's failure to warn of the side effects of Varidase. On appeal by the manufacturer, the appeals court held that the products liability action was not barred by a three-year statute of limitations contained in an Arkansas products liability act and that the evidence was sufficient to award punitive damages. Evidence presented at trial indicated that several side effects were associated with the drug.

Judicial Notice Rule

The judicial notice rule prescribes that well-known facts (e.g., that fractures need prompt attention and that two X-rays of the same patient may show different results) need not be proven, but rather, that they are recognized by the court as fact. If a fact can be disputed, the rule does not apply.

The use of X-rays as a diagnostic aid in cases of fracture can be considered a matter of common knowledge to which a court, in the absence of expert testimony, could take judicial notice. Should a patient have a serious fall and a fracture is indicated, under the foregoing rule it is a matter of common knowledge that the ordinary physician in good standing, in the exercise of ordinary care and diligence, would have ordered X-rays.

The plaintiff in *Arthur v. St. Peter's Hospital*[16] sought treatment in the emergency department of St. Peter's Hospital after an injury to his left wrist. After being examined, he was sent to the radiology department for X-rays of his wrist. He later was released after being advised that there were no fractures. The plaintiff suffered continued swelling and pain. As a result, he decided to seek care from another physician, who subsequently diagnosed a fracture of the navicular bone. The plaintiff sued, and the hospital motioned for summary judgment, stating that the physicians were independent contractors and not employees of the hospital.

Copies of the emergency department record, X-ray report, and billing record contained the logo of the hospital. There was nothing on the records to identify the physicians as being independent contractors. The court took judicial notice that generally, people who seek medical help through the emergency departments of hospitals are unaware of the status of the different professionals working there. Unless the patient had been in some manner put on notice that those physicians with whom he might come into contact during the course of his treatment were independent contractors, it would be natural to assume that they were employees of the hospital.

Medical Books/Hearsay Evidence

Medical books are considered *hearsay* because the authors are not generally available for cross-examination. Although medical books are not admissible as evidence, a physician may testify as how he or she formed an opinion and what part text-books played in forming that opinion. During cross-examination, medical experts may be asked to comment on statements from medical books that contradict their testimony.

Examination of Witnesses

After conclusion of the opening statements, the judge calls for the plaintiff's witnesses. An officer of the court administers an oath to each witness, and direct examination begins. The attorney obtains information from each witness in the form of questions. This is not by the attorney's recitation of the story to the witness. On cross-examination by the defense, an attempt is made to challenge or discredit the plaintiff's witness. Redirect examination by the plaintiff's attorney can follow the cross-examination, if so desired. The plaintiff's attorney may at this time wish to have his or her witness review an important point that the jury may have forgotten during cross-examination. The plaintiff's attorney may ask the same witness more questions in an effort to overcome the effect of the cross-examination. Re–cross-examination may take place if necessary for the defense of the defendant.

A sampling of preliminary questions that a physician might expect to be asked on a personal injury case, for example, may take the following form:

- Name, residence, prior residences?
- Where did you attend medical school?
- Are you licensed in this state?
- Where did you serve your internship?
- Where did you serve your residency?
- Is your practice general or special?
- Are you board certified in one or more specialties?
- How does a physician obtain board certification?
- Are you presently practicing medicine?
- How long have you been in practice?
- During your _____ years of practice have you had occasion to treat a good number of personal injury cases?
- On or about _____ did you have occasion to see _____ on a professional basis?
- Where? Describe his/her condition at the time.
- What, if anything, did you do on that occasion?

- Have you been the attending physician since that date?
- Describe the nature of the examination that you made on _____ and from time to time since then.
- Did you see him/her daily, several times a day at first?
- Did you continue to see him/her? How often?
- Of what, generally, did your treatment consist?
- From your examination and treatment of _____, did you determine what injuries were sustained?
- As a result of your examination, did you find it necessary to seek consultation from another physician or specialist?
- Did there come a time when you found it necessary to transfer the patient to another health care facility?

The credibility of a witness may be impeached if prior statements are inconsistent with later statements or if there is bias in favor of a party or prejudice against a party to a lawsuit. Either attorney to a lawsuit may ask the judge for permission to recall a witness.

After all the witnesses of the plaintiff have testified, the defense may call its witnesses and the process of direct, cross, redirect, and re–cross-examination is repeated until the defense rests.

Hearsay Evidence

Hearsay evidence is based on what another has said or done and is not the result of the personal knowledge of the witness. Hearsay consists of written and oral statements. Where a witness testifies to the utterance of a statement made outside court and the statement is offered in court for the truth of the facts that are contained in the statement, this is hearsay and therefore objectionable. The court in *Costal Health Services, Inc. v. Rozier*[17] held that a "written report" by an ombudsman (who did not testify at trial), concerning injuries and treatment of an 85-year-old patient, was inadmissible as evidence. It contained hearsay accounts of conversations as well as impressions, opinions, and conclusions regarding the nursing facility's negligence when a patient had wandered into another patient's room and was injured by that resident. However, the court found that the testimony about one patient's own account of his violent past, made to the nursing home personnel upon his admission, was admissible as original evidence, not as proof of the actual prior incidents, but to show the defendant's notice of the possibility of violent behavior on the part of that patient.

If a statement is offered not as proof of the facts asserted in the statement but rather only to show that the statement was made, the statement can come into evidence. For example, if it is relevant that a conversation took place, the testimony relating to the conversation may be entered as evidence. The purpose of that testimony would be to establish that a conversation took place and not to prove what was said during the course of the conversation. If testimony is based on personal knowledge, it would be admissible as evidence.

Because of the ability to challenge hearsay evidence successfully, which rests on the credibility of the witness as well as on the competency and veracity of other persons not before the court, it is admitted as evidence in a trial under only very strict rules. The U.S. district court in *Northeast Women's Center v. McMonagle*,[18] in a civil action alleging Racketeer Influenced and Corrupt Organizations Act (RICO) violations and trespass arising from protests at an abortion clinic, found the trial court to have properly excluded testimony of one of the witnesses. The substance of the proposed testimony was based on double hearsay and not the competent testimony of the witness.

There are many exceptions to the hearsay rule that allow testimony that ordinarily would not be admitted. Included in the list of exceptions are admissions made by one of the parties to the action, threats made by a victim, dying declarations, statements to refresh a witness's recollection if he or she is unable to remember the facts that he or she once knew, business records, medical records, and other official records (e.g., certified copies of birth and death records). "Where hearsay evidence is admitted without objection, its probative value is for the jury to determine."[19] The above list of exceptions to hearsay evidence is by no means all-inclusive, and therefore state statutes should be consulted.

A police officer's testimony that he had overheard a drug dealer tell an informant, who was wearing a concealed transmitter, that he could obtain drugs for the informant from a pharmacist friend was properly admitted in a disciplinary proceeding in *Brown v. Idaho State Board of Pharmacy*.[20] The testimony was presented before the Idaho State Board of Pharmacy for proving a dealer's state of mind and explaining his subsequent visit to the pharmacy. The testimony was not subject to hearsay objection.

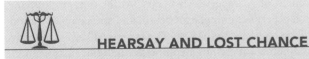

HEARSAY AND LOST CHANCE

Citation: *Stroud v. Golson*, 741 So.2d 182 (La. App. 2d Cir. June 16, 1999)

Facts

On March 29, 1994, Dr. Mikey examined Gloria Stroud. After viewing X-rays, Mikey told Stroud that she may have lung cancer and referred her to Dr. Gullatt. On March 30, 1994, Gullatt examined Mrs. Stroud and referred her to St. Francis Medical Center in Monroe for a CT scan. That same day, a CT scan was performed and its findings interpreted by Dr. Golson. Golson opined that, according to the CT scan, Stroud did not have lung cancer.

Approximately one year later, on April 10, 1995, Stroud was hospitalized at St. Francis for a cerebral hemorrhage caused by an unrelated condition. During this treatment, X-rays and CTs revealed inoperative cancer in Stroud's left lung.

On May 31, 1995, Stroud was discharged from St. Francis. On August 15, 1995, Stroud died as a result of the cancer. She was survived by her husband of 33 years, Clarence Stroud, and her two sons.

The plaintiffs, the decedent's husband and sons, filed the instant suit seeking damages arising from Golson's failure to properly interpret Stroud's CT scan. Before trial, plaintiffs settled with Golson and his insurer, St. Paul Fire and Marine Insurance Company, for $80,000.

On February 23, 1998, a trial by jury was commenced against the PCF, which admitted medical negligence but claimed that Stroud would have died from the fast-acting cancer even if it had been diagnosed in 1994. On February 25, 1998, the jury returned a verdict finding that Stroud lost a less than even chance of survival because of Golson's negligence and awarded plaintiffs $1.5 million in damages. On March 18, 1998, the trial court entered judgment in favor of the plaintiffs consistent with the statutory cap, reducing the award to $400,000, together with legal interest and costs. The defendants appealed.

Issue

Did the jury abuse its discretion in awarding the plaintiffs $1.5 million in damages for the decedent's lost chance of survival? Did the trial judge err when he overruled the hearsay objection regarding Mr. Stroud's testimony?

Holding

The appeals court found no abuse of discretion by the trial court.

Reason

The plaintiffs' expert, Dr. Misfeldt, testified that approximately 25 percent of patients diagnosed with cancer confined to the lung area, as was Stroud's in 1994, are "cured" of disease, noting that the disease was within the most favorable stage for recovery at this time. Misfeldt further explained that when the disease spreads to the mediastinum, as was Stroud's case in 1995, only approximately 5 percent recover. Misfeldt pointed out that the disease was within the least favorable stage for recovery at that time in 1995, causing Stroud to lose a 20 percent chance of survival due to Golson's malpractice.

Stroud suffered a great deal of mental anguish from the hopeless condition with which she was faced and the knowledge that earlier detection was lost because her CT scan was not properly read. Her decision not to undergo the painful and debilitating chemotherapy in 1995, when the odds were so stacked against her recovery, was justified. It is a reasonable conclusion that Stroud would have, in all likelihood, opted for the treatment had the cancer been properly diagnosed in 1994.

The defendant argued that the trial judge erred when he overruled the hearsay objection regarding Mr. Stroud's testimony concerning what Mrs. Stroud's reasons were for declining treatment after her cancer was diagnosed. The testimony at issue is as follows:

> Mr. Thomas: Now, did your wife discuss—You—You and your wife discuss whether or not she should have treatment for her cancer?
>
> Mr. Stroud: Yes, we did.
>
> Mr. Thomas: And were you a part in making a decision with her with why she did not agree to have treatment?
>
> Mr. Stroud: Yes.
>
> Mr. Thomas: Share with the jury what she said about that.
>
> Mr. Stroud: She, ah,—
>
> Mr. Anzelmo: Your Honor, I object to hearsay.
>
> The Court: I understand. But, I think it—It is hearsay but it's reliable. I'll allow it.
>
> Mr. Thomas: Go ahead.
>
> Mr. Stroud: Ah, I had a—My sister passed away in November '94 with lung cancer, and she found out in July of '94 that she had lung cancer. So, she went and took the radium treatments and she weighed 125 pounds and was eating and doing all right until she started taking the radium treatments, and by the end of the radium treatments she could hardly get about, and actually she just laid down and starved herself to death. She weighed 65 pounds when she passed away, and was bed ridden all that time. And the wife felt that it was too far gone in her for any treatments to do any

good, plus what few days she had left she didn't want to be like my sister.

Mr. Stroud's testimony regarding statements his wife made were statements of her then-existing state of mind. The testimony showed the motive behind Stroud's decision not to receive treatment; namely, her belief that the treatments would not be effective, as well as her desire to avoid the severe pain and discomfort that can accompany chemotherapy.

Discussion

1. Do you agree with the jury's $1.5 million damages award?
2. How did the court view hearsay evidence in this case?

Expert Witness Necessary

Expert testimony, as well as scientific data, is used to assist in establishing the standard of care required in any given situation. It is the jury's function to receive testimony presented by witnesses and draw conclusions in the determination of facts. The law recognizes that a jury is composed of ordinary men and women and that some fact-finding will involve subjects beyond their knowledge. When a jury cannot otherwise obtain sufficient facts from which to draw conclusions, an *expert witness* who has special knowledge, skill, experience, or training can be called on to submit an opinion. The expert witness assists the jury when the issues to be resolved in the case are outside the experience of the average juror.

Laymen are quite able to render opinions about a great variety of general subjects, but for technical questions, the opinion of an expert is necessary. At the time of testifying, each expert's training, experience, and special qualifications will be explained to the jury. The experts will be asked to give an opinion concerning hypothetical questions based on the facts of the case. Should the testimony of two experts conflict, the jury will determine which expert opinion to accept. Expert witnesses may be used to assist a plaintiff in proving the wrongful act of a defendant or to assist a defendant in refuting such evidence. In addition, expert testimony may be used to show the extent of the plaintiff's damages or to show the lack of such damages.

In order to qualify as an expert witness in a specified area, the one holding him- or herself out as being an expert must have the appropriate training, experience, and qualifications necessary to explain and/or answer questions based on the facts of a particular case. The pharmacist in *Nail v. Laros*[21] was found not competent to render an expert opinion regarding the proper standard of care required of a physician practicing a medical specialty. The patient, Mrs. Nail, developed a staphylococcal infection following spinal surgery on June 5, 1988. The orthopaedic surgeon, Dr. Laros, treated the patient with the antibiotic Ansef for six days, June 10–16, 1988. The patient was released from the hospital on June 16 without any sign of an infection. On July 11, 1988, the patient, while under the treatment of an orthopaedic surgeon (Dr. Hanley), was discovered through blood tests to have contracted a staphylococcal infection at the operative site. The patient eventually developed osteomyelitis. She brought a lawsuit against Laros for negligence in diagnosing and treating her infection. Nail obtained an affidavit from a pharmacist (Mr. Neff) who stated an opinion that Laros should have treated the patient for a longer period of time on Ansef and that his failure to do so was the proximate cause of Nail's staph infection found by Hanley. The court reasoned that there was nothing in the record to support the pharmacist's claim of being an expert in this case. Neither his education nor his training qualified him to be an expert on equal footing with a board-certified orthopaedic surgeon in diagnosing and treating infections associated with surgical implants. The court of appeals took judicial notice by ruling that the pharmacist cannot legally prescribe medication, and is even prohibited from dispensing a dangerous drug, which by definition includes Ansef, without a valid prescription from a practitioner.

Expert Witness Not Necessary/Surgical Sponge Left in the Patient

Expert testimony was not required in *Powell v. Mullins*,[22] in which a surgical lap sponge was left in the abdomen of a patient during the performance of a Caesarean section. The trial court committed reversible error in directing a verdict in the physician's favor because of the patient's failure to present an expert witness. Testimony of an expert witness generally is not required when an understanding of the physician's alleged lack of skill or due care requires only common knowledge or experience. The Alabama Supreme Court held that it was the physician's responsibility to remove all sponges from inside the patient before closing the incision.

Expert Witness Not Necessary/Patient's Fall

The plaintiff in *McGraw v. St. Joseph's Hospital*[23] walked into the defendant's emergency department complaining of shortness of breath. After several hours of waiting to be seen by medical personnel, the plaintiff was admitted to the hospital. During the early morning hours of May 12 the plaintiff was discovered on the floor near his bed. The plaintiff indicated in his deposition that he fell out of bed. He also testified that on the afternoon of May 21, four nurses and nurse's aides dropped him while attempting to place him in bed.

In medical malpractice cases where lack of care or want of skill is so gross, so as to be apparent, or the alleged breach relates to noncomplex matters of diagnosis and treatment within the understanding of lay jurors by resort to common knowledge and experience, failure to present expert testimony on the accepted standard of care and degree of skill under such circumstances is not fatal to a plaintiff's *prima facie* showing of negligence. Was expert testimony necessary in this case? The defendant takes the position that the common knowledge exception is not applicable here, because liability is premised upon complex medical management issues involving professional management. The court reviewed cases addressing hospital fall incidents and found that a majority of jurisdictions do not require expert testimony in such cases where a

- bed rail is left down contrary to the physician's order and the patient falls and is injured
- patient falls while leaving hospital and there is a duty to provide an escort
- medicated patient is not restrained and he or she falls getting out of bed
- patient falls out of a chair and the hospital is negligent by allowing the patient to sit in the chair
- patient is known to be in weakened condition and is left alone in a shower and falls
- nurse fails to respond to a sedated patient's call and the patient gets out of bed and falls
- patient falls from a table while unattended in the emergency department
- patient falls from bed after warning the nurse that she is dizzy and the nurse assures her that she would brace her

The mere fact a patient falls in a hospital will not generally require expert testimony as to the hospital's negligence. Courts generally make a distinction between medical care and custodial care or routine hospital care. A hospital owes the patient a duty to exercise reasonable care in rendering care and, in the performance of such duty, due regard must be given to the mental and physical condition of the patient of which the hospital, in the exercise of reasonable care, should have knowledge. If a patient requires professional care, then expert testimony as to the standard of care is necessary. The standard of nonmedical, administrative, ministerial, or routine care in a hospital need not be established by expert testimony. A jury is competent from its own experience to determine and apply a reasonable-care standard.

The facts surrounding the plaintiff's fall from his bed on May 12 and being dropped on May 21 are susceptible to a reasonable standard of care that can be determined without an expert by the jury. However, consistent with West Virginia Code, a violation of the standard of care shall be established in medical professional liability cases by testimony of an expert witness, if required by the court. Based upon the current record, the trial judge required an expert for both incidents, although no evidence was proffered that revealed complex management issues involving either incident. The complex management issues were necessary in order to justify requiring expert testimony by the plaintiff.

Notwithstanding the lack of evidence of complex management issues in this case, the plaintiff produced an expert in Dr. Henthorn, who clearly testified that defendant violated the standard of care that it owed to the plaintiff as a result of the plaintiff's fall on May 12. The circuit court was clearly wrong in ruling that the plaintiff did not have an expert on the standard of care, with respect to the May 12 incident. As to the May 21 incident, the trial court may find at a pretrial hearing that expert testimony is necessary on this incident, should the defendant proffer satisfactory evidence that this incident involved complex management issues. This case was reversed and remanded for a determination by the trial court consistent with this opinion.

The patient, Ms. Welte, in *Welte v. Bello*,[24] was admitted to the hospital for surgery for the correction of a deviated septum. Approximately three hours prior to surgery, Ms. Welte conferred with her surgeon about the procedure. She then conferred with her anesthesiologist, Dr. Bello, who informed her that he would be administering sodium pentothal through an IV inserted into a vein in her arm. He told her about the potential risks associated with general anesthesia. Welte read and signed a written "consent to operate, administration of anesthetics, and rendering other medical services. . . ." form. The consent form provided: "I consent to the administration of anesthesia to be applied by or under the direction and control of Bello." Also on the form was the statement that "anesthesia and its complications have been explained and accepted." Both Welte and Bello signed the consent form. After talking with the physicians, Welte was transferred to a presurgical room. While in this room, a nurse inserted a catheter into the vein of Welte's right arm. Welte complained of pain after the IV was inserted. The nurse checked the IV and concluded that it was properly positioned inside the vein. Bello began injecting drugs through a port in the IV. Bello then rechecked the site of the IV and, for the first time, noticed swelling on Welte's arm near the point at which the IV had been inserted. As a consequence of the sodium pentothal infiltration of the tissues surrounding the vein, Welte sustained first-, second-, and third-degree burns, resulting in a large permanent scar.

Welte and her husband commenced two separate malpractice actions, one against the hospital and another against Bello. The separate suits were consolidated for trial. Prior to trial, Bello filed a motion for summary judgment, claiming that Welte had failed to retain a qualified expert to testify against him and, therefore, they would be precluded from offering any expert testimony at trial. Welte argued that the tort claim of failure to obtain an informed consent did not require expert testimony. The trial court concluded that any alleged negligence of the anesthesiologists was not so obvious as to be within the comprehension of a layperson.

The Iowa Supreme Court held that expert testimony was not required to establish a claim against Bello. Citing *Donovan v. State*, "If a doctor operates on the wrong limb or amputates the wrong limb, a plaintiff would not have to introduce expert testimony to establish that the doctor was negligent. On the other hand, highly technical questions of diagnoses and causation which lie beyond the understanding of a layperson require introduction of expert testimony."[25] The chemical burn to Welte's arm was caused by sodium pentothal that the anesthesiologist injected into the patient's vein, which then infiltrated or escaped from the vein into the surrounding tissues. The Iowa Supreme Court found that it was within the common experience of a layperson that such an occurrence in the ordinary course of things would not have occurred if reasonable care had been used. The insertion of a needle into a vein is a common medical procedure. It is a procedure that has become so common that laypersons know certain occurrences would not take place if ordinary care were used. Even if expert evidence were required, the record was sufficient to defeat the summary judgment motion. Even Bello's expert testified in his deposition that in the usual course of events, an IV instituted for purpose of anesthesia does not infiltrate the surrounding tissue.

DEFENSES AGAINST RECOVERY

Once a plaintiff's case has been established, the defendant may put forward a defense against the claim for damages. The defendant's case is presented to discredit the plaintiff's cause of action and prevent recovery of damages. This section deals with the defenses available to defendants in a negligence suit. These are principles of law that may relieve a defendant from liability.

Assumption of the Risk

Assumption of the risk is knowing that a danger exists and voluntarily accepting the risk by exposing oneself to it, knowing that harm might occur. Assumption of the risk may be implicitly assumed, as in alcohol consumption, or expressly assumed, as in relation to warnings found on cigarette packaging.

This defense provides that the plaintiff expressly has given consent in advance, relieving the defendant of an obligation of conduct toward the plaintiff and taking the chances of injury from a known risk arising from the defendant's conduct. For example, one who agrees to care for a patient with a communicable disease and then contracts the disease would not be entitled to recover from the patient for damages suffered. In taking the job, the individual agreed to assume the risk of infection, thereby releasing the patient from all legal obligations.

The following two requirements must be established in order for a defendant to be successful in an assumption of the risk defense: (1) the plaintiff must know and understand the risk that is being incurred, and (2) the choice to incur the risk must be free and voluntary.

The patient in *Faile v. Bycura*[26] was awarded $75,000 in damages by a jury on her allegations that a podiatrist had used inappropriate techniques during an unsuccessful attempt to treat her heel spurs. On appeal, it was held that the trial court erred in striking the podiatrist's defense of assumption of the risk. Evidence established that the patient had signed consent forms that indicated the risks of treatment as well as alternative treatment modalities.

Borrowed Servant and Captain of the Ship Doctrines

The borrowed servant doctrine is a special application of the doctrine of *respondeat superior* and applies when an employer lends an employee to another for a particular employment. Although an employee remains the servant of the employer, under the *borrowed servant doctrine* the employer is not liable for injury negligently caused by the servant while in the special service of another. For example, in certain situations a nurse employed by a hospital may be considered the employee of the physician. In these situations, the physician is the special or temporary employer and is liable for the negligence of the nurse. To determine whether a physician is liable for the negligence of a nurse, it must be established that the physician had the right to control and direct the nurse at the time of the negligent act. If the physician is found to be in exclusive control and if the nurse is deemed to be the physician's temporary special employee, the hospital is not generally liable for the nurse's negligent acts.

In the context of the operating room, the application of the borrowed servant doctrine generally is referred to as the *captain of the ship doctrine*. Under this doctrine, the surgeon is viewed as being the one in command in the operating room. The rationale for this concept was provided in the Minnesota case of *St. Paul-Mercury Indemnity Co. v. St. Joseph Hospital*, when the court stated:

> [t]he desirability of the rule is obvious. The patient is completely at the mercy of the surgeon and relies upon him to see that all the acts relative to the operation are performed in a careful manner.

It is the surgeon's duty to guard against any and all avoidable acts that may result in injury to his patient. In the operating room, the surgeon must be master. He cannot tolerate any other voice in the control of his assistants. In the case at bar, the evidence is clear that the doctor had exclusive control over the acts in question, and therefore the hospital cannot be said to have been a "joint master" or "co-master," even though the nurses were in its general employ and paid by it.[27]

In *Krane v. Saint Anthony Hospital Systems*,[28] the Colorado Court of Appeals held that even if it is assumed that the surgical nurse was the employee of the hospital, she was negligent, and such negligence caused the death of the plaintiff's husband, the so-called captain of the ship doctrine still precludes recovery against the hospital. The factual question that must be determined is whether, at the time of the alleged negligent act, the operating surgeon had assumed such control. If so, the responsibility of the surgeon supersedes that of the hospital. Because it was uncontradicted that the alleged negligent act of the surgical nurse took place over 2 1/2 hours into surgery, there could be no factual dispute that the surgeon had assumed control over the nurse.

Several courts have developed a distinction between a nurse's clerical or administrative acts and those involving professional skill and judgment, which are considered medical acts. The courts use this distinction in allocating liability for the acts of a nurse as between the surgeon and the hospital. If the act is characterized as administrative or clerical, it is the hospital's responsibility; if the act is considered to be medical, it is the surgeon's responsibility. This rule was followed in the Minnesota case of *Swigerd v. City of Ortonville*,[29] in which the court found that the hospital is liable as an employer for the negligence of its nurses in performing acts that are basically administrative. Administrative acts, although constituting a component of a patient's prescribed medical treatment, do not require the application of specialized procedures and techniques or the understanding of a skilled physician or surgeon.

Comparative Negligence

A defense of comparative negligence provides that the degree of negligence or carelessness of each party to a lawsuit must be established by the finder of fact and that each party then is responsible for his or her proportional share of any damages awarded. For example, where a plaintiff suffers injuries of $10,000 from an accident and where the plaintiff is found 20 percent negligent and the defendant 80 percent negligent, the defendant would be required to pay $8,000 to the plaintiff. Thus, with comparative negligence, the plaintiff can collect for 80 percent of the injuries, whereas an application of contributory negligence would deprive the plaintiff of any monetary judgment. This doctrine relieves the plaintiff from the hardship of losing an entire claim when a defendant has been successful in establishing that the plaintiff has contributed to his or her own injuries. A defense that provides that the plaintiff will forfeit an entire claim if he or she has been contributorily negligent is considered too harsh a result in jurisdictions that recognize comparative negligence.

The plaintiff in *Quinones v. Public Administrator*[30] sought to recover damages for the alleged negligence of the defendant's physicians for their failure to treat a fractured ankle. The plaintiff claimed that there was a nonunion of the fracture and that he was advised to put weight on his leg. As a result of this advice, the plaintiff claimed that there was an exacerbation of the original injury requiring two operative procedures, which resulted in the fusion of his left ankle. The defendant claimed that if there was any subsequent injury, it was because of the failure of the plaintiff to return for care. The New York Supreme Court entered a judgment in favor of the defendant hospital, and the plaintiff appealed. The New York Supreme Court, Appellate Division, held that a patient's failure to follow instructions does not defeat an action for malpractice where the alleged improper professional treatment occurred before the patient's own negligence.[31] Damages would be reduced to the degree that the plaintiff's negligence increased the extent of the injury.

Contributory Negligence

Contributory negligence can be defined as any lack of ordinary care on the part of the person injured that, combined with the negligent act of another, caused the injury and without which the injury would not have occurred. When the issue of contributory negligence is raised, the defendant claims that the conduct of the injured person is below the standard of care reasonably prudent persons would exercise for their own safety. A person is contributorily negligent when that person does not exercise reasonable care for his or her own safety. As a general proposition, if a person has knowledge of a dangerous situation and disregards the danger, then the person is contributorily negligent. Actual knowledge of the danger of injury is not necessary for a person to be contributorily negligent. It is sufficient if a reasonable person should have been aware of the possibility of the danger.

In some jurisdictions, contributory negligence, no matter how slight, is sufficient to defeat a plaintiff's claim. Generally, the defense of contributory negligence has been recognized in a medical malpractice action when the patient has: (1) failed to follow a medical instruction, (2) refused or neglected prescribed treatment, or (3) intentionally given erroneous, incomplete, or misleading information that is the basis for medical care or treatment of the patient.

The elements necessary to establish contributory negligence are: (1) that the plaintiff's conduct fell below the required standard of personal care, and (2) that there is a causal connection between the plaintiff's careless conduct and the plaintiff's injury. Thus, the defendant contends that some, if not all, liability is attributable to the plaintiff's own actions. To establish a defense of contributory negligence, the defendant must show that the plaintiff's negligence was an active and efficient contributing cause of the injury. This was not the case in *Bird v. Pritchard*,[32] in which the plaintiff, on July 3, 1970, slipped and fell, cutting her right hand on a mayonnaise jar and thus injuring the ulnar nerve. She was taken to Hocking Valley Memorial Hospital where she requested the services of Dr. Najm, a board-certified general surgeon. However, he was not available. The defendant, an osteopathic surgeon, was available, and he treated the patient's wound. The patient had complained that the fourth and fifth fingers of her right hand were numb. The defendant cleaned the wound and advised the patient to see him on Monday, July 7. The patient did not return to the osteopathic surgeon but went to see Najm that same Monday. A suit was filed, the court of common pleas rendered a judgment for the defendant, and the plaintiff appealed. The court of appeals held that the patient could not be found to have been contributorily negligent or to have assumed the risk. By the time of her scheduled visit, it was impossible to perform primary or secondary repair of the injured nerves that had not been treated on the initial visit when she had fist complained of numbness. For contributory negligence to defeat the claim of the plaintiff, there must not only be negligent conduct by the plaintiff but also a direct and proximate causal relationship between the negligent act and the injury the plaintiff received.

The Delaware Supreme Court affirmed a lower court's dismissal of a wrongful death action against a medical center's emergency department personnel in *Rochester v. Katalan*.[33] The decedent, Mr. Rochester, and a friend had been brought to the emergency department at approximately 6:30 P.M. under the custody of two police officers. Rochester and his friend, claiming to be heroin addicts suffering withdrawal symptoms, requested some form of medication. Rochester stated that he had a habit requiring four to five bags of heroin a day. His actions were symptomatic of withdrawal. He and his friend were loud, abusive, and uncooperative. Rochester complained of abdominal pains, his eyes appeared glassy, and his body was shaking, among other symptoms that he exhibited. The physician on duty in the emergency department asked whether Rochester had ever participated in a methadone clinic program. Rochester indicated that he had, but that he had dropped out of it because he found a new supply source for heroin. The physician then ordered the administration of 40 mg of methadone. Rochester began beating his head against a wall claiming that he was still sick and needed more methadone. The plea was granted, and the physician ordered a second dose of 40 mg of methadone. After eventually calming down, Rochester was taken to a cell by the police officers. The following morning it was impossible to awaken him, and he was later pronounced dead. It was discovered that he had never been an addict or on a methadone program. Rather, the previous night he had been drinking beer and taking Librium. He had not told this to hospital authorities. Rochester's estate sued the physician, and the trial court dismissed the suit. The appellate court affirmed, saying that by Rochester's failure to provide the physician accurate information, he had *contributed to his own death*. On appeal, the plaintiff had argued that the physician and staff could have done more to determine the truth of Rochester's assertions that he was a drug addict. The Delaware Supreme Court held that it already had assumed negligence in that respect. Rochester contributed to his own death by failing to provide a true account of the facts to the emergency department staff. He was guilty of negligent conduct, more accurately "willful" or "intentional" conduct, which was the proximate cause of his death, resulting from multiple drug intoxication. His estate was barred from recovering any monetary damages.

"Generally a relaxed standard of care is required in the contributory negligence situation by persons who are subject to the infirmities of old age."[34] The court in *Powell v. Parkview Estate Nursing Home, Inc.*[35] found that when a resident is unable to physically and mentally care for herself "it logically follows she could not be held to the same degree of accountability as a normally healthy person."[36] The 77-year-old resident, who had been bedridden for a year or more and weighed less than 100 lbs., fell from her bed at 10:30 P.M. The nurse who found her placed her back in bed and raised the side rails. The nurse noted on the resident's chart that the resident apparently did not sustain any serious injuries, although she did suffer from abrasions and cuts on her face. The nurse also noted that the resident "does not complain of pain—hard to determine."[37] The night nurse was asked to observe the resident and was told that if anything came up to notify the administrator of the nursing facility. The following morning a registered nurse determined that the resident's left leg was broken above the ankle and summoned the physician. From the testimony presented from witnesses and the nursing facility records entered into evidence, the trial judge concluded that the side rails were down at the time of the accident. In addition, the night table, which was usually placed close to the resident's bed to prevent her from falling, was not in position. Judgment was rendered for the plaintiff. On appeal, the court held that the defendant's employees were aware that the resident was senile and almost helpless and that both rails should have been raised or the table placed against the bed on the side where the rail was down to prevent the very accident that did occur. The evidence estab-lished that the defendant's employees failed to exercise the care required of them under the law in this instance, and this failure constituted fault. The defendant's argument that the resident was contributorily negligent required that the defendant prove the resident conducted herself in such a way as to constitute negligence. The defendant failed to do that.

The patient, Mr. Cammatte, in *Jenkins v. Bogalusa Community Medical Center*[38] was admitted to Bogalusa Community Medical Center on September 11, 1970, for the treatment of a severe gouty arthritic condition. He had been advised not to get out of bed without first ringing for assistance. On the morning of September 16, 1970, he got out of bed without ringing for assistance and went to a bathroom across the hall. As he returned to his room, he fell and fractured his hip. Cammatte was transferred to Touro Infirmary in New Orleans where he underwent hip surgery and died on October 5, 1970, during recuperation, caused by an apparent pulmonary embolism. The trial court entered judgment for the defendants, and the plaintiffs appealed. The appeals court found that the patient was in full possession of his faculties at the time he fell and fractured his hip. The accident was the result of the patient's knowing failure to follow instructions not to get out of bed without ringing for assistance. The injury in this case was not the result of any breach of the institution's duty to exercise due care.

The rationale for contributory negligence is based on the principle that all persons must be both careful and responsible for their acts. A plaintiff is required to conform to the broad standard of conduct of the reasonable person. The plaintiff's negligence will be determined and governed by the same tests and rules as the negligence of the defendant.

Good Samaritan Laws

The various states have enacted good Samaritan laws, which relieve physicians, nurses, dentists, and other health care professionals, and in some instances, laypersons, from liability in certain emergency situations. Good Samaritan legislation encourages health care professionals to render assistance at the scene of emergencies.

Good Samaritan statutes provide a standard of care that delineates the scope of immunity for those persons eligible under the law. The standards vary widely from state to state and sometimes are ambiguous. In most states, the statement that the person giving aid must act "in good faith" generally qualifies the scope of immunity. Some statutes require that a physician or the person rendering care must act with "due care," without "gross negligence," or without "willful or wanton" misconduct.

Despite problems of interpretation, it is clear that the purpose of the statutes is to encourage volunteer medical assistance in emergency situations. The language that grants immunity also supports the conclusion that the physician, nurse, or layperson who is covered by the act will be protected from liability for ordinary negligence in rendering assistance in an emergency.

Under most statutes, immunity is granted only during an emergency or when rendering emergency care. The concept of emergency usually refers to a combination of unforeseen circumstances that require spontaneous action to avoid impending danger. Some states have sought to be more precise regarding what constitutes an emergency or accident. According to the Alaska statute 09.65.090(a), the emergency circumstances must suggest that the giving of aid is the only alternative to death or serious bodily injury.

Apparently, this provision was inserted to emphasize that the actions of a good Samaritan must be voluntary. To be legally immune under the Good Samaritan laws, a physician or nurse must render help voluntarily and without expectation of later pay.

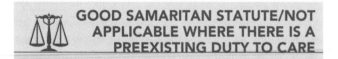

GOOD SAMARITAN STATUTE/NOT APPLICABLE WHERE THERE IS A PREEXISTING DUTY TO CARE

Citation: *Deal v. Kearney*, 851 P.2d 1353 (Alaska 1993)

Facts

On September 16, 1984, after the plaintiff, Mr. Kearney, suffered a life-threatening injury, he was taken by ambulance to the emergency department of Kodiak Island Hospital (KIH). Kearney was examined by the on-call emergency department physician—a family practitioner. It was determined that a surgical consultation was necessary and Deal, a surgeon with staff privileges at the hospital, was called. After ordering certain tests, Deal was of the opinion that Kearney could not survive a transfer to Anchorage. Deal then performed emergency surgery that lasted 9 to 10 hours, ending the following morning.

The plaintiff was eventually transferred to Anchorage. His condition worsened and he suffered loss of circulation and tissue death in both legs. The plaintiff alleged that the hospital was negligent in failing to properly evacuate him to Anchorage.

On October 2, 1989, Lutheran Hospitals and Home Society of America (LHHS) and Mr. Kearney entered into a settlement agreement whereby LHHS paid $510,000 to Kearney. At the same time, LHHS and Kearney released LHHS, Deal, and other health care providers from liability. In return, LHHS as-

signed to Kearney its rights to indemnity, equitable subrogation, and contribution against Deal.

On November 1, 1989, Mr. Kearney, as assignee of the rights of LHHS, brought the present action against Deal, alleging that LHHS had rights of indemnity, contribution, or subrogation against Deal arising from Deal's negligent acts or omissions in the care given Kearney. Deal moved for summary judgment on two grounds. First, Deal argued that the assignment of LHHS's claims to Kearney was invalid. Second, he claimed to be immune from suit under the Good Samaritan statute.

The trial court denied Deal's motion for summary judgment, ruling that the claims brought against him were properly assigned to Kearney, and that the Good Samaritan statute was not applicable to Deal because he was acting under a preexisting duty to render the emergency care to Kearney. Deal petitioned for review, and his petition was granted.

The superior court held that the immunity provided by the Good Samaritan statute is unavailable to physicians with a preexisting duty to respond to emergency situations. The court concluded that Deal was under a preexisting duty in the instant case by virtue of his contract with KIH, the duty being part of the consideration that Deal gave to KIH in exchange for staff privileges at the hospital. The court further found that the Good Samaritan statute did not apply to Deal in any event, because the actions allegedly constituting malpractice occurred during the follow-up care and treatment given Mr. Kearney after surgery. By then, the court reasoned, Deal had become Kearney's treating physician, and was no longer responding to an emergency situation.

Issue

Does the Good Samaritan statute extend immunity to physicians who have a preexisting duty to render emergency care?

Holding

The Alaska Supreme Court held that the Good Samaritan statute does not extend immunity to physicians who have preexisting duty to render emergency care.

Reason

The Alaska Statute 09.65.090(a) states, "A person at a hospital or any other location who renders emergency care or emergency counseling to an injured, ill, or emotionally distraught person who reasonably appears to be in immediate need of emergency aid in order to avoid serious harm or death is not liable for civil damages as a result of an act or omission in rendering emergency aid."

The legislature clearly intended this provision to encourage health care providers, including medical professionals, to administer emergency medical care, whether in a hospital or not, to persons who are not their patients by immunizing them from civil liability. The clear inference of this recommendation is that the statute would not cover those with a preexisting duty. Courts in other cases have held that physicians were entitled to claim immunity under a Good Samaritan statute where they provided emergency medical care in a hospital that was not part of the physicians' express or customary hospital function and therefore did not have a preexisting duty to treat the patients. In summary, the trial court was correct in holding that the Alaska Good Samaritan statute does not extend immunity to physicians who have a preexisting duty to render emergency care.

Discussion

1. Do you agree with the Alaska Statute 09.65.090(a), which provides that a person at a hospital or any other location who renders emergency care or emergency counseling to an injured, ill, or emotionally distraught person who reasonably appears to be in immediate need of emergency aid in order to avoid serious harm or death is not liable for civil damages as a result of an act or omission in rendering emergency aid?
2. What other options might have been available to care for this patient?
3. Do you get the impression that this is a no-win case for the defendants? Explain.

Ignorance of Fact and Unintentional Wrongs

Ignorance of the law excuses no man; not that all men know the law, but because it is an excuse every man will plead, and no man can tell how to confute him.
John Selden (1584–1654)

Ignorance of the law is not a defense; otherwise, the ignorant would be rewarded simply by pleading ignorance. Arguing that a negligent act is unintentional is no defense. If such a defense were acceptable, all defendants would use it.

Intervening Cause

Intervening cause arises when the act of a third party, independent of the defendant's original negligent conduct, is the proximate cause of death or injury. The inquiry is whether "the intervention of the later cause is a significant part of the risk involved in the defendant's conduct, or so reasonably connected with it that the responsibility should not be terminated." If the negligent act of the third party is extraordinary under the circumstances and unforeseeable as a normal and probable consequence of the defendant's negligence, then the third party's negligence supersedes that of the defendant and relieves the defendant of liability.

For example, in *DePesa v. Westchester Square Medical Center*,[39] the trial record reveals that on April 29, 1985, Ruth Durant, who was 49 years old at the time, felt severe pain in her abdomen and went to the emergency department at Westchester Square Medical Center. There, she was prescribed Mylanta and sent home with the advice that she should contact her personal physician if her condition worsened. Durant took the Mylanta, but her condition continued to deteriorate and, after 20 more days, she went to the emergency department at Jacobi Hospital on May 19, 1985. After X-rays and other tests were performed, Durant was admitted and was operated on for a perforated bowel and peritonitis on May 21. Although the evidence indicated that the operation itself was successful, she died at the hospital on May 25, 1985. The autopsy report indicated the presence of yellow fluid in the pleural cavity and peritoneal cavity, and the cause of the death as status post bowel resection, bronchopneumonia, and congestive heart failure.

The case was submitted to the jury with instructions to determine the proportionate liability of the parties. The New York Supreme Court, upon a jury verdict, apportioned negligence 30 percent to decedent, 47 percent to defendant Westchester Square Medical Center, and 23 percent to nonparty Jacobi Hospital, and awarded damages against the defendant. The appellate court unanimously reversed the judgment and the matter was remanded for a new trial.

The appellate court agreed with the defendant Westchester Square Medical Center that the trial court also should have provided an instruction directing the jury to decide whether the postoperative care of decedent by Jacobi Hospital, despite Westchester's negligence, was the proximate and superseding cause of death.

In this case, there was sufficient evidence in the record to present to the jury the factual issue of whether the postoperative care at Jacobi Hospital, although resulting from circumstances set in motion by Westchester's initial negligence, was sufficiently attenuated from Westchester's initial medical misdiagnosis so as to relieve Westchester of liability for the eventual death. Westchester's expert testified, based on the medical evidence, that while the decedent was recovering from surgery, Jacobi Hospital personnel had administered almost double the amount of fluids that the decedent could output, resulting in congestive heart failure and her ultimate demise. Westchester's theory at trial was that the perforation of the bowel occurred at Jacobi Hospital; that Jacobi Hospital administered substantially more fluid to the patient than she could excrete; that these causes of death were independent of Westchester's own negligence in failing to detect bowel conditions; and that such intervening negligence would not have been foreseeable by a reasonably prudent person. Accordingly, the question of intervening causation should have been presented to the jury.

In *Cohran v. Harper*,[40] a patient sued a physician, charging him with malpractice for an alleged Staphylococcus infection that she received from a hypodermic needle used by the physician's nurse. The nurse gave the patient an injection that resulted in osteomyelitis. The grounds of negligence included an allegation that the physician failed to properly sterilize the hypodermic needle that was used to administer a certain dose of penicillin. The evidence showed, without dispute, that a prepackaged sterilized needle and syringe were used in accordance with proper and accepted medical practice. The physician was not liable. There was inadequate proof that either the physician or his nurse was negligent. The court said that even if there was evidence that the needle was contaminated and that the patient's ailment was caused thereby, there was no evidence that either the physician or his nurse or anyone in his office knew, or by the exercise of ordinary care could have discovered, that the prepackaged needle and syringe were so contaminated. The defense of "intervening cause" would have been an adequate defense against recovery of damages if it had been established that the needle was contaminated when packaged.

Statute of Limitations

The *statute of limitations* refers to legislatively imposed time constraints that restrict the period of time after the occurrence of an injury during which a legal action must be commenced. Should a cause of action be initiated later than the period of time prescribed, the case cannot proceed. Whether a suit for personal injury can be brought against a defendant often depends on whether the suit was commenced within a time specified by the applicable statute of limitations. The statutory period begins when an injury occurs, although in some cases (usually involving foreign objects left in the body during surgery) the statutory period commences when the injured person discovers or should have discovered the injury.

Many technical rules are associated with statutes of limitations. Statutes in each state specify that malpractice suits and other personal injury suits must be brought within fixed periods of time. That an injured person is a minor or is otherwise under a legal disability may extend the period within which an action for injury may be brought under the laws of many states. Computation of the period when the statute begins to run in a particular state may be based on any of the following factors:

- the date that the physician terminated treatment
- the time of the wrongful act
- the time when the patient should have reasonably discovered the injury
- the date that the injury is discovered
- the date when the contract between the patient and the physician ended

The running of the statute will not begin if fraud (the deliberate concealment from a patient of facts that might present a cause of action for damages) is involved. The cause of action begins at the time fraud is discovered.

The Supreme Court has ruled that a five-year limitation on bringing certain medical malpractice cases is unconstitutional.[41] The ruling stemmed in part from cases dealing with a serial killer, Donald Harvey. The Court struck down a protection long claimed by medical professionals and hospitals against negligence suits. Mr. Harvey was linked to deaths that occurred 20 years earlier while he was working at a local hospital.

Fraud

In a 1949 Michigan case, *Buchanan v. Kull*,[42] a patient who had undergone a thyroidectomy suffered paralyzed vocal cords. The patient had been told that the injury was due to a lack of calcium. The patient later learned that the vocal cords had been cut. The statute of limitations normally would have run out in this case; however, the presence of fraud did not permit the statute to commence until the patient became aware of the fraud.

Needle Discovered in Patient's Spine

A New Hampshire patient in *Shillady v. Elliot Community Hospital*[43] sued the hospital for negligence in treatment that was administered 31 years earlier. A needle had been left in the patient's spine after a spinal tap in 1940. In 1970, an X-ray showed the needle. The patient had suffered severe pain immediately after the spinal tap, which had decreased over the intervening years to about three "spells" a year. The court held that the six-year statute of limitations does not begin "until the patient learns or in the exercise of reasonable care and diligence should have learned of its presence."[44] Therefore, the defendant's motion to dismiss the case on the grounds that the statute of limitations had run out was not granted.

Untimely Notice

In *Streetman v. University of Texas Health Science Center at San Antonio,*[45] Mr. Streetman died of cancer in January 1995. Prior to being diagnosed with cancer, Mr. Streetman had a history of chronic obstructive lung disease. He visited a veteran's hospital, which the University of Texas Health Science Center at San Antonio (UTHSC) staffed with radiologists, approximately 20 times over the course of five years. During that time, Mr. Streetman had at least two chest X-rays. One of these X-rays was taken on March 31, 1992, and interpreted by Dr. Nguyen. Mr. Streetman's medical records indicate that the X-ray revealed no change from a previous X-ray taken in June 1987. In October 1993, Mr. Streetman was diagnosed with lung cancer. Approximately one year later, in September 1994, a CAT scan revealed that the cancer had spread to Mr. Streetman's spine. Mr. Streetman hired an attorney, who began investigating a potential medical malpractice claim on his behalf and sent notice in October 1994 to UTHSC concerning the potential suit.

In January 1995, Mr. Streetman's attorney received a report from Dr. Flamm. Based upon a review of a portion of Mr. Streetman's medical records, Dr. Flamm concluded that the March 1992 X-ray had been negligently read. In May 1995, after Mr. Streetman had died, his family members brought the present lawsuit against Dr. Nguyen and UTHSC.

Both defendants moved for summary judgment. Nguyen's motion was granted and then severed from the rest of the case. UTHSC's motion was granted on the grounds that the appellants did not provide timely notice to UTHSC under the Texas Tort Claims Act (TTCA) and UTHSC did not have actual knowledge of the claims. The appellants appealed.

The appellants contend that they could not provide timely notice to UTHSC because Mr. Streetman was not diagnosed with metastatic cancer until September 1994. They argued that they provided notice within the six-month time limit after Mr. Streetman discovered the possibility that the cancer could have been detected in March 1992. The appellants did not contest the court's finding that UTHSC did not have actual notice.

To prevail on summary judgment, the movant must show that there are no genuine issues of material fact and that he or she is entitled to judgment as a matter of law. Sovereign immunity to suit against a governmental unit has been waived in limited circumstances by the TTCA.[46] One of the limitations is contained in section 101.101, which, in pertinent part, states:

> (a) A governmental unit is entitled to receive notice of a claim against it under this chapter not later than six months after the day that the incident giving rise to the claim occurred. . . .

The six-month time limit in Section 101.101-(a) ran from the date an X-ray was allegedly misinterpreted, not from the date that the patient discovered that he had metastatic lung cancer, creating the suspicion that his X-rays might have been misdiagnosed. The purpose of the notice provision is to ensure a prompt reporting of claims to enable the governmental unit to investigate the merits of a claim while the facts are fresh and conditions remain substantially the same. Such opportunity to investigate, predicated upon timely reporting of claim of injury, enables the governmental unit to gather the information needed to guard against unfounded claims, settle claims, and prepare for trial.

Sovereign Immunity

Sovereign immunity refers to the common-law doctrine by which federal and state governments historically have been immune from liability for harm suffered from the tortious conduct of employees. For the most part, both federal and state governments have abolished sovereign immunity.

Congress enacted the Federal Tort Claims Act (FTCA), which provides redress for those who have been negligently injured by employees of the federal government acting within their scope of employment. The *Feres doctrine,* which prohibits a person in the armed services from bringing an action against the United States under the FTCA, was first enunciated in *Feres v. United States.*[47] In *Wooten v. United States,*[48] the Veterans Administration Hospital of Memphis, Tennessee, was held negligent for injuries sustained by an 83-year-old heart patient who was found lying outside his room in a hallway of the hospital. This action was brought under the FTCA. The patient had suffered severe head injuries that required surgery. Damages in the amount of $80,000 were awarded the plaintiff. The court held that the evidence was sufficient to raise a duty on the part of hospital personnel attending the patient to use reasonable care to protect him from getting out of bed and injuring himself. This duty was breached, and the patient was injured. The proximate cause of the patient's injuries was related to the hospital's failure to put up the patient's bed rails and its failure to remind him to call a nurse if he needed help. Evidence offered in this case indicated that the Veterans Administration Hospital did not meet the standards of care rendered in other large Memphis hospitals.

The law of the state in which negligence is asserted governs claims made. Action was brought on behalf of a minor in *Steele v. United States,*[49] who received treatment at a U.S. Army hospital and suffered injury because of the optometrist's failure to refer the child to an ophthalmologist for examination. The U.S.

district court held that it was probable that an ophthalmologist would have diagnosed the child's problem and prevented the loss of his right eye. Recovery was permitted against the United States under the FTCA.

NURSE'S NEGLIGENCE/ IMMUNITY DENIED

Citation: *Sullivan v. Sumrall by Ritchey, 618 So.2d 1274 (Miss. 1993)*

Facts

On April 26, 1988, the patient was admitted to the hospital suffering from a severe headache. Her physician ordered a CT scan for the following morning and prescribed Demerol and Dramamine to alleviate pain. Referring to the patient's medical chart, the nurse stated in her deposition that the patient had received injections of Demerol and Dramamine at 6:45 P.M. and 10:00 P.M. on April 26th. The nurse checked on the patient at 11:00 P.M. The patient's temperature and blood pressure were taken at midnight. Her blood pressure was recorded at 90/60, down from 160/80 at 8:00 P.M. At 12:25 A.M., 2 hours and 25 minutes after her last medication, the nurse administered another injection of Demerol and Dramamine because the patient was still complaining of pain. Although hospital rules require consultation with a patient's admitting physician when there is a question regarding the administration of medication, the nurse stated that she *did not call the physician before administering another injection.*

At 4:00 A.M. when the nurse made an hourly check of the patient, she discovered that the patient was not breathing. She issued a Code 99 (an emergency signal for a patient in acute distress). An emergency department physician responded and revived the patient. The patient was diagnosed as having suffered "respiratory arrest, with what appears to be hypoxic brain injury." Her CT scans revealed no bleeding, but other tests "revealed [a] grossly abnormal EEG with diffuse and severe slowing." *Id.* at 1275. The patient was transferred to a nursing facility where she apparently remained in a coma at the time of trial.

The patient's daughter and husband filed a complaint against the hospital, alleging that the hospital had been negligent in monitoring and medicating the patient, in failing to notify a physician when her vital signs became irregular, in failing to properly assess her condition and intervene, and in failing to exercise reasonable care. Later, the complaint was amended to include the nurse.

The defendant nurse filed a motion for summary judgment. She asserted that as a matter of law, she was shielded from liability under the qualified immunity afforded public officials engaged in their performance of discretionary functions. The circuit court denied the motion and the nurse appealed.

Issue

Is a nurse employed by a county hospital shielded by public official qualified immunity from a medical negligence action brought against her individually?

Holding

The Mississippi Supreme Court held that an employee of a county hospital enjoys no qualified immunity.

Reason

There is no qualified immunity for any public hospital employees making treatment decisions. Discretion exercised by medical personnel in making treatment decisions is not the sort of individual judgment sought to be protected by the qualified immunity bestowed upon public officials.

Discussion

1. Do you agree that the nurse should not be shielded from liability on the basis that she is a public official? Explain.
2. What assessment and reassessment issues do you see in this case?
3. Should the dramatic change in the patient's blood pressure have signaled a need to notify the attending physician of the patient's change in health status? Explain.
4. Was the nurse practicing medicine when she administered the second injection without contacting the attending physician?

CLOSING STATEMENTS

After completion of the plaintiff's case and the defendant's defense, the judge calls for closing statements. The defense proceeds first and then the plaintiff. Closing statements provide attorneys an opportunity to summarize for the jury and the court what they have proven. They may point out faults in their opponent's case and emphasize points they wish the jury to remember.

If there appears to be only a question of law at the end of a case, a motion can be made for a directed verdict. The court must decide a motion of this nature. The court will grant the motion if there is no question of fact to be decided by the jury. The directed verdict also may be made on the grounds that the plaintiff has failed to present sufficient facts to prove his or her case or that the evidence fails to establish a legal basis for a verdict in the plaintiff's favor.

JUDGE'S CHARGE TO THE JURY

After the attorneys' summations, the court charges the jury before the jurors recess to deliberate. Because the jury determines issues of fact, it is necessary for the court to instruct the jury with regard to the applicable law. This is done by means of a charge. The charge defines the responsibility of the jury, describes the applicable law, and advises the jury of the alternatives available to it. As an example, statements from the trial judge's oral charge to the jurors in *Estes Health Care Centers v. Bannerman*,[50] in which a nursing facility resident died after transfer to a hospital after suffering burns in a bath, included

> The complaint alleges the defendant Jackson Hospital undertook to provide hospital and nursing care to the deceased, and that the defendant negligently failed to provide proper hospital and nursing care to the plaintiff's intestate.
>
> •　•　•　•　•
>
> The defendants in response to these allegations . . . have each separately entered pleas of the general issue or general denial. Under the law, a plea of the general issue has the effect of placing the burden of proof on the plaintiffs to reasonably satisfy you from the evidence, the truth of those things claimed by them in the bill of the complaint. The defendants carry no burden of proof.
>
> •　•　•　•　•
>
> As to the defendant Jackson Hospital, the duty arises in that in rendering services to a patient, a hospital must use that degree of care, skill, and diligence used by hospitals generally in the community under similar circumstances.
>
> •　•　•　•　•
>
> Negligence is not actionable unless the negligence is the proximate cause of the injury. The law

defines proximate cause as that cause which is the natural and probable sequence of events and without the intervention of any new or independent cause, produces the injury, and without which such injury would not have occurred. For an act to constitute actionable negligence, there must not only be some causal connection between the negligent act complained of and the injury suffered, but connection must be by natural and unbroken sequence, without intervening sufficient causes, so that but for the negligence of the defendant, the injury would not have occurred.

> •　•　•　•　•
>
> If one is guilty of negligence which concurs or combines with the negligence of another, and the two combine to produce injury, each negligent person is liable for the resulting injury. And the negligence of each will be deemed the proximate cause of the injury. Concurrent causes may be defined as two or more causes which run together and act contemporaneously to produce a given result or to inflict an injury. This does not mean that the causes of the acts producing the injury must necessarily occur simultaneously, but they must be active simultaneously to efficiently and proximately produce a result.
>
> •　•　•　•　•
>
> In an action against two or more defendants for injury allegedly caused by combined or concurring negligence of the defendants, it is not necessary to show negligence of all the defendants in order for recovery to be had against one or more to be negligent. If you are reasonably satisfied from the evidence in this case that all the defendants are negligent and that their negligence concurred and combined to proximately cause the injury complained by the plaintiffs, then each defendant is liable to the plaintiffs.[51]

When a charge given by the court is not clear enough on a particular point or when it does not cover different issues in the case, it is the obligation of the attorneys for both sides to request clarification of the charge. When the jury retires to deliberate, the members are reminded not to discuss the case except among themselves.

JURY DELIBERATION AND DETERMINATION

After the judge's charge, the jury retires to the jury room and deliberates as to whether or not the defendant is liable.

The jury returns to the courtroom upon reaching a verdict and their determinations are presented to the court.

If a verdict is against the weight of the evidence, a judge may dismiss the case, order a new trial, or set his or her own verdict. At the time judgment is rendered, the losing party has an opportunity to motion for a new trial. If the new trial is granted, the entire process is repeated; if not, the judgment becomes final, subject to a review of the trial record by an appellate court.

DAMAGES

Monetary damages generally are awarded to individuals in cases of personal injury and wrongful death. Damages generally are fixed by the jury and are nominal, compensatory, hedonic, or punitive.

Nominal damages are awarded as a mere token in recognition that wrong has been committed when the actual amount of compensation is insignificant.

Compensatory damages are estimated reparation in money for detriment or injury sustained (including loss of earnings, medical costs, and loss of financial support).

Hedonic damages are those damages awarded to compensate an individual for the loss of enjoyment of life. Such damages are awarded because of the failure of compensatory damages to compensate an individual adequately for the pain and suffering that he or she has endured as a result of a negligent wrong.

Punitive damages are additional money awards authorized when an injury is caused by gross carelessness or disregard for the safety of others.

Plaintiff's Schedule of Damages

Plaintiffs seek recovery for a great variety of damages. The following are typical:

- personal injuries
- permanent physical disabilities
- permanent mental disabilities
- past and future physical and mental pain and suffering sustained and to be sustained
- loss of enjoyment of life
- loss of consortium where a spouse is injured in the accident
- loss of child's services where a minor child is injured in the accident
- medical and other health expenses reasonably paid or incurred, or reasonably certain to be incurred in the future
- past and future loss of earnings sustained and to be sustained
- permanent diminution in the plaintiff's earning capacity

A plethora of negligence cases have been litigated throughout the nation. The following cases illustrate the types of damages sought by plaintiffs.

Damages/Future Pain and Suffering

In *Luecke v. Bitterman*,[52] an award of $490,000 for future pain and suffering was found reasonable with respect to a 20-year-old patient who, as a result of a physician's negligent application of liquid nitrogen to remove a wart, suffered a 12- by 4-inch third degree burn. The burn resulted in a scar on the right buttock extending to the back of the thigh. The plaintiff suffered excruciating pain and posttraumatic stress disorder.

Punitive Damages/Mighty Engine of Deterrence

Punitive damages are awarded over and above that which is intended to compensate the plaintiff for economic losses resulting from the injury. Punitive damages cover such items as physical disability, mental anguish, loss of a spouse's services, physical suffering, injury to one's reputation, and loss of companionship. Punitive damages were referred to as *that mighty engine of deterrence* in *Johnson v. Terry*.[53]

The court in *Henry v. Deen*[54] held that allegations of gross and wanton negligence incidental to wrongful death in the plaintiff's complaint gave sufficient notice of a claim against the treating physician and physician's assistant for punitive damages. The original complaint, which alleged that the treating physician, the physician's assistant, and the consulting physician agreed to create and did create false and misleading entries in the patient's medical record, was sufficient to allege a civil conspiracy. The decision of the lower court was reversed, and the case was remanded for further proceedings.

In *Estes Health Care Centers v. Bonnerman*, discussed earlier, the court stated:

> While human life is incapable of translation into a compensatory measurement, the amount of an award of punitive damages may be measured by the gravity of the wrong done, the punishment called for by the act of the wrongdoer, and the need to deter similar wrongs in order to preserve human life.[55]

In *Payton Health Care Facilities, Inc. v. Estate of Campbell*,[56] a punitive damage award in the amount of $1.7 million for the wrongful death of a patient from infected decubitus ulcers was found to be justified. The treating physician had agreed to a settlement prior to trial in the amount of $50,000. The deceased, a stroke victim, had been admitted to the Lakeland Health Care Center for nursing and medical care. While at the center the patient developed several severe skin ulcers that eventually necessitated hospitalization in Lakeland General Hospital. The patient's condition had deteriorated to such a state that further treatment was inadequate to prolong his life. Expert testimony had been presented that indicated that the standard of care received by the patient while at the nursing facility was an "outrageous" deviation from acceptable standards of care. There was sufficient evidence of the willful and wanton disregard for rights of others to permit an award of punitive damages against the companies who owned and managed the nursing facility. The cause of death was determined to be bacteremia with sepsis, because of extensive infected necrotic decubitus ulcers, that the patient developed at the nursing facility.

Damages/Surviving Spouse and Children

Damages may be awarded given evidence of a patient's pain and the mental anguish of the surviving husband and children. In *Jefferson Hospital Association v. Garrett*,[57] damages in the amount of $180,000 were found not to be excessive given evidence of the patient's pain and the mental suffering of the surviving spouse and children.

Damages/Emotional Distress

The court of appeals in *Haught v. Maceluch*[58] held that under Texas law the mother was entitled to recover for her emotional distress, even though she was not conscious at the time her child was born. The mother had brought a medical malpractice action, alleging that the physician was negligent in the delivery of her child, causing her daughter to suffer permanent brain injury. The district court entered judgment of $1,160,000 for the child's medical expenses and $175,000 for her lost future earnings. The court deleted a jury award of $118,000 for the mother's mental suffering over her daughter's impaired condition. On appeal, the court of appeals permitted recovery, under Texas law, for mental suffering. The mother was conscious for more than 11 hours of labor and was aware of the physician's negligent acts, his absence in a near-emergency situation, and the overadministration of the labor-inducing drug Pitocin.

Damages/Not Excessive

The plaintiff in *Burge v. Parker*[59] suffered a laceration of his right foot on April 2 and was taken to St. Margaret's Hospital. A physician in the emergency department cleaned and stitched the laceration and released the patient with instructions to keep the foot elevated. Even though reports prepared by the fire medic who arrived on the scene of the accident and by ambulance personnel had indicated the chief complaint as being a fracture of the foot, no X-rays were ordered in the emergency department. The admitting clerk had typed a statement on the admission form indicating possible fracture of the right foot. However, a handwritten note stated the chief complaint as being a laceration of the right foot. The patient returned to the hospital later in the day with his mother, complaining of pain in the right foot. His mother asked if X-rays had been taken. The physician said that it was not necessary. The wound was redressed, and the patient was sent home again with instructions to keep the foot elevated. The pain continued to worsen, and the patient was taken to see another physician on April 5. X-rays were ordered, and an orthopaedic surgeon called for a consultation diagnosed three fractures and a compartment syndrome, a swelling of tissue in the muscle compartments. The swelling increased pressure on the blood vessels, thus decreasing circulation, which tends to cause muscles to die.

Approximately one-half pint of clotted blood was removed from the wound. By April 11, the big toe had to be surgically removed. It was alleged that the emergency department physician had failed to obtain a full medical history, to order the necessary X-rays, and to diagnose and treat the fractures of the foot. As a result, the patient ultimately suffered loss of his big toe. The Macon County Circuit Court awarded damages totaling $450,000 for loss of a big toe, and the physician appealed. The Alabama Supreme Court found the damages not to have been excessive.

In *Tesauro v. Perrige*,[60] Mrs. Tesauro, the appellee, went to Dr. Perrige, the appellant, to have a lower left molar removed. A blood clot failed to form and the appellant administered an injection of alcohol near the affected area. The appellee began to experience pain, burning, and numbness at the site of the injection, on the left side of her face. Several physicians diagnosed her as suffering from muscle spasms caused by a damaged trigeminal nerve. Over a five-year period the appellee was treated by a variety of specialists. In 1989, the plaintiff underwent radical experimental surgery. The surgery corrected the plaintiff's most oppressive symptoms. Although the most painful symptoms have been eliminated, the appellee continued to suffer numbness and burning on the left side of her face. A dental malpractice lawsuit was filed against Dr. Perrige alleging that he was negligent in administering the alcohol injection so close to the trigeminal nerve. The jury returned a verdict in favor of the plaintiffs in the amounts of $2,747,000 to Mrs. Tesauro and $593,000 to Mr. Tesauro for loss of consortium. Perrige, the defendant/appellant, appealed for a new trial to be based on the excessiveness of the jury verdict.

The superior court held that the evidence supported the damage awards. The decision to grant or not to grant a new trial based on the excessiveness of a jury verdict is within the sound discretion of the trial court, and its decision will be upheld on appeal based on a gross abuse of that discretion. In determining excessiveness, a court should consider: (1) the severity of the injury; (2) whether the injury is manifested by objective physical evidence or whether it is revealed only by the subjective testimony; (3) whether the injury is permanent; (4) whether the plaintiff can continue with his or her employment; (5) the size of out-of-pocket expenses; and (6) the amount of compensation demanded in the original complaint.

The superior court determined that the severity of the plaintiff's injury in itself would support the compensatory award. The plaintiff spent five years trying to find a cure for her pain. Although much recovered, the plaintiff continued to suffer from numbness and burning. Her experience clearly fell into the category of severe injury. The severity of the injury had a huge impact on the marital relationship. The compensation awarded to Mr. Tesauro was, therefore, fair and just.

A medical malpractice action was brought against the employer of a physician, alleging that the physician's failure to properly treat an abscess some three weeks after an infant received a live polio vaccine resulted in suppression of the infant's immune system and the infant's contraction of paralytic polio. The jury in the circuit court returned a $16 million verdict in favor of the plaintiffs, and the defendant appealed. The case was transferred from the court of appeals to the state supreme court.[61] Was the $16 million verdict excessive and did the trial court err in denying a new trial based on the alleged excessive verdict?

The Missouri Supreme Court held that there was no basis for a new trial on the grounds of excessiveness of the $16 million verdict. There is no formula for determining the excessiveness of a verdict. Each case must be decided on its own facts to determine what is fair and reasonable. A jury is in the best position to make such a determination. The trial judge could have set aside the verdict if a determination was made that passion and prejudice brought about an excessive verdict. The size of the verdict alone does not establish passion and prejudice. The appellant failed to establish that the verdict was: (1) glaringly unwarranted and (2) based on prejudice and passion. Compensation of a plaintiff is based on such factors as the age of the patient, the nature and extent of injury, diminished earnings capacity, economic condition, and awards in comparable cases. A jury is entitled to consider such intangibles that do not lend themselves to precise calculation, such as past and future pain, suffering, effect on lifestyle, embarrassment, humiliation, and economic loss.

THE WRONG BLOOD

Citation: *Dodson v. Community Blood Ctr.*, 633 *So.2d 252 (La. Ct. App. 1993)*

Facts

The Patients' Compensation Fund (PCF) appealed from an order of the trial court, which awarded damages to a patient who contracted hepatitis following a blood transfusion. The patient was scheduled to undergo surgery at a medical center. In anticipation of the surgery and out of fear of contracting the acquired immune deficiency syndrome (AIDS) through blood transfusions from unknown donors, he arranged to have three known donors donate blood earmarked for his use should transfusion be required.

After surgery, the patient was transfused with two pints of blood. However, the blood used was not the blood obtained from the patient's voluntary donors. The blood had been taken from the hospital's general inventory, which had been obtained from the Community Blood Center. The patient subsequently learned that as a result of the transfusions, he had been infected with what at the time was called non-A non-B hepatitis. It is now referred to as hepatitis C.

Issue

Was the award of $325,000 in general damages to the patient excessive?

Holding

The Louisiana Court of Appeal held that the award of damages was not excessive.

Reason

The PCF contended the trial court erred in assessing general damages. The plaintiffs were awarded the sum of $325,000 in general damages. PCF alleges that the sum of $150,000 in general damages is the maximum to which the plaintiffs are entitled, thus quantum should be reduced accordingly. A review of the record revealed that the patient contracted non-A non-B hepatitis through the blood transfusions received. Based on tests prior to trial, the chronic hepatitis was either resolved or quiescent. The plaintiff had a good prognosis; however, this prognosis was not guaranteed. There remained a chance that the chronic hepatitis may become active in the future.

In reasons for judgment, the trial court found that the patient was a credible witness. He did not exaggerate his symptoms, fears, or worries about his condition. The court believed the patient when he said he felt like a leper and feared infecting his wife, child, and friends with the disease. The trial court arrived at what it determined to be an appropriate award for general damages. After careful review of the record and in light of the vast discretion of the trial court to assess general damages, the court found that there was no abuse of discretion.

Discussion

1. Under what circumstances will an appellate court overturn the decision of a lower court?
2. What are the proper procedures for handling blood and blood products in this case?

Damages Excessive

A jury verdict totaling $12,393,130 was considered an excessive award in *Merrill v. Albany Medical Center*,[62] in which damages were sought with respect to the severe brain damage sustained by a 22-month-old infant as the result of oxygen deprivation. This occurred when the infant went into cardiac arrest during surgery for removal of a suspected malignant tumor from her right lung. Reduction of the amount to $6,143,130 was considered appropriate.

The plaintiffs in *Campbell v. Pitt County Memorial Hospital*[63] brought an action to recover damages for personal injury suffered by an infant. The infant's mother had been admitted to the defendant hospital for delivery of her baby. The defendant physician, Dr. Deyton, determined that the baby was in a footing breech, feet first position. At 1:30 P.M. on the date of delivery, Deyton proceeded with a vaginal delivery despite the position of the baby. For several hours before delivery, the hospital nurses monitoring the baby observed complications that they believed were affecting adversely the condition of the fetus. One of the nurses expressed her concerns to Deyton; however, she did not contact her immediate supervisor or anyone else when Deyton failed to address her concerns. The infant's umbilical cord became wrapped around her legs. The infant sustained brain damage caused by severe asphyxia from the entangled cord. Today, the child suffers from cerebral palsy and requires constant care and supervision. Damages were sought for medical expenses, mental anguish, and trauma. The plaintiffs settled with the defendant physician and his professional association in the amount of $1,500,000, leaving Pitt County Memorial Hospital as the sole defendant. The trial court was found not to have abused its discretion when, after the jury awarded the infant damages in the amount of $4,850,000, it ordered a new trial, finding the damages awarded excessive. The jury award appeared to the court to have been made under the influence of passion and prejudice and was unsupported by the evidence. The defendant's motion for a new trial on this issue was granted. This decision was upheld on appeal to both the court of appeals and the North Carolina Supreme Court.

Joint and Several Liability

The doctrine of *joint and several liability* permits the plaintiff to bring suit against all persons who share responsibility for his or her injury. The doctrine allows the plaintiff to recover monetary damages from any one of or all the defendants. Any one defendant, even though partially responsible for the plaintiff's injury, can be required to pay the full judgment awarded by the jury. Awards tend to fall in greater amounts on defendants with the better insurance. This is the "deep pockets" concept: Whoever has the most pays the greater percentage of the award.

APPEALS

An appellate court reviews a case on the basis of the trial record as well as written briefs and, if requested, concise oral arguments by the attorneys. A brief summarizes the facts of a case, testimony of the witnesses, laws affecting the case, and arguments of counsel. The party making the appeal is the appellant. The party answering the appeal is the appellee. After hearing the oral arguments, the court takes the case under advisement until such time as the judges consider it and agree on a decision. An opinion then is prepared explaining the reasons for a decision.

Grounds for appeal may result from one or more of the following:

- the verdict was excessive or inadequate in the lower court
- evidence was rejected that should have been accepted
- inadmissible evidence was permitted
- testimony was excluded that should have been admissible
- the verdict was contrary to the weight of the evidence
- the court improperly charged the jury

Notice of appeal must be filed with the trial court, the appellate court, and the adverse party. The party wishing to prevent execution of an adverse judgment until such time as the case has been heard and decided by an appellate court also should file a "stay of execution."

The appellate court may modify, affirm, or reverse the judgment or reorder a new trial on an appeal. The majority ruling of the judges in the appellate court is binding on the parties of a lawsuit. If the appellate court's decision is not unanimous, the minority may render a dissenting opinion. Further appeal may be made, as set by statute, to the highest court of appeals. If an appeal involves a constitutional question, it eventually may be appealed to the U.S. Supreme Court.

When the highest appellate court in a state decides a case, a final judgment results, and the matter is ended. The instances when one may appeal the ruling of a state court to the U.S. Supreme Court are rare. A federal question must be involved, and even then the Supreme Court must decide whether it will hear the case. A federal question is one involving the U.S. Constitution or a statute enacted by Congress, so it is unlikely that a negligence case arising in a state court would be reviewed and decided by the Supreme Court.

EXECUTION OF JUDGMENTS

Once the amount of damages has been established and all the appeals have been heard, the defendant must comply with the judgment. If he or she fails to do so, a court order may be executed requiring the sheriff or other judicial officer to sell as much of the defendant's property as necessary, within statutory limitations, to satisfy the plaintiff's judgment.

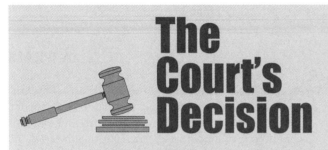

The Court's Decision

The jury found for the plaintiffs on the fraud and battery claims and awarded compensatory damages to Watkins in the amount of $9,660,000. The jury also awarded damages of $1,300,000 to the husband of Watkins for loss of consortium.

Popovich testified that it would have been preferable for the patient to have been awake and responsive when extubated and if the patient was not awake and responsive, it would have been inappropriate to extubate the patient. According to the anesthesia record, Popovich stated that the patient was in trouble at the time she was admitted to the PACU. The evidence presented demonstrated Eliachar represented to Watkins that he would be operating on her. Watkins had specifically asked Eliachar whether he would be performing the surgery. Eliachar performed none of the actual operation on Watkins. When making the representation to the patient, Eliachar knew that he was scheduled to perform simultaneous surgeries on that date; as the performing surgeon of

record, had the responsibility to monitor the patient throughout the entire operation, including postoperative procedures on his patient; and admittedly knew the extubation parameters and would have prevented Watkins's premature extubation had he been the surgeon in the operating room at the time. Eliachar did not return to the operating room prior to the premature extubation of the patient in that same operating room. It was not the responsibility of Guay to supervise the extubation of the patient. Based on this evidence, the elements of fraud were demonstrated and the trial court did not err in denying the motion for directed verdict on that issue.

Eliachar controlled the actions of Guay through his assignment of the procedure to Guay and the supervision of Guay. Also, there was testimony from Guay that he informed Watkins before she was transported to the operating room that he would be performing the operation, yet there is no corroboration of consent to Guay by the patient in the medical record; thus, consent is a question for the trier of fact. The allegedly unconsensual touching by Guay, which is attributable to Eliachar, and then to the defendant hospital, and which permitted Eliachar to be absent at the time of the premature extubation of the patient in the operating room, caused the injury and resulting damages to the patient.

CHAPTER REVIEW

1. *Pleadings* raise questions of law and fact. In a case, if only questions of law are at issue, the judge will decide the case based on the pleadings. If there are questions of fact, a trial will be held to determine those facts. In a negligence action, the first pleading filed with the court is a *complaint*, which identifies the parties to a suit, the cause of action, and the demand for damages.

2. Once a defendant receives a copy of the complaint, the defendant can file a preliminary objection before submitting an *answer*, or response, to the complaint. A formal objection to the lawsuit is called a *demurrer*, and it holds that the evidence presented by the plaintiff is insufficient to sustain an issue or case. The defendant can file a *counterclaim* if he or she has a claim against the plaintiff.

3. Before the trial, facts are investigated in a process called *discovery*. The discovery process helps to prevent surprises during trial. *Examination before trial* is part of the discovery process and allows for witnesses to be examined before the trial. Generally, hospital incident and investigation reports are not protected from discovery. However, communications between client and attorney are protected under attorney-client privilege.

4. A *motion to dismiss* a case can be made before, during, or after the trial. The motion alleges that the plaintiff's complaint does not set forth a claim or cause of action that is recognized by law. If either party to a suit believes that there are no issues of fact in contention, only issues of law, they may make a motion for a *summary judgment*, in which the court is asked to rule without a trial.

5. The *jury* determines the facts in a case and makes a determination of the particular standards of conduct required in all cases in which the judgment of reasonable people might differ. The jury also determines the extent of damages and degree to which the plaintiff's conduct may have contributed to his or her injury.

6. A legal order requiring a person to appear in court or that documents be presented to a court or administrative body is called a *subpoena*. If a witness does not respond to a subpoena, then a *bench warrant*, which orders a witness to appear in court, may be issued.

7. In criminal cases, the *burden of proof* lies with the plaintiff and requires that he or she convince the jury of the truth of his or her case. A *preponderance of credible evidence*—evidence worthy of belief—allows for the award of damages. The principle of *res ipsa loquitur* places the burden of proof on the defendant.

8. Facts proved or disproved during a lawsuit constitute *evidence*. *Direct evidence* is proof that is offered via direct testimony. *Demonstrative evidence* is offered by objects themselves. Written evidence capable of making a truthful statement is considered *documentary evidence*. Written and oral statements that another has said or actions that another person has done that are not the result of personal knowledge of the witness are considered *hearsay evidence*.

9. When the issues to be resolved in the case are outside the understanding or experience of the average juror, an *expert witness* is allowed to offer testimony to assist in explanation of technical matters. The testimony of two experts may conflict, in which case the jury will determine which opinion to accept. An expert witness must have experience and training sufficient to explain the facts or answer the questions of a particular case.

10. After a plaintiff's case has been established, there are several elements that may protect the defendant from recovery of damages:
    - *Assumption of risk* is the knowledge that a danger exists and acceptance of the risk of exposing oneself to it knowing that to do so may result in harm.
    - The *borrowed servant doctrine* applies to cases in which an employee is lent to another for a particular employment. In such cases, the original employer is not responsible for injuries caused by the negligence of the temporary employer.
    - In cases of *comparative negligence*, a plaintiff found negligent and, therefore, partially responsible, is responsible for his or her proportional share of damages awarded.
    - When the defendant claims that the conduct of the plaintiff is below the standard of care that reasonably prudent persons would exercise for their own safety, the issue is one of *contributory negligence*. In such cases, the lack of ordinary care on the part of the plaintiff, combined with another's negligent act, caused the injury.
    - *Good Samaritan laws* encourage volunteer assistance in emergency situations and protect the volunteers from liability for ordinary negligence in rendering assistance in emergency situations.

- When a third party is determined to be the proximate cause of death or injury, independent of the defendant's original negligence, there exists *intervening cause.*
- If a cause of action is initiated beyond a prescribed period of time, the case cannot proceed according to the *statute of limitations.*

11. Damages, which are usually determined by the jury, come in four forms:
    - *Nominal damages* are a token in recognition that a wrong has been committed. In such cases, the amount of compensation is insignificant.
    - *Compensatory damages* are intended as reparation for detriment or injury sustained.
    - *Hedonic damages* are awarded to compensate the plaintiff for the loss of enjoyment of life. This is supplementary to the compensation offered by compensatory damages.
    - *Punitive damages* are additional monetary awards when an injury is caused by gross carelessness or disregard for others' safety.

REVIEW QUESTIONS

1. Describe the trial process, including pretrial motions and the functions of the judge, jury, and attorneys.
2. Describe the kinds of evidence that a plaintiff can present in order to establish a negligent act.
3. What defenses can a defendant present in order to refute a plaintiff's evidence?
4. Describe how *statutes of limitations* favor defendants in a lawsuit.
5. Describe the differences between *nominal, compensatory, hedonic,* and *punitive* damages.

NOTES

1. *Watkins v. Cleveland Clinic Foundation,* 719 N.E.2d 1052 (Ohio App. 1998). (In April 1995).
2. Kern v. Gulf Coast Nursing Home of Moss Point, Inc., 502 So.2d 1198, 1202 (Miss. 1987).
3. Pierce v. Ortho Pharm. Corp., 417 A.2d 505, 509 (N.J. 1980).
4. Steve Cohen, *Malpractice,* NEW YORKER MAGAZINE, Oct. 1, 1990, at 43, 47.
5. 600 A.2d 1063 (D.C. 1991).
6. James W. McElhaney, *Taking Sides,* 78 A.B.A.J. 82 (1992).
7. 349 N.E.2d 516 (Ill. App. Ct. 1976).
8. 245 So.2d 544 (La. Ct. App. 1971).
9. 696 S.W.2d 16 (Tenn. Ct. App. 1985).
10. Roberts v. Ray, 322 S.W.2d 435 (Tenn. Ct. App. 1958).
11. 503 N.Y.S.2d 131 (N.Y. App. Div. 1986).
12. 337 P.2d 974 (Or. 1959).
13. *Id.* at 975.
14. 221 N.W.2d 39 (S.D. 1974).
15. 786 F.2d 859 (8th Cir. 1986).
16. 405 A.2d 443 (N.J. Sup. Ct. 1979).
17. 335 S.E.2d 712 (Ga. Ct. App. 1985).
18. 689 F. Supp. 465 (E.D. Pa. 1988).
19. Spirito v. Temple Corp., 466 N.E.2d 491 (Ind. Ct. App. 1984).
20. 746 P.2d 1006 (Idaho Ct. App. 1987).
21. 854 S.W.2d 250 (Tex. Ct. App. 1993).
22. 479 So.2d 1119 (Ala. 1985).
23. 488 S.E.2d 389 (W. Va. 1997).
24. 482 N.W.2d 437 (Iowa 1992).
25. 445 N.W.2d 763 (Iowa 1989).
26. 346 S.E.2d 528 (S.C. 1986).
27. 4 N.W.2d 637–639 (Minn. 1942).
28. 738 P.2d 75 (Colo. Ct. App. 1987).
29. 75 N.W.2d 217 (Minn. 1956).
30. 373 N.Y.S.2d 224 (N.Y. App. Div. 1975).
31. 320 A.2d 704 (Del. 1974).
32. 291 N.E.2d 769 (Ohio Ct. App. 1973).
33. 320 A.2d 704 (Del. 1974).
34. Garner v. Crawford, 288 So.2d 886 (La. Ct. App. 1975).
35. 240 So.2d 53, 57 (La. Ct. App. 1970).
36. *Id.* at 55.
37. *Id.* at 57.
38. 340 So.2d 1065 (La. Ct. App. 1976).
39. 657 N.Y.S.2d 419 (N.Y. App. Div. 1997).
40. 154 S.E.2d 461 (Ga. Ct. App. 1967).
41. *Kentucky: Malpractice Limit Struck,* 13 NAT'L L.J. 6 (1990).
42. 25 N.W.2d 351 (Mich. 1949).
43. 320 A.2d 637 (N.H. 1974).
44. *Id.*
45. 952 S.W.2d 53 (Tex. App. 1997).
46. TEX. CIV. PRAC. & REM. CODE ANN. § 101.025 (Vernon 1997).
47. 340 U.S. 135 (1950).
48. 574 F. Supp. 200 (W.D. Tenn. 1982).
49. 463 F. Supp. 321 (D. Alaska 1978).
50. 411 So.2d 109 (Ala. 1982).

51. *Id.* at 114–115.

52. 658 N.Y.S.2d 34 (N.Y. App. Div. 1997).

53. No. 537-907 (Wis. Cir. Ct. Mar. 18, 1983).

54. 310 S.E.2d 326 (N.C. 1984).

55. 411 So.2d 109, 113 (Ala. 1982).

56. 497 So.2d 1233 (Fla. Dist. Ct. App. 1986).

57. 804 S.W.2d 711 (Ark. 1991).

58. 681 F.2d 291 (5th Cir. 1982).

59. 510 So.2d 538 (Ala. 1987).

60. 650 A.2d 1079 (Pa. Super. 1994).

61. Callahan v. Cardinal Glennon Hosp., 863 S.W.2d 852 (Mo. 1993).

62. 512 N.Y.S.2d 519 (N.Y. App. Div. 1987).

63. 362 S.E.2d 273 (N.C. 1987).

Corporate Liability

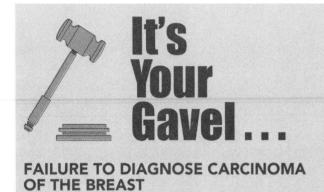

It's Your Gavel...

FAILURE TO DIAGNOSE CARCINOMA OF THE BREAST

The plaintiff/appellee, Condon, in *AA Medical Center v. Condon*,[1] underwent a routine mammogram on July 1, 1988. The mammogram revealed suspicious lesions in her right breast. Dr. Moore performed a biopsy at the AA Medical Center (AAMC). Dr. Williams, who was a pathologist working for Weisburger, MD, PA, a pathology corporation providing contract pathology services to the hospital, performed an evaluation of the tissue. Williams reported noncancerous lesions in the right breast. Moore advised Condon that she did not have cancer. He advised her to undergo frequent mammograms.

Condon, experiencing inflammation of her right breast, consulted with Moore on February 7, 1990. Moore performed another biopsy on February 23, 1990. Condon was advised that the biopsy results indicated invasive carcinoma of the breast. As a result of the diagnosis, Condon underwent a bilateral modified radical mastectomy.

Condon brought a malpractice action against Williams and AAMC. The suit alleged malpractice on the part of Williams for failure to properly diagnose a biopsy as breast cancer. On the eve of the trial, Williams agreed to a $1,000,000 settlement with the plaintiff. The circuit court denied AAMC's request for a summary judgment and entered judgment on a jury verdict in favor of the plaintiff and AAMC appealed, claiming that the release of the agent (Dr. Williams) served to act as a release for the principal (AAMC).

What is your verdict?

INTRODUCTION

This chapter introduces the health care professional to the responsibilities, as well as legal risks, of health care organizations and their governing bodies.

The typical health care organization is incorporated under state law as a freestanding for-profit or not-for-profit corporation. The corporation has a governing body, which is often referred to as a board of directors or board of trustees. The existence of this authority creates certain duties and liabilities for governing boards and their individual members. The governing body has ultimate responsibility for the operation and management of the organization with a necessary delegation of appropriate responsibility to administrative employees and the medical staff. The governing body, or designated persons functioning as the governing body, is legally responsible for establishing and implementing policies regarding the management and operation of the organization.

Not-for-profit health care organizations are usually exempt from federal taxation under Section 501(c)(3) of the Internal Revenue Code of 1986, as amended. Such federal exemption usually entitles the organization to an automatic exemption from state taxes as well. Such tax exemption not only relieves the organization from the payment of income taxes, sales taxes, and the like, but also permits the organization to receive contributions from donors, who then may obtain charitable deductions on their personal tax returns.

Although health care organizations may operate as sole proprietorships or partnerships, most function as corporations. Thus, an important source of law applicable to governing boards and to the duties and responsibilities of their members is found in state corporation laws. An incorporated health care organization is a legal person with recognized rights, duties, powers, and responsibilities. Because the legal "person" is in reality a "fictitious person," there is a requirement that certain humans be designated to exercise the corporate powers and that they be held accountable for corporate decision making. These natural persons comprise the governing body. In an unincorporated organization, one or more natural persons hold the powers and duties. There is no recognized fictitious person.

AUTHORITY OF HEALTH CARE CORPORATIONS

Health care corporations—governmental, charitable, or proprietary—have certain powers expressly or implicitly granted to them by state statutes. Generally, the authority of a corporation is expressed in the law under which the corporation was chartered and in the corporation's articles of incorporation. The existence of this authority creates certain duties and liabilities for governing bodies and their individual members. Members of the governing body of an organization have both express and implied corporate authority.

The governing body is organized to oversee and control all the activities of the corporation. It is therefore essential that the governing body have an appropriate degree of authority. In this way, there will be a rational and practical transition from formulating policy to implementing practice and procedure. Authority is conferred by corporation laws and regulations and by corporate charters.

The governing body is legally responsible for establishing and implementing policies regarding the management and operation of the health care facility. The general responsibilities of the governing body include:

- policy formation
- oversight of the management and operation of the organization
- assurance of the financial viability of the organization
- appointment of a qualified administrator
- provision of a safe physical plant equipped and staffed to maintain services in accordance with any applicable local and state regulations that may apply to federal programs in which the organization participates
- adoption of written policies ensuring the protection of patients' rights
- determination of the frequency of meetings of the governing body and documentation of such meetings
- adoption of a written policy concerning potential conflicts of interest on the part of members of the governing body, the administration, the medical and nursing staff, and other employees who might influence corporate decisions

Express Corporate Authority

Express corporate authority is the authority specifically delegated by statute. A health care corporation derives its authority to act from the laws of the state in which it is incorporated. The articles of incorporation set forth the purpose(s) of the corporation's existence and the powers the corporation is authorized to exercise in order to carry out its purposes.

Implied Corporate Authority

Implied corporate authority is the authority to perform any and all acts necessary to exercise a corporation's expressly conferred authority and to accomplish the purpose(s) for which it was created. Generally, implied corporate authority arises from situations in which such authority is required or suggested as a result of a need for corporate powers not specifically granted in the articles of incorporation. A governing body, at its own discretion, may enact new bylaws, rules, and regulations; purchase or mortgage property; borrow money; purchase equipment; select personnel; adopt corporate resolutions that delineate decision-making responsibilities; etc. These powers can be enumerated in the articles of incorporation and, in such cases, would be categorized as express rather than implied corporate authority.

Ultra Vires Acts

A governing body can be held liable for acting beyond its scope of authority, which is either expressed (e.g., in its articles of incorporation) or implied in law. Acts of this nature are referred to as *ultra vires acts.* The governing body acts in and on behalf of the corporation. If any action is in violation of a statute or regulation, it is illegal. An example of an illegal act would be the employment of an unlicensed person in a position that by law requires a license. The state, through its attorney general, has the power to prevent the performance of an *ultra vires* act by injunction. Governing bodies should have their corporate charters reviewed periodically by legal counsel to make certain that their express powers are consistent with the activities in which they presently engage or plan to undertake in the future.

In certain circumstances, members of an organization's governing body, as well as its corporate officers, may be individually responsible for *ultra vires* acts. This might be true, for example, if a member of a governing body or a corporate officer exceeded the powers of the corporation for individual benefit.

The court of appeals in *Queen of Angels Hospital v. Younger*[2] held that the primary purpose of the corporation was the operation of a hospital and that the corporation could not abandon its operation in favor of neighborhood clinics. The hospital's board intended to use a substantial portion of funds it received from leasing the hospital to establish and operate additional medical clinics. Services provided by the Franciscan Sisters from the inception of the hospital were considered donated with the exception of certain compensated services, and no future remuneration was expected. The sisters' motherhouse had requested funds for a retirement plan. The court of appeals held that the retirement plan was not a proper exercise of either sound business judgment or the fiduciary duties of the Queen of Angels Hospital board. It is clear in this case that a governing body is acting beyond its scope of authority if it diverts funds to support activities not provided for in the hospital's articles of incorporation.

CORPORATE ORGANIZATION AND COMMITTEE STRUCTURE

Ultimate responsibility for the functioning of a health care corporation rests with the governing body. Ideally, the governing body includes representation from both the community and the organization's medical staff. The business of the governing body is generally conducted through a variety of committees. Some of those committees are described below.

Executive Committee

The executive committee is a committee of the governing body that is delegated authority to act on behalf of the full board. It must act within the scope and authority assigned by the governing body. The duties and responsibilities of the committee should be delineated in the corporate bylaws. The functions of the executive committee generally include: acting as a liaison between management and the full board, reviewing and making recommendations on management proposals, and performing special assignments as may be delegated by the full board from time to time. Business transacted and actions taken by the executive committee should be reported at regular sessions of the governing body and ratified. The executive committee generally has all the powers of the governing body, except such powers as the governing body may be prohibited from delegating in accordance with applicable laws.

Bylaws Committee

The bylaws committee reviews and recommends bylaws changes to the governing body. Bylaws generally are amended or rescinded by a majority vote of the governing body.

Finance Committee

The finance committee is responsible for overseeing the financial affairs of the organization and making recommendations to the governing body. The committee is responsible for directing and reviewing the preparation of financial statements, operating budgets, major capital requests, etc. The governing body must approve actions of the committee. Representation on the committee should include the chief executive officer (CEO) and the chief financial officer (CFO).

Joint Conference Committee

The joint conference committee is often an informal committee consisting of an equal number of representatives from both the executive committees of the governing body and medical staff, along with representation from administration and nursing. The committee acts as a forum for discussion of matters of policy and practice pertaining to patient care. The committee generally meets quarterly and reports on its activities to the governing body.

Nominating Committee

The nominating committee is generally responsible for developing and recommending to the governing body criteria for governing body membership. The requirements for membership on a governing body generally include: a willingness to devote the time and energy necessary to fulfill the commitment as a board member; residence in the community or an identifiable association with the community served; demonstration of a knowledge of local health care issues; possession of the traits of good moral character and maturity; and professional, as well as appropriate, life experiences necessary to make managerial decisions in the health care setting.

Planning Committee

The planning committee is responsible for recommending to the governing body the use and development of organizational resources as they relate to the mission and vision of the organization. The committee develops a plan and oversees its implementation throughout the organization. Major issues that the planning committee reviews include the organization's need to: increase market share, expand services, downsize where appropriate, and integrate services across the entire continuum of care in a competitive marketplace. Specifically, the planning committee oversees:

- periodic review of the mission statement
- development of strategic plans and ongoing monitoring
- development of short-term and long-range goals
- maintenance of the organization's physical facilities
- preparation of capital budgets
- oversight of expansion programs
- acquisition of major equipment
- addition of new services
- downsizing and the deletion of services
- regular planning progress reports to the governing body
- program development
- corporate development

The committee generally includes representation from the administration, governing body, medical staff, and nursing. When organizational planning affects the delivery of patient care services, a mechanism for obtaining community input is incorporated into the planning process.

Patient Care Committee

The patient care committee reviews the quality of patient care rendered in the organization and makes recommendations for the improvement of such care. The committee is generally responsible for developing a process to identify patient and family needs and expectations and to establish a process to continuously improve customer relationships. This process should include:

- the development of a tool to identify patient and family needs and expectations

- a methodology for reviewing data
- identification of patterns of concern
- a mechanism for forwarding information to those responsible for implementing change in the organization
- a continuing review, evaluation, and implementation of plans for improving organizational performance

An effective committee should contain membership from the governing body, medical staff, nursing, administration, and appropriate ancillary departments. Actions and/or recommendations are reported to the governing body.

Audit Committee

The audit committee is responsible for the assessment of various functions and control systems of the organization and for providing management with analysis and recommendations regarding activities reviewed. Health care organizations must be vigilant in conducting their financial affairs. As the boards of several investment organizations have experienced in recent years, failure to do so can result in major lawsuits, both civil and criminal. An effective audit committee can be extremely helpful in uncovering and thwarting poor or inept financial decision making. The committee should include members from the governing body and internal auditing staff. Responsibilities of the committee include:

- developing corporate auditing policies and procedures
- recommending independent auditors to the governing body
- reviewing the credentials of the independent auditors and facilitating change in auditors as may be deemed appropriate
- reviewing with independent auditors the proposed scope and general extent of their auditing duties and responsibilities
- reviewing the scope and results of the annual audit with the independent auditors and the organization's management staff
- setting, overseeing, reviewing, and acting on the recommendations of the internal audit staff
- reviewing the internal accounting practices of the corporation, including policies and procedures
- reviewing and evaluating financial statements (e.g., income statements, balance sheets, cash flow reports, investment accounts)
- promoting the prevention, detection, deterrence, and reporting of fraud
- reviewing the means for safeguarding assets, and, as appropriate, the existence of such assets
- ensuring that financial reporting functions are in keeping with generally accepted accounting principles

• reviewing the reliability and integrity of financial and operating information

Failure on the part of an audit committee to question management's representations may be the basis for committee malfeasance, because the committee and the governing body may be held liable for their failure to know what they were responsible for recognizing.

Safety Committee

The safety committee is generally charged with responsibility for overseeing the organization's safety management program. The committee reviews and acts on reports involving the organization's:

• emergency preparedness program/disaster planning
• equipment management program (a program for ensuring user training; new equipment testing; and proper documentation of all repairs, maintenance, and contracted preventative maintenance services, including biomedical, clinical, and electrical equipment)
• life safety program
• risk management program
• safety management program
• utilities management program

DOCTRINE OF *RESPONDEAT SUPERIOR*

Respondeat superior (let the master respond) is the legal doctrine holding employers liable, in certain cases, for the wrongful acts of their agents (employees). This doctrine also has been referred to as *vicarious liability*, whereby an employer is answerable for the torts committed by employees. In the health care setting, an organization, for example, is liable for the negligent acts of its employees, even though there has been no wrongful conduct on the part of the organization. For liability to be imputed to the employer:

1. A master–servant relationship must exist between the employer and the employee; and
2. The wrongful act of the employee must have occurred within the scope of his or her employment.

The question of liability frequently rests on whether persons treating a patient are independent agents (responsible for their own acts) or employees of the organization. The answer to this depends on whether the organization can exercise control over the particular act that was the proximate cause of the injury.

The basic rationale for imposing liability on an employer developed because the employer possesses the right to control the physical acts of its employees. It is not necessary that the employer actually exercise control, but only that it possesses the right, power, or authority to do so.

Generally, the plaintiff's attorney will file suit against both employer and employee. This occurs because the employer is generally in a better financial condition to cover the judgment.

The employer is not without remedy if liability has been imposed against it under *respondeat superior* for an employee's negligent act. Because the law holds negligent persons responsible for their negligent acts, employees are not absolved from liability when a health care facility is held liable through the application of *respondeat superior*. Not only may the injured party sue the employee directly, but also the employer, if sued, may seek indemnification (i.e., compensation for the financial loss caused by the employee's negligent act) from the employee.

EMERGENCY DEPARTMENT PHYSICIAN—HOSPITAL LIABLE

Citation: *Citron v. Northern Dutchess Hosp.*, 603 N.Y.S.2d 639 (N.Y. App. Div. 1993)

Facts

A deceased patient's husband instituted an action against a hospital for negligence, asserting that it failed to have blood products available for his wife, who suffered a ruptured uterus. The patient, 26 weeks pregnant, had complained to her obstetrician about back pain, cramps, and nausea. She was told to go to the hospital's emergency department. It was determined by personnel there that she was suffering from intra-abdominal bleeding. While undergoing surgery performed by her obstetrician, it was learned that her uterus had ruptured. Four hours following surgery, she died of anoxia due to loss of one-half of her total blood. Other than with her obstetrician, she had no physician–patient relationship with any of the emergency department physicians. The trial court jury found in favor of the plaintiff, and the hospital appealed.

Issue

Can a hospital be held vicariously liable for an independent physician's negligent acts, if the patient enters the emergency department and seeks treatment from the hospital, and not a specific physician?

Holding

The New York Supreme Court, Appellate Division, upheld the trial court's decision, finding that the hospital was vicariously liable for the acts of its emergency department physicians, which included treating the deceased without having the necessary blood products available.

Reason

Although neither the patient nor her husband asked for a specific physician once she was admitted to the emergency department, the court found that she could properly assume that the treating physicians and staff of the hospital were acting on behalf of the hospital. Expert testimony had revealed that the failure to provide the decedent with proper blood products was a major factor in her death. The court further held that it was a deviation from accepted practice for the hospital not to have platelets on hand or "available within one hour."

Discussion

1. What steps should the hospital take to prevent further incidents of this nature?
2. What issues do you see as to the assessment and reassessment of the patient's needs?

Radiologist Not Liable for Technician's Negligence

Mr. Oberzan brought a medical malpractice action against a hospital radiologist for injuries allegedly incurred while being prepared by an X-ray technician for a barium enema.[3] Oberzan admitted to the following nine facts:

1. The pretrial questionnaire prepared by the plaintiff alleges that Dr. Smith or his X-ray technician perforated the plaintiff's rectum during the barium enema procedure.
2. Dr. Jones referred the plaintiff to Dr. Smith for the barium enema procedure.
3. The usual procedure for performing barium enemas is that the X-ray technician inserts the enema tip for the barium enema and then gets Dr. Smith to begin the ex-

amination. All patients are in the prone position with the tip in place when Dr. Smith walks into the room.
4. With respect to the plaintiff, when Dr. Smith walked into the room, the plaintiff was already lying in the prone position with the tip already inserted by the technician.
5. In February 1988, Ms. Davis was employed by Maude Norton Hospital as an X-ray technician.
6. As an X-ray technician, Ms. Davis was trained to prep patients for examinations, which would include inserting enema tubes for barium enemas.
7. Ms. Davis inserted the enema tip into the rectum of the plaintiff for the barium enema before Dr. Smith entered the room for the procedure.
8. After Dr. Smith entered the room, the exam began. Immediately after Ms. Davis began injecting the barium, she noticed bleeding at the tip of the rectum.
9. After the procedure was halted, Dr. Smith immediately contacted Dr. Jones to inform him of the bleeding.

Oberzan claimed the physician was vicariously liable for the employee's negligent conduct. The Kansas Supreme Court held that the *respondeat superior* doctrine did not apply to the relationship between the technician employed by the hospital and the radiologist so as to impose vicarious liability on the radiologist. Administrative regulation did not impose a legal duty on the radiologist to personally supervise the enema procedure.

Davis was not an employee of Smith. She was not under his direct supervision and control at the time the injury occurred. Smith did not select Davis to perform the insertion of the enema tip; she was assigned by the hospital. Vicarious liability under *respondeat superior* did not impose liability on Smith. The master–servant relationship was not established because Smith was not exercising personal control or supervision over Davis, a nonemployee, at the time of injury. Oberzan admitted that "[t]he usual procedure for performing barium enemas is that the X-ray technician inserts the enema tip for the barium enema and then gets Dr. Smith to begin the examination."

Mr. Oberzan argued that Kansas law, K.A.R. 28–34–86(a) ("the radiology department and all patient services rendered therein shall be under the supervision of a designated medical staff physician; wherever possible, this physician shall be attending or consulting radiologist"), imposes a duty on radiologists to supervise patient services rendered in a hospital radiology department. However, none of the K.A.R. 28–34–12 subsections require that the preparation of a patient for a barium enema be performed under a physician's direct supervision. The purpose of K.A.R. 28–34–12(c) is to establish an administrative head for the radiology department. Mr. Oberzan cited no authority in support of his position that K.A.R. 28–34–12(c) creates a legal duty for a designated medical staff physician to personally control and supervise all activities that occur in a radiology department. The construction suggested by Mr. Oberzan would create physician liability extending far beyond the intent of the regulation.

 RADIOLOGIST—HOSPITAL NOT LIABLE

Citation: *Hoffman v. Moore Reg'l Hosp., Inc., 441 S.E.2d 567 (N.C. Ct. App. 1994)*

Facts

Mrs. Hoffman was admitted to the hospital by Dr. Neal, her attending physician, with an order for a renal arteriogram. The hospital informed Neal that he could not order the procedure because he did not have staff privileges at the hospital. Therefore, Neal made arrangements with Dr. Daughtridge to order the procedure. After her admission, Hoffman was presented with a consent form for the procedure. The consent listed five radiologists on the form but did not specify which radiologist would perform the procedure. The list of radiologists was composed of members of the Pinehurst radiology group. The group determined which radiologist would cover the hospital each day. Dr. Lina was assigned to perform Hoffman's procedure. Following the renal arteriogram, Lina determined that an angioplasty was necessary. Because of complications during the procedure, Hoffman had to be transferred to University Medical Center. Her condition deteriorated during the following year and she eventually died. Mr. Hoffman then sought to hold the hospital liable for the negligence of the radiologist under the theory of *respondeat superior*. The trial court granted partial summary judgment against the hospital, dismissing the claim that the hospital was liable under the theory of *respondeat superior*.

Issue

Was the hospital liable for the malpractice of Lina under the theory of *respondeat superior*?

Holding

The North Carolina Court of Appeals held that the hospital was not liable for the negligence of Lina under the theory of *respondeat superior*.

Reason

The court of appeals held that Lina was not an employee of the hospital. He was not subject to supervision or control by the hospital. There was no evidence that Hoffman would have sought treatment elsewhere if she had known for a fact that Lina was not an employee.

Discussion

1. Under what conditions could the hospital have been liable for Lina's alleged negligence?
2. Can the patient recover damages from the radiologist who performed the radiologic procedure?
3. Can the patient recover damages from the Pinehurst radiology group?

Joint Tort-Feasors and Vicarious Liability

Joint liability is based on the concept that all joint or concurrent tort-feasors are actually independently at fault for their own wrongful acts. Where a hospital's liability is solely vicarious, it and the physician, for example, could not be considered joint tort-feasors. Thus, when liability of the principal is solely vicarious in nature and is not based upon the principal's independent actionable fault, a release of the agent acts as a release of the principal as a matter of law."[4] If it can be established that a hospital is only vicariously liable, the release of a physician would preclude further recovery against the hospital. "It is unlikely that an agent would ever settle with a plaintiff if he still remained liable to indemnify his principal for any further amount the principal might be compelled to pay to the plaintiff."[5]

"If a plaintiff, under such a hypothetical scheme, were able to find an agent willing to settle, to allow the plaintiff then to proceed additionally against a vicariously liable principal, would, in essence, permit the plaintiff 'two bites out of the same apple.' If the principal could then seek indemnity from the agent, the agent's earlier settlement would be of little solace to him. Such a double exposure would act as a disincentive for agents ever to agree to a settlement."[6]

Independent Contractor

The plaintiff has the burden for establishing an employee–employer relationship. This can be difficult, especially in the case of independent physicians.

In the instance of wrongful conduct by an independent contractor, the doctrine of *respondeat superior* does not apply. An *independent contractor* relationship is established when the principal has no right of control over the manner in which the agent's work is to be performed. The independent contractor therefore is responsible for his or her own negligent acts. However, some cases indicate that an organization may be held liable for an independent contractor's negligence. For example, in *Mehlman v. Powell*,[7] the court held that a hospital may be found vicariously liable for the negligence of an emergency department physician who was not a hospital employee but who worked in the emergency department in the capacity of an independent contractor. The court reasoned that the hospital maintained control over billing procedures, maintained an emergency department in the main hospital, and represented to the patient that the members of the emergency department staff were its employees, which may have caused the patient to rely on the skill and competence of the staff.

The doctrine of *respondeat superior* may impose liability on an organization for a nurse's acts or omissions that result in injury to a patient. Whether such liability attaches depends on whether the conduct of the nurse was wrongful and whether the nurse was subject to the control of the organization at the time the act in question was performed. Determination of whether the nurse's conduct was wrongful in a given situation depends on the standard of conduct to which the nurse is expected to adhere. In liability deliberations, the nurse who is subject to the control of the organization at the time of the negligent conduct is considered an employee and is not the borrowed servant of a staff physician or surgeon.

Corporate Officer/Trustee

An officer or a director of a corporation is not, merely as a result of his or her position, personally liable for the torts of corporate employees. To incur liability, the officer or the director ordinarily must be shown to have in some way authorized, directed, or participated in a tortious act. The administrator of the estate of the deceased in *Hunt v. Rabon*[8] brought a malpractice action against hospital trustees and others for the wrongful death of the decedent during an operation at the hospital. A contractor had incorrectly crossed the oxygen and nitrous oxide lines of a newly installed medical gas system leading to the operating room. The trustees demurred to the complaint on the grounds that it failed to present facts sufficient for an action against them individually as trustees. The lower court sustained the demurrer, and the plaintiff appealed. On appeal, the South Carolina Supreme Court held that the allegations presented were insufficient to hold the trustees liable for the wrongs alleged.

CORPORATE NEGLIGENCE

There are duties that the corporation itself owes to the general public and to its patients. These duties arise from statutes, regulations, principles of law developed by the courts, and the internal operating rules of the organization. A corporation is treated no differently than an individual. If a corporation has a duty to fulfill and fails to do so, it has the same liability to the injured party as an individual would have.

> Corporate negligence is a doctrine under which the hospital is liable if it fails to uphold the proper standard of care owed the patient, which is to ensure the patient's safety and well-being while at the hospital. This theory of liability creates a nondelegable duty which the hospital owes directly to a patient. Therefore, an injured party does not have to rely on and establish the negligence of a third party.[9]

Corporate negligence occurs when a health care corporation fails to perform those duties it owes directly to a patient or to anyone else to whom a duty may extend. If such a duty is breached and a patient is injured as a result of that breach, the organization can be held culpable under the theory of corporate negligence.

Evolution of Corporate Negligence

Hospitals once enjoyed complete tort immunity as charitable institutions. As hospitals evolved into more sophisticated corporate entities that expected fees for its services, their tort immunity receded. Courts first recognized that hospitals could be held liable for the negligence of their employees under the theory of *respondeat superior*. Liability later extended for nonemployees who acted as a hospital's ostensible agents. In *Thompson v. Nason Hospital*,[10] the evolution continued. The Pennsylvania court recognized that hospitals are more than mere conduits through which health care professionals are brought into contact with patients. Hospitals owe some nondelegable duties directly to their patients independent of the negligence of their employees or ostensible agents, such as a duty to:

- use reasonable care in the maintenance of safe and adequate facilities and equipment
- select and retain only competent physicians
- oversee all persons who practice medicine within their walls as to patient care
- formulate, adopt, and enforce adequate rules and policies to ensure quality care for their patients

Darling—A Benchmark Case

The benchmark case in the health care field, which has had a major impact on the liability of health care organizations, was decided in 1965 in *Darling v. Charleston Community Memorial Hospital*.[11] The court here enunciated a corporate negligence doctrine under which hospitals have a duty to provide adequately trained medical and nursing staff. A hospital is responsible, in conjunction with its medical staff, for establishing policies and procedures for monitoring the quality of medicine practiced within the hospital.

The *Darling* case involved an 18-year-old college football player who was preparing for a career as a teacher and coach. The patient, a defensive halfback for his college football team, was injured during a play. He was rushed to the emergency department of a small, accredited community hospital where the only physician on emergency duty that day was Dr. Alexander, a general practitioner. Alexander had not treated a major leg fracture for three years.

The physician examined the patient and ordered an X-ray that revealed that the tibia and the fibula of the right leg had been fractured. The physician reduced the fracture and applied a plaster cast from a point three or four inches below the groin to the toes. Shortly after the cast had been applied, the patient began to complain continually of pain. The physician split the cast and continued to visit the patient frequently while the patient remained in the hospital. Not thinking it was necessary, the emergency department physician did not call in any specialist for consultation.

After two weeks, the student was transferred to a larger hospital and placed under the care of an orthopaedic surgeon. The specialist found a considerable amount of dead tissue in the fractured leg. During a period of two months, the specialist removed increasing amounts of tissue in a futile attempt to save the leg until it became necessary to amputate the leg eight inches below the knee. The student's father did not agree to a settlement and filed suit against the emergency department physician and the hospital. Although the physician later settled out of court for $40,000, the case continued against the hospital.

The documentary evidence relied on to establish the standard of care included: the rules and regulations of the Illinois Department of Public Health under the Hospital Licensing Act; the standards for hospital accreditation of the Joint Commission on Accreditation of Healthcare Organizations; and the bylaws, rules, and regulations of Charleston Hospital. These documents were admitted into evidence without objection. No specific evidence was offered that the hospital had failed to conform to the usual and customary practices of hospitals in the community.

The trial court instructed the jury to consider those documents, along with all other evidence, in determining the hospital's liability. Under the circumstances in which the case reached the Illinois Supreme Court, it was held that the verdict against the hospital should be sustained if the evidence supported the verdict on any one or more of the 20 allegations of negligence. Allegations asserted that the hospital was negligent in its failure to: (1) provide a sufficient number of trained nurses for bedside care of all patients at all times—in this case, nurses who were capable of recognizing the progressive gangrenous condition of the plaintiff's right leg; and (2) failure of its nurses to bring the patient's condition to the attention of the hospital administration and staff so that adequate consultation could be secured and the condition rectified.

Although these generalities provided the jury with no practical guidance for determining what constitutes reasonable care, they were considered relevant to aid the jury in deciding what was feasible and what the hospital knew or should have known concerning hospital responsibilities for the proper care of a patient. There was no expert testimony characterizing when the professional care rendered by the attending physician should have been reviewed, who should have reviewed it, or whether the case required consultation.

Evidence relating to the hospital's failure to review Alexander's work, to require consultation or examination by specialists, and to require proper nursing care was found to be sufficient to support a verdict for the patient. Judgment was eventually returned against the hospital in the amount of $100,000.

The Illinois Supreme Court held that the hospital could not limit its liability as a charitable corporation to the amount of its liability insurance.

> [T]he doctrine of charitable immunity can no longer stand . . . a doctrine which limits the liability of charitable corporations to the amount of liability insurance that they see fit to carry permits them to determine whether or not they will be liable for their torts and the amount of that liability, if any.[12]

In effect, the hospital was liable as a corporate entity for the negligent acts of its employees and physicians. Among other things, the *Darling* case indicates the importance of instituting effective credentialing and continuing medical evaluation and review programs for all members of a professional staff.

Hospitals Provide More than Room and Board

Traditionally, hospitals were organizations that provided the tools and a place where physicians could practice their trade. Now, hospitals are responsible for providing more than room and board; they have a duty and responsibility to properly select and monitor physicians. In *Fridena v. Evans*,[13] the Arizona Supreme Court affirmed that the hospital could be held liable for the negligent supervision of a physician where it has actual or constructive knowledge of the procedures carried on within the hospital. The patient in this case was involved in a motorcycle-automobile accident when she was 15 years old. She suffered a serious injury to her right leg, which required surgery. After surgery by Dr. Fridena, it was noted that the patient's right leg was one and one-half inches shorter than her left leg. The surgeon later attempted to lengthen the leg, which resulted in its being three inches shorter than before. The second operation gave rise to the malpractice suit, resulting in a $300,000 jury award to the patient.

Responsibility for Staff Competency

Hospitals have a duty to ensure the competency of their medical staffs and to evaluate the quality of medical treatment rendered on their premises. A court of appeals in *Elam v. College Park Hospital*[14] held that a hospital is liable to a patient under the doctrine of corporate negligence for the negligent conduct of independent physicians and surgeons who are neither employees nor agents of the hospital.

DUTIES OF HEALTH CARE CORPORATIONS

Along with the corporate authority that is granted to the governing body, duties are attached to its individual members. These responsibilities are considered duties because they are imposed by law and they can be enforced in legal proceedings. Membership on a governing body should not be considered merely a recognition of social or community standing or financial well-being. Governing body members are considered by law to have the highest measure of accountability. They have a fiduciary duty that requires acting primarily for the benefit of the corporation. The general duties of a governing body are both implied and express. Failure of a governing body to fulfill these duties may constitute mismanagement of such a degree that the appointment of a receiver to manage the affairs of the corporation may be warranted.

The duty to supervise and manage is applicable to the trustees as it is to the managers of any other business corporation. In both instances, there is a duty to act as a reasonably prudent person would act under similar circumstances. The governing body must act prudently in administering the affairs of the organization and exercise its powers in good faith.

The basic management functions of the governing body include

- selection of corporate officers and agents
- general control over the compensation of such agents
- delegation of authority to the CEO/administrator and the administrator's subordinates for administrative actions
- selection and monitoring of the medical staff members and the delineation of clinical privileges
- establishment of organizational goals, policies, and procedures
- supervision and vigilance over the welfare and assets of the corporation

Specific management duties peculiar to health care organizations include: (1) determining the policies of the organization in connection with community health needs, (2) maintaining proper professional standards in the organization, (3) assuming a general responsibility for adequate patient care throughout the organization, and (4) providing adequate financing of patient care and assuming business-like control of expenditures.

Duties Specified by Corporate Law

A corporation has certain duties that are specified by the state's corporation laws. These include

- duty to hold meetings
- duty to establish policy
- financial duties
- duty to provide adequate insurance
- duty to pay taxes

The general duty to use due care in the management of the property and assets of an organization and the specific duty to manage its financial aspects include maintenance of the physical plant and appropriating funds for such purpose as necessary. The governing body has a duty to protect the organization from the risk of loss because of fire, other destruction, or liability for the negligence of its employees. The governing body has a duty to pay all taxes that become due on any property so that no penalties are incurred.

Duty To Appoint the Chief Executive Officer

Members of the governing body are responsible for appointing a CEO to act as their agent in the management of the organization. The CEO is responsible for the day-to-day operations of the organization. The individual selected as CEO must possess the competence and the character necessary to maintain satisfactory standards of patient care within the organization.

The responsibilities and authority of the CEO should be expressed in an appropriate job description, as well as in any formal agreement or contract that the organization has with the CEO. State health codes describe the responsibilities of administrators in broad terms. They generally provide that the CEO/administrator shall be responsible for the overall management of the organization; enforcement of any applicable federal, state, and local regulations, as well as the organization's bylaws, policies, and procedures; appointment of, with the approval of the governing body, a qualified medical director; liaison between the governing body and the medical and organization staff; and appointment of an administrative person to act during the CEO's absence from the organization.

The failure to remove an incompetent CEO or any other incapable agent of the organization is as much a breach of a governing body's duty as is its failure to appoint competent employees. Termination of a CEO because of incompetence must be in accordance with organization bylaws, which should set forth the CEO's due process rights. These rights should be included in an appropriately written contract for the CEO.

The general duty of a governing body is to exercise due care and diligence in supervising and managing the organization. This duty does not cease with the selection of a competent CEO. A governing body can be liable if the level of patient care becomes inadequate because of the governing body's failure to supervise properly the management of the organization. CEOs, as is the case with board members, can be personally liable for their own acts of negligence that injure others.

In some health care organizations, the CEO fills a dual role by serving as a member of the governing body in addition to his or her position as the organization's chief executive officer. When the CEO is a board member, he or she frequently serves in the capacity as secretary of the board.

Duty To Ensure that Nursing Facility Administrators Are Licensed

Federal law requires that nursing facility administrators be appropriately licensed.

- *Section 431.702, State Plan Requirement.* A state plan must provide that the state has a program for licensing administrators of nursing homes that meets the requirements of Section 431.703 through 431.713 of this subpart.[15]
- *Section 431.703, Licensing Requirement.* The state licensing program must provide that only nursing homes supervised by an administrator licensed in accordance with the requirement of this subpart may operate in the state.[16]
- *Section 431.713, Continuing Study and Investigation.* The agency or board must conduct a continuing study of nursing homes and administrators within the state to improve: (1) licensing standards and (2) the procedures and methods for enforcing the standards.[17]

To comply with federal requirements, the various states have incorporated licensing requirements in their regulations. Administrators are licensed under the laws of their individual states. Statutes generally provide that the administrator of a nursing facility be licensed in accordance with state law.

States that require administrators to be licensed provide penalties ranging from fines to imprisonment for those ad-

ministrators functioning without a license. A $5,000 fine was imposed on a nursing facility for operating without a licensed administrator for 54 days in *Magnolias Nursing and Convalescent Center v. Department of Health and Rehabilitation Services.*[18] The statute prohibiting operation of a nursing home without a licensed administrator was not considered vague, ambiguous, or unconstitutional.

Duty To Comply with Statutes, Rules, and Regulations

The governing body in general and its agents (assigned representatives) in particular are responsible for compliance with federal, state, and local rules and regulations regarding the operation of the organization. Depending on the scope of the wrong committed and the intent of the governing body, failure to comply could subject the board members and/or their agents to civil liability and, in some instances, to criminal prosecution.

Failure to comply with applicable statutory regulations can be costly. This was the case in *People v. Casa Blanca Convalescent Homes,*[19] in which there was evidence of numerous and prolonged deficiencies in resident care. The nursing home's practice of providing insufficient personnel constituted not only illegal practice but also unfair business practice in violation of Section 17200 of the California Business and Professions Code. The trial court was found to have properly assessed a fine of $2,500 for each of 67 violations, totaling $167,500, where the evidence showed that the operator of the nursing home had the financial ability to pay that amount.

Duty To Comply with Joint Commission on Accreditation of Healthcare Organizations Standards

The governing body, if accredited by the Joint Commission on Accreditation of Healthcare Organizations, is responsible for compliance with applicable standards promulgated by the Joint Commission. Noncompliance could cause an organization to lose accreditation, which in turn would provide grounds for third-party reimbursement agencies (e.g., Medicare) to refuse payment for treatment rendered to patients.

Duty To Provide Propitious Treatment

Health care organizations can be held liable for delays in treatment that result in injuries to their patients. For example, the patient in *Heddinger v. Ashford Memorial Com-*

munity Hospital[20] filed a malpractice action against a hospital and its insurer, alleging that a delay in treating her left hand resulted in the loss of her little finger. Medical testimony presented at trial indicated that if proper and timely treatment had been rendered, the finger would have been saved. The U.S. District Court entered judgment on a jury verdict for the plaintiff in the amount of $175,000. The hospital appealed, and the U.S. Court of Appeals held that even if the physicians who attended the patient were not employees of the hospital but were independent contractors, the risk of negligent treatment was clearly foreseeable by the hospital. The court also held that although the award of damages was high, it was not so excessive as to require appellate reversal.

Duty To Avoid Self-Dealing and Conflict-of-Interest Situations

There should be full disclosure of each board member's dealings with the organization. Transactions between a board member and an organization must be just and reasonable. Governing body members must refrain from self-dealing and avoid conflict of interest situations.

An organization's governing body should require in its bylaws that each director accepting a position on the governing body submit in writing all outstanding voting shares (where applicable) or any relationships or transactions in which the director might or could have a conflict of interest. On those occasions that there are transactions between governing body members and the organization, there should be full disclosure of each board member's dealings with the organization.

Membership on the governing body or its committees should not be used for private gain. Board members are expected to disclose potential conflict-of-interest situations and withdraw from the boardroom at the time of voting on such issues. Board members who suspect a conflict-of-interest situation have a right and a duty to raise pertinent questions regarding any potential conflict. Conflict of interest is presumed to exist when a board member or a firm with which he or she is associated may benefit or lose from the passage of a proposed action.

Membership on the governing body of a nonprofit organization is deemed a public service. Neither the court nor the community expects or desires such public service to be turned to private gain. Thus, the standards imposed on board members regarding the investment of trust funds, self-dealing transactions, or personal compensation may be stricter than are those for directors of business corporations. The essential rules regarding self-dealing are clear. Generally, a contract between the organization and a trustee financially interested in the transaction is voidable by the organization in the event that the interested trustee spoke or voted in favor of the arrangement or did not disclose fully the material facts regarding his or her interest. This resolution of the self-dealing problem is based on the belief that if an interested board member does not participate in the governing body's action and does make full disclosure of his or her interest, the disinterested remaining members of the governing body are able to protect the organization's interests. If the fairness of the transaction is questioned, the burden of establishing fairness falls on the trustee involved.

Underlying the controversy of self-dealing is the knowledge that sometimes the most advantageous contract for an organization would be with one of its trustees or with a company in which the director is interested. These considerations are of great importance when dealings between a charitable corporation and a member of the governing body are involved. A rule denying this opportunity to the corporation would be too severe. However, statutory provisions in some states specifically forbid self-dealing transactions altogether, irrespective of disclosure or the fairness of the deal.

Duty To Provide Adequate Staff

Failure to comply with regulations relating to the professional staff can have serious consequences. Organizations that fail to meet federal standards can lose certification as a provider of health care services. This could lead to the denial of reimbursement under federal entitlement programs.

Calls for Help

Health care organizations must provide for adequate staffing. The court of appeal in *Leavitt v. St. Tammany Parish Hospital*[21] held that the hospital owed a duty to respond promptly to patient calls for help. The hospital breached its duty by having less than adequate staff on hand and by failing to at least verbally answer an assistance light to inquire what the patient needed.

Postoperative Care

The patient in *Czubinsky v. Doctors Hospital*,[22] recovering from anesthesia, went into cardiac arrest and sustained permanent damages. The court of appeals held that the injuries sustained by the patient were the direct result of the hospital's failure to properly monitor and render aid when needed in the immediate postoperative period. The registered nurse assigned to the patient had a duty to remain with her until the patient was transferred to the recovery room. The nurse's absence was the proximate cause of the patient's injuries. Failure of the hospital to provide adequate staff to assist the patient in the immediate postoperative period was an act in dereliction of duty—a failure that resulted in readily foreseeable permanent damages.

Nursing Facility Staffing

Residents in nursing facilities must be under the care and supervision of a physician. Provision should be made by the facility to obtain the services of at least one physician to oversee the quality of medical care.

Federal and state regulations are explicit with regard to the numbers, qualifications, and duties of the nursing staff. The federal rules relating to nursing services that must be provided are found in Omnibus Budget Reconciliation Act (OBRA) and state health regulations.

The states are more exacting than the Medicare regulations in expressing nurse-resident ratios. In *Koelbl v. Whalen*,[23] regulations requiring the employment of sufficient personnel to provide for resident needs in nursing or convalescent homes were found to be sufficiently clear to avoid their being held unconstitutionally vague. State regulations vary in the methods used to establish staffing requirements. State regulations are often developed to ensure that the resident receives treatment, therapies, medications, and nourishment as prescribed in the resident care plans; the resident is kept clean, comfortable, and well groomed; and the resident is protected from accident, infection, etc.

In addition to nurses and physicians, a variety of other health care workers in nursing facilities support the care and services provided to residents. They include dietitians, physical therapists, social workers, activity directors, etc. The members of this group have specialized training and usually are licensed or certified by the state to practice their specialties. They differ from the medical or nursing staff in that they may not be involved with all residents, but rather limit their activities to residents needing their special skills.

Care Given Deceased Was Deficient

In *Montgomery Health Care Facility v. Ballard*,[24] three nurses testified that the facility was understaffed. "One nurse testified that she asked her supervisor for more help but that she did not get it."[25] The estate of a nursing home resident, who had expired as the result of multiple infected bedsores, brought a malpractice action against the nursing home. First American Health Care, Inc., is the parent corporation of the Montgomery Health Care Facility, a nursing home. The trial court entered a judgment on a jury verdict against the home, and an appeal was taken. The Alabama Supreme Court held that reports compiled by the Alabama Department of Public Health concerning deficiencies found in the nursing home were admissible as evidence. Evidence showed that the care given to the deceased was deficient in the same ways as noted in the survey and complaint reports, which indicated that deficiencies in the home included:

> [I]nadequate documentation of treatment given for decubitus ulcers; 23 patients found with decubitus ulcers, 10 of whom developed those ulcers in the facility; dressings on the sores were not changed as ordered; nursing progress notes did not describe patients' ongoing conditions, particularly with respect to descriptions of decubitus ulcers; ineffective policies and procedures with respect to sterile dressing supplies; lack of nursing assessments; incomplete patient care plans; inadequate documentation of doctor's visits, orders or progress notes; a.m. care not consistently documented; inadequate documentation of turning of patients; incomplete "activities of daily living" sheets; "range of motion" exercises not documented; patients found wet and soiled with dried fecal matter; lack of bowel and bladder retaining programs; incomplete documentation of ordered force fluids. . . .[26]

From a corporate standpoint, the parent corporation of the nursing facility could be held liable for the nursing facility's negligence, where the parent company controlled or retained the right to control the day-to-day operations of the home. The defendants had argued that the punitive damage award of $2 million against the home was greater than what was necessary to meet society's goal of punishing them. The Alabama Supreme Court, however, found the award not to be excessive. "The trial court also found that because of the large number of nursing home residents vulnerable to the type of neglect found in Mrs. Stovall's case, the verdict would further the goal of discouraging others from similar conduct in the future."[27]

Duty To Provide Adequate Facilities and Equipment

Health care organizations are under a duty to exercise reasonable care to furnish adequate equipment, appliances, and supplies for use in the diagnosis or treatment of patients. The general rule seems to be that equipment furnished by an organization should be fit for the purposes and uses intended.

Within its duty to provide adequate facilities and equipment, the governing body must exercise reasonable care and skill in supervising and managing facility property. This obligation includes protecting property from destruction and loss.

Health care organizations must be designed, constructed, equipped, and maintained to provide a safe, healthy, functional, sanitary, and comfortable environment for patients, employees, and the public. Buildings and equipment should be maintained and operated to prevent fire and other hazards to personal safety. Patient rooms should be designed and equipped for adequate nursing care, comfort, and privacy. Mechanical, electric, and patient care equipment should be maintained in a safe operating condition.

Driftwood Convalescent Hospital, operated by Western Medical Enterprises, Inc., in *Beach v. Western Medical Enterprises, Inc.,*[28] was fined $2,500 in civil penalties because of nonfunctioning hallway lights and the facility's failure to provide the required type and amount of decubitus preventive equipment necessary for resident care as required by the California Health and Safety Code. The regulations required that equipment "necessary for care to patients, as ordered or indicated" be provided.

> Though no evidence was introduced to show that the decubitus equipment had been ordered by a physician, the phrase "as indicated" supports an inference that when a patient's condition requires certain equipment, the fact that no physician has ordered that equipment does not relieve the hospital (nursing facility) of the responsibility for providing equipment necessary for patient care.[29]

Duty To Provide Adequate Insurance

One basic protection for tangible property is adequate insurance against fire and other risks. This duty extends to keeping the physical plant of the corporation in good repair and appropriating funds for such purpose when necessary.

The duty of the governing body is to purchase insurance against different risks. Organizations face as much risk of losing their tangible and intangible assets through judgments for negligence as they do through fires or other disasters. Where this is true, the duty to insure against the risks of fire is as great as the duty to insure against the risks of negligent conduct.

Duty To Be Financially Scrupulous

Health care organizations searching for alternate sources of income must do so scrupulously and not find themselves in what could be construed as questionable corporate activities.

Smith v. van Gorkum[30] involved a board of directors that authorized the sale of its company through a cash-out merger for a tendered price per share nearly 50 percent over the market price. Although that might sound like a good deal, the governing body did not make any inquiry to determine if it was the best deal available. In fact, it made no decision during a hastily arranged, brief meeting in which it relied solely on the CEO's report regarding the desirability of the move. The Delaware Supreme Court held that the board's decision to approve a proposed cash-out merger was not a product of informed business judgment and that it acted in a grossly negligent manner in approving amendments to the merger proposal.

A triable claim of illegal fee splitting was stated in *Hauptman v. Grand Manor Health Related Facility, Inc.,*[31] by the allegations of a psychiatrist that a nursing home had barred him from continuing to treat its residents unless he joined a professional corporation, the members of which included owners of the nursing home. Under the proposed agreement, the nursing home would retain 20 percent of the fees collected on his behalf. Although Section 6509 (a) of the New York Education Law does not prohibit members of a professional corporation from pooling fees, the statute did not apply to forced conscription into a corporation at the price of surrendering a portion of one's fees unwillingly. Likewise, Title 8, Section 29.1[b][4] of the New York Compilation of Codes and Rules expressly forbids a professional corporation from charging a fee for billing and office expenses based on a percentage of income from a practice. The psychiatrist's allegations also showed possible violation of New York Public Health Law § 2801(b), which prohibited exclusion of a practitioner on grounds not related to reasonable objectives of the organization.

In *Lynch v. Redfield Foundation,*[32] a California bank refused to honor corporate drafts unless all trustees concurred. They could not agree, and funds in a non–interest-bearing account continued to grow in principal from $4,900 to $47,000 over a five-year period. Although two trustees did try to carry on corporate functions despite a dissident trustee, their good faith did not protect them from liability in this case. The money could have been transferred to at least an interest-bearing account without the third trustee's signature. The trustees were held jointly liable to pay to the corporation the statutory rate of simple interest.

Duty To Provide Satisfactory Patient Care

The most important aspect of a governing body's duty to the health care corporation is to operate it with due care and diligence to provide satisfactory patient care. It is only through the fulfillment of this duty that the basic purpose of the organization will be accomplished; this duty includes the maintenance of a satisfactory standard of medical care through supervision of the medical, nursing, and ancillary staffs of the organization.

A staff member or employee has a duty to recognize and report abnormalities in the treatment and condition of patients. If an attending physician fails to act after being informed of such abnormalities, it is incumbent on the organization's staff to so advise management so that appropriate corrective action can be taken.

Although the provision of satisfactory patient care clearly fulfills the purpose of nonprofit organizations, it might be asked whether this duty applies equally to proprietary organizations where the corporation's additional purpose is to provide a return on investment. The duty does apply equally, and the proprietary organization's liability for failure to provide satisfactory care is clear. State licensing laws and regulations impose the same standards on both proprietary and nonprofit organizations, despite the fact that proprietary organizations are permitted to retain a profit.

A LIVING NIGHTMARE: WHAT ARE THE ISSUES?

Mrs. Smith described her admission and care at a major medical center as a living nightmare. She had been admitted with a diagnosis of thoracic outline syndrome resulting in the necessity for surgical removal of the first cervical rib. Mrs. Smith was told that the procedure was relatively simple and that she should expect a quick recovery. Upon admission to the medical center, she observed that a suction jar, which was attached to the wall at the head of the bed, was filled with body fluids. Blood was splattered on the wall behind the bed. There was one sink, located near Mrs. Smith's bed, in the four-bedded room. Surgical residents would enter the room, going from bed to bed examining pre- and postsurgical patients without changing their gloves or washing their hands.

A diabetic patient in one bed had been admitted for the removal of a leg. She had hidden a thermometer and Tylenol in her pocketbook. She was taking Tylenol to reduce her fever, which she feared would cancel her surgery.

Throughout Smith's stay, the room temperature fluctuated between 65 and 90 degrees on any given day. After her surgery, Smith developed a staph infection, pneumonia, and empyema. Her temperature fluctuated between 103 and 106 degrees.

Postoperative nursing care was nonexistent for the first 24 hours following surgery. On or about February 24, 2000, a nurse indicated that there were only two registered nurses on duty to care for 27 surgical patients and that it was difficult to render good patient care.

The attending physician failed to request a consultation from an infectious disease specialist until requested to do so by Smith's spouse. When the specialist, Dr. Berry, eventually did arrive, he stated that drainage tubes should have been inserted much sooner. Berry was overheard commenting, "I am appalled! Why wasn't I called sooner?"

Antibiotics had to be requested by a physician friend of the Smith family. Once antibiotics were requested, there was an ongoing failure to have them administered in a timely fashion. On one occasion, Mr. Smith asked a resident to see if the resident could administer Smith's antibiotic. The resident responded, "That's not my job." Antibiotics had been ordered to be administered at 9:00 A.M. but were not brought to Smith's room until 8:00 P.M. Delays of this nature served only to prolong Smith's stay and were detrimental to her health and early recovery. The situation became so frustrating that on two occasions Mr. Smith called the medical center's CEO in a frantic attempt to obtain his assistance. The calls were never returned. Dr. Plaster, the medical director of the hospital, was called for assistance and was told that his intervention was necessary because of a lack of coordination in Smith's care.

There was a failure to maintain Smith on her antibiotic once it had been prescribed. The IV was pulled out on the morning of February 2 at 5:30 A.M. and was not restarted. It was later determined that Smith should have been maintained on the antibiotic for a longer period of time.

There was also a failure of the residents and interns to follow appropriate safety precautions by washing their hands and changing gloves between patients and changing wound dressings. The spread of a staph infection from one patient to the next was evident. A patient discharged earlier from the room was returned to the hospital with a severe staph infection. It was only a matter of days until every surgical patient in the room developed an infection. Question remains as to what extent the infection may have spread to other patients on the patient care unit.

The fact that the hospital failed to provide Smith with any special care, which is considered standard procedure, was related to Mr. Smith by an infectious disease specialist. He said Smith might not make it through the night. She was so close to death's door that a priest was requested to administer her "last rites."

Smith was discharged with a pocket of fluid between her rib cage and spleen, which was discovered during a sonogram following discharge. The pocket of fluid continues to cause severe pain. What is your verdict?

A year after discharge, in her search for legal redress, Smith's attorney advised: "You look too good. The jury wants to see serious injury. Forget your case." Describe the multifaceted issues of this case and how an organization should address them.

Duty To Require Competitive Bidding

Many states have developed regulations requiring competitive bidding for work or services commissioned by public organizations. The fundamental purpose of this requirement is to eliminate or at least reduce the possibility that such abuses as fraud, favoritism, improvidence, or extravagance will intrude into an organization's business practices. Contracts made in violation of a statute are considered illegal and could result in personal liability for board members, especially if the members become aware of a fraudulent activity and allow it to continue. The mere appearance of favoritism toward one contractor over another could give rise to an unlawful action. For example, a board member's pressing the administrator to favor one ambulance transporter over others because of his or her social acquaintance with the owner is suspect. An organization's governing body should avoid even the appearance of wrongdoing by requiring competitive bidding.

Duty To Provide a Safe Environment for Patients and Employees

It is essential that employers provide a safe environment for both patients and employees. Although one cannot guard against the unforeseeable, a health care organization is liable for injuries resulting from dangers that it knowingly failed to guard against or those that it should have known about and failed to guard against. An organization, for example, generally is not liable for the shooting of an employee in its parking lot unless it knew of or in the course of ordinary care should have known of or could reasonably have foreseen the danger to the employee. In *Mauter v. Toledo Hosp.*,[33] a man shot and killed his estranged wife, a nurse who was an employee of the hospital. The court of appeals held that the hospital had no duty to protect the nurse from that danger.

An organization can be subject to corporate liability if it fails to ensure a patient's safety and well-being. Health care corporations are liable for injuries to both patients and employees rising from environmental hazards.

The license of a nursing facility operator was revoked in *Erie Care Center, Inc. v. Ackerman*[34] on findings of uncleanliness, disrepair, inadequate record keeping, and nursing shortages. The court held that although violation of a single public health regulation may have been insufficient in and of itself to justify revocation of the nursing home's operating license, multiple violations, taken together, established the facility's practice and justified revocation.

Safety Warnings Required/Hospital Created Unsafe Condition

The plaintiff in *Lutheran Hosp. of Ind. v. Blaser*[35] crossed the street one evening after visiting her husband in the hospital and was hit by a car as she was walking up the driveway to the hospital parking lot. She was struck from behind when the car was turning into the parking lot exit. The patient and her husband brought a negligence suit against the hospital as a result of the injuries she suffered.

Drivers in general could not determine that the driveway was not an exit until such time as they were alongside it or were in the process of turning into the driveway. Each night three or four cars mistakenly took the exit for an entrance. Outside visual cues actually drew pedestrians to cross the highway midblock in order to enter the lot. Neither security guards nor the parking lot attendants had attempted to dissuade pedestrians from crossing the street midblock. The superior court found that the funneling of pedestrians and vehicular traffic into the exit driveway created a dangerous condition that the hospital should have reasonably foreseen and the court entered judgment for the plaintiffs. The hospital appealed, claiming that although it maintained the driveway it did not have control over the driveway.

The Indiana Court of Appeals held that the accident was sufficiently foreseeable to require the hospital to protect its invitees from such a mishap. The intervening act of the hit-and-run driver in and of itself does not relieve the hospital of its legal responsibility.

The hospital had a legal duty to exercise reasonable care for the plaintiff's protection. The hospital's failure to post adequate safeguards or warnings to pedestrians and automobiles against the use of the exit driveway as an entrance to the parking lot was the proximate cause of the injuries suffered by the plaintiff. Regardless of whether the hit-and-run driver was confused by inadequate signing or poor illumination, the accident was within the hospital's scope of foreseeability. The hospital was aware of how the driveway was used and yet failed to make any effort to correct the dangerous situation.

The hospital created an unsafe condition and risked a car hitting a pedestrian at the parking lot exit. This was exactly what occurred. Because the subsequent negligent act by the hit-and-run driver was foreseeable by the hospital, the original tort-feasor, the *intervening act* of the negligent driver *does not in and of itself relieve the hospital of its legal responsibility.*

Infection Control

Health care organizations are required to establish and maintain infection control programs that are designed to provide a safe, sanitary, and comfortable environment in which patients reside. Prevention programs should help reduce the risk and transmission of disease and infection between patients, visitors, and the organization's staff.

Chemical Hazards

Employees should be warned of any unusual hazards related to their jobs. For example, pregnant employees may abort because of exposure to anesthetic gases in the operating or delivery room; the fetus of a pregnant employee may suffer cell damage because of exposure to chemotherapeutic agents and radioactive materials.

A generic systems approach and plan to the handling, storage, and disposal of hazardous materials to prevent user exposure should include the following elements:

- development of a hazardous materials (HAZMAT) plan
- policies and procedures (e.g., receipt, storage, and disposal of hazardous materials)
- engineering controls (e.g., vertical laminar flow hood for the preparation of chemotherapeutic medications)
- personal protective clothing and equipment (e.g., masks, gowns, foot and head coverings, and gloves)
- work practices (who, where, when, and how hazardous materials are handled)
- medical surveillance of those who handle hazardous materials (e.g., hazardous materials handling history and exposure follow-up by employee)
- inventory of the location, use, and security of all hazardous materials
- orientation, education, training, annual updates, and meetings
- Material Safety Data Sheets (MSDS) readily available in appropriate locations for all staff

Exposure to Various Caustic Cleaning Solutions

An employee's skin condition was found to be compensable in *Albertville Nursing Home v. Upton*.[36] The employee had developed a severe skin condition on his hands and feet as a result of daily exposure to various caustic cleaning solutions that he used while performing his duties in the nursing facility. The court held that the claimant was entitled to disability benefits for a period of 26 weeks.

The proper test to determine whether a claimant's job caused his or her injury is set out in *Newman Brothers, Inc. v. McDowell*.[37] That test is:

> [i]f in the performance of his job he has to exert or strain himself or is exposed to conditions of risk or hazard and he would not have strained or exerted himself or been exposed to such conditions had he not been performing his job and the exertion or strain or the exposure to the conditions was, in fact, a contributing cause to his injury or death, the test whether the job caused the injury or death is satisfied.[38]

Construction Hazards

The nursing facility's operating certificate in *Slocum v. Berman*[39] was revoked for violations of nursing home regula-

tions relating to construction and safety standards. The most critical issues related to the facility's structure, which was neither "protected wood frame" nor "fire resistive" as required by regulation. This was a violation that adversely affected the "health, safety, and welfare of the occupants."[40] It was determined that the nursing home "could not be made reasonably safe or functionally adequate for nursing home occupancy."[41]

Falls

Restraints

Falls by patients often involve mixed allegations of a failure to restrain, supervise, assist, or attend the patient. Some plaintiffs have argued that, although restraints were applied, they were inadequately applied. The plaintiff in *Smith v. Gravois Rest Haven, Inc.*[42] brought a lawsuit arising out of a fall and subsequent injuries and damages suffered by his 78-year-old mother. The plaintiff's mother required use of a "posey" restraining device because of previous falls in the facility. There was sufficient evidence to establish that the restraints had been improperly applied. Evidence showed that the plaintiff was a frail, elderly woman who had a history of crippling arthritis, among other ailments, and who had been administered a sleeping pill one hour before her fall, making it highly unlikely that she could have untied properly installed restraints and gotten out of bed.

Floors

Slippery floors are often a major source of lawsuits. To reduce liability caused by falls, floors should be maintained properly. To reduce patient falls

- Floors should not contain a dangerous amount of wax.
- Caution signs (e.g., slippery floors) should be used where appropriate.
- Floors should be cared for and maintained properly on rainy and/or snowy days.
- Broken floor tiles should be repaired promptly.
- Foreign matter should be quickly and completely wiped from the floor.
- Signs, ropes, and lights should be used where appropriate.
- Appropriate precautions should be taken for outdoor walkways, to guard against dangers such as icy conditions and construction hazards.

Windows

Health care organizations are required to exercise reasonable care and diligence in safeguarding a patient, measured by the capacity of the patient to provide for his or her own safety. The plaintiffs in *Horton v. Niagara Falls Memorial Medical Center*[43] sought recovery against the hospital for injuries sustained by the plaintiff-patient's fall from a second-story hospital window. The patient had been admitted to the hospital with a fever of unknown origin and was noted to be lacking in coordination and to have blurred vision. The patient had been placed in a private room with a single window that opened to a small balcony encircled by a 2- to 3-foot-high railing. Before the patient's fall, construction workers had notified hospital personnel that the patient was standing on his balcony calling for a ladder. The patient had been confused and disoriented. On learning of the incident, the attending physician advised a nurse to keep the patient under restraint and to keep an eye on him. The patient's wife was called, and she indicated that her mother would come to the hospital in 10 to 15 minutes to watch her husband. The patient fell shortly before the mother's arrival. The Niagara Supreme Court had entered judgment for the plaintiffs and the hospital appealed. The New York Supreme Court, Appellate Division, held that the hospital had a duty to supervise the patient and prevent him from injuring himself.

Beds

Falls from beds are frequent occurrences in health care facilities. Maintaining beds in good repair so that side rails and bed adjustment controls function properly should be part of an ongoing preventative maintenance program.

Duty To Safeguard Patient Valuables

Appropriate procedures should be developed for handling the personal property of patients. A health care facility can be held liable for the negligent handling of a patient's valuables. The following points should be remembered and followed when handling the personal belongings and valuables of patients:

- Send the belongings home when feasible.
- Deposit jewelry, wallets, and other appropriate items in the facility's safe.
- Select one department to handle valuables.
- Provide proper communication between the department handling lost and found articles and the department holding patient valuables for safekeeping.
- Encourage patients to keep with them as little money, jewelry, and other valuables as possible.
- Establish a valuables procedure for deceased patients, patients entering the emergency department, and patients scheduled for a surgical procedure or other diagnostic tests.
- Provide pre-numbered envelopes that list those items placed in each valuables envelope. Verification of the contents should be made between the employee delivering an envelope and the employee accepting the envelope for safekeeping. A receipt should be given to the patient making a deposit. Strikeouts or corrections should not be permitted on the envelope; this will help prevent claims of mishandling.

CEO/ADMINISTRATOR'S ROLE AND RESPONSIBILITY

The administrator is responsible for the supervision of the administrative staff and department heads who assist in the daily operations of the organization. The administrator derives authority from the owner or governing body. The administrator of an organization owned and operated by a governmental agency may be an appointed public official. Administrators, as is the case with governing body members, can be personally liable for their own acts of negligence that injure others.

The administrator must implement the policies of the governing body, as well as interpret policies to the staff. Appropriate action must be taken where noncompliance with rules and regulations occurs. The administrator is responsible for making periodic reports to the governing body regarding policy implementation.

There may be occasions when the administrator believes that following a direction of the governing body may create a danger to the patients or others. If the administrator knows or should have known, as a reasonably prudent administrator, of a danger or unreasonable risk or harm that will be created by certain directed activity but nevertheless proceeds as directed, he or she could become personally liable for any resulting injury. The administrator, therefore, must take appropriate steps to notify the governing body of any danger in carrying out policies that create dangers or unreasonable risks. Good communications with governing body members and suggestions for resolving policy issues will go a long way toward maintaining harmony with the governing body.

Although the administrator cannot assume the functions of the professional staff, he or she must ensure that proper admission and discharge policies and procedures are formulated and carried out. He or she must cooperate with the professional staff in maintaining satisfactory standards of medical care. The administrator must keep abreast of regulatory changes that affect organizational operations. Periodic meetings should be conducted to inform the staff of regulatory changes affecting their duties and responsibilities. The administrator should designate a representative for administrative coverage during those hours he or she is absent from the organization. This individual should be capable of dealing with administrative matters and be able to contact the administrator when major problems arise.

Health care administrators are subject to state laws and administrative regulations that control to some degree the scope of their activities. Nursing facility administrators historically have been subject to greater regulation than other administrators because of federal requirements that states enact licensing laws for nursing home administrators.

Tort Liability of Administrator

The wrongful injury to another by the administrator in the performance of his or her duties makes the administrator liable to the one injured. Because the administrator is subject to the control of the organization, the organization also may be liable for the torts of the administrator that occur within the scope of his or her employment. When performing the duties that he or she was hired to do, the administrator is working for the benefit of the organization and not as an individual. Because the organization gains from the work performed by its employees, the law renders the organization legally responsible for the acts of employees while performing the work of the organization.

Administrator's Liability for the Acts of Others

The administrator is not liable for the negligent acts of other employees, so long as he or she personally took no part in the commission of the negligent act and was not negligent in selecting or directing the person committing the injury. However, under the doctrine of *respondeat superior*, a health care facility can be liable for the employee's negligent acts.

Regulatory Agencies

The duties of the administrator include the correction of any deficiencies found during accreditation surveys by governmental agencies (e.g., Health Care Financing Administration (HCFA)) and nongovernmental agencies (e.g., Joint Commission). During the survey process the surveyor may provide an organization with either written citations or consultative remarks. Consultative remarks are often given in order to highlight an area of concern that should be addressed by the organization. Consultative remarks should be regarded just as significant in identifying areas needing corrective action as written reports that may be given by the surveyor. Many surveyors maintain documentation in their files of consultative remarks that they may have made to organizations that they survey. Such documentation should be viewed as having probative value.

There was an attempt by the Board of Nursing Home Administrators in *Carroll v. Gaddy*[44] to remove the license of a nursing facility administrator for his alleged failure to correct nursing home deficiencies. The South Carolina Department

of Health and Environmental Control (DHEC) found the deficiencies during several inspections of the facility in November 1984 through January 1986. In January 1986, the DHEC recommended to HCFA, the federal Medicare/Medicaid certifying agency, that the facility be decertified. HCFA declined to revoke the facility's certification. Subsequently, the Board of Nursing Home Administrators sought to revoke the administrator's license. The Board conducted a hearing in July and October of 1986, after which the administrator's license was revoked. The trial court reversed the Board's decision, holding that the record did not contain "substantial evidence" to support the Board's decision to revoke the administrator's license.

On appeal by the Board, the South Carolina Supreme Court affirmed the trial court's decision, holding that there was not substantial evidence to support revocation of the administrator's license, despite findings of deficiencies at the facility. Evidence indicated that the administrator was fully cooperative with DHEC inspectors and that he promptly corrected deficiencies. Although the administrator was exonerated, this case illustrates the potential for the abuse of power by administrative agencies.

Case Overviews

A fair number of cases over the years have dealt with administrators and their management of health care organizations. In general, an administrator employed for the duration of satisfactory performance has no property right in the position, as was pointed out in *Bleeker v. Dukakis*.[45] The administrator of the Woodland Nursing Home had been hired through an oral agreement under which his continued employment was contingent upon satisfactory work performance. "The assistant commissioner determined that Woodland was being managed improperly and that the appellant should be replaced."[46] The administrator's appointment was considered to be at the will of the employers even though the nursing facility's policies provided a procedure for warning and an opportunity to correct work performance deficiencies.

Dealing with the legal system can be a harrowing experience, even in those instances where the administrator is eventually exonerated from either negligence or criminal activity. Presented below are a few agonizing moments in the lives of some boards and their administrators.

- An administrator's license was revoked for concealment of the identities of the facility's owners in *Loren v. Board of Examiners of Nursing Home Administrators*.[47] The court found that the record contained substantial evidence to support the board's finding. The administrator had actively participated in a scheme to divert checks belonging to the nursing home to undisclosed partners of the home. The crime of knowingly filing false statements as to the facility's ownership with the intent of defrauding the U.S. government and the state of New York involved moral turpitude and subjected the administrator to disciplinary action.

- An administrator's plea to misdemeanor counts for mismanagement was considered a proper basis for suspending his nursing home license for one year.[48]
- A nursing home's exclusion from a Medicaid rate incentive program was considered rationally related to the encouragement of superior health care after the administrator was indicted for accepting excessive payments from the residents' relatives.[49]
- Although cases of alleged wrongdoing do not always end in a finding for the plaintiff, going through the ordeal is at best a miserable situation for the defendant. The court in *State v. Serebin*[50] held that the evidence of inadequate staffing and diet was found to be insufficient to support homicide charges against the administrator where the resident left the facility and died of exposure.

MEDICAL STAFF

The role of the governing body in setting policy and supervision of the medical staff is extremely important. The governing body should ensure that the medical staff bylaws provide for the following:

- application requirements for clinical privileges and admission to the medical staff
- procedures to be followed in medical emergencies
- procedures for arranging medical consultations
- procedures for the review and appraisal of the quality and appropriateness of medical care rendered by each physician
- procedures and responsibility for maintaining adequate medical records
- procedures for dealing with disruptive physicians and substance abuse (e.g., alcohol and drugs)
- procedures for corrective action (disciplinary actions can take the form of a letter of reprimand, suspension, or termination of privileges)

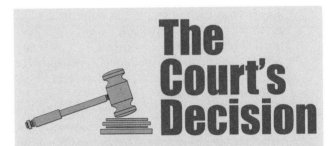

The Court's Decision

The Court of Special Appeals held that, where the liability of AAMC was solely vicarious and based on the negligent conduct of the pathologist as its purported agent, the AAMC and pathologist were not joint tort-feasors. The patient's release of the pathologist acted as a release of AAMC as a matter of law.

CHAPTER REVIEW

1. The governing body of an organization oversees and controls the corporation's activities. This body is legally responsible for establishing and implementing policies for the management and operation of a health care facility.
2. *Articles of incorporation* detail the corporation's purpose and the powers it is authorized to exercise in order to carry out this purpose. *Express corporate authority* is delegated by a statute, while *implied corporate authority* is invoked in cases in which authority not specifically granted in the articles of incorporation is required to carry out its purpose. *Ultra vires acts* are those in which a governing body acts beyond its expressed or implied scope of authority.
3. Traditionally, a number of committees conduct the business of the governing body:
   - Executive committee: has the authority to act on behalf of the full board.
   - Bylaws committee: reviews and recommends bylaws to the governing body
   - Finance committee: oversees financial affairs and makes recommendations to the governing body.
   - Joint conference committee: acts as a forum for discussion of policy and practice matters.
   - Nominating committee: develops and recommends criteria for governing body membership.
   - Planning committee: makes recommendations for the use and development of organizations resources.
   - Patient care committee: reviews the quality of patient care and makes recommendations for its improvement.

- Audit and regulatory compliance committee: assesses various functions and control systems of the organization and provides management with analysis and recommendations for activities reviewed.
  - Safety committee: oversees the organization's safety management program.
4. An employer can be held responsible for the acts of its employees under the legal doctrine *respondeat superior* or *vicarious liability*. The idea that all joint or concurrent tort-feasors are independently at fault for their own wrongful acts is called *joint liability*. An *independent contractor* relationship is one in which the principal has no right of control over the way in which the agent's work is to be performed. To be found liable for the torts of corporate employees, an officer or director of a corporation must have had direct involvement in the tortious act.
5. If a corporation has a duty to fulfill and it fails to do so, it can be found guilty of *corporate negligence*. Under this doctrine, hospitals that fail to uphold proper standards of care are liable. In addition, the failure of a governing body to fulfill its general duties may constitute mismanagement and require that a receiver be appointed to manage the corporation's affairs.
6. Corporations have certain duties specified by the corresponding state's corporation laws. These duties include holding meetings, establishing policies, being financially scrupulous, providing adequate insurance, and paying taxes. The governing body must also appoint a chief executive officer. Public organizations are often required to obtain competitive bids for commissioned services.
7. Among the special duties of hospitals are to provide a safe environment for patients and employees, establish infection control programs, protect employees from and warn them about chemical and construction hazards, and safeguard patients' valuables.
8. The administrator, who is given authority by the owner or governing body, is charged with the supervision of the administrative staff and department heads who assist in the organization's daily operations. In addition, the administrator must implement the governing body's policies and interpret them to staff, and must notify the governing body of potential danger in carrying out policies that create unreasonable risks. The administrator must also keep abreast of regulatory changes and communicate these changes to staff when necessary. If a governmental or nongovernmental agency finds deficiencies within the system, it is the administrator's duty to see that these are corrected.

REVIEW QUESTIONS

1. Describe the organization, responsibilities, duties, and legal risks of a governing body.
2. Describe the meaning of the legal doctrine *respondeat superior*.
3. Describe the term *corporate negligence*.
4. Why is the *Darling* case described as a benchmark case?
5. Does the legal doctrine *respondeat superior* apply to an *independent contractor*? Explain your answer.

NOTES

1. 649 A.2d 1189 (Md. App. 1994).
2. 136 Cal. Rptr. 36 (Cal. Ct. App. 1977).
3. Oberzan v. Smith, 869 P.2d 682 (Kan. 1994).
4. AA Med. Ctr. v. Condon, 649 A.2d 1189, 1193 (Md. App. 1994).
5. *Id.*
6. *Id.* at 1193–1196.
7. 46 U.S.L.W. 2227 (Md. 1977).
8. 272 S.E.2d 643 (S.C. 1980).
9. Thompson v. Nason Hosp., 591 A.2d 703, 707 (Pa. 1991).
10. *Id.*
11. 211 N.E.2d 253 (Ill. 1965).
12. *Id.* at 260.
13. 622 P.2d 463 (Ariz. 1980).
14. 183 Cal. Rptr. 156 (Cal. Ct. App. 1982).
15. 42 C.F.R. § 431.702 (1989).
16. 42 C.F.R. § 431.703 (1989).
17. 42 C.F.R. § 431.713 (1989).
18. 438 So.2d 412 (Fla. Dist. Ct. App. 1983).
19. 206 Cal. Rptr. 164 (Cal. Ct. App. 1984).
20. 734 F.2d 81 (1st Cir. 1984).
21. 396 So.2d 406 (La. Ct. App. 1981).
22. 188 Cal. Rptr. 685 (Cal. Ct. App. 1983).
23. 406 N.Y.S.2d 621 (N.Y. App. Div. 1978).
24. 565 So.2d 221, 224 (Ala. 1990).
25. *Id.* at 224.
26. *Id.* at 223–224.
27. *Id.* at 226.
28. 171 Cal. Rptr. 846 (Cal. Ct. App. 1981).
29. *Id.* at 852.
30. 488 A.2d 858 (Del. 1985).

31. 502 N.Y.S.2d 1012 (N.Y. App. Div. 1986).

32. 88 Cal. Rptr. 86 (Cal. Ct. App. 1970).

33. 571 N.E.2d 470 (Ohio Ct. App. 1989).

34. 449 N.E.2d 486 (Ohio Ct. App. 1982).

35. 634 N.E.2d 864 (Ind. Ct. App. 1994).

36. 383 So.2d 544 (Ala. Civ. App. 1980).

37. 354 So.2d 1138 (Ala. Civ. App. 1987).

38. *Id.* at 1140.

39. 439 N.Y.S.2d 967 (N.Y. App. Div. 1981).

40. *Id.* at 968.

41. *Id.*

42. 662 S.W.2d 880 (Mo. Ct. App. 1983).

43. 380 N.Y.S.2d 116 (N.Y. App. Div. 1976).

44. 368 S.E.2d 909 (S.C. 1988).

45. 665 F.2d 401 (1st Cir. 1981).

46. *Id.* at 402.

47. 430 N.Y.S.2d 402 (N.Y. App. Div. 1980).

48. Feuereisen v. Axelrod, 473 N.Y.S.2d 870 (N.Y. App. Div. 1984).

49. Cliff House Nursing Home, Inc. v. Department of Pub. Health, 463 N.E.2d 578 (Mass. App. Ct. 1984).

50. 338 N.W.2d 855 (Wis. Ct. App. 1983).

Medical Staff

RIGHT PATIENT—WRONG SURGERY

The plaintiff injured his lower back and suffered severe pain and numbness in his leg. He was diagnosed with a herniated disk at L4-L5. His surgeon performed a laminectomy. During a review of the plaintiff's postoperative X-rays, the surgeon noted that he had mistakenly removed the disk at L3-L4. The plaintiff testified that after the surgery his condition progressively worsened.

The plaintiff's expert testified that removal of the healthy disk caused the space between L3-L4 to collapse and the vertebrae to shift and settle. Even the defendant's expert witness testified that the removal of the healthy disk would increase the likelihood that the plaintiff will be more susceptible to future injuries.

The trial court directed a verdict against the defendant based on the defendant's own admission and that of his expert that he was negligent and that his negligence had caused at least some injury to the patient. The defendant appealed.[1]

What is your verdict?

INTRODUCTION

This chapter covers medical staff organization, the credentialing process, and a review of cases focused on the legal risks of physicians. The wide range of authority in treating patients has brought with it a broad range of lawsuits. A medical act, which often transpires over a few minutes' time span, is examined closely by the court years after the occurrence. This chapter discusses many of those areas in which physicians tend to be most vulnerable to lawsuits.

MEDICAL STAFF ORGANIZATION

The medical staff is an integral part of a health care organization with defined responsibilities under its bylaws. The medical staff is formally organized with appropriate officers, committees, and bylaws. The various committees of the medical staff review and analyze at regular intervals their responsibilities, clinical experiences, and opportunities for improvement. The responsibilities of several medical staff committees are described below.

- *Executive committee.* The executive committee oversees the activities of the medical staff. The executive committee is responsible for recommending to the governing body such things as medical staff structure, a process for reviewing credentials and appointing members to the medical staff, a process for delineating clinical privileges, a mechanism for the participation of the medical staff in performance improvement activities, a mechanism by which medical staff membership may be terminated, and a mechanism for fair hearing procedures. The executive committee reviews and acts on the reports of medical staff departmental chairpersons and designated medical staff committees. Actions requiring approval of the governing body are forwarded directly to the governing body or its designated committee. Membership on the executive committee generally includes the chief of staff as chairperson, medical staff officers, departmental chairpersons, the chief executive officer (CEO), and the chief nursing executive.

• *Bylaws committee.* The functioning of the medical staff is described in its bylaws, rules, and regulations, which must be reviewed and approved by the organization's governing body. Bylaws must be kept current and the governing body must approve recommended changes. The bylaws should describe the various membership categories of the medical staff (e.g., active, courtesy, consultative, and allied staff), as well as the process for obtaining privileges.

• *Blood usage committee.* The blood usage committee is responsible for
  – developing blood usage policies and procedures
  – ongoing monitoring of transfusion services
  – reviewing indications for transfusions
  – reviewing blood ordering practices
  – reviewing each transfusion episode
  – reviewing transfusion reactions
  – reporting its findings and recommendations to the medical staff executive committee for review and action

• *Department committee.* Each department of the medical staff (e.g., family practice, obstetrics and gynecology, pediatrics, medicine, pathology, surgery, and radiology) generally has a chairperson. The business of the department is conducted through department meetings.

• *Credentials committee.* The credentials committee oversees the application process for new medical staff applicants, requests for specific clinical privileges, and reappointments to the medical staff. The committee makes its recommendations to the medical executive committee.

• *Infection control committee.* The infection control committee is generally responsible for the development of policies and procedures for investigating, controlling, and preventing infections.

• *Medical records committee.* The medical records committee is responsible for
  – developing policies and procedures as they pertain to the management of medical records, including release, security, and storage
  – determining the format of complete medical records
  – developing and determining the use of forms to be included in medical records

  – reviewing medical records for accuracy, adequacy (completeness), legibility, and timely completion
  – reviewing medical records for clinical pertinence
  – ensuring that medical records reflect the condition and progress of the patient, including the results of all tests and therapy given
  – making recommendations for disciplinary action as necessary

• *Pharmacy and therapeutics committee.* The pharmacy and therapeutics committee is generally charged with responsibility for
  – developing policies and procedures relating to the selection, procurement, distribution, handling, use, and safe administration of drugs, biologicals, and diagnostic testing material
  – developing and maintaining a drug formulary
  – evaluating and approving protocols for the use of investigational or experimental drugs
  – reviewing and tracking medication errors and adverse drug reactions
  – continuously improving the management, control, and effective and safe use of medications through monitoring and evaluation
  – conducting drug usage reviews involving the selection and review of high-risk and high-volume medications utilizing parameters such as appropriateness, safety, effectiveness, medication errors, food-drug interactions, drug-drug interactions, drug-disease interactions, and adverse drug reactions
  – performing other such activities that may be delegated to it by the medical executive committee

• *Quality improvement council.* The quality improvement council functions as a patient care assessment and improvement committee. The council generally consists of representatives from the organization's administration, governing body, medical staff, and nursing. Improvement in quality improvement programs can be ensured by ongoing assessment of the work of the staff, systematic collection of clinically relevant data, and appropriate appraisal and analysis of care and outcome. Quality committees must be willing to evaluate the process of physician decision making and to identify the need for consultation and education.

• *Tissue committee.* The tissue committee reviews all surgical procedures conducted in the institution. Surgical case reviews address the justification and indications for surgical procedures. This review uses preestablished occurrence screens and clinical indicators for each surgical section. Representation on the tissue committee should include the departments of surgery, anesthesiology, pathology, nursing, risk management, and administration.

• *Utilization review committee.* The utilization review committee is responsible for an ongoing monitoring and evaluation program designed to identify utilization issues such as medical necessity and appropriateness of admission and continued stay, as well as delay in the provision of diagnostic, therapeutic, and supportive services. The utilization review committee ensures that each patient is treated at an appropriate level of care. Objectives of the committee include: the timely transfer of those patients requiring alternate levels of care; promotion of the efficient and effective use of the organization's resources; adherence to quality utilization standards of third-party payers; maintenance of high-quality cost-effective care; and identification of opportunities for improvement.

MEDICAL STAFF PRIVILEGES

The governing body is ultimately responsible for the selection of medical staff members and the delineation of clinical privileges. The duty to select members of the medical staff is legally vested in the governing body as the body charged with managing the organization. Medical staff membership is restricted to those professionals who fulfill the requirements as described in an organization's medical staff bylaws. Although cognizant of the importance of medical staff membership, the governing body must meet its obligation to maintain standards of good medical practice in dealing with matters of staff appointment, credentialing, and the disciplining of physicians for such things as disruptive behavior, incompetence, psychological problems, criminal actions, and substance abuse.

Appointment to the medical staff and medical staff privileges should be granted only after there has been a thorough investigation of the applicant. The delineation of clinical privileges should be discipline-specific and based on appropriate predetermined criteria that adhere to national standards.

Masquerading Physician

Failure to properly screen a medical staff applicant's credentials can lead to liability for injuries suffered by patients as a result of that omission. The patient in *Johnson v. Misericordia Community Hospital*[2] brought a malpractice action against the hospital and its liability insurer for alleged negligence in granting orthopaedic privileges to a physician who performed an operation to remove a pin fragment from the patient's hip. The Wisconsin Court of Appeals found the hospital negligent for failing to scrutinize the physician's credentials before approving his application for orthopaedic privileges. The hospital failed to adhere to procedures established under both its own bylaws and state statute. The mea-

sure of quality and the degree of quality control exercised in a hospital are the direct responsibilities of the medical staff. Hospital supervision of the manner of appointment of physicians to its staff is mandatory, not optional. On appeal by the hospital, the Wisconsin Supreme Court affirmed the appellate court's decision, finding that if the hospital had exercised ordinary care, it would not have appointed the physician to the medical staff.

The Screening Process

The purpose of the appointment process is to evaluate the competency of the applicant to determine if he or she is qualified for appointment to the medical staff. The following sections describe the appointment process.

Application

The governing body should establish a policy of nondiscrimination on the basis of race, color, sex, religion, national origin, age, and physical disability. The medical staff application should provide pertinent information regarding the applicant's

- residence
- office location (Geographic requirements should not be unreasonably restrictive. If the applicant does not meet the organization's geographic requirements for residence and office location, provision should be available in the bylaws for exceptions that might be necessary to attract a distinguished consulting staff.)
- medical school
- internship
- residency
- license to practice medicine
- board certification
- fellowship
- medical society membership (Board certification, fellowship, and medical society membership are not legally acceptable criteria for determining eligibility for medical staff appointment.)
- malpractice coverage
- special skills and talents
- privileges requested and specialty
- availability to provide on-call emergency department coverage where applicable
- availability to serve on medical staff and/or organization committees
- other medical staff appointments
- previous disciplinary actions against the applicant
- unexplained breaks in work history
- voluntary and/or involuntary limitations or relinquishment of staff privileges

Each staff member must adhere to the written bylaws governing the medical staff and care of patients. The bylaws should be approved by the medical executive committee and governing body. Each member of the organization's medical staff should be required to sign a statement attesting that the medical staff bylaws have been read and that the physician agrees to abide by the bylaws and other policies and procedures that may be adopted from time to time by the organization.

Physical and Mental Status

Health care organizations must address issues as to a physician's physical and mental capacity prior to and following the granting of medical staff privileges. Credentialed members of the medical staff should undergo a medical evaluation prior to reappointment to the medical staff.

Consent for Release of Information

Consent for release of information from third parties should be obtained from the applicant.

Certificate of Insurance

The applicant should provide evidence of professional liability insurance. The insurance policy should provide minimum levels of insurance coverage, with limits (e.g., $1 million/$3 million) determined by the organization.

State Licensure

Applicants for privileges must have a state license to practice medicine. The individual states have enacted medical practice acts that regulate the practice of medicine. The different states have a legitimate interest in regulating the practice of medicine. This interest includes ensuring the health and welfare of individuals through the regulation and supervision of the practice of medicine. A state may set reasonable standards for determining the qualifications of those who hold themselves out as practitioners of the healing arts, and they also grant the authority to enforce standards to administrative bodies.

A physician's right to practice medicine is subject to the licensing laws contained in the statutes within the state in which the physician resides. The right to practice medicine is not a vested right but is a condition of a right subordinate to the police power of the state to protect and preserve public health. Although a state has power to regulate the practice of medicine, for the benefit of the public health and welfare, this power is restricted. Regulations must be reasonably related to the public health and welfare and must not amount to arbitrary or unreasonable interference with the right to practice one's profession. Health professions commonly requiring licensure include chiropractors, dentists, nurses, pharmacists, physicians' assistants, optometrists, osteopaths, physicians, and podiatrists.

Grounds for the revocation of a license to practice medicine include the following:

- a clear demonstration of the lack of good moral character
- deliberate falsification of a patient's medical record (to protect one's own interests at the expense of the patient)
- intentional fraudulent advertising
- gross incompetence
- sexual misconduct
- substance abuse
- performance of unnecessary medical procedures
- billing for services not performed
- forged operative record

National Practitioner Data Bank

The National Practitioner Data Bank should be queried as to information in its files for all new applicants.

References

References should be checked thoroughly. Failure to do so can lead to corporate liability for a physician's negligent acts. Both written and oral references should be obtained from previous organizations with which the applicant has been affiliated.

An action was brought against a hospital in *Rule v. Lutheran Hospitals & Homes Society of America*[3] for birth injuries sustained during an infant's breech delivery. The action was based on allegations that the hospital had negligently failed to investigate the qualifications of the attending physician before granting him privileges. The jury's verdict of $650,000 was supported by evidence that the hospital administrator failed to check with other hospitals where the physician had practiced. The physician's privileges at one hospital had been limited in that breech deliveries had to be performed under supervision. A finding of causation likewise was permissible on the basis of evidence that there was sufficient time to summon a qualified physician once discovering that the infant was in the breech position.

The Interview Process

The interview process can become ineffective if there are too many reviewing bodies. Too many interview levels can lead to a rubber-stamp mentality, each layer believing that prior interviewing bodies have performed a more thorough interview or thinking that what pertinent information one committee or person fails to discover, the next layer will discover. Potential interviewers include:

- section chief
- department chairperson
- committee (including CEO/administrator and CNO/chief nursing executive)
- medical executive committee

- joint conference committee (this committee should include representatives from both the medical executive committee and the governing body)

The Interview

- Be sure all documents have been received prior to the interview.
- Check to see if there are any unaccounted-for breaks or gaps in education or employment.
- Has any disciplinary action or misconduct investigation been initiated or is pending against the applicant by any licensing body?
- Has the applicant's license to practice medicine in any state ever been denied, limited, suspended, or revoked?
- Has the applicant's medical staff privileges ever been suspended, diminished, revoked, or refused at any health care organization?
- Has the applicant ever withdrawn an application or resigned from any medical staff before a decision was rendered by an organization with regard to application for membership to avoid disciplinary action?
- Has the applicant ever been subject to any disciplinary proceedings at any health care facility?
- Has the applicant ever been named as a defendant in a lawsuit?
- Has the applicant ever been named as a defendant in a criminal proceeding?
- Has a lawsuit ever been filed against the applicant?
- Is the applicant available for emergency coverage?
- Does the applicant have backup and cross-coverage?
- Does the applicant have any special skills or talents?
- Has the applicant reviewed medical staff bylaws, rules, and regulations, and, where applicable, departmental rules and regulations?
- Does the applicant agree to abide by the medical staff bylaws, rules, and regulations and other policies and procedures set by the organization?
- What is the applicant's ability to work with others?
- Has the applicant ever been restricted from participating in any private or government (e.g., Medicare, Medicaid) health insurance program?
- Has the applicant's malpractice insurance coverage ever been terminated by action of the insurance carrier?
- Has the applicant ever been denied malpractice insurance coverage?
- Have there been any settlements and/or judgments against the applicant?
- Does the applicant have any physical or mental impairments that could affect his or her ability to practice the privileges requested?

Governing Body and Final Action

Appointments to the medical staff are made on recommendation to the governing body by the medical staff and

reviewing committees. The governing body has ultimate authority for granting medical staff privileges. This responsibility cannot be delegated. Medical staff membership and delineated clinical privileges are granted by the governing body, based on medical staff recommendations, in accordance with the bylaws, rules, and regulations of the medical staff. The governing body can grant privileges, grant limited privileges, or deny privileges.

DELINEATION OF CLINICAL PRIVILEGES

The delineation of clinical privileges is the process by which the medical staff determines precisely what procedures a physician is authorized to perform. This determination is based on predetermined criteria as to what credentials are necessary to competently perform the privileges requested.

The governing body bears ultimate responsibility for ensuring that applicants to the organization's medical staff are qualified to perform the clinical procedures set forth in the delineation of privileges. Otherwise, an organization may be liable for the negligent acts of its physicians. If an organization is to be responsible for each physician's conduct, it must be permitted to determine the nature and extent of the privileges granted physicians to practice in the organization. In light of the importance of staff appointments to physicians, the courts have prohibited an organization from acting unreasonably or capriciously in rejecting physicians for staff appointments or in limiting their privileges.

HOSPITAL'S DUTY TO ENSURE COMPETENCY

Citation: *Candler Gen. Hosp., Inc. v. Persaud, 442 S.E.2d 775 (Ga. Ct. App. 1994)*

Facts

On or about February 15, 1990, a patient was referred to Dr. Freeman for consultation and treatment of gallstones. Freeman recommended that the patient undergo a laparoscopic laser cholecystectomy.

On February 16, 1990, Freeman requested and was granted temporary privileges to perform the procedure. He submitted a certificate of completion of a laparoscopic laser cholecystectomy workshop, which he took on February 10, 1990. Freeman performed the cholecystectomy on February 20, 1990. Dr. Thomas assisted him.

A complaint by the administrator of the patient's estate, supported by an expert's affidavit, alleged that the cholecystectomy was negligently performed, as a result of which the patient bled to death. The complaint charged the hospital with negligence in permitting Freeman, assisted by Thomas, to perform the procedure on the decedent without having instituted any standards, training requirements, protocols, or otherwise instituted any method for judging the qualifications of a surgeon to perform the procedure. The complaint also alleged that the hospital knew or reasonably should have known that it did not have a credentialing process that could have assured the hospital of the physicians' education, training, and ability to perform the procedure.

The trial court denied the hospital's motion for summary judgment, finding that the plaintiffs' evidence was sufficient to raise a question of fact regarding whether surgical privileges should have been issued by the hospital to Freeman. The hospital appealed.

Issue

Was there a material issue of fact as to whether the hospital was negligent in granting the specific privileges requested by Freeman?

Holding

The Georgia Court of Appeals held that there was a material issue of fact as to whether the hospital was negligent in granting the specific privileges requested, thus precluding summary judgment.

Reason

The court found that a hospital has a direct and independent responsibility to its patients to take reasonable steps to ensure that staff physicians using hospital facilities are qualified for privileges granted. The hospital owed a duty to the plaintiffs' decedent to act in good faith and with reasonable care to ensure that the surgeon was qualified to practice the procedure that he was granted privileges to perform.

Discussion

1. Do you agree that the hospital was negligent in the granting of the privileges requested by Dr. Freeman? Discuss your answer.

2. If the patient had suffered no injuries, do you think the plaintiffs could have recovered any monetary damages?

3. What credentialing issues are evident in this case?

Duty To Select Competent Physicians

The surgeon in *Purcell & Tucson General Hospital v. Zimbelman*[4] performed inappropriate surgery because of his misdiagnosis of the patient's ailment. Prior malpractice suits against the surgeon revealed that the hospital had reason to know or should have known that the surgeon apparently lacked the skill to treat the patient's condition. The court held that the hospital had a clear duty to select competent physicians; to regulate the privileges granted to staff physicians; to ensure that privileges are conferred only for those procedures for which the physician is trained and qualified; and to restrict, suspend, or require supervision when a physician has demonstrated an inability to perform certain procedures. The hospital had assumed the duty of supervising the competence of its physicians. The Department of Surgery was acting for and on behalf of the hospital in fulfilling this duty. If the department was negligent in not taking action against the surgeon or recommending to the governing body that action be taken, the hospital would be negligent. The court noted that it is reasonable to conclude that had the hospital taken some action against the surgeon, the patient would not have been injured.

An action was brought against Morton Canton (who was masquerading as a physician, Dr. LaBella), a hospital, and others in *Insinga v. LaBella*[5] for the wrongful death of a 68-year-old woman whom Canton had admitted. The patient died while she was in the hospital. Canton was found to be a fugitive from justice in Canada where he was under indictment for the manufacture and sale of illegal drugs. He fraudulently obtained a medical license from the state of Florida and staff privileges at the hospital by using the name of LaBella, a deceased physician. Canton was extradited to Canada without being served process. The U.S. District Court for the Southern District of Florida directed a verdict in favor of the hospital. On appeal, the U.S. Court of Appeals for the Eleventh Circuit certified a question to the Florida Supreme Court, asking whether Florida law recognizes the corporate negligence doctrine and whether the doctrine would apply under the facts of this case. The Florida Supreme Court held that the corporate negligence doctrine imposes on hospitals an implied duty to patients to select and retain competent physicians who, although they are independent practitioners, would be providing in-hospital care to their patients through staff privileges. Hospitals are in the best position to protect their patients and consequently have an independent duty to select and retain competent independent physicians seeking staff privileges.

APPEAL PROCESS

An appropriate appeal process should be described in the medical staff bylaws to cover issues such as the initial denial of medical staff privileges, grievances, and disciplinary actions. The governing body should reserve the right to hear any appeals and be the final decision maker within the organization.

A physician whose privileges are either suspended or terminated must exhaust all remedies provided in a hospital's bylaws, rules, and regulations before commencing a court action. The physician in *Eidelson v. Archer*[6] failed to pursue the hospital's internal appeal procedure before bringing a suit. As a result, the Alaska Supreme Court reversed a superior court's judgment for the physician in his action for compensatory and punitive damages.

Medical Staff Bylaws—A Contract

The plaintiff, Dr. Bass, in *Bass v. Ambrosius*,[7] alleged that St. Luke's termination of his staff privileges violated its own bylaws. St. Luke's contended that its bylaws did not constitute a contract between itself and Bass, and, therefore, any violation of those bylaws would not support a breach-of-contract claim. The general rule is that they can. To hold that a hospital did not have to comply with its own bylaws would render them essentially meaningless.

The general rule that hospital bylaws can constitute a contract between the hospital and its staff is consistent with Wisconsin law that an employee handbook written and disseminated by the employer, and whose terms the employee has accepted, constitutes a contract between the employer and the employee. In *Ferraro v. Koelsch*,[8] the handbook was management's statement of what the company offered its employees, and what it expected from its employees in return. It thus contained the essential elements of a binding contract: the promise of employment on stated terms and conditions by the employer and the promise by the employee to continue employment under those conditions. The court noted that a promise for a promise, or the exchange of promises, constitutes consideration to support any contract of this bilateral nature.

The bylaws at issue, required by WIS. ADMIN. CODE § HSS 124.12(5), and approved by St. Luke's board of directors, have the same contractual elements as did the handbook in *Ferraro*. First, the bylaws state that they provide the rules that govern the "physicians and dentists practicing at St. Luke's

Hospital." Second, members of the hospital's medical-dental staff must "continuously meet the qualifications, standards, and requirements set forth in these Bylaws." Third, an appointment to the medical-dental staff confers "only those privileges provided by the letter of appointment and these Bylaws." Fourth, an applicant for appointment to the medical-dental staff must submit a signed application acknowledging that he or she "shall be required to familiarize himself/herself with . . . [the] Bylaws." Finally, and most significant in light of *Ferraro*, an applicant for appointment to the medical-dental staff must submit a signed application attesting that he or she "has read and agreed to accept and abide by the provisions and directives" in the Bylaws. Thus, Bass' application to the medical-dental staff acknowledged over his signature that he would "conduct [his] professional activities according to the bylaws and rules and regulations of both St. Luke's Hospital and the Medical-Dental Staff of St. Luke's Hospital which I have read and understood." In a separate letter, also part of the application process, Bass agreed to "conduct [his] activities according to the bylaws of St. Luke's Hospital, and the bylaws and rules and regulations of the St. Luke's Hospital Medical/Dental Staff which I have read and understood." For its part, St. Luke's promised that the medical-dental staff at the hospital would be guided and governed by rules and regulations consistent with the bylaws, and promised that any adverse action against a member of the medical-dental staff would comply with various procedural safeguards.

There was sufficient evidence to show that the bylaws constituted a contract between Bass and St. Luke's. St. Luke's submitted no evidence that raised a genuine issue of fact in this regard. Accordingly, Bass was entitled to an order holding that St. Luke's had to comply with its bylaws before it could terminate his staff privileges.

PHYSICIAN SUPERVISION AND MONITORING

The medical staff is responsible to the governing body for the quality of care rendered by members of the medical staff. The landmark decision in this area occurred in *Darling v. Charleston Community Memorial Hospital*,[9] in which it was decided that the hospital's governing body had a duty to establish a mechanism for the medical staff to evaluate, counsel, and, when necessary, take action against an unreasonable risk of harm to a patient arising from the patient's treatment by a physician. Physician monitoring is best accomplished through a system of peer review. Most states provide statutory protection from liability for peer review activities when they are conducted in a reasonable manner and without malice.

Responsibility To Know of a Physician's Incompetence

An organization cannot defend itself against a lawsuit on the grounds that the medical staff is independent and self-governing. In *Gonzales v. Nork & Mercy Hospital*,[10] the hospital was found negligent for failing to protect the patient, a 27-year-old man, from acts of malpractice by an independent, privately retained physician. The patient had been injured in an automobile accident and was operated on by Dr. Nork, an orthopaedic surgeon. The plaintiff's life expectancy was reduced as a result of an unsuccessful and allegedly unnecessary laminectomy. It was found that the hospital knew or should have known of the surgeon's incompetence because the surgeon previously had performed many operations either unnecessarily or negligently. In such cases the defendant produced false and inadequate findings as well as false-positive myelograms. He deceived his patients with this information and caused them to undergo surgery. Evidence was presented showing that the surgeon had performed more than three dozen similar operations unnecessarily or in a negligent manner. Even if the hospital was not aware of the surgeon's acts of negligence, an effective monitoring system should have been in place for monitoring his abilities. Consequently, the surgeon and hospital were held jointly liable for damages suffered by the other patients as well.

An organization owes its patients a duty of care, and this duty includes the obligation to protect them from negligent and fraudulent acts of those physicians with a propensity to commit malpractice. The courts will not permit organizations to hide behind the cloak of ignorance in this responsibility.

Disruptive Physicians

Disruptive physicians can have a negative impact on an organization's staff and ultimately affect the quality of patient care. Having the right policies in place as it relates to "conflict resolution" is a must for an effective working environment.

Criteria other than academic credentials (e.g., a physician's ability to work with others) should be considered before granting medical staff privileges. That factor was considered by the court in *Ladenheim v. Union County Hospital District*,[11] which held that the physician's inability to work with other members of the staff was in itself sufficient grounds to deny him staff privileges. The physician's record was replete with evidence of his inability to work effectively with other members of the hospital staff. As stated in *Huffaker v. Bailey*,[12] most other courts have found that the ability to work smoothly with others is reasonably related to the objective of ensuring patient welfare. The conclusion seems justified because health care professionals frequently are required to work together or in teams. A staff member who, because of personality characteristics or other problems, is incapable of getting along with others could severely hinder the effective treatment of patients.

The court in *Pick v. Santa Ana-Tustin Community Hospital*[13] held that the petitioner's demonstrated lack of ability to work with others in the hospital setting was sufficient to support the denial of his application for admission to the medical staff. There was evidence that the petitioner presented a real and substantial danger to patients treated by him and that the patients might receive other than a high quality of medical care.

Suspension and Termination of Privileges

A physician whose privileges are either suspended or terminated must exhaust all remedies provided in a facility's bylaws, rules, and regulations before commencing a court action. The U.S. Court of Appeals in *Northeast Georgia Radiological Associates v. Tidwell*[14] held that a contract with the hospital's radiologists, which incorporated the medical staff bylaws, sustained the plaintiffs' claim to a protected property interest entitling them to a hearing before the medical staff and the hospital authority.

REAPPOINTMENTS

Each physician's credentials and departmental evaluations should be reviewed at least every two years. The medical staff must provide effective mechanisms for monitoring and evaluating the quality of patient care and the clinical performance of physicians. For problematic physicians, consideration should be given to privileges with supervision, a reduction in privileges, suspension of privileges with purpose (e.g., suspension pending further training), or termination of privileges.

MEDICAL DIRECTOR

The responsibilities of a medical director include enforcing the bylaws of the governing body and medical staff; monitoring the quality of medical care in the organization; and serving as a liaison between the medical staff and the organization's governing body and management. Paid medical directors should have clearly written agreements with the facility, including their duties, responsibilities, and compensation arrangements. State nursing home codes often provide for the designation of either a full-time or part-time physician to serve as a medical director.

The medical director of an organization can be liable for failing to perform his or her duties and responsibilities. When a Texas nursing home was indicted by a grand jury in 1981 for the deaths of several residents, the medical director was also indicted.[15] His plea that he merely signed papers and attended meetings did not absolve him of the responsibility to ensure the adequacy and the appropriateness of medical services in the organization.

NEGLIGENT ACTS

The following cases illustrate some of the acts or omissions constituting negligence or malpractice. They are by no means exhaustive and are merely representative of the wide range of potential legal pitfalls in which physicians might find themselves.

Abandonment

The relationship between a physician and a patient, once established, continues until it is ended by the mutual consent of the parties, the patient's dismissal of the physician, the physician's withdrawal from the case, or the fact that the physician's services are no longer needed. A physician who decides to withdraw his or her services must provide the patient with reasonable notice so that the services of another physician can be obtained. Premature termination of treatment is often the subject of a legal action for *abandonment*— the unilateral termination of a physician–patient relationship by the physician without notice to the patient. The following elements must be established in order for a patient to recover damages for abandonment:

- Medical care was unreasonably discontinued.
- The discontinuance of medical care was against the patient's will. Termination of the physician–patient relationship must have been brought about by a unilateral act of the physician. There can be no abandonment if the relationship is terminated by mutual consent or by dismissal of the physician by the patient.
- The physician failed to arrange for care by another physician. Refusal by a physician to enter into a physician–patient relationship by failing to respond to a call or render treatment is not considered a case of abandonment. A plaintiff will not recover for damages unless he or she can show that a physician–patient relationship had been established.

- Foresight indicated that discontinuance might result in physical harm to the patient.
- Actual harm was suffered by the patient.

Aggravation of a Preexisting Condition

Aggravation of a preexisting condition through negligence may cause a physician to be liable for malpractice. If the original injury is aggravated, liability will be imposed only for the aggravation, rather than for both the original injury and its aggravation.

Poor Treatment/Aggravated Preexisting Condition

In *Nguyen v. County of Los Angeles*,[16] an eight-month-old girl went to the hospital for tests on her hip. She had been injected with air for a hip study and suffered a respiratory arrest. She later went into cardiac arrest and was resuscitated but suffered brain damage that was aggravated by further poor treatment. The Los Angeles Superior Court jury found evidence of medical malpractice, ordering payments for past and future pain and suffering as well as medical and total care costs that projected to the child's normal life expectancy.

Patient Fall/Aggravated Preexisting Condition

The plaintiff in *Favalora v. Aetna Casualty & Surety Co.*[17] sued the hospital and the radiologist for injuries she sustained when she fell while undergoing an X-ray examination. The patient's personal physician had admitted her to the hospital for a general checkup and a gastrointestinal (GI) series. She had complained about stomach pains, general fatigue, and fainting. The morning after her admission to the hospital, she was taken from her room in a wheelchair to the radiology department. When preparations for the GI series were complete, two technicians brought the patient to the X-ray room. She then waited for the arrival of the radiologist. When he arrived, she was instructed to walk to the X-ray table and stand on the footboard. The technician instructed her to drink a glass of barium. A second cup of barium was handed to her by the technician who then took the exposed film to a nearby pass box leading to the adjacent darkroom, obtained a new film, and repeated the X-ray process. While the technician was depositing the second set of exposed film in the pass box, the patient suddenly fainted and fell to the floor. The radiologist did not see the plaintiff fall, nor did he detect any evidence of distress. The technician heard a noise, immediately turned on the lights, and found the patient laying on the floor. The radiologist instantly began administering to the patient while the technician summoned additional assistance. The patient was placed on the X-ray table, and X-rays were taken of those portions of her anatomy that indicated the possibility of injury. The X-rays revealed a fracture of the neck and of the right femur that subsequently required open reduction and the insertion of a metal pin by an orthopaedic surgeon. As a result, a preexisting vascular condition was aggravated, causing a pulmonary embolism, which, in turn, necessitated additional surgery. The failure of the radiologist to secure the patient's medical history before the X-ray examination was considered negligence constituting the proximate cause of the patient's injuries.

A defendant generally is required to compensate a patient for only the amount of aggravation caused. However, it is often difficult to determine what monetary damages should be awarded to a plaintiff. In many instances, aggravation is a matter of conjecture.

Prescriptions for Medications/Aggravated Preexisting Condition

Damages were awarded in *Argus v. Scheppegrell*[18] for the wrongful death of a teenage patient with a preexisting drug addiction. It was determined that the physician had wrongfully supplied the patient with prescriptions for controlled substances in excessive amounts, with the result that the patient's preexisting drug addiction had worsened, causing her death from a drug overdose. The Louisiana Court of Appeal held that the suffering of the patient caused by drug addiction and deterioration of her mental and physical condition warranted an award of $175,000. Damages of $120,000 were to be awarded for the wrongful death claims of the parents, who not only suffered during their daughter's drug addiction caused by the physician in wrongfully supplying the prescription, but who also were forced to endure the torment of their daughter's slow death in the hospital.

Anesthesiology

Captain of the Ship/Negligent Insertion of an Endotracheal Tube

Summary dismissal was properly ordered for those portions of a patient's medical malpractice action that sought to hold a surgeon vicariously liable for throat injuries suffered by his patient because of the negligent manner in which an endotracheal tube was inserted during the administration of anesthesia.[19] The patient's allegations that the surgeon had exercised control over the administration of anesthesia were rebutted by evidence to the contrary. Liability of the surgeon could not be premised on the captain of the ship doctrine because that doctrine would not be recognized in West Virginia. The trend in medicine has created situations in which surgeons do not always have the right to control all persons within the operating room. An assignment of liability based on the theory of actual control more realistically reflects the actual relationship that exists in a modern operating room.

Failure To Maintain an Airway

On appeal by the defendant anesthesiologist in *Ward v. Epting*,[20] the issues of deviation from the standard of care and proximate cause were found to have been submitted properly to the jury. The anesthesiologist had failed to establish and maintain an adequate airway and resuscitate properly a postsurgical 22-year-old female patient, which resulted in her death from lack of oxygen. Expert testimony based on autopsy and blood gas tests showed that the endotracheal tube had been removed too soon after surgery and that the anesthesiologist, in an attempt to revive the patient, reinserted the tube into the esophagus. The record contained ample evidence that the anesthesiologist failed to conform to the standard of care and that such deviation was the proximate cause of the patient's death. The plaintiff was awarded $400,000 in damages.

Alternative Procedures

The potential for liability affects the choice of treatment a physician will follow in treating his or her patient. Use of unprecedented procedures that create an untoward result may cause a physician to be found negligent even though due care was followed. A physician will not be held liable for exercising his or her judgment in applying a course of treatment supported by a reputable and respected body of medical experts even if another body of expert medical opinion would favor a different course of treatment. The "two schools of thought" doctrine is only applicable in medical malpractice cases in which there is more than one method of accepted treatment for a patient's disease or injury. Under this doctrine, a physician will not be liable for medical malpractice if he or she follows a course of treatment supported by reputable, respected, and reasonable medical experts.

A physician's efforts do not constitute negligence simply because they were unsuccessful in a particular case. A physician cannot be required to guarantee the results of his or her treatment. The mere fact that an adverse result may occur following treatment is not in and of itself evidence of professional negligence. Innovation in the treatment for minor ailments would be questioned more likely than would innovation in the treatment of a major disease. A physician treating a patient with a new procedure for an ordinary cold runs a greater risk of liability than does a physician treating a patient with a new procedure for an acute and painful disease.

It is assumed by law that medicine has not become so standardized that it is unreasonable for two physicians to have differing opinions on the proper method of treating injuries or illnesses. If there is reason for the difference, the courts have held that neither side can be proven erroneous by the "proof" of the other.

Confidential Communications

Physician–patient privilege imposes on a physician an obligation to maintain the confidentiality of each patient's communications. This obligation applies to all health care professionals. An exception to the rule of confidentiality of patient communications is the implied right to make available to others involved in the patient's care the information necessary to that care. Information received by a physician in a confidential capacity relating to a patient's health should not be disclosed without the patient's consent. Disclosure may be made under compelling circumstances (e.g., suspected child abuse) to a person with a legitimate interest in the patient's health.

Delay in Treatment

A physician may be liable for failing to respond promptly if it can be established that such inaction caused a patient's death.[21] A patient afflicted with lung cancer was awarded damages in *Blackmon v. Langley* because of the failure of the examining physician to inform the patient in a timely manner that a chest X-ray showed a lesion in his lung.[22] The lesion eventually was diagnosed as cancerous. The physician contended that because the evidence showed the patient had less than a 50 percent chance of survival at the time of the alleged negligence, he could not be the proximate cause of injury. The Arkansas Supreme Court found that the jury was properly entitled to determine that the patient suffered and lost more than would have been the case had he been notified promptly of the lesion.

Possibility of Survival Destroyed

On February 5, 1988, Mr. Griffett had been taken to the emergency department with a complaint of abdominal pain.[23] Two emergency department physicians evaluated him and ordered X-rays, including a chest X-ray. Dr. Bridges, a radiologist, reviewed the chest X-ray and noted in his written report that there was an abnormal density present in the upper lobe of Griffett's right lung. Griffett was referred to Dr. Ryan, a gastroenterologist, for follow-up care. Ryan admitted Griffett to the hospital for a 24-hour period and then discharged him without having reviewed the radiology report of the February 5 chest X-ray.

On March 1, 1988, Griffett continued to experience intermittent pain. A nurse in Ryan's office suggested that Griffett go to the hospital emergency department if his pain became persistent.

In November 1989, Dr. Baker examined Griffett, who was complaining of pain in his right shoulder. Baker diagnosed Griffett's condition as being cancer of the upper lobe of his right lung. The abnormal density on the February 5, 1998 chest X-ray was a cancerous tumor that had doubled in size from the time it had been first observed on the February 5 chest X-ray. The tumor was surgically removed in February 1990. However, Griffett died in September 1990.

Dr. Muller, an internist and expert witness for the plaintiff, testified that Griffett *would have had a greater likelihood of survival* if Ryan had made an earlier diagnosis. The defendants objected to Muller's testimony, arguing that the plaintiff failed to establish that Muller was an expert witness capable of testifying as to the proximate cause of Griffett's alleged shorter life span. The trial court initially overruled the defendants' objection to Muller's testimony. Following a verdict by the jury for the plaintiff, the trial court ruled that it had erred by allowing Muller to testify as to causation.

The jury returned a verdict for the plaintiff in the amount of $500,000. On a motion from the defendants, the trial court set aside the verdict, and the plaintiff appealed.

Was Muller qualified to testify as the plaintiff's medical expert? Did the plaintiff prove that the defendant's negligence was the proximate cause of Griffett's death and not just the loss of the mere possibility of survival?

The Virginia Supreme Court held that the plaintiff had sufficiently identified Muller as an expert witness capable of testifying as to the question of causation. Evidence was sufficient to establish that the failure to diagnose lung cancer, in connection with the emergency department visit, was the proximate cause of the patient's death.

Review of the record revealed that Muller demonstrated knowledge of the standards regarding what an internist, who is also a gastroenterologist, should do regarding medical information that is contained in a patient's medical record. The duty to review an X-ray contained in a patient's medical record should not vary between an internist and a gastroenterologist.

The plaintiff presented evidence that showed Ryan's negligence destroyed "any substantial possibility" of Griffett's survival. Muller had testified that within a reasonable degree of medical certainty "there would have been a high likelihood that an operation in 1988 would have resulted in the patient being saved."

Failure To Respond to an Emergency Department Call

Physicians on call for a specific service in an emergency department are expected to respond to requests for emergency assistance when such is considered necessary. Failure to respond is grounds for negligence should a patient suffer injury as a result of a physician's failure to respond.

Issues of fact in *Dillon v. Silver*[24] precluded summary dismissal of an action charging that a woman's death from complications of an ectopic pregnancy occurred because of a gynecologist's refusal to treat her despite a request for aid by a hospital emergency department physician. Although the gynecologist contended that no physician–patient relationship had ever arisen, the hospital bylaws not only mandated that he accept all patients referred to him, but also stated that the emergency department physician had authority to decide which service physician should be called and required the service physician to respond to such a call.

Failure To Follow Up

Failure to follow up can result in a lawsuit if such failure results in injury to a patient. In *Truan v. Smith*,[25] the Tennessee Supreme Court entered judgment in favor of the plaintiffs, who had brought action against a treating physician for damages alleged to have been the result of malpractice by the physician in the examination, diagnosis, and treatment of breast cancer. In January or February 1974, the patient noticed a change in the size and firmness of her left breast, which she attributed to an implant. She later noticed discoloration and pain on pressure. While being examined by the defendant on March 25, 1974, for another ailment, the patient brought her symptoms to the physician's attention but received no significant response, and the physician made no examination of the breast at that time. The patient brought her symptoms to the attention of her physician for the second time on May 6, 1974. She had been advised by the defendant to observe her left breast for 30 days for a change in symptoms, which at the time of the examination included discomfort, discoloration, numbness, and sharp pain. She was given an appointment for one month later. The patient, on the morning of her appointment, June 3, 1974, called the physician's office and informed the nurse that her symptoms had not changed and that she would like to know if she should keep her appointment. The nurse indicated that she would pass on her message to the physician. The patient assumed she would be called back if it was necessary to see the physician. By late June the symptoms became more acute, and the patient made an appointment to see the defendant physician on July 8, 1974. The patient also was scheduled to see a specialist on July 10, 1974, at which time she was admitted to the hospital and was diagnosed as having a malignant mass. A radical mastectomy was performed. Expert witnesses expressed the opinion that the mass had been palpable seven months before the removal, when the defendant undertook to give the plaintiff a complete physical examination, and

that having embarked on a "wait and see" program as an aid in diagnosis, the physician should have followed his patient, who died before the conclusion of the trial. The state supreme court held that the evidence was sufficient to support a finding that the defendant was guilty of malpractice in failing to inform his patient that cancer was a possible cause of her complaints and in failing to make any effort to see his patient at the expiration of the observation period instituted by him.

Failure To Disclose/Informed Consent

The doctrine of informed consent is a theory of professional liability independent from malpractice. A physician's duty to disclose known and existing dangers associated with a proposed course of treatment is imposed by law. The patient in *Leggett v. Kumar*[26] was awarded $675,000 for pain and disfigurement resulting from a mastectomy procedure. The physician in this case failed to advise the patient of treatment alternatives. He also failed to perform the surgery properly.

It is the physician's role to provide the necessary medical facts and the patient's role to make the subjective decision concerning treatment based on his or her understanding of those facts. Before subjecting a patient to a course of treatment, the physician has a duty to disclose information that will enable the patient to evaluate options available and the risks attendant to a specific procedure. A failure to disclose any known and existing risks of proposed treatment when such risks might affect a patient's decision to forgo treatment constitutes a *prima facie* violation of a physician's duty to disclose. If a patient can establish that a physician withheld information concerning the inherent and potential hazards of a proposed treatment, consent is abrogated. Consent for a medical procedure may be withdrawn at any time before the act consented to is accomplished.

In *Gates v. Jensen*,[27] a lawsuit was brought against Dr. Hargiss, an ophthalmologist, and others for failure to disclose to Mrs. Gates that her test results for glaucoma were borderline and that her risk of glaucoma was increased considerably by her high blood pressure and myopia. Hargiss failed to perform a field vision test and to dilate and examine the eye. He wrote off the patient's problem of difficulty in focusing and gaps in vision as being related to difficulties with her contact lenses. Gates visited the clinic 12 times during the following two years with complaints of blurriness, gaps in her vision, and loss of visual acuity. Gates eventually was diagnosed as having open-angle glaucoma. By the time Gates was properly treated, her vision had deteriorated from almost 20/20 to 20/200. The court held that a duty of disclosure to a patient arises whenever a physician becomes aware of an abnormality that may indicate risk or danger. The facts that must be disclosed are those facts the physician knows or should know that a patient needs to be aware of to make an informed decision on the course that future medical care will take.

Once a physician concludes that a particular test is indicated, it should be performed and evaluated as soon as practicable. Delay may constitute negligence. The law imposes on a physician the same degree of responsibility in making a diagnosis as it does in prescribing and administering treatment.

Failure To Order Diagnostic Tests

A plaintiff who claims that a physician failed to order proper diagnostic tests must show the following:

- It is a standard practice to use a certain diagnostic test under the circumstances of the case.
- The physician failed to use the test and therefore failed to diagnose the patient's illness.
- The patient suffered injury as a result.

Failure to order diagnostic tests resulted in the misdiagnosis of appendicitis in *Steeves v. United States*.[28] In this case physicians failed to order the appropriate diagnostic tests for a child who was referred to a Navy hospital with a diagnosis of possible appendicitis. Judgment in this case was entered against the United States, on behalf of the U.S. Navy, for medical expenses and for pain and suffering. The child had been referred by an Air Force dispensary, where a test indicated a high white blood cell count. A consultation sheet had been given to the mother, indicating the possible diagnosis. The physician who examined the child at the Navy hospital performed no tests, failed to diagnose the patient's condition, and sent him home at 5:02 P.M., some 32 minutes after his arrival on July 21. The child was returned to the emergency department on July 22, at about 2:30 A.M., only to be sent home again by an intern who diagnosed the boy's condition as gastroenteritis. Once again, no diagnostic tests were ordered. The boy was returned to the Navy hospital on July 23, at which time diagnostic tests were performed. The patient was subsequently operated on and found to have a ruptured appendix. Holding the Navy hospital liable for the negligence of the physicians who acted as its agents, the court pointed out that a wrong diagnosis will not in and of itself support a verdict of liability in a lawsuit. However, a physician must use ordinary care in making a diagnosis. Only where a patient is examined adequately is there no liability for an erroneous diagnosis. In this instance, the physicians' failure to perform further laboratory tests the first two times the child was brought to the emergency department was found to be a breach of good medical practice.

Efficacy of a Diagnostic Test Questioned

A medical malpractice action was brought against Mambu in *Sacks v. Mambu*,[29] for failure to make a timely diagnosis of Mr. Sack's colon cancer. It was alleged that Mambu was negligent in that he failed to properly screen Sacks for fecal occult blood to determine if there was blood in the colon. Mambu treated Sacks, who presented himself with a complaint of abdominal pains in March 1983. Mambu determined that Sacks was suffering from a urinary tract infection and prescribed an antibiotic. In August 1983, Sacks was hospitalized for removal of his gallbladder. The surgeon on the case did not detect any indication of cancer. Mambu saw the patient regularly following surgery. Because of complaints of fatigue by the patient, Mambu ordered blood tests that revealed a normal hemoglobin, the results of which suggested that Sacks had not been losing blood. However, by late July 1984, Sacks experienced symptoms of jaundice. Mambu ordered an ultrasound test and Sacks was subsequently diagnosed with a tumor of the liver. He was admitted to the hospital and diagnosed with having colon cancer. By the time the cancer was detected, it had invaded the wall of the bowel and had metastasized to the liver. The patient expired in March 1985, seven months following his surgery. The court of common pleas entered judgment on a jury verdict for Mambu and the plaintiff appealed.

The Pennsylvania Superior Court, holding for Mambu, upheld the decision of the trial court. The possibility that Sacks would have died anyway was no defense if Mambu's negligence had been a substantial factor in reducing Sack's opportunity for survival because Mambu would have effectively cut off any chance that Sacks had for survival. The jury had been instructed to address this concern. Had the jury found "the defendant physician negligent in failing to administer a fecal occult blood test, it was the jury's duty to determine whether the doctor's negligence was a proximate cause of the defendant's death." Sacks had an occult blood test administered by his primary care physician, Dr. Weiner, in October 1981. Mambu did not order a fecal occult blood test when he treated the patient in March 1993. The jury determined that the physician's failure to administer the test had not increased the risk of harm by allowing the cancer to metastasize to the liver before discovery and, therefore, was not a substantial factor in causing the patient's death. Although the presence of blood in the stool may be suggestive of polyps, cancer, and a variety of other diseases, not all polyps and cancers bleed. Physicians are therefore in disagreement as to the efficacy of the test.

Failure To Promptly Review Test Results

Can a physician's failure to promptly review test results be the proximate cause of a patient's injuries? The answer is yes—a physician's failure to promptly review test results can be the proximate cause of a patient's injuries. In *Smith v. U.S. Department of Veterans Affairs*,[30] the plaintiff, Smith, was first diagnosed as having schizophrenia in 1972. He had been admitted to the Veterans Administration (VA) hospital psychiatric ward 15 times since 1972. His admissions grew longer and more frequent as time passed. On the occasion of his March 17, 1990, admission, he had been drinking in a bar, got into a fight, and was eventually taken to the VA hospital. Rizk was assigned as Smith's attending physician.

Smith developed an acute problem with his respiration and level of consciousness. It was determined that his psychiatric medications were responsible for his condition. Some medications were discontinued and others reduced. An improvement in his condition was noted.

By March 23, Smith began to complain of pain in his shoulders and neck. He attributed the pain to more than 20 years of service as a letter carrier and to osteoarthritis. His medical record indicated that he had similar complaints in the past. A rheumatology consultation was requested and carried out on March 29. The rheumatology resident conducted an examination and noted that Smith reported bilateral shoulder pain increasing with activity as an ongoing problem since 1979. Various tests were ordered, including an erythrocyte sedimentation rate (ESR).

Smith was incontinent and complained of shoulder pain. By the afternoon he was out of restraints, walked to the shower, and bathed himself. On returning to his room, he claimed that he could not get into bed. He was given a pillow and slept on the floor. By the morning of April 4, Smith was laying on the floor in urine and complaining of numbness. His failure to move was attributed to his psychosis. By evening it was noted that Smith could not lift himself and would not use his hands.

On April 5, a medical student noted that Smith was having difficulty breathing and called for a pulmonary consultation. By evening Smith was either unwilling or unable to grasp a nurse's hand and continued to complain that his legs would not hold him up.

On the morning of April 6, Smith was complaining that his neck and back hurt and that he had no feeling in his legs and feet. Later that day a medical student noted that the results of Smith's ESR was 110 (more than twice the normal rate for a man his age). His white blood count (WBC) was 18.1, also well above the normal rate. A staff member noted on the medical record that Smith had been unable to move his extremities for about five days. A psychiatric resident noted that Smith had been incontinent for three days and had a fever of 101.1 degrees.

On the morning of April 7, Smith was taken to University Hospital for magnetic resonance imaging of his neck. Imaging revealed a mass subsequently identified as a spinal epidural abscess. By the time it was excised, it had been pressing on his spinal cord too long for any spinal function to remain below vertebrae four and five.

The plaintiff brought suit alleging that the physicians' failure to promptly review his test results was the proximate cause of his paralysis. Following a bench trial, the U.S. District Court agreed, holding that the negligent failure of physicians to promptly review laboratory tests results was the proximate cause of the plaintiff's quadriplegia.

Of primary importance was the plaintiff's ESR of 110, the test results being available on the patient care unit by April 2, but which were not seen or at least not noted in the record until April 6. Although witnesses for both sides disagree, there was little disagreement as to the nature and importance of this test. An elevated ESR generally accounts for one of three problems: infection, cancer, or a connective tissue disorder. Most experts agreed that at the very least a repeat ESR should have been ordered. The VA's care of the plaintiff fell below the reasonable standard of care in that no one read the laboratory results until April 6. The fact that the tests were ordered mandates the immediate review of the results. Although it cannot be known with certainty what would have occurred had the ESR been read and acted upon on April 2, it is certain that the plaintiff had a chance to fully recover from his infection. By April 6, that chance was gone.

In the absence of notes from Rizk in the plaintiff's chart, it is impossible to know if Rizk was aware of the plaintiff's symptoms. However, it appears that the absence of notes by Rizk indicated Rizk's care of the plaintiff was negligent, and the failure to review the results of the plaintiff's ESR constituted negligence under the relevant standard of care. That led to the failure to make an early diagnosis of the plaintiff's epidural abscess and was the proximate cause of the patient's eventual paralysis. In light of the fact that a high ESR can manifest in a very serious illness, it was foreseeable that ignoring a high ESR could lead to serious injury.

A mechanism should be in place to expeditiously notify the patient's physician of abnormal test results (e.g., panic values from laboratory tests). Many hospitals use computer systems to help ensure that physicians are notified of critical data so that appropriate care decisions can be implemented.

Failure To Read Nurses' Notes—Breach of Duty

Can a physician breach his or her duty of care by failing to read nursing notes? The answer is yes. In *Todd v. Sauls*,[31] Mr. Todd was admitted to Rapides General Hospital on October 3, 1988, and on October 4, 1988, Dr. Sauls performed bypass surgery. Postoperatively, Todd sustained a heart attack. During the following days Todd did not ambulate well and suffered a weight loss of 19 and 1/2 pounds.

On October 17, the medical record indicated that Todd's sternotomy wound and the mid-lower left leg incision were reddened and his temperature was 99.6. Sauls did not commonly read the nurses' notes but instead preferred to rely on his own observations of the patient. In his October 18 notes, he indicated that there was no drainage. The nurses' notes, however, show that there was drainage at the chest tube site. Contrary to the medical records showing that Todd had a temperature of 101.2 degrees, Sauls noted that the patient was afebrile.

On October 19, Sauls noted that Todd's wounds were improving and he did not have a fever. Nurses' notes indicated redness at the surgical wounds and a temperature of 100 degrees. No White Blood Count (WBC) had been ordered. Again on October 20, the nurses' notes indicated a wound redness and a temperature of 100.8 degrees. No wound culture had yet been ordered. Dr. Kamil, one of Todd's treating physicians, noted that Todd's nutritional status needed to be seriously confronted and suggested that Sauls consider supplemental feeding. Despite this, no follow-up to his recommendation appears and the record is *void of any action by Dr. Sauls to obtain a nutritional consult.*

Todd was transferred to the ICU on October 21 because he was gravely ill with profoundly depressed ventricular function. The following day the nurses' notes describe the chest tube site as draining foul smelling bloody purulence. The patient's temperature was recorded to have reached 100.6 degrees. This is the first time that Sauls had the test tube site cultured. On October 23, the culture report from the laboratory indicated a staph infection and Todd was started on antibiotics for treatment of the infection.

On October 25, at the request of family, Todd was transferred to St. Luke's Hospital. At St. Luke's, Dr. Leatherman, an internist and invasive cardiologist, treated Todd. Dr. Zeluff, an infectious disease specialist, examined Todd's surgical wounds and prescribed antibiotic treatment. Upon admission to St. Luke's, every one of Todd's surgical wounds was infected. Despite the care given at St. Luke's, Todd died on November 2, 1988. The family brought a malpractice suit against the surgeon. The District Court entered judgment on a jury verdict for the defendant and the plaintiff appealed claiming the surgeon breached his duty of care owed to the patient by failing to: (1) aggressively treat the surgical wound infections; (2) read the nurses' observations of infections; and (3) provide adequate nourishment, allowing the patient's body weight to rapidly waste away.

The Louisiana Court of Appeal held that Sauls committed medical malpractice when he breached the standard of care he owed to Todd. Todd was effectively ineligible for a heart transplant, which was his only chance of survival due to the infections and malnourishment caused by Sauls' malpractice. Sauls' testimony convinced the court that he failed to aggressively treat the surgical wound infections, that he chose not to take advantage of the nurses' observations of infection, and that he allowed Todd's body weight to waste away, knowing that extreme vigilance was required because of Todd's already severely impaired heart. The awards of $4,975 for funeral expenses; $19,533.42 for medical expenses; $150,000 for Mrs. Todd; and $50,000 to each of his seven children for loss of love and affection were determined by the court to be appropriate.

In cases where a patient has died, the plaintiff need not demonstrate that the patient would have survived if properly treated. Rather, he need only prove that the patient had a chance of survival and that his chance of survival was lost as a result of the defendant/physician's negligence. The defendant/physician's conduct must increase the risk of a patient's harm to the extent of being a substantial factor in causing the result but need not be the only cause. Sauls' medical malpractice exacerbated an already critical condition and *"deprived Mr. Todd of a chance of survival."*

Leatherman stated that it was the responsibility of the surgeon and cardiologist to pay closer attention to Todd's nutritional status and to have better managed his weight. He emphasized that wounds cannot heal when a patient is malnourished. Leatherman opined that Sauls deviated from the required standard of care he owed to Todd.

Zeluff stated that impaired nutritional status depresses the body's immune system and adversely affects the body's ability to heal wounds. In response to a hypothetical fact situation based on Todd's medical records at Rapides General, Zeluff opined that Sauls further deviated from the standard of care by failing to initiate parenteral or enteral nutrition, by at least October 20.

Dr. Pipkin, an expert cardiac surgeon, corroborated the testimony of Leatherman and Zeluff on the negative effect that malnourishment has on the healing process and the body's ability to fight infection. Pipkin stated that it was Sauls' responsibility to make certain that Todd received adequate calories and proteins. After reviewing the records of Todd, Pipkin found that there was a general wasting of Todd in the postoperative period as evidenced by his steady loss of weight. Pipkin opined that Sauls deviated from the standard of care owed to Todd both with regard to wound infections and malnourishment.

Failure To Seek Consultation

When a practitioner determines or should have determined that a patient's ailment is beyond his or her scope of knowledge or technical skill, or ability or capacity to treat with a likelihood of reasonable success, he or she is under a duty to disclose such determination to the patient. The patient should be advised of the necessity of other or different treatments.

A physician has a duty to consult and/or refer a patient whom he or she knows or should know needs referral to a physician familiar with and clinically capable to treat the patient's particular ailments. Whether the failure to refer constitutes negligence depends on whether referral is demanded by accepted standards of practice. To recover damages, the plaintiff must show that the physician deviated from the standard of care and that the failure to refer resulted in injury.

The California Court of Appeals found that expert testimony is not necessary where good medical practice would require a general physician to suggest a specialist's consultation.[32] The court ruled that because specialists were called in after the patient's condition grew worse, it is reasonable to assume that they could have been called in sooner. The jury was instructed by the court that a general practitioner has a duty to suggest calling in a specialist if a reasonably prudent general practitioner would do so under similar circumstances.

A physician is in a position of trust, and it is his or her duty to act in good faith. If a preferred treatment in a given situation is outside a physician's field of expertise, it is his or her duty to advise the patient. Failure to do so could constitute a breach of duty. Today, with the rapid methods of transportation and easy means of communication, the duty of a physician is not fulfilled merely by using the means at hand in a particular area of practice.

In *Doan v. Griffith*,[33] an accident victim was admitted to the hospital with serious injuries, including multiple fractures of his facial bones. The patient contended that the physician was negligent in not advising him at the time of discharge that his facial bones needed to be realigned by a specialist before the bones became fused. As a result, his face became disfigured. Expert testimony demonstrated that the customary medical treatment of the patient's injuries would have been to realign his fractured bones surgically as soon as the swelling subsided and that such treatment would have restored the normal contour of his face. The appellate court held that the jury reasonably could have found that the physician failed to provide timely advice to the patient on his need for further medical treatment and that such failure was the proximate cause of the patient's condition.

When a physician determines that medication, further office visits, or diet restrictions are indicated, the sufficiency of such instructions to the patient is a subjective, and not an objective, matter. Physicians cannot assume that instructions are adequate just because a reasonably prudent person would understand them. They must make orders clear for each patient, given his or her experience, education, and general knowledge and the nature of the disease. In general, instructions to children must be given to parents as well. If a patient is incompetent, instructions must be given to an appropriate member of the family or other responsible person (e.g., a guardian or committee).

Failure of an attending physician to recognize recommendations by consulting physicians, who determine a different diagnosis and recommend a different course of treatment in a particular case, can result in liability for damages suffered by the patient. This was the case in *Martin v. East Jefferson General Hospital*[34] in which the attending physician had continued to treat the patient for a viral infection despite three other physicians' diagnoses of lupus and their recommendations that the attending physician treat the patient for col-

lagen vascular disease. The trial court found that lupus had been more probable than not the cause of the patient's death and that her chances of recovery had been destroyed by the physician's failure to rule out that diagnosis. Damages totaling $150,000 were awarded to the plaintiff.

The convalescent home resident in *Stogsdill v. Manor Convalescent Home, Inc.*[35] brought an action against the physician, the home, and a co-owner of the home for damages suffered when her leg was amputated as a proximate result of allegedly deficient medical and convalescent care. The resident had developed a decubitus ulcer on her left ankle and gangrene developed sometime before November 7, 1972. There was testimony by one of the nurses at the nursing facility that she had noticed gangrene in August or September. The treating physician, Dr. Hiatt, prescribed certain medications but did not prescribe any antibiotics until November 6, 1972, at which time he prescribed terramycin. Wet soaks, laboratory tests, and vascular studies also were not ordered. The treating physician did not request hospitalization or seek consultation from another physician. On November 7, 1972, the resident's son called another physician to see his mother. He diagnosed the resident's condition as a wet gangrene involving the entire outer surface of the ankle. The resident was taken to the hospital the same day. At the hospital, an orthopaedic surgeon recommended amputation. After building up the patient for surgery with the use of intravenous fluids and feedings, her leg was amputated on November 10, 1972. Dr. Loutfy, a specialist in internal medicine, in response to a hypothetical question, was of the opinion, based on a reasonable degree of medical and surgical certainty, that with proper care and treatment the leg could have been saved. The defendant presented no witnesses at trial.

The trial court directed a verdict for the home and co-owner and assessed damages against the physician in the amount of $40,000 for general damages and $80,000 for punitive damages. The defendant appealed. The appellate court affirmed the directed verdict for the home and co-owner. Testimony was found sufficient to establish that the loss of the leg was proximately caused by Hiatt's negligence.

If a consulting physician has suggested a diagnosis with which the treating physician does not agree, it would be prudent to consider obtaining the opinion of a second consultant who could either confirm or disprove the first consultant's theory. Failure to diagnose and properly treat a suspected illness is an open door to liability.

Failure To Obtain Second Opinion/Abridgement of Privileges

Dr. Goodwich was a licensed physician who specialized in obstetrics and gynecology in *Goodwich v. Sinai Hospital*.[36] Goodwich's clinical practice patterns were subject to question by his peers on a wide variety of medical matters over the years. Dr. Goldstein (Chairman of the Department of Obstetrics and Gynecology) met with him on several occasions in 1988 regarding those concerns. It was suggested to him that he obtain second opinions from board certified obstetricians and gynecologists. Goodwich orally agreed to do so. This agreement was placed in writing to Goodwich on two occasions in 1988. Goodwich failed to comply with the agreement, and Goldstein held a second meeting with him and his attorney in February 1990.

Due to continued noncompliance, Goldstein asked the Director of Quality, Risk, and Utilization Management to determine how often Goodwich failed to obtain a second opinion. The investigation uncovered several instances of noncompliance. Goldstein then met with Goodwich for a third time. Goodwich agreed that he would obtain a second opinion in high-risk obstetrical cases. Goldstein confirmed the agreement in writing on April 23, 1992.

Dr. Goldstein left the hospital in June 1992 and Dr. Taylor was appointed acting Chief of Obstetrics and Gynecology. He asked for a recheck of Goodwich's compliance with the second opinion agreement. By January, the hospital appointed Dr. Currie as the Chief of Obstetrics and Gynecology. Because of Goodwich's continuing failure to obtain second opinions, Currie informed Goodwich in writing that pursuant to Article IV, Sec. 7C of the Bylaws, Rules, and Regulations of the hospital's Medical Staff that his privileges were temporarily abridged. The letter also advised Goodwich that the Medical Executive Committee (MEC) would consider a permanent abridgment of his privileges. The MEC met and abridged Goodwich's privileges for three months. The abridgement of Goodwich's privileges was reported to the Maryland State Board of Physician Quality Assurance and the National Practitioner Data Bank.

Goodwich appealed the MEC decision to two different physician panels and the hospital's Board of Trustees. Both physician panels and the Board of Trustees affirmed the MEC's decision to abridge Goodwich's privileges.

Goodwich sued the hospital for breach of contract, intentional interference with contractual relations, and tortious interference with prospective economic benefit after restrictions were placed on his practice privileges at the hospital. The circuit court entered summary judgment for the hospital on the grounds of statutory immunity. Goodwich appealed. The court of special appeals held that the hospital acted reasonably, as required for immunity under the federal Health Care Quality Improvement Act of 1986. The record was replete with documentation of questionable patient management and continual failure to comply with second opinion agreements.

History and Physical

Failure to obtain an adequate family history and perform an adequate physical examination violates a standard of care

owed to the patient. In *Foley v. Bishop Clarkson Memorial Hospital*,[37] the spouse sued the hospital for the death of his wife. During her pregnancy, the patient was under the care of a private physician. She gave birth in the hospital on August 20, 1964, and died the following day. During July and August, her physician treated her for a sore throat. Several days after her death, one of her children was treated in the hospital for a strep throat infection. There was no evidence in the hospital record that the patient had complained about a sore throat while in the hospital. The hospital rules required a history and physical examination to be written promptly (within 24 hours of admission). No history had been taken, although the patient had been examined several times in regard to the progress of her labor. The trial judge directed a verdict in favor of the hospital. On appeal, the appellate court held that the case should have been submitted to the jury for determination. A jury might reasonably have inferred that if the patient's condition had been treated properly, the infection could have been combated successfully and her life saved. It also might have been reasonably inferred that if a history had been taken promptly when she was admitted to the hospital, the throat condition would have been discovered and hospital personnel alerted to watch for possible complications of the nature that later developed. Quite possibly, this attention also would have helped in diagnosing the patient's condition, especially if it had been apparent that she had been exposed to a strep throat infection. The court held that a hospital must guard not only against known physical and mental conditions of patients, but also against conditions that reasonable care should have uncovered.

Infections

The mere fact that a patient contracted an infection after an operation will not, in and of itself, cause a surgeon to be liable for negligence. The reason for this, according to the Nebraska Supreme Court in *McCall v. St. Joseph Hospital*,[38] is as follows:

> Neither authority nor reason will sustain any proposition that negligence can reasonably be inferred from the fact that an infection originated at the site of a surgical wound. To permit a jury to infer negligence would be to expose every doctor and dentist to the charge of negligence every time an infection originated at the site of a wound. We note the complete absence of any expert testimony or any offer of proof in this record to the effect that a staphylococcus infection would automatically lead to an inference of negligence by the people in control of the operation or the treatment of the patient.[39]

A district court of appeals held in *Gill v. Hartford Accident & Indemnity Co.*[40] that the physician who performed surgery on a patient in the same room as the plaintiff should have known that the infection the patient had was highly contagious. The failure of the physician to undertake steps to prevent the spread of the infection to the plaintiff and his failure to warn the plaintiff led the court to find that hospital authorities and the plaintiff's physician caused an unreasonable increase in the risk of injury. As a result, the plaintiff suffered injuries causally related to the negligence of the defendant.

A jury verdict in the amount of $300,000 was awarded in *Langley v. Michael*[41] for damages arising from the amputation of the plaintiff's infected thumb. Evidence that the orthopaedic surgeon failed to deeply cleanse, irrigate, and debride the injured area of the patient's thumb constituted proof of a departure from that degree of skill and learning ordinarily used by members of the medical profession, and that failure directly contributed to the patient's loss of the distal portion of his thumb.

Lack of Documentation

The importance of maintaining records of treatment rendered to a patient must not be underestimated. It may be many years after a patient has been treated before litigation is initiated; therefore, it is imperative that records of treatment in the physician's office, as well as in the health care facility, be maintained. A jury may consider lack of documentation as sufficient evidence for finding a physician guilty of negligence.

Loss of Chance To Survive

In *Boudoin v. Nicholson, Baehr, Calhoun & Lanasa*,[42] expert testimony supported a finding of loss of chance to survive. A diagnostic radiologist's improper reading of a patient's X-ray resulted in a loss of chance to survive a chest-wall cancer. The radiologist acknowledged that the testimony of some experts at trial supported the finding that the patient suffered some loss of chance of survival due to the delayed detection of his tumor.

Boudoin had suffered a minor shoulder injury while lifting something at his job as a pipefitter. Because the pain did not subside after a few days, on May 19 he went to see Dr. Nicholson, the family practitioner who had treated him since he was 18. Based upon Boudoin's complaint of pain in the outer chest and a physical examination, Dr. Nicholson took a chest X-ray that, in his opinion, showed nothing remarkable. A cardiogram was also normal, so Dr. Nicholson diagnosed Boudoin's injury as a muscle strain and prescribed accordingly. Nevertheless, he sent the X-ray to be evaluated by a diagnostic radiologist, Hendler. The radiology report returned to Nicholson read in part:

> CHEST: Cardiac, hilar and mediastinal shadows do not appear unusual. Both lung fields and angles appear clear. A 3.5 cm. broad based benign osteo-

matous projection is noted at the level of the vertebral border of the inferior aspect of the left scapula.

> IMPRESSION: 1—No evidence of active pulmonary or cardiac pathology.

Boudoin did not contact Nicholson again until January 1989, when he complained of discomfort in his neck as well as pain in his right shoulder blade and arm. Nicholson again ruled out serious injury through a cervical X-ray, resulting in a diagnosis of cervical spasm, degenerative discs, and bilateral spondylosis. On April 18, 1989, Boudoin returned to Nicholson complaining of night sweats, weight loss, and pain in his left chest. A chest X-ray showed a large abnormal mass, so Boudoin was given both the 1988 X-ray and the one just taken, and was immediately sent to see a pulmonologist, Dr. Rosenberg. On his way to Rosenberg's office, Boudoin went to J.C. Penney's, where his wife, Rosalie, worked. On the verge of tears, he told his wife that the doctor had "found something" on his lungs and that he had to see a lung specialist. Mrs. Boudoin clocked out and accompanied her husband to the pulmonologist's office, where he delivered the two X-rays and underwent various examinations and tests. While Boudoin was undergoing a breathing test, Rosenberg called Mrs. Boudoin into his office and showed her the tumor as it appeared on the X-rays taken eleven months apart, and also had her read Hendler's May 1988 report. Although Rosenberg told Mrs. Boudoin that the tumor could have been removed easily when it was as small as it first appeared, she did not attach any importance to the discussion. As she testified at trial, from the moment her husband had told her about Nicholson's discovery, her attention was focused on his life and survival, rather than the past. Although the tumor initially appeared to be on Boudoin's left lung, innumerable tests and examinations in the next few weeks established that the cancer was in the pleura, the tissue lining the chest wall; it was definitely malignant. Although a bone scan of the ribs indicated those on the left had a different absorption rate than those on the right, no sign of metastasis was found in the lymph nodes of the chest or other tissues. Dr. Rigby surgically removed the tumor, now measuring 20 by 17.5 by 7 centimeters, on May 10, 1989, along with a large portion of the chest wall and four ribs. Because a four or five millimeter metastatic deposit was found in Boudoin's right diaphragm, a section of that tissue also was removed, but there was no sign of cancer on the lungs. A metal plate was implanted to replace the structural support lost with the removal of the ribs. After recovering from his surgery, Boudoin underwent concurrent radiation and chemotherapies from June through August 1989 with a final course of chemotherapy in September. X-rays and examinations done every other month through March 1990 showed no signs of recurrence. Four months later, however, abnormalities were detected, and a second surgery was performed on July 20, 1990. The surgeon now found a tumor that was so extensive that "we were never able to get entirely beyond it, and it did not allow access to the intrapleural cavity." The only tissue removed during the surgery was a biopsy sample, which confirmed a malignant recurrence. Boudoin and his family were informed that even with chemotherapy, the prognosis was very poor. Further treatment was restricted to alleviating pain until Boudoin's death on December 18, 1990.

Dr. Hendler appealed an award of $560,000 to the widow and adult children of Mr. Boudoin, based upon a jury's finding that the physician's improper reading of Boudoin's X-ray resulted in a loss of chance to survive a chest-wall cancer. The appeals court affirmed the finding of liability and causation but reduced the amount of the award.

Medications

With thousands of brand and generic drugs in use, it is no surprise that medication error is one of the leading causes of patient injuries. Physicians should encourage the limited and judicious use of all medications and document periodically the reason for their continuation. They should be alert to any contraindications and incompatibilities between prescription and over-the-counter drugs and herbal supplements.

Recognizing common causes for and developing practices that reduce the likelihood of errors can reduce medication errors. The negligent administration of medications is often due to the following errors: the wrong medication; the wrong patient; the wrong dose; the wrong route; and/or the wrong site.

Wrong Dosage

Expert testimony in *Leal v. Simon*,[43] a medical malpractice action, supported the jury's determination that the physician had been negligent when he reduced the dosage of a resident's psychotropic medication, Haldol. The resident, a 36-year-old retarded individual who had been institutionalized his entire life, was a resident in an intermediate care facility. The drug had been used for controlling the resident's self-abusive behavior. Expert medical testimony showed that the physician failed to familiarize himself with the resident's history, failed to secure the resident's complete medical records, and failed to wean the resident off the medication slowly.

Abuse in Prescribing Controlled Substances

The Board of Regents in *Moyo v. Ambach*[44] determined that a physician had prescribed methaqualone fraudulently and with gross negligence to 20 patients. The Board of Regents found that the physician did not prescribe methaqualone in good faith or for sound medical reasons. His abuse in prescribing controlled substances constituted the fraudulent practice of medicine. Expert testimony established that it was common knowledge in the medical community that methaqualone was a widely abused and addictive drug. Meth-

aqualone should not have been used for insomnia without first trying other means of treatment. On appeal, the court found that there was sufficient evidence to support the board's finding.

Misdiagnosis

Misdiagnosis is the most frequently cited injury event in malpractice suits against physicians. Although diagnosis is a medical art and not an exact science, early detection can be critical to a patient's recovery. Misdiagnosis may involve the diagnosis and treatment of a disease different from that which the patient actually suffers or the diagnosis and treatment of a disease that the patient does not have. Misdiagnosis in and of itself will not necessarily impose liability on a physician, unless deviation from the accepted standard of care and injury can be established.

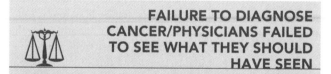

FAILURE TO DIAGNOSE CANCER/PHYSICIANS FAILED TO SEE WHAT THEY SHOULD HAVE SEEN

Citation: *Corley v. State Department of Health & Hospitals, 749 So.2d 926 (La. App. 1999)*

Facts

In 1978, Mr. Corley was diagnosed with neurofibromatosis and had four neurofibromas removed from his head, arm, hip, and leg by a physician in Texarkana. Thereafter, a few months prior to his return to Louisiana in 1988, Corley, who had no other known health problems, began experiencing low back pain.

On February 11, 1988, Corley sought medical treatment from Dr. Gremillion, a family practitioner. Corley complained that he had been experiencing low back pain and abdominal discomfort for approximately four months. He also noted that he had intermittent right shoulder pain and trouble sleeping. At Corley's request, Gremillion ordered a total work-up that included X-rays of the lower spine, chest, kidneys, and gall bladder, as well as an upper gastrointestinal (GI) series. Gremillion also prescribed Flexeril, a muscle relaxer, and Anaprox, an antiinflammatory pain medication. Gremillion, feeling that a specialist should see Corley, then gave him a written referral to E.A. Conway Medical Center in Monroe for an orthopaedic evaluation.

On March 2, 1988, Corley, accompanied by Sheila Corley, reported to the E.A. Conway emergency department. The Corleys presented admitting personnel with all of Corley's records from Gremillion, including the X-rays and other test reports. Dr. Fuller, an emergency department physician, took a history from Corley and reviewed Gremillion's notes and the X-ray reports. He also conducted a routine physical examination and had X-rays made of Corley's lower back. Notwithstanding the presence of several growths and café au lait spots on Corley's back and torso, Fuller was unaware that his patient had neurofibromatosis.

Fuller found everything to be within normal limits and it was his impression that Corley was suffering from low back pain based on minimal subjective complaints of pain. Fuller continued Corley on the medication prescribed by Gremillion and made an appointment for him with the Orthopedic Clinic on March 16, 1988.

On that date, a fourth year resident, Dr. Bridges, saw Corley in the Orthopedic Clinic. Bridges does not recall looking at or reading the X-rays or reports from Corley's previous examinations. Bridges conducted a physical exam, which was normal, and started Corley on a conservative course of treatment for low back pain. Bridges' notes from this date indicate his awareness of Corley's neurofibromatosis.

Dr. Mehta next saw Corley on April 20, 1988. Mehta's notes reflect that his physical exam of Corley was normal, but that he felt that Corley had a posture problem and referred him to physical therapy for correction of his posture. Again, the notes do not reflect whether Mehta reviewed any of Corley's previous medical records, X-rays, or reports.

On September 14, 1988, Corley was seen by fourth year surgical resident Dr. White. On that date, Corley noted that his pain had worsened and was occasionally affecting his walking. White's examination yielded no objective findings of low back pain, but he did notice several café au lait spots indicative of neurofibromatosis so he ordered a CT scan of Corley's low back to rule out any neurofibroma changes in the nerve roots. Dr. Ellis, a radiologist at E.A. Conway, interpreted the CT scan as showing arthritis consistent with fibrosis or spinal stenosis and possible edema of the right L-5 nerve root, which, according to White, may or may not have been the cause of Corley's back pain. White did not review any of the previous medical records, X-rays, or reports. Corley's last visit to E.A. Conway was September 21, 1988. On that date, White reviewed the results of the CT scan with Corley, continued him on an antiinflammatory drug, and encouraged him to continue his back exercises. White instructed Corley to return to the clinic in three months.

Thereafter, on October 26, 1988, Corley, plagued by constant back pain and beginning to experience difficulty breathing, consulted Dr. Maxwell, a chiropractor, who did a full spinal X-ray that revealed a markedly diminished right lung area. Maxwell sent Corley to his father, also a chiropractor, who confirmed that there was a potential problem with Corley's right lung and recommended that he see a pulmonary specialist.

On October 31, 1988, Corley presented to Gremillion complaining of chest congestion and shortness of breath. Gremillion diagnosed him with bronchitis and implemented treatment accordingly. Corley returned to Gremillion on November 14, 1988, with complaints of shortness of breath and marked weight loss. Subsequent diagnostic testing confirmed the presence of a very large mass in Corley's right chest.

Prior to his death on January 23, 1990, Corley received radiation and chemotherapy treatment.

Corley's surviving spouse and son instituted a malpractice action seeking wrongful death and survival damages.

The trial court rendered judgment in favor of the plaintiffs and against E.A. Conway in the amount of $400,000. It is from this judgment that defendants, the state and E.A. Conway, have appealed.

Issue

The primary issue on appeal is whether the trial court committed error in finding that the physicians at E.A. Conway deviated from the applicable standard of care by failing to properly diagnose Corley's condition, a large cancerous mass in his mediastinum, during the course of their treatment of his low back pain.

Finding

The physicians at E.A. Conway Medical Center fell below the standard of care when they failed to properly diagnose Walter Corley's condition.

Reason

The evidence was in Gremillion's X-rays and medical report when Corley first arrived at E.A. Conway. Simply put, these physicians *failed to see what they should have seen.*

When Corley did not respond to conservative treatment, there had to be another explanation for his low back pain. The physicians ignored this and did not expand their inquiry, which they should have done under a differential diagnosis assessment. For this, Corley was deprived of a significant chance of survival.

A physician is required to take a "thorough" history based upon a patient's presenting signs and symptoms. A physician is required to perform a physical examination based upon the patient's presenting signs and symptoms. If the findings from the medical history and physical exam support a diagnosis, one should be made and treatment instituted.

When, in treating a patient, a diagnosis cannot be made, at that time a *differential diagnosis* should be made, which includes all reasonable, plausible, and foreseeable causes for the signs and symptoms noted in the patient. After forming a differential diagnosis, it is the physician's duty to rule out all imminent, serious, and life-threatening causes for the signs and symptoms. This includes performing or ordering diagnostic tests or studies that will assist in ruling in or out imminent, serious, and life-threatening causes.

Physicians are obligated to rule out these imminent, serious, and life-threatening causes first. Failure to eliminate these causes can subject a patient to a foreseeable risk of harm and would further constitute a breach of the applicable standards of care.

Discussion

1. Why is it important to be able to make differential diagnoses?
2. Why did the appellate court find that the trial court had not erred in finding that the physicians deviated from the applicable standard of care in their diagnosis and treatment of Corley?

Appendicitis

Misdiagnosis does not always end in a verdict for the plaintiff. Summary judgment was properly entered in dismissing an action alleging that a physician had been negligent in failing to diagnose a pregnant patient's appendicitis in *Fiedler v. Steger.*[45] The testimony of expert witnesses for both parties established that diagnosis of appendicitis during pregnancy is difficult, that it probably would not have been diagnosed on the dates in question, and that the appendix had probably ruptured postpartum.

Diabetic Acidosis

A case before the Mississippi Supreme Court, *Hill v. Stewart,*[46] involved a patient who became ill and was admitted to the hospital. The physician was advised of the patient's recent weight loss, frequent urination, thirst, loss of vision, nausea, and vomiting. Routine laboratory tests were ordered including a urinalysis, but not a blood glucose test. On the following day, a consultant diagnosed the patient's condition as severe diabetic acidosis. Treatment was given, but the patient failed to respond to the therapy and died. The attending physician was sued for failing to test for diabetes and for failing to diagnose and treat the patient on the first day in the hospital. The attending physician said in court that he had suspected diabetes and admitted that when diabetes is suspected, a urinalysis and a blood sugar test should be performed. An expert medical witness testified that failure to do so would be a departure from the skill and care required of a general practitioner. The expert also stated that the patient in this case probably would have had a good chance of survival if treated properly. The state supreme court reversed the directed verdict for the physician by a lower court and remanded the case for retrial. There was sufficient evidence presented to permit the case to go to the jury for decision.

Once a physician concludes that a particular test is indicated, it should be performed and evaluated as soon as practicable. Delay may constitute negligence. The law imposes on a physician the same degree of responsibility in making a diagnosis as it does in prescribing and administering treatment.

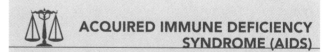

ACQUIRED IMMUNE DEFICIENCY SYNDROME (AIDS)

Citation: *Doe v. McNulty, 630 So.2d 825 (La. Ct. App. 1993)*

Facts

The plaintiff, Jane Doe, had been exposed to the human immunodeficiency virus (HIV) as the result of sexual contact. The plaintiff consulted her defendant physicians but they failed to diagnose her condition as being positive for either HIV or AIDS. The disease weakened her immune system and she developed pneumocystis carinii pneumonia (PCP) and was admitted to a hospital.

The patient was eventually diagnosed with AIDS. The patient's infectious disease expert, Dr. Hill, claimed that proper diagnosis prior to her acute episode would have provided greater opportunity for improved long-term treatment. Hill stated that the patient would not have contracted PCP for another year and this would have added another year to her life expectancy and ability to work. The defendants admitted that they negligently failed to timely diagnose the patient's condition.

The defendants' expert witness, Dr. Lutz, testified from his review of the patient's medical record that the patient's diagnosis could not have been determined based on the symptoms as described in the record. Lutz had never examined the patient and based his determination on the documentation contained in the medical record. Lutz did, however, agree that if the patient's immune system had not been totally destroyed, preventive treatment could have resulted in a longer life span.

The civil district court entered judgment on a jury verdict of $700,000 in general damages, which included pain and suffering, mental anguish, disability, and the loss of the enjoyment of life, and $314,000 for medical and special damages. The defendant appealed.

Issue

Did the defendant's failure to timely diagnose the plaintiff's condition cause her to lose one year of life? Did the jury commit obvious error in awarding $700,000 in general damages and $314,000 in medical damages?

Holding

The Louisiana Court of Appeal held that the evidence supported the jury's finding of causation and that the award of $700,000 was not excessive.

Reason

The medical defendants agreed that they negligently failed to timely diagnose the patient's condition. The plaintiff's expert witness testified repeatedly that within the "reasonable medical probability" standard and the "more-likely-than-not" standard, if the plaintiff had been properly diagnosed and treated no later than August 18, 1990, which was the date the medical defendants should have diagnosed and treated her, then she would have not contracted pneumocystis carinii pneumonia. She would have worked, as well as lived, for another year.

Discussion

1. On what basis should a physician determine the appropriateness of his or her patient's specific clinical needs (e.g., medical history)?
2. When does the physician–patient relationship terminate? Does it terminate at the moment of discharge? Explain.

Mitral Valve Malfunction

In *Lauderdale v. United States*,[47] the federal government was held liable under the Federal Tort Claims Act for the death of a patient whose mitral valve malfunction was misdiagnosed at a military medical clinic. Under applicable Alabama law, the physician failed to conduct the necessary tests to determine the cause of a suspected heart problem. The physician never indicated to the patient that the problem was severe, that the treatment with digoxin was tentative, and that his well-being mandated that he return in a week. The patient subsequently died. He was found not to have been contributorily negligent by failing to return to the clinic. The patient had not been told sufficiently of the urgency of a return visit. This failure was considered the proximate cause of the patient's death because his illness might have been treated successfully.

Skull Fracture

In *Ramberg v. Morgan*,[48] a police department physician, at the scene of an accident, examined an unconscious man who had been struck by an automobile. The physician concluded that the patient's insensibility was a result of alcohol intoxication, not the accident, and ordered the police to remove him to jail instead of the hospital. The man, to the physician's knowledge, remained semiconscious for several days and finally was taken from the cell to the hospital at the insistence of his family. The patient subsequently died, and the autopsy revealed massive skull fractures. The court found that any physician should reasonably anticipate the presence of head injuries when a person is struck by a car. Failure to refer an accident victim to another physician or a hospital is actionable neglect of the physician's duty. Although a physician does not ensure the correctness of the diagnosis or treatment, a patient is entitled to such thorough and careful examination as his or her condition and attending circumstances permit, with such diligence and methods of diagnosis as usually are approved and practiced by medical people of ordinary or average learning, judgment, and skill in the community or similar localities.

Testicular Cancer

The hospital in *Brickner v. Osteopathic Hospital*[49] was held vicariously liable for a surgical resident's failure to diagnose testicular cancer during exploratory surgery performed under the supervision of a staff physician. The hospital was not insulated from liability under the borrowed servant doctrine even though the supervising surgeon had authority over the resident during the operation. The hospital never relinquished control over the resident, who was required under the hospital's training program to assist in diagnosis and who could have taken a biopsy without express instructions of the operating surgeon. Liability was not precluded because of the hospital's lack of actual control over the resident's medical decision not to perform a biopsy. The resident was performing a service for which he had been employed.

Mistaken Identity/Wrong Patient–Wrong Surgery

In *Southwestern Kentucky Baptist Hospital v. Bruce*,[50] a patient admitted for conization of the cervix was taken mistakenly to the operating room for a thyroidectomy. The physician was notified early during surgery that he had the wrong patient on the operating room table. The operation was terminated immediately. The thyroidectomy was not completed, and the incision was sutured. The patient filed an action for malpractice and recovered $10,000 from the physician and $90,000 from the hospital. That the patient mistakenly answered to the name of another patient who had been scheduled for a thyroidectomy did not excuse the failure of the surgeon, the anesthesiologist, and the surgical technician to determine the identity of the patient by examining her identification bracelet. The Kentucky Supreme Court held that the verdict was not excessive in view of the injuries, which consisted of a four-inch incision along the patient's neck, which became infected and required cosmetic surgery.

Obstetrics/Gynecology

One of the most vulnerable medical specialties with significant risk exposure to malpractice suits is obstetrics/gynecology. Obstetrical negligence claims often stem from errors in physician judgment, whereas gynecologic claims are often the result of inadequate technical performance. The following cases illustrate why the risks are high.

Failure To Perform a Caesarean Section

A medical malpractice action was brought against two obstetricians, a pediatrician, and the hospital in *Ledogar v. Giordano*[51] because of a newborn infant's prenatal and post-natal hypoxia, which allegedly caused brain damage resulting in autism. The record contained sufficient proof of causation to support a verdict in favor of the plaintiff when an expert obstetrician testified that both obstetricians were negligent in failing to perform a Caesarean section at an earlier time, that the hospital staff departed from proper medical standards of care by not monitoring the fetal heartbeat at least every 15 minutes, and that, with a reasonable degree of medical certainty, it was probable that the fetus had suffered hypoxia during labor.

Failure To Attend Delivery—Fetus Decapitated

The plaintiff in *Lucchesi v. Stimmel*[52] brought an action against a physician for intentional infliction of emotional distress, claiming that the physician had failed to be present during unsuccessful attempts to deliver her premature fetus and that he thereafter had failed to disclose to her that the fetus was decapitated during attempts to achieve delivery by pulling on the hip area to free the head. The judge instructed the jury that it could conclude that the physician had been guilty of extreme and outrageous conduct for staying at home and leaving the delivery in the hands of a first-year intern and a third-year resident, neither of whom was experienced in breech deliveries.

Failure To Perform Timely Caesarean Section

The attending physician in *Jackson v. Huang*[53] was negligent in failing to perform a timely Caesarean section. The attending physician had applied too much traction when he was faced with shoulder dyscotia, a situation in which a baby's shoulder hangs under the pubic bone, arresting the progress of the infant through the birth canal. As a result, the infant suffered permanent injury to the brachial plexus nerves of his right shoulder and arm. On appeal of this case, there was no error found in the trial court's finding of fact when such finding was supported by testimony of the plaintiff's expert witness. The trial judge accepted the testimony of Dr. Forte, the expert witness, who testified that the defendant did possess the necessary skill and knowledge relevant to the practice of obstetrics and gynecology. The defendant, because of prolonged labor and weight of the baby, should have anticipated the possibility of shoulder dyscotia and performed a timely Caesarean section.

Emergency Assistance

An obstetrician who responds to an emergency call by a surgeon to assist in the completion of a tubal ligation most likely will be immune from a negligence claim under the state's good Samaritan law if he or she had a good-faith belief that the patient was in a life-threatening situation. Such was the case in *Pemberton v. Dharmani*,[54] where the court of appeals held that the Michigan Good Samaritan statute:

merely requires a good-faith belief by health care personnel that they are attending a life-threatening emergency in order to be cloaked with the immunity provided by the statute, regardless of whether a life-threatening emergency actually exists. To construe the statute otherwise would controvert the purpose of the statute and render it meaningless. Healthcare personnel would be discouraged from giving treatment in emergency situations if an actual life-threatening situation were required to exist before they would be cloaked with immunity. Treatment may be even delayed in a given case, worsening the condition of the patient by waiting until the patient is in an obviously life-threatening situation before rendering treatment.[55]

Wrongful Death/Unborn Fetus

A medical malpractice action was filed against the physician in *Modaber v. Kelley*[56] for personal injuries and mental anguish caused by the stillbirth of a child. The circuit court entered judgment on a jury verdict against the obstetrician, and an appeal was taken. The Virginia Supreme Court held that the evidence was sufficient to support a finding that the obstetrician's conduct during the patient's pregnancy caused direct injury to the patient. Evidence at trial showed that the physician failed to treat the mother's known condition of toxemia, including the development of high blood pressure and the premature separation of the placenta from the uterine wall, and that the physician thereafter had failed to respond in a timely fashion when the mother went into premature labor. The court also held that injury to the unborn child constituted injury to the mother and that she could recover for the physical injury and mental anguish associated with the stillbirth. The court found that the award of $750,000 in compensatory damages was not excessive.

Premature Discharge

The premature discharge of a patient is risky business. The intent of discharging patients more expeditiously is to reduce costs. As pointed out by Dr. Nelson, an obstetrician and board member of the American Medical Association, such decisions "should be based on medical factors and ought not be relegated to bean counters."[57]

Psychiatry

The major risk areas of psychiatry include commitment, electroshock, duty to warn, and suicide. Matters relating to admission, consent, and discharge are governed by statute in most states.

Commitment

One of the more difficult issues for physicians is how to handle the different situations that might arise with individuals requiring involuntary commitment for psychiatric care and evaluation. The recent emphasis on patient rights has had a major impact on the necessity to perform an appropriate assessment prior to commitment. The various state statutes often provide requirements granting an individual's rights to legal counsel and other procedural safeguards (e.g., patient hotline) governing the admission, retention, and discharge of psychiatric patients.

Most states have enacted administrative procedures that must be followed. The various statutes often require that two physicians certify the need for commitment. Physicians who participate in the commitment of a patient should do so only after first examining the patient and reaching their own conclusions. Reliance on another's examination and recommendation for commitment could give rise to a claim of malpractice. Commitment is generally necessary in those situations in which a person may be in substantial danger of injuring another person or property.

Involuntary. In *In re Detention of Meistrell*,[58] proof of dangerousness was found adequate to support an order of involuntary commitment. There was testimony that on two occasions the patient had jumped off a teeter-totter, causing his two small children to fall to the ground. A substantial risk of physical harm to others also was demonstrated by testimony that the patient had threatened his wife's ex-husband.

Continuation of Commitment. In *In re Todd*,[59] a psychiatrist filed a petition for additional detention of a person previously ordered admitted to a state hospital for pretrial psychiatric examination. The circuit court, after hearing testimony from the appellant's son, a social worker at the hospital, and the psychiatrist, ordered detention, and the detainee appealed. The episode that gave rise to the involuntary commitment occurred when the appellant threw eggs at a house and various businesses and broke some windows at a house with a tire iron. She lightly bumped a police car and was charged with second-degree property damage. During her involuntary detention, she refused to take her medications, which were necessary because of her illness. The psychiatrist indicated his concern that she might harm her invalid husband on release. Additional detention was considered necessary until such time as the detainee's illness could be controlled by drugs. The court of appeals held that the testimony of the psychiatrist established clear and convincing evidence to meet a required standard that the detainee's actions presented risk of serious harm to herself or others.

Involuntary Commitment Invalid. In *In re Carl*,[60] a New York Supreme Court found a patient to be mentally ill and authorized his involuntary retention. On appeal, however, the New York Supreme Court, Appellate Division, held that the state had not shown by clear and convincing evidence that the patient's instability caused him to pose a substantial threat of physical injury to himself or others. The examining physician's testimony indicated that the patient did not pose a direct threat of physical harm to himself or others but that it was questionable whether he would be able to provide for the essentials of life. The patient had testified that he was aware of food needs, of where to get food, and how he would pay for it. He indicated that he would not sleep outside and that he had a bed in a rooming house where he had been paying rent for two years.

Commitment by Spouse. In *Bencomo v. Morgan*[61] the plaintiff's husband filed a petition to have his wife declared incompetent. In a letter supporting the petition, the defendant physician, who had treated the wife 10 years previously, stated that she was badly in need of a psychiatric examination. The plaintiff/wife attempted to sue the physician for libel and slander. The court held that the plaintiff had no cause for action because it was her husband who initiated the commitment procedures.

Commitment by Parent. In *Parham v. J.R.*,[62] the U.S. Supreme Court held that the risk of error inherent in a parental decision to have a child institutionalized for mental health care is sufficiently great that an inquiry should be made by a neutral fact finder to determine whether statutory requirements for admission are satisfied. Although a formal or quasi-formal hearing is not required and an inquiry need not be conducted by a legally trained judicial or administrative officer, such inquiry must probe a child's background, using all available sources. It is necessary that a decision maker have the authority to refuse to admit a child who does not satisfy medical standards for admission. A child's continuing need for commitment also must be reviewed periodically by a similarly independent procedure.

Patient Due Process Rights. The principles of due process were violated in *Birl v. Wallis*[63] when an involuntarily committed patient was conditionally released and reconfined without notice and opportunity for a hearing. Remand was required to permit the drafting of reconfinement procedures that would protect the patient's due process rights.

Electroshock

Most states have laws and regulations governing the use of electroshock and other treatments for psychiatric patients. Failure to abide by these statutory and regulatory guidelines may result in liability to the organization and treating physician.

Duty To Warn

In *Tarasoff v. Regents of the University of California*,[64] a former patient allegedly killed a third party after revealing his homicidal plans to his therapist. His therapist made no effort to inform the victim of the patient's intentions. The California Supreme Court held that when a therapist determines or reasonably should determine that a patient poses a serious danger of violence to others, there is a duty to exercise reasonable care to protect the foreseeable victims and to warn them of any impending danger. Discharge of this duty also may include notifying the police or taking whatever steps are reasonably necessary under the circumstances.

Under Nebraska law, the relationship between a psychotherapist and a patient gives rise to an affirmative duty to initiate whatever precautions are reasonably necessary to protect the potential victims of a patient. This duty develops when a therapist knows or should know that a patient's dangerous propensities present an unreasonable risk of harm to others.[65]

Exceptions to Duty To Warn

In *Shaw v. Glickman*,[66] the Maryland Court of Special Appeals held that a plaintiff could not recover against a psychiatric team on the theory that they were negligent in failing to warn the plaintiff of the patient's unstable and violent condition. The court held that making such a disclosure would have violated statutes pertaining to privilege against disclosure of communications relating to treatment of mental or emotional disorders. The court found that a psychiatrist may have a duty to warn the potential victim of a dangerous mental patient's intent to harm. However, the duty could be imposed only if the psychiatrist knew the identity of the prospective victim.

The psychiatrist in *Currie v. United States*[67] was found not to have had a duty to seek the involuntary commitment of a patient who evidenced homicidal tendencies. Absent control over the patient, the federal government could not be held liable for a murder that the patient committed at his former place of employment. The psychiatrist had warned the patient's former employer and law enforcement officials about his dangerousness.

There was no duty on the part of the hospital or treating psychiatrists in *Sharpe v. South Carolina Department of Mental Health*[68] to warn the general public of the potential danger that might result from a psychiatric patient's release from a state hospital. There was no identifiable threat to a decedent who was shot by the patient approximately two months after the patient's release from voluntary commitment under a plan of outpatient care. In addition, there was nothing in the record that indicated that the former patient and the decedent had known each other prior to the patient's release.

Suicide

The attendant in *Fernandez v. State*[69] left a patient alone in her room for five minutes when the patient appeared to be asleep. During the attendant's absence, the patient injured herself in a repeated suicide attempt. The court found that even if the hospital had assumed a duty to observe the patient continually, such a five-minute absence would not constitute negligence. Therefore, the hospital could not be held liable for the patient's injuries.

However, in a case in which a patient with a 14-year history of mental problems escaped from a hospital and committed suicide by jumping off a roof,[70] the record showed the patient was to be checked every 15 minutes. There was no evidence that such checks had been made. The appellate court ruled that the facts showed a *prima facie* case of negligence.

In *Eady v. Alter*,[71] the New York Supreme Court, Appellate Division, held that an intern's notation on the hospital record that the patient tried to jump out the window was sufficient to establish a *prima facie* case against the hospital. The patient succeeded in committing suicide by jumping out the window approximately 10 minutes after having been seen by the intern. Testimony had been given that the patient was restrained inadequately after the reported attempted suicide.

Failure To Provide Appropriate Evaluation

The plaintiff's 21-year-old son, in *Vasilik v. Federbush*,[72] was at his father's home on April 25, seeking help in overcoming his heroin addiction. On April 26, the son was acting noticeably withdrawn and began vomiting. The plaintiff took his son to a local hospital to be evaluated for drug withdrawal symptoms. The son tested negative for the presence of drugs in his blood and he was discharged on the same day with instructions to attend a drug rehabilitation program.

The next afternoon, April 27, the plaintiff noticed that his son was not in his room, but he was able to locate him after a search by car. Unbeknownst to the plaintiff at the time, his son had slashed his wrist with a kitchen knife and jumped out of a bedroom window in unsuccessful attempts at suicide. That evening, after his son went to sleep, and after the plaintiff became aware that his son had attempted suicide, the plaintiff called the office of a drug rehabilitation program for help. He was advised that, because of his son's attempts at suicide, his son could not be admitted to the rehabilitation program. The plaintiff was advised that when his son awoke, the plaintiff should take him to the defendant hospital's Crisis Center.

On April 28, the plaintiff took his son to the Crisis Center and brought with him the knife his son had used to attempt suicide. They were sent to the hospital's emergency department. The plaintiff explained to the emergency department nurse that his son had attempted suicide. The son's wrist was bandaged, and the plaintiff and his son then proceeded to the Crisis Center. There, the son was interviewed by defendant Van Doren, a nurse, and by defendant Dr. Federbush, a physician. After about 40 minutes, the plaintiff was admitted to the interview room. Federbush and Van Doren advised the plaintiff that his son was not suicidal but was instead "acting out" and looking for attention. Hospitalization was not offered and the plaintiff was advised to follow up with a drug rehabilitation program. The hospitalization records contain no information as to voluntary hospitalization being recommended or offered, nor do the records reflect that the son refused any offer of voluntary hospitalization.

The plaintiff and his son returned to the plaintiff's home, and his son went to bed. When the plaintiff checked his son at about 6:00 A.M., he was gone. The plaintiff telephoned the home of his ex-wife and was relieved to learn that his son was there. The plaintiff agreed to pick him up before the mother left for work. A few minutes later, however, the mother called and told the plaintiff that their son had left her house. The plaintiff got into his car and immediately went to look for his son. While searching for his son, he noticed flashing lights on nearby Route 80. When he went to investigate, he saw paramedics administering cardiopulmonary resuscitation (CPR) to his son. He began screaming and was restrained by the police. The plaintiff was told that his son had jumped in front of a dump truck. While at the scene, the plaintiff observed the paramedics placing a blanket over his son's body.

The plaintiff instituted a lawsuit against the defendants alleging negligence, malpractice, and negligent infliction of emotional distress.

At trial, defendant Federbush testified that voluntary admission to the hospital would be automatically discussed as part of the treatment plan at the Crisis Center. Interrogatory answers by the defendants indicated that the son was offered voluntary admission, but that the son had declined the offer. At trial, Dr. Federbush testified that the deceased declined voluntary admission to the hospital. However, in a deposition prior to trial, he had testified that he could not recall whether the son had declined voluntary admission or not. On cross-examination, Federbush conceded that he had never specifically recommended hospitalization to the son.

Defendant nurse Van Doren testified that voluntary hospitalization was explained as an option to the plaintiff and his son, but was not recommended. That option, if in fact offered, was not recorded in the written hospital record.

The plaintiff's medical experts testified that (1) because of the son's two suicide attempts, he needed hospitalization; (2) additional steps should have been taken prior to ruling out major depression; (3) in all probability, the son would not have killed himself had he been hospitalized earlier and put on medications; and (4) his son's prior suicide attempts should have been taken more seriously. They opined that the failure to hospitalize the son and keep him under close supervision was a deviation from accepted standards of medical practice. The defendants' expert testified to the contrary, but conceded on cross-examination that the son had at least three high-risk factors for suicide.

In short, the trial largely turned on the contest between the experts. The jury, by its verdict, accepted the opinions of the plaintiff's experts. The court found, after a review of the record, no reason to disturb the jury's verdict. It was clearly not against the weight of the evidence. The plaintiff, as administrator of the estate of his late son, recovered a verdict of $425,000 against the defendants for their failure to provide appropriate evaluation and hospitalization of his son.

Prior to trial, the court dismissed the plaintiff's claim for damages for emotional distress. The state supreme court, in *Gendek v. Poblete*,[73] clarified the requirements for maintaining a claim for infliction of emotional distress based on malpractice. In *Gendek* the court stated that, to conform to public policy principles, the court would insist that an immediate, close, and clear involvement or connection be present between a person suffering emotional distress and the conduct of the professional health care providers whose fault has contributed to the grave or fatal injuries of a related loved one.

In this case, it was an undisputed fact that the tragic suicide did not come immediately after the misdiagnosis, but rather on the next day, some 15 hours later. The court found that 15 hours does not meet *Gendek's* requirement of an immediate connection. In addition, the plaintiff did not witness the occurrence of the tragic event, but instead happened upon the scene some minutes later and sadly witnessed the unsuccessful resuscitation efforts. Under the circumstances, the trial judge was correct in dismissing the emotional distress claim.

Surgery

Wrong-Sided Surgery

In *Hoffman v. Wells*,[74] the Georgia Supreme Court determined that hospital employees were not responsible for the plaintiff's injuries that resulted from the physician's performance of a surgical procedure on the wrong hand. The Georgia Supreme Court relied on the fact that the determination to proceed with the surgery was a medical decision made by the physician in the operating room. Further, the nursing staff informed the physician that the patient's admissions chart and consent form indicated that the surgery was scheduled to be performed on the patient's right hand. The physician nevertheless performed the surgery on the left hand. The court noted that the hospital owes a duty of reasonable care to its patients and is liable for the injuries negligently inflicted upon its patients by the nurses and other *employees* of the hospital.

Foreign Objects

Physicians who change an organization's procedures governing surgical operations can be liable for those acts should they result in patient injury, even if they are performed by an organization's employees. In *Martin v. Perth Amboy General Hospital*[75] a patient sued the hospital, cardiovascular surgeon, and nurses for leaving a laparotomy pad in his stomach. The surgeon, Dr. Lev, who performed the operation, was assisted by two other physicians as well as by a scrub nurse and a circulating nurse. Before the laparotomy pads were brought into the operating room, a strip of radiopaque material was embedded between the folds of the laparotomy pads that would show on an X-ray if a pad was left in the abdomen. Rings were attached to the laparotomy pads to prevent errors in counts made by the nurses; however, before the pads were used, the nurses, at the direction of the operating surgeon, removed the rings. For some unknown reason, the sponge count at the end of the operation indicated that no sponges were missing.

Lev contended that the charge against him adopted the captain of the ship doctrine, which is not recognized by the state of New Jersey. If Lev had not ordered the rings to be removed by the nurses, the court would have agreed that the charge was contrary to state judicial decisions. By exercising control over the nurses to the extent of directing them to remove the rings and thus eliminating the safeguards provided by the hospital to ensure a proper count by its employees, the surgeon became the nurses' "temporary or special employer" with regard to their duties involving the laparotomy pads used during the operation. Thus, the surgeon was equally liable with the hospital for the nurses' subsequent negligence in counting the pads.

The most common methods of preventing operating room objects from being left in a surgical wound are

- sponge or instrument counts
- attachments on lap pads and on drains and tubings
- X-rays taken at the time of the operation, sometimes made more effective by the use of radiopaque threads in sponges and pads (X-rays are also one of the postoperative methods of detecting foreign objects left in an operative wound.)

THE BROKEN NEEDLE

Citation: *Williams v. Kilgore, 618 So.2d 51 (Miss. 1992)*

Facts

On March 31, 1964, the patient-plaintiff was admitted to the University Medical Center for treatment of metastatic malignant melanoma on her left groin. On April 6, 1964, an unknown resident performed a bone marrow biopsy. The needle broke during the procedure and a fragment lodged in the patient. The patient was told that the needle would be removed the following day, when surgery was to be performed to remove a melanoma from her groin. The operating surgeons, Dr. Peede and Dr. Kilgore, were informed of the presence of the needle fragment prior to surgery. A notation by Peede stated that the needle fragment had been removed.

Although the needle fragment had not been removed, the patient remained asymptomatic until she was hospitalized for back pain in September 1985. During her hospitalization, the patient learned that the needle fragment was still in her lower back.

On October 7, 1985, the needle fragment was finally removed. The physician's discharge report suggested that there was a probable linkage between the needle fragment and recurrent strep infections that the patient had been experiencing. Although the patient's treating physicians had known as early as 1972 that the needle fragment had not been removed, there was no evidence that the patient was aware of this fact.

The defendant physicians argued that the statute of limitations had tolled under Mississippi Code, thus barring the case from proceeding to trial. The circuit court entered a judgment for the physicians, and the plaintiff appealed.

Issue

Was the plaintiff's malpractice action time barred?

Holding

The Mississippi Supreme Court held that the plaintiff's action was not time barred and was, therefore, remanded for trial.

Reason

A patient's cause for action begins to accrue and the statute of limitations begins to run when the patient can reasonably be held to have knowledge of the disease or injury. In this instance, the patient began to experience infections and back pain in 1985. Moreover, this is the date she discovered that the needle was causing her problems, never having been informed previously that the needle from the 1964 biopsy procedure remained lodged within her.

Discussion

1. Under what circumstances would the plaintiff's action have been time barred?
2. What is your impression of Dr. Peede's claim that the needle fragment had been removed?
3. What is the efficacy of X-rays following the alleged removal of the needle fragment?

Improper Performance of a Procedure

In *Ozment v. Wilkerson*,[76] Mrs. Wilkerson was suffering from Crohn's disease, a chronic ailment that affects the colon and small intestine. Part of the treatment for the disease is to allow the patient's gastrointestinal system to rest, and that means that the patient cannot eat. The patient is given a concentrated caloric solution intravenously. To deliver the needed nutritional solution, Dr. Ozment needed to place a central venous catheter into Mrs. Wilkerson's body. His practice had always been to insert such a catheter into the right atrium. He inserted a needle into Wilkerson's right subclavian vein and threaded a guide wire through that vein and on into the superior vena cava. Ozment then inserted the catheter over the guide wire, and removed the guide wire. Either the catheter or the guide wire punctured Mrs. Wilkerson's pericardial sac. The puncture resulted in a condition known as cardiac tamponade, caused by the accumulation of fluids in the pericardial sac. Wilkerson required emergency surgery to correct this condition and to repair the puncture. The surgery left a large and permanent scar over Wilkerson's sternum; the scar is typical of those left by open-heart surgery. The defendants, following a jury verdict favorable to the plaintiffs, filed an appeal.

The Alabama Supreme Court held that expert testimony supported the jury's finding that the catheter was inserted incorrectly. The plaintiff's expert, Dr. Moore, testified that the tip of the catheter should be placed in the superior vena cava and should not extend into the heart. Moore also stated that placing the tip of the catheter in the atrium, or against the wall of the atrium, was a deviation from the standard of care, skill, and diligence ordinarily exercised by a similarly situated physician in the same line of practice under the same or similar circumstances. Moore further testified that having the tip of the catheter lodged against the wall of the atrium presented a great danger to Wilkerson. He explained that Ozment should have withdrawn the catheter a little and rechecked the X-ray to see if the bent area had been straightened and if the tip was clearly above the level of the right atrium. Moore also stated that the intravenous central line perforated the right atrium and had caused cardiac tamponade, the condition that caused Wilkerson to have to undergo the emergency surgery. Moore's testimony provided sufficient evidence from which the jury could determine that Ozment had inserted the catheter incorrectly and had thereby breached his duty of care to Wilkerson.

Timely Diagnosis

A physician can be liable for reducing a patient's chances for survival. The timely diagnosis of a patient's condition is as important as the need to diagnose a patient's injury or disease properly. Failure to do so can constitute malpractice if a patient suffers injury as a result of such failure.

WRONGFUL DEATH

Citation: *Powell v. Margileth, 524 S.E.2d 434 (Va. 2000)*

Facts

On January 9, 1992, Dr. Massey, a specialist in otolaryngology, measured a node in Mr. Powell's neck as 4 cm x 3 cm and ordered a CT scan. The CT scan conducted January 11, 1992, indicated that the size of the left cervical mass was due to an enlarged internal jugular node, which most likely was an abscess.

On January 14, 1992, Massey aspirated fluid from the enlarged node. Although he discussed the CT scan with Powell and ordered cultures, he did not suggest a need for an examination to rule out cancer.

Because Powell had told Massey that he had experienced some exposure to cats, Massey referred Powell to Dr. Margileth, an infectious disease specialist experienced in the diagnosis and treatment of cat scratch disease. On January 27, 1992, Margileth performed tests for tuberculosis and cat scratch disease and measured the swelling in the left anterior superior neck. He advised Powell that he had cat scratch disease and prescribed antibiotics. The results of the CT scan had been furnished to Margileth.

On February 18, 1992, Massey palpitated the nodule in Powell's neck which measured 4 cm x 2.8 cm. Massey performed another examination on April 7, 1992, during the course of which he suggested the possibility of cancer.

In June 1992, Powell discovered a second lump in his neck and in July went for help to the Veterans Administration (VA) Medical Center Hospital. A needle aspiration of the two lumps resulted in the diagnosis of cancer, representing a progression from stage III in January 1992 when the CT scan was conducted to stage IV in July 1992. Powell underwent radiation therapy, surgery, and other treatment but died of cancer three years later at the age of 40.

The trial court held that there was not sufficient evidence that would allow a jury of reasonable persons to conclude that the defendant's breach of the standard of care: (1) proximately caused Powell's injuries; (2) adversely altered the required method of treatment; or (3) adversely affected Powell's rate of survival.

Issue

Did the trial court err in granting the defendant's motion to strike the plaintiff's evidence?

Holding

The appeals court ruled that there was adequate evidence that would allow a jury of reasonable persons to conclude that the defendant's breach of the standard of care proximately caused the decedent's injuries. The case was remanded for a new trial.

Reason

There was sufficient evidence that would allow this case to go to trial based on the testimony of qualified experts. Dr. Holder, one of the plaintiff's expert witnesses, testified that the defendant's misdiagnosis of cat scratch disease caused his patient delay in diagnosis and treatment of his cancer from January until July, and that if Powell had been informed of the possibility of cancer in January, and options were offered in terms of biopsy for fine needle aspirations, then Powell would have had a diagnosis of cancer probably the first week of February. Asked whether the delay was a direct and proximate cause of the failure of Margileth to comply with the required standard of care, Holder answered, "Yes, it was."

Dr. Ali, who had treated Powell at the VA Hospital, testified as an expert in the staging, treatment, and surgery of cancer. Asked what would have been Powell's percentage chance of survival for five years if he had received Powell as a patient based on the January 11, 1992 CT scan report, which identifies the cancer as stage III, Ali said that Powell would have had approximately a "75 percent chance" of surviving five years compared with the "15 to 20 percent chance" he had in July 1992.

Dr. Tercilla, a professor at Medical College of Virginia, was qualified as an expert in the staging and treatment of cancer, estimating prognosis at the cancer stage, and medical treatment caused by failure to make a timely diagnosis. Tercilla testified that, in his opinion, if Powell had been treated in January as opposed to July Powell would have had a higher likelihood of being in control of this disease than he had when he presented at the VA hospital in July.

Absent a recurrence, the witness agreed in all likelihood that Margileth's patient "would still be alive."

Dr. Kipreos, a pathologist at the VA center, was asked her opinion whether, "if Margileth would have requested a fine needle aspirate at the Mary Washington Hospital pathology laboratory" in January 1992, would Powell's cancer have been diagnosed at that time. In reply, the witness said that it was her opinion that it would have been diagnosed at that time.

Discussion

1. Discuss how the outcome in this case might have been different if a consultant had been involved early on in the patient's care and treatment.
2. Discuss the role of expert testimony in this case.

Treatment Outside the Field of Competence

A physician should practice discretion when treating a patient outside his or her field of expertise or competence. The standard of care required in a malpractice case will be that of the specialty in which a physician is treating, whether or not he or she has been credentialed in that specialty.

In a California case, *Carrasco v. Bankoff*,[77] a small boy suffering third-degree burns over 18 percent of his body was admitted to a hospital. During his initial confinement, there was little done except to occasionally dress and redress the burned area. At the end of a 53-day confinement, the patient was suffering hypergranulation of the burned area and muscular-skeletal dysfunction. The surgeon treating him was not a board-certified plastic surgeon and apparently not properly trained in the management of burn cases. At trial, the patient's medical expert, a plastic surgeon who had assumed responsibility for care after the first hospitalization, outlined

the accepted medical practice in cases of this nature. The first surgeon acknowledged this accepted practice. The court held that there was substantial evidence to permit a finding of professional negligence because of the defendant surgeon's failure to perform to the accepted standard of care and that such failure resulted in the patient's injury.

Radiology

Diagnostic errors often account for radiology claims. Several cases involving X-rays are discussed below.

Misinterpretation of X-rays

The deceased, Jane Fahr, in *Setterington v. Pontiac General Hospital*,[78] was concerned about a lump in her thigh. She had a CT scan taken at Pontiac General Hospital in August 1987. The radiologist, Dr. Mittner, did not mention that the lump could be cancerous. In reliance on the radiologist's report, Dr. Sanford, the plaintiff's treating physician, regarded the condition as a hematoma and believed that a biopsy was not warranted. In late January 1988, Fahr returned to Pontiac General Hospital for another CT scan as the lump seemed to be enlarging. The radiologist, Dr. Khalid, did not include the possibility of a malignant tumor in his report. As a result, Sanford continued to believe that Fahr had a hematoma. In early September 1988, Fahr returned to Sanford who had another CT scan performed. Dr. Kayne, the radiologist, found an enlarged hematoma. In a follow-up discussion with Sanford, Kayne assured Sanford that the lump did not appear to be dangerous or invasive. As a result, Sanford concluded that Fahr had a hematoma with a leaking blood vessel. In October 1988, the tumor was biopsied and the cancer diagnosed. By December 1988, chest scans revealed metastasis. Fahr died on July 6, 1990, at the age of 32. Setterington, Fahr's personal representative, brought a malpractice action against Sanford and Pontiac General Hospital, alleging that they failed to timely diagnose and treat Fahr.

The jury found that the radiologists were agents of defendant Pontiac General Hospital and breached the standard of care. The jury also concluded that the breach was a proximate cause of Fahr's death. The jury returned a verdict for the plaintiff in the amount of $251,554.62. The trial court denied the plaintiff's motion for new trial as to damages, as well as the defendant's motion for new trial.

The defendant argued that plaintiff failed to produce evidence that the malpractice was a proximate cause of Fahr's death. Dr. Golomb testified that there is a five-year survival rate for 60 percent of the patients who undergo the treatment he recommended at the stage of plaintiff's cancer in the fall of 1987. However, he did not testify that the plaintiff would have fallen within the 60 percent group. The defendant asserted that there was no evidence that Fahr would have survived even with the proper diagnosis and treatment. Golomb testified that, had Fahr received an accurate diagnosis of cancer in August 1987 and received treatment, she would have had a 60 percent chance of survival. Hence, the defendant was factually incorrect in asserting that there was no proximate cause testimony.

The defendant argued that the claim as to Kayne and Khalid should not have been presented to the jury. The record reveals that the defendant moved for a directed verdict on three grounds: (1) that the radiologists were not the defendant's agents, (2) that the radiology report had not misled Sanford, and (3) that the testimony of Golomb that the plaintiff would have had a 40 percent chance of dying in any event was insufficient to establish proximate cause. The court found that the evidence as to the malpractice of Khalid and Kayne supported the jury's finding that each was professionally negligent. Kayne failed to diagnose the cancer in September 1988. With a proper diagnosis there could have been a full month or more of treatment before metastasis was visible in December. Therefore, there was sufficient evidence to support the conclusion that the malpractice of Kayne was a proximate cause of the metastasis and Fahr's death. As to Khalid, whose malpractice was seven months earlier, the conclusion is even stronger.

A critical question is whether, at the time of her admission to the hospital, Fahr was looking to the hospital for treatment of physical ailments or merely viewing the hospital as the site where her physician would treat her for her problems. A relevant factor in this determination involves the resolution of the question of whether the hospital provided the plaintiff with the radiologists or whether the plaintiff and the radiologists had a patient–physician relationship independent of the hospital setting. Here, the evidence supports the jury's finding that an agency relationship existed between the radiologists and the hospital. Fahr did not have a patient–physician relationship with the radiologists independent of the hospital setting. Rather, the radiologists just happened to be on duty when Fahr arrived at the hospital. Moreover, the evidence showed that the radiology department is held out as part of the hospital, leading patients to understand that the services are being rendered by the hospital.

Inadequate X-ray Examination

The failure to order a proper set of X-rays is as legally risky as the failure to order any X-rays. In *Betenbaugh v. Princeton Hospital*,[79] the plaintiff had been taken to the hospital because she injured the lower part of her back. One of the defendant physicians directed that an X-ray be taken of her sacrum. No evidence of a fracture was found. When the patient's pain did not subside, the family physician was consulted. He found that the films taken at the hospital did not include the entire lower portion of the spine and sent her to a radiologist for further study. On the basis of additional X-

rays, a diagnosis of a fracture was made, and the patient was advised to wear a lumbosacral support. Two months later, the fracture was healed. The radiologist who had taken X-ray films on the second occasion testified that it was customary to take both an anterior-posterior and a lateral view when making an X-ray examination of the sacrum. In his opinion, the failure at the hospital to include the lower area of the sacrum was a failure to meet the standard required. The family physician testified that if the patient's fracture had been diagnosed at the hospital, appropriate treatment could have been instituted earlier, the patient would have suffered less pain, and recovery time would have been reduced. The evidence was sufficient to support findings that the physicians and the hospital were negligent by not having taken adequate X-rays and that such negligence was the proximate cause of the patient's additional pain and delay in recovery.

Failure To Consult with Radiologist

The internist in *Lanzet v. Greenberg*[80] failed to consult with the radiologist after his conclusion that the patient suffered from congestive heart failure. This factor most likely contributed to the death of the patient while on the operating table.

Failure To Read X-rays

The patient in *Tams v. Lotz*[81] had to undergo a second surgical procedure to remove a laparotomy pad that had been left negligently in the patient during a previous surgical procedure. The trial court was found to have properly directed a verdict with respect to the patient's assertion that the surgeon who performed the first operation had failed to read a postoperative X-ray report, which allegedly would have put him on notice both that the pad was present and that there was a need for emergency surgery to remove the pad, therefore averting the need to remove a portion of his intestine.

The plaintiff in *Killebrew v. Johnson*[82] had filed a complaint to recover damages from the physician, alleging that he was negligent by failing to inform himself of the results of X-rays ordered to determine the possible location of an intrauterine contraceptive device. The superior court granted the physician's motion for judgment. The court of appeals held that the testimony of the plaintiff's medical witness and the treating physician's admission that he did not inform himself of the contents of the X-rays or the X-ray reports were sufficient to place before the jury the applicable standard of care.

The failure of a radiologist to read an X-ray properly does not necessarily constitute negligence. This is especially true in those cases in which the treatment rendered to the patient would have been the same regardless of the radiologist's findings.

Failure To Notify of X-ray Results

The court of appeals in *Washington Healthcare Corp. v. Barrow*[83] held that evidence was sufficient to sustain a finding that the hospital was negligent in failing to provide a radiology report demonstrating pathology on a patient's lung in a timely manner. An X-ray of the patient taken on April 4, 1982, disclosed a small nodular density in her right lung. Within a year, the cancerous nodule had grown to the size of a softball.

The most significant testimony at trial was that of Theresa James, a medical student who worked for Dr. Oweiss, the defendant, until April 23, 1982. James testified that her job entailed combing through Oweiss's mail and locating abnormal X-ray reports, which she then would bring to his attention. Emphasizing that she had come to know the patient personally, James said that she would have been upset if she had come across an abnormal report on her. James claimed that she received no such report while working for the physician, thus accounting for 19 days after the X-ray was taken. James stated that the X-ray reports were usually received within four or five days after being taken. Dr. Odenwald, who dictated the patient's report on April 4, 1982, gave testimony to corroborate her testimony. Odenwald, of Groover, Christie and Merritt, PC, (GCM), who operated the radiology department at the Washington Hospital Center (WHC), stated that the X-ray reports usually were typed and mailed the same day that they were dictated. The jury could have determined that if the report did not reach Oweiss by April 23, 1982, then it did not reach him by May 3, 1982. The patient's record eventually was found; however, it was not in the patient's regular folder. One could infer that the record therefore was negligently filed.

Questions also arise as to why Oweiss did nothing to follow up on the matter in ensuing months. Oweiss testified that he did receive the report by May 3, 1982, and that he informed Mrs. Barrow of its contents. Barrow stated that although her folder was on the physician's desk at the time of her visit, he did not relay to her any information regarding an abnormal X-ray. Oweiss, however, was severely impeached at trial, and the jury chose not to believe him. Considering the entire record, there was reasonable probability that WHC was negligent and that Oweiss had not received the report. The plaintiff had settled with Oweiss, the patient's personal physician, in the amount of $200,000 during pendency in the district court, and the action against him was dismissed with prejudice. The record did not support WHC's request of indemnification from Oweiss. The trial court had directed a verdict in favor of GCM, leaving WHC as the sole defendant. The court of appeals remanded WHC's cross-claim for indemnification from GCM for further findings of fact and conclusions by the trial court.

Delay in Conveying X-ray Report to Attending Physician

On April 20, 1995, Mr. Carrasco[84] was taken to the Tri City Community Hospital (Tri City) emergency department by ambulance, complaining of back pain. He was admitted for observation, then released on April 21. He was complaining of back pain at the time of his release.

On April 22, Carrasco returned to Tri City complaining of continued back pain and the inability to stand. A chest X-ray taken on April 22 revealed a "significantly widened mediastinum" and "an increase in the size of the cardiac silhouette." On April 24, a radiologist reported that the X-ray revealed: "In the setting of back pain, consideration should be given for aortic dissection."

Sometime on April 24, Carrasco's condition deteriorated, and he was air lifted to Methodist Hospital in San Antonio. A CT scan revealed an aneurysm of the thoracic aorta. Carrasco underwent emergency surgery, and the surgeons found a ruptured aneurysm of the thoracic aorta. The following day, Carrasco suffered another pericardial effusion. Emergency surgery was undertaken again, and a new bleeding site into the pericardium was found. Carrasco coded and died.

The appellants sued Tri City and the emergency department physician. Tri City filed a motion for summary judgment, asserting that the appellants failed to present any evidence of proximate cause between Tri City's alleged breach of the standard of care and the appellants' injuries. The trial court granted summary judgment on this ground, and the appellants appealed.

A no-evidence summary judgment is improperly granted if the respondent brings forth "more" than a scintilla of probative evidence to raise a genuine issue of material fact. *Less than a scintilla of evidence* exists when the evidence is so weak as to do no more than create a mere surmise or suspicion of a fact. *More than a scintilla of evidence* exists when the evidence rises to a level that would enable reasonable and fair-minded people to differ in their conclusions.

The appeals court had to determine whether the evidence constituted more than a scintilla of probative evidence sufficient to raise a genuine issue of material fact as to the proximate cause element of the appellants' cause of action.

The appellants alleged that Tri City's care fell below the required standard by failing to properly record Carrasco's complaints and failing to timely report the results from the X-ray taken April 22. In its motion for summary judgment, Tri City asserted that the appellants had failed to produce any evidence that these alleged actions proximately caused Carrasco's death. The appellants filed a response to which two affidavits of Dr. Youmans were attached, together with the medical records from Tri City.

In his affidavits, Youmans asserted that Carrasco's chance for success would have been significantly better if the aneurysm was operated on under an elective basis as opposed to a postrupture emergent basis. Youmans stated that there was no doubt that Carrasco would have had a better chance for survival if the diagnosis of the aneurysm had been established on April 22, or even two days previously when he was seen in the emergency department on April 20. Although the X-ray report was not dictated until April 24, there was no attempt by Tri City personnel to convey what should have been emergency-type information to the attending physicians on the day of admission. Youmans expressed his opinion that Tri City had the responsibility of seeing to it that the reports of the grossly abnormal chest X-rays were conveyed to the attending physician on an emergent basis.

Tri City stated that the affidavits did not suggest that the failure to properly diagnose the patient was the result of the failure to convey the emergency-type information or that the attending physician would have made the correct diagnosis with the information. Because the X-ray report states: "In the setting of back pain, consideration should be given for aortic dissection," and because the diagnosis that led to Carrasco's surgery was an aneurysm of the thoracic aorta, this is some evidence that the X-ray report would have led the attending physician to a correct diagnosis. In addition, after noting Tri City's failure to convey the emergency-type information on the day of admission, Youmans stated: "Subsequently, the correct diagnosis apparently was not suspected until the time the patient coded on April 24." This statement links Tri City's failure to convey the X-ray information with the misdiagnosis. At the very least, the evidence rises to a level that would enable reasonable and fair-minded people to conclude that the absence of the X-ray report caused the improper diagnosis.

Because Carrasco's condition did not deteriorate until April 24, an inference can be made that the rupture occurred sometime on April 24. If the X-ray results had been relayed on April 22, the day of admission, the surgery could have been elective instead of emergent.

Youmans' affidavit provided more than a scintilla of evidence that Tri City's failure to ensure that the X-ray was read and relayed to the attending physician on the day of admission was a proximate cause of the appellants' injuries. The trial court's judgment was reversed, and the cause was remanded for trial.

PHYSICIAN–PATIENT RELATIONSHIP

The suggestions below, if followed, will help to decrease the probability of malpractice suits:

- Do not guarantee treatment outcome.
- Provide for cross-coverage during days off.
- Maintain timely, complete, and accurate records. Do not make erasures.
- Personalize your treatment. A patient is more inclined to sue an impersonal physician than one with whom he or she has developed a good relationship.
- Do not overextend your practice.
- Provide sufficient time and care to each patient. Take the time to explain treatment plans and follow-up care to the patient, his or her family, and other professionals caring for your patient.
- Avoid prescribing over the telephone.
- Do not become careless because you know the patient.
- Request consultations when indicated and refer if necessary.
- Seek the advice of counsel should you suspect the possibility of a malpractice claim.

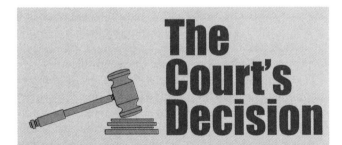

The Illinois Appellate Court held that the evidence was sufficient to support a determination that the defendant's negligence had caused the plaintiff's pain and suffering.

CHAPTER REVIEW

1. A health care organization's bylaws set forth, among other things, the responsibilities of the medical staff. The committees of the staff review and analyze their responsibilities, clinical experiences, and opportunities for improvement. The selection of medical staff is the responsibility of the governing body.

2. In cases in which a medical staff member's credentials were not screened properly, the health care organization can be held liable for injuries to patients as a result of the lack of investigation. The screening and appointment process involves many stages. These include the application; an evaluation of the applicant's physical and mental status; the applicant's release of information from third parties; the applicant's provision of a certificate of insurance; provision of evidence of an applicant's state licensure; a query of the National Practitioner Data Bank for information on the applicant; evaluation of the applicant's references; a thorough interview of the applicant; and approval by the governing body.

3. The medical staff must determine what procedures a physician is authorized to perform. This determination, known as *delineation of privileges*, is based on a set criteria for credentials required to perform with competence the privileges requested.

4. To commence a court action for issues such as initial denial of medical staff privileges, grievances, and disciplinary actions, a physician must first exhaust all remedies set forth in the hospital's bylaws, rules, and regulations.

5. Physician monitoring is most effectively practiced through peer review. The governing body of a hospital has a duty to create a means through which medical staff can evaluate, counsel, and, when appropriate, take action against a physician whose actions pose an unreasonable risk of harm to a patient. However, a health care organization cannot use as a defense the argument that the medical staff is an independent, self-governing body.

6. A physician will not be held liable for exercising best judgment in following a course of treatment that is supported by a reputable, respected body of medical experts. However, a physician is at risk for liability if he or she uses an unprecedented procedure that results in harm. Additionally, physicians cannot be required to guarantee the success of treatment methods or courses of treatment. If a physician's failure to act caused a patient's death, the physician may be held liable.

7. The doctrine of *informed consent* provides that a physician must disclose to the patient known and existing dangers associated with a course of treatment. If it can be proven that a physician did not disclose information regarding hazards of a treatment, then consent is revoked.

8. In some cases, a physician can be held liable for failure to order diagnostic tests, promptly review test results, read nurses' notes, seek consultation, obtain a second opinion, obtain an adequate family history and perform an adequate physical examination, maintain proper documentation, allow a patient a chance to survive, prescribe appropriate medications, or provide an accurate diagnosis.

9. Among the duties held by mental health professionals is the *duty to warn*. If a therapist determines or should reasonably determine that a patient poses a serious threat of violence or danger to a third party, the therapist must exercise reasonable care to protect the third party and warn him or her of the impending danger.

10. In a malpractice case, the standard of care applied will be that pertaining to the specialty in which the physician is treating, regardless of whether or not that physician is credentialed in that specialty.

REVIEW QUESTIONS

1. Discuss the importance of *delineating clinical privileges.*
2. Why is it important that the governing body approve the appointment and reappointment of physicians to the medical staff?
3. What, if any, sanctions should be imposed upon a physician who fails to respond to the emergency department? Discuss your answer.
4. When is a physician considered to have abandoned his or her patient?
5. Under what circumstances should a hospital be held liable for a physician's negligent performance of surgery?
6. Under what conditions should a physician be suspended from the medical staff?
7. Do you think that there are certain standards of care required of a gastroenterologist on which an internist would not be qualified to render an opinion? Explain.
8. Should physicians guarantee outcomes? Explain.
9. When two physicians have opposing views as to a patient's medical needs, what course of action should the patient's attending physician follow?
10. Does a poor outcome necessarily indicate a negligent act? Explain.

NOTES

1. Bombagetti v. Amine, 627 N.E.2d 230 (Ill. App. Ct. 1993).
2. 301 N.W.2d 156 (Wis. 1981).
3. 835 F.2d 1250 (8th Cir. 1987).
4. 500 P.2d 335 (Ariz. Ct. App. 1972).
5. 543 So.2d 209 (Fla. 1989).
6. 645 P.2d 171 (Alaska 1982).
7. 520 N.W.2d 625 (Wis. App. 1994).
8. 368 N.W.2d 666, 668, 674 (1985).
9. 211 N.E.2d 253 (Ill. 1965).
10. No. 228566 (Cal. Super. Ct. Sacramento Co. 1976).
11. 394 N.E.2d 770 (Ill. App. Ct. 1979).
12. 540 P.2d 1398, 1400 (Or. 1975).
13. 130 Cal. App. 3d 970 (1982).
14. 670 F.2d 507 (5th Cir. 1982).
15. 42 C.F.R. § 482.12(a)(7).
16. No. C538628 (L.A. Co. Cal. Super. Ct.).
17. 144 So.2d 544 (La. Ct. App. 1962).
18. 489 So.2d 392 (La. Ct. App. 1986).
19. Thomas v. Raleigh, 358 S.E.2d 222 (W. Va. 1987).
20. 351 S.E.2d 867 (S.C. Ct. App. 1987).
21. John v. Jarrard, 927 F.2d 551 (11th Cir. 1991).
22. 737 S.W.2d 455 (Ark. 1987).
23. Griffett v. Ryan, 443 S.E.2d 149 (Va. 1994).
24. 520 N.Y.S.2d 751 (N.Y. App. Div. 1987).
25. 578 S.W.2d 73 (Tenn. 1979).
26. 570 N.E.2d 1249 (Ill. App. Ct. 1991).
27. 595 P.2d 919 (Wash. 1979).
28. 294 F. Supp. 466 (D.S.C. 1968).
29. 632 A.2d 1333 (Pa. Super. Ct. 1993).
30. 865 F. Supp. 433 (N.D. Ohio 1994).
31. 647 So.2d 1366 (La. App. 3d Cir. 1994).
32. Valentine v. Kaiser Found. Hosps., 15 Cal. Rptr. 26 (Cal. Ct. App. 1961) (dictum).
33. 402 S.W.2d 855 (Ky. Ct. App. 1966).
34. 582 So.2d 1272 (La. 1991).
35. 343 N.E.2d 589 (Ill. 1976).
36. 653 A.2d 541 (Md. App.1995).
37. 173 N.W.2d 881 (Neb. 1970).
38. 165 N.W.2d 85 (Neb. 1969).
39. *Id.* at 89.
40. 337 So.2d 420 (Fla. Dist. Ct. App. 1976).
41. 710 S.W.2d 373 (Mo. Ct. App. 1986).
42. 698 So.2d 469 (La. App. 4 Cir. 1997).
43. 542 N.Y.S.2d 328 (N.Y. App. Div. 1989).
44. 523 N.Y.S.2d 645 (N.Y. App. Div. 1988).
45. 713 P.2d 773 (Wyo. 1986).
46. 209 So.2d 809 (Miss. 1968).
47. 666 F. Supp. 1511 (Ala. 1987).
48. 218 N.W.2d 492 (Iowa 1928).
49. 746 S.W.2d 108 (Mo. Ct. App. 1988).
50. 539 S.W.2d 286 (Ky. 1976).
51. 505 N.Y.S.2d 899 (N.Y. App. Div. 1986).
52. 716 P.2d 1013 (Ariz. 1986).
53. 514 So.2d 727 (La. Ct. App. 1987).
54. 469 N.W.2d 74 (Mich. Ct. App. 1991).
55. *Id.* at 76.
56. 348 S.E.2d 233 (Va. 1986).
57. Anita Manning, *AMA Calls Drive-Thru Birth Risky*, USA TODAY, June 21, 1995, at 1.
58. 733 P.2d 1004 (Wash. Ct. App. 1987).
59. 767 S.W.2d 589 (Mo. Ct. App. 1988).
60. 511 N.Y.S.2d 144 (N.Y. App. Div. 1987).
61. 210 So.2d 236 (Fla. Dist. Ct. App. 1968).
62. 442 U.S. 584 (1979).
63. 619 F. Supp. 481 (D. Ala. 1985)
64. 551 P.2d 334 (Cal. 1976).
65. *See* Lipari v. Sears, Roebuck & Co., 497 F. Supp. 185 (D. Neb. 1980).
66. 415 A.2d 625 (Md. Ct. Spec. App. 1980).
67. 836 F.2d 209 (4th Cir. 1987).
68. 354 S.E.2d 778 (S.C. Ct. App. 1987).
69. 356 N.Y.S.2d 708 (N.Y. App. Div. 1974).
70. Fatuck v. Hillside Hosp., 356 N.Y.S.2d 105 (N.Y. App. Div. 1974).
71. 380 N.Y.S.2d 737 (N.Y. App. Div. 1976).
72. 742 A.2d 591 (N.J. Super. Ct. App. Div. 1999).
73. 654 A.2d 970 (1995).
74. 397 S.E.2d 696 (Ga. 1990).
75. 250 A.2d 40 (N.J. Super. Ct. App. Div. 1969).
76. 646 So.2d 4 (Ala. 1994).
77. 33 Cal. Rptr. 673 (Cal. Ct. App. 1963).
78. 568 N.W.2d 93 (Mich. App. 1997).
79. 235 A.2d 889 (N.J. 1967).
80. 594 A.2d 1309 (N.J. 1991).
81. 530 A.2d 1217 (D.C. 1987).
82. 404 N.E.2d 1194 (Ind. Ct. App. 1980).
83. 531 A.2d 226 (D.C. 1987).
84. Gomez v. Tri City Community Hosp., 4 S.W.3d 281 (Tex. App. 1999).

CHAPTER 8

Nursing and the Law

PATIENT'S CHANCE OF SURVIVAL DIMINISHED

On the afternoon of May 20, the patient, Mr. Ard, began feeling nauseous. He was in pain and had shortness of breath. Although his wife rang the call bell several times, it was not until sometime later that evening that someone responded and gave Ard medication for the nausea. The nausea continued to worsen and Ard vomited. Mrs. Ard then noticed that her husband was having difficulty breathing. He was reeling from side to side in bed. Believing that her husband was dying, she continued to call for help. She estimated that she rang the call bell for 1 hour and 15 minutes before anyone responded. A code was eventually called. Unfortunately, Mr. Ard did not survive the code. There was no documentation on the medical records, on May 20, between 5:30 P.M. and 6:45 P.M. that would indicate that

any nurse or physician checked on Ard's condition. This finding collaborated Mrs. Ard's testimony regarding this time period.

A wrongful death action was brought against the hospital and the district court granted judgment for Mrs. Ard. The hospital appealed.

Ms. Krebs, an expert in general nursing, stated that it should have been obvious to the nurses from the physicians' progress notes that the patient was a high risk for aspiration. This *problem was never addressed in the nurses' care plan* or in the nurses' notes.

On May 20, Ard's assigned nurse was Ms. Florscheim. Krebs stated that Florscheim did not perform a full assessment of the patient's respiratory and lung status. There was nothing in the record indicating that she completed such an evaluation after he vomited. Krebs also testified that a nurse did not conduct a swallowing assessment at any time. Although Florscheim testified that she checked on the patient around 6:00 P.M. on May 20, there was no documentation in the medical record.

Ms. Farris, an expert in intensive care nursing, testified for the defense. She disagreed with Krebs that there was a breach of the standard of care. However, on cross-examination, she admit-

181

ted that if a patient was in the type of distress described by Mrs. Ard and no nurse checked on

him for 1 hour and 15 minutes, then that would fall below the standard of care.[1]

What is your verdict?

HISTORICAL PERSPECTIVE

Florence Nightingale's service in caring for the sick and injured was faithfully industrious. To appreciate her work, it must be remembered that for more than a century before her organization of nursing service, health care facilities resembled the worst type of prisons. The ill were at the mercy of attendants who were both heartless and unsympathetic. By 1854, during the Crimean War, her opportunity came. The English government, disturbed by reports of conditions among the sick and wounded soldiers, selected Florence Nightingale as the one person capable of improving patient care. On her arrival at the military hospital in Crimea, she found that the sick were lying on canvas sheets in the midst of dirt and vermin. There was no laundry, and beds were made of straw. With boundless energy and a small band of nurses she had assembled, she proceeded to establish order and cleanliness. She organized diet kitchens, a laundry service, and departments of supplies, often using her own funds to finance her projects. Ten days after her arrival, the newly established kitchens were feeding 1,000 soldiers. Within three months, 10,000 were receiving clothing, food, and medicine. It is said that as a result of her work, the death rate was reduced from 40 percent to 2 percent.[2] Ms. Nightingale has been credited with observing:

> A good nursing staff will perform their duties more or less satisfactorily under every disadvantage. But while doing so, their head will always try to improve their surroundings, in such a way as to liberate them from subsidiary work, and enable them to devote their time more exclusively to the care of the sick.[3]

As a result of her tremendous organizational skills, Florence Nightingale is considered by many to be the first true health care administrator. The culmination of her work came in 1860, after her return to England. There she founded the Nightingale School of Nursing at the St. Thomas Hospital. From this school, a group of 15 nurses graduated in 1863. They later became the pioneer heads of training schools throughout the world.

In 1886, the Royal British Nurses' Association (RBNA) was formed. The RBNA worked toward the establishment of a standard of technical excellence in nursing. A charter granted to the RBNA in 1893 denied nurses a register, although it did agree to the maintenance of a list of persons who could apply to have their name entered thereon as nurses.[4]

A unique opportunity presented itself to the nurse leaders of the 1890s. Mrs. Bedford Fenwick, a nurse leader in the English nurse registration movement, came to Chicago in 1893 to arrange the English nursing exhibit to be displayed in the Women's building at the Worlds Fair. As part of the Congress on Hospitals and Dispensaries, a nursing section included papers on establishing standards in hospital training schools, the establishment of a nurses' association, and nurse registration.[5]

Nursing today is significantly different than it was in the days of Florence Nightingale. It requires a wider variety of skills and specialized knowledge. As nursing tasks become more complex, the element of risk to the patient increases, as well as the nurse's potential exposure to malpractice. This chapter provides an overview of some of the more common risks encountered by nurses.

THE PRACTICE OF NURSING

Although nurses traditionally have followed the instructions of attendant physicians, physicians realistically have long relied on nurses to exercise independent judgment in many situations.[6]

Each state has its own Nurse Practice Act that defines the practice of nursing. Although most states have similar definitions of nursing, differences generally revolve around the scope of practice permitted. The scope of practice of a licensed practical nurse is generally limited to routine patient care under the direction of a registered nurse or a physician.

A registered nurse is one who has passed a state registration examination and has been licensed to practice nursing. The scope of practice of a registered professional nurse includes, for example, patient assessment, analyzing laboratory reports, patient teaching, health counseling, executing medical regimens, and operating medical equipment as prescribed by a physician, dentist, or other licensed health care provider.

A nurse practitioner is a registered nurse who has completed additional training beyond basic nursing education.

The nurse practitioner provides primary health care services in accordance with state nurse practice laws or statutes. The scope of practice of a nurse practitioner is discussed later in this chapter.

"Professional nursing . . . is in a period of rapid and progressive change in response to the growth of biomedical knowledge, changes in patterns of demand for health services, and the evolution of professional relationships among nurses, physicians and other health professions."[7] Although the actual authority of nurses to act varies considerably from state to state, the expanding scopes of nursing functions and licensure are illustrated clearly in the following examples:

- 1901—New York began to organize for passage of nurse practice legislation.
- 1903—North Carolina enacted the first nurse registration act.
- 1905—The development of the hospital economics course at Teachers College, Columbia University, ushered in a new era in preparation of nurse leaders in America. This one-year certificate course was extended to a two-year post–basic training program in 1905. The commitment of key nursing leaders to advancing educational preparation for nurse faculty fostered the subsequent development of baccalaureate education in nursing during the first quarter of the 20th century.
- 1937—The American Nurses Association (ANA) began recommending that nurses use their professional organization to "improve every phase of their working lives."
- 1938—New York enacted the first exclusive practice act. This act required mandatory licensure of everyone who performed nursing functions as a matter of employment.
- 1946—The ANA convention adopted an economic security program and called for collective action on such items as a 40-hour workweek and higher minimum wages.
- 1952—By 1952, all states, including the District of Columbia and U.S. territories, had enacted nurse practice acts.
- 1955—The ANA approved a model definition for nursing practice.
- 1957—The California Nurses' Association met with representatives of medical and hospital associations to draw up a statement supporting nurses in performing venipunctures.
- 1966—The Michigan Heart Association favored the use of defibrillators by coronary care nurses.
- 1968—The Hawaii nursing, medical, and hospital associations approved nurses performing cardiopulmonary resuscitation.
- 1970—The ANA amended its model definition for nursing practice to include "nursing diagnosis."

- 1971—Idaho revised its nurse practice act by allowing diagnosis and treatment as part of the scope of practice for nurse practitioners (NPs).
- 1972—New York expanded its nurse practice act and adopted a broad definition of nursing.
- 1973—The first ANA Guidelines for NPs were written for geriatric NPs. These were later modified and adapted to apply to other practitioners.
- 1975—Missouri Revised Statutes (1975) authorized a nurse to make an assessment of persons who are ill and to render a "nursing diagnosis." The 1975 Act not only described a much broader spectrum of nursing functions, it qualified this description with the phrase, "including, but not limited to."
- 1980—The ANA published a model nurse practice act for state legislators—to provide for consistency in individual state nurse practice acts.
- 1985—New York revised its definition of nursing by providing that a registered professional nurse who has the appropriate training and experience may provide primary health care services as defined under the statutory authority of the Public Health Law and as approved by the hospital's governing authority. The term "primary health care services" means taking histories and performing physical examinations, selecting clinical laboratory tests and diagnostic radiology procedures, and choosing regimens of treatment. These provisions do not alter a physician's responsibility for patient care.
- 1989—New York allowed NPs to diagnose, treat, and write prescriptions within their area of specialty with minimum physician supervision.
- 1990—The ANA again amended its model definition for nursing practice to include the advance NP as well as the registered nurse (RN).

THE BROADENING SCOPE OF PRACTICE

The *scope of practice* refers to the permissible boundaries of practice for health care professionals, as is often defined in state statutes, which define the actions, duties, and limits of nurses in their particular roles. The role of the nurse continues to expand because of a shortage of primary physicians in certain rural and inner-city areas, ever-increasing specialization, improved technology, public demand, and expectations within the profession itself.

A nurse who exceeds his or her scope of practice as defined by state nurse practice acts can be found to have violated licensure provisions or to have performed tasks that are reserved by statute for another health care professional. Because of increasingly complex nursing and medical procedures, it is sometimes difficult to distinguish the tasks that are clearly reserved for the physician from those that may be performed by the professional nurse. Nurses, however, generally have not encountered lawsuits for exceeding their scope of practice unless negligence is an issue.

Nursing Diagnosis

The defendant physicians in *Cignetti v. Camel*[8] ignored a nurse's assessment of a patient's diagnosis, which contributed to a delay in treatment and injury to the patient. The nurse had testified that she told the physician that the patient's signs and symptoms were not those associated with indigestion. The defendant physician objected to this testimony, indicating that such a statement constituted a medical diagnosis by a nurse. The trial court permitted the testimony to be entered into evidence. Section 335.01(8) of the Missouri Revised Statutes (1975) authorizes an RN to make an assessment of persons who are ill and to render a *nursing diagnosis*. On appeal, the Missouri Court of Appeals affirmed the lower court's ruling, holding that evidence of negligence presented by a hospital employee, for which an obstetrician was not responsible, was admissible to show the events that occurred during the patient's hospital stay.

NURSE LICENSURE

The common organizational pattern of nurse licensing authority in each state is to establish a separate board, organized and operated within the guidelines of specific legislation, to license all professional and practical nurses. Each board is in turn responsible for the determination of eligibility for initial licensing and relicensing; for the enforcement of licensing statutes, including suspension, revocation, and restoration of licenses; and for the approval and supervision of training institutions. A licensing board has the authority to suspend a license; however, it must do so within existing rules and regulations.

Requirements for Licensure

Formal professional training is necessary for nurse licensure in all states. The course requirements vary, but all courses must be completed at board-approved schools or institutions. Each state requires that an applicant pass a written examination, which is generally administered twice annually. A licensing board may draft examinations, or a professional examination service or national examining board may prepare them. Some states waive their written examination for applicants who present a certificate from a national nursing examination board. Graduate nurses are generally able to

practice nursing under supervision while waiting for the results of their examination.

The four basic methods by which boards license out-of-state nurses are (1) reciprocity, (2) endorsement, (3) waiver, and (4) examination.

Reciprocity. A formal or informal agreement between states whereby a nurse licensing board in one state recognizes licensees of another state if the board of that state extends reciprocal recognition to licensees from the first state. To have reciprocity, the initial licensing requirements of the two states must be essentially equivalent.

Endorsement. Although some nurse licensing boards use the term *endorsement* interchangeably with *reciprocity*, the two words have different meanings. In licensing by endorsement, boards determine whether out-of-state nurses' qualifications are equivalent to their own state requirements at the time of initial licensure. Many states make it a condition for endorsement that the qualifying examination taken in another state be comparable with their own. As with reciprocity, endorsement becomes much easier when uniform qualification standards are applied by the different states.

Waiver and Examination. Licensing out-of-state nurses can be accomplished by waiver and examination. When applicants do not meet all the requirements for licensure but have equivalent qualifications, the specific prerequisites of education, experience, or examination may be waived. Some states will not recognize out-of-state licensed nurses and make it mandatory that all applicants pass a licensing examination.

Most states grant temporary licenses for nurses. These licenses may be issued pending a decision by a licensing board on permanent licensure or may be issued to out-of-state nurses who intend to be in a jurisdiction for a limited time.

Graduates of schools in other countries are required to meet the same qualifications as are nurses trained in the United States. Many state boards have established special training, citizenship, and experience requirements for students educated abroad, and others insist on additional training in the United States. Nurses who have completed their studies in a foreign country are required to pass an English proficiency examination and/or a licensing examination administered in English. A few states have reciprocity or endorsement agreements with some foreign countries.

Suspension and Revocation

Nurse licensing boards have the authority to suspend or revoke the license of a nurse who is found to have violated specified norms of conduct. Such violations may include procurement of a license by fraud; unprofessional, dishonorable, immoral, or illegal conduct; performance of specific actions prohibited by statute; and malpractice.

Suspension and revocation procedures are most commonly contained in the licensing act; in some jurisdictions, however, the procedure is left to the discretion of the board or is contained in the general administrative procedure acts. For the most part, suspension and revocation proceedings are administrative, rather than judicial, and do not carry criminal sanctions.

Liability for Practicing without a License

Health care organizations are required to verify that each nurse's license is current. The mere fact that an unlicensed practitioner was hired would not generally in and of itself impose additional liability unless a patient suffered harm as a result of the unlicensed nurse's negligence.

AMERICAN NURSES ASSOCIATION

The American Nurses Association (ANA) is a national professional organization of graduate RNs in the United States and its territories. ANA membership is available to all graduate nurses who are licensed in any jurisdiction of the United States. The purpose of the ANA is to "foster high standards of nursing practice and to promote the professional and educational advancement of nurses and the welfare of nurses to the end that all people may have better nursing care. The association helps provide health protection for the American people, aids nurses to become more effective members of their profession, and promotes quality health care."[9]

NATIONAL LEAGUE FOR NURSING

The National League for Nursing (NLN) is a membership organization of individuals and agencies organized for the purpose of fostering development and improvement of hospital, public health, and other organized nursing services and nursing education through the coordinated action of nurses, allied professional groups, citizens, agencies, and schools so that the nursing needs of the people will be met. The philosophy of the NLN is to bring together professional and paraprofessional health care workers and consumers to work toward improving nursing services and nursing education. The NLN is involved in nursing research, recruitment of students, testing services, workshops, conferences, seminars, consultation services, accreditation of nursing schools, fellowship aid, publications, and films. The NLN is funded through membership dues and grantors such as the American Hospital Association, the W.K. Kellogg Foundation, and the Rockefeller Fund.

NURSE PRACTICE ROLES

Nurse-Anesthetist

Administration of anesthesia by a nurse anesthetist requires special training and certification. Nurse-administered anesthesia was the first expanded role for nurses requiring certification. Oversight and availability of an anesthesiologist are required by most organizations.

Major risks for nurse anesthetists include: improper placement of an airway; failure to recognize significant changes in a patient's condition; and the improper use of anesthetics (e.g., wrong anesthetic, wrong dose, wrong route).

CLASSIC BATTLE OF THE EXPERTS—SUPERVISION BY AN ANESTHESIOLOGIST REQUIRED

Citation: *Denton Reg'l Med. Ctr. v. LaCroix, 947 S.W.2d 941 (Tex. Ct. App. 1997)*

Facts

Appellees Mr. and Mrs. LaCroix went to the hospital (DRMA) for the birth of their first child, Lawryn. LaCroix was admitted to the hospital under the care of her obstetrician, Dr. Dulemba. She underwent a Caesarean section. Mr. LaCroix was in the operating room for the Caesarean section. Before the Caesarean section began, LaCroix complained several times of breathing difficulty. When Dr. McGehee, the pediatrician, arrived, he noticed that Mrs. LaCroix appeared to be in respiratory distress and heard her say, "I can't breathe." McGehee asked nurse Blankenship, a nurse anesthetist, if LaCroix was okay, and she responded that LaCroix was just nervous. Mr. LaCroix testified that soon after that his wife's eyes "got big" and she whispered again to him that she could not breathe. Mr. LaCroix shouted, "She can't breathe. Somebody please help my wife." Blankenship asked that Mr. LaCroix be removed from the operating room because LaCroix was having what appeared to her to be a seizure.

Blankenship could not establish an airway with an airbag and mask because LaCroix's teeth were clenched shut from the seizure. She told one of the nurses: "Get one of the anesthesiologists here now!" Dr. Green, who was in his car, was paged. When he received the page, he immediately drove to the Women's Pavilion. Dulemba was already making the Caesarean-section incision when the seizure occurred, and he told Blankenship that LaCroix's blood was dark, as opposed to bright red, oxygenated blood. When Lawryn was delivered, she was not breathing, and McGehee had to resuscitate her. Meanwhile, to intubate LaCroix to establish an airway for her, Blankenship had to paralyze her, using the drug Anectine, and put her to sleep, using sodium pentothal, a general anesthetic. She was then able to intubate LaCroix; however, it was an *esophageal intubation*, rather than tracheal. After Dulemba, who was still working inside LaCroix's abdomen, pointed out that he thought that the intubation was esophageal, Blankenship removed the tube and successfully intubated LaCroix.

While Dulemba was closing the Caesarean-section incisions, LaCroix's blood pressure and pulse dropped, and Blankenship gave her ephedrine to try to raise her blood pressure. LaCroix then became asystole—she went into full cardiac arrest and her heart stopped beating. A physician and nurse from the hospital's emergency department had responded to a code for assistance and came into the operating room. McGehee testified that the *emergency department physician* said that he did not know how to resuscitate pregnant women and *left without providing any medical care*. Dulemba and a nurse began cardiopulmonary resuscitation (CPR) on LaCroix, and McGehee, once he was finished treating Lawryn, took control of the code and directed nurses to give LaCroix atropine and epinephrine to resuscitate her. LaCroix's heart resumed beating after one dose of epinephrine.

LaCroix suffered irreversible brain injury caused by hypoxia (deprivation of oxygen to the brain). She was totally and permanently disabled from independent living.

Blankenship and Dr. Hafiz settled with the LaCroixes by paying $500,000 and $750,000, respectively, for a total settlement of $1.25 million. Dr. Hafiz was the Denton Anesthesiology Associates, PA (DAA) anesthesiologist on call for the Women's Pavilion on the day of LaCroix's incident.

The trial court entered a judgment against the hospital awarding the LaCroixes approximately $8.8 million in damages.

Issue

Was the evidence legally and factually sufficient to hold the hospital liable for medical negligence under a theory of direct corporate liability, notwithstanding the jury's failure to find the treating physicians and nurse negligent?

Holding

The evidence was sufficient to hold the hospital liable for medical negligence under a theory of direct corporate liability. The evidence established that the hospital owed a duty to the plaintiff to have an anesthesiologist provide or supervise all anesthesia care, including having an anesthesiologist personally present or immediately available in the operating suite. The hospital's breach of this duty had proximately caused the patient's brain damage.

Reason

It was undisputed that an anesthesiologist never saw LaCroix until she had suffered brain damage. It was agreed by all the defendants that the LaCroixes had a right to know that LaCroix was going to be receiving anesthesia care from a certified registered nurse anesthetist (CRNA). It was undisputed that no physician ever countersigned in LaCroix's medical chart any of the medical treatments that were signed by Blankenship. The hospital's policies and procedures required that the CRNA's supervising physician sign for the CRNA. Around 1:30 P.M., Dulemba decided that a Caesarean section was warranted because of an occasionally low fetal pulse and LaCroix's slow cervical dilation. Although the Caesarean section was an emergency in that it was unscheduled, it was not a "stat" emergency Caesarean section that had to be done immediately. On her own and without a physician's order, Blankenship began LaCroix on Nesacaine, a Caesarean section epidural anesthetic. Blankenship gave LaCroix a total of 20 cc of Nesacaine.

Blankenship testified that she cannot administer anesthesia without the medical direction of a physician and that she administered anesthesia and other drugs to LaCroix under Dulemba's medical direction and supervision. Dulemba testified that he did not give Blankenship medical direction for her anesthesia care. He said that he would never supervise a CRNA because he is not qualified to do so.

The evidence showed that the practice of anesthesia is a specialized practice of medicine by a physician—an anesthesiologist. Nurse anesthetists may administer anesthesia, but only under the medical direction or supervision of a physician.

In determining the standard of care, the hospital's internal bylaws, policies, and procedures, as well as the standards of the Joint Commission on Accreditation of Healthcare Organizations can be utilized in determining the required standard of care. These factors alone, however, do not determine the governing standard of care. The anesthesia department policies and procedures provided that a CRNA could provide "anesthetic patient care only under the direct and personal supervision of a physician."

The responsible anesthesiologist must perform a preanesthetic evaluation, in which the anesthesiologist:

1. Reviews the chart.
2. Interviews the patient to:
   - Discuss medical history including anesthetic experiences and drug therapy.
   - Perform any examinations that would provide information that might assist in decisions regarding risk and management.
3. Orders test and medications essential to the conduct of anesthesia.
4. Obtains consultations as necessary.
5. Records impressions on the preanesthesia summary along with a brief discussion of planned anesthesia management, techniques, and American Society of Anesthesiologists (ASA) patient classification.

CRNAs will document the visit and discuss the evaluation of their patients with the supervising anesthesiologist or the operating physician; the anesthesiologist or the operating physician will document the discussion by signing (with the nurse anesthetist) the preanesthetic summary.

When the LaCroixes arrived at the Women's Pavilion with LaCroix in labor, they were presented with and signed an anesthesia consent form that had the names of Drs. Green, Pourzan, and Hafiz preprinted on it. None of the physicians knew that the hospital was doing the anesthesia consent for patients at the Women's Pavilion in that manner. LaCroix *never received a preanesthetic evaluation* by an anesthesiologist, and no anesthesiologist ever explained the anesthesia consent form.

The LaCroixes contended that the evidence was sufficient to establish that the *hospital owed a duty to have an anesthesiologist supervise anesthesia care*, including having an anesthesiologist personally present or immediately available in the operating suite, and that the hospital's breach of this duty proximately caused LaCroix's brain damage. The hospital's anesthesia department policies and procedures re-

quired that an anesthesiologist perform the preanesthesia evaluation, that an anesthesiologist discuss with the patient the anesthesia plan, and that an anesthesiologist supervise a CRNA by being "physically present or immediately available in the operating suite."

The hospital, which opened the Women's Pavilion in 1986, initially entered into an exclusive contract with DAA to provide anesthesia care for the Women's Pavilion. The May 31, 1990, contract was a renewal of DAA's initial exclusive contract with the hospital. Mr. Ciulla was in charge of the DAA contract. According to Ciulla, he renewed the contract in conjunction with the hospital's medical staff.

Ciulla admitted that before he renewed the contract with DAA, anesthesiologists who practiced at the hospital had warned him that DAA's CRNAs were not being properly supervised in the Women's Pavilion. Both Dr. Via, chairman of the hospital's anesthesiology department in 1991, and Ciulla testified that Via and other anesthesiologists had complained to Ciulla about the lack of proper CRNA supervision in the Women's Pavilion. Via said that in renewing the contract with DAA, Ciulla did nothing to address the complaints that had been made.

According to Ciulla, he renewed the contract in conjunction with the hospital's medical staff. According to Via, the hospital's medical executive committee recommended to Ciulla that he not renew DAA's contract and that he seek another anesthesia group for the Women's Pavilion. The hospital's board of directors renewed the contract anyway.

Four months before the LaCroixes went to the hospital to have their baby, Via wrote a memo (dated September 10, 1990) to Ciulla complaining that DAA's anesthesiologists were still not supervising DAA's CRNAs in the Women's Pavilion.

Via wrote a memo describing the dissatisfaction of the staff anesthesiologists who voiced concern regarding the medical supervision, or lack thereof, of nurse anesthetists administering anesthetics at DRMC.

Administrators at DRMC not only failed to heed these concerns but seemingly promoted the practice by their inaction and the contractual arrangements in the Women's Pavilion. It became apparent that the contracted anesthesiologists frequently were not present in that facility while nurse employees were providing anesthetics. This practice recently was estimated to occur between 50 and 75 percent of the time. Additionally, on several occasions nurse employees of DAA provided anesthetics in the main operating room of DRMC without supervision by their employers.

Dr. Redick, a Duke University medical professor of anesthesiology and associate professor of obstetrics, testified that LaCroix's brain damage was caused by a "high block" that resulted from being given too high a dosage of Nesacaine and that her respiratory distress was not recognized and treated quickly enough. Dr. Temple shared this opinion. Both physicians opined that if an anesthesiologist had supervised the administration of anesthesia, the high block would not have occurred, or would have been recognized and treated more promptly, and that the hospital's failure to have an anesthesiologist present and performing, or directly supervising, LaCroix's anesthesia care was a direct cause of her brain damage. McGehee also testified that LaCroix "failed to receive the proper treatment" and that her situation "should have been prevented." The hospital and Dr. Green and Dr. Pourzan presented several expert witnesses who testified that LaCroix had an unpredictable "anaphylactic" reaction (a severe allergic reaction) to the Nesacaine and that the presence of an anesthesiologist would not have affected the outcome because the anaphylactic reaction that caused LaCroix's cardiopulmonary arrest could not have been prevented.

However, Redick and Temple testified that an anesthesiologist would have determined through preanesthesia evaluation that LaCroix was a high-risk patient for airway problems; would have known to allow for LaCroix's labor epidural sensitivity, blood volume depletion, age, weight, and height; and would have reduced the dosage and thus avoided the hypotensive episode and respiratory distress that caused LaCroix's hypoxic brain damage.

Evidence was sufficient to support a finding that the hospital owed a duty to have an anesthesiologist provide or supervise all of the anesthesia care and that its breach of this duty was the direct cause of the patient's brain injury. The duty the hospital owed to LaCroix and the medical cause of LaCroix's brain injury were at the center of a *classic battle of the experts*, and the jury was free to accept or reject either side's theory.

Discussion

1. Describe the many reasons why this outcome occurred and how similar events can be prevented in the future.

2. Discuss hospital policy issues as they relate to:
   - contracts (i.e., supervision of CRNAs)
   - competency (i.e., CRNAs and emergency department physicians)
   - anesthesia assessments (i.e., preanesthesia, preinduction, and postanesthesia)
   - patient consent
   - medical staff dissatisfaction with anesthesia services
3. What other issues can you identify in this case?

Nurse Practitioner

NPs are RNs who have completed the necessary education to engage in primary health care decision making. Nurse practitioners receive specialized training in diagnosing and treating illnesses and providing health care maintenance. The American Nurses Association certifies NPs. The NP is trained in the delivery of primary health care and the assessment of psychosocial and physical health problems such as the performance of routine examinations and the ordering of routine diagnostic tests. A physician may not delegate a task to an NP when regulations specify that the physician must perform it personally or when the delegation is prohibited under state law or by an organization's own policies.

The potential risks of liability for the NP are as real as the risks for any other nurse. The standard of care required most likely will be set by statute. If not, the courts will determine the standard based on the reasonable person doctrine (i.e., what would a reasonably prudent NP do under the given circumstances?). The standard would be established through the use of expert testimony of other NPs in the field. Although case law in this area is limited, NPs are required to meet the standards recognized in the field as reflecting the current status of the art. Because of potential liability problems and pressure from physicians, hospitals have been historically reluctant to use NPs to the full extent of their training. Such reluctance has been diminishing as the competency of NPs has been well demonstrated in practice.

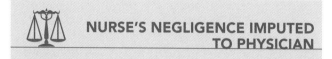

NURSE'S NEGLIGENCE IMPUTED TO PHYSICIAN

Citation: *Adams v. Krueger*, 856 P.2d 864 (Idaho 1993)

Facts

The plaintiff initially went to a physician's office for diagnosis and treatment. An NP who was employed by the physician performed her initial assessment. The NP diagnosed the plaintiff as having genital herpes. The physician prescribed an ointment to help relieve the patient's symptoms. The plaintiff eventually consulted with another physician who advised her that she had a yeast infection, not genital herpes.

The plaintiff and her husband then filed an action against the initial treating physician and his NP for their failure to correctly diagnose and treat her condition. The action against the physician was based on his failure to review the NP's diagnosis and treatment plan.

The court gave instructions to the jury that the plaintiff would recover nothing if it found the plaintiff more than 50 percent negligent. The jury found the plaintiff 49 percent negligent, the physician 10 percent negligent, and the NP 41 percent negligent.

The trial court found in favor of the plaintiff and the defendants appealed. The court of appeals affirmed and further appeal was made.

Issue

Did the trial court err by imputing the nurse's negligence to the physician?

Holding

The Idaho Supreme Court held that the negligence of the nurse was properly imputed to the physician.

Reason

The Idaho Supreme Court held that the physician and NP stood in a master–servant relationship and that the nurse acted within the scope of her employment. Consequently, her negligence was properly attributed to her employer/physician.

Discussion

1. Do you agree with the court's decision? Explain.
2. What might the physician/employer do to limit his liability in the future for the negligent acts of his professional employees?
3. If the NP has malpractice insurance, can the physician recover any of his losses from her insurance carrier?

Clinical Nurse Specialist

A clinical nurse specialist (CNS) is a professional RN with an advanced academic degree, experience, and expertise in a clinical specialty (e.g., obstetrics, pediatrics, and psychiatry). The CNS functions in a leadership capacity as a clinical role model, assisting the nursing staff to continuously evaluate patient care. Further, the CNS acts as a resource for the management of patients with complex needs and conditions. The CNS participates in staff development activities related to his or her clinical specialty, and makes recommendations to establish standards of care for those patients. The CNS functions as a change agent by influencing attitudes, modifying behavior, and introducing new approaches to nursing practice. The CNS collaborates with other members of the health care team in developing and implementing the therapeutic plan of care for patients.

Nurse Midwife

Nurse midwives provide comprehensive prenatal care including delivery for patients who are at low risk for complications. For the most part, they manage normal prenatal, intrapartum, and postpartum care. Provided that there are no complications, normal newborns are also cared for by a nurse midwife. Nurse midwifes often provide primary care for women's issues from puberty to post menopause.

Nursing Assistants

A nursing assistant is an aide who has been certified and trained to assist patients with activities of daily living. The nursing assistant provides basic nursing care to non-acutely ill patients and assists in the maintenance of a safe and clean environment under the direction and supervision of an RN or licensed practical nurse (LPN). The nursing assistant helps with positioning, turning, and lifting and performs a variety of tests and treatments. The nursing assistant establishes and maintains interpersonal relationships with patients and other hospital personnel while ensuring confidentiality of patient information.

Failure To Follow Procedures

Mr. Ovitz, a 73-year-old man who had suffered a stroke and who was a resident of the Moon Lake Convalescent Center, died after immersion in a tub of hot water that had been prepared by a nursing assistant.[10] Ovitz had paralysis of his left side and could articulate only the words "yes" and "no." The nursing assistant checked the water with his hand and bathed the resident. Later in the day, a nurse noticed that the resident's leg was bleeding and his skin was sloughing off.

The paramedics were contacted, and they transferred the resident to the Evanston Hospital after determining that the patient had suffered a third-degree burn. Dr. Drueck, the surgeon in charge at Evanston Hospital, observed that Ovitz had suffered third degree burns over 40 percent of his body, primarily on his back, buttocks, both sides, genitals, and lower legs. Ovitz's knees were not burned, nor were there splatter burns. The burns were consistent with immersion in a discrete body of water.

Ovitz developed pneumonia during his hospitalization and died on January 15, 1984. There was testimony from Drueck that the cause of death was due to complications following the burns. Moon Lake's bathing policy, "Prevent accidents—do not make water too hot (95° to 100° F.)," indicates it recognized the importance of safe water temperatures with elderly residents who are susceptible to burns. Moon Lake's daily temperature logs for November 1983 also indicate that it knew that the water temperature in the system at times fluctuated above its bathing policy, at times exceeding 110° F. Yet, Moon Lake failed to take adequate measures to protect elderly residents from accidents from excessive water temperatures.

Written procedure was violated when the nursing assistant left the resident unattended in his bath. The appellate court held that revocation of the facility's license was warranted in this case.

Patient Falls

A nursing assistant in *Kern v. Gulf Coast Nursing Home of Moss Point, Inc.*,[11] was attempting to give a resident a whirlpool bath. The resident had been placed in a special rolling seat and was being lifted by a hydraulic lifting device that was used to place residents in the whirlpool. In the process of lifting the resident, the seat, which had been connected to the lift, disconnected. The resident fell to the floor, hitting her head and breaking her hip. The trial court entered a verdict in the amount of $20,000 for the plaintiff and the plaintiff appealed, stating that the award was "inadequate." The Mississippi Supreme Court held that the *verdict was not so low as to shock the conscience of the court.*

Nurse Managers

The chief nursing executive (CNE) is a qualified RN who has administrative authority, responsibility, and accountability for the function, activities, and training of the nursing staff. CNEs are generally responsible for: maintaining standards of practice; maintaining current policy and procedure manuals; making recommendations for staffing levels based on need; coordinating and integrating nursing services with other patient care services; selecting nursing staff members; and developing orientation and training programs.

Although a nurse manager is liable for his or her own negligent acts, the employer is liable for the negligent acts of all employees, including managers. Managers are not liable under the doctrine of *respondeat superior* for the negligent acts of those being supervised. They have the right to direct the nurses who are being supervised. In a health care facility, the managers' powers are derived directly from the facility's right of control.

A manager who knowingly fails to supervise an employee's performance or assigns a task to an individual whom he or she knows, or should know, is not competent to perform, can be held personally liable if injury occurs. The employer will be liable under the doctrine of *respondeat superior* as the employer of both the manager and the individual who performed the task in a negligent manner. The manager is not relieved of personal liability even though the employer is liable under *respondeat superior*.

In determining whether a nurse with supervisory responsibilities has been negligent, the nurse is measured against the standard of care of a competent and prudent nurse in the performance of supervisory duties. Those duties include the setting of policies and procedures for the prevention of accidents in the care of patients.

A manager ordinarily may rely on the fact that a subordinate is licensed or certified as an indication of the subordinate's capabilities in performing tasks within the ambit of the license or certificate. Nonetheless, where the individual's past actions have led the manager to believe that the person is likely to perform a task in an unsatisfactory manner, assigning the task to that person can lead to liability for negligence on the part of the manager because the risk of harm to the patient is knowingly increased.

Failure To Supervise

Nursing managers must properly supervise the care rendered to patients by their subordinates. Failure to do so can lead to disciplinary action by a state regulatory agency. This was the case in *Hicks v. New York State Department of Health*,[12] in which the court held that evidence was sufficient to support a finding that a practical nurse was guilty of resident neglect for failing to ensure that a resident was properly cared for during her assigned shift. The record demonstrated that the petitioner was responsible for ensuring that the nursing aides' tasks were properly accomplished by conducting a visual check of each resident while making rounds at the end of her shift. The nurse's record indicated that a security guard found HC lying in the dark, half in his bed and half still restrained in an overturned wheelchair. HC was in his undershirt with his briefs partially off, and his pants, shirt, and socks on the floor near the door. The nurse's record also indicated that HC was covered in urine and stool. The Commissioner of Health denied the petitioner's request to expunge the patient neglect report and assessed a penalty of $200, of which the petitioner was required to pay $50.

Special Duty Nurse

A special duty nurse is a nurse employed by a patient or patient's family to perform nursing care for the patient. An organization is generally not liable for the negligence of a special duty nurse unless a master–servant relationship can be determined to exist between the organization and the special duty nurse. If a master–servant relationship exists between the organization and the special duty nurse, the doctrine of *respondeat superior* may be applied to impose liability on the organization for the nurse's negligent acts.

Like a staff physician, a special duty nurse may be required to observe certain rules and regulations as a precondition to working in the organization. The observance of organization rules is insufficient, however, to establish a master–servant relationship between the organization and the nurse. Under ordinary circumstances the patient employs the special duty nurse, and the organization has no authority to hire or fire the nurse. The organization does, however, have the responsibility to protect the patient from incompetent or unqualified special duty nurses.

Float Staff

Float staff is staff that is rotated from unit to unit based on staffing needs. Floaters can benefit an understaffed unit, but they also may present a liability as well if they are assigned to work in an area outside their expertise. If a patient is injured because of a floater's negligence, the standard of care required of the floater will be that required of a nurse on the assigned patient care unit.

Agency Personnel

Health care organizations are at risk for the negligent conduct of agency personnel. Because of this risk, it is important to be sure that agency workers have the necessary skills and competencies to carry out the duties and responsibilities assigned by the organization.

Student Nurses

Student nurses are entrusted with the responsibility of providing nursing care to patients. When liability is being assessed, a student nurse serving at a health care facility is considered an agent of the facility. This is true even if the student is at the facility on an affiliation basis. Student nurses are personally liable for their own negligent acts, and the facility is liable for their acts on the basis of *respondeat superior*. A registered professional nurse, who is either the direct agent of the student's nursing school or one who has been designated by the school to serve in that capacity, must supervise students.

A student nurse is held to the standard of a competent professional nurse when performing nursing duties. The courts, in several decisions, have taken the position that anyone who performs duties customarily performed by professional nurses is held to the standards of professional nurses. Each and every patient has the right to expect competent nursing services even if students provide the care as part of their clinical training. It would be unfair to deprive a patient of compensation for an injury simply because the nurse was a student.

Nurse's Aide

Patient Neglect

The record in *Jones v. Axelrod*[13] indicated that a nurse's aide, while transferring a "total care" nursing home patient to her bed from a wheelchair, left the patient sitting on the edge of the bed. The patient subsequently fell to the floor. The aide acknowledged that the patient required restraints. The supervisor testified that the act of leaving the patient unrestrained and unattended on the edge of the bed was improper and inconsistent with safe procedure. Sufficient evidence supported a determination by the commissioner of health that the conduct of the nurse's aide constituted patient neglect.

Patient Fall and Aide's Discharge

In *Bowe v. Charleston Area Medical Center*,[14] a nurse's aide brought an action against a medical center for retaliatory discharge and breach of contract. The nurse's aide had assisted a patient to the bathroom and placed him on the commode. She left him unattended for about 10 minutes. When she returned, the patient was found lying on the floor in a pool of blood. The patient had apparently hit his head on the sink when he fell.

Following an investigation of the incident, the hospital found that the aide had been grossly negligent and terminated her employment. The personnel director had authorized the employee's termination because of a provision in the employee handbook that makes gross negligence a dischargeable offense. The aide claimed that she had been terminated in retaliation because of complaints she had made about the lack of patient care on the oncology unit to which she had been assigned. Her head nurse and the employee responsible for patient complaints could substantiate no evidence of her complaints. In addition, there was no evidence in the employee's personnel file that would indicate that she had filed a grievance over patient care. Upon jury verdict, the circuit court entered judgment for the plaintiff. The plaintiff was awarded $36,238.17 in lost wages and $15,000 for mental suffering. The circuit court added an additional $5,218.30 in interest, and the medical center appealed.

The West Virginia Supreme Court of Appeals held that: (1) the evidence established that patient neglect by the plaintiff prompted an investigation that led to her subsequent discharge, and (2) the disclaimer in the employee handbook adequately shielded the employer from any contractual liability based on the employee handbook.

The evidence showed that the aide, contrary to the medical center's policy, had assisted a patient in getting on a commode and then left him unattended, resulting in a fall and his subsequent death. Leaving the patient unattended for 10 minutes on the commode was clearly against hospital policy. The nurse's aide failed to establish that her discharge was a retaliatory act or that it contravened some public policy. The evidence presented during the development of the present case substantially cast doubt as to whether the plaintiff had ever actually made any complaints about patient care.

The hospital's disclaimer specifically stated that the employee handbook was not intended to create any contractual rights. Employment was subject to termination at any time by either the employee or employer. The disclaimer in the employee handbook read:

> Because of court decisions in some states, it has become necessary for us to make it clear that this handbook is not part of a contract, and no employee of the Medical Center has any contractual right to the matters set forth in this handbook. In addition, your employment is subject to termination at any time by either you or by the Medical Center.[15]

NEGLIGENT ACTS

The following cases illustrate some of the acts or omissions constituting negligence. They are by no means exhaustive and are merely representative of the wide range of potential legal pitfalls in which nurses might find themselves.

Administration of Medications

Nurses are required to handle and administer a vast variety of drugs that are prescribed by physicians and dispensed by an organization's pharmacy. Medications may range from aspirin to esoteric drugs that are administered through intravenous (IV) solutions. Medications must be administered in the prescribed manner and dose to prevent serious harm to patients.

The practice of pharmacy includes the ordering, preparation, dispensing, and administration of medications. These activities may be carried out only by a pharmacist with a state license or by a person exempted from the provisions of a state's pharmacy statutes. Nurses are exempted from the various pharmacy statutes when administering a medication on the oral or written order of a physician.

Administration without Prescription

In *People v. Nygren*,[16] evidence was considered sufficient to establish probable cause for charging the director of nursing and a charge nurse with second-degree assault in the administration of unprescribed doses of Thorazine to a resident at a time when he was incapable of providing consent. The trial court was found to have erred in dismissing the information before the prosecution's first witness had completed his testimony. There was probable cause to believe that the defendants had committed the offense charged and that it would have been established if the prosecution had been permitted to present its witnesses, two of which would have testified that the nurses administered the unprescribed doses of the drug. The treating physician had told the special investigator from the attorney general's office that Thorazine never had been prescribed for the resident while he was in the nursing facility. The resident was mentally retarded and incapable of consenting to administration of the drug. Medical evidence of the amount of Thorazine in the resident's blood was consistent with stupor and impairment of physical and mental functions.

Wrong Medication

The injection of the wrong medication can lead to a malpractice suit. In *Abercrombie v. Roof*,[17] a solution was prepared by an employee and injected into the patient by a physician. The physician made no examination of the fluid, and the patient suffered permanent injuries as a result of the injection. An action was brought against the physician for malpractice. The patient claimed that the fluid injected was alcohol and that the physician should have recognized its distinctive odor. In finding for the physician, the court stated that he was not responsible for the misuse of drugs prepared by an employee, unless the ordinarily prudent use of his faculties would have prevented injury to the patient.

Wrong Dosage

A nurse is responsible for making an inquiry if there is uncertainty about the accuracy of a physician's medication order in a patient's record. In the Louisiana case *of Norton v. Argonaut Insurance Co.*,[18] the court focused attention on the responsibility of a nurse to obtain clarification of an apparently erroneous order from the patient's physician. The medication order, as entered in the medical record, was incomplete and subject to misinterpretation. Believing the order to be incorrect because of the dosage, the nurse asked two physicians present on the patient care unit whether the medication should be given as ordered. The two physicians did not interpret the order as the nurse did and therefore did not share the same concern. They advised the nurse that the attending physician's instructions did not appear out of line. The nurse did not contact the attending physician but instead administered the misinterpreted dosage of medication. As a result, the patient died from a fatal overdose of the medication.

The court upheld the jury's finding that the nurse had been negligent in failing to get in contact with the attending physician before administering the medication. The nurse was held liable, as was the physician who wrote the ambiguous order that led to the fatal dose. In discussing the standard of care expected of a nurse who encounters an apparently erroneous order, the court stated that not only was the nurse unfamiliar with the medication in question, but she also violated the rule generally followed by members of the nursing profession in the community, which requires that the prescribing physician be called when there is doubt about an order. The court noted that it is the duty of a nurse to make absolutely certain what the physician intended, regarding both dosage and route. The evidence leaves no doubt that although nurses do at times consult any available physician when unsure of another physician's orders, the nurses who testified agreed that the better practice is to *consult the prescribing physician regarding questionable orders.* This clarification was not sought from the physician who wrote the order. This departure from the standard of competent nursing practice provided the basis for holding the nurse liable for negligence.

The nurse in *Harrison v. Axelrod*[19] was charged with patient neglect in that she administered the wrong dosage of the drug Haldol to a patient on seven occasions while she was employed at a nursing facility. The patient's physician had prescribed a 0.5 milligram dosage of Haldol. The patient's medication record indicated that the nurse had been administering dosages of 5 milligrams, which were being sent to the patient care unit by the pharmacy. A Department of Health investigator testified that the nurse had admitted that she administered the wrong dosage, and that she was aware of the facility's medication administration policy, "which she breached by failing to check the dosage supplied by the pharmacy against the dosage ordered by the patient's doctor." The nurse denied that she made these admissions to the investigator. The Commissioner of the Department of Health made a determination that the administration of the wrong dosage of Haldol on seven occasions constituted patient neglect.

The New York Supreme Court, Appellate Division, held that the evidence established that the nurse administered the wrong dosage of the prescribed drug Haldol to the patient.

This was a breach of the facility's medication administration policy and was sufficient to support the determination of patient neglect.

MEDICATION OVERDOSE/ *RES IPSA LOQUITUR*

Citation: *Harder v. Clinton, Inc., 948 P.2d 298 (Okla. 1997)*

Facts

Ms. Kayser was admitted to the Heritage Care Center (a nursing home) on July 14, 1992. On the evening of September 30, she was transferred to the Clinton Regional Hospital after ingesting an overdose of Tolbutamide, a diabetic medication. She was diagnosed as having a hypoglycemic coma caused by the lowering of her blood sugar from ingestion of the medication. An IV device was inserted in the dorsum area of her right foot to treat the coma. Gangrene later developed in the same foot, which eventually required an above-the-knee amputation.

Ms. Harder, Kayser's sister, brought a suit against the nursing home, as Kayser's guardian, for harm caused to Kayser by an overdose of the wrong prescription administered to her while she was in the Center's care and custody. At the close of Harder's case, which followed a *res ipsa loquitur* pattern of proof, the trial court directed a verdict for the nursing home. The trial court ruled that Harder's evidence fell short of establishing a negligence claim because her proof failed to show all the requisite foundational elements for *res ipsa loquitur*.

Issue

Did the trial court err when it directed a verdict for the nursing home based on its ruling that Harder had not satisfied the requirements for a *res ipsa loquitur* submission?

Holding

By the evidence adduced at trial, Harder met the standards for submission of her claim based on the doctrine of *res ipsa loquitur* pattern of proof.

Reason

In light of the circumstances that surround the injurious event, it seems reasonably clear that Kayser's ingestion of a Tolbutamide overdose would not have taken place in the absence of negligence by the nursing home's staff. The record shows that Kayser had not been prescribed any diabetes medication while a resident at the nursing home and that she had never been prescribed that type of hypoglycemic drug. It is uncontradicted that Kayser was at the nursing home when she ingested the prescribed medication. There is no direct evidence that anyone else supplied to her the harm-dealing dosage or that the substance in question was kept in her room (or elsewhere within her control). Neither is there indication that any other cause contributed to the coma. According to Dixon, the nursing home is responsible for the administration of medication to its residents. The administration of the wrong medication in an amount so excessive as to harm a resident is below the applicable standard of care.

Harder's evidence laid the requisite *res ipsa loquitur* foundation facts from which it could be inferred that the injury—from an overdose of the wrong prescription—was one that would not ordinarily occur in the course of controlled supervision and administration of prescribed medicine in the absence of negligence. Nothing in the record negates any of the critical elements for application of *res ipsa loquitur;* Harder clearly met her probative initiative by establishing the necessary components for invoking the rule. The responsibility for producing proof that would rebut the inferences favorable to Harder's legal position was thus shifted to the defendant.

Discussion

1. How would you have argued this case if you were the defendant nursing home?
2. What procedures would you consider implementing in order to reduce the likelihood of similar events from occurring in the future?

Wrong Route

The nurse in *Fleming v. Baptist General Convention*[20] negligently injected the patient with a solution of Talwin and Atarax subcutaneously, rather than intramuscularly. The patient suffered tissue necrosis as a result of the improper injection. The suit against the hospital was successful. On appeal, the court held that the jury's verdict for the plaintiff found adequate support in the testimony of the plaintiff's expert witness on the issues of negligence and causation.

Failure To Administer Medication

In *Kallenberg v. Beth Israel Hospital*,[21] a patient died after her third cerebral hemorrhage because of the failure of the physicians and staff to administer necessary medications. When the patient was admitted to the hospital, her physician determined that she should be given a specific drug to reduce her blood pressure and make her condition operable. For an unexplained reason, the drug was not administered. The patient's blood pressure rose, and after the final hemorrhage, she died. The jury found the hospital and physicians negligent in failing to administer the drug and ruled that the negligence had caused the patient's death. On appeal, the appellate court found that the jury had sufficient evidence to decide that the negligent treatment had been the cause of the patient's death.

Failure To Discontinue Medication

A health care organization will be held liable if a nurse continues to inject a solution into a patient after noticing its ill effects. In the Florida case of *Parrish v. Clark*,[22] the court held that a nurse's continued injection of saline solution into an unconscious patient's breast after the nurse noticed ill effects constituted negligence. Once something was observed to be wrong with the administration of the solution, the nurse had a duty to discontinue its use.

Wrong Patient

A patient's identification bracelet must be checked prior to administering any medication. To ensure that the patient's identity corresponds to the name on the patient's bracelet, the nurse should address the patient by name when approaching the patient's bedside to administer any medication. Should a patient unwittingly be administered another patient's medication, the attending physician should be notified and appropriate documentation placed on the patient's chart.

Negligent Injection

Emergency Department

On February 22, 1988, the plaintiff in *Pellerin v. Humedicenters, Inc.*,[23] went to the emergency department at Lakeland Medical Center complaining of chest pain. An emergency department physician, Dr. Gruner, examined her and ordered a nurse to give her an injection consisting of 50 mg of Demerol and 25 mg of Vistaril. Although the nurse testified she did not recall giving the injection, she did not deny giving it, and her initials are present in the emergency department record. The nurse admitted that she failed to record the site and mode of injection in the emergency department records. She said she may have written this information in the nurse's notes, but no such notes were admitted into evidence.

The plaintiff testified that she felt pain and a burning sensation in her hip during the injection. According to testimony by Gruner, a burning sensation upon injection of Vistaril is common. However, the burning persisted afterward and progressively worsened over the next several weeks. The pain spread to an area approximately 10 inches in diameter around the injection site. She could not sleep on her right side, work, perform household chores, or participate in sports without experiencing pain. She also testified that she had a lump around the injection site and that her skin was numb in that area.

The appeals court found that there was sufficient evidence to support a jury finding that the nurse had breached the applicable standard of care in administering an injection of Vistaril into Pellerin's hip. The record indicated that the patient suffered from pain and a lump in her hip area. An expert testified that hitting a subcutaneous nerve while administering an injection was more likely than missing one, and he believed that the needle itself probably caused the nerve damage, thereby causing the patient's pain. In addition, there was expert testimony that it was possible for a lump to form in the patient's hip, because an injection of Vistaril into subcutaneous tissue could damage the nerve and cause a lump. The jury awarded the plaintiff $90,304.68 in total damages.

The record amply supported the jury's verdict. The nurse admitted that she failed to record the site and mode of injection in the emergency department records. According to the testimony of two experts in nursing practice, failing to record this information is below the standard of care for nursing. Although these omissions could not have affected the administration of the injection, they tend to indicate that in this instance the nurse did not follow accepted procedure while performing her job.

Permanent Injuries

In *Nueces v. Long Island College Hospital*,[24] the plaintiff brought an action against the hospital seeking to recover damages resulting from a negligently administered injection. The New York Supreme Court entered judgment on a jury verdict for the patient and the hospital appealed.

Contrary to the hospital's contention, a review of the evidence demonstrated that the jury's verdict was supported by sufficient evidence. There existed a rational basis for the jury's findings of negligence on the part of the hospital's agent in the administration of an injection to the plaintiff's left buttock proximately causing her permanent injuries. Because the parties' respective medical experts differed concerning the nature and cause of the plaintiff's injuries, the matter was properly left to the jury.

Negligent Injection of Tetracycline

In *Bernardi v. Community Hospital Association*,[25] a seven-year-old patient was in the hospital after surgery for the drainage of an abscessed appendix. The attending physician had left a written postoperative order requiring an injection of tetracycline every 12 hours. During the evening of the first day after surgery, the nurse, employed by the hospital and acting under this order, injected the prescribed dosage of tetracycline in the patient's right gluteal region. It was claimed that the nurse negligently injected the tetracycline into or adjacent to the sciatic nerve, causing the patient to permanently lose the normal use of the right foot. The court did not hold the physician responsible. It concluded that if the plaintiff could prove the nurse's negligence, the hospital would be responsible for the nurse's act under the doctrine of *respondeat superior*. The physician did not know which nurse administered the injection because he was not present when the injection was given, and he had no opportunity to control its administration. The hospital was found liable under *respondeat superior*. The hospital was the employer of the nurse. Only it had the right to hire and fire her. Only it could assign the nurse to certain hours, designated areas, and specific patients.

Failure To Note an Order Change

Failure to review a patient's record before administering a medication to ascertain whether an order has been modified may render a nurse liable for negligence. The case of *Larrimore v. Homeopathic Hospital Association*[26] concerned a female patient who had been receiving a drug by injection over a period of time. The physician wrote an instruction on the patient's order sheet changing the method of administration from injection to oral medication. When a nurse on the patient unit who had been off duty for several days was preparing to medicate the patient by injection, the patient objected and referred the nurse to the physician's new order. The nurse, however, told the patient she was mistaken and gave the medication by injection. Perhaps the nurse had not reviewed the order sheet after being told by the patient that the medication was to be given orally; perhaps the nurse did not notice the physician's entry. Either way, the nurse's conduct was held to be negligent. The court went on to say that the jury could find the nurse negligent by applying ordinary common sense to establish the applicable standard of care.

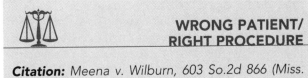

**WRONG PATIENT/
RIGHT PROCEDURE**

Citation: Meena v. Wilburn, 603 So.2d 866 (Miss. 1992)

Facts

The plaintiff bumped her right leg and injured it. The injury was a "nick" that developed into an ulcer because of poor blood circulation. Due to the plaintiff's diabetic condition, the ulcer did not heal. She visited her physician, who referred her to Dr. Maples, a vascular surgeon. Maples performed surgery.

Two days following surgery, Dr. Meena was at the hospital covering for one of his partners, Dr. Petro, who had asked him to remove the staples from one of his patients, 65-year-old Slaughter. Slaughter shared a semi-private room with the plaintiff. Meena testified that he went and picked up Slaughter's chart at the nurse's desk and asked one of the nurses as to which bed Slaughter was in. Meena claimed that he was led to believe that she was in the bed next to the window. He picked up the chart and asked Greer, a nurse, to accompany him to the plaintiff's room. Shortly thereafter, Meena received an emergency call at the nursing station. He said that he asked Greer to take out the staples, because he had to respond to an emergency call at another hospital. Greer conceded during her testimony that, before removing staples from a patient, a nurse should read the chart, be familiar with the chart, look at the patient's wrist band, and compare the arm band to the chart—all of which she failed to do. Greer rationalized her failure: "When the doctor I work for is standing at the foot of a patient's bed, I would have no doubt—no reason to doubt what he tells me to do."

Greer began to remove the plaintiff's staples. She soon realized that there was a problem. The plaintiff's skin split open—revealing the layer of fat under the skin. Greer stopped the procedure and left the room to check the medical records maintained at the nursing station. She realized that she had removed staples from the wrong patient. At that point, she encountered Maples and explained to him what had happened. Maples immediately restapled the skin.

Following discharge, the plaintiff's health began to falter and she developed a fever of 101° F. The tissue where the staples had been removed had become infected. Dr. Evans ultimately readmitted her to the hospital; she remained there for approximately 22 days—during which time she underwent more surgery and received intensive care for the infection. The plaintiff testified that she continued to experience pain upon being discharged from the hospital in May 1988. Her condition gradually improved and, presumably, she had recovered completely with the exception of some scarring and skin "indention."

In June 1988, a complaint was filed against Meena and Greer. After four days of trial, the jury returned a verdict against Meena and assessed damages in the amount of $125,000. The jury declined to hold the nurse liable for the plaintiff's injuries. Meena's motion for a new trial was denied and an appeal was taken.

Issue

Was the jury's exoneration of the nurse, who removed the surgical staples, grounds for a new trial on the issue of the physician's liability?

Holding

The Mississippi Supreme Court held that the jury's exoneration of Greer was not grounds for a new trial on the issue of the physician's liability.

Reason

Meena contended that the Mississippi Supreme Court should reverse and remand the case for a new trial because the jury was bound to return a verdict against both defendants, inasmuch as the defendants were sued as joint tort-feasors.

The plaintiff argued that the court has often held that it would not reverse a case simply because one joint tort-feasor was deemed liable and the other was exonerated. Two relevant cases are as follows:

In *Golden Flake Snack Foods v. Thornton*, 548 So.2d 382 (Miss. 1989). . . . Mississippi's law on joint and several liability is such that the instant case need not be reversed for the failure to include the defendant Hope Thornton in the verdict. One may recognize that misery wants company, but this court does not have to assign company to those in misery. The jury had the prerogative of including or not including Hope Thornton in the verdict; after a review, they did not. This court is loath to find fault, certainly not intentional fault with 12 men and women tried and true. *Id.* at 383–384.

In *Capital Transport Co. v. McDuff*, 319 So.2d 658, 660–61 (Miss. 1975), the court held that "For some time it has been the established law in this state that a case will not be reversed simply because a master is held liable where the servant is exonerated. . . ."

The court, under authority of its previous holdings in *Golden Flake* and *Capital Transport*, held that Meena's contention that the jury improperly returned a verdict against him but not the nurse was rejected.

Discussion

1. Do you agree with the court's decision? Explain.
2. Should liability have been apportioned between the nurse and the physician?
3. What are the issues in this case that are applicable to all health care providers?
4. Do you think that the patient had cause to file further proceedings against the nurse who failed to follow hospital procedures?

Burns

Burns by hot-water bottles, sitz baths, and heating pads often result in lawsuits. The plaintiff in *Quinby v. Morrow*[27] sought damages against the hospital, the instrument nurse, and the surgeon for third-degree burns sustained by her during a tonsillectomy. A hot metal gag had been placed in the patient's mouth, causing the severe burn. There was testimony that it was the duty of the circulating nurse, a hospital employee not named in the suit, to have a basin of water available to cool sterilized surgical instruments before their use. The surgeon testified that the basin was missing or at least not in its usual place and that this was a serious omission. The jury returned a verdict holding the hospital liable for $30,000. The surgeon and the instrument nurse were found not liable. These verdicts were affirmed by the appellate court, which held that evidence was sufficient to allow the jury to affix responsibility to the hospital, based on the acts of the circulating nurse, and to exonerate the surgeon and the instrument nurse.

The negligent use of a Bovie plate led to liability in *Monk v. Doctors Hospital*,[28] in which a nurse had been instructed by the physician to set up a Bovie machine. The nurse placed the contact plate of the Bovie machine under the patient's right calf in a negligent manner and the patient suffered burns. The patient introduced instruction manuals, issued by the manufacturer, supporting a claim that the plate was placed improperly. These manuals had been available to the hospital. The trial court directed a verdict in favor of the hospital and the physician. The appellate court found that there was sufficient evidence from which the jury could conclude that the Bovie plate was applied in a negligent manner. There was also sufficient evidence, including the manufacturer's

manual and expert testimony, from which the jury could find that the physician was independently negligent.

Failure To Follow Established Nursing Procedures

The following cases present potential hazards to nurses who fail to follow established nursing procedures.

Infection Control

Failure to follow proper infection control procedures (e.g., proper hand-washing techniques) can result in cross-contamination between patients, staff, and visitors. Staff members who administer to patients, moving from one patient to another without washing their hands after changing dressings and carrying out routine procedures, can expose an organization to lawsuits.

The patient in *Helmann v. Sacred Heart Hospital*[29] had sustained chest injuries, a left hip dislocation, and multiple fractures in the area of the left hip socket and was paralyzed from the waist down. The patient was returned to his room after hip surgery. The patient's roommate complained of a boil under his right arm. Eight days later, a culture was taken of drainage from the wound. Three days later, the laboratory identified the infection as Staphylococcus aureus. The infected roommate was transferred immediately to an isolation room. Until this time, ward nurses and hospital attendants administered to both patients regularly, moving from one patient to another without washing their hands as they changed dressings and carried out routine procedures. On the day the roommate was placed in isolation, the plaintiff's wound erupted, discharging a large amount of purulent drainage. A culture of the drainage showed it to have been caused by the presence of Staphylococcus aureus. The infection penetrated into the patient's hip socket, destroying tissue and requiring a second operation. In the second operation, the patient's hip was fused in a nearly immovable position. The court ruled that there was sufficient circumstantial evidence from which the jury could have found that the patients were infected with the same Staphylococcus aureus strain and that the infection was caused by the hospital's negligence in that its personnel failed to follow sterile techniques in ministering to its two patients.

In staphylococcus infection cases, one must demonstrate negligence of the defendant and injury resulting from that negligence. The burden of proof is on the plaintiff to establish a causal relationship between the injury and the hospital's deviation from the accepted standard of care. Negligence on the nurse's part can arise from failure to follow appropriate isolation procedures. Sterile technique must be followed when it is suspected that a patient has an infection, even though it has not been confirmed. Negligence often arises from failure to make a proper diagnosis and/or to treat properly.

Breaching a Standard—IV Sites

The plaintiffs in *Morris v. Children's Hospital Medical Center*[30] alleged in their complaint that, while hospitalized at Children's Hospital Medical Center, the patient suffered a laceration to her arm as a result of treatment administered by the defendants and their agents that fell below the accepted standard of care. Mrs. Morris alleged from personal observation that the laceration to her daughter's arm was caused by the jagged edges of a plastic cup that had been split and placed on her arm to guard the IV site. A nurse, in her affidavit, who stated her qualifications as an expert, expressed her opinion that the practice of placing a split plastic cup over an IV site as a guard constituted a breach of the standard of nursing care. Was the RN competent to give expert testimony on liability issues?

An appeals court held that the RN was competent to give expert testimony on liability issues. Expert testimony is not essential to state a claim in ordinary negligence. Such testimony is, however, admissible in evidence if the witness is qualified as an expert and the expert's specialized knowledge will aid the trier of fact in understanding the evidence. The RN, by affidavit, attested to her qualifications and her familiarity with the standards of nursing care and expressed her opinion that the practice alleged to have caused the child's injury was not in conformity with the accepted standards of nursing care.

Decubitus Ulcers

The staff of health care facilities must be properly trained in the prevention and treatment of ulcers. An organized protocol and consistent plan of care should be implemented in order to help prevent ulcer formation and to aid in the healing process.

The failure of nurses to follow adequate nursing procedures in treating decubitus ulcers was found to be a factor leading to the death of a nursing facility resident in *Montgomery Health Care v. Ballard*.[31] Two nurses testified that they did not know that decubitus ulcers could be life threatening. One nurse testified that she did not know that the patient's physician should be called if there were symptoms of infection. Such allegations would indicate that there was a lack of training and supervision of the nurses treating the patient. The seriousness of such failure was driven home when the court allowed $2 million in punitive damages.

The occurrence of pressure ulcers can be reduced by

- observing the general condition of the patient's skin for
  - redness
  - blanching
  - soft/dry/rough, etc.
  - rashes/irritation
  - bruises
  - scabs
  - freedom from above
- taking measures to prevent skin breakdown
- using Rx for pressure ulcers
- using padding for pressure points and bony prominences, including padding on bed and chair
- doing a proper, gentle massage to bony areas several times a day
- giving regular assistance for resident to turn or shift weight (e.g., bedrails, footboards, trapeze)
- keeping bed linens, clothing, and underpads smooth and free from wrinkles
- keeping elastic bandages or hose smooth and wrinkle free
- keeping elastic bandages wrapped smoothly with appropriate overlap
- including dietary/nutritional support for skin integrity

Failure To Follow Instructions

Supervisor's Instructions

Failure of a nurse to follow the instructions of a supervising nurse to wait for her assistance before performing a procedure can result in the revocation of the nurse's license. The nurse in *Cafiero v. North Carolina Board of Nursing*[32] failed to heed instructions to wait for assistance before connecting a heart monitor to an infant. The incorrect connection of the heart monitor resulted in an electrical shock to the infant. The board of nursing, under the Nursing Practice Act, revoked the nurse's license. The board had the authority to revoke the nurse's license even though her work before and after the incident had been exemplary. The dangers of electric cords are within the realm of common knowledge. The record showed that the nurse failed to exercise ordinary care in connecting the infant to the monitor.

Two Standards—Which Is Right?

Given two standards of care, should a hospital adopt the least restrictive standard? This generally would not be a good idea. For example, in *Edwards v. Brandywine Hosp.*,[33] the plaintiff/appellant, Mr. Edwards, went to the emergency department complaining of pain in his hip. He was admitted and a "heparin lock" (a device that allows multiple IV fluids to be introduced at a common point) was placed in his left hand. The heparin lock was left in place for three or four days. This was in violation of regulations promulgated by the Pennsylvania Department of Health requiring hospitals to develop written standards regarding such antiseptic practices as changing IV catheter sites. The regulations state that these standards should comply with standards described in the American Hospital Association's publication entitled *Infec-*

tion Control in the Hospital (1979), which recommends that IV catheter sites be changed every 48 hours in order to reduce the risk of infection. The hospital was subject to corporate liability for adopting a 72-hour rule.

Following discharge, Edwards noticed a red spot at the site of the heparin lock. He had returned that day to the hospital for physical therapy. His therapist referred him to the emergency department for evaluation. The emergency department physician examined Edward's hand and took a specimen of pus from the site of the heparin lock and sent it to the laboratory for evaluation. Edwards was provided with oral antibiotics and sent home. The laboratory results showed that Edwards had a staphylococcus infection. The emergency department physician entered this information on the patient's record.

Edwards returned to the hospital a few days later and was admitted with leg pains. A second laboratory test was ordered, which again showed the presence of a staph infection. The patient was treated over a period of time with IV antibiotics and eventually discharged with a good bill of health, only to return a week later with pain and a fever. The physicians believed that the staph infection had spread to his artificial hip. Following treatment and various hospitalizations over the next several years, Edwards' physicians decided to remove his artificial hip and treat him with massive doses of antibiotics. In order to be ambulatory, Edwards now needs the aid of assistive devices (e.g., crutches).

A suit was brought against the physicians and hospital. The trial court took notice of the health department's regulation regarding catheter site changing and ruled that the hospital's admitted failure to move the heparin lock for at least three days constituted negligence *per se*. The physicians settled with the plaintiff, leaving the hospital as the only defendant. At the close of the plaintiff's case, the trial court granted the defendant's motion for a directed verdict. The trial court held that although the negligence *per se* ruling established the hospital's breach of a duty to care, the plaintiff could not prove causation.

> The court reasoned that to establish legal causation, Edwards had to prove that staphylococcus bacteria entered his body at the heparin lock site at least 48 hours after the lock was installed, because it was only after 48 hours that the hospital became negligent in not moving the catheter. The court held that there is simply no evidence as to when this organism entered Edwards even if I did assume that it did enter through the heparin lock site. The jury would have to speculate as to when organism entered the body and this I would not permit.[34]

The superior court reversed the trial court's directed verdict for the defendant, finding that the evidence presented at trial by the plaintiff was sufficient to allow the claim of causa-

tion to go to the jury. Evidence included: (1) failure to change placement of the catheter within 48 hours; (2) testimony from an infectious diseases expert who testified to the same causal relationship; and (3) a discharge report that noted Mr. Edwards' staph infection was thought to be secondary to an abscess at the heparin lock site.

The kind of causation evidence the trial court expects cannot be produced. No witness could possibly testify that she saw a Staphylococcus aureas bacterium crawl into Mr. Edwards' hand through the heparin lock site on his third day in the hospital and then multiply into the infection that spread to his artificial hip. Yet the trial court's ruling implied that such showing was necessary to get to the jury.

Once a plaintiff has introduced evidence that a defendant's negligent act or omission increased the risk of harm to a person in the plaintiff's position, and that harm in fact was sustained, it becomes a question for the jury as to whether or not that increased risk was a substantial factor in producing the harm.

Is there an issue of corporate negligence? Yes. The plaintiff claimed that the hospital was subject to corporate liability for adopting a 72-hour rule for changing placement of IV catheters. The plaintiff had introduced evidence showing that a 48-hour rule was appropriate, but that the hospital had adopted a rule allowing IVs to remain in place at the same site for 72 hours. If Edwards could prove that the 72-hour rule was inadequate, that the hospital should have known that it was inadequate, and that following this rule caused him harm, then he has made out a proper claim for corporate negligence.

Should the nurse have been faulted for following hospital policy? No. A nurse following hospital rules cannot be faulted. If hospital policy required changing the site of the catheter every 48 hours and the nurse failed to do so, then the nurse could be held negligent and the hospital liable under the theory of *respondeat superior*.

When faced with the dilemma of two standards for rendering patient care, an organization may find it more attractive to adopt the one least restrictive or labor intensive. This could prove to be a costly decision for both the patient and the organization by increasing (1) the risk of patient injury and (2) the organization's exposure to corporate liability for any injury suffered from following the less restrictive standard.

Failure To Monitor Patient's Vital Signs

In *McCann v. ABC Insurance Co.*,[35] an attempt to deliver a baby by forceps was unsuccessful. The obstetrician, Dr. Merrill, testified that he auscultated (listened to the baby's heart tone) immediately after the failed forceps delivery and the baby's heart rate was normal. The baby was then delivered by Caesarean section. At birth the baby was not breathing and had no detectable heartbeat. The baby was resuscitated with oxygen and was transferred to another hospital where he went into an irreversible coma. He was in a clinically brain-dead state within 24 hours. Evidence adduced at trial established that during delivery the baby suffered a severe hypoxic event that caused the baby's death.

The plaintiffs instituted a lawsuit against the obstetrician and the hospital. The trial court granted a motion for a directed verdict at the end of the trial, dismissed Merrill, and an appeal was taken.

The cause of the hypoxic event was unknown. Not one expert called to testify could identify a cause of the hypoxic event. The plaintiffs' cause of action was dependent upon whether the plaintiffs could show that Merrill or the hospital was negligent in failing to timely diagnose the existence of the hypoxic event so that an attempt could be made to deliver the baby more quickly and thus increase the baby's chance of survival. The sole claim against Merrill was the allegation that he failed to properly monitor the baby's heartbeat or make sure that the nurse properly monitored the baby's heartbeat after the fetal monitor had been removed. Evidence presented indicated that the standard of care would require that fetal heartbeats be monitored every 10 minutes following removal of the fetal monitor. The evidence presented indicated that this did not occur. Both the defendants' and plaintiffs' medical experts agreed that Merrill did not breach the standard of care required in treating Mrs. McCann. The plaintiffs' expert testified by deposition that the duty to monitor was a nursing responsibility. The Louisiana Patient's Compensation Fund (the entity responsible for excess amount owed by the hospital) argued that there was a lack of expert testimony on the issue of Merrill's negligence. No medical testimony was introduced to rebut any of the medical testimony that established that the nurse had the duty to auscultate the baby.

Testimony was needed to show that Merrill breached the standard of care required in treating McCann. Because the plaintiffs failed to provide such testimony, the trial court was found to have correctly granted the directed verdict.

> Plaintiffs' cause of action against . . . Hospital was predicated primarily upon its failure to have policies and procedures regarding the continuous monitoring of fetal heart tones and its failure to adequately and continuously monitor the unborn infant. The basic thrust of the case was that none of the parties auscultated the baby every 10 minutes after the fetal monitoring device was removed, as required by the standards of the American College of Obstetrics and Gynecology (ACOG). Thus the issue in this case is not whether the baby would have died from other causes even if the Caesarean section had been performed faster, but rather the issue is whether the

baby had lost a chance of survival. . . . [Because] the nurses' negligent inaction has terminated any chance of survival, conjecture as to other possible causes of death is inadmissible.[36]

NURSES' FAILURE TO REPEAT VITAL SIGNS

Citation: *Porter v. Lima Mem'l Hosp., 995 F.2d 629 (6th Cir. 1993)*

Facts

A medical malpractice action was filed on behalf of Liesl Fitzenrider, an infant who was injured in an automobile accident and subsequently developed paralysis—allegedly because of the physician's and hospital's failure to diagnose a spinal cord injury.

The automobile in which Liesl was traveling spun out of control and she was thrown to the floor of the car. The rescue squad personnel examined the infant and found nothing seriously wrong. A rescue squad member then held Liesl in his arms while she was transported with her mother, Mrs. Porter, to Lima Memorial Hospital, the hospital nearest to the scene of the accident.

The rescue squad took Liesl to the Lima emergency department, where she lay on a hospital table awaiting examination by Dr. Singh, an emergency department physician. Ms. Ogelsbee, an RN, took Liesl's vital signs and recorded them on the medical chart. She reported them to Singh, upon his arrival, for examination and treatment. At this point, the only observable sign of injury was a small bruise or hematoma on the right side of Liesl's head. Ogelsbee also reported this to Singh, and he then assumed primary responsibility for treating Liesl. Singh found all of Liesl's extremities functioning normally and ordered several laboratory tests and numerous X-rays. He did not, however, order any spinal X-rays and failed to diagnose spinal instability. Ogelsbee did not repeat the vital signs during or after Singh's examination, claiming that she received no physician's instruction in this regard. After reviewing the X-rays and laboratory tests, Singh discharged Liesl and provided her mother with written instructions concerning her head injuries.

After Singh discharged Liesl, she and her mother remained at the hospital while awaiting a ride home. During a period of more than two hours, Liesl apparently displayed no additional signs of serious injury as observed by her mother. Her mother did report a short period of irregular breathing to one of the nurses at Lima. The nurse examined Liesl, determined that nothing was wrong, and returned Liesl to her mother. Mrs. Porter made no further inquiries; she testified that the nurse told her that "babies just breathe funny." When she reached her home, the mother noted that Liesl's condition was worsening and she then took Liesl to Defiance Hospital, where physicians determined, for the first time, that Liesl's legs were not moving. They ordered numerous X-rays and laboratory tests, and eventually another hospital staff physician diagnosed a subluxation at her first and second lumbar vertebrae, which resulted in Liesl's paralysis from the waist down. Experts who testified in the trial agreed that Liesl suffered paralysis sometime after Dr. Singh's examination and before her arrival, hours later, at Defiance Hospital.

The experts also appeared to agree that Singh was the primary person who could have prevented the spinal injury by diagnosing Liesl's unstable spine before it became critically injured. Singh settled for $2,500,000.

The proximate cause of Liesl's injury was the crucial issue upon which Lima's asserted liability depended. There was evidence that both Singh and the nurses breached a duty of care, and this evidence of negligence was sufficient to survive Lima's motion for a new trial. The pertinent question was whether the nurses' conduct proximately caused Liesl's paralysis. After the mother settled with the physician, the district court denied the hospital's motion for judgment, notwithstanding the verdict in favor of the mother, but ordered a new trial at which the jury found the hospital not liable for the infant's injuries. Both the hospital and the mother appealed.

Issue

Did the Lima nurses' conduct proximately cause the infant's paralysis?

Holding

The United States Court of Appeals for the Sixth Circuit held that the nurses' failure to repeat vital signs was legally insufficient to establish a connection between the failure to repeat vital signs and the eventual paralysis.

Reason

After the accident, Liesl was not immobilized while being transported to Lima. Singh did not di-

rect that she be immobilized at any time while examining, testing, and treating her, but notes that she was moving her extremities. Liesl demonstrated no signs of paralysis while he was examining her, and this would seem to eliminate any failure of this kind, which may have previously occurred, as a proximate cause of the paralysis. The experts on both sides generally agreed that the Lima nurses had no independent duty, apart from a physician's instructions, to immobilize the infant.

The plaintiff's expert, Dr. Hall, changed his original, unequivocal opinion that the Lima nurses acted appropriately in the care of Liesl, but he made it clear, nonetheless, that the physician was the ultimate person responsible from the standpoint of proximate cause:

> Q. Now, Doctor [Hall], generally speaking, it's the role and responsibility of the emergency room physician to determine the patient's medical diagnosis and then to order the necessary and appropriate medical treatment, is it not?
>
> A. Yes, it is.
>
> Q. And, Doctor, in this case, where the emergency room doctor did not diagnose any spinal cord injury and discharged the baby after examining and X-raying the infant, you're not criticizing the nurses for not diagnosing and treating the spinal cord injury, are you?
>
> A. That's correct.
>
> Q. And that's because it was Dr. Singh's role and responsibility to do that, correct?
>
> A. Yes.
>
> Q. And what you're telling the jury is that, in your opinion, it was Dr. Singh who was responsible for treating Liesl's spinal cord injury, or at least he was responsible for ordering Liesl to be immobilized and hospitalized for further care and work up, isn't that the thrust of your testimony in this case?
>
> A. Yes.
>
> Q. So you are not saying that the conduct of the nurses or other hospital personnel caused any permanent harm or injury [to Liesl Fitzenrider], are you?
>
> A. That's correct. *Id.* at 634.

Dr. Aranosian, another of the plaintiff's experts, opined that the Lima nurses should have repeated vital signs. Like Hall, however, he believed it was Singh's failure rather than the nurses' failure to repeat vital signs or to immobilize Liesl that proximately caused Liesl's injuries:

Q. And it's your testimony that Dr. Singh should have ordered Liesl to be immobilized after she arrived at the emergency room, isn't that correct?

A. Yes, sir.

Q. And it's your opinion that, as far as responsibility for ordering immobilization in the emergency room in 1979, that would be the duty of the emergency room physician involved in the care of the patient, isn't that true?

A. Yes, sir.

Q. And it's also true—now, generally speaking, I will go on. Now, generally speaking, isn't it the real objective and responsibility of the emergency room physician to determine the patient's medical diagnosis and then to order the necessary and appropriate medical treatment?

A. Yes, sir.

Q. And, Doctor, in this case, where the emergency room doctor did not diagnose any spinal cord injury and then discharged the baby after examining and X-raying the infant, you certainly are not criticizing the nurses for not diagnosing and treating the spinal cord injury, are you?

A. Well, that's correct. I mean, the nurse would not make the diagnosis on the child. That's correct.

Q. And that's because it was Dr. Singh's role and responsibility to determine the medical diagnosis and then order the necessary and appropriate medical treatment, isn't that correct?

A. Yes, sir. *Id.* at 634.

Still another of the plaintiff's experts, Dr. Voeller, was even more specific in stating he did not think the vital signs had any causal relationship to the paralysis.

Discussion

1. Describe the importance of patient assessment and documentation.
2. What was the importance of collaboration between the nurse and physician in this case?

Failure To Report Physician Negligence

An organization can be liable for the failure of nursing personnel to take appropriate action when a patient's per-sonal physician is clearly unwilling or unable to cope with a situation that threatens the life or health of the patient. In a California case, *Goff v. Doctors General Hospital,*[37] a patient was bleeding seriously after childbirth because the physician failed to suture her properly. The nurses testified that they were aware of the patient's dangerous condition and that the physician was not present in the hospital. Both nurses knew the patient would die if nothing was done, but neither contacted anyone except the physician. The hospital was liable for the nurses' negligence in failing to notify their supervisors of the serious condition that caused the patient's death. Evidence was sufficient to sustain the finding that the nurses who attended the patient and who were aware of the excessive bleeding were negligent and that their negligence was a contributing cause of the patient's death. The measure of duty of the hospital toward its patients is the exercise of that degree of care used by hospitals generally. The court held that nurses who knew that a woman they were attending was bleeding excessively were negligent in failing to report the circumstances so that prompt and adequate measures could be taken to safeguard her life.

Failure To Question Patient Discharge

A nurse has a duty to question the discharge of a patient if he or she has reason to believe that such discharge could be injurious to the health of the patient. Jury issues were raised in *Koeniguer v. Eckrich*[38] by expert testimony that the nurses had a duty to attempt to delay the patient's discharge if her condition warranted continued hospitalization. By permissible inferences from the evidence, the delay in treatment that resulted from the premature discharge contributed to the patient's death. Summary dismissal of this case against the hospital by a trial court was found to have been improper.

SWOLLEN BEYOND RECOGNITION

Citation: *NKC Hosps., Inc. v. Anthony, 849 S.W.2d 564 (Ky. Ct. App. 1993)*

Facts

The decedent was in her first pregnancy under the primary care of Dr. Hawkins, her personal physician and an obstetrician. Mrs. Anthony was in good health, 26 years of age, employed, and about 30 weeks along in her noneventful pregnancy.

On September 5, 1989, Anthony's husband took her to the emergency department. She was experiencing nausea, vomiting, and abdominal pain, and because of her pregnancy, she was referred to the hospital's obstetrical unit. In the obstetrical unit, Anthony came under the immediate care of Ms. Moore, a nurse, who performed an assessment.

Hawkins was called later that evening. She issued several orders, including an IV start, blood work, urinalysis, and an antinausea prescription. Later that night, a second call was made to Hawkins, giving her the test results and informing her that the patient was in extreme pain. Believing that Anthony had a urinary tract infection, antibiotics were ordered along with an order for her discharge from the hospital.

That same night a third call was made to Hawkins because of the pain Anthony was experiencing, as observed by Moore. Mr. Anthony also talked with Hawkins about his wife's pain. Moore became concerned about Hawkins' discharge order. Although aware of Moore's evaluation, Hawkins prescribed morphine sulfate but was unrelenting in her order of discharge.

Dr. Love, the resident physician on duty, did not see or examine the patient, although a prescription for the morphine was ordered and administered pursuant to the telephoned directions of Hawkins. It is not clear from the record, but it is assumed the morphine prescription was written by Love. At approximately 2:00 A.M., the morphine was administered to Anthony. She rested comfortably for several hours, but awakened in pain again. At 6:00 A.M., the patient was discharged in that condition.

During trial testimony, Ms. Hale, a nursing supervisor, admitted that it was a deviation from the standard of nursing care to discharge a patient in significant pain. Moore, who was always concerned with the patient's pain, had *grave reservations about her discharge* in that condition. She suggested that Love examine Anthony. She even consulted her supervisor, Nurse Hale. The major allegation of the hospital's negligence in this case is the undisputed fact that at no time, prior to her discharge, was Anthony ever clinically seen or examined by a physician.

At approximately 10:00 A.M., Anthony was readmitted to the hospital. Upon readmission, Hawkins began personal supervision of her patient. It was determined that Anthony had a serious respiratory problem. The next day the patient was transferred to the hospital's intensive care unit.

The following day, the baby was delivered by Caesarean section. It was belatedly determined at that time that Anthony's condition was caused by a perforation of the appendix at the large bowel, a condition not detected by anyone at the hospital during her first admission. Almost three weeks later, while still in Norton Hospital, Anthony died of acute adult respiratory distress syndrome (ARDS), a complication resulting from the delay in the diagnosis and treatment of her appendicitis.

A medical negligence judgment was brought against the hospital. At trial, Dr. Fields, an expert witness for the estate of Anthony, board certified in obstetrics and gynecology, testified in no uncompromising terms that the hospital deviated from the standard of care. Pertinent testimony of Fields is as follows:

Q. Had Margaret [Anthony] received care at Norton's Hospital which was within, which would have been within the standard of care, what would have been the outcome?

A. She would have had a prompt appendectomy performed following ruling out of various other conditions, such as kidney infection, and the appendix would have been removed, the antibiotic therapy instituted promptly in the intravenous fashion, her dehydrated state would have been corrected, she would never have suffered the pulmonary complication known as acute adult respiratory distress syndrome.

Q. Within a degree of medical probability, sir, would she be alive today?

A. Yes.

Q. Was the discharge of Margaret Anthony from the hospital on the early morning hours of September 6, 1989, a deviation from the standard of care for the hospital?

A. Yes, sir. *Id.* at 566.

Fields' testimony tagged Norton Hospital with negligence as its actions were below the standard of care for any institution that he was familiar with. Every patient who presents herself to the labor and delivery area, the emergency department, or any area of the hospital should be seen by a physician before anything is undertaken, and certainly before she is allowed to leave the institution. Further, to provide the patient with medication in the form of a prescription without the physician ever seeing the patient was below any standard of care that Fields' was acquainted with. The jury was instructed on the comparative negligence of Hawkins and the hospital. An award of more than $2 million was returned, with the apportionment of causation attributable to Hawkins as 65 percent and to the hospital as 35 percent. The hospital argued that the trial court erred in failing to grant its motions for directed verdict and for judgment notwithstanding the verdict because of the lack of substantial causation in linking the negligence of the hospital to Anthony's death.

Issue

Was the negligence of the hospital superseded by the negligence of the patient's primary care physician, and was the award excessive?

Holding

The Kentucky Court of Appeals held that negligence of the hospital was not superseded by the negligence of the patient's primary care physician, and that the award for 20 days of pain and suffering prior to the patient's death was not excessive.

Reason

The hospital's negligence is based on acts of omission, by failing to check Anthony's lungs or to have her examined by a physician, and on positive acts of negligence, such as discharging her in pain. The hospital certainly should have foreseen the injury to Anthony because its own staff was questioning the judgments of Hawkins, while at the same time failing to follow through with the standard of care required of it. All qualified health care providers, within the range of care for the patient, were under a duty to exercise their senses and intelligence to investigate and inspect for potential dangers to her. They did not. Their voluntary ignorance of her condition will grant no relief because voluntary ignorance is negligence. The defense that the hospital's nurses were only following a "chain of command" by doing what Hawkins ordered is not persuasive. The nurses were not the agents of Hawkins. *All involved had their independent duty to Mrs. Anthony.*

The evidence presented a woman conscious of her last days on earth, swollen beyond recognition, tubes exiting almost every orifice of her body, in severe pain, and who deteriorated to the point where she could not verbally communicate with loved ones. Among the last things she did was write out instructions about the care for her newborn child. The trial court, when confronted with a motion for a new trial on excessive damages, must evaluate the award mirrored against the facts. It is said, if the trial judge does not blush, the award is not excessive. *No question, the award was monumental, but so was the injury.*

Discussion

1. Was Dr. Hawkins' "telephone" assessment of the patient appropriate?
2. How would you apportion negligence among the attending physician, resident, obstetrical nurse, nursing supervisor, and hospital?
3. What are the lessons that should be learned from this case?
4. What educational issues are apparent?

Failure To Note Changes in a Patient's Condition

Failure to note changes in a patient's condition can lead to liability on the part of the nurse and the organization. The recovery room nurse in *Eyoma v. Falco,*[39] who had been assigned to monitor a postsurgical patient, left the patient and failed to recognize that the patient had stopped breathing. Nurse Falco had been assigned to monitor the patient in the recovery room. She delegated that duty to another nurse and failed to verify that the other nurse accepted that responsibility.

> Nurse Falco admitted she never got a verbal response from the other nurse, and when she returned there was no one near the decedent. She acknowledged that Dr. Brotherton told her to watch the decedent's breathing, but claimed she was not told that decedent had been given narcotics. She maintained that upon her return she checked the decedent and observed his respirations to be eight per minute.
>
> Thereafter, Brotherton returned and inquired about the decedent's condition. Falco informed the doctor that the patient was fine. However, upon his personal observation, Brotherton realized that the decedent had stopped breathing.
>
> •　　•　　•　　•
>
> Decedent, because of oxygen deprivation, entered a comatose state and remained unconscious for over a year until his death.[40]

The jury held the nurse to be 100 percent liable for the patient's injuries. The court held that there was sufficient evidence to support the verdict.

Failure To Report Changes in a Patient's Condition

Nurses have the responsibility to observe the conditions of patients under their care and report any pertinent findings to the attending physician.

Prompt Notification Required

In *Cuervo v. Mercy Hospital, Inc.*,[41] Evelio Cuervo was admitted to Mercy Hospital by Dr. Iglesias to undergo routine diagnostic cardiac tests. Iglesias had surgical privileges at Mercy Hospital and was authorized to perform a cardiac catheterization.

After performing the catheterization on Cuervo, Iglesias decided to perform a PTCA (balloon angioplasty) procedure; Iglesias was not authorized to perform this procedure. Unfortunately, in carrying out this procedure, Iglesias inserted the catheters into the wrong artery in Cuervo's right leg. This compromised the blood flow to the leg, causing loss of pulse and sensation. This error was compounded when Mercy Hospital's nurses on Cuervo's floor were unable to reach Iglesias for six hours and never attempted to reach Dr. Milian, the backup physician, to alert them of Cuervo's deteriorating condition.

The following day, Dr. Pena attempted an arteriogram to treat the right leg. Regrettably, Pena accessed the wrong artery in the left leg, compromising the blood flow to that leg as well. Shortly thereafter, Cuervo began to lose pulse and sensation in his left leg. Mercy Hospital's nurses never reported this condition to the physicians. Sometime later, Milian performed surgery to attempt to restore circulation to the right leg; the surgery was unsuccessful. Two hours later, surgery was performed on the left leg; the surgery failed to restore circulation to that leg. Thereafter, both legs required amputation.

Cuervo sued the physicians and Mercy Hospital, asserting that the hospital was negligent based on the nurses' failure to promptly notify a physician of his condition, and asserting corporate negligence against the hospital based on the unauthorized procedure. Cuervo's experts testified at deposition that but for the nursing staff's failure to contact a physician when the symptoms were first detected, the amputations would not have been necessary. Relying on the same experts' testimony, Mercy Hospital filed a motion for summary judgment, asserting that any acts or omissions of its nurses were not the proximate cause of Cuervo's injuries, and that the allegations in support of the corporate negligence count were also not the legal cause of Cuervo's injuries. Mercy Hospital's motion for summary judgment did not raise any issue as to whether the hospital breached its duty to Cuervo by allowing a medical doctor to perform unauthorized procedures or by failing to provide adequate nursing care. Mercy Hospital's motion solely disputed "causation." The court granted the motion and entered final summary judgment in the hospital's favor.

The court of appeal reversed the summary judgment because genuine issues of material fact remained unresolved regarding causation. The trier of fact must generally resolve proximate cause questions based on all the facts and the circumstances presented.

Particularly in a case such as this, where both parties rely on testimony from the same experts to draw diametrically opposed conclusions, the jury should be given opportunity to weigh the evidence and determine whether Mercy Hospital's conduct was the proximate cause of Cuervo's injuries. The summary judgment was reversed and the case was remanded for a jury trial.

Physician's Failure To Respond

An organization's policies and procedures should prescribe the guidelines for staff members to follow when confronted with a physician or other health care professional whose action or inaction jeopardizes the well-being of a patient. Guidelines in place, but not followed, are of no value, as the following case illustrates. The plaintiff in *Utter v. United Hospital Center, Inc.*[42] suffered an amputation that the jury determined resulted from the failure of the nursing staff to properly report the patient's deteriorating condition. The nursing staff, according to written procedures in the nursing manual, was responsible for reporting such changes. It was determined that deviation from hospital policy constituted negligence.

In *Goff v. Doctors General Hospital*,[43] the court held that nurses who knew that a woman they were attending was bleeding excessively were negligent in failing to report the circumstances so that prompt and adequate measures could be taken to safeguard her life.

Need To Report All Patient Symptoms

In *Citizens Hospital Association v. Schoulin*,[44] an accident victim sued the hospital and the attending physician for their negligence in failing to discover and properly treat his injuries. The court held that there was sufficient evidence to sustain a jury verdict that the hospital's nurse was negligent in failing: to inform the physician of all the patient's symptoms, to conduct a proper examination of the plaintiff, and to follow the directions of the physician. Thus, as the nurse was the employee of the hospital, the hospital was liable under the doctrine of *respondeat superior*.

In *Hiatt v. Grace*,[45] on appeal by the hospital and the nurse, the Kansas Supreme Court held that there was sufficient evidence to authorize the jury to find that the nurse was negligent in failing to timely notify the physician that delivery of the plaintiff's child was imminent. This delay resulted in an unattended childbirth with consequent injuries. The trial court had awarded the plaintiff $15,000.

Failure To Report Defective Equipment

Failure to report defective equipment can cause a nurse to be held liable for negligence if the failure to report is the proximate cause of a patient's injuries. The defect must be known and not hidden from sight.

Failure To Take Correct Telephone Orders

Failure to take correct telephone orders can be just as serious as failure to follow, understand, and/or interpret correctly a physician's orders. Telephone orders are necessary because of the nature of a physician's practice. Nurses must be alert in transcribing orders because there are periodic contradictions between what physicians claim they ordered and what nurses allege they ordered. Orders should be repeated, once transcribed, for verification purposes. Verification of an order by another nurse on a second telephone is helpful, especially if an order is questionable. Any questionable orders must always be verified with the physician initiating the order. Physicians must authenticate their verbal orders. This should be a firm rule of the organization. Nurses who disagree with a physician's order should not carry out an obviously erroneous order. In addition, they should confirm the order with the prescribing physician and report to the supervisor any difficulty in resolving a difference of opinion with the physician.

Nursery—Switching of Infants

The inadvertent or negligent switching of babies born at the same time can lead to liability for damages. Damages in the amount of $110,000 were awarded for the inadvertent switching of two babies born at the same time in *De Leon Lopez v. Corporacion Insular de Seguros.*[46]

Patient Falls

Patients are highly susceptible to falling and the consequences of falling are generally more serious with older age groups. Among senior citizens, falls represent the fifth leading cause of death, and the mortality rate from falls increases significantly with age. For those aged 75 years and older, the mortality rate from falls is five times higher than for those in the 65- to 74-year age group, and the rate increases so that persons older than 80 years have an even greater chance of experiencing a fatal fall.

Failure To Restrain

Standards for the application of both physical and chemical restraints have been evolving over the past decade and they are becoming more stringent. Because of patient rights issues, injuries, and the improper and indiscreet use of restraints, organizations are attempting to develop restraint-free environments.

In *St. Elizabeth Hospital v. Graham,*[47] a suit for damages was brought by the plaintiff, Floyd Graham, against St. Elizabeth Hospital claiming that Graham was negligently injured while recuperating from a severe head injury sustained six days earlier.

On February 11, 1989, Graham apparently was driving alone in his truck late at night when his vehicle left the road and struck an embankment. Graham's head struck a part of his truck. The blow resulted in a comminuted depressed skull fracture as well as a basilar skull fracture. In a comatose condition, he was transported to St. Elizabeth. Dr. Hirschauer performed a craniotomy on Graham. Graham was taken to the Neuro Intensive Care Unit where he remained until February 18. He was then transferred to the hospital's neurological unit. He was discharged on March 4, 1989.

Graham instituted litigation seeking actual and punitive damages, alleging that the hospital was guilty of ordinary negligence and gross negligence, principally in failing to restrain him or to use restraints to keep him from falling out of a recliner chair in the Neuro ICU on February 17, 1989. The verdict declared the hospital guilty of ordinary negligence but not gross negligence. The damage award to Graham was in the sum of $1,250,000 in actual or compensatory damages and prejudgment interest in excess of $216,000.

The hospital stated that the trial court erred in entering judgment on the jury verdict for the plaintiff because there was no evidence to support the jury's findings that the defendant hospital was guilty of negligence proximately causing injuries to Graham.

Several nurses who were employees of the hospital testified. Some worked in the Neuro ICU on the day of Graham's fall and some had worked or were working in the Neuro ICU in February 1989. The employee-nurses testified that they had knowledge of the nursing service policies of their employer regarding safety and restraints. Some nurses admitted that it was not necessary to have a physician's order to apply appropriate restraints.

The evidence of the nurses demonstrated that they had discretion to apply restraints to confused and disoriented patients or to patients who did not possess sufficient physical control to avoid falling and thus sustain new, further injuries and damages, or aggravating previous injuries. Graham was such a patient. The hospital's policies and rules were for the purpose of the furtherance of the patient's safety and the prevention or aggravation of injury or a new injury. The jury had the benefit of the testimony of the charge nurse and the managing nurse for the Neuro ICU. Graham had fallen from a recliner chair.

After reviewing the hospital records of Graham and also reviewing the nursing policy standards of the hospital, a licensed RN with experience in neuro intensive care units testified that the employees of the hospital had violated the hospital's own standard of care by not restraining Graham in the recliner chair.

An expert neurologist offered an oral deposition. A videotape of the same expert was played. The videotape and the deposition contained evidence of probative force and evaluation demonstrating the defendant's negligence in failing to restrain the plaintiff while in the recliner chair. A jury issue was competently raised. The neurologist testified that it would be more difficult for a patient such as Graham to fall and to injure or to re-injure himself while wearing a posey vest while being positioned in a recliner chair. This neurologist opined that in light of the problems and in light of the general physical condition of Graham while in the Neuro ICU, Graham should not have been placed in a recliner chair without restraints. His testimony went further to say that any patient in a Neuro ICU suffering from problems, disabilities, and complications such as those of Graham should not be placed in a recliner chair without restraints. These medical opinions were based on reasonable medical probability.

This same witness, Dr. Haufrect, gave his expert opinion that the placing of Graham in a recliner chair without restraints was a failure to exercise the degree of care that a reasonably prudent neuro intensive care nurse or institution would have exercised in the same or similar circumstances.

The record reflects additional evidence on this point. As an example, the record reflects that Graham was confused postoperatively. He was not following instructions and was somewhat combative. Graham was not well oriented, nor was he coordinated in his arms. He had sustained a moderately severe concussion. These factors required the application and monitoring of restraints so that the patient would not fall. Following intermediate appellate review, the court overruled the appellant's point of error.

Medication/Patient Fall

The plaintiff *in Polonsky v. Union Hospital*[48] suffered a fall and fractured her hip after the administration of a sleeping medication commonly known by the trade name Dalmane. The superior court awarded damages in the amount of the statutory limit of $20,000, and the hospital appealed. The appeals court held that from the Dalmane warning provided by the drug manufacturer and the hospital's own regulation regarding bedside rails, without additional medical testimony, the jury could draw an inference that the hospital's nurse had failed to exercise due care when she failed to raise the bed rails after administering Dalmane.

The fall of a patient is not always attributable to negligence. The New York Court of Appeals held that the evidence in *Stoker*

v. Tarentino[49] did not support discipline of a nurse on a charge that a wheelchair resident was improperly left alone in the bathroom. The negligence charge against the petitioner was predicated on a wheelchair resident having been left alone in the bathroom after the petitioner assisted another nurse in moving the resident from the bed to the wheelchair to the bathroom. All the nurses who testified agreed that there was no order, written or verbal, requiring the nurse to remain with the resident while she was in the bathroom. Policies and procedures of the nursing facility and the health department contained no instructions concerning toilet procedures with respect to wheelchair residents. The court held that disciplinary action against the nurse should be annulled and expunged from the petitioner's personnel file.

Emergency Department/Examination Tables

A judgment for the plaintiff was affirmed in *Petry v. Nassau Hospital*,[50] which was an action to recover damages for personal injuries suffered by the plaintiff's wife. The patient had been placed on a narrow examination table in the emergency department of the defendant hospital and fell from the table. The table had no sides, and the patient had been left unattended by the nurse in charge.

Suicidal Patients

Organizations have a duty to exercise reasonable care to protect suicidal patients against foreseeable harm to themselves. This duty exists whether the patient is voluntarily admitted or involuntarily committed. In *Abille v. United States*,[51] the district court held that evidence supported a finding that the attending physician had not authorized a change in status of a patient, who had been admitted to a U.S. Air Force hospital in Alaska and was diagnosed as being suicidal, to permit him to leave the ward without an escort. The nursing staff allowed him to leave the ward, and he found a window from which he jumped. This constituted a breach of the standard of due care under Alaska law, where the act or omission occurred.

Staffing

Health care organizations must continuously monitor their staffing needs in order to provide adequate care. The organization's leaders define for their respective areas the qualifications and job expectations of staff, and a system to evaluate the degree to which expectations are satisfied.

Under federal law, nursing facilities must have sufficient nursing staff to provide nursing and related services adequate to attain and maintain the highest practicable physical, mental, and psychosocial well-being of each resident, as determined by resident assessments and individual plans of care. Nursing facilities must provide 24-hour nursing services that are sufficient to meet the total nursing needs in accordance with patient care plans.[52] Unfortunately, there is a severe national shortage of nurses specializing in gerontology.[53] As nursing facilities are increasingly filled with older, disabled residents with ever-increasing complex care needs, the demands for highly educated and trained nursing personnel continue to grow.[54] The nursing profession itself acknowledged this situation in a position statement on long-term care prepared by the New York State Nurse's Association, which states that "long term care is becoming increasingly complex and requires attention and direction from the nursing profession."[55]

Health officials reported to the House Select Committee on Aging that the nation's shortage of nurses hit long-term care providers hardest. Inadequate career ladders and wage scales lower than those found in acute care hospitals make it difficult for long-term care facilities to attract nurses.

The nursing facility in *Our Lady of the Woods v. Commonwealth of Kentucky Health Facilities*[56] was closed because of deficiencies found during an inspection of the facility, the most serious of which was the lack of continuous nursing care on all shifts. The court held that evidence that the nursing facility lacked continuous services required by regulation was sufficient to sustain an order to close the facility. The appellants in this case had been notified of the deficiencies and were ordered to correct them. Many witnesses testified concerning the deficiencies and even the administrator admitted to the most serious violation—lack of continuous nursing services. The hearing officer, although noting that the quality of care provided to the facility's residents was satisfactory, concluded:

> The facts clearly reveal that the respondent has long violated one of the "essential functions of a nursing home" by not providing continuous graduate nursing supervision. To contend that such supervision can be provided from afar (by an "on-call" nurse) is to contend that a resident will never be confronted with a medical problem of such immediacy that his health or even his life would not be endangered while awaiting the arrival of the "on-call" professional. Such contention is unacceptable; the facility violated on a protracted basis one of its most substantive mandates. Absent proof that an adequate nursing staff could not be obtained (there is no such proof herein), it must be concluded that there is no justification for this violation.[57]

The court held that "deference is given to the trier of the fact and agency determinations are to be upheld if the decision is supported by substantial, reliable, and probative evidence in the record as a whole."[58]

Surgical Suite

Sponge and/or Instrument Miscounts

There are many cases involving foreign objects left in patients during surgery. The hospital in *Ross v. Chatham County Hospital Authority*[59] was properly denied summary dismissal of an action in which a patient sought to recover damages for injuries suffered when a surgical instrument was left in the patient's abdomen during surgery. This incident occurred as a result of the failure of the operating room personnel to conduct an instrument and sponge count after surgery. The borrowed servant doctrine did not insulate the hospital from the negligence of its nurses because the doctrine only applies to acts involving professional skill and judgment. Foreign objects negligently left in a patient's body constitute an administrative act. A standard nursing check-off procedure should be used to account for all sponges and/or instruments used in the operating room. Preventative measures of this nature will reduce a hospital's risk of liability.

The decedent's estate in *Holger v. Irish*[60] sued a surgeon and the hospital that employed the nurses who assisted the surgeon during the operation performed upon the deceased. During the course of performing colon surgery, the surgeon placed laparotomy sponges in the decedent's abdomen. After he had removed the sponges at the end of surgery, the two nurses assisting him counted them and verified that they had all been removed. Two years later, a sponge was discovered in the patient's abdomen. It was removed, and the 92-year-old patient died. The jury decided in favor of the defendants, and the decedent's estate appealed. The court of appeals reversed, and the Oregon Supreme Court reviewed the case.

The Oregon Supreme Court held that the surgeon was not vicariously liable, as a matter of law, for the negligence of the operating room nurses.

There was no evidence presented that the nurses were the defendants' employees, or that they were under the supervision or control of the defendant regarding their counting of the sponges. It was their sole responsibility to count the sponges. The nurses had been hired and trained by the hospital, which paid for their services.

Improper Sterilization

The patient in *Howard v. Alexandria Hosp.*[61] brought a medical malpractice action against a hospital, seeking damages arising out of an operation performed on her with unsterile instruments. During her stay in the recovery room following surgery, the operating surgeon reported to the patient that she had been operated on with unsterile instruments. Allegedly, the nurse in charge of the autoclave used to sterilize the instruments did not properly monitor the sterilization process. Because of the patient's fear of a variety of diseases, she was administered several human immunodeficiency virus (HIV) tests, one of which was taken six months following her discharge from the hospital. The patient was evaluated by an infectious disease specialist and was administered antibiotics intravenously. Following her discharge, the patient was placed on several medications and as a result developed symptoms of pseudomembranous enterocolitis. Testimony was entered that described the patient's symptoms as resulting from the administration of the antibiotics. One expert testified that the patient had reason to be concerned for at least six months following the surgical procedure because of her risk of being infected with one of a variety of diseases. The hospital argued that the patient suffered no physical injury from the surgical procedure and the instruments utilized during the procedure.

The circuit court, entering summary judgment for the hospital, granted a motion by the hospital to strike the evidence on the grounds that no physical injury had been shown.

The Virginia Supreme Court held that the patient had suffered injury resulting from measures taken to avoid infection following discovery of the use of unsterile instrumentation, even though the patient did not sustain any infection from use of the instruments. The case was reversed and remanded for a new trial on all issues.

Injury can be either physical or mental. It is clear that because of the hospital's use of inadequately sterilized instruments, the plaintiff sustained positive physical and mental injury. As the direct result of the wrong, IV tubes and needles invaded the plaintiff's body. She experienced physical pain and the discomforts of headache, nausea, vomiting, fever, chills, and unusual sweating. In sum, to argue that the plaintiff established mere emotional disturbance absent physical injury was found to ignore the evidence in this case.

Control of Patient's Tourniquet

In *Tye v. Wilson*,[62] the plaintiff, husband of the decedent, sued the hospital, physicians, and an RN for medical malpractice he claimed caused his wife's death. Following surgery, the patient began to bleed internally and suffered hypovolemic shock. The plaintiff alleged that the physicians failed to stop the bleeding. Because the patient was not sedated, she accidentally dislodged her endotracheal tube, causing her death.

The nurse filed a motion to dismiss the complaint. She argued that a physician, whom she claimed was not competent to testify that she was negligent, prepared an affidavit setting forth a negligent act by her. The trial court rejected her motion, but allowed her to file an appeal.

The Georgia Court of Appeals held that the affidavit of a medical doctor relating to the standard of care in treating and monitoring an intubated patient was sufficient to support a malpractice claim against a nurse.

The expert stated that he was familiar with the standard of care acceptable to the medical profession generally. The court found that was enough to include the nursing profession. The medical doctor's opinion was that the patient's injury was caused by the negligent application and control of a patient's tourniquet during her operation. There was nothing to suggest that physicians and nurses are trained differently with regard to treating intubated patients.

Negligent Procedure/Cutting an IV Tube

A nurse employed by the defendant in *Ahmed v. Children's Hospital of Buffalo*[63] amputated nearly one third of the index finger of plaintiffs' one-month-old daughter while cutting an IV tube with a pair of scissors. Surgery was performed to reattach the amputated portion. The reattachment was unsuccessful and, about a week later, the amputated portion was removed.

The jury awarded the plaintiffs $87,000 for past pain and suffering and $50,000 for future damages. The defendant moved to set aside the verdict and sought a new trial, claiming that damages were excessive.

It was the jury's function to assess the credibility of witnesses and to evaluate the testimony regarding the child's pain, suffering, and disability. In rejecting much of the testimony proffered by the plaintiffs, the trial court improperly invaded the jury's province to evaluate the nature and extent of the injury. The appellate court found that the jury's award of damages does not deviate materially from what would be reasonable compensation. The jury's verdict was reinstated.

Apnea Monitor Disconnected by Nurses

In *Odom v. State Department of Health and Hospitals*,[64] the appeals court held that the decedent's cause of death was directly related to the absence of being placed under the watch of a heart monitor. Jojo was born 12 weeks prematurely, at the Huey P. Long Medical Center (HPL). His mother placed him for adoption. Jojo remained in a premature nursery and was eventually placed into two different foster homes prior to his admission to Pinecrest. While a Pinecrest resident, Mr. and Mrs. Odom adopted Jojo.

Jojo was unable to feed himself and was nourished via gastrostomy tube. Because he suffered from obstructive apnea due to a malformation of his head, neck, and trachea, his breathing became dependent on a trach tube. Following an episode of respiratory distress, he sustained a tracheostomy at Cabrini Hospital on June 24, 1992. Subsequent to an episode of extubation on July 2, 1992, he was transported from Cabrini to the Children's Hospital where a new trach tube was installed.

Simultaneous to his discharge from Children's Hospital on August 19, 1992, a physician, Dr. Baroni, issued a home care plan regarding the tracheostomy. Among other things, the plan specified that the trach collar should be changed once daily, the trach itself should be changed at least every

Wednesday, and that a spare trach should always be kept at Jojo's bedside. The plan also required that an apnea monitor be maintained on Jojo "while sleeping or unattended." Children's Hospital recommended that the apnea monitor be set to alarm within predetermined parameters.

The plan recommended that Pinecrest keep a log of information to include, among other things, "secretion type and changes," "respiratory rate," and "pulse." In fact, the apnea monitor was set to alarm when Jojo's heart rate decreased below 60 beats per minute or accelerated over 132 beats per minute and when respirations slowed to fewer than 12 per minute or increased to more than 32 per minute. Pinecrest also instituted a trach and apnea monitor chart to be filed by the nurses on a daily basis. The apnea monitor chart, in particular, was implemented to check whether the nurses kept the monitor turned on at all times. Indeed, testimony showed that the monitor's alarm would go off frequently, sometimes for no reason, other times because Jojo would simply hold his breath so that the nurses would attend to him. The nurses would become "aggravated" with the alarm and would turn off the monitor. Finally, a daily activity schedule, implemented pursuant to Pinecrest physicians' orders, reflected that the apnea monitor was to be "on at all times."

At Pinecrest, Jojo was assigned to Home 501. Home 501 was consistently staffed with two LPNs, one RN, and three to four resident training specialists (RTS) for each of the three eight-hour shifts to be filled during the day. The first shift ran from 6 A.M. until 2 P.M., the second from 2 P.M. until 10 P.M., and the third from 10 P.M. until 6 A.M. During the 2–10 shift on the afternoon of August 19, 1994, 501 was staffed with one RN, Ms. Fowler, one LPN, Ms. Johnson, and three RTS, Ms. Ogle, Mr. Lambert, and Ms. Means.

While making a round, Means found Jojo with his trach out of the stoma but still tightly attached to his neck. Means called to Johnson for help. Ogle and Johnson responded rapidly. Johnson immediately sent Means to call Fowler for help and *asked if anyone knew CPR.* Ogle answered that she thought she did and started CPR through Jojo's mouth, unaware that Jojo had a trach. She was unable to feel a pulse or see him breathe. Johnson stated that she tried to put the trach back in but was unsuccessful. She asserts that she helped Ogle with CPR and recalls that Jojo's lips and nail beds had turned blue. She did not remember seeing any spare trach on Jojo's bedside table, as was required.

Ms. Savoy, Ms. Gjesdal, and an RN, Ms. Wiley, responded from other homes. Wiley immediately took the CPR efforts under her control. First, she noticed that Jojo was breathless. She immediately reinserted the trach but with difficulty, because it was snugly tied around Jojo's neck. She noticed that Jojo was still hooked to a monitor. She started CPR, and upon noticing that Jojo pinked back up, she increased her resuscitation efforts.

Never, at any time, did anyone hear the heart monitor's alarm sound. Means asserts that the monitor was on, because she saw that the monitor's red lights, indicating the heart rate and breathing rate, were blinking. She stated that she took the monitor's leads off of Jojo to put the monitor out of the way, but the alarm did not sound.

CPR efforts continued while Jojo was placed on a stretcher and sent by ambulance to HPL. Jojo was pronounced dead at HPL's emergency department at 7:02 P.M.

The Odoms filed suit against Pinecrest. At the end of a jury trial, the Odoms filed a motion for directed verdict on the issue of liability, which the trial court granted.

The Odoms filed a petition against Pinecrest, alleging that Jojo's death was caused by the negligence and fault of Pinecrest, its servants, and employees. The following wrongful acts or omissions were asserted:

- failure to instruct, train, and supervise properly its employees in the management and care of resident patients/clients like decedent
- failure to monitor
- improper staffing
- neglectful supervision
- utilizing an improper tie device on the tracheotomy apparatus
- disconnecting and/or rendering inoperable or useless decedent's heart monitor

The trial court's reasons for judgment are enlightening in that it stated the monitor should have been on but was, however, disconnected by the staff and that was the cause in fact of Jojo's injury. The Daily Activity Schedule prepared by Pinecrest's own physicians required that Jojo be placed on the heart monitor 24 hours per day. The record reflects that the monitor followed Jojo everywhere, even to school. There was no merit in Pinecrest's argument that the monitor was supposed to be on only when Jojo was sleeping or unattended, because Jojo was, in fact, located in his bed and had not been attended to for at least 20 minutes preceding the discovery of the incident. Even assuming that Pinecrest's argument is correct, the nurses still were under a duty to place Jojo on a heart monitor while he lay in bed unattended.

The appeals court found that the record supported the trial court's findings and conclusions.

The evidence adduced at trial regarding this issue is overwhelming. It is undisputed that the nurses did not hear the monitor's alarm sound at all times pertinent to the events. Means testified that the monitor was on, because she saw the red lights blinking. She stated that the lights were still on after the failed resuscitation efforts and that she disconnected the cables from Jojo to move the monitor out of the way, and, yet, the alarm still did not sound. The other nurses are not sure whether the monitor was on. Johnson stated in her deposition that she did not check whether it was on, but she asserted that it was on during her testimony.

Mr. Rolka, electronic engineer at Corometrics, the maker of the apnea monitor, testified that he tested the monitor actually used on Jojo after the accident and that it was functioning within the required parameters. Thus, his testimony eliminates any other possibilities except that the monitor was turned off or that it was on but not reset after the alarm sounded at some time during the day.

The disappearance of the apnea monitor and trach care check lists was odd. The trial court found that it created an adverse presumption against Pinecrest, stating that the staff had not kept the monitor on Jojo and that it aggravated some of the people that were taking care of him so much that they started that check list to make sure that people would do that. The paperwork was created to make sure that the monitor was on. There was overwhelming evidence upon which the trial court relied to find that the monitor was turned off, in breach of the various physicians' orders with which the nurses should have complied.

The appeals court agreed with the trial court's conclusion. The monitor was supposed to be on Jojo to warn the nurses of any respiratory distress episodes that he may experience. Dr. Reams issued a forensic pathologist's report that determined the cause of Jojo's death to be hypoxia, secondary to respiratory insufficiency, secondary to apnea episodes. Thus, Jojo's cause of death was directly related to the absence of being placed under the watch of a heart monitor.

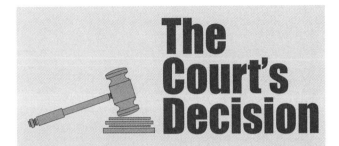

The Court's Decision

The court concluded there was ample evidence to support the trial judge's conclusion that the nursing staff breached the standard of care. Testimony indicated that Ard "*would have had a much better chance of survival if he had been transferred to the intensive care unit.*" The court raised the general damages award from $50,000 to $150,000.

CHAPTER REVIEW

1. Most states have similar definitions of nursing, but each state has its own individual Nurse Practice Act, which defines the practice of nursing and outlines a nurse's authority to act in that state. The *scope of practice* defines the actions, duties, and limits of various health care professionals.
2. The nurse licensure process differs slightly from state to state, but each requires that applicants have received formal professional training and can pass a written examination.
3. There are several positions in which nurses who have undergone the requisite training and certification can enjoy expanded roles. These include nurse-anesthetist, CNS, nurse midwife, nursing assistants, NP, nurse manager, and special duty nurse. The *chief nursing executive* is an RN who oversees the operations of the nursing staff. A patient or patient's family can employ a *special duty nurse* to perform nursing care.
4. Among the most common acts for which nurses can be found negligent are improper or inappropriate administration of medication; negligent injection; failure to note an order change; burning a patient; failure to follow established nursing procedures; failure to follow instructions; failure to monitor a patient's vital signs; failure to report physician negligence; failure to question a patient discharge that could result in injury to the patient; failure to notice or to report changes in a patient's condition; failure to report defective equipment; failure to transcribe telephone orders correctly; switching of infants; and failure to take appropriate steps to prevent a patient from falling.
5. Federal law requires that nursing facilities have sufficient nursing staff to provide appropriate nursing and related services. However, the nation is in the midst of a nursing shortage, particularly in the area of gerontology.

REVIEW QUESTIONS

1. Should nurses be held liable to the same standard of care as a physician? Discuss your answer.

2. If a nurse disagrees with a physician's written orders and is sure that he or she is right, should he or she violate the orders? Explain your answer.

3. If a nurse knows that a piece of equipment is defective, but the hospital is in bankruptcy, should he or she attempt to fix the machine? Discuss your answer.

4. If a nurse believes that a patient's change in condition is not life threatening, should he or she still record the change?

NOTES

1. Ard v. East Jefferson Gen. Hosp., 636 So.2d 1042 (La. Ct. App. 1994).

2. M.T. MACEACHERN, HOSPITAL ORGANIZATION AND MANAGEMENT 17 (1962).

3. Byrnes, *Non-Nursing Functions: The Nurses State Their Case*, 82 AM. J. NURSING 1089 (1982).

4. C. Howse, *Registration: A Minor Victory*, 85(49) NURSING TIMES, Dec. 6, 1989, at 32.

5. D.J. MASON & S.W. TALBOTT, POLITICAL HANDBOOK FOR NURSES 11–12 (1985).

6. Fraijo v. Hartland Hosp., 160 Cal. Rptr. 252 (Ct. App. 1979).

7. DEP'T OF HEALTH, ED. & WELFARE, PUB. NO. (HSM) 73-2037, EXTENDING THE SCOPE OF NURSING PRACTICE: A REPORT OF THE SECRETARY'S COMMITTEE TO STUDY ROLES FOR NURSES 8 (1971).

8. 692 S.W.2d 329 (Mo. Ct. App. 1985).

9. E. SPALDING, PROFESSIONAL NURSING: TRENDS/RESPONSIBILITIES/RELATIONSHIPS 351 (1959).

10. Moon Lake Convalescent Center v. Margolis, 535 N.E.2d 956 (Ill. App. Ct. 1989).

11. 502 So.2d 1198 (Miss. 1987).

12. 570 N.Y.S.2d 395 (N.Y. App. Div. 1991).

13. 519 N.Y.S.2d 738 (N.Y. App. Div. 1987).

14. 428 S.E.2d 773 (W. Va. 1993).

15. Id. at 779.

16. 696 P.2d 270 (Colo. 1985).

17. 28 N.E.2d 772 (Ohio 1940).

18. 144 So.2d 249 (La. Ct. App. 1962).

19. 599 N.Y.S.2d 96 (N.Y. App. Div. 1993).

20. 742 P.2d 1087 (Okla. 1987).

21. 357 N.Y.S.2d 508 (N.Y. App. Div. 1974).

22. 145 So.2d 848 (Fla. 1933).

23. 696 So.2d 590 (La. App. 1997).

24. 609 N.Y.S.2d 592 (N.Y. App. Div. 1994).

25. 443 P.2d 708 (Colo. 1968).

26. 181 A.2d 573 (Del. 1962).

27. 340 F.2d 584 (2d Cir. 1965).

28. 403 F.2d 580 (D.C. Cir. 1968).

29. 381 P.2d 605 (Wash. 1963).

30. 597 N.E.2d 1110 (Ohio Ct. App. 1991).

31. 565 So.2d 221 (Ala. 1990).

32. 403 S.E.2d 582 (N.C. Ct. App. 1991).

33. 652 A.2d 1382 (Pa. Super. 1995).

34. Id. at 1385.

35. 640 So.2d 865 (La. App. 4 Cir. 1994).

36. *Id.* at 872.

37. 333 P.2d 29 (Cal. Ct. App. 1958).

38. 422 N.W.2d 600 (S.D. 1988).

39. 589 A.2d 653 (N.J. Super. App. Div. 1991).

40. *Id.* at 655.

41. 694 So.2d 98 (Fla. App. 1997).

42. 236 S.E.2d 213 (W. Va. 1977).

43. 333 P.2d 29 (Cal. Ct. App. 1958).

44. 262 So.2d 303 (Ala. 1972).

45. 523 P.2d 320 (Kan. 1974).

46. 931 F.2d 116 (1st Cir. 1991).

47. 883 S.W.2d 433 (Tex. App.-Beaumont 1994).

48. 418 N.E.2d 620 (Mass. App. Ct. 1981).

49. 478 N.E.2d 184 (N.Y. 1985).

50. 48 N.Y.S.2d 227 (N.Y. App. Div. 1944).

51. 482 F. Supp. 703 (N.D. Cal. 1980).

52. 42 C.F.R. § 483.20 (1989).

53. U.S. CONGRESS, OFFICE OF TECHNOLOGY ASSESSMENT, PUB. NO. OTA-BA-306, LIFE-SUSTAINING TECHNOLOGIES AND THE ELDERLY 364 (1987).

54. *Educating and Licensing Nursing Home Administrators: Public Policy Issues,* 30 THE GERONTOLOGIST 582 (1990).

55. N.Y. STATE NURSES' ASSOC., POSITION STATEMENT ON LONG TERM CARE 3 (1990).

56. 655 S.W.2d 14 (Ky. Ct. App. 1982).

57. *Id.* at 16.

58. *Id.* at 17.

59. 367 S.E.2d 793 (Ga. 1988).

60. 851 P.2d 1122 (Or. 1993).

61. 429 S.E.2d 22 (Va. 1993).

62. 430 S.E.2d 129 (Ga. Ct. App. 1993).

63. 661 N.Y.S.2d 164 (N.Y. App. Div. 1997).

64. 733 So.2d 91 (La. App. 3 Cir. 1999).

Liability by Departments and Health Care Professionals

DYING AT THE HOSPITAL'S DOOR: A CHILD LOST, TROUBLING QUESTIONS*

While frustrating dialogue was occurring among a child's parent, a 911 dispatcher, and hospital personnel, the child's condition was deteriorating as the communications broke down. Twelve hours later, the four-year-old girl was brain dead, and she expired three days later. Although there are several central issues involved in this story, the conversation that took place is particularly important:

Parent to 911 dispatcher:

Dispatcher: 911, Is this an emergency?

Parent: Yes, it's an emergency. I need an ambulance. I have a three-year-old daughter that's passed out on me.

Dispatcher: OK. Where do you need the ambulance?

Parent: I'm right in front of the emergency exit in . . . Hospital.

Dispatcher: You're right in front of the emergency exit?

Parent: Yes, that's exactly where I am. And they won't do a . . . thing in this place.

Dispatcher to emergency department:

Dispatcher: There's a guy that says he's right outside your emergency exit. And he needs an ambulance. He says his three-year-old daughter is dehydrated.

Hospital: This is a guy who wants to be seen quicker. We're busy. So he figured if he called 911 he'd be seen quicker.

Dispatcher: Well, he's saying he needs an ambulance right away. Is somebody going to go out there, or not?

Hospital: There's nothing we can do.[1]

What is your verdict?

---

*MIAMI HERALD Volume/Edition by RONNIE GREEN. Copyright 1995 by MIAMI HERALD. Reproduced with permission of MIAMI HERALD in the format Textbook via Copyright Clearance Center.

INTRODUCTION

This chapter presents an overview of selected departments and health care professions. Although it describes a variety of legal issues, there is no intensive review of any specific department or profession. Many of the cases presented in this chapter could have been discussed in more than one chapter. However, they were placed here to illustrate that no health care profession is exempt from the long arm of the legal system. Health care professionals are held to the prevailing standard of care required in their profession, which includes proper assessments, reassessments, diagnosis, treatment, and follow-up care.

AMBULATORY CARE CENTERS

Poor Communications

In 1987, the patient-plaintiff in *Follett v. Davis*[2] had her first office visit with Dr. Davis. In the spring of 1988, the plaintiff discovered a lump in her right breast and made an appointment to see Davis. The clinic had no record of her appointment. The clinic's employees directed her to radiology for a mammogram. The plaintiff was not offered an examination by Davis or any other physician at the clinic. In addition, she was not scheduled for a physician's examination as a follow-up to the mammogram. A technician examined the plaintiff's breast and confirmed the presence of a lump in her right breast. After the mammogram, clinic employees told her that she would hear from Davis if there was any problem with her mammogram.

The radiologist explained in his deposition that the mammogram was not normal. Davis received and reviewed the mammogram report and considered it to be negative for malignancy. He did not know of the new breast lump because none of the clinic employees had informed him about it. The clinic, including Davis, never contacted the plaintiff about her lump or the mammogram. On April 6, 1990, the plaintiff called the clinic and was told that there was nothing to worry about unless she heard from Davis. On September 24, 1990, the plaintiff returned to the clinic after she had developed pain associated with that same lump. A mammogram performed on that day gave results consistent with cancer. Three days later, Davis made an appointment for the plaintiff with a clinic surgeon for a biopsy and treatment. She kept her appointment with the surgeon. Nevertheless, this was her last visit with the clinic, as she subsequently transferred her care to other physicians.

In October 1990, the biopsy confirmed the diagnosis of cancer. In August 1992, the plaintiff filed her complaint with the Department of Insurance.

The Indiana Court of Appeals held that the doctrine of continuing wrong was applicable so that the period of limitations did not begin to run until the patient's last visit to the clinic.

The plaintiff claimed that the wrong she suffered was a continuing wrong. The doctrine of continuing wrong is simply a legal concept used to define when an act, omission, or neglect took place. The statutory period of limitations begins to run at the end of the continuing wrongful act. The evidence shows that, after she had found a lump in her breast, she went to Davis, her regular obstetrician/gynecologist, and the clinic for aid. Davis and the clinic, through the clinic's employees and agents, undertook to treat her ailment. That undertaking ended only when the clinic's surgeon performed the biopsy and therefore was continuous in nature. When the sole claim of medical malpractice is a failure to diagnose, the omission cannot as a matter of law extend beyond the time the physician rendered a diagnosis. When the plaintiff last visited Davis on September 24, 1990, and last visited the clinic on September 27, 1990, the evidence most favorable to her demonstrated that, had clinic procedures been followed, Davis or another physician at the clinic would have had occasion to diagnose her problem before either of those dates. On August 20, 1992, the plaintiff timely filed her proposed complaint within two years of the last visits to Davis and the clinic.

ANESTHESIA

 OXYGEN MASK CATCHES FIRE DURING SURGERY

Citation: *Gold v. Ishak, 720 N.E.2d 1175 (Ind. App. 1999)*

Seventy-eight-year-old Margaret Frostick was admitted to Porter Memorial Hospital for surgery. Dr. Kalmbach ordered monitored anesthesia care, a type of anesthesia commonly referred to as a "mac," to be used in the procedure. The "mac" keeps a patient in a sedated state but still allows the patient to be responsive, so that vital signs can be closely watched and oxygen can be administered. Supplemental oxygen was given to Frostick through a mask in order to prevent complications.

In performing the surgery, Kalmbach used an electrocautery unit provided by the hospital. During the surgery, Drs. Kalmbach, Ishak, Venditti, Jr., and hospital employees Grace Dytrt, a nurse, and Barbara Fugate, a surgical technologist, were present. Kalmbach was standing on Frostick's right side and Fugate was on Frostick's left side. Ishak was standing at the head of the bed and Dytrt was at the foot of the bed.

The circulating nurse, who was employed by the hospital, used a skin preparation on Frostick called PhisoHex. Kalmbach placed towels on Frostick's face, and then, with the assistance of a circulating nurse, placed drapes around her that separated the electrocautery unit from the oxygen mask. The drapes were placed in such a manner that Kalmbach could not see Frostick's face or the oxygen mask from where he stood during the surgery. Ishak, the anesthesiologist, who was sitting at the head of the table, was the only person who could see Frostick's face.

During the procedure, a "popping" sound came from the electrocautery unit used by Kalmbach. Venditti then checked the settings on the unit. Kalmbach continued the procedure because everything appeared fine. A second "popping" sound was heard and Frostick began squirming under the towels and became very agitated. Fugate testified that she saw an unusually large spark. At that point, Ishak, Venditti, and Fugate realized that the oxygen mask was on fire. Ishak or Venditti removed the burning mask from Frostick's face.

Frostick presented a claim of negligent treatment to a medical review panel, which concluded that the medical providers had complied with the requisite standards of care in treating Frostick. Frostick filed a complaint against the medical providers for medical malpractice. The trial court refused to apply the doctrine of *res ipsa loquitur*.

Issue

Did the trial court err in refusing to apply the doctrine of *res ipsa loquitur*?

Holding

The trial court was found to have erred by refusing to apply the doctrine of *res ipsa loquitur*.

Reason

Gold (administrator of Frostick estate) has shown that the injuring instrumentality was under the management or exclusive control of the medical providers. A fire under these circumstances is such that in the ordinary course of things it would not happen if the medical providers used proper care in relation to the electrocautery unit and oxygen mask.

Expert testimony is not required because a fire occurring during surgery where an instrument that emits a spark is used near a source of oxygen is not beyond the realm of the layperson to understand. Although mere use of the electrocautery unit combined with the use of supplemental oxygen may not itself fall below the standard of care, it is easily understandable to the common person that careless use of the two could cause a fire and result in bodily injury.

The evidence presented at trial clearly shows that Gold has established the elements necessary for the inference of *res ipsa loquitur*.

Discussion

1. What precautions should the hospital take to prevent further such events from occurring in the operating suite?
2. To whom should fault be assigned: the physicians, the hospital, or both the hospital and the physicians? Discuss your answer.

CHIROPRACTOR

Standard of Care Required

A chiropractor is required to exercise the same degree of care, judgment, and skill exercised by other reasonable chiropractors under like or similar circumstances. He or she has a duty to determine whether a patient is treatable through chiropractic means and to refrain from chiropractic treatment when a reasonable chiropractor would or should be aware that a patient's condition will not respond to chiropractic treatment. Failure to conform to the standard of care can result in liability for any injuries suffered.

Inflating Insurance Claims

The North Carolina Court of Appeals held that a chiropractor's license was properly suspended for six months in *Farlow v. North Carolina State Board of Chiropractic Examiners*[3] for inflating the insurance claims of victims of an automobile accident. Dr. Farlow had prescribed a course of treatment for several patients that was not justified by the injuries they had received. The treatment had been prescribed to inflate insurance claims.

DENTISTRY

The Wrong Tooth

Dr. Smith told Ms. O'Neal that tooth number 14, an upper left molar, should be extracted. She advised Dr. Smith that another dentist had warned her that tooth number 14 should not be pulled because it was embedded in the sinus. Smith responded that all of her top teeth were in the sinus and that extraction was no problem. O'Neal relented to Smith's judgment and tooth number 14 was extracted. Complications developed in the extraction process, resulting in an oral antral perforation of the sinus cavity wall. Four days after the extraction, Dr. Smith began root canal work, even though the antral opening wound was not healed. In performing these additional procedures, Smith used both high- and low-speed drills, capable of flinging bacteria and other debris about the mouth. Three weeks after the extraction, a tissue mass developed in the tooth socket. The patient was referred to Dr. Herbert, an oral surgeon.

Dr. Herbert testified that the degree of infection inhibited proper healing and closure of the extraction site. After several more months, in January 1985, O'Neal was referred to Dr. Berman, an ear, nose, and throat specialist. Because of the continual deterioration, Berman performed a surgical procedure that sealed the extraction site. The surgery required hospitalization.

O'Neal brought a malpractice action against Dr. Smith.[4] The trial court entered judgment in favor of O'Neal. Smith appealed, arguing that the evidence was factually insufficient to support the judgment.

Dr. Miedzinski, an expert witness for the appellee, testified that Smith was negligent for not referring the patient to an oral surgeon for the necessary extraction, because of the known risks of roots embedded in the sinus floor. Smith was also negligent for not referring the patient to a specialist when the antral perforation first occurred and later by not referring her to a specialist when the fistula and the infection manifested itself. Smith's expert witness also testified that it is good medical practice to refer a patient to an oral surgeon or other specialist when complications arise from a sinus molar extraction.

The dentist's expert testimony was found sufficient to support a jury finding that the defendant was negligent in the treatment of his patient. The expert testified that the defendant was negligent by extracting the upper left molar without first attempting endodontic treatment to save the tooth. The patient was not experiencing pain on the left side of her mouth and the tooth did not present an emergency.

Dental Assistant/Failure To Supervise

The plaintiff in *Hickman v. Sexton Dental Clinic*[5] brought a malpractice action against a dental clinic for a serious cut under her tongue. The dental assistant, without being supervised by a dentist, placed a sharp object into the patient's mouth, cutting her tongue while taking impressions for dentures. The court of common pleas entered a judgment on a jury verdict in favor of the plaintiff, and the clinic appealed. The court of appeals held that the evidence presented was sufficient to infer without the aid of expert testimony that there was a breach of duty to the patient. The testimony of Dr. Tepper, the clinic dentist, was found pertinent to the issue of the common knowledge exception in which the evidence permits the jury to recognize breach of duty without the aid of expert testimony. Tepper presented the following testimony regarding denture impressions:

> Q. You also stated that you have taken, I believe, thousands?
> A. Probably more than that.
> Q. Of impressions?
> A. Yes, sir.
> Q. This never happened before?
> A. No, sir, not a laceration.
> Q. Would it be safe and accurate to say that if someone's mouth were to be cut during the impression process, someone did something wrong?
> A. Yes, sir.[6]

Unauthorized Treatment

Unauthorized treatment can result in successful suits against medical practitioners. The plaintiff in *Gaskin v. Goldwasser*[7] brought a suit against an oral surgeon, alleging dental malpractice. The oral surgeon had removed 19 of the teeth remaining in the plaintiff's mouth. The defendant admitted that 5 of the 19 teeth were removed without the consent of the patient. The circuit court entered a judgment for the plaintiff on a jury verdict for damages resulting from the extraction of the five lower teeth. On appeal, the appellate court held that the patient was entitled to have the allegation of willful and wanton misconduct and battery for unauthorized removal of the five lower teeth submitted to the jury. The case was remanded for a new trial.

Dental Hygienist/Unlawful Administration of Nitrous Oxide

This case[8] arises from a complaint by a dental hygienist against a former employer, Lowenberg and Lowenberg Corporation. The dental hygienist alleged that the defendant allowed dental hygienists to administer nitrous oxide to patients. Under state law, dental hygienists may not administer nitrous oxide. The Department of Education's Office of Professional Discipline investigated the complaint by using an undercover investigator. The investigator made an appointment for teeth cleaning. At the time of her appointment, she requested that nitrous oxide be administered. Agreeing to the investigator's request, the dental hygienist administered the nitrous oxide. There were no notations in the patient's chart indicating that she had been administered nitrous oxide.

The hearing panel found the dental hygienist guilty of administering nitrous oxide without being properly licensed. In addition, the hearing panel found that the dental hygienist had failed to accurately record in the patient's chart that she had administered nitrous oxide.

The New York Supreme Court, Appellate Division, held that the investigator's report provided sufficient evidence to support the hearing panel's determination. There is adequate evidence in the record to support a finding that the dentist's conduct was such that it could reasonably be said that he permitted the dental hygienist to perform acts that she was not licensed to perform.

Failure To Prescribe Antibiotics

In *Pasquale v. Miller*,[9] the plaintiff brought a suit against the defendant, Dr. Miller, for dental malpractice. On March 22, 1986, Miller treated the plaintiff for swollen gums. Miller removed tissue from her gums and used sutures to control the bleeding. Although it was common practice to prescribe antibiotics prior to or following gum surgery, Miller failed to prescribe antibiotics in either case. The following May, after the plaintiff had experienced a persistent fever, she was diagnosed as having contracted subacute bacterial endocarditis. The plaintiff was treated in the hospital for nearly a month. Dr. Miller claimed that the bacterial infection could have resulted from a number of causes. The trial court, upon a jury verdict, found for the plaintiff. An appeals court held that the evidence supported a finding of causation.

The plaintiff's expert witnesses testified that her endocarditis was related to the dental surgery and that one of the risks of not prescribing an antibiotic is that bacteria can flow through the bloodstream to the heart. The jury could and did reject testimony from Miller that endocarditis could have been caused by something other than failure to administer antibiotics prior to or following gum surgery.

Infection Control/Failure To Wear Protective Gloves

In *Kirschner v. Mills*,[10] there was sufficient evidence to support a charge that a dentist had failed to wear protective gloves while performing a medical examination on a patient. That charge was supported by the testimony of the patient, whom a hearing panel found to be direct, forthright, and credible, that the dentist did not wear gloves during the ex-

amination. The violation of accepted practice was also supported by the testimony of the dentist's own expert, a dentist, who opined that it was necessary to wear gloves "anytime you put your hands on a patient."

EMERGENCY DEPARTMENT

Emergency departments are high-risk areas that tend to be a main source of lawsuits for hospitals. Results of the Harvard Medical Practice Study revealed that the hospital emergency department is "a real hot spot" for negligence.[11] In this study, 70 percent of adverse events occurring in the emergency department were because of negligence. Hospital emergency departments heavily used by patients as primary care clinics are a major source of adverse events because of poor follow-up care. Suits that end up in a courtroom are few in comparison with the out-of-court settlements from negligence in rendering medical care in emergency departments.

Both federal and state regulations, as well as the standards set by the Joint Commission on Accreditation of Healthcare Organizations, may be considered by the courts in finding a duty of hospital emergency departments to provide emergency care to those who present themselves with the need for such care.

Lidocaine Administered 44 Times Normal Dosage

In *Riffe v. Vereb Ambulance Service, Inc.*,[12] a wrongful death action was filed by appellants against Vereb Ambulance Service, St. Francis Hospital, and Valerie Custozzo. The complaint alleged that, while responding to an emergency call, defendant Custozzo, an emergency medical technician employed by Vereb Ambulance Service, began administering lidocaine to Anderson, as ordered over the telephone by the medical command physician at the defendant hospital. While in route to the hospital, Anderson was administered lidocaine 44 times the normal dosage. Consequently, normal heart function was not restored and Anderson was pronounced dead at the hospital shortly thereafter.

The superior court held that the liability of medical technicians could not be imputed to the hospital. The court noted the practical impossibility of the hospital carrying ultimate responsibility for the quality of care and treatment given patients by emergency medical services (EMS). The focus of training and monitoring of such services must lie with the EMS regional and local councils pursuant to and subject to regulations promulgated by the Department of Health.

Although hospitals, as facilities, participate in the overall operation of EMS services, the hospital command facility derives its function from the law and regulations relating to the operation of EMS. The networking of EMS and command facilities is such that they have a common interrelated function that is apart from the administration of the hospitals to which they are attached. Because EMS may be involved with several hospitals depending on specialization, and even allowing for patients' directions, a hospital's legal responsibility for the operation of any given EMS becomes too tenuous.

Failure To Admit

On October 31, 1987, Mrs. Roy went to the emergency department, complaining of chest pains. The attending emergency department physician was Dr. Gupta. Upon examination, Roy exhibited normal vital signs. She showed no obvious physical abnormalities. Gupta performed an electrocardiogram that showed ischemic changes indicating a lack of oxygen to the heart tissue. He applied a transdermal nitroglycerin patch and gave her a prescription for nitroglycerin. After monitoring her progress, he sent her home. Several hours later she returned to the emergency department, experiencing more chest pains. She was admitted to the hospital and it was determined that she was having a heart attack. Three days later, Roy died of a massive myocardial infarction.

On October 29, 1990, a bench trial was held.[13] The trial court found Gupta negligent in failing to hospitalize Roy or failing to inform her of the serious nature of her situation so that she would agree to hospitalization. The trial court also found that had Roy been hospitalized on her first visit, her chances of survival would have been greatly increased.

The Louisiana Court of Appeal held that Gupta was negligent by failing to advise Roy that she should be hospitalized for chest pains.

Dr. Caskey and Dr. d'Autremont, two expert witnesses, testified that it is common practice to enter in a patient's record whether a recommendation of hospitalization was made. Gupta made no such notation in Roy's chart. All of the medical expert witnesses, except Dr. Kilpatrick, a defense witness, testified that Roy should have been admitted. Kilpatrick testified that such a decision varied greatly among physicians. The trial court disregarded his testimony because he was too hostile in his responses to be of any assistance.

In his reasons for judgment, it was evident the trial judge was not convinced by Dr. Gupta's explanation of why Roy was not hospitalized. He focused on Gupta's failure to have X-rays taken during the first visit, which might have allowed him to determine whether the ischemic changes were due to her hypertension medication or indicated the beginnings of a heart attack. The relative simplicity of the technique and its obvious availability lent credence to the trial judge's belief that the requisite attention was not paid to Roy's complaints.

The law does not require proof that proper treatment would have been the difference between Roy's living or dying. It only requires proof that proper treatment would have increased her chances of survival. Even though the expert testimony of d'Autremont was guarded in this area, the inference can be drawn from her testimony that although nothing could ensure Roy's survival, admittance on the first visit would have at least increased her chances. This is a difficult area in which to make factual determinations, and the degree of specialization requires the trier of fact to rely heavily on the testimony of the experts. The trial judge was present and able to determine the credibility and sincerity of all who testified.

Documentation Sparse and Contradictory

The plaintiff-administrator in *Feeney v. New England Medical Center, Inc.,*[14] commenced an action against the emergency department physician, the nurse on duty, and hospital, alleging that the death of his son was caused by medical malpractice.

An ambulance team found 26-year-old Mr. Feeney intoxicated, sitting on a street corner in South Boston. Feeney admitted to alcohol abuse but denied that he used drugs. He was physically and verbally combative and had trouble walking and speaking intelligibly. His condition interfered with the team's conducting an examination and he was transported by ambulance to the hospital.

Documentation at the hospital between 10:45 P.M. and 11:30 P.M. was sparse and contradictory. The minimum standard for nursing care required monitoring the patient's respiratory rate every 15 minutes. It was doubtful that this occurred. This would more likely have permitted the nursing staff to observe changes in the patient's breathing patterns and/or the onset of respiratory arrest. As to the emergency department physician, he failed to evaluate the patient and to initiate care within the first few minutes of Feeney's entry into the emergency facility. The emergency physician had an obligation to determine who was waiting for physician care and how critical the need was for that care. Had the standards been maintained, respiratory arrest might have been averted. According to the autopsy report, respiratory arrest was the sole cause of death.

The failure to provide adequate care could be rationally attributed to the staff nurse assigned to the area in which the patient lay, as well as to the physicians in charge. The hospital was implicated on the basis of the acts or omission of its staff.

Emergency Medical Treatment and Active Labor Act

In 1986, Congress passed the Emergency Medical Treatment and Active Labor Act (EMTALA), which forbids Medicare-participating hospitals from "dumping" patients out of emergency departments. The Act provides that:

> [i]n the case of a hospital that has a hospital emergency department, if any individual (whether

or not eligible for benefits under this subchapter) comes to the emergency department and a request is made on the individual's behalf for examination or treatment for a medical condition, the hospital must provide for an appropriate medical screening examination within the capability of the hospital emergency department, including ancillary services routinely available to the emergency department, to determine whether or not an emergency medical condition . . . exists.[15]

Emergency Medical Condition Defined

The term *emergency medical condition* has been defined under EMTALA as:

(A) a medical condition manifesting itself by acute symptoms of sufficient severity (including severe pain) such that the absence of immediate medical attention could reasonably be expected to result in—(i) placing the health of the individual (or, with respect to a pregnant woman, the health of the woman or her unborn child) in serious jeopardy, (ii) serious impairment to bodily functions, or (iii) serious dysfunction of any bodily organ or part; or (B) with respect to a pregnant woman who is having contractions—(i) that there is inadequate time to effect a safe transfer to another facility before delivery, or (ii) that transfer may pose a threat to the health or safety of the woman or the unborn child.[16]

EMTALA Limited to Actions against Hospital

The decedent in *Ballachino v. Anders*[17] went to the hospital on May 15, 1990, with complaints of chest pain and repeated episodes of loss of consciousness. The physicians allegedly negligently failed to provide an appropriate medical screening examination and failed to determine whether or not an emergency medical condition existed. The patient's survivor and representative brought an action against the hospital and physicians alleging violations of EMTALA and medical malpractice. EMTALA requires that a Medicare provider hospital provide an appropriate medical screening examination to determine whether an emergency medical condition exists for any individual who presents to the emergency department seeking examination or treatment. If the hospital determines that an emergency medical condition exists, then it must either stabilize the patient or provide for transfer of the patient to a facility capable of meeting the patient's medical needs.

The U.S. District Court for the Western District of New York held that there is no private right of action against the individual physicians under EMTALA. However, the representative's complaint did state a claim against the hospital under EMTALA.

EMTALA provides no private right of action against individual physicians. The enforcement provision of EMTALA is explicitly limited to actions against a Medicare-participating hospital. Although the physicians were alleged to have acted in concert in rendering professional medical and surgical care and treatment to the decedent while at the hospital, the physicians importantly are nowhere alleged to have provided any "emergency screening examination." The plaintiff clearly alleged that the defendants negligently failed to provide an appropriate medical screening examination and failed to determine whether an emergency medical condition existed for the decedent. The court was faced with the question of whether any emergency screening examination occurred at all. The plaintiff also alleged that the hospital failed in its stabilization and transfer procedures. The district court determined that all of the allegations taken together stated an EMTALA claim against the hospital.

Stabilizing the Patient

Patients can be transferred only after they have been medically screened by a physician, stabilized, and cleared for transfer by the receiving institution. Stabilized means, "with respect to an emergency medical condition . . . to provide such medical treatment of the condition as may be necessary to assure, within reasonable medical probability, that no material deterioration of the condition is likely to result from or to occur during the transfer of the individual from a facility."[18] A patient should not be transferred from the emergency department to another health care facility unless:

(A)(i) the individual (or a legally responsible person acting on the individual's behalf) after being informed of the hospital's obligations . . . and of the risk of transfer, in writing requests a transfer to another medical facility, (ii) a physician . . . has signed a certification that based on the information available at the time of transfer, the medical benefits reasonably expected from the provision of appropriate medical treatment at another medical facility outweigh the increased risks to the individual and, in the case of labor, to the unborn child from effecting the transfer, or (iii) if a physician is not physically present in the emergency department at the time an individual is transferred, a qualified medical person . . . has signed a certification . . . after a physician . . . in consultation with the person, has made the determination . . . and subsequently countersigns the certification; and (B) the transfer is an appropriate transfer . . . to that facility.[19]

Discharge Appropriate

In *Holcomb v. Humana Med. Corp.*,[20] the administratrix of the estate of a deceased patient, Mrs. Smith, sued the hospital, alleging a violation of EMTALA. Smith had entered the emergency department on May 4, 1990, a week after giving birth, with a complaint of a fever, aching, sore throat, and coughing. Both a physician's assistant and a physician examined Smith. The examination revealed that Smith had a temperature of 104.3° F, a pulse of 146, respirations of 32, and a blood pressure of 112/64. Diagnostic tests ordered included a white blood cell count, urine analysis, and chest X-ray. After reviewing the results of Smith's complaints and medical history, physical examination, and test results, the physician diagnosed the patient as having a viral infection. The physician ordered Tylenol and intravenous (IV) fluids as treatment. Smith was maintained in the emergency department overnight. The physician conducted a second physical examination during the night. By morning, Smith's vital signs had returned to normal. She was discharged with instructions for bed rest, fluids, and a request to return to the hospital if her condition worsened. After returning home, Smith reported that she was feeling better, but then took a turn for the worse and was admitted to Jackson Hospital on May 6, 1990. She was diagnosed with endometritis and subsequently died on May 9, 1990.

Was the patient inappropriately discharged from the emergency department under provisions of EMTALA?

The U.S. District Court for the Middle District of Alabama held that there was no EMTALA violation. The patient was appropriately examined and screened. The care rendered was standard for any patient based on the complaints given. In addition, the plaintiff failed to demonstrate that an emergency condition existed at the time that the patient was discharged.

Emergency Department/Screening and Discharge Appropriate

Fifteen-year-old Nydia Marshall, in *Marshall v. East Carroll Parish Hospital Service District*,[21] was brought by ambulance to the hospital emergency department on October 18, 1994, because she "wouldn't move" while at school after the bell rang. Upon her arrival, hospital personnel took her history and vital signs. She was unable to communicate verbally while at the emergency department, but cooperated when removing her clothing and watched movement of persons coming in and out of the emergency department. She was examined by Dr. Horowitz, who also had several medical tests performed on her.

Horowitz diagnosed Nydia as having a respiratory infection and discharged her. He informed Nydia's mother, Ms. Marshall, that her daughter's failure to communicate was of unknown etiology, and advised her to continue administering the medications that had been prescribed by the family physician on the previous day and to return to the emergency department if the condition deteriorated. The complaint alleged that, later that same day, Nydia's symptoms continued to worsen, and she was taken to the emergency department at

a different hospital, where she was diagnosed as suffering from a cerebrovascular accident consistent with a left middle cerebral artery infarction.

This action claimed that the hospital violated EMTALA by failing to provide Nydia with an appropriate medical screening examination and failing to stabilize her condition prior to discharge. The hospital moved for summary judgment and submitted supporting affidavits from Horowitz and a registered nurse who had participated in Nydia's treatment in the hospital's emergency department.

The district court granted summary judgment for the hospital on the grounds that no material fact issues were in dispute. EMTALA provides in relevant part:

> In the case of a hospital that has a hospital emergency department, if any individual . . . comes to the emergency department and a request is made on the individual's behalf for examination or treatment for a medical condition, the hospital must provide for an appropriate medical screening examination within the capability of the hospital's emergency department, including ancillary services routinely available to the emergency department, to determine whether or not an emergency medical condition . . . exists.[22]

The Act defines an "emergency medical condition," in pertinent part, as:

> (A) a medical condition manifesting itself by acute symptoms of sufficient severity (including severe pain) such that the absence of immediate medical attention could reasonably be expected to result in
>
> (i) placing the health of the individual (or, with respect to a pregnant woman, the health of the woman or her unborn child) in serious jeopardy,
>
> (ii) serious impairment to bodily functions, or
>
> (iii) serious dysfunction of any bodily organ or part. . . .[23]

And, if the hospital determines that the individual has an "emergency medical condition," then the hospital must provide either:

> (A) within the staff and facilities available at the hospital, for such further medical examination and such treatment as may be required to stabilize the medical condition, or
>
> (B) for transfer of the individual to another medical facility. . .[24]

Marshall contends that hospital personnel knew that Nydia had an emergency medical condition and were very concerned about the cursory examination provided by Horowitz; that Horowitz should have performed a funduscopic examination, cranial nerve testing, motor strength testing, and deep tendon reflex testing; and that Nydia should have been admitted to the hospital for observation of her unexplained altered mental status. In essence, Marshall is contending that Horowitz committed malpractice by failing to accurately diagnose an emergency medical condition.

The appeals court agreed with other courts that have interpreted that EMTALA was *not intended to be used as a federal malpractice statute, but instead was enacted to prevent "patient dumping," which is the practice of refusing to treat patients who are unable to pay.*

Accordingly, an EMTALA "appropriate medical screening examination" is not judged by its proficiency in accurately diagnosing the patient's illness, but rather by whether it was performed equitably in comparison with other patients with similar symptoms. If the hospital provided an appropriate medical screening examination, it is not liable under EMTALA even if the physician who performed the examination made a misdiagnosis that could subject him or her and his or her employer to liability in a medical malpractice action brought under state law. A hospital's failure to diagnose a patient's condition may be actionable under state medical malpractice law, but not under EMTALA. Questions regarding whether a physician or other hospital personnel failed to properly diagnose or treat a patient's condition are best resolved under existing and developing state negligence and medical malpractice theories of recovery. In the absence of any allegation that the defendant departed from its standard emergency department procedures in treating a patient, questions related to a patient's diagnosis remain the exclusive province of local negligence and malpractice law. Therefore, *a treating physician's failure to appreciate the extent of the patient's injury or illness, as well as a subsequent failure to order additional diagnostic procedures, may constitute negligence or malpractice, but cannot support an EMTALA claim for inappropriate screening.* EMTALA does not impose any duty on a hospital requiring that the screening result in a correct diagnosis.

To avoid summary judgment, Marshall was required to present evidence showing a material fact issue as to whether the hospital provided an EMTALA-appropriate medical screening examination. But, an "appropriate medical screening examination" is not defined by EMTALA. Most of the courts that have interpreted the phrase have defined it as a screening examination that the hospital would have offered to any other patient in a similar condition with similar symptoms. EMTALA is implicated only when individuals who are perceived to have the same medical condition receive disparate treatment. The essence of this requirement is that there be some screening procedure, and that it be administered evenhandedly. When a hospital does not follow its own standard procedures, the plaintiff(s) must prove that the hospital treated a patient differently from other patients. *The Act is not intended to ensure that each emergency department patient obtains a correct diagnosis, but rather to ensure that each is accorded the same level of treatment regularly provided to patients in similar medical circumstances.* An appropriate medical screening is interpreted to mean a screening that the hospital would have offered to any paying patient. It is the plaintiff's burden to show that the hospital treated her differently from other patients; the hospital is not required to show that it had a uniform screening procedure.

The affidavits submitted by the hospital as part of its evidence in support of summary judgment both stated that Nydia was given an appropriate medical screening examination that would have been performed on any other patient, and that she was not diagnosed as having an emergency medical condition. Marshall contends that these assertions were refuted by Ms. Middlebrooks' affidavit. In her affidavit, Ms. Middlebrooks stated that she witnessed a disagreement between a nurse and Horowitz over whether Nydia should be admitted or transferred to another hospital, rather than discharged, and that during her 14-year employment at the hospital she had seen several other patients with symptoms similar to Nydia's who had all been admitted for observation and further testing and treatment.

As a result, and in the light of the summary judgment record, because there is no material fact issue as to whether Horowitz conducted an appropriate medical screening examination or as to his determination that Nydia did not have an emergency medical condition, the hospital was entitled to judgment, as a matter of law, that it did not have a duty under EMTALA to provide further medical treatment, to stabilize her condition prior to discharge, or to transfer her to another facility. A duty to stabilize does not arise unless the hospital has actual knowledge of the individual's unstabilized emergency medical condition. The hospital's duty to stabilize the patient does not arise until the hospital first detects an emergency medical condition. Stabilization and transfer provisions of EMTALA "are triggered only after a hospital determines that an individual has an emergency medical condition." The hospital *has no duty under EMTALA to stabilize a condition that was not ascertained in appropriate screening examination.*

Transfer Prior to Stabilizing Patient— Wrongful Death

The plaintiff in *Huckaby v. East Ala. Med. Ctr.*[25] brought an action against the hospital alleging that the patient was transferred from the hospital's emergency department before her condition was stabilized. The patient went to the hospital on September 19, 1990, suffering from a stroke. The complaint alleged that the patient's condition was critical and materially deteriorating. The attending emergency department physician, Dr. Wheat, informed the patient's family that she needed the services of a neurosurgeon, but that the *hospital had problems in the past with getting neurosurgeons to accept patients.* Upon the recommendation of Wheat, the patient was transferred to another hospital where she expired soon after arrival. The plaintiff alleged that Wheat did not inform the family regarding the risks of transfer and that the transfer of the patient in an unstable condition was the proximate cause of her death.

Did the plaintiff have a cause of action under EMTALA?

The U.S. District Court held that the plaintiff stated a cause of action under EMTALA for which monetary relief could be granted. For the plaintiff to overcome the defendant's motion to dismiss the case, the plaintiff had to demonstrate that, under EMTALA, the patient (1) went to the defendant's emergency department, (2) was diagnosed with an emergency medical condition, (3) was not provided with adequate screening, and (4) was discharged and transferred to another hospital before her emergency condition was stabilized. The plaintiff met this standard.

Refusal To Consent to Treatment

Patients have a right to refuse treatment. If a patient rejects treatment, he or she should be asked to sign a release. The hospital should take all reasonable steps to: (1) inform the individual of the benefits and risks of treatment, and (2) secure the individual's written informed consent to refuse examination and treatment. If the individual refuses to sign such a consent, documentation of the refusal should be maintained by the hospital.

Enforcement—Physician Ought To Vote with His Feet

Failure to follow EMTALA can result in civil penalties. In addition, any individual who suffers personal harm as a direct result of a participating hospital's violation of a requirement may, in a civil action against the participating hospital, obtain those damages available for personal injury under the law of the state in which the hospital is located.

In *Burditt v. U.S. Department of Health and Human Services*,[26] EMTALA was violated by a physician when he ordered a woman with dangerously high blood pressure (210/130) and in active labor with ruptured membranes transferred from the emergency department of one hospital to another hospital 170 miles away. The physician was assessed a penalty of $20,000. Dr. Louis Sullivan, Secretary of the Department of Health and Human Services at that time, issued a statement: "This decision sends a message to physicians everywhere that they need to provide quality care to everyone in need of emergency treatment who comes to a hospital. This is a significant opinion and we are pleased with the result."[27] The American Public Health Association, in filing an *amicus curiae*, advised the appeals court that *if Burditt wants to ensure that he will never be asked to treat a patient not of his choosing, then he ought to vote with his feet by affiliating only with hospitals that do not accept Medicare funds or do not have an emergency department.*[28]

State Regulations

Legislation in many states imposes a duty on hospitals to provide emergency care. The statutes implicitly, and sometimes explicitly, require hospitals to provide some degree of emergency service.

If the public is aware that a hospital furnishes emergency services and relies on that knowledge, the hospital has a duty to provide those services to the public. Two Mexican children, burned in a fire at home, were refused admission or first aid by a local hospital. A lawsuit was filed, claiming that additional injury occurred as a result of the failure to render care.[29] The trial court dismissed the suit. The Arizona Court of Appeals found the defendants liable, claiming that it was the custom of the hospital to render aid in such a case. On appeal, the Arizona Supreme Court also held the defendants liable. It reasoned that state statutes and licensing regulations mandate that a hospital may not deny a patient emergency care.

The New York State Emergency Medical Services Act of 1983 provides that every general hospital shall admit any person who is in need of immediate hospitalization. Any licensed medical practitioner who refuses to treat a person arriving at a general hospital for emergency medical treatment will be guilty of a misdemeanor and subject to up to one year in prison and a fine. Emergency medical technicians, paramedics, and ambulance drivers are expected to report any refusals by general hospitals to treat emergency patients. Patients may be transferred after they have been stabilized if it is deemed by the attending physician to be in the best interest of the patient.

General Duty

The courts recognize a general duty to care for all patients presenting themselves to hospital emergency departments. Not only must hospitals accept, treat, and transfer emergency department patients if such is necessary for the patients' well-being, but they must adhere to the standards of care they have set for themselves, as well as to national standards.

Scope of Care

The objectives of emergency care are the same regardless of severity. No matter how trivial the complaint, each patient must be examined. Treatment must begin as rapidly as possible, function is to be maintained or restored, scarring and deformity are to be minimized, etc. Every patient must be treated regardless of ability to pay.

As the Sixth Circuit points out, there are many reasons other than indigence that might lead a hospital to give less than standard attention to a person who arrives at the emergency room. These might include: prejudice against the race, sex, or ethnic group of the patient; distaste for the patient's condition (e.g., acquired immune deficiency syndrome [AIDS] patients); personal dislike or antagonism between medical personnel and the patient; disapproval of the patient's occupation; or political or cultural opposition. If a hospital refused treatment to persons for any of these reasons, or gave cursory treatment, the evil inflicted would be quite akin to that discussed by Congress in the legislative history, and the patient would fall squarely in the statutory language.[30]

Physician Looked at the Wrong Record

Terry Trahan, in *Trahan v. McManus*,[31] was taken to the hospital after being injured in an automobile accident. Lawrence and Marie Trahan, Terry's parents, were informed about the accident. They were asked to come to the hospital to retrieve their son. After being informed of the accident, Mrs. Trahan drove to the hospital's emergency department. Mrs. Trahan consulted with Dr. McManus, the emergency department physician who treated Terry. McManus assured Mrs. Trahan that it would be all right to take her son home as there was nothing more that could be done for him at the hospital. McManus advised Mrs. Trahan to put Terry to bed and to see that he got lots of rest.

Upon ordering the discharge, however, McManus had not realized that he had made a grave and ultimately fatal mistake. *McManus had looked at the wrong chart* in determining Terry's status and consequently was ignorant of Terry's true condition. Terry had three broken ribs as a result of the accident. This injury was not diagnosed although X-rays were taken. The chart McManus had looked at indicated that the patient's vital signs were normal. In fact, Terry's blood pressure was 90/60, indicative of shock, when he was admitted to the hospital. Forty-five minutes after being admitted, Terry's blood pressure had dropped to 80/50, and his respiration rate had doubled. Terry's vital signs clearly indicated that he was suffering from internal hemorrhaging.

In the seven hours following his discharge, Terry's condition continued to worsen. Terry complained to his parents about severe pain. He could not turn from his back to his side without the aid of his father. Several hours after being brought home from the hospital, Lawrence Trahan noticed that Terry's abdomen was swelling. Marie Trahan immediately called the hospital. Mr. Trahan asked Terry if he wanted to sit up. Terry replied, "Well, we can try." Those were Terry's final words. Terry slumped in his father's arms and his head fell forward. When Mr. Trahan attempted to lift Terry's head, Terry's face was white. Mr. Trahan immediately laid his son down on the bed, realizing for the first time that his son was not breathing and had no pulse. Mr. Trahan attempted cardiopulmonary resuscitation (CPR) as Mrs. Trahan called for an ambulance. Mr. Trahan continued CPR until the ambulance arrived a few minutes later. Terry Trahan was pronounced dead on arrival at the hospital.

Subsequently, during a medical review panel proceeding in which the Trahans participated, McManus admitted liability by tendering his $100,000 limit of liability, pursuant to the Medical Malpractice Act.

The Trahans filed their own claim against McManus. Subsequently, McManus filed exceptions of no right and no cause of action, claiming that remedies are not available to the parents when a spouse and child survive a decedent. The trial judge granted defendants' exception of no right and no cause of action. The court of appeal reversed the trial court's judgment and remanded the case for trial.

A 12-person jury returned a verdict absolving McManus of any liability, finding that Terry's injuries would have occurred despite the physician's failure to use reasonable care in his treatment of Terry. The Trahans brought a second appeal.

To reverse the judge or jury on its finding of fact, the court of appeals had to find, after a review of the record, that there is no factual basis for its finding, and that the finding is clearly wrong. A trial court's reasonable determinations and inferences of fact are not to be disturbed solely because a reviewing court may feel that its own evaluations are more reasonable than those of the fact finder. Although the trial court is in a better position to evaluate and assess the credibility of witnesses, the overriding determination for the court of appeals is whether these determinations are reasonable. Where there are two permissible views of the evidence, the fact finder's choice between them cannot be manifestly erroneous or clearly wrong.

It was conceded by all parties that Terry's ultimate death was due to the negligent discharge by McManus. The court of appeals determined the event that caused Terry's death was the physician's negligent discharge of Terry. The trial court's judgment was reversed and the case was remanded for trial.

McManus discussed the two reasons that he would not have released Terry from the hospital; namely, the sharp drop in blood pressure coupled with a sharp increase in respiration. These symptoms had been duly noted on Terry's chart. McManus testified that he had not seen these notations because he had looked at someone else's chart. McManus stated that Terry's symptoms indicated hypovolemic shock or a decrease of blood volume.

In the autopsy report, the pathologist concluded that Terry's death was due to hypovolemic shock secondary to massive intra-abdominal and retroperitoneal hemorrhage. According to the pathologist, Terry was an otherwise healthy 36-year-old male.

The primary inquiry in determining negligence on the part of a defendant is whether any causal connection exists between the harm to the plaintiff and the defendant's negligent conduct. In reaching this determination, the defendant's conduct need not be the sole cause of the harm, but must be a necessary antecedent to the harm suffered. Put simply, if the plaintiff can show he probably would not have suffered damages absent the defendant' conduct, he has satisfied his burden of proving cause-in-fact.

The court found that the jury's determination was erroneous when it concluded that the physician's actions were not the cause-in-fact of Terry's death. This determination was based on the following uncontroverted facts that were adduced at trial: (1) McManus's belief that Terry could have been saved had he not been wrongfully discharged; (2) proof that McManus's negligent conduct was a necessary antecedent to Terry's death; and (3) evidence that Terry would probably not have died absent McManus's conduct. The record is completely devoid of any facts or allegations indicating that Terry died from a cause or causes unrelated to McManus's admittedly negligent discharge. The record is replete with testimony, including McManus's own admissions, that he acted negligently when he discharged Terry, that his actions led to Terry's death, and that there was treatment available that could have made a difference. The court found that the jury was clearly wrong in deciding that a direct causal connection did not exist between McManus's act of negligently discharging Terry and Terry's death.

Emergency Department Call Rosters

What Common Sense Made Evident

Hospitals are expected to notify specialty on-call physicians when their particular skills are required in the emergency department. A physician who is on call and fails to respond to a request to attend a patient can be liable for injuries suffered by the patient because of his or her failure to respond. In *Thomas v. Corso*,[32] a Maryland court sustained a verdict against the hospital and physician. The patient had been brought to the hospital emergency department after he was struck by a car. A physician did not attend to him even though he had dangerously low blood pressure and was in shock. There was some telephone contact between the nurse in the emergency department and the physician who was providing on-call coverage. The physician did not act upon the hospital's call for assistance until the patient was close to death. The court reasoned that *expert testimony was not even necessary to establish what common sense made evident*: that a patient who had been struck by a car may have suffered internal injuries and should have been evaluated and treated by a physician. Lack of attention in such cases is not reasonable care by any standard. The concurrent negligence of the nurse, who failed to contact the on-call physician after the patient's condition had worsened, did not relieve the physician of liability for his failure to come to the emergency department at once. Rather, under the doctrine of *respondeat superior*, the nurse's negligence was a basis for holding the hospital liable as well.

Failure To Respond

Treatment rendered by hospitals is expected to be commensurate with that available in the same or similar communities or in hospitals generally. In *Fjerstad v. Knutson*,[33] the South Dakota Supreme Court found that a hospital could be held liable for the failure of an on-call physician to respond to a call from the emergency department. An intern who attempted to contact the on-call physician and was unable to do so for three and one-half hours treated and discharged the patient. The hospital was responsible for assigning on-call physicians and ensuring that they would be available when called. The patient died during the night in a motel room as a result of asphyxia resulting from a swelling of the larynx, tonsils, and epiglottis that blocked the trachea. Testimony from the medical director of laboratories indicated that the emergency department's on-call physician was to be available for consultation and was assigned that duty by the hospital. Expert testimony also was offered that someone with the decedent's symptoms should have been hospitalized and that such care could have saved the decedent's life. The jury could have believed that an experienced physician would have taken the necessary steps to save the decedent's life.

Timely Response

Hospitals are not only required to care for emergency patients, but they also are required to do so in a timely fashion. In *Marks v. Mandel*,[34] a Florida trial court was found to have erred in directing a verdict against the plaintiff. It was decided that the relevant inquiry in this case was whether the hospital and the supervisor should bear ultimate responsibility for failure of the specialty on-call system to function properly. Jury issues had been raised by evidence that the standard for on-call systems was to have a specialist attending the patient within a reasonable time period of being called.

Unavailability of On-Call Physician

In *Millard v. Corrado*,[35] the Missouri Appellate Court found that "on call" physicians owe a duty to reasonably foreseeable emergency patients to provide reasonable notice to appropriate hospital personnel when they will be unavailable to respond to calls. This duty exists independently of any duties flowing from a physician–patient relationship. Physicians who cannot fulfill their "on call" responsibilities must provide notice as soon as practicable once they learn of the circumstances that will render them unavailable. Imposing a duty on "on call" physicians to notify hospital personnel of their unavailability does not place an unreasonable burden on the medical profession. In this case, a mere telephone call would have significantly reduced the four-hour time period between an accident and life-saving surgery. Whatever slight inconvenience may be associated with notifying the hospital of the on-call physician's availability is trivial when compared with the substantial risk to emergency patients absent any notice requirement.

Telephone Medicine Can Be Costly

The Inevitable Sense of Loss

The diagnosis and treatment of emergency department patients via the telephone can be costly. *Futch v. Attwood*[36] points this out quite clearly. In this case a suit was brought against Dr. Charles Attwood and American Legion Hospital seeking damages for the wrongful death action arising from negligent medical care rendered to the decedent, the plaintiff's minor daughter, Lauren Futch. Dr. Attwood, a pediatrician, had treated Lauren for her diabetes from the time that he first diagnosed it in February 1988, when Lauren was two and one-half years old, to when, on or about February 29, 1990, some two years later, Lauren died from complications arising from her diabetic condition.

The trial court allocated $98,000 for the conscious pain and suffering of Lauren. The defendant complained that the award of $98,000 was excessive.

The record shows that on the morning of February 28, 1990, a nauseated Lauren awoke her mother. She had vomited two or three times and her glucose/blood sugar reading was high. Wanda administered her daughter's morning insulin injection and intended to feed her child a light breakfast before bringing Lauren to see Attwood at about 9:45 A.M. According to the plaintiff, Attwood, having initially diagnosed Lauren as diabetic two years earlier, did not check Lauren's blood sugar or her urine to determine whether or not ketones were present; had he done so, young Lauren's condition could have been quickly corrected by the simple administration of insulin. Instead of administering insulin, however, Attwood prescribed the use of Phenergan suppositories to address Lauren's symptoms. Lauren's symptoms of nausea continued and she was taken the hospital emergency department. Hospital personnel eventually contacted Attwood. When Attwood returned the call, he again prescribed a Phenergan injection. The plaintiff observed that Attwood did not go to the hospital and had not been given Lauren's vital signs when he suggested such an injection, and further failed to order any blood or urine tests.

Wanda returned home with Lauren at approximately 8:00 P.M. and put Lauren to bed, waking around midnight to administer the prescribed medication, whereupon she found Lauren sleeping but breathing through her mouth rather than her nose. The child woke, but went right back to sleep. Early the next morning, Wanda awoke and found Lauren with labored breathing. While attempting to wake up the four-year-old, the only responses, according to plaintiff's brief, were "Huh" followed by moaning. Wanda telephoned Attwood and informed him of her daughter's far-worsened condition and Attwood admitted Lauren to the hospital at 6:30 A.M. that morning.

Hospital records revealed Lauren's being "acutely ill" at the time of admission, her glucose level raised to 507 with her blood acid revealing diabetic ketoacidosis. At approximately 9:13 A.M., Lauren went into respiratory arrest as a result of her brain swelling and rupturing into the opening at the base of her neck. Lauren was immediately transported by helicopter to Children's Hospital in New Orleans and diagnosed with ketoacidotic coma, cerebral edema (swelling of the brain), bilateral pulmonary edema (swelling of both lungs), and was pronounced dead at 5:07 P.M. on March 2, 1990. The record shows that during Lauren's short life, she and her mother were virtually inseparable literally 24 hours per day, except when Wanda was at school. All of this changed in Lauren's last few days when she was rushed to New Orleans. During Lauren's two and one-half days of illness, every moment seemed worse than the previous. The *mother had to witness her daughter's decline in health* at Crowley. Next, she had to drive to New Orleans, where her protracted wait was punctuated only by various traumatic episodes, including Lauren's respiratory intubation, then by her respiratory failure and consequent "code blue," complete with the scurrying in and out of numerous medical staff to see Lauren behind doors closed to Wanda, and, finally, Wanda's being asked to consider whether she would prefer to "pull the plug" on her daughter or to watch her linger indefinitely. Confronted with this dilemma, the young mother opted not to punish her daughter with more torment. She decided to let her go, and did. For Wanda, the period following Lauren's death has been marked by the inevitable sense of loss of one who had since her coming to this world been virtually joined at her mother's hip, and by the guilt of one whose unrelenting loss always compels her to ask what she might have done differently to have saved her child's life. In view of these facts, the appeals court could not find that the trial court had erred in concluding what sum was fair to both parties.

Prevention of Lawsuits in the Emergency Department

Emergency department lawsuits can be reduced by implementing and enforcing some fundamental common-sense policies, procedures, and programs:

- Develop and implement appropriate emergency department policies and procedures, including:
  - the necessity to treat each patient courteously and promptly
  - a requirement that all patients are to be treated—regardless of ability to pay
  - established treatment priorities—emergency cases to be treated first, followed by urgent and less serious cases
  - on-call roster procedures
  - consultation requirements for specialists
  - consent procedures for both adults and minors
  - disaster procedures
  - transfer procedures
- Communicate with the patient and the patient's family to ensure that a complete and accurate picture of the patient's symptoms and complaints is obtained.
- Communicate among health care professionals. This is imperative. Each professional gains a certain amount of information from a patient's history. Such information must be communicated to the attending physician. Both the nurse and the physician must assume that each has certain pieces of information necessary for the proper treatment of the patient. A poor listener and a poor communicator have no place in the care of emergency department patients.
- Provide continuing education programs for all staff members.
- Institute a preventive maintenance program for emergency department equipment.
- Do not take lightly any patient's complaint. This may well be the single most fatal mistake of emergency departments.
- Those professionals who cannot accept the concept that all patients, regardless of ailment, must be treated need to search for placement outside the emergency department.

Hospitals Removed from Sterile World of Altruistic Agencies

On January 24, 1994, McBride, in *Simmons v. Tuomey Regional Medical Center*,[37] was involved in an accident while driving his moped. Upon learning of the accident, Simmons rushed to the scene, where she found emergency service personnel attending to an injury to the back of her father's head. McBride was taken to Tuomey where Simmons signed an admission form for her father. The admission form contained the following provision:

THE PHYSICIANS PRACTICING IN THIS EMERGENCY ROOM ARE NOT EMPLOYEES OF TUOMEY REGIONAL MEDICAL CENTER. THEY ARE INDEPENDENT PHYSICIANS, AS ARE ALL PHYSICIANS PRACTICING IN THIS HOSPITAL.

While in Tuomey's emergency department, Dr. Cooper and Dr. Anderson examined McBride. Despite McBride's confused state, the physicians decided to treat his contusions and release him from the hospital with the instruction to refrain from drinking alcohol. The physicians, apparently attributing McBride's confusion to intoxication, did not treat his head injury.

The next day, McBride returned to Tuomey where his head injury was diagnosed as a subdural hematoma. Ultimately, McBride was transported to Richland Memorial Hospital. Approximately six weeks later, McBride died of complications from a subdural hematoma.

When Simmons brought this suit, Tuomey moved for summary judgment by alleging that it was not liable because the physicians were independent contractors. Tuomey relied on its June 1987 contract with Coastal Physicians Services, which set forth the procedures by which Coastal would provide emergency department physicians to Tuomey. The carefully worded contract referred numerous times to the physicians as "independent contractors" and stated that Tuomey agreed not to exercise "any control over the means, manner, or methods by which any Physician supplied by [Coastal] carries out his duties." The trial court accorded great weight to the Coastal-Tuomey contract when it granted Tuomey's motion for summary judgment. Simmons appealed, arguing the trial court erred in granting summary judgment on the issues of actual agency, apparent agency, and nondelegable duty.

The operation of emergency departments is such an important activity to the community that hospitals should be liable for the negligence of emergency department caregivers. Few things are more comforting in today's society than knowing that immediate medical care is available around-the-clock at any hospital. As the Texas Court of Appeals astutely observed:

> Emergency rooms are aptly named and vital to public safety. There exists no other place to find immediate medical care. The dynamics that drive paying patients to a hospital's emergency rooms are known well. Either a sudden injury occurs, a child breaks his arm or an individual suffers a heart attack, or an existing medical condition worsens, a diabetic lapses into a coma, demanding immediate medical attention at the nearest emergency room. The catch phrase in legal nomenclature, "time is of the essence," takes on real meaning. Generally, one cannot choose to pass by the nearest emergency room, and after arrival, it would be improvident to depart in hope of finding one that provides services through employees rather than independent contractors. The patient is there and must rely on the services available and agree to pay the premium charged for those services.[38]

The public not only relies on the medical care rendered by emergency departments, but also considers the hospital as a single entity providing all of its medical services. A set of commentators observed

> [T]he hospital itself has come to be perceived as the provider of medical services. According to this view, patients come to the hospital to be cured, and the doctors who practice there are the hospital's instrumentalities, regardless of the nature of the private arrangements between the hospital and the physician. Whether or not this perception is accurate seemingly matters little when weighed against the momentum of changing public perception and attendant public policy.[39]

The change in public reliance and public perceptions, as well as the regulations imposed on hospitals, has created an absolute duty for hospitals to provide competent medical care in their emergency departments. The hospital has lost its perch as an institution functioning in the public interest and therefore deserving of support in the form of insulation from liability. Hospitals have contributed to the shift in public perception through commercial advertisements. By actively soliciting business, hospitals have effectively removed themselves from the sterile world of altruistic agencies. The Alaska Supreme Court, the first American court to recognize a nondelegable duty in the hospital context, wrote, "Not only is [finding a nondelegable duty] consonant with the public perception of the hospital as a multifaceted health care facility responsible for the quality of medical care and treatment rendered, it also treats tort liability in the medical arena in a manner that is consistent with the commercialization of American medicine."[40] The real effect of finding a duty to be nondelegable is to render not the duty, but the liability, not delegable; the person subject to a nondelegable duty is certainly free to delegate the duty, but will be liable to third parties for any negligence of the delegatee, regardless of any fault on the part of the delegator.

Given the cumulative public policies surrounding the operation of emergency departments and the legal requirement that hospitals provide emergency services, hospitals must be accountable in tort for the actions of caregivers working in their emergency departments. The court in this case agreed with a New York court, which wrote:

> In this Court's opinion it is public policy, and not traditional rules of the law of agency or the law of torts, which should underlie the decision to hold hospitals liable for malpractice which occurs in their emergency rooms. In this regard the observation of former U.S. Supreme Court Justice Oliver Wendell Holmes is apt: "The true grounds of decision are consideration of policy and of social advantage, and it is vain to suppose that solutions can be attained merely by logic and the general propositions of law which nobody disputes. Propositions as to public policy rarely are unanimously accepted, and still more rarely, if ever, are capable of unanswerable proof."[41]

The appeals court held that hospitals have a nondelegable duty to render competent service to the patients of their emergency departments. The trial court's grant of summary judgment was reversed and the case was remanded for further proceedings.

ENVIRONMENT OF CARE

Each organization is responsible for providing a safe environment for patients, staff, and visitors. Responsibility for this function is often assigned to an organization's plant services/engineering department. Among other duties, the department is responsible for the provision of heat, water, electricity, and refrigeration and for maintenance of the organization's equipment and physical plant. The duties of the department often vary from one organization to the next, depending on the size of a particular organization's facilities.

Fire Safety

Wrongful Death

In *Stacy v. Truman Medical Center*,[42] the patients' families brought wrongful death actions against the medical center and one of its nurses. The wrongful death actions resulted from a fire in the decedents' room at the medical center. On the day of the fire, Ms. Stacy visited her brother, Stephen Stacy. When she arrived, Stephen, who suffered from head injuries and was not supposed to walk around, was in a chair smoking a cigarette with the permission of one of the nurses. No one told Stacy not to let him smoke. Stacy also lit a cigarette and because she did not see an ashtray in the room, she used a juice cup and a plastic soup tray for her ashes.

At approximately 5:00 P.M., a nurse came in and restrained Stephen in his chair with ties to prevent him from sliding out of the chair. Before Stacy left, she lit a cigarette, held it to Stephen's mouth, and extinguished it in the soup tray. When Stacy left, she believed there were one or two cigarette butts in the soup container. Ms. Stacy testified that she did not think she dumped the soup tray into the wastebasket but that she could have.

Shortly after 5:00 P.M., a fire started in a wastebasket in the room. There was no smoke detector in the room. Another patient, Mr. Wheeler, was in the bed next to the windows. When Ms. Schreiner, the nurse in charge, discovered the fire, she did not think Mr. Wheeler was in immediate danger. She unsuccessfully tried to untie Stephen from his restraints. Then she attempted to put out the fire by smothering it with a sheet. When her attempts to extinguish the fire failed, she ran to the door of the room and yelled for help, which alerted Nurses Cominos and Rodriguez. After calling for help, Ms. Schreiner resumed her attempts to smother the flames with bed linens. Subsequently, she and others grabbed Stephen by the legs and pulled him and his chair toward the hallway. In the process, Stephen's restraints burned through, and he slid from the chair to the floor. Schreiner and her assistants pulled him the remaining few feet out of the room and into the hallway. Schreiner tried to get back into the room but was prevented by the intense smoke, flames, and heat.

After initially entering the room, both Rodriguez and Cominos returned to the nurse's station to sound alarms and to call security. Neither attempted to remove Mr. Wheeler from the room. Both ran directly past a fire extinguisher, but neither grabbed it before returning to the room. After Stephen was removed from the room, Cominos entered the room with a fire extinguisher and tried to rescue Wheeler. Because of the intense smoke and heat, however, she was unable to reach Wheeler. Wheeler died in the room from smoke inhalation. Stephen survived for several weeks, then died as a result of complications from infections secondary to burns.

The medical center's policy in case of fire provided for the removal of patients from the room and out of immediate danger first. In its fire training programs, the medical center used the acronym of "RACE" to supply a chronology of steps to take in case of a fire.

> R—Rescue or remove the patient first.
> A—An alarm should be sounded second.
> C—Contain the fire third.
> E—Extinguish the fire last.

The medical center also had a training movie depicting a trash can fire that was started by smoking that showed how to pull a patient out of bed by the sheets and drag the patient across the floor at the first recognition of a fire.

The medical center's written smoking policy at the time of the fire stated: "No smoking shall be permitted in the Truman Medical Center Health Care Facility except in those areas specifically designated and posted as smoking areas." The patient's room was not posted as a designated smoking area on the date of the fire. The smoking policy further stated: "In the event violations of this policy are observed, the person violating the policy must be requested to discontinue such violation. This shall be the responsibility of all employees and particularly supervisory and security employees." Nurse Cominos admitted that she was a supervisor and that she violated this portion of the smoking policy on the date of the fire by observing smoking and the use of a juice cup for an ashtray.

On appeal, the Missouri Supreme Court held that a causal connection between the medical center's negligence and the patients' deaths was sufficiently established. The medical center owed a duty of reasonable care to all of its patients. The medical center argued that there was no evidence to causally link the alleged negligence in allowing smoking without an approved ashtray to the death of Wheeler. There was evidence that the fire started in the trash can from discarded smoking materials. The jury was free to believe from the evidence presented that had Ms. Stacy been given a hospital-approved ashtray, she would have discarded her cigarette in a proper ashtray and that the fire would not have occurred.

The individual in charge of fire safety training at the medical center, Lieutenant Campbell, testified that the hospital's policy was to first remove a patient from the room and out of immediate danger in case of fire. Testimony was also offered that the particular training received by the medical center's nurses was below the standard of care and that attempting to put the fire out with linens would also be indicative of a lack of training. The medical center's expert, Fire Captain Gibson, testified that throwing dry sheets on the fire would have added to the problem by fueling the fire. The jury could have found that if the medical center's nurses would have been properly trained, they would have followed their training and prevented Wheeler's death by removing him from the room, in accordance with their training acronym "RACE."

Hazardous Materials

One of the responsibilities of health care organizations is to oversee the handling and disposal of the institution's waste products. The wash-up of medical wastes on East Coast beaches placed the seriousness of waste disposal in the public spotlight. Judges, attorneys, and regulators are continuing to grapple with the problem. There are "an estimated 20,000 hazardous waste dump sites in the country, with ever-widening chemical contamination . . . and no end in sight of the constant parade of state and federal rules in this area. . . ."[43] The fear of AIDS has only served to exacerbate the problem and has led to costly legislation and government scrutiny.

The regulation and cleanup of hazardous waste, along with tort liability arising from exposure to toxic substances, are major environmental problems facing the health care industry. Pollution issues have generated costly legislative and regulatory responses on the federal (e.g., the Environmental Protection Agency [EPA], the Occupational Safety and Health Administration [OSHA], and the Centers for Disease Control and Prevention [CDC]), state, and local levels. Many lawsuits have resulted in the areas of enforcement, toxic torts, and products liability. Health care organizations—through their representative councils and their state and national associations—and physicians—through their medical societies and associations—should become more involved in the regulatory process to identify what wastes should be regulated and the methods most appropriate for hazardous waste disposal.

The federal Medical Waste Tracking Act passed in late 1988 established a pilot program to be administered by the EPA for tracking medical waste in three states—Connecticut, New Jersey, and New York—and made the program optional for other states.

Under new standards, OSHA requires the labeling of containers of regulated wastes and the identification of restricted areas containing hazardous wastes. OSHA also regulates the handling, transportation, and disposal of hazardous waste.

Refuse generated by health care facilities can be divided into five separate categories:

1. infectious
2. biohazardous
3. hazardous
4. radioactive
5. general (solid) waste

Each category poses its own particular problems with no easy solutions available for any or all forms of waste. However, potential polluters must keep in mind that existing fines are stiff. One Minnesota hospital paid a $35,000 fine for improper incineration, and violators in states implementing tracking systems face fines of up to $25,000 per day for each violation and criminal penalties of up to $50,000 per day per violation.

Compliance

Health care organizations and physicians must be aware of what regulations apply to them. Each health care organizations should develop a plan of action and organize an effective program by working through an appropriate committee, such as the safety committee, to review the needs of both the organization and the physicians. Membership should include the facility's director of environmental services and representation from finance, administration, medical staff, laboratory, radiology, housekeeping, nursing, and engineering. The committee should

- Identify infectious wastes (e.g., cultures, blood and blood byproducts, needles, and pathological wastes).
- Review and develop appropriate protocols for disposal of wastes.
- Review the various methods of disposal (e.g., carting, incineration, recycling) from a cost point of view.

- Review recycling options (disposal methods vary depending on the kind of waste).
- Identify waste-handling costs when purchasing.
- Develop employee safety programs to determine what handling, storage, and disposal procedures should be implemented for employee, patient, and public safety.
- Develop a monitoring system to ensure that the different classifications of wastes are disposed of properly and that the organization complies with the ever-expanding body of law regulating the disposal of medical waste.

Insurance

Both health care organizations and physicians should review their insurance policies to determine if they have

- liability coverage for cleanup and disposal of hazardous wastes, environmental impairment, property damage claims, future injury claims, and demands for medical monitoring by claimants
- comprehensive general liability
- pollution exclusion clauses
- provisions covering the number of occurrences

Health care providers without such coverage should evaluate the need for its inclusion in their policies.

Medical Equipment

Bed Improperly Set Up Worsening Patient's Condition—Manufacturer Responsible

The plaintiff in *Parris v. Uni Med, Inc.*[44] was admitted to St. Francis Hospital with a decubitus ulcer. While there, he used a Mediscus (a hospital bed marketer and distributor) bed, which was designed with 21 separate air pockets to prevent decubitus ulcers. Upon discharge on May 31, 1987, the pressure ulcer was only barely apparent.

On June 15, 1987, the plaintiff was readmitted. Before he was placed in the Mediscus bed, it was set up in only five minutes. At the time of the June admission, his pressure ulcer was healing. Four days later, a nurse noted that the ulcer condition had worsened and a new pressure ulcer had formed. The nurse noticed that the dressing on the first site was touching the metal frame on the bed, thus putting pressure on his sacral area every time he sat. The nurse called Uni Med and a company employee made adjustments to the bed. In spite of observed improvement in the pressure ulcers at the time of discharge, the patient deteriorated to such an extent that surgery was required. Evidence showed that the beds were not monitored regularly and that the nurses were not trained to turn the patients or adjust or regulate the beds.

The plaintiff, a 37-year-old paraplegic, brought an action against Uni Med, Inc., for pressure ulcers he sustained during his hospital stay. The jury found that the inadequate pressure setting on the bed was caused by its being improperly set up, thus causing worsening of the condition of the ulcers, necessitating surgery.

On appeal, the Missouri Court of Appeals found that: (1) the hospital bed was not set up properly, (2) the failure to set it up properly caused the patient's pressure ulcers and subsequent surgery, and (3) nurses were properly qualified as experts regarding testimony regarding pressure ulcers.

Evidence demonstrated that the bed had been set up hastily; continuous pressure of two hours on one area of skin can cause pressure ulcers; and nurses had not been properly trained to use the bed. The court also found that Uni Med had no monitoring system, and that the patient's original pressure ulcer had been healing prior to the hospital visit and then worsened after coming into contact with the bed frame.

Preventative Maintenance—Hospital Responsible

The plaintiff, Ms. Thibodeaux, in *Thibodeaux v. Century Manufacturing Co.*,[45] a nurse's aide at the Rosewood nursing facility, sued Century Manufacturing Company after she was injured while operating a Saf-Kary chair lift, which was manufactured by Century. The plaintiff was injured when the chair fell and smashed her finger when the chair's lifting arm failed. The failure occurred when a patient was being lifted from a whirlpool bath. The plaintiff alleged that Century manufactured a defective chair lift that was the cause of her injuries.

Century argued that the chair lift was not defective in design and that the failure of the chair was caused by air in the Saf-Lift hydraulic system, resulting from the nursing facility's lack of maintenance. The plaintiff's expert witness testified that after inspecting the equipment, he found that the accident was caused by the safety lock failing to prevent the chair from disconnecting from the lift. Century theorized that this want of maintenance caused the whole lift apparatus, including the chair still connected to the lifting arm of the lift column, to rapidly descend on Irene's finger. Approximately four months before the accident, a Century-licensed service technician performed an inspection of the equipment. He found leaks of hydraulic fluid, deteriorating seals and rings, a corroded lift base, and an air-contaminated lifting column. He took the chair lift out of service and recommended that Rosewood not use it until repairs were made to restore it to safe operation. These findings were communicated to Rosewood in writing. Rosewood did not make the repairs. The court, on a jury verdict, found that the sole cause of the accident was due to poor maintenance on the part of the nursing facility. The plaintiff appealed.

The Louisiana Court of Appeal held that the evidence supported the conclusion that the accident was caused by the nursing home's failure to properly maintain the equipment and that the injury was not the result of poor design. Virtually all products are subject to wear and tear and therefore need periodic maintenance. The nursing facility had been warned by the manufacturer of the need for repairs on the chair lift. The nursing facility failed to heed that warning.

Safety

Preventative Maintenance

In *Palka v. Servicemaster Management Services*,[46] Servicemaster Management Services contracted in 1987 with Ellis Hospital, at the rate of $91,207 biweekly, to develop and implement a maintenance program for the hospital. Servicemaster's duties included the training, management, and direction of all support service employees, including the maintenance department. There had been preexisting wall-mounted fans that had been inspected for safety prior to Servicemaster taking over. The plaintiff, Ms. Palka, a registered nurse employed by the hospital, was injured when one of the fans fell from the wall onto her. She sued Servicemaster for negligence. The jury rendered a verdict for the plaintiff, and Servicemaster appealed, alleging that they had no duty to her. The appellate division reversed and dismissed the complaint. The nurse then appealed.

The court of appeals reversed the decision of the appellate division, and reinstated the jury verdict for the plaintiff.

Servicemaster, by its contract with the hospital, assumed a duty to act. Although no specific mention of fan maintenance, including inspection of them, was made in the contract, the director of operations for Servicemaster testified that part of their duties was "to create a safe and clean environment" for employees and patients, to reduce safety hazards, and to engage in "preventative maintenance and casualty control or casualty prevention," which is defined as inspection and checking to see if something needs to be repaired before it falls. He further testified that it was Servicemaster's responsibility to train hospital employees how and when to perform maintenance on all electrical and mechanical equipment. The duty to be obeyed is defined by the risk reasonably to be perceived. The court analyzed the wrongfulness of Servicemaster's action or inaction, and the nurse's reasonable expectation of the care owed and the basis for her expectation. The court found that all persons, including the nurse, who entered the hospital had a reasonable expectation that someone was in charge of maintenance and inspection of both the premises and the equipment. The contract between Servicemaster and the hospital clearly affected the safety of everyone who came onto the hospital premises. All of those people were entitled to rely on the nonnegligent maintenance service and repair responsibilities. Service-master contracted with the hospital to perform certain services and performed those services negligently, which caused Palka's injury. Palka was part of a known and identifiable group of hospital employees, patients, and visitors who were to be protected by proper safety and maintenance protocols assumed exclusively by Servicemaster.

Visitor Slip and Fall—Hospital Not Liable

The plaintiff in *Borota v. University Medical Center,*[47] a hospital visitor, brought an action against University Medical Center to recover for injuries she suffered as a result of slipping on a puddle of milk in the hospital corridor. The plaintiff claimed that the spill appeared fresh and that there were several spots of milk on the floor and on the walls. She also noted that the corridor was well lit. The trial court granted summary judgment for the hospital, and the plaintiff appealed.

The Arizona Court of Appeals held that the plaintiff did not establish constructive notice that would indicate that the hospital was aware of the spilled milk. Although it is the responsibility and duty of a hospital to keep its premises reasonably safe for invitees, the hospital does not ensure their safety. The hospital is not liable for the injuries sustained by the plaintiff unless she can establish that either the hospital's employees caused the spill and failed to clean it on a timely basis or that the milk was there for such a long period of time that the hospital had constructive notice that the spill was there and failed to clean it. The plaintiff failed to show evidence that the milk was spilled by a hospital employee. As to constructive notice, the plaintiff was unable to show that the hospital was aware of the spill. She testified herself that the spill appeared to be fresh.

Lobby Slip and Fall—Hospital Liable

The plaintiff in *Blitz v. Jefferson Parish Hospital Service District*[48] brought a slip-and-fall suit against a hospital, alleging that her fall was caused by loose vinyl stripping in the front entrance of the hospital. The plaintiff was at the hospital to register for cataract surgery that was scheduled for the following day. She was wearing flat shoes with wedge heels with a height of approximately one-half inch. The front lobby of the hospital was covered by joined sections of carpeting, except for an area surrounding the centrally located information desk, which had terrazzo flooring. Vinyl stripping covered the space between the carpeting and terrazzo. The plaintiff testified that as she walked across the lobby her foot got caught in the vinyl stripping. She contends that the vinyl stripping was loose, so that the front of the sole of her shoe was caught between the vinyl stripping and the carpeting. The plaintiff testified that it felt like her foot was caught in a bear trap. She contended further that the vinyl stripping was defectively installed and maintained. An expert testified that there was an insufficient amount of vinyl adhesive on the

underside of the vinyl trim stripping in contact with the top of the terrazzo floor. The expert concluded that either an inadequate amount of adhesive was applied during the original installation or that the efficiency of the adhesive originally applied was unacceptably reduced by chemical action on it from the wax that was applied during frequent maintenance of the terrazzo.

The plaintiff filed suit against the hospital and was awarded $80,000 after a bench trial. The hospital service appealed, contending that the finding of liability was erroneous and that the trial judge erred in refusing to accept several defense witnesses as experts.

The court of appeal held that the evidence supported a liability determination. Hospital witnesses were apparently neither as credible nor as acceptable as the plaintiff's witnesses. The court was reluctant to substitute its findings of fact for those of the trial judge. The determination of liability was supported by adequate evidence and was not clearly erroneous.

Parking Lot Slip and Fall—Hospital Liable

The plaintiff, Harkins, in *Harkins v. Natchitoches Parish Hospital,*[49] tripped on a piece of black vinyl garden border material, hidden in the grass, and seriously injured herself. Although the plaintiff had surgery, she never regained full use of her right shoulder. Prior to her fall, Harkins was completely independent and able to care for herself and her apartment. Since the fall, she requires assistance in cleaning her apartment and managing her daily life's activities because of the partial loss of use of her right shoulder. This loss of use is permanent, and it continues to be painful to her. The trial court awarded her $50,000.

On appeal, the court held that a hospital owes a duty to its visitors to exercise reasonable care commensurate with the particular circumstances. It must prove that it acted reasonably to discover and correct a dangerous condition reasonably anticipated in its business activity. The plaintiff was required to prove that she tripped and fell and was injured because of some defect at the hospital's premises, creating a presumption of negligence on the hospital's part. If she met this burden of proof, then the hospital had to exculpate itself from that presumption.

Harkins established that she fell because she tripped on the black vinyl plastic gardening border, which was partially hidden by the grass. It was up to the hospital to exculpate itself from this presumption of liability. This it failed to do. It offered no proof to show that it acted with reasonable care under the circumstances, by having a hidden black vinyl gardening border in an area near its entrance that was regularly traversed by persons using the hospital's facilities. The hospital chose to defend itself by contending that Harkins had made inconsistent statements about the location where she tripped, and attempted to prove that the location of the accident actually occurred at the curb of the median, some 10 feet away from the plastic gardening border, based upon Harkins' statements to the emergency department physician and nurse.

The trial judge found that Ms. Harkins tripped on the gardening border on the grassy median. Given all of the evidence, this had a reasonable basis. Especially considering the fact that Harkins was in substantial pain from a separated shoulder while she was in the emergency department, her making a miscalculation about the exact location of where she tripped is entirely understandable. The appeals court agreed with the trial judge that it seemed reasonable to believe that the groundskeeper knew the piece of vinyl border material was present and took no action to remove it or place warning signs that it existed. The failure to either remove the vinyl or place warning signs was a failure to exercise reasonable care.

Fall from Emergency Department Gurney

On June 14, 1986, Mr. Hussey, in *Hussey v. Montgomery Memorial Hospital*,[50] suffered permanent brain damage when he fell from a gurney at the defendant hospital. He had been ill and was taken to the hospital by his wife. Upon arrival, he was seated on a gurney in the emergency department. The gurney had no side rails. Shortly thereafter, Hussey fell from the gurney and was rendered unconscious. As a result of the fall, Hussey suffered severe head injury and was comatose and unresponsive. He experienced continuous seizures. After being treated by a physician in the hospital's emergency department, the physician advised Mrs. Hussey that her husband's condition was caused by swelling in the brain, which was the result of his striking his head on the floor. Hussey was moved by ambulance to another hospital, where he was diagnosed with a dislocated clavicle, laceration of the skin, and two fractures of the lateral wall of the right orbit. He underwent surgery for the dislocated clavicle.

The plaintiffs alleged that during the 10-day period after the fall and again on July 10, 1986, they questioned Dr. Andrews, the attending physician, as to whether there was any permanent brain damage or injury. On each occasion, Andrews answered that there was not and would not be any brain damage. Two months after the fall, the plaintiffs consulted with an attorney concerning a possible claim against the defendant hospital, but the plaintiffs decided not to pursue a lawsuit at that time because they feared doing so might impair the plaintiff husband's ability to receive medical treatment.

For the next three and one-half years, Hussey continued to see his medical providers. He was kept on medication for his nerves. No physicians ever disclosed to the plaintiffs that Hussey had suffered a brain injury or that he may suffer permanent brain impairment.

By April 1990, Hussey's behavior became severely erratic and unpredictable to the point that Mrs. Hussey took him to Sandhills Center for Mental Health. Hussey was examined and transferred to the Dartmouth Clinic. Dr. Lee informed the plaintiffs that the test results indicated "permanent and residual brain impairment." On June 12, 1990, the plaintiffs filed a complaint alleging negligence against the hospital. The hospital filed a motion to dismiss on the grounds that the action was barred by the three-year statute of limitations.

The trial judge granted the hospital's motion for summary judgment and the plaintiffs appealed. The court of appeals held that the action was time barred.

Where the injury is latent, the claim is held not to accrue until the plaintiff discovers the injury. Where causation of an injury is unknown, the action accrues when both the injury and its cause have been (or should have been) discovered. The statute of limitations accrued on June 14, 1986, the date of Hussey's fall. The head injury was not latent. The court acknowledged that the plaintiffs questioned hospital personnel on occasions immediately after the fall to attempt to ascertain the extent of the plaintiff husband's injuries, and that on those occasions, the plaintiffs were told by hospital personnel that there was not and would not be any brain damage or injury. Nonetheless, Hussey had a cause of action on the date he fell from the gurney. Upon falling from the gurney, he suffered a severe head injury and was rendered unconscious. A treating physician in the emergency department advised Hussey's wife that swelling in the brain caused her husband's condition. The probable cause of the accident was the hospital's negligence. On the date of the fall, it was apparent that there had been wrongdoing, most likely attributable to the hospital. The ultimate injuries sustained by Hussey were a direct result of the June 14, 1986, fall caused by the hospital's wrongdoing that occurred on that date.

Loading Dock Unsafe

In *Glowacki v. Underwood Memorial Hospital*,[51] a nurse, while employed as a pediatric transport nurse for a hospital, was transporting a critically ill infant from the hospital. An isolette was needed for this purpose. This piece of equipment weighed approximately 200 pounds and was on wheels. Part of the nurse's responsibilities was to wheel it out to the ambulance, lower its wheels and then lift it up, with the help of the ambulance driver, into the ambulance. The ambulance arrived at the hospital and drove to the emergency department area where it backed up to the loading platform. The back of the ambulance made contact with hard rubbery pieces that jutted out from a wooden bumper. The bumper was separated from the concrete loading platform by intermittent rubber blocks, which left an open space of approximately three and one-half inches between the bumper and the dock. The nurse stepped from the ambulance directly onto the concrete platform. The nurse and the driver began the process of lifting the isolette up into the ambulance. The distance or height to the back of the ambulance appeared to have been approximately one foot. During this process, the nurse's foot became wedged into the space between the wooden bumper and the concrete platform. The nurse alleged that the space was as wide as her shoe.

A civil engineer testified at trial as an expert on behalf of the nurse. He distinguished the situation in the instant case because this was a "people-loading," not a "cargo-loading," facility. Because those who used this dock would have to pay more attention to their patients than to their own feet, he opined that it was unsafe to have a hole or gap in the bumper system.

The hospital produced a civil engineer who confirmed that there was no standard in the industry applicable to hospital bumpers. He admitted that any design should consider the nature of traffic going over it. It was his opinion that the system in the instant case did not create an unreasonable hazard of tripping or falling. The hospital's director of plant operations conceded that the hospital was aware of the spaces in the bumper system, but indicated there had never been a report of an incident since it was built.

The court charged the jury on principles of ordinary negligence and the liability of a property owner to business invitees for a dangerous condition on its property. The jury was also charged on contributory negligence and ultimate outcome. The jury returned a verdict finding that an unsafe condition existed on the hospital's platform, that the hospital was negligent, and that the negligence was a proximate cause of the nurse's accident. However, the court also found the nurse negligent. Her negligence was found to be a proximate cause of the accident. Thus, the court found the hospital 85 percent negligent and the nurse 15 percent negligent.

The defendant argued that the court erred in denying its motion for a new trial on damages because the verdict of $908,000 constituted a miscarriage of justice, was against the weight of the evidence, and was the result of passion, prejudice, sympathy, or mistake. The appeals court disagreed. A trial judge should not interfere with the quantum of damages assessed by a jury unless it is so disproportionate to the injuries and resulting disabilities as to shock the conscience and to convince the judge that to sustain the award would be manifestly unjust. The nurse's symptomatology from the day following the accident to the date of trial eight years later never changed. The defendant's argument that a "low back sprain" is not worth $908,000 ignores the principle that any established predetermined scale does not gauge consequential damages in personal injury cases. The trial judge correctly charged the jury on the elements of damages demonstrated by the nurse and her experts to be implicated by

reason of her substantial permanent injury and disability. The nurse's medical proofs were capable of supporting a jury finding that her back injury was one involving the spine and intervertebral discs and not merely a low back sprain.

Security

FAILURE TO PROVIDE ADEQUATE SECURITY

Citation: *Hanewinckel v. St. Paul's Property & Liab., 611 So.2d 174 (La. App. 1992)*

Facts

The plaintiff, a 52-year-old nurse anesthetist, arrived at the hospital at approximately 5:25 A.M. She began to back into a parking lot space, and before she shut off her engine, a man, approximately 30 years old, jumped into her car and sat in the driver's seat. He began to drive off, and the plaintiff asked him what he was doing. When he said that he was going to rape her, she jumped from the car. Before she could get away, her attacker caught her and started to beat her about the face and head. As he was dragging her, she was fighting him, and an employee pulling into the parking lot saw what was happening and alerted security. They found her car running with the lights on, but could not see her because of the fog. When they searched the area, they found her and rescued her. The assailant fled and was never found. She suffered a broken left wrist, 12 teeth either knocked out or broken, severe bruises on her face, and cuts on her legs and knees. She also suffered mental distress from which she had not recovered.

The nurse sued the owner of the parking lot and the security force for breach of their duty to protect her from a criminal attack committed on the premises. The trial court found that the defendant had a duty to provide reasonable and adequate security in the parking area, and that it had breached this duty, which resulted in injury to the plaintiff. The plaintiff was awarded $733,000 and the defendant appealed.

Issue

Did the hospital have a legal duty to protect the employee from harm? Did the hospital breach a duty by failing to patrol the area, thus causing her injury?

Holding

The court of appeals affirmed the decision for the plaintiff, finding that the hospital had breached its duty to the employee by failing to patrol the parking lot.

Reason

The hospital took on the responsibility to maintain the security force for the parking lot. As such, the hospital had assumed liability, giving a warranty that, through employment of a security service, their work would be carried out in a nonnegligent manner. The evidence indicated that other witnesses had seen the attacker in or near the parking lot five hours earlier in the day, yet no security personnel had spotted him. Further, there were not enough people on duty that day to patrol the parking lot properly. If they had been patrolling properly, the court concluded that the criminal would have been discovered and the attack prevented. The purpose of the security force was to protect everyone coming onto hospital grounds from attack. The court found further that the security force breached its duty by negligently failing to provide adequate security, which should have included random patrolling of all of the areas. Once the attacker was reported to security, nothing other than a brief walk through the lot was done.

Discussion

1. Examine the "duty to care" and "breach of duty" with regard to the security force and the attack and injuries suffered by the nurse.
2. What are the implications of this case for health care organizations?

LABORATORY

An organization must provide for clinical laboratory services to meet the needs of its patients. Each health care organization is responsible for the quality and timeliness of the services provided. Because it is often necessary to contract out certain tests, the organization should be sure that it is contracting for services with a reputable licensed laboratory.

An organization's laboratory provides data that are vital to a patient's treatment. Among its many functions, the laboratory monitors therapeutic ranges, measures blood levels for toxicity, places and monitors instrumentation on patient units, provides education for the nursing staff (e.g., glucose monitoring), provides valuable data utilized in research studies, provides data on the most effective and economical antibiotic for treating patients, serves in a consultation role, and provides valuable data as to the nutritional needs of patients.

Mismatched Blood

A laboratory technician in *Barnes Hospital v. Missouri Commission on Human Rights*[52] had been discharged because of inferior work performance. On three occasions, the employee allegedly had mismatched blood. The employee filed a complaint with the Commission on Human Rights, alleging racial discrimination as a reason for his discharge by the hospital. The hospital appealed, and the circuit court reversed the Commission's order. The technician appealed to the Missouri Supreme Court, which held that the evidence did not support the ruling of racial discrimination by the Missouri Commission on Human Rights.

Refusal To Work with Certain Blood Specimens

A laboratory technician was found to have been properly dismissed from her job for refusing to perform chemical examinations on vials with AIDS warnings attached in *Stepp v. Review Board of the Indiana Employment Security Division.*[53] The court of appeals held that the employee was dismissed for just cause and that the laboratory did not waive its right to compel employees to perform assigned tasks.

Reference Lab

LOST CHANCE OF SURVIVAL/ FAILURE TO DETECT CELLULAR CHANGES IN PAP SMEAR

Citation: *Sander v. Geib, Elston, Frost Prof'l Ass'n, 506 N.W.2d 107 (S.D. 1993)*

Facts

As part of her care, the patient had several gynecological examinations, including Pap smears, in

1977, 1978, 1980, 1984, 1986, and 1987. The patient's physician performed the examinations. Specimens for the Pap test were submitted to a laboratory for evaluation. The laboratory procedure consisted of a clerk assigning each specimen a number when it was received. A cytotechnologist would then screen the specimen. If the specimen was determined to be abnormal, it would be marked for review by a pathologist. Out of the Pap tests that were determined to be normal, only 1 in 10 was actually viewed by a pathologist. The pathologist made recommendations based on the classification of the Pap tests. A biopsy would be recommended if the Pap test was determined to be Class IV.

Except for the Pap test in 1987, which showed premalignant cellular changes, all of the patient's other Pap tests were determined to be negative. In 1986, the laboratory made a notation to the patient's physician that "moderate inflammation" was present. The patient's physician, who was treating her with antibiotics for a foot inflammation, thought that the medication would also treat the other inflammation. In September 1987, the patient returned to her physician complaining of pain, erratic periods, and tiredness. After completing a physical, her physician took a Pap test, which he sent to the laboratory. He also referred her to a gynecologist. The pathologist recommended a biopsy. Biopsies and further physical examinations revealed squamous cell carcinoma that had spread to her pelvic bones or to one-third of her vagina. Her Pap tests were reexamined by the laboratory, which reported that the 1986 smear showed that malignancy was highly likely. The patient was referred to the University of Minnesota to determine whether she was a viable candidate for radiation treatment. The cancer, however, had spread, and the patient was not considered a candidate for radiation treatment as she had no chance of survival. When the university reviewed all of the available slides, they found cellular changes back to 1984.

The patient sued in 1988, alleging that the laboratory failed to detect and report cellular changes in her Pap tests in time to prevent the spread of the cancer. Before trial, the patient died. Her husband and sister were substituted as plaintiffs, and the complaint was amended to include a wrongful death action. After trial, a jury awarded $3.7 million in damages, which were reduced to $1 million by the circuit court. The jury found against the laboratory and the laboratory appealed.

Issue

Was it erroneous for the trial court to submit to the jury the 1988 negligence claim based on the 1984 slide?

Holding

The South Dakota Supreme Court upheld the jury verdict and restored the $3.7 million damage award.

Reason

The court determined that evidence relating to negligence claims pertaining to Pap tests taken more than two years before filing the action were admissible because the patient had a continuing relationship with the clinical laboratory as a result of her physician's submitting her Pap tests to the laboratory over a period of time.

Discussion

1. What changes in procedure should the laboratory take to help ensure that Pap tests are properly classified?
2. How might continuous quality improvement activities improve the laboratory's operations?

MEDICAL IMAGING

Failure To Restrain/Patient Fall

The plaintiff in *Cockerton v. Mercy Hospital Medical Center*[54] was admitted to the hospital for the purpose of surgery to correct a problem with her open bite. Her physician ordered postsurgical X-rays for her head and face to be taken the next day. A hospital employee took the plaintiff from her room to the X-ray department by wheelchair. A nurse had assessed her condition as slightly "oozy" and drowsy. She was wearing a urinary catheter. An IV and a nasogastric tube were still in place.

An X-ray technician took charge of the plaintiff in the X-ray room. It was her third day on the job. After the plaintiff was taken inside the X-ray room, she was transferred from a wheelchair to a portable chair for the procedure. Upon being moved, the plaintiff complained of nausea, and the technician observed that the plaintiff's pupils were dilated. The technician did not use the restraint straps to secure the plaintiff to the chair. At some point during the procedure, the plaintiff had a fainting seizure. The technician called for help. When another hospital employee entered the room, the technician was holding the plaintiff in an upright position.

She appeared nonresponsive. The plaintiff only remembered being stood up and having a lead jacket thrown across her back and shoulders. The technician maintains that the plaintiff did not fall.

At the time the plaintiff left the X-ray room, her level of consciousness was poor. She was brought back to the ward and the nasogastric tube was removed. The plaintiff's physician noticed a deflection of the plaintiff's nose, but had difficulty assessing it because of the surgical procedure from the day before. Because the plaintiff had fainted in X-ray, an incident report was completed at the request of the plaintiff's physician. The following day, the deflection of the plaintiff's nose was much more evident. A specialist was contacted and an attempt was made to correct the deformity. The specialist made an observation that it would require a substantial injury to the nose to deflect it to that severity.

The plaintiff instituted proceedings against the hospital, alleging that the negligence of the nurses or technicians allowed her to fall during the procedure and subsequently caused injury. The trial court did not require expert testimony concerning the standard of care given by the technician. The jury concluded that the hospital was negligent in leaving the plaintiff unattended or failing to restrain her, which proximately caused her fall and injury. The jury rendered a verdict of $48,370, and the hospital appealed.

Is expert testimony required where the health care provider's lack of care is so obvious as to be within the comprehension of a layperson, and to require only common knowledge and experience to understand?

The Iowa Court of Appeals held that the patient was not required to present expert testimony on the issue of the hospital's negligence.

Ordinarily, evidence of negligence in a medical malpractice action must be proven by expert testimony. The court rejected the hospital's argument that the X-ray procedure could not be categorized as routine or ministerial care. The conduct in question was simply the way the technician handled the plaintiff during the X-ray examination. In arguing for a professional standard, the hospital pointed to the elaborate training requirements for an X-ray technician, as required by the Iowa Administrative Code. However, the fact that an X-ray technician must meet certain requirements under the Iowa Administrative Code does not make all of the technician's conduct professional in nature. The applicable standard requires that of reasonable care.

The X-ray technician testified that during the X-ray, the plaintiff appeared to have a "seizure episode." She also testified that she left the plaintiff unattended for a brief period of time and that she did not use the restraint straps that were attached to the portable X-ray chair. Using the restraint straps would have secured the plaintiff to the portable chair during the X-ray examination.

The plaintiff's physician testified that there had been no problems with the septum during surgery, and that he had never had a complication such as the plaintiff's injury occur during surgery. While the plaintiff was in recovery immediately following surgery, the physician observed no injuries to her nose. The patient did not leave her bed until she was taken to the X-ray room the next morning. Following the X-ray examination, her nose appeared "grotesque" and injured. Taking the evidence in the light most favorable to the plaintiff, the court found that substantial evidence existed to establish a causal connection between the hospital's conduct and the plaintiff's injury.

WRONGFUL DEATH

Citation: *Schopp v. Our Lady of the Lake Hospital, Inc., 739 So.2d 338, 98 1382 (La. App. 1 Cir. 6/25/99)*

Facts

Sophie Schopp stumbled coming from her bathroom and fell, striking her head on August 2, 1993. She was treated in the emergency department of Our Lady of the Lake Hospital (OLOL). She was unable to get up and lay on the floor until approximately 8:00 A.M., when a home health aide, Daisy Montgomery, came to her home for her daily visit. Her doors were locked, but Schopp told Montgomery to go across the street and get a key, which she did. Emergency medical services arrived shortly thereafter and took Schopp to OLOL. Her friend and neighbor, Eloise Guwang, followed in her car. Schopp's friend, Fran Haper, also came to OLOL that morning.

Schopp was taken for skull X-rays, and when she returned, the X-ray technologist, Coates, told Haper and Guwang that there had been "a little accident." Haper testified that Coates said that the X-ray plate fell on her head. He pointed to Schopp's head and showed Haper where it had fallen on her. Haper stated she saw no mark or bruise and thought nothing more of it. Guwang testified, however, that she pushed back Schopp's hair and saw a blue mark on the left side of her forehead. Guwang testified that she knew Schopp was hurt. According to Guwang, Schopp told her that Coates and Smith were "cutting up" when Smith let the X-ray cartridge slip, and it fell on her head. Schopp did not tell Guwang from what distance the cartridge fell.

Coates testified that Schopp was laying on the X-ray table when the accident occurred. He saw the cassette begin to tip. He reached and caught it at the same time it hit her head. He stated that the cassette "barely tapped her on the head." He asked her if she was okay, and she replied that she did not know. He stated that he asked her "more out of politeness than necessarily concern," because he knew the cassette did not hurt her. They then took the X-ray and took her back to the emergency department, where he told her "family" that the cassette had bumped her. He told them to tell the physician if she had any pain.

Smith asked Schopp if she was all right. Schopp did not respond at first, then said she did not know. Smith denied that she and Coates were "cutting up." She was concerned that Schopp might have been hurt and knew that they had to file an incident report with OLOL.

Dr. Allain was the emergency department physician on duty on August 2 when Schopp arrived at OLOL. He found her to be awake and alert but in considerable pain, primarily from a bruise to her left elbow. She also had a bruise around her right eye. He ordered X-rays of her elbow and skull. The X-rays were negative, but after consulting with Dr. Morris, her internist, he decided to admit her overnight for observation. After she was admitted, a female X-ray technologist came to him kind of scared and said that they dropped a plate on her and that it fell on her face.

Morris received a panic call from a nurse at the hospital who told him an X-ray cartridge had been dropped on Schopp and that she had had an injury to her cranium, she had an excruciating headache, and she did not look good. Morris ordered a CT scan for Schopp. About an hour later, he arrived at the hospital and went to Schopp's room. She was not herself; she recognized him and could speak, but the "distinctness of her mentality" was gone. She told him that an X-ray cassette had been dropped on her, then lifted her hand to her head and said, "It hit me here." He noticed swelling and puffiness in the area where she pointed.

The CT scan showed that Schopp had a large acute subdural hematoma. Dr. Perone, a board-certified neurosurgeon, performed surgery to evacuate the hematoma. Although Schopp seemed to improve initially following the surgery, her health declined thereafter, and she died on August 16, 1993.

Schopp's sons filed suit against OLOL (defendant) and two of defendant's X-ray technologists, Coates and Smith. The plaintiffs later dismissed Coates and Smith but proceeded to jury trial against the defendant. The jury rendered a verdict in favor of the plaintiffs and an appeal was taken for wrongful death.

Issue

Was Schopp's death caused by the negligence of hospital staff dropping an X-ray cassette on her head while undergoing a skull X-ray?

Holding

The defendant contended that the trial court erred in giving a jury charge regarding aggravation of a preexisting condition. After the jury retired for deliberations, the defendant objected to the charge, and the trial judge stated that he had intended to omit that instruction. Because this case was tried and argued throughout as an either/or case (i.e., either the hematoma was caused by the fall or by the X-ray cartridge), the court found this error to be harmless.

Reason

The defendant contended that the cassette only brushed or tapped Schopp's head and thus could not have caused a hematoma. It relied on the testimony of Smith and Coates. The plaintiffs, on the other hand, relied on the statements of the nurse who called Morris, Smith's statement to Allain, and Schopp's statement to Morris that the cartridge had been "dropped" on her head. The defendant also contended that Perone's operative note that there was no bruise on the left side of Schopp's head shows that even if the cartridge was dropped on her head, it was not done with enough force to cause a hematoma. Perone's notation is contradicted, however, by Guwang's testimony that she saw a blue mark on the left side of Schopp's head and Morris's testimony that he saw swelling and puffiness in the area where Schopp indicated that the cartridge had hit her.

The defendant also contended that the testimony of its experts was more credible than that of Morris. Perone testified that, in his opinion,

Schopp's subdural hematoma was caused by her fall at home. He explained that although she hit the right side of her head in the fall, it is common for blood vessels on the opposite side of the brain to stretch and tear as the atrophied brain of an elderly person moves around inside his or her skull during a fall. This phenomenon is called a contrecoup injury. He admitted that his opinion was based primarily on the description of the X-ray incident given by Coates and Smith, but he believed that even if they had dropped an X-ray cartridge on her, the blow could not have caused a subdural hematoma. He stated that the cartridge would had to have been dropped from higher than the ceiling to cause the size hematoma that she had.

Because Perone was chief of staff at OLOL at the time of trial and the defendant was afraid that he might be perceived as biased in its favor, the defendant also presented the video testimony of Dr. Hurst, a Lafayette neurosurgeon. Hurst testified that the most likely cause of the hematoma was the fall at home. He stated that the cartridge would have to be dropped on Schopp from a height of a meter or more to present enough force to cause a subdural hematoma, and that according to the technologist's version of the incident, the cartridge fell only two millimeters, or less than one inch. He believed the technologists' version of the incident rather than the history that Schopp gave to Morris. He stated that in Morris's discovery deposition, Morris stated that Schopp was lethargic and delirious when he first saw her. Based on that statement, he had some "credibility difficulty" with Morris's testimony regarding Schopp's history that the cartridge was dropped on her head.

Morris gave very moving testimony regarding Schopp's injury. He was emphatic that he had the education and experience to give an opinion as to causation. He stated that although he did not operate, he made the diagnoses that led to surgery. He pointed out he was the one who diagnosed the subdural hematoma. He stated that there was no doubt in his mind that the incident in the X-ray room caused the hematoma. He believed that the cartridge was dropped on Schopp's head based on her statements to him and the alarmed tone in the nurse's voice when she called him to report the X-ray incident. He saw the soft tissue swelling on Schopp's head and noted the hematoma was in the exact place she had shown him where the cartridge struck her. He stated that to him, this was "an obvious cause and effect."

In this case, there were two versions of the X-ray-room incident: either the cartridge tilted less than an inch and barely brushed Schopp's head, leaving no mark, or it was dropped from some distance and struck her with enough force to leave a soft-tissue injury. The jury believed the second version. There were also two opinions as to causation: that of Perone and Hurst, based on the first version of the incident, and that of Morris, based on the second. The jury must have believed Morris's opinion. Based on review of the entire record, including the transcript, the video and written depositions, the medical records, and the X-ray stand and cartridge, the appeals court found this was a permissible view.

Discussion

1. Do you agree with the court's findings? Discuss your answer.
2. What are the lessons to be learned from this case for employees?

NUTRITIONAL SERVICES

Health care organizations must provide each patient with a nourishing, palatable, well-balanced diet that meets the daily nutritional and special dietary needs of each patient. The dietitian has general responsibility for this function. Failure to do so can lead to negligence suits. The daughter of the deceased in *Lambert v. Beverly Enterprises, Inc.*[55] filed an action claiming that her father had been mistreated. The notice of intent to sue indicated that the deceased suffered various injuries and from malnutrition as a direct result of the acts or omissions of personnel and that the plaintiff's father suffered actual damages that included substantial medical expenses and mental anguish due to the injuries he sustained. A motion to dismiss the case was denied.

PARAMEDIC

Many states have enacted legislation that provides civil immunity to paramedics who render emergency life-saving services. The plaintiff in *Malone v. City of Seattle*[56] alleged that the defendant was negligent in providing care to the plaintiff after an automobile accident. The plaintiff, on appeal, contended that the trial court wrongfully instructed the jury regarding a 1971 civil immunity statute. The following is an excerpt from the relevant Washington statute:

No act or omission of any physician's trained mobile intensive care paramedic . . . done or omitted in good faith while rendering emergency lifesaving service . . . to a person who is in immediate danger of loss of life shall impose any liability upon the trained mobile intensive care paramedic . . . or upon a . . . city or other local governmental unit. . . .[57]

One of the issues raised was whether the legislature intended the statute to apply only to the rendition of cardiopulmonary emergency treatment by a paramedic. The court of appeals indicated that although the definition contained in the statute places special emphasis on the paramedic's training in all aspects of cardiopulmonary resuscitation, the Act does not limit the paramedic to cardiopulmonary resuscitation. The Act implicitly recognizes that paramedics may encounter different emergencies.

In *Morena v. South Hills Health Systems,*[58] the Pennsylvania Supreme Court held that paramedics were not negligent in transporting a victim of a shooting to the nearest available hospital, rather than to another hospital located five or six miles farther away where a thoracic surgeon was present. The paramedics were not capable, in a medical sense, of accurately diagnosing the extent of the decedent's injury. Except for the children's center and the burn center, there were no emergency trauma centers specifically designated for the treatment of particular injuries.

PHARMACY

Among nonoperative adverse events, medication errors are the leading cause of medical injury. Antibiotics, chemotherapeutic drugs, and anticoagulants are the three categories of drugs responsible for most drug-related adverse events. The prevention of medication errors requires recognition of common causes and the development of practices to help reduce the incidence of errors. With thousands of drugs, many of which look alike and sound alike, it is understandable why medication errors are so common. The following listing describes some of the more common type of medication errors:

- prescription errors
  - wrong drug
  - wrong dose
  - wrong route
  - transcription errors (often due to illegible handwriting)
- administration errors
  - failure to administer the medication
  - administration to the wrong patient
- wrong time
  - failure to administer the medication
  - failure to administer the medication at the appropriate time

- improper preparation
  - failure to properly formulate the medication
  - preparation of an expired drug

The practice of pharmacy essentially includes preparing, compounding, dispensing, and retailing medications. These activities may be carried out only by a pharmacist with a state license or by a person exempted from the provisions of a state's pharmacy statutes. The entire stock of drugs in a pharmacy is subject to strict government regulation and control. The pharmacist is responsible for developing, coordinating, and supervising all pharmacy activities and reviewing the drug regimens of each patient.

Government Control of Drugs

The power and authority to regulate drugs, their products, packaging, and distribution rest primarily with federal and state governments. Consequently, there are often two sets of regulations and standards governing the same activity. In general, states have attempted to conform their laws to the federal laws. For example, most states have adopted the Uniform Controlled Substances Act (UCSA). This uniform law is based on and is in conformity with the federal Controlled Substances Act. Several states have modified the UCSA in various ways, frequently setting more stringent standards than are required under the federal law.

Federal Controls

Federal laws and regulations applicable to drugs include the Controlled Substances Act and the Federal Food, Drug and Cosmetic Act.

Controlled Substances Act

The Comprehensive Drug Abuse Prevention and Control Act of 1970, commonly known as the Controlled Substances Act, was signed into law on October 27, 1970, as Public Law No. 91–513. This law replaced virtually all preexisting federal laws dealing with narcotics, depressants, and stimulants.

Federal Food, Drug and Cosmetic Act

The Federal Food, Drug and Cosmetic Act (FDCA) applies to drugs and devices carried in interstate commerce and to goods produced and distributed in federal territory. The Act's requirements apply to almost every drug that would be dispensed from a pharmacy, because nearly all drugs and devices, or their components, are eventually carried in interstate commerce.

Section 502 of the Act sets forth the information that must appear on the labels or the labeling of drugs and devices. The label must contain, among other special information: (1) the name and place of business of the manufacturer, packer, or distributor; (2) the quantity of contents; (3) the name and quantity of any ingredient found to be habit-forming, along with the statement "Warning—may be habit-forming"; (4) the established name of the drug or its ingredients; (5) adequate directions for use; (6) adequate warnings and cautions concerning conditions of use; and (7) special precautions for packaging.

The regulation implementing the labeling requirements of Section 502 exempts prescription drugs from the requirement that the label bear "adequate directions for use for laymen" if the drug is in the possession of a pharmacy or under the custody of a practitioner licensed by law to administer or prescribe legend drugs.[59] This particular exemption applies only to prescription drugs meeting the other requirements. Ordinary household remedies in the custody or possession of a practitioner or pharmacist would not fall under the labeling exemption.

If the drug container is too small to bear a label with all the required information, the label may contain only the quantity or proportion of each active ingredient and the lot or control number. The prescription legend may appear on the outer container of such drug units. The lot or control number may appear on the crimp of a dispensing tube, and the remainder of the required label information may appear on other labeling within the package.

Besides the label itself, each legend drug must be accompanied by labeling, on or within the sealed package from which the drug is to be dispensed, bearing full prescribing information including indications; dosage; routes, methods, and frequency of administration; contraindications; side effects; precautions; and any other information concerning the intended use of the drug necessary for the prescriber to use the drug safely. This information usually is contained in what is known in the trade as the "package insert."

State Regulations

Besides federal laws affecting the manufacture, use, and handling of drugs, the different states have controlling legislation. All states regulate the practice of pharmacy, as well as the operation of pharmacies. State regulations generally provide that: (1) each health care organization must ensure the availability of pharmaceutic services to meet the needs of patients; (2) pharmaceutic services must be provided in accordance with all applicable federal and state laws and regula-

tions; (3) pharmaceutic services must be provided under the supervision of a pharmacist; (4) space and equipment must be provided within the organization for the proper storage, safeguarding, preparation, dispensing, and administration of drugs; (5) each organization must develop and implement written policies and procedures regarding accountability, distribution, and assurance of quality of all drugs; and (6) each organization must develop and follow current written procedures for the safe prescription and administration of drugs.

State laws require that pharmacies be licensed and that they be under the supervision of a person licensed to practice pharmacy. The pharmacist usually can be either an employee of the organization or a consultant. The authority of an organization to operate a pharmacy is conditioned on compliance with licensing requirements affecting the pharmacy premises and its personnel. The statutes applying to pharmacies usually empower regulatory agencies, such as the state pharmacy board, to issue rules and regulations as necessary.

Each organization is subject to liability for the negligent acts of its professional and nonprofessional employees in the handling of drugs and medications within the organization. Both the pharmacist and the organization are subject to criminal liability, as well as civil liability, for the violation of statutory directives. Most states have regulations that dictate in detail the dispensing, distribution, administration, storage, control, and disposal of drugs within health care organizations.

Compounding Oral Medications

Oral medications (e.g., tablets) may be more subject to errors than other forms of medication. Improper dosing, incorrect or misunderstood directions for use, improper compounding, and inaccurate measurements of oral medications can result in medication errors.

Distribution, Dispensing, and Administration of Drugs

Distribution is the movement of a legend drug from a community pharmacy or institutional pharmacy to a nursing service area, while in the originally labeled manufacturer's container, labeled according to federal and state statutes and regulations.

The *dispensing* of medications is the processing of a drug for delivery or for administration to a patient pursuant to the order of a health care practitioner. It consists of checking the directions on the label with the directions on the prescription or order to determine accuracy; selecting the drug from stock to fill the order; counting, measuring, compounding, or preparing the drug; placing the drug in the proper container; and adding to a written prescription any required notations.

The *administration* of medications is an act in which a single dose of a prescribed drug is given to a patient by an authorized person in accordance with federal and state laws and regulations governing such act. The complete act of administration includes removing an individual dose from a previously dispensed, properly labeled container (including a unit dose container), verifying it with the physician's order, giving the individual dose to the proper patient, and recording the time and dose given.

Licensed persons, in accordance with state regulations, may administer medications. Each dose of a drug administered must be recorded on the patient's clinical records. A separate record of narcotic drugs must be maintained. The record must contain a separate sheet for each narcotic of different strength or type administered to the patient. The narcotic record must contain the following information: date and time administered, physician's name, signature of person administering the dose, and the balance of the narcotic drug on hand.

In the event that an emergency arises that requires the immediate administration of a particular drug, the patient's record should be documented properly, showing the necessity for administration of the drug on an emergency basis. Procedures should be in place for handling emergency situations.

Storage of Drugs

Drugs must be stored in their original containers and must be labeled properly. The label should indicate the patient's full name, physician, prescription number, strength of the drug, expiration date of all time-dated drugs, and the address and telephone number of the pharmacy dispensing the drug. The medication containers must be stored in a locked cabinet at the nurses' station. Medications containing narcotics or other dangerous drugs must be stored under double lock (e.g., a locked box within the medicine cabinet). The keys to the medicine cabinet and narcotics box must be in the possession of authorized personnel. Medications for "external use only" must be marked clearly and kept separate from medications for internal use. Medications that are to be taken out of use must be disposed of according to federal and state laws and regulations.

Drug Substitution

Drug substitution may be defined as the dispensing of a different drug or brand in place of the drug or brand ordered. Several states prohibit this, and penal sanctions, including loss of license, are imposed for violation of the law.

Health care organizations use a "formulary system," whereby physicians and pharmacists create a formulary list-ing drugs used in the institution. The formulary contains the brand names and generic names of drugs. Under the formulary system, a physician agrees that his or her prescription, which calls for a brand name drug, may be filled with the generic equivalent of that drug (i.e., a drug that contains the same active ingredients in the same proportions).

Authorization for using a generic equivalent should be given by the physician at the time he or she prescribes a formulary drug and should be evidenced by a written consent on the face of the prescription. When a formulary system is in use, the prescribing physician can require the use of a particular brand name drug, when he or she deems it necessary or desirable, by expressly prohibiting the use of the formulary system.

A pharmacist can be subject to liability for the mishandling or misuse of drugs. Failure to meet and maintain required standards in the handling of drugs can lead to criminal or civil liability and even to the revocation of a pharmacist's license.

Medicaid Fraud

The court of appeals in *State v. Beatty*[60] upheld a lower court's finding that the evidence submitted against the defendant pharmacist was sufficient to sustain a conviction for Medicaid fraud. The state was billed for medications that were never dispensed, was billed for more medications than some patients received, and, in some instances, was billed for the more expensive trade name drugs when cheaper generic drugs were dispensed.

The pharmacists in *People v. Kendzia*[61] were convicted of mishandling drugs, and they appealed. The New York Supreme Court, Appellate Division, held that the evidence supported a finding that the pharmacists sold generic drugs in vials with brand name labels and was sufficient to support a conviction. Investigators, working undercover, were provided with Medicaid cards and fictitious prescriptions requiring brand name drugs to be dispensed as written. Between April and October 1979, the investigators had taken the prescriptions to the pharmacy where they were filled with generic substitutions in vials with the brand name labels.

Inaccurate Records

The operator of a pharmacy, in a disciplinary proceeding before the California Board of Pharmacy, was found negligent because of inaccurate record keeping.[62] The pharmacist had failed to keep accurate records of dangerous drugs, report thefts by employees, and report a burglary of pharmacy drugs. Such reporting was required by state statute.

Decreasing Medication Misadventures/Helpful Tips

- Be sure that your handwriting is legible—print if necessary.
- For clarity—do not use felt-tip pens.
- Abbreviations should be used according to hospital policy.
- Do not write ambiguous orders.
- Always add a zero prior to a decimal.
- Hold orders should be accompanied by a time frame.
- Know about the medication that you are prescribing.
- Be sure medications have been properly diluted before prescribing.
- Be sure that medications are being administered by proper route.

Expanding Role of the Pharmacist

Historically, the role of the pharmacist was centered on the management of the pharmacy and the accurate dispensing of drugs. Pharmacists now, among other duties, maintain patient medication profiles and monitor patient profiles, looking for incompatibilities between drugs and food-drug interactions. In *Baker v. Arbor Drugs, Inc.*,[63] a Michigan court imposed a duty on a pharmacist to monitor a patient's medications. Three different prescriptions were prescribed by the same physician and filled at the same pharmacy. The pharmacy maintained a computer system that detected drug interactions. The pharmacy advertised to consumers that it could, through the use of a computer monitoring system, provide a medication profile of a customer for adverse drug reactions. Because the pharmacy advertised and used the computer system to monitor the medications of a customer, the pharmacist voluntarily assumed a duty of care to detect the harmful drug interaction that occurred.

The pharmacist is playing an ever-expanding interdisciplinary collaborative role on the clinical side of health care. For example, pharmacists often maintain a separate telephone line in hospitals for caregivers and practitioners to use to ask queries and discuss such issues as treatment plans for patients and proper dosing. Pharmacists are playing an important role when they respond and participate in reviving patients in cardiac arrest. Their knowledge of drugs, potential drug interactions, and proper dosing can be the difference between life and death. Some hospitals have reported improved code outcomes when pharmacists attend and participate in patient codes.

A Pennsylvania court held that a pharmacy failed to exercise due care and diligence because the patient was not warned about the maximum dosage.[64] This failure resulted in an overdose, causing the patient permanent injuries. Expert testimony focused on the fact that a pharmacist who receives inadequate instructions as to the maximum recommended

dosage of a medication has a duty to ascertain if the patient is aware of the limitations concerning the use of the drug or, alternatively, to contact the prescribing physician as to the inadequacy of the prescription. In *Hooks v. McLaughlin*,[65] the Indiana Supreme Court held that a pharmacist had a duty to refuse to refill prescriptions at an unreasonably faster rate than prescribed pending directions from the prescribing physician. The Indiana Code provides that a pharmacist is immune from civil prosecution or civil liability if he or she, in good faith, refuses to honor a prescription because, in his or her professional judgment, the honoring of the prescription would aid or abet an addiction of habit.[66]

The duties and responsibilities of pharmacists have moved well beyond the concept of filling prescriptions and dispensing drugs. Schools of pharmacy have recognized the ever-expanding role of the pharmacist into the clinical aspects of patient care; so much so, that the educational requirements are getting more stringent, with emphasis on clinical education and application.

PHYSICAL THERAPY

Physical therapy is the art and science of preventing and treating neuromuscular or musculoskeletal disabilities through the evaluation of an individual's disability and rehabilitation potential; the use of physical agents—heat, cold, electricity, water, and light; and neuromuscular procedures that, through their physiologic effect, improve or maintain the patient's optimum functional level. Because of different physical disabilities brought on by various injuries and medical problems, physical therapy is an extremely important component of a patient's total health care.

Contracted Services

The physical therapist in *Armintor v. Community Hospital of Brazosport*[67] was properly enjoined from entering the hospital's premises after termination of an oral contract to furnish services to hospital patients in need of physical therapy. Substantial evidence supported the court's finding that the hospital's attempt to establish a hospital-based physical therapy program would have been disrupted if the independent therapist had been permitted to continue treating patients. The court considered the exclusion of a therapist an administrative matter within the board's discretion. The therapist's entering the hospital without the permission of a staff physician would constitute trespass and would be in violation of hospital policy.

Neglect

In *Zucker v. Axelrod*,[68] a physical therapist had been charged with resident neglect for refusing to allow an 82-

year-old nursing facility resident to go to the bathroom before starting his therapy treatment session. Undisputed evidence at a hearing showed that the petitioner refused to allow the resident to be excused to go to the bathroom. The petitioner claimed that her refusal was because she assumed that the resident had gone to the bathroom before going to therapy and that the resident was undergoing a bladder training program. The petitioner had not mentioned when she was interviewed after the incident or during her hearing testimony that she considered bladder training a basis for refusing to allow the resident to go to the bathroom. It is uncontroverted that the nursing facility had a policy of allowing residents to go to the bathroom whenever they wished to do so. The court held that the finding of resident neglect was supported sufficiently by the evidence.

PHYSICIAN'S ASSISTANT

One of the solutions to the shortage of physicians in certain rural and inner-city areas has been to train allied health professionals such as physician's assistants (PAs) to perform the more routine and repetitive medical functions. A physician may delegate to a PA such tasks as suturing minor wounds, administering injections, and performing routine history and physical examinations. A physician may not delegate a task when regulations specify that the physician must perform it personally or when the delegation is prohibited under state law or by the facility's own policies.

PAs are responsible for their own negligent acts. If a PA is an employee of a health care organization, the organization can be held liable for the PA's negligent acts on the basis of *respondeat superior*. A physician, as an employer of a PA, also can be held liable on the basis of *respondeat superior*.

To limit the potential risk of liability to a PA, the physician should monitor and supervise the PA's work closely. Guidelines and procedures also should be established to provide a standard mechanism for reviewing a PA's performance.

PODIATRIST

Negligent Surgery

The podiatrist in *Strauss v. Biggs*[69] was found to have failed to meet the standard of care required of a podiatrist, and that failure resulted in injury to the patient. The podiatrist, by his own admission, stated that his initial incision in the patient's foot had been misplaced. The trial court was found not to have erred in permitting the jury to consider additional claims that the podiatrist had acted improperly by failing to refer the patient, stop the procedure after the first incision, inform the patient of possible nerve injury, and provide proper postoperative treatment. Testimony of the patient's

experts was adequate to show that such alleged omissions had violated the standard of care.

RESPIRATORY THERAPIST

Failure To Report

The court in *Poor Sisters of St. Francis v. Catron*[70] held that the failure of nurses and an inhalation therapist to report to the supervisor that an endotracheal tube had been left in the plaintiff longer than the customary period of three or four days was sufficient to allow the jury to reach a finding of negligence. The patient experienced difficulty speaking and underwent several operations to remove scar tissue and open her voice box. At the time of trial, she could not speak above a whisper and breathed partially through a hole in her throat created by a tracheotomy. The hospital was found liable for the negligent acts of its employees and the resulting injuries to the plaintiff.

Improper Procedure

The respiratory therapist in *State University v. Young*[71] was suspended for using the same syringe for drawing blood from a number of critically ill patients. The therapist had been warned several times of the dangers of that practice and that it violated the state's policy of providing high-quality care.

SEXUAL IMPROPRIETIES

A significant number of cases address health care professionals who have been involved in sexual relationships with their patients. Such cases are being litigated, in many instances, in both civil and criminal arenas. Health care professionals finding themselves in such unprofessional relationships must seek help for themselves as well as refer their patients to other appropriate professionals. Besides being subject to civil and criminal litigation, health care professionals also are subject to having their licenses revoked for sexual improprieties.

Dentist

Revocation of a dentist's license on charges of professional misconduct was properly ordered in *Melone v. State Education Department*[72] on the basis of substantial evidence that while acting in a professional capacity, the dentist had engaged in physical and sexual contact with five different male patients within a three-year period. Considering the dentist's responsible position, the extended time period during which the sexual contacts occurred, the age and impressionable nature of the victims (7 to 15 years of age), and the possibility of lasting effects on the victims, the penalty was not shocking to the court's sense of fairness.

Nurse

A nurse's sexual relations with a patient can give rise to disciplinary action resulting in the nurse's loss of license. In *Heineche v. Department of Commerce*,[73] a male nurse lost his license after having a sexual relationship with a patient, even though she was no longer a patient at the hospital where he had met her. The fact that the nurse resigned from the hospital and was living with the patient was not a defense sufficient to support such behavior.

Physician

A hospital technologist in *Copithorne v. Framingham Union Hospital*[74] alleged that a staff physician raped her during the course of a house call. The technologist's claim against the hospital had been summarily dismissed for lack of proximate causation. On appeal, the dismissal was found to be improper when the record indicated that the hospital had received notice of allegations that the physician had assaulted patients on and off the hospital's premises. The hospital had instructed the physician to have another individual present when visiting female patients and had instructed nurses "to keep an eye on him." The physician's sexual assault was foreseeable. There was evidentiary support for the proposition that failure to withdraw the physician's privileges had caused the rape when the technologist asserted that it was the physician's good reputation in the hospital that had led her to seek his services.

Psychiatrist

The sexual relationship a psychiatrist had with the spouse of a patient was found to be improper in *Richard v. Larry*.[75] California Civil Code Section 43.5, abolishing causes of action for alienation of affection, criminal conversation, and seduction of a patient over the age of consent, did not bar damages for emotional distress caused by the alleged professional negligence of the psychiatrist who had sexual relations with the plaintiff's wife. The psychiatrist owed a special duty to use due care for his patient's health. The statute was not intended to lower the standard of care that psychiatrists owed their patients. Besides an action against the psychiatrist, allegations that the psychiatrist was an agent of the hospital stated a cause of action against the hospital.

On April 10, 1998, the Bureau of Professional Medical Conduct charged the petitioner in *Goldberg v. De Buono*,[76] a licensed physician and psychiatrist, with moral unfitness, gross negligence and incompetence, negligence on more than one occasion, and incompetence by reason of his alleged sexual relationship with a patient. Following a hearing, a Hearing Committee of the State Board for Professional Medical Conduct sustained the specifications of moral unfitness, gross negligence, and negligence and recommended revocation of the petitioner's license. The petitioner commenced an Article 78 proceeding to annul the Committee's determination and revocation of petitioner's license.

The New York Supreme Court, Appellate Division, rejected the petitioner's assertion that the Committee erred in crediting the testimony of patient A and her daughter. Issues of credibility, even as to witnesses with psychiatric illnesses, are exclusively for the administrative factfinder to determine. Moreover, it is noteworthy that the petitioner conceded his sexual relationship with patient A but contended that the physician–patient relationship had been terminated at the time the sexual relationship occurred. Inasmuch as respondent's medical expert testified that the relationship was not terminated and the petitioner's relationship with patient A constituted a serious deviation from accepted standards of practice, the court was satisfied that the Committee's determination was supported by substantial evidence.

Psychologist

A defense that sexual improprieties with clients did not take place during treatment sessions is unacceptable conduct. The Board of Psychologist Examiners in *Gilmore v. Board of Psychologist Examiners*[77] revoked a psychologist's license for sexual improprieties. The psychologist petitioned for judicial review. She argued that therapy had terminated before the sexual relationships began. The court of appeals held that evidence supported the board's conclusion that the psychologist had violated an ethical standard in caring for her patients. When a psychologist's personal interests intrude into the practitioner–client relationship, the practitioner is obliged to re-create objectivity through a third party. The board's findings and conclusions indicated that the petitioner failed to maintain that objectivity.

SURGERY

Improper Positioning of Arm

The plaintiff in *Wick v. Henderson*[78] had pain in her left arm upon awakening from surgery. An anesthesiologist told her that her arm was "stressed" during surgery. According to the plaintiff's evidence, she sustained an injury to the ulnar nerve in her left upper arm.

A malpractice action was filed against the hospital and the anesthesiologist. The plaintiff sought recovery on theory of *res ipsa loquitur*. There was testimony that the main cause of the injury was the mechanical compression of the nerve by improper positioning of the arm during surgery. The trial court granted the defendants a directed verdict, resulting in dismissal of the case. The Iowa Supreme Court held that the *res ipsa loquitur* doctrine applied.

The plaintiff must prove two foundational facts in order to invoke the doctrine of *res ipsa loquitur*. First, that the defendants had exclusive control and management of the instrument that caused the plaintiff's injury, and second, that it was the type of injury that ordinarily would not occur if reasonable care had been used. As to control, it should be enough that the plaintiff can show an injury resulting from an external force applied while she lay unconscious in the hospital. It is within common knowledge and experience of a layperson that an individual does not enter the hospital for gallbladder surgery and leave with ulnar nerve injury.

Sciatic Nerve Injury

The plaintiff in *Lacombe v. Dr. Walter Olin Moss Regional Hospital*[79] was admitted to the hospital for surgery. Upon regaining consciousness in the recovery room, the plaintiff began complaining of severe pain in her right buttock, shooting down the back of her right leg. The plaintiff was eventually diagnosed with sciatic nerve injury. It is undisputed that the injury is permanent. A medical malpractice claim was filed against the hospital and the physicians involved in the surgery. A medical review panel rendered a decision finding no breach of the standard of care. The plaintiff then filed a malpractice suit against the hospital and physicians. By the time of trial, all of the defendants except the hospital had been dismissed from the litigation. After trial, the trial judge rendered judgment in favor of the plaintiff. The trial judge found that, applying the doctrine of *res ipsa loquitur* to the evidence, the plaintiff had proven her case. Accordingly, he found the hospital responsible under the theory of *respondeat superior* for the negligent conduct of its agents (the personnel who prepared the plaintiff for surgery and the physicians who conducted the operation).

The hospital contended that the trial court incorrectly applied the doctrine of *res ipsa loquitur*. The facts established by the plaintiff must also reasonably permit the jury to discount other possible causes and to conclude it was more likely than not that the defendant's negligence caused the injury. The Fourteenth Judicial District awarded damages to Mrs. Lacombe, and the hospital appealed.

The Louisiana Court of Appeals held that the evidence warranted an inference of *res ipsa loquitur*. Expert testimony established that the plaintiff was suffering from a sciatic nerve injury and that the injury was permanent. Experts on both sides agreed that sciatic nerve injury was not a known risk of this surgery. The testimony indicated that the plaintiff went into the hospital without the injury and came out with it. The various experts expressed three theories as to the cause of the injury: (1) her position during surgery put pressure on the nerve, (2) the nerve was nicked or caught in a suture during surgery, or (3) either immediately prior to or after surgery, an injection of medication was made directly into the nerve. The actual cause of the nerve injury, however, could not be established. After reviewing the record, the court agreed with the trial court that the evidence warranted an inference that negligence on the part of the defendant caused the injury. Additionally, none of the theories put forward as to the cause of the injury negated the inference.

CERTIFICATION OF HEALTH CARE PROFESSIONALS

The certification of health care professionals is the recognition by a governmental or professional association that an individual's expertise meets the standards of that group. The standards established by professional associations generally exceed those required by government agencies. Some professional groups establish their own minimum standards for certification in those professions that are not licensed by a particular state. Certification by an association or group is a self-regulation credentialing process.

LICENSING OF HEALTH CARE PROFESSIONALS

Licensure can be defined as the process by which some competent authority grants permission to a qualified individual or entity to perform certain specified activities that would be illegal without a license. As it applies to health care personnel, licensure refers to the process by which licensing boards, agencies, or departments of the several states grant to individuals who meet certain predetermined standards the legal right to practice in a health care profession and to use a specified health care practitioner's title. The commonly stated objectives of licensing laws are to limit and control admission to the different health care occupations and to protect the public from unqualified practitioners by promulgating and enforcing standards of practice within the professions.

The authority of states to license health care practitioners is found in their regulating power. Implicit in the power to license is the authority to collect license fees, establish standards of practice, require certain minimum qualifications and competency levels of applicants, and impose on applicants other requirements necessary to protect the general public welfare. This authority, which is vested in the legislature, may be delegated to political subdivisions or to state boards, agencies, and departments. In some instances, the scope of the delegated power is made specific in the legislation; in others, the licensing authority may have wide discretion in performing its functions. In either case, however, the authority granted by the legislature may not be exceeded.

HELPFUL ADVICE FOR ALL HEALTH CARE PROFESSIONALS

- Do not criticize the professional skills of others. Use appropriate, available reporting mechanisms when the skill of another is to be challenged.
- Maintain complete and adequate medical records.
- Provide each patient with medical care comparable with national standards.
- Seek the aid of consultants when indicated.
- Obtain consent for diagnostic and therapeutic procedures.
- Do not indiscriminately prescribe medications, blood tests, diagnostic tests, and treatments.
- Inform the patient of the risks, benefits, and alternatives to proposed medical and surgical procedures.

- Practice in the specialty in which you have been trained.
- Participate in continuing education programs.
- Keep all patient information confidential.
- Check all patient equipment regularly and monitor it for safety through an equipment management program.
- In terminating a professional relationship with a patient, give adequate written notice to the patient.
- Authenticate all telephone orders.
- Obtain a qualified substitute when you will be absent from your practice.
- Investigate patient incidents promptly.
- Be a good listener and allow each patient sufficient time to express fears and anxieties.

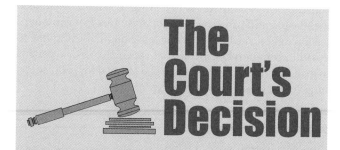

The parents were offered an out-of-court settlement totaling $200,000.

CHAPTER REVIEW

1. Health care professionals, regardless of field, are required to adhere to the prevalent standards of care required within their professions. This includes proper assessment, reassessment, diagnosis, treatment, and follow-up care.
2. Many lawsuits against hospitals arise from care administered in emergency departments. The vast majority of these lawsuits are the result of negligence. Many of these claims charge poor follow-up care and are brought by patients who use emergency departments as primary care clinics.
3. Some of the most common issues around which emergency department lawsuits are centered are improper and inappropriate administration of medication; failure to admit a patient; sparse or contradictory medical documentation; failure to render care; and inappropriate discharge or transfer.
4. In many states, hospitals are required by law to provide emergency care. Licensed medical practitioners who refuse to treat a person who has arrived at a general hospital for emergency medical treatment will be guilty of a misdemeanor and will be subject to a maximum of one year in prison and a fine.
5. When their skills are required in the emergency department, hospitals are required to notify specialty physicians who are on call. A physician who is on call and does not respond to such a notification can be found liable for injuries to the patient resulting from this lack of response.
6. Health care organizations usually rely on a plant services or engineering department to meet the requirements for the provision of a safe environment for patients, staff, and visitors. Failure to provide such an environment can make the organization liable if it results in injury. Such incidents include slips and falls, lack of fire safety, improper disposal of hazardous materials, improper functioning of medical equipment, and failure to provide adequate security.

7. Health care organizations are responsible for the quality and timeliness of the services provided by their clinical laboratories. When services are contracted out, organizations must be sure that they are contracting with reputable and licensed laboratories.

8. Dietitians are responsible for the provision to patients of nourishing, palatable, well-balanced diets. Each diet must meet the daily nutritional and special dietary needs of the respective patient.

9. Medication errors are common due to many factors, including the vast number of drugs available and their similar names and appearances. These errors constitute a leading cause of injury. In addition to federal laws regarding the manufacture, use, and handling of drugs, states also have legislation designed to regulate pharmacies.

10. In addition to their regular duties to manage the pharmacy and accurately dispense medications, pharmacists are now required to maintain patient medical profiles and monitor these profiles for incompatibilities between drugs and food-drug interactions.

11. Physical therapists evaluate patients' disabilities and potential for rehabilitation for the purpose of preventing and treating neuromuscular or musculoskeletal disabilities.

12. Physician's assistants (PAs) are often called upon to perform appropriate routine or repetitive medical functions. PAs will be held responsible for their own negligent actions and, in addition, their employers and physicians also can be held responsible.

13. Health care professionals who are involved in sexual improprieties are subject to civil and criminal litigation and may have their licenses revoked.

14. Licensure of health care professionals is the process through which licensing boards, agencies, or departments grant to individuals who meet certain criteria the legal right to practice in a health care profession and use the title of a health care practitioner.

REVIEW QUESTIONS

1. What was the reasoning for enacting the Emergency Medical Treatment and Active Labor Act?
2. A sexual impropriety committed by a health care practitioner should be handled in the institution, not in court. Comment.
3. When a patient refuses to consent to treatment, the staff should pursue the course of treatment if it is life saving. Discuss.
4. Should medical advice be dispensed on the telephone? Explain your opinion.
5. Discuss the various safety issues that confront hospitals on a daily basis.

NOTES

1. Ronnie Green, *Dying at the Hospital's Door: A Child Lost, Troubling Questions*, The Miami Herald, Apr. 16, 1995, at 14A.
2. 636 N.E.2d 1282 (Ind. Ct. App. 1994).
3. 322 S.E.2d 696 (N.C. Ct. App. 1985).
4. Smith v. O'Neal, 850 S.W.2d 797 (Tex. Ct. App. 1993).
5. 367 S.E.2d 453 (S.C. 1988).
6. *Id.* at 455–456.
7. 520 N.E.2d 1085 (Ill. App. Ct. 1988).
8. Lowenberg v. Sobol, 594 N.Y.S.2d 874 (N.Y. App. Div. 1993).
9. 599 N.Y.S.2d 58 (N.Y. App. Div. 1993).
10. 711 N.Y.S.2d 65 (N.Y. Sup. Ct., App. Div., 3d Dep't, 2000).
11. The Robert Wood Johnson Foundation, *Negligent Medical Care: What Is It, Where Is It, and How Widespread Is It?* ABRIDGE, Spring 1991, at 7.
12. 650 A.2d 1076 (Pa. Super. 1994).
13. Roy v. Gupta, 606 So.2d 940 (La. Ct. App. 1992).
14. 615 N.E.2d 585 (Mass. App. Ct. 1993).
15. 42 U.S.C.A. § 1395dd(a) (1992).
16. 42 U.S.C.A. § 1395dd(e)(1) (1992).
17. 811 F. Supp. 121 (W.D. N.Y. 1993).
18. 42 U.S.C.A. § 1395dd(3)(A) (1992).
19. 42 U.S.C.A. § 1395dd(c)(1) (1992).
20. 831 F. Supp. 829 (M.D. Ala. 1993).
21. 134 F.3d 319 (5th Cir. 1998).
22. 42 U.S.C. § 1395dd(a) (1992).
23. 42 U.S.C. § 1395dd(e)(1) (1992).
24. 42 U.S.C. § 1395dd(b)(1) (1992).
25. 830 F. Supp. 1399 (M.D. Ala. 1993).
26. 934 F.2d 1362 (5th Cir. Tex. 1991).
27. *Courts Uphold Law, Regulations against Patient Dumping*, NATION'S HEALTH, Aug. 1991, at 1.
28. *Id.* at 17.
29. Guerrero v. Copper Queen Hosp., 537 P.2d 1329 (Ariz. 1975).
30. Cleland v. Bronson Health Care Group, 917 F.2d 266, 272 (6th Cir. 1990.)

31. 689 So.2d 696 (La. App. 1997).

32. 288 A.2d 379 (Md. 1972).

33. 271 N.W.2d 8 (S.D. 1978).

34. 477 So.2d 1036 (Fla. Dist. Ct. App. 1985).

35. 14 S.W.3d 42 (Mo. App. 1999).

36. 698 So.2d 958 (La. App. 1997).

37. 498 S.E.2d 408 (1998).

38. Baptist Mem'l Hosp. Sys. v Sampson, 969 S.W.2d 945, 947 (Tex. 1998).

39. Martin C. McWilliams, Jr. & Hamilton E. Russell, III, *Hospital Liability for Torts of Independent Contractor Physicians*, 47 S.C. L. REV. 431, 473 (1996).

40. Jackson v. Powei, 743 P.2d 1376, 1385 (Alaska 1987).

41. Martell v. St Charles Hosp., 523 N.Y.S.2d 342, 352 (N.Y. Sup. Ct. 1987).

42. 836 S.W.2d 911 (Mo. 1992).

43. M. LAUCHHEIMER, HAZARDOUS WASTE AND TOXIC TORTS 1 (1989).

44. 861 S.W.2d 694 (Mo. Ct. App. 1993).

45. 625 So.2d 351 (La. Ct. App. 1993).

46. 634 N.E.2d 189 (N.Y. 1994).

47. 861 P.2d 679 (Ariz. Ct. App. 1993).

48. 636 So.2d 1059 (La. Ct. App. 1994).

49. 696 So.2d 19, 83–97 (La. App. 1997).

50. 441 S.E.2d 577 (N.C. Ct. App. 1994).

51. 636 A.2d 527 (N.J. Super. Ct. App. Div. 1994).

52. 661 S.W.2d 534 (Mo. 1983).

53. 521 N.E.2d 350 (Ind. Ct. App. 1988).

54. 490 N.W.2d 856 (Iowa Ct. App. 1992).

55. 753 F. Supp. 267 (W.D. Ark. 1990).

56. 600 P.2d 647 (Wash. Ct. App. 1979).

57. 1971 WASH. LAWS § 1783.

58. 462 A.2d 680 (Pa. 1983).

59. 21 C.F.R. § 1.106.

60. 308 S.E.2d 65 (N.C. Ct. App. 1983).

61. 478 N.Y.S.2d 209 (N.Y. App. Div. 1984).

62. Banks v. Board of Pharmacy, 207 Cal. Rptr. 835 (Cal. Ct. App. 1984).

63. 544 N.W.2d 727 (Mich. Ct. App. 1996).

64. Riff v. Morgan Pharmacy, 508 A.2d 1247 (Pa. Super. Ct. 1986).

65. 642 N.E.2d 514 (Ind. 1994).

66. IND. CODE § 25-26-13-16(b)(3) (1993).

67. 659 S.W.2d 86 (Tex. Ct. App. 1983).

68. 527 N.Y.S.2d 937 (N.Y. App. Div. 1988).

69. 525 A.2d 992 (Del. 1987).

70. 435 N.E.2d 305 (Ind. Ct. App. 1982).

71. 566 N.Y.S.2d 79 (N.Y. App. Div. 1991).

72. 495 N.Y.S.2d 808 (N.Y. App. Div. 1985).

73. 810 P.2d 459 (Utah 1991).

74. 520 N.E.2d 139 (Mass. 1988).

75. 243 Cal. Rptr. 807 (Cal. Ct. App. 1988).

76. 711 N.Y.S.2d 81 (N.Y. App. Div. 2000).

77. 725 P.2d 400 (Or. Ct. App. 1986).

78. 485 N.W.2d 645 (Iowa 1992).

79. 617 So.2d 612 (La. Ct. App. 1993).

CHAPTER 10

Information Management and Health Care Records

It's Your Gavel...

FATAL HANDWRITING MIX-UP

Vasquez, a 42-year-old man, died as a result of a handwriting mix-up on the medication prescribed for his heart. The pharmacist had misread the physician's handwriting. Vasquez had been given a prescription for 20 mg of Isordil to be taken four times per day. The pharmacist misread the physician's handwriting and filled the prescription with Plendil, a drug for high blood pressure, which is usually taken at no more than 10 mg per day. As a result, the heart patient was given the wrong medication at eight times the recommended dosage. Two weeks later he was dead from an apparent heart attack. The likelihood of similar occurrences is a growing danger as the number and variety of medications increase with similar names and look-alikes.[1]

What is your verdict?

INTRODUCTION

The effective and efficient delivery of patient care requires that an organization determine its information needs. Organizations that do not centralize their information needs will often suffer the problem of scattered databases (e.g., duplication of data gathering, inconsistent reports, and inefficiencies in the use of economic resources). The objectives of information management are to: identify the information needs of the organization in providing patient care services; evaluate existing data for accuracy, availability, accessibility, security, necessity, and performance; develop action plans to enhance and improve organizational performance in patient care, governance, management, and support processes to meet the goals of the organization; improve turnaround time of results; reduce unnecessary duplication of data entries; provide timely access to information throughout the organization; provide patient-centered information systems and technology; and provide for the collection, generation, and analysis of data.

MANAGING INFORMATION

The goals of an information management plan include

- determining customer needs, both internal and external (e.g., third-party payers)
- monitoring needs (ongoing)
- establishing priorities
- improving accuracy
- providing uniformity of data collections and definitions

- developing an integrated patient care record
- limiting duplication of entries
- delivering timely and accurate information
- providing easy access to information
- maintaining the security and confidentiality of information
- enhancing patient care activities
- improving collaboration across the organization through information sharing
- disaster planning for the recovery of information
- orienting and training staff on the information management system
- providing an annual review of the information plan to include its scope, organization, objectives, and effectiveness

The development and maintenance of information management systems are major activities that take place across all organizations, regardless of their mission or size. Many of the records that are required to be maintained for informational purposes include financial, medical, personnel, purchasing, and safety records. Information management is a process intended to facilitate the flow of information within and between departments and caregivers.

MEDICAL RECORDS

Health care organizations are required to maintain a medical record for each patient in accordance with accepted professional standards and practices. The primary emphasis in this section lies with medical records—documentation of the facts of a patient's illness, symptoms, diagnosis, and treatment.

Medical record requirements are often provided for in each state's public health laws. These laws contain provisions mandating that organizations maintain a complete medical record for each patient that contains all pertinent information regarding the daily care and treatment of that patient. Because medical records are the principal means of communication between health care professionals in matters relating to patient care, documentation of the facts of a patient's illness, symptoms, diagnosis, and treatment is an extremely important tool in furnishing modern health care.

The main purposes of the medical record are to provide a planning tool for patient care; to record the course of a patient's treatment and the changes in a patient's condition; to document the communications between the practitioner responsible for the patient and any other health care professional who contributes to the patient's care; assist in protecting the legal interests of the patient, the organization, and the practitioner; provide a database for use in statistical reporting, continuing education, and research; and provide information necessary for third-party billing and regulatory agencies. Medical records must be complete, accurate, current, readily accessible, and systematically organized.

Medical Records and the Nurse

The nurse is generally the one medical professional the patient sees more than any other. Consequently, the nurse is in a position to monitor the patient's illness, response to medication, display of pain and discomfort, and general condition. The patient's care, as well as the nurse's observations, should be recorded on a regular basis. The nurse should comply promptly and accurately with the orders the physician writes in the record.

NURSES FAILED TO RECORD PATIENT'S CONDITION

Citation: *Gerner v. Long Island Jewish Hillside Med. Ctr., 609 N.Y.S.2d 898 (N.Y. App. Div. 1994)*

Facts

On March 8, 1971, the plaintiff gave birth to her infant son at the defendant medical center. Dr. Geller, a private physician, arrived six hours later as the attending pediatrician with resident privileges. On March 11, 1971, Geller, having noted and confirmed a slightly jaundiced condition, ordered phototherapy. After three days of such treatment and monitoring, the child's bilirubin count fell to a normal level, and Geller ordered the patient discharged. Geller continued to treat the child over the next four years. The child today is brain damaged, with permanent neurological dysfunction.

The plaintiff alleged medical malpractice on the part of both the medical center and the private attending physician for failing to diagnose and treat the jaundice in a timely manner. Following examinations before trial, the medical center's motion for summary judgment was granted. The plaintiff and Geller appealed.

Issue

Were there questions of fact as to whether there were indications in the first six hours after the infant's birth, before the private attending pediatrician arrived, that should have alerted the hospital delivery and nursery staff of possible hyperbilirubinemia, precluding summary judgment for the hospital?

Holding

The New York Supreme Court, Appellate Division, held that questions of fact precluded summary judgment for the hospital.

Reason

Two factual issues were left unresolved. The first is whether there were indications, in the first six hours after birth, that should have alerted the hospital delivery and nursery staff of possible hyperbilirubinemia. According to the hospital's expert, one such overlooked indicator was a blood incompatibility between the mother and child. Because the hospital acted alone as the plaintiff's medical practitioner over those first six hours, it would have to bear sole responsibility for any malpractice committed during that time period.

The second issue is whether the medical center should be exempt from sharing any responsibility for malpractice over the course of the next six days (until the infant's discharge) by reason of the fact that, for the balance of that period, the infant was technically under the care of a private attending physician. A number of allegations are raised as to negligence attributed solely to hospital staff during that period. For example, *notes of attending nurses* at the nursery *failed to record any jaundiced condition,* or any reference to color, until the third day after birth, despite the parents' complaints to hospital personnel about the baby's yellowish complexion. Additionally, Geller ordered a complete blood count and bilirubin test on the morning of March 11, as soon as he learned of the first recorded observation by a nurse of a jaundiced appearance. Test results, which showed a moderately elevated bilirubin count, were not reported by the laboratory until 10 hours after the blood sample was drawn, and it took another 3 hours before Geller's order for phototherapy was carried out. An issue is thus raised as to whether the 13-hour delay in commencement of the treatment had any permanent effect. Normally, a hospital is shielded from liability for the negligence of a private attending physician practicing at its facility. However, myriad cases hold that a hospital may be held concurrently liable with a private practitioner for the independent negligence of the former's medical staff. During pretrial discovery, the hospital failed to dispel allegations of its own negligence concurrent with Geller's attendance to the patient.

Discussion

1. What is the importance of documentation as it relates to this case?
2. What is the importance of assessment and reassessment as it relates to patient care in general?

Coordinating Patient Care

When two or more practitioners treat a patient, they are required to coordinate their findings and communicate in a manner that best serves their patient's well-being. The extent of a practitioner's involvement determines what effort he or she must take to satisfy his or her obligation to communicate.[2]

Contents of the Medical Record

The medical record must be a complete, accurate, up-to-date report of the medical history, condition, and treatment of each patient. It is composed of at least two distinct parts, each of which is made up of several types of forms. The first part is compiled on admission and includes the admission record, which describes pertinent data regarding the patient's age, address, reason for admission, social security number, marital status, religion, addresses, and any other information necessary to meet both federal and state requirements. The first part also includes the general consent and authorization-for-treatment forms allowing the health care facility to perform routine diagnostic testing, etc.

The second part, the clinical record, includes

- the medical history and physical examination, including diagnosis, and findings that support the diagnosis
- initial assessments (e.g., nursing, functional, nutritional, and discharge planning)
- anesthesia assessments
- operative reports
- delivery records
- diagnostic and therapeutic orders, including all medications, treatments, diet, and restorative and special medical procedures required for the safety and well-being of the patient
- progress records describing significant changes in a patient's condition, written at the time of each visit
- medication and treatment record
- nurses' notes containing observations made by nursing personnel

- records of vital signs
- consultation notes and reports
- dental reports
- discharge planning/social service notes and reports
- recreational, occupational, and activity therapy notes and reports
- physical therapy notes and reports
- nutritional notes and reports
- laboratory and X-ray reports
- fluid intake and output charts
- discharge summaries

Licensure rules and regulations contained in state statutes generally describe the requirements and standards for the maintenance, handling, signing, filing, and retention of medical records.

Failure to maintain a complete and accurate medical record reflecting the treatment rendered may affect the ability of the organization and/or physician to obtain third-party reimbursement (e.g., from Medicare, Medicaid, or Blue Cross). Under federal and state laws, the medical record must reflect accurately the treatment for which the organization or physician seeks payment. Thus, the medical record is important to the organization for medical, legal, and financial reasons.

Legal Requirements

Health care organizations are required to maintain medical records under a variety of statutes and regulations. The scope and detail of record requirements vary from state to state. Licensure rules and regulations contained in state statutes generally describe the requirements and standards for maintaining, handling, completing, authenticating, filing, and retaining medical records. In addition to state regulations, minimum standards for record keeping have been established by the federal government for health care organizations receiving federal funding.

Ideally, the individual in charge of medical records should be a health information management administrator (HIMA), who is licensed by the American Health Information Management Association (AHIMA) as a registered health information administrator (RHIA). The HIMA is responsible for ensuring that the facility complies with all regulations and amendments affecting medical records.

Diagnosis-Related Groups

Diagnosis-related groups (DRGs) refer to a methodology developed by professors at Yale University for classifying patients in categories according to age, diagnosis, and treat-

ment resource requirements. It is the basis for the Department of Health and Human Services' prospective payment system, contained in the 1983 Social Security Amendments for reimbursing inpatient hospital costs for Medicare beneficiaries. The key source of information for determining the course of treatment of each patient and the proper DRG assignment is the medical record. Reimbursement is based on preestablished average prices for each DRG. As a result of this reimbursement methodology, poor record keeping can precipitate financial disaster for a hospital. The potential financial savings for Medicare are substantial. Under this system of payment, if hospitals can provide quality patient care at a cost under the price established for a DRG, they keep the excess dollars paid. This is an incentive for hospitals to keep costs under control. There is, however, a continuing fear that patients may, to their detriment, be discharged too early, for financial reasons. This in turn leads to costly malpractice suits.

Incomplete Records

Grounds for Suspension of Medical Staff Privileges

Various licensing regulations require prompt completion of records after the discharge of patients. Persistent failure to conform to a medical staff rule requiring the physician to complete records promptly was held in *Board of Trustees Memorial Hospital v. Pratt*[3] to provide a basis for suspension of staff privileges.

Charting by Exception

On April 9, 1986, Dr. Borras, in *Lama v. Borras*,[4] while operating on Mr. Lama, discovered that the patient had an extruded disc and attempted to remove the extruded material. Either because Borras failed to remove the offending material or because he operated at the wrong level, the patient's original symptoms returned several days after the operation. Borras concluded that a second operation was necessary to remedy the recurrence.

On May 15, Borras operated again on the patient. Borras did not order pre- or postoperative antibiotics. It is unclear whether the second operation was successful in curing the herniated disc. On May 17, a nurse's note indicated that the bandage covering the patient's surgical wound was "very bloody," which, according to expert testimony, indicates the possibility of infection. On May 18, the patient was experiencing local pain at the site of the incision, another symptom consistent with an infection. On May 19, the bandage was soiled again. A more complete account of the patient's evolving condition was not available because the *hospital instructed nurses to engage in charting by exception*, a system whereby nurses did not record qualitative observations for each of the day's three shifts, but instead made such notes only when necessary to chronicle important changes in a patient's condition.

On May 21, Dr. Piazza, an attending physician, diagnosed the patient's problem as discitis—an infection of the space between discs—and responded by initiating antibiotic treatment. Lama was hospitalized for several additional months while undergoing treatment for the infection.

After moving from Puerto Rico to Florida, Lama filed a tort action in U.S. District Court for the District of Puerto Rico. Although the plaintiff did not claim that the hospital was vicariously liable for any negligence on the part of Borras, he alleged that the hospital had failed to prepare, use, and monitor proper medical records.

The jury returned a verdict awarding the plaintiff $600,000 in compensatory damages. The district court ruled that the evidence was legally sufficient to support the jury's findings and an appeal was taken.

The U.S. Court of Appeals for the First Circuit held that the evidence supported a jury conclusion that the hospital had been negligent in maintaining a charting by exception method of recording notes in the patient's record.

The hospital did not contest the plaintiff's allegation that a regulation of the Puerto Rico Department of Health, in force in 1986, requires qualitative nurses' notes for each nursing shift. Nor did the hospital dispute the charge that, during the patient's hospital stay, the nurses attending to him did not supply the required notes for every shift but instead followed the hospital's policy of charting by exception. The question was whether there was sufficient evidence for the jury to find that the violation of the regulation was a proximate cause of harm to Lama.

The hospital questioned the plaintiff's proof of causation in two respects. First, the hospital claimed that the plaintiff did not prove that the charting by exception policy was a proximate cause of the delayed detection of the patient's infection. Second, the hospital argued that there was no causal relationship between the belated diagnosis of the infection and any unnecessary harm suffered.

There was evidence from which the jury could have inferred that, as part of the practice of charting by exception, the nurses did not regularly record certain information important to the diagnosis of an infection, such as the changing characteristics of the surgical wound and the patient's complaints of postoperative pain. Indeed, one former nurse at the hospital who attended to the patient testified that, under the charting by exception policy, she would not report a patient's pain if she either did not administer any medicine or simply gave the patient an aspirin-type medication (as opposed to a narcotic). Further, because there was evidence that the patient's hospital records contained some scattered possible signs of infection that deserved further investigation (e.g., an excessively bloody bandage and local pain at the site of the wound), the jury could have reasonably inferred that

the intermittent charting failed to provide the sort of continuous danger signals that would be the most likely to spur early intervention by the physician.

The hospital claimed that even if faulty record keeping was a cause of the delayed diagnosis, the plaintiff failed to demonstrate a link between the timing of the diagnosis and the harm the patient eventually suffered. It appeared that Lama acquired a wound infection as early as May 17 (when a nurse noted a "very bloody" bandage) or May 19 (when Lama complained of pain at the site of the wound). The wound infection then developed into discitis on or about May 20 (when Lama began experiencing excruciating back pain). Although there may have been no way to prevent the initial wound infection, the key question then becomes whether early detection and treatment of the wound infection could have prevented the infection from reaching the disc interspace in the critical period prior to May 20. Time is an extremely important factor in handling an infection. A 24-hour delay in treatment can make a difference, and a delay of several days carries a high risk that the infection will not be properly controlled. The jury could have reasonably inferred that the diagnosis and treatment were delayed at least 24 hours (May 19 to 20), and perhaps 72 hours (May 17 to 20). As a result, the jury could have reasonably concluded that the delayed timing of the diagnosis and treatment of the wound infection was a proximate cause of the patient's discitis.

Legal Proceedings and the Medical Record

The ever-increasing frequency of personal injury suits mandates that health care organizations maintain complete, accurate, and timely medical records. Their importance as evidentiary tools in legal proceedings cannot be overemphasized. The integrity and completeness of the medical record are extremely important in reconstructing the events surrounding any alleged negligence in the care of the patient. Medical records aid police investigations, provide information for determining the cause of death, and indicate the extent of injury in workers' compensation or personal injury proceedings.

When health care professionals are called as witnesses in a proceeding, they are permitted to refresh their recollections of the facts and circumstances of a particular case by referring to the medical record. Courts recognize that it is impossible for a medical witness to remember the details of every patient's treatment. The record therefore may be used as an aid in relating the facts of a patient's course of treatment.

The medical record itself may be admitted into evidence in legal proceedings. For medical record information to be admitted into evidence, the court must be assured that the information is accurate, that it was recorded at the time the event took place, and that it was not recorded in anticipation of a specific legal proceeding. Although it is recognized that witnesses may refresh their memories and that records may be admitted into evidence, there is nevertheless a need for assurance that the information is trustworthy.

When a medical record is introduced into evidence, its custodian, usually the medical records administrator, must testify as to the manner in which the record was produced and the way in which it is protected from unauthorized handling and change. Whether such records and other documents are admitted or excluded is governed by the facts and circumstances of the particular case, as well as by the applicable rules of evidence. Admission of a business record requires "the testimony of the custodian or other qualified witness."[5]

> [A] writing is not admissible . . . merely because it may appear upon its face to be a writing made by a physician in the regular course of his practice. It must first be shown that the writing was actually made by or under the direction of the physician at or near the time of his examination of the individual in question and also that it was his custom in the regular course of his professional practice to make such a record.[6]

The records purportedly relating to a patient's treatment in *Belber v. Lipson*[7] were not admissible as business records because the witness who had possession of them had no personal knowledge of the circumstances under which the records were prepared.

Whatever the situation, the record must be complete, accurate, and timely. If it can be shown that the record is inaccurate or incomplete or that it was made long after the event it purports to record, its credibility as evidence will be diminished.

Confidential Communications

The Clinton administration issued new privacy regulations requiring that: "Patients must give permission to release medical information. . . . Health plans, hospitals, employers or doctors that violate the rules face penalties, including up to $250,000 in fines and 10-year prison terms for selling information that is supposed to be private."[8]

The duty of an organization's employees and staff to maintain confidentiality encompasses both verbal and written communications. This requirement also applies to consultants, contracted individuals, students, and volunteers. Information about a patient, regardless of the method in which it is acquired, is confidential and should not be disclosed without the patient's permission. Those who come into possession of the most intimate personal information about patients have both a legal and an ethical duty not to reveal confidential communications. The legal duty arises because the law recognizes a right to privacy. To protect this right, there is a corresponding duty to obey. The ethical duty is broader and applies at all times.

All health care professionals who have access to medical records have a legal, ethical, and moral obligation to protect the confidentiality of the information in the records. The communications between a physician and his or her patient and the information generated during the course of the patient's illness are generally accorded the protection of confidentiality. However, "patient confidentiality seems to have lost its meaning in the current health care environment, some experts say. Yet the dearth of litigation stemming from medical record disclosures clearly indicates that patients are not likely to sue over their loss of confidentiality."[9] Health care professionals have a clear legal and moral obligation to maintain this confidentiality. As noted above, medical records, with proper authorization, may be used for the purposes of research, statistical evaluation, and education. The information obtained from medical records must be dealt with in a confidential manner; otherwise, an organization could incur liability.

Breach of Physician–Patient Confidentiality

During her initial appointment with Dr. Sonneland, Ms. Berger revealed information about her medical and personal history.[10] When questioned about her personal history, Berger said that she had previously been married to Dr. Hoheim, a physician in Montana. She described her relationship with her ex-husband as extremely strained. After meeting with Berger, Sonneland contacted Hoheim and discussed Berger's use of pain medications. Based on information provided by Sonneland, Hoheim filed a motion in a Montana court seeking to modify the custody orders relating to the couple's two children. Berger sought damages for Sonneland's alleged breach of physician–patient confidentiality.

The Washington Legislature has acknowledged the confidential nature of the physician–patient relationship by adopting the Washington Uniform Health Care Information Act,[11] and by establishing the physician–patient privilege.[12] The physician–patient privilege prevents a physician from testifying in a civil action about information the physician acquired when treating the patient, unless the patient consents. The purpose of this privilege is to: (1) promote proper treatment by facilitating full disclosure of information, and (2) to protect the patient from embarrassment or scandal that might result if the intimate details of medical treatment were revealed.

The court granted Sonneland's motion for summary judgment based on the absence of damage evidence. The court reasoned that RCW 7.70 supported a cause of action for breach of physician–patient confidentiality, but concluded that Berger had failed to present a *prima facie* case because she failed to establish, through medical testimony, any objective symptoms of emotional distress. Berger moved for reconsideration, urging the court to apply invasion of privacy principles rather than principles related to the tort of negligent infliction of emotional distress.

Sonneland saw Berger as a new patient. As part of his interview with Berger, Sonneland learned the identity of her ex-husband and obtained confidential information concerning her prior use of and/or present need for pain medicine. Sonneland then contacted Hoheim, who subsequently filed an affidavit stating that Ms. Berger had requested narcotic pain medicine from Sonneland and that Sonneland had written a prescription for her. These facts are sufficient to establish that Sonneland disclosed confidential information related to health care and obtained within the physician–patient relationship.

Physicians recognize the importance of confidentiality and assume that it is an integral part of their relationships with patients and other treating physicians. All physicians take the Hippocratic Oath that honors the confidentiality of information obtained from a patient. This close confidential relationship is also recognized by the ethical guidelines of the American Medical Association. The American Medical Association has incorporated this duty in its Principles of Medical Ethics. Principle IV provides that a physician shall respect the rights of patients and shall safeguard patient confidences within the constraints of the law.

Physicians cannot administer effective treatment if patients avoid treatment or withhold information based on a fear that their physician might disclose information obtained as part of the treatment process. Likewise, patients enter the physician–patient relationship assuming that information acquired by the physician will be held in confidence and that the physician will not disclose confidential communications or information related to treatment unless the patient consents or disclosure is required by law. Mutual trust and confidence are essential to the physician–patient relationship, and from these elements flow the physician's obligations to fully inform the patient of his or her condition, to continue to provide medical care once the physician–patient relationship has been established, to refer the patient to a specialist if necessary, and to obtain the patient's informed consent to the medical treatment proposed.

Here, the trial court correctly decided that RCW 7.70 supported an action against the physician for the unauthorized disclosure of confidential information.

Society has an interest in protecting the confidential nature of the physician–patient relationship. When a physician discloses confidential information without authority, he or she invades two distinct interests of the patient: (1) the patient's interest in the security of the confidential relationship and his or her corresponding expectation of secrecy; and (2) the patient's specific interest in avoiding whatever injuries will result from circulation of the information. Invasion of the first interest will most likely affect the patient's willingness to disclose confidential information in the future and invasion of the second interest could result in a variety of injuries to the patient. For this reason, the duty of confidentiality is not meant to protect against one specific type of injury to the patient, but instead discourages any injury that might result from a physician's unauthorized disclosure of information. Emotional distress might be one result of an unauthorized disclosure by a physician, but a patient may also suffer a tarnished reputation or damage to a relationship.

A patient seeking damages for a physician's unauthorized disclosure of confidential information related to health care should be entitled to those damages necessary to compensate the patient for the harm caused by the physician's disclosure. To hold otherwise deprives this tort action of the ability to compensate victims. An action alleging a breach of physician–patient confidentiality is analogous to invasion of privacy and plaintiffs are entitled to recover damages, including emotional damages, for the harm caused by the physician's unauthorized disclosure.

The courts have increasingly begun to recognize an action for breach of physician–patient confidentiality as an independent tort.

The appeals court held that a tort action exists under RCW 7.70.030(1) for damages resulting from the unauthorized disclosure of confidential information related to health care and obtained within the physician–patient relationship. One who has established a cause of action for breach of physician–patient confidentiality is entitled to recover damages for (1) the harm to his or her interests in confidentiality resulting from the unauthorized disclosure; (2) his or her mental distress proved to have been suffered if it is of a kind that normally results from such an unauthorized disclosure; and (3) special damage of which the unauthorized disclosure is a legal cause.

Taking the evidence in the light most favorable to Berger, the evidence here is sufficient to raise a question of fact as to whether Berger was injured by Sonneland's unauthorized disclosure of confidential information related to health care and obtained within the physician–patient relationship. For this reason, the judgment of the superior court was reversed and the matter was remanded for further proceedings.

Privileged Communications

The Federal Health Care Quality Improvement Act of 1986[13] insulates certain medical peer review activities affecting medical staff privileges from antitrust liability. Peer review is protected so long as it is taken in the reasonable belief that it is conducted in the furtherance of quality care. In enacting this legislation, Congress recognized that without such antitrust immunity, effective peer review may not be possible.

The burden to establish "privilege" is on the party seeking to shield information from discovery. The party asserting the privilege has the obligation to prove, by competent evidence, that the privilege applies to the information sought.

JOINT COMMISSION ON ACCREDITATION OF HEALTHCARE ORGANIZATIONS ACCREDITATION REPORTS PRIVILEGED FROM DISCOVERY

Citation: *Humana Hosp. Corp. v. Spears-Petersen, 867 S.W.2d 858 (Tex. Ct. App. 1993)*

Facts

The underlying suit in this petition involved a plaintiff, Ms. Garcia, who was scheduled to undergo an epidural steroid injection but instead was administered a lumbar epidural steroid injection by the defendant, Dr. Garg. The plaintiff sued Garg on the basis of negligence, lack of informed consent, battery, and fraud. Garcia also sued Humana Corporation for negligence in credentialing, supervising, and monitoring Garg's clinical privileges. The plaintiff's attorney requested documents from Humana, including reports prepared by the Joint Commission on Accreditation of Healthcare Organizations.

The Joint Commission is a voluntary organization that surveys various health care organizations for the purpose of accreditation. The organization's governing body consists of members representing such organizations as the American Medical Association, the American College of Physicians, and the American Hospital Association.

Humana objected to releasing Joint Commission reports and filed for a protective order preventing disclosure. The Joint Commission reports contained recommendations describing the hospital's noncompliance with certain of its published standards. Humana argued that the Joint Commission reports are privileged information under Texas statute. Under Texas law, the records and proceedings of a medical committee are considered confidential and are not subject to a court subpoena. The plaintiff argued that the Joint Commission is not a medical committee as defined in the Texas statute. The hospital's chief operating officer testified that the Joint Commission surveys and accredits hospitals across the country. The accreditation is voluntary, and the hospital chooses to have the accreditation survey. During the survey, the Joint Commission looks at certain standards it has developed for hospitals to abide by in maintaining quality care. The hospital's executive committee is charged in its bylaws with keeping abreast of the accreditation process. Humana argued that release of the Joint Commission's recommendations would do more than "chill" the effectiveness of such accreditation. The plaintiff argued further that even if the information was privileged, it had already been disclosed to a third party, the hospital, thus waiving its rights to nondisclosure. The trial court denied Humana's motion for a protective order that, if granted, would have permitted it to withhold from discovery any information pertaining to credentialing, monitoring, or supervision practices of the hospital regarding its physicians. Humana appealed.

Issue

Are accreditation reports prepared by the Joint Commission privileged from discovery?

Holding

The Texas Court of Appeals held that the accreditation reports were privileged because: (1) the Joint Commission was a "joint committee" as created by statute creating a privilege from discovery for hospital review committee deliberations, (2) the disclosure of the Joint Commission's report to the hospital did not result in waiver of the privilege, and (3) the reports reflected a deliberative process by the Joint Commission and were therefore privileged.

Reason

The purpose of privileged communications is to encourage open and thorough review of a hospital's medical staff and operations of a hospital with the objective of improving the delivery of patient care. The plaintiff argued that the Joint Commission is not a medical committee as defined in the Texas statute. The court of appeals found that:

the determinative factor is not whether the entity is known as a "committee," or a "commission," or by any other particular term, but whether it is organized for the purposes contemplated by the statute and case law. We think it is clear from the evidence we have detailed that the Joint Commission is a joint committee made up of representatives of various medical organizations and thus fits within the statutory definition. . . . Further, it is organized, as are the various in-house medical committees that indisputably come within the statute, for the laudable purposes of improving patient care. Both the statute and case law recognize that the open, thorough, and uninhibited review that is required for such committees to achieve their purpose can only be realized if the deliberations of the committee remain confidential. *Id.* at 862.

As to the Joint Commission's disclosing its report to the hospital, the only disclosure was to the hospital as the intended beneficiary of the committee's findings. The only disclosure made to the outside world was the accreditation certificate, which merely declares that the hospital has been awarded accreditation by the Joint Commission.

Discussion

1. How might the Joint Commission's new "public disclosure policy" to make available certain information to the public affect the "privilege" of other information surrounding the accreditation process (e.g., interviews, notes, minutes, and reports)?
2. Does privilege from discovery extend to all documents maintained in the normal course of business? Explain.

Self-Evaluation—Privileged Information

In *Estate of Hussain v. Gardner*,[14] discovery was sought regarding the statements given by a physician to the hospital's internal peer review committee regarding the plaintiff's management and treatment of a patient. In this medical malpractice action, the plaintiff alleged that the defendant physician deviated from accepted medical standards in the care and treatment of the plaintiff's decedent during surgical procedures. The New Jersey Superior Court held that the statements given by the defendant were protected.

In *Wylie v. Mills*,[15] the court adopted the privilege used in several federal jurisdictions that prevents disclosure of confidential, critical evaluative, and/or deliberative material whenever the public interest in confidentiality outweighs an individual's need for full discovery. In applying the privilege to information contained in a corporate report on an accident in which an employee was involved, the court held that

self-evaluation privilege protected the report from discovery. In reaching this conclusion, the court stressed the importance of self-critical analysis in recognizing past problems and trying to eliminate future problems. Without such protection, candid expressions of opinion or suggestions as to future policy would not be forthcoming due to a fear that these statements may be used against the employer in a subsequent litigation. The standard used for disclosure of confidential investigative records sets forth the following factors, which should be taken into consideration: (1) the extent to which the information may be available from other sources; (2) the degree of harm that the litigant will suffer from its unavailability; and (3) the possible prejudice in the agency's investigation. The court adopted the holding that the plaintiffs had not made a strong showing of a particularized need that outweighs the public interest in the confidentiality of the quality assessment committee. Because information is available from other sources, the court found that the information sought by the plaintiff was readily discoverable.

Ordinary Business Documents

Privileged communications statutes do not protect from discovery the records maintained in the ordinary course of doing business and rendering inpatient care. Such documents often can be subpoenaed after showing cause.

Attorney–Client Privilege

Attorney–client privilege generally will preclude discovery of memorandums written to an organization's general counsel by the organization's risk management director. In *Mlynarski v. Rush Presbyterian-St. Luke's Medical Center*,[16] a memorandum written by the risk management coordinator to the hospital's general counsel was barred from discovery. There was undisputed evidence that the risk management coordinator had consulted with and assisted counsel in determining the legal action to pursue and the advisability of settling a claim that she had been assigned to investigate. Information contained in the memorandum was available from witnesses whose names and addresses were made available to the plaintiff. If the hospital later at trial decided to attempt to impeach those witnesses based on the coordinator's testimony, privilege would be waived and the hospital would be required to produce the relevant reports.

Peer Review Documents/Confidentiality Exceptions

The identity of peer review committee members and individuals who may have given information to such committees is not always considered privileged. A state, for example, is entitled to access peer review reports relating to a physician suspected of criminal negligence.[17] In a civil action, a hospital may be required to identify all persons who have knowledge of an underlying event that is the basis of a malpractice action, whether or not they were members of a peer review committee.[18]

The surgeon in *Robinson v. Magovern*[19] brought an action under the Sherman Antitrust Act, as well as under state law, seeking recovery because he had been denied hospital privileges. The plaintiff moved in the U.S. District Court for an order compelling the defendants and certain third-party witnesses to respond to discovery requests and deposition questions. The defendants had objected, claiming that the information sought was privileged and that the Pennsylvania Peer Review Protection Act seeks to foster candor and discussion at medical review committee meetings through grants of immunity and confidentiality. The court held that although there was a powerful interest in confidentiality embodied in the Pennsylvania Peer Review Protection Act, the Act would not be applied to shield from discovery events surrounding the denial of staff privileges, including what occurred at meetings of the hospital's credentials committee and executive committee. The need for evidence was greater than the need for confidentiality in this case. The defendants' objections were overruled, and the motion to compel was granted.

The physician in *Ott v. St. Luke Hospital of Campbell County, Inc.*[20] had brought a civil rights suit because his application for medical staff privileges was denied. The physician contended that he was not invited to several peer review committee meetings or given an opportunity to be heard. The hospital filed for a protective order that would bar discovery of the proceedings of the peer review committee. The hospital argued that such committees would become ineffective if their deliberations were discoverable and that the privilege claimed by the hospital is recognized in Section 311.377 of the Kentucky Revised Statutes Annotates (1990). The U.S. District Court held that where there was no real showing that the peer review committee's functions would be impaired substantially, and where the benefit gained for correct disposal of the litigation by denying privilege was overwhelming, the hospital would not be permitted to assert privilege. The hospital's motion was therefore denied. The court reasoned that the efficiency of such committees may be fostered by an atmosphere of openness, and there may be less likelihood of reliance on bias, hearsay, and prejudice. A potential Louis Pasteur (French chemist and microbiologist), Joseph Lister (British surgeon), or Philipp Semmelweis (Hungarian physician) who advocates salutary changes in procedures may be excluded simply because he or she makes waves. The court indicated that it cannot permit the discharge of its responsibility to conduct a search for the truth to be thwarted by rules of privilege in the absence of strong countervailing public policies.

Committee Minutes Not Privileged

The plaintiff, a patient, brought an action against a hospital seeking to recover for injuries he sustained as a result of a nosocomial infection he allegedly contracted at the hospi-

tal.[21] The plaintiff claimed that his infection was due to an act or omission on the part of the hospital in failing to protect him from such infections. During the discovery phase of the proceedings, the plaintiff filed a motion for production of documents seeking studies done by the hospital regarding the percentage of nosocomial infection rates per patients admitted. The hospital objected to this request and the plaintiff obtained an order to compel the hospital to produce the documents. The court of appeal, on review, reversed the trial court's ruling, determining that statutes rendering hospital records confidential barred the information from disclosure.

The Louisiana Supreme Court, however, held that the records sought by the plaintiff were not entirely privileged from disclosure. The reliance of the court of appeal on La. R.S. 13:3715.3(A) and 44:7(D) was partially misplaced. These provisions were intended to provide confidentiality to the records and proceedings of hospital committees, not to insulate from discovery certain facts merely because they have come under the review of any particular committee. Such an interpretation could cause any fact that a hospital chooses to unilaterally characterize as involving information relied on by one of its committees formed to regulate and operate the hospital to be barred from an opposing litigant's discovery regardless of the nature of that information. The plaintiff sought facts relating to nosocomial infection rates in the defendant's hospital. A nosocomial infection is the same malady that gave rise to the plaintiff's injuries. Such facts would be highly relevant to the plaintiff's case or highly likely to lead to such evidence.

When a plaintiff seeks information relevant to his or her case that is not information regarding the action taken by a committee or its exchange of honest self-critical study, but merely factual accountings of otherwise discoverable facts, such information is not protected by any privilege as it does not come within the scope of information entitled to that privilege. This does not mean that the plaintiff is entitled to the entire study, as such study may contain evidence of policy making, remedial action, proposed courses of conduct, and self-critical analysis that the privilege seeks to protect in order to foster the ability of hospitals to regulate themselves unhindered by outside scrutiny and unconcerned about the possible liability ramifications their discussions might bring about. As such, the trial court must make an *in camera* inspection of such records and determine to what extent they may be discoverable.

Staff Privileging Documents Discoverable— Illinois

In *May v. Wood River Township Hospital*,[22] the patient's guardian sued the hospital and physicians, alleging that the hospital was negligent in providing care to the patient and in granting staff privileges to Dr. Marrese. The circuit court granted the guardian's motion to compel, ordering the hospital to answer certain interrogatories, and the hospital appealed.

The hospital submitted a memorandum of law and an affidavit of the current president in support of its opposition to the interrogatories and in support of its motion. Attached to the affidavit were copies of the hospital's bylaws in force at that time. The affidavit stated that all documents concerning the granting of associate staff privileges to Marrese were "being kept in the course of internal quality control,"[23] and that the granting and reviewing of staff privileges at the hospital is done to maintain and improve the quality of patient care. The trial court denied the hospital's motion for a protective order and granted the plaintiff's motion to compel, ordering the hospital to answer all of the plaintiff's interrogatories "regarding any material or information generated by anyone on the hospital's executive committee or from any other source so long as it was information generated or made before the date when Marrese was granted Associate Staff privileges."[24]

The trial court ruled that nothing related to work done, communications between executive committee members during their meetings, or discussions related to Marrese is protected by the Code of Civil Procedure, nor are the minutes of the committee protected so long as this information existed or was created before the actual decision to grant privileges to Marrese. The court further stated that no privilege exists under the Code as to a review of a physician's qualification for medical staff privileges before said physician is actually on the hospital's staff.

The plaintiff argued that peer review was not involved in the instant case because the materials sought in discovery concerned actions taken by the executive committee prior to the time Marrese was granted staff privileges. The hospital urged on appeal, however, that no Illinois case has interpreted the Code as being inapplicable to the credentialing process.

Was the information held by the hospital generated prior to Marrese's application for hospital privileges, along with his application for privileges, outside the scope of the Code of Civil Procedure and privileged from discovery?

The Illinois Appellate Court held that the Code of Civil Procedure did not protect information generated prior to the physician's application for staff privileges or his application for the privileges. The information generated prior to Marrese's application for privileges, as well as his application for privileges, is outside the scope of the Code of Civil Procedure and not privileged. The same is true of a whole host of materials that might be considered by the committee, for example:

- The fact that staff privileges were granted, denied, or revoked at other hospitals.
- The fact that licenses to practice medicine were awarded, denied, suspended, or revoked in a given state.
- The fact that an applicant has been sued or has never been sued for malpractice.

These matters are facts that would exist independent of a peer review process. These facts cannot be privileged simply because a committee devoted to quality control or peer review considered them. That which is nonprivileged cannot be converted to being privileged simply by handing the facts to a committee.

On the other hand, if the committee sought to generate new opinions or information for consideration by the committee, a privilege could attach. For example, if the committee interviewed a colleague of Marrese's to elicit an opinion on Marrese's ability as a physician, that opinion could be privileged. If, however, the same opinion had been stated earlier in a deposition in a malpractice case and the committee reviewed the deposition, no privilege could attach to conceal the deposition from the discovery process, nor should the fact that it was considered be immune from discovery.

Staff Privileging Documents Not Discoverable—South Carolina

The underlying action in *McGee v. Bruce Hospital System*[25] involved a medical malpractice wrongful death claim. This matter was before the court pursuant to a circuit court order granting the plaintiffs a motion to compel and instructing the defendant, Bruce Hospital System, to produce the credentialing files and clinical privileges for each of the defendant physicians. The defendant physicians contended that such documentation is protected by the confidentiality statute, S.C. CODE ANN. § 40–71–20 (Supp. 1992), which provides that:

> all proceedings of and all data and information acquired by the committee referred to in § 40–71–10 in the exercise of its duties are confidential. . . . These proceedings and documents are not subject to discovery, subpoena, or introduction into evidence in any civil action except upon appeal from the committee action. *Information, documents, or records which are otherwise available from original sources are not immune from discovery or use in a civil action merely because they were presented during the committee proceedings . . .* nor shall any complainant or witness before the committee be prevented from testifying in a civil action as to matters of which he has knowledge apart from the committee proceedings or revealing such matters to third persons.[26]

The trial judge found that the materials sought were discoverable. The South Carolina Supreme Court held that: (1) applications for staff privileges and supporting documents of appropriate training were protected by the confidentiality statute, (2) the confidentiality statute did not preclude discovery of general policies and procedures for staff monitoring, and (3) the patient could discover a listing of clinical privileges either granted or denied by the hospital. The overriding public policy of the confidentiality statute is to encourage health care professionals to monitor the competency and professional conduct of their peers in order to safeguard and improve the quality of patient care. The underlying purpose behind the confidentiality statute is not to facilitate the prosecution of civil actions, but to promote complete candor and open discussion among participants in the peer review process. As stated in *Cruger v. Lone:*[27]

> [t]he policy of encouraging full candor in peer review proceedings is advanced only if all documents considered by the committee . . . during the peer review or credentialing process are protected. Committee members and those providing information to the committee must be able to operate without fear of reprisal. Similarly, it is essential that doctors seeking hospital privileges disclose all pertinent information to the committee. Physicians who fear that information provided in an application might someday be used against them by a third party will be reluctant to fully detail matters that the committee should consider.[28]

The court found that the public interest in candid professional peer review proceedings should prevail over a litigant's need for information from the most convenient source. The confidentiality statute does, however, provide that documents otherwise available from the original source do not become privileged merely because they are presented to a medical staff committee.

Section 40–71–20 of the South Carolina statute does not preclude the discovery of the general policies and procedures for staff monitoring. The information contained in the written rules, regulations, policies, and procedures for the medical staff would not compromise the statutory goal of candid evaluation of peers in the medical profession.

The court found that the outcome of the decision-making process is not protected. Permitting discovery of the effect of the committee proceedings does not inhibit open discussion. In the court's view, the confidentiality statute was intended to protect the review process, not to restrict the disclosure of the result of the process. Accordingly, the plaintiffs were entitled to a listing of clinical privileges either granted or denied by the hospital.

Ownership and Release of Medical Records

Medical records are the property of the organization and are maintained for the benefit of the patient. Ownership resides with the organization or professional rendering treatment. Although medical records generally have been protected from public scrutiny by a general practice of nondisclosure, this practice has been waived under a limited number of specifically controlled situations.

Several jurisdictions recognize the principle that an individual has a right to privacy and to be protected from the mass dissemination of information pertaining to his or her personal or private affairs. The right of privacy generally includes the right to be kept out of the public spotlight.

Requests by Patients

Health care professionals and health care organizations, as a rule, have not released medical records to patients. The courts, however, have taken the view that patients have a legally enforceable interest in the information contained in their medical records and, therefore, have a right to access their records.

Some states have enacted legislation permitting patients access to their records. Patients may generally have access to review and/or obtain copies of their records, X-rays, and laboratory and diagnostic tests. Access to information includes that maintained or possessed by a health care organization and/or a health care practitioner who has treated or is treating a patient. Organizations and physicians can withhold records if it is determined that the information could reasonably be expected to cause substantial and identifiable harm to the patient (e.g. patients in psychiatric hospitals, institutions for the mentally disabled, or alcohol- and drug-treatment programs).

Failure to release a patient's record can lead to a legal action. The patient in *Pierce v. Penman*[29] brought a lawsuit seeking damages for severe emotional distress when physicians repeatedly refused to turn over her medical records. The defendants had rendered different professional services to the plaintiff for approximately 11 years. The patient moved and found a new physician, Dr. Hochman. She signed a release authorizing Hochman to obtain her records from the defendant physicians. Hochman wrote a letter for her records but never received a response. The defendants claimed that they never received the request. The patient changed physicians again and continued in her efforts to obtain a copy of the records. Eventually the defendants' offices were burglarized, and the plaintiff's records were allegedly taken. The detective in charge of investigating the burglary stated that he never was notified that any records were taken. The court of common pleas awarded the patient $2,500 in compensatory damages and $10,000 in punitive damages. On appeal, the superior court upheld the award. The physicians' contention that they relied on the advice of legal counsel did not insulate them from liability for punitive damages.

Requests by Third Parties

The medical record is a peculiar type of property because there is a wide variety of third-party interest in the information contained in medical records. Health care organizations may not generally disclose information without patient consent. Policies regarding the release of information to third parties should be formulated to address the rights of patients, insurance carriers processing claims, physicians, medical researchers and educators, governmental agencies, etc.

Psychiatric Records

The psychotherapist-patient privilege that exists under the Federal Rules of Evidence can be overcome if the evidentiary need for a psychiatric history outweighs a privacy interest. This was the case in *United States v. Diamond*,[30] in which the privacy interests regarding the psychiatric history of the person, who initiated a criminal investigation against another individual, were outweighed by the interests of the accused. Because the credibility of the witness was the central issue at trial, his psychiatric history was relevant.

Criminal Investigations

There are several exceptions to the restriction on disclosing information obtained in a confidential relationship. For example, disclosure may be required when a patient is the victim of a crime. The hospital in *In re Brink*[31] sought to quash a grand jury request for the medical records pertaining to the blood tests administered to a person under investigation. The court of common pleas held that the physician-patient privilege did not extend to medical records subpoenaed pursuant to a grand jury investigation. A proceeding before a grand jury is considered secret in nature; therefore, a patient's interests in preserving the confidentiality of his or her records are protected.

Patient records are generally obtainable during investigation into alleged criminal actions such as Medicaid fraud. The grand jury in *People v. Ekong*[32] was permitted to obtain certain patient files and records that were in the possession of the physician who was under investigation for Medicaid fraud. The physician had contended that he could not release the files because of physician-patient privilege.

Drug and Alcohol Abuse Records

The federal Drug Abuse and Treatment Act of 1972[33] and the federal regulations promulgated thereunder provide that patient records relating to drug and alcohol abuse treatment must be held confidential and not disclosed except as provided in these laws. Unlike other medical records, drug- and alcohol-abuse records cannot be released until the court has determined whether a claimed need for the records outweighs the potential injury to the patient, to the patient–physician relationship, and to the treatment services being rendered. Because of these strict requirements, the courts have been reluctant to order the release of these records unless absolutely necessary.

Privacy Act of 1974

The Privacy Act of 1974, codified at 5 U.S.C. 552, was enacted to safeguard individual privacy from the misuse of federal records, to give individuals access to records concerning themselves that are maintained by federal agencies, and to establish a Privacy Protection Safety Commission. Section 2 of the Privacy Act reads as follows:

> The Congress finds that (1) the privacy of an individual is directly affected by the collection, maintenance, use, and dissemination of personal information by Federal agencies; (2) the increasing use of computers and sophisticated information technology, while essential to the efficient operations of the Government, has greatly magnified the harm to individual privacy that can occur from any collection, maintenance, use, or dissemination of personal information; (3) the opportunities for an individual to secure employment, insurance, and credit, and his right to due process, and other legal protections are endangered by the misuse of certain information systems; (4) the right to privacy is a personal and fundamental right protected by the Constitution of the United States; and (5) in order to protect the privacy of individuals identified in information systems maintained by Federal agencies, it is necessary and proper for the Congress to regulate the collection, maintenance, use, and dissemination of information by such agencies. [b] The purpose of this Act is to provide certain safeguards for an individual against an invasion of personal privacy by requiring Federal agencies, except as otherwise provided by law, to (1) permit an individual to determine what records pertaining to him are collected, maintained, used, or disseminated by such agencies; (2) permit an individual to prevent records pertaining to him obtained by such agencies for a particular purpose from being used or made available for another purpose without his consent; (3) permit an individual to gain access to information pertaining to him in Federal agency records, to have a copy made of all or any portion thereof, and to correct or amend such records; (4) collect, maintain, use, or disseminate any record of identifiable personal information in a manner that assures that such action is for a necessary and lawful purpose, that the information is current and accurate for its intended use, and that adequate safeguards are provided to prevent misuse of such information. . . .

Computerized Medical Records

Computers have invaded the health care industry. They are found in the admitting office, the business office, and even the operating room. They are in the laboratory, pharmacy, X-ray, and medical records departments. They are fast and accurate and have an almost endless capacity to store data.

The medical record is no longer comprised of handwritten entries, but rather includes fetal monitoring strips, electrocardiogram (ECG) strips, electroencephalogram (EEG) strips, and electronic output from the laboratory, pharmacy, and radiology services, etc.

Clinical Applications

At Brigham and Women's Hospital in Boston, "more than 85,000 orders a week are being written in general medicine, surgery, and orthopaedics. Laboratory and pharmacy results, pulmonary function, EEG, and 50 other results-generating areas are based around the system. A very strong aspect of the order-entry capability is its use of medical logic and medical-expertise technology. Eighty-three times on an average day, the system flags cases where there have been duplicate physician orders, which results in the physician canceling that order. Three times a day, on average, the system signals a patient-allergy alert, resulting in an order cancellation."[34]

Advantages

The age of the computer has arrived. They have become an economic necessity and are assisting health care providers in improving the quality of health care. Computers

- Retrieve demographic information and consultants' reports, as well as laboratory, radiology, and other test results.
- Improve productivity and quality.
- Have economic benefits in reducing costs.
- Support clinical research.
- Play an ever-increasing role in the education process.
- Can be interactive, allowing for computer-assisted diagnosis.
- Allow for computer-generated prescriptions (integrated computer systems and clinical pharmacy services are associated with reducing the incidence of medication errors).
- Can generate reminders for follow-up testing.
- Can assist in the decision-making process.
- Are helpful when standardizing treatment protocols.
- Are capable of assisting in the identification of drug-drug and food-drug interactions.
- Are used in telecommunications around the world on a real-time basis transporting picture graphics (e.g., computed tomography scans) between nations.

Disadvantages

Although computers are an economic necessity, they are not perfect. Problems associated with computerization include the loss of confidentiality and the unauthorized disclosure of information, thus requiring the development of sophisticated security systems, equipment reliability, and questions relating to the accuracy and reliability of data input by computer operators.

Another potential shortcoming of computerized medical records is the lack of system responsiveness. A system must respond quickly to any request for information. Although most forms of human-computer communication have had a history of responding too slowly for effectiveness and patient safety, computer hardware is now only limited by our ability to use it effectively.

System Design

Health care organizations undergoing computerization must determine user needs, design an effective system, select appropriate hardware and software, develop user training programs, develop a disaster recovery plan (e.g., provide for emergency power systems and backup files), provide for data security, etc. Experienced computer consulting firms can save health care organizations thousands of dollars with their expertise. Computers are not difficult to understand, but minor mistakes can cost major dollars and be health and life threatening.

Legal Issues

As computers become more widely used in the health care industry, the potential for computer-related liability will increase. Computer-generated output is often entered as evidence in malpractice suits.

As to confidentiality, protecting a patient's medical information is an ongoing challenge. Although there are a variety of federal laws that protect credit information, there are few laws protecting the computerized medical record. In *Whalen v. Roe*,[35] the applicant, the New York Commissioner of Health, had been enjoined by a three-judge court from enforcing certain provisions of the New York State Public Health Law that required the name and address of each patient receiving a schedule II controlled substance to be reported to the applicant. Schedule II drugs are those considered to have a high potential for abuse but also have an accepted medical use. Under the law, a physician prescribing a schedule II drug does so on a special serially numbered prescription form, one copy of which goes to the New York Commissioner of Health, who transfers the data, including the name and address of the user, from the prescription form to a centralized computer file. The respondent claimed that mandatory disclosure of the name of a patient receiving schedule II drugs violated the patient's right of privacy and interfered with the physician's right to prescribe treatment for his patient solely on the basis of medical considerations. The court held that the patient identification requirement had been the product of an orderly and rational legislative decision about the state's broad police powers. The statute does not impair any private interest on its face and does not impair the right of physicians to practice medicine free from unwarranted state interference.

Cybercrime

The rapid growth of the Internet has led to an explosion of high-technology crime and related illegal activities. Increases in cybercrime have led to a need for high-end technology products and services to combat these problems. U.S. companies are currently spending more than $13 billion annually to protect their networks and critical infrastructures from cyber-based threats.

To address the growing market for products and services, and the need to train professionals in high-tech security, Anne Arundel Community College and the Windermere Group, an Annapolis, Md.–based information technology company specializing in information security and white collar crime detection and prevention, have established a partnership to create *The Maryland Cybercrime Center of Excellence.* The mission of the center is to provide specialized training encompassing the technological and legal aspects of this problem, which places individuals, corporations, health care facilities, and other institutions at risk. The offerings of the center will be available both nationally and internationally.

 RELEASE OF CONFIDENTIAL INFORMATION

Citation: *Proenza Sanfiel v. Department of Health, 749 So.2d 525 (Fla. App. 1999)*

Facts

Sanfiel, a psychiatric nurse, had his professional license suspended for five years after he intentionally disclosed confidential patient information to the news media. Sanfiel testified that he knew the information he possessed was confidential patient information, and that he understood the danger in disclosing psychiatric records to unauthorized persons. He also knew that a nurse could be disciplined for disclosing such information, yet he intentionally released information to the news media.

Sanfiel appealed a final order issued by the State Board of Nursing following disciplinary proceedings. The order suspended Sanfiel's psychiatric nursing license and placed him on probation for five years for disclosing confidential patient information.

Issue

Was the State Board of Nursing authorized to suspend Sanfiel's license because of his conduct involving patients not under his care?

Holding

Sanfiel's professional license was properly suspended for a five-year period after he intentionally disclosed confidential patient information to the news media.

Reason

Sanfiel obtained a computer, which was previously owned by Charter Behavioral Health System, a psychiatric hospital in Orlando. Charter's patient records were contained in the computer. Sanfiel testified that he reviewed this information and recalled that Charter was being investigated for defrauding the government. He contacted local law enforcement and the state attorney's office to initiate a criminal investigation. The agencies declined, telling him that the matter was outside their jurisdictions. Sanfiel then called the news media and allowed them to see the information concerning the patients. He asked that the patients' names be blurred to protect their identity. He believed that the information on the computer should have been erased before the computer was donated as surplus. He told reporters that the hard drive contained the names of psychiatric patients, their admission dates, types of addiction, treatments, and psychiatric disorders. The story was broadcast along with the patients' names and diagnoses shown on the computer screen. One of the journalists located and interviewed a patient identified from Sanfiel's computer. The patient was distressed over the fact that his confidential medical information was being exposed to the public. An unknown number of other patients also were contacted by the news media.

The state Agency for Health Care Administration ("AHCA") immediately began investigating and ordered an emergency suspension of Sanfiel's nursing license. When the representative for AHCA asked for the hard drive with the patients' confidential information, Sanfiel refused to surrender it. When representatives from Charter asked that the computer be returned, Sanfiel again refused, but suggested he would be willing to return the computer and the information for $20,000. Charter obtained an injunction prohibiting Sanfiel from disclosing confidential patient information.

Sanfiel does not dispute that he made the disclosure or that as a psychiatric nurse he knew that the information on the computer was confidential. He admitted that he was aware that a nurse could be disciplined for disclosing confidential psychiatric information to unauthorized persons. However, he argues that he could not be punished because he was acting in a private capacity and not as a nurse to the patients whose records were contained on the computer.

The Board's authority to discipline Sanfiel is derived from Chapters 455 and 464, Florida Statutes. Chapter 455 contains general provisions for the regulation of all professions, while Chapter 464 specifically addresses nursing. Sanfiel may not have been practicing nursing in January 1997, but he was licensed and his license was active and evidently in good standing.

Under section 464.108(1)(l), Florida Statutes (1997), Sanfiel could be disciplined for "[k]nowingly violating any provision of this chapter, a rule of the board or the department, or a lawful order of the board . . . or failing to comply with a lawfully issued subpoena of the department." The Board determined that Sanfiel violated Florida Administrative Code "by violating the confidentiality of information or knowledge concerning a patient." An agency's interpretation of a statute or rule that it has authority to administer should receive deference from a reviewing court and should not be overturned unless it is clearly erroneous. So long as the agency's interpretation "is within the range of possible and reasonable," it should be affirmed.

Rule 59S-8.005 states in part that unprofessional conduct includes violating the confidentiality of information or knowledge concerning a patient. The Board reasonably interpreted this provision to apply to the circumstances present in this case. Sanfiel testified that he knew the information he possessed was confidential patient information, and that he understood the danger in disclosing psychiatric records to unauthorized persons. He knew that a nurse could be disciplined for disclosing such information, yet he intentionally released the information to the news media. It is reasonable to characterize Sanfiel's actions as unprofessional conduct even though Sanfiel was acting in a "private" capacity. Therefore, the Board's determination was not disturbed.

Discussion

1. Do you agree with the court's findings?

2. Do Charter patients have any recourse for the unauthorized release of their medical information?

3. What steps should Charter take to prevent similar occurrences in the future?

Retention of Records

The length of time medical records must be retained varies from state to state. The organization, with the advice of an attorney, should determine how long records should be maintained, taking into account patient needs, statutory requirements, future need for such records, and the legal considerations of having the records available in the event of a lawsuit.

A California court revoked the license of a nursing facility for failure to keep adequate records (along with other violations of the law). In *Yankee v. State Department of Health*,[36] the facility claimed that the word "adequate" was unclear and therefore the requirement was invalid. The court stated that the word "adequate" is not so uncertain as to render a penal statute invalid.

Retention of X-rays

Mr. Rodgers, in *Rodgers v. St. Mary's Hosp. of Decatur*,[37] filed a medical malpractice action alleging the wrongful death of his wife, who died at the hospital two days after giving birth to their son. Named as defendants in the medical malpractice action were Mrs. Rodgers' obstetricians, her radiologists, and the hospital.

Rodgers filed a complaint for damages against the hospital alleging that the hospital breached its statutory duty to preserve for five years all of the X-rays taken of his wife. He claimed that the X-rays were crucial to proving his case against the obstetricians and radiologists. On motion of the hospital, the circuit court dismissed the complaint. Rodgers amended his complaint and brought a medical malpractice action against the hospital, a day after he reached an $800,000 settlement with the obstetricians. In his complaint, Rodgers alleged that his wife's death was caused by a condition that appeared on an X-ray that the hospital had a duty to preserve. He alleged that the hospital's failure to preserve the X-ray was a breach of its duty arising from the X-Ray Retention Act and from the hospital's internal regulations. Rodgers asserted that because the hospital failed to preserve the X-ray, he was unable to prove his case against the radiologists. The circuit court entered judgment in favor of the hospital, and Rodgers appealed.

The Illinois Supreme Court held that a private cause of action existed under the X-Ray Retention Act, and that Rodgers stated a claim under the Act.

The X-Ray Retention Act provides that "Hospitals which produce photographs of the human anatomy by the X-ray or roentgen process on the request of licensed physicians for use by them in the diagnosis or treatment of a patient's illness or condition shall retain such photographs or films as part of their regularly maintained records for a period of 5 years."

The hospital argued that the statute is merely an administrative regulation to be enforced exclusively by the Public Health Department. The court disagreed. Nothing in the statute suggested that the legislature intended to limit the available remedies to administrative ones.

The hospital also argued that the loss of one X-ray out of a series of six should not be considered a violation of the statute. The court disagreed, finding that the statute requires that all X-rays be preserved, not just some of them. The court concluded that Rodgers had stated a cause of action against the hospital for failure to preserve the X-ray for use in litigation. Whether the missing X-ray proximately caused Rodgers to lose his case against the radiologists and to settle for less than the full amount of the judgment is a question for the trier of fact.

Medical Record Battleground

The medical record must not be used as a battleground against another professional or the health care organization. The medical record is a document that cannot be erased once a recording has been made. It should not be used as an instrument for registering a complaint against another health care professional or the organization. Those individuals who use a patient's medical record unwisely may have vented their emotions for the moment but at the same time may have provided the basis for having to justify their actions to another professional, to the organization, or to a jury. It should be remembered that comments written during a time of anger may have been based on inaccurate information, which, in turn, could be damaging to one's credibility and future statements.

Falsification of Records

The intentional alteration, falsification, or destruction of medical records, to avoid liability for one's medical negligence, is generally sufficient to show actual malice, and punitive damages may be awarded whether or not the act of altering, falsifying, or destroying records directly causes compensable harm. The evidence in *Dimora v. Cleveland Clinic Foundation*[38] had showed that the patient had fallen

and broken five or six ribs; yet, upon examination, the physician noted in the progress notes that the patient was smiling and laughing pleasantly, exhibiting no pain upon deep palpation of the area. Other testimony indicated that she was in pain and crying. This discrepancy between the written progress notes and the testimony of the witnesses who observed the patient was sufficient to raise a question of fact as to the possible falsification of documents by the physician to minimize the nature of the incident and the injury of the patient due to the possible negligence of the hospital personnel. The testimony of the witnesses, if believed, would have been sufficient to show that the physician falsified the record or intentionally reported the incident inaccurately in order to avoid liability for the negligent care of the patient.

Falsification of medical and/or business records is grounds for criminal indictment, as well as for civil liability. In *People v. Smithtown General Hospital*,[39] a motion to dismiss indictments against a physician and a nurse charged with falsifying business records in the first degree was denied. In each indictment, it was charged that the defendant was in violation of a duty imposed on him or her by law or by the nature of his or her position. The surgeon was charged because he omitted to make a true entry in his operative report; the nurse was charged because she failed to make a true entry in the operating room log.

Employees at a rest home attempted to cover up the death of an elderly woman who had wandered away from the rest home and was found frozen to death in a drainage ditch.[40] The deceased patient had been brought back into the home. She was dressed in a nightgown and placed in her bed. On the basis of the account given by the employees, a physician signed a death certificate stating that the 77-year-old patient had died in her sleep. An anonymous tip to the county examiner's office prompted an autopsy. The patient was found to have frozen to death.

Tampering with Medical Record Entries

Tampering with records sends the wrong signal to jurors and can shatter one's credibility. Altered records can create a presumption of negligence. The court in *Matter of Jascalevich*[41] held "We are persuaded that a physician's duty to a patient cannot but encompass his affirmative obligation to maintain the integrity, accuracy, truth and reliability of the patient's medical record. His obligation in this regard is no less compelling than his duties respecting diagnosis and treatment of the patient since the medical community must, of necessity, be able to rely on those records in the continuing and future care of that patient. Obviously, the rendering of that care is prejudiced by anything in those records which is false, misleading or inaccurate. We hold, therefore, that a deliberate falsification by a physician of his patient's medical record, particularly when the reason therefor is to protect his own interests at the expense of his patient's, must be regarded as gross malpractice endangering the health or life of his patient."[42]

The State Board of Medical Examiners in a disciplinary hearing in *State Board of Medical Examiners v. McCroskey*[43] issued a letter of admonition to Dr. McCroskey based upon a series of incidents arising out of the care of patient's stab wound. Although the patient's condition was initially thought to be stable, he bled to death several hours after his admission to the hospital. McCroskey was the attending surgeon on the date of the incident and, therefore, responsible for the accurate completion of the patient's medical record. McCroskey declined to accept the letter of admonition and a formal disciplinary hearing was held.

McCroskey had erased and wrote over a preoperative note made by another physician concerning the patient's estimated blood loss. Specifically, the original record entry was completed by a surgical resident on the date of the patient's death and stated that the patient's blood loss just prior to surgery was "now greater than 3000 cc." Sometime after the autopsy, McCroskey changed the record to read that the patient's blood loss was "now greater than 2000 cc."[44] After listening to conflicting expert testimony, the Administrative Law Judge (ALJ) concluded that the physician had not violated generally accepted standards of medical practice by adding the note to the patient's medical record days or weeks after the patient's death and then backdating the note to the date of the death.

On review of the ALJ's decision, the Board accepted the ALJ's evidentiary finding that many physicians date a medical record entry to reflect the date of the medical event, rather than the date on which the entry was made. The Board disagreed, however, with the ALJ's conclusion that this fact brought McCroskey's conduct within generally accepted standards of medical practice. Instead, the Board determined that backdating a medical record entry falls below accepted standards of documentation. Having thus found two acts that fell below generally accepted standards of medical practice, the Board concluded that McCroskey committed unprofessional conduct under section 12–36–117(1)(p), and issued a letter of admonition. On appeal, the court of appeals held that the board erroneously rejected the ALJ's findings.

On further appeal by the board, the Colorado Supreme Court held that the findings of the Board were supported by substantial evidence. The backdating of a minor or trivial item may not warrant discipline, whereas backdating another entry on a patient's chart may be a more serious matter. Because of the expertise of the Board, it was in a position to determine the seriousness of the physician's conduct by placing the events in their proper factual context.

> All three of the inquiry panel's witnesses testified that the generally accepted standard of practice requires that a medical record entry be dated

with the date it is made. Even one of McCroskey's witnesses acknowledged that misdating the medical record was "certainly something that should not have been done." McCroskey did not simply backdate a trivial note in a patient's medical record. Instead McCroskey's actions took place in the context of a patient's death, which resulted in a corner's autopsy, peer review activities, publicity, and several legal actions. McCroskey was the attending physician responsible for the accuracy of the patient's medical record, and yet he engaged in conduct that cast doubt upon the medical record's integrity. Under these circumstances, the Board was justified in considering McCroskey's conduct to violate the standard of care.[45]

Rewriting and Replacing Notes

The temptation is always present to clarify and explain one's activities in the care of a patient. In a well-publicized case that involved the death of a child, the nurse had replaced her original notes with a second set of notes that were much more detailed and indicated that she had seen the patient more frequently than was reported in her original notes.[46] Rewriting one's notes in a patient's medical record always leaves a bad taste in a juror's mouth. It is more believable to explain why you did not chart all activities than it is why you rewrote and replaced your original notes.

Illegible Entries/Penmanship

Illegible handwriting is as ancient as the first stylus. Unfortunately, poor penmanship can cause injury to patients. The American Medical Association is urging physicians to print, type, or computerize prescriptions. Prescription errors because of poor handwriting can lead to extended length of stays and in some cases the death of patients. A Harvard study found that "penmanship was among the causes of 220 prescription errors out of 30,000 cases."[47] Although errors may occur in less than 1 percent of cases, even one is too many.

FALSIFYING RECORDS

Citation: *Moskovitz v. Mount Sinai Med. Ctr.*, 635 N.E.2d 331 (Ohio 1994)

Facts

In 1978, the patient, Mrs. Moskovitz, was treated by Dr. Gabelman for a tumor on her left leg. The tumor was removed and found to be benign. In 1984, Gabelman completely and successfully removed a second mass. In 1985, the patient was referred to Dr. Figgie, an orthopaedic surgeon, for treatment of a degenerative arthritic condition in her knees. In October 1985, Figgie performed surgery. The patient underwent additional knee surgery performed by Figgie in May 1986.

On October 2, 1986, Moskovitz visited Figgie's office, complaining of a lump on her leg. Figgie did not recommend a biopsy of the lesion. Figgie had been aware that tumors had been removed from the patient's left leg in 1978 and 1984.

On November 3, Moskovitz was admitted to University Hospitals for a right knee revision. Prior to surgery, she was examined by Mr. Magas, a registered nurse. Magas' written report of the examination, signed by Figgie, noted the existence of a firm nodule measuring one centimeter by one centimeter on Moskovitz's left Achilles tendon. Figgie performed the right knee revision on November 5. Following surgery, Moskovitz was examined by Dr. Balourdas, a resident physician at University Hospitals. A discharge summary prepared by Balourdas (and signed by Figgie) noted the existence of a "left Achilles tendon mass, [1] x 1 cm. nodule." The report indicated that the mass had been present for some time.

On November 10, 1987, Figgie removed the mass. On November 13, the tumor was found to be an epithelioid sarcoma, a rare form of malignant soft-tissue cancer. A bone scan revealed that the cancer had metastasized to Moskovitz's shoulder and right femur.

Following the diagnosis of cancer, Moskovitz's care was transferred to Figgie's partner at University Orthopaedic, Dr. Makley, an orthopaedic surgeon specializing in oncology. Makley received Figgie's original office chart, which contained seven pages of notes documenting Moskovitz's course of treatment from 1985 through November 1987. Makley thereafter referred Moskovitz to radiation therapy at University Hospitals. Apparently, in November 1987, without Figgie's knowledge, Makley sent a copy of page seven of Figgie's office notes to the radiation department at University Hospitals.

In December 1987, Figgie, or someone on his behalf, requested that Makley return Figgie's office chart pertaining to the care of Moskovitz. In December 1987, Makley was the primary treating physician and Dr. Figgie was no longer directly involved in the patient's care.

Makley's secretary forwarded the chart to Figgie's office. Figgie's secretary then sent a copy of the chart to Dr. Ashenberg, Moskovitz's psychologist. The copy was received by Ashenberg sometime between December 14 and 18, 1987.

In January 1988, Makley's secretary requested that Figgie's office return the chart to Makley. At this time, it was discovered that the original chart had mysteriously vanished. On October 21, 1988, Moskovitz filed a complaint for discovery seeking to ascertain information relative to a potential claim for medical malpractice. Moskovitz died on December 5, 1988, as a result of the cancer. Prior to her death, her testimony was preserved by way of videotaped deposition.

Makley, in his January 30, 1989, deposition, produced a copy of page seven of Figgie's office chart. That copy was identical to the copy ultimately recovered by the plaintiff's counsel from the radiation department records at University Hospitals. The copy produced by Makley contained a typewritten entry dated September 21, 1987, which states: "Mrs. Moskovitz comes in today for her evaluation on the radiographs reviewed with Dr. York. He was not impressed that this [the mass on Moskovitz's left leg] was anything other than a benign problem, perhaps a fibroma. We [Figgie and York] will therefore elect to continue to observe." However, the photostatic copy revealed that a line had been drawn through the sentence "We will therefore elect to continue to observe." The copy further revealed that beneath the entry Figgie had interlineated a handwritten notation: "As she does not want excisional Bx [biopsy] we will observe." The September 21, 1987, entry was followed by a typewritten entry dated September 24, 1987, which states: "I [Figgie] reviewed the X-rays with Dr. York. I discussed the clinical findings with him. We [Figgie and York] felt this to be benign, most likely a fibroma. He [York] said that we could observe and I concur." At some point, Figgie had also added to the September 24, 1987, entry a handwritten notation, "see above," referring to the September 21, 1987, handwritten notation that Moskovitz did not want an excisional biopsy. *Id.* at 336.

Figgie, at his deposition on March 2, 1989, produced records, including a copy of page seven of his office chart. As his original chart had been lost in December 1987 or January 1988, Figgie had this copy made from the copy of the chart that had been sent to Ashenberg in December 1987. The September 21, 1987, entry in the records produced by Figgie did not contain the statement "We will therefore elect to continue to observe." Apparently, that sentence had been deleted (whited out) on the original office chart from which Ashenberg's copy (and, in turn, Figgie's copy) had been made, in a way that left no indication on the copy that the sentence had been removed from the original records.

During his deposition, Figgie maintained that he did not discover the mass on the left Achilles tendon until February 23, 1987, and that Moskovitz had continually refused a workup or biopsy.

During discovery, another copy of page seven of Figgie's office chart, identical to the copy produced by Makley during his deposition, was recovered from the radiation department records at University Hospitals. This copy had been received by the radiation department in November 1987, when Moskovitz was referred to radiation therapy by Makley. It became apparent that the final sentence in the September 21, 1987, entry had been deleted from Figgie's original office chart sometime between November 1987, when the radiation department obtained a copy of the record, and mid-December 1987, when Ashenberg received a copy of the record from Figgie's office. Presumably, that alteration occurred in December 1987 while the original chart was in the possession of Figgie.

Eventually, Figgie's entire office chart was reconstructed from copies obtained through discovery. The reconstructed chart contains no indication that a workup or biopsy was recommended by Figgie and refused by Moskovitz at any time prior to August 10, 1987.

In her videotaped deposition, Moskovitz claimed that she never refused to have the tumor biopsied. The panel found in favor of all the defendants participating in that proceeding with the exception of Figgie. The panel made the following findings regarding Figgie:

> 3. The evidence supported a finding that plaintiffs' [sic] decedent had a very good chance of long-term survival if the tumor was found to be malignant at a time when it was less than one centimeter in size. The evidence supported the fact that the tumor had not grown in size as of May 7, 1987. If Dr. Figgie had performed a biopsy prior to this date, the cancer would not have metastasized and the decedent would have recovered.

> 4. Dr. Figgie's office chart, which is the primary reference material in analyzing a physician's conduct, is filled with contradictions and inconsistencies.

> 5. Even if Dr. Figgie was first informed of the growth on February 23, 1987, he still fell below acceptable standards of care because he did not conduct further investigation till [sic] X-rays performed in September 1987. All handwritten entries which appear on or prior to September 24, 1987, indicating that a biopsy was recommended or that the decedent refused further work-up were subsequent changes of the records done to justify Figgie's conduct. The sentence "We will therefore elect to continue to observe" on the September 21, 1987 entry was whited out and the handwritten entry "as she does not want excisional biopsy we will observe" was a subsequent alteration of the records. *Id.* at 338.

The jury believed the decedent had a very good chance of long-term survival if the tumor was found to be malignant before it exceeded one centimeter in size. The trial court entered judgment in accordance with the jury's verdict.

The court of appeals upheld the finding of liability against Figgie on the wrongful death and survival claims. The court of appeals found that the appellant was not entitled to punitive damages as a matter of law. The court of appeals reversed the judgment of the trial court as to the award of damages and remanded the case for a new trial only on the issue of compensatory damages.

Issue

Is an intentional alteration or destruction of medical records to avoid liability sufficient to show actual malice? Can punitive damages be awarded whether or not the act of altering or destroying records directly causes compensable harm?

Holding

The Ohio Supreme Court held that the evidence regarding the physician's alteration of the patient's records supported an award of punitive damages, regardless of whether the alteration caused actual harm.

Reason

The jury's award of punitive damages was based on Figgie's alteration or destruction of medical records. Figgie's alteration of records was inextricably intertwined with the claims advanced by the appellant for medical malpractice, and the award of compensatory damages on the survival claim formed the necessary predicate for the award of punitive damages based on the alteration of medical records.

The purpose of punitive damages is not to compensate a plaintiff, but to punish and deter certain conduct. If the act of altering and destroying records to avoid liability is to be tolerated in society, the court could think of no better way to encourage it than to hold that punitive damages were not available in this case. Figgie's conduct of altering records should not go unpunished. The court warned others to refrain from similar conduct through an award of punitive damages.

Figgie's alteration of records exhibited a total disregard for the law and the rights of Moskovitz and her family. Had the copy of page seven of Figgie's office chart not been recovered from the radiation department records at University Hospitals, the appellant would have been substantially less likely to succeed in this case. The copy of the chart and other records produced by Figgie would have tended to exculpate Figgie for his medical negligence while placing the blame for his failures on Moskovitz.

A unanimous panel of arbitrators determined that records were altered with bad motive, and that Figgie was the responsible party. With all due respect to the court of appeals' majority, the state supreme court believed that the appellate court simply substituted its judgment for that of the jury and, thereby, invaded the province of the finder of fact.

The court reversed the judgment of the court of appeals on the issue of punitive damages. An intentional alteration or destruction of medical records to avoid liability for medical negligence is sufficient to show actual malice, and punitive damages may be awarded whether or not the act of altering, falsifying, or destroying records directly causes compensable harm.

Discussion

1. Do you consider the evidence sufficiently adequate to establish that the surgeon intentionally altered, falsified, or destroyed the patient's medical records to avoid liability for medical negligence? Explain.
2. If you found it necessary to clarify an entry that you made in a patient's medical record, what procedure would you follow?
3. Is the use of correction fluid the preferred way to clarify your entries?

Discharge Notes Inaccurately Reported To Avoid Liability

Ms. Dimora,[48] a 79-year-old woman, had difficulty in ambulating, requiring an attendant while using a walker. Her condition was noted numerous times on her chart and she had been evaluated as high risk for falls.

On November 5, 1993, Dimora was preparing to be discharged from the Clinic. After using the toilet with the assistance of a student nurse, she lost her balance and fell backward. The fall resulted in Dimora breaking five or six ribs. The fall was noted both in the nursing notes and discharge summary by the attending physician. Upon examination, Dimora was found to have good strength in all four extremities, was without pain of movement, and had a five centimeter by eight centimeter abrasion on the right posterior thorax. The area was noted to be nontender with deep palpitation. Ice and lotion were applied to the abraded area. No X-rays were taken at the Clinic after the fall, and no further treatment was administered by the Clinic. Dimora's broken ribs were not diagnosed until the following day, when X-rays were taken at Marymount Hospital.

Dimora's daughter, granddaughter, and caregiver testified that when they arrived at the hospital to pick up Dimora, she was crying and complaining of pain. Dimora's daughter testified that one of the nurses said that her mother had fallen when she was left alone in the bathroom.

The claim of the appellee for punitive damages alleges that the Clinic, through its agents and/or employees, intentionally falsified Dimora's medical records or inaccurately and improperly reported the fall incident to avoid liability for its medical malpractice or negligence.

The defendant moved for a directed verdict claiming that the plaintiff had failed to demonstrate alteration of the record and malice on the part of the Clinic, asserting, therefore, that the claim for punitive damages must fail. The trial court denied this motion. The jury awarded a verdict in favor of Dimora in the amount of $25,000 for compensatory damages and $25,000 in punitive damages.

Did the trial court err in denying the applicant's motion for a directed verdict on the appellee's claim for punitive damages, alleging that the appellee failed to present evidence of alteration of the record or, farther, failed to demonstrate fraud and actual malice?

The judgment of the trial court was affirmed.

At trial, testimony presented by witnesses for the appellee indicated that the right side of Dimora's body was red, bruised, and painful after the fall. Three witnesses testified that Dimora was crying and in pain approximately 45 minutes after the incident while she was still in the hospital. Testimony was offered that broken ribs would be painful upon deep palpation. Pictures were offered into evidence indicating large areas of bruising on Dimora's body on the day after the event.

In contrast to the evidence presented by the appellee, the progress note of the examining physician at issue here states in part:

> Pt was in transport between walker and toilet seat according to student nurse. Pt was at walker and lost balance backward. The SN acted by holding the pt from the L side and gradually lowering her to the floor, and called for help. Pt was lifted back into wheelchair. On exam, pt has full use of all 4 extremities with good strength and no pain with movement. A small 5 x 8 cm area on the pts r posterior thorax was slightly scraped. It was not tender to deep palpations and no crepitus was noted. There were no other lacerations bumps or abrasions noted. Head was traumatic. The abrasion on the thorax was treated with lotion and ice. The pt was smiling and laughing pleasantly during the exam.

Appellant contends that this record accurately reflects the incident. However, the testimony presented by the appellee is in apparent conflict with the description of the incident, the injury, and Dimora's demeanor. The evidence showed that Dimora had fallen and broken five or six ribs; yet, upon examination, the physician noted that she was smiling and laughing pleasantly with no pain upon deep palpation of the area. Other testimony indicated that she was in pain and crying. The discrepancy between the written progress notes and the testimony of the witnesses who observed Dimora was sufficient to raise a question of fact as to the possible falsification of documents by the physician to minimize the nature of the incident and the injury of the patient due to the possible negligence of hospital personnel. The testimony of the witnesses, if believed, would be sufficient to show that the physician falsified the record or intentionally reported the incident inaccurately to avoid liability for the negligent care. Such conduct is the type of intentional and deceptive behavior more indicative of actual malice. If such evidence is believed, the jury could award punitive damages. With the proper caution exercised in instructing the jury as to when punitive damages are proper, the issue of punitive damages should have been submitted to the jury.

Charting—Some Helpful Advice

The medical record is the most important document in a negligence action. Both plaintiff and defendant use it as a basis for their action and defense. The following advice on documentation should prove to be helpful in charting:

- The medical record describes the care rendered to each patient. It should be sufficiently complete to allow those not treating a patient to review the record and assume continuing care when necessary.
- Medical records entries should be timely, legible, clear, and meaningful to each patient's course of treatment. Handwriting has long been a major problem in interpreting the events surrounding the care of patients. Illegible medical records not only damage one's ability to defend oneself, but also can have an adverse effect on the credibility of other health care professionals who read the record and act on what they read.
- The medical record should be complete. This is often a problem with progress notes when there is little new information to report. Progress notes should describe the symptoms or condition being addressed, the treatment rendered, the patient response, and the patient's status at the time treatment is discontinued.
- Long, defensive, or derogatory notes should not be written. Only the facts should be related. Criticism, complaints, emotional comments, and extraneous remarks have no place in the medical record. Such remarks can in and of themselves precipitate a malpractice suit.
- Erasures and correction fluid should not be used to cover up entries. Do not tamper with the chart in any form. A single line should be drawn through a mistaken entry, the correct information entered, and the correction signed and dated.
- Charts related to pending legal action should be placed in a separate file under lock and key. Legal counsel should be notified immediately of any potential lawsuit.
- A medical record has many authors. Entries made by others must not be ignored. Good patient care is a collaborative interdisciplinary team effort. Entries made by health care professionals provide valuable information in treating the patient.

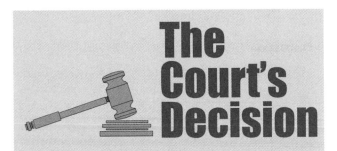

The Court's Decision

A West Texas jury ordered the physician, drugstore, and pharmacist to pay $225,000 to the family.

CHAPTER REVIEW

1. Information management is the process of facilitating the flow of information within and among departments and caregivers.

2. Health care organizations are required to maintain medical records for their patients in accordance with accepted professional standards and practices, and the requirements for these records are often set forth within states' public health laws. Medical records are to be complete and must contain all relevant information on the daily care and treatment of the patient. Records should be complete, accurate, current, readily accessible, and organized systematically.

3. An *admission record* contains data including age, address, reason for admission, social security number, marital status, religious affiliation, addresses, and other information required under federal and state requirements. It includes general consent and authorization-for-treatment forms. Patient-specific medical information is recorded in the *clinical record*.

4. Third-party reimbursement may be denied to an organization or physician who has failed to maintain a complete and accurate medical record. To receive federal funding, health care organizations must meet minimum federal standards for record keeping.

5. *Diagnosis-related groups* (DRGs) are a method of classifying patients by categories according to age, diagnosis, and treatment resource requirements. DRGs are the basis for the Department of Health and Human Service's prospective payment system and are assigned using information detailed in a patient's medical record. Failure to keep complete and accurate records could result in trouble obtaining reimbursement.

6. Records can be used as important evidentiary tools. The integrity and completeness of a medical record can be crucial in reconstructing the events surrounding alleged negligence.

7. The employees and staff of health care organizations are required to maintain the confidentiality of verbal and written communications. This is in accordance with both laws protecting a patient's right to privacy and ethical standards for health care professionals.

8. Lack of trust and confidence in a physician can destroy the integrity of the physician–patient relationship and negatively affect the quality and appropriateness of the treatment administered. Patients can be awarded damages if it is proven that a physician disclosed confidential information without authorization and that this disclosure resulted in harm to the patient.

9. Information can be shielded from discovery if *privilege* can be established by the party that seeks to protect the information.

10. Medical records are maintained for the benefit of the patients and are considered the property of the health care organization. Generally, health care professionals and health care organizations do not release medical records to patients. Most courts, however, take the view that patients have a right to access their records and some states have issued legislation granting this access.

11. The restriction on disclosing patient information can be lifted under certain circumstances including the information's relevance in a criminal investigation.

12. The integration of computers into the health care industry has tremendous impact on issues surrounding the confidentiality of medical records. Although they improve the ease and efficiency with which data are compiled and shared, they also pose a risk to confidentiality.

13. The requirements for the length of time medical records must be retained differ among states. In determining the length of time these records should be retained, patient needs, statutory requirements, future need for the records, and legal considerations of record availability in the event of a lawsuit should be considered.

14. The intentional alteration, falsification, or destruction of medical records to avoid liability for negligence is usually sufficient to show malice. Punitive damages may be awarded whether or not the act resulted in compensable harm. Falsification of medical or business records is grounds for both criminal indictment and civil liability.

REVIEW QUESTIONS

1. What is information management as it relates to health care?
2. What are the basic purposes of the medical record?

3. Discuss the advantages and disadvantages of computer-generated medical records.
4. A medical record is the sole property of the patient and should never be released. Discuss your opinion on this statement.
5. What is the reasoning for the establishment of statutes that protect an organization's peer review information?
6. Should statements given by a defendant to a hospital's internal peer review committee be discoverable by a plaintiff? Explain.
7. What records or parts thereof should be protected from discovery?
8. Should information gathered prior to a physician's application for staff privileges be privileged from discovery? Explain.
9. What records should a hospital maintain?
10. How long should patient records and X-rays be maintained?

NOTES

1. *Doctor Held Liable for Fatal Handwriting Mix-up*, USA TODAY, Oct. 21, 1999.

2. Jennings v. Case, 10 S.W.3d 625 (Tenn. App. 1999).

3. 262 P.2d 682 (Wyo. 1953).

4. 16 F.3d 473 (1st Cir. 1994).

5. FEDERAL RULES OF EVIDENCE, 28 § 803(6) (1988).

6. Masterson v. Pennsylvania R.R., 182 F.2d 793, 797 (3d Cir. 1950).

7. 905 F.2d 549 (1st Cir. 1990).

8. Julie Appleby, *Rules to Protect Medical Privacy*, USA TODAY, Dec. 20, 2000, at 1.

9. Ellen Weisman, *Liability for Medical Record Disclosure Is Real But Rare*, HOSPITALS, Aug. 20, 1990, at 32.

10. Berger v. Sonneland, 1 P.3d 1187 (2000)

11. RCW 70.02.

12. RCW 5.60.060.

13. 42 U.S.C.A. §§ 11101–11152 (1989).

14. 624 A.2d 99 (N.J. Super. Ct. App. Div. 1993).

15. 478 A.2d 1273 (N.J. Super. Ct. App. Div. 1984).

16. 572 N.E.2d 1025 (Ill. App. Ct. 1991).

17. People v. Superior Court, 286 Cal. Rptr. 478 (Cal. Ct. App. 1991).

18. Moretti v. Lowe, 592 A.2d 855 (R.I. 1991).

19. 521 F. Supp. 842 (W.D. Pa. 1981).

20. 522 F. Supp. 706 (E.D. Ky. 1981).

21. Smith v. Lincoln Gen. Hosp., 605 So.2d 1347 (La. 1992).

22. 629 N.E.2d 170 (Ill. App. Ct. 1994).

23. *Id.*

24. *Id.* at 171.

25. 439 S.E.2d 257 (S.C. 1993).

26. *Id.* at 259 (emphasis added).

27. 599 So.2d 111 (Fla. 1992).

28. *Id.* at 171.

29. 515 A.2d 948 (Pa. Super. Ct. 1986).

30. No. 91–1467 (2d Cir. June 1, 1992).

31. 536 N.E.2d 1202 (Ohio Com. Pl. 1988).

32. 582 N.E.2d 233 (Ill. App. Ct. 1991).

33. 21 U.S.C. § 1175 (1972).

34. John P. Glaser, *Brigham and Women's Wager on Huge PC Network Pays Solid Returns*, HEALTH MANAGEMENT TECHNOLOGY, Oct. 1994, at 7.

35. 423 U.S. 1313 (1975).

36. 328 P.2d 556 (Cal. Ct. App. 1958).

37. 597 N.E.2d 616 (Ill. 1992).

38. 683 N.E.2d 1175 (Ohio App. 1996).

39. 402 N.Y.S.2d 318 (N.Y. Sup. Ct. 1978).

40. *Deceit Found In Fatality At Rest Home*, N.Y. TIMES, Feb. 5, 1995, at 35.

41. 442 A.2d 635 (N.J. Super. Ct. 1982).

42. In re Jascalevich, 182 N.J.Super. 445, 442 A.2d 635, 644–45 (1982).

43. 880 P.2d 1188 (Colo. 1994).

44. *Id.* at 1192.

45. *Id.* at 1196.

46. Ronnie Greene, *Examiner: Treatment "Appropriate,"* THE MIAMI HERALD, April 16, 1995, at 14A.

47. Esme M. Infante, *Doctors' Rx: Write Right*, USA TODAY, June 14, 1994, at 1.

48. Dimora v. Cleveland Clinic Found., 683 N.E.2d 1175 (Ohio App. 8 Dist. 1996).

Patient Consent

It's Your Gavel...

THE LONG WAIT

On August 10, 1988, Mrs. Mathews had gone unassisted to the emergency department of the hospital complaining of a burning pain in her upper chest that had radiated down her right side that evening, as well as the previous evening. Upon arriving at the hospital's emergency department at about 11:25 P.M., Matthews was triaged by a nurse who took her vital signs, recorded her medical history, and made an assessment of her immediate medical needs. Although slightly elevated, Matthews' vital signs were within normal limits. The triage nurse classified Matthews as a "category two" patient, a non-threatening condition. It was explained to her that she would have a long wait, as the emergency department was very busy. A social services representative had testified that he had spoken to Matthews between six and eight times during her wait in the emergency department. He indicated that she was in no apparent distress during those times that he had spoken to her. Following a four-and-one-half-hour wait, Matthews decided to leave the emergency department without being treated. The social services representative stated that he told Matthews that a treatment room was ready for her and that she would be attended to shortly. Matthews said that she had already waited long enough and she was leaving. The social services representative stated that he had pleaded with her to stay but she refused, claiming that she would see her own physician in the morning. Matthews went to work the following day without having seen her physician. She died on August 12, 1988. A malpractice action was brought against DeKalb County Hospital Authority arising out of the death of Matthews. The DeKalb Superior Court granted the hospital's motion for summary judgment, and an appeal was taken.[1] Was the patient's subsequent death following her visit to the hospital's emergency department due to the hospital's negligence?

What is your verdict?

INTRODUCTION

Consent must be obtained from the patient, or from a person authorized to consent on the patient's behalf, before any medical procedure can be performed. Every individual has a right to refuse to authorize a touching. Touching of another without authorization to do so could be considered a battery.

Not every touching results in a battery. When a person voluntarily enters a situation in which a reasonably prudent person would anticipate a touching (e.g., riding in an elevator or rushing through a crowded subway), consent is implied. Consent is not required for the normal, routine, everyday touching and bumping that occur in life.

In the process of caring for patients, it is inevitable that they will be touched and handled. Most touching in the health care setting is considered routine. Typical routine touchings might include bathing, administering medications, dressing changes, etc.

This chapter reviews the many issues surrounding consent in the health care setting.

Whose Decision Is It?

The operation you get often depends on where you live. One patient underwent a mastectomy only to learn that a less destructive alternative procedure was available in a region near her home. The procedure, a lumpectomy, has the same survival rate as a mastectomy. The patient claims the surgeon never informed her as to the alternative.

CONSENT—A DEFINITION

Consent is the voluntary agreement by a person who possesses sufficient mental capacity to make an intelligent choice to allow something proposed by another to be performed on him- or herself. Consent changes a touching that otherwise would be nonconsensual to one that is consensual. Consent can be either express or implied.

Express consent can take the form of a "verbal" agreement or it can be accomplished through the execution of a "written" document authorizing medical care.

Implied consent is determined by some act or silence, which raises a presumption that consent has been authorized.

PATIENT SELF-DETERMINATION ACT

On December 1, 1991, the Patient Self-Determination Act of 1990[2] took effect in hospitals, skilled nursing facilities, home health agencies, hospice organizations, and health maintenance organizations serving Medicare and Medicaid patients. The Act protects the rights of patients to make decisions regarding their own health care. The Act provides that each individual has a right under state law (whether statutory or as recognized by the courts of the state) to make decisions concerning his or her medical care, including the right to accept or refuse medical or surgical treatment. The Act provides that:

. . . a provider of services or prepaid or eligible organization (as the case may be) maintain written policies and procedures with respect to all adult individuals receiving medical care by or through the provider or organization

(A) to provide written information to each such individual concerning

(i) an individual's rights under State law (whether statutory or as recognized by the courts of the State) to make decisions concerning such medical care, including the right to accept or refuse medical or surgical treatment and the right to formulate advance directives (as defined in paragraph (3)), and

(ii) the written policies of the provider or organization respecting the implementation of such rights;

(B) to document in the individual's medical record whether or not the individual has executed an advance directive;

(C) not to condition the provision of care or to otherwise discriminate against an individual based on whether or not the individual has executed an advance directive;

(D) to ensure compliance with requirements of State law (whether statutory or as recognized by the courts of the State) respecting advance directives at facilities of the provider or organization; and

(E) to provide (individually or with others) for education for staff and the community on issues concerning advance directives.

Subparagraph (C) shall not be construed as requiring the provision of care which conflicts with an advance directive.

(2) The written information described in paragraph (1)(A) shall be
provided to an adult individual

(A) in the case of a hospital, at the time of the individual's admission as an inpatient,

(B) in the case of a skilled nursing facility, at the time of the individual's admission as a resident,

(C) in the case of a home health agency, in advance of the individual coming under the care of the agency,

(D) in the case of a hospice program, at the time of initial receipt of hospice care by the individual from the program, and

(E) in the case of an eligible organization (as defined in section 1876 (b)) or an organization provided payments under section 1833

(a)(1)(A), at the time of enrollment of the individual with the organization.

(3) In this subsection, the term "advance directive" means a written instruction, such as a living will or durable power of attorney for healthcare, recognized under State law (whether statutory or as recognized by the courts of the State) and

relating to the provision of such care when the individual is incapacitated.[3]

INFORMED CONSENT

Informed consent is a legal concept that provides that a patient has a right to know the potential risks, benefits, and alternatives of a proposed procedure. Consent is based on information that would ordinarily be provided to a patient under like circumstances by health care providers engaged in a similar practice in the locality or in similar localities. Informed consent is predicated on the duty of the physician to disclose to the patient sufficient information to enable the patient to evaluate a proposed medical or surgical procedure before submitting to it. Informed consent requires that a patient have a full understanding of that to which he or she has consented. An authorization from a patient who does not understand to what he or she is consenting is not effective consent.

Hospitals generally do not have an independent duty to obtain informed consent or to warn patients of the risks of a procedure to be performed by a physician not an agent of the hospital. It is the treating physician who has the education, expertise, skill, and training necessary to treat a patient and determine what information a patient should have in order to give informed consent. Nurses and other nonphysician hospital employees do not normally possess the knowledge of a particular patient's medical history, diagnosis, or other circumstances that would enable the employee to fully disclose all pertinent information to the patient.

Assessing the Patient's Decision-Making Capacity

A patient is considered competent to make medical decisions regarding his or her care unless a court determines otherwise. Generally speaking, the determination of a patient's decision-making capacity is made by medical personnel. The clinical assessment of decision-making capacity should include the patient's ability to

- understand the risks, benefits, and alternatives of a proposed test or procedure
- evaluate the information provided by the physician
- express his or her treatment options/plan
- voluntarily make decisions regarding his or her treatment plan without undue influence by family, friends, or medical personnel

Nurses and Informed Consent

In *Giese v. Stice*,[4] the plaintiff, Ms. Giese, alleged that she underwent separate breast implantation procedures on April 29, 1991, and January 3, 1992, at Clarkson. Giese alleged that during the procedures, Dr. Stice was assisted by nurses and other personnel employed by Clarkson and that the implants used in those procedures were procured by Clarkson and billed to her through Clarkson. There is no allegation of any agency relationship between Clarkson and Stice, and no allegation that the breast implants were defective in any manner. The patient contended that a representative of the hospital's purchasing department should have counseled her prior to surgery regarding possible side effects associated with the implants.

In general, a hospital has no duty to: advise the patient as to a surgical procedure to be employed; advise the patient as to the risks, benefits, and alternatives to the recommended procedure; or obtain a patient's informed consent to surgery merely because the physician had directed a nurse to have the patient sign a consent form.

The plaintiff, Roberta Davis, in *Davis v. Hoffman*,[5] a resident of New York, experienced pain in her lower abdomen and consulted Dr. Hoffman. He diagnosed her to be suffering from a fibroid uterus and prescribed a dilation and curettage procedure designed to remove the fibroids. Hoffman further suggested a laparoscopy and hysteroscopy to search for cancer. The physician's nurse, Puchini, conducted a presurgical interview with the plaintiff in which she described a video hysteroscopy, a dilation and curettage procedure, a resectoscopic removal of submucous fibroids, a laparoscopy, and a laser myomectomy. The plaintiff claimed that she specifically informed Hoffman and Puchini that she did not consent to a hysterectomy. They responded that they would awaken her during the operation to obtain her consent before proceeding to a hysterectomy. At no time did they inform the plaintiff that Hoffman intended to perform a hysterectomy. The plaintiff underwent a procedure that resulted in a hysterectomy, during which no one awakened her to discuss and explore possible alternatives. Claiming that the hysterectomy caused her substantial injuries, the plaintiff brought an action for lack of informed consent against Hoffman, Puchini, and the hospital.

In response to the plaintiff's allegation that the hospital committed battery by lack of informed consent to the hysterectomy, the hospital asserted that Pennsylvania law places no duty on a hospital to obtain a patient's consent to an operation. The hospital argued that Pennsylvania courts have applied the doctrine of informed consent only to physicians, not to hospitals.

The plaintiff responded that the hospital gratuitously undertook to obtain her consent prior to the operation. Although the consent form authored and printed by the hospital was used, there was no suggestion that the deficiency in consent was in any way causally inadequate in the form. Rather, any failure was attributed to the omissions in the way the form was filled in, or in the way the patient was not informed as to what was to be the next phase of the operation. Thus, the form was causally irrelevant and could not be a basis for finding liability.

Because nurses do not have a duty to obtain informed consent, the plaintiff had not stated a claim for battery by lack of informed consent against Puchini. Pennsylvania law generally imposes no duty on persons other than surgeons to obtain informed consent before performing surgery.

Physicians and Informed Consent

Risks, Benefits, and Alternatives

The patient in *Stover v. Surgeons*[6] suffered damage to her heart valves as a result of childhood rheumatic fever. Dr. Ford, one of a group of physicians that the patient consulted after her condition had worsened, informed the patient that she needed a heart valve replacement. Testimony from Ford revealed that he briefly reviewed the details of the surgery with the patient. She indicated that she was told only that mechanical valves outlasted natural tissue valves. She further stated that she was never informed about the risks associated with installing mechanical valves, including the Beall valve that was implanted in her. Thromboemboli, strokes, and the lifelong use of anticoagulants, which are common side effects of valve replacements, were never discussed with her. Dr. Zikria performed the surgery, and could not recall discussing any risks other than clotting risks associated with the implantation. After the surgery, the patient suffered severe, permanent brain damage from multiple episodes of thromboemboli directly caused by valve implantation. She then sued for lack of informed consent, and the jury returned a verdict for her. The physicians appealed.

The Pennsylvania Superior Court held that the physicians had to discuss alternative prostheses with the patient, where it represented medically recognized alternatives. Evidence that the heart valve actually implanted was no longer in general use at the time of operation was relevant and material to the issue of informed consent.

Although the physicians argued that the choice of prosthesis should belong to them, the court held that if there are other recognized, medically sound alternatives, the patient must be informed about the risks and benefits of them in order to make a sound treatment judgment, including the desire to execute a waiver of consent. The agreement between the physician and the patient is contractual. Therefore, in order for valid consent to occur, there must be a finding that both parties understood the nature of the procedure, including what any possible as well as expected results would be. The consent is not valid if the patient did not understand the operation to be performed, its seriousness, the disease or incapacity, and possible results. Physicians must disclose risks that a reasonable person would consider material to his or her decision of whether to undergo treatment. In the instant case, the physicians failed to inform the patient about the recognized risks of the valve that was implanted.

Finally, the court reasoned that there were alternative valves available that were never discussed with the patient. To arrive at an informed decision concerning her treatment, it was material for her to have been told about the alternatives, risks, and benefits.

DUTY TO INFORM REQUIRES THE EXERCISE OF DELICATE MEDICAL JUDGMENT

Citation: *Mathias v. St. Catherine's Hosp., Inc.,* 569 N.W.2d 330 (Wis. App. 1997)

Facts

Ms. Mathias, a patient of Dr. Witt's at St. Catherine's Hospital, delivered a full-term son by Caesarean section on February 2, 1993, while she was under general anesthesia. While in the operating room, Witt indicated that he needed a particular instrument that would be used in a tubal ligation. The nurses, Ms. Snyder and Ms. Perri, employees of St. Catherine's, looked at Mathias' chart. Snyder informed Witt that she did not see a signed consent form for that procedure. In deposition testimony, Snyder stated that Witt replied, "Oh, okay."

Witt performed a tubal ligation. Three days after the procedure had been done, a nurse brought Mathias a consent form for the procedure. This nurse told Mathias that the form was "just to close up our records." The nurse testified in her deposition that she signed Perri's name on that same consent form and backdated it to February 2, 1993, the day the surgery was performed. As the trial court noted in its oral decision granting summary judgment, these actions after the surgery are immaterial to the issue of the hospital's duty to Mathias. The trial court granted summary judgment dismissing St. Catherine's from their medical malpractice action and from an order denying reconsideration. Mr. and Ms. Mathias appealed the summary judgment contending that the hospital owed a duty to Mathias to prevent her physician from performing a tubal ligation for which there was no signed consent form.

Issue

Did the hospital owe a duty to Mathias to prevent her physician from performing a tubal ligation for which there was no consent? Did the trial court err in granting summary judgment to St. Catherine's?

Holding

St. Catherine's fulfilled its duty of ordinary care to Mathias and therefore is not liable. The trial court's grant of summary judgment was affirmed.

Reason

The duty to advise a patient of the risks of treatment lies with the physician and not the hospital. This duty is codified in WIS. STAT. § 448.30, which requires:

> Any physician who treats a patient shall inform the patient about the availability of all alternate, viable medical modes of treatment and about the benefits and risks of these treatments. The physician's duty to inform the patient under this section does not require disclosure of:

1. information beyond what a reasonably well-qualified physician in a similar medical classification would know
2. detailed technical information that in all probability a patient would not understand
3. risks apparent or known to the patient
4. extremely remote possibilities that might falsely or detrimentally alarm the patient
5. information in emergencies where failure to provide treatment would be more harmful to the patient than treatment
6. information in cases where the patient is incapable of consenting

This statute is the cornerstone of the hospital's duty in this case. The court noted that the legislature limited the application of the duty to obtain informed consent to the treating physician. Although the record is littered with semantic arguments about whether this is a case of nonconsent or lack of informed consent, what the Mathiases sought was to extend the duty of ensuring informed consent to the hospital.

The duty to inform rests with the physician and requires the exercise of delicate medical judgment. It is the physician—not the hospital—who has the duty of obtaining informed consent. The surgeon, not the hospital, has the education, training, and experience necessary to advise each patient of risks associated with a proposed procedure. The physician is in the best position to know the patient's medical history and to evaluate and explain the risks of a particular operation in light of the particular medical history.

Discussion

1. Do you agree with the court's finding that the hospital had no legal duty to ensure that Witt obtain informed consent from Mathias? Explain.
2. What finding would the Joint Commission on Accreditation of Healthcare Organizations make during an accreditation survey if its hospital surveyors found that Mathias had undergone surgery without informed consent? Should the hospital be penalized by the Joint Commission for the surgeon's failure to obtain informed consent? Explain.
3. What issues do you see in another nurse's decision to sign Perri's name on the consent form and then backdate it to February 2, 1993?

Invasive vs. Noninvasive Alternatives—My Decision

The plaintiff-patient in *Matthies v. Mastromonaco*[7], an elderly woman living alone in a senior citizens residence, fell and fractured her hip. The patient was taken to the hospital and seen by an orthopaedic surgeon. The defendant reviewed the patient's history, condition, and X-rays, and decided that, rather than utilizing a pinning procedure for her hip involving the insertion of four steel screws, it would be better to adopt a conservative course of treatment, bed rest.

Prior to her injury, the plaintiff had maintained an independent style of living. She did her own grocery shopping and other household duties, and had been able to climb steps unassisted.

Expert testimony at trial indicated that bed rest was an inappropriate treatment. The defendant was of the opinion that given the frail condition of the patient and her age, she would be best treated in a nursing home, and therefore, was of the opinion that conservative treatment was the best alternative for the patient. At the heart of the informed consent issue was the plaintiff's assertion that she would not have consented to bed rest if she had been informed of the probable effect on the quality of her life.

The New Jersey Supreme Court held that it is necessary to obtain a patient's informed consent to one of several alternatives courses of treatment; the *physician should explain medically reasonable invasive and noninvasive alternatives*, including the risks and likely outcomes of those alternatives, even when the chosen course is noninvasive.

In informed consent analysis, the decisive factor is not whether a treatment alternative is invasive or noninvasive, but whether the physician adequately presents the material facts so that the patient can make an informed decision. That conclusion does not imply that a physician must explain in detail all treatment options in every case. For example, a physician need not recite all the risks and benefits of each potential appropriate antibiotic when writing a prescription for treatment of an upper respiratory infection. Conversely, a physician could be obligated, depending on the circumstances, to discuss a variety of treatment alternatives, such as chemotherapy, radiation, or surgery, with a patient diagnosed with cancer. Distinguishing the two situations are the limitations of the reasonable patient standard, which need not unduly burden the physician–patient relationship. The standard obligates the physician to disclose only that information material to a reasonable patient's informed decision.[8]

If the patient's choice is not consistent with the physician's recommendation, the physician has the option of withdrawing from the case. The patient then has the option to seek another physician who is comfortable with the alternative treatment preferred by the patient.

No Consent—Why Did You Let Them Do That to Me?

Four children, in *Riser v. American Medical Intern, Inc.*,[9] brought a medical malpractice action against Dr. Lang, a physician who performed a femoral arteriogram on their 69-year-old mother, Mrs. Riser, who subsequently died 11 days following the procedure. Riser had been admitted to De La Ronde Hospital experiencing impaired circulation in her lower arms and hands. The patient had multiple medical diagnoses, including diabetes mellitus, end-stage renal failure, and arteriosclerosis. Her physician, Dr. Sottiurai, ordered bilateral arteriograms in order to determine the cause of the patient's impaired circulation. Because De La Ronde Hospital could not accommodate Sottiurai's request, Riser was transferred to Dr. Lang, a radiologist at St. Jude Hospital. Lang performed a femoral arteriogram as opposed to the bilateral brachial arteriogram ordered by Sottiurai. The procedure seemed to go well and the patient was prepared for transfer back to De La Ronde Hospital. However, shortly after the ambulance departed the hospital, the patient suffered a seizure in the ambulance and was returned to St. Jude. Riser's condition deteriorated and she died 11 days later. The plaintiffs claimed in their lawsuit that Riser was a poor risk for the procedure. The district court ruled for the plaintiffs, awarding damages in the amount of $50,000 for Riser's pain and suffering and $100,000 to each child. Lang appealed.

The Louisiana Court of Appeal held that Lang breached the standard of care by subjecting the patient to a procedure that would have no practical benefit to the patient, that Lang failed to obtain informed consent from the patient, and that the damage award was not excessive.

Testimony revealed that Lang had breached the standard of care by performing a procedure that he knew or should have known would have had no practical benefit to the patient or her referring physician. The defendant himself, as well as the expert witnesses in this case, testified that it is a breach of the standard of care for any physician to subject a patient to a particular test or procedure that has any risk of injury, however small, associated with it if that physician knows or reasonably should know that the procedure will be of no benefit to the patient.

As to informed consent, a reasonably prudent person in the position of Riser would have refused to undergo the procedure if he or she had known of the strong possibility of a stroke. Informed consent requires that the physician reveal to the patient all material risks. The patient's consent to an arteriogram was vitiated by Lang's failure to disclose such a possibility. The consent form itself did not contain express authorization for Lang to perform the femoral arteriogram. Sottiurai ordered a brachial arteriogram, not a femoral arteriogram. Riser was under the impression that she was about to undergo a brachial arteriogram, not a femoral arteriogram. Two consent forms were signed; neither form authorized the performance of a femoral arteriogram. Mrs. O'Neil, one of Riser's daughters, claimed that her mother said following the arteriogram, "Why did you let them do that to me?"[10] Although Lang claims that he explained the procedure to Riser and O'Neil, the trial court, faced with this conflicting testimony, chose to believe the plaintiffs. The appeals court found no error in the trial court's decision. The defendants argued that the plaintiffs had not established a causal connection between the arteriogram and the stroke. There was conflicting testimony between the pathologists who testified at trial as to the cause of the patient's death. The judge chose to believe the pathologist's testimony that it was more probable than not that the stroke resulted from the arteriogram performed by Lang.

Information To Be Disclosed Can Vary

A physician should provide as much information about treatment options as is necessary based on a patient's personal understanding of the physician's explanation of the risks of treatment and the probable consequences of the treatment. The needs of each patient can vary depending on age, maturity, and mental status.

Some courts have recognized that the condition of the patient may be taken into account to determine whether the patient has received sufficient information to give consent. The individual responsible for obtaining consent must weigh the importance of giving full disclosure to the patient against the likelihood that such disclosure will seriously and adversely affect the condition of the patient.

Objective Test and Full Disclosure

Janet Warren, in *Warren v. Schecter*,[11] was diagnosed as having a stomach ulcer in December 1981. She was initially treated by Dr. Feldman, who referred her to Dr. Schecter, a surgeon. Schecter sought to perform surgery to remove the portions of the stomach containing the ulcer, which was not healing completely. One of the significant risks of gastric surgery is decreased calcium absorption, leading to early and severe metabolic bone disease (osteoporosis, osteomalacia, or bone pain). Studies have reported that up to 38 percent of patients develop early severe osteoporosis following such surgery. It was Schecter's role as the surgeon to advise Warren of the risks of surgery in order to obtain her informed consent. Schecter did not believe osteoporosis, osteomalacia, and bone pain were risks of the surgery and he did not discuss those substantial risks with her. Schecter did advise Warren that she might experience bowel obstructions. Schecter also informed Warren of other risks, including "dumping syndrome," involving nausea, and the slight risk of death from the administering of anesthesia during any operation. Based on the limited risks disclosed to Warren, she consented to the surgery, which Schecter performed on September 10, 1982.

The surgery recommended by Schecter was elective. Warren had nonsurgical options for her ulcers, namely, to discontinue the use of Advil and aspirin, to cease smoking, and to continue with her ulcer medications. Following the surgery, Warren developed dumping syndrome, a side effect that occurs in about 1 percent of the patients who undergo this procedure. Warren also developed alkaline reflux gastri-

tis, a condition involving the movement of alkaline fluid back into the stomach.

After Warren was diagnosed with these complications, she returned to Schecter, who recommended surgery. The purpose of the second surgery was to relieve the pain and discomfort from the first surgery. The second surgery would enhance the risk of bone disease. However, Schecter again failed to advise Warren of the risk of metabolic bone disease.

The first manifestation of bone disease occurred on May 4, 1990, when Warren fractured her back from the mere act of turning over in bed. Until then, there had been no objective evidence of bone disease and no symptoms. Warren was taken to the UCLA Hospital emergency department, where she was advised that she had suffered a fracture of one of the lumbar vertebrae. At that time, she first learned that severe metabolic bone disease was a common side effect of the surgeries she had undergone. Saleh at UCLA advised Warren that the surgeries had caused the osteoporosis that had led to the fracture. A bone density scan confirmed that Warren's bones were brittle. Since the onset of bone disease, Warren's condition continued to deteriorate.

In January 1991, Warren filed an action for medical negligence, alleging that Schecter was liable under an informed consent theory for performing surgery without advising her of the risk of bone disease. Warren claimed that had Schecter warned her of the risk of metabolic bone disease, she would not have consented to surgery. The jury found on special verdict that: (1) Schecter did not disclose to Warren all relevant information that would enable her to make an informed decision regarding surgery, (2) a reasonably prudent person in Warren's position would not have consented to surgery if adequately informed of all the significant perils, and (3) Schecter's negligence was a cause of injury to Warren.

On appeal, the plaintiff was found entitled to compensation for all damages proximately resulting from the physician's failure to give full disclosure of the risks of surgery. The patient was entitled to recover not only for the undisclosed complications, but also for the disclosed complications, because she would not have consented to any surgery had the true risk been disclosed, and, therefore, she would not have suffered those complications.

A plaintiff meets the burden of establishing a causal relationship between the physician's failure to inform and the injury to the plaintiff by demonstrating that a prudent person in the plaintiff's position would have declined the procedure if adequately informed of the risks. The *objective standard*, which in effect equates the plaintiff with a reasonable person, is appropriate because it protects the defendant-physician from the self-serving testimony of a plaintiff who inevitably will assert at trial that he or she would have refused the procedure if duly advised of the risk. The objective test required of the plaintiff does not prevent the physician from showing, by way of defense, that even though a reasonably prudent person might not have undergone the procedure if properly informed of the perils, this particular plaintiff still would have consented to the procedure. In sum, it was not Warren's burden to establish that she would not have consented to the surgery even if adequately informed. Under the objective standard, Warren had only to prove that a prudent person in her position would not have consented if adequately informed of the risks. Schecter failed to provide Warren with the risks and benefits of the surgical procedures prior to obtaining her consent for the operations and Warren testified that she would not have consented to either surgery if duly advised of the risk.

OBJECTIVE TEST PREFERRED

Citation: *Ashe v. Radiation Oncology Assocs.*, 9 S.W.3d 119 (Tenn. 1999)

Facts

The plaintiff, Ms. Ashe, was diagnosed with breast cancer in 1988. She ultimately underwent a double mastectomy and chemotherapy as treatment for her breast cancer. In 1993, she began experiencing problems with a cough and a fever. She returned to her oncologist, Dr. Kuzu, where she presented a variety of symptoms, including fever, cough, weight loss, and decreased appetite. A chest X-ray and a computed tomography (CT) scan revealed the presence of a mass in the medial left apex of her left lung.

The record indicates that the lung tumor could possibly have been metastatic cancer from the breast. Ashe underwent surgery, and the upper portion of her left lung was removed. She underwent chemotherapy and was referred to the defendant, Dr. Stroup, for consideration of radiation therapy. Stroup testified that chemotherapy alone would be indicated if the lung tumor were metastasized breast cancer. He, however, opined that radiation therapy would be indicated if the lung cancer were primary as opposed to secondary cancer.

Stroup prescribed radiation treatment for Ashe. She received a daily dose of 200 centigray for 25 days. He described the dose as a "midplane dose." Ashe sustained "radiation myelitis" caused by a permanent radiation injury to her spinal cord. She is now a paraplegic.

Stroup did not inform Ashe that the radiation treatment might result in a permanent injury to her spinal cord. According to Stroup, the risk that she would sustain a spinal cord injury was less than 1 percent. Ashe proffered the testimony of her expert, Dr. Perez, who opined that the risk of spinal cord injury was 1 to 2 percent. Perez testified that the applicable standard of care required physicians to warn patients about the risk of radiation injury to the spinal cord.

Ashe filed the present action alleging claims for medical malpractice and lack of informed consent. At trial, she testified that *she would not have consented* to radiation therapy had she been informed of the risk of paralysis. On cross-examination, defense counsel pointed out that the plaintiff did equivocate in her deposition on the issue of consent. Her deposition testimony indicated that she did not know what she would have done had she been warned about the risk of spinal cord injury. She then testified on redirect examination as follows:

> True, but the risk of being paralyzed and put in a wheelchair for the rest of your life was not one of the items, if there was any discussed, because had he said that within a six-month period—which they said that would be the time frame for it to happen—had he said, "Patty, if you do this there is a risk that you will be in a wheelchair six months from now," I would have told him, "I will take my chances." I would not have it done.

The trial court found that the plaintiff's trial testimony conflicted with her deposition testimony regarding whether she would have consented to the procedure had she been warned of the risk of spinal cord injury. The trial court, therefore, struck the trial testimony and granted the defendant a directed verdict on the informed consent claim. The plaintiff's malpractice claim went to the jury. The jury was unable to reach a verdict, and a mistrial was declared.

The plaintiff appealed to the court of appeals. The court of appeals held that as part of the plaintiff's informed consent claim she was required to prove that a reasonable person knowing of the risk for spinal cord injury would have decided not to have the procedure performed. The court held that the discrepancy between the trial and deposition testimony went to the issue of credibility and that the trial testimony should not have been stricken.

The court of appeals reversed the trial court's grant of a directed verdict on the informed consent claim and remanded the case for a new trial.

Issue

What is the appropriate standard to be employed when assessing the issue of causation in a medical malpractice informed consent case?

Finding

The "objective" standard best balances a patient's right to self-determination with the need for a realistic framework for rational resolution of the issue of causation. The standard to be applied in informed consent cases is whether a reasonable person in the patient's position would have consented to the procedure or treatment in question if adequately informed of all significant perils.

Reason

In Tennessee, a plaintiff must prove by expert testimony that the defendant did not supply appropriate information to the patient in obtaining his or her informed consent to the procedure out of which the plaintiff's claim allegedly arose in accordance with the recognized standard of acceptable professional practice in the profession and in the specialty, if any, that the defendant practices in the community in which he practices or in similar communities.

Tennessee Code requires that the plaintiff prove the recognized standard of acceptable professional practice, that the defendant acted with less than ordinary and reasonable care in accordance with that standard, and that the plaintiff sustained injuries as a result of the defendant's negligent act or omission. Accordingly, the plaintiff in an informed consent medical malpractice case has the burden of proving: (1) what a reasonable medical practitioner in the same or similar community would have disclosed to the patient about the risk posed by the proposed procedure or treatment; and (2) that the defendant departed from the norm.

The issue with which the court was confronted was whether an objective, subjective, or a hybrid subjective/objective test shall be employed when assessing causation in informed consent cases. The issue is one of first impression in Tennessee. The majority of jurisdictions having addressed this issue follow an objective standard.

Subjective Standard

Causation under the *"subjective standard"* is established solely by patient testimony. Patients must testify and prove that they would not have consented to the procedures had they been advised of the particular risk in question. Accordingly, resolution of causation under a subjective standard is premised on the credibility of a patient's testimony.

Proponents of the subjective test argue that a patient should have the right to make medical determinations regardless of whether the determination is rational or reasonable. Opponents, however, focus on the unfairness of allowing the issue of causation to turn on the credibility of the hindsight of a person seeking recovery after experiencing an undesirable result. The subjective test potentially places the physician in jeopardy of the patient's hindsight and bitterness. Moreover, the adoption of a subjective standard could preclude recovery in an informed consent case in which the patient died as a result of an unforewarned collateral consequence.

Objective Standard

Causation in informed consent cases is better resolved on an objective basis "in terms of what a prudent person in the patient's position would have decided if suitably informed of all perils bearing significance." The *objective view* recognizes that neither the plaintiff nor the fact-finder can provide a definitive answer as to what the patient would have done had the patient known of the particular risk prior to consenting to the procedure or treatment. Accordingly, the patient's testimony is relevant under an objective approach, but the testimony is not controlling.

The objective test appropriately respects a patient's right to self-determination. The finder of fact may consider and give weight to the patient's testimony as to whether the patient would have consented to the procedure upon full disclosure of the risks. When applying the objective standard, the finder of fact may also take into account the characteristics of the plaintiff, including the plaintiff's idiosyncrasies, fears, age, medical condition, and religious beliefs. Accordingly, the objective standard affords the ease of applying a uniform standard and yet maintains the flexibility of allowing the finder of fact to make appropriate adjustments to accommodate the individual characteristics and idiosyncrasies of an individual patient. The standard to be applied in informed consent cases is whether a reasonable person in the patient's position would have consented to the procedure or treatment in question if adequately informed of all significant perils.

The jury should not have been precluded from deciding the issue of informed consent. Under the objective analysis, the plaintiff's testimony is only one factor when determining the issue of informed consent. The issue is not whether Ashe would herself have chosen a different course of treatment. The issue is whether a reasonable patient in Ashe's position would have chosen a different course of treatment. The jury, therefore, should have been allowed to decide whether a reasonable person in Ashe's position would have consented to the radiation therapy had the risk of paralysis been disclosed.

Discussion

1. Discuss the difference between the "objective test" and the "subjective test" as it relates to the concept of informed consent.
2. Would the outcome of this case have been different if a "subjective test" was applied? Discuss your answer.

Hospitals—In Some Instances—Have a Duty To Provide Informed Consent

Mr. Keel, in *Keel v. St. Elizabeth Medical Center, Ky.*,[12] filed a medical malpractice action. He alleged that the hospital performed a medical procedure without his informed consent. He went to the medical center for a CT scan, which was to include the injection of a contrast dye material. Prior to the test, Keel was given no information concerning any risks attendant to the procedure. The dye was injected and the scan was conducted. However, the plaintiff developed a thrombophlebitis at the site of the injection.

The plaintiff argued that expert medical testimony was not required in order to prove the absence of informed consent. The hospital argued that the question of informed consent, like the question of negligence, must be determined against the standard of practice among members of the medical profession.

The circuit court granted summary judgment to the hospital on the grounds that the plaintiff failed to present expert testimony on the issue. The plaintiff appealed.

The Kentucky Supreme Court held that expert testimony was not required to establish lack of informed consent, and

that the hospital had a duty to inform the patient of the risks associated with the procedure. Responsibility did not lie solely with the patient's personal physician. The circuit court's summary judgment for the hospital was reversed and the matter was remanded for further proceedings.

In most cases, expert medical evidence will likely be a necessary element of a plaintiff's proof in negating informed consent. In view of the special circumstances of this case, the court found it significant that St. Elizabeth offered Keel no information whatsoever concerning any possible hazards of this particular procedure, while at the same time the hospital admits that it routinely questions every patient about to undergo a dye injection as to whether he or she has had any previous reactions to contrast materials. Failure to adequately inform the patient need not be established by expert testimony where the failure is so apparent that laypersons may easily recognize it or infer it from evidence within the realm of common knowledge. A juror might reasonably infer from the nontechnical evidence that St. Elizabeth's utter silence as to the risks amounted to an assurance that there were none. The hospital's own questions to patients regarding reactions to the CT scan procedure demonstrated that the hospital recognized the substantial possibility of complications. These inconsistencies are apparent without recourse to expert testimony.

Adequacy of Consent

When questions do arise as to whether adequate consent has been given, some courts take into consideration the information that is ordinarily provided by other physicians. A physician must reveal to his or her patient such information as a skilled practitioner of good standing would provide under similar circumstance. A physician must disclose to the patient the potential of death, serious harm, and other complications associated with a proposed procedure.

Scope of Duty

The scope of a physician's duty to disclose, as noted in *Wooley v. Henderson*,[13] is to be measured by those communications that a reasonable medical practitioner in that branch of medicine would make under the same or similar circumstances. The plaintiff ordinarily must establish this standard by expert medical evidence. The plaintiff would have to show that a reasonable person in the position of the plaintiff would have declined the treatment after being informed of a risk that could result in harm.

Full Disclosure Exception

A patient suffering from hypertension could very well receive a modified disclosure if the attending physician has reason to believe that a full explanation of a contemplated treatment could aggravate the hypertension, which, in turn, could have a detrimental effect on the body systems already impaired by age or illness. A modified disclosure consistent with the patient's condition may be adequate if it can be shown that other physicians in the community also would have made a modified disclosure.

Beyond the Scope of Consent

The plaintiff in *Ramos v. Pyati*[14] brought a medical malpractice action, alleging that the physician performed surgery on his hand outside the scope of surgery to which he consented. The plaintiff had injured his thumb while at work. He was referred to the defendant after seeing three other physicians. The plaintiff was diagnosed as having a ruptured thumb tendon. The plaintiff consented to a surgical repair of the thumb. During surgery, the defendant discovered that scar tissue had formed, causing the ends of the tendons in the thumb to retract. As a result, the surgeon decided to use a donor tendon to make the necessary repairs to the thumb. He chose a tendon from the ring finger. On discovering additional disability from the surgery, the plaintiff filed a suit alleging that his hand was rendered unusable for his employment as a mechanic and that the defendant had breached his duty by not advising him of the serious nature of the operation, by not exercising the proper degree of care in performing the operation, and by failing to discontinue surgery when he knew or should have known that the required surgery would most likely cause a greater disability than the already injured condition of the thumb. The plaintiff testified that although he signed a written consent form authorizing the surgery on his thumb, he did not consent to a graft of his ring finger tendon or any other tendon. The plaintiff's expert witness testified that the ring finger is the last choice of four other tendons that could have been selected for the surgery. The circuit court entered a judgment for the plaintiff, and the defendant appealed. The appellate court upheld the judgment for the plaintiff, finding that the plaintiff had not consented to use of the ring finger tendon for repair of the thumb tendon.

RIGHT TO REFUSE TREATMENT

Patients have a right to be secure from any touching, and they are free to reject recommended treatment. A competent patient's refusal to consent to a medical or surgical procedure must be adhered to, whether the refusal is grounded on lack of confidence in the physician, fear of the procedure, doubt as to the value of a particular procedure, or mere whim. The U.S. Supreme Court stated that the "notion of bodily integrity has been embodied in the requirement that informed consent is generally required for medical treatment" and the "logical corollary of the doctrine of informed consent is that the patient generally possesses the right not to consent, that is, to refuse treatment."[15] The common law doctrine of informed consent is viewed as generally encompassing the right of a competent individual to refuse medical treatment.

The question of liability for performing a medical or surgical procedure without consent is separate and distinct from any question of negligence or malpractice in performing a procedure. Liability may be imposed for a nonconsensual touching of a patient, even if the procedure improved the patient's health. The eminent Justice Cardozo, in *Schloendorff v. Society of New York Hospital*, stated:

> Every human being of adult years and sound mind has a right to determine what shall be done with his own body and a surgeon who performs an operation without his patient's consent commits an assault, for which he is liable in damages, except in cases of emergency where the patient is unconscious and where it is necessary to operate before consent can be obtained.[16]

The courts perform a balancing test to determine whether or not to override a competent adult's decision to refuse medical treatment. The courts balance state interests, such as preservation of life, protection of third parties, prevention of suicide, and the integrity of the medical profession against a patient's rights of bodily integrity and religious freedom. The most frequently used state right to intervene in a patient's decision-making process is for the *protection of third parties*. In *In re Fetus Brown*,[17] the State of Illinois asserted that its interest in the well-being of a viable fetus outweighed the patient's rights to refuse medical treatment. The state argued that a balancing test should be used to weigh state interests against patient rights. The appellate court held that it could not impose a legal obligation upon a pregnant woman to consent to an invasive medical procedure for the benefit of her viable fetus.

RIGHT TO CHOOSE OR REFUSE TREATMENT— MAY A HOSPITAL ASSERT STATE INTERESTS?

Citation: *Matter of Dubreuil, 629 So.2d 819 (Fla. 1993)*

Facts

A patient was in the advanced stage of pregnancy when she was admitted through the emergency department of the hospital. At the time of her admission, she signed a standard consent form that included her agreement to have a blood transfusion if necessary. The next day she was going to have a Caesarean section, but she would not consent to a blood transfusion because of her religious beliefs. During the course of the delivery, after she had lost a significant amount of blood, it was determined that she needed a transfusion to save her life, but she would not give her consent. Her estranged husband was contacted, and upon his arrival at the hospital, he gave his consent for the transfusion. After the first transfusion, physicians determined that she would need more blood, so they petitioned the circuit court for an emergency hearing to determine if they could give the transfusion in spite of the patient's lack of consent. Although no testimony was given at the hearing, there was a telephone call advising the court that the patient had just regained consciousness and that she continued to withhold her consent.

The trial court decided to allow the hospital to administer blood as they felt it was necessary. The patient moved for a rehearing, and the circuit court denied it. The patient then sought review by the Florida Supreme Court, arguing that her federal and state constitutional rights of privacy, self-determination, and religious freedom had been denied.

Issue

May a hospital assert state interests in order to defeat a patient's decision to refuse emergency medical treatment? Did the patient's refusal of a blood transfusion constitute abandonment of her minor children, thus giving the state an interest that outweighed her constitutional rights of privacy and religion?

Holding

The district court's decision is quashed.

Reason

A competent person has the right to choose or refuse medical treatment, including all decisions relevant to his or her health. That right merges with the right to refuse a blood transfusion while exercising one's religious beliefs. A health care provider must comply with the patient's wishes unless supported

by a court order to do otherwise. Here, the state interest was the protection of the children as innocent third parties. However, in this case there would have been no abandonment, because under Florida law, when there are two living parents, they share equally in the responsibilities of parenting. Had the patient died, her husband would have assumed the care of the children.

Discussion

1. What are the competing rights of the state and patient with regard to refusing blood transfusions because of the patient's religious beliefs?
2. Do you agree with the court's decision? Explain.

PROOF OF CONSENT

Oral Consent

Oral consent, if proved, is as binding as written consent, for there is, in general, no legal requirement that a patient's consent be in writing. However, an oral consent is more difficult to corroborate.

Written Consent

Written consent provides visible proof of a patient's wishes. Because the function of a written consent form is to preserve evidence of informed consent, the nature of the treatment, the risks, benefits, and consequences involved should be incorporated into the consent form. States have taken the view that consent, to be effective, must be "informed consent." An informed consent form should include the following elements:

- the nature of the patient's illness or injury
- the procedure or treatment consented to
- the purpose of the proposed treatment
- the risks and probable consequences of the proposed treatment
- the probability that the proposed treatment will be successful
- any alternative methods of treatment and their associated risks and benefits
- the risks and prognosis if no treatment is rendered
- an indication that the patient understands the nature of any proposed treatment, the alternatives, the risks involved, and the probable consequences of the proposed treatment

- the signatures of the patient, physician, and witnesses
- the date the consent is signed

Health care professionals have an important role in the realm of informed consent. They can be instrumental in averting major lawsuits by being observant as to a patient's doubts; changes of mind; confusion; or misunderstandings expressed by a patient regarding any proposed procedures he or she is about to undergo.

General Consent

Many physicians and health care organizations have relied on consent forms worded in such general terms that they permit the physician to perform almost any medical or surgical procedure believed to be in the patient's best interests. There is little difference between a surgical patient who signs no authorization and one who signs a form consenting to whatever procedure the physician deems advisable.

A general written consent should be executed at the time of a patient's admission. This form records the patient's consent to routine services, general diagnostic procedures, medical treatment, and the everyday routine touchings of the patient. The danger from its use arises from the potential of unwarranted reliance on it for specific, potentially high-risk procedures or treatments.

Temporary Consent

General emergency care consent forms provided by school officials, teachers, or camp counselors when they bring injured students or campers to the emergency department for treatment provide limited protection in the care of a particular child. This consent indicates a parent's desire and intent to have the school official, teacher, or counselor seek emergency treatment when necessary. Such consent allows the health care facility to initiate emergency treatment while an attempt is being made to reach the family for consent.

Special Consent

A special consent form should be executed when a proposed treatment program may involve some unusual risk(s) to the patient. A list of procedures and treatments requiring special written consent should be maintained and appropriate consent forms used by the nursing and medical staff. The special consent form should be signed, dated, and witnessed at the time the physician explains to the patient the procedure that he or she plans to perform. For special consents to

be effective, they should be signed within a reasonable time prior to a scheduled procedure or treatment.

WHO MAY CONSENT

Consent of the patient ordinarily is required before treatment. However, when the patient is either physically unable or legally incompetent to consent and no emergency exists, consent must be obtained from a person who is empowered to consent on the patient's behalf. The person who authorizes treatment of another must have sufficient information to make an intelligent judgment on behalf of the patient.

SPOUSAL CONSENT

Citation: Greynolds v. Kurman, 632 N.E.2d 946 (Ohio Ct. App. 1993)

Facts

On July 29, 1987, Mr. Greynolds suffered from a transient ischemic attack (TIA). A TIA is a sudden loss of neurological function caused by vascular impairment to the brain. As a result of the TIA, Greynolds had garbled speech and expressive and perceptive aphasia (a medical term used to describe the loss of the power of expression by speech, writing, or signs, or of comprehending spoken or written language). Greynolds was taken to a hospital's emergency department where he was met by Dr. Litman, a cardiologist. At Litman's request, he was examined by Dr. Rafecas, a cardiologist. Rafecas determined that because of Greynolds' past medical history, which included previous TIAs, he was at a high risk for a stroke, and sought to pinpoint the exact source of vascular insufficiency to the brain.

On August 3, 1987, after receiving the results of noninvasive tests, Rafecas ordered a cerebral angiogram. Dr. Kurman performed the angiogram. Greynolds suffered a stroke during the procedure that left him severely disabled.

Greynolds and his wife filed a medical malpractice action against Rafecas and Kurman, asserting that Rafecas had negligently recommended the procedure and that Kurman had performed the procedure without obtaining the informed consent of the patient.

Kurman argued that the trial court erred by refusing to enter judgment for him consistent with the answer to jury interrogatory number three:

> Interrogatory No. 1: Do you find there was a failure to obtain informed consent?
>
> Answer: Yes.
>
> Interrogatory No. 2: If you answered Interrogatory No. 1 yes, then state specifically in what manner Dr. Kurman's care fell below the recognized standards of the medical community?
>
> Answer: Mr. Greynolds was not in our estimation capable of comprehending the consent form. Therefore, Dr. Kurman should have obtained consent from the next-of-kin, specifically, Mrs. Greynolds.
>
> Interrogatory No. 3: If you answered yes to interrogatory No. 1 and you found that Mr. Greynolds did not consent to the procedure, do you find that a reasonable person would have consented to the procedure?
>
> Answer: Yes. *Id.* at 949.

Kurman moved the trial court to grant him a judgment notwithstanding the verdict because the jury's answer to interrogatory number three was inconsistent with the jury's general verdict. The trial court overruled Kurman's motion and entered judgment for the plaintiffs. Kurman appealed.

Issue

Was there sufficient evidence to support a judgment for the plaintiffs?

Holding

The court of appeals held that the evidence was sufficient to support a judgment in favor of the patient and his wife.

Reason

In determining whether a judgment in a civil case is supported by sufficient evidence, the court examines whether the judgment is supported by credible evidence going to all the essential elements of the case. The jury needed to determine that the risks involved in the cerebral angiogram were not disclosed to Greynolds, that the risks involved in the procedure materialized and caused his stroke, and that a reasonable person in the position of Greynolds would have decided against having the angiogram had the risks associated with the procedure been disclosed to him. The jury concluded that Greynolds did not consent to the angiogram because he "was not . . . capable of comprehending the consent form," and further noted that Kurman should have sought consent from the next of kin, specifically, the spouse. Given the evidence of Greynolds' condition when he signed the consent forms, his past medical history, and the fact that he was at an increased risk to suffer complications during an angiogram, the court found that there was sufficient evidence to support a finding of lack of informed consent.

Discussion

1. What would constitute informed consent?
2. Who should describe the risks associated with a procedure to the patient?

Competent Patients

A competent adult patient's wishes concerning his or her person may not be disregarded. The court in *In re Melideo*[18] held that every human being of adult years has a right to determine what shall be done with his or her own body and cannot be subjected to medical treatment without his or her consent. When there is no compelling state interest that justifies overriding an adult patient's decision, that decision should be respected.

In *Fosmire v. Nicoleau*,[19] the New York Supreme Court, Suffolk County, issued an order authorizing blood transfusions for a patient who had refused them. The plaintiff applied for an order vacating the supreme court's order. The New York Supreme Court, Appellate Division, held that the patient's constitutional rights of due process were violated by the supreme court's issuing an order authorizing blood transfusions in the absence of notice or opportunity for the patient or her representatives to be heard. The right of a competent patient to refuse medical treatment, even if premised on fervently held religious beliefs, is not unqualified and may be overridden by compelling state interests. However, a state's interest in preserving a patient's life is not inviolate and in and of itself may not, under certain circumstances, be sufficient to overcome the patient's express desire to exercise her religious belief and forgo blood transfusion. The appellate division held in part that the state's interest would be satisfied if the other parent survived.

The court of appeals went further by stating that the citizens of the state have long had the right to make their own medical care choices without regard to their medical condition or status as parents. The court of appeals held that a competent adult has both a common-law and statutory right under Sections 2504 and 2805-d of the Public Health Law to refuse lifesaving treatment. Citing the state's authority to compel vaccination to protect the public from the spread of disease, to order treatment for persons who are incapable of making medical decisions, and to prohibit medical procedures that pose a substantial risk to the patient alone, the court of appeals did note that the right to choose was not absolute.

In the final analysis, if there is no compelling state interest to justify overriding a patient's intelligent and knowing refusal to consent to a medical procedure because of his or her religious beliefs, states are reluctant to override such a decision.

Guardianship

A guardian is an individual who by law is invested with the power and charged with the duty of taking care of a patient by protecting the patient's rights and managing the patient's estate. Guardianship is often necessary in those instances in which a patient is incapable of managing or administering his or her private affairs because of physical and/or mental disabilities or because he or she is under the age of majority.

Temporary guardianship can be granted by the courts if it is determined that such is necessary for the well-being of the patient. Temporary guardianship was granted by the court in *In re Estate of Dorone*.[20] In this case, the physician and administrator petitioned the court on two occasions for authority to administer blood. A 22-year-old male patient brought to the Lehigh Valley Hospital Center by helicopter after an automobile accident was diagnosed as suffering from an acute subdural hematoma with a brain contusion. It was determined that the patient would die unless he underwent a cranial operation. The operation required the administration of blood to which the parents would not consent because of their religious beliefs. After a hearing by telephone, the court of common pleas appointed the hospital's administrator as temporary guardian, authorizing him to consent to the performance of blood transfusions during emergency surgery. A more formal hearing did not take place because of the emergency situation that existed. Surgery was required a second time to remove a blood clot, and the court once again granted the administrator authority to authorize administration of blood. The superior court affirmed the orders, and the parents appealed. The Pennsylvania supreme court held that the judge's failure to obtain direct testimony from the patient's parents and others concerning the patient's religious beliefs was not in error when death was likely to result from withholding blood. The judge's decisions granting guardianship and the authority to consent to the administration of blood were considered absolutely necessary in the light of the facts of this case. Nothing less than a fully conscious contemporary decision by the patient himself would have been sufficient to override the evidence of medical necessity.

Consent for Minors

When a medical or surgical procedure is to be performed on a minor, the question arises whether the minor's consent alone is sufficient and, if not, from whom consent should be obtained. The courts have held, as a general proposition, that the consent of a minor to medical or surgical treatment is ineffective and that the physician must secure the consent of the minor's parent or someone standing *in loco parentis*; otherwise, he or she will risk liability. Although parental consent should be obtained before treating a minor, treatment should not be delayed to the detriment of the child.

Parental consent is not necessary when the minor is married or otherwise emancipated. Most states have enacted statutes making it valid for married and emancipated minors to provide effective consent. Several courts have held the consent of a minor to be sufficient authorization for treatment in certain situations. In any specific case, a court's determination that the consent of a minor is effective and that parental consent is unnecessary will depend on such factors as the minor's age, maturity, mental status, and emancipation and the procedure involved, as well as public policy considerations.

In *Carter v. Cangello*,[21] the California Court of Appeals held that a 17-year-old girl who was living away from home, in the home of a woman who gave her free room and board in exchange for household chores, and who made her own financial decisions, legally could consent to medical procedures performed on her. The court made this decision knowing that the girl's parents provided part of her income by paying for her private schooling and certain medical care. The physician was privileged under statute to act on the minor's consent to surgery, and such privilege insulated him from liability to the parents for treating their daughter without their consent.

Many states have recognized by legislation that treatment for such conditions as pregnancy, venereal disease, and drug dependency does not require parental consent. State legislatures have reasoned that a minor is not likely to seek medical assistance when parental consent is demanded. Insisting on parental consent for the treatment of these conditions would increase the likelihood that a minor would delay or do without treatment to avoid explanation to the parents.

Incompetent Patients

The ability to consent to treatment is a question of fact. The attending physician, who is in the best position to make the determination, should become familiar with his or her state's definition of legal incompetence. In any case in which a physician doubts a patient's capacity to consent, the consent of the legal guardian or next of kin should be obtained. If there are no relatives to consult, application should be made for a court order that would allow the procedure. It may be the duty of the court to assume responsibility of guardianship for a patient who is *non compos mentis*. The most frequently cited conditions indicative of incompetence are mental illness, mental retardation, senility, physical incapacity, and chronic alcohol or drug abuse.

A person who is mentally incompetent cannot legally consent to medical or surgical treatment. Therefore, consent of the patient's legal guardian must be obtained. When no legal guardian is available, a court that handles such matters must be petitioned to permit treatment.

Subject to applicable statutory provisions, when a physician doubts a patient's capacity to consent, even though the patient has not been judged legally incompetent, the consent of the nearest relative should be obtained. If a patient is conscious and mentally capable of giving consent for treatment, the consent of a relative without the consent of the competent patient would not protect the physician from liability.

Implied Consent

Although the law requires consent for the intentional touching that involves medical or surgical procedures, exceptions do exist with respect to emergency situations. Implied consent will generally be presumed when immediate action is required to prevent death or permanent impairment of a patient's health. If it is impossible in an emergency to obtain the consent of the patient or someone legally authorized to give consent, the required procedure may be undertaken without liability for failure to procure consent.

Unconscious patients are presumed under law to approve treatment that appears to be necessary. It is assumed that such patients would have consented if they were conscious and competent. However, if a patient expressly refuses to consent to certain treatment, such treatment may not be instituted after the patient becomes unconscious. Similarly, conscious patients suffering from emergency conditions retain the right to refuse consent.

If a procedure is necessary to protect one's life or health, every effort must be made to document the medical necessity for proceeding with medical treatment without consent. It must be shown that the emergency situation constituted an immediate threat to life or health.

In *Luka v. Lowrie*,[22] involving a 15-year-old boy whose left foot had been run over and crushed by a train, consultation by the treating physician with other physicians was an important factor in determining the outcome of the case. On the boy's arrival at the hospital, the defending physician and four house surgeons decided it was necessary to amputate the foot. The court said it was inconceivable that, had the parents been present, they would have refused consent in the face of a determination by five physicians that amputation would save the boy's life. Thus, despite testimony at the trial that the amputation may not have been necessary, professional consultation before the operation supported the assertion that a genuine emergency existed and could be implied consent.

Consent also can be implied in nonemergency situations. For example, a patient may voluntarily submit to a procedure, implying consent, without any explicitly spoken or written expression of consent. In the Massachusetts case of *O'Brien v. Cunard Steam Ship Co.*,[23] a ship's passenger who joined a line of people receiving injections was held to have implied his consent to a vaccination. The rationale for this decision is that individuals who observe a line of people and who notice that injections are being administered to those at the head of the line should expect that if they join and remain in the line, they will receive an injection. The voluntary act of entering the line and the plaintiff's opportunity to see what was taking place at the head of the line were accepted by the jury as manifestations of consent to the injection. The *O'Brien* case contains all the elements necessary to imply consent from a voluntary act: the procedure was a simple vaccination, the proceedings were visible at all times, and the plaintiff was free to withdraw up to the instant of the injection.

Whether a patient's consent can be implied is frequently asked when the condition of a patient requires some deviation from an agreed-on procedure. If a patient expressly prohibits a specific medical or surgical procedure, consent to the procedure cannot be implied. The same consent rule applies if a patient expressly prohibits a particular extension of a procedure even though the patient voluntarily submitted to the original procedure.

RELIGIOUS BELIEFS

As part of their religious beliefs, Jehovah's Witnesses generally have refused the administration of blood, even in emergency situations. Case law over the past several decades has developed to a point where any person, regardless of religious beliefs, has the right to refuse any medical treatment.

The plaintiff, Bonita Perkins, in *Perkins v. Lavin*,[24] was a Jehovah's Witness. She gave birth to a baby at defendant hospital on September 26, 1991, and was discharged two or three days later. After going home, she began hemorrhaging and returned to the hospital. She specifically informed the defendant's employees that she was not to be provided any blood or blood derivatives and completed and signed a form to that effect:

I request that no blood or blood derivatives be administered to (plaintiff) during this hospitalization, notwithstanding that such treatment may be deemed necessary in the opinion of the attending physician or his assistants to preserve life or promote recovery. I release the attending physician, his assistants, the hospital and its personnel from any responsibility whatever for any untoward results due to my refusal to permit the use of blood or its derivatives.[25]

Due to the plaintiff's condition, it became necessary to perform an emergency dilation and curettage on her. She continued to bleed and her condition deteriorated dramatically. Her blood count dropped, necessitating administration of blood products as a lifesaving measure. Her husband, who was not a Jehovah's Witness, consented to a blood transfusion, which was administered. The plaintiff recovered and filed an action against the defendant for assault and battery and intentional infliction of emotional distress. The plaintiff's claim as to assault and battery was sustained. The claim as to the intentional infliction of emotional distress was overruled.

The plaintiff specifically informed the defendant that she would consider a blood transfusion an offensive contact. Although both parties have noted that the plaintiff's husband provided his consent for the transfusion, the defendant has not argued that his consent was sufficient to overcome plaintiff's direction that she was not to receive a transfusion. The plaintiff submitted sufficient evidence to the trial court to establish that there was, at least, a genuine issue whether the defendant intentionally invaded her right to be free from offensive contact. Because of the plaintiff's recognition that the defendant acted to save her life, a jury may find that she is entitled to only nominal damages.

REFUSAL OF TREATMENT

Adult patients who are conscious and mentally competent have the right to refuse medical care to the extent permitted by law even when the best medical opinion deems it essential to life. Such a refusal must be honored whether it is grounded in religious belief or mere whim. Every person has the legal right to refuse to permit a touching of his or her body. Failure to respect this right can result in a legal action for assault and battery. If a patient refuses consent, every effort should be made to explain the importance of the procedure. Coercion through threat, duress, or intimidation must be avoided.

RELEASE FORM

A patient's refusal to consent to treatment, for any reason, religious or otherwise, should be noted in the medical record, and a release form should be executed. The completed release provides documented evidence of a patient's refusal to consent to a recommended treatment. A release will help protect the organization and physicians from liability should a suit arise as a result of a failure to treat. The best possible care must be rendered to the patient at all times within the limits imposed by the patient's refusal.

Should a patient refuse to sign the release, this should be noted in the patient's medical record. Advice of legal counsel should be sought in those cases in which refusal of treatment poses a serious threat to a patient's health.

With the advice of legal counsel, the organization should formulate a policy regarding treatment when consent has been refused. An administrative procedure should be developed to facilitate application for a court order when one is necessary and there is sufficient time to obtain one. Even though a signed consent may not unequivocally constitute proof that informed consent was obtained from a patient, it does create a presumption that it was, thereby shifting the burden of responsibility to the patient to prove that it was not.

EXCULPATORY AGREEMENT

An *"exculpatory agreement"* is an agreement that relieves one from liability when he or she has acted in good faith. Exculpatory agreements in the medical setting are generally considered invalid.

In *Cudnik v. William Beaumont Hospital,*[26] Mr. Cudnik underwent radiation therapy in March and April 1985, after undergoing surgery for prostate cancer. Before receiving therapy, he signed a consent document that provided in part:

> Further, my physician has fully explained to me the possibilities of reactions and the possible side effects of the treatment. I understand that there is no guarantee given to me as to the results of radiation therapy. Understanding all of the foregoing, I hereby release the physicians and staff of the Department of Radiation Oncology and William Beaumont Hospital from all suits, claims, liability, or demands of every kind and character which I or my heirs, executors, administrators [sic] or assigns hereafter can, shall, or may have arising out of my participation in the radiation therapy treatment regimen.[27]

In early 1989, Cudnik returned to the hospital complaining of back discomfort, whereupon he was diagnosed as suffering from a postradiation ulcer burn at the site where he previously received radiation treatment. An action was brought against the hospital claiming that the negligent administration of radiation therapy contributed to Cudnik's death. The defendant moved for summary judgment and the Oakland Circuit Court granted the hospital's motion after concluding that the exculpatory agreement between the parties precluded the plaintiff's claims. The plaintiff appealed, claiming that the hospital should be held vicariously liable for the medical malpractice of its employees or agents.

As a general proposition, the parties to a contract may enter into an exculpatory agreement provided that it does not violate the law or contravene public policy. The question in this case is whether the plaintiff's claim of medical malpractice is precluded by the exculpatory agreement between the two parties. The court of appeals held in this case that the exculpatory agreement executed by the patient prior to receiving radiation therapy was invalid and unenforceable to absolve a medical care provider from liability for medical malpractice. The agreement in this case is clearly against public policy.

The majority of jurisdictions that have addressed this question have held that exculpatory agreements in medical situations are unenforceable because medical treatment involves a particularly sensitive area of public interest. The performance of medical services is of great importance to the public, and is a matter of practical necessity for some members of the public.

The results of this case by no means are an indication that hospitals should discontinue the use of patient consent forms. It merely points out that true negligence is actionable and that exculpatory agreements are generally invalid. The patient does, however, have the right to know the potential benefits, risks, alternatives, and outcomes of the proposed and agreed-upon treatment plan.

Some exculpatory agreements in the medical setting are considered valid. An exception to the general rule invalidating exculpatory agreements for medical malpractice involves experimental procedures. Experimental procedures may require a different standard, because, by their very nature, they require a deviation from generally accepted medical practices. For example, in a case involving the patient's last hope of survival, the New York Supreme Court held that "the parties may covenant to exempt the physician from liability for those injuries which are found to be the consequences of the nonnegligent, proper performance of the procedure."[28] The *Cudnik* case does not appear to involve an experimental procedure.

STATUTORY CONSENT

Many states have adopted legislation concerning emergency care. An emergency in most states eliminates the need for consent. When a patient is clinically unable to give consent to a lifesaving emergency treatment, the law implies consent on the presumption that a reasonable person would consent to lifesaving medical intervention.

When an emergency situation does arise, there may be little opportunity to contact the attending physician, much less a consultant. The patient's records, therefore, must be complete with respect to the description of his or her illness and condition, the attempts made to contact the physician as well as relatives, and the emergency measures taken and procedures performed. If time does not permit a court order to be obtained, a second medical opinion, when practicable, is advisable.

CONSENT AND JUDICIAL INTERVENTION

Judicial intervention is periodically necessary for emergency matters when a court is not in session. A judge should be contacted only after alternative methods have been exhausted and the matter cannot wait for a determination during the normal working hours of the court. Some courts (e.g., Massachusetts trial courts) require an attorney to initiate the call to the justice and to certify that there are no alternatives, other than a judicial response, available in the matter.

DEFENSE AND FAILURE TO INFORM

The burden of establishing proof on a complaint of lack of informed consent is on the plaintiff. The plaintiff must establish that: (1) a reasonably prudent person in the patient's position would not have undergone the treatment or diagnosis if fully informed; and (2) the lack of informed consent is the proximate cause of the injury or condition for which recovery is sought.

In a lawsuit, testimony would be necessary to establish the extent of the patient's actual knowledge and understanding of the treatment rendered. It is possible for a patient, after treatment, to claim a lack of advance knowledge about the nature of a physician's treatment. And it is possible that a jury will believe the patient and impose liability on the physician and/or the organization.

Several defenses are available to defendants who have been sued on the basis of failure to provide their patients with sufficient information to make an informed decision. Some of the defenses include:

- The risk not disclosed is too commonly known to warrant disclosure.
- The patient assured the medical practitioner that he or she would undergo the treatment, procedure, or diagnosis regardless of the risk involved, or the patient assured the medical practitioner that he or she did not want to be informed of the matters to which he or she would be entitled to be informed.
- Consent by or on behalf of a patient was not reasonably possible.
- The medical practitioner, after considering all of the attendant facts and circumstances, used reasonable discretion

as to the manner and extent to which such alternatives or risks were disclosed to the patient because the practitioner reasonably believed that the manner and extent of such disclosure could reasonably be expected to adversely and substantially affect the patient's condition.

A patient's condition during surgery may be recognized as different from that which had been expected and explained, requiring a different procedure than the one to which the patient initially had consented. The surgeon may proceed to treat the new condition; however, the patient must have been aware of the possibility of extending the procedure. The patient in *Winfrey v. Citizens & Southern National Bank*[29] brought a suit against the deceased surgeon's estate, alleging that during exploratory surgery the surgeon had performed a complete hysterectomy without the patient's consent. The superior court granted summary judgment for the surgeon's estate, and the patient appealed. The court of appeals held that even though the patient may not have read the consent document, when no legally sufficient excuse appeared, she was bound by the terms of the consent document that she voluntarily executed. The plain wording of the binding consent authorized the surgeon to perform additional or different operations or procedures that he might consider necessary or advisable in the course of the operation. Relevant sections of the consent signed by the patient included the following:

1. I authorize the performance on (patient's name) of the following operation/laparoscopy, possible laparotomy....
2. I consent to the performance of operations and procedures in addition to or different from those now contemplated, which the above named doctor or his associates or assistants may consider necessary or advisable in the course of the operation....

• • • •

7. I acknowledge that the nature and purpose of the operation, possible alternative methods of treatment, the risks involved, and the possibility of complications have been fully explained to me.[30]

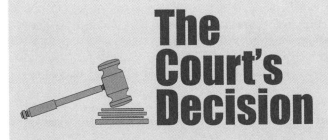

The Court's Decision

The Georgia Court of Appeals held that the patient's voluntary termination of her relationship with the hospital's emergency department personnel effectively severed any relationship between the hospital's act of classifying the patient as a category two patient who could wait to see a physician and her subsequent death two days later. Accordingly, the hospital could not be held liable for the death of the patient.

To recover damages in a tort action, a plaintiff must prove that the defendant's negligence was both the "cause in fact" and the "proximate cause" of the injury. The requirement of proximate cause constitutes a limit on legal liability; it is a policy decision that, for a variety of reasons (e.g., intervening act, the defendant's conduct, and the plaintiff's injury), is too remote for the law to consider recovery. Matthews left the hospital on her own cognizance at a time when the hospital's emergency department physician was about to see her. She went to work the following morning without seeing her own physician, as she had indicated that she would. The elements that a plaintiff must establish in a malpractice case are duty to care, breach of duty, injury, and causation. The fact that Matthews voluntarily terminated her relationship with the emergency department personnel at DeKalb General effectively severed any causal relationship that might have existed between DeKalb General's act of classifying Matthews as a category two patient and her death.

CHAPTER REVIEW

1. Patients have rights to make decisions regarding their own health care under the Patient Self-Determination Act of 1990. These rights include the ability to refuse or accept medical or surgical treatment.

2. *Consent* is voluntary agreement by a person to allow something proposed by another to be performed on him- or herself. A person can consent to something only if he or she has sufficient mental capacity to make an intelligent choice. A verbal or written agreement provides *express consent*. In cases in which an act or silence indicates that performance of an act has been authorized, the consent is referred to as *implied consent*. Consent may be given either by an individual or by someone authorized to consent on the individual's behalf.

3. The legal concept that protects a patient's right to know the potential risks, benefits, and alternatives of a proposed procedure is referred to as *informed consent*. Most often, the duty to inform the patient and to decide what information the patient should be given falls to the treating physician, who has the expertise, education, skill, and training necessary to treat the patient. It is up to the individual responsible for obtaining consent to decide whether to give full disclosure to the patient, or whether this degree of disclosure would seriously and adversely affect the patient's condition. Modified disclosure can be supported if it can be proven that other physicians in the community also would have made a modified disclosure.

4. Most often, medical personnel are the ones who have to make decisions regarding a patient's competence and concurrent ability to make medical decisions regarding his or her care.

5. Under the *subjective standard*, causation is established solely by patient testimony. Conversely, the *objective standard* resolves the issue of causation in terms of what a prudent person in the patient's position would have decided if suitably informed of all perils bearing significance.

6. Liability for performing a medical or surgical procedure without consent is distinct from a question of negligence or malpractice in performing the procedure. A physician can be found liable for imposing nonconsenual treatment, even if that treatment improved the patient's health.

7. Oral consent, although binding, is often difficult to corroborate, whereas written consent provides visible proof of a patient's wishes.

8. *Temporary consent* is an agreement that allows the health care facility to initiate emergency treatment while an attempt is being made to reach the family or other appropriate party for consent. Temporary consent is often provided by people, like schools officials, teachers, and camp counselors, who work with children.

9. *Special consent* forms are obtained when a proposed treatment exposes a patient to unusual risks. These forms should be signed, dated, and witnessed at the time that the physician explains the procedure and associated risks to the patient.

10. Generally, the consent of a minor is not sufficient to proceed with medical or surgical treatment. However, parental consent, or the consent of another party standing *in loco parentis*, is not required if the minor is married or otherwise emancipated.

11. If an individual is found incompetent to give consent, and if there are no relatives or other parties from whom to obtain consent, an application should be made for a court order that would allow the procedure.

12. Implied consent is generally presumed when immediate action is required to prevent death or permanent impairment of a patient's health. In such cases, documentation justifying the need to treat before obtaining consent should be maintained.

13. Over the past few decades, case law has developed in such a way that any person, regardless of religious beliefs, has the right to refuse any medical treatment. If a patient refuses treatment, that refusal should be noted in the patient's medical record and a release form should be executed.

14. An *exculpatory agreement* is an agreement that relieves one from liability when he or she has acted in good faith. However, these are generally considered invalid in the medical setting.

REVIEW QUESTIONS

1. Who should be responsible for reviewing with the patient the risks, benefits, and alternatives of a proposed diagnostic test or treatment?

2. Describe what information a patient should be provided prior to undergoing a risky procedure in order for consent to be "informed."
3. Why is it important to obtain consent from a patient prior to proceeding with a risky procedure?
4. Can a patient give consent and then withdraw it?
5. Can a parent refuse to consent to a lifesaving procedure for his or her child? Discuss your answer.
6. How much information is sufficient in order for informed consent to be effective?
7. Discuss the implications of the following statement: "Patients are generally persons unlearned in the medical sciences and, therefore, except in rare instances, the knowledge of patient and physician is *not in parity.*"

NOTES

1. Matthews v. DeKalb County Hosp. Auth., 440 S.E.2d 743 (Ga. Ct. App. 1994).
2. Public Law 101–508, November 5, 1990, sections 4206 and 4751 of the Omnibus Budget Reconciliation Act.
3. 42 U.S.C. 1395cc(a)(1).
4. 567 N.W.2d 156 (Neb. 1997).
5. 972 F. Supp. 308 (D.C. Pa. 1997).
6. 635 A.2d 1047 (Pa. Super. Ct. 1993).
7. 733 A.2d 456 (1999).
8. *Id.* at 461.
9. 620 So.2d 372 (La. Ct. App. 1993).
10. *Id.* at 380.
11. 67 Cal. Rptr. 2d 573 (Cal. App. 1997).
12. 842 S.W.2d 860 (Ky. 1992).
13. 418 A.2d 1123 (Me. 1980).
14. 534 N.E.2d 472 (Ill. App. Ct. 1989).
15. Cruzan v. Director, Missouri Dep't of Health, 497 U.S. 261, 269 (1990).
16. 105 N.E. 92, 93 (N.Y. 1914).
17. 689 N.E.2d 397 (Ill. App. Ct. 1997).
18. 390 N.Y.S.2d 523 (N.Y. Sup. Ct. 1976).
19. 536 N.Y.S.2d 492 (N.Y. App. Div. 1989).
20. 534 A.2d 452 (Pa. 1987).
21. 164 Cal. Rptr. 361 (Cal. Ct. App. 1980).
22. 136 N.W. 1106 (Mich. 1912).
23. 28 N.E. 266 (Mass. 1891).
24. 648 N.E.2d 839 (Ohio App. 9 Dist. 1994).
25. *Id.* at 840.
26. 525 N.W.2d 891 (Mich. App. 1994).
27. *Id.* at 893.
28. Colton v. New York Hosp., 414 N.Y.S.2d 866 (1979).
29. 254 S.E.2d 725 (Ga. Ct. App. 1979).
30. *Id.* at 727.

It's Your Gavel...

ALLEGED ABUSE: IMMUNITY PROVIDED PSYCHOLOGIST

Two children were placed in the temporary custody of a foster family. One child was referred to a licensed psychologist for evaluation. After two interviews the psychologist formed the professional opinion that the child had been sexually molested. Based in part on statements made by the child, the psychologist further believed that the perpetrator of the suspected molestation was the father. At a hearing before the juvenile court, the court determined that the evidence did not support a finding that the child had been abused by his father. Custody was returned to the parents.

The child's parents subsequently initiated an action for medical malpractice against the psychologist. The psychologist claimed immunity from liability as provided by a state child abuse reporting statute. The trial court and the parents appealed, arguing that the immunity provisions of the statute do not apply to the psychologist because she was not a "mandatory reporter" under that statute.[1]

What is your verdict?

INTRODUCTION

This chapter provides an overview of a variety of reporting requirements mandated by both federal and state regulatory agencies. It is through such reporting that appropriate measures can be taken to safeguard the health of the nation's population. Most states have legislative reporting requirements for diseases that pose a threat to public health and safety.

Rules and regulations are designed to encourage the health care professional to report and to protect the health care professional from liability. Although most statutory reporting requirements do not contain an express immunity from liability for disclosure without the permission of the person affected, as a general rule, a person making a report in good faith and under statutory command is protected.

CHILD ABUSE

The physically abused or neglected child presents a medical, social, and legal problem. What constitutes an abused child is difficult to determine because it is often impossible to ascertain whether a child was injured intentionally or accidentally.

What Is Child Abuse?

An abused child is one who has suffered intentional serious mental, emotional, sexual, and/or physical injury inflicted by a parent or other person responsible for the child's care. Some states extend the definition to include a child suffering from starvation. Other states include moral neglect in the definition of abuse. Others mention immoral associations; endangering a child's morals; and the location of a child in a disreputable place or in association with vagrant, vicious, or immoral persons. Sexual abuse also is enumerated as an element of neglect in the statutes of some states.

An abused child is generally defined as a person younger than 18 years of age whose parent or other person legally responsible for his or her care: inflicts, or allows to be inflicted, upon a child, physical injury by nonaccidental means that causes or creates a substantial risk of death, serious or protracted disfigurement, protracted impairment of physical or emotional health, or protracted loss or impairment of the function of any bodily organ; commits, or allows to be committed, a sex offense against a child; and/or allows, permits, or encourages a child to engage in an act considered unlawful.

Who Should Report?

Presently, all states have enacted laws to protect abused children. Most states protect the persons required to report cases of child abuse. In a few states, certain identified individuals who are not required to report instances of child abuse, but who do so, are protected. Child abuse laws may or may not provide penalties for failure to report. The individuals covered by the various statutes range from physicians to any person. Persons in the health care setting who are required to report or cause a report to be made when they have reasonable cause to suspect that a child has been abused include administrators, physicians, interns, registered nurses, chiropractors, social service workers, psychologists, dentists, osteopaths, optometrists, podiatrists, mental health professionals, and volunteers in residential facilities

Detecting Abuse

An individual who reports child abuse should be aware of the physical and behavioral indicators of abuse and maltreatment that appear to be part of a pattern (e.g., bruises, burns, and broken bones). In reviewing the indicators of abuse and maltreatment, the reporter does not have to be absolutely certain that abuse or maltreatment exists before reporting. Rather, abuse and maltreatment should be reported whenever they are suspected, based on the existence of the signs of abuse and maltreatment and in light of the reporter's train-

ing and experience. Behavioral indicators include, but are not limited to, substantially diminished psychological or intellectual functioning, as failure to thrive, no control of aggression, self-destructive impulses, decreased ability to think and reason, acting out and misbehavior, or habitual truancy. Such impairment must be clearly attributable to the unwillingness or inability of the person responsible for the child's care to exercise a minimum degree of care toward the child.

Good-Faith Reporting

Any report of suspected child abuse must be made with a good-faith belief that the facts reported are true. The definition of *good faith* as used in a child abuse statute may vary from state to state. However, when a health care practitioner's medical evaluation indicates reasonable cause to believe a child's injuries were not accidental and when the health care practitioner is not acting from his or her desire to harass, injure, or embarrass the child's parents, making the report will not result in liability.

Statutes generally require that when a person covered by a statute is attending a child and suspects child abuse, the staff member must report such concerns. Typical statutes provide that an oral report be made immediately, followed by a written report. Most states require the report to contain the following information:

- the child's name and address
- the persons responsible for the child's care
- the child's age
- the nature and extent of the child's injuries (including any evidence of previous injuries)
- any other information that might be helpful in establishing the cause of the injuries, such as photographs of the injured child and the identity of the alleged perpetrator

A minor child and his mother brought an action for damages against physicians for failing to diagnose disease and filing erroneous child abuse reports in *Awkerman v. Tri-County Orthopedic Group*.[2] The Wayne County Circuit Court granted the physicians' motions for partial summary judgment, and the plaintiffs appealed. The Michigan Court of Appeals held that the child abuse reporting statute provides immunity to persons who file child abuse reports in good faith even if the reports were filed because of negligent diagnosis of the cause of the child's frequent bone fractures, which eventually was diagnosed as osteogenesis imperfecta. The court of appeals also held that damages for shame and humiliation were not recoverable pursuant to Michigan statute. Immunity from liability did not extend to damages for malpractice that may have resulted from the failure to diagnose the child's disease as long as all the elements of negligence were present.

ELDER ABUSE

Elder abuse is the harmful treatment of people and includes abandonment; emotional, financial (e.g., theft or misuse of an elder's money or property by a person in a position of trust), verbal, mental, sexual, or physical abuse, corporal punishment; and involuntary restraint and seclusion. *Neglect* is the failure to provide the care necessary to avoid physical harm (e.g., the failure of staff to turn a patient periodically to prevent pressure sores) or mental anguish.

Most states have enacted statutes mandating the reporting of elder abuse. In general, elder abuse is less likely to be reported than child abuse. Physical and emotional neglect, as well as verbal and financial abuse, are perceived as the most prevalent forms of elder abuse. Seniors often fail to report incidents of abuse because they fear retaliation and not being believed. Threats of placement in a nursing home or shame that a family member may be involved often prevents the elder from seeking help. In addition, proving such charges is often difficult.

Signs of Abuse or Neglect

- Unexplained or unexpected death
- Development of "pressure sores"
- Heavy medication and sedation used in place of adequate nursing staff
- Occurrence of broken bones
- Sudden and unexpected emotional outbursts, agitation, or withdrawal
- Bruises, welts, discoloration, burns, and so on
- Absence of hair and/or hemorrhaging below scalp
- Dehydration and/or malnourishment without illness-related cause
- Hesitation to talk openly
- Implausible stories
- Unusual or inappropriate activity in bank accounts
- Signatures of checks, etc., that do not resemble the patient's signature
- Power of attorney given or recent changes or creation of will when the person is incapable of making such decisions
- Missing personal belongings such as silverware or jewelry
- Senior has an untreated medical condition
- The senior may not be given the opportunity to speak for him- or herself, or see others, without the presence of the caregiver (suspected abuser).

Policies and Procedures

Policies and procedures should be developed that include prohibition of mistreatment; description of reporting procedures regarding alleged abuse; maintenance of evidence of alleged abuse; investigation of alleged abuse; and preventing further potential abuse while an investigation is in progress.

Documentation

Caregivers who suspect abuse are expected to report their findings. Symptoms and conditions of suspected abuse should be defined clearly and objectively.

- *Witnesses*—Reporters of abuse must describe statements made by others as accurately as possible; what actions were taken, by whom, when, where, etc. Information should be included on how witnesses may be contacted.
- *Photographs*—It may be necessary to photograph wounds or injuries. A hospital emergency room or the police department can be asked to photograph emergency situations.

COMMUNICABLE DISEASES

Most states have enacted laws that require the reporting of actual or suspected cases of communicable diseases. The need for statutes requiring the reporting of communicable diseases is clear: If a state is to protect its citizens' health through its power to quarantine, it must ensure the prompt reporting of infection or disease.

BIRTHS AND DEATHS

All births and deaths are reportable by statute. Births occurring outside of a health care facility should be reported by the legally qualified physician in attendance at a delivery or, in the event of the absence of a physician, by the registered nurse or other attendant. The physician who pronounces death must sign the death certificate. Statutes requiring the reporting of births and deaths are necessary to maintain accurate census records.

SUSPICIOUS DEATHS

Greater than a state's interest in the recording of all births and deaths is the state's desire to review suspicious deaths that may be the result of some form of criminal activity. Unnatural deaths must be referred to the medical examiner for review. Such cases include violent deaths, deaths caused by unlawful acts or criminal neglect, and deaths that may be considered suspicious or unusual. The medical examiner may make an investigation of such cases and issue an autopsy report. The purpose of a medical examiner's investigation is to determine the actual cause of death and thereby provide assistance for any further criminal investigation that may be considered necessary.

REPORTING PROFESSIONAL MISCONDUCT—NATIONAL PRACTITIONER DATA BANK

The Health Care Quality Improvement Act of 1986 (HCQIA)[3], signed by President Reagan on November 14, 1986, was enacted to encourage greater efforts in professional peer review and to restrict the ability of incompetent practitioners who move from state to state attempting to avoid discovery of previous substandard performance or unprofessional conduct. The law established the National Practitioner Data Bank, to be operated under the authority of the Secretary of the Department of Health and Human Services (HHS). Responsibility for data bank implementation resides in the Bureau of Health Professions, Health Resources and Services Administration of the HHS. The Act authorizes the data bank to be used to collect and release information on the professional competence and conduct of physicians, dentists, and other health care practitioners. Reporting and disclosure requirements for the National Practitioner Data Bank also are set out in regulations.[4]

After several delays and changes since it was mandated by Congress in 1986, the National Practitioner Data Bank became operational September 1, 1990. The regulations are intended to encourage good-faith professional review activities. The data bank was established because of the increasing occurrence of medical malpractice and the need to improve the quality of medical care; the need to restrict the ability of incompetent physicians who move from state to state without disclosure or discovery of their previous damaging or incompetent performance; and the overriding need to provide incentive and protection for physicians engaging in professional peer review.[5]

The National Practitioner Data Bank presents a number of challenges to health care institutions. A major one is to educate the medical staff so that the data bank will not erode medical staff participation in risk management. The purpose of the data bank is not punishment, but rather prevention and deterrence.

Reporting Requirements

The regulations establish reporting requirements applicable to hospitals; health care entities; boards of medical ex-

aminers; professional societies of physicians, dentists, or other health care practitioners that take adverse licensure or professional review actions (e.g., reduction, restriction, suspension, revocation, or denial of clinical privileges or membership in a health care entity of 30 days or longer); and individuals and entities (including insurance companies) making payments as a result of medical malpractice actions or claims. A medical malpractice action or claim has been defined as a written complaint or claim demanding payment based on a health care practitioner's provision of or failure to provide health care services, including the filing of a cause of action based on tort law, brought in any state or federal court or other adjudicative body.

Required Queries and Medical Staff Privileges

Health care organizations must query the data bank every two years on the renewal of staff privileges of physicians and dentists. The data bank serves as a flagging system whose principal purpose is to facilitate a more comprehensive review of professional credentials. As a nationwide flagging system, it provides another resource to assist state licensing boards, hospitals, and other health care entities in conducting extensive independent reviews of the qualifications of health care practitioners they seek to license or hire or to whom they wish to grant clinical privileges.

Who Should Report?

For those health care providers who question whether they are covered under this law, HHS defines the term *entity* broadly, rather than to attempt to focus on the myriad health care organizations, practice arrangements, and professional societies, to ensure that the regulations include all entities within the scope of the statute. A health care entity is an entity that provides health care services and engages in professional review activity through a formal peer review process for the purpose of furthering quality health care, or a committee of that entity. Health care practitioners include all health care practitioners authorized by a state to provide health care services by whatever formal mechanism the state uses (e.g., certification, registration, and licensure).

Data Bank Queries

Data bank queries can be made by state licensing boards, hospitals, other health care entities, and professional societies, which have entered or may be entering employment or affiliation relationships with a physician, dentist, or other health care practitioner who has applied for clinical privileges or appointment to a medical staff. A plaintiff's attorney is permitted to obtain information from the data bank when a malpractice action has been filed and the practitioner on whom information has been sought is named in the suit.

Data Bank Query Fees

Under data bank rules, there is a nominal fee for data bank queries each time a physician and dentist apply for medical staff privileges at their facilities.[6]

Penalties for Failing To Report

Hospitals or other health care entities that fail to report adverse professional review actions limiting the clinical privileges of physicians or dentists lasting more than 30 days can lose immunity protection provided by Title IV of the HCQIA for a three-year period.

Confidentiality of Data Bank Information

Information reported to the data bank is considered strictly confidential. Individuals and entities that knowingly and willfully report to or query the data bank under false pretenses or fraudulently access the data bank computer directly are subject to civil penalties. The data bank follows the following guidelines on disclosure:

> Information reported to the Data Bank is considered confidential and shall not be disclosed outside the Department of Health and Human Services, except as specified in Sec. 60.10, Sec. 60.11 and Sec. 60.[7] Persons and entities which receive information from the Data Bank either directly or from another party must use it solely with respect to the purpose for which it was provided. Nothing in this paragraph shall prevent the disclosure of information by a party which is authorized under applicable State law to make such disclosure. . . . Any person who violates [the above] shall be subject to a civil money penalty of up to $10,000 for each violation. . . .[8]

RISK MANAGEMENT/INCIDENT REPORTING

The purpose of a risk management program is to reduce the number of patient injuries and minimize the exposure of an organization to lawsuits. An effective risk management program includes a monitoring system that identifies potential risks to patients and staff. Information gathered is used to improve patient care and treatment practices. A successful risk management program requires a high degree of trust and collaboration between the medical staff and organization.

Incident reports contain statements made by employees and physicians regarding a noteworthy deviation from what is considered acceptable patient care. Some state health codes provide that hospitals and nursing facilities must investigate incidents regarding patient care and require that certain incidents must be reported in a manner prescribed by regulation. Reportable incidents often include such things as those incidents that have resulted in a patient's serious injury or death, an event such as fire or loss of emergency power, certain infection outbreaks, and strikes by employees.

Incident reports should not be placed in the medical record. They should be directed to counsel for legal advice. This will help prevent discovery on the basis of client-attorney privilege. There is conflicting case law in that some courts will not permit incident reports to be discovered whereas others will allow discovery. A Florida appeals court ruled that incident reports prepared in anticipation of litigation are not discoverable, even though the information contained in the report was not available by any other means.[9] In *Berg v. Des Moines General Hospital Co.,*[10] the Iowa Supreme Court ruled that, because of the time lapse between the actual incident and the inability of the nurses to recall the incident, discovery of the written incident report was allowed.

Hospital Incident/Occurrence Reports Discoverable

Occurrence reports in *Columbia/HCA Healthcare Corp. v. Eighth Judicial District Court*[11] were found to have been prepared in the ordinary course of the hospital's business, and were therefore not protected by the work product doctrine. The hospital's petition implicitly admitted that it required its personnel to fill out preprinted forms in the event of an unexpected occurrence. Occurrence reports consisted of a four-page form, which was completed by a hospital employee who had information regarding an unusual event that occurred at the hospital. The hospital further admitted that the purpose, at least in part, for creating occurrence reports was to improve the quality of care given at the hospital. The hospital documents did not become privileged by injecting an attorney into the investigative process. The investigation occurred in the ordinary course of business. The Nevada legislature never intended to exempt occurrence reports from discovery under NEV. REV. STAT. § 49.265.

Occurrence reports, which the hospital admitted are nothing more than factual narratives, contain the very type of information that will most likely be uncovered through traditional discovery procedures. In those instances where the information can be obtained only through the occurrence report, prospective plaintiffs should not be denied access. Allowing NEV. REV. STAT. § 49.265 to become an impenetrable bulwark of damaging factual information defeats the very purposes of Nevada's evidence code for which NEV. REV. STAT. § 49.265 is a part: "The purposes of this [evidence code is] to secure fairness in administration . . . to the end that truth may be ascertained and proceedings justly determined".[12] The court concluded that the occurrence reports are neither work product nor protected by the peer review privilege embodied in NEV. REV. STAT. § 49.265

State Reportable Incidents

Various states require, by law, that certain incidents be reported. For example, New York State Public Health Law requires hospitals to investigate incidents regarding patient care and report them to the department of health.

> Hospitals shall report such incidents within 24 hours of when the incident occurred or when the hospital has reasonable cause to believe that such an incident has occurred and shall take no more than seven calendar days to determine whether an incident defined . . . is reportable and subject to the requirements of this section. The hospital shall give written notification within seven calendar days of the initial notification. This notification shall be submitted in a format specified by the department and shall record the nature, classification and location of the incident; medical record numbers of all patients directly affected by the incident; the full name and title of physicians and hospital staff directly involved in the incident as well as their license, permit, certification or registration numbers; the effect of the incident on the patient; follow-up treatments and evaluations planned; the expected completion date for the hospital's investigation and identification information required by the department.[13]

Incidents that must be reported within 24 hours of occurrence include: patient deaths in circumstances other than those related to the natural course of illness; fires or internal disasters in the facility; equipment malfunction or equipment user error during treatment or diagnosis of a patient that did or could have adversely affected a patient or personnel; poisoning occurring within the facility; reportable infection outbreaks; patient elopements and kidnappings; strikes by personnel; disasters or other emergency situations external to the organization's environment that affect facility operations; and unscheduled termination of any services vital to the continued safe operation of the facility.

Individuals designated to report incidents must do so if required by a state's statute. The director of nursing at a nursing facility in *Choe v. Axelrod*[14] was fined $150 for failure to report an instance of patient neglect. An anonymous telephone call had been placed with the department of health regarding two incidents of alleged patient neglect. In one incident, a patient had been left unattended in a shower by an orderly, and the patient sprayed himself with hot water, which resulted in second-degree burns on his forehead. On a second occasion, a similar incident occurred, but no one was injured. On investigation by the department of health, a determination was made that both incidents constituted patient neglect and that failure to report these incidents was a violation of New York Public Health Law. After a hearing by an administrative law judge, the charge in the first incident was sustained and in the second incident was dismissed. The director of nurses petitioned to annul the administrative determination. She contended that the department of health failed to establish a *prima facie* case of patient neglect, that the incident was an unavoidable accident, and that the department of health's proof was based on hearsay evidence. The court held that evidence supported a finding that the director of nurses had failed to report an incident of patient neglect as required by statute. On the question of hearsay evidence:

> It is . . . well established that an agency can prove its case through hearsay evidence. . . . In the final analysis, the evidence showed that the patient was left unattended, albeit momentarily, O'Brien (the orderly) was disciplined for that act, and petitioner did not report the incident. The finding is thus supported by the kind of evidence on which reasonable persons are accustomed to rely in serious affairs.[15]

Although it may not always be clear as to when an incident report should be filed, appropriate procedures should be in place addressing how questionable events should be handled.

SENTINEL EVENT REPORTING/JOINT COMMISSION

The Joint Commission on Accreditation of Healthcare Organizations implemented a policy requiring health care organizations to self-report sentinel events. The Joint Commission has defined a *sentinel event* as "an unexpected occurrence involving death or serious physical or psychological injury, or the risk thereof. Serious injury specifically includes loss of limb or function. The phrase, or the risk thereof, includes any variation for which recurrence would carry a significant chance of a serious adverse outcome."[16] The sentinel event policy of the Joint Commission applies only to events that meet the following criteria: (1) the event has resulted in an unanticipated death or major permanent loss of function, not related to the natural course of the patient's illness or underlying condition; or (2) the event is one of the following (even if the outcome was not death or major permanent loss of function):

- suicide
- infant abduction or discharge to the wrong family
- rape
- hemolytic transfusion reaction involving administration of blood or blood products having major blood group incompatibilities[17]

Sentinel events that are not reportable include: any near miss; full return of bodily function to the same level as prior to the adverse event by discharge or within two weeks of the initial loss of said function; any sentinel event that has not affected the recipient of care; and medication errors that do not result in death or major permanent loss of function. Top sentinel event occurrences include: patient suicides; medication errors; deaths due to delay in treatment; operative/postoperative complications; and surgical procedures on the wrong site.

Organizations are expected to conduct a *root cause analysis* when sentinel events occur. *Root cause analysis* is "a process for identifying the basic or causal factors that underlie variation in performance, including the occurrence or possible occurrence of a sentinel event."[18] The basic purpose of root cause analysis is to improve organizational performance outcomes. Organizations that decline to share any information regarding a sentinel event with the Joint Commission are at risk for being placed on Accreditation Watch (monitoring an organization because of a sentinel event) and, ultimately, risk the loss of accreditation.

Organizations are concerned with the possibility that root cause analyses could be subject to discovery by plaintiff attorneys and could be used against them in civil trials. To address this concern and minimize the risks of additional liability exposure, the Joint Commission continues to work with state hospital associations, as well as state and federal legislators, to prevent the disclosure of the substance of root cause analyses.

CORPORATE COMPLIANCE PROGRAMS

The federal government's initiative to investigate and prosecute health care organizations for criminal wrongdoing, coupled with strong sanctions imposed after conviction, is resulting in health care organizations hiring attorneys to assist them in establishing internal mechanisms for prevent-

ing, detecting, and reporting criminal conduct. Sentencing incentives are in place for organizations that establish effective corporate compliance programs. The following paragraphs describe the elements of an effective corporate compliance program.

An "effective program to prevent and detect violations of the law" means a program that has been reasonably designed, implemented, and enforced so that it generally will be effective in preventing and detecting criminal conduct. Failure to prevent or detect the instant offense, by itself, does not mean that the program was not effective. The hallmark of an effective program to prevent and detect violations of law is that the organization exercised due diligence in seeking to prevent and detect criminal conduct by its employees and other agents. Due diligence requires at a minimum that the organization must have taken the following types of steps:

(1) The organization must have established compliance standards and procedures to be followed by its employees and other agents that are reasonably capable of reducing the prospect of criminal conduct.

(2) Specific individual(s) within high-level personnel of the organization must have been assigned overall responsibility to oversee compliance with such standards and procedures.

(3) The organization must have used due care not to delegate substantial discretionary authority to individuals whom the organization knew, or should have known through the exercise of due diligence, had a propensity to engage in illegal conduct.

(4) The organization must have taken steps to communicate effectively its standards and procedures to all employees and other agents, e.g., by requiring participation in training programs or by disseminating publications that explain in a practical manner what is required.

(5) The organization must have taken reasonable steps to achieve compliance with its standards, e.g., by utilizing monitoring and auditing systems reasonably designed to detect criminal conduct by its employees and other agents and by having in place and publicizing a reporting system whereby employees and other agents could report criminal conduct by others within the organization without fear of retribution.

(6) The standards must have been consistently enforced through appropriate disciplinary mecha-

nisms, including, as appropriate, discipline of individuals responsible for the failure to detect an offense. Adequate discipline of individuals responsible for an offense is a necessary component of enforcement; however, the discipline that will be appropriate will be case specific.

(7) After an offense has been detected, the organization must have taken all reasonable steps to respond appropriately to the offense and to prevent similar offenses—including any necessary modifications to its program to prevent and detect violations of the law.[19]

The Court's Decision

The Georgia Court of Appeals held that the statute's grant of immunity from liability extended to the psychologist. The evidence did not establish bad faith on the part of the psychologist so as to deprive her of such immunity. The statute provides that any person participating in the making of a report, or participating in any judicial proceeding or any other proceeding resulting in a report of suspected child abuse, is immune from any civil or criminal liability that might otherwise be incurred or imposed, provided such participation pursuant to the statute is made in good faith. The grant of qualified immunity covers *every person who, in good faith*, participates over time in the making of a report to a child welfare agency. Proof of negligent reporting or bad judgment is not proof that the psychologist refused to fulfill her professional duties, out of some harmful motive, or that she consciously acted for some dishonest purpose. There was no competent evidence that the psychologist acted in bad faith.

CHAPTER REVIEW

1. An *abused child* is defined as one who has suffered intentional and serious mental, emotional, sexual, and/or physical injury inflicted by a parent or other person charged with the child's care. Some states include in their definitions moral neglect, immoral associations, endangering of a child's morals, and the location of a child in a disreputable place in association with vagrant, vicious, or immoral persons.
2. Child abuse laws differ from state to state, but in most states, persons required to report cases of child abuse are protected. When reviewing the indicators of abuse and maltreatment, the person reporting the abuse does not have to be absolutely certain that abuse or maltreatment has taken place before he or she reports, but reports must be made with a good-faith belief that the facts reported are true.
3. Generally, senior abuse is less likely to be reported than child abuse and proving senior abuse charges is often difficult. However, most states have enacted statues that require the reporting of elder abuse.
4. The prompt reporting of infection or disease is necessary in order for states to protect citizens' health by invoking the power to quarantine.
5. All births and deaths are reportable by statute. Birth certificates must be signed by a physician or, when appropriate, attendant, and death certificates must be signed by the physician who pronounces the death. All unnatural deaths are to be referred to the medical examiner to determine the actual cause of death and provide related assistance for further criminal investigation, when necessary.
6. The *National Practitioner Data Bank* is used to collect and release information on the professional competence and conduct of physicians, dentists, and other health care practitioners. The data bank was established as part of the

Health Care Quality Improvement Act of 1986. Health care organizations are required to query the data bank every two years on the renewal of staff privileges of physicians and dentists.

7. Information in the data bank is considered strictly confidential. Data bank queries can be made by state licensing boards, hospitals, other health care organizations, and professional societies that have entered or may be entering into employment or affiliation relationships with a physician, dentist, or other health care practitioner who has applied for clinical privileges or appointment to a medical staff.

8. Risk management programs should include monitoring systems to identify potential risks to patients and staff, and the information gathered should be used to improve patient care and treatment practices. *Incident reports* include statements from employees and physicians regarding significant or noteworthy deviation from acceptable patient care. Some states require the reporting of specific incidents.

9. According to the Joint Commission on Accreditation of Healthcare Organizations, a *sentinel event* is an unexpected occurrence involving death or serious physical or psychological injury, or the risk thereof. The Joint Commission has implemented a policy that requires organizations to self-report sentinel events that meet certain criteria. Organizations reporting sentinel events must conduct *root cause analyses* to determine why the events occurred.

REVIEW QUESTIONS

1. When a health care provider reports child abuse, should the defendant be able to know the identity of his or her accuser?
2. Should a health care provider be sanctioned for reporting abuse if it proves to be false?
3. If an elderly patient, who is incompetent, complains of having been abused, should it be reported?
4. What is the purpose of conducting a "root cause analysis" following a "sentinel event"?
5. What are the basic elements of an effective corporate compliance program?

NOTES

1. Michaels v. Gordon, 439 S.E.2d 722 (Ga. Ct. App. 1993).
2. 373 N.W.2d 204 (Mich. Ct. App. 1985).
3. PUB. L. NO. 99-660, tit. IV (1986).
4. 45 C.F.R. § 60.1 (1991).
5. 42 U.S.C. § 11101 (1991).
6. There is a guidebook that is meant to serve as a resource for the users of the National Practitioner Data Bank. It is one of a number of efforts to inform the U.S. health care community about the data bank and what is required to comply with the requirements established by the HCQIA. The data bank Help Line (1-800-767-6732) is a toll-free telephone service that provides health care entities and health care practitioners with information about the data bank.
7. 456 N.W.2d 173 (Iowa 1990).
8. 45 C.F.R. § 60.13 (1991).
9. 551 So.2d 532 (Fla. Dist. Ct. App. 1990).
10. 456 N.W.2d 173 (Iowa 1990).
11. 936 P.2d 844 (Nev. 1997).
12. NEV. REV. STAT. § 47.030.
13. N.Y. COMP. CODES R. & REGS. tit. 10(c), § 405.8 (1988).
14. 534 N.Y.S.2d 739 (N.Y. App. Div. 1988).
15. *Id.* at 741.
16. *2001 Hospital Accreditation Standards*, Joint Commission on Accreditation of Healthcare Organizations, 2001, at 21.
17. JOINT COMMISSION ON ACCREDITATION OF HEALTHCARE ORGANIZATIONS, *Sentinel Event Alert*, Issue 3 (May 1, 1998), at 2–3.
18. *2001 Hospital Accreditation Standards*, Joint Commission on Accreditation of Healthcare Organizations, 2001, at 54.
19. 56 Fed. Reg. 22,762 (May 16, 1991).

CHAPTER 13

Issues of Procreation

It's Your Gavel...

OBSTRUCTING ACCESS TO ABORTION CLINICS

Abortion clinics and others sought enforcement of an injunction precluding anti-abortion groups, their leaders, and others from blockading or obstructing access to abortion clinics.

On January 16, 1992, the order required defendants to appear before the court to show cause why each of them should not be cited for contempt for violating and inducing others to violate a July 31, 1990, injunction in the above matter.

On January 22, defendants Mr. Tucci, Mr. Terry, and Mr. Mahoney spoke at a rally. Tucci was introduced as a leader of Operation Rescue National and spoke about how the group had successfully closed down clinics that day. He also solicited funds for his organization. Terry said, "they needed contributions to keep their work going." On January 24, 1992, at a hearing on the matter, Mr. Gannett, representing himself *pro se*, admitted that he participated in the Operation Rescue events and intervened at one of the "rescue" blockades. The defendants appeared before the court at two hearings to show cause why they should not be cited in contempt for violating the court's July 31, 1990, injunction.[1] Can anti-abortion leaders and groups be fined for violating an injunction barring them from blockading or obstructing access to abortion clinics? Can anti-abortion groups be ordered to pay damages to compensate an abortion clinic for property damage resulting from an abortion clinic blockage that violated an injunction?
What is your verdict?

INTRODUCTION

With more than one million abortions performed annually in the United States, it is certain that the conflict between "pro-choice" and "pro-life" advocates will continue to blemish America's landscape.

This chapter reviews a variety of issues of procreation. Primary emphasis is placed on abortion. Discussed to a lesser extent are issues relating to sterilization; artificial insemination; and wrongful birth, wrongful life, and wrongful conception.

ABORTION

U.S. Supreme Court Decisions

Abortion is the premature termination of pregnancy. It can be classified as spontaneous or induced. It may occur as an incidental result of a medical procedure, or it may be an elective decision on the part of the patient. In addition to having substantial ethical, moral, and religious implications, abortion has proven to be a major political issue and will continue as such in the future. More laws will be proposed, more laws will be passed, and more lawsuits will wind their way up to the Supreme Court.

1973—Roe v. Wade

Roe v. Wade gave strength to a woman's right to privacy in the context of matters relating to her own body, including how a pregnancy would end.[2] However, the Supreme Court also has recognized the interest of the states in protecting potential life and has attempted to spell out the extent to which the states may regulate and even prohibit abortions.

In *Roe v. Wade*, the U.S. Supreme Court held the Texas penal abortion law unconstitutional, stating: "[s]tate criminal abortion statutes . . . that except from criminality only a lifesaving procedure on behalf of the mother, without regard to the stage of her pregnancy and other interests involved, is violating the Due Process Clause of the Fourteenth Amendment."[3]

First Trimester. During the first trimester of pregnancy, the decision to undergo an abortion procedure is between the woman and her physician. A state may require that abortions be performed by a physician licensed pursuant to its laws. However, a woman's right to an abortion is not unqualified because the decision to perform the procedure must be left to the medical judgment of her attending physician. "For the stage prior to approximately the end of the first trimester, the abortion decision and its effectuation must be left to the medical judgment of the pregnant woman's attending physician."[4]

Second Trimester. In *Roe v. Wade*, the Supreme Court stated, "[f]or the stage subsequent to approximately the end of the first trimester, the State, in promoting its interest in

the health of the mother, may, if it chooses, regulate the abortion procedure in ways that are reasonably related to maternal health."[5] Thus, during approximately the fourth to sixth months of pregnancy, the state may regulate the medical conditions under which the procedure is performed. The constitutional test of any legislation concerning abortion during this period would be its relevance to the objective of protecting maternal health.

Third Trimester. The Supreme Court reasoned that by the time the final stage of pregnancy has been reached, the state has acquired a compelling interest in the product of conception, which would override the woman's right to privacy and justify stringent regulation even to the extent of prohibiting abortions. In the *Roe* case, the Court formulated its ruling as to the last trimester in the following words: "[f]or the stage subsequent to viability, the State in promoting its interest in the potentiality of human life, may, if it chooses, regulate, and even proscribe, abortion except where it is necessary, in appropriate medical judgment for the preservation of the life or health of the mother."[6]

Thus, during the final stage of pregnancy, a state may prohibit all abortions except those deemed necessary to protect maternal life or health. The state's legislative powers over the performance of abortions increase as the pregnancy progresses toward term.

1973—Doe v. Bolton

The Supreme Court then went on to delineate what regulatory measures a state lawfully may enact during the three stages of pregnancy. In the companion decision, *Doe v. Bolton*,[7] where the Court considered a constitutional attack on the Georgia abortion statute, further restrictions were placed on state regulation of the procedure. The provisions of the Georgia statute establishing residency requirements for women seeking abortions and requiring that the procedure be performed in a hospital accredited by the Joint Commission on Accreditation of Healthcare Organizations were declared constitutionally invalid. In considering legislative provisions establishing medical staff approval as a prerequisite to the abortion procedure, the Court decided that "interposition of the hospital abortion committee is unduly restrictive of the patient's rights and needs that . . . have already been medically delineated and substantiated by her personal physician. To ask more serves neither the hospital nor the State."[8]

The Court was unable to find any constitutionally justifiable rationale for a statutory requirement of advance approval by the abortion committee of the hospital's medical staff. Insofar as statutory consultation requirements are concerned, the Court reasoned that the acquiescence of two co-practitioners has no rational connection with a patient's needs and, further, unduly infringes on the physician's right to practice.

Thus, by using a test related to patient needs, the Court in *Doe v. Bolton* struck down four pre-abortion procedural requirements commonly imposed by state statutes: (1) residency, (2) performance of the abortion in a hospital accredited by the Joint Commission, (3) approval by an appropriate committee of the medical staff, and (4) consultations.

1976—Danforth v. Planned Parenthood

The Supreme Court ruled in *Danforth v. Planned Parenthood*[9] that it is unconstitutional to require all women younger than the age of 18 years to obtain parental consent in writing prior to obtaining an abortion. The Court, however, failed to provide any definitive guidelines as to when and how parental consent may be required if the minor is too immature to fully comprehend the nature of the procedure.

1977—Maher v. Roe

In *Maher v. Roe*,[10] the Supreme Court considered the Connecticut statute that denied Medicaid benefits for first-trimester abortions that were not medically necessary. The Court rejected the argument that the state's subsidy of medical expenses incident to pregnancy and childbirth created an obligation on the part of the state to subsidize the expenses incident to nontherapeutic abortions. The Supreme Court voted six to three that the states may refuse to spend public funds to provide nontherapeutic abortions for women.

1979—Colautti v. Franklin

The Supreme Court in *Colautti v. Franklin*[11] voted six to three that the states may seek to protect a fetus that a physician has determined could survive outside the womb. Determination of whether a particular fetus is viable is, and must be, a matter for judgment of the responsible attending physician. State abortion regulations that impinge on this determination, if they are to be constitutional, must allow the attending physician the room that he or she needs to make the best medical judgment.

1979—Bellotti v. Baird—Parental Consent

The Supreme Court in *Bellotti v. Baird*[12] ruled eight to one that a Massachusetts statute requiring parental consent before an abortion could be performed on an unmarried woman younger than the age of 18 years was held to be unconstitutional. Justice Stevens, joined by Justices Brennan, Marshall, and Blackmun, concluded that the Massachusetts statute was unconstitutional, because under that statute as written and construed by the Massachusetts Supreme Judicial Court, no minor, no matter how mature and capable of informed decision making, could receive an abortion without the consent of either both parents or a superior court judge, thus making the minor's abortion subject in every instance to an absolute third-party veto.

1980—Harris v. McRae

In *Harris v. McRae*,[13] the Supreme Court upheld five to four the Hyde Amendment, which restricts the use of federal funds for Medicaid abortions. Under this case, the different states are not compelled to fund Medicaid recipients' medically necessary abortions for which federal reimbursement is unavailable, but may choose to do so.

1981—H. L. v. Matheson

The Supreme Court in *H. L. v. Matheson*,[14] by a six to three vote, upheld a Utah statute that required a physician to "notify, if possible" the parents or guardian of a minor on whom an abortion was to be performed. In this case, the physician advised the patient that an abortion would be in her best medical interest but, because of the statute, refused to perform the abortion without notifying her parents. The Supreme Court ruled that although a state may not constitutionally legislate a blanket, unreviewable power of parents to veto their daughter's abortion, a statute setting out a mere requirement of parental notice when possible does not violate the constitutional rights of an immature, dependent minor.

1983—City of Akron v. Akron Center for Reproductive Health

The Supreme Court in *City of Akron v. Akron Center for Reproductive Health*[15] voted six to three that the different states cannot (1) mandate what information physicians give abortion patients or (2) require that abortions for women more than three months pregnant be performed in a hospital. With respect to a requirement that the attending physician must inform the woman of specified information concerning her proposed abortion, it is unreasonable for a state to insist that only a physician is competent to provide the information and counseling relative to informed consent. A state may not adopt regulations to influence a woman's informed choice between abortion and childbirth.

With regard to a second-trimester hospital requirement, this could significantly limit a woman's ability to obtain an abortion. This is especially so in view of the evidence that a second-trimester abortion may cost more than twice as much in a hospital as in a clinic.

1989—Webster v. Reproductive Health Services

Webster v. Reproductive Health Services[16] began the Court's narrowing of abortion rights by upholding a Missouri statute providing that no public facilities or employees should be used to perform abortions and that physicians should conduct viability tests before performing abortions.

1991—Rust v. Sullivan

Federal regulations that prohibit abortion counseling and referral by family planning clinics that receive funds under

Title X of the Public Health Service Act were found not to violate the constitutional rights of pregnant women or Title X grantees in a five to four decision by the Supreme Court in *Rust v. Sullivan.*[17] Proponents of abortion counseling argue that the regulations impermissibly burden a woman's privacy right to abortion. Prohibiting the delivery of abortion information, even as to where such information could be obtained, the regulations deny a woman her constitutionally protected right to choose under the First Amendment. The question arises: How can a woman make an informed choice between two options when she cannot obtain information as to one of them? In *Sullivan*, however, the Supreme Court found that there was no violation of a woman's or provider's First Amendment rights. The Court has extended the doctrine that government need not subsidize the exercise of the fundamental rights to free speech. The plaintiff argued that the government may not condition receipt of a benefit on the relinquishment of constitutional rights.

The White House directed the Department of Health and Human Services (HHS) to make an exception to the "gag rule," which bars abortion counseling at federally funded clinics, by revising the rule to allow physicians to discuss and provide medical information regarding abortions to their patients. The U.S. Circuit Court of Appeals held that the revised gag rule, making an exception for physicians in abortion counseling, was adopted illegally. The court held that the White House must provide opportunity for public comment prior to ordering an exception to the rule. As anticipated, the gag rule was rescinded during the first week of the Clinton administration.

1992—Planned Parenthood v. Casey

In *Planned Parenthood v. Casey,*[18] the Supreme Court affirmed Pennsylvania law restricting a woman's right to abortion. The Court was one vote shy of overturning *Roe v. Wade.* The Supreme Court ruling, as enunciated in *Roe v. Wade,* reaffirmed:

- the constitutional right of women to have an abortion before viability of the fetus, as first enunciated in *Roe v. Wade*
- the state's power to restrict abortions after fetal viability, so long as the law contains exceptions for pregnancies that endanger a woman's life or health
- the principle that the state has legitimate interests from the outset of the pregnancy in protecting the health of the woman and the life of the fetus

The Supreme Court rejected the trimester approach in *Roe v. Wade*, which limited the regulations states could issue on abortion depending on the development stage of the fetus. In place of the trimester approach, the Court will evaluate the permissibility of state abortion rules based on whether they unduly burden a woman's ability to obtain an abortion. A rule is an undue burden if its purpose or effect is to place a substantial obstacle in the path of a woman seeking an abortion before the fetus attains viability. The Supreme Court ruled that it is "not an undue burden" to require that

- a woman be informed of the nature of the abortion procedure and the risks involved
- a woman be offered information on the fetus and on the alternatives to abortion
- a woman give her informed consent before the abortion procedure
- parental consent for a minor seeking an abortion, providing for a judicial bypass option if the minor does not wish or cannot obtain parental consent
- a 24-hour waiting period before any abortion can be performed

1998—Women's Medical Professional Corp. v. Voinovich

The Supreme Court in *Women's Medical Professional Corp. v. Voinovich*[19] denied *certiorari* for the first partial-birth case to reach the federal appellate courts. This case involved an Ohio statute that banned the use of the intact dilation and extraction (D&X) procedure in the performance of any pre- or postviability abortion. The Sixth Circuit Court of Appeals held that the statute banning any use of the D & X procedure was unconstitutionally vague. It is likely that a properly drafted statute will eventually be judged constitutionally sound.

CIRCUIT COURT DECISIONS

Partial Birth Abortion

Arkansas

The partial-birth abortion, also referred to as the D&X procedure, is a late-term abortion involving partial delivery of the baby prior to it being aborted. A "partial-birth" abortion law in Arkansas was found to impose an undue burden on women seeking abortion by prohibiting commonly used abortion procedures. The defendants in *Little Rock Family Planning Services v. Jegley*[20] appealed a district court decision holding Arkansas's Partial-Birth Abortion Ban Act of 1997 unconstitutional.

The central difficulty with the Arkansas statute was that it covered too much. The statute made it a crime to perform an abortion in which the person performing the abortion partially vaginally delivers a living fetus before taking the life of the fetus and completing the delivery. The term "partial-birth abortion," however, is commonly understood to refer to a particular procedure also known as intact dilation and extraction (D&X). The accepted description of this procedure is much more specific and much narrower than the definition of "partial-birth abortion" given in the Arkansas law. As defined by the American College of Obstetricians and Gynecologists (ACOG), an intact D&X combines four elements, in the following order:

1. deliberate dilatation of the cervix, usually over a sequence of days
2. instrumental conversion of the fetus to a footling breech
3. breech extraction of the body excepting the head
4. partial evacuation of the intracranial contents of a living fetus to effect vaginal delivery of a dead but otherwise intact fetus

The key difference between the definition in the Arkansas statute and the definition given by ACOG was made clear by the third numbered element of a D&X as defined by ACOG. The definition contemplates removal from the womb of the fetus's entire body except for the head. The Arkansas statute, on the other hand, required only that a fetus be "partially" delivered. The word "partially" referred to any part of the fetus, or, at least, any substantial part. It was not limited to delivery of the entire fetus except for the head. "Partial" delivery occurs as part of other recognized abortion procedures, methods that are concededly constitutionally protected.

The word "partially" cannot, by the ordinary process of construction, be converted into "all of the fetus except for the head." The statute actually enacted contains a much broader prohibition, and was therefore invalid.

On April 1, 1997, Arkansas's Governor signed into law Act 984, the Partial-Birth Abortion Ban Act of 1997. The Act provides:

> (a) Whoever knowingly performs a partial-birth abortion and thereby takes the life of a human fetus shall be guilty of a Class D felony.

> •   •   •   •

> (c) It is an affirmative defense to a prosecution under this section, which must be proved by a preponderance of the evidence, that the partial-birth abortion was performed by a physician who reasonably believed:
> (1) The partial-birth abortion was necessary to save the life of the woman upon whom it was performed; and
> (2) No other form of abortion would suffice for that purpose.[21]

Arkansas Code defines "partial-birth abortion" as an abortion in which the person performing the abortion par-

tially vaginally delivers a living fetus before taking the life of the fetus and completing the delivery or as defined by the United States Supreme Court.[22]

The Act provided that, in addition to committing a felony, a physician who knowingly performed a "partial-birth abortion" would be subject to disciplinary action by the State Medical Board.

The district court held the Act unconstitutional because it was unconstitutionally vague, imposed an undue burden on women seeking abortions, and it did not adequately protect the health and lives of pregnant women. The circuit court agreed, holding the Act unconstitutional.

The plaintiffs used two methods of abortion that they believed were directly affected by the Act: the suction-curettage procedure and the dilation and evacuation (D&E) procedure. Any physician who performed a D&X procedure would have been affected by the Act, as would the physician's patients. The Act also would have affected physicians who perform the D&E procedure and, in some instances, the suction-curettage procedure.

The most common method used for abortions performed up to 12 weeks' gestation is the suction-curettage procedure. During this procedure, the physician gradually dilates the cervix and then inserts a clear plastic tube, known as a cannula, through the vagina into the uterus. The cannula is attached to a vacuum device that is used to remove the fetus. Although the D&E procedure is the most common method of second-trimester abortions, suction curettage can also be used in some second trimester abortions, with the use of a larger cannula. A fetus removed by suction curettage at this stage does not usually remain intact. Part of the fetus may remain in the uterus while another part is being drawn into and through the vagina. Some physicians may also perform second-trimester abortions with a combination of suction and the use of forceps.

In a D&E procedure, the physician inserts forceps into the uterus, grasps a part of the fetus, commonly an arm or a leg, and draws that part out of the uterus into the vagina. Using the traction created between the mouth of the cervix and the pull of the forceps, the physician dismembers the fetal part that has been brought into the vagina, and removes it from the woman's body. The rest of the fetus remains in the uterus while dismemberment occurs, and is often still living.

In both the suction-curettage procedure and the D&E procedure, as well as in the D&X procedure, fetal death will occur after the physician has started the procedure. In all three procedures, part of a living fetus may be brought out of the uterus into the vagina. In a suction-curettage procedure where the fetus does not remain intact, part of the fetus, which is still living, may be drawn into the vagina before fetal demise occurs. In a D&E procedure, part of the fetus is brought into the vagina before it is dismembered, leading to fetal demise. In a D&X procedure, fetal demise will occur sometime after the cranial contents have been evacuated. The physician does not generally know exactly when fetal death occurs. It is generally, however, after part of the fetus is brought out of the uterus into the vagina.

The state argued that the Act was "aimed at" prohibiting the D&X procedure, and that the Act prohibits only that procedure. The state argued that the Act does not prohibit any other abortion procedure.

The language of the Act, however, encompassed more than the D&X procedure. The Act prohibited an abortion in which the person performing the abortion partially vaginally delivers a living fetus before taking the life of the fetus and completing the delivery or as defined by the United States Supreme Court. [23] The problem here was the word "partially." A physician who, as part of a D&E procedure, or as part of a suction-curettage procedure, brings an arm or a leg or some other part of a living fetus out of the uterus into the vagina would have violated the Act.

The state argued that the Act's scienter requirement limits the Act's scope to prohibiting only the D&X procedure. This argument failed. The Act prohibited "knowingly" performing a "partial-birth abortion." Using the definition of "partial-birth abortion" provided in the Act, any physician who knowingly partially vaginally delivered a living fetus, then takes the life of the fetus, and completes delivery, would have violated the Act. Because both the D&E procedure and the suction-curettage procedure used in second-trimester abortions often include what the Act prohibits, physicians performing those procedures would have violated the Act.

New Jersey

New Jersey's partial-birth abortion statute was void for vagueness, in that it did not define the proscribed conduct with certainty and could be easily construed to ban the safest, most common and readily available conventional abortion procedures. The statute also was unconstitutional as creating an undue burden on a woman's right to obtain an abortion, in that its broad language covered many conventional, constitutionally permissible methods of abortion and it failed to contain a health exception. [24]

STATE REGULATION

The effect of the Supreme Court's 1973 decisions in *Roe* and *Doe* was to invalidate all or part of almost every state abortion statute then in force. The responses of state legislatures to these decisions were varied, but it is clear that many state laws had been enacted to restrict the performance of abortions as much as possible. Although *Planned Parenthood v. Casey* was expected to clear up some issues, it is evident that the states have been given more power to regulate the performance of abortions.

24-Hour Waiting Period Not Burdensome

The 1993 Utah Abortion Act Revision, Senate Bill 60, provides for informed consent by requiring that certain information be given to the pregnant woman at least 24 hours prior to the performance of an abortion. The law allows for exceptions to this requirement in the event of a medical emergency. The Utah Women's Clinic, in *Utah Women's Clinic, Inc. v. Leavitt*,[25] filed a 106-page complaint, which could more properly be described as a press release, challenging the constitutionality of the new Utah law. The plaintiffs' case was referred to the magistrate judge, who determined that the 24-hour waiting period does not impose an undue burden on the right to an abortion. Finding that Senate Bill 60 is constitutionally proper, the magistrate judge recommended that the plaintiffs' request for injunctive relief be denied. On appeal, the U.S. District Court for the district of Utah held that the Utah abortion statute's 24-hour waiting period and informed consent requirements do not render the statute unconstitutionally vague.

In 1992, the Supreme Court in *Planned Parenthood of Southeastern Pennsylvania v. Casey*[26] determined that in asserting an interest in protecting fetal life, a state may place some restrictions on previability abortions, so long as those restrictions do not impose an "undue burden" on the woman's right to an abortion. The Court determined that the 24-hour waiting period, the informed consent requirement, and the medical emergency definitions did not unduly burden the right to an abortion and were therefore constitutional. In the instant case, because Senate Bill 60 is less restrictive than the Pennsylvania abortion statute, the plaintiffs may not prevail unless they can show material differences between the circumstances of Utah and Pennsylvania. The plaintiffs did not meet this burden. A review of the plaintiffs' complaint in the instant case shows no factual allegations materially different from those already considered by the Court in *Casey*. The plaintiffs had no case from the beginning.

Under *Casey*, there is no viable legal cause of action. It would be extremely difficult in light of the *Casey* decision, if not impossible, to bring a good-faith facial challenge to the constitutionality of Utah's 24-hour waiting period and informed consent requirements. In an emergency situation, there is never a requirement of informed consent or a 24-hour waiting period. The plaintiffs' contention that Senate Bill 60, "when read together with provisions from Utah's 1991 abortion law, does not clearly provide that a woman can obtain an immediate abortion when necessary in a medical emergency," is without merit.

"The abortion issue is obviously one that invokes strong feelings on both sides. Individuals are free to urge support for their cause through debate, advocacy, and participation in the political process. The subject also might be addressed in the courts so long as there are valid legal issues in dispute.

Where, however, a case presents no legitimate legal arguments, the courthouse is not the proper forum. Litigation, or the threat of litigation, should not be used as economic blackmail to strengthen one's hand in the political battle. Unfortunately, the court sees little evidence that this case was filed for any other purpose."[27]

"Senate Bill 60, the duly enacted law of the people of Utah, has not been enforced for nearly nine months. That will change today. The court hereby adopts the report and recommendation of the magistrate judge, lifts the injunction, and dismisses plaintiffs' case in its entirety with prejudice."[28]

Consent

Spouse

A Florida statute had required written consent of the husband before a wife could be permitted to obtain an abortion. The husband's interest in the baby was held to be insufficient to force his wife to face the mental and physical risks of pregnancy and childbirth.[29]

In *Doe v. Zimmerman*,[30] the court declared unconstitutional the provisions of the Pennsylvania Abortion Control Act, which required that the written consent of the husband of a married woman be secured before the performance of an abortion. The court found that these provisions impermissibly permitted the husband to withhold his consent either because of his interest in the potential life of the fetus or for capricious reasons. The natural father of an unborn fetus in *Doe v. Smith*[31] was found not to be entitled to an injunction to prevent the mother from submitting to an abortion. Although the father's interest in the fetus was legitimate, it did not outweigh the mother's constitutionally protected right to an abortion, particularly in the light of the evidence that the mother and father had never married. The father had demonstrated substantial instability in his marital and romantic life. The father was able to beget other children and, in fact, did produce other children.

In the 1992 decision of *Planned Parenthood v. Casey*, the Supreme Court ruled that spousal consent would be an undue burden on the woman.

Parental

The trial court in *In re Anonymous*[32] was found to have abused its discretion when it refused a minor's request for waiver of parental consent to obtain an abortion. The record indicated that the minor lived alone, was within one month of her 18th birthday, lived by herself most of the time, and held down a full-time job.

Incompetent Persons

An abortion was found to have been authorized properly by a family court in *In re Doe*[33] for a profoundly retarded woman. She had become pregnant during her residence in a group home as a result of a sexual attack by an unknown person. The record had supported a finding that if the woman had been able to do so, she would have requested the abortion. The court properly chose welfare agencies and the woman's *guardian ad litem* (a guardian appointed to prosecute or defend a suit on behalf of a party incapacitated by infancy, mental incompetence, etc.) as the surrogate decision makers, rather than the woman's mother. The mother apparently had little contact with her daughter over the years.

Employee Refusal To Participate in Abortions

Individuals have a right to refuse to participate in abortions and can abstain from involvement in abortions as a matter of conscience or religious or moral conviction. In a Missouri case, *Doe v. Poelker*,[34] the city was ordered to obtain the services of physicians and personnel who had no moral objections to participating in abortions. The city also was required to pay the plaintiff's attorneys' fees because of the wanton disregard of the indigent woman's rights and the continuation of a policy to disregard and/or circumvent the U.S. Supreme Court's rulings on abortion.

Funding

Several states have placed an indirect restriction on abortion through the elimination of funding. Under the Hyde Amendment, the U.S. Congress, through appropriations legislation, has limited the types of medically necessary abortions for which federal funds may be spent under the Medicaid program. Although the Hyde Amendment does not prohibit states from funding nontherapeutic abortions, this action by the federal government opened the door to state statutory provisions limiting the funding of abortions.

In *Beal v. Doe*,[35] the Pennsylvania Medicaid plan was challenged on the basis of denial of financial assistance for nontherapeutic abortions. The Supreme Court held that Title XIX of the Social Security Act (the Medicaid program) does not require the funding of nontherapeutic abortions as a condition of state participation in the program.[36] The state has a strong interest in encouraging normal childbirth, and nothing in Title XIX suggests that it is unreasonable for the state to further that interest. The Court ruled that it is not inconsistent with the Medicaid portion of the Social Security Act to refuse to fund unnecessary (although perhaps desirable) medical services.

A Michigan statute, Section 400.109a of the Michigan Compiled Laws, which prohibited the use of Medicaid funds to pay for an abortion for a minor who became pregnant as a result of a rape, was held to be unconstitutional. The statute violated the state's equal protection clause under the state's constitution.[37]

The West Virginia Supreme Court of Appeals held that the state may fund abortions for Medicaid recipients who do not qualify for reimbursement under the Hyde Amendment.[38] By contrast, the Michigan Supreme Court held that a Michigan statute barring funds to pay for an abortion unless it is necessary to save the woman's life does not violate the state constitution's equal protection clause.[39]

Continuing Controversy

While *pro choice* advocates are arguing the rights of women to choose, they are also pointing out the fact that legalized abortions are safer. In 1972, for example, the year before *Roe v. Wade* was upheld, the number of deaths from abortions in the United States is estimated to have reached the thousands. By 1985, the figure was six.[40] In addition, "pro choice" advocates argue that women who have a right to an abortion when pregnancy threatens the life of the mother also have the right to an abortion when pregnancy is the result of incest or rape.

Right-to-Life advocates argue that life comes from God and that no one has a right to deny the right to life.

There will most likely be a continuing stream of court decisions, as well as political and legislative battles, well into the 21st century. Given the emotional, religious, and ethical concerns, as well as those of women's rights groups, it is unlikely that this matter will be resolved anytime soon.

Physicians Feeling the Heat

Physicians are feeling the heat and are concerned about the ongoing abortion controversy. In *Beverly v. Choices Women's Medical Center*,[41] a physician, whose picture was published in an abortion calendar without the physician's consent, brought a civil rights action against the for-profit medical center for publication of her picture. The calendar was disseminated to the public by the center. The center, among other things, performs abortions from which it derives approximately 50 percent of its income. The plaintiff was awarded $50,000 in compensatory damages and $25,000 in punitive damages. The physician testified that the publication of her picture caused her to suffer physical and mental injury. She also testified as to the effect of the publication on her lifestyle and career decisions.

Did Police Officers Use Excessive Force against Protesters?

In March 1989, the San Diego police became aware that Operation Rescue planned to stage several anti-abortion demonstrations in the city.[42] The purpose of the demonstrations was to disrupt operations at the target clinic and ultimately to cause the clinic to cease operations. In each of the three demonstrations at issue, protesters converged on a medical building, blocking entrances, filling stairwells and corridors, and preventing employees and patients from entering.

For each arrest, the officers warned the demonstrators that they would be subjected to pain-compliance measures if they did not move, that such measures would hurt, and that they could reduce the pain by standing up, eliminating the tension on their wrists and arms. The officers then forcibly moved the arrestees by tightening Orcutt police nonchakus (two sticks of wood connected at one end by a cord used to grip a demonstrator's wrist) around their wrists until they stood up and walked. All arrestees complained of varying degrees of injury to their hands and arms, including bruises, a pinched nerve, and one broken wrist. Several subsequently filed suit, claiming that the police violated the Fourth Amendment by using excessive force in executing the arrests. The judge allowed the case to proceed to the jury in order to determine whether any particular uses of force were unconstitutional. After viewing a videotape of the arrests, the jury concluded that none involved excessive force and returned a verdict for the city. An appeal was taken as to whether the police officers used excessive force in arresting the demonstrators, in light of the testimony of the officers and demonstrators and the videotape of the arrest.

The U.S. Court of Appeals for the Ninth Circuit held that the police did not use excessive force. Determining whether the force used to effect a particular seizure is reasonable under the Fourth Amendment requires a careful balancing of the nature and quality of the intrusion on the individual's Fourth Amendment interests against the countervailing governmental interests at stake. The reasonableness inquiry in an excessive force case is an objective one. Are the officers' actions objectively reasonable in light of the facts and circumstances confronting them? In addition to hearing the testimony of numerous officers and demonstrators, the jury watched the entire videotape of the arrests. As the district court noted, the videotape created an extensive evidentiary record: "thanks to videotaped records of the actual events, plus the testimony of witnesses on both sides, the jury had more than a sufficient amount of evidence presented to them from which they could formulate their verdicts. The extensive use of video scenes of exactly what took place removed much argument and interpretation of the facts themselves."[43]

The police did not threaten or use deadly force and did not deliver physical blows or cuts. The force consisted of physical pressure administered on the demonstrators' limbs in increasing degrees, resulting in pain. The city clearly had a legitimate interest in quickly dispersing and removing the lawbreakers with the least risk of injury to police and others. The arrestees were part of a group of more than 100 protesters operating in an organized and concerted effort to invade private property, obstruct business, and hinder law enforcement. Although many of these crimes were misdemeanors, the city's interest in preventing their widespread occurrence was significant.

PICKETING PHYSICIANS' RESIDENCIES: A PRIVACY ISSUE

Citation: *Murray v. Lawson, 642 A.2d 338 (N.J. 1994). 264 N.J.Super. 11, 624 A.2d 1 (1993).*

Facts

Two physicians brought separate actions to obtain injunctions against anti-abortion protesters who had been picketing their residences. In the first case, the defendant discovered the personal address of Dr. Murray and visited the house, where the physician's 14-year-old son answered the door. The defendant told the son to tell his father to stop performing abortions. A month later, the defendant told the police that he and 50 other people were going to picket the physician's home. After being warned about the picketing, Murray sent his family away. However, he stayed in the house that day, managing, from his home, two of his patients who were in labor. The picketers walked on the sidewalk in front of Murray's home, carrying posters stating among other things, that he "scars and kills women and their unborn children." They also told neighbors that he was a killer. Murray filed suit seeking damages and injunctive relief, testifying that the picketing deprived him and his family of their family time, harmed his ability to practice because he had to manage his patients from home, and caused his wife to suffer from nervousness and depression. After the hearing, the medical center where Murray had performed abortions was burned to the ground. In spite of a telephone bomb threat, police never determined who called in the threat or burned the building. After the bomb threat, the defendant and another picketer protested in front of the Murray house. Murray called the police, who arrived and told him to stay in the house. He came out, however, and took a swing at the defendant. He was later convicted of assault. The chancery division ordered a permanent injunction prohibiting the defendant and all others from picketing within 300 feet of the Murray home. The defendants appealed, claiming that the injunction impinged upon their freedom of speech. The appellate division affirmed, finding that the injunction

set a reasonable time, place, and manner restriction, thereby not violating free speech.

In the second case, Dr. Boffard performed abortions at a clinic, which had been subjected to protests two years prior to the protests at Murray's home. In 1990, the protesters appeared at the front of Boffard's residence. The picketers carried signs, some of which read, "Thou Shalt Not Kill." Other signs contained pictures of bloody fetal parts. The demonstrators yelled at the physician's wife that her husband was a murderer.

Subsequently, a suit was brought in the chancery division to enjoin the defendants from picketing. The court issued a temporary restraining order prohibiting picketing within 200 feet of the physician's home, from referring to Boffard as a killer, and from depicting fetuses on posters. The court made the injunction permanent five months later, stopping the picketing within "the immediate vicinity" of Boffard's home. Again, as in the *Murray* case, the appellate division upheld the injunction. Both cases were appealed to the New Jersey Supreme Court.

Issue

Did the defendants' free speech rights outweigh the plaintiffs' residential privacy interests?

Holding

The New Jersey Supreme Court upheld the injunction in the *Murray* case, but remanded the Boffard injunction for a more precise definition of the spatial scope of the ban, finding that "within the immediate vicinity" was too vague.

Reason

Residential privacy represents a sufficient public policy interest to justify injunctive restrictions. Moreover, the chancery division had the power to enjoin the nonviolent, noncriminal activity of the defendants to protect the plaintiffs' residential privacy. The court determined that the injunctions in both cases were content-neutral because they could be justified without referring to the content of the defendants' speech. They prohibited any and all picketing, regardless of the type of speech, within a certain distance of the residences. The court further held that because a state has a significant interest in protecting the residential privacy of its citizens, it is justified in imposing injunctive relief.

STERILIZATION

Sterilization is the termination of the ability to produce offspring. Sterilization often is accomplished by either a vasectomy for men or a tubal ligation for women. A *vasectomy* is a surgical procedure in which the vas deferens is severed and tied to prevent the flow of the seminal fluid into the urinary canal. A *tubal ligation* is a surgical procedure in which the fallopian tubes are cut and tied, preventing passage of the ovum from the ovary to the uterus. Sterilizations are often sought because of

- economic necessity to avoid the additional expense of raising a child
- therapeutic purposes to prevent harm to a woman's health (e.g., to remove a diseased reproductive organ)
- genetic reasons to prevent the birth of a defective child

Elective Sterilization

Voluntary or elective sterilizations on competent individuals present few legal problems, so long as proper consent has been obtained from the patient and the procedure is performed properly. Civil liability for performing a sterilization of convenience may be imposed if the procedure is performed in a negligent manner. The physician in *McLaughlin v. Cooke*[44] was found negligent for mistakenly cutting a blood vessel in the patient's scrotum while he was performing a vasectomy. Excessive bleeding at the site of the incision was found to have occurred because of the physician's negligent postsurgical care. On appeal, the jury's finding of negligence was held to have been supported properly by testimony that the physician's failure to intervene sooner and to remove a hematoma had been the proximate cause of tissue necrosis, which later required the removal of the patient's testicle.

The parents in *Goforth v. Porter Medical Associates, Inc.*,[45] brought a medical malpractice action for expenses resulting from the negligence of the physician in performing a sterilization on August 2, 1980. The physician assured the plaintiff that she was sterile. The patient subsequently became pregnant and delivered a child on October 9, 1981. The plaintiff argued that as a result of the physician's negligence, she incurred $2,000 in medical bills and will incur $200,000 for the future care of the child. The district court dismissed the case. On appeal, the Oklahoma Supreme Court held that the parents could not recover the expenses of raising a healthy child; however, they could maintain an action for expenses resulting from the negligent performance of a sterilization and the unplanned pregnancy.

Regulation of Sterilization of Convenience

Like abortion, voluntary sterilization is the subject of many debates over its moral and ethical propriety. Some health care institutions have adopted policies restricting the performance of such operations at their facilities. The U.S. Court of Appeals for the First Circuit has ruled in *Hathaway v. Worcester City Hospital*[46] that a governmental hospital may not impose greater restrictions on sterilization procedures than on other procedures that are medically indistinguishable from sterilization with regard to the risk to the patient or the demand on staff or facilities. The court relied on the Supreme Court decisions in *Roe v. Wade*[47] and *Doe v. Bolton*,[48] which accorded considerable recognition to the patient's right to privacy in the context of obtaining medical services. The extent to which hospitals may prohibit or substantially limit sterilization procedures is not clear, but it appears likely that such hospitals will be allowed considerable discretion in this matter.

At least one state, Kansas, has enacted legislation declaring that hospitals are not required to permit the performance of sterilization procedures and that physicians and hospital personnel may not be required to participate in such procedures or be discriminated against for refusal to participate. Such legislation, which more frequently is enacted in relation to abortion procedures, often is referred to by the term *conscience clause* and was not found objectionable in Supreme Court decisions striking down most state abortion laws.

Therapeutic Sterilization

If the life or health of a woman may be jeopardized by pregnancy, the danger may be avoided by terminating her ability to conceive or her husband's ability to impregnate. Such an operation is a therapeutic sterilization—one performed to preserve life or health. The medical necessity for sterilization renders the procedure therapeutic. Sometimes a diseased reproductive organ has to be removed to preserve the life or health of the individual. The operation results in sterility, although this was not the primary reason for the procedure. Such an operation technically should not be classified as a sterilization because the sterilization is incidental to the medical purpose.

Involuntary/Eugenic Sterilization

The term *eugenic sterilization* refers to the involuntary sterilization of certain categories of persons described in statutes, without the need for consent by, or on behalf of, those subject to the procedures. Persons classified as mentally deficient, feeble-minded, and, in some instances, epileptic are included within the scope of the statutes. Several states also have included certain sexual deviates and persons classified as habitual criminals. Such statutes ordinarily are said to be designed to prevent the transmission of hereditary defects to succeeding generations, but several statutes also have recognized the purpose of preventing procreation by individuals who would not be able to care for their offspring.

Although there have been many judicial decisions to the contrary, the U.S. Supreme Court in *Buck v. Bell*[49] specifically upheld the validity of such eugenic sterilization statutes, provided that certain procedural safeguards are observed.

Several states have laws authorizing eugenic sterilization. The decision in *Wade v. Bethesda Hospital*[50] strongly suggests that in the absence of statutory authority, the state cannot order sterilization for eugenic purposes. At the minimum, eugenic sterilization statutes provide the following:

- a grant of authority to public officials supervising state institutions for the mentally ill or prisons and to certain public health officials to conduct sterilizations
- a requirement of personal notice to the person subject to sterilization and, if that person is unable to comprehend what is involved, notice to the person's legal representative, guardian, or nearest relative
- a hearing by the board designated in the particular statute to determine the propriety of the prospective sterilization; at the hearing, evidence may be presented, and the patient must be present or represented by counsel or the nearest relative or guardian
- an opportunity to appeal the board's ruling to a court

The procedural safeguards of notice, hearing, and the right to appeal must be present in sterilization statutes to fulfill the minimum constitutional requirements of due process. An Arkansas statute was found to be unconstitutional in that it did not provide for notice to the incompetent patient and opportunity to be heard, or for the patient's entitlement to legal counsel.[51]

Current statutes do not authorize castration and often specifically prohibit it. Most eugenic sterilization statutes provide for vasectomy or salpingectomy. This prohibition against castration, along with provisions granting immunity only to persons performing or assisting in a sterilization that conforms to the law, is an added safeguard for persons subject to sterilization. Civil or criminal liability for assault and battery may be imposed on one who castrates or sterilizes another without following the procedure required by law.

ARTIFICIAL INSEMINATION

Generally, artificial insemination is the injection of seminal fluid into a woman to induce pregnancy. The term also may include insemination that takes place outside of the woman's body, as with so-called test-tube babies. If the semen of the woman's husband is used to impregnate her, the technique is called homologous artificial insemination, but if the semen comes from a donor other than the husband, the procedure is identified as heterologous artificial insemination.

The absence of answers to many questions concerning heterologous artificial insemination may have discouraged couples from seeking to use the procedure and physicians from performing it. Some of the questions concern the procedure itself; others concern the status of the offspring and the effect of the procedure on the marital relationship.

Consent

The Oklahoma heterologous artificial insemination statute specifies that husband and wife must consent to the procedure.[52] It is obvious that the wife's consent must be obtained; without it, the touching involved in the artificial insemination would constitute a battery. Besides the wife's consent, it is important to obtain the husband's consent to ensure against liability accruing if a court adopted the view that without the consent of the husband, heterologous artificial insemination was a wrong to the husband's interest for which he could sustain a suit for damages.

The Oklahoma statute also deals with establishing proof of consent. It requires the consent to be in writing and to be executed and acknowledged by the physician performing the procedure and by the local judge who has jurisdiction over the adoption of children, as well as by the husband and wife.

In states without specific statutory requirements, medical personnel should attempt to avoid such potential liability by establishing the practice of obtaining the written consent of the couple requesting the heterologous artificial insemination procedure.

Confidentiality of the Procedure

Another problem that directly concerns medical personnel involved in heterologous artificial insemination birth is preserving confidentiality. This problem is met in the Oklahoma heterologous artificial insemination statute, which requires that the original copy of the consent be filed pursuant to the rules for the filing of adoption papers and is not to be made a matter of public record.[53]

WRONGFUL BIRTH, WRONGFUL LIFE, AND WRONGFUL CONCEPTION

There is substantial legal debate regarding the impact of an improperly performed sterilization. Suits have been brought on such theories as wrongful birth, wrongful life, and wrongful conception. Wrongful life suits are generally unsuccessful, primarily because of the court's unwillingness, for public policy reasons, to permit financial recovery for the "injury" of being born into the world.

However, some success has been achieved in litigation by the patient (and his or her spouse) who allegedly was sterilized and subsequently proved fertile. Damages have been awarded for the cost of the unsuccessful procedure; pain and suffering as a result of the pregnancy; the medical expense of the pregnancy; and the loss of comfort, companionship services, and consortium of the spouse. Again, as a matter of public policy, the courts have indicated that the joys and benefits of having the child outweigh the cost incurred in the rearing process.

There have been many cases in recent years involving actions for wrongful birth, wrongful life, and wrongful conception. Such litigation originated with the California case in which a court found that a genetic testing laboratory can be held liable for damages from incorrectly reporting genetic tests, leading to the birth of a child with defects.[54] Injury caused by birth had not been previously actionable by law. The court of appeals held that medical laboratories engaged in genetic testing owe a duty to parents and their unborn child to use ordinary care in administering available tests for the purpose of providing information concerning potential genetic defects in the unborn. Damages in this case were awarded on the basis of the child's shortened life span.

Wrongful Birth

In a *wrongful birth* action, the plaintiffs claim that but for a breach of duty by the defendant(s) (e.g., improper sterilization), the child would not have been born. A wrongful birth claim can be brought by the parent(s) of a child born with genetic defects against a physician who or a laboratory that negligently fails to inform them, in a timely fashion, of an increased possibility that the mother will give birth to such a child, therefore precluding an informed decision as to whether to have the child.

Recovery for damages was permitted for wrongful birth but not wrongful life in *Smith v. Cote*.[55] The physician in this case was negligent in that he failed to test in a timely fashion for the mother's exposure to rubella and to advise her of the potential for birth defects. She therefore was entitled to maintain a cause of action for wrongful birth. However, for compelling reasons of public policy, the mother would not be permitted to assert on the child's behalf a claim for damages on the basis of wrongful life.

In *Proffitt v. Bartolo*,[56] the parents of a handicapped child stated a cause of action for wrongful birth against a physician who allegedly failed to properly interpret a rubella test performed during the mother's first trimester of pregnancy, thereby precluding the option of abortion. The physician had a duty to advise the parents so that they would have an opportunity to exercise the option of an abortion. If it could be established that the physician breached such a duty and that the parents would have terminated the pregnancy, the necessary causal connection would be demonstrated, and the parents would be entitled to recover for their extraordinary costs of raising the handicapped child and for any emotional harm that they might have suffered as a result of their child's handicap.

The Alabama Supreme Court in *Keel v. Banach*[57] held that a cause of action for wrongful birth is recognized in Alabama, and compensable losses are any medical and hospital expenses incurred as a result of the physician's negligence, physical pain suffered by the mother, loss of consortium, and mental and emotional anguish suffered by the parents. The basic rule of tort compensation is that the plaintiffs should be placed in the position where they would have been without the defendant's negligence. A jury could conclude that the defendants, in failing to inform the mother of the possibility of giving birth to a child with multiple congenital deformities, directly deprived her and her husband of the option to accept or reject a parental relationship with the child and thus caused them to experience mental distress.

The Alabama Supreme Court said that it agreed with the Illinois Supreme Court, finding:

> [m]any courts have accepted wrongful birth as a cause of action on the theory that it is a logical and necessary extension of existing principles of tort law. . . . Some courts have recognized the cause of action because of the expanding ability of medical technology to accurately detect and predict genetic or other congenital abnormalities before conception or birth. Imposing liability on individual physicians or other health care providers, these courts say, vindicates the societal interest in reducing and preventing the incidence of such defects. . . . Other courts have expressed concern that refusing to recognize this cause of action would frustrate the fundamental policies of tort law: to compensate the victim, to deter negligence, and to encourage due

care. . . . The Alabama legislature passed a new Medical Liability Act in 1987, regarding medical negligence causes of action. Nowhere in that Act are wrongful birth cases excluded as they are in the laws passed in Missouri and Minnesota.[58]

The state of Georgia did not recognize a cause of action for wrongful birth filed by the parent of child born with Down's Syndrome in *Etkind v. Suarez*.[59] Throughout her pregnancy, Dr. Etkind was a patient of Dr. Suarez. After giving birth to a child with Down's Syndrome, she and her husband filed suit against Suarez and his partnership, asserting a "wrongful birth" claim. Such a claim "is brought by the parents of an impaired child and alleges basically that, but for the treatment or advice provided by the defendant, the parents would have aborted the fetus, thereby preventing the birth of the child." The trial court granted the defendants' motion for judgment on the pleadings. A cause of action for wrongful birth is not recognized in Georgia.

In a New Jersey case, *Canesi ex rel. v. Wilson*,[60] the New Jersey Supreme Court reviewed the dismissal of an action for wrongful birth on the claim of the parents that, had the mother been informed of the risk that a drug, Provera, which she had been taking before she learned that she was pregnant, might cause the fetus to be born with congenital anomalies, such as limb reduction, she would have decided to abort the fetus. It was alleged that the physicians failed to disclose the risks associated with the drug. The physicians' argued that the informed consent doctrine requires that the plaintiffs establish that the drug in fact caused the birth anomalies. The court rejected the argument, and distinguished the wrongful birth action from one based on informed consent:

> In sum, the informed consent and wrongful birth causes of action are similar in that both require the physician to disclose those medically accepted risks that a reasonably prudent patient in the plaintiff's position would deem material to her decision. What is or is not a medically acceptable risk is informed by what the physician knows or ought to know of the patient's history and condition. These causes of action, however, have important differences. They encompass different compensable harms and measures of damages. In both causes of action, the plaintiff must prove not only that a reasonably prudent patient in her position, if apprised of all material risks, would have elected a different course of treatment or care. In an informed consent case, the plaintiff must additionally meet a two-pronged test for proximate causation: she must prove that the undisclosed risk actually materialized and that it was medically caused by the treatment. In a wrongful birth case,

on the other hand, a plaintiff need not prove that the doctor's negligence was the medical cause of her child's birth defect. Rather, the test of proximate causation is satisfied by showing that an undisclosed fetal risk was material to a woman in her position; the risk materialized, was reasonably foreseeable and not remote in relation to the doctor's negligence; and, had plaintiff known of that risk, she would have terminated her pregnancy. The emotional distress and economic loss resulting from this lost opportunity to decide for herself whether or not to terminate the pregnancy constitute plaintiff's damages.[61]

In addressing the issue of proximate cause, the court noted:

> . . . the nature of the wrongful birth does not depend on whether a defendant caused the injury or harm to the child. Rather, the appropriate inquiry was viewed as to whether the defendant's negligence was the proximate cause of the parent's loss of the option to make an informed and meaningful decision either to terminate the pregnancy or to give birth to a potentially defective child.

> •   •   •   •

> The appropriate proximate cause question, therefore, is not whether the doctor's negligence caused the fetal defect; the congenital harm suffered by the child is not compensable. Rather the determination to be made is whether the doctor's inadequate disclosure deprived the parents of their deeply personal right to decide for themselves whether to give birth to a child who could possibly be afflicted with a physical abnormality. There is sufficient evidence in the record of this case to enable the jury to make that determination.[62]

With the increasing consolidation of hospital services and physician practices, a case could be made for finding a hospital liable for the physician's failure to obtain informed consent where the hospital actually owns or controls the physician's practice or where both the hospital and the physician's practice are owned or controlled by another corporation that sets policy for both the hospital and the physician's practice.

Wrongful Life

A *wrongful life* claim is brought by the parent(s) or child who claims to have suffered harm as a result being born. The plaintiffs generally contend that the physician or laboratory negligently failed to inform the child's parents of the risk of bearing a genetically defective infant and hence prevented the parents' right to choose to avoid the birth.[63] Because there is no recognized legal right not to be born, wrongful life cases are generally not successful.

> [L]egal recognition that a disabled life is an injury would harm the interests of those most directly concerned, the handicapped. Disabled persons face obvious physical difficulties in conducting their lives. They also face subtle yet equally devastating handicaps in the attitudes and behavior of society, the law, and their own families and friends. Furthermore, society often views disabled persons as burdensome misfits. Recent legislation concerning employment, education, and building access reflects a slow change in these attitudes. This change evidences a growing public awareness that the handicapped can be valuable and productive members of society. To characterize the life of a disabled person as an injury would denigrate both this new awareness and the handicapped themselves.[64]

A cause of action for wrongful life was not cognizable under Kansas law in *Bruggeman v. Schimke*.[65] A child born with congenital birth defects was not entitled to recover damages on the theory that physicians had been negligent when, after a prior sibling was born with congenital anomalies, they mistakenly advised the parents that the first child's condition was not because of a known chromosomal or measurable biochemical disorder. In view of the fundamental principle of law that human life is valuable, precious, and worthy of protection, a legal right not to be born rather than to be alive with deformities could not be recognized. The Kansas Supreme Court held that there was no recognized cause for wrongful life.

A wrongful life action was brought against the physicians in *Speck v. Finegold* on behalf of an infant born with defects.[66] The court held that regardless of whether the claim was based on wrongful life or otherwise, no legally cognizable cause of action was stated on behalf of the infant even though the defendants' actions of negligence were the proximate cause of her defective birth. The parents could recover pecuniary expenses that they had borne and would bear for care and treatment of their child and that resulted in the natural course of things from the commission of the tort. The tort in this case was the failure of the urologist to perform a vasectomy properly and the failure of the obstetrician/gynecologist to perform an abortion properly. Recovery for negligence was allowed because the plaintiff parents did set forth a duty owed to them by the physicians and breached by the physicians with resulting injuries to the plaintiffs. Claims for emotional disturbance and mental distress were denied.

In *Pitre v. Opelousas General Hospital*,[67] the parents of a child born with a congenital defect filed a malpractice suit seeking damages for themselves and their child, alleging that the surgeon had been negligent in performing a tubal ligation. The suit also claimed that the hospital and the physician failed to inform Mrs. Pitre that the operation was unsuccessful. A pathology report had revealed that the physician had severed fibromuscular tissue, rather than fallopian tissue, during the surgical procedure. The parents were not informed of this finding. The mother became pregnant and gave birth to an albino child. The court of appeals dismissed the child's claim for wrongful life and struck all the parents' individual claims with the exception of expenses associated with the pregnancy and the husband's loss of consortium. On a writ of certiorari to review the ruling, the Louisiana Supreme Court held that the physician owed a duty to warn the parents regarding the failure of the tubal ligation, the physician did not have a duty to protect the child from the risk of albinism, and the parents were entitled to damages relating to the pregnancy and the husband's consortium. Special damages relating to the child's deformity were denied.[68]

Wrongful Conception/Wrongful Pregnancy

Wrongful conception or *wrongful pregnancy* refers to a claim for damages sustained by the parents of an unexpected child based on an allegation that conception of the child resulted from negligent sterilization procedures or a defective contraceptive device.[69] Damages sought for a negligently performed sterilization might include

- pain and suffering associated with pregnancy and birth
- expenses of delivery
- lost wages
- father's loss of consortium
- damages for emotional or psychological pain
- suffering resulting from the presence of an additional family member in the household
- the cost and pain and suffering of a subsequent sterilization
- damages suffered by a child born with genetic defects

The most controversial item of damages claimed is that of raising a normal healthy child to adulthood. The mother in *Hartke v. McKelway*[70] had undergone a sterilization for therapeutic reasons to avoid endangering her health from pregnancy. The woman became pregnant as a result of a failed sterilization. She delivered a healthy child without injury to herself. It was determined that "the jury could not rationally have found that the birth of this child was an injury to this plaintiff. Awarding child rearing expense would only give Hartke a windfall."[71]

However, the costs of raising a normal healthy child in *Jones v. Malinowski*[72] were recoverable. The plaintiff had three previous pregnancies. The first pregnancy resulted in a breech birth; the second child suffered brain damage; and the third child suffered from heart disease. For economic reasons, the plaintiff had undergone a bipolar tubal laparoscopy, which is a procedure that blocks both fallopian tubes by cauterization. The operating physician misidentified the left tube and cauterized the wrong structure, leaving the left tube intact. As a result of the negligent sterilization, Mrs. Malinowski became pregnant. The court of appeals held the costs of raising a healthy child are recoverable and that the jury could offset these costs by the benefits derived by the parents from the child's aid, comfort, and society during the parents' life expectancy. The jury was instructed not to consider that the plaintiffs "might have aborted the child or placed the child out for adoption [since] . . . as a matter of personal conscience and choice parents may wish to keep an unplanned child."[73]

The cost of raising a healthy newborn child to adulthood was recoverable by the parents of the child conceived as a result of an unsuccessful sterilization by a physician employee at Lovelace Medical Center. The physician in *Lovelace Medical Center v. Mendez*[74] found and ligated only one of the patient's two fallopian tubes and then failed to inform the patient of the unsuccessful operation. The court held that:

> the Mendezes' interest in the financial security of their family was a legally protected interest which was invaded by Lovelace's negligent failure properly to perform Maria's sterilization operation (if proved at trial), and that this invasion was an injury entitling them to recover damages in the form of the reasonable expenses to raise Joseph to majority.[75]

Some states bar damage claims for emotional distress and the costs associated with the raising of healthy children but will permit recovery for damages related to negligent sterilizations. In *Butler v. Rolling Hills Hospital*,[76] the Pennsylvania Superior Court held that the patient stated a cause of action for the negligent performance of a laparoscopic tubal ligation. The patient was not, however, entitled to compensation for the costs of raising a normal healthy child. "In light of this Commonwealth's public policy, which recognizes the paramount importance of the family to society, we conclude that the benefits of joy, companionship, and affection which a normal, healthy child can provide must be deemed as a matter of law to outweigh the costs of raising that child."[77]

As the Court of Common Pleas of Lycoming County, Pennsylvania, in *Shaheen v. Knight*, stated:

> Many people would be willing to support this child were they given the right of custody and adoption, but according to plaintiff's statement, plaintiff does not want such. He wants to have the child and wants the doctor to support it. In our opinion, to allow such damages would be against public policy.[78]

Prevention of Wrongful Birth, Wrongful Life, and Wrongful Conception Lawsuits

The occurrence of a pregnancy is not necessarily the result of negligence. Although slight, there is known to be a given failure rate. Physicians can prevent lawsuits by informing each patient both orally and through written consent as to the likelihood of an unsuccessful sterilization, as well as the inherent risks in the procedure.

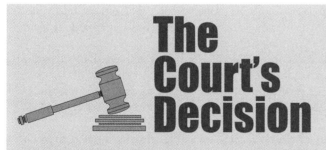

The Court's Decision

The United States District Court for the District of Columbia held that leaders and groups would be fined for violating the injunction. In addition, anti-abortion groups are liable to abortion clinics for property damages resulting from blockades.

The defendants violated those provisions of the injunction "barring all defendants and those acting in concert with them 'from inducing, encouraging, directing, aiding, or abetting others' to trespass on, blockade, or obstruct access to or egress from facilities at which abortions are performed and other medical services are rendered." *Id.* at 734. In blockading the clinics, the defendants violated District of Columbia trespass law, which states, "Any person who, without lawful authority, shall enter, or attempt to enter, any public or private dwelling . . . against the will of the lawful occupant or of the person lawfully in charge thereof . . . shall be guilty of a misdemeanor" (D.C. CODE § 22–3102).

The participants in the blockades were under court order not to trespass on the clinics and were ordered by clinic personnel and the police at the time of the blockades to leave the property. Their presence on the property clearly constituted trespass. The July 31, 1990, revised injunction explicitly stated that, in order to coerce compliance, if the terms of the injunction were violated, there would be a "fine to be paid to the medical facility or facilities that are or become the target of the violation." *Id.* at 735.

Because of the dual compensatory and coercive nature of civil contempt proceedings, future contempt fines were intended to be payable to the plaintiff clinics "as additional deterrence, and because plaintiffs have demonstrated that defendants' activities cause damage to the blockaded clinics." *Memorandum*, July 31, 1990, at 13. The court had established a schedule of sanctions in order to deter future violations of the revised injunction order. These orders warned defendants that in the event of future violations, sanctions would be imposed.

CHAPTER REVIEW

1. *Abortion* is defined as the premature termination of a pregnancy, either spontaneous or induced. *Roe v. Wade* is the Supreme Court's ruling that, within certain guidelines, allows women to make decisions regarding how their pregnancies will end. According to *Roe v. Wade*:
   - during the first trimester, an abortion decision is between a woman and her physician
   - in the second trimester, the state may regulate the medical conditions under which an abortion or performed
   - a state can prohibit all abortions except those deemed necessary to protect maternal life or health during the third trimester—the final stage of pregnancy
2. States' and women's rights regarding reproductive decision have been further shaped and defined by a number of landmark rulings. In the 1992 ruling in the case of *Planned Parenthood v. Casey*, the Supreme Court nearly overturned *Roe v. Wade*. It did reject the trimester approach in favor of the Court evaluating the permissibility of state abortion rules based on whether they unduly burden a woman's ability to obtain an abortion. A rule is considered an *undue burden* if its purpose or effect is to place a substantial obstacle in the path of a woman seeking an abortion before the fetus is viable.
3. A *partial birth abortion* is a late-term abortion that involves partial delivery of the baby prior to its being aborted. An Arkansas statute failed to prohibit this manner of abortion largely due to its broad coverage. The act was determined to be unconstitutional because it was unconstitutionally vague, imposed an undue burden on women seeking abortions, and did not adequately protect the health and lives of pregnant women.
4. In *Utah Women's Clinic, Inc. v. Leavitt*, the court determined that imposition of a 24-hour waiting period—except in the event of a medical emergency—does not impose an undue burden on the right to an abortion.
5. Issues of required consent vary from state to state. In Florida, a wife must have the written consent of her husband in order to obtain an abortion. However, in *Doe v. Zimmerman*, the court declared unconstitutional a similar provision in the Pennsylvania Abortion Control Act.
6. Individuals have a right to refuse to participate in abortions for reason of conscience or religious or moral conviction.
7. Several states have placed restrictions on abortions by reducing funding for the procedures. The Hyde Amendment, through which the U.S. Congress has limited the types of medically necessary abortions for which federal funds can be spent under the Medicaid program, opened the door to such provisions within states.
8. Physicians feel the effects of the abortion controversy. There are cases in which physicians have filed successful litigation regarding physical and mental injuries suffered as a result of the controversy.
9. *Sterilization* is defined as the termination of the ability to produce offspring.
10. A *vasectomy* is a surgical procedure performed on men in which the vas deferens is severed and tied to prevent the flow of seminal fluid into the urinary canal.

11. A *tubal ligation* is a surgical procedure performed on women in which the fallopian tubes are cut and tied. This prevents the passage of the ovum from the ovary to the uterus.

12. As long as proper consent is obtained and the procedure performed properly, *elective sterilizations* present few legal problems. A *therapeutic sterilization* is performed to preserve life or health. *Eugenic sterilization*—the involuntary sterilization of certain categories of persons—is often performed to prevent the transmission of hereditary defects and, in some states, is performed to prevent procreation by persons who would not be able to care for their offspring.

13. *Artificial insemination* most often takes the form of the injection of seminal fluid into a woman to induce pregnancy. *Homologous artificial insemination* is when the husband's semen is used in the procedure. *Heterologous artificial insemination* is when the semen is from a donor other than the husband.

14. *Wrongful birth* actions claim that, but for breach of duty by the defendant, a child would not have been born. *Wrongful life* suits—those in which a parent or child claims to have suffered harm as a result of being born—are generally unsuccessful. *Wrongful conception/pregnancy* actions claim that damages were sustained by parents of an unexpected child based on the allegation that the child's conception was the result of negligent sterilization procedures or a defective contraceptive device. Physicians can avoid liability in wrongful conception/pregnancy actions by obtaining oral and written consent that indicates that the physician has disclosed the inherent risks of the sterilization procedure.

REVIEW QUESTIONS

1. Do you agree that individual states should be able to place reasonable restrictions or waiting periods? Who should determine what is reasonable?
2. Should a married woman be allowed to abort without her husband's consent?
3. Give two arguments for and two arguments against partial birth abortions.
4. Why is the medical issue of abortion an example of legislating morality?
5. Do you agree that eugenic sterilization should be allowed? Why or why not?
6. Describe the distinctions among wrongful birth, wrongful life, and wrongful conception. Why is there such diversity in opinions from the different states?

NOTES

1. NOW v. Operation Rescue, 816 F. Supp. 729 (D. D.C. 1993).
2. 410 U.S. 113 (1973).
3. *Id.* at 164.
4. *Id.*
5. *Id.*
6. *Id.*
7. 410 U.S. 179 (1973).
8. *Id.* at 198.
9. 428 U.S. 52 (1976).
10. 432 U.S. 464 (1977).
11. 99 S. Ct. 675 (1979).
12. 443 U.S. 622 (1979).
13. 448 U.S. 297 (1980).
14. 101 S. Ct. 1164 (1981).
15. 103 S. Ct. 2481 (1983).
16. 492 U.S. 490 (1989).
17. 111 S. Ct. 1759 (1991).
18. Planned Parenthood v. Casey, 112 S. Ct. 2792 (1992).
19. 118 S. Ct. 1347 (1998).
20. 192 F.3d 794 (8th Cir. 1999).
21. Ark. Code Ann. § 5–61–203 (1997).
22. Ark. Code Ann. § 5–61–202 (1997).
23. Ark. Code Ann. § 5–61–202 (1997).
24. Planned Parenthood of Cent. N.J. v. Farmer, 220 F.3d 127 (3d Cir. 2000).
25. 844 F. Supp. 1482 (D. Utah 1994).
26. 112 S. Ct. 2791 (1992).
27. 844 F. Supp. 1482 (D. Utah 1994) at 1494.
28. *Id.* at 1495.
29. Poe v. Gerstein, 517 F.2d 787 (5th Cir. 1975).
30. 405 F. Supp. 534 (M.D. Pa. 1975).
31. 486 U.S. 1308 (1988).
32. 515 So.2d 1254 (Ala. Civ. App. 1987).
33. 533 A.2d 523 (R.I. 1987).
34. 515 F.2d 541 (8th Cir. 1975).
35. 432 U.S. 438 (1977).
36. *Id.*
37. Doe v. Director of Dep't of Social Serv., 468 N.W. 2d 862 (Mich. Ct. App. 1991).
38. Boley v. Miller, No. 20158 (W. Va. May 15, 1992) (unpublished).
39. Doe v. Director of Mich. Dep't of Social Serv., No. 91092 (Mich. June 9, 1992) (unpublished).
40. *Abortion: A World View*, Self, Nov. 1992, at 54.
41. 565 N.Y.S.2d 833 (N.Y. App. Div. 1991).
42. Forrester v. City of San Diego, 25 F.3d 804 (9th Cir. 1994)

43. *Id.* at 807.
44. 774 P.2d 1171 (Wash. 1989).
45. 755 P.2d 678 (Okla. 1988).
46. 475 F.2d 701 (1st Cir. 1973).
47. 410 U.S. 113 (1973).
48. 410 U.S. 179 (1973).
49. 224 U.S. 200 (1927).
50. 337 F. Supp. 671 (E.D. Ohio 1971).
51. McKinney v. McKinney, 805 S.W.2d 66 (Ark. 1991).
52. Okla. Stat. Ann. 10, §§ 551–553.
53. Okla. Stat. Ann. 10, §§ 551–553.
54. 165 Cal. Rptr. 477 (Cal. Ct. App. 1980).
55. 513 A.2d 341 (N.H. 1986).
56. 412 N.W.2d 232 (Mich. Ct. App. 1987).
57. 624 So.2d 1022 (Ala. 1993).
58. *Id.* at 1031.
59. 519 S.E.2d 210 (Ga. 1999)
60. 730 A.2d 806 (N.J. 1999).
61. *Id.* at 18.
62. *Id.*
63. Smith v. Cote, 513 A.2d 344 (N.H. 1986).
64. *Id.* at 353.
65. 718 P.2d 635 (Kan. 1986).
66. 408 A.2d 496 (Pa. Super. Ct. 1979).
67. 530 So.2d 1151 (La. 1988).
68. *Id.*
69. Cowe v. Forum Group, Inc., 575 N.E.2d 630, 631 (Ind. 1991).
70. 707 F.2d 1544 (D.C. Cir. 1983).
71. *Id.* at 1557.
72. 473 A.2d 429 (Md. 1984).
73. *Id.* at 431.
74. 805 P.2d 603 (N.M. 1991).
75. *Id.* at 612.
76. 582 A.2d 1384 (Pa. Super. Ct. 1990).
77. *Id.* at1385.
78. 11 Pa. D. & C.2d 41, 46 (Lycoming Co. Ct. Com. Pl. 1957).

Patient Rights and Responsibilities

A MOTHER'S RIGHT—A CHILD'S DEATH

Mrs. Harrell, a Jehovah's Witness, was six months pregnant when physicians discovered a life-threatening blood condition that could rapidly deteriorate and place both her life and the life of the fetus in jeopardy. Because of her religious beliefs, Harrell objected to a blood transfusion. After an emergency hearing where the Harrells could not summon an attorney, the court ruled that a blood transfusion could be given to Harrell if it was necessary to save the life of the fetus and that after the child was born, a blood transfusion could be given to the child if necessary to save the child's life. The child was delivered by Caesarean section and died two days later. No blood transfusion was given to Harrell or to the child. As a result, St. Mary's Hospital and the state claimed that the appeal of the trial court's order is moot. Because of the hospital's serious misunderstanding about its standing to bring such proceedings, the court addressed the issue of standing as capable of repetition yet evading review.

Article I, section 23 of the Florida Constitution guarantees that a competent person has the constitutional right to choose or refuse medical treatment, and that right extends to all relevant decisions concerning one's health. In cases where these rights are litigated, a party generally seeks to invoke the power of the state, through the exercise of the court's judicial power, either to enforce the patient's rights or to prevent the patient from exercising those rights. The state has a duty to ensure that a person's wishes regarding medical treatment are respected. That obligation serves to protect the rights of the individual from intrusion by the state unless the state has a compelling interest great enough to override this constitutional right (e.g., protection of innocent third parties). The means to carry out any such compelling state interest must be narrowly tailored in the least intrusive manner possible to safeguard the rights of the individual.

Harrell argued that the hospital should not have intervened in her private decision to refuse a blood transfusion. She claimed that the state had never been a party in this action, had not asserted any interest, and that the hospital had no authority to assume the state's responsibilities.[1]

What is your verdict?

INTRODUCTION

This chapter discusses both the rights and responsibilities of patients. Every individual possesses certain rights guaranteed by the U.S. Constitution and its amendments, including freedom of speech, religion, and association and the right not to be discriminated against on the grounds of race, color, creed, or national origin. The Supreme Court has interpreted the Constitution as also guaranteeing certain other rights not expressly mentioned, such as the right to privacy and the right to self-determination. An individual's rights are not automatically waived upon entering a health care facility.

In addition to rights, patients have responsibilities. Such responsibilities include the necessity to disclose all information relevant to one's medical condition and being considerate of the rights of others.

PATIENT RIGHTS

Every patient has the right to choose the medical care that he or she wishes to receive. Health care organizations must respect each patient's personal dignity and his or her fundamental right to make critical treatment decisions. Each patient has the right to refuse treatment, or to discontinue treatments already in progress.

As medical technology becomes more advanced, these decisions can become more and more difficult. Should I have the surgery or not? Do I want to be maintained on a respirator? Who will decide for my father, now that he is suffering from Alzheimer's?

Frequently, these decisions involve not just medical questions, but moral and ethical questions as well—questions about the quality versus the longevity of life, about religious beliefs and personal values.

Patient rights may be classified as either legal, those emanating from law, or human statements of desirable principles, such as the right to health care or the right to be treated with human dignity. Both staff and patients should be aware and understand not only their own rights and responsibilities but also the rights and responsibilities of others.

Patient Self-Determination Act

The continuing trend of consumer awareness, coupled with increased governmental regulations, makes it advisable for caregivers to understand the scope of patient rights and how to ensure them. The Patient Self-Determination Act of 1990 (PSDA),[2] for example, made a significant advance in the protection of the rights of patients to make decisions regarding their own health care. Health care organizations may no longer merely passively permit patients to exercise their rights but must "protect and promote" such rights. The PSDA provides that each individual has a right under state law (whether statutory or as recognized by the courts of the state) to make decisions concerning his or her medical care, including the right to accept or refuse medical or surgical treatment and the right to formulate advance directives.

ADMISSION

At the time of admission, the patient should be informed in writing of his or her rights and responsibilities. If necessary, each patient has a right to have those rights explained.

Health care organizations must not discriminate by reason of race, creed, color, sex, religion, or national origin. Those that do discriminate violate constitutionally guaranteed rights. They also may be in violation of federal, state, and local laws. Discrimination in some states can be considered a misdemeanor and also may carry a civil penalty. Federal and state funds may be withheld from those institutions that practice discrimination.

Most federal, state, and local programs specifically require, as a condition for receiving funds under such programs, an affirmative statement on the part of the organization that it will not discriminate. For example, the Medicare and Medicaid programs specifically require affirmative assurances by health care organizations that no discrimination will be practiced.

Right To Refuse Treatment

In *Matter of Dubreuil*,[3] a patient was in the advanced stage of pregnancy when she was admitted through the emergency department of the hospital. At the time of her admission, she signed a standard consent form that included her agreement to have a blood transfusion if necessary. The next day, she was going to have a Caesarean section, but she would not consent to a blood transfusion because of her religious beliefs. During the course of the delivery, after she had lost a significant amount of blood, it was determined that she needed a transfusion to save her life, but she would not give her consent. Her estranged husband was contacted, and upon his arrival at the hospital, he gave his consent for the transfusion. After the first transfusion, physicians determined that she would need more, so they petitioned the circuit court for an emergency hearing to determine if they could give the transfusion in spite of the patient's lack of consent. Although no testimony was given at the hearing, there was a telephone call advising the court that the patient had just regained consciousness and that she continued to withhold her consent.

The trial court decided to allow the hospital to administer blood as they felt it was necessary. The patient moved for a rehearing, and the circuit court denied it. The patient then sought review by the Florida Supreme Court, arguing that her federal and state constitutional rights of privacy, self-determination, and religious freedom had been denied.

The Florida Supreme Court found that a competent person has the right to choose or refuse medical treatment, including all decisions relevant to his or her health. That right merges with the right to refuse a blood transfusion while exercising one's religious beliefs. A health care provider must comply with the patient's wishes unless supported by a court order to do otherwise. Here, the state interest was the protection of children as innocent third parties. However, in this case there would have been no abandonment, because under Florida law, when there are two living parents, they share equally in the responsibilities of parenting. Had the patient died, her husband would have assumed the care of the children.

Federal and State Regulations

Civil rights are rights ensured by the U.S. Constitution and by the acts of Congress and the state legislatures. Generally, the term includes all the rights of each individual in a free society.

Congress and the federal courts have dealt with discriminatory practices in health care organizations. Discrimination in the admission of patients and segregation of patients on racial grounds are prohibited in any organization receiving federal financial assistance. Pursuant to Title VI of the Civil Rights Act of 1964, the guidelines of the Department of Health and Human Services (HHS) prohibit the practice of racial discrimination by any organization or agency receiving money under any program supported by HHS. This includes all "providers of service" receiving federal funds under Medicare legislation.

According to the Fourteenth Amendment to the Constitution, a state cannot act to deny any person equal protection of the laws. If a state or a political subdivision of a state, whether through its executive, judicial, or legislative branch, acts in such a way as to deny unfairly to any person the rights accorded to another, the amendment has been violated.

Government Organizations

Whether a person is entitled to admission to a particular governmental institution depends on the statute establishing that institution. Governmental hospitals, for example, are by definition creatures of some unit of government; their primary concern is service to the population within the jurisdiction of that unit. In all cases, connection with the unit operating the hospital is necessary to entitle one to use the hospital's facilities. Some of the statutes cover all inhabitants of the geographic area and, in addition, are broad enough to apply to any person within the area who falls ill or suffers traumatic injury and requires hospital care.

Although persons who are not within the statutory classes have no right of admission, hospitals and their employees owe a duty to extend reasonable care to those who present themselves for assistance and are in need of immediate attention. With respect to such persons, governmental hospitals are subject to the same rules that apply to private hospitals.

The patient in *Stoick v. Caro Community Hospital*[4] brought a medical malpractice action against a government physician in which she alleged that the physician determined that she was having a stroke and required hospitalization but that he refused to hospitalize her. The plaintiff's daughter-in-law called the defendant, Caro Family Physicians, P.C., where the patient had a 1:30 P.M. appointment. She was told to take the patient to Caro Community Hospital. On arriving at the hospital, there was no physician available to see the patient, and a nurse directed her to Dr. Loo's clinic in the hospital. On examination, Loo found right-sided facial paralysis, weakness, dizziness, and an inability to talk. He told the patient that she was having a stroke and that immediate hospitalization was necessary. Loo refused to admit her because of a hospital policy that only the patient's family physician or treating physician could admit her. The plaintiff went to her physician, Dr. Quines, who instructed her to go to the hospital immediately. He did not accompany her to the hospital. At the hospital she waited approximately one hour before another physician from Caro Family Physicians arrived and admitted her. Loo claimed that he did not diagnose the patient as having a stroke and that there was no bad faith on his part. The circuit court granted the physician's motion for summary judgment on the grounds of governmental immunity. The court of appeals reversed, holding that the plaintiff did plead sufficient facts constituting bad faith on the part of Loo. His failure to admit or otherwise treat the patient is a ministerial act for which governmental immunity does not apply and may be found by a jury to be negligence.

Privacy in Care and Treatment

The right to privacy in care and treatment is one of the most difficult to protect in a health care setting. The limitations of space and finances make it difficult to preserve a patient's privacy. Nevertheless, the organization has a responsibility to provide as much privacy as is possible.

Confidentiality of Information

Patients have a right to expect that information regarding their care and treatment will be kept confidential. Caregivers must be careful not to discuss any aspect of a patient's case with others not involved in the case.

DISCHARGE

A patient may not be detained in a health care facility because of his or her inability to pay for services rendered. An unauthorized detention of this nature could subject a facility to charges of false imprisonment.

A minor should be released only to a parent or authorized guardian. An incompetent should be released in the care of an appropriate family member or guardian. At times, patients will refuse discharge if they are homeless. These cases should be handled on an individual basis with the assistance of a case manager or social worker.

Discharge Orders

When discharging a patient, a physician should issue and sign all discharge orders. If there is no need for immediate care, the patient should be advised to seek follow-up care with his or her family physician.

Release from Hospital Contraindicated

The plaintiff in *Somoza v. St. Vincent's Hospital*[5] was admitted to the hospital during the 29th week of her pregnancy. She was admitted under the care of her private attending physician, defendant Dr. Svesko. She presented herself to the hospital with complaints of severe abdominal pain. Upon the plaintiff's admission to the hospital, Dr. Gutwein (a resident physician at the hospital) examined her. According to the notations she made on the plaintiff's chart, Dr. Gutwein independently formed the impression that the plaintiff might be suffering from either left pyelonephritis, premature labor, or polyhydramnios. Gutwein recorded a written plan and orders requiring that the plaintiff be hooked up to a fetal monitor. She also was to undergo a number of diagnostic tests, including a renal pelvic sonogram. The results of the sonogram were abnormal and the radiologist recommended a follow-up sonogram. However, the attending physician did not order a follow-up. Despite the abnormal sonogram and various findings on the physical examinations, Svesko decided to release the plaintiff from the hospital because her pain had subsided. He orally conveyed this order to Gutwein. According to Gutwein, she did not formulate an opinion as to the correctness of the decision to discharge because she was of the opinion that it was not her place to make such a decision. Instead, pursuant to Svesko's instruction, on her early morning rounds, Gutwein simply signed an order discharging the plaintiff from the hospital. Four days later, the plaintiff returned to the hospital suffering severe pain and soon thereafter delivered twin girls. The twins were diagnosed as suffering from cerebral palsy resulting from their premature birth. The plaintiff brought a medical malpractice action against the hospital and Svesko arising out of the premature birth of the twins. The defendants filed a motion for summary judgment and it was denied. The defendants appealed.

The state supreme court held that there were material issues of fact as to whether the mother's symptoms exhibited during her physical assessment contraindicated her release from the hospital and that ordinary prudence required further inquiry by the resident physician, Gutwein.

The plaintiffs presented an affidavit by expert witness Dr. Sherman, who stated that "the failure of the hospital staff to discharge without another physical examination, in my opinion, with a reasonable degree of medical certainty, is a departure from good and accepted medical practice. The resident clearly had an obligation to examine even a private patient in the face of a changing cervix and not just to discharge her pursuant to some attending physician's order."[6] A hospital whose staff carries out a physician's order may be held responsible where the hospital staff knows, or should know, that the orders are so clearly contraindicated by normal practice that ordinary prudence requires inquiry into the correctness of the orders. In this case, the plaintiff's release from the hospital was so clearly contraindicated by normal practice that ordinary prudence required further inquiry by Gutwein into the correctness of the discharge order.

FAILURE TO OVERRIDE A PHYSICIAN'S DECISION

Citation: *Greer v. Bryant, 621 A.2d 999 (Pa. Super. Ct. 1993)*

Facts

While at the Philadelphia College of Osteopathic Medicine (PCOM) and under the care of her physician, Dr. Bryant, Mrs. Greer was diagnosed with "pre-eclampsia," a condition characterized by high blood pressure in the mother that poses a risk to the unborn child. On September 20, the patient suffered symptoms of fetal distress and was examined by the hospital's interns and residents. Tests ordered at the time of her visit revealed that the fetus was suffering from "decelerations," a periodic lowering of the heartbeat. Following her examination, Greer was instructed to return to the hospital on September 23. During that visit, it was noted that the fetus was experiencing "poor beat to beat variability." Greer was once again sent home with instructions to return to the hospital on September 27. However, on September 26, Greer, experiencing severe pains, called the hospital emergency department. She was told to wait until her scheduled appointment the following day. Her appointment was subsequently canceled because of inclement weather. Upon the insistence of her sister, Greer went to the hospital on September 27, where she delivered her child. The infant, suffering from "severe meconium aspiration" (inhalation by the fetus of its own fecal matter while in utero), died several days later.

The plaintiff alleged that the hospital, through its negligence, had contributed to her child's death. Greer sued Bryant and PCOM separately. She alleged that based on the prenatal test results during her September 23 visit to PCOM, she should have been delivered on that date by Bryant. Questions were raised as to whether Bryant was aware of the test results. The plaintiff argued that, even if the test results had been communicated to Bryant and he decided to send her home, the residents should have recognized the serious condition of the fetus and, if necessary, sought approval from their superiors to keep her at the hospital.

Bryant made an offer to settle and the plaintiff accepted. The Court of Common Pleas, upon jury verdict, entered judgment for the mother, finding PCOM 41 percent liable to the plaintiff. PCOM appealed.

Issue

Was Bryant properly notified that the fetus was suffering heart decelerations, and did the plaintiff's expert witness, Dr. Gabrielson, exceed her scope of opinion in her medical report by stating that the plaintiff should have been admitted and the child delivered despite the private physician's instructions to send her home?

Holding

The Pennsylvania Superior Court found that the jury could find that the hospital's staff was negligent by not reporting the fetal distress of the unborn child to Bryant and that the plaintiff's expert witness did not exceed her scope of opinion in her medical report.

Reason

Although a resident and intern claimed that they had called Bryant, neither could testify as to the content of their conversation with him. Bryant testified that he did not recall receiving any telephone calls. He stated that if he had been aware of the decelerated heart rate, he would have ordered delivery of the child. "Since many of the critical events occurred on September 23, the jury could have determined that PCOM's employees' crucial nonfeasance occurred on that date . . . we must assume that the jury drew this inference." *Id.* at 1002.

Gabrielson, in three written reports and through oral testimony, testified that if the test results had not been reported to Bryant, such conduct, in her opinion, fell below the required standard of care. PCOM argued that this new *"failure to override* [Dr. Bryant's possible orders to send Rachel home] *theory"* was not contained in the reports and that they were unfairly surprised by the opinion. The superior court did not agree. The following is an excerpt from a report, which presents questioning of Gabrielson by the plaintiff's counsel:

> 3. Ms. Greer was sent to Osteopathic Hospital on three occasions for non-stress and contraction stress testing. On the second occasion. . .it was noted that the baby's heart rate showed poor variability. . . . Could you explain the significance of this finding with regard to the health and well-being of the fetus?
>
> A. The episode of bradycardia observed on September 20 was a very ominous sign and very suggestive of cord compression probably resulting from oligo-hydramnios. This would result in fetal distress with meconium passage and aspiration. It could result in sudden intrauterine death.
>
> 4. Once the fetal distress was detected, did the hospital act appropriately by sending Ms. Greer home?
>
> A. No.
>
> 5. What measures, if any, should have been taken to ensure the health and well-being of the fetus?
>
> A. Ms. Greer should have been admitted and delivered. *Id.* at 1004.

The question of hospital negligence in sending the plaintiff home was within the fair scope of Gabrielson's oral testimony and written reports.

"PCOM's decision to send Rachel home was contemplated and counsel should have anticipated that the 'failure to override theory' was looming." *Id.* at 1004.

Discussion

1. What steps should hospitals take when a patient is faced with life-threatening test results and the attending physician makes a determination to send the patient home?
2. What effect, if any, should such cases have upon the training of students and residents?
3. What action should a nurse take when faced with questionable actions by physicians and residents?
4. What policies and procedures should be in place to address similar issues in other patient care settings (emergency departments and ambulatory care centers)?

TRANSFER

Patients must have access to the appropriate level and type of care that they need. This will at times necessitate the transfer of the patient to another health care organization that has the special services that the patient requires. For this reason, it is important for each organization to execute transfer agreements with other health care organizations.

The patient's right to choose a receiving facility must be honored whenever possible. The Medicaid patient in *Macleod v. Miller*[7] was entitled to an injunction preventing his involuntary transfer from the nursing home. The patient had not been accorded a pretransfer hearing as was required by applicable regulations. In addition, it was determined that the trauma of transfer might result in irreparable harm to the patient. The appeals court remanded the case to the trial court with directions to enter an order prohibiting the defendants from transferring the plaintiff pending exhaustion of his administrative remedies.

The 97-year-old resident in *Henson v. Department of Consumer and Regulatory Affairs*[8] petitioned for review of a decision by the Department of Consumer and Regulatory Affairs to involuntarily discharge her from a community residence facility. The resident had lived in the facility for eight years. The basis for the agency's decision was that the resident's discharge was essential to be in accordance with her prescribed level of care, pursuant to D.C. Code Annotated Section 32–1421(a). The only evidence presented by the facility was three medical certification forms completed by Dr. Choisser, the treating physician. Two forms indicated in an ambiguous check-off system that the resident required an intermediate level of care. This was contradicted by a letter written by Choisser that stated, "I see no reason why she should not continue to reside in Chevy Chase House with complete safety. . . . It is my opinion that a change in her residence, at this stage in her life, would prove harmful to her emotionally, and I strongly suggest that she be left as she is."[9] The court held that the need for the discharge was not proven by clear and convincing evidence.

PATIENT BILL OF RIGHTS

The patient must be informed by the organization regarding his or her rights and responsibilities. An organization's description of patient rights and responsibilities should be viewed as a document with legal significance whether or not the state in question has adopted a similar code. The rights of patients must be respected at all times. Each patient is an individual with unique health care needs. The patient has a right to make decisions regarding his or her medical care, including the decision to discontinue treatment, to the extent permitted by law. Patients have a right to:

1. Receive an explanation of their rights.
2. Receive assistance in understanding their rights, including an interpreter.
3. Receive treatment without discrimination as to race, color, religion, sex, national origin, disability, sexual orientation, or source of payment.
4. Receive considerate and respectful care in a clean and safe environment free of unnecessary restraints.
5. Receive emergency care if needed.
6. Be informed of the names and positions of the caregivers who will be in charge of their care in the hospital.
7. Know the names, positions, and functions of any hospital staff involved in their care and refuse treatment, examination, or observation by them.
8. Receive complete information about their diagnosis, treatment, and prognosis.
9. Receive all the information they need to give informed consent for any proposed procedure or treatment. This information shall include the possible risks and benefits of the procedure or treatment
10. Receive all the information they need to give informed consent for an order not to resuscitate. They also have the right to designate an individual to give this consent if they are too ill to do so.
11. Refuse treatment and be told what effect this may have on their health.
12. Refuse to consent or decline to participate in research.

13. Expect privacy while in the hospital and confidentiality of all information and records regarding their care.
14. Participate in all decisions about their treatment and discharge from the hospital.
15. Review their medical records without charge and obtain a copy of their medical records.
16. Receive an itemized bill and explanation of all charges.
17. Complain, without fear of reprisal, about the care and services they are receiving.
18. Know the hospital's relationships with outside parties that may influence a patient's treatment and care. These relationships may be with educational institutions, insurers, and other health care providers.
19. Know about hospital resources, such as patient representatives or ethics committees, that can help them resolve problems and questions about their hospital stay and care.

PATIENT RESPONSIBILITIES

Patients have responsibilities as well as rights.

Historical Perspective

The following is an excerpt from Cornwall General Hospital's "Rules for Patients," which were posted in that hospital in 1897:

1. Patients on admission to the Hospital must have a bath, unless orders to the contrary are given by the Attending Medical Attendant.

. . . .

6. Patients must be quiet and exemplary in their behaviour and conform strictly to the rules and regulations of the Hospital, and carry out all orders and prescriptions of the various officers of the establishment.

. . . .

8. No male patient shall, under any pretense whatever, enter the apartments or wards for the females, nor shall a female patient enter the apartments or wards for males, without express orders from the Medical Attendant or Lady Superintendent.

. . . .

10. Every patient shall retire to bed at 9 P.M. from First May to First November, and at 8 P.M. from No-

vember to May; and those who are able shall rise at 6 A.M. in the Summer and 7 A.M. in the Winter.

11. Such patients as are able, in the opinion of the physicians and surgeons, shall assist in nursing others, or in such services as the Lady Superintendent may require.

. . . .

13. Patients must not take away bottles, labels or appliances when leaving the Hospital.

14. No patients shall enter into the basement story, operating theater, or any of the officers' or attendants' rooms, except by permission of an officer of the Hospital.

. . . .

17. Any patient bringing spirituous liquors into the Hospital or the grounds, or found intoxicated, will be discharged.

18. Whenever patients misbehave or violate any of the standing rules of the Hospital, the Attending Physician may remove or discharge them, as provided by clauses 91 and 93 of Rules for Medical Staff.

Contemporary Perspective

Today, patient responsibilities are stated somewhat differently than they were in 1897. Patient responsibilities include the following:

- fully disclosing all information relevant to one's medical condition (the court of appeals in *Fall v. White*[10] affirmed the superior court's ruling that the patient had a duty to provide the physician with accurate and complete information and to follow the physician's instructions for further care or tests)
- providing accurate, timely, and complete information regarding complaints, past illnesses, hospitalizations, and medications
- reporting unexpected changes in condition to the treating practitioner(s)
- making it known whether one clearly understands the contemplated plan of care, course of treatment, and what is expected of oneself
- following the treatment plan recommended by the practitioner (this may include following the instructions of nurses and allied health personnel)
- following the institution's rules and regulations
- refraining from the self-administration of medications not prescribed by the attending physician

- keeping appointments and, when unable to do so, notifying the responsible practitioner or health care facility
- accepting the consequences of refusing treatment or not following instructions
- being considerate of the rights of others, including health care personnel in assisting in the control of noise, smoking, and the number of visitors
- being respectful of the property of other persons and of the health care facility
- recognizing the effect of life-style as it affects one's personal health

No constitutional right is absolute. Even the First Amendment rights to free speech will not protect a person who shouts "Fire" in a crowded room and causes injury to others. By analogy, the patient exercising his or her right to free speech might disturb fellow patients. The right to speak then is conflicting with the right to privacy, which includes the right to peace and quiet.

 RESPONSIBILITY TO DISCLOSE INFORMATION

Citation: *Oxford v. Upson County Hosp., Inc.,* 438 S.E.2d 171 (Ga. Ct. App. 1993)

Facts

Ms. Oxford brought a lawsuit against the Upson County Hospital and nurses claiming that their medical malpractice caused her injury from a fall in the hospital's bathroom. Oxford had been admitted to the hospital after having been diagnosed with gastroenteritis and dehydration. Nothing on her chart indicated that she had experienced dizziness. Testimony at the trial indicated that Oxford had told her nurse that she had to go to the bathroom. Oxford did not inform the nurse that she felt dizzy. After the nurse escorted her to the bathroom, Oxford fainted while sitting on the toilet. As she fainted, she hit her head on the bathroom wall.

Two nurse experts testified that it is a *patient's responsibility to communicate to the staff any symptoms* the patient is experiencing. Oxford had told her physician prior to her hospitalization about feeling dizzy, but he had not related this information to the hospital's staff.

After a jury verdict for the hospital, Oxford appealed, arguing that the trial court's jury charges on causation, failure to exercise ordinary care, and comparative negligence were wrong.

Issue

Was there sufficient evidence to warrant the judge's charges to the jury?

Holding

The Georgia Court of Appeals affirmed the jury verdict and found that the judge's charges on the issues had been sufficient.

Reason

The court followed its determination in *Carreker v. Harper,* 196 Ga.App. 658, 659, 396 S.E.2d 587 (1990), that when a patient fails to disclose all information related to her condition and fails to exercise ordinary care for her safety by seeking medical attention for her worsening condition, a charge of comparative negligence is applicable. In this case, the court did not require that Oxford diagnose herself, but she should have told the staff about her symptoms so that they could have treated her using their professional judgment.

Discussion

1. What precautions should the admitting physician and nurses take to help prevent similar injuries from occurring in the future?
2. Do you agree with the appellate court's decision?

PATIENT ADVOCACY

Because patients are often helpless and unable to speak for themselves, all caregivers, whether they are volunteers or paid staff, should consider themselves as patient advocates. Patient advocacy can be accomplished by caregivers providing care in their particular areas of responsibility and expertise. Many states have established, by legislation, ombuds programs. Ombudspersons are responsible for the investigation of reports of resident abuse in nursing facilities.

The concept of ombudsman originated in Sweden when that country moved from a monarchy to a democratic form of government. The Swedes felt the need for an agency or an office to be established to act as a go-between the average citizen and the government; someone who would be there to answer questions, to advocate on behalf of the citizens, someone who could receive and resolve complaints from the citizenry in regard to government policies and programs.

The Swedish concept of ombudsman was eventually adopted in the United States. The primary impetus for the program came from the Nixon Administration, and gradually the program has spread throughout the country. It was not until 1978 that the Older Americans Act Amendments (Pub.L. No. 95-478) mandated that every state have an ombudsperson program and that a certain amount of the Older Americans Act funds from Title III-B (the Social Services Section) had to be allocated to the ombudsperson program.

The Court's Decision

The court concluded that a health care provider must not be forced into the position of having to argue zealously against the wishes of its own patient, seeking deference to the wishes or interests of nonpatients—in this case, the patient's husband, her brothers, the children, and the state itself. *Patients do not lose their right to make decisions affecting their lives when they enter into the care of a health care facility.* A health care provider's function is to provide medical treatment in accordance with the patient's wishes and best interests, not supervening the wishes of a competent adult. A health care provider must comply with the wishes of a patient to refuse medical treatment unless ordered to do otherwise by a court of competent jurisdiction. A health care provider cannot act on behalf of the state to assert state interests.

In situations like these, health care providers generally have sought judicial intervention to determine their rights and obligations to avoid liability. Health care providers, when terminating life support in accordance with a patient's wishes, are relieved of potential civil and criminal liability as long as they act in good faith, and that no prior court approval of the health care provider's action is required. *When a health care provider, acting in good faith, follows the wishes of a competent and informed patient to refuse medical treatment, the health care provider is acting appropriately and cannot be subjected to civil or criminal liability.*

CHAPTER REVIEW

1. The Patient Self-Determination Act of 1990 made a significant advance in the protection of patients' right to make decisions regarding their own health care. This Act requires that health care organizations not only observe these rights, but also to protect and promote them.
2. Patients should be informed of their rights and responsibilities at the time of admission. If a patient does not understand these rights and responsibilities, they should be explained to the patient.
3. Health care organizations that discriminate on racial grounds are not eligible to receive federal financial assistance.
4. *Government hospitals* operate with the mission of delivering care to a population within the jurisdiction of the government unit with which the hospital is associated. However, these hospitals are still required to extend reasonable care to patients in need of immediate assistance.
5. When discharging a patient, a physician must be sure to issue and sign all discharge orders. Patients cannot be held at a facility because of inability to pay. Minors and incompetents should be released only into the care of an appropriate family member or guardian.
6. If a patient is to be transferred, *transfer agreements* with the receiving health care organization must be executed. Whenever possible, patients should have the right to select the receiving facility.

7. Patients have rights, but they also have responsibilities. These responsibilities help health care providers treat patients in the most appropriate way possible and help maintain order within the facility.

8. Caregivers should consider themselves *patient advocates* because of their position to help patients who are often helpless and unable to speak for themselves. Many states have established *ombudsman* programs responsible for the investigation of reports of resident abuse in nursing facilities.

9. A health care provider who acts in good faith to follow the wishes of a competent and informed patient to refuse medical treatment is acting appropriately and cannot be subjected to civil or criminal liability.

REVIEW QUESTIONS

1. Describe those circumstances in which a state might have a right to interfere with a patient's decision to forgo emergency care.

2. When considering a person's religious beliefs, should the state have a right to interfere with a mother's decision to refuse a blood transfusion? Why?

3. Should a hospital be able to raise whatever interest the state itself may have in seeking to compel an unwilling patient to undergo a routine, lifesaving medical procedure? Explain.

4. Describe why a patient's responsibilities are as important as his or her rights.

5. Discuss the ramifications of the following statement: *It is the patient's responsibility to communicate to the staff any symptoms that he or she is experiencing.*

NOTES

1. *Harrell v. St. Mary's Hosp., Inc.*, 678 So.2d 455 (Fla. Dist. Ct. App. 1996).
2. 42 U.S.C. 1395cc(a)(1).
3. 629 So.2d 819 (Fla. 1993).
4. 421 N.W.2d 611 (Mich. Ct. App. 1988).
5. 596 N.Y.S.2d 789 (N.Y. App. Div. 1993).
6. *Id.* at 791
7. 612 P.2d 1158 (Colo. Ct. App. 1980).
8. 560 A.2d 543 (D.C. 1989).
9. *Id.* at 545.
10. 449 N.E.2d 628 (Ind. Ct. App. 1983).

CHAPTER

15

Acquired Immune Deficiency Syndrome

It's Your Gavel...

AMERICA'S MOST FEARED DISEASE

The patient-plaintiff had a blood specimen drawn and sent to SmithKline Laboratories for testing for human immunodeficiency virus (HIV). The laboratory informed the physician that his patient tested positive for HIV.

On June 13, 1988, the patient was informed that he had acquired immune deficiency syndrome (AIDS). Not believing that his symptoms mimicked those of an individual with AIDS, the patient was retested for HIV. On three separate occasions (July 1, 1988, July 15, 1988, and July 22, 1988) involving two separate laboratories, he tested negative for the virus. In September 1990, the plaintiff later filed a lawsuit against his physician and SmithKline for the negligent interpretation and reporting of his blood samples as being HIV positive.

The circuit court ruled that the plaintiff stated a claim upon which relief could be granted in alleging that the defendants caused him to suffer major depression. The defendants appealed.[1]

What is your verdict?

INTRODUCTION

AIDS is considered to be the deadliest epidemic in human history. The first case of AIDS appeared in the literature in 1981.[2] A report from the United Nations AIDS Programme estimated that at least 36.1 million people would be living with the HIV infection by the end of the year 2000, and three million would have died in that same year. More than 21 million people have died from AIDS thus far.[3]

AIDS generally is accepted as a syndrome—a collection of specific, life-threatening, opportunistic infections and mani-

festations that are the result of an underlying immune deficiency. It is caused by HIV and is the most severe form of the HIV infection. HIV is considered to be a highly contagious bloodborne virus.

AIDS is a fatal disease that destroys the body's capacity to ward off bacteria and viruses that ordinarily would be fought off by a properly functioning immune system. Although there is no effective long-term treatment of the disease, indications are that proper management of the disease can improve the quality of life and delay progression of the disease. Internationally, AIDS is posing serious social, ethical, economic, and health problems.

SPREAD OF AIDS

AIDS is spread by direct contact with infected blood or body fluids, such as vaginal secretions, semen, and breast milk. At the present time, there is no evidence that the virus can be transmitted through food, water, or casual body contact. HIV does not survive well outside the body. Although there is presently no cure for AIDS, early diagnosis and treatment with new medications can help HIV-infected persons remain healthy for longer periods. High-risk groups include homosexual men, intravenous drug users, and those who require transfusions of blood and blood products, such as hemophiliacs.

Blood Transfusions

The administration of blood is considered to be a medical procedure. It results from the exercise of professional medical judgment that is composed of two parts: (1) diagnosis, deciding the need for blood; and (2) therapy, the actual administration of blood.

Suits often arise as a result of a person with AIDS claiming that he or she contracted the disease as a result of a transfusion of contaminated blood or blood products. In blood transfusion cases, the standards most commonly identified as having been violated concern blood testing and donor screening. An injured party generally must prove that a standard of care existed, that the defendant's conduct fell below the standard, and that this conduct was the proximate cause of the plaintiff's injury.

The most common occurrences that lead to lawsuits in the administration of blood involve

- transfusion of mismatched blood
- improper screening and transfusion of contaminated blood
- unnecessary administration of blood
- improper handling procedures (i.e., inadequate refrigeration and storage procedures)

In *Roberts v. Suburban Hospital Association,*[4] the Maryland Court of Special Appeals held that a blood transfusion constituted provision of a service (i.e., the rendering of health care rather than the sale of a product) and was subject to the exhaustion of Maryland's Health Claims Arbitration Act. It followed then that the complaint should have been dismissed for failure to follow the required administrative remedy. The *Roberts* case involved the contraction of AIDS by a hemophiliac through the transfusion of contaminated blood. The court stated: "A transfusion is not just a sale of blood which the patient takes home in a package. The transfusion of the blood—the injecting of it into the patient's bloodstream, is what he really needs and pays for, and that involves the application of medical skill."[5]

The risk of HIV infection and AIDS through a blood transfusion has been reduced significantly through health history screening and blood donations testing. All blood donated in the United States has been tested for HIV antibodies since May 1985. Blood units that do test positive for HIV are removed from the blood transfusion pool.

A summary dismissal against a hospital and the American Red Cross was ordered properly in *Kozup v. Georgetown University,*[6] in which it was alleged that the death of a premature infant was due to causes related to AIDS contracted through a blood transfusion given in January 1983, without the parent's informed consent. The case was dismissed on the basis that no reasonable jury would have found that the possibility of contracting AIDS from a blood transfusion in 1983 was a material risk. Dismissal also was justified on the basis that the transfusion was the only method of treating the child for a life-threatening condition.

A hemophiliac patient in *McKee v. Miles Laboratories*[7] had contracted AIDS from a coagulation protein, which was provided by the defendants, and subsequently died. The defendants moved for summary judgment as to the merits of the case, contending that at the time the plaintiff's decedent contracted AIDS, there were no tests that would have revealed the presence of the AIDS virus. The plaintiff argued that there was a genuine issue of material fact as to whether an alternative testing method was available when the decedent contracted AIDS in 1983. The district court held that the provision of blood and blood byproducts was a service and not a sale and that the lack of any test to purify or screen blood or blood byproducts for the AIDS virus demonstrated that the supplier did not violate industry standards.

The methods available for testing for AIDS during the early 1980s were analyzed carefully in *Kozup,* in which the court determined it was not until 1984 that the medical community reached a consensus as to the proposition that AIDS was transmitted by blood. The district court in *McKee* held there was no need to rehash the same chronological medical history of AIDS that *Kozup* so methodically composed.

The plaintiff in *McKee* appealed the district court's decision to the U.S. Court of Appeals for the Sixth Circuit in *McKee v. Cutter Laboratories.*[8] The court of appeals upheld the district court's decision that the manufacturer was not negligent.

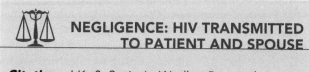

NEGLIGENCE: HIV TRANSMITTED TO PATIENT AND SPOUSE

Citation: *J.K. & Susie L. Wadley Research Inst. v. Beeson,* 835 S.W.2d 689 (Tex. Ct. App. 1992)

Facts

In January 1983, a blood center knew that blood from homosexual or bisexual males should not be accepted under any circumstances. The blood center's written policy provided that donors who volunteer that they are gay should not be permitted to donate blood.

On April 22, 1983, Dr. Kraus, a cardiologist, discovered that Mr. B, the patient, had severe blockage of two major arteries in his heart and recommended cardiac bypass surgery. During surgery, B received seven units of blood by transfusion. In May 1987, B had chest pain and trouble breathing. On June 5, 1987, B was hospitalized. Kraus consulted with two specialists in pulmonary medicine about the unusual pneumonia evident in X-rays of B's lungs. Because there was a possibility that the lung infection was secondary to AIDS, B was tested for HIV. Although B had not yet been formally diagnosed, physicians started him on therapy for AIDS.

B was formally diagnosed as HIV positive. His wife was then tested for HIV, and she learned that she was also HIV positive. On July 2, 1987, B expired. On April 21, 1989, the plaintiffs, Mrs. B and her son, filed suit against the blood center, alleging that her husband contracted HIV from the transfusion of a unit of blood donated at the blood center on April 19, 1983, by a donor identified at trial as Doe. The parties stipulated at trial that Doe was a sexually active homosexual male with multiple sex partners.

The plaintiffs amended their original petition to contend that the blood center's negligence in testing and screening blood donors caused Mrs. B's contraction of HIV. At trial, the jury awarded the plaintiffs $800,000 in damages. Following the trial court's denial of the blood center's motion for judgment notwithstanding the verdict, the blood center filed an appeal. The blood center argued that the trial court erred in denying its motion for judgment notwithstanding the verdict because the evidence of causation was legally insufficient to support the jury verdict.

Issue

Did the evidence support a finding that the blood center's negligence was the proximate cause of B's contraction of HIV?

Holding

The Texas Court of Appeals held that the evidence supported a finding that the blood center's negligence in the collection of blood was the proximate cause of B's HIV infection.

Reason

If there is more than a scintilla of evidence to support the jury's answers to causation, the blood center's no evidence challenge must fail. The question of causation is a fact question for the jury. The issue of proximate cause includes two essential elements: (1) foreseeability and (2) cause-in-fact. Both elements must be present and both may be established by direct or circumstantial evidence.

Foreseeability is satisfied by showing that the actor, as a person of ordinary intelligence, should have anticipated the danger to others by its negligent act. *Cause-in-fact* means that the act or omission was a substantial factor in bringing about the injury and without which no harm would have occurred.

Doe testified that he did not know that he was at a high risk for AIDS and that he would never have given blood if he had known that he was at risk for AIDS. This evidence provided some indication that the blood center's screening procedure did not effectively educate donors. The jury could reasonably infer that the *blood center's failure to effectively educate* Doe and to ask Doe specific questions caused him to donate blood rather than to defer. There was more than a scintilla of evidence to support a finding that the blood center, despite its knowledge about the dangers of HIV-contaminated blood, failed to reject gay men, that the blood center's donor screening was inadequate, and that these omissions were substantial factors in causing Mr. and Mrs. B's HIV infections.

The blood center's own technical director admitted that there was "strong evidence" that the blood accepted from Doe was contaminated with HIV. This statement was based on the fact that Doe's blood was broken into two components, with red blood cells given to another recipient six months later, and that both Bs were subsequently diagnosed as HIV positive less than six months apart from one another.

Discussion

1. What precautions should the blood center have taken to prevent this unfortunate event?
2. What is meant by foreseeability as it relates to this case?
3. What does cause-in-fact refer to as it relates to this case?

Sexual Transmission

Heterosexual relations are becoming a main conduit for the spread of AIDS. Heterosexual transmission is the predominant mode of infection and is increasing.

AIDS AND HEALTH CARE WORKERS

The ever-increasing likelihood that health care workers will come into contact with persons carrying the AIDS virus demands that health care workers comply with approved safety procedures. This is especially important for those who come into contact with blood and body fluids of HIV-infected persons.

SUSPENSION OF SURGICAL PRIVILEGES

An AIDS-infected surgeon in New Jersey was unable to recover on a discrimination claim when the hospital restricted his surgical privileges. In *Estate of Behringer v. Medical Center at Princeton,*[9] the New Jersey Superior Court held that the hospital acted properly in initially suspending a surgeon's surgical privileges, thereafter imposing a requirement of informed consent and ultimately barring the surgeon from performing surgery. The court held that in the context of informed consent, the risk of a surgical accident involving an AIDS-positive surgeon and implications thereof would be a legitimate concern to a surgical patient that would warrant disclosure of the risk. "The 'risk of harm' to the patient includes not only the actual transmission of HIV from the surgeon to patient but the risk of a surgical accident, i.e., a scalpel cut or needle stick, which may subject the patient to post-surgery HIV testing."[10]

CONFIDENTIALITY

Guidelines drafted by the Centers for Disease Control and Prevention (CDC) call on health care workers who perform "exposure-prone" procedures to undergo tests voluntarily to determine whether they are infected. The guidelines also recommend that patients be informed. Both health care workers and patients claim mandatory HIV testing violates their Fourth Amendment right to privacy. The dilemma is how to balance these rights against the rights of the public in general to be protected from a deadly disease.

State laws have been developed that protect the confidentiality of HIV-related information. Also, some states have developed informational brochures and consent, release, and partner notification forms. The unauthorized disclosure of confidential HIV-related information can subject an individual to civil and/or criminal penalties.

Information regarding a patient's diagnosis as being HIV positive must be kept confidential and should be shared with other health care professionals only on a need-to-know basis. Each person has a right to privacy as to his or her personal affairs. The plaintiff surgeon, in the *Estate of Behringer v. Medical Center at Princeton,*[11] was entitled to recover damages from the hospital and its laboratory director for the unauthorized disclosure of his condition during his stay at the hospital. The hospital and the director had breached their duty to maintain confidentiality of the surgeon's medical records by allowing placement of the patient's test results in his medical chart without limiting access to the chart, which they knew was available to the entire hospital community. "The medical center breached its duty of confidentiality to the plaintiff, as a patient, when it failed to take reasonable precautions regarding the plaintiff's medical records to prevent the patient's AIDS diagnosis from becoming a matter of public knowledge."[12]

The hospital in *Tarrant County Hospital District v. Hughes*[13] was found to have properly disclosed the names and addresses of blood donors in a wrongful death action alleging that a patient contracted AIDS from a blood transfusion administered in the hospital. The physician-patient privilege expressed in the Texas Rules of Evidence did not apply to preclude such disclosure because the record did not reflect that any such relationship had been established. The disclosure was not an impermissible violation of the donors' right of privacy. The societal interest in maintaining an effective blood donor program did not override the plaintiff's right to receive such information. The order prohibited disclosure of the donors' names to third parties.

In *Doe v. University of Cincinnati,*[14] a patient who was infected with HIV-contaminated blood during surgery brought an action against a hospital and a blood bank. The trial court granted the patient's request to discover the identity of the blood donor, and the defendants appealed. The court of appeals held that the potential injury to a donor in revealing his identity outweighed the plaintiff's modest interest in learning of the donor's identity. A blood donor has a constitutional right to privacy not to be identified as a donor of blood that contains HIV. At the time of the plaintiff's blood transfusion in July 1984, no test had been developed to determine the existence of AIDS antibodies. By May 27, 1986, all donors donating blood through the defendant blood bank were tested for the presence of HIV antibodies. Patients who received blood from donors that tested positive were to be notified through their physicians. In this case, the plaintiff's family was notified because of the plaintiff's age and other disability.

Any new HIV-related regulations must address the rights and responsibilities of both patients and health care workers. Although this will require a delicate balancing act, it must not be handled as a back burner issue by legislators.

COMPELLING NEED FOR DISCLOSURE OF PHYSICIAN'S HIV STATUS

Citation: *Application of Milton S. Hershey Med. Ctr., 639 A.2d 159 (Pa. 1993)*

Facts

The physician, John Doe, was a resident in obstetrics and gynecology (OB/GYN) at the Milton S. Hershey Medical Center. In 1991, he cut his hand with a scalpel while he was assisting another physician. Because of the uncertainty that blood had been transferred from Doe's hand wound to the patient through an open surgical incision, he agreed to have a blood test for HIV. His blood tested positive for HIV and he withdrew himself from participation in further surgical procedures. The date and means by which Doe contracted HIV could not be determined. The Hershey Medical Center and Harrisburg Hospital, where Doe also participated in surgery, identified those patients who could be at risk. Hershey identified 279 patients and Harrisburg identified 168 patients who fell into this category. Because the hospital records did not identify those surgeries in which physicians may have accidentally cut themselves, the hospitals filed petitions in the Court of Common Pleas, alleging that there was, under the Confidentiality of HIV-Related Information Act [35 P.S. § 7608(a)(2)], a "compelling need" to disclose information regarding Doe's condition to those patients who conceivably could have been exposed to HIV. Doe argued that there was no compelling need to disclose the information and that he was entitled to confidentiality under the Act.

The court issued an order for the selective release of information by providing the name of Doe to physicians and residents in the OB/GYN, by providing the name of Doe to physicians with whom he had participated in a surgical procedure or obstetrical care, by providing a letter to the patients at risk describing Doe as a resident in OB/GYN, and by setting forth the relevant period of such service. The physicians were reminded that they were prohibited under the HIV Act from disclosing Doe's name. The superior court affirmed the decision of the trial court.

Issue

Was there a compelling need to release selective information regarding Doe's HIV-positive status as determined by the trial court?

Holding

The Pennsylvania Supreme Court held that a compelling need existed for at least a partial disclosure of the physician's HIV status.

Reason

There was no question that Doe's HIV-positive status fell within the HIV Act's definition of confidential information. There were, however, exceptions within the HIV Act that allowed for disclosure of the information. In this case, there was a compelling reason to allow disclosure of the information. Although a definition of compelling reason is not included in the Act, a balancing analysis needs to be applied. The "court shall weigh the need for disclosure against the privacy interest of the individual and the public interests which may be harmed by disclosure" [35 P.S. § 7608(c)]. All the medical experts who testified agreed that there was some risk to exposure and that some form of notice should be given to the patients at risk. Even the expert witness presented by Doe agreed that there was at least some conceivable risk of exposure and that giving a very limited form of notice would not be unreasonable. Failure to notify the patients at risk could result in the spread of the disease to other noninfected individuals through sexual contact and through exposure to other body fluids. Doe's name was not revealed to the patients, only the fact that a resident physician who participated in their care had tested HIV-positive. "No principle is more deeply embedded in the law than that expressed in the maxim *Salus populi suprema lex*, . . . (the welfare of the people is the supreme law), and a more compelling and consistent application of that principle than the one presented would be quite difficult to conceive." *Id.* at 163.

MEDICAL RECORDS

Health care institutions must be sure to adopt appropriate and effective policies and procedures for protecting the rights of patients with HIV. As with mental health records, a higher degree of confidentiality generally is expected of the treating institution because of the negative impact on persons who have contracted HIV.

AIDS AND THE RIGHT TO KNOW

Health Care Professionals

Health care professionals and others working with AIDS patients have a right to know when they are caring for patients with highly contagious diseases. There are times when the duty to disclose outweighs the rights of confidentiality. The U.S. Court of Appeals for the Tenth Circuit in *Dunn v. White*[15] declared there is no Fourth Amendment impediment to a state prison's policy of testing the blood of all inmates for HIV. Under the U.S. Supreme Court's drug-testing decisions, the proper analysis is to balance the prisoner's interest in being free from bodily intrusion inherent in a blood test against the prison's institutional rights in combating the disease. The U.S. Court of Appeals held that in or out of prison, a person has only a limited privacy interest in not having his or her blood tested. The court cited *Schmerber v. California*,[16] which rejected a Fourth Amendment challenge to the blood testing of a suspected drunken driver. Against the prisoner's minimal interest, prison authorities have a strong interest in controlling the spread of HIV.

Sexual Partner

A person has a right to know when his or her partner has tested positive for HIV. Physicians are expected to counsel an HIV-positive patient to notify his or her sexual or needle-sharing partners or to seek help in doing so from public health officials. If a patient refuses to do so, a physician may, without the patient's consent, notify a sexual partner known to be at risk of HIV infection.

AIDS—THE RIGHT TO TREATMENT

More and more health care organizations are expressing in their ethics statements that HIV-infected patients have a right not to be discriminated against in the provision of treatment. The Ethics Committee of the American Academy of Dermatology, for example, states that "it is unethical for a physician to discriminate against a class or category of patients and to refuse the management of a patient because of medical risk, real or imagined."[17] Patients with HIV infection, therefore, should receive the same compassionate and competent care given to other patients.

MANDATORY TESTING

The U.S. District Court found that routine testing of firefighters and paramedics for the AIDS virus does not violate an individual's Fourth Amendment or constitutional privacy rights.[18] Because the tested employees are a high-risk group for contracting and transmitting HIV to the public, the city has a compelling interest and legal duty to protect the public from contracting the virus. Firefighters and paramedics are in a higher-risk category than hospital personnel because they work in a noncontrolled setting. *Skinner v. Railway Executives Association* confirmed "society's judgment that blood tests do not constitute an unduly extensive imposition on an individual's privacy and bodily integrity."[19] However, "mandatory testing by a governmental agency for the sole purpose of obtaining a baseline to determine whether an employee contracted AIDS on the job, and thereby to determine the validity of any future worker's compensation claim, is not valid. Mandatory AIDS testing of employees can be valid only if the group of employees involved is at risk of contracting or transmitting AIDS to the public."[20]

NEWS MEDIA AND CONFIDENTIALITY

The Pennsylvania Superior Court in *Stenger v. Lehigh Valley Hospital Center*[21] upheld the court of common pleas' order denying the petition of The Morning Call, Inc., which challenged a court order closing judicial proceedings to the press and public in a civil action against a hospital and physicians. A patient and her family had all contracted AIDS after the patient received a blood transfusion. The access of the media to pretrial discovery proceedings in a civil action is subject to reasonable control by the court in which the action is pending. The protective order limiting public access to pretrial discovery material did not violate the newspaper's First Amendment rights. The discovery documents were not judicial records to which the newspaper had a common-law right of access. Good cause existed for nondisclosure of information about the intimate personal details of the plaintiffs' lives, disclosure of which would cause undue humiliation.

DISCRIMINATION

Discrimination against persons who have contracted the AIDS virus often is found to be in violation of their constitutional rights. The sufferings and hardships of those who have contracted the disease extend to family as well as friends. The infringements of those infected with HIV include discrimination in access to health care, education, employment, housing, insurance benefits, and military service. Those who believe that they have been discriminated against can contact their state's human rights commission.

Access to Health Care

The American Civil Liberties Union in New York City charged in a report that nursing homes discriminate against AIDS patients. "The report is based on a study of 13,000 AIDS discrimination incidents that occurred between 1983 and 1988. The report shows that 'public accommodations'—including nursing homes—accounted for 16 percent of the incidents."[22] A Long Island man stricken with AIDS spent the final three years of his life searching for a nursing home. He died in Nassau County Medical Center after he had been rejected by 22 different homes. The Health Systems Agency, along with the efforts of some state and local officials, were able to "persuade nursing homes in Nassau and Suffolk counties to open their doors to people with AIDS."[23]

The need for nursing home care for AIDS patients is growing, particularly for those who are homeless or have no family support system. An AIDS survey conducted by mail in Oregon revealed that 79 percent of hospitals, 26 percent of skilled nursing facilities, and 69 percent of home health agencies responding had adequate resources to care for AIDS patients.[24] In response to the need for nursing home care, some health departments are encouraging the development of specialized HIV/AIDS nursing homes that will combine medical services and drug treatment for AIDS patients who have become infected through drug abuse.

Education

A school's refusal to admit students with HIV generally is considered an unnecessary restriction on an individual's liberty. However, there are circumstances where it would be unreasonable to infer that Congress intended to force institutions to accept or readmit persons who pose a significant risk of harm to themselves or others. For example, in *Doe v. Washington University*,[25] the university disenrolled a dental student based on his positive HIV status—"the circumstance surrounding plaintiff's HIV status presented little alternative to those charged with evaluating plaintiff's ability to qualify as a dental student."[26]

Employment

AIDS-related employment issues involve a two-sided coin, with employment discrimination on one side and the refusal of employees to care for AIDS patients on the other. The growing consensus of case law indicates employment-related discrimination is unlawful. The California Court of Appeals, Second District, in *Raytheon v. Fair Employment & Housing Commission*,[27] determined an employee with AIDS who was admitted to and treated in a hospital was unlawfully denied his right to return to work after treatment in the hospital. The court held that AIDS is a protected physical handicap under California's Fair Employment and Housing Act and that the employer failed to prove its defense of protecting the health and safety of its other workers. The employer had ignored the advice of county health officials and communicable disease authorities that there was no risk to other employees at the plant.

Employees who have contracted the AIDS virus and whose symptoms warrant should not be placed in positions that threaten the health and safety of patients and employees. The court in *School Board of Nassau County v. Airline* noted that "a person who poses a significant risk of communicating an infectious disease will not be otherwise qualified for his or her job if reasonable accommodations will not eliminate the risk."[28]

Situations may arise from time to time in which employees may refuse to treat AIDS patients. There are two basic approaches that can be taken in dealing with such problems. The most beneficial course of action for the employee and the institution would be to embark on a thorough program of educating the staff. The alternative and less desirable response to the problem may require that disciplinary steps be initiated against the employee. Such action could be justified on the basis that a health care organization has a right to manage its work force by assigning staff in a responsible manner to carry out its mission of caring for the sick.

In the final analysis, many competing issues (e.g., humanitarian, legal, moral, ethical, and religious) pertain to the rights of patients and caregivers who have contracted the AIDS virus, as well as those who have not, and employers. As the search for answers continues, the debates and controversies will be heated. It is hoped that solutions will be forthcoming that will meet the needs of those who have been infected with the AIDS virus and those who are involved with providing health care to them.

Insurance Benefits

In *Weaver v. Reagan*,[29] Medicaid recipients who were denied benefits for AZT (zidovudine; trade name Retrovir) treatments were found to be entitled to summary judgment in their class action suit to require Missouri's authorities to provide Medicaid coverage for the cost of AZT treatments. In this case, the U.S. Court of Appeals for the Eighth Circuit decided that states must provide Medicaid coverage for the drug AZT to HIV-infected individuals who are eligible for Medicaid and whose physicians had certified that AZT was a medically necessary treatment. The state had argued that its reliance on the Food and Drug Administration's approval statement in limiting coverage for AZT treatments was a reasonable exercise of its discretion. The Eighth Circuit disagreed.

NEGLIGENCE

Administration of Wrong Blood

The plaintiff, Mrs. Bordelon, in *Bordelon v. St. Francis Cabrini Hospital*,[30] was admitted to the hospital to undergo a hysterectomy. Prior to surgery, she provided the hospital with her own blood in case it was needed during surgery. During surgery Bordelon did indeed need blood but was administered donor blood other than her own. Bordelon filed a lawsuit claiming that the hospital's failure to provide her with her own blood resulted in her suffering mental distress. The hospital filed a peremptory exception claiming that there was no cause of action. The Ninth Judicial District Court dismissed the suit because the plaintiff did not allege that she suffered any physical injury.

On appeal by the plaintiff, the court of appeal held that the plaintiff did in fact state a cause of action for mental distress. It is well established in law that a claim for negligent infliction of emotional distress unaccompanied by physical injury is a viable claim of action. It is indisputable that HIV can be transmitted through blood transfusions even when the standard procedure for screening for the virus is in place. Mrs. Bordelon's fear was easily associated with receiving someone else's blood, and therefore a conceivable consequence of the defendant's negligent act.[31] The hospital acquired a duty to ensure that Bordelon receive her own blood when it accepted that as a condition of her hospitalization. It is undisputed that the hospital had a "duty" to administer the plaintiff's own blood. The hospital breached that duty by administering the wrong blood.

Recordkeeping

A service member brought an action under the Federal Tort Claims Act in *Johnson v. United States*,[32] alleging that on or about October 8, 1986, Army physicians and medical personnel negligently and wrongly advised her that she had AIDS after she had donated blood to a public blood drive sponsored by the Army hospital, which resulted in her having an unnecessary and unwanted abortion. In November 1986, prior to being notified of this error, the plaintiff discovered that she was pregnant. On November 21, 1986, physicians at Army Reed advised the plaintiff that her child would most certainly be born with AIDS and would not live beyond five years. The physicians indicated that under these circumstances it would be better for the plaintiff to have an abortion than to carry the child to term. As a result of this counseling, and for no other reason, the plaintiff had an abortion on December 4, 1986. It was not until February 3, 1987, nearly four months later, that a physician at Walter Reed Hospital told the plaintiff that there had been an error in the paperwork, and she did not have AIDS.

The United States had moved to have the case dismissed on the grounds that the action was barred by the *Feres* doctrine. Under this doctrine, the United States is not liable under the Federal Tort Claims Act for injuries that arise out of or are in the course of activity incident to service. The district court held that the donation of blood was not "incident to service," and therefore, the *Feres* doctrine did not bar the action.

Surgery

The *Feres* doctrine did not bar a serviceman's claim in *C.R.S. v. United States*.[33] The serviceman had been infected with the AIDS virus during surgery performed on him while he was on active duty. He allegedly spread the virus to both his wife and daughter. The policy rationale for the *Feres* doctrine was not appropriate for barring the claims made in this case.

CRIMINAL ACTIONS

On June 24, 1987, the defendant in *United States v. Moore*,[34] an inmate at the Federal Medical Center in Rochester, was convicted by a jury of assault and battery with a deadly or dangerous weapon. The indictment indicated that he had tested positive for the HIV antibody and later had assaulted two federal correctional officers with his mouth and teeth. The defendant motioned the U.S. District Court for a judgment of acquittal and for a new trial. Evidence at trial showed that AIDS can be transmitted through body fluids such as blood and semen. The defendant had been informed that he had both the AIDS virus and the hepatitis antibody and that he potentially could transmit the diseases to other persons. He bit one officer on the leg twice, leaving a 4-inch saliva stain. He bit the second officer, leaving a mark that was visible five months later at trial. Expert testimony at trial indicated that any human bite can cause a serious infection and that blood is sometimes present in the mouth, particularly if an individual has ill-fitting teeth or gum problems. In the defendant's motion for a new trial, he claimed that the court erred in denying his requested Jury Instruction 12, which would have prohibited the officers' testimony as to medical instructions they were given to avoid infecting their families from being entered into evidence. The evidence was considered probative of the dangerousness of the bites inflicted by the defendant, and the probative value outweighed any prejudicial effect. The defendant's motions for a judgment of acquittal and a new trial were denied.

REPORTING REQUIREMENTS

Because of the social stigma associated with AIDS, there is a tendency to underreport the incidence of the disease. This is particularly true in developing countries, where the problem is compounded by the lack of efficient reporting systems. For example, in Africa, for every person with AIDS, between 50 and 100 more are estimated to be infected with HIV. The social stigma is not endemic to African countries. In the United States, health information is merely more readily available because of sophisticated reporting systems.

AIDS is a reportable communicable disease in every state. Physicians and hospitals must report every case of AIDS—with the patient's name—to government public health authorities. Cases reported to local health authorities are also reported to the CDC, with the patients' names encoded by a system known as Soundex. CDC records come under the general confidentiality protections of the federal Privacy Act of 1974. However, the statute permits disclosures to other federal agencies, under certain circumstances.

AIDS EMERGENCY ACT

AIDS has been reported in all 50 states. Because the incidence of HIV affects different localities of the United States disproportionately, the Senate and House of Representatives enacted the Ryan White Comprehensive AIDS Resources Emergency Act of 1990. The purpose of the Act is to:

> provide emergency assistance to localities that are disproportionately affected by the human immunodeficiency virus epidemic and to make financial assistance available to States and other public or private nonprofit entities to provide for the development, organization, coordination and operation of more effective and cost efficient systems for the delivery of essential services to individuals and families with the HIV disease.[35]

Under the HIV Care Grants section of the Act, a state may use grant funds

1. To establish and operate HIV care consortia within areas most affected by HIV disease that shall be designated to provide a comprehensive continuum of care to individuals and families with HIV disease.
2. To provide home- and community-based care services for individuals with HIV disease.
3. To provide assistance to ensure the continuity of health insurance coverage for individuals with HIV disease.
4. To provide treatments that have been determined to prolong life or prevent serious deterioration of health to individuals with HIV disease.[36]

OCCUPATIONAL SAFETY AND HEALTH ACT

The Occupational Safety and Health Act (OSHA) requires that health care organizations implement strict procedures to protect employees against the AIDS virus. OSHA requires strict adherence to guidelines developed by the CDC. Complaints investigated by OSHA can result in the issuance of fines for failure to comply with regulatory requirements.

AIDS EDUCATION

The ever-increasing likelihood that health care workers will come into contact with persons carrying HIV demands the development of and compliance with approved safety procedures. This is especially important for those who come into contact with blood and body fluids of HIV-infected persons. The CDC expanded its infection control guidelines and has urged hospitals to adopt "universal precautions" to protect their workers from exposure to patients' blood and other body fluids. Hospitals are following universal precautions in the handling of body fluids, which is the accepted standard for employee protection.

A wide variety of AIDS-related educational materials is available on the market. One of the most important sources of AIDS information is the CDC. The process of staff educa-

tion in preparing to care for patients with AIDS is extremely important and must include a training program on prevention and transmission in the work setting. Educational requirements specified by OSHA for health care employees include epidemiology, modes of transmission, preventive practices, and universal precautions.

The Court's Decision

On appeal, the West Virginia Supreme Court of Appeals ruled that the plaintiff had stated a claim for the negligent infliction of emotional distress. The supreme court found that, "Given the well known fact that AIDS had replaced cancer as the *most feared disease in America* and, as defendant SmithKline candidly acknowledges, a diagnosis of AIDS is a death sentence, conventional wisdom mandates that fear of AIDS triggers genuine—not spurious—claims of emotional distress." *Id.* at 775.

CHAPTER REVIEW

1. Acquired immune deficiency syndrome (AIDS) is a fatal disease that destroys the body's ability to fight bacteria and viruses. AIDS is caused by the human immunodeficiency virus (HIV), and it is considered to be the deadliest epidemic in human history. HIV is spread through direct contact with infected blood or body fluids.

2. There have been many cases in which a plaintiff has charged that he or she contracted AIDS as a result of the transfusion of contaminated blood or blood products. In such cases, the plaintiff must prove that there was a deviation from an established standard of care and that the deviation was the proximate cause of injury.

3. Historically, there have been conflicts centered on the CDC-issued guidelines that recommend regular HIV testing for health care workers who perform high-risk procedures and further recommend that patients be informed if their health care workers are infected. The argument has been made that mandatory HIV testing violates workers' and patients' rights to privacy. Information about a patient's HIV-positive status is to be distributed on only a need-to-know basis.

4. Patients with HIV are entitled to the same level of treatment and compassion as all other patients. They have a right not to be discriminated against in the provision of treatment.

5. Because firefighters and paramedics are at high risk for contracting and transmitting HIV to the public, the U.S. District Court ruled that routine HIV/AIDS testing does not violate their Fourth Amendment or constitutional rights to privacy. Mandatory testing of employees is valid only if that group of employees is at high risk for contracting or transmitting HIV to the public.

6. Although employment discrimination is unlawful, employers must try to achieve balance between protecting the rights of employees and the health and safety of patients and other employees.

7. Physicians and hospitals are required to report every case of AIDS because of its status as a communicable disease. Failure to report cases can result in compounded problems to treat the disease.

8. Employees are to be protected from HIV/AIDS under the Occupational Safety and Health Act.

9. The high rate of exposure to HIV/AIDS among health care workers requires that health care organizations comply with approved safety procedures. The CDC has expanded its infection control guidelines and has encouraged hospitals to adopt universal precautions to protect workers.

REVIEW QUESTIONS

1. Should a physician who refuses to treat an AIDS patient be suspended from an organization's medical staff?
2. Discuss whether or not AIDS treatment should be covered by insurance.
3. Should a hospital be permitted to publish the identity of AIDS patients in order to protect other patients and staff?

NOTES

1. Bramer v. Dotson, 437 S.E.2d 775 (W. Va. 1993).
2. Cantwell, *AIDS: The Mystery and the Solutions*, L.A. (1986), at 54.
3. JOINT UNITED NATIONS PROGRAMME ON HIV/AIDS, AIDS EPIDEMIC UPDATE: DECEMBER 2000, UNAIDS/00.44E - WHO/CDS/CSR/EDC/2000.9. <http://www.unaids.org>
4. 532 A.2d 1081 (Md. Ct. Spec. App. 1987).
5. *Id.* at 1088.
6. 663 F. Supp. 1048 (D.D.C. 1987).
7. 675 F. Supp. 1060 (D.C. Ky. 1987).
8. 866 F.2d 219 (6th Cir. 1989).
9. 592 A.2d 1251 (N.J. Super. Ct. Law Div. 1991).
10. *Id.* at 1255.
11. 592 A.2d 1251 (N.J. Super. Ct. Law Div. 1991).
12. *Id.* at 1255.
13. 734 S.W.2d 675 (Tex. Ct. App. 1987).
14. 538 N.E.2d 419 (Ohio Ct. App. 1988).
15. No. 88–2194 (10th Cir. Aug. 1, 1989) (unpublished).
16. 384 U.S. 757 (1966).
17. ETHICS COMMITTEE OF THE AMERICAN ACADEMY OF DERMATOLOGY, ETHICS IN MEDICAL PRACTICE, 1992, at 6.
18. Anonymous Fireman v. Willoughby, No. C88–1182 (D.C. N. Ohio Dec. 31, 1991) (unpublished).
19. 489 U.S. 602, 625 (1989).
20. *Anonymous Fireman*, No. C88–1182.
21. 554 A.2d 954 (Pa. Super. Ct. 1989).
22. *Long-Term Care*, HOSP., Nov. 20, 1990, at 20.
23. *The High Cost of the State's "Little Cuts,"* NEWSDAY, Mar. 31, 1991, at 7.
24. White & Berger, *Response of Hospitals, Skilled Nursing Facilities, and Home Health Agencies in Oregon to AIDS: Reports of Nursing Executives*, 81(4) AM. J. PUB. HEALTH 495 (1991).
25. 780 F. Supp. 628 (E.D. Mo. 1991).
26. *Id.* at 628.
27. No. B035809 (Cal. Ct. App. Aug. 7, 1989) (unpublished).
28. 107 S. Ct. 1131 (1987).
29. 886 F.2d 194 (8th Cir. 1989).
30. 640 So. 2d 476 (La. App. 3d Cir. 1994).
31. *Id.* at 479.
32. 735 F. Supp. 1 (D.D.C. 1990).
33. 761 F. Supp. 665 (D.C. Minn. 1991).
34. No. Crim. 4–87–44 (D. Minn. Sept. 3, 1987) (unpublished).
35. PUB. L. NO. 101–381, 1990 U.S. CODE CONG. & AD. NEWS (104 Stat.) 576.
36. *Id.* at 586.

Health Care Ethics

LIFE OR DEATH: THE RIGHT TO CHOOSE

Upon admission to the hospital, Vega, a Jehovah's Witness, executed a release requesting that no blood or its derivatives be administered to her during her hospitalization. Vega's husband also signed the release. She delivered a healthy baby. Following the delivery, Vega bled heavily. Her obstetrician, Dr. Sood, recommended a dilation and curettage (D&C) to stop the bleeding. Although Vega agreed to permit Sood to perform the D&C, she refused to allow a blood transfusion. Prior to undergoing the procedure, she signed a second release refusing any transfusions and releasing the hospital from liability. Despite the D&C, Vega continued to hemorrhage.

Vega's physicians tried a number of alternatives to the transfusion, but her condition continued to worsen. Eventually, when she was having difficulty breathing, her physicians placed her on a respirator in the intensive care unit. Vega and her husband maintained throughout these events that, although she might die without blood transfusions, it was against their religious beliefs to allow the use of blood. Because Sood and the other physicians involved in Vega's care believed that it was essential that she receive blood in order to survive, the hospital filed a complaint against Vega requesting that the court issue an injunction that would permit the hospital to administer blood transfusions.

The trial court convened an emergency hearing at the hospital. Although Vega's attorney, who was en route to the hospital, had not yet arrived, the court appointed Vega's husband as her guardian *ad litem* and began hearing testimony. Vega's physicians testified that they had exhausted all nonblood alternatives and that, with reasonable medical certainty, she would die without blood transfusions. Her husband testified that, on the basis of his religious beliefs as a Jehovah's Witness, he continued to support his wife's decision to refuse transfusions and believed that she would take the same position if she were able to participate in the hearing.

The court, relying on the state's interests in preserving life and protecting innocent third parties, and noting that Vega's life could be saved by a blood transfusion, granted the hospital's request for an injunction permitting it to administer blood transfusions to her. Vega was then given blood transfusions, recovered, and was discharged from the hospital.

Vega appealed to the appellate court. The hospital moved to dismiss the appeal on the ground of mootness, and the appellate court granted the hospital's motion.

Vega argued that if her refusal of blood transfusions interfered with certain state interests, it should be the state itself, not a private hospital,

that asserts the state's interests. The hospital responded that, because it was charged with Vega's care, it had a direct stake in the outcome of the controversy and was a proper party to bring this action.

Was this case moot because the patient recovered and was discharged from the hospital? Did the hospital have standing to challenge Vega's refusal of lifesaving blood transfusions? Did the issuance of the injunction, followed by the administration of the blood transfusions, violate Vega's common law right of bodily self-determination?[1]
What is your verdict?

INTRODUCTION

This chapter provides the reader with an overview of current health care ethics issues, as well as a framework for thinking, assessing, and making difficult decisions.

Ethics is that branch of philosophy that deals with values relating to human conduct with respect to the rightness and wrongness of actions and the goodness and badness of motives and ends. Ethics encompasses the decision-making process of determining the ultimate values and standards by which actions are judged. It involves how individuals decide to live, how they exist in harmony with the environment, and how they live with each other when so few have so much and so many have so little.

The scope of health care ethics encompasses numerous issues including the right to choose or refuse treatment and the right to limit the suffering one will endure. The incredible advances in technology and the resulting capability to extend life beyond the point of what some may consider a reasonable quality of life have complicated the process of health care decision making. The scope of health care ethics is not limited to philosophical issues but embraces economic, medical, political, and legal dilemmas. The numerous ethical questions involve the entire life span, from the right to be born to the right to die.

One of the most tension-producing issues facing health care providers is *end of life issues*. Although it is well settled that competent terminally ill patients may refuse life-sustaining treatment, physician-assisted suicide remains a major point of contention. Ethics committees have moved from the background to the forefront of this and other ethical considerations. Moreover, they have a central consultative role in offering suggestions to assist patients and their caregivers in resolving ethical dilemmas. The competing

concerns of morality, patient autonomy, legislation, and states' interests swirl around those involved in the decision-making process.

ETHICS COMMITTEE

A *bio-ethics committee* is a multidisciplinary committee, which serves as a hospital resource to patients, families and staff, offering an objective counsel when dealing with difficult health care issues and decisions. An ethics committee is an educational and consultative committee whose role is to analyze ethical dilemmas and to advise and educate health care providers, patients, and families. The goal of the ethics committee must be to assist the patient and family, as appropriate, in coming to consensus with the options that best meet the patient's goal for care. The ethics committee enhances but does not replace the important patient/family–physician relationship, but affords support for decisions made within the relationship.

Ethics committees had their origins in the 1976 landmark *Quinlan* case,[2] where parents were granted permission by the New Jersey Supreme Court to remove their daughter Karen from a ventilator after she had been in a coma for a year. She died 10 years later at the age of 31, having been in a persistent vegetative state the entire time.

The *Quinlan* court looked to the prognosis committee to verify Karen's medical condition. It then factored in the committee's opinion with all other evidence to reach the decision to allow withdrawing her life-support equipment. To date, ethics committees, which are commonly composed of religious leaders, health care professionals, attorneys, and ethicists, do not have sole surrogate decision-making authority. However, they play an ever-expanding role in the development of policy and procedural guidelines to assist in resolving the ethical dilemmas.

Seniors, because of their advancing age, are often treated as though they are incapable of making their own treatment decisions. This faulty thinking is an infringement upon their right to self-determination. All patients have a right to be informed as to the diagnosis, prognosis, proposed intervention, risks of that intervention, availability of other options and their risks, and the consequences of no intervention. After receiving this information, all individuals are legally empowered to either consent to or refuse the intervention, even if that refusal should lead to serious harm or death.

Committee Function

The functions of ethics committees are multifaceted and include: development of policy and procedure guidelines to assist in resolving ethical dilemmas; staff and community education; conflict resolution; case reviews, support, and consultation; and political advocacy. The degree to which an ethics committee serves each of these functions varies in different health care organizations.

Policy and Procedure Development

The ethics committee is a valuable resource for developing hospital policies and procedures to assist health care professionals in making difficult decisions.

Educational Role

The ethics committee typically provides education on current ethical concepts and issues to committee members, organization staff, and the community at large.

Consultative Role

The ethics committee often consults with caregivers, patients, and patient families to assist in making difficult treatment decisions. Always mindful of its basic orientation towards the patient's best interests, the committee provides options and suggestions for resolution of ethical conflict in actual cases. Consultation with an ethics committee is not mandatory, but is conducted at the request of a physician, patient, family member, or other health care professional.

The ethics committee strives to provide viable alternatives that will lead to the optimal resolution of dilemmas confronting the continuing care of the patient. It is important to remember that an ethics committee functions in an advisory capacity and should not be considered a substitute proxy for the patient.

Requests for an ethics committee consultation often involve

- clarification of issues regarding decision-making capacity, informed consent, and advanced directives

- do not resuscitate orders
- withdrawal of treatment
- assistance in conflict resolution

Consultations must be conducted in a timely manner. The ethics committee member initially contacted should consider

- Who requested the consultation?
- What is the issue?
- Is there a problem that needs referral to another service?
- What specifically is being requested of the ethics committee (e.g., clarification of the problem or mediation)?

When conducting a consultation, all patient records must be reviewed and discussed with the attending physician, family members, and other caregivers involved in the patient's treatment. If an issue is common and easily resolved, a designated member of the ethics committee should be able to consult on the case without the need for a full committee meeting. If the problem is unusual, problematic, delicate, or has important legal ramifications, a full committee meeting should be called. Other individuals that can be invited to an ethics committee case review, as appropriate, include: the patient, if competent; relatives; agent or surrogate decision maker; and caregivers.

Evaluation of a case consultation should take into consideration

- current medical status, diagnosis, and prognosis
- benefits and burdens of recommended treatment, or alternative treatments
- effect of no treatment
- life expectancy, treated and untreated
- views of caregivers and consultants
- pain and suffering
- quality-of-life issues

Patient preferences must take into consideration the patient's

- value system
- personal assessment of quality of life
- current expressed choices
- advance directives
- competency to make decisions
- ability to process information rationally to compare risks, benefits, and alternatives to treatment
- ability to articulate major factors in decisions and reasons for them
- ability to communicate

The patient must have all the information necessary to allow a reasonable person to make a prudent decision on his or her own behalf. The patient's choice must be voluntary and free from coercion by family, physicians, or others.

Family members must be identified and the following facts taken into consideration when making decisions:

- Do they understand the situation?
- Is there any conflict of interest?
- Are they in agreement with what is believed to be the patient's wishes?
- Does the patient have an advance directive?
- Has the patient appointed an agent?
- Are there any religious proscriptions?
- Are there any financial concerns?
- Are there any legal factors (applicable state statutes and case law)?

The ethical issues under review must be delineated as clearly as possible. Options must be clarified and questions answered, such as

- Are recommendations consistent with appropriate medical goals for the patient under the circumstances?
- Are the recommendations consistent with the patient's preferences or best interests?
- Is there a conflict between the patient's preferences, best interests, and the medical indications and how can it be resolved?
- Are recommendations consistent with ethical principles?

When the ethics committee is engaged in the consulting process, its recommendations should be offered as suggestions, imposing no obligation for acceptance on the part of the patient, organization, its governing body, medical staff, attending physicians, or other persons. Exhibit 16–1 presents a suggested form for documenting an ethics committee consultation.

Political Advocacy Role

The ethics committee is health care's sleeping giant. Because of its potential to bring about change, its "mission" must not be limited to end-of-life issues. Its "vision" must not be restricted to issues internal to the organization, but must include external matters that affect internal operations.

END-OF-LIFE ISSUES

Freedom To Die?

> *No right is held more sacred, or is more carefully guarded, by the common law, than the right of every individual to the possession and control of his own person, free from all restraint or interference of others, unless by clear and unquestioned authority of law.*[3]

The human struggle to survive and dreams of immortality have been instrumental in pushing humankind to develop means to prevent and cure illness. Advances in medicine and related technologies that have resulted from human creativity and ingenuity have given society the power to prolong life. However, the process of dying also can be prolonged. Those victims of long-term pain and suffering, as well as patients in vegetative states and irreversible comas, are the most directly affected. Rather than watching hopelessly as a disease destroys a person or as a body part malfunctions, causing death to a patient, physicians now can implant artificial body organs. Exotic machines and antibiotics are weapons in a physician's arsenal to help extend a patient's life. Such situations have generated vigorous debate. This section reviews many of those issues that inevitably come as one approaches the end of life.

Any glimmer of uncertainty as to a patient's desires in an emergency situation should be resolved "in favor of preserving life." The question here is whether the patient made a fully informed and knowing decision to refuse blood if this meant her death. The patient in *Matter of Hughes*[4] signed a standard blank hospital form entitled *"Refusal to Permit Blood Transfusion."* There was no indication on the form that the consequences of her refusal had been explained to her in the context of the elective surgical procedure she was about to undergo. The form should have contained an unequivocal statement that under any and all circumstances, blood is not to be used and an acknowledgment that the consequences of the refusal were fully explained. The form should fully release the physician, all medical personnel, and the hospital from liability should complications arise from the failure to administer blood, thereby resolving any doubt as to the physician's responsibility to his patient. If Hughes would have refused to sign such a form, her physician could then decide whether to continue with Hughes's treatment or aid her in finding a physician who would carry out her wishes.

The court emphasized that this case arose in the context of elective surgery. This was not an emergency situation where the physician and patient did not have time to fully discuss the potential risks, benefits, and alternatives of the planned surgery and the conflict arising over the patient's religious beliefs. Patients have an obligation to make medical preferences known to the treating physician, including the course to follow, if life-threatening complications should arise. This protects the patient's right to freedom of religion and self-determination. In addition, it is helpful to the hospital when faced with the dilemma of trying to preserve life whenever possible and honoring the patient's wishes to forgo sustaining treatment.

Right to Self-Determination/Chronology of Significant Events

1976   The New Jersey Supreme Court granted the parents of Karen Ann Quinlan permission to remove her from a ventilator.

Exhibit 16–1 Request for Ethics Committee Consultation

Date: _____ Time: _____ Caller: _____

Reason for Call: _____ Action Taken: _____

Patient: _____ Age: _____ Medical Record #: _____

Consultation requested by: _____ Relationship (e.g., caregiver or spouse): _____

Attending Physician: _____

Other Physicians involved: _____

Is the patient participating in the consultation? ☐ Yes ☐ No

If no, does the patient have decision-making capacity? ☐ Yes ☐ No, explain _____

Is there a surrogate/legal guardian? ☐ Yes ☐ No

If yes, name of guardian: _____ Phone #: _____

Have the patient's wishes been expressed in this manner? ☐ Yes ☐ No

Other consultation participants (list all persons involved):
☐ Family/relationship
☐ Physician/s
☐ RNs
☐ Case Manager
☐ Administrator
☐ Ethics Committee Members

☐ Social Worker
☐ Patient Advocate
☐ Other
☐ Chaplain or other religious leader

Medical Treatment Care Information

Diagnosis: _____ Prognosis: _____

Course of illness/hospitalization (related to consultation issues): _____

Contacts with administrative/legal representatives: _____

What are the ethical issues/dilemmas (include treatment options along with their risks, benefits, and alternatives)?

Is there any additional information needed in Fact Finding to assist in the decision-making process? ☐ Yes ☐ No

Are there other persons who should be given information or asked for their input? ☐ Yes ☐ No

If so, have any been contacted? ☐ Yes ☐ No

Recommendations: _____

Notification of Recommendations: _____

Consultation Noted on Medical Record: ☐ Yes ☐ No Disposition: _____

Form completed by: _____ Date/Time: _____

California passed the first living will legislation permitting a person to sign a declaration stating that, if there is no hope of recovery, no heroic measures need to be taken to prolong life. This provision is now available in every state.

1980 The Hemlock Society is formed to advocate for physician-assisted dying for the terminally ill, mentally competent patient.

1983 California passed the first durable power of attorney legislation permitting an advance directive to be made describing the kind of health care that one would desire when facing death by designating an agent to act on the patient's behalf.

1990 The Supreme Court ruled that the parents of Nancy Cruzan, a 32-year-old woman who had been unconscious since a 1983 car accident, could have her feeding tube removed.[5]

Dr. Jack Kevorkian used a suicide machine to assist Janet Adkins, a 54-year-old woman with Alzheimer's disease, end her life at her request.

Congress passed the Patient Rights Self-Determination Act. The Act requires federally funded health care organizations to explain to patients that they have a right to complete an advance directive.

Timothy Quill, a primary care physician, published an article in which he described how he had prescribed a lethal dose of sedatives to end the life of a young woman whose suffering from leukemia had become unbearable.

Derek Humphry's popular text, *Final Exit: The Practicalities of Self Deliverance and Assisted Suicide for the Dying,* is published.

1994   Oregon vote legalized physician-assisted dying. The law took three years to become effective.

1996   The Second and Ninth U.S. Circuit Courts of Appeals ruled that there is a constitutional right under the Fourteenth Amendment for a terminally ill person to receive help from a physician in dying.

1997   Kevorkian was charged with murder in five cases of physician-assisted suicide and was acquitted.

Supreme Court overturns both 1996 circuit decisions, ruling that it is up to the states to enact laws regarding medically assisted death.

Oregon voters reaffirm their support for the Death with Dignity Act by a 60 percent majority.

1998   Kevorkian administered a lethal injection to Thomas Youk, a 52-year-old man with Lou Gehrig's disease, on national television.

1999   Kevorkian was convicted of second-degree murder for Youk's death and is sentenced to 10 to 20 years in prison.

Twenty-three terminally ill patients were reported as receiving lethal doses of medication since passage of Oregon's Death with Dignity Act.

Protection and advocacy system lacked standing to bring action to enjoin family members from terminating a disabled patient's nutrition and hydration.[6]

Euthanasia

When patients and their families perceive a deterioration of the quality of life and no end to unbearable pain, it is then that conflict arises between health care professionals, who are trained to save lives, and patients and their families, who wish to end the suffering. This conflict centers on the concept of euthanasia and its place in the modern world. There seems to be an absence of controversy only when a patient who is kept alive by modern technology is still able to appreciate and maintain control over his or her life.

Any discussion of euthanasia obliges a person to confront humanity's greatest fear—*death.* The courts and legislatures

have faced it and have made advances in setting forth some guidelines to assist decision makers in this arena. However, much more must be accomplished. Society must be protected from the risks associated with permitting the removal of life-support systems. Society cannot allow the complex issues associated with this topic to be simplified to the point where it is accepted that life can be terminated based on subjective quality-of-life considerations. The legal system must ensure that the constitutional rights of the patient are maintained, while at the same time protect society's interests in preserving life, preventing suicide, and maintaining the integrity of the medical profession. For example, can competent adult patients who ask that no extraordinary lifesaving measures be taken recover damages for finding themselves alive after unwanted resuscitative measures? During a medical emergency, it seems too much to ask a caregiver to first look in a patient's medical record for an advance directive before tending to the immediate needs of the patient. In the final analysis, the boundaries of patient rights remain very uncertain.

From its inception, euthanasia has evolved into an issue with competing legal, medical, and moral implications, which continue to generate debate, confusion, and conflict. Currently, there is a strong movement advocating death with dignity, which excludes machines, monitors, and tubes. Figures 16–1 and 16–2 illustrate and summarize the numerous ramifications of euthanasia discussed in this chapter.

Even the connotation of the word *euthanasia* has changed with time depending upon who is attempting to define it. Originating from the Greek word *euthanatos,* euthanasia, meaning "good death" or "easy death," was accepted in situations in which people had what were considered to be incurable diseases. Euthanasia is defined broadly as "the mercy killing of the hopelessly ill, injured or incapacitated."[7]

In the religions of Confucianism and Buddhism, suicide was an acceptable answer to unendurable pain and incurable disease. The Celtics went a step farther, believing that those who chose to die of disease or senility, rather than committing suicide, would be condemned to hell. Such acceptance began to change during the nineteenth century when Western physicians refused to lessen suffering by shortening a dying patient's life. Napoleon's physician, for example, rejected Napoleon's plea to kill plague-stricken soldiers, insisting that his obligation was to cure rather than to kill people.

In the late 1870s, writings on euthanasia began to appear, mainly in England and the United States. Although such works were written, for the most part, by lay authors, the public and the medical community began to consider the issues raised by euthanasia. Then defined as "the act or practice of painlessly putting to death persons suffering from incurable conditions or diseases," it was considered to be a merciful release from incurable suffering. By the beginning of the twentieth century, however, there were still no clear answers or guidelines regarding the use of euthanasia. Unlike

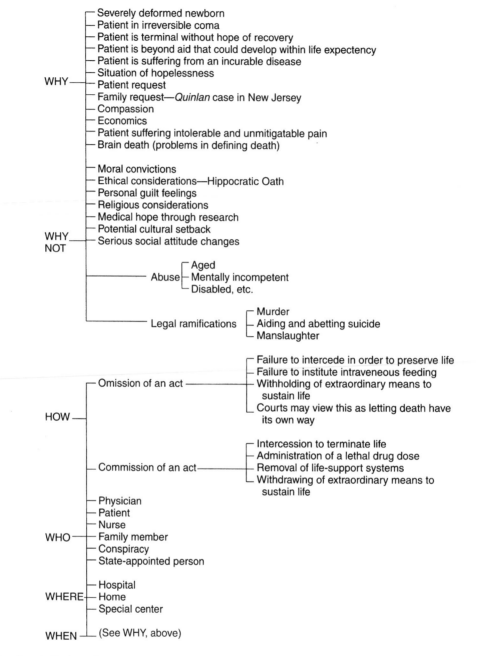

Figure 16-1 Considerations in Euthanasia

in prior centuries when society as a whole supported or rejected euthanasia, different segments of today's society apply distinct connotations to the word, generating further confusion. Some believe euthanasia is meant to allow a painless death when one suffers from an incurable disease, yet is not dying. Others, who remain in the majority, perceive euthanasia as an instrument to aid only dying people in ending their lives with as little suffering as possible.

It has been estimated that of the two million Americans who die each year, 80 percent die in hospitals or nursing homes, and 70 percent of those die after a decision to forgo life-sustaining treatment has been made. Although such decisions are personal in nature and based on individual moral values, they must comply with the laws applicable to the prolonging of the dying process. Courts have outlined the ways in which the government is allowed to participate in the decision-making process. Yet the misconceptions and lack of clear direction regarding the policies and procedures have resulted in wide disparity among jurisdictions, both in legislation and in judicial decisions. As a result, the American

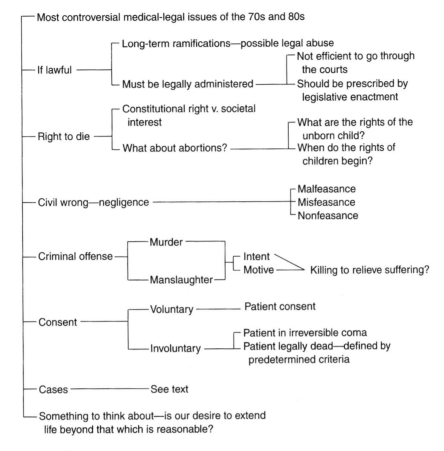

Figure 16–2 Legal Ramifications of Euthanasia

Medical Association, the American Bar Association, legislators, and judges are actively attempting to formulate and legislate clear guidelines in this sensitive, profound, and as yet not fully understood area. To ensure compliance with the law, while serving the needs of their patients, it is incumbent on health care providers to keep themselves informed of the legislation enacted in this ever-changing field.

To properly address the topic of euthanasia, it is necessary to understand the precise meaning of the recognized forms. Rhetorical phrases such as *right to die, right to life,* and *death with dignity* have obfuscated, rather than clarified, the public's understanding of euthanasia. The dividing of euthanasia into two categories, active or passive, is, for many, the most controversial aspect of this topic.

Active or Passive Euthanasia

Active euthanasia is commonly understood to be the intentional commission of an act, such as giving a patient a lethal drug that results in death. The act, if committed by the patient, is thought of as suicide. Moreover, because the patient cannot take his or her own life, any person who assists in the causing of the death could be subject to criminal sanction for aiding and abetting suicide.

Passive euthanasia occurs when life-saving treatment (such as a respirator) is withdrawn or withheld, allowing the patient diagnosed as terminal to die a natural death. Passive euthanasia is generally accepted pursuant to legislative acts and judicial decisions.[8] These decisions, however, generally are based on the facts of a particular case. Regardless of the definitional differences though, the end result in both active and passive euthanasia is the same.

The distinctions are important when considering the duty and the liability of a physician who must decide whether to continue or initiate treatment of a comatose or terminally ill patient. Physicians are obligated to use reasonable care to preserve health and to save lives, so unless fully protected by the law, they will be reluctant to abide by a patient's or family's wishes to terminate life-support devices.

Although there may be a duty to provide life-sustaining equipment in the immediate aftermath of cardiopulmonary arrest, there is no duty to continue its use once it has become futile and ineffective to do so in the opinion of qualified medical personnel. Two physicians in *Barber v. Superior Court*[9] were charged with the crimes of murder and conspiracy to commit murder. The charges were based on their acceding to requests of the patient's family to discontinue life-support equipment and intravenous tubes. The patient had suffered a cardiopulmonary arrest in the recovery room after surgery. A team of physicians and nurses revived the patient and placed him on life-support equipment. The patient had suffered severe brain damage that placed him in a comatose and vegetative state, from which, according to tests and examinations by other specialists, he was unlikely to recover. The patient, on the written request of the family, was taken off life-support equipment. The patient's family (his wife and eight children) made the decision together after consultation with the physicians. Evidence had been presented that the patient, before his incapacitation, had expressed to his wife that he would not want to be kept alive by machine or "become another Karen Ann Quinlan." There was no evidence indicating that the family was motivated in their decision by anything other than love and concern for the dignity of their loved one. The patient continued to breathe on his own. Showing no signs of improvement, the physicians again discussed the patient's poor prognosis with the family. The intravenous lines were removed, and the patient died sometime thereafter.

A complaint was then filed against the two physicians. The magistrate who heard the evidence determined that the physicians did not kill the deceased, because their conduct was not the proximate cause of the patient's death. The superior court determined as a matter of law that the evidence required the magistrate to hold the physicians to answer and ordered the complaint reinstated. The court of appeals held that the physicians' omission to continue treatment, although intentional and with knowledge that the patient would die, was not an unlawful failure to perform a legal duty. The evidence amply supported the magistrate's decision. The superior court erred in determining that as a matter of law the evidence required the magistrate to hold the physicians to answer. The peremptory writ of prohibition to restrain the Superior Court of Los Angeles from taking any further action in this matter, other than to vacate its order reinstating the complaint and to enter a new and different order denying the people's motion, was granted.

Other states have been confronted increasingly with the question of whether it is ever right for a physician to provide a patient with aid in dying. On July 26, 1991, a Monroe County, New York, grand jury answered "Yes" when it failed to indict Dr. Timothy Quill for giving a leukemia patient sleeping pills to enable her to take her own life. Dr. Quill, an associate chief of medicine at a hospital in Rochester, New York, wrote an article in the *New England Journal of Medicine* focusing on the suffering of terminal patients. Moreover, he discussed how physicians could relieve an individual's suffering. He is not alone in his support of physician-assisted suicide. In the best-selling book, *The Final Exit*, Derek Humphry, executive director of the Hemlock Society (a nationally known organization advocating the right to die), describes methods of self-assisted suicide for terminally ill people.

Voluntary or Involuntary Euthanasia

Both active and passive euthanasia may be either voluntary or involuntary. *Voluntary euthanasia* occurs when the suffering incurable makes the decision to die. To be considered voluntary, the request or consent must be made by a legally competent adult and be based on material information concerning the possible ramifications and alternatives available. The term *legally competent* was addressed in a right-to-refuse-treatment case, *Lane v. Candura*.[10] The case involved a patient who twice refused to permit surgeons to amputate her leg to prevent gangrene from spreading. The patient's daughter sought to be appointed as a legal guardian to enable her to consent to her mother's surgery. The appellate court, finding no evidence indicating that Mrs. Lane was incapable of appreciating the nature and consequence of her decision, overturned the trial court's holding of incompetence. Therefore, even though Lane's decision ultimately would lead to her death, she was found to be competent, and thus, she was allowed to reject medical treatment.

The *Lane* court and others have defined legal competence as the mental ability to make a rational decision. A patient must exhibit perception and appreciation of all relevant facts and then make decisions based on those facts. In the active euthanasia context, the patient would be demonstrating that by voluntarily requesting euthanasia, he or she would be selecting death over life.[11]

In the case of *In re Lydia Hall Hospital*,[12] a patient, who was terminally ill and requiring dialysis, was taken off all medication to ensure that his mind would be clear when psychiatrists examined him to determine whether he was competent. Case law asserts that the standard of proof required for a finding of an incurable's incompetence is that of clear and convincing evidence.[13] This is a higher standard than the normal fair preponderance of the credible evidence required in civil proceedings.

Involuntary euthanasia, however, occurs when a person other than the incurable makes the decision to terminate the life of an incompetent or an unconsenting competent person's life.

The patient's lack of consent could be due to mental impairment or comatose unconsciousness. Important value questions face courts grappling with making decisions regarding involuntary euthanasia:

- Who should decide to withhold or withdraw treatment?
- On what factors should the decision be based?
- Are there viable standards to guide the courts?
- Should criminal sanctions be imposed on a person assisting in ending a life?
- When does death occur?

Constitutional Considerations

To analyze the important questions regarding whether life-support treatment can be withheld or withdrawn from an incompetent patient, it is necessary to consider first what rights a competent patient possesses. Both statutory law and case law have presented a diversity of policies and points of view. Some courts point to common law and the early case of *Schloendorff v. Society of New York Hospital*[14] to support their belief in a patient's right to self-determination. The *Schloendorff* court stated:

> Every human being of adult years has a right to determine what shall be done with his own body; and the surgeon who performs an operation without his patient's consent commits an assault for which he is liable for damages.[15]

This right of self-determination was emphasized in *In re Storar*[16] when the court announced that every human being of adult years and sound mind has the right to determine what shall be done with his or her own body.

The *Storar* case was a departure from the New Jersey Supreme Court's rationale in the case of *In re Quinlan*.[17] The *Quinlan* case was the first to significantly address the issue of whether euthanasia should be permitted when a patient is terminally ill. The *Quinlan* court, relying on *Roe v. Wade*,[18] announced that the constitutional right to privacy protects a patient's right to self-determination. The court noted that the right to privacy "is broad enough to encompass a patient's decision to decline medical treatment under certain circumstances, in much the same way as it is broad enough to encompass a woman's decision to terminate pregnancy under certain conditions."[19]

Most cases today follow the right to privacy argument. The *Quinlan* court, in reaching its decision, applied a test balancing the state's interest in preserving and maintaining the sanctity of human life against Karen's privacy interest. It decided that, especially in light of the prognosis (physicians determined that Karen Quinlan was in an irreversible coma), the state's interest did not justify interference with her right to refuse treatment. Thus, Karen Quinlan's father was appointed her legal guardian, and the respirator was shut off. Opponents of euthanasia argue that before the *Quinlan* decision, any form of euthanasia was defined as murder by the U.S. legal system. Although acts of euthanasia did take place, the law was applied selectively, and the possibility of criminal sanction against active participants in euthanasia was enough to deter physicians from assisting a patient in committing euthanasia.

Despite intense criticism by legal and religious scholars, the *Quinlan* decision paved the way for courts to consider extending the right to decline treatment to incompetents as well. State courts recognize the right but differ on how this right is to be exercised.

In the same year as the *Quinlan* decision, the case of *Superintendent of Belchertown State School v. Saikewicz*[20] was decided. There, the court, using the balancing test enunciated in *Quinlan*, approved the recommendation of a court-appointed *guardian ad litem* that it would be in Saikewicz's best interests to end chemotherapy treatment. Saikewicz was a mentally retarded, 67-year-old patient suffering from leukemia. The court found from the evidence that the prognosis was dim, and even though a "normal person" would probably have chosen chemotherapy, it allowed Saikewicz to die without treatment to spare him the suffering.

Although the court also followed the reasoning of the *Quinlan* opinion in giving the right to an incompetent to refuse treatment, based on either the objective *"best interests" test* or the subjective *"substituted judgment" test*, which it favored because Mr. Saikewicz always had been incompetent, the court departed from *Quinlan* in a major way. It rejected the *Quinlan* approach of entrusting a decision concerning the continuance of artificial life support to the patient's guardian, family, attending physicians, and a hospital "ethics committee." The *Saikewicz* court asserted that even though a judge might find the opinions of physicians, medical experts, or hospital ethics committees helpful in reaching a decision, there should be no requirement to seek out the advice. The court decided that questions of life and death with regard to an incompetent should be the responsibility of the courts, which would conduct detached but passionate investigations. The court took a "dim view of any attempt to shift the ultimate decision-making responsibility away from duly established courts of proper jurisdiction to any committee, panel, or group, ad hoc or permanent."[21]

This main point of difference between the *Saikewicz* and *Quinlan* cases marked the emergence of two different policies on the incompetent's right to refuse treatment. One line of cases has followed *Saikewicz* and supports court approval before physicians are allowed to withhold or withdraw life support. Advocates of this view argue that it makes more sense to leave the decision to an objective tribunal than to extend the right of a patient's privacy to a number of interested parties, as was done in *Quinlan*. They also attack the *Quinlan* method as being a privacy decision effectuated by popular vote.[22]

Six months after *Saikewicz*, the Massachusetts Appeals Court narrowed the need for court intervention in *In re Dinnerstein*[23] by finding that "no code" orders are valid to prevent the use of artificial resuscitative measures on incompetent terminally ill patients. The court was faced with the case of a 67-year-old woman who was suffering from Alzheimer's disease. It was determined that she was permanently comatose at the time of trial. Further, the court decided that *Saikewicz*-type judicial proceedings should take place only when medical treatment could offer a reasonable expectation of effecting a permanent or temporary cure of or relief from the illness.

The Massachusetts Supreme Judicial Court attempted to clarify its *Saikewicz* opinion with regard to court orders in *In re Spring*.[24] It held that such different factors as the patient's mental impairment and his or her medical prognosis with or without treatment must be considered before judicial approval is necessary to withdraw or withhold treatment from an incompetent patient. The problem in all three cases is that there is still no clear guidance as to exactly when the court's approval of the removal of life-support systems would be necessary. *Saikewicz* seemed to demand judicial approval in every case. *Spring*, however, in partially retreating from that view, stated that it did not have to articulate what combination of the factors it discussed, thus making prior court approval necessary.

The inconsistencies presented by the Massachusetts cases have led most courts since 1977 to follow the parameters set by *Quinlan*, requiring judicial intervention. In cases where physicians have certified the irreversible nature of a patient's loss of consciousness, an ethics committee (actually a neurologic team) could certify the patient's hopeless neurologic condition. Then a guardian would be free to take the legal steps necessary to remove life-support systems. The main reason for the appointment of a guardian is to ensure that incompetents, like all other patients, maintain their right to refuse treatment. Most holdings indicate that because a patient has the constitutional right of self-determination, those acting on the patient's behalf can exercise that right when rendering their best judgment concerning how the patient would assert the right. This *substituted judgment doctrine* could be argued on standing grounds, whereby a second party has the right to assert the constitutional rights of another when that second party's intervention is necessary to protect the other's constitutional rights. The guardian's decision is more sound if based on the known desires of a patient who was competent immediately before becoming comatose.

Courts adhering to the *Quinlan* rationale have recognized that fact, and in 1984 the highest state court of Florida took the lead and accepted the living will as persuasive evidence of an incompetent's wishes. In *John F. Kennedy Memorial Hospital v. Bludworth*,[25] the Florida Supreme Court allowed an incompetent patient's wife to act as his guardian, and, in accordance with the terms of a living will he executed in 1975, she was told to substitute her judgment for that of her husband. She asked to have a respirator removed. The court declined the necessity of prior court approval, finding that the constitutional right to refuse treatment that had been decided for competents in *Satz v. Perlmutter*[26] extended to incompetents. The court required the attending physician to certify that the patient was in a permanent vegetative state, with no reasonable chance for recovery, before a family member or guardian could request termination of extraordinary means of medical treatment.

In keeping with *Saikewicz*, the decision maker would attempt to ascertain the incompetent patient's actual interests and preferences. Court involvement would be mandated only to appoint a guardian in one of the following cases:

- family members disagree as to the incompetent's wishes
- physicians disagree on the prognosis
- the patient's wishes cannot be known because he or she always has been incompetent
- evidence exists of wrongful motives or malpractice
- no family member can serve as a guardian[27]

Defining Death

The decision in *John F. Kennedy Memorial Hospital v. Bludworth* increased the desire of the public, courts, and religious groups to know when a patient is considered to be legally dead and what type of treatment can be withheld or withdrawn. Most cases dealing with euthanasia speak of the necessity that a physician diagnose a patient as being either in a persistent vegetative state[28] or terminally ill.[29]

Traditionally, the definition of death adopted by the courts has been the *Black's Law Dictionary* definition: "cessation of respiration, heartbeat, and certain indications of central nervous system activity, such as respiration and pulsation."[30] At present, however, modern science has the capacity to sustain vegetative functions of those in irreversible comas. Machinery can sustain heartbeat and respiration even in the face of brain death. "With 10,000 patients existing in the twilight state at this time,"[31] every appellate court that has ruled on the question has recognized that the irreversible cessation of brain function constitutes death.

Ethicists who advocate the prohibition on taking action to shorten life agree that "where death is imminent and inevitable, it is permissible to forgo treatments that would only provide a precarious and painful prolongation of life, as long as the normal care due to the sick person in similar cases is not interrupted."[32]

Relying on the 1968 Harvard Criteria set forth by the Ad Hoc Committee of the Harvard Medical School To Examine the Definition of Brain Death, the American Medical Association in 1974 accepted that death occurs when there is "irreversible cessation of all brain functions including the brain stem."[33] Most states now recognize brain death by statute or judicial decision. New York, for example, in *People v. Eulo*,[34] in rejecting the traditional cardiopulmonary definition of death, announced that the determination of brain death can be made according to acceptable medical standards. The court also repeated its holding in *In re Storar*[35] that clear and convincing evidence of a person's desire to decline extraordinary medical care may be honored and that a third person may not exercise this judgment on behalf of a person who has not or cannot express the desire to decline treatment. Following the *Bludworth* logic, the court noted that health care professionals acting within the cases should not face liability.

The clear and convincing evidence standard was defined more succinctly by the New York Court of Appeals in *In re Westchester County Medical Center ex rel. O'Connor*.[36] There the court determined that artificial nutrition could be withheld from O'Connor, a stroke victim who was unable to converse or feed herself. The court held that "nothing less than unequivocal proof of a patient's wishes will suffice when the decision to terminate life support is at issue."[37] The factors outlined by the court in determining the existence of clear and convincing evidence of a patient's intention to reject the prolongation of life by artificial means were:

- the persistence of statements regarding an individual's beliefs
- the desirability of the commitment to those beliefs
- the seriousness with which such statements were made
- the inferences that may be drawn from the surrounding circumstances

The Missouri Supreme Court applied the *Westchester* ruling and held that the family of a woman who was in a persistent vegetative state since 1983 could not order physicians to remove artificial nutrition.[38] In 1983, Nancy Cruzan sustained injuries in a car accident, in which her car overturned, after which she was found face down in a ditch without respiratory or cardiac function. Although unconscious, her breathing and heartbeat were restored at the site of the accident. On examination at the hospital to which she was taken, a neurosurgeon diagnosed her as having suffered cerebral contusions and anoxia. It was estimated that she had been deprived of oxygen for 12 to 14 minutes. After remaining in a coma for three weeks, Cruzan went into an unconscious state. At first she was able to ingest some food orally. Thereafter, surgeons implanted a gastrostomy feeding and hydration tube, with the consent of her husband, to facilitate feeding her. She did not improve, and until December 1990, she lay in a Missouri state hospital in a persistent vegetative state that was determined to be irreversible, permanent, progressive, and ongoing. She was not dead, according to the accepted definition of death in Missouri, and physicians estimated that she could live in the vegetative state for an additional 30 years. Because of the prognosis, Cruzan's parents asked the hospital staff to cease all artificial nutrition and hydration procedures. The staff refused to comply with their wishes without court approval. The state trial court granted authorization for termination, finding that Cruzan had a fundamental right—grounded in both the state and federal constitutions—to refuse or direct the withdrawal of death-prolonging procedures. Testimony at trial from a former roommate of Cruzan indicated to the court that she had stated that if she were ever sick or injured, she would not want to live unless she could live halfway normally. The court interpreted that conversation, which had taken place when Cruzan was 25 years old, as meaning that she would not want to be forced to take nutrition and hydration while in a persistent vegetative state.

The case was appealed to the Missouri Supreme Court, which reversed the lower court decision. The court not only doubted that the doctrine of informed consent applied to the circumstances of the case, it moreover would not recognize a broad privacy right from the state constitution that would support the right of a person to refuse medical treatment in every circumstance. Because Missouri recognizes living wills, the court held that Cruzan's parents were not entitled to order the termination of her treatment, because "no person can assume that choice for an incompetent in the absence of the formalities required under Missouri's Living Will statutes or the clear and convincing, inherently reliable evidence absent here."[39] The court found that Cruzan's statements to her roommate did not rise to the level of clear and convincing evidence of her desire to end nutrition and hydration.

In June 1990, the U.S. Supreme Court heard oral arguments and held that:

- The U.S. Constitution does not forbid Missouri from requiring that there be clear and convincing evidence of an incompetent's wishes as to the withdrawal of life-sustaining treatment.
- The Missouri Supreme Court did not commit constitutional error in concluding that evidence adduced at trial did not amount to clear and convincing evidence of Cruzan's desire to cease hydration and nutrition.
- Due process did not require the state to accept the substituted judgment of close family members, absent substantial proof that their views reflected those of the patient.[40]

In delivering the opinion of the Court, Justice Rehnquist noted that although most state courts have applied the common-law right to informed consent or a combination of that right and a privacy right when allowing a right to refuse treatment, the Supreme Court analyzed the issues presented in the *Cruzan* case in terms of a Fourteenth Amendment liberty interest, finding that a competent person has a constitutionally protected right grounded in the due process clause to refuse lifesaving hydration and nutrition. Missouri provided for the incompetent by allowing a surrogate to act for the patient in choosing to withdraw hydration and treatment. Moreover, it put into place procedures to ensure that the surrogate's action conforms to the wishes expressed by the patient when he or she was competent. Although recognizing that Missouri had enacted a restrictive law, the Supreme Court held that right-to-die issues should be decided pursuant to state law, subject to a due process liberty interest, and in keeping with state constitutional law. After the Supreme Court rendered its decision, the Cruzans returned to Missouri probate court, where on November 14, 1990, Judge Charles Teel authorized physicians to remove the feeding tubes from Cruzan. The judge determined that testimony presented to him early in November demonstrated clear and convincing evidence that Nancy would not have wanted to live in a persistent vegetative state. Several of her co-workers had testified that she told them before her accident that she would not want to live "like a vegetable." On December 26, 1990, two weeks after her feeding tubes were removed, Nancy Cruzan died.

Legislative Response

After the *Cruzan* decision, states began to rethink existing legislation and draft new legislation in the areas of living wills, durable powers of attorney, health care proxies, and surrogate decision making. Pennsylvania and Florida were two of the first states to react to the *Cruzan* decision. The new Pennsylvania law is applied to terminally ill or permanently unconscious patients. The statute, the Advance Directive for Health Care Act,[41] deals mainly with individuals who have prepared living wills. It includes in its definition of life-sustaining treatment the administration of hydration and nutrition by any means if it is stated in the individual's living will. The statute mandates that a copy of the living will be given to the physician to be effective. Further, the patient must be incompetent or permanently unconscious. If there is no evidence of the presence of a living will, the Pennsylvania probate codes allow an attorney-in-fact who was designated in a properly executed durable power of attorney document to give permission for "medical and surgical procedures to be utilized on an incompetent patient."[42]

The Supreme Court stated in *Cruzan* that only 15 percent of the population has signed any living wills or other types of medical directives. In the light of that, more states will have to address the problem of surrogate decision making for an incompetent. Legislation would not only have to include direction to consider evidence of an incompetent's wishes that had been expressed when he or she was competent, it also would have to include provisions for consideration and protection of an incompetent who never stated what he or she would want done if in a terminally ill or persistent vegetative state.

Unless there is some national uniformity in the legislation, patients and their families will shop for states that will allow them to have medical treatment terminated or withdrawn with as few legal hassles as possible. For example, on January 18, 1991, a Missouri probate court judge authorized a father to take his 20-year-old brain-damaged daughter, Christine Busalacchi, from the Missouri Rehabilitation Center to Minnesota for testing by a pro-euthanasia physician, Dr. Cranford. Cranford, who practices at the Hennepin County Medical Center, has been at the center of controversy in

Minnesota. In January 1991, Pro Life Action Ministries demanded Cranford's resignation, claiming that he "desires to make Minnesota the killing fields for the disabled."[43] He, however, views himself as an advocate of patients' rights. However the situation involving Cranford is resolved, it is clear that the main reason Busalacchi sought authorization to take his daughter to Minnesota is that he believed that he would have to deal with fewer legal impediments there to allow his daughter to die.

Because of the continuing litigation concerning the right-to-die issue, it is clear that the public must be educated about the necessity of expressing their wishes concerning medical treatment while they are competent. Uniformity with regard to the legal instruments available for demonstrating what a patient wants should be a common goal of legislators, courts, and the medical profession. If living wills, surrogates, and durable powers of attorney were to be enacted pursuant to national rather than individual state guidelines, the result should be a greater ease in resolving the myriad conflicting issues in this area. Some states have addressed the problem by statutorily providing for these instruments, thereby enabling individuals to have a say in the medical care they should receive if they become unable to speak for themselves.

Chief Justice Dore of the Washington Supreme Court voiced his opinion that a legislative response to right-to-die issues could be better addressed by the legislature.

> The United States Supreme Court, in *Cruzan*, questioned whether a federally protected right to forgo nutrition and hydration existed. The *Cruzan* Court confronted the same philosophical issues that we face today and wisely recognized and deferred to the Legislature's superior policy-making abilities. As was the case in *Cruzan*, our legislature is far better equipped to evaluate this complex issue and should not have its power usurped by the court.[44]

The Patient Self-Determination Act of 1990

As a result of implementation of the Patient Self-Determination Act of 1990 (PSDA),[45] which went into effect on December 1, 1991, health care organizations participating in the Medicare and Medicaid reimbursement programs must address patient rights regarding life-sustaining decisions and other advance directives. Health care organizations have a responsibility to explain to patients, staff, and families that patients do have a legal right to direct their own medical and nursing care as it corresponds to existing state law, including right-to-die directives. A person's right to refuse medical treatment is not lost when the person's mental or physical status changes. When a person is no longer competent to exercise his or her right of self-determination, the right still exists but the decision must be delegated to a surrogate decision maker. Those organizations that do not comply with a patient's directives or those of a legally authorized decision maker on treatment are exposing themselves to the risk of a lawsuit.

The PSDA provides that patients have a right to formulate advance directives and to make decisions regarding their health care. Self-determination includes the right to accept or refuse medical treatment. Health care providers (including hospitals, nursing homes, home health agencies, health maintenance organizations, and hospices) receiving federal funds under Medicare are required to comply with the new regulations. Providers are not entitled to reimbursement under the Medicare program if they fail to meet PSDA requirements.

Each state is required under PSDA to provide a description of the law in the state regarding advance directives to providers, whether such directives are based on state statutes or judicial decisions. Providers must ensure that written policies and procedures with respect to all adult individuals regarding advance directives are established:

> (A) to provide written information to each such individual concerning—
>
> (i) an individual's rights under State law (whether statutory or as recognized by the courts of the State) to make decisions concerning such medical care, including the right to accept or refuse medical or surgical treatment and the right to formulate advance directives . . . , and
>
> (ii) written policies of the provider organization respecting the implementation of such rights;
>
> (B) to document in the individual's medical record whether or not the individual has executed an advance directive;
>
> (C) not to condition the provision of care or otherwise discriminate against an individual based on whether or not the individual has executed an advance directive;
>
> (D) to ensure compliance with requirements of State law (whether statutory or recognized by the courts of the State) respecting advance directives at the facilities of the provider or organization; and
>
> (E) to provide (individually or with others) for education for staff and the community on issues concerning advance directives.[46]

Although the PSDA is being cheered as a major advancement in clarifying and nationally regulating this often obscure area of law and medicine, there are continuing problems and new issues that must be addressed.

Advance Directives: Advance directives allow the patient to state in advance the kinds of medical care that he or she considers acceptable or not acceptable. The patient can appoint an agent to make those decisions on his or her behalf. Patients should be asked at the time of admission if they have an advance directive. If a patient does not have an advance directive, the organization should provide the patient with information as to what an advance directive is and the opportunity to execute a directive. Every patient should clearly understand that an advance directive is a guideline for caregivers as to his or her wishes for what medical care he or she would and would not want to receive in the event he or she becomes incapacitated and unable to make decisions. This interaction should be documented in the patient's medical record. If the patient has an advance directive, a copy should be requested for insertion into the patient's record. If the patient does not have a copy of the advance directive with him or her, the substance thereof should be documented and flagged in the patient's medical record. Documentation should include the location of the advance directive; the name and telephone number of the designated health care agent; and any information that might be helpful in the immediate care situation (e.g., patient's desire for food and hydration). The purpose of such documentation should not be considered as a need to recreate a new directive, but should be considered as a desire to adhere to a patient's wishes in the event some untoward event occurs while waiting for a copy of the directive.

The patient can execute a new directive at any time if he or she so desires. Patient and family education should be provided as to the existence of the directive and its contents. The patient should be periodically queried as to whether he or she wishes to make any changes with regard to an advance directive.

Substituted Judgment/Guardianship: Guardianship is a legal mechanism by which the court declares a person incompetent and appoints a guardian. The court transfers the responsibility for managing financial affairs, living arrangements, and medical care decisions to the guardian.

The right to refuse medical treatment on behalf of an incompetent person is not limited to legally appointed guardians but may be exercised by health care proxies or surrogates such as close family members or friends. When a patient has not expressed instructions concerning his or her future health care in the event of later incapacity but has merely delegated full responsibility to a proxy, designation of a proxy must have been made in writing.

SPOUSE'S RIGHT AS GUARDIAN QUESTIONED BY RELATIVES

Citation: *In re Martin, 517 N.W.2d 749 (Mich. Ct. App. 1994)*

Facts

Mr. Martin sustained debilitating injuries as the result of an automobile accident. He suffered severe subcortical brain damage significantly impairing his physical and cognitive functioning. His injuries left him totally paralyzed on the left side. He could not speak or eat and had no bladder or bowel control. Martin remained conscious and had some awareness of his surroundings. He could communicate to a very minimal degree through head nods.

The trial court determined that Martin did not have nor would he ever have the ability to have the requisite capacity to make decisions regarding the withdrawal of life-support equipment. The evidence demonstrated that Martin's preference would have been to decline life support equipment given his medical condition and prognosis. The trial court's decision was based on the following four-part test for determining if a person has the requisite capacity to make a decision whether the person: (1) has sufficient mind to reasonably understand the condition, (2) is capable of understanding the nature and effect of the treatment choices, (3) is aware of the consequences associated with those choices, and (4) is able to make an informed choice that is voluntary and not coerced. The trial court also determined that Mrs. Martin, the patient's spouse, was a suitable guardian for him.

Mrs. Martin petitioned to withdraw her husband's life support. Martin's mother and sister counterpetitioned to have Mrs. Martin removed as the patient's guardian.

Issue

Was there sufficient evidence to support a finding that the patient lacked requisite capacity to make decisions regarding the removal of life-sustaining treatment? Was there sufficient evidence to show that the patient had a medical preference to decline life-sustaining treatment under circumstances such as those that occurred following his injury? Was Mrs. Martin a suitable individual to represent her husband with respect to making a decision as to withdrawing life-sustaining medical treatment?

Holding

The Michigan Court of Appeals held that the evidence was sufficient to support a finding that the patient lacked capacity to make decisions regarding the withholding or withdrawal of life-sustaining treatment. As to the patient's desire not to be placed on life-supporting equipment, there was sufficient evidence to show that the patient had a medical preference to decline treatment under circumstances such as those that occurred. There was also sufficient evidence to show that the patient's spouse was a suitable guardian.

Reason

The test for determining if Martin had the requisite capacity to make a decision regarding the withholding or withdrawal of life-supporting medical treatment was clear and convincing—he did not have sufficient decision-making capacity. The evidence was just as clear that he never would regain sufficient decision-making capacity that would enable him to make such a decision. It was the general consensus of all of the experts that Martin's condition and cognitive level of functioning would not improve in the future.

Testimony from two of Martin's friends described statements made by him that he would never want to be maintained in a coma or in a vegetative state. In addition, Mrs. Martin described numerous statements made to her by Martin prior to the accident that he would not want to be maintained alive given the circumstances described above. The trial court found that Mrs. Martin was credible. The court of appeals found no reason to dispute the trial court's finding as to Mrs. Martin's credibility.

Contrary to allegations made by the patient's mother and sister, the evidence was clear that Mrs. Martin's testimony was credible. There was no evidence that Mrs. Martin had anything but her husband's best interest at heart. There were allegations, but no evidence of, financial considerations or pressure from another individual that would show that Mrs. Martin's testimony was influenced by other individuals.

Discussion

1. Knowing that the patient had some ability to interact with his environment, discuss the four-part test for determining the patient's ability to make a decision.
2. Do you agree with the court's decision? Explain.
3. Should the concern of the mother and sister have carried more weight in removing custody from Mrs. Martin?
4. What influence do you believe the mother and sister might have had on Mrs. Martin?

Durable Power of Attorney: Power of attorney is a legal device that permits one individual known as the "principal" to give to another person called the "attorney-in-fact" the authority to act on his or her behalf. The attorney-in-fact is authorized to handle banking and real estate affairs, incur expenses, pay bills, and handle a wide variety of legal affairs for a specified period of time. The power of attorney may continue indefinitely during the lifetime of the principal so long as that person is competent and capable of granting power of attorney. If the principal becomes comatose or mentally incompetent, the power of attorney automatically expires, just as it would if the principal dies.

Because a *power of attorney* is limited by the competency of the principal, some states have authorized a special legal device for the principal to express intent concerning the durability of the power of attorney, to allow it to survive disability or incompetency. The *durable power of attorney* is more general in scope, and the patient does not have to be in imminent danger of death, as is necessary in a living will situation. Although it need not delineate desired medical treatment specifically, it must indicate the identity of the principal's attorney-in-fact and that the principal has communicated his or her health care wishes to the attorney-in-fact. Although the laws vary from state to state, all 50 states and the District of Columbia have durable power of attorney statutes. This legal device is an important alternative to guardianship, conservatorship, or trusteeship. Because a durable power of attorney places a considerable amount of power in the hands of the attorney-in-fact, the power of attorney should be drawn up by an attorney in the state the client resides.

Health Care Proxy: A health care proxy allows a person to appoint a *health care agent* to make treatment decisions in the event he or she becomes incapacitated and unable to make decisions for him- or herself. The agent must be made aware of the patient's wishes regarding nutrition and hydration in order to be allowed to make a decision concerning withholding or withdrawing them. In contrast to a living will, a health care proxy does not require a person to know about and consider in advance all situations and decisions that could arise. Rather, the appointed agent would know about and interpret the expressed wishes of the patient and then make decisions about the medical care and treatment to be administered or refused. The *Cruzan* decision indicates that the Supreme Court views advance directives as clear and convincing evidence of a patient's wishes regarding life-sustaining treatment.

Although most of the statutes fail to cover incompetents, cases such as *Quinlan* and *Saikewicz* created a constitutionally protected obligation to terminate the incurable incompetent's life when guardians use the doctrine of substituted judgment. Further, some states provide for proxy consent in the form of durable power of attorney statutes. Generally, these involve the designation of a proxy to speak on the incompetent incurable's behalf. They represent a combination of the intimate wishes of the patient and the medical recommendations of the physicians.

Oral declarations are accepted only after the patient has been declared terminally ill. Moreover, the declarant bears the responsibility of informing the physician to ensure that the document becomes a part of the medical record. The California statute provides that the document be re-executed after five years. Other statutes differ in the length of time of effectiveness. Most states allow the document to be effective until revoked by the individual. To revoke, the patient must sign and date a new writing, destroy the first document him- or herself, direct another to destroy the first document in his or her presence, or orally state to the physician an intent to revoke. The effect of the directive varies among jurisdictions. However, there is unanimity in the promulgation of regulations that specifically authorize health care personnel to honor the directives without fear of incurring liability. The highest court of New York in *In re Eichner*[47] complied with the request of a guardian to withdraw life-support systems from an 83-year-old brain-damaged priest. The court reached its result by finding the patient's previously expressed wishes to be determinative.

Before exercising an incompetent patient's right to forgo medical treatment, the surrogate decision maker must satisfy the following conditions:

- The surrogate must be satisfied that the patient executed a document (e.g., Durable Power of Attorney for Health Care and Health Care Proxy) knowingly, willingly, and without undue influence, and that the evidence of the patient's oral declaration is reliable.
- The patient must not have reasonable probability of recovering competency so that the patient could exercise the right.
- The surrogate must take care to ensure that any limitations or conditions expressed either orally or in written declarations have been considered carefully and satisfied.

Determining Incapacity

Before declaring an individual incapacitated, the attending physician must find with a reasonable degree of medical certainty that the patient lacks capacity. A notation should be placed in the patient's medical record describing the cause, nature, extent, and probable duration of incapacity. Before withholding or withdrawing life-sustaining treatment, a second physician must confirm the incapacity determination and make an appropriate entry on the medical record before honoring any new decisions by a health care agent.

Agent's Rights

A health care agent's rights are no greater than what those of a competent patient would be. However, the agent's rights are limited to any specific instructions included in the proxy document. An agent's decisions take priority over any other person except the patient. The agent has the right to consent or refuse to consent to any service or treatment, routine or otherwise; to refuse life-sustaining treatment; and to access "all" the patient's medical information to make informed decisions. The agent must make decisions based on the patient's moral and religious beliefs. If a patient's wishes are not known, decisions must be based on a good-faith judgment of what the patient would have wanted.

Living Will

A *living will,* also referred to in many states as a "directive" or "declaration," is the instrument or legal document that describes those treatments an individual wishes or does not wish to receive should he or she become incapacitated and unable to make medical decisions for him- or herself. Typically, a living will allows a person, when competent, to inform caregivers in writing of his or her wishes with regard to withholding and withdrawing life-supporting treatment, including nutrition and hydration. The living will is helpful to health care professionals in that it provides guidance about a patient's wishes for treatment, provides legally valid instructions about treatment, and protects the patient's rights and the provider that honors them.

The living will should be signed and dated by two witnesses who are not blood relatives or beneficiaries of property. A living will should be discussed with the patient's physician and a signed copy should be placed in the patient's medical record. A copy also should be given to the individual designated to make decisions in the event the patient is unable to do so. A person who executes a living will when healthy and mentally competent cannot predict how he or she will feel at the time of a terminal illness. Therefore, it should be updated regularly so that it accurately reflects a patient's wishes. The written instructions become effective when a patient is either in a terminal condition, permanently unconscious, or suffering irreversible brain damage.

Feeding Tubes

Theologians and ethicists have long recognized a distinction between ordinary and extraordinary medical care. The theological distinction is based on the belief that life is a gift from God that should not be destroyed deliberately by humans. Therefore, extraordinary therapies that extend life by imposing grave burdens on the patient and family are not required. A patient, however, has an ethical and moral obligation to accept ordinary or life-sustaining treatment. Although the courts have accepted decisions to withhold or withdraw extraordinary care, especially the respirator, from those who are comatose or in a persistent vegetative state with no possibility of emerging, they have been unwilling until now to discontinue feeding, which they have considered ordinary care.

However, in 1985, the New Jersey Supreme Court heard the case of *In re Claire C. Conroy.*[48] The case involved an 84-year-old nursing home patient whose nephew petitioned the court for authority to remove the nasogastric tube that was feeding her. The court overturned the appellate division decision and held that life-sustaining treatment, including nasogastric feeding, could be withheld or withdrawn from incompetent nursing home patients who will, according to physicians, die within one year, in three specific circumstances:

1. when it is clear that the particular patient would have refused the treatment under the circumstances involved (the subjective test)
2. when there is some indication of the patient's wishes (but he or she has not "unequivocally expressed" his or her desires before becoming incompetent) and the treatment "would only prolong suffering" (the limited objective test)
3. when there is no evidence at all of the patient's wishes, but the treatment "clearly and markedly outweighs the benefits the patient derives from life" (the pure objective test based on pain)[49]

A procedure involving notification of the state Office of the Ombudsman is required before withdrawing or withholding treatment under any of the three tests. The ombudsman must make a separate recommendation.

The court also found tubal feeding to be a medical treatment, and as such, it is as intrusive as other life-sustaining measures. The court in its analysis emphasized duty, rather than causation, with the result that medical personnel acting in good faith will be protected from liability. If physicians follow the *Quinlan/Conroy* standards and decide to end medical treatment of a patient, the duty to continue treatment ceases. Thus, the termination of treatment becomes a lawful act.

Although *Conroy* presents case-specific guidelines, there is concern that the opinion will have far-reaching repercussions. There is fear that decisions to discontinue treatment will not be based on the "balancing of interests" test, but rather that a "quality of life" test similar to that used by Hitler will be used to end the lives of severely senile, very old, decrepit, and burdensome people.

Those quality of life judgments would be most dangerous for nursing home patients in which age would be a factor in the decision-making process. "Advocates of 'the right to life' fear that the 'right to die' for the elderly and handicapped will become a 'duty to die.'"[50] In both the *Saikewicz* and *Spring* cases, age was a determining factor weighing against life-sustaining treatment. Further, in *In re Hier*,[51] the court found that Mrs. Hier's age of 92 years made the "proposed gastrostomy substantially more onerous or burdensome . . . than it would be for a younger, healthier person." Moreover, a New York Superior Court held that the burdens of an emergency amputation for an elderly patient outweighed the benefit of continued life.[52] Finding that prolonging her life would be cruel, the court stated that life had no meaning for her. Although some courts have recognized the difference, other courts must still address the difference between *Quinlan*-type patients and elderly, confined, and conscious patients who can interact but whose mental or physical functioning is impaired.

However, in a New Jersey case, the ombudsman denied a request to remove feeding tubes from a comatose nursing home patient.[53] In applying the *Conroy* tests, the ombudsman decided that Hilda Peterson might live more than one year, the period that *Conroy* used as a criterion for determining whether life support can be removed.

To further complicate this issue, on March 17, 1986, the American Medical Association changed its Code of Ethics on comas. Now physicians may ethically withhold food, water, and medical treatment from patients in irreversible comas or persistent vegetative states with no hope of recovery—even if death is not imminent.[54] Although physicians can consider the wishes of the patient and family or the legal representatives, they cannot cause death intentionally. The wording is permissive, so those physicians who feel uncomfortable withdrawing food and water may refrain from doing so. The American Medical Association's decision does not comfort those who fear abuse or mistake in euthanasia decisions, nor does it have any legal value as such. There are physicians, nurses, and families who are unscrupulous and have their own, and not the patient's, interests in mind. Even with the *Conroy* decision and the American Medical Association's Code of Ethics change, the feeding tube issue is not settled.

On April 23, 1986, the New Jersey Superior Court ruled that the husband of severely brain-damaged Nancy Jobes could order the removal of her life-sustaining feeding tube, which would ultimately cause the 31-year-old comatose patient, who had been in a vegetative state in a hospice for the past six years, to starve to death.[55] Dr. Fred Plum created and defined the term persistent vegetative state as one in which:

> . . . the body functions entirely in terms of its internal controls. It maintains temperature. It maintains digestive activity. It maintains heart beat and pulmonary ventilation. It maintains reflex activity of muscles and nerves for low level conditioned responses. But there is no behavioral

evidence of either self-awareness or awareness of the surroundings in a learned manner.[56]

Medical experts testified that the patient could, under optimal conditions, live another 30 years. Relieving the nursing home officials from performing the act on one of its residents, the court ruled that the patient may be taken home to die (with the removal to be supervised by a physician and medical care to be provided to the patient at home).

The nursing home had petitioned the court for the appointment of a "life advocate" to fight for continuation of medical treatment for Jobes, which, it argued, would save her life. The court disallowed the appointment of a life advocate, holding that case law does not support requiring the continuation of life-support systems in all circumstances. Such a requirement, according to the court, would contradict the patient's right of privacy.

The court's decision applied "the principles enunciated in *Quinlan* and . . . *Conroy*" and the "ruling by the American Medical Association's Council on Judicial Affairs that the provision of food and water is, under certain circumstances, a medical treatment like any other and may be discontinued when the physician and family of the patient feel it is no longer benefiting the patient."[57]

The Illinois Supreme Court in *In re Estate of Longeway*,[58] agreed with the logic of the *Jobes* decision and other sister state rulings regarding the characterization of artificial nutrition and hydration as medical treatment. The Illinois court found that the authorized guardian of a terminally ill patient in an irreversible coma or persistent vegetative state has a common-law right to refuse artificial nutrition and hydration. The court found that there must be clear and convincing evidence that the refusal is consistent with the patient's interest. The court also required the concurrence of the patient's attending physician and two other physicians. "Court intervention is also necessary to guard against the remote, yet real possibility that greed may taint the judgment of the surrogate decision maker."[59] Dissenting, Judge Ward said, "The right to refuse treatment is rooted in and dependent on the patient's capacity for informed decision, which an incompetent patient lacks."[60]

Also, Elizabeth Bouvia, a mentally competent cerebral palsy victim, won her struggle to have feeding tubes removed even though she was not terminally ill.[61] The California Court of Appeals announced on April 16, 1986, that she could go home to die. The court found that Bouvia's decision to "let nature take its course" did not amount to a choice to commit suicide with people aiding and abetting it. The court stated that it is not "illegal or immoral to prefer a natural, albeit sooner, death than a drugged life attached to a mechanical device."[62] The court's finding that it was a moral and philosophic question, not a legal or medical one, leaves one wondering if the courts are opening the door to permitting "legal starvation" to be used by those who are not terminally ill but who do wish to commit suicide.

Assisted Suicide

There are those in the health care field who are using their knowledge to develop new instruments of death to assist those who are terminally ill and want to end their lives. Dr. Jack Kevorkian of Michigan announced in October 1989 that he had developed a device that would end one's life quickly, painlessly, and humanely. He described his invention as a metal pole with bottles containing three solutions that feed into a common intravenous line. When the intravenous line is inserted into the patient's vein, a harmless saline solution will flow to clean the line of air. The patient then can flip a switch causing an anesthetic to render the patient unconscious. Sixty seconds later, a lethal dose of potassium chloride will flow into the patient, causing heart seizure and death. The news of this invention motivated the medical community and society at large to repeat their fear that individuals would abuse the practice of euthanasia, which Kevorkian refers to as a "medicide," despite any safeguards that are in place. Kevorkian assisted Janice Adkins, a 54-year-old Alzheimer's disease patient, in committing suicide on June 4, 1990. In December 1990, he was charged with first-degree murder, but the charge was later dismissed because Michigan had no law against assisted suicide. He was ordered, however, not to help anyone else commit suicide or to give advice about it. On February 6, 1991, he violated the court order by giving advice about the preparation of the drug to a terminally ill cancer patient.[63] Additional murder charges were lodged against Kevorkian in October 1991, when he instructed two Michigan women in the use of his "suicide machine." In dismissing the charges against him on July 21, 1992, Oakland County Circuit Court Judge David Breck stated that "some people with intractable pain cannot benefit from treatment." While emphasizing that Michigan has no law against assisting suicide, the judge also expressed his belief that physician-assisted suicide remains an alternative for patients experiencing "unmanageable pain."[64]

The Michigan House approved legislation placing a temporary ban on assisted suicide on November 24, 1992. The Senate approved the temporary ban after Kevorkian helped a sixth terminally ill patient kill herself. On December 15, 1992, Michigan Governor John Engler signed the law just hours after two more women committed suicide with Kevorkian's aid.

The new law, which became effective on April 1, 1993, made assisting suicide a felony punishable by up to four years in prison and a $2,000 fine. Under the new law, assisted suicide was banned for 15 months. During this time period a special commission studied assisted suicide and submitted its recommendations to the Michigan legislature for review and action. The new law apparently raised constitutional questions and was challenged by the Civil Liberties Union of Michigan because of the claim that it fails to recognize that the terminally ill have the right to end their lives painlessly and with dignity.

Kevorkian faced prosecution for murdering two people and for assisting in the suicides of three others. As a result, he appealed a Michigan Supreme Court ruling that found there is no right to assisted suicide.[65] The U.S. Supreme Court rejected his argument that assisted suicide is a constitutional right. The high court's decision allowed the State of Michigan to move forward and prosecute Kevorkian on the pending charges. At the time of the high court's ruling, Kevorkian had attended his twenty-second suicide, involving a retired clergyman, less than a month after he was left facing murder charges in Michigan.[66] As of March 1998, Kevorkian had aided in or witnessed 100 suicides.

In March 1995, a federal appeals court upheld the State of Washington's ban on assisted suicide.

But, in 1994, Oregon became the first state to allow physician-assisted suicide. In March 1998, the first known suicide under the new law occurred. During the first year, 23 patients obtained medication, but only 15 ended their lives with it. Entitled *The Death with Dignity Act*, it allows the physician to prescribe but not administer the lethal drugs to the requester who must be terminally ill with fewer than six months to live. The prescription fee of $28 is borne by the taxpayer. Two physicians must examine the patient to confirm the diagnosis and prognosis. The patient must have made a witnessed request both orally and in writing. All prescriptions must be reported to the state health department.

Then, in June 1997, the U.S. Supreme Court, in two unanimous and separate decisions, ruled that the laws in Washington and New York prohibiting assisted suicide are constitutional.

 CRIMINALIZING ASSISTED SUICIDE

Citation: *Quill v. Vacco,* 117 S. Ct. 2293 (1997)

Facts

Plaintiffs-appellants Dr. Quill, Dr. Klagsbrun, and Dr. Grossman challenged the constitutionality of two New York State statutes penalizing assisted suicide. The physicians contended that each statute is invalid to the extent that it prohibits them from acceding to the requests of terminally ill, mentally competent patients for help in hastening death. In granting summary judgment in favor of defendants-appellees, the district court considered and rejected challenges to the statutes predicated upon the due process and equal protection clauses of the Fourteenth Amendment. The Court of Appeals for the Second Circuit affirmed in part, and reversed in part.

The petitioners were New York public officials, and the respondents were physicians who practiced in New York and three gravely ill patients who died before the case reached the Supreme Court.

Ms. Doe was a 76-year-old retired physical education instructor who was dying of thyroid cancer; Mr. Kingsley was a 48-year-old publishing executive suffering from acquired immunodeficiency syndrome (AIDS); and Mr. Barth was a 28-year-old former fashion editor under treatment for AIDS. Each of these respondents alleged that she or he had been advised and understood that she or he was in the final stages of a terminal illness, and that there was no chance of recovery. Each had sought to hasten death in a certain and humane manner and for that purpose sought necessary medical assistance in the form of medications prescribed by her or his physician, which were to be self-administered.

The physician-respondents alleged that they encountered, in the course of their medical practices, mentally competent, terminally ill patients who requested assistance in the voluntary self-termination of life. Many of these patients apparently experienced chronic, intractable pain and/or intolerable suffering and sought to hasten their deaths for those reasons. Barth was one of the patients who sought the assistance of Grossman. Each of the physician plaintiffs had alleged that under certain circumstances it would be consistent with the standards of his medical practice to assist in hastening death by prescribing drugs for patients to self-administer for that purpose. The physicians alleged that they were unable to exercise their best professional judgment to prescribe the requested drugs, and the other plaintiffs alleged that they were unable to receive the requested drugs, because of the prohibitions contained in sections 125.15(3) and 120.30 of the New York Penal Law, all respondents being residents of New York. Section 125.15 of the New York Penal Law provides in pertinent part: "A person is guilty of manslaughter in the second degree when . . . He intentionally . . . aids another person to commit suicide." A violation of this provision is classified as a class C felony. *Id.*

Section 120.30 of the New York Penal Law provides: "A person is guilty of promoting a suicide attempt when he intentionally . . . aids another person to attempt suicide." A violation of this provision is classified as a class E felony. *Id.*

The respondents argued that "[t]he Fourteenth Amendment guarantees the liberty of mentally competent, terminally ill adults with no chance of recovery to make decisions about the end of their lives." It also included an allegation that the Fourteenth Amendment guarantees the liberty of physicians to practice medicine consistent with their best professional judgment, including using their skills and powers to facilitate the exercise of the decision of competent, terminally ill adults to hasten inevitable death by prescribing suitable medications for the patient to self-administer for that purpose.

The respondents further urged that the relevant portions of the New York Penal Law deny the patient-plaintiffs and the patients of the physician-plaintiffs the equal protection of the law by denying them the right to choose to hasten inevitable death, while terminally ill persons whose treatment includes life support are able to exercise this choice with necessary medical assistance by directing termination of such treatment.

The respondents requested judgment declaring the New York statutes complained of constitutionally invalid and therefore in violation of 42 U.S.C. § 1983 "as applied to physicians who assist mentally competent, terminally ill adults who choose to hasten inevitable death." The plaintiffs also sought an order permanently enjoining the defendants from enforcing the statutes and an award of attorneys' fees.

The district court disagreed and concluded that the type of physician-assisted suicide at issue in this case does not involve a fundamental liberty interest protected by the Due Process Clause of the Fourteenth Amendment. The court of appeals for the second circuit reversed. It determined that New York law does not treat equally all competent persons who are in the final stages of fatal illness and wish to hasten their deaths. It further held that the statutes were not rationally related to any legitimate state interest.

Turning to the equal protection issue, the district court identified a reasonable and rational basis for the distinction drawn by New York law between the refusal of treatment at the hands of physicians and physician-assisted suicide:

[I]t is hardly unreasonable or irrational for the State to recognize a difference between allowing nature to take its course, even in the most severe situations, and intentionally using an artificial death-producing device. The State has obvious legitimate interests in preserving life, and in protecting vulnerable persons. The State has the further right to determine how these crucial interests are to be treated when the issue is posed as to whether a physician can assist a patient in committing suicide. *Id.* at 84–85.

Accordingly, the court held that the plaintiffs have not shown a violation of the Equal Protection Clause of the Fourteenth Amendment.

Issue

Do the New York State statutes criminalizing assisted suicide violate the equal protection clause of the Fourteenth Amendment?

Holding

New York's prohibition on assisting suicide does not violate the equal protection clause.

Reason

The Supreme Court found that neither the assisted suicide ban nor the law permitting patients to refuse medical treatment treats anyone differently from anyone else, or draws any distinctions between persons. It explained that there is a distinction between letting a patient die and making one die. Most legislatures have allowed the former, but have prohibited the latter. The Supreme Court disagreed with the respondents' claim that the distinction is arbitrary and irrational.

In its decision, the Supreme Court determined that New York had valid reasons for distinguishing between refusing treatment and assisting suicide. Those reasons included: prohibiting intentional killing and preserving life; preventing suicide; maintaining the physician's role as his or her patient's healer; and protecting vulnerable people from indifference, prejudice, and psychological and financial pressure to end their lives. All of those reasons, the Court decided, constitute valid and important public interests fulfilling the constitutional requirement that a legislative classification bear a rational relation to a legitimate end.

Discussion

1. For what reasons did the Supreme Court disagree with the Second Circuit and find that New York's statute prohibiting assisted suicide did not violate the equal protection clause?
2. Describe what you think the Supreme Court meant when it stated that there is a difference between letting and making a person die. Cite examples to explain the difference.

In the Washington case, *Washington v. Glucksberg,*[67] the Court applied the same "rationally related to the state's interest in preserving life" test (which includes: preventing suicide and studying, identifying, and treating its causes; protecting vulnerable groups; and preventing the state from allowing euthanasia). The Court held that assisted suicide is not a liberty protected by the Constitution's due process clause. A majority of states now ban assisted suicide. These rulings, however, do not affect the right of patients to refuse treatment. It is clear that this emotionally charged issue is not settled. Legislative, judicial, and public debates continue to rage.

A Florida court ruled that a man dying of AIDS had a right to physician-assisted suicide under the privacy issues of the state's constitution. The court emphasized that the patient had to administer the lethal dose of medication, which was prescribed by his physician. Prosecutors were enjoined from bringing criminal charges against the physician.[68]

Do Not Resuscitate Orders

Do Not Resuscitate (DNR) orders are those given by a physician, indicating that in the event of a cardiac or respiratory arrest, no resuscitative measures should be used to revive the patient. A DNR order is an extremely difficult decision to make for both the patient and family. It is generally made when one's quality of life has been so diminished that "heroic" rescue methods are no longer in the patient's best interests.

DNR orders must be in writing, signed, and dated by the physician. Appropriate consents must be obtained from the patient or his or her health care agent. Many states have acknowledged the validity of DNR orders in cases involving terminally ill patients in which the patients' families make no objections to such orders.

DNR orders must comply with statutory requirements, be of short duration, and be reviewed periodically to determine whether the patient's condition or other circumstances (e.g., change of mind by the patient or family) surrounding the "no code" orders have changed. Presently, it is generally accepted that if a patient is competent, the DNR order is considered to be the same as other medical decisions in which a patient may choose to reject life-sustaining treatment. In the case of an incompetent, absent any advance written directives, the best interests of the patient would be considered. In

Payne v. Marion General Hospital,[69] the Indiana Court of Appeals overturned a lower court decision in favor of a physician. The physician had issued a no code status on Mr. Payne despite evidence given by a nurse that up to a few minutes before his death Payne could communicate. The physician had determined that Payne was incompetent, thereby rendering him unable to give informed consent to treatment. Because Payne left no written directives, the physician relied on one of Payne's relatives who asked for the DNR order. The court found that there was evidence that Payne was not incompetent and should have been consulted before a DNR order was given. Further, the court reviewed testimony that one year earlier Payne had suffered and recovered from the same type of symptoms, leading to the conclusion that there was a possibility that he could have survived if resuscitation had continued. There was no DNR policy in place at the hospital to assist the physician in making his decision. To avoid this type of problem, health care providers should adopt policies with respect to the issuance of no code orders.

AUTOPSY

Autopsies, or postmortem examinations, are conducted to ascertain the cause of a person's death, which, in turn, may resolve several legal issues. An autopsy may reveal whether death was the result of criminal activity, whether the cause of death was one for which payment must be made in accordance with an insurance contract, whether the death is compensable under workers' compensation and occupational disease acts, or whether death was the result of a specific act or a culmination of several acts. Aside from providing answers to these specific questions, the information gained from autopsies adds to medical knowledge. As such, medical schools have an interest in autopsies for educational purposes.

In those instances when the death of a patient is the result of criminal activity or unusual or suspicious circumstances, the patient's death must be reported to the medical examiner. Deaths resulting from natural causes within 24 hours of admission to a hospital do not need to be reported as long as the patient was in the hospital at the time of death and as long as an appropriate physician signs the death certificate and records the cause of death.

Deaths that occur during a surgical procedure are generally reportable events to the medical examiner. If an autopsy for medical evaluation is desired by the hospital, consent must be obtained from the next of kin. An unauthorized autopsy may disturb persons whose religious beliefs prohibit such a procedure as well as those persons who have a general aversion to the procedure. When autopsies are performed without statutory authorization and without the consent of the decedent, the surviving spouse, or an appropriate relative, liability may be imposed.

Damages awarded in cases of liability through interference with the rights of a surviving spouse or near relative with regard to the body of a decedent are based on the emotional and mental suffering that result from such interference. For damages to be awarded, the conduct of the alleged wrongdoer must be sufficiently disturbing to a person of ordinary sensibilities as to cause emotional harm. Cases involving the wrongful handling of dead bodies may be classified into four groups: (1) mutilation of a body, (2) unauthorized autopsy, (3) wrongful detention, and (4) unauthorized use or publication of photographs taken after death.

To limit lawsuits regarding the disposition of dead bodies, appropriate handling and release procedures should be established. Legal counsel should review such procedures. Interfering with rights to a body can result in liability. For example, in the case of *Lott v. State*,[70] two bodies were mistagged. The body of a person of the Roman Catholic faith was prepared for Orthodox Jewish burial, and the person of the Orthodox Jewish faith was prepared for Roman Catholic burial. This negligent conduct interfered with burial plans and caused mental anguish, for which liability was imposed.

Autopsy Consent Statutes

Recognizing both the need for information that can be secured only through the performance of a substantial volume of autopsies and the valid interests of relatives and friends of the decedent, most states have enacted statutes dealing with autopsy consent. Such legislation seems intended to have a twofold effect: first, to protect the rights of the decedent's relatives, and second, to guide those performing autopsies in establishing procedures for consent to autopsy. Most autopsy consent statutes establish an order for obtaining consent to autopsy based on the degree of family relationship.

Authorization by the Decedent

Most autopsy consent statutes provide that persons may authorize an autopsy prior to death. Ordinarily such consent must be in writing. There may be legal as well as practical problems in obtaining authorization for an autopsy from a patient before death if the state does not statutorily provide for such authorization.

In states where there is neither an autopsy consent statute nor a statute permitting donation that may be construed to include autopsy, it is unwise to rely exclusively on the authorization of a decedent to perform an autopsy. This is especially true when relatives of the deceased who assume custody of the body for burial object to an autopsy. Although the courts have upheld the wishes of the deceased with respect to the place of internment or the manner of disposition of the remains (i.e., by burial or cremation), it is possible that the courts will not afford the same weight to the decedent's wishes concerning an autopsy. In such instances, compelling reasons presented by certain next of kin of the decedent, especially the surviving spouse, may prevail over the wishes of the decedent.

Authorization by Person Other Than Decedent

Generally, the primary right to custody of a deceased person belongs to the surviving spouse. When there is no spouse, the right passes (in the absence of statutes furnishing a preference order of responsibility for burial and consent for autopsy) to the adult children of the deceased, parents, adult brothers and sisters, grandparents, uncles and aunts, and finally cousins. A court may find that a surviving spouse's unwillingness to assume responsibility for burial is sufficient to permit the right to custody of the body to devolve on a relative who is willing to assume such responsibility.

In *Callsen v. Cheltenham York Nursing Home*,[71] the relatives of the decedent, Mrs. Callsen, sued the defendants regarding the transfer of her body to a teaching hospital for dissection purposes. The defendants claimed immunity from liability under good-faith provisions of the Uniform Anatomical Gift Act. An amended complaint named 22 separate defendants. The complaint recited that Callsen was the mother of the plaintiffs and that prior to her death she resided at the Cheltenham York Nursing Home. The nursing home maintained records of family and friends who visited her. On May 27, 1990, the nursing home transferred Callsen (who expired on or about June 9, 1990) to the Einstein Medical Center. The medical center was notified that there was no family information for Callsen. Plaintiffs allege that the medical center made no further efforts to contact family members or friends.

The plaintiffs also alleged in their amended complaint that following Callsen's death, no efforts were made to locate and notify family members regarding the transfer of the decedent's remains. The family did not discover her whereabouts until about 10 days after her death, and by that time, the body had been partially dissected. The plaintiffs also claim that the defendants were negligent in failing to follow the statutory procedures for disposition of a deceased person's remains and that their conduct was grossly negligent and outrageous. The common pleas court sustained preliminary objections and dismissed the complaint and an appeal was taken. The question arises whether or not there were triable issues of fact as to whether appropriate efforts were made to locate the patient's family.

The commonwealth court held that demurrer, based on a claim of good-faith immunity, should not have been sustained in light of triable issues of fact as to whether appropriate efforts to locate the patient's family had been made. Although the nursing facility had access to names of family members, the nursing facility agreement did not record their names. One of the facility's nurses had reported to Einstein Medical Center that there was "no family information" for the decedent. The complaint does not disclose what efforts, if any, were made to locate the relatives or to notify any of them as to the proposed disposition of the decedent's remains. The court held that the ultimate decision as to the presence or absence of the exercise of good faith by any of the three parties must await the filing of further pleadings, the completion of any necessary discovery, and possible motions for summary judgment.

Scope and Extent of Consent

Legal issues may arise as a result of an autopsy even if consent has been obtained from the person authorized by law to grant such consent. If autopsy procedures go beyond the limits imposed by the consent or if the consent to an autopsy is obtained by fraud or without the formal requisites, liability may be incurred. It is a fundamental principle that a person who has the right to refuse permission for the performance of an act also has the right to place limitations or conditions on consent.

It is especially important that the hospital and its personnel adhere to any limitations or conditions placed on the permission to autopsy; if such limitations are exceeded, the physician or the hospital has no defense on the ground of emergency or medical necessity.

Although consent to autopsy also may encompass authorization for removal of body parts for examination, a separate question may arise concerning disposal of tissues and organs on completion of the examination: May the hospital and its personnel dispose of such material in a routine manner or use it for the hospital's own purposes, or must the hospital return the tissue and organs to the body before burial? In *Hendriksen v. Roosevelt Hospital*,[72] permission had been granted for a complete autopsy including an examination of the central nervous system by a scalp incision. Yet the court held that liability might be imposed on the hospital if the jury found that the hospital retained parts of the body. Pursuant to a New York statute requiring the authorization of the next of kin, consent was given for dissection; however, the court held that this statute should be construed narrowly and that special consent would have to be obtained to retain the internal organs of the decedent.

Consent given with the understanding that organs and tissue could be removed and retained for examination would seem to authorize the hospital to dispose of such materials in a suitable manner or to use them after the autopsy. However, the *Hendriksen* decision raises doubts on this matter. Where the party giving consent expressly stipulates that parts severed from the body are to be returned to the body for burial, conduct deviating from this provision may result in liability. Also, it would appear that consent to autopsy does not include authorization to mutilate or disfigure the body. Therefore, when autopsy involves the removal of exterior body parts and the physical appearance of the body cannot be restored without return of such parts, the hospital may be subject to liability for exceeding the scope of the authorization if the removed parts are not returned. In general, hospitals should periodically review protocols for obtaining consent, limitations placed on an autopsy, and the disposition of body parts.

Fraudulently Obtained Consent

It is a long-accepted principle that consent obtained through fraud or material misrepresentation is not binding and that the person whose consent is so obtained stands in the same position as if no consent had been given. This principle can apply to autopsies when facts are misrepresented to the person who has the right to consent to induce his or her consent. If a physician or a hospital employee states, as fact, something known to be untrue to gain consent, the autopsy would be unauthorized, and liability might follow.

Determination of Death

The time of a patient's death must be determined by a physician in attendance at the donor's death, or a physician certifying death, who shall not be a member of the team of physicians engaged in the transplantation procedure.

Consideration of legal duties regarding the use, handling, and disposition of dead bodies cannot be divorced from the legal questions involved in determining when death occurs. In many contexts, such as deciding rights to the property of the deceased person, the determination of death does not involve the hospital or its personnel. However, when permission has been granted for use of a patient's body or organs for the benefit of another or science in general, determination of the point of death becomes critical. New technology, specifically medical advancement in artificially sustaining life and transplanting vital organs, raises both legal and moral questions regarding the viability of the traditional methods of determining death.

Unclaimed Dead Bodies

Persons entitled to possession of a dead body must arrange for release of the body for transfer to an undertaker for final disposal. The recognition by the courts of a quasi-property right in the body of a deceased person imposes a duty on a health care facility to make reasonable efforts to give notice to persons entitled to claim the body. When there are no known relatives or friends of the family who can be contacted by the facility to claim the body, the facility has a responsibility to dispose of the body in accordance with law. Most states have statutes providing for the disposal of such bodies.

Unclaimed bodies generally are buried at public expense; a public official, usually a county official, has the duty to bury or otherwise dispose of such bodies. Most states have statutes providing for the disposal of unclaimed bodies by delivery to institutions for educational and scientific purposes. The public official in charge of the body has a duty to notify the government agency of the presence of the body. The agency then arranges for the transfer of the body in accordance with the statute. If no such agency exists under the statute, the health care facility or a public official may be authorized to allow a medical school or other institution or person, designated by the statute as an eligible recipient of unclaimed dead bodies, to remove the body for scientific use.

Certain categories of persons usually are excluded from these provisions permitting the distribution of bodies for educational and scientific use. For public health reasons, the statutes usually do not permit distribution of the bodies of persons who have died from contagious diseases.

Although most of these statutes explicitly require notification of relatives and set time limits for holding the body to allow relatives an opportunity to claim the body, strict compliance with the statutory provisions is often impossible because of the very nature of the problems that arise in the handling of dead bodies and in the required procedures themselves.

Noncompliance in such instances would not appear to cause liability. An example of such a provision is the requirement that relatives be notified immediately on death and that the body be held for 24 hours subject to claim by a relative or friend. The procedure of locating and notifying relatives may consume the greater part of the 24-hour period after death. If relatives who are willing to claim the body are located, the body should be held for a reasonable time to allow them to arrange custody for burial.

ORGAN DONATIONS

Federal regulations require that hospitals have, and implement, written protocols regarding the organization's organ procurement responsibilities. The regulations impose specific notification duties, as well as other requirements concerning informing families of potential donors. It encourages discretion and sensitivity in dealing with the families and in educating hospital staff on a variety of issues involved with donation matters, in order to facilitate timely donation and transplantation.

Organ transplantation is the result of the need for treating patients with end-stage organ disease and who face organ failure. Developments in medical science have enabled physicians to take tissue from persons immediately after death and use it to replace or rehabilitate diseased or damaged organs or other parts of living persons. Interest in organ transplantation began about 25 years ago when attempts were made to transplant kidneys between twins.[73] Improving success rates have been because of improved patient selection, improved clinical and operative management and skills, and immunosuppressant drugs developed to aid in decreasing the incidence of tissue rejection (e.g., cyclosporin A, which acts to suppress the production of antibodies that attack transplanted tissue). Progress in this field of medicine has created the problem of obtaining a sufficient supply of replacement body parts. There is a corresponding cry for more organs as the success rate in organ transplantation increases. Out of the fear of people buying and selling organs, the National Organ Procurement Act was enacted in 1984, making it illegal to buy or sell organs. Throughout the country, there are tissue banks and other facilities for the storage and preservation of organs and tissue that can be used for transplantation and for other therapeutic services.

The ever-increasing success of organ transplants and the demand for organ tissue require the close scrutiny of each case, making sure that established procedures have been followed in the care and disposal of all body parts. Section 1138, Title XI, of the Omnibus Budget Reconciliation Act of 1986 requires hospitals to establish organ procurement protocols or face a loss of Medicare and Medicaid funding. Physicians, nurses, and other paramedical personnel assigned with this responsibility often are confronted with several legal issues. Liability can be limited by complying with applicable regulations. Organs and tissues to be stored and preserved for future use must be removed almost immediately after death. Therefore, it is imperative that an agreement or arrangement for obtaining organs and tissue from a body be completed before death, or very soon after death, to enable physicians to remove and store the tissue promptly.

Persons aware of the shortage of dead bodies needed for medical education and transplantation may wish to make arrangements during their lifetimes for the use of their bodies after death for such purposes. A surviving spouse may, however, object to such disposition. In such cases, the interest of the surviving spouse or other family member could supersede that of the deceased.

The American Bar Association has endorsed a Uniform Anatomical Gift Act drafted by the Commission on Uniform State Laws. This statute has been enacted by all 50 states and has many detailed provisions that apply to the wide variety of issues raised in connection with the making, acceptance, and use of anatomic gifts. The Act allows a person to make a decision to donate organs at the time of death and allows potential donors to carry an anatomical donor card. State statutes regarding donation usually permit the donor to execute the gift during his or her lifetime.

The right to privacy of the donor and his or her family must be respected. Information should not be disseminated regarding transplant procedures that publish the names of the donor or donee without adequate consent.

States have enacted legislation to facilitate donation of bodies and body parts for medical uses. Virtually all the states have based their enactments on the Uniform Anatomical Gift Act, but it should be recognized that in some states there are deviations from this Act or additional laws dealing with donation.

Uniform Anatomical Gift Act

Individuals who are of sound mind and 18 years of age or older are permitted to dispose of their own bodies or body parts by will or other written instrument for medical or dental education, research, advancement of medical or dental science, therapy, or transplantation. Among those eligible to receive such donations are any licensed, accredited, or approved hospitals; accredited medical or dental schools; surgeons or physicians; tissue banks; or specified individuals who need the donation for therapy or transplantation. The statute provides that when only a part of the body is donated, custody of the remaining parts of the body shall be transferred to the next of kin promptly after removal of the donated part.

A donation by will becomes effective immediately on the death of the testator, without probate, and the gift is valid and effective to the extent that it has been acted on in good faith. This is true even if the will is not probated or is declared invalid for testimonial purposes.

Failure To Obtain Consent

Although failure to obtain consent for removal of body tissue can give rise to a lawsuit, not all such claims are successful. In *Nicoletta v. Rochester Eye & Human Parts Bank*,[74] the father of a deceased patient brought an action against a hospital for alleged emotional injuries resulting from the removal of his son's eyes for donation after a fatal motorcycle accident. The hospital was immune from liability under the provisions of the Uniform Anatomical Gift Act because the hospital had neither actual nor constructive knowledge that the woman who had authorized the donation was not the decedent's wife. The hospital was entitled to the immunity afforded by the "good-faith" provisions of Section 4306(3) of the act in which its agents had made reasonable inquiry as to the status of the purported wife, who had resided with the decedent for 10 years and was the mother of their two children. The hospital had no reason to believe that any irregularity existed. The father, who was present at the time his son was brought to the emergency department, failed to object to any organ donation and failed to challenge the authority of the purported wife to sign the emergency department authorization.

There are several methods by which a donation may be revoked. If the document has been delivered to a named donee, it may be revoked by

- a written revocation signed by the donor and delivered to the donee
- an oral revocation witnessed by two persons and communicated to the donee
- a statement to the attending physician during a terminal illness that has been communicated to the donee
- a written statement that has been signed and on the donor's person or in the donor's immediate effects

If the written instrument of donation has not been delivered to the donee, it may be revoked by destruction, cancellation, or mutilation of the instrument. If the donation is made by a will, it may be revoked in the manner provided for revocation or amendment of wills. Any person acting in good-faith reliance on the terms of an instrument of donation will not be subject to civil or criminal liability unless there is actual notice of the revocation of the donation.

EXPERIMENTATION

The Nuremberg Code and the Declaration of Helsinki provided guidelines for the development of federal regulations for medical research and the protection of human subjects in the United States. Federal regulations control federal grants that apply to experiments involving new drugs, new medical devices, or new medical procedures. Generally, a combination of federal and state guidelines and regulations ensures proper supervision and control over experimentation that involves human subjects. For example, federal regulations require hospital-based researchers to obtain the approval of an institutional review board. This board functions to review proposed research studies and conduct follow-up reviews on a regular basis.

Federal and state regulations impose several other requirements on experiments involving human subjects. Institutions conducting medical research on human subjects must

- Fully disclose the inherent risks to the patient.
- Make a proper determination that the patient is competent to consent.
- Identify treatment alternatives.
- Obtain written consent from the patient.

Institutional Review Board (IRB)

An organization's IRB is a committee responsible for reviewing, monitoring, and approving clinical investigations of drugs and medical devices involving human subjects. The IRB is responsible for ensuring that the rights of each individual are protected and that all research is conducted within appropriate state and federal guidelines (e.g., Food and Drug Administration (FDA) guidelines).

Informed Consent

A written consent form must be obtained from each patient who participates in a clinical investigation. The consent form must not contain any coercive or exculpatory language through which the patient is forced to waive his or her legal rights, including the release of the investigator, sponsor, or organization from liability for negligent conduct.

A government report released on April 19, 1995, indicated that physicians implanted experimental devices in patients at 80 different hospitals without informing them that they were part of an experiment.[75] One physician had implanted a prosthetic device with a chemical coating to promote the growth of bone tissue in 238 patients. The physician had reported using the implant in only 37 patients. The report did not name the devices, hospitals, or physicians.

The necessity of informed consent cannot be overemphasized. In *Friter v. Iolab Corp.*,[76] the hospital had contracted with the FDA to participate in a clinical study involving the implantation of experimental intra-ocular lenses. They were so experimental that they had not yet obtained FDA approval. Hence, the FDA promulgated regulations requiring the hospital to obtain informed consent, using a very detailed, five-page consent form, setting forth with particularity the possibility of the existence of unknown risks, as the lenses were still being tested. The court held in this case that the failure to obtain informed consent is actionable.

Experimental Drugs

Federal regulations require that the nature of experimental drugs and possible adverse consequences must be explained to the patient. Failure to obtain consent for the administration of experimental drugs can give rise to a lawsuit. The district court in *Blanton v. United States*[77] held that when a new drug of unknown effectiveness was administered to a patient at a Navy medical center, despite the availability of other drugs of known effectiveness, the hospital violated the accepted medical standards and its duty of due care, so that in the absence of the patient's consent to the experiment, the United States was liable for the resulting injury.

Food and Drug Administration

The FDA, under enormous criticism over the years because of the red tape involved in the approval of new drugs, issued rules to speed up the approval process. The rules permit the use of experimental drugs outside a controlled clinical trial if the drugs are used to treat a life-threatening condition. However, clinical trials of new drugs and medical devices have been referred to as endangered because manufacturers have been taking their devices overseas for faster approvals. An unpublished survey by the Health Industry Manufacturers Association, which represents more than 700 medical device companies, indicates that there is a major exodus among makers of devices that are required to go through clinical trials.[78] The devices include pacemakers, joint implants, and cardiac catheters. Some companies have already moved some clinical trials of devices offshore.

Nursing Facilities

The Health Care Financing Administration survey process includes a review of the rights of any nursing facility residents participating in experimental research. Surveyors will review the records of residents identified as participating in a clinical research study. They will determine whether informed consent forms have been executed properly. The form will be reviewed to determine if all known risks have been identified. Appropriate questions may be directed to both the staff and residents or the residents' guardians.

Possible questions to ask staff include:

- Is the facility participating in any experimental research?
- If yes, what residents are involved? (Interview a sample of these residents.)[79]

Residents or guardians may be asked questions such as:

- Are you participating in the study?
- Was this explained to you well enough so that you understand what the study is about and any risks that might be involved?[80]

Patients participating in research studies should fully understand the implications of their participation. Health care organizations involved in research studies should have appropriate protocols in place that protect the rights of patients. Consent forms should describe both the risks and benefits involved in the research activity.

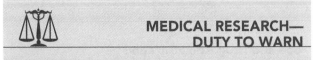

MEDICAL RESEARCH— DUTY TO WARN

Citation: *Blaz v. Michael Reese Hosp. Found., 74 F. Supp. 2d 803 (D.C. Ill. 1999)*

Facts

About 5,000 patients at Michael Reese Hospital and Medical Center, located in Chicago, Illinois, were treated with X-ray therapy for some benign conditions of the head and neck from 1930 to 1960. Among them was Joel Blaz, now a citizen of Florida, who received this treatment for infected tonsils and adenoids while a child in Illinois in 1947–48. He has suffered various tumors, which he now attributes to this treatment. Blaz was diagnosed with a neural tumor in 1987.

In 1974, Michael Reese set up a Thyroid Follow-Up Project to gather data and conduct research among the people who had been subjected to the X-ray therapy. In 1975, the Program notified Blaz by mail that he was at increased risk of developing thyroid tumors because of the treatment. In 1976, someone associated with the Program gave him similar information by phone and invited him to return to Michael Reese for evaluation and treatment at his own expense, which he declined to do.

Dr. Arthur Schneider was put in charge of the Program in 1977. In 1979, Schneider and Michael Reese submitted a research proposal to the National Institutes of Health (NIH) stating that a study based on the Program showed "strong evidence" of a connection between X-ray treatments of the sort administered to Blaz and various sorts of tumors: thyroid, neural, and other. In 1981, Blaz received but did not complete or return a questionnaire attached to a letter from Schneider in connection with the Program. The letter stated that the purpose of the questionnaire was to "investigate the long term health implications" of childhood radiation treatments and to "determine the possible associated risks." It did not say anything about "strong evidence" of a connection between the treatments and any tumors.

In 1996, after developing neural tumors, Blaz sued Michael Reese's successor, Galen Hospital, Illinois, and Dr. Schneider, alleging, among other things, that they failed to notify and warn him of their findings that he might be at greater risk of neural tumors in a way that might have permitted their earlier detection and removal or other treatment.

Issue

Is there a duty to warn the subject of previously administered radiation treatments when there is a strong connection between those treatments and certain sorts of tumors?

Finding

The physician had a duty to warn.

Reason

The general criteria for the existence of a legal duty established by the Illinois Supreme Court are: (1) whether the harm reasonably was foreseeable; (2) the likelihood of injury; (3) the magnitude of the burden of guarding against it; and (4) the consequences of placing that burden upon the defendant.

Under this framework, it is clear that a duty to warn exists. The harm alleged, neural and other tumors, would here be reasonably foreseeable as a likely consequence of a failure to warn, and was in fact foreseen by Schneider. A reasonable physician, indeed any reasonable person, could foresee that if someone were warned of "strong evidence" of a connection between treatments to which he had been subjected and tumors, he would probably seek diagnosis or treatment and perhaps avoid these tumors, and if he were not warned he probably would not seek diagnosis or treatment, increasing the likelihood that he would suffer from such tumors. Other things being equal, therefore, a reasonable physician would warn the subject of the treatments.

Discussion

1. What is the reasoning for requiring physicians to describe the benefits, risks, and alternatives to experimental treatments?

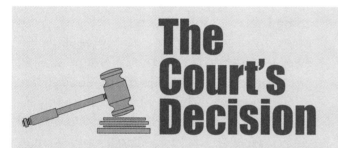

The Court's Decision

The court determined that the case was not moot. Insofar as the hospital's claims are founded on its own interests, rather than those of the state, the court agreed with the hospital that it had standing to bring those claims. The court concluded, however, that under the circumstances of this case, the hospital's legitimate interest in protecting its patients does not extend that far.

The hospital later conceded that this case is not moot because it is capable of repetition. Notwithstanding the hospital's concession and the resulting lack of dispute between the parties, the court considered the issue of mootness.

A challenge to the issuance of an injunction permitting the administration of nonconsensual blood transfusions will virtually always become moot long before appellate litigation can be concluded or initiated. Of necessity, a medically necessary blood transfusion must be accomplished, if at all, as soon as reasonably possible after its need becomes apparent to the patient's health care provider. Once a court order is issued permitting such a transfusion against the patient's will, and the court lifts any stay of that order, as it will inevitably do, it cannot be expected that the health care provider that sought the order will await the outcome of an appeal before complying with the order. Any order that is challenged on appeal is, by its very nature, of such limited duration that it is virtually certain that it will become moot before appellate litigation can be concluded.

The hospital had a legitimate interest in receiving official guidance in resolving the ethical dilemma it faced—whether to practice medicine by *trying to save a patient's life* despite that patient's refusal to consent to treatment, *or* to practice medicine in accordance with the patient's wishes and likely *watch the patient die*, knowing nonetheless that it had the power to save her life. The hospital had conflicting interests, and was in the role not of opposing its patient, but of a party seeking the court's guidance in determining its obligations under the circumstances.

Conferring standing only on the state and denying it to the hospital, in this case, however, would have had the practical effect of requiring the hospital to abandon its own legitimate interests. Such action would have effectively insulated the patient's choice from any official scrutiny because it would have been extremely difficult for the state to initiate judicial proceedings in time to do any good, and even if the state could have done so, it would likely have been unfamiliar both with the medical options available and with the facts and circumstances surrounding the patient's desires. The hospital was the best informed and most feasible candidate, under these circumstances, to set the judicial machinery in motion. The court concluded that, for these reasons, the hospital had standing to challenge Vega's refusal of blood transfusions.

Vega claimed that the state's interest in the welfare of her child is not sufficiently compelling as to outweigh her interest in refusing blood transfusions. Vega maintained that the trial court's injunction, issued at the behest of the hospital, violated her common-law right of self-determination, her federal constitutional right to bodily self-determination, her federal constitutional right to free exercise of religion, and her state constitutional right of religious liberty. The court concluded that, under the circumstances of this case, the issuance of the injunction, followed by the administration of blood transfusions, violated Ms. Vega's common-law right of bodily self-determination.

Once the infant was born, Vega's decision to refuse a blood transfusion posed no risk to the infant's physical health. Vega's claim centers on her common-law right of bodily self-determination. The only question, therefore, is whether the hospital and the trial court were obliged to respect Vega's decision to refuse blood transfusions, even though her decision would likely have led to her death.

Although the hospital's interests are sufficient to confer standing on it in this case, they are not sufficient to take priority over Vega's common-law right to bodily integrity, even when the assertion of that right threatens her own life. The hospital had no common-law right or obligation to thrust unwanted medical care on a patient who, having been sufficiently informed of the consequences, competently and clearly declined that care. The hospital's interests were sufficiently protected by Vega's informed choice, and neither it nor the trial court was entitled to override that choice. Vega's common-law right of bodily self-determination was entitled to respect and protection. The trial court improperly issued an injunction that permitted the hospital to administer blood transfusions to Vega.

CHAPTER REVIEW

1. The branch of philosophy that deals with values related to human contact in regard to right and wrong actions and good and bad motives and ends is called *ethics*. It encompasses the process through which society's ultimate values and standards are determined. In relation to health care, ethics includes not only philosophical, but also economic, medical, political, and legal, dilemmas.
2. A *bio-ethics committee* is one designed to educate and advise health care providers, patients, and families and to analyze ethical dilemmas. Such a committee serves as a hospital resource designed to offer objective counsel. The

committee performs functions such as developing policy and procedure guidelines to assist in resolving ethical dilemmas, educating staff and community, resolving conflicts, reviewing cases, offering support and consultation, and offering political advocacy.

3. When there exists an element of uncertainty regarding a patient's wishes in an emergency situation, the situation should be resolved in a way that favors the preservation of life.

4. *Euthanasia* is the mercy killing of the hopelessly ill, injured, or incapacitated. The debate over euthanasia is complex, and the legal system must maintain a balance between ensuring that the patient's constitutional rights are protected and protecting society's interests in preserving life, preventing suicide, and maintaining the integrity of the medical profession.
   * *Active euthanasia* is the intentional commission of an act that will result in death.
   * *Passive euthanasia* is when a potentially life-saving treatment is withdrawn or withheld.

5. A physician's willingness to abide by a patient's wishes can be limited by the lack of protection from liability should he or she participate in active or passive euthanasia.

6. Euthanasia can be voluntary or involuntary. *Voluntary euthanasia* occurs when a competent adult patient with an incurable condition who has been informed of the possible ramifications and alternatives available gives request or consent. *Involuntary euthanasia* is when a person other than the incurable decides to terminate the life of an incompetent or an unconsenting competent person's life.

7. The invention of machinery that can sustain heartbeat and respiration has called into question the idea of what constitutes death. Most states recognize brain death, by statute or judicial decision, as constituting death.

8. Because of the debate surrounding right-to-die issues, patients should be counseled to make decisions regarding their wishes while they are competent. Living wills, designation of surrogates, health care proxies, and powers of attorney are legal steps that allow patients to express their wishes.

9. According to the *Patient Self-Determination Act* of 1990, health care organizations have a responsibility to explain to patients, staff, and families that patients have legal rights to direct their medical and nursing care as it corresponds to existing state law. This includes right-to-die directives.

10. A primary difference between health care proxies and living wills is that proxies do not require that a person know about and consider in advance every situation and decision that could arise. Instead, the appointed agent would have to interpret the patient's wishes based on the information given at the time that the patient is incapacitated and unable to make decisions for him- or herself.

11. Dr. Jack Kevorkian is probably the most famous figure in the debate surrounding assisted suicide. The Supreme Court ruled that there exists no constitutional right to assisted suicide and this decision allowed the state of Michigan to prosecute him for helping patients commit suicide.

12. *Do not resuscitate* orders are given by physicians and indicate that, in the event of a cardiac or respiratory arrest, no resuscitative measures should be used to revive the patient. These orders must be in writing and must be signed and dated by the physician. Additionally, the patient or his or her health care agent must give appropriate consents.

13. *Autopsies* are postmortem examinations conducted to ascertain the cause of death. Most states have enacted autopsy consent statutes that establish an order to obtain consent to autopsy based on the degree of family relationship.

14. The *Uniform Anatomical Gift Act* allows a person to make a decision to donate organs at the time of death and allows potential donors to carry an anatomical donor card. It also provides that if only part of a body is donated, custody of the remaining parts will be transferred to the next of kin promptly after the removal of the donated part.

15. In most states, a combination of federal and state guidelines and regulations ensures the proper supervision and control over experimentation involving human subjects. An organization's institutional review board is responsible for reviewing, monitoring, and approving clinical investigations of drugs and medical devices that involve human subjects. Written consent must be obtained from patients participating in clinical investigations.

REVIEW QUESTIONS

1. Discuss the ever-expanding role of ethics committees, including internal operational issues and external influences that affect internal operations.
2. How can social workers and hospital chaplains help families cope with serious illness and grief?
3. What are the differences between allowing a patient to die and physician-assisted suicide?

4. Examine the statement: "the inherent risk is that society's faith in doctors as healers would become subverted if doctors participate in physician-assisted suicide."
5. Constitutionally, what gives patients the right to self-determination?
6. What is "standing" with regard to who can bring an action, and who has standing in litigating the right to die?
7. Why is it important that a written consent be obtained from each patient who participates in a clinical trial?

NOTES

1. Stamford Hosp. v. Vega, 674 A.2d 821 (Conn. Super. Ct. 1996).
2. In re Quinlan, 355 A.2d 647 (N.J. 1976).
3. Union Pac. Ry. Co. v. Botsford, 141 U.S. 250, 251 (1891).
4. 611 A.2d 1148 (N.J. Super Ct. 1992).
5. Cruzan v. Director of the Mo. Dep't of Health, 497 U.S. 261 (1990).
6. Protection & Advocacy Sys., Inc. v. Presbyterian Healthcare Servs., 989 P.2d 890 (N.M. App. 1999).
7. J. Podgers, *Matters of Life and Death*, A.B.A.J. May 1992, at 60.
8. In re Estate of Brooks, 205 N.E.2d 435 (Ill. 1965); Superintendent of Belchertown State Sch. v. Saikewicz, 370 N.E.2d 417 (Mass. 1977); In re Quinlan, 355 A.2d 647 (N.J. 1976).
9. 147 Cal. App. 3d 1006 (Cal. Ct. App. 1983).
10. 376 N.E.2d 1232 (Mass. App. Ct. 1979).
11. State Dep't of Human Servs. v. Northern, 563 S.W.2d 197, 209 (Tenn. Ct. App. 1978).
12. 455 N.Y.S.2d 706 (N.Y. Sup. Ct. 1981).
13. *Id.* at 712 (*citing* In re Storar, 438 N.Y.S.2d 266 (N.Y. 1981)).
14. 105 N.E. 92 (N.Y. 1914).
15. *Id.* at 93.
16. 438 N.Y.S.2d 266, 272 (N.Y. 1981).
17. In re Quinlan, 355 A.2d 647 (N.J. 1976).
18. 410 U.S. 113 (1973).
19. *Quinlan*, 355 A.2d at 663.
20. 370 N.E.2d 417 (Mass. 1977).
21. *Id.* at 434.
22. Gelford, *Euthanasia and the Terminally Ill Patient*, 63 Neb. L. Rev. 741, 747 (1984).
23. 380 N.E.2d 134 (Mass. 1978).
24. 405 N.E.2d 115 (Mass. 1980).
25. 452 So.2d 925 (Fla. 1984).
26. 362 So.2d 160 (Fla. Dist. Ct. App. 1978).
27. John F. Kennedy Mem'l Hosp. v. Bludworth, 452 So.2d 921, 925 (Fla. 1984) (*citing* In re Welfare of Colyer, 660 P.2d 738 (Wash. 1983), in which the court found prior court approval to be "unresponsive and cumbersome").
28. Severns v. Wilmington Med. Ctr., 425 A.2d 156 (Del. Ch. 1980) (incompetent's right to refuse medical treatment may be expressed through a guardian when the patient is in a chronic vegetative state); Leach v. Akron Gen. Med. Ctr., 426 N.E.2d 809 (Ohio Com. Pl. 1980) (right to privacy includes right of terminally ill patient in a vegetative state to determine his or her own course of treatment).
29. Satz v. Perlmutter, 379 So.2d 359 (Fla. 1980) (constitutional right to privacy supports decision of competent adult suffering from a terminal illness to refuse extraordinary treatment); Superintendent of Belchertown State Sch. v. Saikewicz, 370 N.E.2d 417 (Mass. 1977) (right to refuse medical treatment for terminal illness extends to incompetent patients).
30. Schmitt v. Pierce, 344 S.W.2d 120 (Mo. 1961).
31. Coyle, *Fast Furious Questioning Marks Session on Coma Case*, Nat'l L. J., Dec. 18, 1989, at 8; Wallis, *To Feed or Not To Feed?*, Time, Mar. 31, 1986, at 60.
32. Connery, *Prolonging Life: The Duty and Its Limits, Moral Responsibility in Prolonging Life's Decisions*, in To Treat or Not To Treat 25 (1984).
33. *Statement of Medical Opinion Re: "Brain Death,"* A.M.A. House of Delegates Res. (June 1974).
34. 482 N.Y.S.2d 436 (1984).
35. 438 N.Y.S.2d 266 (1981).
36. 534 N.E.2d 886 (N.Y. 1988).
37. *Id.* at 891.
38. Cruzan v. Harman, 760 S.W.2d 408 (Mo. 1988).
39. *Id.* at 425.
40. Cruzan v. Director of the Mo. Dep't of Health, 497 U.S. 261 (1990).
41. Pa. S.646, Amendment A3506, Printer's No. 689, Oct. 1, 1990.
42. 20 Pa. Cons. Stat. Ann. § 5602(a)(9) (1988).
43. *Hospital Wants To Let Wife Die*, Newsday, Jan. 11, 1991, at 13.
44. Farnam v. Crista Ministries, 807 P.2d 830, 849 (Wash. 1991).
45. 42 U.S.C. § 1395 (1992).
46. 42 U.S.C. § 1395cc (1992).
47. 420 N.E.2d 64 (N.Y. 1981).
48. 486 A.2d 1209 (N.J. Sup. Ct. 1985).
49. *Id.*
50. U.S. Congress, Off. of Technology Assessment, Pub. No. OTA-BA-306, Life-Sustaining Technologies and the Elderly 48 (1987).
51. 464 N.E.2d 959 (Mass. 1984).
52. In re Beth Israel Med. Ctr., 519 N.Y.S.2d 511, 517 (N.Y. Sup. Ct. 1987).
53. Sullivan, *Ombudsman Bars Food Tube Removal*, N.Y. Times, Mar. 7, 1986, at 82.
54. *AMA Changes Code of Ethics on Comas*, Newsday, Mar. 17, 1986, at 2.
55. In re Jobes, 529 A.2d 434 (N.J. 1987).
56. *Id.* at 438.
57. *Man Wins Right To Let Wife Die*, Newsday, Apr. 24, 1986, at 3.
58. 549 N.E.2d 292 (Ill. 1989).
59. *Id.* at 790.
60. *Id.* at 793.
61. Bouvia v. Superior Court (Glenchur), 225 Cal. Rptr. 297 (Cal. Ct. App. 1986).
62. *Id.* at 306.
63. *Dr. Death at Work*, Newsday, Feb. 7, 1991, at 12.
64. *Kevorkian Charges Dropped*, Newsday, July 22, 1992, at 4.
65. Hobbins v. Attorney Gen. of Mich., No. 94–1473 (Mich. 1994); Kevorkian v. Michigan, No. 94–1490 (Mich. 1994).

66. *22nd Death for "Dr. Death,"* USA Today, May 9, 1995, at 2A.

67. 117 S. Ct. 2258 (1997).

68. McIver v. Krischer, No. CL-96-1504-AF (Jan. 31, 1997) (stay issued February 11, 1997).

69. 549 N.E.2d 1043 (Ind. Ct. App. 1990).

70. 225 N.Y.S.2d 434 (N.Y. Ct. Cl. 1962).

71. 624 A.2d 663 (Pa. Comm. Ct. 1993).

72. 297 F. Supp. 1142 (S.D.N.Y. 1969).

73. U.S. Dep't of Health & Human Services, Task Force on Organ Donation and Transplantation (1986).

74. 519 N.Y.S.2d 928 (N.Y. Sup. Ct. 1987).

75. Tim Friend, *Patients Not Told Devices Experimental,* USA Today, Apr. 19, 1995, at 1.

76. 607 A.2d 1111 (1992).

77. 428 F. Supp. 360 (D.D.C. 1977).

78. Tim Friend, *Clinical Trials in U.S. Called "Endangered,"* USA Today, May 10, 1995, at 1–2.

79. 2 C.F.R. § 488.115 (1989).

80. *Id.*

Malpractice Insurance

CRIMINAL ACTS AND BENEFITS EXCLUSION

A physician was convicted for the sexual assault of a minor. He was then sued in federal court for civil damages. The insurer had issued medical malpractice policies to the physician. Under the policies, the insurer agreed to pay on behalf of the insured all sums that the insured became legally obligated to pay as damages because of bodily injury or personal injury re-

sulting from rendering or failing to render, during the policy period, professional services by the insured. The policies contained an express exclusion barring liability of the insurer for any acts of the insured arising out of the performance of a criminal act. The physician argued that the federal complaint pleads malpractice covered by his malpractice insurance. The insurer argued that liability resulting from the federal complaint is not covered because the physician's acts did not constitute rendering or failing to render professional services by the insured.

Did sexual assault constitute rendering professional services within the coverage provisions of the physician's insurance policy? Can a malpractice insurer be required to indemnify a physician for liability resulting from the sexual assault of a minor?[1]

What is your verdict?

INTRODUCTION

I never was ruined but twice—once when I gained a lawsuit, and once when I lost one.
Francois Marie de Voltaire (1694–1778)

This chapter introduces the reader to some of the basic concepts related to malpractice insurance. The cost of malpractice insurance continues to be a major concern for the health care industry. Medical professional insurance, as in

all insurance, is subject to the cyclical nature of the insurance market. Problems intrinsic in malpractice insurance include the uncertainty of the U.S. legal system, the effects of inflation on ultimate claim values, emerging technology, and new treatments.

Health care organizations and professionals in the mid-1970s and mid-1980s experienced difficult times in obtaining medical liability insurance coverage. Competition between insurers was minimal, with high premiums and adequate umbrella coverage often difficult to obtain.

Many commercial insurance carriers discontinued underwriting professional liability coverage in the middle to late 1970s. As a result, some states required insurance carriers to join a consortium of insurance companies to underwrite malpractice insurance. These consortiums were referred to as joint underwriting associations.

Between those hard markets was a soft market that brought steady premium reduction and greater availability of coverage. In 1986, there was another softening of the market. By 1988, insurers of medical professional liability coverage provided increased flexibility of programs, premium reductions, and broadened coverage. Premiums then began to stabilize in the 1990s. On a long-term basis, the cyclic underwriting pattern of the insurance industry could very well result in a return once again to a crisis in the medical malpractice insurance market.

THE INSURANCE POLICY

Insurance is a contract that creates legal obligations on the part of both the insured and the insurer. It is a contract in which the insurer agrees to assume certain risks of the insured for consideration or payment of a premium. Under the terms of the contract, also known as the insurance policy, the insurer promises to pay a specific amount of money if a specified event takes place. An insurance policy contains three necessary elements: (1) identification of the risk covered, (2) the specific amount payable, and (3) the specified occurrence.

Insurance companies are required by the laws of the different states to issue only policies that contain certain mandated provisions and to maintain certain financial reserves to guarantee to policyholders that their expectations will be met when coverage is needed. The basic underlying concept of insurance is the spreading of risk. By writing coverage for a large enough pool of individuals, the company has determined actuarially that a certain number of claims will arise within that pool, and if the premium structure has been established correctly and the prediction of claims made accurately, the company ought to be able to meet those claims and return a profit to its shareholders.

Risk Categories

A risk is the possibility that a loss will occur. The main function of insurance is to provide security against this loss. Insurance does not prevent or hinder the occurrence of the loss, but it does compensate for the damages.

An insured individual may be exposed to three categories of risk: (1) risk of property loss or damage, (2) risk of personal injury or loss of life, and (3) risk of incurring legal liability. *Property risk* is the possibility that an insured's property may be damaged or destroyed by fire, flood, tornado, hurricane, or other catastrophe. *Personal risk* is the possibility that the insured may be injured in an accident or may become ill; the possibility of death is a personal risk covered in the typical life insurance plan. *Legal liability risk* is the possibility that the insured may become legally liable to pay money damages to another and includes accident and professional liability insurance.

Policy Types

The two basic kinds of malpractice policies are (1) *occurrence policies*, which cover all incidents that arise during a policy year, regardless of when they are reported to the insurer; and (2) *claims-made policies*, which cover only those claims made or reported during the policy year, regardless of when they occurred.

LIABILITY OF THE PROFESSIONAL

An individual who provides professional services to another person may be legally responsible for any harm the person suffers as a result of negligence. Many professionals protect themselves from their exposure to a legal loss by acquiring a professional liability insurance policy.

Do Nurses Need Insurance?

Should nurses carry malpractice insurance? From a legal standpoint, the answer is *yes*. Even though an organization, as a nurse's employer, can be held responsible for the negligence of a nurse pursuant to the doctrine of *respondeat superior*, a nurse could be held liable for his or her own negligence. From a cost-benefit standpoint, the answer is also *yes*. Malpractice insurance premiums for nurses continue to be relatively reasonable. Malpractice insurance coverage is especially important if a nurse is working:

- as a volunteer at a clinic or health fair not sponsored by his or her employer
- as an independent contractor providing a service in a patient's home
- for an independent agency or nurse registry
- for an organization that is covered by an insurance policy that has an exclusionary provision by which the insurance company disclaims liability for malpractice actions brought against the insured organization

If a private agency has inadequate insurance coverage, there is always a possibility that recovery will be sought against a nurse's estate.

There are disadvantages to nurses obtaining malpractice insurance. First, acquisition of malpractice coverage by nurses could encourage naming nurses as defendants in malpractice suits. Second, an increase in complaints against nurses could cause a rise in insurance premiums, eventually placing the cost of malpractice insurance outside their financial means.

The court in *Jones v. Medox, Inc.*,[2] held that only the nurse's insurance carrier, Globe Insurance, was liable for injuries sustained by the plaintiff while at Doctors Hospital; these injuries resulted from an injection administered by the nurse. Medox, Inc., a corporation providing temporary medical personnel to Doctors Hospital, employed Ms. Jones. After settlement of the claim against the nurse, the hospital, and the nurse's employer, the nurse and her insurer brought an action against Doctors Hospital, Medox, Inc., and their insurers. The trial court granted summary judgment in favor of the hospital and its insurer and dismissed the claim against Medox, Inc., and its insurer.

A nurse's insurance policy was primary with respect to the first $100,000 of a settlement that resulted from a malpractice action against the nurse in *American Nurses Association v. Passaic General Hospital*.[3] The National Fire Insurance Company had issued an insurance policy covering the contractual obligation of the American Nurses Association to its members. The New Jersey Supreme Court held that the judgment against the nurse in excess of $100,000 was properly apportioned equally between the hospital's liability insurer and the association's liability insurer.

Private Duty Nurse

A private duty nurse is not an employee of an institution but rather is engaged by the patient (or the patient's family) to provide services to that patient. As such, the nurse should obtain personal coverage. The patient engaging the nurse would be well advised to ask about the availability of such coverage, as would the institution in which the nurse is providing professional care for that patient.

Even though a patient employs a special duty nurse, an organization can be liable for damages resulting from a nurse's negligent conduct. The existence of an employer–employee relationship, which determines the applicability of *respondeat superior*, is a matter to be determined by the jury.

An organization also can be liable for damages awarded in a malpractice action if a nurse and his or her registry have inadequate insurance to cover a jury award. In such instances, an organization then would have a right to seek recovery from the nurse and the registry.

Students

The potential for liability is not limited to licensed professionals. Students engaged in learning a profession who en-

gage in activities involving the care and treatment of others face potential liability for their acts. For this reason, these individuals often obtain personal insurance coverage or assure themselves of such coverage through the institution in which they are employed or the institution in which they are enrolled to obtain their education.

THE INSURANCE AGREEMENT

A health care facility, nurse, physician, and other health care practitioners who are covered by an insurance policy must recognize the rights and duties inherent in the policy. The professional should be able to identify the risks that are covered, the amount of coverage, and the conditions of the contract.

Although the policies of different insurance companies may vary, the standard policy usually provides that the insurance company will pay on behalf of the insured all sums that the insured shall become legally obligated to pay as damages because of injury arising out of malpractice error or mistake in rendering or failing to render professional services. A standard liability insurance policy has five distinct parts:

1. insurance agreement
2. defense and settlement
3. policy period
4. amount payable
5. conditions of the policy

The insurer, under the terms of the policy, has a legal obligation to pay any sum that has been agreed to or determined by a court, up to the policy limit, including legal fees. Under a professional liability policy, the professional is protected from damages arising from rendering or failing to render professional services. Thus, a professional who performs a negligent act resulting in legal liability or who fails to perform a necessary act (thereby incurring damages) is personally protected from paying an injured party. The insurer makes payment of damages to the injured party.

Defense and Settlement

In the defense and settlement portion of the insurance policy, the insured and the insurance company agree that the company will defend any lawsuit against the insured arising from performance or nonperformance of professional services. The insurance company is delegated the power to effect a settlement of any claims as it deems necessary. In a professional liability policy, the duty of the insurer under this clause is limited to the defense of lawsuits against the insured that are a consequence of professional services.

The insurance company fulfills its obligation to provide a defense by engaging the services of an attorney on behalf of the insured. The obligation of the attorney is to the insured directly, because the insured is the attorney's client. Here is, to some extent, a divided loyalty because the attorney looks to the insurance company to obtain business. Nevertheless, the attorney–client relationship exists between only the attorney and the insured, and the insured has the right to expect the attorney to fulfill the requirements of such a relationship.

If an insurance company has established the right to obtain a settlement of any claim prior to trial, the company's only obligation is to act reasonably and not to the detriment of the insured.

Policy Period

The period of the policy is stated in the insurance contract. Under an *occurrence policy*, the contract provides protection only for claims that occur during the time frame within which the policy is stated to be in effect. Any incident that occurs before or after the policy period would not be covered under the insuring agreement. Occurrence policies provide coverage for all claims that may arise out of a policy period. The actual reporting time has no bearing on the validity of the claim, so long as it is filed before the applicable statute of limitations tolls. Although the reporting time has no bearing on the validity of the claim from the standpoint of coverage under the policy, the conditions of the policy will require notice within a specified time. Failure to provide such notice could void the insurer's obligation under the policy if it can be demonstrated that the carrier's position was compromised as a result of filing an untimely claim or report.

A *claims-made policy* provides coverage for only those claims instituted during the policy period. Notice of a claim is required during the policy period. Failure to give notice of a claim to the insurer in a claims-made policy until after the policy expires can result in denial by the insurance company to cover the claim.

Coverage—The Amount Payable

The amount to be paid by an insurer is determined by the amount of damages incurred by the injured party. The insurance company and the injured party may negotiate a settlement prior to or during trial. Some states have provisions mandating that consent of the court must be obtained prior to the settlement of a negligence claim on behalf of a minor.

In any event, the insurance company will pay the injured party no more than the maximum limit stated in the insurance policy. The insured professional must personally pay any damages that exceed the policy limits. For example, under a policy with a maximum coverage of $1 million for each claim and $3 million for aggregate claims (the total amount payable to all injured parties), the insured must pay any amount over $1 million on each individual claim and any amount over $3 million in a policy period.

Punitive Damages

A claim for punitive damages awarded in a malpractice suit was submitted to an insurance carrier for payment but was subsequently denied by the carrier.[4] The insurance carrier cited Florida public policy, which prohibits coverage of punitive damage awards.

Intentional Torts

An action was brought by a comprehensive liability insurer for declaratory judgment as to its duty to defend the insured in civil actions alleging slander, interference with business relations, and violations of the federal antitrust laws in *St. Paul Insurance Co. v. Talladega Nursing Home.*[5] The federal district court ruled for the insurer and the nursing facility appealed. The Fifth Circuit held that the insurer has no duty to defend or provide coverage for alleged intentional torts. Under Alabama law, all contracts insuring against loss from intentional wrongs are void as being against public policy.

Conditions of an Insurance Policy

Each insurance policy contains a number of important conditions. Failure to comply with these conditions may cause forfeiture of the policy and nonpayment of claims against it. Generally, insurance policies contain the following conditions:

- *notice of occurrence*—When the insured becomes aware that an injury has occurred as a result of acts covered under the contract, the insured must notify the insurance company promptly. The form of notice may be either oral or written, as specified in the policy.
- *notice of claim*—Whenever the insured receives notice that a claim or suit is being instituted, prompt notice must be sent by the insured to the insurance company. This provides the insurance company with an opportunity to investigate the facts of a case. The policy will specify what papers are to be forwarded to the company. The mere failure to advise in a timely manner may be in and of itself a breach of the insurance contract, entitling the insurer to decline coverage. It may not matter that the insurer has in no way been prejudiced by the late notification. The mere fact that the insured has failed to carry out obligations under the policy may be sufficient to permit the insurer to avoid its obligations. When the

insurer has refused to honor a claim because of late notice and the insured wishes to challenge such refusal, an action can be brought, asking a court to determine the reasonableness of the insurer's position.

- *assistance of the insured*—The insured must cooperate with the insurance company and render any assistance necessary to reach a settlement.
- *other insurance*—If the insured has pertinent insurance policies with other insurance companies, the insured must notify the insurance company so that each company may pay the appropriate amount of the claim.
- *assignment*—The protections contracted for by the insured may not be transferred unless the insurance company grants permission. Because the insurance company was aware of the risks the insured would encounter before the policy was issued, the company will endeavor to avoid protecting persons other than the policyholder.
- *subrogation*—This is the right of a person who pays another's debt to be substituted for all rights in relation to the debt. When an insurance company makes a payment for the insured under the terms of the policy, the company becomes the beneficiary of all the rights of recovery the insured has against any other persons who also may have been negligent. For example, if several nurses were found liable for negligence arising from the same occurrence and the insurance company for one nurse pays the entire claim, the company will be entitled to the rights of that nurse and may collect a proportionate share of the claim from the other nurses.
- *changes*—The insured cannot make changes in the policy without the written consent of the insurance company. Thus, an agent of the insurance company ordinarily cannot modify or remove any condition of the liability contract. Only the insurance company, by written authorization, may permit a condition to be altered or removed.
- *cancellation*—A cancellation clause spells out the conditions and procedures necessary for the insured or the insurer to cancel the liability policy. Written notice usually is required. The insured person's failure to comply with any terms of the policy can result in cancellation and possible nonpayment of a claim by the insurance company. As a legal contract, failure to meet the terms and conditions of an insurance policy can result in a breach of contract and voidance of coverage.

MEDICAL LIABILITY INSURANCE

The fundamental tenets of insurance law and their application to the typical liability insurance policy are pertinent to the provisions of medical professional liability insurance as applied to individuals and institutions. Professional liability policies vary in the broadness, the exclusions from coverage, and the interpretations a company places on the language of the contract.

There are three medical professional liability classes:

1. individuals including (but not limited to) physicians, surgeons, dentists, nurses, osteopaths, chiropractors, opticians, physiotherapists, optometrists, and different types of medical technicians (This category may include medical laboratories and blood banks.)
2. health care institutions, such as hospitals, extended care facilities, homes for the aged, institutions for the mentally ill, and other health care facilities where bed and board are provided for patients or residents
3. outpatient facilities and clinics where there are no regular bed or board facilities (These institutions may be related to industrial or commercial enterprises; however, they are to be distinguished from facilities operated by dentists or physicians, which usually are covered under individual professional liability contracts.)

The insuring clause usually will provide for payment on behalf of the insured if an injury arises from either of the following:

- malpractice, error, or mistake in rendering or failing to render professional services in the practice of the insured's profession during the policy period
- acts or omissions on the part of the insured during the policy period as a member of a formal accreditation or similar professional board or committee of a health care facility or a professional society

Although injury is not limited to bodily injury or property damage, it must result from malpractice, error, mistake, or failure to perform acts that should have been performed.

The most common risks covered by medical professional liability insurance are

- negligence
- assault and battery as a result of failing to obtain consent to a medical or surgical procedure
- libel and slander
- invasion of privacy for betrayal of professional confidences

Coverage may vary from company to company, but standards of policy coverage generally are followed. Rates will differ for individuals by profession and specialty and by type of health care facility (e.g., nursing facility and hospital).

MEDICAL MALPRACTICE INSURANCE ASSOCIATIONS

The difficulty that health care organizations and physicians had in obtaining malpractice insurance in many states during the early 1980s resulted in the formation of medical malpractice insurance associations. The purpose of these associations is to provide a market for institutions or physicians who are unable to obtain medical malpractice insurance in the open market at a reasonable price. Legislation was introduced requiring all insurance carriers engaged in writing personal liability insurance within a particular state to provide malpractice coverage through these associations (similar to "assigned risk" pools for problem automobile drivers).

Most physician-owned liability insurance companies are not-for-profit enterprises. In general, their policies are set by physician boards of directors, but their business operations are managed by professional insurance executives. Most of these companies were established by and retain close ties to medical societies. Most physician-owned companies were established in order to maintain access to malpractice insurance when commercial insurers withdrew from the market in the late 1970s.[6]

SELF-INSURANCE

Exorbitant malpractice insurance premiums often have produced situations in which the premium cost of insurance has approached and, on occasion, reached the face amount of the policy. Because of the extremely high cost of maintaining such insurance, some institutions have sought alternatives to this conventional means of protecting against medical malpractice. One alternative is self-insurance. When a health care facility self-insures its malpractice risks, it no longer purchases a policy of malpractice insurance but instead periodically sets aside a certain amount of its own funds as a reserve against malpractice losses and expenses. An institution that self-insures generally retains the services of a self-insurance consulting firm and of an actuary to determine the proper level of funding that the institution should maintain.

A self-insurance program need not involve the elimination of insurance coverage in its entirety. A health care organization may find it prudent to purchase excess coverage whereby the organization self-insures the first agreed-on dollar amount of risk and the insurance carrier insures the balance. For example, in a typical program the organization may self-insure the first $1 million of professional liability risk per year. Because most claims will be disposed of within such limitation, the cost of excess insurance may be quite reasonable.

Before a corporation makes a decision to self-insure, not only must it determine the economic aspects of such a decision and the necessary funding levels to maintain an adequate reserve for future claims, but it also must determine whether there are any legal impediments to such a program. A corporation that has obtained funding from governmental sources or that has issued bonds or other obligations containing certain covenants may find itself unable to self-insure because of these prior commitments. Health care organizations should consult legal counsel to review appropriate and applicable documentation before making the self-insurance decision.

TRUSTEE COVERAGE

Trustees should be covered by liability insurance just as physicians and other health care professionals. Such coverage is generally provided for by the organization. Such coverage is helpful in attracting qualified board members. Before an insurer writing a trustee policy (generally known as directors' and officers' liability insurance) will respond to defend or pay a claim on behalf of a trustee, it must be shown that the trustee acted in good faith and within the scope of his or her responsibilities. Ordinarily, coverage would not be afforded when a trustee is accused of acting improperly in his or her relationship with the corporation. Also, insurance coverage for officers' and directors' liability generally excludes as a covered event the failure to obtain other necessary insurance for the institution (e.g., fire insurance).

Insurance coverage for officers and directors of a corporation should include indemnification, to the extent possible by law, for all liabilities and expenses including:

- counsel fees and expenses that are reasonably incurred as the result of any legal proceeding stemming from lawsuits that might arise in connection with an officer's or director's position with the corporation
- funds paid in satisfaction of judgments
- fines and penalties
- coverage that extends to actions taken while in office or thereafter, by reason of being or having been a director or officer of the corporation, excepting when the officer or director has not acted in good faith or in the reasonable belief that an officer's or director's action was not in the best interest of the corporation

MANDATED MEDICAL STAFF INSURANCE COVERAGE

Physicians often are required by health care organizations to carry their own malpractice insurance. Physicians who fail to maintain such coverage can be suspended from a hospital's medical staff. A federal district court in *Pollack v. Methodist Hospital*[7] ruled that a hospital has the legal right to suspend a staff physician for failing to comply with its requirement that physicians carry medical malpractice insurance coverage. The decision resulted from a suit brought against Methodist Hospital in New Orleans by a physician whose staff privileges were suspended because he failed to comply with a newly adopted hospital requirement that all staff physicians provide proof of malpractice coverage of at least $1 million. The court rejected the physician's charges that the requirement violated his civil rights and antitrust laws.

As held in *Wilkinson v. Madera Community Hospital*,[8] a health care organization can require its medical staff to show evidence of professional liability insurance. The physician in this case was refused reappointment because he failed to maintain malpractice insurance with a "recognized insurance company" as required by the hospital.

INVESTIGATION AND SETTLEMENT OF CLAIMS

An injured party may request settlement of a claim prior to instituting legal action. As a first step toward settlement of a claim, the insurance carrier may have an investigator interview a claimant regarding the details of the alleged occurrence that led to the injury. After an investigation, the insurance company may agree to a settlement if liability is questionable and the risks of proceeding to trial are too great. Should settlement negotiations fail, an attorney may be employed by the injured party to negotiate a settlement. If the attorney fails to obtain a settlement, either the claim can be dropped or legal action commenced.

Once a claim is settled, a general release, signed by the plaintiff, surrenders the right of action against the defendant. If the claimant is married, a general release also should be obtained from the spouse because there may be a cause of action due to loss of the injured spouse's services (e.g., companionship). A parent's release surrenders only a parental claim. Approval of a court may be necessary to release a child's claim. Release by a minor, in some instances, may be repudiated by the minor on reaching majority. A general release can be voided if the releasee

- is intoxicated, under the influence of drugs, in shock, or in extreme pain that prevents sufficient understanding of a general release and therefore prevents or voids its execution
- does not understand the language of the release
- has not had the opportunity to obtain appropriate legal consultation
- has been the victim of mental or physical duress
- has executed the release as a result of misrepresentation or fraud
- is mentally incompetent and cannot give a valid release (In this instance, a court-appointed guardian is required to execute a release on behalf of a mental incompetent, and a court must pass on the terms of any settlement.)

The Court's Decision

Sexual assault did not constitute rendering professional services within coverage provisions of the physician's insurance policy. The New Mexico Supreme Court held that the malpractice insurer was not required to indemnify a physician for liability resulting from the sexual assault of a minor. The physician's conviction was admitted into evidence not to prove negligence but to prove that the physician's misconduct constituted criminal acts within exclusions of liability policies.

CHAPTER REVIEW

1. As with all insurance, medical malpractice insurance is affected by the cyclical nature of the insurance market. Specific issues that affect malpractice insurance are the changing legal system, inflation's effects on claim values, new technology, and new treatments.

2. *Insurance* is a contract in which the company providing the insurance agrees to assume some of the risks of the insured party for consideration or the payment of a premium. There are three primary components of an insurance policy:
   1. identification of the covered risks
   2. specification of the amounts payable
   3. specification of the occurrence
3. By creating a large pool of individuals, an insurance company can balance its risk—the possibility that loss will occur—enough that it should be able to both cover claims and return a profit to shareholders.
4. There are three primary categories of risk:
   1. The possibility that the insured's property may be damaged or destroyed by catastrophe is *property risk.*
   2. *Personal risk* is the possibility that the insured will be injured in an accident or will become seriously ill.
   3. *Legal liability* is the possibility that the insured will be found legally liable to pay damages to another.
5. *Occurrence policies* cover all accidents during a policy year, regardless of when they are reported, while *claims-made policies* cover claims made or reported during the policy year, no matter when they occurred.
6. Nurses may want to obtain malpractice insurance because even though their employers can be held responsible for negligence, nurses also can be held liable for their own negligence. However, drawbacks include the encouragement of naming nurses in malpractice suits and a concurrent rise in insurance premiums.
7. Standard liability policies have five parts:
   1. The *insurance agreement* specifies that the insurer has a legal obligation to pay any sum that has been agreed or determined by a court, up to the limit of the policy, including legal fees.
   2. The *defense and settlement* portion contains the agreement between the insured and the insurance company that the company will defend any lawsuit against the insured that arises from the performance or nonperformance of professional services. The insurance company also obtains the power to enact a settlement of any claims it deems necessary or appropriate.
   3. The *policy period* sets forth the duration of the policy period and the circumstances under which claims will be processed.
   4. The policy also details *coverage*, or the maximum amount that the insurance company will pay an injured party.
   5. The policy will include several *conditions*. If the insured does not comply with these conditions, forfeiture of the policy and nonpayment of claims against it could result.
8. Most medical professional liability insurance covers risks such as negligence; assault and battery that result from failing to obtain consent to a medical or surgical procedure; libel and slander; and invasion of privacy for betrayal of professional confidences.
9. *Self-insurance* is a practice in which a health care organization periodically sets aside a certain amount of money to cover malpractice losses and expenses. These organizations often seek the advice of self-insurance consulting firms and actuaries to estimate the proper level of funding for these expenses.
10. When a claim is settled, the plaintiff signs a *general release*, which states that the plaintiff surrenders the right of action against the defendant.

REVIEW QUESTIONS

1. Describe the conditions of an insurance policy as described in this chapter.
2. Explain the differences in liability for supervising nurses, private duty nurses, and students.
3. Under what circumstances should a health care professional be self-insured?
4. Should a health care provider who has been sued lose staff privileges? Discuss your answer.
5. Why do insurance carriers require "timely" notice of a claim?

NOTES

1. New Mexico Physicians Mut. Liab. Co. v. LaMure, 860 P.2d 734 (N.M. 1993).
2. 430 A.2d 488 (D.C. 1981).
3. 484 A.2d 670 (N.J. 1984).
4. American Nursing Ctr.-Greenbrook v. Heckler, 592 F. Supp. 1311, 1312 (D.D.C. 1984).
5. 606 F.2d 631 (5th Cir. 1979).
6. U.S. Dep't of Health & Human Servs., Task Force on Medical Liability and Malpractice 3 (1987).
7. 392 F. Supp. 393 (E.D. La. 1975).
8. 192 Cal. Rptr. 593 (Cal. Ct. App. 1983).

Labor Relations

It's Your Gavel...

UNFAIR LABOR PRACTICES

Ms. Welton worked in a nursing facility's dietary department. She attended a union organization meeting on July 5 and signed a union authorization card. At a hearing before an administrative law judge (ALJ), she testified that the day after the meeting her supervisor took her aside at work and asked whether she or anyone from the dietary department had attended the meeting. Before the ALJ, Welton's supervisor denied having any conversation with Welton about the union meeting. The National Labor Relations Board (NLRB) found that the questioning of Welton constituted unlawful interrogation.

Mr. Hopkins worked as a janitor for the nursing facility. In April 1990, he was laid off as a result of the financial problems the facility was then experiencing. He was rehired in late June. Following his return, Hopkins also attended the meeting on July 5 and signed an authorization card. He testified before the ALJ that his supervisor approached him at work and questioned him as to whether any of the nurses or aides harassed him about the union. The Board credited Hopkins' and Welton's version of the events, noting that they were not employed by the facility at the time and had nothing to gain by fabricating their testimony.

On July 18, the facility circulated a memorandum to all employees that stated, "This is to advise that the NLRB has tentatively set a hearing on Wednesday, July 25th, to decide who can vote in a union election. Our position is that supervisors, RNs, and LPNs cannot vote. We will keep you advised."

On July 19, the facility held a mandatory meeting for all registered nurses (RNs), licensed practical nurses (LPNs), and supervisors. The facility's administrator, Mr. Wimer, the facility's attorney, Mr. Yocum, and the chief executive officer, Mr. Colby, of the facility's affiliated hospital, conducted the meeting. Yocum told the nurses that, in the facility's opinion, all RNs and LPNs were supervisors who could not vote in the upcoming election but must remain loyal to the facility. When asked by Sands, a union supporter, what he meant by loyalty, Yocum replied that all RNs and LPNs were prohibited from engaging in union activities. When asked by Sands why the facility opposed the union, Yocum responded, "Well, for one thing, they cost too . . . much money. . . . Do you think those dues come out of thin air?"

The Board concluded that the facility, through Yocum, violated the National Labor Relations Act by telling LPNs present at the meeting that they could not vote in the upcoming union election or participate in union activities, and that engaging in such activities could subject them to dismissal.[1]
What is your verdict?

INTRODUCTION

The relationship between employers and employees is regulated by both state and federal laws. Health care organizations are not exempt from the impact of these laws and therefore are required to take into account such matters as employment practices (wages, hours, and working conditions), union activity, workers' compensation laws, occupational safety and health laws, and employment discrimination laws.

Federal or state regulation generally pervades all areas of employer–employee relationships. The most significant piece of federal legislation dealing with labor relations is the National Labor Relations Act (NLRA). Although federal laws generally take precedence over state laws when there is a conflict between the state and the federal laws, state laws are applicable and must be considered, especially when state standards are often more stringent than federal legislation. This chapter provides an overview of those laws affecting the health care industry.

UNIONS AND HEALTH CARE ORGANIZATIONS

Through the mid-1930s, union organizational activity in the health care industry was minimal, and it continued that way with relatively slow growth until the late 1950s. Union activity has been successful most often in those geographic areas in which unions have been active in other industries.

Many labor organizations now are involved heavily in attempts to become the recognized collective bargaining representatives in health care organizations. There are craft unions, which devote their primary organizing efforts to skilled employees, such as carpenters and electricians, and industrial unions and unions of governmental employees, which seek to represent large groups of unskilled or semi-skilled employees. Professional and occupational associations, such as state nurses' associations, historically known for their social and academic efforts, have involved themselves in collective bargaining for their professions. To the extent that the professional organizations seek goals directly concerned with wages, hours, and other employment conditions and engage in bargaining on behalf of employees, they perform the functions of labor unions.

FEDERAL LABOR ACTS

National Labor Relations Act of 1935

The NLRA[2] was enacted by Congress in July 1935, to govern the labor-management relations of business firms engaged in interstate commerce. The act is generally known as the Wagner Act, after Senator Robert R. Wagner of New York. The Act defines certain conduct of employers and employees as unfair labor practices and provides for hearings on complaints that such practices have occurred. The NLRA was modified by the Taft-Hartley amendments of 1947 and the Landrum-Griffin amendments of 1959.

Jurisdiction

Nearly all proprietary health care organizations, for some time, have been subject to the provisions of the NLRA. The NLRB, which is entrusted with enforcing and administering the Act, has jurisdiction over matters involving proprietary and not-for-profit health care organizations with gross revenues of at least $250,000 per year and nurses' associations and health care–related organizations with gross revenues of more than $100,000 per year.

The NLRB's basic method of operation is to investigate claims or complaints of unfair practices submitted by the employer or employees, or both. The Board reviews the claim, determining whether there have been unfair labor practices, and recommends a remedy.

Most questions submitted to the Board involve claims by employees that their rights of self-organization or of choosing their collective bargaining representative have been interfered with by the employer. Employers also may submit complaints to the NLRB (e.g., when two unions are seeking recognition and one of them intimidates employees by making allegations that a sweetheart relationship exists between the employer and the competing union in an effort to disrupt the certification process).

An exemption for governmental institutions was included in the 1935 enactment of the NLRA, and charitable health care institutions were exempted in 1947 by the Taft-Hartley Act amendments to the NLRA. However, a July 1974 amendment to the NLRA extended coverage to employees of nonprofit health care institutions that previously had been exempted from its provisions. In the words of the amendment, a health care facility is "any hospital, convalescent hospital, health maintenance organization, health clinic, nursing home, extended care facility, or other institution devoted to the care of the sick, infirm or aged."[3]

The amendment also enacted unique, special provisions for employees of health care organizations who oppose unionization on legitimate religious grounds. These provisions allow a member of such an institution to make periodic contributions to one of three nonreligious charitable funds selected jointly by the labor organization and the employing institution rather than paying periodic union dues and initiation fees. If the collective bargaining agreement does not specify an acceptable fund, the employee may select a tax-exempt charity.

Elections

The NLRA sets out the procedures by which employees may select a union as their collective bargaining representative to negotiate with health care organizations over employment and contract matters. A health care organization may choose to recognize and deal with the union without resorting to the formal NLRA procedure. If the formal process is adhered to, the employees vote on union representation in an election held under NLRB supervision.

The NLRA provides that the representative, having been selected by a majority of employees in a bargaining unit, is the exclusive bargaining agent for all employees in the unit. The scope of the bargaining unit is often the subject of dispute, for its boundaries may determine the outcome of the election, the employee representative's bargaining power, and the level of labor relations stability.

When the parties cannot agree on the appropriate unit for bargaining, the NLRB has broad discretion to decide the issue. But the NLRB's discretion is limited to determining appropriate units for only those employees who are classified as professional, supervisory, clerical, technical, or service and maintenance employees when they are included in units outside their particular category. This is the case unless there has been a self-determination election in which the members of a certain group vote, as a class, to be included within the larger bargaining unit. For example, nurses and other professional employees can be excluded from a bargaining unit composed of service and maintenance employees unless the profession-

als are first given the opportunity to choose separate representation and reject it. Supervisory nurses also have been held entitled to a bargaining unit separate from the unit composed of general duty nurses.

Although the NLRA does not require employee representatives to be selected by any particular procedure, the Act provides for the NLRB to conduct representation elections by secret ballot. The NLRB may conduct such an election when a petition for certification has been filed by an employee; a group of employees; an individual; a labor union acting on the employees' behalf; or an employer. When the petition is filed, the NLRB must investigate and direct an election if it has reasonable cause to believe a question of representation exists. After an election, if any party to it believes that certain conduct created an atmosphere that interfered with employee free choice, that party may file objections with the NLRB.

Unfair Labor Practices

The NLRA prohibits health care organizations from engaging in certain conduct classified as employer unfair labor practices. For example, discriminating against an employee for holding union membership is not permitted. The NLRA stipulates that the employer must bargain in good faith with representatives of the employees; failure to do so constitutes an unfair labor practice. The NLRB may order the employer to fulfill the duty to bargain.

If the employer dominates or controls the employees' union or interferes and supports one of two competing unions, the employer is committing an unfair labor practice. Such employer support of a competing union is illustrated clearly in a situation in which two unions are competing for members in the same facility, as well as for recognition as the employees' bargaining organization. If the organization permits one of the unions to use its facilities for its organizational activities but denies the use of the facilities to the other union, an unfair labor practice is committed. Financial assistance to one of the competing unions also constitutes an unfair labor practice.

The NLRA also places duties on labor organizations and prohibits certain employee activities that are considered unfair labor practices. Coercion of employees by the union constitutes an unfair labor practice; such activities as mass picketing, assaulting nonstrikers, and following groups of nonstrikers away from the immediate area of the facility plainly constitute coercion and will be ordered stopped by the NLRB. Breach of a collective bargaining contract by the labor union is another example of an unfair labor practice.

Norris-LaGuardia Act

Congress enacted the Norris-LaGuardia Act[4] to limit the power of the federal courts to issue injunctions in cases involving or growing out of labor disputes. The Act's strict standards must be met before such injunctions can be issued. Essentially, a federal court may not apply restraints in a labor dispute until after the case is heard in open court and the finding is that unlawful acts will be committed unless restrained and that substantial and irreparable injury to the complainant's property will follow (*United States v. Hutcheson*, 312 U.S. 219 (1941)).

The Norris-LaGuardia Act is aimed at reducing the number of injunctions granted to restrain strikes and picketing. An additional piece of legislation designating procedures limiting strikes in health care institutions is the 1974 amendment to the NLRA.

This amendment sets out special procedures for handling labor disputes that develop from collective bargaining at the termination of an existing agreement or during negotiations for an initial contract between a health care institution and its employees. The procedures were designed to ensure that the needs of patients would be met during any work stoppage (strike) or labor dispute in such an institution.

The amendment provides for creating a board of inquiry if a dispute threatens to interrupt health care in a particular community. The board is appointed by the director of the Federal Mediation and Conciliation Service (FMCS) within 30 days after notification of either party's intention to terminate a labor contract. The board then has 15 days in which to investigate and report its findings and recommendations in writing. Once the report is filed with the FMCS, both parties are expected to maintain the status quo for an additional 15 days.

The board's findings provide a framework for arbitrators' decisions, while recognizing both the community's need for continuous health services and the good-faith intentions of labor organizations to avoid a work stoppage whenever possible and to accept arbitration when negotiations reach an impasse.

The amendment also mandates certain notice requirements by labor groups in health care institutions: (1) the institution must be given 90 days' notice before a collective bargaining agreement expires, and (2) the FMCS is entitled to 60 days' notice. Previously, only 60 days' notice to the employer and 30 days' notice to the FMCS were required. However, if the bargaining agreement is the initial contract between the parties, only 30 days' notice need be given to the FMCS.

More significantly, 10 days' notice is required in advance of any strike, picketing, or other concerted refusal to work, regardless of the source of the dispute. This allows the NLRB to determine the legality of a strike before it occurs and also gives health care institutions ample time to ensure the continuity of patient care. At the same time, any attempt to use this period to undermine the bargaining relationship is implicitly forbidden.

The 10-day notice may be concurrent with the final 10 days of the expiration notice. Any employee violation of these provisions amounts to an unfair labor practice and automatically may result in the discharge of the employee. Also,

injunctive relief may be available from the courts if circumstances warrant.

In summary, the amendment's provisions are designed to ensure that every possible approach to a peaceful settlement is explored fully before a strike is called.

Labor-Management Reporting and Disclosure Act of 1959

The Labor-Management Reporting and Disclosure Act of 1959[5] places controls on labor unions and the relationships between unions and their members. Also, it requires that employers report payments and loans made to officials or other representatives of labor organizations or any promises to make such payments or loans. Expenditures made to influence or restrict the way employees exercise their rights to organize and bargain collectively are illegal unless the employer discloses them. Agreements with labor consultants, under which such persons undertake to interfere with certain employee rights, also must be disclosed.

Reports required under the Act must be filed with the secretary of labor and are then made public. Both charitable and proprietary health care organizations that make such payments or enter into such agreements must file reports. Penalties for failing to make the required reports or for making false reports include fines up to $10,000 and imprisonment for one year.

Fair Labor Standards Act

The Fair Labor Standards Act (FLSA)[6] establishes minimum wages and maximum hours of employment. The employees of all governmental, charitable, and proprietary health care organizations are covered by this Act. Employers must conform to the minimum wage and overtime pay provisions. However, bona fide executive, administrative, and professional employees are exempted from the wage and hour provisions.

The law permits employers to enter into agreements with employees, establishing a work period of 14 consecutive days as an alternative to the usual 7-day week. If the alternative period is chosen, the employer must pay the overtime rate only for hours worked in excess of 80 hours during the 14-day period. The alternative 14-day work period does not relieve a facility from paying overtime for hours worked in excess of 8 hours in any one day even if no more than 80 hours are worked during the period.

Equal Pay Act of 1963

The Equal Pay Act (EPA) of 1963[7] is essentially an amendment to the FLSA and was passed to address wage disparities based on sex. The EPA prohibits sex discrimination in the payment of wages for women and men performing substantially equal work in the same establishment. Under the EPA, a lawsuit may be filed by the Equal Employment Opportunity Commission (EEOC) or by individuals on their own behalf. If a complainant is paid full back wages under EEOC supervision or if the EEOC takes legal action first, then a private suit may not be filed.

The EPA is applicable everywhere that the minimum wage law is applicable and is enforced by the EEOC. The EPA, simply stated, requires that employees who perform equal work receive equal pay. There are situations in which wages may be unequal so long as they are based on factors other than sex, such as in the case of a formalized seniority system or a system that objectively measures earnings by the quantity or quality of production.

The EPA of 1963 and Title VII of the Civil Rights Act of 1964 were violated when a female nurse's aide was paid less than male orderlies were paid for similar work in *Odomes v. Nucare, Inc.*[8] The nursing facility had argued that the orderlies performed heavy lifting chores and provided a form of security for the mostly all-female shift. "Uncontradicted testimony of the orderlies who testified for Mrs. Odomes was that they did little or nothing that the nurse's aides didn't do."[9] The security aspects of an orderly's job were at best his presence on the shift and his periodic checking of the facility's premises. The facility argued that the orderlies were involved in a training program that justified higher pay. The court considered this an "illusory post-event justification for unequal pay for equal work."[10]

The Supreme Court stated in *Corning Glass Works v. Brennan* that

> Congress' purpose in enacting the Equal Pay Act was to remedy what was perceived to be a serious and endemic problem of employment discrimination in private industry. The fact that the wage structure of many segments of American industry has been based on an ancient but outmoded belief that a man, because of his role in society, should be paid more than a woman even though his ideas are the same.[11]

Equal Employment Opportunity Act of 1972

Title VII of the Civil Rights Act of 1964, as amended by the Equal Employment Opportunity Act of 1972,[12] prohibits private employers and state and local governments from discriminating on the basis of age, race, color, religion, sex, or national origin. An exception to prohibited employment practices may be permitted when religion, sex, or national origin is a bona fide occupational qualification necessary to the operation of a particular business or enterprise.

The Act also exempts hospitals operated by religious corporations or societies, but only with respect to employees directly concerned with religious activities. Almost all employment in hospitals operated by religious bodies is unrelated to religious activity.

Many states have enacted protective laws with respect to the employment of women. The EEOC guidelines on sex discrimination make it clear that state laws limiting the employment of women in certain occupations are superseded by Title VII and are no defense against a charge of sex discrimination.

Racial Discrimination

In *Buckley Nursing Home v. Massachusetts Commission against Discrimination*,[13] a complaint alleging racial discrimination was filed against a nursing facility by Ms. Young, a black applicant for a nurse's aide position. Ms. Young had responded to a newspaper advertisement for a nurse's aide position. She had filed an application on March 1, 1974, and was interviewed by the acting supervisor of nursing. The applicant called to inquire about the position on several occasions and eventually was told that the position had been filled. The advertisement ran again in the newspaper, and the applicant again called in response to the advertisement. Young was told that her application was on file and that she would be called as needed. The facility hired four full-time and one part-time nurse's aides for the evening shift between March 1, 1974, and July 1, 1974.

> On the upper right hand corner of Young's application, there is a hand-written notation "no openings," even though during the relevant time periods there were openings and other persons were hired for the evening shift. That notation does not appear on any other application, and none of Buckley's witnesses could identify who wrote it or when it appeared.

> •　　•　　•　　•

> Despite testimony to the contrary, the commission found that there was discussion about Young's race and that Buckley decided not to hire her on that basis.

> •　　•　　•　　•

> The commission thus concluded that Buckley's reason for not hiring Young (that she was not the

best qualified applicant for the job) was a pretext and that she would have been hired but for her race.[14]

The commission awarded Young $6,986 plus interest for lost wages and $2,000 for emotional distress. Besides the monetary award to Young, the nursing facility had been instructed by the commission to develop a minority recruitment program. On appeal by the facility, the trial court upheld the commission's decision. On further appeal, the appeals court held that the evidence was sufficient to support a reasonable inference that the nursing facility's rejection of the applicant occurred after consideration of her race.

Age Discrimination in Employment Act of 1967

Persons 40 years of age or older are protected by the Age Discrimination in Employment Act (ADEA) of 1967,[15] as amended, which prohibits age-based employment discrimination. The purpose of this law is to promote employment of older persons on the basis of their ability without regard to their age. The law prohibits arbitrary age discrimination in hiring, discharge, pay, term, conditions, or privileges of employment. The ADEA covers private employers with 20 or more employees, state and local governments, employment agencies, and most labor unions. The Age Discrimination and Claims Assistance Amendment of 1990 extends the suit filing period for ADEA charges meeting certain criteria. There are strict time frames in which charges of age discrimination must be filed.

Occupational Safety and Health Act of 1970

Congress enacted the Occupational Safety and Health Act (OSH Act) of 1970[16] to establish administrative machinery for the development and enforcement of standards for occupational health and safety. The legislation was enacted based on congressional findings that personal injuries and illnesses arising out of work situations impose a substantial burden on and are substantial hindrances to interstate commerce in terms of lost production, wage loss, medical expenses, and disability compensation payments. Congress declared that its purpose and policy were to ensure, so far as possible, every working man and woman in the nation safe and healthful working conditions and to preserve human resources

1. by encouraging employers and employees in their efforts to reduce the number of occupational safety and health hazards at their places of employment, and stimulating employers and employees to institute new and to perfect existing programs for providing safe and healthful working conditions;

2. by providing that employers and employees have separate but dependent responsibilities and rights with respect to achieving safe and healthful working conditions;

3. by authorizing the Secretary of Labor to set mandatory occupational safety and health standards applicable to businesses affecting interstate commerce, and by creating an Occupational and Health Review Commission for carrying out adjudicatory functions under the Act;

4. by building upon advances already made through employer and employee initiative for providing safe and healthful working conditions;

5. by providing for research in the field of occupational safety and health, including the psychological factors involved, and by developing innovative methods, techniques, and approaches for dealing with occupational safety and health problems;

6. by exploring ways to discover latent diseases, establishing causal connections between diseases and work in environmental conditions, and conducting other research relating to health problems, in recognition of the fact that occupational health standards present problems often different from those involved in occupational safety;

7. by providing medical criteria that will assure, insofar as practicable, that no employee will suffer diminished health, functional capacity, or life expectancy as a result of his or her work experience;

8. by providing for training programs to increase the number and competence of personnel engaged in the field of occupational safety and health;

9. by providing for the development and promulgation of occupational safety and health standards;

10. by providing an effective enforcement program which shall include a prohibition against giving advance notice of any inspection and sanctions for any individual violating this prohibition;

11. by encouraging the States to assume the fullest responsibility for the administration and enforcement of their occupational safety and health laws by providing grants to the States to assist in identifying their needs and responsibilities in the area of occupational safety and health, to develop plans in accordance with the provisions of this Act, to improve the administration and enforcement of state occupational safety and health laws, and conducting experimental and demonstration projects in connection therewith;

12. by providing for appropriate reporting procedures with respect to occupational safety and health which procedures will help achieve the objectives of this Act and accurately describe the nature of the occupational safety and health problem;

13. by encouraging joint labor-management efforts to reduce injuries and disease arising out of employment.[17]

The employer must comply with the occupational and health standards under the Act and employees must follow the rules, regulations, and orders issued under the Act that are applicable to their actions and conduct on the job. The duties of employers and employees under the Act are as follows:

a. Each employer—
1. shall furnish to each of his employees employment and a place of employment which is free from recognized hazards that are causing or are likely to cause death or serious physical harm to his employees;
2. shall comply with occupational safety and health standards promulgated under this Act.
b. Each employee shall comply with occupational safety and health standards and all rules, regulations, and orders pursuant to this Act which are applicable to his own actions and conduct.[18]

Promulgation and Enforcement of OSH Act Standards

The Occupational Safety and Health Administration (OSHA) is responsible for administering the Act, issuing standards, and conducting on-site inspections to ensure compliance with the Act. OSHA develops and promulgates occupational safety and health standards for the workplace. It develops and issues regulations, conducts investigations and inspections to determine the status of compliance, and issues citations and proposes penalties for noncompliance. Inspections are conducted without advance notice.

Employers are responsible for becoming familiar with those standards applicable to their businesses and for ensuring that employees have and use personal protective equipment when required for safety. Employees must comply with all rules and regulations that are applicable to their work environment. Where OSHA has not promulgated specific standards, the employer is responsible for following the Act's general duty clause. The general duty clause states that each employer must furnish a place of employment that is free from recognized hazards that are causing or likely to cause death or serious physical harm.

OSHA inspectors have called for stiffer penalties for health and safety violations to deter violations. "OSHA inspectors surveyed by Congress' General Accounting Office said further criminal enforcement authority was needed to enforce this nation's workplace health and safety standards."[19]

Recordkeeping

Employers of 11 or more employees are required to maintain records of occupational injuries and illnesses. The purpose of maintaining records is to permit the Bureau of Labor Statistics to help define high-hazard industries and to inform employees of the status of their employer's record.

Education

Employers are responsible for keeping employees informed about OSHA and about the various safety and health matters with which they are involved. OSHA requires that employers post certain material at a prominent location in the workplace (e.g., Job Safety and Health Protection workplace poster informing employees of their rights and responsibilities under the Act).

Infectious Body Fluids

OSHA issued standards on December 2, 1991, that are to be followed by employers to protect employees from bloodborne infections. Universal precautions are mandatory and employees who are likely to be exposed to body fluids must be provided with protective clothing (e.g., masks, gowns, and gloves). In addition, postexposure testing must be available to employees who have been exposed to body fluids.

Employee Complaints

Employees should inform their supervisors if they suspect or detect a dangerous situation in the workplace. Employers are expected to address reported hazards in the workplace. Employees or their representatives have the right to file complaints with an OSHA office and request a survey when they believe that conditions in the workplace are unsafe or unhealthy. If a violation of the Act is found at the time of a survey, the employer may receive a citation stating a time frame within which the violation must be corrected.

State Regulation

The states have statutes charging employers with the duty to furnish employees with a safe working environment. The city and county in which a health care facility is located also may prescribe rules regarding the health and safety of employees. Many communities have enacted sanitary and health codes that require certain standards.

Legal Liability

From a liability point of view, an employer can be held legally liable for damages suffered by employees through exposure to dangerous conditions that are in violation of OSHA standards. Proof of an employee's exposure to noncompliant conditions is generally necessary to find an employer liable.

Rehabilitation Act of 1973

The essential purpose of the Rehabilitation Act of 1973[20] is to afford protection to handicapped employees. The law basically is administered by the Department of Health and Human Services (HHS), which derives its jurisdiction from the fact that health care organizations participate in such federal programs as Medicare, Medicaid, and Hill-Burton. The law therefore is applied to both public and private organizations, because both participate in these programs.

Section 503 of the Act applies to government contractors whose contracts exceed $2,500 in value. Section 504, which applies to employers who are recipients of federal financial assistance, states, "[n]o . . . qualified handicapped individual in the United States . . . shall solely by reason of his handicap, be excluded from participation in, be denied the benefits of, or be subjected to discrimination under any program as actively receiving federal financial assistance." Section 504 applies to virtually every area of personnel administration, including recruitment, advertising, processing of applications, promotions, rates of pay, fringe benefits, and job assignments.

Since July 1977, all institutions receiving federal financial assistance from HHS have been required to file assurances of compliance forms. Each employer must designate an individual to coordinate compliance efforts. A grievance procedure should be in place to address employee complaints alleging violation of the regulation. All employment decisions must be made without regard to physical or mental handicaps that are not disqualifying (e.g., an employer is not obligated to employ a person with a highly contagious disease that can be easily transmitted to others).

Employers receiving federal funds are required to perform a self-evaluation as to their compliance with Section 504 of the Rehabilitation Act of 1973. If discriminatory practices are identified through the self-evaluation process, remedial steps are to be taken to eliminate the effects of any discrimination. Records of the evaluation are to be maintained on file for at least three years after the review for public inspection.[21]

Limitations on Number of Bargaining Units: 1989

A major area of concern for health care institutions is the number of bargaining units allowed in any one institution. Rules and regulations issued on April 21, 1989, by the NLRB allow up to eight collective bargaining units in health care organizations as opposed to the three normally allowed before the regulations. The American Hospital Association brought an action to enjoin the NLRB from enforcing the newly promulgated regulation recognizing up to eight bargaining units in *American Hospital Association v. NLRB.*[22] A federal district court enjoined enforcement of the rule. The NLRB and intervening unions appealed. The Seventh Circuit held that the rule was not arbitrary and was within the authority of the NLRB. No rule is necessary to confer the rights already conferred by statute entitling guards and professional employees to form separate bargaining units.

In making unit determinations, the NLRB is required to strike a balance among the competing interests of unions, employees (whose interests are not always identical with those of unions), employers, and the broader public. The statute can be read to suggest that the tilt should be in favor of unions and toward relatively many, rather than relatively few, units.

This balancing act is not spelled out in the statute, thus requiring an NLRB decision. The decision is particularly difficult and delicate in the health care industry because the work force of a hospital, nursing home, or rehabilitation center tends to be small and heterogeneous.

On appeal, the U.S. Supreme Court, on April 23, 1991, by unanimous decision, upheld an NLRB rule allowing hospital workers to form up to eight separate bargaining units, including those for

- physicians
- registered nurses
- other professionals
- technical employees
- clerical employees
- skilled maintenance employees
- other nonprofessional employees
- security guards[23]

Management must strive to maintain open lines of communications with employees and strive to improve working conditions. An honest and open relationship with employees will go a long way toward maintaining a union-free environment.

Americans with Disabilities Act of 1990

Findings of the U.S. Congress demonstrate that some 43 million Americans have one or more physical or mental disabilities. The number of disabled Americans is increasing as the population grows older. Society has tended to isolate and segregate individuals with disabilities. Despite some improvements, discrimination against individuals with disabilities continues to be a serious and pervasive social problem. Discrimination continues in such crucial areas as employment, housing, public accommodations, education, transportation, and health services. Unlike individuals who have experienced discrimination on the basis of race, color, sex, national origin, religion, or age, those who have been disabled have had no legal recourse to redress such discrimination. Individuals with disabilities continually encounter different forms of discrimination, including outright intentional exclusion; the discriminatory effects of architectural, transportation, and communication barriers; the failure to make modifications to existing organizations and practices; exclusionary qualification standards and criteria; segregation; and relegation to lesser services, programs, activities, benefits, jobs, or other opportunities.

Census data, national polls, and other studies have documented that people with disabilities, as a group, occupy an inferior status in society. The nation's proper goals regarding individuals with disabilities are to ensure equality of opportunity, full participation, independent living, and economic self-sufficiency for such individuals.

As a result of the continuing discrimination against the disabled, Congress enacted Title 1 of the Americans with Disabilities Act (ADA) of 1990.[24] The Act prohibits job discrimination in hiring, promotion, or other provisions of employment against qualified individuals with disabilities by private employers, state and local governments, employment agencies, and labor unions. On July 26, 1991, the EEOC issued final regulations implementing Title 1 of the ADA. It is the purpose of the ADA to

- Provide a clear and comprehensive national mandate for the elimination of discrimination against individuals with disabilities.
- Provide clear, strong, consistent, enforceable standards addressing discrimination against individuals with disabilities.
- Ensure that the federal government plays a central role in enforcing the standards established in the Act on behalf of individuals with disabilities.
- Invoke the sweep of congressional authority, including the power to enforce the Fourteenth Amendment and to regulate commerce to address the main areas of discrimination faced day to day by people with disabilities.[25]

The general rule of discrimination under Title I of the Act provides that "no covered entity shall discriminate against a qualified individual with a disability because of the disability of such individual in regard to job application procedures, the hiring, advancement, or discharge of employees, employee compensation, job training, and other terms, conditions, and privileges of employment."[26]

A defense to a charge of discrimination under the Act would require a showing that the screening out of a specific disability was job-related and consistent with business necessity and that performance cannot be accomplished by "reasonable" accommodation.

Tips for Employers

- Train management personnel as to the requirements of the ADA (e.g., it is unlawful to ask an applicant whether he or she is disabled; however, it is okay to ask a prospective employee if he or she is able to perform job-related functions).

- Review and revise the employment application and job descriptions, as necessary, to bring them into compliance with ADA requirements.
- Bring the physical environment into compliance with ADA requirements.
- Post a notice on the employee bulletin board(s) describing the purposes of the ADA.

STATE LAWS

The federal labor enactments serve as a pattern for many state labor laws that comprise the second labor regulation system touching health care organizations. State labor acts vary from state to state. Therefore, it is important that each institution familiarize itself not only with federal regulations but also with state regulations affecting labor relations within the institution.

State Labor-Management Relations Act

Because the NLRA excludes from coverage health care organizations operated by the state or its political subdivisions, regulation of labor-management relations in these organizations is left to state law. Unless the constitution in such a state guarantees the right of employees to organize and imposes the duty of collective bargaining on the employer, health care organizations do not have to bargain collectively with their employees. However, in states that do have labor relations acts, the obligation of an organization to bargain collectively with its employees is determined by the applicable statute.

State laws vary considerably in their coverage, and often employees of state and local governmental organizations are covered by separate public employee legislation. Some of these statutes cover both state and local employees, whereas others cover only state or only local employees.

Some of the states that have labor relations acts granting employees the right to organize, join unions, and bargain collectively have specifically prohibited strikes and lockouts and have provided for compulsory arbitration whenever a collective bargaining contract cannot otherwise be executed amicably. Anti-injunction statutes would not forbid injunctions to restrain violations of these statutory provisions.

The doctrine of federal preemption, as applied to labor relations, displaces the states' jurisdiction to regulate an activity that is arguably an unfair labor practice within the meaning of the NLRA. Nonetheless, the U.S. Supreme Court has ruled that states can still regulate labor relations activity that also falls within the jurisdiction of the NLRB when deeply rooted local feelings and responsibility are affected.

Union Security Contracts and Right-To-Work Laws

Labor organizations frequently seek to enter union security contracts with employers. Such contracts are of two types: (1) the *closed shop* contract, which provides that only members of a particular union may be hired, and (2) the "*union shop*" contract, which makes continued employment dependent on membership in the union, although the employee need not have been a union member when applying for the job.

More than one-third of all the states have made such contracts unlawful. Statutes forbidding such agreements generally are called *right-to-work* laws on the theory that they protect everyone's right to work even if a person refuses to join a union. Several other state statutes or decisions purport to restrict union security contracts or specify procedures to be completed before such agreements may be made.

Wage and Hour Laws

When state minimum wage standards are higher than federal standards, the state's standards are applicable.

Child Labor Acts

Many states prohibit the employment of minors younger than a specified age and restrict the employment of other minors. Child labor legislation commonly requires that working papers be secured before a child may be hired, forbids the employment of minors at night, and prohibits minors from operating certain types of dangerous machinery.

This kind of legislation rarely exempts charitable institutions, although some exceptions may be made with respect to the hours when student nurses may work.

Workers' Compensation

Workers' compensation is a program by which an employee can receive certain wage benefits because of work-related injuries. An employee who is injured while performing job-related duties is generally eligible for workers' compensation. Workers' compensation programs are administered by the states.

State legislatures have recognized that it is difficult and expensive for employees to recover from their employers and therefore have enacted workers' compensation laws. Employers are required to provide workers' compensation as a benefit. Workers' compensation laws give the employee a legal way to receive compensation for injuries on the job. The acts do not require the employee to prove that the injury was the result of the employer's negligence. Workers' compensation laws are based on the employer–employee relationship and not on the theory of negligence.

The scope of workers' compensation varies widely. Some states limit an employee's compensation to the amount recoverable by the workers' compensation law, and further lawsuits against the employer are barred. Other states permit employees to choose whether to accept the compensation provided by law or to institute a lawsuit against the employer. Some acts go farther and provide a system of insurance that may be under the supervision of state or private insurers.

Physical Injury

The courts have been somewhat liberal in allowing workers' compensation benefits to be paid to employees injured while on duty, even when challenged by the employer under seemingly justifiable circumstances. The employee, for example, in *Fondulac Nursing Home v. Industrial Commission*[27] was found to be entitled to workers' compensation despite orders that she was not to lift patients because of a back injury. When a patient was being transferred from her wheelchair to her bed and began to fall, the nurse attempted to prevent the fall, injuring herself. The nurse acted within her scope of employment by attempting to prevent the fall to her own detriment and her employer's best interests by protecting the patient from injury.

Job Stress

Workers' compensation has been awarded for depression related to job stress. In *Elwood v. SAIF*,[28] a registered nurse filed a workers' compensation claim for an occupational disease based on depression. The referee and the workers' compensation board affirmed the insurer's denial of the claim and the claimant sought judicial review. The questions that needed to be answered to determine job stress were

- What were the "real" events and conditions of plaintiff's employment?
- Were those real events and conditions capable of producing stress when viewed objectively, even though an average worker might not have responded adversely to them?
- Did the plaintiff suffer a mental disorder?
- Were the real stressful events and conditions the major contributing cause of plaintiff's mental disorder?

The record established that many events and conditions of her employment, including her termination, were real and capable of producing stress when viewed objectively. The claimant's treating physician advised her that she was suffering from anxiety, depression, and stress and advised her to seek a psychiatric evaluation. The court held that the claimant established that her condition was compensable.

Influenza Vaccination

A hospital employee's reaction to an influenza vaccination given by an emergency department employee while he or she is on duty will most likely be a compensable injury under workers' compensation. A housekeeping employee in *Monette v. Manatee Memorial Hospital*[29] suffered a serious reaction to the influenza vaccination administered to her while on duty and was entitled to workers' compensation.

LABOR RIGHTS

Rights and responsibilities run concurrently. Employee rights include

- the right to organize and bargain collectively
- the right to solicit and distribute union information during nonworking hours (i.e., mealtimes and coffee breaks)
- the right to picket (Picketing is the act of patrolling, by one or more persons, of a place related to a labor dispute. It varies in purpose and form. It may be conducted by employees or nonemployees and, like strikes, some picketing may be legislatively or judicially disapproved and subject to regulation.)
- the right to strike (A strike may be defined as the collective quitting of work by employees as a means of inducing the employer to assent to employee demands. Employees possess the right to strike, although this right is not absolute and is subject to limited exercise. The 1974 amendments to the NLRA have added requirements with respect to strikes and picketing in an attempt to reduce the interruption of health care services. The NLRB is urged to give top priority to settling labor-management disputes resulting in the loss of health care personnel or medical services.)

Employees granted the above rights have the concomitant responsibility to perform their work duties properly. A nursing home housekeeper, for example, was terminated properly after repeated oral and written reprimands concerning her improper cleaning of rooms in *Ford v. Patin*.[30] Her substandard performance, despite repeated warnings, evidenced willful and wanton disregard of her employer's interest and constituted misconduct within purview of Section 23:1601(2) of the Louisiana Revised Statutes Annotated.

MANAGEMENT RIGHTS

As with labor, management also has certain rights and responsibilities. Specific management rights are reviewed here.

Right To Receive Strike Notice

Management has a right to a 10-day advance notice of a bargaining unit's intent to strike.

Right To Hire Replacement Workers

Although management may not discharge employees in retaliation for union activity, concomitant with the employees' right to strike is management's right to hire replacement workers in the event of a strike. The nursing home in *Charlesgate Nursing Center v. State of Rhode Island*[31] brought an action against the state, seeking a determination that a state statute prohibiting strike-affected employers from using the services of a third party to recruit replacement workers during a strike was unconstitutional. Employees of the nursing home went on strike June 2, 1988, and Charlesgate hired temporary replacement workers to provide continued services for its patients. The temporary employees were hired through employment agencies. The actions of Charlesgate and the agencies had violated Sections 28–10–10 and 28–10–12 of the General Laws of Rhode Island (1956) (1986 Re-enactment), which read:

> 28–10–10. Recruitment prohibited—It shall be unlawful for any person, partnership, agency, firm or corporation, or officer or agent thereof, to knowingly recruit, procure, supply or refer any person who offers him or herself for employment in the place of an employee involved in a labor strike or lockout in which such person, partnership, agency, firm, or corporation is not directly interested.
>
> 28–10–12. Agency for procurement—It shall be unlawful for any person, partnership, firm or corporation, or officer or agent thereof, involved in a labor strike or lockout to contract or arrange with any other person, partnership, agency, firm or corporation to recruit, procure, supply, or refer persons who offer themselves for employment in the place of employees involved in a labor strike or lockout for employment in place of employees involved in such labor strike or lockout.

Citing these statutes, the labor unions involved in the strike notified nursing pools throughout the state that it was unlawful to provide Charlesgate with replacement workers. At the same time, the unions urged the City of Providence and the Rhode Island Attorney General to prosecute Charlesgate, at which time Charlesgate filed its suit claiming that the Rhode Island statutes were unconstitutional.

Although the strike was settled before any actions by the city and the Attorney General, the case was not required to be dismissed. The federal district court held that the statute was unconstitutional because it prohibited activity that Congress had intended to leave open to strike-affected employers as a peaceful weapon of economic self-help.

Right To Restrict Union Activity to Prescribed Areas

Management has the right to reasonably restrict union organizers to certain locations in the health care facility and to certain time periods to avoid interference with facility operations.

Right To Prohibit Union Activity during Working Hours

Management has the right to prohibit union activities during employee working hours.

Right To Prohibit Supervisors from Participating in Union Activity

Management has the right to prohibit supervisors from engaging in union organizational activity. A nursing supervisor brought a lawsuit for wrongful discharge against a nursing facility and its director of nursing. She was dismissed for her activities in attempting to form an organization to represent the nurses. The circuit court granted summary judgment for the defendants and the appeals court affirmed. On review, the Wisconsin Supreme Court held in *Arena v. Lincoln Lutheran of Racine*[32] that after the NLRB had determined that the nurse in this case was a "supervisor" rather than an "employee" within the meaning of the NLRA, federal labor law preempted the state court from determining whether the nurse's discharge for engaging in concerted activities was wrongful under Wisconsin law. Employees who are supervisors as defined in the NLRA are treated differently than professional employees. The definition of the term supervisor found in Section 2(11) provides: "The term 'supervisor' means any individual having authority, in the interest of the employer, to hire, transfer, suspend, lay off, recall, promote, discharge, assign, reward, or discipline other employees, or responsibly to direct them, or to adjust their grievances, or effectively to recommend such action, if in connection with the foregoing the exercise of such authority is not merely a routine or clerical nature, but requires the use of independent judgment."

The petitioner alleged in her complaint that she had become concerned with certain policies that included nurses being treated in an arbitrary manner. The petitioner had held a meeting outside of Racine with the nurses to discuss their concerns and the possibility of forming an association to represent the collective interests of the nurses. The NLRA did not protect the nursing supervisor because she was a supervisor rather than an employee. Congress excluded supervisors from protection afforded rank-and-file employees engaged in concerted activity for their mutual benefit to assure management of the undivided loyalty of its supervisory personnel by making sure that no employer would have to retain as its agent one who is obligated to a union.

Seven registered nurses at a small 72-bed nursing home were found not to function as supervisors and were, therefore, eligible for a separate bargaining unit in *NLRB v. Res-Care, Inc.*[33] Although the nurses had the authority to assign nurses' aides, their exercise of this authority was merely routine and did not require independent judgment. The nurses were not shown to have any authority to hire, discipline, and/or fire any of the nursing aides. Such authority, if present, would have indicated some sort of supervisory status. Allowing seven nurses to form their own collective bargaining unit rather than merging them into a unit consisting of nurses' aides and other workers was not found to be improper nor was it an undue proliferation of bargaining units at the facility.

Certification of 17 registered nurses as an employee bargaining unit in *NLRB v. American Medical Services*[34] was shown to be improper. The nursing home had contended that a very low ratio of supervisors to employees would occur if the NLRB's decision was upheld. Substantial evidence had been presented to the court showing that the nurses exercised substantial supervisory powers, including the authority to issue work assignments and discipline employees.

> Taft-Hartley applied some brakes, so that the balance of power between companies and unions would not shift wholly to the union side. The exclusion of supervisors is one of the brakes. If supervisors were free to join or form unions and enjoy the broad protection of the Act for concerted activity, see Sec. 7, 29 U.S.C. Sec. 157, the impact of a strike would be greatly amplified because the company would not be able to use its supervisory personnel to replace strikers. More important, the company with or without a strike could lose control of its work force to the unions, since the very people in the company who controlled hiring, discipline, assignments, and other dimensions of the employment relationship might be subject to control by the same union as the employees they were supposed to be controlling on the employer's behalf.[35]

EQUAL EMPLOYMENT OPPORTUNITY— AFFIRMATIVE ACTION PLAN

Health care organizations are required to comply with all applicable HHS regulations "including but not limited to those pertaining to nondiscrimination on the basis of race, color, or national origin (45 C.F.R. part 80), nondiscrimination on the basis of handicap (45 C.F.R. part 84), nondiscrimination on the basis of age (45 C.F.R. part 91), protection of human subjects of research (45 C.F.R. part 46), and fraud and abuse (42 C.F.R. part 455). Although these regulations are not in themselves considered requirements under this part, their violation may result in the termination or suspension of or the refusal to grant or continue payment with federal funds."[36] To comply with the spirit of these regulations and Executive Order 11246, health care organizations should have an equal employment opportunity or affirmative action plan in place.

An affirmative action program includes such things as the collection and analysis of data on the race and sex of all applicants for employment and a statement in the personnel policy and procedure manuals and employee handbooks that would read, for example, "Health Care Facility, Inc., is an equal opportunity/affirmative action employer and does not discriminate on the basis of race, color, religion, sex, national origin, age, handicap, or veteran status."

PATIENT RIGHTS DURING LABOR DISPUTES

Just as labor and management have different rights and responsibilities, the same is true for patients. For example, patients' rights take precedence over employee and management rights when a patient's right to privacy or well-being is in jeopardy because of labor disputes.

INJUNCTIONS

An *injunction* is an order by a court directing that a certain act be performed or not performed. Persons who fail to comply with court orders are said to be in "contempt of court." The earliest use of injunctions in labor relations was by employers to stop strikes or picketing by employees. Today, the general rule limits the availability of injunctive relief to halt work stoppages. The federal government and many states have enacted anti-injunction acts. These acts restrict the power of the courts to limit injunctions in labor disputes by setting strictly defined standards that must be met before injunctions can be granted to restrain activities such as strikes and picketing.

ADMINISTERING A COLLECTIVE BARGAINING AGREEMENT

Once a collective bargaining agreement has been negotiated "in good faith," it should be administered with care and good faith as well. The first-line supervisors are responsible for administering the agreement at the grass roots level. They should familiarize themselves with the provisions of the

agreement. Formal orientation programs can be provided by an organization's human resources department. Special emphasis should be placed on the use of corrective discipline, as provided under the contract, and on how to respond to grievances. The organization's management, through its human relations department, maintains the ultimate responsibility in the facility for the fair and effective administration of its union contract(s).

Maintaining propitious records of all grievances, grievance meetings, and grievance resolutions is the responsibility of supervisors and management. Regardless of whether a grievance is meritorious and settled by management or whether it is spurious and therefore denied, clear and complete records should be maintained. An ability to document resolutions of particular problems, as well as management's approach to grievances, is especially important if arbitration is required to settle a grievance.

Arbitration procedures are set in motion when the union files a demand for arbitration either with the employer or with the arbitration agency named in the contract. The arbitration hearing is a relatively informal proceeding at which labor and management frequently choose to be represented by counsel. The arbitrator's decision is binding on both parties.

The arbitrator's decision can be upset by showing any of the following:

- The arbitrator has clearly exceeded his or her authority under the collective bargaining agreement.
- The decision is the product of fraud or duress.
- The arbitrator has been guilty of impropriety.
- The award violates the law or requires a violation of the law.

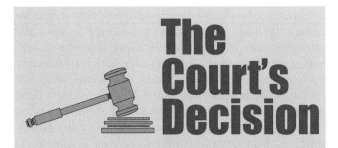

The U.S. Court of Appeals for the Seventh Circuit found that the employer's interrogation of nursing facility employees about a union meeting constituted an unfair labor practice. On the record as a whole, substantial evidence supported the board's conclusions that the questioning of Welton and Hopkins amounted to unlawful interrogation.

CHAPTER REVIEW

1. The National Labor Relations Act (NLRA) of 1935 is the most significant federal legislation concerning labor relations. It defines unfair labor practices and provides for hearings on complaints regarding such practices.

2. The National Labor Relations Board (NLRB) is responsible for administering and enforcing the NLRA. The Board reviews claims submitted by employers or employees, determines whether unfair labor practices have taken place, and suggests a remedy.

3. The NLRA includes procedures through which employees can choose a union as a collective bargaining representative to negotiate employment and contract concerns with their employer. However, an employer does not necessarily have to follow the NLRA procedure when dealing with the union.

4. The Norris-LaGuardia Act was enacted by Congress to limit the power of the federal courts to issue injunctions in cases that involve or have grown out of labor disputes. It is aimed specifically at reducing the number of injunctions granted to restrain strikes and picketing. In 1974, an amendment designating procedures that limit strikes in health care organizations was added to the NLRA. Among other provisions, this amendment requires that 10 days' notice of a strike be given. The allows the NLRB to determine the legality of the strike and gives the organization time to put in place provisions that will protect the level of patient care.

5. The Fair Labor Standards Act (FLSA) established minimum wages and maximum hours of employment. The Equal Pay Act, essentially an amendment to the FLSA, prohibits sex discrimination in the payment of wages. Further, the Equal Employment Opportunity Act of 1972 prohibits private employers, as well as state and local governments, from discriminating based on age, race, color, religion, sex, or national origin. An act that further addresses age discrimination is the Age Discrimination in Employment Act of 1967.

6. The Occupational Safety and Health Act of 1970 was enacted by Congress to ensure, to the extent to which such legislation can, that every working man and woman in the country have safe and healthful working conditions and to preserve human resources. Employers are required to follow the Act's general duty clause, which states that all employers must provide a place of employment that is without recognized hazards that cause or are likely to cause death or serious physical harm. For health care organizations, the city and county in which a facility is located may prescribe additional rules regarding the health and safety of employees.

7. The Rehabilitation Act of 1973 provides protection from discrimination to handicapped employees and is applied to both public and private organizations. The Americans with Disabilities Act of 1990 is legislation that further protects the rights of the disabled. The Act prohibits job discrimination in hiring, promotion, and other requirements of employment against qualified individuals with disabilities.

8. There are two kinds of union security contracts:
   1. *Closed shop contracts* provide that only members of a particular union may be hired.
   2. *Union shop contracts* hold that continued employment is dependent on membership in the union.
   More than one-third of states hold that such contracts are unlawful.

9. *Workers' compensation* is a reimbursement program for employees with work-related injuries. These programs are administered on a state-by-state basis.

10. Management has certain important, specific rights, including the right to hire replacement workers in the event of a strike and the right to prohibit supervisors from participating in organized union activity.

11. Most health care organizations have an equal employment opportunity or affirmative action plan. Affirmative action programs include the collection and analysis of data on the race and sex of all applicants for employment and a nondiscrimination statement in personal policy and procedure manuals and employee handbooks.

12. An *injunction* is an order by a court that instructs that a certain act be performed or not performed. Today, the rule limits the availability of injunctive relief to halt work stoppages. *Anti-injunction acts* restrict the courts' power to limit injunctions in labor disputes.

13. Arbitration procedures begin when a union files a demand for arbitration either with the employer or with the arbitration agency named in the contract. The decision of the arbitrator is binding on both parties.

REVIEW QUESTIONS

1. Provide a general overview of the NLRA.
2. Use the hospital as a setting and give two examples of what would violate the NLRA.

3. How do patients' rights come into play during a strike by nurses?
4. What is the purpose of OSHA?
5. Why was the Norris-LaGuardia Act enacted by Congress?
6. Where is the Equal Pay Act applicable? What is the purpose of the EPA?

NOTES

1. NLRB v. Shelby Mem'l Hosp. Ass'n, 1 F.3d 550 (7th Cir. 1993).

2. 29 U.S.C. § 151.

3. NLRA § 2(14) (1974).

4. Norris-LaGuardia Act 29 U.S.C. ch. 6 (1932)

5. Labor-Management Reporting and Disclosure Act of 1959, Pub. L. No. 86–257 (29 U.S.C. ch. 11)

6. Fair Labor Standards Act of 1938, 29 U.S.C. ch. 8.

7. Equal Pay Act of 1963, 29 U.S.C. ch. 8.

8. 653 F.2d 246 (6th Cir. 1981).

9. *Id.* at 250.

10. *Id.* at 247.

11. 417 U.S. 188, 195 (1974).

12. Equal Employment Opportunity Act of 1972, 42 U.S.C. § 2000e *et seq.*

13. 478 N.E.2d 1292 (Mass. App. Ct. 1985).

14. *Id.* at 1295.

15. Age Discrimination in Employment Act of 1967, 29 U.S.C. ch. 14.

16. Occupational Safety and Health Act of 1970, 29 U.S.C. § 651.

17. PUB. L. NO. 91–596, § 2, 84 Stat. 1590 (Dec. 29, 1970); *see also* 29 U.S.C.A. § 651 (1990).

18. *Id.* at § 5, 84 Stat. 1593; *Id.* at § 654.

19. *OSHA's Inspectors Call for Stiffer Penalties for Violations*, NATION'S HEALTH, Jan. 1991, at 7.

20. Rehabilitation Act of 1973, 29 U.S.C. ch. 14.

21. 45 C.F.R. § 4.6[c].

22. 899 F.2d 651 (7th Cir. 1990).

23. *Supreme Court Upholds NLRB Bargaining-Unit Rule*, A.H.A. NEWS, Apr. 29, 1991, at 1.

24. Americans with Disabilities Act of 1990, PUB. L. NO. 101–336, 104 Stat. 327 (July 26, 1990).

25. *Id.* at 329.

26. *Id.* at 331–332.

27. 460 N.E.2d 751 (Ill. 1984).

28. 676 P.2d 922 (Or. Ct. App. 1984).

29. 579 So.2d 195 (Fla. Dist. Ct. App. 1991).

30. 534 So.2d 1003 (La. Ct. App. 1988).

31. 723 F. Supp. 859 (D.R.I. 1989).

32. 437 N.W.2d 538 (Wis. 1989).

33. 705 F.2d 1461 (7th Cir. 1983).

34. *NLRB v. American Medical Services, Inc.*, 705 F.2d 1472, 1474–75 (7th Cir.1983).

35. NLRB v. Res-Care, Inc., 705 F.2d 1461, 1465 (7th Cir.1983).

36. 42 C.F.R. § 483.75 (1989).

CHAPTER 19

Employment, Discipline, and Discharge

NURSE DISCHARGED FOR SUGGESTING PATIENT CHANGE PHYSICIANS

The patient began losing weight and having hallucinations. A nurse documented the patient's difficulties and attempted on several occasions to call the patient's physician. The physician failed to return her calls.

Because of the patient's deteriorating condition, the family contacted the nurse. After the nurse advised the patient's family as to her concerns, a member of the patient's family asked her what they should do. The nurse advised that she would reconsider their choice of physicians. The defendant-nursing facility terminated the nurse because she had advised the patient's family to consider changing physicians.

The nurse brought a lawsuit for wrongful discharge in violation of public policy. The complaint was dismissed by a trial court and an appeal was taken. The public policy that the plaintiff claimed was violated was based on language in the Nursing Practice Act (NPA) of North Carolina.

The appellate court summarized the nurse's public policy exception of the at-will doctrine as follows: the NPA and regulations of the Board of Nursing describe the practice of nursing as assessing a patient's health, which entails a responsibility to communicate, counsel, and provide accurate guidance to clients and their families; the nurse's comments that resulted in her termination were proffered in fulfillment of the foregoing responsibilities; and termination of the nurse for fulfilling her responsibilities as a practicing nurse in North Carolina violated state public policy and is a factual question for jury determination.

The defendant asserted that the NPA and the wording of the nursing board regulations relied on by the nurse did not express a policy prohibiting the discharge and that, in any event, the nurse had no duty to advise the patient's family. The court gave considerable attention to language in the NPA and the regulations that recognized nursing to include teaching and counseling about a patient's health care and of providing information to patients and their families, including making referrals to appropriate resources.[1]

What is your verdict?

INTRODUCTION

Man never fastened one end of a chain around the neck of his brother that God did not fasten the other end round the neck of the oppressor.

Lamartine

Fairly balancing the rights of the employee and the needs of the organization is an extremely complex objective. This chapter provides some direction in this balancing act.

For the health care worker, an unexpected termination may mean a significant setback in career progression, financial hardship, and loss of self-esteem. For the organization and its community, a termination means a lack of stability in the management structure and possible disruption and realignment of services provided. A growing consensus is that high turnover rates are unhealthy and provide a disservice to an industry already plagued with cost constraints and other pressures.

Wrongful discharge claims are difficult, time-consuming, and expensive lawsuits to defend. Employers who experience favorable court decisions in wrongful discharge claims often have unfavorable repercussions because of bad press and the negative effects a discharge has on employee morale.

EMPLOYMENT AT WILL

An at will prerogative without limits could be suffered only in an anarchy, and there not for long, it certainly cannot be suffered in a society such as ours without weakening the bond of counter balancing rights and obligations that holds such societies together.

Sides v. Duke Hospital[2]

The common-law "employment-at-will" doctrine provides that employment is at the will of either the employer or the employee and that employment may be terminated by the employer or the employee at any time for any or no reason, unless there is a contract in place that specifies the terms and duration of employment. Historically, termination of employees for any reason was widely accepted. However, contemporary thinking does not support this concept.

In recent years the rule that employment for an indefinite term is terminable by the employer whenever and for whatever cause he chooses without incurring liability has been the subject of considerable scholarly debate, and judicial and legislative modification. Consequently, there has been a growing trend toward a restricted application of the at-will employment rule whereby the right of an employer to discharge an at-will employee

without cause is limited by either public policy considerations or an implied covenant of good faith and fair dealing.[3]

In *Sides v. Duke Hospital*, the North Carolina Court of Appeals found it to be an

obvious and indisputable fact that in a civilized state where reciprocal legal rights and duties abound, the words "at will" can never mean "without limit or qualification," as so much of the discussion and the briefs of the defendants imply; for in such a state the rights of each person are necessarily and inherently limited by the rights of others and the interests of the public. An at will prerogative without limits could be suffered only in an anarchy, and there not for long, it certainly cannot be suffered in a society such as ours without weakening the bond of counter balancing rights and obligations that holds such societies together.

•   •   •   •

If we are to have law, those who so act against the public interest must be held accountable for the harm inflicted thereby; to accord them civil immunity would incongruously reward their lawlessness at the unjust expense of their innocent victims.[4]

The concept of the employment-at-will doctrine is embroiled in a combination of legislative enactments and judicial decisions. Some states have a tendency to be more employer-oriented, such as New York, whereas others, such as California, emerge as being much more forward thinking and in harmony with the constitutional rights of the employee.

The employment at will common law doctrine is not truly applicable in today's society and many courts have recognized this fact. In the last century, the common law developed in a laissez-faire climate that encouraged industrial growth and improved the right of an employer to control his own business, including the right to fire without cause an employee at will. . . . The twentieth century has witnessed significant changes in socioeconomic values that have led to reassessment of the common law rule. Businesses have evolved from small and medium size firms to gigantic corporations in which ownership is separate from management. Formerly there was a clear delineation between employers, who frequently were owners of their own businesses, and employees. The employer in the old sense has been replaced by a superior in the corporate hierarchy who is himself an employee.[5]

As discussed below, exceptions to the employment-at-will doctrine involve contractual relationships, public policy issues, defamation, retaliatory discharge, and fairness. Besides public policy issues in general, it would seem that the doctrine has little applicability in modern society.

PUBLIC POLICY ISSUES

The public policy exception to the employment-at-will doctrine provides that employees may not be terminated for reasons that are contrary to public policy. Public policy originates with legislative enactments that prohibit, for example, the discharge of employees on the basis of handicap, age, race, color, religion, sex, national origin, pregnancy, filing of safety violation complaints with various agencies (e.g., the Occupational Safety and Health Administration), or union membership. Any attempt to limit, segregate, or classify employees in any way that would tend to deprive any individual of employment opportunities on these bases is contrary to public policy.

Public policy also can arise as a result of judicial decisions that address those issues not covered by statutes, rules, and regulations. "[I]t can be said that public policy concerns what is right and just and what affects the citizens of the state collectively. It is to be found in the state's constitution and statutes and, when they are silent, in its judicial decisions."[6]

> Public policy favors the exposure of crime, and the cooperation of citizens possessing knowledge thereof is essential to effective implementation of that policy. Persons acting in good faith who have probable cause to believe crimes have been committed should not be deterred from reporting them by the fear of unfounded suits by those accused.[7]

In those instances in which state and federal laws are silent, not all courts concur with the use of judicial decisions as a means for determining public policy. A California court has determined that a public policy exception to the at-will employment doctrine must be based on constitutional or statutory provisions rather than judicial policy making.[8]

Age

According to the U.S. Supreme Court in *Texas Department of Community Affairs v. Burdine*, a *prima facie* case of age discrimination requires that evidence sufficient to support a finding for the complainant must establish all of the following:

- The complainant is in a protected age group.
- The complainant is qualified for his or her job.

- The complainant was discharged.
- The discharge occurred in circumstances that give rise to the inference of age discrimination.[9]

A *prima facie* case of age discrimination was not established in *Pena v. Brattleboro Retreat*,[10] in which a 63-year-old female administrator of a psychiatric nursing facility alleged that she was dismissed as administrator so that a younger administrator could take over her position. The evidence established that the younger assistant administrator, a woman in her early 30s, had been hired at the suggestion of the administrator so that she could eventually take over the position of administrator on the administrator's retirement. A federal district court found in favor of the administrator on jury verdict, and an appeal was taken. The Second Circuit held that the former administrator had failed to prove either explicit or constructive discharge. A *constructive discharge* occurs when the employer, rather than acting directly, deliberately makes an employee's working conditions so intolerable that the employee is forced into an involuntary resignation.

> The Retreat's treatment of Mrs. Pena cannot be described as intolerable. Mrs. Pena was simply asked to train her successor for a year and a half, rather than the six months she herself envisioned. This was no more than a change in job responsibilities based on a reasonable business decision on the part of the Retreat. Mrs. Pena was faced with no loss of pay or change in title.[11]

The Retreat claimed that Mrs. Pena resigned on her own because of her inability to adjust to the Retreat's business decisions. The Age Discrimination in Employment Act does not protect employees who resign in protest against business decisions.

Sex

In *Jones v. Hinds General Hospital*,[12] a *prima facie* case of sex discrimination was established by evidence showing that a hospital laid off female nursing assistants while retaining male orderlies who performed the necessary functions. The court, however, held that Title VII of the Civil Rights Act was not violated by the hospital's use of gender as a basis for laying off its employees. Gender was a bona fide occupational qualification for orderlies because a substantial number of male patients objected to the performance of catheterizations and surgical preparation by female assistants.

Historical Perspective of Sexual Harassment

1964   The Civil Rights Act of 1964 was enacted, prohibiting job discrimination on the basis of sex.

1975   The first reported sexual harassment decision was rendered in which two women claimed that they had suffered repeated verbal and physical advances by a supervisor. The court ruled that the Civil Rights Act of 1964 did not cover such claims.

1977   A federal appeals court ruled that sexual harassment is discrimination under the Civil Rights Act of 1964, when a woman alleged that her position was abolished because she refused a supervisor's sexual advances.

1980   The Equal Employment Opportunity Commission (EEOC) issued landmark sexual harassment guidelines that prohibit unwelcomed sexual advances or requests that are made as a condition of employment. The guidelines also prohibit conduct that creates a hostile work environment.

1986   The U.S. Supreme Court upheld the validity of EEOC guidelines in those instances when harassment creates an abusive or hostile work environment.

1991   A Florida district court ruled that nude pinups in the workplace can constitute harassment. A California federal appeals court ruled that a hostile work environment should be evaluated from a "reasonable woman standard" and not a reasonable person standard.

1993   The U.S. Supreme Court held that a hostile work environment need not be psychologically injurious but only perceived as abusive.

Pregnancy

An employer may not discriminate against an employee because of pregnancy. The X-ray technician in *Hayes v. Shelby Memorial Hospital*[13] brought an employment discrimination action against the hospital. The technician was fired by the hospital when it learned that she was pregnant. The federal district court found that the hospital had violated the Pregnancy Discrimination Act. In affirming the lower court's decision, the appellate court held that the hospital failed to consider less discriminatory alternatives to firing the technician.

Race

Discharge of an employee on the basis of racial bias is actionable under state and federal laws. Title VII of the Civil Rights Act of 1964 "requires the elimination of artificial, arbitrary, and unnecessary barriers to employment that operate invidiously to discriminate on the basis of race."[14] An at-will employee's claim of racially motivated retaliatory discharge for filing a discrimination complaint can be actionable in tort as a violation of public policy.

The Civil Service Commission was found to have acted improperly in suspending a black licensed practical nurse as a result of a physical altercation with a white coworker in *Theodore v. Department of Health & Human Services.*[15] The white nurse had been accidentally struck by a crib being pushed by the black nurse. Evidence at trial supported the black nurse's contentions that she had apologized for the accident. The white nurse struck the first blow and spoke inflammatory slurs. The black nurse's reaction had been defensive. The facts revealed no grounds for suspension or disciplinary action against the black nurse.

The Bethany Methodist Corporation's medical and skilled nursing care facility had terminated a black certified nursing assistant because of its determination that she had abused a patient on four separate occasions in *Billups v. Methodist Hospital of Chicago.*[16] The appellate court upheld a lower court order entering a summary judgment in favor of the defendant. The plaintiff did not offer traditional forms of indirect evidence to prove racial discrimination, such as statistics or evidence of comparable situations. There was no evidence in the record suggesting that Bethany terminated black employees more frequently for physically abusing a patient, while retaining nonblack employees.

Reporting Patient Abuse

An employer may not discharge an employee for fulfilling societal obligations or in those instances in which the employer acts with a socially undesirable motive.[17] A tort claim for wrongful discharge was stated in *McQuary v. Air Convalescent Home*[18] by allegations that the plaintiff was discharged wrongfully from her position at the nursing facility in retaliation for threatening to report to state authorities instances of alleged patient mistreatment. Such mistreatment purportedly involved violation of a patient's rights under the Nursing Home Patient's Bill of Rights. To prevail, the discharged employee was not required to prove that patient abuse actually had occurred but only that she acted in good faith.

This conclusion is consistent with established Oregon law. Statutes which protect employees against retaliation do not require that the alleged violation which the employee claims be ultimately proved. See, e.g., ORS 652.355 (protects an employee who merely consults an attorney or agency about a wage claim); ORS 654.062(5) (protects any employee who makes a complaint under the Oregon Safe Employment Act); ORS 659.030(1)(f) (prohibits discrimination against an employee who filed a civil rights complaint); ORS 633.120(3) (prohibits discrimination against an employee for filing an unfair labor practices complaint). We have, in fact, upheld awards for retaliation despite holding that the original complaint did not show discrimination.

· · · ·

Similar considerations of public policy lead to our conclusion that an employee who reports a violation of a nursing home patient's statutory rights in good faith should be protected from discharge for that action.[19]

This case, which had been dismissed in the lower court, was reversed and remanded for trial.

Whistleblowing

Whistleblowing has been defined as an act of someone "who, believing that the public interest overrides the interest of the organization he serves, publicly blows the whistle if the organization is involved in corrupt, illegal, fraudulent, or harmful activity."[20]

[A]ccording to the public policy exception, an employer may not rely on the at-will doctrine as a basis for escaping liability for discharging an employee because of the doing of, or the refusing to do, such an act. Moreover, statutes in several jurisdictions protect an employee from an employer's retaliation for engaging in certain types of protected activities, such as whistleblowing.[21]

 PAVING HER WAY TO HEAVEN

Citation: *Kirk v. Mercy Hosp. Tri-County, 851 S.W.2d 617 (Mo. Ct. App. 1993)*

Facts

The plaintiff was employed as a charge nurse with supervisory duties. A short time after one of her patients had been admitted to the hospital, the plaintiff diagnosed that the patient was suffering from toxic shock syndrome. Knowing that if left untreated death would result, the plaintiff believed that the physician would order antibiotics. After a period of time had passed without having received those orders from the physician, she discussed the patient's situation with the director of nursing. She was informed by the director to document, *report the facts, and stay out of it.*

The plaintiff discussed the patient's condition and lack of orders with the chief of staff. Although the chief of staff took appropriate steps to treat the patient, the patient died. After the nursing director was informed by a member of the patient's family that the plaintiff offered to obtain the medical records, and was later told that the plaintiff was heard to say that the physician was *"paving her way to heaven,"* the director terminated the plaintiff.

After her termination, the plaintiff received a service letter from the hospital that directed her to refrain from making any further false statements about the hospital and its staff. The trial court entered a summary judgment for the defendant, stating that there were no triable issues of fact, and there was no public policy exception to the plaintiff's at-will termination. Further, the court could not find any law or regulation prohibiting the hospital from discharging her as a nurse. The plaintiff appealed.

Issue

Was there a public policy exception to the Missouri employment-at-will doctrine?

Holding

The Missouri Court of Appeals reversed the granting of summary judgment and remanded the case for trial, holding that the Nursing Practice Act provided a clear mandate of public policy that the nurses had a duty to provide the best possible care to patients.

Reason

Public policy clearly mandates that a nurse has an *obligation to serve the best interests of patients.* Therefore, if the plaintiff refused to follow her supervisor's orders to stay out of a case where the patient was dying from a lack of proper medical treatment, there would be no grounds for her discharge under the public policy exception to the employment-at-will doctrine. Pursuant to the Nursing Practice Act, the plaintiff risked discipline if she ignored improper treatment of the patient. Her persistence in attempting to get the proper treatment for the patient was her absolute duty. The hospital could not lawfully require that she stay out of a case that would have obvious injurious consequences to the patient. Public policy, as defined in case law, holds that no one can lawfully do that which tends to be injurious to the public or against the public good.

Discussion

1. Explain how a public policy would be analyzed and then determined to apply in an employment-at-will case.
2. What was the public policy mandate in this case?

INTERFERENCE WITH EMPLOYMENT ACTIVITIES

Liability for discrimination is not limited strictly to employer–employee relationships, but can be applied in situations in which discriminatory practices can affect the ability of a nonemployee to obtain a job with a third party. This occurred in *Pardazi v. Cullman Medical Center*,[22] in which the court held that the physician stated a claim for relief under Title VII of the Civil Rights Act of 1964, based on the allegation that the hospital's denial of staff privileges interfered with his employment relationship with a third party. Dr. Pardazi, a medical practitioner, had entered into an employment contract with an Alabama corporation that required Pardazi to become a staff member of the defendant hospital. Pardazi argued that the hospital's discriminatory practices in denying his appointment denied him the right of an attorney at rehearing, extended his observation period from four months to one year (a deviation from the medical staff bylaws), and interfered with his employment opportunities. The lower court's summary judgment for the hospital was reversed and the case remanded.

DEFAMATION ACTIONS

Dismissal was ordered properly for claims of wrongful termination and defamation in *Eli v. Griggs County Hospital & Nursing Home*,[23] in which a nurse's aide was terminated on the basis of an incident in the hospital dining room. In the presence of patients and visitors, she cursed her supervisor and complained that personnel were working short-staffed. Given the nature of her employment and the high standard of care that persons reasonably expected from a nursing care facility, such behavior justified her termination on a charge of reported breach of patient-specific and facility-specific information. No defamation resulted from the entry of such

charges in the aide's personnel file because the record established that the charges were true.

RETALIATORY DISCHARGE

There is a tendency for those in power to abuse that power through threats, abuse, intimidation, and retaliatory discharge, all of which are cause for legal action. Employees who become the targets of a vindictive supervisor often have difficulty in proving a bad-faith motive. In an effort to reduce the probability of wrongful discharge, some states, such as Connecticut,[24] Maine,[25] Michigan,[26] and Montana,[27] have enacted legislation that protects employees from terminations found to be arbitrary and capricious. The Montana Supreme Court upheld state legislation that protects workers against arbitrary discharge, while at the same time limiting the damages they can win.

Employees have brought claims alleging abusive discharge in violation of public policy. This type of action is usually found to be sound in tort, and thus in certain circumstances punitive damages have been awarded. The burden of proof for establishing some hidden motive for discharge from employment rests on discharged employees.

> The National Labor Relations Act and other labor legislation illustrate the governmental policy of preventing employers from using the right of discharge as a means of oppression. . . . Consistent with this policy, many states have recognized the need to protect employees who are not parties to a collective bargaining agreement or other contract from abusive practices by the employer. . . . Those states have recognized a common law cause of action for employees-at-will who were discharged for reasons that were in some way "wrongful." The courts in those jurisdictions have taken various approaches: some recognizing the action in tort, some in contract.[28]

The court in *Khanna v. Microdata Corp.*[29] held that substantial evidence supported a finding that the employer fired the employee in bad-faith retaliation for bringing a lawsuit against the employer, thus violating an implied covenant of good faith and fair dealing.

> Under the traditional common-law rule, codified in section 2922 of the [California] Labor Code, an employment contract of indefinite duration is in general terminable at the will of either party. During the past several decades, however, judicial authorities in California and throughout the United States have established the rule that,

under both common law and the statute, an employer does not enjoy an absolute or totally unfettered right to discharge even an at-will employee.[30]

A cause of action was stated for the employer's breach of an implied-in-fact covenant to terminate only for good cause.

In *Shores v. Senior Manor Nursing Center*,[31] a formerly employed nurse's assistant brought an action against the nursing facility on the basis of retaliatory discharge. The circuit court dismissed the complaint for failure to state a cause of action and the decision was appealed. The appellate court held that the allegation of the former nursing facility employee that she was discharged in retaliation for reporting to the nursing home administrator that the charge nurse was performing her nursing functions improperly, which allegedly violated the Nursing Home Care Reform Act, stated a cause of action for retaliatory discharge. The circuit court was reversed, and the case was remanded for further proceedings.

Dismissal of an employee shortly after a request for a grievance hearing regarding a salary discrepancy with another employee can raise an issue of liability for retaliatory discharge. The physician in *Jones v. Westside-Urban Health Center*[32] was found to have established a *prima facie* case of retaliatory discharge in which the record indicated that he had been fired from the hospital five days after his request for a grievance hearing on an alleged salary discrepancy.

 RETALIATORY DISCHARGE AND EMOTIONAL DISTRESS

Citation: *Dalby v. Sisters of Providence, 865 P.2d 391 (Or. Ct. App. 1993)*

Facts

Ms. Dalby, a pharmacy technician, alleged that she was discharged for reporting to her supervisor on several occasions that there were inaccuracies in the drug inventory and that recordkeeping regarding these inaccuracies was in violation of Oregon administrative rules. Dalby alleged that rather than comply with the regulations, her supervisor retaliated against her because of her insistence that her employer comply with the rules.

Retaliatory actions against Dalby included accusations of stealing cocaine from the hospital's drug inventory. Dalby learned that the sheriff's department had been asked to arrest her for stealing the cocaine. The sheriff's department refused to make

the arrest. Dalby also alleged that her supervisor refused to talk to her except for job-related purposes and that hospital attendance policies were rigidly applied against her. As a result of the defendant's actions, Dalby resigned her position.

Dalby's former employer argued that the allegations did not demonstrate constructive discharge, which included that the employer deliberately created or deliberately maintained the working conditions with the intention of forcing the employee to leave the employment, and that the employee left the employment because of the working conditions.

The circuit court dismissed Dalby's claim, and she appealed.

Issue

Did the plaintiff state a cause of action for wrongful discharge and emotional distress?

Holding

The Oregon Court of Appeals, assuming the plaintiff's allegation to be true, reversed and remanded the case, holding that the pharmacy technician had stated a cause of action for wrongful discharge and the intentional infliction of emotional distress.

Reason

Dalby made a good-faith report as to the hospital's noncompliance with the drug inventory and recordkeeping requirements required under Oregon regulations. Her report fulfilled an important "societal obligation." An employer may not discharge an employee for making such reports. The conduct of the employer, including false accusations that she had taken cocaine, gave rise to an action for the infliction of emotional distress.

Discussion

1. Regardless of the final disposition of this case by the trial court, what issues remain open for review by management and the governing body?
2. What control mechanisms should there be in place to ensure oversight in the drug inventory?

FAIRNESS—THE ULTIMATE TEST

"Is it fair?" is the ultimate question that a supervisor must ask when considering a termination. In general, bad-faith and inexplicable terminations are subject to the scrutiny of the courts. Some courts and legislative enactments have overturned the view that employers have total discretion to terminate workers who are not otherwise protected by collective bargaining agreements or civil service regulations. Montana legislation grants every employee the right to sue the employer for wrongful discharge. The mere fact that an employment contract is terminable at will does not give the employer an absolute right to terminate it in all cases. The court in *Cleary v. American Airlines*[33] held that the longevity of the employee's services, together with the express policy of the employer, operated as a form of estoppel, precluding any discharge of the employee by the employer without good cause, and thus, the employee stated a cause of action for wrongful discharge.

There is an implied covenant of good faith and fair dealing in every contract that neither party will do anything that will injure the right of the other to receive benefits from the agreement. The employee in *Pugh v. See's Candies*[34] was found to have shown a *prima facie* case of wrongful termination in violation of an implied promise that the employer would not act arbitrarily in dealing with the employee. *The employer's right to terminate an employee is not absolute.* It is limited by fundamental principles of public policy and by expressed or implied terms of agreement between the employer and the employee.

Procedural issues are as important as issues of discrimination. In *Renny v. Port Huron Hospital*,[35] the Michigan Supreme Court found, as did the jury, that the employee's discharge hearing was not final and binding because it did not comport with elementary fairness. The court found that there was sufficient evidence for the jury to find that the employee had not been discharged for just cause. The existence of a just-cause contract is a question of fact for the jury when the employer establishes written policies and procedures and does not expressly retain the right to terminate an employee at will. That the hospital followed the grievance procedure with the plaintiff is evidence that a just-cause contract existed on which the plaintiff relied.

The employee handbook provided for a grievance board as a fair way to resolve work-related complaints and problems. This was not a mandatory procedure to which the hospital's employees had to submit. The employee was not bound by the grievance board's determination that her discharge was proper, in that evidence supported a finding that she was not given adequate notice of who the witnesses against her would be. She was not permitted to be present when the witnesses testified, and she was not given the right to present certain evidence.

There was sufficient evidence for the jury to conclude that the plaintiff had suffered damages. Evidence presented indicated that her subsequent professional employment did not equal her earnings before discharge and that she had experienced increased expenses because of the loss of her health insurance as well as other financial losses that she suffered as a result of her discharge.

An employee who believes that he or she has been unfairly discharged will most likely seek access to the following information in defense of his or her claim:

- minutes of pertinent meetings
- written reports, typed or handwritten
- personnel file
- tapes
- letters, cards, and handwritten notes written on the employee's behalf from the public
- personnel handbook
- personnel and departmental policies and procedures books
- oral testimony from fellow employees and supervisors

Employers must document carefully and fairly any disciplinary proceedings that might be subject to discovery by a disgruntled employee. Failure to do so could place the organization or supervisor at a disadvantage should a complaint reach the courts.

UNEMPLOYMENT COMPENSATION

Fair dealing in termination also should include fair dealing with the terminated employee who files for unemployment benefits. In *Mankato Lutheran Home v. Miller*,[36] a nursing assistant was found not to be disqualified from receiving unemployment benefits because of a single episode of profanity directed toward her supervisor while she was ill, frustrated, and, in part, provoked by actions of her supervisor. The nursing assistant had no prior record of misconduct in five years of employment; however, her illness and frustration at having to work after she repeatedly had indicated that she was not feeling well increased over the course of several hours until she exploded emotionally. She had asked her supervisor, Ms. Darkow, if she could go home but was refused because of the probability of being unable to replace her in the middle of a shift.

> At about 5:30 A.M. Darkow entered a patient's room where Miller was helping a resident get dressed. When she asked how Miller was feeling, Miller became upset and said, "What the hell do you care, you don't think I'm sick anyway. I could drop over dead and still have to do these . . . people." Darkow retorted that Miller should not have come to work if she was so sick, and Miller yelled back, "I never had this . . . pain until I came to this . . . hole."[37]

Although the assistant's outburst was directed toward her supervisor, one of two residents in the room who heard the incident was upset by it. The episode in this case did not represent a disregard for the employer's interests or of the nursing assistant's duties and responsibilities.

Fair dealing does not always imply that every discharged employee should be entitled to unemployment benefits. For example, in *Forbis v. Wesleyan Nursing Home*,[38] unemployment compensation was denied because of an employee's discharge resulting from theft of a patient's clock. The theft constituted willful and wanton disregard for the nursing home's interests. The Employment Security Commission on its investigation made the following findings of fact:

> 2. The claimant was discharged . . . for theft [of] patient property.
> 3. [A] patient accused the claimant of taking the patient's clock.
> 4. Upon being confronted with the patient's accusation, the claimant produced the missing clock from her pocket and admitted taking it.[39]

In another case, a nursing assistant was properly denied unemployment benefits as a result of being terminated for poor work attendance, even though her most recent absence had been excused.[40] The employee's record indicated that the center had shown great tolerance in allowing the employee to continue employment for as long as it did.

Voluntary termination because of a change in working conditions will not necessarily make an employee eligible for unemployment benefits. In *Montclair Nursing Home v. Wills*,[41] a licensed practical nurse was found not to be eligible for unemployment benefits when she resigned after reassignment to a night shift. Voluntary termination because of a change in working hours was not considered sufficient cause to grant unemployment benefits, absent an "improper" purpose or motive in the change in the employee's work hours.

TERMINATION

A decision to terminate an employee should be reviewed carefully by a member of management familiar with the issues of wrongful discharge. Oral counseling, written counseling, written counseling with suspension, and written counseling with termination are the textbook responses to disciplinary action and discharge. Whatever form of discipline is used, it should be designed to produce a more effective and productive employee.

The employer's right to terminate an employee is not absolute. It is limited by fundamental principles of public policy and by express or implied terms of agreement between the employer and the employee.

> Formulating a standard for substantive fairness in employee dismissal law requires accommodat-

ing a number of different interests already afforded legal recognition. The legal interest of employees to be protected against certain types of unfair and injurious action . . .are at the core of any employee dismissal proposal. Arrayed against these interests are employer and societal interests in effective management of organizations, which require that employees not be shielded from the consequences of their poor performance or misconduct, and that supervisors not be deterred from exercising their managerial responsibilities by the inconvenience of litigating employees' claims.[42]

Before termination of an employee, the employer should review the following questions:

- Was the termination:
  - a violation of any policy or procedure outlined in an administrative manual, the employee handbook, the human resource department's policies and procedures, or any other health care facility policies and procedures or regulations
  - arbitrary and capricious
  - discriminatory on the basis of age, disability, race, creed, color, religion, gender, national origin, or marital status
  - a violation of any contract, oral or written
  - a violation of any public policy, federal, state, or local
  - consistent with the reasons for discharge
  - discriminatory against the employee for filing a lawsuit
  - fixed before any appeal actions that might be available to the employee (If an appeal was granted, was the employee given an opportunity to be represented by counsel?)
- Was there:
  - retaliatory action because of a refusal to perform an illegal act or a questioning of a management practice
  - defamation of character
  - a conspiracy
  - a personal vendetta
  - threat or intimidation
  - unlawful activity
  - an attempt to bribe
  - a denial of constitutional rights to freedom of speech
  - an interference with an employee's rights as secured by the laws or Constitution of the United States

Employment Disclaimers

A *disclaimer* is the denial of a right that is imputed to a person or that is alleged to belong to him or her. Although a disclaimer is often a successful defense for employers in wrongful discharge cases, it should not be considered a license to discharge at will and at the whim of the supervisor in an arbitrary and capricious manner.

Employers can help prevent successful lawsuits for wrongful discharge that are based on the premise that an employee handbook or departmental policy and procedure manual is an implied contract by incorporating disclaimers in published manuals, such as that described in *Battaglia v. Sisters of Charity Hospital*,[43] in which a personnel manual could not be interpreted to limit the hospital's power to terminate an at-will employee. Language in the manual indicated that the personnel manual was not a contract; that it could be modified, amended, or supplemented; and that the hospital retained the right to make all necessary management decisions for the delivery of patient care services and the selection, direction, compensation, and retention of employees.

Handbooks that do not contain disclaimers can alter an employee's at-will status. An appeals court in *Trusty v. Big Sandy Health Care Center*[44] noted that the handbook did not contain any disclaimer or any other language that employment was at will. The court held that there was sufficient evidence to establish that the handbook had altered the employee's at-will status and determined that the employee could bring a wrongful discharge suit.

Disclaimers must be clear to the employee. The court in *Harvet v. Unity Medical Center*[45] held in a wrongful discharge suit that the hospital's employee handbook was sufficiently definite to form an employment contract.

> Unity's handbook contained detailed provisions on conduct and procedures for discipline. As the trial court observed, "there can be no question that [respondent's] handbook provisions are sufficiently definite to form a contract." The handbook represents much more than Unity's general statement of policy. Moreover, the terms of the handbook were sufficiently definite to allow a fact finder to determine whether there had been a breach.

> • • • •

> Respondent contends the handbook contained the following reservations on the part of the employer indicating it was not being offered as a contract: "Exceptions to any personnel policy or procedure may be permitted on a documented form showing of good and sufficient cause."

> • • • •

> In the present case the trial court correctly found, "the clause does not clearly tell employees that the handbook is not part of an employment contract."[46]

The employer's disclaimers were considered clear in *Simonson v. Meader Distribution Co.*,[47] in which an employee filed a breach of contract suit alleging a dismissal was outside company-adopted disciplinary guidelines. The court held that the company could and did reserve the discretion to discipline employees outside adopted guidelines. The policy manual contained the following three specific reservations of management discretion:

1. Management reserves the right to make any changes at any time by adding to, deleting, or changing any existing policy.
2. The rules set out below are as complete as we can reasonably make them. However, they are not necessarily all-inclusive, because circumstances that we have not anticipated may arise. Some currently unanticipated circumstances may warrant the application of discipline, including discharge.
3. Management may vary from the above policies if, in its opinion, the circumstances require.[48]

Health care organizations can be successful when confronted with wrongful discharge suits based on breach of contract by placing similar language in their personnel manuals.

Job Description

The job description is not intended to be an employment contract, nor does it dissolve the "at will" employment relationship. It is a record of the basic purpose, typical level of authority, typical source of action, and representative function or duties of the job. It is designed to provide management and others with a clear understanding of the level of the job and its working relationships, skills, and requirements in relation to other jobs.

Termination for Cause

A termination-for-cause-only clause in an employment contract is binding. An employment contract in *Eales v. Tanana*[49] that provided that an employee hired up to retirement age could be terminated only for cause was upheld by the court.

Violation of No-Smoking Policy

Unemployment compensation was properly denied a nursing assistant for breach of a no-smoking rule in *Selan v. Commonwealth Unemployment Compensation Board of Review*.[50] The nursing facility's personnel handbook clearly provided that smoking was allowed only in specified areas.

- Smoking can be very offensive. It also creates a health and fire problem.
- You must refrain from smoking in offices, resident areas, elevators, corridors, or any area where it might be hazardous. In fact, you should not smoke in the public view. All "no smoking signs" must be observed. Your Department Director will inform you of the areas in which you are permitted to smoke.
- Smoking is permitted during break times and at meal times in these designated smoking areas.
- Smoking is permitted in vehicles only if residents are not present.
- Use ashtrays to keep The Home clean and to prevent fires. Special care must be exercised when oxygen or other inflammable gases may be present.

The nursing home assistant admitted that she was smoking but argued that she did not break the facility's smoking rules. The court disagreed. Evidence was sufficient to show that the employee knowingly violated Methodist Home's rule by smoking in a patient's bathroom. Deliberate violation of a reasonable employer rule, without due cause, constitutes willful misconduct warranting disqualification for unemployment compensation.

Termination and Financial Necessity

No breach of employment contract occurred in *Wilde v. Houlton Regional Hospital*[51] when, because of financial difficulties, a hospital terminated the employment of two nurses, a ward clerk, and a dietary supervisor. Even if the employees were correct in contending that their indefinite contracts of employment had been modified by virtue of a "dismissal for cause" provision in the employee's handbook and by management's oral assurances that they were permanent, full-time employees whose jobs were secure so long as they performed satisfactorily, the employees' discharge for financial or other legitimate business reasons did not offend the employment contracts as thus modified. A private employer had an essential business prerogative to adjust its work force as market forces and business necessity required, and the layoffs in question violated no compelling public policy.

> [T]he appellants have failed to set forth specific facts showing that they were discharged for any reasons other than financial difficulties and overstaffing. The record does not suggest, for example, that financial difficulties were a pretext for discharges that were actually motivated by Houlton Regional's bad faith or retaliatory purpose.[52]

Termination and Hostile Attitude

The chief X-ray technician in *Paros v. Hoemako Hospital*[53] was dismissed because of a chronic argumentative and hostile attitude inconsistent with the performance of supervisory duties. The trial court entered a summary judgment in favor of the hospital and the administrator. On appeal, the appeals court held that the discharge was properly based on good cause and precluded recovery for breach of contract and wrongful discharge.

Termination and Improper Billing Practices

The hospital in *Jagust v. Brookhaven Memorial Association*[54] was found to have properly dismissed a staff physician from his administrative position as director of the hospital's family practice residency program without a hearing. The hospital learned that the physician had engaged in improper billing practices by submitting bills for services that he never rendered. The physician was an employee at will as far as his administrative position was concerned. Neither the hospital's administrative procedure manual nor the employee handbook stated that the employee was subject to discharge for cause. Procedural protection was provided in the medical staff bylaws; however, the bylaws pertained to medical staff privileges and not administrative positions.

Termination and Poor Work Performance

In *Yerry v. Ulster County*,[55] a nurse's aide had been terminated from a county infirmary for misconduct in that, among other things, she failed to timely report bumping and injuring a resident's leg, failed to properly feed a resident as ordered by the resident's physician, and on another occasion, fed a resident food that burned the resident's mouth. The court held that eyewitness testimony and believable hearsay were sufficient to sustain the findings of the hearings officer who recommended her termination.

> As to the imposition of discipline, when petitioner's serious performance deficiencies are considered in light of her experience and the grave responsibility her work demanded in caring for helpless and dependent patients, the court found that the penalty imposed was not disproportionate to the offenses. She showed an insensitivity and a lack of ability that made her unsuitable for the work and this constituted a danger to the well-being of the infirmary's elderly residents.[56]

The plaintiff in *Silinzy v. Visiting Nurse Association*[57] brought an action claiming racial discrimination and retaliatory discharge. The court granted a motion for summary judgment by the defendant-employer. The district court held that the plaintiff failed to establish a *prima facie* case of racial discrimination and retaliatory discharge. The plaintiff's poor job performance was the reason for her discharge. The defendant was found to have produced ample evidence that the plaintiff was not performing her job adequately. Numerous complaints regarding her negative attitude and poor job performance, from a variety of sources, were documented.

Termination and Alcoholism

Discharge of an employee because of alcoholism is not necessarily a discriminatory practice. The hospital's discharge of a staff physician for alcoholism in *Soentgen v. Quain & Ramstad Clinic*[58] was found not to be a discriminatory practice. The physician had been discharged on a bona fide occupational qualification reasonably necessary for a physician.

Termination and Damages

An employee who is wrongly discharged may maintain a cause of action in contract or tort, or both. In a tort action for wrongful discharge, the court can award punitive damages. This remedy is not available under the law of contract.

A California Supreme Court decision that prohibits plaintiffs from seeking punitive and emotional distress damages from former employers in wrongful dismissal cases applies retroactively to thousands of cases pending in that state's courts. In *Newman v. Emerson Radio Corp.*,[59] the court, by a 4–3 vote, decided that its December 29 decision in *Foley v. Interactive Data Corp.*[60] applies to all wrongful dismissal cases pending as of January 30. The California Supreme Court held in *Foley* that a wrongful discharge claim asserting a breach of an implied covenant of good faith and fair dealing may give rise to contract, but not tort, damages. As a result of this ruling, punitive damages will not ordinarily be available to wrongfully discharged plaintiffs.

The Montana Supreme Court held that a Montana statute that limits the damages recoverable in wrongful discharge suits to four years' wages and benefits does not violate the state constitution.[61] According to the court, the state constitution's guarantee of "full legal redress" affords the plaintiff, a former nursing home administrator, only a right to judicial access to obtain remedies, not a fundamental right to full redress. The statute abolishes common-law causes of action for discharge and creates a statutory action. It is the first of its kind in the nation. Punitive damages are available only on clear and convincing evidence that the employer acted with actual malice or committed actual fraud.

EFFECTIVE HIRING PRACTICES

It is possible for employers to reduce their exposure to liability for wrongful discharge by developing appropriate guidelines. The best way for the human resources manager to prevent negligent hiring litigation for the employer is to be-

come familiar with the risks and avoid hiring workers who are likely to become problem employees. The organization should

- Develop clear policies and procedures on hiring, disciplining, and terminating employees.
- Include appropriate language in the organization's policies and procedures reserving the right to add, delete, and or revise the same.
- Develop an application that realistically determines an applicant's qualifications before hiring.
- Take appropriate precautions to prevent the hiring of those who might be a hazard to others.
- Review each applicant's background and past work behavior.
- Become familiar with any state laws that might be applicable when hiring an individual with a past criminal record.
- Develop a two-tiered interview system for screening applicants. (The interviews should be conducted first by an appropriately trained member of the human resources department and then by the supervisor of the service to which the applicant is applying.)
- Solicit references with the applicant's permission using a release form, and follow up with a telephone call for further information.
- Define clear personnel policies and procedures in the form of a personnel handbook and present a job description to each new employee. (Signed documentation should be maintained in the employee's personnel folder indicating that the employee received, read, and understood the employee handbook and job description.)
- Develop constructive performance evaluations that reinforce good behavior and provide instruction in those areas needing improvement. (The performance evaluation should include a written statement regarding the employee's performance.)
- Develop a progressive disciplinary action policy.
- Provide in-service education programs for supervisors on such subjects as employee interviews, evaluations, and discipline. (Various colleges, universities, and consultants provide in-service education programs for employers.)
- Be mindful of the importance of developing appropriate employment contract language, as well as administrative manuals and employee handbooks.

Employers must communicate clearly to prospective employees that their employment is at will and can be terminated at any time by either the employer or the employee. During the course of employment, handbooks and personnel manuals must provide a fair and unambiguous standard for employee discipline and termination.

The Court's Decision

The North Carolina Court of Appeals held that the nurse stated a claim for wrongful discharge in violation of public policy. Although there may be a right to terminate at-will employment for no reason, or for an arbitrary or irrational reason, there can be no right to terminate such employment for an unlawful reason or purpose that contravenes public policy.

CHAPTER REVIEW

1. *Employment at will* is a doctrine by which employment is by will of either the employer or the employee and that employment may be terminated at any time and for any or no reason. Exceptions to this doctrine include employment contracts, public policy issues, defamation, regulatory discharge, and fairness.
2. Public policy begins with legislative enactments that prohibit the firing of an employee based on factors such as race, age, color, religion, sex, national origin, handicap, pregnancy, filing complaints with various agencies, or membership in a union. Public policy also can result from judicial decisions that address issues not covered by statutes, rules, and regulations.
3. When someone who believes that the public interest overrides the interest of the organization he or she serves reveals that the organization is involved in corrupt, illegal, fraudulent, or harmful activity, it is referred to as *whistleblowing*.
4. Employees who believe that they have suffered *retaliatory discharge* are entitled to bring legal action against their former employer. The burden of proof, however, lies on the discharged employee.
5. The fact that an employment contract is terminable at will does not, in all cases, allow an employer the absolute right to terminate the contract. Many bad-faith and inexplicable terminations are subject to the scrutiny of the courts. Before terminating an employee, the employer should be sure that a member of management familiar with the issues of wrongful discharge has reviewed the decision to terminate.
6. Employers are required to deal fairly with terminated employees who file for unemployment benefits.
7. The denial of a right that is imputed to a person or that is alleged to belong to a person is a *disclaimer*. A disclaimer can sometimes be used by employers as a successful defense in wrongful discharge cases.
8. Termination of employees for financial or other legitimate business reasons does not constitute a breach of employment contract.
9. Employers can reduce exposure to liability for wrongful discharge by establishing and maintaining effective hiring practices. Such practices can help the employer to avoid hiring employees who are likely to pose problems.

REVIEW QUESTIONS

1. Is the employment-at-will concept appropriate in today's society?
2. What are the pros and cons of the employment-at-will doctrine?
3. Describe the elements that are necessary for an employee handbook to form a valid contract, granting enforceable rights to an employee.
4. Why do supervisors often find it difficult to prepare written performance appraisals?
5. What should be included in a management training program to assist managers in preparing fair and objective performance appraisals?
6. What measures can an organization take to improve the competence of its staff?
7. Why is it important that the qualifications of a particular position be commensurate with defined job responsibilities?
8. Should there be a correlation between the job description and performance evaluation? Explain.

NOTES

1. Deerman v. Beverly Cal. Corp., 518 S.E.2d 804 (N.C. App. 1999).

2. 328 S.E.2d 818 (N.C. Ct. App. 1985).

3. 44 A.L.R. 4th 1136 (1986).

4. Sides v. Duke Hosp., 328 S.E.2d 818 (N.C. Ct. App. 1985).

5. Pierce v. Ortho Pharm. Corp., 417 A.2d 505, 509 (N.J. 1980).

6. Palmateer v. International Harvester Co., 421 N.E.2d 876, 878 (Ill. 1981).

7. Joiner v. Benton Community Bank, 411 N.E.2d 229, 231 (Ill. 1980).

8. Gantt v. Sentry Ins., 824 P.2d 680, 687–688 (Cal. 1992).

9. 450 U.S. 248, 253 (1981).

10. 702 F.2d 322 (2d Cir. 1983).

11. *Id.* at 325.

12. 666 F. Supp. 933 (D. Miss. 1987).

13. 726 F.2d 1543 (11th Cir. 1984).

14. Griggs v. Duke Power Co., 401 U.S. 424 (1971).

15. 515 So.2d 454 (La. Ct. App. 1987).

16. 922 F.2d 1300 (7th Cir. 1991).

17. Delaney v. Taco Time Int'l, 681 P.2d 114 (Or. 1984). This case involved an employer found liable by the Oregon Supreme Court for the wrongful discharge of an at-will employee who was discharged for fulfilling a societal obligation in that he refused to sign a false and arguably tortious statement that cast aspersions on the work habits and moral behavior of a former employee.

18. 684 P.2d 21 (Or. Ct. App. 1984).

19. *Id.* at 24.

20. WHISTLEBLOWING: THE REPORT OF THE CONFERENCE OF PROFESSIONAL RESPONSIBILITY 6 (1972); *see also* Annotation, 99 A.L.R. Fed. 778.

21. Annotation, 99 A.L.R. Fed. 775.

22. 838 F.2d 1155 (11th Cir. 1988).

23. 385 N.W.2d 99 (N.D. 1986).

24. CONN. GEN. STAT. ANN. § 31–51m(a) (West 1987).

25. ME. REV. STAT. ANN. 26, §§ 831–840 (West 1987).

26. MICH. COMP. LAWS ANN. §§ 15.361–369 (West 1981).

27. MONT. CODE ANN. § 39-2-901 (1987).

28. Pierce v. Ortho Pharm. Corp., 417 A.2d 505, 509 (N.J. 1980).

29. 215 Cal. Rptr. 860 (Cal. Ct. App. 1985).

30. *Id.* at 865.

31. 518 N.E.2d 471 (Ill. App. Ct. 1988).

32. 760 F. Supp. 1575 (D.C. Ga. 1991).

33. 168 Cal. Rptr. 722 (Cal. Ct. App. 1980).

34. 171 Cal. Rptr. 917 (Cal. Ct. App. 1981).

35. 398 N.W.2d 327 (Mich. 1986).

36. 358 N.W.2d 96 (Minn. Ct. App. 1984).

37. *Id.* at 98.

38. 325 S.E.2d 651 (N.C. Ct. App. 1985).

39. *Id.* at 652.

40. Love v. Heritage House Convalescent Ctr., 463 N.E.2d 478 (Ind. Ct. App. 1983).

41. 371 N.W.2d 121 (Neb. 1985).

42. H. H. PERRITT, EMPLOYEE DISMISSAL LAW AND PRACTICE 354 (1984).

43. 508 N.Y.S.2d 802 (N.Y. App. Div. 1986).

44. No. 89-CA-2272-MR (Ky. Ct. App. Mar. 22, 1991).

45. 428 N.W.2d 574 (Minn. Ct. App. 1988).

46. *Id.* at 577.

47. 413 N.W.2d 146 (Minn. Ct. App. 1987).

48. *Id.* at 147.

49. 663 P.2d 958 (Alaska 1983).

50. 415 A.2d 139 (Pa. Commw. Ct. 1980).

51. 537 A.2d 1137 (Me. 1987).

52. *Id.* at 1138.

53. 681 P.2d 918 (Ariz. Ct. App. 1984).

54. 541 N.Y.S.2d 41 (N.Y. Ct. App. Div. 1989).

55. 512 N.Y.S.2d 592 (N.Y. App. Div. 1987).

56. *Id.* at 593.

57. 777 F. Supp. 1484 (E.D. Mo. 1991).

58. 467 N.W.2d 73 (N.D. 1991).

59. 772 P.2d 1059 (Cal. 1989).

60. 765 P.2d 373 (Cal. 1988).

61. Meech v. Hillhaven W., Inc., 776 P.2d 488 (Mont. 1989).

CHAPTER 20

Managed Care and Organizational Restructuring

It's Your Gavel...

TOO LITTLE TOO LATE

The plaintiff, the deceased's wife, alleged that the primary care physician had delayed in submitting a request for services of an "out-of-plan cardiologist" to the health maintenance organization (HMO). This act, coupled with further delay by the denial of the request, led to the deceased's death. After the referral to a nonparticipating cardiologist had been denied, the deceased accepted a referral and appointment with a participating cardiologist for the following day. *Too little too late.* The deceased suffered a massive myocardial infarction that resulted in his death the same day that the referral was made. The claims brought against the defendant-Yung were for medical malpractice, breach of contract, and breach of fiduciary duty.

The trial court refused to grant the defendant's motion for dismissal based on Employee Income Security Act (ERISA) preemption. The appellate division reversed and dismissed the complaint.[1]

What is your verdict?

INTRODUCTION

Health care has come a long way from the days when answering a knock at the front door was met with a genuine, black leather bag–carrying, independent-practicing, family physician. The physician knew you and every member of your family and, most likely, delivered you, as well as your mother and father. The only charge for a home visit may have been your mother's home-baked apple pie. This scene has changed dramatically over the years. The health care setting is a bombardment of mergers, buyouts, up- and downsizing, health maintenance organizations (HMOs), cost controls, regulations, and regulators monitoring regulators.

The latest buzzword is *managed care organizations* (MCOs), which represent a major shift away from the domination of the fee-for-service system toward networks of providers supplying a full range of services. *Managed care* is the process of structuring or restructuring the health care system in terms of financing, purchasing, delivering, measuring, and documenting a broad range of health care services and products. Managed care is nothing new to the U.S. health care delivery system; it has been around in some form for decades.

The relationships that are being restructured are those among employers, physicians, a wide variety of health care organizations, payers, and consumers. The two major and objected-to constraints of MCOs are their (1) limitations on the choice of providers by the consumer and (2) requirements for prior authorization in order to obtain services. As reviewed in this chapter, managed care comes in a variety of packages.

COMMON MODELS OF MANAGED CARE ORGANIZATIONS

Health Maintenance Organizations

HMOs are organized health care systems that are responsible for both the financing and the delivery of a broad range of comprehensive health services to an enrolled population. They are the most highly regulated form of MCOs. HMOs act both as insurer and provider of health care services. They charge employers a fixed premium for each subscriber. An independent practice association (IPA)-model HMO provides medical care to its subscribers through contracts it establishes with independent physicians. In a staff-model HMO, the physicians would normally be full-time employees of the HMO. Individuals who subscribe to an HMO are often limited to the panel of physicians who have contracted with the HMO to provide services to its subscribers.

Preferred Provider Organizations

Preferred provider organizations (PPOs) are entities through which employer health benefit plans and health insurance carriers contract to purchase health care services for covered beneficiaries from a selected group of participating providers. About half of the states have specific PPO laws that directly regulate such entities. Common characteristics of PPOs include

- select provider panel
- negotiated payment rates
- rapid payment terms
- utilization management (programs to control the utilization and cost)
- consumer choice (allow covered beneficiaries to use non-PPO providers for an additional out-of-pocket charge [point-of-service option])

In PPOs, a payer, such as an insurance company, provides incentives to its enrollees to obtain medical care from a panel of providers with whom the payer has contracted a discounted rate.

Exclusive Provider Organizations

Exclusive provider organizations (EPOs) limit their beneficiaries to participating providers for any health care ser-

vices. EPOs use a gatekeeper approach to authorizing nonprimary care services. The primary difference between an HMO and an EPO is that the former is regulated under HMO laws and regulations, whereas the latter is regulated under insurance laws and regulations. Characteristics of EPOs include

- Primary care physicians are reimbursed through capitation payments or other performance-based reimbursement methods.
- Primary care physicians act as gatekeepers.

Open-Access or Point-of-Service HMOs

HMO members covered under these types of benefit plans may decide whether to use HMO benefits or indemnity-style benefits for each instance of care. In other words, the member is allowed to make a coverage choice at the point of service.

Self-Insured and Experience-Rated HMOs

Under experience-rated benefit options, an HMO receives monthly premium payments much as it would under traditional premium-based plans. Typically, to arrive at a final premium rate, there is a settlement process in which the employer is credited with some portion, or all, of the actual utilization and cost of its group. Then refunds or additional payments are calculated and made to the appropriate party.

Specialty HMOs

These HMOs provide limited components of health care coverage. Dental HMOs have become more common as an option to indemnity dental insurance coverage.

Independent Practice Associations

An IPA is a legal entity composed of physicians organized for the purpose of negotiating contracts to provide physician services. For example, an IPA might contract with an HMO or a physician hospital organization (PHO). The physicians maintain their own practices and do not share services, such as claims, billing, scheduling, accounting, etc.

Group Practice

A physician group that has only one or a small number of service delivery locations is a group practice. It is completely integrated economically, sharing costs and revenues. Group practices often are either specialty or primary care dominated.

Group Practice without Walls

A group practice without walls (GPWW) is a physician organization formed for the purpose of sharing some administrative and management costs while continuing to practice at their own locations rather than at a centralized location.

Physician Hospital Organizations

A PHO is a legal entity consisting of a joint venture of physicians and a hospital. It is formed to facilitate managed care contracting, to improve cost management and services, and to create new health care resources in the community.

Medical Foundations

In a medical foundation, the foundation employs or contracts with physicians to provide care to the foundation's patients.

Management Service Organizations

A management service organization (MSO) is an entity that provides administrative and management services to physicians. The organization performs services, such as practice management, marketing, managed care contracting, accounting, billing, and personnel management. The MSO can be hospital affiliated, a hospital-physician joint venture, physician owned, or investor owned.

Vertically Integrated Delivery System

A vertically integrated delivery system (IDS) is any organization or group of affiliated organizations that provides physician and hospital services to patients. The goal of hospital-physician integration is to provide a full range of services to patients. A vertically IDS achieves this goal, providing services ranging from primary outpatient care to tertiary inpatient care. More elaborate systems provide additional services, such as home health care, long-term care, rehabilitation, and mental health care.

HORIZONTAL CONSOLIDATIONS

A *horizontal merger* involves similar or identical businesses at the same level of the market. There is no single qualitative or quantitative factor from which it can be determined whether such a group merger is permissible. Recognizing a congressional intent to preserve competition by preventing undue market concentration, the courts have focused primarily on the possibility that consolidation will substantially lessen competition.

FEDERALLY QUALIFIED HMOs

Many HMOs are federally qualified. Federal qualification, which is entirely voluntary, requires HMOs to meet federal standards for legal and organizational status, financial viability, marketing, and health service delivery systems, as delineated in the federal HMO Act and its implementing regulations. The disadvantage of federal qualification—beyond the fees involved—is that a federally qualified HMO has less flexibility in its benefits package and in developing premium rates.

The standards for federal qualification were introduced in 1973, when Congress enacted Title XIII of the Public Health Service Act, commonly known as the HMO Act.[2] This law was intended to foster the growth of HMOs, which were considered to be a cost-effective method of health care delivery.

The law was amended in 1976 to ease some of the restrictions on open enrollment, community rating, and medical staffing. It was amended again in 1978 on financial disclosure, and in 1981 for solvency protection. In 1986, certain HMO grant and loan programs were abolished.[3]

The most dramatic amendments, however, occurred in 1988. They permitted federally qualified HMOs to provide up to 10 percent of their physician services through non-HMO-affiliated physicians and authorized reasonable deductibles for those services. They also repealed the dual-choice requirement, effective in 1995; broadened the definition of restrictive state laws; required disclosure of rate-making methods and data; addressed nondiscrimination in the financing of employee plans; deleted the requirement that one-third of the policy-making body be composed of HMO members; and repealed the requirement that the policy-making body include equitable representation from underserved communities.

Federally qualified HMOs must provide or arrange for basic health services for their members as needed and without limitation as to time, cost, frequency, extent, or kind of services actually provided. Basic health services include

- physician services, including consultant and referral services by a physician
- inpatient and outpatient services, including short-term rehabilitation services and physical therapy
- medically necessary emergency health services
- 20 outpatient visits per member per year for short-term, evaluative, or crisis intervention mental health services
- medical treatment and referral services
- diagnostic laboratory and diagnostic and therapeutic radiology services

- home health services
- preventive health services, including immunizations and well-child care from birth

STATE LAWS

Most states have enacted comprehensive HMO laws. HMO laws are often based on the National Association of Insurance Commissioners' Model HMO Act (NAIC Model HMO Act). State laws generally specify what type of entities can apply for a certificate of authority to operate an HMO. Typically, the state insurance department is the primary regulatory body.

Generally, state HMO laws require that an application for a certificate of authority be accompanied by a description of the proposed marketing plan that the regulator must approve. HMO laws generally specify that a schedule of charges and amendments must be filed and approved by the commissioner.

The majority of state HMO laws require that the provision of basic health services include emergency care, inpatient care, physician care, and outpatient care. State HMO laws contain several provisions designed to protect enrollees in the event that the HMO becomes insolvent. These include deposit, capital, reserve, and net worth requirements. State laws pertaining to HMOs generally require that

- The HMO cannot cancel or refuse to renew an enrollee solely because of the individual's health.
- If an individual terminates employment or membership in a group, that person must be permitted to convert to a direct payment basis.
- Grievance procedures must be in place.

State HMO laws usually condition issuance of a certificate of authority on the submission and approval of a quality assurance program.

CASE MANAGEMENT FIRMS

Case management firms assist employers and insurers in managing catastrophic cases. They identify cases that will become catastrophic, negotiate services and reimbursement with providers who can treat the patient's condition, develop a treatment protocol for the patient, and monitor the treatment.

THIRD-PARTY ADMINISTRATORS

Third-party administrator firms perform administrative activities, such as claims processing, for self-funded or managed care plans.

UTILIZATION REVIEW

Utilization review (UR) is a process whereby a third-party payer evaluates the medical necessity of a course of treatment. Generally, UR is performed prospectively, concurrently, or retrospectively. In *prospective review*, the payer determines whether to pay for treatment before the treatment is initiated. If the review reveals that the treatment is not medically necessary, the payer then indicates its decision not to pay for the medical care. *Concurrent review* is performed during the course of treatment. Concurrent review entails monitoring whether medical care continues to be appropriate and necessary. If it is not, the payer will not pay for additional care. *Retrospective review* is performed after treatment has been completed. If the review indicates that medical care was not necessary, the insurer can deny the claim.

Most insurance companies and MCOs rely on prospective and concurrent utilization review to determine whether care is necessary, as well as what level of care is appropriate. Utilization review has become an accepted and essential part of cost containment.

Case management is an increasingly important aspect of utilization management. It involves identifying at an early stage those patients who can be treated more cost effectively in an alternative setting or at a lower level of care without negatively affecting the quality of care. Case management usually is employed in catastrophic or high-cost cases.

Utilization Management Firms

Utilization management firms perform utilization management activities for managed care entities, insurers, or employers. Mental health and dental care are two common types of such firms. In recent years, the regulation of utilization by private review agents or utilization review organizations (UROs) has increased dramatically.

Just as health care entities have a corporate duty to select and monitor physicians carefully, they also have a duty to carefully select the URO with which they contract. That duty entails investigating the URO before contracting with it to ensure that its procedures are adequate and its personnel are qualified to perform UR activities.

Negligent UR Decisions

MCOs that perform UR may be found liable for undesirable patient outcomes because of defects or failures in the UR process or because of a negligent UR decision. The first reported case involving liability for UR was *Wickline v. State of California*.[4] In that case, the court stated that a third-party payer of health care services can be held legally accountable when medically inappropriate decisions result from defects in the design or implementation of cost containment mechanisms. Liability in the UR process can arise from several sources, including failure to gather information adequately before making a decision as to medical necessity, failure to initiate a meaningful dialogue between UR personnel and the treating physician, failure to inform members of their right to appeal an adverse UR decision, and failure to issue a timely UR decision.

LIABILITY FOR NONPARTICIPATING PHYSICIANS

MCOs may be liable for the medical malpractice of non-employee participating physicians under an *ostensible or apparent agency theory* if (1) the patient reasonably views the entity rather than the individual physician as the source of care, and (2) the entity engages in conduct that leads the patient reasonably to believe that the source of care is the entity or that the physician is an employee of the entity.

The doctrine of corporate negligence clearly applies to staff-model HMOs in which the HMO employs the physicians and provides the facility within which they offer care. If an HMO employs physicians, such as in a staff-model HMO, the HMO can be held liable for the negligence of its employees under the doctrine of *respondeat superior.*

EMPLOYEE RETIREMENT INSURANCE SECURITY ACT

The Employee Retirement Insurance Security Act of 1974 (ERISA) was designed to ensure that employee welfare benefit plans conform to a uniform body of benefits law. ERISA preempts state law affecting employee benefit plans. The law does not, however, regulate the contents of the welfare benefit plans. For example, it does not mandate that specific benefits be provided to beneficiaries. To qualify as an employee benefit plan, the plan must be maintained by an employer or employee organization for the benefit of its employees. ERISA requires that every plan (1) describe procedures for the allocation of responsibilities for its operation and administration, and (2) specify the basis on which payments are made to and from the plan.

REDUCING EXPOSURE TO LIABILITY

Employers, managed care entities, and providers can reduce liability exposure by complying with all formalities; considering contracting through the plan itself; and defining clearly discretionary responsibilities. Employers should seek and employ competent advisers. A managed contract should be developed between the employer and the selected fiduciary. The contract should ensure that

- the fiduciary is responsible for monitoring its discretionary authority
- the fiduciary is committed to supplying the employer with data on the various aspects of its performance
- proper indemnities are negotiated on behalf of the employer and its employees
- hold-harmless clauses are provided for employees for payment for services rendered
- financial disclosures are made as appropriate
- sufficient reinsurance, fiduciary insurance, and liability insurance are maintained and proof is supplied to the employer
- confidentiality agreements are established and observed
- quality assurance programs are maintained
- claims and appeal procedures are available and assurances given as to the program's operation and improvement
- a description is provided of the fiduciary's utilization control mechanism, methods for preadmission review of elective procedures, continuous stay review procedures, systems for retrospective review of ancillary services provided, retrospective review of surgical procedures, quality assurance programs, and mechanisms for denial of coverage or charges, as well as the method used for dispute resolution

HEALTH CARE QUALITY IMPROVEMENT ACT OF 1986

The Health Care Quality Improvement Act of 1986 (HCQIA) was enacted in part as a response to numerous antitrust suits against participants in peer review and credentialing activities. Congress passed the Act to encourage continued participation in these activities. The purpose of the HCQIA is to provide those persons giving information to professional review bodies and those assisting in review activities limited immunity from damages that may arise as a result of adverse decisions that affect a physician's medical staff privileges. The immunity does not extend to civil rights litigation or suits filed by the United States or an attorney general of a state.

In 1989, the Ethics in Patient Referral Act (frequently referred to as the Stark bill for its author, Rep. Fortney [Pete] Stark [D-Cal.]) was enacted as part of the Omnibus Budget Reconciliation Act of 1989. Effective January 1, 1992, the Act prohibits physicians who have ownership interest or compensation arrangements with a clinical laboratory from referring Medicare patients to that laboratory. The law also requires all Medicare providers to report the names and provider numbers of all physicians or their immediate relatives with ownership interests in the provider entity prior to October 1, 1991. Failure to comply with the disclosure requirements exposes providers to a civil monetary penalty of up to $10,000 per day.

MANAGED CARE AND LEGAL ACTIONS

Insurer and Tort-Feasor

The plaintiff in *Karsten v. Kaiser Foundation Health Plan*[5] brought a legal action against her HMO for malpractice. The plaintiff alleged that Kaiser's negligent care caused her to deliver a premature stillborn fetus. Although Kaiser denied any wrongdoing, the jury awarded the plaintiff $210,000 in damages. At trial, the plaintiff introduced hospital bills incurred as a result of the incident in question. Kaiser had paid these bills prior to trial. Although Kaiser agreed that, based on its contract with the plaintiff, it was required to pay these bills regardless of fault, Kaiser objected to the medical bills as part of the plaintiff's compensatory damages because they had already been paid by Kaiser.

The issue under Virginia law was, does the collateral source rule allow the plaintiff to recover compensatory damages for medical bills previously satisfied by her HMO?

The U.S. District Court held that, under Virginia law, the collateral source rule allows a member to receive from the HMO compensatory damages for medical bills that the HMO previously paid under the HMO contract, when the HMO was also liable to the plaintiff as a tort-feasor.

The court focused on the nature of each payment Kaiser was being asked to make. The first payment made by Kaiser was for the plaintiff's medical bills. The defendant made this payment in its capacity as the plaintiff's insurer. The defendant is now being asked to pay these same medical expenses as compensatory damages. In other words, the plaintiff is receiving the benefit of her bargain with the defendant as insurer, and she is receiving compensation for her injuries arising out of the defendant's malpractice. Even though the defendant is being asked to pay the same damages twice, it is patent that the nature of the two payments is different.

Open Enrollment

Federal HMO regulations require federally qualified HMOs to hold an open enrollment period of not less than 30 days per year, during which the HMO must accept individual applicants for coverage regardless of their health status. Not all state HMO laws require open enrollment periods; however, a few state laws do.

Emergency Care

HMOs can refuse benefit coverage to patients if they determine retrospectively that a patient's condition did not require emergency department care. Of course, hindsight is 20/20. Determining whether one's chest pains are because of diet or a coronary condition requires expensive testing. To refuse a patient care before determining the etiology of a patient's condition could be financially disastrous to the organization. In addition, federal law prohibits hospital emergency departments from turning away patients seeking emergency care. Unfortunately, *retrospective denial* places the burden on the provider to seek reimbursement from the patient if the insurer denies the charges.

Benefit Denials

The California Supreme Court has ruled that insurers must inform beneficiaries of their right to contest a benefit denial. The court, in *Davis v. Blue Cross of N. California*,[6] held that the insurer had breached its duty of good faith and fair dealing by failing to timely or adequately apprise an insured of his rights under the policy's arbitration clause.

The insured in *Katskee v. Blue Cross/Blue Shield*[7] brought action against the health insurer for breach of contract. In January 1990, on recommendation of her gynecologist, Dr. Roffman, the appellant consulted with Dr. Lynch regarding her family's history of breast and ovarian cancer, and particularly her health in relation to such a history. After examining the appellant and investigating her family's medical history, Lynch diagnosed her as suffering from a genetic condition known as breast-ovarian carcinoma syndrome. Lynch then recommended that the appellant have a total abdominal hysterectomy and bilateral salpingo-oophorectomy, which involves the removal of the uterus, the ovaries, and the fallopian tubes. Roffman concurred with Lynch's diagnosis and agreed that the recommended surgery was the most medically appropriate treatment available.

Initially, Blue Cross/Blue Shield sent a letter to the appellant and indicated that it might pay for the surgery. Two weeks before the surgery, Dr. Mason, the chief medical officer for Blue Cross/Blue Shield, wrote to the appellant and stated that Blue Cross/Blue Shield would not cover the cost of the surgery. Nonetheless, the appellant had the surgery. She filed an action for breach of contract, seeking to recover $6,022.57 in costs associated with the surgery. Blue Cross/Blue Shield filed a motion for summary judgment. The district court granted the motion. It found that there was no genuine issue of material fact and that the policy did not cover the appellant's surgery. Specifically, the court stated that

1. The appellant did not suffer from cancer, and although her high-risk condition warranted the surgery, it was not covered by the policy.
2. The appellant did not have a bodily illness or disease that was covered by the policy.
3. Under the terms of the policy, Blue Cross/Blue Shield reserved the right to determine what is medically necessary.

The appellant filed a notice of appeal to the Nebraska Court of Appeals contending that the district court erred in finding that no genuine issue of material fact existed and in granting summary judgment in favor of appellee. Blue Cross/Blue Shield denied coverage because it concluded that appellant's condition did not constitute an illness, and thus the treatment she received was not medically necessary.

An insurance policy is to be construed, as any other contract, to give effect to the parties' intentions at the time the contract was made. The issue was whether the insured's breast-ovarian carcinoma syndrome was an illness, defined as a bodily disorder or disease within meaning of the health insurance policy.

The Nebraska Supreme Court held that the insured's breast-ovarian carcinoma syndrome was an illness within meaning of the health insurance policy, notwithstanding insurer's contention that the syndrome was merely predisposition to cancer. The court found that whether a policy is ambiguous is a matter of law for the court to determine. A general principle of construction, which the courts apply to ambiguous insurance policies, holds that an ambiguous policy will be construed in favor of the insured. The language used in the policy at issue in the present case was not reasonably susceptible to differing interpretations, and thus not ambiguous. The issue then becomes whether appellant's condition—breast-ovarian carcinoma syndrome—constituted an illness.

Blue Cross/Blue Shield argued that the appellant did not suffer from an illness because she did not have cancer. Blue Cross/Blue Shield characterized the appellant's condition only as a "predisposition to an illness." The record on summary judgment included the depositions of Lynch, Roffman, and Mason. According to Lynch's testimony, some forms of cancer occur on a hereditary basis. Breast and ovarian cancer are such forms of cancer. Women diagnosed with the syndrome have at least a 50 percent chance of developing breast and/or ovarian cancer, whereas unaffected women have only a 1.4 percent risk of developing breast or ovarian cancer. The procedure for detecting the onset of ovarian cancer is ineffective. Generally, by the time ovarian cancer is capable of being detected, it has already developed to a very advanced stage, making treatment relatively unsuccessful. Lynch and Roffman agreed that the standard of care for treating women

with breast-ovarian carcinoma syndrome ordinarily involves surveillance methods. However, for women at an inordinately high risk for ovarian cancer, such as the appellant, the standard of care may require radical surgery that involves the removal of the uterus, ovaries, and fallopian tubes. Blue Cross/Blue Shield did not provide any evidence disputing the premise that the origin of this condition is in the genetic makeup of the individual and that in its natural development it is likely to produce devastating results.

The appellant's condition was considered a deviation from what is considered a normal, healthy, physical state or structure. The abnormality or deviation from a normal state arises, in part, from the genetic makeup of the woman. The existence of this unhealthy state results in the woman's being at substantial risk of developing cancer. The recommended surgery is intended to correct that morbid state by reducing or eliminating the risk.

Blue Cross/Blue Shield did not dispute the nature of the syndrome, the method of diagnosis, or the accuracy of the diagnosis. The medical evidence regarding the nature of breast-ovarian carcinoma syndrome persuaded the court that the appellant suffered from a bodily disorder or disease and, thus, suffered from an illness as defined by the insurance policy. Blue Cross/Blue Shield was, therefore, not entitled to judgment as a matter of law.

False and Misleading Statements

The plaintiff in *Drolet v. Healthsource, Inc.*[8] was a beneficiary of a health care plan administered by her employer, the Mitre Corporation. The plaintiff brought a class action complaint alleging that Healthsource New Hampshire, Inc., and its parent corporation, Healthsource, Inc., are liable under ERISA for several materially false and misleading statements that Healthsource New Hampshire, Inc. allegedly made to the plan's beneficiaries. The defendants moved to dismiss the complaint, claiming that the plaintiff lacked standing to pursue her claim and that her complaint failed to state a claim for relief because neither defendant qualifies as a fiduciary under ERISA.

The benefits provided by the plan require a member to choose a "primary care physician" to be responsible for providing the member with routine medical care and coordinating the member's specialty care referrals. In defining the term *primary care physician*, the agreement emphasized that the physician has a contractual relationship with Healthsource, which does not interfere with the exercise of the physician's independent medical judgment. The plaintiff contended that the physician–patient relationship is compromised by various undisclosed financial incentives that are provided to the plan's physicians to reduce expenditures on specialty care services. Among these incentives, the plaintiff alleged, are "Referral Funds" that permit a physician to earn up to 33 percent in additional income by minimizing the use of specialty services such as diagnostic tests, referrals, and hospitalizations. The plaintiff relied on Healthsource New Hampshire's alleged misrepresentations in arguing that the company breached the fiduciary duty it allegedly owed to Mitre plan's participants and beneficiaries under ERISA. The plaintiff also argued that Healthsource was liable for Healthsource New Hampshire's acts because it "controls the policies and practices" of Healthsource New Hampshire and has the power to grant or deny, or to order its subsidiaries to grant or deny, health care benefits.

The plaintiff satisfactorily alleged in her complaint that Healthsource New Hampshire had the discretionary authority and control over the plan to qualify it as a fiduciary. Healthsource New Hampshire conceded at the hearing on a motion to dismiss the case that it exercises final control over benefits' appeals. The plaintiff also adequately alleged that Healthsource controls the policies and practices of Healthsource New Hampshire to such an extent that it also exercises control over the management and policies of the plan.

A fiduciary owes a duty of loyalty to its beneficiaries that includes the obligation to deal fairly and honestly with plan members. This duty not to mislead is derived both from the common law of trusts and ERISA's statutory language. The duty to disclose material information is the core of a fiduciary's responsibility, animating the common law of trusts long before the enactment of ERISA. Therefore, if Healthsource New Hampshire made material misrepresentations in the Group Subscriber Agreement and other plan documents, it can be enjoined under ERISA to prevent further breaches of its fiduciary duty. Regulations limit Healthsource's obligation to disclose; they do not authorize Healthsource New Hampshire, as a fiduciary, from making misrepresentations to beneficiaries when it voluntarily provides information not required to be disclosed.

ANTITRUST

Market Power

Whenever an MCO possesses significant market power or deals with a group that has significant market power, antitrust implications should be considered. To determine market power, it is necessary first to identify the market in which the entity exercises power. For antitrust purposes, the relevant market has two components: (1) a product component and (2) a geographic component.

Product Market

The relevant product market involves the product or service at issue and all substantially acceptable substitutes for it. The relevant product market for MCOs is the market for health care financing. Broadly defined, this market includes traditional insurers, HMOs, PPOs, IPAs, etc., and their subscriber members.

Market power results from the ability to cut back the market's total supply and then raise prices because of consumer demand for the product. Generally, the market in health care financing is competitive because the customers can switch companies readily, new suppliers can enter the market quickly, and existing suppliers can expand their sales rapidly.

Geographic Market

The relevant geographic market is the market area in which the seller operates, and to which the purchaser can practically turn for supplies. The primary factors that courts have examined to determine the geographic scope of the market for hospital services are

- patient flow statistics
- location of physicians who admit patients
- determinations of health planners
- public perception

Price Fixing

Price fixing is considered a *per se* violation of the antitrust laws. Price fixing occurs when two or more competitors come together to decide on a price that will be charged for services or goods.

The provider-controlled MCO is at significant antitrust risk when setting provider reimbursement and bargaining with payers. There is a danger that provider-controlled organizations will be viewed as a horizontal conspiracy between competitors that acts as a mechanism for price fixing.

Even without organizational control, providers may have practical control of the plan. The Federal Trade Commission (FTC) has identified the following factors as indicative of control:

- power to vote on plan reimbursement or coverage proposals
- representation on, or selection of, key plan policy-making committees

- delegated authority, including veto or approval power over plan policies
- power to appoint or approve plan management
- financing of plan operations
- interlocking directors, officers, or executives
- absence of other strong interest groups in the governing body[9]

One of the leading cases involving price fixing is *Maricopa County Medical Society v. Arizona University*,[10] a U.S. Supreme Court case that involved the exercise of provider control over the level of physician reimbursement. Because the physicians had no financial stake in the success of the plan, the Supreme Court found that the maximum fee schedule set by the physicians constituted illegal price fixing.

In *Maine v. Alliance Healthcare, Inc.*,[11] an entity composed of four hospitals and their affiliated physician groups was formed to contract with managed care plans. The state attorney general charged that the entity was engaged in price fixing because it allegedly forced HMOs to pay physicians on a fee-for-service instead of a capitation basis. In the resulting consent decree, the entity agreed to cease collectively negotiating prices for its members. In *Hassan v. Independent Practice Assoc.*, the court found that a capitated IPA arrangement was appropriate when

- Physicians shared the risk of loss through acceptance of capitation payments.
- The plan did not dictate what participating physicians could charge to nonplan patients, including those belonging to competing health carriers.
- The plan constituted a new product, namely, guaranteed comprehensive physician services, for a prepaid premium different from fee-for-services.[12]

In this context, the court held that the maximum reimbursement rates established by the IPA were lawful as a necessary part of the joint venture's integration of resources.

Provider Exclusion

Providers who are excluded from managed care systems may bring group boycott charges alleging that the exclusion constitutes an illegal restraint of trade. Traditionally, group boycotts have been considered inherently anticompetitive and, therefore, characterized as *per se* violations of the Sherman Act.[13] In *Northwest Wholesale Stationers, Inc. v. Pacific Stationery and Printing Co.*, the U.S. Supreme Court identified three characteristics as indicative of *per se* illegal boycotts:

1. The boycott cuts off access to a supply, facility, or market necessary to enable the victim firm to compete.
2. The defendant possesses a dominant market position.
3. The practices are not justified by plausible arguments that they enhance overall efficiency or competition.[14]

Today, that designation is principally reserved for cases in which competitors agree with each other not to deal with a supplier or distributor if it continues to serve a competitor whom they seek to injure.

Antitrust and Market Share

Competition between HMOs can bring about actions in antitrust. For example, in *U.S. Healthcare, Inc. v. Healthsource, Inc.*,[15] several HMOs, U.S. Healthcare, Inc., U.S. Healthcare of Massachusetts, Inc., and U.S. Healthcare of New Hampshire, Inc. (collectively U.S. Healthcare), brought an action against Healthsource, Inc. (also an HMO), alleging that an exclusive dealing clause in Healthsource's service agreements with physicians violated antitrust laws. Both sides are engaged in providing medical services through HMOs in New Hampshire.

Healthsource, founded in 1985, an IPA-model HMO, was the first HMO established in New Hampshire. Aware that other HMOs were considering marketing in New Hampshire, Healthsource, in order to maintain its market share, offered its panel of physicians greater compensation if they agreed to an exclusive contract. Healthsource's new agreement provided the following optional paragraph:

> 11.01 Exclusive Services of Physicians. Physician agrees during the term of this agreement not to serve as a participating physician for any other HMO plan; this shall not, however, prevent Physician from providing professional courtesy coverage arrangements for brief periods of time or emergency services to members of other HMO plans.[16]

U.S. Healthcare entered the New Hampshire market by applying for and obtaining a license on February 21, 1991, to market its HMO in New Hampshire.

The U.S. District Court sustained the exclusive service provision and entered judgment for Healthsource. U.S. Healthcare appealed, claiming a *per se* violation of the Sherman Antitrust Act, in that the exclusivity clause consisted of a group boycott.

The U.S. Court of Appeals held that the exclusive dealing clause in Healthsource's service agreements with physicians did not give rise to a *per se* violation of the Sherman Antitrust Act.

The Court of Appeals found that there was no evidence of a horizontal agreement among Healthsource's physicians. The exclusivity agreement challenged by U.S. Healthcare was vertical in form. It is "clear that a purely vertical arrangement, by which (for example) a supplier or dealer makes an arrangement, exclusively to supply or serve a manufacturer, is not a group boycott. . . . Were the law otherwise, every distributor or retailer who agreed with a manufacturer to handle only one brand of television or bicycle would be engaged in a group boycott of other manufacturers."[17]

The Court of Appeals held that the competitors of Healthsource, Inc., failed to establish violation of the Sherman Antitrust Act under the rule of reason. U.S. Healthcare asserted that the exclusivity clause completely foreclosed U.S. Healthcare and any other nonstaff HMO from operation in New Hampshire. This argument was weak in that the financial incentive to remain in an exclusive status is questionable because of variation from physician to physician, based on patient load. Physicians with the least number of patients would be the least constrained to remain with Healthsource, and, therefore, would be more likely candidates for competing HMOs. Although the number of physicians tied to Healthsource represented 25 percent of the total number of primary care physicians practicing in the state of New Hampshire, a significant number of physicians were not tied to an exclusive arrangement with Healthsource. Physicians who signed into the exclusivity contract were not tied in permanently. U.S. Healthcare could have competed for Healthsource physicians by offering greater financial incentives to switch over. In addition, there is a constant stream of new physicians entering the marketplace. These physicians are a source for recruitment for any competitor. Absent the showing of a properly defined market in which Healthsource could approach monopoly size, there was no reason to consider the geographic dimension of the market. If health care financing is the product market, as the magistrate judge determined, plainly Healthsource had no monopoly or anything close to it, given the number of other providers in New Hampshire, such as insurers, staff HMOs, Blue Cross/Blue Shield, and individual physicians. This was equally so whether the geographic market was southern New Hampshire (as U.S. Healthcare claims) or the whole state (as the magistrate judge found).

Per Se Rule

The *per se* rule applies to restraints in trade that are so inimical to competition and so unjustified that they are presumed to be unreasonable and, therefore, are illegal. Examinations of *per se* violations include price fixing, horizontal market allocation, tying, and group boycotts.

CORPORATE REORGANIZATION

Traditionally, hospitals have functioned as independent, freestanding corporate entities or as units or divisions of multihospital systems. Until recently, a freestanding hospital functioned as a single corporate entity with most programs and activities carried out within such entity to meet increasing competition.

Dependence on government funding and related programs (e.g., Medicare, Medicaid, and Blue Cross) and the continuous shrinkage occurring in such revenues have forced hospitals to seek alternative sources of revenue. Greater competition from nonhospital sources also has contributed to this need to seek alternative revenue sources. It has become apparent that traditional corporate structures may no longer be appropriate to accommodate both normal hospital activities and those additional activities undertaken to provide alternative sources of revenue.

The typical hospital is incorporated under state law as a freestanding, for-profit, or not-for-profit corporation. The corporation has a governing body. Such governing body has overall responsibility for the operation and management of the hospital with a necessary delegation of appropriate responsibility to administrative employees and the medical staff.

Not-for-profit hospitals are usually exempt from federal taxation under Section 501(c)(3) of the U.S. Internal Revenue Code of 1986 as amended. Such federal exemption usually entitles the organization to an automatic exemption from state taxes as well. Such tax exemption not only relieves the hospital from the payment of income taxes, sales taxes, and the like, but also permits the hospital to receive contributions from donors who then may obtain charitable deductions on their personal tax returns.

Given the need to obtain income and to meet competition, hospitals have begun to consider establishing business enterprises. They also may consider other nonbusiness operations, such as the establishment of additional nonexempt undertakings (e.g., hospices and long-term care facilities). Because hospitals have resources including the physical plant, administrative talent, and technical expertise in areas that are potentially profitable, the first option usually considered is direct participation by the hospital in health-related business enterprises. There are, however, regulatory and legal pressures that present substantial impediments.

Taxation

Income earned by tax-exempt organizations from nonexempt activities is subject to unrelated business income taxes under the Internal Revenue Code. These taxes are similar to those paid by profit-making organizations. In addition, tax-exempt status may be lost if a substantial portion of the corporation's activities are related to nonexempt activities and/or if the benefits of the tax-exempt status accrue to individuals who control the entity either directly or indirectly (private inurement). Care also must be taken to avoid the use of facilities exempt from real estate taxation for nonexempt enterprises because this may lead to a partial or complete loss of such exemption.

Third-Party Reimbursement

Medicare, Medicaid, Blue Cross, and other third parties that reimburse hospitals directly for patient care require that no reimbursement be available for activities unrelated to the provision of such care. Thus, costs associated with unrelated activities must be deducted from costs submitted to third-party payers for reimbursement. The "carving out" of these costs can be detrimental to the hospital unless alternative revenues are found.

Certificate of Need

Generally, hospitals may not add additional programs or services nor may they expend monies for the acquisition of capital in excess of specified threshold limits without first obtaining approval from appropriate state regulatory agencies. The process by which this approval is granted generally is referred to as the certificate of need (CON) process.

The National Health Planning and Resources Development Act of 1974, Public Law No. 93–641, sought to encourage state review of all plans calling for the construction, expansion, or renovation of health facilities or services by conditioning receipt of certain federal funds on the establishment of an approved, state CON program. Most states responded to this law by instituting state CON programs that complied with federal standards. Although the federal law is now history, CON programs remain in effect in a dwindling number of states. Some states continue to maintain control over Medicaid expenditures for hospital and nursing home care by controlling the number of beds through the CON process. This process can be lengthy and expensive. Further, it may not always result in approval of the request to offer the new program or service or to make the capital expenditure.

Health care providers have criticized CON requirements because they require review of those expenditures "by or on behalf of a health care facility" but may allow groups of physicians or independent laboratories to make large expenditures for equipment or services without triggering the state review mechanism.

Disapprovals of CONs often occur because they do not comply with state health plans that are designed to limit programs and services and prevent overbedding in predefined geographic areas. Some CON applicants have attempted to seek revisions in state health plans to obtain approval of their projects. *Nursing Home of Dothan v. Alabama State Health Planning & Development Agency*[18] was one such case. The nursing home had filed a CON application with the State Health Planning Agency (SHPA) to construct a 110-bed nursing home. SHPA informed Dothan that the state health plan failed to indicate a need for additional beds and advised Dothan to seek an amendment to the state health plan before proceeding with the CON process. The defendant filed the proposed amendment with the State Health Coordinating Council, which approved the defendant's request for additional beds. The amendment, which required the governor's approval, was rejected by him. On appeal of the circuit court's finding for SHPA, denying Dothan's proposed amendment to the state health plan and subsequent denial of the CON application, the appeals court held that the governor properly disapproved the requested amendment.

Disapproval of a CON application also can be based on the financial feasibility of the project. A CON proposal to construct a long-term care nursing facility with 65 percent Medicaid beds was found to have been properly denied in *National Health Corp. v. South Carolina Department of Health & Environmental Control*.[19] The Department of Health and Environmental Control's decision was considered proper, reasonable, and consistent with applicable laws and regulations. The unsuccessful applicant, National Health Corp. (NHC), had failed to establish its project's financial feasibility because of the unavailability of Medicaid funding. Discrepancies also existed between its budgets and its cost reports.

The record contains clear evidence that Medicaid funds would not be available for the NHC beds. The Board also found that inconsistencies in four budgets submitted by NHC and the discrepancies between those budgets and the cost reports submitted by NHC to State Health and Human Services Finance Commission raised serious questions regarding the financial feasibility of the NHC project.[20]

The agency's competitor had shown the financial feasibility of its project and was, therefore, granted a CON.

There can be disagreement among justices within the same court as to whether an applicant has established the criteria for need within a specific geographic area. The record in *Heritage of Yankton, Inc. v. South Dakota Department of Health*[21] was found to have supported denial of a CON application for additional beds based on the argument that there was no need for additional beds in the service area. The department of health was found not to have acted arbitrarily and capriciously in denying the application. It provided valid reasons for rejecting new information submitted at a rehearing. The department of health rejected an argument that a bed shortage in the county demonstrated a need for more beds.

The department argued that it had never considered county boundaries in determining bed need, and that the population of the facility's service area is the proper area for consideration. In view of its policy to maintain high occupancy rates in all facilities, the department also rejected Heritage's claim that the department's formula forces the elderly to be separated from their families and home communities.

Justice Henderson stated in a dissenting opinion:

> This health care facility submitted three items of new evidence which had not been previously considered. This consisted of population projections for the area and an in-and-out migration data with information pertaining to the existence of alternative services. The Department, summarily, expressed that it refused to consider this new evidence. Instead of opening its mind and then opening the door of reconsideration with relevant evidence, the Department of Health chose to be unyielding with its grip on the single formula and methodology it employed. If this health facility's evidence had been reconsidered, an open mind would see that there was an extensive need for beds existing in the city of Yankton and Yankton county.

· · · · ·

> I cannot in good conscience, join the majority opinion which prevents elderly citizens from having a bed, with medical care and treatment, administered compassionately, in a community where their children and grandchildren reside. I would elevate reality over a single methodology and accordingly dissent.
>
> "[T]herefore never send to know for whom the bell tolls; it tolls for thee." John Donne (1573–1631), *Devotions upon Emergent Occasions,* Meditation XVII. My mind drifts to Ernest Hemingway. And a clod of dirt. Chipped away at the shores of Europe by the sea. "If a clod be washed away by the sea, Europe is the less. . . ." *Supra.* All from whence Hemingway's great novel was born. And, yes, not a person is turned away from a bed of repose, in his older years, but South Dakota is lesser in spirit. A refrain also comes to my mind: "And crown thy good, with Brotherhood, from sea to shining sea."[22]

Financing

Even when a hospital has determined that it can and should add a program or service and when it is allowed to do

so, it may lack the necessary capital financing. The hospital could join with private investors (who may, in fact, be members of the medical staff) to gain greater access to capital. Care must be taken, however, that no venture that includes physicians who refer to the hospital can be construed as providing an incentive or a reward for such referrals. Federal antifraud and abuse laws and regulations and similar state regulations impose severe penalties for such violations.

Recognizing the problems enumerated above and further recognizing the need to develop alternative sources of revenue, hospitals have determined that the establishment of an additional or a restructured organization is necessary. Besides the need to develop alternative sources of capital, some restructurings come about simply because of the evolution of a multi-institutional system. Thus, when hospitals merge or consolidate, restructuring is virtually automatic. Also, when several hospitals fall under common ownership or when additional health enterprises are undertaken, restructuring usually evolves as more institutions are added to the system. In these instances, general legal principles applicable to corporations, as well as proper management considerations, will control the development of the appropriate corporate structure.

RESTRUCTURING ALTERNATIVES

Assuming the existence of a single, not-for-profit tax-exempt hospital, any restructuring undertaken normally involves the creation of at least one additional not-for-profit tax-exempt entity. This entity may be referred to as a parent or holding company or foundation. Its general function is to serve as the corporate vehicle to receive the ultimate benefits from the revenue-producing activities and to confer some or all of these benefits on the hospital. Under current rules regarding income taxation, income received directly (by providing goods or services) or indirectly (by means of dividends or other investment income) does not give rise to any tax obligation if the receiver of such benefit is exempt from taxation under any of several subsections of Section 501(c) of the Internal Revenue Code, provided that exempt activities are the organization's main source of income and expense.

Parent Holding Company Model

Under this model, a new not-for-profit corporation is formed in conformity with the laws of the state in which the hospital is located. This corporation then can seek to obtain a tax exemption under the Internal Revenue Code. The overall purposes of the corporation are general in nature but involve a promotion of the health and welfare of the public and also may directly involve benefit to a named hospital or hospitals. In some states, when one organization exists to benefit a licensed hospital, such organization must itself be approved through a CON or similar process. The government of the parent holding company usually is derived from the governing body of the hospital. Qualifications for certain categories of exempt status under the Internal Revenue Code may require overlapping governing bodies between the hospital and the new entity. Section 509(a) of the Internal Revenue Code deals with the qualification of a tax-exempt entity as a "private and/or non-private" foundation. Nonprivate is the preferred status, and the qualification for such status may depend in part on the relationship between the entity seeking tax exemption and the already exempt entity (i.e., the hospital).

Because there is no stock involved in a not-for-profit corporation (the ownership of which would confer control by one corporation over another), control of the not-for-profit hospital by the not-for-profit parent holding company generally arises when the parent holding company is the sole member of the hospital corporation. Membership carries with it the right to elect directors and thus creates the necessary linkage for the parent-subsidiary relationship.

As a tax-exempt entity, the parent holding company also may own one or more for-profit subsidiaries. Although such ownership cannot represent most activities of the parent holding company, the ownership of such entities would not in and of itself disqualify the parent holding company from achieving and maintaining a tax-exempt status. It is through the subsidiaries that for-profit activities are carried on. The for-profit ventures (which may be independent corporations, joint ventures with other investors, etc.) are tax-paying entities. The net revenues (after payment of taxes) are paid out as dividends to the entity owning the stock or other ownership interest (the parent holding company), which, being tax exempt, pays no taxes on the receipt of such dividends. The parent holding company may then, as a donation, confer benefits directly on the hospital or any other entity intended to benefit from the parent holding company. Again, it is important to monitor closely the activities of this corporation so that its participation in or ownership of for-profit entities does not destroy its tax-exempt status. The Internal Revenue Service is becoming increasingly concerned about this issue and has stepped up its auditing activities dramatically.

Controlled Foundation

An alternative structure to the parent holding company model is one in which the new, not-for-profit entity is controlled directly by the hospital. Instead of the parent holding company's being a member of the hospital corporation, the reverse is true. The hospital is the member of the new entity. The structure described earlier to carry out for-profit activities would then fall under the controlled foundation. In many states, the regulators would view such a controlled foundation as nothing more than the alter ego of the hospital and therefore impose on this entity all regulatory restrictions, reimbursement restrictions, and the like.

Independent Foundation

The establishment of a separate not-for-profit corporation and the substructure below it for carrying out for-profit activities may be accomplished independent of the hospital. Even though members of the hospital's governing body are involved in the creation of the new not-for-profit entity, the two corporations themselves may not necessarily be linked. This "brother-sister" relationship frequently is found to be desirable when the governing body of a hospital does not favor the creation of a parent organization to control the hospital but nevertheless seeks to create a viable structure within which for-profit activities may be carried on outside the hospital. A concern frequently expressed in this brother-sister relationship is that the new entity, not being controlled directly by the hospital, or in the alternative, not controlling the hospital, may "run away" and not necessarily ultimately benefit the hospital as was originally intended. Whether such a concern will materialize is naturally dependent on the degree to which the governing bodies of the two organizations overlap and the degree to which each organization remains responsive to the other. The use of this model also may have certain reimbursement advantages regarding earnings on donated monies. If reimbursement regulations ever change to offset charitable gifts from reimbursable activities, an independent organization also may prove useful.

GENERAL CONSIDERATIONS

The organizational structures described above are not intended to alter the way a hospital is managed or the way care is delivered. The driving force behind the creation of alternative structures is the desire to develop alternative sources of revenue and/or to streamline management of multi-institutional systems. In many states, substantial changes in the governance of a hospital require regulatory approval. The establishment of the alternative structures previously described normally does not require such regulatory approval as long as the hospital continues to be governed by a governing body and continues to carry out its functions in accordance with applicable laws, rules, and regulations.

Once restructuring has taken place, many additional entities will require legal and accounting attention. These entities (normally corporations) must maintain minutes, books, and records; file tax returns; and make other such filings as are required by state laws and by federal and state income tax laws and regulations. It is important that the structures be viewed as running independently, one from the other. This includes the establishment of separate bank accounts, the holding of regular meetings among officers and directors, and the maintenance of appropriate minutes. Too often the activities and records of one entity are difficult to discern from those of another, and then the benefits of the separate organizations may be lost. The concept of "piercing the corporate veil" may come into play when each corporate entity is not maintained separately and apart from every other entity. The corporate veil will be pierced when a court determines that the activities of the corporation are indistinguishable from the activities of either another corporation or the corporation's directors, officers, or members.

The parent corporation in *Boafo v. Hospital Corp. of America*[23] was held not liable for injuries sustained by a patient at a subsidiary hospital. Even though the parent corporation shared some officers with the subsidiary and furnished it with substantial administrative services, there was no basis for piercing the corporate veil of the parent, absent some showing that the subsidiary was a sham formed for the purpose of promoting fraud, defeating justice, concealing crime, or evading contractual or tort responsibility.

Although the hospital was a wholly owned subsidiary of a national management corporation, it was a fully capitalized corporate entity that was insured, owned the hospital property, autonomously managed and operated the hospital on a day-to-day basis, maintained its own payroll, and employed its own employees. Therefore, there was no basis for holding the parent corporation liable.

MEDICAL STAFF AND RESTRUCTURING

Any discussion of corporate reorganization undertaken by a hospital must necessarily involve the medical staff. Although a reorganization may have little or no direct impact on the medical staff, the perception of major change requires, at the very least, a full explanation and involvement in the process.

Many hospitals have come to realize that the medical staff presents a fertile area for developing relationships and projects leading to additional revenues. Projects such as imaging centers, laboratories, durable medical equipment businesses, and the like may be organized in conjunction with one or more members of the medical staff. Other likely candidates to participate in joint ventures include existing laboratories, home care companies, durable medical equipment companies, drug companies, surgical supply houses, and the like. As previously noted, ventures involving physicians are coming under significantly greater scrutiny and regulation. Laws and regulations have been designed to curb the practice of physicians and other health care professionals referring patients to facilities or enterprises in which they have a financial interest.

Joint ventures with physician groups are not without risk, as was shown in *Arango v. Reyka*,[24] in which a hospital entered into a joint venture with an anesthesiology group and thus was vicariously liable for the malpractice of the members of that group. The hospital billed patients for anesthesiology services, retained 12 percent of all collections, owned and furnished anesthesiology equipment and medications used by the group, scheduled patients, and referred to the group as the hospital's department of anesthesiology. As a result, there existed a common purpose to provide anesthesiology services to hospital patients. Control was shared between the hospital and the group over the provision of anesthesia services, and there was a joint interest in the financial benefits and profits generated by the combination of their resources and services. That the physicians had an obligation to maintain control over their medical judgment did not prevent the creation of a joint venture contract.

Development of a business involving equity participation must be considered in the light of state and federal securities laws and other relevant laws, rules, and regulations to determine that there is full compliance. Shares of stock, shares in linked partnerships, and other similar equity participation interests may fall within the definition of a public offering of securities requiring filings and/or registrations under state and federal securities laws.

FUND-RAISING

A not-for-profit hospital generally raises funds. Any new not-for-profit corporation formed as part of restructuring also may be able to engage in fund-raising if such entity obtains a tax exemption under the Internal Revenue Code.

Also, as part of a reorganization and despite the creation of a new entity as indicated, hospitals frequently determine that it is desirable to create an additional foundation, the sole purpose of which is fund-raising for the hospital. This, therefore, may lead to as many as three organizations with both the capability and the intent to engage in fund-raising to benefit the hospital. Obvious confusion may arise in the minds of the public being asked to give to these organizations. A coordinated approach to fund-raising is critical to avoid such confusion.

Any organization engaged in fund-raising may have local filing requirements at the state or other governmental level. Care must be taken that the public is informed completely as to the ultimate beneficiary of such fund-raising and the manner in which the monies raised will be spent. A donor to a charity may have a claim against that charity if the donor can show that he or she was misled as to the ultimate beneficiary of the gift or as to the purposes for which the gift would be used. Members of the public may be reluctant to donate when capital is to be used to fund for-profit enterprises. The overall charitable purposes of the entity must be carried out, and the activities may not be so concentrated on the operation or participation in for-profit ventures that either the tax exemption is jeopardized or it is determined (usually by the state attorney general) that the funds have been raised improperly from the public.

REGULATORY AUTHORITY CHECKLIST

In considering restructuring, the following regulatory authority checklist may be helpful:

- Not-for-profit corporations
  - not-for-profit corporation law
  - Internal Revenue Code (exemption and taxpayer identification number)
  - state and local tax laws on exemptions (including real property)
  - attorney general or similar charitable registration requirements
  - bylaws, organization minutes, and minutes of first governing body meeting
  - bank account
- For-profit corporations
  - business corporation law
  - taxpayer identification number
  - bylaws, organization minutes, minutes of first governing body meeting, and issuance of stock
  - bank account
- Hospitals
  - reimbursement regulations
  - certificate of need regulations
  - governing body bylaws and relationship to additional corporations
  - fraud and abuse laws, rules, and regulations

ANTICOMPETITION

Because an organization exerts a certain amount of influence and dominance over its patient population, the participation in for-profit enterprises to which an organization's patients are referred may give rise to anticompetitive activities and antitrust claims. Patients must be permitted a free choice in connection with goods and services. For example, if an organization (through its reorganized structure) participates in a durable medical equipment (DME) business and seeks to recommend such business to its patients on discharge, such patients must be allowed to choose an alternate supplier. Patients must be advised that they are not required to use the vendor recommended by the organization. An or-

ganization should disclose its relationship to the DME company so that the patient knows the organization's involvement in advance of making a choice.

Care must be taken that local vendors and merchants who have a traditional relationship with the organization or with the patients are not so affected by the proposed for-profit activity that ill will is generated within the community, and a potential legal claim regarding anticompetitive activity evolves.

Restructuring requires a multidisciplinary approach. The issues to be considered include legal, financial, accounting, tax, regulatory, and reimbursement concerns. These disciplines must provide input on an ongoing basis, not merely at inception. Changing requirements and interpretations—especially in the areas of taxation and Medicare/Medicaid fraud and abuse regulations—mandate a continuous process of review and modification so that desired goals are not subverted by legal and financial problems.

> Nonetheless, a word of caution. Today's ventures require additional planning for the possibility that some, or part, of an enterprise might ultimately be found illegal. Therefore, potential buyers, and hopefully arrangements with them, as well as appropriate dissolution and unwinding provisions, now more than ever, need to be part of the fabric and documentation of any new joint venture. As well, the documentation of existing ventures must be reviewed in the light of current considerations and where necessary, needed revisions crafted.[25]

The FTC determined that the Hospital Corporation of America (HCA), a proprietary hospital chain, violated Section 7 of the Clayton Act, as amended, 15 U.S.C. § 18 (1982), by acquiring two hospital corporations, Hospital Affiliates International, Inc., and Health Care Corporation, in the Chattanooga area for $700 million. HCA already owned one hospital in the area. Hospital Affiliates International held management contracts with two other area hospitals.[26] This in effect gave HCA control of more than 5 of the 11 hospitals in the Chattanooga area. The management contract with one of the hospitals was canceled after the FTC began investigating HCA's acquisition of Hospital Affiliates. HCA sought judicial review by petitioning the court of appeals to set aside the decision of the FTC. The court of appeals held that there was substantial evidence to support the commission's determination that the acquisitions were likely to foster collusive practices harmful to consumers.

Restructuring is an undertaking that requires careful planning and legal and accounting advice, and should be undertaken not because it is "fashionable" but rather because it will provide the hospital with opportunities not available under its current structure.

SAFE-HARBOR REGULATIONS

The safe-harbor regulations describe how health care providers should structure financial arrangements in order to be exempt from prosecution by the Department of Justice and the FTC. The safe-harbor regulation covers (1) investment interests, (2) space rentals, (3) equipment rentals, (4) personal services and mandatory contracts, (5) sales of practice, (6) referral services, (7) warranties, (8) discounts, (9) employees, (10) group purchasing organizations, and (11) waivers of beneficiary coinsurance and deductibles (for inpatient hospital services under a prospective payment system). "Under the rules, providers must be under no obligation to refer business to the venture. In addition, providers' financial return must be in proportion to the amount of their investment and not tied to their business referrals."[27]

The Medicare and Medicaid Patient and Program Protection Act (MMPPPA) specifically directed the Secretary of the Department of Health and Human Services (HHS), in consultation with the Attorney General, to publish regulations specifying payment practices that would not be treated as a criminal offense under the antikickback provisions. Illegal remunerations (kickbacks) are a felony offense. The statute provides that once those rules have been promulgated, any payment practice specified in such regulations will not be considered illegal. Failure to fall squarely within a safe harbor, however, does not necessarily mean that the practice is illegal. It simply indicates that it is not automatically safe. Failure to comply with the regulations can result in civil or criminal sanctions, as well as exclusion from Medicare and Medicaid programs.

The regulations establishing safe harbors were published July 9, 1991, and became effective on that date.[28] The following briefly describes the safe harbors and some of the requirements that must be met in order to fall within the safe harbor:

- Investments in large publicly traded entities—No violation is inherent in a payment that is a return on an investment interest made to an investor as long as requirements, such as the following, are met: payment to an investor as return on investment must be directly proportional to the amount of that investor's capital investment.
- Investments in smaller ventures—No violation is inherent in a payment that is a return on an investment interest made to an investor.
- Lease of space and equipment—The Office of the Inspector General (OIG) has characterized as two different safe harbors two kinds of lease arrangements—those for space and those for equipment. Despite this characterization, however, the rules for the two safe harbors are very similar: rental payments made by lessees to lessors for use of space or equipment received is safe-harbor protected.

- Personal services and management contracts—Safe-harbor protection applies to payments made by a principal to an agent as compensation for the services of the agent.
- Sale of practitioner practice—Payments made to a practitioner by another practitioner in order to purchase a practice are protected.
- Referral services—Any payment or exchange of anything of value between a referral service and a referral service participant is protected.
- Warranties—This safe harbor covers warranties that meet the definition of that term in the Magnuson-Moss Warranty-Federal Trade Commission Improvement Act,[29] as well as agreements by a manufacturer or supplier to replace another manufacturer's or supplier's defective item on terms equal to the agreement if replaced.
- Standards for buyers—Any payment or exchange of anything of value under a warranty provided by a manufacturer or supplier of an item to the buyer of the item receives safe harbor protection.
- Standards for manufacturers and suppliers—To qualify for this safe-harbor protection, a manufacturer or supplier must meet certain requirements, such as reporting any price reduction that was obtained as part of the warranty.
- Discounts—Discounts are a reduction in the amount a seller charges a buyer (who buys either directly or through a wholesaler or a group purchasing organization) for a good or service based on an arm's-length transaction.[30] The term discount may include a rebate check or credit. It does not include any cash payment nor does it include furnishing one good or service without charge or at a reduced charge in exchange for any agreement to buy a different good or service.
- Standards for buyers—A hospital that receives a discount for a purchased good or service must comply with requirements such as the discount being earned based on purchases of that same good or service bought within a single fiscal year.
- Standards for sellers—The person or entity that sells discounted goods or services to a hospital must comply with requirements, such as the seller must fully and accurately report such discount on the invoice or statement submitted to the buyer and inform the buyer of its obligations to report such discount.
- Employees—This safe harbor allows an employer to pay an employee, who has a bona fide employment relationship with the employer, for providing covered items or services.
- Group purchasing organizations (GPOs)—A GPO is an entity authorized to act as a purchasing agent for a group of individuals or entities who are furnishing services for which payment may be made under Medicare or a state health care program, and who are neither wholly owned by the GPO nor subsidiaries of a parent

corporation that wholly owns the GPO (either directly or through another wholly owned entity).

- Waiver of beneficiary coinsurance and deductibles—Hospitals may waive co-payments or deductibles for inpatient hospital care for which Medicare pays under the prospective payment system.
- Managed care—Two additional safe harbors for managed care plans were published in the Federal Register on November 5, 1992. The safe harbors are intended to protect certain business and payment relationships between health care plans, providers, and enrollees that allow them to compete in the marketplace for managed care.
- Coverage, costsharing, or premiums offered to enrollees—Under this safe harbor, managed care plans may offer incentives to beneficiaries, including additional coverage of any item or service to an enrollee, reduction of some or all of the enrollee's obligations to pay the health plan or a contract health care provider for cost-sharing amounts (such as coinsurance, deductible, or co-payment amounts), or reduction of the premium amounts attributable to items or services covered by the health plan, Medicare, or a state health plan.
- Price reductions providers offer to health plans—This safe harbor protects certain price-reduction agreements between health care plans and health care providers. Contract health care providers may offer a reduction in price to health plans as long as both the health plan and the contract health care provider comply with all of the applicable standards.

STATEMENTS OF ANTITRUST ENFORCEMENT POLICY IN THE HEALTH CARE AREA

The Department of Justice and the FTC issued six policy statements, which address the following antitrust safety zones:

1. hospital mergers

2. hospital joint ventures involving high-technology or other expensive medical equipment
3. physicians' provision of information to purchasers of health care services
4. hospital participation in exchanges of price and cost information
5. joint purchasing arrangements among health care providers
6. physician network joint ventures[31]

The policy statements are designed to provide education and instruction to the health care community on issues related to mergers and joint ventures. The policy statements give health care providers guidance in the form of antitrust safety zones, which describe the circumstances under which the agencies will not challenge conduct as violative of the antitrust law as a matter of prosecutorial discretion. The statements set forth in outline format the analysis the agencies will utilize to review conduct that falls outside the antitrust safety zones. The policy statements, for the first time, commit the agencies to responding to requests for business reviews or advisory opinions from the health care community no later than 90 days following the receipt of all information regarding any matters addressed in the statements, with the exception of requests regarding mergers falling outside the antitrust safety zone.[32]

Under the Health Insurance Portability and Accountability Act of 1996 (HIPPA), HHS is now required to provide formal guidance to individual parties with respect to the antikickback statute. HHS, in collaboration with the Department of Justice, must issue written opinions relating to the following: what constitutes prohibited remuneration; whether an arrangement violates the antikickback and safe harbors statutory scheme; what constitutes an inducement to limit or reduce services to Medicare and Medicaid beneficiaries in a managed care plan; and whether any activity exposes a provider to criminal or civil liability.

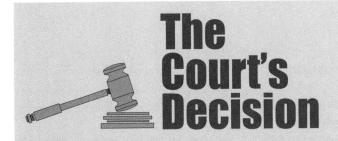

The Court's Decision

The New York Court of Appeals reinstated the plaintiff's complaint. The Court of Appeals summed up its view of the case and its ruling in the following language: The issue before us is whether ERISA's preemption clause bars the plaintiff's claims against her husband's primary care physician, Yung. All of these claims fall within the traditional domain of State regulation. Yung, therefore, bears the "considerable burden" of overcoming the presumption that Congress did not intend to preempt them. In an attempt to surmount that formidable hurdle, Yung alleges that ERISA preempts these claims because they "relate to" the administration of the US Healthcare HMO.

The Appellate Division agreed, holding that Yung was protected by ERISA preemption because he had acted in a "purely administrative" capacity, and not as an actual provider of medical care. The plaintiff's claims against Yung do not relate to an employee benefit plan.

The Pennsylvania Supreme Court looked closely at the allegations against Yung and explained why, in its analysis, the allegations did not "relate to" the administration of an employee benefit plan. Here, the plaintiff alleges that Yung, as a direct provider of medical services, violated the duties and standard of care owed to this his patient by improperly assessing the nature and extent of his condition and by failing to take reasonable steps to provide for his timely treatment by a specialist. Viewed pragmatically, these claims are not preempted by ERISA. The plaintiff's allegations of negligent medical care do not "relate to" the administration of an ERISA plan merely because they refer to Yung's delay in submitting the US Healthcare form seeking a referral to Dr. Green. The plaintiff does not allege that Yung is responsible for delay caused by US Healthcare's decision-making process with respect to coverage or benefits. Her claim against Yung is that he failed to take timely action to treat her husband.

The plaintiff did not challenge any administrative determination relating to an employee benefit plan or the extent of rights and benefits under such a plan, but focused entirely on the alleged failing by the physician to promptly submit the necessary paperwork to the HMO. Thus, the claims that the physician breached his duty to the deceased did not relate to ERISA plan administration and were to be determined under state law.

The Pennsylvania Supreme Court in *Pappas v. Asbel*,[33] said:

> Claims that an HMO was negligent when it provided contractually-guaranteed medical benefits in such a dilatory fashion that the patient was injured indisputably are intertwined with the provision of safe medical care. We believe that it would be highly questionable for us to find that these claims were preempted when the United States Supreme Court has stated that there was no intent on the part of Congress to preempt state laws concerning the regulation of the provision of safe medical care. *Id.* at 893.

The Pennsylvania Supreme Court acknowledged that by allowing negligence claims, there will be a financial impact on HMOs. The court did not consider this enough to countermand the conclusion that these claims are not preempted. As noted by the *DeBuono* court, an additional increase in the costs imposed on an ERISA will not mandate a finding of preemption.[34]

CHAPTER REVIEW

1. The process of structuring or restructuring health care systems' financing, purchasing, delivering, measuring, and documenting a broad range of services and products is called *managed care.*
2. *Health maintenance organizations* (HMOs) are the most highly regulated form of *managed care organizations (MCOs)* and are health systems that are responsible for the financing and delivery of a wide range of comprehensive services to their enrolled populations.
   - *Independent practice association (IPA) models* provide care to subscribers through contracts with independent physicians.
   - *Staff models* normally contract with physicians as full-time employees.

3. Entities through which employer health benefit plans and health insurance carriers contract to purchase services for covered beneficiaries from a selected group of providers are called *preferred provider organizations (PPO)*. *Exclusive provider organizations (EPOs)* limit beneficiaries to participating providers.

4. *Open-access* and *point-of-service* plans allow members to decide whether to use HMO benefits or the more traditional indemnity benefits at each instance of care.

5. *IPAs* are legal entities of physicians who have organized to negotiate contracts to provide their services. *Group practices* are physician groups that have only one or a small number of service delivery locations, while in a *group practice without walls (GPWW)*, physicians organize to share administrative and management costs but practice at their own locations.

6. *Management service organizations (MSOs)* provide services such as practice management, marketing, managed care contracting, billing, and personnel management for physicians. *Vertically integrated delivery systems (IDS)* provide physician and hospital services to patients. IDSs can be one organization or several affiliated organizations.

7. *Federal qualification* of HMOs is voluntary, and those that are federally qualified must provide or arrange for basic services for members as needed and without limitations on time, cost, frequency, extent, or nature of services provided.

8. Most state HMO laws require that an application for a certificate of authority be accompanied by a description of proposed marketing plans. A regulator must approve this plan. Also, most laws specify that a schedule of charges and amendments be filed and approved by the commissioner.

9. *Utilization review (UR)* is a process through which a third-party payer assesses the medical necessity of a course of treatment. *Prospective review* is the determination of whether to pay for a treatment before the treatment is administered, *concurrent review* takes place during the treatment, and *retrospective review* takes place after the treatment.

10. Employers, managed care entities, and providers can do several things to reduce the risk of liability, including complying with formalities, contracting through the plan itself, and defining clearly discretionary responsibilities.

11. Congress passed the *Health Care Quality Improvement Act (HCQIA)* of 1986 to encourage continued participation in peer review and credentialing activities. The Act grants immunity to persons who supply to professional review bodies information that may result in adverse decisions against a physician.

12. A fiduciary is obligated to deal fairly and honestly with plan members. The duty not to mislead is derived both from the common law of trusts and the statutory language in the *Employee Retirement Income Security Act (ERISA)* of 1974.

13. The market, as related to antitrust purposes, has two components: (1) a *product market* that involves the product or service at issue and all substantially acceptable substitutes for it, and (2) a *geographic market* that is the area in which the seller operates and to which the purchaser can practically turn for supplies.

14. *Price fixing* is when two or more competitors collude to decide on the price that will be charged for services or goods. For MCOs, there is a danger that provider-controlled organizations will be seen as a horizontal conspiracy between competitors that acts as a mechanism for price fixing.

15. Dependence on government funding and related programs, the continuous shrinkage in such revenues, and increased competition from nonhospital sources have contributed to the need to seek alternative resources for revenue. The need to obtain income and meet competition has caused hospitals to consider establishing business enterprises.

16. A *certificate of need (CON)* is granted by a state regulatory agency and allows hospitals to add programs or services or expend monies for the acquisition of capital in excess of specified threshold limits. Health care providers have criticized CON requirements because they require the review of expenditures by or on behalf of a health care facility but may permit groups of physicians or independent laboratories to make large expenditures without triggering state review mechanisms.

17. Restructuring of a single not-for-profit tax-exempt hospital normally involves the formation of at least one additional not-for-profit tax-exempt entity, which may be referred to as a parent or holding company or foundation. The creation of this additional entity is so that it can serve as the corporate vehicle to receive the ultimate benefits for the revenue-producing activities and can confer some or all of those benefits to the hospital.

18. If a business involving equity participation is to be developed, state and federal securities laws, along with other relevant laws, rules, and regulations, must be considered in order to ensure full compliance.

19. Patients must be allowed free choice of goods and services in order for organizations to protect themselves from anticompetitive activities and antitrust claims. Patients must be advised that they are not required to use a vendor that an organization recommends and also should be informed of the organization's relationship to the company in advance of the patient's decision.

20. The regulations that describe how health care providers should structure financial arrangements in order to be exempt from prosecution by the Department of Justice and the FTC are called *safe-harbor regulations*.

21. The Department of Justice and the FTC issued six policy statements designed to educate and instruct health care community members on issues surrounding mergers and joint ventures. These statements outline the analysis the agencies will use to review conduct that falls outside antitrust safety zones.

REVIEW QUESTIONS

1. Describe some of the more common models of MCOs.
2. What are the advantages and disadvantages of HMOs?
3. What does the *Safe Harbor Act* regulate?
4. What is meant by the "parent holding company model?"
5. What is the purpose of *utilization review*?

NOTES

1. Nealy v. US Healthcare HMO, 1999 NY LEXIS 208 (N.Y. Mar. 25, 1999).
2. 42 U.S.C. § 300 (1995).
3. *See* 42 U.S.C. § 300e (1995) (Historical and Statutory Notes).
4. 239 Cal. Rptr. 810 (Cal. Ct. App. 1986).
5. 808 F. Supp. 1253 (E.D. Va. 1992).
6. 600 P.2d 1060 (Cal. 1979).
7. 515 N.W.2d 645 (Neb. 1994).
8. 968 F. Supp. 757 (D.C. N.H. 1997).
9. 46 Fed. Reg. 48,982 (1981).
10. 457 U.S. 332 (1982).
11. 1991–1 Trade Cas. (CCH) ¶ 69,339.
12. 698 F. Supp. 679 (D. Mich. 1988).
13. Eastern States Retail Lumber Dealers Ass'n v. United States, 234 U.S. 600 (1914).
14. 472 U.S. 284 (1985).
15. 986 F.2d 589 (1st Cir. 1993).
16. *Id.* at 592.
17. *Id.* at 594.
18. 542 So.2d 935 (Ala. Civ. App. 1989).
19. 380 S.E.2d 841 (S.C. Ct. App. 1989).
20. *Id.* at 845.
21. 432 N.W.2d 68 (S.D. 1988).
22. *Id.* at 76–77.
23. 338 S.E.2d 477 (Ga. Ct. App. 1985).
24. 507 So.2d 1211 (Fla. Dist. Ct. App. 1987).
25. Weissburg, *Joint Ventures: To Be or Not To Be*, FED'N OF AM. HEALTH SYS. REV., May–June 1989, at 50.
26. Hospital Corp. of Am. v. Federal Trade Comm'n, 807 F.2d 1381 (7th Cir. 1986).
27. 56 Fed. Reg. 35,952 (codified at 42 C.F.R. § 1001.951–953).
28. *HHS's Final "Safe-Harbor" Regulations Limit Referrals*, A.H.A. NEWS, July 29, 1991, at 1.
29. The term *written warranty* is defined as: (A) any written affirmation of fact or written promise made in connection with the sale of a consumer product by a supplier to a buyer which relates to the nature of the material or workmanship and affirms or promises that such material or workmanship is defect free or will meet a specified level of performance over a specified period of time, or (B) any undertaking in writing in connection with the sale by a supplier of a consumer product to refund, repair, replace, or take other remedial action with respect to such product in the event that product fails to meet the specifications set forth in the undertaking, which written affirmation, promise, or undertaking becomes part of the basis of the bargain between a supplier and a buyer for purposes other than resale of such product.
30. Safe Harbor, 42 C.F.R. § 1001.951–953.
31. U.S. DEPT. OF JUSTICE AND FED. TRADE COMM'N, STATEMENTS OF ANTITRUST ENFORCEMENT POLICY IN THE HEALTH CARE AREA, Sept. 15, 1993, at 1.
32. *Id.* at 1–2.
33. 724 A.2d 889 (Pa. 1998).
34. *Id.* at 894.

Tort Reform and Reducing the Risks of Malpractice

Given the difficulties in the present tort system, we often become victims of the failures of medicine as opposed to beneficiaries of its many successes. Physicians have lost in that they have changed, limited, or closed their practices after having spent the most vigorous years of their lives training for such work. Patients have lost in that the physicians of their choice, with whom they have developed trusting relationships, are no longer available to care for them. It is certain that the system requires sensible reform.

Author Anonymous

INTRODUCTION

The tort system has proven to be inadequate in the prevention of medical malpractice. Damage awards as a deterrent to malpractice have failed to hold the number of claims to a reasonable level. Exorbitant jury awards and malpractice insurance premiums, costing billions of dollars annually, are bringing health care organizations ever closer to a day of reckoning with financial disaster.

Physicians who wish to practice medicine and survive have accepted the concept of practicing defensive medicine. Defensive (self-protective) medicine is believed to be one of the most harmful effects produced by the threat of malpractice litigation. Such medicine is practiced to forestall potential litigation and provide an advantageous legal defense should a lawsuit be instituted. Defensive medicine often results in undertreatment, by avoiding high-risk tests and procedures, or overtreatment, such as the excessive use of diagnostic tests. "The message the tort system is sending to doctors is not so much deterrence, in terms of practicing good medicine, but more just 'drive defensively,' because any patient you may see may be a litigant."[1]

This chapter reviews selected schemes for tort reform and suggested programs for coping with the malpractice crisis.

ARBITRATION AND MEDIATION

Among the many factors contributing to the malpractice crisis is the high cost of litigation. Trial by jury is lengthy and expensive. If case disputes can be handled out of court, the process and expense of a lawsuit can be significantly reduced. Arbitration and mediation are basically mechanisms for simplifying and expediting the settlement of claims.

Arbitration is the process by which parties to a dispute voluntarily agree to submit their differences to the judgment of an impartial mediation panel for resolution. It is used as a means to evaluate, screen, and resolve medical malpractice disputes before they reach the courts. Arbitration can be accomplished by mutual consent of the parties or statutory provisions. A decision made at arbitration may or may not be binding, depending on prior agreement between the parties or statutory requirements.

Mediation is the process whereby a third party, the mediator, attempts to bring about a settlement between the parties of a complaint. The mediator cannot force a settlement.

STRUCTURED AWARDS

Structured awards are set up for the periodic payment of judgments by establishing a reversible trust fund for specified parts of awards due plaintiffs. The purpose of a structured award is to provide compensation during a plaintiff's lifetime. It would eliminate an unwarranted windfall to the plaintiff's beneficiaries in the event of death. Some states have sought to deal with award limitations by mandating so-called structured recoveries when awards exceed a certain dollar amount.

Structured recoveries provide that money awarded to the plaintiff be placed in a trust fund and invested appropriately so that those funds will be available to the plaintiff over a long period. The rationale behind such legislation is that an immediate award of a large sum of money is not necessary for a plaintiff to be well taken care of after suffering injuries. The prudent investment of a smaller amount of money can produce a recovery commensurate with the needs and the rights of the plaintiff. This, in turn, requires a smaller cash outlay by the defendant or the defendant's insurance company, thereby holding down the costs of malpractice insurance and the ultimate cost of medical care to the consumer.

PRETRIAL SCREENING PANELS

Pretrial screening panels are designed to evaluate the merits of medical injury claims to encourage the settlement of claims outside the courtroom. "Panels render an opinion on provider liability and, in some cases, on damages. In most states, the panel's decision on the merit of the claim is admissible in court."[2] Unlike binding arbitration, the decision of a screening panel is not binding and is imposed as a condition precedent to trial, whereas arbitration is conducted in lieu of a trial. Mandatory screenings of alleged negligence cases are useful in discouraging frivolous lawsuits from proceeding to trial.

The Alaska Supreme Court in *Keyes v. Humana Hospital Alaska*[3] held that a statute creating mandatory pretrial review of medical malpractice claims by an expert advisory panel did not impermissibly infringe on the plaintiff's constitutional right to a trial by jury. The statute was a reasonable legislative response to the medical malpractice insurance crisis.

The constitutionality of a Virginia statute in *Speet v. Bacaj*[4] provided that admission of a medical review panel's opinion into evidence did not infringe on the plaintiff's right to a trial by jury as guaranteed by the Virginia Constitution.

COLLATERAL SOURCE RULE

The *collateral source rule* is a common-law principle that prohibits a court or jury from taking into account when setting an award that part of the plaintiff's damages covered by other sources of payment (e.g., health insurance, disability, and compensation). Several states have modified the collateral source rule so that evidence regarding other sources of payment to the plaintiff may be introduced for purposes of reducing the amount of the ultimate award to the plaintiff. The jury then would be permitted to assign the evidence such weight as it chooses. The award could be reduced to the extent that the plaintiff received compensation from other sources.

Imposition of the collateral source rule can result in recoveries to plaintiffs far in excess of their economic loss. Such excessive payments contribute significantly to the high cost of malpractice insurance and the high cost of medicine to the public. When evidence regarding collateral sources of payment is allowed to be introduced to mitigate the damages payable to a plaintiff, excessive recoveries may be discouraged.

RECOVERY OF EXPENSES IN EXCESS OF MEDICAID PAYMENTS NOT ALLOWED

Citation: Terrell v. Nanda, 759 So.2d 1026 (2d Cir. 2000).

Facts

Mr. Taylor suffered a ruptured disc during an automobile accident. On October 26, 1994, Taylor underwent surgery. The surgery was performed at Louisiana State University Medical Center (LSUMC). After surgery, Taylor began to experience numbness and difficulty moving his lower extremities. An emergency surgery was performed to correct these problems. The procedure was unsuccessful, and Taylor's condition deteriorated to quadriplegia. As a result of the quadriplegia, Taylor developed pulmonary and respiratory complications, necessitating the installation of a pacemaker. He also became ventilator dependent. Taylor was treated at LSUMC until January 1995, at which time he was transferred to LifeCare Hospital, as a Medicaid patient, for long-term rehabilitation treatment. Taylor remained at LifeCare until his death on May 22, 1995.

Taylor's family-plaintiffs filed suit for damages against LSUMC and Taylor's treating physicians, Dr. Nanda and Dr. Zizzi, alleging medical malpractice. The claims against Nanda and Zizzi were later dismissed. The Medical Review Panel determined that *LSUMC breached the applicable standard of care*, particularly in *failing to conduct or record neurological checks* from the end of the first surgery until more than three hours later. The plaintiffs and LSUMC reached a partial settlement for $630,000. This settlement did not pertain to the plaintiffs' claim for medical expenses contractually written off by LifeCare pursuant to Medicaid requirements.

Evidence showed that Taylor's medical expenses at LifeCare totaled $1,110,922.82 and that Medicaid paid LifeCare $164,084.82. The difference of $946,838 was contractually written off by LifeCare as required by Medicaid. Because LifeCare accepted Taylor as a Medicaid patient, LifeCare was required by both federal and state law to accept the Medicaid payment as payment in full and was prohibited from collecting further payment from Taylor. The evidence also showed that upon applying for Medicaid, Taylor and his family were informed that they would not be charged for Taylor's treatment and would incur no liability for his medical expenses.

The plaintiffs relied upon the collateral source rule as support for their claim that the contractually adjusted medical expenses are an item of damages to which they are entitled. The trial court denied the plaintiffs' motion for recovery of the contractually adjusted medical expenses in the amount of $946,838. In denying the plaintiffs' claim, the trial court found that it would be unconscionable to permit the taxpayers to bear the expense of providing free medical care to a person and then allow that person to recover damages for medical expenses from a tort-feasor and pocket the windfall.

The plaintiffs contended that the trial court erred in denying recovery of the contractually adjusted medical expenses and that this error is in contravention of Louisiana law applying the collateral source rule to medical expenses contractually adjusted as required by the Medicaid/Medicare laws. The plaintiffs asserted that, through application of the "collateral source" rule, they were entitled to an award of $946,838, the amount of medical expenses incurred by Mr. Taylor in the course of his treatment at LifeCare.

Issue

Can the plaintiffs collect the amount of medical expenses contractually written off by LifeCare pursuant to its contract with Medicaid?

Finding

The collateral source rule does not allow a medical malpractice plaintiff to recover expenses in excess of Medicaid payments.

Reason

By application of the collateral source rule, Louisiana courts have held that a plaintiff's recovery cannot be diminished by amounts paid by Medicare. Although Louisiana courts have applied the collateral source rule to allow recovery of amounts paid by a

variety of sources, Louisiana courts have not squarely addressed the issue presented in this case, namely, whether a plaintiff may recover as damages those medical expenses contractually adjusted or written off pursuant to the requirements of the Medicaid program.

Taylor entered LifeCare as a Medicaid patient fully aware that he would incur no liability for the expenses. The collateral source rule does not allow for recovery of expenses in excess of the Medicaid payments. A plaintiff may ordinarily recover reasonable medical expenses, past and future, which he incurs as a result of injury. The term "incur" is defined as "to become liable for." As a Medicaid patient, the medical expenses incurred by Taylor were those paid by Medicaid. There was no liability on the part of Taylor and there is no liability on the part of the plaintiffs for expenses above those paid by Medicaid. The Medicaid payment to LifeCare was payment in full for Taylor's expenses. Application of the collateral source rule would generally allow for recovery from the tort-feasor of those medical expenses paid by Medicaid. Otherwise, the tort-feasor would receive a windfall due to benefits received by the plaintiff from the contribution or procuration of other sources.

Discussion

1. Why was recovery of expenses in excess of Medicaid payments not allowed?
2. Do you agree with the court's ruling?

CONTINGENCY FEE LIMITATIONS

A *contingency fee* is payment for services rendered by an attorney predicated on the favorable outcome of a case. Payment is based on a preestablished percentage of the total award. Some states set this percentage by statute. Under a contingency agreement, if there is no award to the plaintiff, then the attorney receives no payment for services rendered.

Physicians argue that the contingency fee arrangement serves to encourage an inordinate number of lawsuits. Attorneys reason that if they or their clients must bear the initial cost of a lawsuit, only those with obvious merit will be brought forward. The contingency fee structure allows those unable to bear the cost of litigation to initiate a suit for damages. Limiting contingency fees on a sliding scale basis, with the percentage decreasing as the award to the plaintiff increases, and/or providing for a lesser fee if a claim is settled prior to trial, seems to have some merit.

FRIVOLOUS CLAIMS

Health care providers, in some instances, have filed countersuits after being named in what they believe to be malicious, libelous, slanderous, frivolous, and nonmeritorious medical malpractice suits. Remedies for such actions vary from one jurisdiction to the next. For a physician to prevail in a suit against a plaintiff or plaintiff's attorney, the physician must show that

- the suit was frivolous
- the motivation of the plaintiff was not to recover for a legitimate injury
- the physician has suffered damages as a result of the suit

There have been arguments that defendants should be allowed to recover court costs and damage awards from both the plaintiff(s) and the attorneys for frivolous claims and counterclaims. The courts thus far have not looked favorably on countersuits for frivolous and unscrupulous negligence actions. Some state legislatures have taken limited action in this area. An Arkansas statute, for example, provides that in any civil action in which the court finds that there was a complete absence of a judicial issue of either law or fact raised by the losing party or his or her attorney, the court shall award, with certain stipulations, an attorney fee in an amount not to exceed $5,000 or 10 percent of the amount in controversy, whichever is less, to the prevailing party.[5]

In *Berlin v. Nathan*,[6] a radiologist, a surgeon, and a hospital were sued for alleged malpractice by a patient who sought $250,000 because the defendants did not diagnose a fracture of her little finger. The radiologist missed the break, but he claimed that it was not evident on the X-ray taken at the hospital and that there was no error on his part. Further, the finger was placed in a splint just as if it had been broken, so the treatment was correct regardless of the diagnosis. The radiologist countersued, so that the malpractice suit and countersuit were tried together. When the jury was selected, the patient withdrew the malpractice suit, but the radiologist persisted with his case. The jury awarded the radiologist $2,000 as compensation and $6,000 in punitive damages, presumably convinced that the patient and her attorneys acted improperly in bringing the lawsuit and that the attorneys were negligent in their investigation of the patient's case before filing suit.

When the case was taken to an appellate court, the decision of the lower court was reversed on the grounds that the physician had failed to plead special damages and (because the countersuit had been filed prematurely) had failed to plead a favorable result in the original suit. The appellate court went on to say that a showing of special damages is essential in a case of this type in order that the public's right to free access to the court system not be impeded by the threat of counterlitigation. The court reasoned that persons who believe they have legitimate claims should not be dissuaded from using the court system solely because of the fear of liability in the event their claim is unsuccessful.

The appellate court holding in the *Berlin* case represents the majority judicial view across the country regarding countersuits. Courts generally do not find in favor of the countersuing party because they fear that persons who otherwise would bring malpractice suits will be discouraged simply because of a concern over the possibility of a countersuit.

Frivolous and unscrupulous malpractice actions have caused physicians to place limitations on their scope of practice. Many obstetricians/gynecologists, for example, have dropped the high-risk obstetrics portion of their practices to reduce their malpractice premiums. There is also an ever-increasing reluctance by physicians to perform heroic measures on accident victims because of the high risks of malpractice exposure.

JOINT AND SEVERAL LIABILITY

The doctrine of *joint and several liability* provides that a person causing an injury concurrently with another person can be held liable for the entire judgment awarded by a court. It is proposed by some that each defendant in a multidefendant action should be limited to payment for the percentage of fault ascribed to him or her. Some states have taken action to modify the doctrine. A 1986 Wyoming statute, for example, provides that each defendant to a lawsuit is liable only for that proportion of the total dollar amount of damages according to the percentage of the amount of fault attributed to him or her.[7] A Minnesota statute provides that a defendant whose fault is 15 percent or less may be jointly liable for a percentage of the whole award not greater than four times his or her percentage of fault.[8]

MALPRACTICE CAPS/AWARD LIMITATIONS

The impetus for malpractice caps is due, in part, because jury awards often vary substantially from one jurisdiction to the next within the same state. As a result, negligence attorneys often prefer to try personal injury cases in those jurisdictions in which a jury is likely to grant a higher award. Different states are attempting to stem the tide of rising malpractice costs by passing laws that impose restrictions on limiting the total dollar damages allowable in malpractice actions. Although there have been challenges to statutes limiting awards, it would appear that limitations on malpractice recoveries are not unconstitutional. The Idaho Supreme Court in *Jones v. State Board of Medicine*[9] held that the state's limitation on malpractice recoveries ($150,000) need not necessarily be unconstitutional. The court held that there was no inherent right to an unlimited amount of damages and that the state had a legitimate interest in controlling excessive medical costs caused by large malpractice recoveries, and thus the statute could be held constitutional.

The California Supreme Court in *Fein v. Permanente Medical Group*[10] found that provisions in the Medical Injury Compensation Reform Act of 1975, Section 3333.2 of the Civil Code, that limit noneconomic damages for pain and suffering in medical malpractice cases to $250,000 are not unconstitutional. The legislature did not place limits on a plaintiff's right to recover for economic damages, such as medical expenses and lost earnings resulting from an injury.

A Virginia statute that places a cap of $750,000 on damages recoverable in a malpractice action was found not to violate the Seventh Amendment separation of powers principles or the Fourteenth Amendment due process or equal protection clauses.[11]

NO-FAULT SYSTEM

A *no-fault system* compensates injured parties for economic losses regardless of fault. It is intended to compensate more claimants with smaller awards. A no-fault system compensates victims of medical injury whether or not they can prove medical negligence. Proponents of the no-fault approach cite as its advantages swifter and less expensive resolution of claims and more equitable compensation for patients.

A no-fault system of compensation has its drawbacks. Opponents to the no-fault system are concerned about the loss of whatever deterrence effect the present tort system exerts on health care providers. The system's lower administrative costs can be an incentive to file lawsuits and, therefore, may not produce the desired outcome of reducing the incidence of malpractice claims.

PEER REVIEW ORGANIZATIONS

Public Law No. 92–603 of the Social Security Amendments of 1972 and Public Law No. 94–182 of the Social Security Act of 1975 created a nationwide review agency known as Professional Standard Review Organizations (PSROs) under Title XI of the Social Security Act. Their purpose is to ensure that medical care provided to patients is of high quality and reflects the most appropriate and efficient use of an organization's health care services.

PSRO norms, standards, and criteria were to be used as guidelines of acceptable medical care to measure the standard of care rendered to beneficiaries of Medicare, Medicaid, and maternal and child health programs. PSROs compiled and studied physician profiles of care to determine whether services rendered in a given area were consistent with the standards of learning and skill of the average reputable physician, either nationwide or in communities similar to those under examination.

In 1982, Congress repealed the PSRO program, replacing it with the Peer Review Improvement Act.[12] Under this Act, peer review organizations (PROs) perform functions similar to those of the PSROs. Hospitals must have agreements with PROs as a condition of receiving Medicare payments under the prospective payment system (PPS), as required by the Deficit Reduction Act of 1984.[13] PROs can deny reimbursement for substandard care. They also can recommend that a practitioner be suspended from the Medicare and Medicaid programs, as well as be fined for a pattern of poor performance.

Peer review documents generally are protected from discovery so long as they are maintained in compliance with a formalized quality assurance program. The U.S. Supreme Court in *Patrick v. Burget*,[14] by an 8–0 vote, reversed the decision of the Ninth Circuit Court of Appeals, which had held that the peer review process was exempt from antitrust scrutiny under the so-called state action doctrine.

> Because we conclude that no state actor in Oregon actively supervises hospital peer-review decisions, we hold that the state action doctrine does not protect the peer-review activities challenged in this case from application of the federal antitrust laws. In so holding we are not unmindful of the policy argument that respondents and their amici have advanced for reaching the opposite conclusion. They contend that effective peer review is essential to the provision of quality medical care and that any threat of antitrust liability will prevent physicians from participating openly and actively in peer-review proceedings. This argument, however, essentially challenges the wisdom of applying the antitrust laws to the sphere of medical care, and as such is properly directed to the legislative branch. To the extent that Congress has declined to exempt medical peer review from the reach of the antitrust laws, peer review is immune from antitrust scrutiny only if the state effectively has made this conduct its own. The State of Oregon has not done so.[15]

Compliance with the Health Care Quality Improvement Act (HCQIA) is the only way health care organizations and their medical staffs can hope to protect credentialing and peer review activities from antitrust liability. The Supreme Court endorsed the act in the *Patrick* opinion, holding that the HCQIA, which was enacted well after the events at issue in this case and is not retroactive, essentially immunizes peer review action from liability if the action was taken in the reasonable belief that it was in the furtherance of quality health care.

A physician who resigned after evaluation of his suspected alcohol, drug, or emotional problem filed a complaint against the hospital and the assistant administrator for slander, coercion, intentional infliction of emotional distress, and intentional interference with his employment contract as medical director of the hospital's department of perinatology.[16] Alcohol had been detected on the physician's breath while he was performing certain medical procedures. A chemical dependency specialist conducted interviews with members of the hospital's staff who had contact with the plaintiff. According to the witnesses, the plaintiff was subject to mood swings, became abrupt and tactless with patients, boasted of becoming intoxicated, and occasionally would leave work and return "wired." The plaintiff had been described as bizarre and paranoid. In conducting the interviews with the hospital staff, the witnesses believed that something was wrong with the plaintiff, but they were reluctant to speak because of their fondness for him.

Acting on the advice of the chemical dependency specialist, the vice president of medical staff affairs for the hospital formed a committee that met for the purpose of confronting the physician regarding the alleged behavior problem. The physician reluctantly agreed to an evaluation by a physician experienced in treating impaired physicians. The plaintiff was evaluated later that day at a nearby hospital. The record is silent as to the results of that evaluation, except to indicate that the plaintiff did not require hospitalization. The circuit court dismissed the complaint, and the physician appealed. On appeal, the appellate court held that the Hospital Licensing Act provided the defendants with absolute immunity from liability for the hospital peer review committee's investigation of the physician's conduct.

MEDICAL MISCONDUCT

Some states require the reporting of a physician who is guilty of professional misconduct. Medical misconduct generally includes: obtaining a license fraudulently; practicing a profession fraudulently, beyond its authorized scope, with gross incompetence; practicing a profession while the ability to practice is impaired by alcohol, drugs, physical disability, or mental disability; refusing to provide professional service to a person because of such person's race, creed, color, or national origin; permitting, aiding, or abetting an unlicensed person to perform activities requiring a license; and being convicted of committing an act constituting a crime.

The penalties that may be imposed on a licensee found guilty of medical misconduct include: suspension of the license to practice; revocation of the license to practice; limitation on registration or issuance of any further licenses; and imposition of a fine.

The physician in *Gunduy v. Commissioner of Education*[17] appealed the commissioner of education's decision to revoke his license for being convicted under federal law on seven counts of an indictment. The physician was involved in the possession and distribution of large amounts of amphetamines and furnished false information in required reports and records. The court confirmed the commissioner's decision and noted that professionals have considerable responsibility not to abuse the trust that licensure places on them by violating the laws controlling dangerous drugs.

REGULATION OF INSURANCE PRACTICES

Many believe that the regulation of insurance practices is necessary to prevent windfall profits. Both the medical profession and the legal profession believe that insurance carriers have raised premiums disproportionately to their losses and that, despite their claims of substantial losses, they have reaped substantial profits.

SETTING STANDARDS OF MEDICAL CARE

Setting and following preestablished medical standards can help reduce the number of lawsuits in any given medical specialty. "Many of the specialty societies either have drafted or are drafting practice guidelines for their medical area of expertise. For example, the American Society of Anesthesiologists developed guidelines for intraoperative monitoring in 1986. During the following year, no lawsuits were brought for hypoxic injuries; in previous years hypoxic injury suits averaged six per year."[18]

NATIONAL HEALTH CARE REFORM

The medical malpractice crisis continues to be a major dilemma for the health care industry. Although there have been many approaches to resolving the crisis, there appears to be no one magic formula. The solution most likely will require a variety of efforts, including tort reform.

The ever-increasing proliferation of regulations by policymakers, which have been designed to control costs and improve the quality of care, has alienated health care providers and added fuel to the practice of defensive medicine.

Physicians who are on the front lines often have been excluded from the decision-making processes that threaten their autonomy and financial security. A concerted effort must be made to include them in policy development and implementation. The present system of punishment for all because of the inadequacies of the few has proven to be costly and far from productive. The key to improving quality and controlling costs is cooperation, not alienation. Policymakers have failed in this arena and must return to a commonsense approach in policy development by including those who are on the front lines of medicine.

RISK MANAGEMENT

Risk management is a systematic program designed to reduce preventable injuries and accidents and minimize the financial severity of claims. It involves the identification of potential accidents with an emphasis on claims prevention. In risk management, steps are taken on a team effort basis to improve the quality of care and eliminate or minimize the number of accidents that become potential lawsuits. Liability insurers have been strong proponents of risk management; in many cases, insurers have cut premiums for physicians and health care organizations who adopt sanctioned risk management practices.

Risk management must include a heightened sensitivity to providing a safe environment and addressing the emotional needs of patients. The input of the provider–patient relationship cannot be overemphasized when the provider–patient relationship is intense and inescapable. Individuals, not incidents, bring lawsuits. Good relationships with patients are very important in preventing malpractice suits. Public relations for health care professionals are a challenge. It is not only good medical practice but it is at the very core of the problem of medical malpractice.

Increasing insurance costs and general financial constraints have pressured hospitals to assume leadership in the prevention of medically related injuries. Risk management programs should include the following components:

- a grievance or complaint mechanism designed to process and resolve as promptly and effectively as possible grievances by patients or their representatives
- collection of data with respect to negative health care outcomes (whether or not they give rise to claims)
- medical care evaluation mechanisms, which shall include a tissue committee or medical audit committee to periodically assess the quality of medical care being provided
- education programs for staff personnel engaged in patient care activities dealing with patient safety, medical injury prevention, the legal aspects of patient care, problems of communication and rapport with patients, and other relevant factors known to influence malpractice claims and suits

Elements of a Risk Management Program

Valuable components of a risk management program include

- early intervention and sympathetic care after accidental injury to a patient

- preparation of incident reports
- prompt identification and investigation of specific incidents of patient injuries and, when possible, intervention
- definition of the cause of each incident
- generation and maintenance of a risk database from which hazardous trends and areas may be identified and corrected
- evaluation of the frequency and severity of incident exposure
- formulation and implementation of corrective actions to reduce risk and exposure to liability
- training and education of employees and clinicians to assist in reducing exposure
- continuing attention of a safety committee
- use of a suggestion box
- a public relations program (employees should be trained in completing timely incident reports that document the facts and that are not used to cover up unfortunate incidents but to train personnel and identify problems)

Risk Management Committee

A risk management committee with representation from the organization's governing body, administration, and medical staff should be established. The committee should be chaired by a person trained in medical audits and the risk management process. The risk manager should be responsible for the development and coordination of strategic prevention programs. Information from all committees (e.g., pharmacy, transfusion, infections, safety, audit, utilization, tissue, medical records, personnel, credentials, continuing education, product review, etc.) regarding potential liability hazards should be funneled into this committee for review, evaluation, and appropriate action. This committee serves to monitor all potential hazards. The organization's attorney should be readily available for legal counsel.

Because an organization's governing body has ultimate responsibility for adequate patient care, that group's involvement in the risk management process is mandatory. The governing body must be just as concerned with reviewing the competence of the medical staff as it is with the financial aspects of institutional operations. Public expectations place a broad responsibility on organizations to ensure quality care whether that care involves administrative, nursing, or physician activities.

CONTINUOUS QUALITY IMPROVEMENT

Continuous quality improvement (CQI) is an approach to improving quality on a continuing basis. CQI is introduced here because of its value in reducing the risks of malpractice.

This section presents the practical side and components of CQI, the success factors, the advantages and benefits, and how to implement CQI teams.

CQI is a term given to the philosophy of management introduced into the U.S. business world in 1980 by an American statistician, Dr. W. E. Deming. Dr. Deming was rediscovered by his own country when an NBC news documentary entitled "If Japan Can—Why Can't We?" was broadcast on June 24, 1980. A portion of the documentary highlighted Dr. Deming's efforts in helping to make Japanese management and products what some would call the best in the world. Dr. Deming had been at work with Japanese organizations since post–World War II. His concepts on improving quality, however, failed to catch the attention of the business world in the United States. Through his years of research, Dr. Deming formulated step-by-step procedures for improving quality and decreasing costs. Since that time, there have been numerous variations on the CQI process of improving quality. CQI comes in a diversity of packages that contain sound business practices that have been developed over the years. The following lists the numerous labels ascribed to the quality improvement process:

- TQM—total quality management
- PM—participative management
- PI—performance improvement
- QCs—quality circles
- TQI—total quality improvement
- CQI—continuous quality improvement
- MOB—management by objectives
- IOP—improving organizational performance

CQI involves improving performance at every functional level of an organization's operation, using available resources (human and capital). It combines fundamental management techniques, innovative improvement efforts, and specialized technical skills in a structure focused on continuously improving processes. CQI relies on people and involves everyone. CQI is concerned with providing a quality product, getting to market on time, providing the best service, reducing costs, broadening market share, and organizational growth. The benefits of CQI are well documented and include reduced customer complaints and turnover; increased ability to attract new customers; and improved productivity, services, and quality.

Paradigm Shift

Most health care organizations have recognized the need for a paradigm shift from the autocratic style of management to a more humanistic participative style of management. The hierarchical autocratic organization is not appropriate for modern society's highly competitive marketplace. The fruits of the autocratic style of management, which include high staff turnover, low morale, resistance to change, limited creativity, lack of excitement and challenge, rigidity, entrenchment in the status quo, low ownership and accountability, and a passive following, have served only to slow the wheels of progress.

Selecting a CQI Process

Although many health care organizations are still in the process of overcoming eighteenth-century European and American ideas regarding management wherein the workers were literally expendable, numerous successes are occurring toward improving the quality of care through collaboration and involvement. The shift toward the concepts of CQI in the health care industry is particularly important because of the Joint Commission on Accreditation of Healthcare Organizations' emphasis on improving organizational performance. The Joint Commission provides that health care organizations must have a planned, systematic, organizationwide approach to designing, measuring, assessing, and improving their performance.

CQI Implementation

The ultimate successes of CQI require commitment by the organization's leadership. In the health care setting, leadership includes the administration, governing body, medical staff, and nursing staff. From the leadership, involvement must be expanded to include the entire organization.

The organization's plan should be designed to provide a systematic and ongoing process for monitoring and evaluating patient care, identifying opportunities for improvement, and identifying high-risk areas having the potential for adverse outcomes and increased exposure to litigation.

Steering Committee

To be successful in implementing a CQI program, an organization's leaders should establish a steering committee or coordinating council with senior leaders of the organization at the helm. This committee is responsible for providing direction, designing and implementing a CQI program, overseeing the progress of the organization's CQI program, assessing the strengths and weaknesses of the organization, determining the right strategy for the organization, creating and tracking management indicators, and providing the appropriate resources necessary to make the CQI program successful.

Training

Education in the principles of CQI must occur at every level of the organization. An effective CQI program requires

- an understanding of the organization's mission and vision
- change to be the norm and not the exception
- communications and information dissemination
- continuous evaluation, measurement, and improvement
- identification of customer requirements
- constant feedback from all levels of the organization
- self-assessment
- empowerment of a CQI team to act (if the team is not supported by the organization it will lead to disintegration)
- active involvement by all employees
- authority and autonomy to be commensurate with duties
- a periodic reporting mechanism to the governing body
- an annual evaluation of the organization's performance improvement plan

Facilitators

Facilitators act as helpers in the CQI process. They should be highly knowledgeable in the brainstorming process and have an in-depth understanding about human behavior with little or no stake in the outcome of a team's decision-making process. A good facilitator will ensure equal participation from the group members and will aid in maximizing the number of ideas from the group. The facilitator must be trained in CQI and basic management skills. The facilitator is not a "boss." The role of the facilitator includes that of teacher/trainer and consultant. The facilitator supports, provides oversight, assists CQI teams in obtaining the information and resources necessary to complete their tasks, and provides the group with direction.

Persons experienced in implementing CQI programs should train facilitators. A training agenda should include

- a historical overview of CQI concepts
- examples of the processes and principles involved
- highlights of the benefits of a CQI program
- small group behavior, processes, and dynamics
- participative management theory
- theories of motivation
- communications skills
- body language
- methodologies for problem solving
- changing behavior
  - the stone wall
  - staying calm under confrontation
  - working with difficult people
  - minimizing the negative effects of difficult behavior

- turning conflict into stepping stones for harmony
  - being a catalyst for changing difficult behavior
  - overcoming the fear of confrontation
  - recognizing the important difference between occasional difficult behavior and behavior that has become a lifestyle
- data collection methodologies
- cost analysis and forecasting
- statistical analysis and report writing skills
- public speaking skills

CQI Teams

CQI teams are multidisciplinary groups of individuals that meet regularly to identify opportunities for improvement, generate ideas as to how to make improvements, select and implement a preferred improvement, and audit the progress of and refine improvements. The advantages of CQI teams include

- development of a problem-solving ethic
- more effective use of an organization's resources
- increased productivity
- improvement in quality and patient satisfaction
- participation and personal pride in the organization
- improved morale and job satisfaction
- team building
- the cultivation of professional growth
- improvement of leadership performance
- improvement in market share and increased revenues

CQI Data Collection/Indicators and Screens

Volume Indicators

Volume indicators provide data that demonstrate the scope and frequency of services provided over time (e.g., admission/discharge data, number of procedures, and outpatient visits). Volume indicators also provide valuable information for monitoring the incidence of adverse outcomes (e.g., infection rates following surgical procedures, adverse drug reactions, and medication errors). The information and data gathered by an organization are of significant importance as they relate to budgeting, resource allocation, and strategic planning.

Clinical Indicators

Clinical indicators are used to screen the care provided to patients by clinical specialty. The screens are generally confined to those related to high-volume or high-risk problems that may be unique to the clinical specialty. Each specialty uses such indicators to aid in the identification of opportunities for improving care practices. These opportunities are identified when collected data elements cross a preestablished threshold set by the clinical department or service. Once the threshold has been crossed, those cases are then examined and the reason for variation is determined.

Occurrence Screens

Occurrence screens are predetermined indicators used to signal the need for evaluation of some aspect of patient care. Screens may describe the processes in the delivery of care, clinical events, complications, or outcomes for which data can be collected in order to compare actual results with criteria related to the screen. Events such as unexpected deaths, returns to the surgical suite, or adverse drug reactions should prompt for investigation to determine whether the events could be traced to structural problems (e.g., availability of resources) or process problems (e.g., timeliness and skills in the delivery of health care).

Focused Reviews

Focused reviews are concentrated reviews of key areas in a department or clinical specialty determined by their high volume, high risk, or history of identified problems. Focused reviews might target a representative sample of high-volume diagnoses or procedures over a finite time period or a review of all cases of low-volume but high-risk care.

Clinical Pertinence Review of Medical Records

The clinical pertinence review of medical records is a CQI process that monitors and evaluates the clinical pertinence, completeness, accuracy, timeliness, and legibility of documentation as reflected in the medical record. The purpose of such a review is to identify opportunities for improvement in the record documentation process.

Successful CQI Programs

Listed below are but a few of the numerous areas in which health care organizations have been successful in implementing the CQI process:

- improving response time for thrombolytic therapy
- tracking and reducing employee needle sticks
- recognizing abnormal vital signs and changes in a patient's condition
- improving response time (e.g., cardiopulmonary arrest)
- improving charting (charting objectively, descriptively, and clinically)
- providing patient-family education
- utilizing resources in a cost-effective manner
- improving safety
- improving customer satisfaction
- reducing postoperative hypothermia
- designing and implementing clinical pathways
- providing security and confidentiality of computer-generated information
- using antibiotics effectively and efficiently
- improving pain management
- developing and implementing nutritional screens and assessments
- improving the healing process and patient diet
- improving patient records and pertinent documentation
- reducing the use of restraints
- documenting patient rights and advance directives

The implementation of CQI in health care organizations will improve the quality of patient care and reduce the untoward events that result in lawsuits. Success will come with true commitment by each organization's leadership. Such commitment requires the full participation of all caregivers. The evolution of a truly successful CQI program involves the transition from CQI as a plan to CQI as a process, and ultimately to CQI as an organizational culture.

CHAPTER REVIEW

1. Arbitration and mediation are methods through which parties can settle claims out of court. *Arbitration* is a process wherein parties agree to submit their differences to the judgment of an impartial mediation panel for resolution. It is conducted in lieu of trial. *Mediation* is a process wherein a third party attempts to bring about a settlement between the parties.
2. *Structured awards* are set up to provide compensation over a plaintiff's lifetime. They provide that money awarded to a plaintiff be placed in trust and invested appropriately, thereby making the funds available to the plaintiff over a long period of time.
3. *Pretrial screening panels* are used to encourage out-of-court settlement. The panels give an opinion on provider liability and, in some cases, damages.
4. The common-law principle that prohibits a court or jury from, when setting an award, taking into account the part of the plaintiff's damages that would be covered by other sources of payment is called *collateral source rule.*

5. A *contingency fee* is payment for an attorney's services predicated on the favorable outcome of the case. This arrangement allows those otherwise unable to bear the cost of litigation to initiate a suit, but many physicians argue that contingency fees encourage an inordinate number of lawsuits.

6. The concept of *joint and several liability* holds that a person who caused an injury concurrently with another person can be held liable for the full judgment awarded by a court.

7. Some states are attempting to limit the rising costs of malpractice by limiting the total dollar damages that can be awarded in malpractice actions.

8. Professional Standard Review Organizations (PRSOs) were charged with ensuring that medical care is of high quality and reflects the most appropriate and efficient use of an organization's health care services. In 1982, Congress repealed the PRSO program and replaced it with the Peer Review Improvement Act, under which peer review organizations (PROs) perform a similar function of ensuring quality of care. Hospitals must have agreements with a PRO in order to receive Medicare payments under the prospective payment system (PPS).

9. If found guilty of professional misconduct, a licensee could suffer the suspension of his or her license to practice, the revocation of that license, limitation on the registration or issuance of further licenses, and/or the imposition of a fine.

10. *Risk management* involves the identification of potential accidents with an emphasis on claims prevention. Teams take steps to improve the quality of care and eliminate or minimize the number of accidents that could result in lawsuits. A risk management committee should include representation from the organization's governing body, administration, and medical staff. The purpose of this committee is to monitor all potential hazards.

11. *Continuous quality improvement* (CQI) is a process that involves improving performance at every functional level of an organization's operation by using available human and capital resources. CQI can hold significant value in the reduction of malpractice risks. For a CQI program to be successful, education in the basic principles behind it must occur at every level of the organization. Facilitators act as helpers in the CQI process by providing support, oversight, and direction, and by assisting teams in obtaining the information and resources necessary to complete their tasks. The teams are multidisciplinary groups that meet regularly to identify opportunities for improvement, generate ideas as to how these improvements could be made, select and implement preferred improvements, and assess the progress of and refine improvements.

REVIEW QUESTIONS

1. Should there be limits placed on malpractice awards? Support your opinion.
2. How does a structured award work?
3. Which of the schemes for tort reform discussed above do you consider most helpful in addressing the malpractice insurance crisis?
4. Describe the continuous quality improvement (CQI) process as it applies to health care organizations.

NOTES

1. The Robert Wood Johnson Found., *The Tort System for Medical Malpractice: How Well Does It Work, What Are the Alternatives?* ABRIDGE, Spring 1991, at 2.
2. The Robert Wood Johnson Found., *Legal Reform,* ABRIDGE, Spring 1991, at 3.
3. 750 P.2d 343 (Alaska 1988).
4. 377 S.E.2d 397 (Va. 1989).
5. ARK. CODE ANN. § 16–22–309 (Michie 1987).
6. 381 N.E.2d 1367 (1978).
7. WYO. STAT. § 1–1–109 (1986).
8. MINN. STAT. § 604.02 (1988).
9. 555 P.2d 399 (Idaho 1976).
10. 695 P.2d 665 (Cal. 1985).
11. Boyd v. Bulala, 877 F.2d 1191 (4th Cir. 1989).
12. Tit. XI, § 143, part B.
13. Pub. L. No. 98-369.
14. 486 U.S. 94 (1988).
15. *Id.* at 105.
16. Cardwell v. Rockford Mem'l Hosp. Ass'n, 539 N.E.2d 1322 (Ill. App. Ct. 1989).
17. 460 N.Y.S.2d 664 (N.Y. App. Div. 1983).
18. The Robert Wood Johnson Found., *Preventing Negligence,* ABRIDGE, Spring 1991, at 8.

Zero Tolerance

According to the theory of aerodynamics, and as may be readily demonstrated through experiments, the bumblebee can't fly. This is because the size, the weight, and the shape of the body in relation to its wingspan, make flying impossible. BUT, the bumblebee, being ignorant of these scientific truths, goes ahead and flies anyway—and makes a little honey every day.

Author Unknown

INTRODUCTION

Because the human body is a complex walking-talking-thinking machine that is well integrated and inter- and intradependent on the perfect functioning of each of its parts, perfect patient care must then be the ultimate goal of an interdisciplinary, collaborative, multitasking effort among health care providers, toward the ultimate goal of analyzing the body's systems, placing them all in their proper perspective, and prioritizing the patient's needs based on an individualized systems analysis and treatment. Mediocrity cannot be an acceptable standard for achieving goals often thought by skeptics to be beyond humankind's reach.

There is no room for human error in the delivery of quality patient care! For the patient, organizations must adopt a *zero tolerance* mentality for poor judgment and careless mistakes.

Health care organizations must reduce the number of human process errors that are often the "root cause" of poor outcomes. Desired outcomes must be closely aligned with predictability. This can occur more frequently if redundant (backup) systems, procedures, and processes are in place for safe and effective patient care. The development of redundant systems will reduce the likelihood of human process errors.

The health care industry should follow the example of other large organizations that respond in a proactive manner. The National Aeronautics and Space Administration (NASA), for example, has numerous redundant systems in place each time a shuttle is launched into space for the safety of the astronauts. Meaningful redundant systems must be in place in hospitals as well, for patient safety.

Many hospitals have a variety of redundant systems to improve patient outcomes. For example, a patient about to undergo surgery must have a variety of assessments and clinical tests prior to undergoing the surgical procedure. The organization must ensure that the right patient is in the right surgical suite and is about to undergo the correct procedure on the correct body part at the right time. The right patient would require appropriate identification by checking the patient's wristband; being recognized by the operating surgeon, staff, and anesthesiologist; and addressing the patient by name prior to the administration of anesthesia. Identification of the surgical site should include participation by the patient's marking of the surgical site prior to surgery. These represent simple procedures critical to desired outcomes.

It is important to review sentinel events occurring in health care organizations and to conduct root cause analyses, seeking answers as to why a particular outcome occurred and how to prevent similar events from repeating themselves. More important, the "how to prevent" an undesirable outcome is as valuable as the "why" a bad outcome occurred in the first place. More focus on "how" to do it right the first time will lessen the likelihood of having to ask "why" things went wrong.

Redundant systems can improve outcomes. The following pages provide a variety of questions that have been designed to be thought provoking and should lead to deeper inquiry into designing meaningful redundancy in systems.

LEADERSHIP

- What are the organization's mission, vision, and values?
- How have the organization's mission/vision/values changed over time?
- How does the planning process relate to the organization's mission, vision, and values?
- How are the organization's mission, vision, values, and long-range plans communicated to the organization and community?
- What is the scope of services provided by the organization?
- How is the scope of services determined?
- How does the leadership effectuate collaboration among the organization's leaders (e.g., governing body, administration, medical staff, and nursing)?
- How does the organization plan services for
  - specific patient populations (e.g., indigent patients)?
  - directing and staffing services?
  - coordinating and integrating services?
  - improving services?
- What are the characteristics of the governing body?
  - How does one become a member?
  - Does the composition of the governing body include community representation?
  - What is the organization's process for orienting and educating new board members?
  - Is there a systems board, single board, or both?
  - Is there a community advisory board, and if so, how does one become a member?
  - What are the purpose and function of the community advisory board?
  - What is the governing body's process for evaluating/reviewing and improving its effectiveness?
  - What are the mechanisms used to educate the organization's leadership?
- How intensely does the governing body probe into the "who, what, where, when, why, and how" of organizational successes and failures?
- Does the organization practice patient-focused care?
- Does the purchase of cheaper products compromise the quality of patient care?
- How does the organization's leadership know if clinical outcomes are improving?
  - Who is monitoring the improvement and effectiveness of treatment modalities?
- What is the organization's mechanism for addressing conflict resolution?
- Has the organization implemented a conflict-of-interest policy?
- How does the organization assure itself that the same level of care is being delivered across the organization?
- How does the organization assure itself that the appropriateness of care is not based on cost alone?
- Does the organization have a corporate compliance program in place for the prevention of fraud and abuse?
- Does the program provide for a corporate compliance officer?
- What redundant systems does the organization have in place to improve patient outcomes?
- How does management evaluate its effectiveness?
- How does the governing body assure and reassure itself that it is doing the right thing?
  - Does the governing body conduct a self-assessment?
  - What is the organization's process/mechanism for conducting the evaluation?
  - What areas have been identified as needing improvement?
  - What initiatives has the governing body undertaken to improve its effectiveness during the past 12 months?
- How does the governing body monitor the effectiveness of the organization's leadership?
- How is accountability for the organization's leadership evaluated?

PLANNING

- Does the organization have a clear strategy and strategic plan that charts the course and direction of the organization in response to community need?
- What is the organization's planning process/plan for planning (e.g., how does an idea become reality)?
- Is planning conducted on a collaborative basis?
- How are community needs assessed?
  - What is the organization's plan for identifying and addressing community needs?
  - How does the organization improve services as a result of patient input?
  - What is the organization's mechanism for obtaining community feedback (e.g., satisfaction surveys)?
  - Are satisfaction surveys used in the planning process?
- Do planning documents address patient care needs, including needs identified by the medical staff?
- How are priorities set?
  - Are needs prioritized on a collaborative basis?
  - Does prioritizing include administration, governing body, nursing, and medical staff?
  - Are power brokers driving their own agenda in prioritizing organizational needs?
  - How do the organization's leaders and community leaders collaborate to design and prioritize the need for new services?
- How do services relate to the organization's mission, vision, and values?

- How do services relate to identified needs?
- How does the organization ensure that services are relative to community need?
- Does the organization obtain patient and family input as to how the organization is meeting the care needs of its patients?
- How does the governing body assess clinical quality in the organization?

RESOURCE ALLOCATION

- What is the organization's process for developing budgets (capital, human resource, and expense)?
- What processes are in place for the organization to position itself for economic survival?
- What is the mechanism for leadership participation in resource allocation for
  - human resources?
  - equipment purchases?
  - capital acquisitions?
  - new services?
- How are priorities set for allocation of financial resources?
  - Who has input into setting resource allocation priorities (e.g., governing body, administration, medical staff, and/or nursing)?
- What is the process for defining and approving new services?
- How do department directors participate in the organization's ongoing decision-making processes for
  - planning?
  - budgeting?
  - staffing?
- What financial data does the organization provide to its managers?
- What are the organization's parameters for feedback on variance reporting?
- How are funds allocated for
  - orientation, training, and education of staff?
  - patient and family education?
- What is the relationship of patient care services to patient care needs?
- What is the organization's process for approving expenditures?
- What aggregate data does the organization's leadership and managers use to support decision-making processes, operations, and performance improvement activities?
- What services does the organization contract out?
- How does the organization ensure effective communications in the delivery of patient care as it relates to
  - age-specific barriers?

  - language barriers?
  - cultural and religious barriers?

PERFORMANCE IMPROVEMENT (PI)

- Is the leadership committed to PI?
  - Have commitment and buy-in to PI flowed throughout the organization?
- What is the organization's process/methodology for PI?
- Does the organization have a PI coordinating committee?
  - Describe the membership of the committee.
  - Is membership interdisciplinary?
- What is the organization's process for involvement across disciplines?
- Does the organization have collaborative practice teams?
- How does the organization ensure that all staff participate in PI processes?
- How are training and education provided to the staff?
- Describe the organization's success in integrating evening/weekend shifts into the PI process.
- How does the organization integrate offsite care centers (e.g., ambulatory care) into the organization's PI process?
- Is consideration given to involving patients and family in the PI process (e.g., focus groups)?
- How does the organization identify opportunities for improvement?
- How does the organization decide what to review and improve (high-risk, high-volume, problem-prone activities)?
- What is the organization's methodology for establishing priorities for PI (how are priorities set)?
- How does the organization go about chartering PI teams?
- How has PI improved the health of the community?
- Do PI teams periodically review and revisit the results of their activities?
- Are measurement and assessment major components of the PI process?
- In what measurement systems does the organization participate?
- What happens when measurement data suggest opportunities for improvement?
- Describe organizational successes that have come about as a result of PI activities.
- What is the organization doing to evaluate the effectiveness and appropriateness of its PI program?
- How does the organization know that it is improving clinical outcomes?

- What evidence/documentation does the organization have to demonstrate that internal processes are continuously and systematically measured, assessed, and improved?
- How does the organization measure or validate its successes?
- What data does the organization trend for PI activities?
- What clinical databases does the organization have in place for benchmarking?
- Is intensive assessment conducted when variables of measurement are unacceptable?
- How does the organization collect data?
- How are data assessed?
- How does the organization assess its success with critical pathways?
- How are PI processes improved?
- What effect has PI had on teamwork?

HUMAN RESOURCES

Screening New Employees

- What is the organization's process for verification of licensure?
- Are job descriptions reflective of each staff member's duties and responsibilities?
- What are the technical skills of the position?
- Is the position applied for a part of the applicant's career path or just another job?
- Does the applicant appear motivated?
- Does the applicant exhibit a sense of excitement about the position?
- Are the applicant's communications skills appropriate for the position applied for?

Staffing

- How does the organization know that it is adequately staffed?
  - What data does the organization collect that indicate the organization is appropriately staffed?
  - How does the organization's leadership know that staffing is appropriate?
  - How does the organization's leadership know that it has the right mix of employees?
  - How does the organization determine the mix, numbers, and qualifications of staff?
  - What is the downside of productivity in the organization?

- What programs does the organization's leadership have in place to promote recruitment, retention, development, and recognition of staff?
- What effect has reengineering had on staff?

Orientation

- What topics are included in the organization's general orientation program?
- How are employees oriented to the culture of the organization?
- How are agency and contracted staff oriented to the organization?
- Are volunteers oriented to the organization?
  - Are volunteers oriented to the volunteer service?
- Does the orientation program provide education relative to
  - mission, vision, and values?
  - review of organizational and department policies and procedures?
  - safety issues?
  - equipment management?
  - the organization's PI process?

Performance Evaluations

- How does the governing body assure itself that the competency review process is effective?
- Do competency reports to the governing body include contracted and other agency staff?
- What mechanisms does the organization have in place to monitor the competency of individuals whose jobs have been reengineered?
- How is the performance of senior management staff evaluated?
- How does the competency evaluation relate to the job description?
- How are age-specific competencies evaluated?
  - Does the organization utilize both a self-testing module (e.g., Erickson's Growth and Development) and observation?
  - Are age-specific criteria applicable to the job classification?

Education and Training

- How does the organization assess the education and training needs of staff?

- How does the organization assess the effectiveness and appropriateness of training and education programs?
- What mechanisms are in place to promote job-related education and advancement goals of staff members?

INFECTION CONTROL

- Airborne Pathogens
  - Are air vents (supply and exhaust) scheduled for cleaning on a regular basis?
  - Are mattress pads with tears and holes (e.g., bed, transport stretcher, and examination and surgical table pads) replaced as necessary?
  - Are food products in containers labeled as to contents, including expiration dates?
- What are the organization's infection control policies and procedures as they relate to gowning, masks, and glove changes between patients?
- Are furniture, equipment, and toys disinfected between patients with appropriate germicidal solutions?
- Is ventilator-associated pneumonia being tracked?
- Are central line–associated bloodstream infections being tracked?
- Are equipment-associated infections being tracked?
- Are nosocomial infections being tracked for each patient care unit? What is done with this information?
- Are physicians being provided with current information as to drug of choice in treating infections?

INFORMATION MANAGEMENT

- How does the organization address its information technology needs?
- Does the organization have an interdisciplinary committee structure for assessing and reassessing needs?
  - What leaders are represented on the committee?
  - What are the functions of the committee?
  - Does the committee address satisfaction?
  - Does the committee address timeliness of information?
  - Does the committee address clinical needs?
- Is there an ongoing process for assessment and reassessment of information needs in the organization?
  - Does the pharmacy have a software package that alerts the pharmacist to potential food-drug interactions, drug-drug interactions, drug-herbal interactions, and inappropriate dosing on a real time basis?
  - What alerts are provided to the professional staff on patient care units (e.g., panic lab values, medication alerts)?

- Has the organization implemented a physician order entry system? If not, what are the organization's plans to implement such a system?
  - Are information systems in place to collect data for evaluating clinical care?
- What is the methodology for prioritizing needs?
- How are information technology funds allocated between clinical and administrative needs?
- Has the organization committed appropriate funds for upgrading technology systems?
- How does the organization maintain systems security and confidentiality?

PATIENT ASSESSMENT

- Is there an interdisciplinary collaborative team that addresses the totality of patient care needs?
- How does the organization ensure that collaboration is effective?
- What is the organization's process for assessing the needs of patients with multisystem breakdown?
- Given an aging population, how do caregivers collaborate in planning a patient's treatment plan?
- What is the organization's policy for conducting screenings and assessments for
  - histories and physicals?
  - nursing assessment and reassessments?
  - nutritional screens, assessments, and reassessments?
  - functional screens, assessments, and reassessments?
  - respiratory assessments and reassessments?
  - spiritual assessments and reassessments?
  - discharge planning?
  - pain assessments and reassessments?
- Are second opinions obtained, literature searched, and other resources utilized in search of current, timely, and accurate diagnoses and treatment of patients?

Nutritional Care

- What is the organization's policy for nutritional care?
- How is the diet manual developed and approved?
- How are the criteria for nutritional screens developed and approved?
  - Who participates in determining screening criteria?
  - Who performs nutritional screens?
  - What is the role of the nurse in identifying patients at nutritional risk?

- How is staff competency to screen patients assessed?
- What is the organization's process for screening and assessing patients at nutritional risk?
  - Is every patient's nutritional status screened?
  - What criteria has the organization established for determining high-risk patients?
  - Is the patient consulted as part of the screening?
  - Are nutritional assessments conducted on a timely basis?
  - Are family members interviewed, as appropriate, for their input?
- Are patients periodically reassessed for nutritional needs as determined by the patient's condition?
- Are all patients at nutritional risk evaluated by a dietitian?
  - Is the nutritional plan of care conducted on an interdisciplinary collaborative basis?
- Do initial nutritional screenings address patients at nutritional risk? Do risk factors include
  - enteral or parenteral feeding?
  - patient age, height, weight and diagnosis?
  - sudden weight gain or loss?
  - special dietary needs?
  - medications that might affect nutritional status (e.g., chemotherapy)?
  - assistance needed with food preparation or feeding at home?
  - patient observation?
  - skin color and condition (e.g., breakdown/wounds)?
  - cachexia, temporal wasting, or appearance of weight-height discrepancy?
  - severe nausea/vomiting?
  - diarrhea/constipation?
  - difficulty chewing/swallowing?
  - recent change in appetite (e.g., < 50–75% of meals consumed for five days or more)?
  - high-risk surgery patient (e.g., multiple surgeries, geriatric patient)?
  - human immunodeficiency virus (HIV) positive?
  - new diabetic?
- Is a physician's order necessary to conduct an in-depth nutritional assessment?
- How is the potential for food–drug interactions monitored?
- Who is responsible for modified diet counseling?
- How are patients on special diets monitored to ensure that they have the appropriate food tray?
- How are diet changes monitored?
- How is the appropriateness of diet prescriptions monitored?
- How are the appropriateness and effectiveness of nutritional care monitored?

- Is the organization's mechanism for ordering, preparing, dispensing, administering, and monitoring of total parenteral nutrition defined by the medical staff?
- What are the responsibilities for nutritional care by the various caregivers (e.g., nurse, nutritionist, pharmacist, and speech therapist/pathologist)?
- Does the nurse ensure that each patient receives appropriate assistance with feeding?
- Is each patient's intake and output monitored?
- Does the pharmacist prepare and dispense parenteral nutrition solutions?
- Can speech pathologists recommend a nutritional consult for patients considered at nutritional risk?
- Do speech pathologists evaluate patients with dysphagia?
  - Do speech pathologists make recommendations for adaptive swallowing techniques and diet consistency? Will the following observations trigger a speech-pathologist consult:
  - severe dysarthria
  - "wet" voice
  - drooling
  - poor cough reflex
- Documentation
  - Are screenings and assessments documented on approved forms?
  - Are fluid intake and output documented on approved forms?
- Is nutrition counseling provided at the request of the patient, physician, nurse, or at the discretion of the dietitian?
- Is responsibility for nutrition education determined by a multidisciplinary team based on patient need?
- Is education provided by a nurse for basic instruction and by a clinical dietitian/nutritionist for complex or specialized diet counseling?

Rehabilitation Services

- How are functional screens conducted?
- If it is determined that a full assessment is necessary, within what time frame must it be completed?
- Is a physician's order necessary for a full assessment?
- Who provides patient/family education?
- Does the organization provide for weekend coverage to ensure continuity of care?

EMERGENCY DEPARTMENT

- Are patients triaged, assessed, and treated within a reasonable period of time?

- Does the emergency department have an "express care" treatment area?
  - What are the criteria for admission and discharge?
  - Is response time by physicians on the on-call list timely?
- Are all patients assessed and treated by a physician prior to discharge?
- What is the organization's mechanism for obtaining consultations?
- What is the door-to-needle time for the administration of thrombolytics?
- If admission is necessary, is the designated attending physician responsible for
  - accepting the patient as an admission?
  - suggesting a specified consulting physician?
  - requesting that the emergency department physician hold the patient for further assessment until the patient's private physician can assess the patient?
  - requesting transfer to a more appropriate facility for care (e.g., burn center)?
- What are the specific competencies required of staff who work in the emergency department?
- Is adequate staff available to care for patients?
- In the event a patient's past admissions are microfilmed, are pertinent sections or specific portions of previous records readily available as needed?
- Are medical records maintained for each patient treated in the emergency department?
- Are medical records maintained for each patient who prearranges to meet his or her physician in the emergency department for both urgent and non-urgent care?
- Are copies of the medical records of a patient seen in the emergency department sent to both the patient's treating and family physician?
- If a patient has been treated in other settings within the organization (e.g., ambulatory care settings), how are records from those settings accessed?
- What is the process for providing patient education in the emergency department prior to discharge?
- How are patients discharged from the emergency department notified of abnormal test results?
- What documentation is maintained regarding notification of patients as to test results?
- Who is responsible for follow-up with patients who have abnormal tests?
- What are the issues and perceptions identified by patients as to the care being rendered in the emergency department?
- What transfer agreements does the organization have in place to effectuate a timely transfer of a patient in need of an alternate level of care?

- What evaluation tools does the organization utilize to improve the care rendered in the emergency department?
- How is staff educated
  - regarding abuse and neglect?
  - about age-specific competencies?
- What is the process for obtaining informed consent?
- How are advanced directives handled for end-of-life patients?
- Are observation beds maintained in the emergency department?
- What is the organization's policy for treat and divert?
- Is there an isolation room?
- Who reads X-rays when there is no radiologist available in the hospital?
- What are the criteria for referral and transfer of emergency department patients?

ENVIRONMENTAL SAFETY

General Safety

- Does the organization have a safety program?
- Has the organization designated a safety officer to be responsible for the overall activities of the safety program?
- Does the organization have a safety committee?
- Is there an in-house program for addressing employee safety complaints?
- How are employees informed as to the activities of the safety committee?

Fire Safety

- Are exits clearly marked?
  - Are exit signs clear as to direction of egress?
  - Are exit signs illuminated?
- Does the organization have a designated smoking area?
- Do fire-rated doors
  - have a self-closing device?
  - have a positive latching mechanism?
- Are fire-rated doors smoke tight with vertical gaps no greater than 1/8 inch and undercuts no greater than 3/4 inch?
- Are designated smoking areas appropriately ventilated?
  - Is air exhausted to the outside?
- Are there current safety policies and procedures for each department?
- Are fire drills conducted? How often?
- Are fire circuits tested? Are portable fire extinguishers maintained according to appropriate safety codes?

- Are through-the-wall penetrations sealed to prevent the spread of smoke?
- Is there a clear space 18 inches below sprinkler heads?
- Do linen and trash chutes have positive latching?
- Are fire extinguishers mounted in readily accessible locations throughout the organization?
  - Are fire extinguishers properly maintained?
  - Have employees been trained in the proper handling and use of fire extinguishers?
- Have employees been trained in proper fire evacuation procedures?
- Is the fire department acquainted with the facility?

Utilities

- Are electrical panels secure/locked, labeled, and provided with preventive maintenance?
- Are emergency generators properly tested?
- Are primary and secondary shutoff valves for utility systems labeled?
- Medical gas vacuum
  - How is air conditioned prior to exhaust (e.g., air wash)?
  - Is the air intake a minimum of 10 feet from the nearest exhaust?
- Are exit corridors blocked with storage?
- How are air-handling systems monitored for replacement of air filters?
  - Is there both visual and mechanical monitoring?
- Is there is a reliable, adequate emergency power system to provide electricity to all critical areas?

Security

- Have security issues been addressed throughout the organization?
  - Have sensitive areas been identified (e.g., nursery, operating rooms, pediatrics, and emergency department) and appropriate precautions taken to protect patients, staff, and visitors?
  - What security precautions have been taken to protect these areas (e.g., combination locks, cameras, security rounds, mirrors, visitor control/identification tags, alarms, wristband/ankle/umbilical cord alarms, closed units, and staff education)?

Hazardous Materials

- What hazardous materials does the organization handle?

- Are hazardous materials inventoried by location?
- Is there a written hazard communication program that addresses staff education needs?
- Are Material Safety Data Sheets (MSDS) readily available to employees?
- What precautions are taken for the storage of hazardous materials to minimize the risks of leakage, explosion, and fire?
- What precautions are taken in handling and storing hazardous materials?
- Are combustible materials stored in covered metal receptacles and removed from the worksite?
- Are flammable liquids kept in closed containers when not in use?
- Are storage containers and piping connections vapor and liquid tight?
- Are hazardous materials stored in a safe, secure, and appropriately ventilated environment?
- Do storage rooms for flammable and combustible liquids have explosion-proof lights?
- Are "No Smoking" signs posted in hazardous areas?
- Is there a hazardous materials (HAZMAT) response team?
- How are hazardous spills handled?
- Are reports of incidents related to spills maintained?
- What is the organization's process for disposing of hazardous materials?

Medical Equipment

- Does the organization maintain written criteria as to the selection of medical equipment?
- Is equipment tested prior to use?
- Who is responsible for training the "end user"?
- Do medical equipment policies and procedures provide for
  - selecting and acquiring equipment?
  - having available written criteria to identify, evaluate, and inventory medical equipment?
  - assessing/minimizing clinical and physical risks associated with medical equipment by providing preventive and corrective maintenance services?
  - monitoring and acting on medical equipment hazard notices and recalls?
  - monitoring and reporting incidents that may have caused or contributed to an injury?
  - reporting and investigating equipment management problems?
- How are equipment failures reported?

- What procedures does the organization follow in the event of loss of water, power, medical gas, heat, and cooling?
- How is equipment testing documented?
  - How are user errors reported?
  - How are programs evaluated?
  - Are there any trends?
  - Are actions taken as appropriate?
  - Are outside maintenance contracts monitored?

Personal Protective Equipment

- Has the work environment been assessed to determine if there are hazards that require the use of personal protective equipment?
- Do employees use properly fitted protective equipment?
- Are protective goggles and face masks worn in hazardous areas while working with hazardous materials, including all body fluids?
- Are hard hats worn where there is danger of falling objects?
  - Are hard hats inspected periodically for damage to the shell and suspension system?

LABORATORY

- What regulatory bodies accredit the lab?
- What tests are conducted outside the lab?
- Are outside lab testing sites approved by the medical staff?
  - Where is their approval documented?
- Do designated lab personnel review test results and compare those results with clinical presentation and history?
- Is lab staff integrated into the clinical decision-making process?
- Does lab staff participate in the activities of the pharmacy and therapeutics committee?
- Does the lab
  - have representation on the pharmacy and therapeutics committee?
  - report panic values to the patient care units and attending physicians?
  - monitor therapeutic ranges?
  - check blood levels for toxicity?
  - determine therapeutic levels?
  - provide data vital to evaluating the nutritional status of patients?
  - provide drugs in—data out information?
  - provide organism–drug interactions?

- conduct culture and sensitivity studies?
- act in a consultative role?
- provide information as to physician ordering practices?
- participate in PI activities with other disciplines on a collaborative basis?
- describe the PI activities that lab personnel participate in with other disciplines?
- How does the lab, pharmacy, and dietary staff work collaboratively to improve patient care?
- If test results do not fit a patient's clinical picture or expected outcomes, what happens?
- Are lab personnel reviewing test results for drug interactions through testing procedures (e.g., patients can produce antibodies to drugs that can cross-react with lab tests)?
- Does communication between the lab and pharmacy facilitate the production of more useful data from lab tests and allow better utilization of lab resources to improve patient care and decrease direct costs to the patient and provider?
  - Is there documentation of draw times on specimens for therapeutic drug monitoring so that the drug level determined at a known point in time can be related to the specific dose given at a specific time? (Without such a relationship in time, interpretation of serum drug levels to drug dosage would be questionable.)
- What is the importance of having the admitting diagnosis and comments placed on lab slips?
  - A glucometer ordered with the admitting diagnosis of urosepsis septic shock clues the lab to the fact that the patient may be on antibiotics, which can interfere with test results. A patient in septic shock may have abnormal glucose results on the glucometer. Such results would be followed up with a lab glucose to verify glucometer readings.
- How is monitoring of the various shifts conducted?
- Why should patient assessment include questions of what medications are being administered?
- How are autopsy criteria developed?
- How are pre- and post-operation path report discrepancies addressed?

MEDICAL STAFF

- What are the organization's processes for credentialing physicians and other health care practitioners (e.g., acupuncturists)?
- Is information collected from the National Practitioner Data Bank utilized in the credentialing process?
- How does the organization review and evaluate the competency of the members of the medical staff?

- What mechanism does the organization have in place for ongoing evaluation and reevaluation/appointment and reappointment?

MEDICATION USE

Control of Medications

- Who is responsible for overseeing the storage and control of medications maintained on patient care units?
- What risk reduction activities does the organization have in place to reduce the likelihood of adverse drug reactions and medication errors?
- What disciplines have been credentialed to prescribe medications (e.g., physician's assistants and nurse practitioners)?
- How are controlled substances monitored, inventoried, and wasted (is wasting witnessed and documented)?
- What is the organization's mechanism for monitoring the effect of medications on patients?

Medication Errors

- What is the organization's process for monitoring, tracking, and trending medication errors?
- Are medication errors tracked and trended by profession (e.g., nurse, pharmacist, and physician)?
  - How is the information gathered utilized to reduce the likelihood of medication errors?
- What are the common causes/trends and patterns for medication errors?
  - Are errors trended by patient care unit?
- What processes does the organization have in place to reduce the likelihood of transcription errors?
- What is the organization's frequency of
  - transcription errors?
  - dosing errors (including age-related dosing for neonates, infants, adolescents, adult, and geriatric populations)?
  - administration errors?
  - double dosing?
  - administering medications not ordered?
  - untimely administration of medications?
  - administering a medication to the wrong patient?
  - packaging errors by pharmacy staff?
  - packaging errors by drug manufacturers?
  - errors due to illegible and/or ambiguous handwriting?
  - administering medications to the wrong patient?
  - administering the wrong drug?
  - administering medications at the wrong frequency?
  - not administering medications at the designated time?
  - medications not being administered?
  - unordered medications being administered?
  - administering medication after it has been discontinued?
  - administering medications after the expiration date?
  - administering medications prior to the designated start date?
  - administering medications without obtaining consent?
- Is consent obtained for the use of investigational drugs and high-risk medications?
- What is the frequency of "missed" doses?
- What educational processes have been implemented to reduce the likelihood of medication errors?

Adverse Drug Reactions

- How do reported adverse drug reactions compare with like organizations?
- Is there a mechanism in place for monitoring side effects?
- Is there a mechanism in place for reducing the frequency of adverse drug reactions?

Emergency Medications

- How are emergency medications obtained when the pharmacy is closed?
- How are medications obtained that are not included in the hospital's formulary?

Investigational Drugs

- Is informed consent obtained from patients prior to the use of investigational drugs?
- Describe the organization's procedure for reviewing and approving research protocols.
- Does the organization have a mechanism in place for approving and overseeing the use of investigational drugs in the organization?
- How are investigational drug protocols and criteria developed and approved?

Look-Alike Drugs

- How are potentially dangerous look-alike drugs separated in the pharmacy?
- Are look-alike medications repackaged or relabeled in the pharmacy?

Sample Drugs

- Does the organization permit the dispensing of sample medications?
- What information is maintained in patient records in the event a sample drug is recalled?
- Does the organization maintain a medication log for tracking the dispensing of sample drugs?
- Does the log include the following pertinent information: medication dispensed; date medication was dispensed; patient name; patient record number; dosage and amounts given; medication control/lot numbers for purposes of recall; expiration date; and physician signature?

Medications from Home

- Are patients permitted to self-administer medications (e.g., insulin)?
- Where are self-administered medications stored?
- How is monitoring conducted?

Crash Cart Medications

- Who is responsible for stocking medications in crash carts?
- Who is responsible for ensuring that medications have not expired?
- Who is responsible for ensuring the integrity of "crash carts" (e.g., that appropriate medications, equipment, and supplies are available when needed)?
- Are logs maintained?
- Does the organization maintain the appropriate equipment on crash carts for treating both children and adults?
- Are staff members appropriately trained in the testing and use of equipment contained in or on the crash cart?
- How are staff members who participate in codes evaluated?
- Do pharmacists attend codes?
- What value might be added if pharmacists attended codes?
  - calculations based on age, weight, and height?
  - drip rates?
  - mixing?
- Is there a collaborative approach to reviewing the organization's procedures after a code?
- What mechanisms are in place for reviewing medications administered during a code?

Medications and Patient Education

- Is education conducted on a collaborative basis?
  - What is the role of the nurse?
  - What is the role of the pharmacist?
  - What is the role of the physician?
  - What is the role of the dietitian?
- How is education provided in ambulatory care settings?

Medication Use Improvement Activities/Safe Administration of Medications

- What is the organization's process for evaluating high-risk, high-volume, problem-prone, and high-cost medications?
- Does the organization have a multidisciplinary medication use improvement team?
- What are the team's goals?
  - promoting a nonpunitive approach to reducing medication errors?
  - increasing detection and reporting of medication errors?
  - understanding the cause of errors?
  - educating staff as to the cause and prevention of errors?
- How is information on medication monitoring obtained?
- How has the organization's cost-reduction activities affected patient care?
- Describe the kinds of aggregate data available for performance improvement activities.

Multiple Medications

- What systems does the organization have in place to minimize the likelihood of drug-drug interactions?
- What is the protocol for handling patients on multiple medications?
- What stat lab tests does the organization have in place for patients who have overdosed?

PASTORAL CARE SERVICES

- How are the spiritual needs of patients addressed?
- How do patients know such services are available?
- Do organizational policies and procedures address the psychosocial, spiritual, and cultural variables that influence one's understanding and perception of illness?
- How are referrals made by caregivers for spiritual assessment, reassessment, and follow-up?

- What evidence/documentation is placed in the patient's medical record to indicate that the patient's spiritual needs have been addressed?

PATIENT COMPLAINT PROCESS

- What is the organization's patient complaint process?
- How does the patient know about the process?
- How are complaints addressed in the organization?

PATIENT CARE UNIT

- What are the size, special characteristics, census data, staffing patterns, and results of patient satisfaction surveys?
- How are medications stored?
- Where and what hazardous materials are stored, handled, and disposed of?
- What happens if there is a power failure?
- What is the organization's smoking policy?
- Are bathrooms safe (e.g., equipped with hand rails and call buttons)?
- How is patient assessment integrated into the patient's medical record by the various disciplines?
- How are formulary updates communicated to the staff?
- Describe patient record documentation, including admission records, history and physicals, anesthesia reports, operative reports, consents, medication records, patient/family education documentation, physician's orders, progress notes, rehabilitative service records, respiratory therapy, test result reporting records (e.g., lab, ECG, EEG, imaging reports), nurses' notes, advance directives, restraints, discharge planning, etc.
- Are there unique safety concerns specific to the unit (e.g., special isolation procedures)?
- Are there age-specific requirements that pertain to the patient population? What are they?
- Describe how patient rights are addressed.
- How are confidentiality issues addressed?
- Are tests results available in a timely manner?
- Is there evidence of patient/family education?
  - Is there an assessment of a patient's readiness/willingness, ability, and need to learn?
  - Are patients provided information as to medications, diet, allergies, blood type, and medical equipment appropriate to their care needs?
- What are the security issues specific to the unit?
- What PI activities are conducted on the unit?
- In specialty units such as the intensive care unit and the coronary care unit

- Are there monitors in all patient rooms?
- Is there visual observation of patients at all times?
- Are there admission criteria to the unit by diagnosis?
- Are there discharge criteria?
- Is there a consultation policy?
- Are there specific triggers to generate a consultation (e.g., infection)?
- What are the age groups of patients treated on the unit?

PATIENT AND FAMILY EDUCATION

- How are the learning needs of patients and families addressed?
- How is patient education provided?
- What is the organization's mechanism for documentation on the patient record?
- How are the following issues addressed:
  - medication use?
  - medical equipment use?
  - food-drug interactions?
  - access to community resources?
  - how to obtain further care, if necessary?
  - responsibilities of patient and family?
  - resources available for patient/family education?
- Is the teaching reaching the patient?
  - Does the patient understand the message?
  - What is the likelihood that the patient and family will comply with instructions?
  - How is reinforcement of education conducted?
- Is there an interdisciplinary approach to patient and family education?
- What is the physician's role in patient and family education?
- What are the key factors to assessment and readiness to learn?
- How do you evaluate the effectiveness of patient education resources?
- What resources are available for patient and family education?
- What are your options or opportunities for follow-up and reinforcement of education?

PATIENT RIGHTS

- How are advance directives addressed?
  - Are patients queried to determine if they have an advance directive?

– What happens if the patient has an advance directive? Is a copy placed in the patient's individual record?

– What happens if the patient has no advance directive? Is the patient provided information and an opportunity to execute an advance directive?

• How does the organization address ethical issues?

• Does the organization have a code of ethical behavior?

– Does the code address admissions, discharge, transfer, billing practices, referrals, and relationships with other health care professionals?

• Does the organization have an ethics committee?

– What are the functions of the ethics committee?

– Does committee membership include representation from both community and providers?

– How are the patients and staff educated as to the existence and functions of the ethics committee?

– How is the committee accessed for consultation?

• Are patients provided a statement as to their rights and responsibilities upon admission?

• Do patients have a right to review their medical records?

• How are complaints addressed?

• What are the organization's policies and procedures for asking patients and families about organ donations?

RADIOLOGY

• How are radiologists credentialed for special procedures?

• Who interprets diagnostic images?

• How is the staff monitored for radiation safety?

• What is the mechanism for approving the department's policies and procedures?

• How are staff competencies evaluated?

• Is staff educated to be watchful for abuse and neglect?

• What happens if computed tomography (CT) or magnetic resonance imaging (MRI) equipment is not operational?

• Who provides the patient with education as to the procedure(s) that he or she is about to undergo?

• How is a code managed in the radiology department?

• What hazardous materials do the staff handle?

– How are hazardous materials disposed?

• How are radiographic contrast media stored, controlled, distributed, administered, and monitored?

RESOURCE CENTER

• What resources are available to the staff?

• How are needs assessed?

• Are resources available to patients and families?

• In what PI activities does the medical librarian participate?

RESPIRATORY CARE

• What is your scope of services?

• How do you sterilize equipment and reusable supplies?

• Do you have ventilator protocols?

• How do you provide for staff education?

STERILE SUPPLY

• What is the mandated dress code for decontamination?

• Is decontamination performed elsewhere in the organization (e.g., labor and delivery, and emergency department)?

• Are staff members cross-trained for each area?

• How does the organization handle implants?

• Describe the monitoring process of the sterilizers.

• Describe the flow of activities when contaminated instruments are received.

• Is biological testing being conducted and records being maintained?

SURGERY

Surgical Privileges

• What is the process for credentialing surgeons as to which procedures they can perform?

• Who ensures that all appropriate assessments have been completed prior to surgery (e.g., history and physical and anesthesia)?

• Does the organization have assessment criteria for emergent and nonemergent surgical cases?

• What patient education is in place prior to surgery?

Consent for Anesthesia and Surgery

• What is the organization's procedure for ensuring that patients have been informed as to the risks, benefits, and alternatives of anesthesia, surgical procedures, and administration of blood or blood products?

• Who is responsible for informing the patient of the risks, benefits, and alternatives to anesthesia, surgical procedures, and the administration of blood or blood products?

• Who verifies that consent forms (e.g., anesthesia, surgery, and blood) have been executed and placed in the patient's record)?

• Does the organization have a process by which there is correlation of pathology and imaging findings?

Correct-Sided Surgery

- What is the organization's process for ensuring that it selected the correct site and correct surgical procedure for the right patient?
- Who is responsible for ensuring that the appropriate equipment, supplies, and staffing are available prior to induction (administration of anesthesia)?
  - Is surgical equipment properly cleaned and stored following each procedure?
  - Is blood stored in the operating room suite?
  - Is blood stored at appropriate temperatures?
  - How are temperatures monitored?

Anesthesia

- Who is responsible for developing and updating the organization's conscious sedation policy?
- Do nurse anesthetists administer conscious sedation and/or general anesthesia?
  - What is the process for credentialing nurse anesthetists?
  - How is competency reviewed?
  - Who monitors their work?
  - Is backup coverage readily available from an anesthesiologist?
  - Are there any limitations as to what forms of anesthesia can be administered?
- Are surgical nurses ACLS certified?
- How are patients monitored?
  - Is monitoring the same at all locations?
- Does the organization have a mechanism in place for reviewing and monitoring unplanned returns to the operating suite?
- What are the discharge criteria for the post-anesthesia recovery unit?
- What redundant systems does the organization have in place for electrical failures, equipment breakdown, and backup staffing?

Postoperative Infections

- Are surgical site infections being tracked?
- What processes does the organization have in place to follow up with patients who have postoperative infections?

- How does the organization identify postoperative infections in day surgery patients?
- Is there routine consultative care by an infectious disease specialist available when a patient develops an infection?
- How does the organization's infection rate compare with that of other organizations?
- Is there appropriate separation of clean and soiled supplies and instrumentation?
- Who is responsible for ensuring that each operating suite has been properly cleaned prior to the next procedure?
- Are postsurgical infections being tracked?

WEB SITES

The following Web sites should prove helpful in improving patient care and organizational performance:

- www.ismp.org—This site provides information on medication safety articles.
- www.careplans.com—This site provides information on the patient care planning process.
- www.best4health.org—This site is a *Best Practice Network* used to promote information sharing in health care by nurses, physicians, and other health care professionals. This network facilitates the exchange of ideas, encourages collaboration in results-oriented problem solving, and enables health care professionals to share best practices.
- www.hcwp.org/meddirfm—This site provides samples of Medical Staff Bylaws, Patient Care Policies (e.g., Conscious Sedation, Criteria for Monitoring Patients Receiving IV Conscious Sedation, and Informed Consent), and Medical Staff Policies.
- www.wlm-web.com/hcnet—This site is an independent Web site for health care professionals to share policies and procedures.
- www.jcaho.org—This site contains information regarding the Joint Commission, the nation's leading organization that develops standards and other performance measures, awards accreditation decisions, and provides education and consultation to health care organizations around the world.

CHAPTER REVIEW

1. The development of redundant, or backup, systems, procedures, and processes reduces the likelihood of errors in human processes.
2. The review of sentinel events and the implementation of a system of root cause analysis help organizations determine why an event happened, as well as ways in which similar events can be prevented.

Glossary

Abandonment: Unilateral severance by the physician of the professional relationship between him- or herself and the patient without reasonable notice at a time when the patient still needs continuing care.

Abortion: Premature termination of pregnancy at a time when the fetus is incapable of sustaining life independent of the mother.

Admissibility (of evidence): Refers to the issue of whether a court, applying the rules of evidence, is bound to receive or permit introduction of a particular piece of evidence.

Advance directives: Written instructions expressing an individual's health care wishes in the event that he or she becomes incapacitated and is unable to make such decisions for him- or herself.

Adverse drug reaction: Unusual or unexpected response to a normal dose of a medication. An injury caused by the use of a drug in the usual, acceptable fashion.

Affidavit: A voluntary statement of facts, or a voluntary declaration in writing of facts, that a person swears to be true before an official authorized to administer an oath.

Agency: A relationship between parties in which one party authorizes the other party to act for or to represent him or her (e.g., an agent acting for or on behalf of an insurance company). In a malpractice suit, a plaintiff may name both parties as codefendants, even though only one of the parties may have treated the patient.

Americans with Disabilities Act (ADA): Federal Act that bars employers from discriminating against disabled persons in hiring, promotion, or other provisions of employment.

Appellant: Party who appeals the decision of a lower court to a court of higher jurisdiction.

Appellee: Party against whom an appeal to a higher court is taken.

Assault: Intentional act that is designed to make the victim fearful and produces reasonable apprehension of harm.

Assignment: Transfer of rights, responsibilities, or property from one party to another.

Attestation: Act of witnessing a document in writing.

Autonomy: Right of an individual to make his or her own independent decisions.

Battery: Intentional touching of one person by another without the consent of the person being touched.

Best evidence rule: Legal doctrine requiring that primary evidence of a fact (such as an original document) be introduced or that an acceptable explanation be given before a copy can be introduced or testimony given concerning the fact.

Bona fide: In good faith; openly, honestly, or innocently; without knowledge or intent of fraud.

Borrowed servant doctrine: Refers to a situation in which an employee is temporarily under the control of someone other than his or her primary employer. It may involve a situation where an employee is carrying out the specific instructions of a physician. The traditional example is that of a nurse employed by a hospital who is "borrowed" and under the control of the attending surgeon during a procedure in the operating room. The temporary employer of the borrowed servant can be held responsible for the negligent acts of the borrowed servant under the doctrine of *respondeat superior*. This rule is not easily applied, especially if the acts of the employee are for the furtherance of the objectives of the employer. The courts apply a narrow application if the employee is fulfilling the requirement of his or her position.

Captain of the ship doctrine: A doctrine making the physician responsible for the negligent acts of other professionals because he or she had the right to control and oversee the totality of care provided to the patient.

Caregiver: One who provides care to a patient.

Case citation: Means of describing where the court's opinion in a particular case can be located. It identifies the parties in the case, the text in which the case can be found, the court writing the opinion, and the year in which the case was decided. For example, the citation "*Bouvia v. Superior Court (Glenchur)*, 225 Cal. Rptr. 297 (Ct. App. 1986)" is described as follows:

- "*Bouvia v. Superior Court (Glenchu)*" identifies the basic parties involved in the lawsuit.
- "225 Cal. Rptr. 297" identifies the case as being reported in volume 225 of the California Reporter at page 297.
- "Ct. App. 1986" identifies the case as being in the California Court of Appeals in 1986.

Case law: Aggregate of reported cases on a particular legal subject as formed by the decisions of those cases.

Certiorari: Writ that commands a lower court to certify proceedings for review by a higher court. This is the common method of obtaining review by the U.S. Supreme Court.

Charitable immunity: Legal doctrine that developed out of the English court system that held charitable institutions blameless for their negligent acts.

Chemical device: Use of medications to control patient behavior.

Civil law: Body of law that describes the private rights and responsibilities of individuals. It is that part of law that does not deal with crimes. It involves actions filed by one individual against another (e.g., actions in tort and contract).

Clinical privileges: On qualification, the diagnostic and therapeutic procedures that an institution allows a physician to perform on a specified patient population. Qualification includes a review of a physician's credentials, such as medical school diploma, state licensure, and residency training.

Closed shop contract: Labor-management agreement that provides that only members of a particular union may be hired.

Common law: Body of principles that has evolved and continues to evolve and expand from court decisions. Many of the legal principles and rules applied by courts in the United States had their origins in English common law.

Complaint: In a negligence action, the first pleading that is filed by the plaintiff's attorney. It is the first statement of a case by the plaintiff against the defendant and states a cause of action, notifying the defendant as to the basis for the suit.

Congressional Record: Document in which the proceedings of Congress are published. It is the first record of debate officially reported, printed, and published directly by the federal government. Publication of the Record began March 4, 1873.

Consent: *See* Informed consent.

Counterclaim: Defendant's claim in opposition to the plaintiff's claim.

Crime: Act against society in violation of the law. Crimes are prosecuted by and in the name of the state.

Criminal negligence: Reckless disregard for the safety of others. It is the willful indifference to an injury that could follow an act.

Critical pathway: A series of sequential steps in a process that is required to ensure a satisfactory outcome.

Defamation: Injury of a person's reputation or character caused by the false statements of another made to a third person. Defamation includes both libel and slander.

Defendant: In a criminal case, the person accused of committing a crime. In a civil suit, the party against whom the suit is brought, demanding that he or she pay the other party legal relief.

Demurrer: Formal objection by one of the parties to a lawsuit that the evidence presented by the other party is insufficient to sustain an issue or case.

Deposition: A method of pretrial discovery that consists of statements of fact taken by a witness under oath in a question and answer format as it would be in a court of law with opportunity given to the adversary to be present for cross-examination. Such statements may be admitted into evidence if it is impossible for a witness to attend a trial in person.

Directed verdict: When a trial judge decides either that the evidence and/or law is clearly in favor of one party or that the plaintiff has failed to establish a case and that it is pointless for the trial to proceed further, the judge may direct the jury to return a verdict for the appropriate party. The conclusion of the judge must be so clear and obvious that reasonable minds could not arrive at a different conclusion.

Discharge summary: That part of a medical record that summarizes a patient's initial complaints, course of treatment, final diagnosis, and suggestions for follow-up care.

Discovery: To ascertain that which was previously unknown through a pretrial investigation; it includes testimony and documents that may be under the exclusive control of the other party. Discovery facilitates out-of-court settlements.

Do-not-resuscitate (DNR): Directive of a physician to withhold cardiopulmonary resuscitation in the event a patient experiences cardiac or respiratory arrest.

Durable power of attorney: Legal instrument enabling an individual to act on another's behalf. In the health care setting, it includes the authority to make medical decisions for another.

Euthanasia: Act conducted for the purpose of causing the merciful death of a person who is suffering from an incurable condition.

Evidence: Proof of a fact, which is legally presented in a manner prescribed by law, at trial.

Expert witness: Person who has special training, experience, skill, and knowledge in a relevant area and who is allowed to offer an opinion as testimony in court.

Facility: In the context of this text, a "facility," in most instances, is referring to health care facilities in general, unless within the context of its usage it is referring to particular institutions, such as acute care hospitals or nursing facilities/homes.

Federal question: Legal question involving the U.S. Constitution or a statute enacted by Congress.

Felony: Serious crime usually punishable by imprisonment for a period of longer than one year or by death.

Good Samaritan laws: Laws designed to protect those who stop to render aid in an emergency. These laws generally provide immunity for specified persons from any civil suit arising out of care rendered at the scene of an emergency, provided that the one rendering assistance has not done so in a grossly negligent manner.

Governing body: Official body of an institution vested with the legal responsibility for its operation.

Grand jury: Jury called to determine whether there is sufficient evidence that a crime has been committed to justify bringing a case to trial. It is not the jury before which the case is tried to determine guilt or innocence.

Grand larceny: Theft of property valued at more than a specified amount (usually $50), thus constituting a felony instead of a misdemeanor.

Grievance: The process undertaken to resolve a labor-management dispute when there is an allegation by a union member that management has failed in some way to meet the terms of a labor agreement.

Guardian: Person appointed by a court to protect the interests of and make decisions for a person who is incapable of making his or her own decisions.

Habeas corpus: Writ to challenge the legality of imprisonment or detention.

Health: According to the World Health Organization, "[a] state of complete physical, mental, and social well-being and not merely the absence of disease or infirmity."

Health Care Financing Administration (HCFA): Federal agency that coordinates the federal government's participation in the Medicare and Medicaid programs.

Health care proxy: Document that delegates the authority to make one's own health care decisions to another adult, known as the health care agent, when one has become incapacitated or is unable to make his or her own decisions.

Hearsay rule: Rule of evidence that restricts the admissibility of evidence that is not the personal knowledge of the witness. Hearsay evidence is admissible only under strict rules.

Holographic will: Will handwritten by the testator.

Home health agency: Any public agency or private organization, or a subdivision of such an agency or organization, whether operated for profit or not, that provides home health services. Home health care involves an array of services provided to patients in their homes or foster homes because of acute illness, exacerbation of chronic illness, and disability. Such services are therapeutic and/or preventive.

Home health care: Home health care is an alternative for those who fear leaving the secure environment of their home. Such care is available through home health agencies. These agencies provide a variety of services for the elderly living at home. Such services include part-time or intermittent nursing care; physical, occupational, and speech therapy; medical social services, home health aide services, nutritional guidance; medical supplies other than drugs and biologicals prescribed by a physician; and the use of medical appliances. Depending on individual needs, these services are available on a daily, weekly, or even monthly basis.

Hospice: Long-term care facility for terminally ill persons. It is provided in a setting more economical than that of a hospital or nursing home. Hospice care generally is sought after a decision has been made to discontinue aggressive efforts to prolong life. A hospice program includes such characteristics as support services by trained individuals, family involvement, and control of pain and discomfort.

Hydration: Intravenous addition of fluids to the circulatory system.

Impeachment: Legislative proceeding designed to remove an executive or judicial officer from office because of misconduct.

Incompetent: Individual determined by a court to be incapable of making rational decisions on his or her own behalf.

Independent contractor: One who agrees to undertake work without being under the direct control or direction of the employer.

Indictment: Formal written accusation, found and presented by a grand jury, charging a person therein named with criminal conduct.

Informed consent: Legal concept that provides that a patient has the right to know the potential risks, benefits, and alternatives of a proposed procedure prior to undergoing a particular course of treatment.

Injunction: Court order either requiring a person to perform a certain act or prohibiting the person from performing a particular act.

In loco parentis: Legal doctrine that permits the courts to assign a person to stand in the place of parents and possess their legal rights, duties, and responsibilities toward a child.

Interrogatories: List of questions sent from one party in a lawsuit to the other party to be answered under oath.

Joint Commission on Accreditation of Healthcare Organizations: A not-for-profit independent organization dedicated to improving the quality of health care in organized health care settings. The major functions of the Joint Commission include the development of organizational standards, awarding accreditation decisions, and providing education and consultation to health care organizations.

Judge: Officer who guides court proceedings to ensure impartiality and enforces the rules of evidence. The trial judge determines the applicable law and states it to the jury. The appellate judge hears appeals and renders decisions concerning the correctness of the actions of the trial judge, the law of the case, and the sufficiency of the evidence.

Judicial notice: Act by which a court, in conducting a trial or forming a decision, will of its own motion and without evidence recognize the existence and truth of certain facts bearing on the controversy at bar (e.g., serious falls require X-rays).

Jurisdiction: Right of a court to administer justice by hearing and deciding controversies.

Jurisprudence: Philosophy or science of law on which a particular legal system is built.

Larceny: Taking of another person's property without consent with the intent to permanently deprive the owner of its use and ownership.

Legal wrong: Invasion of a protected right.

Liability: As it relates to damages, an obligation one has incurred or might incur through a negligent act.

Libel: False or malicious writing that is intended to defame or dishonor another person and is published so that someone other than the one defamed will observe it.

Living will: Document in which an individual expresses in advance his or her wishes regarding the application of life-sustaining treatment in the event that he or she is incapable of doing so at some future time.

Malfeasance: Execution of an unlawful or improper act.

Malpractice: Professional misconduct, improper discharge of professional duties, or failure to meet the standard of care of a professional that results in harm to another. The negligence or carelessness of a professional person, such as a nurse, pharmacist, physician, or accountant.

Mandamus: Action brought in a court of competent jurisdiction to compel a lower court or administrative agency to perform or not to perform a specific act.

Mayhem: Crime of intentionally disfiguring or dismembering another.

Medicaid: Medical assistance provided in Title XIX of the Social Security Act. Medicaid is a state-administered program for the medically indigent.

Medicare: Medical assistance provided in Title XVIII of the Social Security Act. Medicare is a health insurance program administered by the Social Security Administration for persons aged 65 years and older and for disabled persons who are eligible for benefits. Medicare Part A benefits provide coverage for inpatient hospital care, skilled nursing facility care, home health care, and hospice care. Medicare Part B benefits provide coverage for physician services, outpatient hospital services, diagnostic tests, various therapies, durable medical equipment, medical supplies, and prosthetic devices.

Medication error: Any error in the medication process that might occur from the time a medication is ordered until the time it is administered.

Misdemeanor: Unlawful act of a less serious nature than a felony, usually punishable by a jail sentence for a term of less than one year and/or a fine.

Misfeasance: Improper performance of an act.

National Labor Relations Board (NLRB): Formed under the Wagner Act, the National Labor Relations Board serves to determine who should be in an official bargaining unit when a new unit is formed and who should be included in the unit and adjudicate unfair labor charges.

Negligence: Omission or commission of an act that a reasonably prudent person would or would not do under given circumstances. It is a form of heedlessness or carelessness that constitutes a departure from the standard of care generally imposed on members of society.

Non compos mentis: "Not of sound mind"—suffering from some form of mental defect.

Nonfeasance: Failure to act, when there is a duty to act, as a reasonably prudent person would in similar circumstances.

Nuncupative will: Oral statement intended as a last will made in anticipation of death.

Occupational Safety and Health Act (OSH Act): Congress enacted the Occupational Safety and Health Act (OSH Act) of 1970, 29 U.S.C § 651, to establish administrative machinery for the development and enforcement of standards for occupational health and safety. [A Web site is available on the Internet at http://www.OSHA.gov].

Ombudsman: Person who is designated to speak and act on behalf of a patient/resident, especially in regard to his or her daily needs.

Opined: To give or express as an opinion.

Opinion of the court: In an appellate court decision, the reasons for the decision. One judge writes the opinion for the majority of the court. Judges who agree with the result, but for different reasons, may write concurring opinions explaining their reasons. Judges who disagree with the majority may write dissenting opinions.

Perjury: Willful act of giving false testimony under oath.

Plaintiff: Party who brings a civil suit seeking damages or other legal relief.

Police power: Power of the state to protect the health, safety, morals, and general welfare of the people.

Privileged communication: Statement made to an attorney, physician, spouse, or anyone else in a position of trust. Because of the confidential nature of such information, the law protects it from being revealed even in court. The term is applied in two distinct situations. First, the communications between certain persons, such as physician and patient, cannot be divulged without the consent of the patient. Second, in some situations the law provides an exemption from liability for disclosing information where there is a higher duty to speak, such as statutory reporting requirements.

Probate: Judicial proceeding that determines the existence and validity of a will.

Probate court: Court with jurisdiction over wills. Its powers range from deciding the validity of a will to distributing property.

Process: A series of related actions to achieve a defined outcome. Ordering and/or administering medications are processes.

Prognosis: Informed judgment regarding the likely course and probable outcome of a disease.

Protocol: A set of rules governing a required process or procedure.

Proximate: In immediate relation with something else. In negligence cases, the careless act must be the proximate cause of injury.

Real evidence: Evidence furnished by tangible things (e.g., medical records and equipment).

Rebuttal: Giving of evidence to contradict the effect of evidence introduced by the opposing party.

Regulatory agency: Arm of the government that enforces legislation regulating an act or activity in a particular area, for example, the federal Food and Drug Administration.

Release: Statement signed by one person relinquishing a right or claim against another.

Remand: Referral of a case by an appeals court back to the original court, out of which it came, for the purpose of having some action taken there.

Res gestae: "The thing done"—all the surrounding events that become part of an incident. If statements are made as part of the incident, they are admissible in court as *res gestae* despite the hearsay rule.

Res ipsa loquitur: "The thing speaks for itself"—a doctrine of law applicable to cases where the defendant had exclusive control over the thing that caused the harm and where the harm ordinarily could not have occurred without negligent conduct.

Res judicata: "The thing is decided"—that which has been acted on or decided by the courts.

Respondeat superior: "Let the master answer"—an aphorism meaning that the employer is responsible for the legal consequences of the acts of the servant or employee who is acting within the scope of his or her employment.

Restraint: Restraints can be either "physical" or "chemical." A physical restraint involves a device (e.g., safety belts, safety bars, geriatric chairs, and bed rails) that restricts or limits voluntary movement and that cannot be removed by the patient.

Slander: False oral statement, made in the presence of a third person, that injures the character or reputation of another.

Standard of care: Description of the conduct that is expected of an individual in a given situation. It is a measure against which a defendant's conduct is compared.

Stare decisis: "Let the decision stand"—the legal doctrine that prescribes adherence to those precedents set forth in cases that have been decided.

Statute of limitations: Legal limit on the time allowed for filing suit in civil matters, usually measured from the time of the wrong or from the time when a reasonable person would have discovered the wrong.

Statutory law: Law that is prescribed by legislative enactments.

Stipulation: Agreement, usually in writing, by attorneys on opposite sides of an issue as to any matter pertaining to the proceedings. A stipulation is not binding unless agreed on by the parties involved in the issue.

Subpoena ad testificandum: Court order requiring one to appear in court to give testimony.

Subpoena duces tecum: Court order that commands a person to come to court and to produce whatever documents are named in the order.

Subrogation: Substitution of one person for another in reference to a lawful claim or right.

Suit: Court proceeding in which one person seeks damages or other legal remedies from another.

Summary judgment: Generally, an immediate decision by a judge, without jury deliberation.

Summons: Court order directed to the sheriff or other appropriate official to notify the defendant in a civil suit that a suit has been filed and when and where to appear.

Surrogate decision maker: Individual who has been designated to make decisions on behalf of an individual determined incapable of making his or her own decisions.

Tertiary care: Highly specialized care generally provided in a major medical center, often a teaching hospital.

Testimony: Oral statement of a witness given under oath at a trial.

Tort: Civil wrong committed by one individual against another. Torts may be classified as either intentional or unintentional. If a tort is classified as a criminal wrong (e.g., assault, battery, and false imprisonment), the wrongdoer could be held liable in a criminal action as well as a civil action.

Tort-feasor: Person who commits a tort.

Trial court: Court in which evidence is presented to a judge or jury for decision.

Union shop contract: Labor-management agreement making continued employment contingent on joining the union.

Venue: Geographic district in which an action is or may be brought.

Verdict: Formal declaration of a jury's findings of fact, signed by the jury foreperson and presented to the court.

Waiver: Intentional giving up of a right, such as allowing another person to testify to information that ordinarily would be protected as a privileged communication.

Will: Legal declaration of the intentions a person wishes to have carried out after death concerning property, children, or estate. A will designates a person or persons to serve as the executor(s) responsible for carrying out the instructions of the will.

Witness: Person who is called to give testimony in a court of law.

Writ: Written order that is issued to a person or persons, requiring the performance of some specified act or giving authority to have it done.

Wrongful birth: Applies to the cause of action of the parents who claim that the negligent advice or treatment deprived them of the choice of aborting conception or of terminating the pregnancy.

Wrongful life: Refers to a cause of action brought by or on behalf of a defective child who claims that but for the defendant (e.g., a laboratory's negligent testing procedures or a physician's negligent advice or treatment of the child's parents), the child would not have been born.

Index of Cases

Index